# *Easy Learning*
# German
# Dictionary

# BEGINNER'S
# GERMAN
# DICTIONARY

 HarperResource

*An Imprint of* HarperCollins*Publishers*

# Easy Learning
# German
# Dictionary

HarperCollinsPublishers

second edition 2001

© HarperCollins Publishers 1997, 1998, 2001

**latest reprint 2002**

HarperCollins Publishers
Westerhill Road, Bishopbriggs, Glasgow G64 2QT
Great Britain

**www.collinsdictionaries.com**

Collins® and Bank of English® are registered trademarks of
HarperCollins Publishers Limited

ISBN 0-00-472402-X

---

HarperCollins Publishers, Inc
10 East 53rd Street, New York, NY 10022

ISBN 0-06-273753-8

Library of Congress Cataloging-in-Publication Data has been applied for

www.harpercollins.com

---

*general editor*
Horst Kopleck

*editors*
**Veronika Schnorr**
Christine Bahr     Elizabeth Morris
Philip Mann     Martin Crellin     Elspeth Anderson

*editorial coordination*
Vivian Marr, Maree Airlie, Joyce Littlejohn
*second edition*
Sharon J. Hunter, Caitlin McMahon

*computing staff*
Ann Rautenbach

*concept development*
Michela Clari, Ray Carrick

*illustrations*
Richard Anderson

*series editor*
Lorna Sinclair Knight

---

**Corpus Acknowledgements**
We would like to acknowledge the assistance of the many hundreds of individuals and
companies who have kindly given permission for copyright material to be used in the
Bank of English. The written sources include many national and regional newspapers in
Britain and overseas; magazine and periodical publishers; and book publishers in Britain,
the United States and Australia. Extensive spoken data has been provided by radio and
television broadcasting companies; research workers at many universities and other
institutions; and numerous individual contributors. We are grateful to them all.

A catalogue record for this book is available from the British Library

Printed and bound in Italy by Amadeus S.p.A.

# CONTENTS

# INTRODUCTION

*Collins Easy Learning German Dictionary* is an innovative dictionary designed specifically for anyone starting to learn German. We are grateful to everyone who has contributed to the development of the Easy Learning series, and acknowledge the help of the examining boards in providing us with word lists and exam papers, which we carefully studied when compiling this dictionary.

**Note on trademarks**
Words which we have reason to believe constitute trademarks have been designated as such. However, neither the presence nor the absence of such designation should be regarded as affecting the legal status of any trademark.

# DICTIONARY SKILLS

Using a dictionary is a skill you can improve with practice and by following some basic guidelines. This section gives you a detailed explanation of how to use the dictionary to ensure you get the most out of it.

The answers to all the checks in this section are on page 16.

## ▶ MAKE SURE YOU LOOK IN THE RIGHT SIDE OF THE DICTIONARY

The German-English side comes first, followed by the English-German. The middle pages of the book have a blue border so that you can see where one side finishes and the other starts.

> **1**  Which side of the dictionary would you look up to translate *"das Fahrrad"*?

## ▶ FINDING THE WORD YOU WANT

When you are looking for a word, for example **froh**, look at the first letter – **f** – and find the **F** section in the German-English side. At the top of each page, you'll find the first and last words on that page. When you find the page with the words starting with **fr**, scan down the page until you find the word you want. Remember that even if a word has an umlaut on it, for example *für*, it makes no difference to the alphabetical order.

> **2**  On which page will you find the word – *"gestern"*?
> **3**  Which comes first – *"Bruder"* or *"Brötchen"*?

## ▶ MAKE SURE YOU LOOK AT THE RIGHT ENTRY

An entry is made up of a **word**, its <u>translations</u> and, often, example phrases to show you how to use the translations. If there is more than one entry for the same word, then there is an information box to tell you so. Look at the following example entries:

**flat** ADJECTIVE

> see also **flat** NOUN
>
> [1] flach ◊ *flat shoes* flache Schuhe
> ◆ **a flat roof** ein Flachdach NEUT
> [2] platt *(tyre)* ◊ *I've got a flat tyre.* Ich habe
> einen platten Reifen.

**flat** NOUN

> see also **flat** ADJECTIVE
>
> die Wohnung ◊ *She lives in a flat.* Sie wohnt
> in einer Wohnung.

4 **Which entry for "*flat*" should you look at if you want to translate the phrase "*My car has a flat tyre*"?**

**Always pay attention to information boxes – they tell you if there is more than one entry for the same word, give you guidance on grammatical points, or tell you about differences between German and British life.**

## ▶ CHOOSING THE RIGHT TRANSLATION

The main translation of a word is shown on a new line and is underlined to make it stand out from the rest of the entry. If there is more than one main translation for a word, each one is numbered. If an entry continues over the page there is a signpost to indicate this ☞.

Often you will see phrases in *italics*, preceded by a white diamond ◊. These help you choose the translation you want because they show how the translation they follow can be used.

5 **Use the phrases given at the entry "*hard*" to help you translate: "*This bread is hard*".**

Words often have more than one meaning and more than one translation, for example, a **pool** can be a puddle, a pond or a swimming pool; **pool** can also be a game. When you are translating from English into German, be careful to choose the German word that has the particular meaning you want. The dictionary offers you a lot of help with this. Look at the following entry:

**pool** NOUN
[1] (*puddle*)
die <u>Pfütze</u>
[2] (*pond*)
der <u>Teich</u> (PL die Teiche)
[3] (*for swimming*)
das <u>Schwimmbecken</u> (PL die Schwimmbecken)
[4] (*game*)
das <u>Poolbillard</u> ◊ *Shall we have a game of pool?* Sollen wir eine Partie Poolbillard spielen?
◆ **the pools** (*football*) das Toto ◊ *to do the pools* Toto spielen

The underlining points out all the main translations, the numbers tell you that there is more than one possible translation and the words in brackets in *italics* help you choose which translation you want.

> 6  How would you translate "*I like playing pool*"?

**Never take the first translation you see without looking at the others. Always look to see if there is more than one translation underlined.**

Phrases in **bold type** preceded by a black diamond ◆ are phrases which are particularly common or important. Sometimes these phrases have a completely different translation from the main translation; sometimes the translation is the same. For example:

**cancer** NOUN
der <u>Krebs</u> (GEN des Krebses) ◊ *He's got cancer.* Er hat Krebs.
◆ **I'm Cancer.** Ich bin Krebs.

**abgemacht** ADJECTIVE
<u>agreed</u> ◊ *Wir trafen uns zur abgemachten Zeit.* We met at the agreed time.
◆ **Abgemacht!** OK!

When you look up a word, make sure you look beyond the main translations to see if the entry includes any **bold phrases**.

> 7  Look up "*fahren*" to help you translate the sentence "*Ich werde morgen mit dem Zug fahren*".

## ▶ MAKING USE OF THE PHRASES IN THE DICTIONARY

Sometimes when you look up a word you will find not only the word, but the exact phrase you want. For example, you might want to say "*What's the date today?*" Look up **date** and you will find the exact phrase and its translation.

Sometimes you have to adapt what you find in the dictionary. If you want to say "*I play darts*" and look up **dart** you will find:

**dart** NOUN
der <u>Pfeil</u> (PL die Pfeile)
◆ **to play darts** Darts spielen

8

You have to substitute *ich spiele* for the infinitive form *spielen*. You will often have to adapt the infinitive in this way, adding the correct ending to the verb for **ich**, **du**, **er** etc and choosing the present, future or past form. For help with this, look at the German verb tables in the middle of the dictionary. **Spielen** is a regular verb so it follows the same pattern as **machen**, which is set out on page 344.

8  How would you say *"We played football"*?

Phrases containing nouns and adjectives may also need to be adapted. You may need to make the noun genitive, plural or dative plural, or the adjective feminine, neuter or plural. Remember that some nouns have irregular genitive or plural forms and that this information is shown in the entry.

9  How would you say *"The red flowers are beautiful"*?

## ▶ DON'T OVERUSE THE DICTIONARY

It takes time to look up words so try to avoid using the dictionary unnecessarily, especially in exams. Think carefully about what you want to say and see if you can put it another way, using the words you already know. To rephrase things you can:

◇  Use a word with a similar meaning. This is particularly easy with adjectives, as there are a lot of words which mean *good*, *bad*, *big* etc and you're sure to know at least one.

◇  Use negatives: if the cake you made was a total disaster, you could just say that it wasn't very good.

◇  Use particular examples instead of general terms. If you are asked to describe the sports facilities in your area, and time is short, you could say something like "In our town there is a swimming pool and a football ground."

10  How could you say *"The Black Forest is huge"* without looking up the word *"huge"*?

You can also guess the meaning of a German word by using others to give you a clue. If you see the sentence *"ich lese ein gutes Buch"*, you may not know the meaning of the word **lese**, but you know it's a verb because it's preceded by **ich**. Therefore it must be something you can do to a book: **read**. So the translation is: *I'm reading a good book.*

11  Try NOT to use your dictionary to work out the meaning of the sentence *"Das Mädchen schreibt ihrer Brieffreundin einen Brief auf Deutsch"*.

# PARTS OF SPEECH

If you look up the word **flat**, you will see that there are two entries for this word as it can be a noun or an adjective. It helps to choose correctly between the entries if you know how to recognize these different types of words.

## ▶ NOUNS

Nouns often appear with words like *a, the, this, that, my, your* and *his*.
They can be singular (abbreviated to SING in the dictionary):

      *his* **dog**        *her* **cat**        *a* **street**

or plural (abbreviated to PL in the dictionary):

    *the* **facts**      *those* **people**      *his* **shoes**      *our* **holidays**

They can be the subject of a verb:

                    **Vegetables** are good for you

or the object of a verb:

                    I play **tennis**

> *I bought my mother a box of chocolates.*
>
> **12 Which three words in this sentence are nouns?**
> **13 Which of the nouns is plural?**

German nouns all start with a capital letter and can be either masculine, feminine or neuter (abbreviated to MASC, FEM or NEUT in the dictionary).
Masculine nouns are shown by **der**:

        *der* Hund          *der* Zug          *der* Arm

feminine nouns are shown by **die**:

*die* Katze          *die* Milch          *die* Tür

neuter nouns are shown by **das**:

*das* Auto          *das* Kind          *das* Sofa

The plural form of **der**, **die** and **das** is **die**. The plural of most feminine German nouns is made by adding **en** or **n**:

*die* Katzen          *die* Türen          *die* Familien

Many German nouns, however, do not add **en** or **n** in the plural, so the plural of these nouns is shown in the entry:

*die Hunde*     *die Häuser*     *die Autos*     *die Wagen*     *die Mütter*

In German **der**, **die** and **das** (and also **ein** and **eine**) may change when the noun they precede is used in another case, for example in the accusative, genitive or dative case (abbreviated to ACC, GEN and DAT in the dictionary). It is important to learn when you should use each case in German.

The **nominative** case is used to show the subject of a sentence – *the dog* is chasing the cat. All German nouns are shown in the nominative case in the dictionary:

*Ich* esse ein Eis.          *Die Katze* schläft.          *Der Ball* ist im Garten.

The **accusative** case is used to show the direct object of a sentence – I love *chocolate* – and after certain prepositions e.g. durch, ohne:

Ich sehe **den Hund.**          Sie liebt **mich.**          Wir gingen durch **den Wald.**

The **genitive** case is used to show that something belongs to somebody – my *father's* hat – and after certain prepositions e.g. wegen:

das Auto **des Mannes**          der Hund **meiner Mutter**          wegen **des** schlechten **Wetters**

The **dative** case is used to show the indirect object of a sentence – she told *me* the news – and after certain prepositions e.g. mit, aus:

Ich gebe **dem Lehrer** das Heft.          Er schreibt **mir** einen Brief.          Sie spielen mit **dem Ball.**

The rules for the changes to **der**, **die**, **das**, **ein** and **eine** are shown here:

|     | MASC SING | FEM SING | NEUT SING | PL |
|-----|-----------|----------|-----------|-----|
| NOM | der | die | das | die |
| ACC | den | die | das | die |
| GEN | des | der | des | der |
| DAT | dem | der | dem | den |

|  | MASC SING | FEM SING | NEUT SING |
|---|---|---|---|
| NOM | ein | eine | ein |
| ACC | einen | eine | ein |
| GEN | eines | einer | eines |
| DAT | einem | einer | einem |

Masculine and neuter singular German nouns usually add **es** or **s** when they are used in the genitive case:

*des* Vaters    *des* Hundes    *des* Autos

feminine and plural German nouns do not change in the genitive:

*der Mutter*    *der Tür*    *der Katzen*    *der Männer*

Sometimes, however, the genitive form is irregular, and this is shown in the entry:

*des Jazz*    *des Herrn*    *des Abiturienten*

An **n** is added to the plural form of German nouns in the dative case, unless the plural form already ends in **n**:

*den* Kindern    *den* Häusern    *den* Katzen    *den* Lehrerinnen

> *Ich gebe meinem Bruder ein Buch.*
>
> 14 Which two words in the sentence are nouns – are they singular or plural?
> 15 What is the genitive form of "Bruder"?
> 16 Use your dictionary to find the plural form of "Buch". Then work out the dative plural form.

## ▶ PRONOUNS

Words like *I, me, you, he, she, him, her* and *they* are pronouns. They can be used instead of nouns. You can refer to a person as *he* or *she* or to a thing as *it*.

> *I showed him the new computer.*
>
> 17 Which words are pronouns in this sentence?

## ▶ ADJECTIVES

**Flat** can be an adjective as well as a noun. Adjectives describe nouns: your tyre can be **flat**, you can have a pair of **flat** shoes.

> *I'm afraid of the dark.*
> *The girl has dark hair.*
>
> 18 In which sentence is "dark" an adjective?

German adjectives can be masculine, feminine or neuter, singular or plural. The ending of the adjective may also change depending on whether the noun is preceded by **ein, eine** etc or by **der, die** or **das**:

der **kleine** Hund    ein **kleines** Kind
**kleine** Kinder    die **kleinen** Katzen

Adjectives are also affected by the case i.e. **nominative, accusative** etc of the noun they describe:

des **kleinen** Hundes    der **kleinen** Katze
einem **kleinen** Mädchen   den **kleinen** Kindern

The endings of German adjectives follow the rules shown here:

|  | MASC SING(der) | FEM SING(die) | NEUT SING(das) | PL(die) |
|------|----------------|----------------|-----------------|----------|
| NOM | kleine | kleine | kleine | kleinen |
| ACC | kleinen | kleine | kleine | kleinen |
| GEN | kleinen | kleinen | kleinen | kleinen |
| DAT | kleinen | kleinen | kleinen | kleinen |

|  | MASC SING(ein) | FEM SING(eine) | NEUT SING(ein) | PL |
|------|----------------|----------------|-----------------|----------|
| NOM | kleiner | kleine | kleines | kleine |
| ACC | kleinen | kleine | kleines | kleine |
| GEN | kleinen | kleinen | kleinen | kleiner |
| DAT | kleinen | kleinen | kleinen | kleinen |

Only the basic form of the adjective is shown in the dictionary. So, if you want to find out what kind of girls **die schönen Mädchen** are, look under **schön**.

Some adjectives, called **invariable adjectives**, don't change whether they are masculine, feminine, neuter or plural or describing a noun in a different case. This is shown in the dictionary:

**pink** ADJECTIVE
<u>rosa</u>
 *rosa is invariable.*
 ◊ *a pink shirt* ein rosa Hemd

**19** What is the feminine accusative singular form of "schwarz"?
**20** What is the basic form of the adjective in the sentence "*Peter ist ein braves Kind*"?

## ► VERBS

*She's going to record the programme for me.*
*His time in the race was a new world record.*

**Record** is a verb in the first sentence, and a noun in the second.

One way to recognize a verb is that it frequently comes with a pronoun such as **I**, **you** or **she**, or with somebody's name. Verbs can relate to the present, the past or the future. They have a number of different forms to show this: **I'm going** (present), **he will go** (future), and **Nicola went** (past). Often verbs appear with **to: they promised to go**. This basic form of the verb is called the infinitive.

In this dictionary verbs are preceded by "to", so you can identify them at a glance. No matter which of the four previous examples you want to translate, you should look up to **go**, not **going** or **went**. If you want to translate I **thought**, look up to **think**.

---

I came        she's crying        they've done it        he's out

**21 What would you look up to translate the verbs in these phrases?**

---

Verbs have different endings in German, depending on whether you are talking about **ich**, **du**, **wir** etc: **ich mache**, **du machst**, **wir machen** etc. They also have different forms for the present, past (imperfect and perfect tenses), future etc; **wir machen** (*we do* = present), **wir machten** (*we did* = imperfect), **wir haben gemacht** (*we have done* = perfect), **wir werden machen** (*we will do* = future). **machen** is the infinitive and is the form that appears in the dictionary.

Sometimes the verb changes completely between the infinitive form and the **ich**, **du**, **er** etc form. For example, *to give* is **geben**, but *he gives* is **er gibt**, and *ich bin gegangen* comes from the verb **gehen** (*to go*).

On pages 344-356 of the dictionary, you will find tables of the most important forms of German verbs. And on pages 357-360 you will find a list of the most important forms of other German irregular verbs. Any irregular forms of verbs are also shown in the entry.

---

to **bowl** VERB
  *see also* **bowl** NOUN
  (*in cricket*)
  werfen (PRESENT wirft, IMPERFECT warf, PERFECT
hat geworfen)

**heben** VERB (IMPERFECT **hob**, PERFECT **hat
  gehoben**)
  to lift

**22** Look up the dictionary to find the imperfect and perfect tenses of "laufen".

## ▶ ADVERBS

An adverb is a word which describes a verb or an adjective:

> Write **soon**.        *Check your work* **carefully**.
> The film was **very** good.

In the sentence *"The swimming pool is open daily"*, **daily** is an adverb describing the adjective **open**. In the phrase *"my daily routine"*, **daily** is an adjective describing the noun **routine**. We use the same word in English for both adjective and adverb forms, and the same word is used in German too. In many cases the same German word is used to translate an adjective and an adverb in English. Sometimes, however, the translations are different and you will need to know the difference between an adjective and an adverb to be able to choose the correct German translation.

> Take the sentence "The menu changes daily".
>
> **23** Is "*daily*" an adverb or an adjective here?

## ▶ PREPOSITIONS

Prepositions are words like **for**, **with** and **across**, which are followed by nouns or pronouns:

> *I've got a present* **for** *David.*    *Come* **with** *me.*    *He ran* **across** *the road.*

In German, all prepositions are followed by nouns or pronouns in a certain case, for example, **mit** is followed by nouns or pronouns in the dative case. The case which follows a preposition is shown in the entry:

**ab** PREPOSITION, ADVERB
> *The preposition **ab** takes the dative.*

**1** from ◇ *Kinder ab zwölf Jahren* children from the age of twelve ◇ *ab morgen* from tomorrow

**2** off ◇ *Die Straße geht nach links ab.* The road goes off to the left. ◇ *Der Knopf ist ab.* The button has come off. ◇ *Ab nach Hause!* Off you go home!
- ◆ **ab sofort** as of now
- ◆ **ab und zu** now and then

**above** PREPOSITION, ADVERB
über ◇ *above forty degrees* über vierzig Grad
> *Use the accusative to express movement or a change of place. Use the dative when there is no change of place.*

◇ *He put his hands above his head.* Er hielt die Hände über den Kopf. ◇ *The lamp is hanging above the table.* Die Lampe hängt über dem Tisch.
- ◆ **the flat above** die Wohnung darüber
- ◆ **mentioned above** oben erwähnt
- ◆ **above all** vor allem

> *The party's over.*
> *The shop's just over the road.*
>
> **24** Which sentence shows a preposition followed by a noun?
> **25** What case does the preposition "*durch*" take?
> **26** Use your dictionary to help you translate "*He is going into the garden*".

## ▶ ANSWERS

1. the German side
2. on page 123
3. **Brötchen** comes first
4. the first (ADJECTIVE) entry
5. **Dieses Brot ist hart.**
6. **Ich spiele gern Poolbillard.**
7. **I'm going by train tomorrow.**
8. **Wir spielten Fußball.**
9. **Die roten Blumen sind schön.**
10. **Der Schwarzwald ist sehr groß.**
11. **The girl is writing a letter to her pen friend in German.**
12. **mother, box** and **chocolates** are nouns
13. **chocolates** is plural
14. **Bruder** and **Buch** are nouns – they are both singular
15. **Bruders**
16. **Bücher** – **Büchern** is the dative plural form
17. **I** and **him** are pronouns
18. in the second sentence
19. **schwarze**
20. **brav**
21. to **come**, to **cry**, to **do**, to **be**
22. the imperfect tense is **lief**, the perfect tense is **ist gelaufen**
23. **daily** is an adverb
24. the second sentence
25. **durch** takes the accusative case
26. **Er geht in den Garten.**

# A

**der Aal** NOUN (PL die **Aale**)
eel

**ab** PREPOSITION, ADVERB
*The preposition ab takes the dative.*
[1] from ◊ *Kinder ab zwölf Jahren*
children from the age of twelve ◊ *ab morgen* from tomorrow
[2] off ◊ *Die Straße geht nach links ab.*
The road goes off to the left. ◊ *Der Knopf ist ab.* The button has come off. ◊ *Ab nach Hause!* Off you go home!
♦ **ab sofort** as of now
♦ **ab und zu** now and then

**abbiegen** VERB (IMPERFECT **bog ab,** PERFECT **ist abgebogen**)
[1] to turn off ◊ *Sie bog an der Kreuzung nach links ab.* At the crossroads she turned off to the left.
[2] to bend ◊ *Die Hauptstraße biegt nach rechts ab.* The main road bends to the right.

**die Abbildung** NOUN
illustration

**abbrechen** VERB (PRESENT **bricht ab,** IMPERFECT **brach ab,** PERFECT **hat abgebrochen**)
[1] to break off ◊ *Sie brach einen blühenden Zweig ab.* She broke off a flowering branch.
[2] to pull down ◊ *Das alte Gebäude muss abgebrochen werden.* The old building will have to be pulled down.
[3] to stop ◊ *Es ist schon spät, wir sollten abbrechen.* It's late now; we ought to stop.
[4] to abort ◊ *Das dauert zu lang, du solltest das Programm abbrechen.* It's taking too long; you should abort the program.

**abbuchen** VERB (PERFECT **hat abgebucht**)
to debit ◊ *Der Betrag wird von Ihrem Konto abgebucht.* The amount will be debited from your account.

**der Abend** NOUN (PL die **Abende**)
evening ◊ *Sie macht jeden Abend einen Spaziergang.* She goes for a walk every evening. ◊ *guten Abend* good evening
♦ **zu Abend essen** to have dinner
♦ **heute Abend** this evening

**das Abendbrot** NOUN
supper

**das Abendessen** NOUN (PL die **Abendessen**)
dinner ◊ *Zum Abendessen gibt es Spaghetti.* There's spaghetti for dinner.

**abends** ADVERB
in the evening

**das Abenteuer** NOUN (PL die **Abenteuer**)
adventure

**aber** CONJUNCTION, ADVERB

[1] but ◊ *Er wollte mit uns mitkommen, aber seine Eltern haben es nicht erlaubt.*
He wanted to come with us, but his parents wouldn't let him.
[2] however ◊ *Ich möchte nach Ägypten reisen. Ich habe aber kein Geld.* I'd like to go to Egypt. However, I haven't got any money.
♦ **Das ist aber schön!** That's really nice.
♦ **Nun ist aber Schluss!** Now that's enough!

**abfahren** VERB (PRESENT **fährt ab,** IMPERFECT **fuhr ab,** PERFECT **ist abgefahren**)
to leave ◊ *Wir fahren morgen sehr früh ab.* We're leaving very early tomorrow.
◊ *Wann fährt dein Zug ab?* When does your train leave?

**die Abfahrt** NOUN
departure

**der Abfall** NOUN (PL die **Abfälle**)
rubbish

**der Abfalleimer** NOUN (PL die **Abfalleimer**)
rubbish bin

**abfällig** ADJECTIVE
disparaging

**abfliegen** VERB (IMPERFECT **flog ab,** PERFECT **ist abgeflogen**)
to take off ◊ *Die Maschine ist mit Verspätung abgeflogen.* The plane was late taking off.
♦ **Um wie viel Uhr fliegt ihr ab?** What time does your plane leave?

**der Abflug** NOUN (PL die **Abflüge**)
[1] departure ◊ *Wir müssen eine Stunde vor Abflug am Flughafen sein.* We have to be at the airport one hour before departure.
[2] takeoff ◊ *Die Maschine stürzte kurz nach dem Abflug ab.* The plane crashed shortly after takeoff.

**abfragen** VERB (PERFECT **hat abgefragt**)
[1] to test orally ◊ *die Vokabeln abfragen* to give an oral vocabulary test
[2] to call up ◊ *Sie können die Abfahrtszeiten am Computer abfragen.* You can call up departure times on the computer.

**das Abführmittel** NOUN (PL die **Abführmittel**)
laxative

**das Abgas** NOUN (GEN des **Abgases,** PL die **Abgase**)
exhaust fumes

**abgeben** VERB (PRESENT **gibt ab,** IMPERFECT **gab ab,** PERFECT **hat abgegeben**)
[1] to hand in ◊ *Die Klassenarbeiten müssen am Ende der Stunde abgegeben werden.* Tests must be handed in at the end of the lesson.

**2** to pass ◊ *Er gab den Ball an den Mittelstürmer ab.* He passed the ball to the centre-forward.

♦ **sich mit jemandem abgeben** to associate with somebody

♦ **sich mit etwas abgeben** to bother with something ◊ *Mit solch dummen Fragen will ich mich nicht abgeben.* I don't want to bother with such stupid questions.

♦ **jemandem etwas abgeben** to let somebody have something

♦ **Du würdest eine wunderbare Lehrerin abgeben.** You would make a wonderful teacher.

**abgelegen** ADJECTIVE
remote

**abgemacht** ADJECTIVE
agreed ◊ *Wir trafen uns zur abgemachten Zeit.* We met at the agreed time.

♦ **Abgemacht!** OK!

**abgeneigt** ADJECTIVE
disinclined

**abgesehen** ADJECTIVE

♦ **es auf jemanden abgesehen haben** to be out to get somebody

♦ **es auf etwas abgesehen haben** to be after something

♦ **abgesehen von ...** apart from ...
◊ *Abgesehen von ein paar Fehlern war der Aufsatz sehr gut.* The essay was very good, apart from a few mistakes.

**abgewöhnen** VERB (PERFECT **hat abgewöhnt**)

♦ **sich etwas abgewöhnen** to give something up ◊ *Ich will mir das Rauchen abgewöhnen.* I want to give up smoking.

der **Abhang** NOUN (PL die **Abhänge**)
slope

**abhängen (1)** VERB (PERFECT **hat abgehängt**)

**1** to take down ◊ *Weil ihr das Bild nicht mehr gefiel, hängte sie es ab.* She took the picture down because she didn't like it any more.

**2** to unhitch ◊ *Er hängte den Wohnwagen ab, bevor er in die Stadt fuhr.* He unhitched the caravan before he drove into town.

**3** to shake off ◊ *Den Räubern gelang es, die Polizei abzuhängen.* The robbers managed to shake off the police.

**abhängen (2)** VERB (IMPERFECT **hing ab,** PERFECT **hat abgehangen**)

♦ **von jemandem abhängen** to depend on somebody

♦ **von etwas abhängen** to depend on something ◊ *Es hängt vom Wetter ab, ob das Fußballspiel stattfindet.* Whether or not the football match goes ahead depends on the weather.

**abhängig** ADJECTIVE

♦ **abhängig von** dependent on

**abheben** VERB (IMPERFECT **hob ab,** PERFECT **hat abgehoben**)

**1** to answer ◊ *Es scheint niemand zu Hause zu sein, es hebt nämlich keiner ab.* There doesn't seem to be anyone at home as nobody's answering the phone.

**2** to withdraw ◊ *Ich muss Geld vom Sparbuch abheben.* I'll have to withdraw some money from my savings account.

**3** to take off ◊ *Wir sahen zu, wie das Flugzeug abhob.* We watched the plane take off.

**4** to lift off ◊ *Die Rakete hob senkrecht ab.* The rocket lifted off vertically.

♦ **sich von etwas abheben** to stand out against something ◊ *Das Muster hebt sich gut vom Hintergrund ab.* The pattern stands out well against this background.

**abholen** VERB (PERFECT **hat abgeholt**)

**1** to collect ◊ *Der Müll wird einmal in der Woche abgeholt.* Rubbish is collected once a week.

**2** to pick up ◊ *Ich hole dich um sieben ab.* I'll pick you up at seven. ◊ *Der Krankenwagen hat den Verletzten abgeholt.* The ambulance picked up the injured man.

das **Abitur** NOUN
A levels

der **Abiturient** NOUN (GEN des **Abiturienten,** PL die **Abiturienten**)
A level student

die **Abiturientin** NOUN
A level student

**abkürzen** VERB (PERFECT **hat abgekürzt**)
to abbreviate ◊ *Man kann "bitte wenden" mit b. w. abkürzen.* You can abbreviate "please turn over" to PTO.

♦ **den Weg abkürzen** to take a short cut

die **Abkürzung** NOUN

**1** abbreviation ◊ *Die Abkürzung für Europäische Union ist EU.* The abbreviation for European Union is EU.

**2** short cut ◊ *Wir haben eine Abkürzung genommen.* We took a short cut.

**abladen** VERB (PRESENT **lädt ab,** IMPERFECT **lud ab,** PERFECT **hat abgeladen**)
to unload

**ablaufen** VERB (PRESENT **läuft ab,** IMPERFECT **lief ab,** PERFECT **ist abgelaufen**)

**1** to expire ◊ *Ihr Pass ist leider abgelaufen.* Unfortunately, your passport has expired.

**2** to drain away ◊ *Der Abfluss ist verstopft, und deshalb läuft das Wasser nicht ab.* The waste pipe is blocked, and that's why the water won't drain away.

♦ **Erzähl mir, wie der Abend abgelaufen ist.** Tell me how the evening went.

**ablehnen** VERB (PERFECT **hat abgelehnt**)

**1** to turn down ◊ *Sie hat das Amt der Klassensprecherin abgelehnt.* She turned down being class representative. ◊ *Mein*

**A**

Antrag auf ein Stipendium wurde abgelehnt. My application for a grant was turned down.
2 to disapprove of ◇ *Ich lehne eine solche Arbeitseinstellung ab.* I disapprove of such an attitude to work.

**ablenken** VERB (PERFECT **hat abgelenkt**)
to distract ◇ *Lenk ihn nicht von seiner Arbeit ab.* Don't distract him from his work.
♦ **Sie hat in letzter Zeit viel Sorgen. Versuch mal, sie etwas abzulenken.** She's had a lot of worries recently. Try to take her mind off things.
♦ **vom Thema ablenken** to change the subject

**abliefern** VERB (PERFECT **hat abgeliefert**)
1 to drop off ◇ *Wir haben die Kinder wieder wohlbehalten zu Hause abgeliefert.* We dropped the children off at home safe and sound.
2 to hand in ◇ *Bis wann musst du das Referat abliefern?* When do you have to hand your assignment in by?
♦ **etwas bei jemandem abliefern** to take something to somebody ◇ *Wir haben die gefundene Uhr beim Fundbüro abgeliefert.* We took the watch we found to the lost property office.

**abmachen** VERB (PERFECT **hat abgemacht**)
1 to take off ◇ *Weißt du, wie man den Deckel abmacht?* Do you know how to take the lid off?
2 to agree ◇ *Wir haben abgemacht, dass wir uns um sieben Uhr treffen.* We agreed to meet at seven.
3 to sort out ◇ *Ihr solltet das untereinander abmachen, wer heute aufräumt.* Sort out amongst yourselves who's going to clear up today.

die **Abmachung** NOUN
agreement

die **Abnahme** NOUN
decrease ◇ *eine weitere Abnahme der Teilnehmerzahlen* a further decrease in attendance

**abnehmen** VERB (PRESENT **nimmt ab**, IMPERFECT **nahm ab**, PERFECT **hat abgenommen**)
1 to remove ◇ *Bei diesem Auto kann man das Verdeck abnehmen.* You can remove the hood on this car.
♦ **Als das Telefon klingelte, nahm sie ab.** When the telephone rang, she answered it.
♦ **jemandem etwas abnehmen** to take something away from somebody ◇ *Ihr wurde der Führerschein abgenommen.* They took away her driving licence.
2 to decrease ◇ *Die Zahl der Teilnehmer hat stark abgenommen.* The number of participants has decreased dramatically.

3 to lose weight ◇ *Ich muss dringend abnehmen.* I really must lose weight.
◇ *Ich habe schon zwei Kilo abgenommen.* I've already lost two kilos.
4 to buy ◇ *Wenn Sie mehr als zehn Stück abnehmen, bekommen Sie einen Rabatt.* If you buy more than ten you get a discount.
♦ **Hat sie dir diese Geschichte wirklich abgenommen?** Did she really buy that story?

das **Abonnement** NOUN (PL die **Abonnements**)
subscription

**abonnieren** VERB (PERFECT **hat abonniert**)
to subscribe to

**abräumen** VERB (PERFECT **hat abgeräumt**)
to clear away ◇ *Sie räumte die Teller ab.* She cleared away the plates.
♦ **den Tisch abräumen** to clear the table

**abreagieren** VERB (PERFECT **hat abreagiert**)
♦ **etwas an jemandem abreagieren** to take something out on somebody
♦ **sich abreagieren** to calm down

die **Abreise** NOUN
departure

**abreisen** VERB (PERFECT **ist abgereist**)
to leave

**Abs.** ABBREVIATION (= *Absender*)
sender

die **Absage** NOUN
refusal

**absagen** VERB (PERFECT **hat abgesagt**)
1 to call off ◇ *Die Vorstellung wurde abgesagt.* The performance was called off.
2 to turn down ◇ *eine Einladung absagen* to turn down an invitation

der **Absatz** NOUN (GEN des **Absatzes**, PL die **Absätze**)
1 heel ◇ *Die Absätze von deinen Schuhen sind ganz schief.* The heels of your shoes are worn down.
2 paragraph ◇ *Hier solltest du einen Absatz machen.* You need to start a new paragraph here.
3 sales ◇ *Der Absatz an elektrischen Geräten ist gestiegen.* Sales of electrical appliances have risen.

**abschaffen** VERB (PERFECT **hat abgeschafft**)
1 to abolish ◇ *Wann wurde in Deutschland die Todesstrafe abgeschafft?* When was the death sentence abolished in Germany?
2 to get rid of ◇ *Ich werde mein Auto abschaffen.* I'm going to get rid of my car.

**abscheulich** ADJECTIVE
abominable

**abschicken** VERB (PERFECT **hat abgeschickt**)
to send off

der **Abschied** NOUN (PL die **Abschiede**)
parting

☞

♦ **von jemandem Abschied nehmen** to say goodbye to somebody

der **Abschleppdienst** NOUN (PL die **Abschleppdienste**)
breakdown service

**abschleppen** VERB (PERFECT **hat abgeschleppt**)
to tow ◊ *ein Auto abschleppen* to tow a car

♦ **jemanden abschleppen** to pick somebody up ◊ *Paul hat auf der Party versucht, Petra abzuschleppen.* Paul tried to pick Petra up at the party.

**abschließen** VERB (IMPERFECT **schloss ab**, PERFECT **hat abgeschlossen**)
[1] to lock ◊ *Ich schließe meinen Schreibtisch immer ab.* I always lock my desk.

♦ **Bist du sicher, dass du abgeschlossen hast?** Are you sure you locked up?
[2] to conclude ◊ *einen Vertrag abschließen* to conclude a contract

**abschließend** ADJECTIVE, ADVERB
in conclusion ◊ *Abschließend möchte ich noch Folgendes sagen: ...* In conclusion I would like to say this: ...

die **Abschlussprüfung** NOUN
final exam

**abschneiden** VERB (IMPERFECT **schnitt ab**, PERFECT **hat abgeschnitten**)
[1] to cut ◊ *Kannst du mir bitte eine Scheibe Brot abschneiden?* Can you cut me a slice of bread, please?
[2] to do ◊ *Sie hat in der Prüfung sehr gut abgeschnitten.* She did very well in the exam.

**abschrecken** VERB (PERFECT **hat abgeschreckt**)
to deter ◊ *Diese Maßnahmen sollen Jugendliche davon abschrecken, Drogen zu nehmen.* These measures are intended to deter young people from taking drugs.

**abschreiben** VERB (IMPERFECT **schrieb ab**, PERFECT **hat abgeschrieben**)
to copy ◊ *Er wurde dabei erwischt, wie er von seinem Nachbarn abgeschrieben hat.* He was caught copying from his neighbour. ◊ *Schreibt diesen Satz bitte in eure Hefte ab.* Please copy this sentence into your exercise books.

**absehbar** ADJECTIVE
foreseeable ◊ *in absehbarer Zeit* in the foreseeable future

♦ **Das Ende ist absehbar.** The end is in sight.

**abseits** ADVERB
apart ◊ *Sie stand etwas abseits von den anderen.* She was standing somewhat apart from the others.

der **Absender** NOUN (PL die **Absender**)
sender

**absetzen** VERB (PERFECT **hat abgesetzt**)

[1] to drop off ◊ *Ich setze dich am Bahnhof ab. I'll drop you off at the station.*
[2] to take off ◊ *Willst du nicht deinen Motorradhelm absetzen?* Don't you want to take your helmet off?
[3] to drop ◊ *Dieser Sprachkurs musste vom Programm abgesetzt werden.* This language course has had to be dropped from the syllabus.

♦ **die Pille absetzen** to stop taking the pill

die **Absicht** NOUN
intention ◊ *Das war nicht meine Absicht.* That was not my intention.

♦ **mit Absicht** on purpose

**absichtlich** ADJECTIVE, ADVERB
deliberate ◊ *eine absichtliche Beleidigung* a deliberate insult

♦ **etwas absichtlich tun** to do something deliberately

**absolut** ADJECTIVE, ADVERB
absolute

♦ **Das ist absolut unmöglich.** That's absolutely impossible.

♦ **Ich habe absolut keine Lust.** I really don't feel like it.

**abspülen** VERB (PERFECT **hat abgespült**)
to rinse ◊ *Er spülte die Teller ab.* He rinsed the plates.

♦ **Geschirr abspülen** to wash up

der **Abstand** NOUN (PL die **Abstände**)
distance ◊ *Abstand halten* to keep one's distance

**abstellen** VERB (PERFECT **hat abgestellt**)
[1] to put down ◊ *Der Koffer ist so schwer, ich muss ihn kurz abstellen.* The case is so heavy that I'll have to put it down for a moment.
[2] to park ◊ *Wir haben das Auto am Stadtrand abgestellt.* We parked the car on the outskirts of town.
[3] to switch off ◊ *Kannst du bitte das Radio abstellen?* Can you switch the radio off, please?

die **Abstimmung** NOUN
vote

**abstrakt** ADJECTIVE, ADVERB
[1] abstract ◊ *abstrakte Kunst* abstract art
[2] in an abstract way ◊ *Er drückt sich sehr abstrakt aus.* He expresses himself in a very abstract way.

**abstreiten** VERB (IMPERFECT **stritt ab**, PERFECT **hat abgestritten**)
to deny

**abstürzen** VERB (PERFECT **ist abgestürzt**)
[1] to fall ◊ *Mathis ist beim Klettern abgestürzt.* Mathis fell while climbing.
[2] to crash ◊ *Die Maschine ist kurz nach dem Start abgestürzt.* The plane crashed shortly after takeoff.

das **Abteil** NOUN (PL die **Abteile**)
compartment

die **Abteilung** NOUN

[1] department ◊ *Sie wurde in eine andere Abteilung versetzt.* She was transferred to another department.
[2] ward ◊ *In welcher Abteilung liegt Mathis?* Which ward is Mathis in?

die **Abtreibung** NOUN
abortion

**abtrocknen** VERB (PERFECT **hat abgetrocknet**)
to dry

**abwärts** ADVERB
down

der **Abwasch** NOUN
washing-up ◊ *den Abwasch machen* to do the washing-up

**abwaschen** VERB (PRESENT **wäscht ab**, IMPERFECT **wusch ab**, PERFECT **hat abgewaschen**)
[1] to wash ◊ *Du solltest dir das Gesicht abwaschen!* You ought to wash your face. ◊ *Wer muss heute das Geschirr abwaschen?* Who's turn is it to wash the dishes today?
♦ **Ich muss noch schnell abwaschen, dann können wir gehen.** I'll just have to wash up, then we can go.
[2] to wash off ◊ *Wasch dir mal die Soße vom Gesicht ab!* Wash that gravy off your face.

das **Abwasser** NOUN (PL die **Abwässer**)
sewage

die **Abwechslung** NOUN
change ◊ *zur Abwechslung* for a change

**abwerten** VERB (PERFECT **hat abgewertet**)
to devalue

**abwertend** ADJECTIVE, ADVERB
derogatory ◊ *sich abwertend über etwas äußern* to talk in a derogatory way about something

**abwesend** ADJECTIVE
absent

die **Abwesenheit** NOUN
absence

**abwischen** VERB (PERFECT **hat abgewischt**)
to wipe ◊ *Er wischte die Tafel ab.* He wiped the board.

**abzählen** VERB (PERFECT **hat abgezählt**)
to count

das **Abzeichen** NOUN (PL die **Abzeichen**)
badge

**abziehen** VERB (IMPERFECT **zog ab**, PERFECT **hat/ist abgezogen**)
*For the perfect tense use haben when the verb has an object and sein when there is no object.*
[1] to take out ◊ *Er zog den Zündschlüssel ab.* He took out the ignition key.
[2] to withdraw ◊ *Sie haben ihre Truppen aus der Stadt abgezogen.* They have withdrawn their troops from the town.
[3] to deduct ◊ *Die Steuer wird*

*vom Gehalt abgezogen.* Tax is deducted from earnings.
♦ **Er ist beleidigt abgezogen.** He went away in a huff.

**abzüglich** PREPOSITION
*The preposition **abzüglich** takes the genitive.*
less ◊ *das Gehalt abzüglich der Steuern* earnings less tax

die **Achsel** NOUN
shoulder

**acht** NUMBER
see also **die Acht** NOUN
eight
♦ **acht Tage** a week

die **Acht** NOUN
see also **acht** NUMBER
eight ◊ *Schreibe eine Acht.* Write the figure eight.
♦ **auf etwas Acht geben** to pay attention to something ◊ *Du solltest etwas mehr auf die Rechtschreibung Acht geben!* You should pay a bit more attention to spelling.
♦ **auf jemanden Acht geben** to keep an eye on somebody ◊ *Würden Sie mal bitte auf meinen Sohn Acht geben?* Would you keep an eye on my son for a minute, please?
♦ **Gib Acht, da kommt uns ein Auto entgegen!** Look out, there's a car coming towards us.
♦ **sich in Acht nehmen** to beware ◊ *Du solltest dich vor ihr in Acht nehmen!* You should beware of her.
♦ **etwas außer Acht lassen** to disregard something

**achte** ADJECTIVE
eighth ◊ *Sie wiederholte den Satz ein achtes Mal.* She repeated the sentence for an eighth time. ◊ *Er kam als Achter.* He was the eighth to arrive.

**achten** VERB
to respect ◊ *Ich achte deine Meinung.* I respect your opinion. ◊ *Sie ist sehr geachtet.* She's highly respected.
♦ **auf etwas achten** to pay attention to something ◊ *Du solltest auf die Verkehrsschilder achten.* You should pay attention to the road signs.
♦ **auf jemanden achten** to take notice of somebody ◊ *Achte nicht auf ihn!* Don't take any notice of him!

die **Achterbahn** NOUN
roller coaster

**achthundert** NUMBER
eight hundred

**achtmal** ADVERB
eight times

die **Achtung** NOUN
respect ◊ *Ich habe große Achtung vor ihr.* I've great respect for her.
♦ **Achtung!** Look out!

♦ **Achtung Stufe!** Mind the step.
♦ **Achtung, Achtung, hier eine Durchsage!**
Your attention, please. Here is an
announcement.
♦ **Alle Achtung!** Well done!
**achtzehn** NUMBER
eighteen
**achtzig** NUMBER
eighty
der **Acker** NOUN (PL die **Äcker**)
field
der **ADAC** NOUN (GEN des **ADAC**)
(= *Allgemeiner Deutscher Automobil-
Club*)
AA (*motoring organization*)
**addieren** VERB (PERFECT **hat addiert**)
to add
der **Adel** NOUN
nobility
die **Ader** NOUN
vein
das **Adjektiv** NOUN (PL die **Adjektive**)
adjective
der **Adler** NOUN (PL die **Adler**)
eagle
**adlig** ADJECTIVE
noble
**adoptieren** VERB (PERFECT **hat adoptiert**)
to adopt
die **Adoption** NOUN
adoption
die **Adoptiveltern** PL NOUN
adoptive parents
das **Adoptivkind** NOUN (PL die **Adoptivkinder**)
adopted child
die **Adresse** NOUN
address
**adressieren** VERB (PERFECT **hat adressiert**)
to address ◊ *An wen soll ich den Brief
adressieren?* To whom should I address
the letter?
die **Adria** NOUN
the Adriatic
der **Advent** NOUN
Advent
der **Adventskalender** NOUN (PL die
**Adventskalender**)
Advent calendar
der **Adventskranz** NOUN (PL die
**Adventskränze**)
Advent wreath
das **Adverb** NOUN (PL die **Adverbien**)
adverb
das **Aerobic** NOUN
aerobics
der **Affe** NOUN (GEN des **Affen**, PL die **Affen**)
monkey
**Afrika** NEUT NOUN
Africa
♦ **aus Afrika** from Africa
♦ **nach Afrika** to Africa
der **Afrikaner** NOUN (PL die **Afrikaner**)
African
die **Afrikanerin** NOUN
African
**afrikanisch** ADJECTIVE
African
**AG** ABBREVIATION (= *Aktiengesellschaft*)
plc
**Ägypten** NEUT NOUN
Egypt ◊ *nach Ägypten* to Egypt
der **Ägypter** NOUN (PL die **Ägypter**)
Egyptian
die **Ägypterin** NOUN
Egyptian
**ägyptisch** ADJECTIVE
Egyptian
**ähneln** VERB
♦ **jemandem ähneln** to resemble
somebody ◊ *Sie ähnelt ihrer Mutter.* She
resembles her mother.
♦ **Sie ähneln sich.** They are alike.
**ahnen** VERB
[1] to know ◊ *Ich habe geahnt, dass er
nicht kommen würde.* I knew he wouldn't
come. ◊ *Das konnte ich doch nicht
ahnen!* How was I supposed to know
that?
[2] to sense ◊ *Das Tier hat die Gefahr
geahnt und ist schnell verschwunden.*
The animal sensed the danger and
quickly disappeared.
**ähnlich** ADJECTIVE
similar ◊ *Unsere Kleider sind sehr
ähnlich.* Our dresses are very similar.
♦ **Er ist seinem Vater sehr ähnlich.** He's
very like his father.
♦ **Das sieht ihr ähnlich!** That's typical of
her.
die **Ähnlichkeit** NOUN
similarity
die **Ahnung** NOUN
[1] idea ◊ *Ich habe keine Ahnung, ob er
kommt.* I've no idea whether he's coming.
♦ **Er hat von Computern keine Ahnung.** He
doesn't know the first thing about
computers.
[2] hunch ◊ *Er hatte eine Ahnung, dass
etwas Schlimmes geschehen würde.* He
had a hunch that something terrible
would happen.
**ahnungslos** ADJECTIVE
unsuspecting
der **Ahorn** NOUN (PL die **Ahorne**)
maple
das **Aids** NOUN (GEN des **Aids**)
AIDS (= Acquired Immune Deficiency
Syndrome) ◊ *Gerd ist an Aids gestorben.*
Gerd died of AIDS.
der **Akademiker** NOUN (PL die **Akademiker**)
university graduate
die **Akademikerin** NOUN
university graduate
**akademisch** ADJECTIVE

academic
der **Akkusativ** NOUN (PL die **Akkusative**)
accusative
die **Akne** NOUN
acne ◊ *Sie hat Akne.* She's got acne.
die **Akte** NOUN
file
♦ **etwas zu den Akten legen** to file something away
die **Aktentasche** NOUN
briefcase
die **Aktie** NOUN
share ◊ *in Aktien investieren* to invest in shares
die **Aktiengesellschaft** NOUN
public limited company
die **Aktion** NOUN
⊞ campaign ◊ *eine Aktion für den Frieden* a campaign for peace
② operation ◊ *Wir alle nahmen an der Aktion teil.* We all took part in the operation.
♦ **in Aktion treten** to go into action ◊ *In solchen Fällen tritt die Feuerwehr in Aktion.* In cases like these, the fire brigade goes into action.
**aktiv** ADJECTIVE
active
die **Aktivität** NOUN
activity
**aktuell** ADJECTIVE
① topical ◊ *ein aktuelles Thema* a topical issue
② up-to-date ◊ *ein aktueller Fahrplan* an up-to-date timetable
*Be careful! aktuell does not mean actual.*
der **Akzent** NOUN (PL die **Akzente**)
① accent ◊ *Sie spricht mit einem amerikanischen Akzent.* She speaks with an American accent.
② emphasis ◊ *Der Akzent unserer Ausstellung liegt auf Benutzerfreundlichkeit.* The emphasis in our exhibition is on user-friendliness.
**albern** ADJECTIVE
silly
♦ **sich albern benehmen** to act silly
der **Albtraum** NOUN (PL die **Albträume**)
nightmare
das **Album** NOUN (PL die **Alben**)
album
die **Algebra** NOUN
algebra
der **Alkohol** NOUN
alcohol
**alkoholfrei** ADJECTIVE
nonalcoholic
der **Alkoholiker** NOUN (PL die **Alkoholiker**)
alcoholic
die **Alkoholikerin** NOUN
alcoholic
**alkoholisch** ADJECTIVE

alcoholic
das **All** NOUN
space ◊ *Sie haben eine Rakete ins All geschossen.* They've sent a rocket into space.
**alle** ADJECTIVE, PRONOUN
*see also* **alles** PRONOUN
① all the ◊ *Alle Schüler sollten kommen.* All the pupils should come.
② all ◊ *Nicht alle Afrikaner sind schwarz.* Not all Africans are black.
③ all of them ◊ *Wir haben alle gesehen.* We saw all of them.
♦ **Sie kamen alle.** They all came.
♦ **wir alle** all of us
♦ **Ich habe alle beide eingeladen.** I've invited both of them.
④ every ◊ *alle vier Jahre* every four years ◊ *alle fünf Meter* every five metres
♦ **Die Milch ist alle.** The milk's all gone.
♦ **etwas alle machen** to finish something up
die **Allee** NOUN (PL die **Alleen**)
avenue
**allein** ADJECTIVE, ADVERB, CONJUNCTION
① alone ◊ *Sie lebt allein.* She lives alone. ◊ *Du allein kannst das entscheiden.* You alone can decide.
② on one's own ◊ *Sie hat das ganz allein geschrieben.* She wrote that all on her own. ◊ *Seit ich allein bin, habe ich mehr Zeit.* Since I've been on my own, I've had more time.
♦ **Er fühlt sich allein.** He feels lonely.
♦ **nicht allein** not only
♦ **allein stehend** single
**allerbeste** ADJECTIVE
very best ◊ *Felix ist mein allerbester Schüler.* Felix is my very best pupil.
**allerdings** ADVERB
① though ◊ *Der Urlaub war schön, allerdings etwas kurz.* The holiday was nice, though it was rather short. ◊ *Ich werde kommen, kann allerdings nicht lange bleiben.* I'll come. I can't stay long, though.
② certainly ◊ *Das ist allerdings schwierig.* That's certainly difficult.
die **Allergie** NOUN
allergy
**allergisch** ADJECTIVE
allergic ◊ *Sie ist allergisch gegen Katzen.* She's allergic to cats.
das **Allerheiligen** NOUN
All Saints' Day

ℹ *Allerheiligen (November 1st) is a public holiday in those parts of Germany where most of the population are Roman Catholics.*

**allerhöchstens** ADVERB
at the very most

**allerlei** ADJECTIVE
<u>all sorts of</u> ◊ *allerlei Sachen* all sorts of things

**allerletzte** ADJECTIVE
<u>very last</u> ◊ *zum allerletzten Mal* for the very last time

**allerseits** ADVERB
<u>on all sides</u> ◊ *Dieser Vorschlag fand allerseits Zustimmung.* This suggestion met with approval on all sides.
♦ **Prost allerseits!** Cheers, everyone!

**alles** PRONOUN
│ *see also* **alle** ADJECTIVE, PRONOUN │
<u>everything</u> ◊ *Sie haben alles aufgegessen.* They've eaten everything up.
♦ **alles, was er sagt** everything he says
♦ **alles in Allem** all in all
♦ **Alles Gute!** All the best!

**allgemein** ADJECTIVE
<u>general</u>
♦ **im Allgemeinen** in general

**allmählich** ADJECTIVE, ADVERB
① <u>gradual</u> ◊ *eine allmähliche Besserung* a gradual improvement
② <u>gradually</u> ◊ *Es wird allmählich wärmer.* It's gradually getting warmer.
♦ **Allmählich solltest du das wissen.** You should know that by now.

der **Alltag** NOUN
<u>everyday life</u>

**allzu** ADVERB
<u>all too</u> ◊ *allzu oft* all too often
♦ **allzu viel** far too much

die **Alm** NOUN
<u>alpine pasture</u>

die **Alpen** PL NOUN
<u>Alps</u>

das **Alphabet** NOUN (PL die **Alphabete**)
<u>alphabet</u>

**alphabetisch** ADJECTIVE
<u>alphabetical</u> ◊ *alphabetisch geordnet* arranged in alphabetical order

der **Alptraum** NOUN (PL die **Alpträume**)
<u>nightmare</u>

**als** CONJUNCTION
① <u>when</u> ◊ *Als ich ein Kind war ...* When I was a child ...
② <u>as</u> ◊ *Sie kam, als ich gerade gehen wollte.* She arrived as I was about to leave. ◊ *Ich als Lehrerin weiß, ...* As a teacher, I know ...
♦ **gerade, als ...** just as ...
♦ **als ob** as if ◊ *Er tat, als ob er nichts bemerkt hätte.* He acted as if he hadn't noticed anything.
③ <u>than</u> ◊ *Sie ist älter als ich.* She's older than me. ◊ *Ich kam später als er.* I came later than he did.
♦ **lieber als ...** rather than ... ◊ *Ich mag Süßes lieber als Salziges.* I like sweet things rather than savoury things.
♦ **nichts als Ärger** nothing but trouble

**also** ADVERB, CONJUNCTION, EXCLAMATION
① <u>then</u> ◊ *Was sollen wir also tun?* What shall we do, then? ◊ *Du willst also nicht mit.* You don't want to come along, then. ◊ *Du hast es also gewusst.* You did know then.
② <u>so</u> ◊ *Es war schon spät, also bin ich nach Hause gegangen.* It had got late, so I went home.
③ <u>well</u> ◊ *Also ich gehe jetzt!* Well, I'm off now. ◊ *Also, Sie fahren immer geradeaus ...* Well, keep going straight on ...
♦ **Also gut!** Okay then.
♦ **Also, so was!** Well really!
♦ **Na also!** There you are then!
*Be careful! The German word **also** does not mean also.*

**alt** ADJECTIVE
<u>old</u> ◊ *Wie alt bist du?* How old are you? ◊ *Felix ist zehn Jahre alt.* Felix is ten years old. ◊ *Sein Auto ist älter als unseres.* His car is older than ours. ◊ *Das ist meine ältere Schwester.* That's my elder sister. ◊ *Mein ältester Bruder heißt Thomas.* My eldest brother's called Thomas.
♦ **alles beim Alten lassen** to leave everything as it was

der **Altar** NOUN (PL die **Altäre**)
<u>altar</u>

das **Alter** NOUN (PL die **Alter**)
① <u>age</u> ◊ *In deinem Alter sollte man das wissen.* You ought to know that at your age.
② <u>old age</u> ◊ *Im Alter sind die Menschen oft einsam.* People are often lonely in old age.
♦ **im Alter von** at the age of

die **Altersgrenze** NOUN
<u>age limit</u>

das **Altglas** NOUN (GEN des **Altglases**)
<u>used glass</u>

der **Altglascontainer** NOUN (PL die **Altglascontainer**)
<u>bottle bank</u>

**altmodisch** ADJECTIVE
<u>old-fashioned</u>

das **Altpapier** NOUN
<u>waste paper</u>

die **Altstadt** NOUN (PL die **Altstädte**)
<u>old town</u>

die **Alufolie** NOUN
<u>tinfoil</u>

das **Aluminium** NOUN
<u>aluminium</u>

der **Alzheimer** NOUN
<u>Alzheimer's</u> ◊ *Sie hat Alzheimer.* She's got Alzheimer's.

**am = an dem**
♦ **am fünften März** on the fifth of March
♦ **am höchsten** the highest
♦ **am schönsten** the most beautiful

die **Ameise** NOUN
 ant
**Amerika** NEUT NOUN
 America
 ♦ **aus Amerika** from America
 ♦ **in Amerika** in America
 ♦ **nach Amerika** to America
der **Amerikaner** NOUN (PL die **Amerikaner**)
 American
die **Amerikanerin** NOUN
 American
**amerikanisch** ADJECTIVE
 American
die **Ampel** NOUN
 traffic lights ◊ *Die Ampel ist grün.* The
 traffic lights are at green.
die **Amsel** NOUN
 blackbird
das **Amt** NOUN (PL die **Ämter**)
 office ◊ *Welches Amt ist für Kindergeld
 zuständig?* Which office deals with child
 benefit?
**amtlich** ADJECTIVE
 official
**amüsant** ADJECTIVE
 amusing
**amüsieren** VERB (PERFECT **hat amüsiert**)
 to amuse ◊ *Diese Geschichte hat uns
 sehr amüsiert.* The story amused us very
 much.
 ♦ **sich amüsieren** to enjoy oneself ◊ *Wir
 haben uns blendend amüsiert.* We
 enjoyed ourselves immensely.
**an** PREPOSITION, ADVERB

 | see also **am** |

 *Use the accusative to express movement
 or a change of place. Use the dative
 when there is no change of place.*
 [1] on ◊ *Das Wort stand an der Tafel.* The
 word was written on the blackboard.
 ◊ *Der Lehrer schrieb das Wort an die
 Tafel.* The teacher wrote the word on the
 blackboard.
 [2] to ◊ *Er ging ans Fenster.* He went to
 the window. ◊ *Wir waren gestern am
 Meer.* We went to the seaside yesterday.
 ◊ *Wir wollen morgen ans Meer fahren.*
 We want to go to the seaside tomorrow.
 ◊ *Ich habe einen Brief an meine Mutter
 geschrieben.* I've written a letter to my
 mother.
 ♦ **eine Frage an dich** a question for you
 ♦ **an diesem Ort** in this place
 ♦ **unten am Fluss** down by the river
 [3] by ◊ *Ihr Haus liegt an der Autobahn.*
 Their house is by the motorway.
 ♦ **Köln liegt am Rhein.** Cologne is on the
 Rhine.
 ♦ **am neunten November** on the ninth of
 November
 ♦ **an diesem Tag** on this day
 ♦ **an Ostern** at Easter
 ♦ **an etwas denken** to think of something

 ♦ **reich an Nährstoffen** rich in nutrients
 ♦ **an etwas sterben** to die of something
 ♦ **an und für sich** actually ◊ *Das ist an und
 für sich ganz einfach.* Actually, it's quite
 simple.
 ♦ **an die hundert** about a hundred
 ♦ **von heute an** from today onwards
 ♦ **Das Licht ist an.** The light's on.
 ♦ **ohne etwas an** with nothing on
die **Ananas** NOUN (PL die **Ananas**)
 pineapple
**anbauen** VERB (PERFECT **hat angebaut**)
 [1] to build on ◊ *eine Garage ans Haus
 anbauen* to build a garage onto the
 house
 [2] to cultivate ◊ *Reis anbauen* to
 cultivate rice
**anbei** ADVERB
 enclosed
**anbieten** VERB (IMPERFECT **bot an**, PERFECT **hat
 angeboten**)
 to offer ◊ *Ich bot ihr eine Tasse Kaffee
 an.* I offered her a cup of coffee.
 ♦ **Kann ich dir etwas zum Trinken
 anbieten?** Can I get you something to
 drink?
 ♦ **anbieten, etwas zu tun** to volunteer to
 do something ◊ *Er hat angeboten, mir
 beim Umzug zu helfen.* He volunteered
 to help me move house.
der **Anblick** NOUN (PL die **Anblicke**)
 sight
**anbrechen** VERB (PRESENT **bricht an**, IMPERFECT
 **brach an**, PERFECT **ist/hat angebrochen**)
 *For the perfect tense use **haben** when
 the verb has an object and **sein** when
 there is no object.*
 [1] to break into ◊ *Für den Kauf müsste
 ich meine Ersparnisse anbrechen.* To buy
 it, I'd have to break into my savings.
 [2] to dawn ◊ *Ein neues Zeitalter ist
 angebrochen.* A new age has dawned.
 [3] to break ◊ *wenn der Tag anbricht*
 when day breaks
**anbrennen** VERB (IMPERFECT **brannte an**,
 PERFECT **ist angebrannt**)
 to burn ◊ *Der Kuchen ist angebrannt.*
 The cake's burnt.
**andauernd** ADJECTIVE, ADVERB
 [1] continual ◊ *diese andauernden
 Unterbrechungen* these continual
 interruptions
 [2] constantly ◊ *Er stört andauernd.* He's
 constantly interrupting.
das **Andenken** NOUN (PL die **Andenken**)
 [1] memory ◊ *Zum Andenken an eine
 schöne Zeit.* In memory of a wonderful
 time.
 [2] souvenir ◊ *Ich habe mir aus dem
 Urlaub einige Andenken mitgebracht.* I
 brought a few souvenirs back from my
 holiday.
**andere** ADJECTIVE, PRONOUN

**andererseits → anfreunden**

**1** other ◊ *Nein, nicht dieses Buch, gib mir bitte das andere.* No, not that book, please give me the other one.

**2** different ◊ *Er hat jetzt eine andere Freundin.* He's got a different girlfriend now.

**3** another ◊ *ein anderes Mal* another time ◊ *Wir werden das an einem anderen Tag machen.* We'll do that another day.

◆ **kein anderer** nobody else

◆ **die anderen** the others ◊ *Martin ist noch da, die anderen sind schon gegangen.* Martin's still here, the others have already left.

◆ **andere** other ones ◊ *Wenn Ihnen dieses Kleid nicht gefällt, haben wir auch andere.* If you don't like this dress, we also have other ones.

◆ **etwas anderes** something else ◊ *von etwas anderem sprechen* to talk about something else

**andererseits** ADVERB
on the other hand ◊ *Einerseits ..., andererseits ...* On the one hand ..., on the other hand ...

**andermal** ADVERB
◆ **ein andermal** some other time

**ändern** VERB
to alter ◊ *Ich habe das Kleid ändern lassen.* I've had the dress altered.

◆ **So ist das nun mal, ich kann's nicht ändern.** That's the way it is. I can't do anything about it.

◆ **sich ändern** to change ◊ *Sie hat sich in letzter Zeit sehr geändert.* She's changed a lot recently. ◊ *Wenn sich die Lage nicht ändert ...* If the situation doesn't change ...

**anders** ADVERB
differently ◊ *So geht das nicht, du musst das anders machen.* Not like that – you have to do it differently.

◆ **anders als** different from ◊ *Sie ist ganz anders als ihr Bruder.* She's quite different from her brother. ◊ *Sie hat das anders als ich übersetzt.* She translated it differently from me.

◆ **Wer anders?** Who else?

◆ **jemand anders** somebody else

◆ **irgendwo anders** somewhere else

◆ **anders aussehen** to look different

**anderthalb** ADJECTIVE
one and a half

**die Änderung** NOUN
alteration

**andeuten** VERB (PERFECT **hat angedeutet**)
to hint ◊ *Sie hat angedeutet, dass sie weiß, wer es war.* She's hinted that she knows who it was.

**die Andeutung** NOUN
hint ◊ *Sie hat eine Andeutung gemacht, dass sie es weiß.* She hinted that she knew.

**anerkennend** ADJECTIVE, ADVERB
appreciative

◆ **Sie sprach sehr anerkennend von seiner Leistung.** She spoke very appreciatively of his work.

**die Anerkennung** NOUN

**1** appreciation ◊ *Ihre Leistung fand nicht die entsprechende Anerkennung.* Her work didn't get the appreciation it deserved.

**2** recognition ◊ *Dieser neue Staat hofft auf Anerkennung durch die Bundesrepublik.* This new country is hoping for recognition by the Federal Republic.

**anfahren** VERB (PRESENT **fährt an**, IMPERFECT **fuhr an**, PERFECT **hat/ist angefahren**)

**1** to hit ◊ *Er hat einen Fußgänger angefahren.* He hit a pedestrian.

**2** to start up ◊ *beim Anfahren* when starting up

**der Anfall** NOUN (PL die **Anfälle**)
fit ◊ *Sie hatte einen epileptischen Anfall.* She had an epileptic fit. ◊ *Wenn er das erfährt, bekommt er einen Anfall.* If he finds out, he'll have a fit.

**der Anfang** NOUN (PL die **Anfänge**)
beginning ◊ *von Anfang an* right from the beginning

◆ **am Anfang** at the beginning

◆ **zu Anfang** first

◆ **Anfang Mai** at the beginning of May

**anfangen** VERB (PRESENT **fängt an**, IMPERFECT **fing an**, PERFECT **hat angefangen**)

**1** to begin ◊ *Es fängt an zu regnen.* It's beginning to rain. ◊ *Märchen fangen mit dem Satz an: "Es war einmal".* Fairy tales begin with the words: "Once upon a time".

**2** to start ◊ *Der Film hat schon angefangen.* The film's already started. ◊ *Hast du den Aufsatz schon angefangen?* Have you already started your essay?

◆ **Damit kann ich nichts anfangen.** It doesn't mean anything to me.

◆ **Das fängt ja gut an!** That's a good start!

**der Anfänger** NOUN (PL die **Anfänger**)
beginner

**anfassen** VERB (PERFECT **hat angefasst**)

**1** to touch ◊ *Fass den Hund besser nicht an!* You'd better not touch the dog.

**2** to treat ◊ *Du solltest die Kinder nicht immer so rau anfassen!* You shouldn't treat the children so roughly.

◆ **mit anfassen** to lend a hand ◊ *Kannst du mal mit anfassen, den Schrank wegzuschieben?* Can you lend a hand shifting this cupboard to one side?

◆ **sich anfassen** to feel ◊ *Samt fühlt sich weich an.* Velvet feels soft.

**sich anfreunden** VERB (PERFECT **hat sich angefreundet**)

1 to make friends ◊ *Ich habe mich in den Ferien mit einer Engländerin angefreundet.* I made friends with an English girl during the holidays.

2 to become friends ◊ *Die beiden haben sich angefreundet.* The two of them have become friends.

**anfühlen** VERB (PERFECT **hat angefühlt**)
to feel ◊ *Fühl mal meine Stirn an, ich glaube, ich habe Fieber.* Feel my forehead, I think I've got a temperature. ◊ *Der Stoff fühlt sich weich an.* The material feels soft.

die **Anführungszeichen** NEUT PL NOUN
inverted commas

die **Angabe** NOUN
1 information ◊ *Die Angaben waren falsch.* The information was wrong.
2 serve (*tennis*) ◊ *Wer hat Angabe?* Whose serve is it?
♦ **Das ist doch alles nur Angabe!** That's nothing but show.

**angeben** VERB (PRESENT **gibt an,** IMPERFECT **gab an,** PERFECT **hat angegeben**)
1 to give ◊ *Geben Sie bitte Ihre Personalien an.* Please give your personal details.
2 to state ◊ *Sie hat angegeben, dass sie zu dem Zeitpunkt zu Hause war.* She stated that she was at home at the time.
3 to indicate ◊ *Alle Raststätten sind auf der Karte angegeben.* All service areas are indicated on the map.
4 to show off ◊ *Glaub ihm kein Wort, er gibt nur an.* Don't believe a word he says – he's just showing off.

der **Angeber** NOUN (PL die **Angeber**)
show-off

**angeblich** ADJECTIVE, ADVERB
1 alleged ◊ *Sie ist die angebliche Täterin.* She's the alleged culprit.
2 allegedly ◊ *Angeblich hat sie es getan.* Allegedly, she did it.

das **Angebot** NOUN (PL die **Angebote**)
offer ◊ *Ich nehme dein Angebot an.* I accept your offer.
♦ **ein Angebot an etwas** a selection of something ◊ *Das Kaufhaus hat ein großes Angebot an Kleidern.* The department store has a large selection of dresses.
♦ **Angebot und Nachfrage** supply and demand

**angeheitert** ADJECTIVE
tipsy

**angehen** VERB (IMPERFECT **ging an,** PERFECT **hat/ist angegangen**)
*For the perfect tense use **haben** when the verb has an object and **sein** when there is no object.*
1 to concern ◊ *Diese Angelegenheit geht mich nichts an.* This matter doesn't concern me.

♦ **Was geht dich das an?** What business is it of yours?
2 to tackle ◊ *Ich weiß noch nicht so richtig, wie ich das Thema angehen soll.* I'm not really sure how to tackle the subject.
3 to light ◊ *Das Holz war zu nass, also ist das Feuer nicht angegangen.* The wood was too wet, so the fire wouldn't light.
4 to go on ◊ *Das Licht ging an.* The light went on.
♦ **was ... angeht** as regards ... ◊ *Was die Ferien angeht, haben wir noch nichts entschieden.* As regards the holidays, we still haven't decided anything.

**angehend** ADJECTIVE
prospective

der die **Angehörige** NOUN (GEN des/der **Angehörigen,** PL die **Angehörigen**)
relative ◊ *Er ist ein Angehöriger von mir.* He's a relative of mine.

die **Angel** NOUN
1 fishing rod
2 hinge (*Türangel*)
*Be careful! The German word **Angel** does not mean **angel**.*

die **Angelegenheit** NOUN
1 matter ◊ *Ich werde diese Angelegenheit prüfen.* I'll look into the matter.
2 affair ◊ *Das ist meine Angelegenheit.* That's my affair.

**angeln** VERB
1 to catch ◊ *Er hat eine große Forelle geangelt.* He caught a large trout.
2 to fish ◊ *Sonntags geht Alex immer angeln.* Alex always goes fishing on Sundays.

die **Angelrute** NOUN
fishing rod

**angenehm** ADJECTIVE, ADVERB
pleasant
♦ **Der Motor ist angenehm leise.** The engine is pleasantly quiet.
♦ **Angenehm!** Pleased to meet you.

**angesehen** ADJECTIVE
respected

der die **Angestellte** NOUN (GEN des/der **Angestellten,** PL die **Angestellten**)
employee ◊ *Er ist nur ein kleiner Angestellter.* He's just a lowly employee.
♦ **Sie ist Angestellte bei der Firma Boll & Co.** She works at Boll & Co.

**angewiesen** ADJECTIVE
♦ **auf jemanden angewiesen sein** to be dependent on somebody
♦ **auf etwas angewiesen sein** to be dependent on something

**angewöhnen** VERB (PERFECT **hat angewöhnt**)
♦ **jemandem etwas angewöhnen** to teach somebody something ◊ *Sie sollten Ihrem*

*Sohn bessere Manieren angewöhnen.*
You ought to teach your son better
manners.

♦ **sich etwas angewöhnen** to get into the
habit of doing something ◊ *Ich habe es
mir angewöhnt, jeden Morgen um
sieben Uhr aufzustehen.* I've got into the
habit of getting up at seven every
morning.

die **Angewohnheit** NOUN
<u>habit</u> ◊ *Das ist so eine Angewohnheit
von ihr.* That's a habit of hers.

**angreifen** VERB (IMPERFECT **griff an**, PERFECT **hat
angegriffen**)
[1] <u>to attack</u> ◊ *Ich wurde von einem Hund
angegriffen.* I was attacked by a dog.
[2] <u>to criticize</u> ◊ *Sie wurde wegen dieser
Aussage von ihren Freunden
angegriffen.* She was criticized by her
friends for what she said.

der **Angriff** NOUN (PL die **Angriffe**)
<u>attack</u>
♦ **etwas in Angriff nehmen** to make a start
on something

die **Angst** NOUN (PL die **Ängste**)
<u>fear</u>
♦ **vor jemandem Angst haben** to be afraid
of somebody
♦ **vor etwas Angst haben** to be afraid of
something
♦ **Ich habe Angst vor der Prüfung.** I'm
worried about the exam.
♦ **Angst um jemanden haben** to be worried
about somebody
♦ **Mir ist angst.** I'm afraid.
♦ **jemandem Angst machen** to scare
somebody

**ängstlich** ADJECTIVE, ADVERB
[1] <u>scared</u> ◊ *Nun sei doch nicht so
ängstlich, der Hund tut dir nichts!*
There's no need to be scared, the dog
won't harm you.
[2] <u>anxious</u> ◊ *"Wird er wieder gesund?",
fragte sie ängstlich.* "Will he get well
again?", she asked anxiously.

**anhaben** VERB (PRESENT **hat an**, IMPERFECT
**hatte an**, PERFECT **hat angehabt**)
<u>to have on</u> ◊ *Sie hatte heute das rote
Kleid an.* She had her red dress on today.
♦ **jemandem nichts anhaben können** to
have nothing on somebody ◊ *Ich bin
unschuldig, die Polizei kann mir nichts
anhaben.* I'm innocent, the police have
got nothing on me.

**anhalten** VERB (PRESENT **hält an**, IMPERFECT
**hielt an**, PERFECT **hat angehalten**)
[1] <u>to stop</u> ◊ *Können wir bitte anhalten,
mir ist schlecht.* Can we stop please? I
feel sick. ◊ *Kannst du bitte das Auto
anhalten?* Can you stop the car please?
[2] <u>to last</u> ◊ *Das wird nicht lange
anhalten.* It won't last long.
♦ **die Luft anhalten** to hold one's breath

der **Anhalter** NOUN (PL die **Anhalter**)
<u>hitchhiker</u>
♦ **per Anhalter fahren** to hitchhike

**anhand** PREPOSITION
*The preposition* **anhand** *takes the
genitive.*
<u>with the help of</u> ◊ *Wir werden das
anhand der Unterlagen prüfen.* We'll
check that with the help of the
documents.

der **Anhang** NOUN (PL die **Anhänge**)
<u>appendix</u>

der **Anhänger** NOUN (PL die **Anhänger**)
[1] <u>supporter</u> ◊ *Er ist Anhänger von
Borussia Dortmund.* He's a Borussia
Dortmund supporter.
[2] <u>trailer</u> (*on car*)
[3] <u>label</u> ◊ *Mach einen Anhänger mit
deinem Namen und deiner Adresse an
deinen Koffer.* Put a label with your
name and address on your case.
[4] <u>pendant</u> ◊ *Sie trug eine Kette mit
Anhänger.* She was wearing a chain with
a pendant.

die **Anhängerin** NOUN
<u>supporter</u> ◊ *Sie ist Anhängerin von
Borussia Dortmund.* She's a Borussia
Dortmund supporter.

**anhören** VERB (PERFECT **hat angehört**)
<u>to listen to</u> ◊ *Wir haben CDs angehört.*
We listened to CDs.
♦ **jemandem etwas anhören** to hear
something in somebody's voice ◊ *Man
hat ihr ihre Aufregung angehört.* You
could hear the excitement in her voice.
♦ **sich anhören** to sound ◊ *Der Vorschlag
hört sich gut an.* That sounds a good
suggestion.

der **Anker** NOUN (PL die **Anker**)
<u>anchor</u>

der **Anklang** NOUN
♦ **bei jemandem Anklang finden** to meet
with somebody's approval

die **Ankleidekabine** NOUN
<u>changing cubicle</u>

**anklicken** VERB (PERFECT **hat angeklickt**)
<u>to click on</u> (*computer*) ◊ *ein Icon
anklicken* to click on an icon

**ankommen** VERB (IMPERFECT **kam an**, PERFECT
**ist angekommen**)
<u>to arrive</u> ◊ *Wir kommen morgen
Nachmittag an.* We'll arrive tomorrow
afternoon. ◊ *Ist der Brief schon
angekommen?* Has the letter arrived yet?
♦ **bei jemandem gut ankommen** to go
down well with somebody ◊ *Das Stück
ist bei den Zuschauern gut
angekommen.* The play went down well
with the audience.
♦ **bei jemandem schlecht ankommen** to go
down badly with somebody ◊ *Der Witz
ist offensichtlich schlecht angekommen.*
The joke clearly went down badly.

**A**

♦ **es kommt darauf an** it depends ◊ *Es kommt darauf an, wie das Wetter ist.* It depends what the weather's like.

♦ **Es kommt auf jeden einzelnen von uns an.** It depends on each and every one of us.

♦ **wenn es darauf ankommt ...** when it really matters ...

♦ **Bei diesem Beruf kommt es auf Genauigkeit an.** What matters in this job is accuracy.

♦ **es darauf ankommen lassen** to wait and see

**ankreuzen** VERB (PERFECT **hat angekreuzt**)
to mark with a cross

**ankündigen** VERB (PERFECT **hat angekündigt**)
to announce

die **Ankunft** NOUN (PL die **Ankünfte**)
arrival

die **Ankunftszeit** NOUN
arrival time

die **Anlage** NOUN
[1] gardens ◊ *Wir sind in der Anlage spazieren gegangen.* We went for a walk in the gardens.
[2] plant ◊ *Das ist eine neuartige Anlage zum Recycling von Kunststoff.* That's a new plastics recycling plant.
[3] investment ◊ *Wir raten zu einer Anlage in Immobilien.* We would advise investment in real estate.

der **Anlass** NOUN (GEN des **Anlasses**, PL die **Anlässe**)
occasion ◊ *ein festlicher Anlass* a festive occasion

♦ **ein Anlass zu etwas** cause for something ◊ *Das ist ein Anlass zum Feiern.* That's cause for celebration.

♦ **aus Anlass** on the occasion of ◊ *Aus Anlass ihres fünfzigsten Geburtstags ...* On the occasion of her fiftieth birthday ...

♦ **Anlass zu etwas geben** to give cause for something ◊ *Ihr Sohn gibt keinen Anlass zu Klagen.* Your son doesn't give cause for complaint.

der **Anlasser** NOUN (PL die **Anlasser**)
starter (*of car*)

die **Anleitung** NOUN
instructions

der **Anlieger** NOUN (PL die **Anlieger**)
resident ◊ *"Anlieger frei"* "residents only"

**anmachen** VERB (PERFECT **hat angemacht**)
[1] to put on ◊ *Mach bitte das Licht an.* Please put the light on.
[2] to light ◊ *Wir haben ein Feuer angemacht.* We lit a fire.
[3] to dress ◊ *Sie macht den Salat immer mit Zitrone an.* She always dresses her salads with lemon.
[4] to chat up ◊ *Ich glaube, der Typ versucht, dich anzumachen.*

I think that bloke is trying to chat you up.

das **Anmeldeformular** NOUN (PL die **Anmeldeformulare**)
registration form

**anmelden** VERB (PERFECT **hat angemeldet**)
to announce ◊ *Sie hat für morgen ihren Besuch angemeldet.* She's announced that she'll visit us tomorrow.

♦ **jemanden anmelden (1)** to make an appointment for somebody ◊ *Er hat seinen Sohn für morgen beim Zahnarzt angemeldet.* He's made a dental appointment for his son for tomorrow.

♦ **jemanden anmelden (2)** to put somebody's name down ◊ *Habt ihr Maximilian schon im Gymnasium angemeldet?* Have you already put Maximilian's name down for grammar school?

♦ **sich anmelden (1)** to make an appointment ◊ *Ich muss mich beim Zahnarzt anmelden.* I must make an appointment with the dentist.

♦ **sich anmelden (2)** to put one's name down ◊ *Sie hat sich für einen Judokurs angemeldet.* She's put her name down for a judo course.

♦ **Alle Besucher müssen sich beim Pförtner anmelden.** All visitors must report to the gatehouse.

♦ **Haben Sie sich schon beim Einwohnermeldeamt angemeldet?** Have you already registered with the residents' registration office?

> *i* *Anyone moving to a new address in Germany is required by law to register* (**sich anmelden**) *at the residents' registration office* (**Einwohnermeldeamt**).

die **Anmeldung** NOUN
registration ◊ *Schluss für Anmeldungen ist der erste Mai.* The deadline for registrations is the first of May.

**annehmen** VERB (PRESENT **nimmt an,** IMPERFECT **nahm an,** PERFECT **hat angenommen**)
[1] to accept ◊ *Sie wollte das Geschenk nicht annehmen.* She didn't want to accept the present. ◊ *Danke für die Einladung, ich nehme gerne an.* Thank you for the invitation, which I'm happy to accept.
[2] to take ◊ *Er hat den Namen seiner Frau angenommen.* He took his wife's name.

♦ **ein Kind annehmen** to adopt a child
[3] to believe ◊ *Die Polizei nimmt an, dass er der Täter war.* The police believe he did it.

☞

4 to suppose ◊ *Nehmen wir einmal an, es wäre so.* Let's suppose that was the case.

♦ **angenommen** ... supposing ... ◊ *Angenommen, er kommt nicht.* Supposing he doesn't come.

**anordnen** VERB (PERFECT **hat angeordnet**)
1 to arrange ◊ *Er ordnete die Blumen zu einem hübschen Gesteck an.* He arranged the flowers into a pretty bouquet.
2 to order ◊ *Wer hat das angeordnet?* Who ordered that?

**anprobieren** VERB (PERFECT **hat anprobiert**)
to try on

die **Anrede** NOUN
form of address ◊ *Für verheiratete und unverheiratete Frauen benutzt man die Anrede "Frau".* "Frau" is the form of address used for married and unmarried women.

der **Anruf** NOUN (PL die **Anrufe**)
phone call

der **Anrufbeantworter** NOUN (PL die **Anrufbeantworter**)
answering machine

**anrufen** VERB (IMPERFECT **rief an,** PERFECT **hat angerufen**)
to phone ◊ *Hat jemand angerufen?* Did anyone phone? ◊ *Ich muss mal eben meine Eltern anrufen.* I must just phone my parents. ◊ *Ruf mal bei Wengels an, vielleicht ist sie dort.* Phone the Wengels; perhaps she's there.

**ans** = **an das**

**anschalten** VERB (PERFECT **hat angeschaltet**)
to switch on

**anschauen** VERB (PERFECT **hat angeschaut**)
to look at ◊ *Schau mich an!* Look at me.
♦ **Willst du dir mal die Fotos anschauen?** Do you want to have a look at the photos?
♦ **Den Film will ich mir unbedingt anschauen.** I must go and see that film.

**anscheinend** ADVERB
apparently

der **Anschlag** NOUN (PL die **Anschläge**)
1 notice ◊ *Sie machte einen Anschlag am schwarzen Brett.* She put a notice on the notice board.
2 attack ◊ *Es gab einen Anschlag auf den Präsidenten.* There's been an attack on the President.

**anschließen** VERB (IMPERFECT **schloss an,** PERFECT **hat angeschlossen**)
1 to connect ◊ *Das Telefon ist noch nicht angeschlossen.* The telephone hasn't been connected yet.
2 to follow ◊ *Wir können an den Vortrag gern noch eine Diskussion anschließen.* We can of course follow the lecture with a discussion.

♦ **sich jemandem anschließen** to join somebody ◊ *Wir gehen ins Kino, willst du dich uns nicht anschließen?* We're going to the cinema. Won't you join us?
♦ **Ich schließe mich dieser Meinung an.** I endorse this view.

**anschließend** ADJECTIVE, ADVERB
1 subsequent ◊ *die daran anschließende Diskussion* the subsequent discussion
2 adjacent ◊ *das anschließende Grundstück* the adjacent plot of land
3 afterwards ◊ *Wir waren essen, und anschließend sind wir ins Kino gegangen.* We had a meal and afterwards went to the cinema.

der **Anschluss** NOUN (GEN des **Anschlusses,** PL die **Anschlüsse**)
connection ◊ *Sie haben Anschluss an einen Zug nach Paris.* You have a connection with a train to Paris.
♦ **im Anschluss an** following ◊ *Im Anschluss an die Ansprache findet ein Empfang statt.* Following the speech there will be a reception.
♦ **Anschluss finden** to make friends ◊ *Sie hat in der neuen Klasse schnell Anschluss gefunden.* She quickly made friends in her new class.

sich **anschnallen** VERB (PERFECT **hat sich angeschnallt**)
to fasten one's seat belt

die **Anschrift** NOUN
address

**ansehen** VERB (PRESENT **sieht an,** IMPERFECT **sah an,** PERFECT **hat angesehen**)
| *see also* **das Ansehen** NOUN |
1 to look at ◊ *Sieh mich an!* Look at me.
♦ **Willst du dir mal die Fotos ansehen?** Do you want to have a look at the photos?
♦ **Den Film will ich mir unbedingt ansehen.** I must go and see that film.
♦ **Man hat ihr ihre Enttäuschung angesehen.** You could see the disappointment in her face.
2 to regard ◊ *Sie wird als eine Expertin auf diesem Gebiet angesehen.* She's regarded as an expert in this field.
♦ **Sieh mal einer an!** Well, fancy that!

das **Ansehen** NOUN
| *see also* **ansehen** VERB |
1 respect ◊ *Sie genießt großes Ansehen bei ihren Kollegen.* She enjoys great respect among her colleagues.
2 reputation ◊ *Ein solches Benehmen könnte unserem Ansehen schaden.* Behaviour like that could damage our reputation.

die **Ansicht** NOUN
view ◊ *eine Postkarte mit der Ansicht des Matterhorns* a postcard with a view of the Matterhorn ◊ *Wenn Sie meine Ansicht in dieser Sache hören wollen ...* If

you want to hear my view on this business ...
♦ **zur Ansicht** on approval
♦ **meiner Ansicht nach** in my view
die **Ansichtskarte** NOUN
  picture postcard
die **Ansichtssache** NOUN
  matter of opinion
**ansprechen** VERB (PRESENT **spricht an,** IMPERFECT **sprach an,** PERFECT **hat angesprochen**)
  [1] to approach ◊ *Mich hat ein wildfremder Mann angesprochen.* I was approached by a complete stranger.
  [2] to appeal to ◊ *Diese Art von Malerei spricht mich nicht an.* This style of painting doesn't appeal to me.
  [3] to ask ◊ *Ich werde Herrn Arnold ansprechen, ob er uns vielleicht hilft.* I'll ask Mr Arnold if he'll maybe help us.
  [4] to mention ◊ *Sie hat dieses Problem bis jetzt noch nicht angesprochen.* She hasn't mentioned this problem yet.
  ♦ **auf etwas ansprechen** to respond to something ◊ *Der Patient spricht auf die Medikamente nicht an.* The patient isn't responding to the drugs.
der **Anspruch** NOUN (PL die **Ansprüche**)
  demand ◊ *Sie war den Ansprüchen ihres Berufs nicht gewachsen.* She wasn't up to the demands of her job.
  ♦ **hohe Ansprüche haben** to demand a lot
  ♦ **hohe Ansprüche an jemanden stellen** to demand a lot of somebody
  ♦ **Anspruch auf etwas haben** to be entitled to something ◊ *Ich habe Anspruch auf eine Erklärung.* I'm entitled to an explanation.
  ♦ **etwas in Anspruch nehmen** to take advantage of something ◊ *Wir sollten dieses Angebot in Anspruch nehmen.* We should take advantage of this offer.
  ♦ **Ihr Beruf nimmt sie sehr in Anspruch.** Her job's very demanding.
**anständig** ADJECTIVE
  decent ◊ *ein anständiges Essen* a decent meal
  ♦ **Ich bin eine anständige Frau!** I'm a respectable woman.
  ♦ **sich anständig benehmen** to behave oneself
**anstarren** VERB (PERFECT **hat angestarrt**)
  to stare at
**anstatt** PREPOSITION, CONJUNCTION
  *The preposition* **anstatt** *takes the genitive.*
  instead of ◊ *Sie kam anstatt ihres Bruders.* She came instead of her brother.
  ♦ **anstatt etwas zu tun** instead of doing something
**anstecken** VERB (PERFECT **hat angesteckt**)

♦ **Er hat die halbe Klasse mit seiner Grippe angesteckt.** He gave half the class his flu.
♦ **Lachen steckt an.** Laughter is infectious.
♦ **sich anstecken** to catch something
  ◊ *Pass auf, dass du dich nicht ansteckst.* Be careful you don't catch anything. ◊ *Ich habe mich bei ihm angesteckt.* I caught it from him.
♦ **sich etwas anstecken** to pin something on ◊ *Ich habe mir das Abzeichen des Sportvereins angesteckt.* I pinned my sports club badge on.
**ansteckend** ADJECTIVE
  infectious ◊ *eine ansteckende Krankheit* an infectious disease
  ♦ **Herpes ist ansteckend.** Herpes is contagious.
**anstelle** PREPOSITION
  *The preposition* **anstelle** *takes the genitive.*
  instead of ◊ *Anstelle der Mutter hat seine Tante unterschrieben.* His aunt has signed instead of his mother.
  ♦ **Pralinen anstelle von Blumen** chocolates instead of flowers
**anstellen** VERB (PERFECT **hat angestellt**)
  [1] to turn on ◊ *Kannst du mal bitte den Fernseher anstellen?* Can you turn the television on, please?
  [2] to employ ◊ *Sie ist bei einem Versandhaus angestellt.* She's employed by a mail-order company.
  [3] to do ◊ *Wie soll ich es bloß anstellen, dass er es erlaubt?* What can I do to get him to allow it? ◊ *Was stellen wir denn heute Nachmittag an?* What shall we do this afternoon?
  [4] to be up to ◊ *Was hat der Lümmel denn schon wieder angestellt?* What has that rascal been up to this time?
  ♦ **sich anstellen (1)** to queue ◊ *Musstet ihr euch für die Karten lange anstellen?* Did you have to queue for long for the tickets?
  ♦ **sich anstellen (2)** to act ◊ *Sie hat sich wirklich dumm angestellt.* She acted really stupidly.
  ♦ **Stell dich nicht so an, natürlich kannst du das.** Don't make such a fuss. Of course you can do it.
**anstrengen** VERB (PERFECT **hat angestrengt**)
  ♦ **Die Reise hat mich sehr angestrengt.** The journey took a lot out of me.
  ♦ **Streng deinen Kopf an!** Use your head!
  ♦ **sich anstrengen** to make an effort
**anstrengend** ADJECTIVE
  tiring
die **Anstrengung** NOUN
  effort
die **Antarktis** NOUN
  the Antarctic ◊ *in der Antarktis* in the Antarctic

der **Anteil** NOUN (PL die **Anteile**)
share ◊ *Ich möchte meinen Anteil am Gewinn haben.* I would like to have my share of the profit.
♦ **Anteil nehmen an (1)** to sympathize with ◊ *Ich nehme Anteil an deinem Pech.* I sympathize with you in your bad luck.
♦ **Anteil nehmen an (2)** to take an interest in ◊ *Der Patient nimmt keinen Anteil an seiner Umgebung.* The patient takes no interest in his surroundings.

die **Antenne** NOUN
aerial

**Anti-** PREFIX
anti-

**antiautoritär** ADJECTIVE
anti-authoritarian

das **Antibiotikum** NOUN (PL die **Antibiotika**)
antibiotic

**antik** ADJECTIVE
antique

die **Antiquitäten** FEM PL NOUN
antiques

der **Antrag** NOUN (PL die **Anträge**)
[1] application ◊ *Sie stellte einen Antrag auf Arbeitslosenunterstützung.* She put in an application for unemployment benefit.
[2] motion ◊ *der Antrag der Opposition* the motion put by the opposition
♦ **Ich stelle den Antrag, dass wir diesen Punkt erst später behandeln.** I move that we deal with this point later.

**antun** VERB (IMPERFECT **tat an**, PERFECT **hat angetan**)
♦ **jemandem etwas antun** to do something to somebody ◊ *Das kannst du deinen Eltern nicht antun!* You can't do that to your parents.
♦ **jemandem ein Unrecht antun** to wrong somebody ◊ *Uns ist ein großes Unrecht angetan worden.* We've been cruelly wronged.
♦ **sich Zwang antun** to force oneself ◊ *Tu dir keinen Zwang an!* Don't force yourself!
♦ **sich etwas antun** to kill oneself ◊ *Wenn ich durchfalle, dann tue ich mir was an.* If I fail, I'll kill myself.

die **Antwort** NOUN
answer ◊ *jemandem eine Antwort geben* to give somebody an answer

**antworten** VERB
to answer ◊ *Antworte bitte!* Please answer.
♦ **auf etwas antworten** to answer something ◊ *Sie konnte auf diese Frage nicht antworten.* She couldn't answer the question.
♦ **jemandem antworten** to answer somebody ◊ *Wo warst du? Antworte mir gefälligst!* Where have you been? Answer me, will you!

der **Antwortschein** NOUN (PL die **Antwortscheine**)
reply coupon

der **Anwalt** NOUN (PL die **Anwälte**)
lawyer

die **Anwältin** NOUN
lawyer

die **Anweisung** NOUN
instruction ◊ *Folgen Sie bitte den Anweisungen Ihres Führers.* Please follow your guide's instructions.
♦ **Anweisung haben, etwas zu tun** to have instructions to do something

**anwenden** VERB (IMPERFECT **wendete** or **wandte an**, PERFECT **hat angewendet** or **angewandt**)
[1] to use ◊ *Welche Software wenden Sie an?* What software do you use? ◊ *Sie wenden eine neue Technik zum Recycling von Kunststoff an.* They use a new recycling technique for plastic.
[2] (*law, rule*)
to apply
♦ **Gewalt anwenden** to use violence

**anwesend** ADJECTIVE
present

die **Anwesenheit** NOUN
presence

die **Anzahl** NOUN
number ◊ *je nach Anzahl der Teilnehmer* according to the number of participants ◊ *eine große Anzahl an Fehlern* a large number of mistakes

**anzahlen** VERB (PERFECT **hat angezahlt**)
♦ **fünfzig Mark anzahlen** to pay fifty marks deposit
♦ **ein Auto anzahlen** to put down a deposit on a car

die **Anzahlung** NOUN
deposit ◊ *eine Anzahlung leisten* to pay a deposit

das **Anzeichen** NOUN (PL die **Anzeichen**)
sign

die **Anzeige** NOUN
advertisement ◊ *Ich habe ihn über eine Anzeige kennen gelernt.* I met him through an advertisement.
♦ **Anzeige gegen jemanden erstatten** to report somebody to the police
♦ **Ich möchte Anzeige wegen Diebstahls erstatten.** I wish to report a theft.

**anzeigen** VERB (PERFECT **hat angezeigt**)
[1] to show ◊ *Der Tachometer zeigt die Geschwindigkeit an.* The speedometer shows the speed.
[2] to report ◊ *Ich werde Sie wegen Ruhestörung anzeigen!* I'll report you for breach of the peace. ◊ *Ich habe einen Diebstahl anzuzeigen.* I wish to report a theft.

**anziehen** VERB (IMPERFECT **zog an**, PERFECT **hat angezogen**)

**1 to put on** ◊ *Ich muss mir nur noch die Schuhe anziehen.* I just have to put my shoes on.

**2 to dress** ◊ *Kannst du bitte die Kinder anziehen?* Can you dress the children, please? ◊ *Er war sehr schick angezogen.* He was dressed very elegantly.

♦ **sich anziehen** to get dressed

**3 to attract** ◊ *Der Zoo zieht viele Besucher an.* The zoo attracts a lot of visitors.

♦ **sich von jemandem angezogen fühlen** to feel attracted to somebody

♦ **sich von etwas angezogen fühlen** to feel attracted to something

**4 to tighten** (*screw*)

der **Anzug** NOUN (PL die **Anzüge**)
suit

**anzünden** VERB (PERFECT **hat angezündet**)
to light ◊ *Ich habe mir eine Zigarette angezündet.* I lit a cigarette.

die **AOK** NOUN (= *Allgemeine Ortskrankenkasse*)
German health insurance

der **Apfel** NOUN (PL die **Äpfel**)
apple

das **Apfelmus** NOUN (GEN des **Apfelmuses**)
apple purée

der **Apfelsaft** NOUN (PL die **Apfelsäfte**)
apple juice

die **Apfelsine** NOUN
orange

die **Apfeltasche** NOUN
apple turnover

die **Apotheke** NOUN
chemist's ◊ *in der Apotheke* at the chemist's

der **Apotheker** NOUN (PL die **Apotheker**)
pharmacist ◊ *Er ist Apotheker.* He's a pharmacist.

der **Apparat** NOUN (PL die **Apparate**)
**1 gadget** ◊ *Mit diesem Apparat kann man Dosen zerkleinern.* You can crush tins with this gadget.

**2 camera**

**3 telephone** ◊ *Wer war am Apparat?* Who was on the telephone?

♦ **Am Apparat!** Speaking!

**4 set**

das **Appartement** NOUN (PL die **Appartements**)
flat

der **Appetit** NOUN
appetite

♦ **Ich habe keinen Appetit.** I'm not hungry.

♦ **Guten Appetit!** Enjoy your meal!

die **Aprikose** NOUN
apricot

der **April** NOUN (GEN des **April** or **Aprils,** PL die **Aprile**)
April ◊ *im April* in April ◊ *am dritten April* on the third of April ◊ *Ulm, den 3. April 2001* Ulm, 3 April 2001 ◊ *Heute ist*

*der dritte April.* Today is the third of April.

♦ **April, April!** April Fool!

der **Araber** NOUN (PL die **Araber**)
Arab

die **Araberin** NOUN
Arab

**arabisch** ADJECTIVE

♦ **arabische Länder** Arab countries

♦ **die arabische Sprache** Arabic

die **Arbeit** NOUN
**1 job** ◊ *Das ist eine sehr anstrengende Arbeit.* That's a very tiring job. ◊ *Er sucht eine Arbeit auf dem Bau.* He's looking for a job on a building site.

**2 work** ◊ *Ich habe im Moment viel Arbeit.* I've got a lot of work at the moment. ◊ *Die Arbeiten an unserem neuen Haus gehen gut voran.* Work on our new house is progressing well.

♦ **Sie hat keine Arbeit.** She's out of work.

♦ **Das war eine Arbeit!** That was hard work.

**3 dissertation** ◊ *Sie schreibt eine Arbeit über englische Ortsnamen.* She's writing a dissertation on English place names.

**4 test** ◊ *Ich habe in der Arbeit eine Fünf geschrieben.* I got an "E" in the test. ◊ *Morgen schreiben wir in Mathe eine Arbeit.* We've got a maths test tomorrow.

♦ **in Arbeit sein** to be in hand ◊ *Ihre Reparatur ist in Arbeit.* Your repair work is in hand.

**arbeiten** VERB
to work ◊ *Sie arbeitet hart.* She works hard. ◊ *Er arbeitet als Elektriker bei der Firma Müller.* He works as an electrician for Müller's. ◊ *Seine Nieren arbeiten nicht richtig.* His kidneys don't work properly.

♦ **sich durch etwas arbeiten** to work one's way through something ◊ *Nach dem Urlaub musste ich mich durch Berge von Post arbeiten.* After my holiday I had to work my way through piles of mail.

der **Arbeiter** NOUN (PL die **Arbeiter**)
worker

die **Arbeiterin** NOUN
worker

der **Arbeitgeber** NOUN (PL die **Arbeitgeber**)
employer

der **Arbeitnehmer** NOUN (PL die **Arbeitnehmer**)
employee ◊ *Als Arbeitnehmer hat man gewisse Rechte.* As an employee you have certain rights.

das **Arbeitsamt** NOUN (PL die **Arbeitsämter**)
job centre

die **Arbeitsbedingungen** PL NOUN
working conditions

die **Arbeitserlaubnis** NOUN (PL die **Arbeitserlaubnisse**)
work permit

**arbeitslos** ADJECTIVE

☞

unemployed
der **Arbeitslose** NOUN (GEN des/der
die **Arbeitslosen,** PL die **Arbeitslosen)**
unemployed person ◊ *Ein Arbeitsloser
hat die Stelle bekommen.* An
unemployed person got the job.
♦ **die Arbeitslosen** the unemployed
die **Arbeitslosigkeit** NOUN
unemployment
die **Arbeitslosenhilfe** NOUN
unemployment benefit
der **Arbeitsort** NOUN (PL die **Arbeitsorte)**
place of work
der **Arbeitsplatz** NOUN (GEN des
**Arbeitsplatzes,** PL die **Arbeitsplätze)**
[1] job ◊ *Suchen Sie einen neuen
Arbeitsplatz?* Are you looking for a new
job?
[2] desk ◊ *Frau Marr ist im Moment nicht
an ihrem Arbeitsplatz.* Ms Marr isn't at
her desk at the moment.
das **Arbeitspraktikum** NOUN (GEN des
**Arbeitspraktikums,** PL die **Arbeitspraktika)**
work experience ◊ *Sie absolviert gerade
ihr Arbeitspraktikum.* She's doing work
experience.
die **Arbeitszeit** NOUN
working hours
♦ **gleitende Arbeitszeit** flexitime
das **Arbeitszimmer** NOUN (PL die
**Arbeitszimmer)**
study
der **Architekt** NOUN (GEN des **Architekten,** PL die
**Architekten)**
architect ◊ *Er ist Architekt.* He's an
architect.
die **Architektur** NOUN
architecture
die **ARD** ABBREVIATION (= *Arbeitsgemeinschaft
der Rundfunkanstalten Deutschlands)*
German TV channel
**Argentinien** NEUT NOUN
Argentina ◊ *nach Argentinien* to
Argentina
der **Ärger** NOUN
[1] anger ◊ *Er hat seinen Ärger über die
Verspätung an mir ausgelassen.* He took
out his anger at the delay on me.
[2] trouble ◊ *Wenn du das machst,
bekommst du Ärger.* If you do that, you'll
get into trouble.
♦ **Ärger mit etwas haben** to have trouble
with something ◊ *Hast du wieder Ärger
mit deinem Computer?* Are you having
trouble with your computer again?
**ärgerlich** ADJECTIVE
[1] annoying ◊ *Diese dauernden
Störungen sind sehr ärgerlich.* These
constant interruptions are very annoying.
[2] angry ◊ *Ich bin auf ihn ärgerlich.* I'm
angry with him. ◊ *Er ist über die
Verzögerung ärgerlich.* He's angry at the
delay.

♦ **jemanden ärgerlich machen** to annoy
somebody
**ärgern** VERB
to annoy ◊ *Du sollst deine Schwester
nicht immer ärgern!* Don't keep annoying
your sister.
♦ **sich ärgern** to be annoyed ◊ *Ich habe
mich über diesen Fehler sehr geärgert.* I
was very annoyed about that mistake.
die **Arktis** NOUN
the Arctic ◊ *in der Arktis* in the Arctic
der **Arm** NOUN (PL die **Arme)**
| see also **arm** ADJECTIVE |
arm
♦ **jemanden auf den Arm nehmen** to pull
somebody's leg ◊ *Du willst mich wohl
auf den Arm nehmen?* You're pulling my
leg.
**arm** ADJECTIVE
| see also **der Arm** NOUN |
poor ◊ *Er ist ärmer als ich.* He's poorer
than me.
das **Armband** NOUN (PL die **Armbänder)**
bracelet
die **Armbanduhr** NOUN
wristwatch
die **Armee** NOUN
army
der **Ärmel** NOUN (PL die **Ärmel)**
sleeve
der **Ärmelkanal** NOUN
the English Channel
die **Armut** NOUN
poverty
**arrangieren** VERB (PERFECT **hat arrangiert)**
to arrange ◊ *Sie hat ein Treffen der
beiden arrangiert.* She arranged for them
both to meet.
die **Art** NOUN (PL die **Arten)**
[1] way ◊ *Ich mache das auf meine Art.* I
do that my way.
[2] kind ◊ *Ich mag diese Art Obst nicht.* I
don't like this kind of fruit. ◊ *Häuser aller
Art* all kinds of houses
[3] species ◊ *Diese Art ist vom
Aussterben bedroht.* This species is in
danger of extinction.
♦ **Es ist nicht seine Art, das zu tun.** It's not
like him to do that.
der **Artikel** NOUN (PL die **Artikel)**
article
die **Arznei** NOUN
medicine
das **Arzneimittel** NOUN (PL die **Arzneimittel)**
drug
der **Arzt** NOUN (PL die **Ärzte)**
doctor ◊ *Helmut ist Arzt.* Helmut's a
doctor.
die **Ärztin** NOUN
doctor ◊ *Jutta ist Ärztin.* Jutta's a doctor.
**ärztlich** ADJECTIVE
medical

**A**

♦ **Die Wunde muss ärztlich behandelt werden.** The wound will have to be treated by a doctor.

das **As** NOUN *see* **Ass**

die **Asche** NOUN (PL die **Aschen**)
ash

der **Aschenbecher** NOUN (PL die **Aschenbecher**)
ashtray

der **Aschermittwoch** NOUN
Ash Wednesday ◊ *am Aschermittwoch* on Ash Wednesday

der **Asiat** NOUN (GEN des **Asiaten**, PL die **Asiaten**)
Asian

die **Asiatin** NOUN
Asian

**asiatisch** ADJECTIVE
Asian

**Asien** NEUT NOUN
Asia
♦ **aus Asien** from Asia
♦ **nach Asien** to Asia

**aß** VERB *see* **essen**

das **Ass** NOUN (GEN des **Asses**, PL die **Asse**)
ace ◊ *das Herzass* the ace of hearts

der **Assistent** NOUN (GEN des **Assistenten**, PL die **Assistenten**)
assistant

die **Assistentin** NOUN
assistant

der **Ast** NOUN (PL die **Äste**)
branch

das **Asthma** NOUN
asthma ◊ *Sie hat Asthma.* She's got asthma.

die **Astrologie** NOUN
astrology

der **Astronaut** NOUN (GEN des **Astronauten**, PL die **Astronauten**)
astronaut ◊ *Er ist Astronaut.* He's an astronaut.

die **Astronomie** NOUN
astronomy

das **Asyl** NOUN (PL die **Asyle**)
asylum ◊ *um Asyl bitten* to ask for asylum
♦ **ein Obdachlosenasyl** a hostel for the homeless

der **Asylbewerber** NOUN (PL die **Asylbewerber**)
asylum-seeker

die **Asylbewerberin** NOUN
asylum-seeker

der **Atem** NOUN
breath ◊ *außer Atem* out of breath

**atemlos** ADJECTIVE
breathless

die **Athletik** NOUN
athletics

der **Atlantik** NOUN
the Atlantic ◊ *eine Insel im Atlantik* an island in the Atlantic

der **Atlas** NOUN (GEN des **Atlasses**, PL die **Atlasse** *or* **Atlanten**)
atlas

**atmen** VERB
to breathe

die **Atmosphäre** NOUN
atmosphere

das **Atom** NOUN (PL die **Atome**)
atom

**atomar** ADJECTIVE
atomic

die **Atombombe** NOUN
atom bomb

die **Atomwaffen** FEM PL NOUN
atomic weapons

**atomwaffenfrei** ADJECTIVE
nuclear-free

**attraktiv** ADJECTIVE
attractive ◊ *attraktiv aussehen* to look attractive

**ätzend** ADJECTIVE
[1] rubbish ◊ *Die Musik ist ätzend.* The music's rubbish.
[2] corrosive
[3] caustic

**au!** EXCLAMATION
ouch!
♦ **Au ja!** Oh yes!

**auch** ADVERB
[1] also ◊ *Gummienten verkaufen wir auch.* We also sell rubber ducks.
[2] too ◊ *Das ist auch schön.* That's nice, too.
♦ **Ich auch.** Me too.
♦ **Ich auch nicht.** Me neither.
♦ **Er kommt. – Sie auch.** He's coming. – So is she.
♦ **auch nicht** not ... either ◊ *Nein, das Kleid gefällt mir auch nicht.* No, I don't like that dress either.
♦ **Auch das noch!** That's all we needed!
[3] even ◊ *Auch wenn das Wetter schlecht ist.* Even if the weather's bad. ◊ *ohne auch nur zu fragen* without even asking
♦ **Du siehst müde aus. – Bin ich auch.** You look tired. – I am.
♦ **wer auch** whoever ◊ *Wer das auch gesagt hat, ich glaube es nicht.* I don't believe it, whoever said it.
♦ **was auch** whatever ◊ *Was du auch sagst, ich finde es schön.* Whatever you say, I think it's nice.
♦ **wie dem auch sei** be that as it may ◊ *Wie dem auch sei, ich gehe jetzt trotzdem.* Be that as it may, I'm still going.
♦ **wie sehr er sich auch bemühte** however much he tried

**auf** PREPOSITION, ADVERB
[1] on
*Use the accusative to express movement or a change of place. Use the dative when there is no change of place.*

☞

◇ *Stell die Suppe bitte auf den Tisch.*
Please put the soup on the table. ◇ *Die
Suppe steht auf dem Tisch.* The soup's
on the table.
◆ **Auf dem Land ist die Luft besser.** The air
is better in the country.
◆ **Wir fahren morgen aufs Land.** We're
going to the country tomorrow.
◆ **auf der ganzen Welt** in the whole world
◆ **auf Deutsch** in German
◆ **bis auf ihn** except for him
◆ **auf einmal** at once
◆ **auf seinen Vorschlag hin** at his
suggestion
[2] open ◇ *Das Fenster ist auf.* The
window's open. ◇ *Die Geschäfte sind am
Sonntag nicht auf.* The shops aren't open
on Sunday.
[3] up ◇ *Ist er schon auf?* Is he up yet?
◇ *Ich bin schon seit sieben Uhr auf.* I've
been up since seven.
◆ **auf und ab** up and down
◆ **auf und davon** up and away

**aufatmen** VERB (PERFECT **hat aufgeatmet**)
to heave a sigh of relief

**aufbauen** VERB (PERFECT **hat aufgebaut**)
to build up

**aufbekommen** VERB (IMPERFECT **bekam auf,**
PERFECT **hat aufbekommen**)
[1] to get open ◇ *Ich bekomme das
Fenster nicht auf.* I can't get the window
open.
[2] to be given homework ◇ *Wir haben
heute nichts aufbekommen.* We weren't
given any homework today.

**aufbewahren** VERB (PERFECT **hat
aufbewahrt**)
to keep ◇ *Sie bewahrt ihre Ersparnisse in
einer Blechdose auf.* She keeps her
savings in a tin.

**aufblasen** VERB (PRESENT **bläst auf,** IMPERFECT
**blies auf,** PERFECT **hat aufgeblasen**)
to inflate

**aufbleiben** VERB (IMPERFECT **blieb auf,** PERFECT
**ist aufgeblieben**)
[1] to stay open ◇ *Donnerstags bleiben
die Geschäfte länger auf.* The shops stay
open longer on Thursdays.
[2] to stay up ◇ *Heute dürft ihr
ausnahmsweise länger aufbleiben.*
Today you can stay up late for once.

**aufbrechen** VERB (PRESENT **bricht auf,**
IMPERFECT **brach auf,** PERFECT **hat/ist
aufgebrochen**)

*For the perfect tense use **haben** when
the verb has an object and **sein** when
there is no object.*

[1] to break open ◇ *Die Diebe haben den
Safe aufgebrochen.* The thieves broke
the safe open.
[2] to open up ◇ *Die Wunde ist wieder
aufgebrochen.* The wound has opened
up again.

[3] to set off ◇ *Wann seid ihr
aufgebrochen?* When did you set off?

**aufbringen** VERB (IMPERFECT **brachte auf,**
PERFECT **hat aufgebracht**)
[1] to open ◇ *Ich bringe das
Konservenglas nicht auf.* I can't open the
jar.
[2] to raise ◇ *Wie soll ich nur das Geld für
die Reparatur aufbringen?* However am I
going raise the money for the repairs?
◆ **Verständnis für etwas aufbringen** to be
able to understand something

**aufeinander** ADVERB
on top of each other ◇ *Leg die
Handtücher aufeinander.* Put the towels
on top of each other.
◆ **aufeinander schießen** to shoot at one
another
◆ **aufeinander vertrauen** to trust each
other

der **Aufenthalt** NOUN (PL die **Aufenthalte**)
[1] stay ◇ *Während unseres Aufenthalts
in London ...* During our stay in
London ...
[2] stop ◇ *Der Zug hat fünf Minuten
Aufenthalt in Ulm.* The train has a five-
minute stop in Ulm.

**aufessen** VERB (PRESENT **isst auf,** IMPERFECT **aß
auf,** PERFECT **hat aufgegessen**)
to eat up

**auffallen** VERB (PRESENT **fällt auf,** IMPERFECT **fiel
auf,** PERFECT **ist aufgefallen**)
to be conspicuous
◆ **jemandem auffallen** to strike somebody
◇ *Es fiel mir auf, dass sie sich recht
seltsam benahm.* It struck me that she
was behaving rather strangely.

**auffällig** ADJECTIVE
conspicuous
◆ **auffällig gekleidet sein** to be dressed
strikingly

**auffangen** VERB (PRESENT **fängt auf,** IMPERFECT
**fing auf,** PERFECT **hat aufgefangen**)
to catch

**aufführen** VERB (PERFECT **hat aufgeführt**)
[1] to perform ◇ *ein Stück aufführen* to
perform a play
[2] to list ◇ *Alle Fachausdrücke sind im
Anhang aufgeführt.* All technical terms
are listed in the appendix.
◆ **sich aufführen** to behave

die **Aufführung** NOUN
performance

die **Aufgabe** NOUN
[1] task ◇ *Vier Kinder zu erziehen ist eine
schwierige Aufgabe.* Bringing up four
children is a difficult task.
[2] question ◇ *Ich konnte die zweite
Aufgabe in der Mathearbeit nicht lösen.* I
couldn't solve the second question in the
maths test.

**3** homework ◊ *Hast du deine Aufgaben schon gemacht?* Have you done your homework yet?

**aufgeben** VERB (PRESENT **gibt auf,** IMPERFECT **gab auf,** PERFECT **hat aufgegeben**)
**1** to give up ◊ *Du solltest das Rauchen aufgeben.* You should give up smoking.
**2** to post ◊ *Ich habe das Paket an dich vor drei Tagen aufgegeben.* I posted the parcel to you three days ago.
**3** to check in ◊ *Du kannst den Koffer ja vor der Reise aufgeben.* You can check in your suitcase before you travel.
♦ **eine Anzeige aufgeben** to place an advertisement
♦ **Ich gebe auf!** I give up.

**aufgehen** VERB (IMPERFECT **ging auf,** PERFECT **ist aufgegangen**)
**1** to rise ◊ *Der Mond ist aufgegangen.* The moon has risen.
**2** to open ◊ *Die Tür ging auf, und Christoph kam herein.* The door opened and Christoph came in.
**3** to become clear ◊ *Mir ist inzwischen aufgegangen, warum sie das gesagt hat.* It has since become clear to me why she said that.
♦ **Zwanzig durch sechs geht nicht auf.** Six into twenty doesn't go.

**aufgelegt** ADJECTIVE
♦ **gut aufgelegt sein** to be in a good mood
♦ **schlecht aufgelegt sein** to be in a bad mood
♦ **zu etwas aufgelegt sein** to feel like something ◊ *Ich bin zu einem Spaziergang aufgelegt.* I feel like a walk.

**aufgeregt** ADJECTIVE
excited

**aufgeschlossen** ADJECTIVE
open-minded

**aufgrund** PREPOSITION

*The preposition **aufgrund** takes the genitive.*

**1** because of ◊ *Das Spiel ist aufgrund des schlechten Wetters ausgefallen.* The game was cancelled because of the bad weather.
**2** on the basis of ◊ *Sie wurde aufgrund von Indizien überführt.* She was convicted on the basis of circumstantial evidence.

**aufhaben** VERB (PRESENT **hat auf,** IMPERFECT **hatte auf,** PERFECT **hat aufgehabt**)
**1** to have on ◊ *Sie hatte einen roten Hut auf.* She had a red hat on.
**2** to have homework to do ◊ *Wir haben heute in Englisch nichts auf.* We haven't got any English homework to do today.

**aufhalten** VERB (PRESENT **hält auf,** IMPERFECT **hielt auf,** PERFECT **hat aufgehalten**)
**1** to detain ◊ *Ich möchte dich nicht aufhalten.* I don't want to detain you.

**2** to check ◊ *Wie kann die Vergrößerung des Ozonlochs aufgehalten werden?* How can the growth of the ozone hole be checked?
**3** to hold open ◊ *Kannst du mir bitte die Tür aufhalten?* Can you hold the door open for me, please?
♦ **Sie hielt die Hand auf.** She held out her hand.
♦ **Halt die Augen auf, ob du sie sehen kannst.** Keep your eyes peeled. You might see them.
♦ **sich aufhalten (1)** to live ◊ *Sie hat sich lange im Ausland aufgehalten.* She lived abroad for a long time.
♦ **sich aufhalten (2)** to stay ◊ *Ich möchte mich nicht lange aufhalten.* I don't want to stay long.
♦ **sich mit etwas aufhalten** to waste time over something ◊ *Mit solchen Kinderspielen halte ich mich doch nicht auf.* I'm not wasting my time over such childish games.

**aufhängen** VERB (PERFECT **hat aufgehängt**)
to hang up (*washing*)
♦ **sich aufhängen** to hang oneself ◊ *Er hat gedroht, sich aufzuhängen.* He's threatened to hang himself.

**aufheben** VERB (IMPERFECT **hob auf,** PERFECT **hat aufgehoben**)
**1** to pick up ◊ *Sie hob das Heft, das auf den Boden gefallen war, auf.* She picked up the exercise book which had fallen on the floor.
**2** to keep ◊ *Sie hat alle seine Briefe aufgehoben.* She's kept all his letters.
♦ **gut aufgehoben sein** to be well looked after ◊ *Unsere Tochter ist bei ihrer Oma gut aufgehoben.* Our daughter's being well looked after at her granny's.

**aufheitern** VERB (PERFECT **hat aufgeheitert**)
♦ **jemanden aufheitern** to cheer somebody up ◊ *Versuch, sie etwas aufzuheitern.* Try to cheer her up a bit.

**aufhören** VERB (PERFECT **hat aufgehört**)
to stop ◊ *Der Regen hat aufgehört.* The rain's stopped.
♦ **aufhören, etwas zu tun** to stop doing something ◊ *Hör endlich auf, dich dauernd zu beklagen.* Will you stop complaining all the time!

**aufklären** VERB (PERFECT **hat aufgeklärt**)
to solve ◊ *Die Polizei hat den Mord aufgeklärt.* The police have solved the murder.
♦ **jemanden aufklären (1)** to explain to somebody ◊ *Kannst du mich bitte aufklären, wie man das machen muss.* Can you please explain to me how this should be done.
♦ **jemanden aufklären (2)** to tell somebody the facts of life ◊ *Meine Eltern haben mich aufgeklärt, als ich zehn war.* My

☞

parents told me the facts of life when I was ten.

♦ **sich aufklären** to clear up ◊ *Das Wetter klärt sich auf.* The weather's clearing up.

♦ **Das Rätsel hat sich aufgeklärt.** The mystery has been solved.

der **Aufkleber** NOUN (PL die **Aufkleber**)
sticker

**auflassen** VERB (PRESENT **lässt auf,** IMPERFECT **ließ auf,** PERFECT **hat aufgelassen**)
[1] to leave open ◊ *Lass bitte das Fenster auf.* Please leave the window open.
[2] to keep on ◊ *Kann ich meine Mütze auflassen?* Can I keep my hat on?

**auflegen** VERB (PERFECT **hat aufgelegt**)
to hang up ◊ *Sie hat einfach aufgelegt.* She simply hung up.

**auflesen** VERB (PRESENT **liest auf,** IMPERFECT **las auf,** PERFECT **hat aufgelesen**)
to pick up ◊ *etwas von der Straße auflesen* to pick something up off the street

**auflösen** VERB (PERFECT **hat aufgelöst**)
[1] to dissolve ◊ *Du solltest die Tablette in Wasser auflösen.* You should dissolve the tablet in water.
[2] to break up ◊ *Die Polizei hat die Demonstration aufgelöst.* The police broke up the demonstration.

♦ **sich auflösen** to dissolve ◊ *Der Zucker hatte sich schnell im Tee aufgelöst.* The sugar had quickly dissolved in the tea.

♦ **wenn sich der Nebel aufgelöst hat** when the fog has lifted

♦ **Die Menschenmenge löste sich auf.** The crowd dispersed.

♦ **in Tränen aufgelöst sein** to be in tears

**aufmachen** VERB (PERFECT **hat aufgemacht**)
[1] to open ◊ *Kannst du bitte die Tür aufmachen?* Can you open the door, please? ◊ *Wann machen die Geschäfte auf?* When do the shops open?
[2] to undo ◊ *Ich schaffe es nicht, den Reißverschluss aufzumachen.* I can't undo the zip.

♦ **sich aufmachen** to set out ◊ *Wir machten uns nach London auf.* We set out for London.

**aufmerksam** ADJECTIVE
attentive

♦ **jemanden auf etwas aufmerksam machen** to point something out to somebody ◊ *Ich habe ihn auf das Schloss aufmerksam gemacht.* I pointed the castle out to him.

die **Aufmerksamkeit** NOUN
attention ◊ *Darf ich um Ihre Aufmerksamkeit bitten!* May I have your attention?

♦ **Wir sollten ihnen eine kleine Aufmerksamkeit mitbringen.** We ought to take them a little something.

**aufmuntern** VERB (PERFECT **hat aufgemuntert**)
to cheer up

die **Aufnahme** NOUN
[1] welcome ◊ *Wir fanden eine sehr freundliche Aufnahme in unserer Partnerstadt.* We were given a very friendly welcome in our twin town.
[2] recording ◊ *Wir haben uns die Aufnahme des Konzerts angehört.* We listened to a recording of the concert.
[3] photograph ◊ *Möchtest du die Aufnahmen sehen, die ich in den Ferien gemacht habe?* Would you like to see the photographs I took on holiday?

die **Aufnahmeprüfung** NOUN
entrance test

**aufnehmen** VERB (PRESENT **nimmt auf,** IMPERFECT **nahm auf,** PERFECT **hat aufgenommen**)
[1] to take ◊ *Wie hat sie die Nachricht aufgenommen?* How did she take the news?
[2] to record ◊ *Wenn das Lied im Radio kommt, muss ich es unbedingt aufnehmen.* If they play the song on the radio, I really must record it.
[3] to photograph ◊ *Diesen tollen Sonnenuntergang muss ich aufnehmen.* I must photograph this wonderful sunset.
[4] to admit ◊ *Was muss man tun, um in den Tennisklub aufgenommen zu werden?* What do you have to do to be admitted to the tennis club?

♦ **es mit jemandem aufnehmen können** to be able to compete with somebody

**aufpassen** VERB (PERFECT **hat aufgepasst**)
to pay attention ◊ *Ich habe heute im Unterricht nicht aufgepasst.* I didn't pay attention in class today.

♦ **auf jemanden aufpassen** to look after somebody ◊ *Ich muss auf meinen kleinen Bruder aufpassen.* I have to look after my little brother.

♦ **auf etwas aufpassen** to look after something ◊ *Kannst du mal eben auf meinen Koffer aufpassen?* Can you look after my suitcase for a moment?

♦ **Aufgepasst!** Look out!

**aufpumpen** VERB (PERFECT **hat aufgepumpt**)
to pump up

**aufräumen** VERB (PERFECT **hat aufgeräumt**)
to tidy up ◊ *Ich darf erst raus, wenn ich mein Zimmer aufgeräumt habe.* I can't go out until I've tidied up my room.

**aufrecht** ADJECTIVE
upright

**aufrechterhalten** VERB (PRESENT **erhält aufrecht,** IMPERFECT **erhielt aufrecht,** PERFECT **hat aufrechterhalten**)
to maintain

**aufregen** VERB (PERFECT **hat aufgeregt**)
to excite

A

♦ **sich aufregen** to get excited

**aufregend** ADJECTIVE
exciting

**aufs** = **auf das**

der **Aufsatz** NOUN (GEN des **Aufsatzes**, PL die **Aufsätze**)
essay ◊ *Wir haben heute in Deutsch einen Aufsatz geschrieben.* We wrote an essay in today's German lesson.

**aufschieben** VERB (IMPERFECT **schob auf**, PERFECT **hat aufgeschoben**)
[1] to push open ◊ *Man kann diese Tür aufschieben.* You can push this door open.
[2] to put off ◊ *Wir haben unsere Abreise noch einmal aufgeschoben.* We put off our departure once again.

**aufschlagen** VERB (PRESENT **schlägt auf**, IMPERFECT **schlug auf**, PERFECT **hat aufgeschlagen**)
[1] to open ◊ *ein Buch aufschlagen* to open a book ◊ *Schlagt Seite 111 auf.* Open your books at page 111.
[2] to pitch ◊ *Sie schlugen ihre Zelte auf.* They pitched their tents.
[3] (*prices*)
to go up ◊ *Butter ist wieder aufgeschlagen.* The price of butter has gone up again.
[4] (*tennis*)
to serve ◊ *Du schlägst auf.* It's your turn to serve.

**aufschließen** VERB (IMPERFECT **schloss auf**, PERFECT **hat aufgeschlossen**)
to unlock ◊ *Schließ bitte die Tür auf!* Please unlock the door. ◊ *Sie schloss auf und ging hinein.* She unlocked the door and went in.

**aufschlussreich** ADJECTIVE
informative

der **Aufschnitt** NOUN (PL die **Aufschnitte**)
cold meat

**aufschreiben** VERB (IMPERFECT **schrieb auf**, PERFECT **hat aufgeschrieben**)
to write down

**aufsehen** VERB (PRESENT **sieht auf**, IMPERFECT **sah auf**, PERFECT **hat aufgesehen**)
see also das **Aufsehen** NOUN
to look up ◊ *Als die Tür aufging, sah sie von ihrer Arbeit auf.* When the door opened she looked up from her work.

das **Aufsehen** NOUN
see also **aufsehen** VERB
stir ◊ *Ihre Kleidung hat Aufsehen erregt.* Her outfit caused a stir.
♦ **Aufsehen erregend** sensational

**aufsein** VERB see **auf**

**aufsetzen** VERB (PERFECT **hat aufgesetzt**)
to put on ◊ *Setz dir eine Mütze auf!* Put a hat on.
♦ **Ich setze das Teewasser auf.** I'll put the kettle on.

♦ **sich aufsetzen** to sit up ◊ *Der Patient setzte sich auf.* The patient sat up.

die **Aufsicht** NOUN
supervision
♦ **die Aufsicht haben** to be in charge

**aufstehen** VERB (IMPERFECT **stand auf**, PERFECT **ist/hat aufgestanden**)
Use **sein** for **to get up** and **haben** for **to be open**.
[1] to get up ◊ *Wann bist du heute Morgen aufgestanden?* When did you get up this morning? ◊ *Sie stand auf und ging.* She got up and left.
[2] to be open ◊ *Die Tür hat aufgestanden, also ging ich hinein.* The door was open, so I went in.

**aufstellen** VERB (PERFECT **hat aufgestellt**)
[1] to pitch ◊ *Wir haben unser Zelt am Waldrand aufgestellt.* We pitched our tent at the edge of the woods.
[2] to stand up ◊ *Der Sonnenschirm ist umgefallen, ich muss ihn wieder aufstellen.* The sunshade has fallen over. I'll have to stand it up again.
[3] to set up ◊ *Sie stellte die Schachfiguren auf.* She set up the chess pieces.
♦ **eine Liste aufstellen** to draw up a list
♦ **einen Rekord aufstellen** to set a record
♦ **die Mannschaft aufstellen** to pick the team
♦ **jemanden für ein Spiel aufstellen** to pick somebody for a game
♦ **sich aufstellen** to line up ◊ *Stellt euch bitte in Zweierreihen auf!* Please line up in twos.

**auftauchen** VERB (PERFECT **ist aufgetaucht**)
to appear

**auftauen** VERB (PERFECT **hat/ist aufgetaut**)
For the perfect tense use **haben** when the verb has an object and **sein** when there is no object.
[1] to thaw ◊ *Der Schnee taute auf.* The snow thawed.
[2] to defrost ◊ *Ich habe die Pizza im Mikrowellenherd aufgetaut.* I've defrosted the pizza in the microwave. ◊ *Sobald das Fleisch aufgetaut ist, kann ich es zubereiten.* As soon as the meat has defrosted I can cook it.

**aufteilen** VERB (PERFECT **hat aufgeteilt**)
to divide up ◊ *Wir wurden in drei Gruppen aufgeteilt.* We were divided up into three groups.

der **Auftrag** NOUN (PL die **Aufträge**)
orders ◊ *Ich habe den Auftrag, Sie davon zu unterrichten, dass ...* I have orders to inform you that ...
♦ **Wir haben dem Architekten den Auftrag erteilt, einen Bauplan zu zeichnen.** We instructed the architect to draw up some building plans.

☞

♦ **im Auftrag von** on behalf of ◊ *Ich komme im Auftrag der Firma Haehnle & Co.* I'm here on behalf of Haehnle and Co.

**auftreten** VERB (PRESENT **tritt auf,** IMPERFECT **trat auf,** PERFECT **ist aufgetreten**)
[1] to appear ◊ *Dieser Schauspieler tritt erst im dritten Akt auf.* This actor doesn't appear until the third act.
[2] to occur ◊ *Sollten Probleme auftreten, wende dich an uns.* If any problems occur, get in touch with us.
[3] to behave ◊ *Er ist ziemlich unbeliebt, weil er immer so überheblich auftritt.* He's quite unpopular because he always behaves so arrogantly.

**aufwachen** VERB (PERFECT **ist aufgewacht**)
to wake up

**aufwachsen** VERB (PRESENT **wächst auf,** IMPERFECT **wuchs auf,** PERFECT **ist aufgewachsen**)
to grow up

**aufwecken** VERB (PERFECT **hat aufgeweckt**)
to wake up

**aufzählen** VERB (PERFECT **hat aufgezählt**)
to list

**aufziehen** VERB (IMPERFECT **zog auf,** PERFECT **hat aufgezogen**)
[1] to draw ◊ *Zieh die Vorhänge auf und lass das Licht herein!* Draw the curtains and let some light in.
[2] to wind ◊ *Ich habe vergessen, die Uhr aufzuziehen.* I forgot to wind the clock.
♦ **jemanden aufziehen** to tease somebody ◊ *Sie haben mich wegen meiner roten Haare aufgezogen.* They teased me about my red hair.
♦ **Kinder aufziehen** to bring up children

der **Aufzug** NOUN (PL die **Aufzüge**)
lift ◊ *Wir sind mit dem Aufzug nach oben gefahren.* We went up in the lift.

das **Auge** NOUN (PL die **Augen**)
eye ◊ *Sie hat dunkle Augen.* She's got dark eyes.
♦ **unter vier Augen** in private

der **Augenblick** NOUN (PL die **Augenblicke**)
moment
♦ **im Augenblick** at the moment

die **Augenbraue** NOUN
eyebrow

der **August** NOUN (GEN des **Augustes** or **August,** PL die **Auguste**)
August ◊ *im August* in August ◊ *am fünften August* on 5 August ◊ *Ulm, den 5. August 2000* Ulm, 5 August 2000 ◊ *Heute ist der fünfte August.* Today is the fifth of August.

die **Aula** NOUN (PL die **Aulen**)
assembly hall

**aus** PREPOSITION, ADVERB
*The preposition* **aus** *takes the dative.*
[1] out of ◊ *Sie nahm ein Bonbon aus der Tüte.* She took a sweet out of the bag.
◊ *aus dem Fenster* out of the window

[2] from ◊ *Wenn er aus der Schule kommt, ist er immer sehr müde.* When he comes home from school he's always very tired. ◊ *Ich komme aus Deutschland.* I come from Germany. ◊ *Er ist aus Berlin.* He's from Berlin.
[3] made of ◊ *Die Vase ist aus Porzellan.* The vase is made of china.
♦ **aus Erfahrung** from experience
♦ **aus Spaß** for fun
♦ **Ich habe ihr aus Freundschaft geholfen.** I helped her out of a sense of friendship.
♦ **Aus ihr wird nie etwas.** She'll never get anywhere.
[4] finished ◊ *wenn das Kino aus ist* when the film's finished ◊ *Komm sofort nach Hause, wenn die Schule aus ist.* Come straight home when school has finished.
♦ **Wann ist die Schule aus?** When does school finish?
[5] off ◊ *Der Fernseher ist aus.* The television's off.
♦ **Licht aus!** Lights out!
♦ **Sie können meinen Mann nicht sprechen, er ist aus.** You can't speak to my husband. He's out.
♦ **von sich aus** of one's own accord
♦ **von ihm aus** as far as he's concerned

**ausatmen** VERB (PERFECT **hat ausgeatmet**)
to breathe out

**ausbeuten** VERB (PERFECT **hat ausgebeutet**)
to exploit

**ausbilden** VERB (PERFECT **hat ausgebildet**)
to train ◊ *Er bildet Lehrlinge aus.* He trains apprentices. ◊ *Sie ist ausgebildete Krankenschwester.* She's a qualified nurse.

die **Ausbildung** NOUN
training ◊ *eine solide Ausbildung* a decent training

der **Ausbildungsplatz** NOUN (GEN des **Ausbildungsplatzes,** PL die **Ausbildungsplätze**)
training job

die **Ausdauer** NOUN
stamina

**ausdenken** VERB (IMPERFECT **dachte aus,** PERFECT **hat ausgedacht**)
♦ **sich etwas ausdenken** to think something up ◊ *Da hast du dir aber was Witziges ausgedacht.* You've certainly thought up something imaginative.

der **Ausdruck (1)** NOUN (PL die **Ausdrücke**)
expression ◊ *Sie hat in der Schule ein paar schlimme Ausdrücke gelernt.* She's learned a few nasty expressions at school. ◊ *Als Ausdruck meiner Dankbarkeit habe ich ihr Blumen geschenkt.* I gave her flowers as an expression of my gratitude. ◊ *Ich kann am Ausdruck in deinem Gesicht sehen,*

*dass dir das nicht passt.* I can see by your expression that it doesn't suit you.

der **Ausdruck (2)** NOUN (PL die **Ausdrucke**)
printout ◇ *Kannst du mir von der Datei einen Ausdruck machen?* Can you do me a printout of the file?

**ausdrucken** VERB (PERFECT **hat ausgedruckt**)
to print out ◇ *Soll ich dir die Namen ausdrucken?* Shall I print out the names for you?

**ausdrücken** VERB (PERFECT **hat ausgedrückt**)
to express ◇ *Ich weiß nicht, wie man das auf Englisch ausdrückt.* I don't know how to express it in English.

**ausdrücklich** ADJECTIVE
explicit ◇ *Sie hat dir das ausdrücklich verboten.* She explicitly forbade you to do it.

**auseinander** ADVERB
apart ◇ *weit auseinander* far apart
♦ **Auseinander, ihr beiden!** Break it up, you two!
♦ **auseinander schreiben** to write separately
♦ **auseinander halten** to distinguish
♦ **auseinander nehmen** to take to pieces

die **Ausfahrt** NOUN
exit ◇ *Wir müssen an der nächsten Ausfahrt raus.* We have to take the next exit.

**ausfallen** VERB (PRESENT **fällt aus,** IMPERFECT **fiel aus,** PERFECT **ist ausgefallen**)
[1] to be cancelled ◇ *Der Sportunterricht fällt heute aus.* PE has been cancelled today.
[2] to break down ◇ *Die Heizung ist mal wieder ausgefallen.* The heating has broken down again.
♦ **Wenn der Strom ausfällt, dann sind alle Dateien weg.** If there's a power cut all the files are lost.
♦ **Die Mathearbeit ist furchtbar schlecht ausgefallen.** The results of the maths test were really awful.
[3] to fall out ◇ *Ihm sind die Haare ausgefallen, als er noch ziemlich jung war.* His hair fell out when he was still quite young.

der **Ausflug** NOUN (PL die **Ausflüge**)
outing ◇ *einen Ausflug machen* to go on an outing

**ausfragen** VERB (PERFECT **hat ausgefragt**)
to question

die **Ausfuhr** NOUN
export

**ausführen** VERB (PERFECT **hat ausgeführt**)
to carry out ◇ *Sie hat ihren Plan ausgeführt.* She carried out her plan.
♦ **jemanden ausführen** to take somebody out ◇ *Er hat mich zum Essen ausgeführt.* He took me out for a meal.
♦ **einen Hund ausführen** to take a dog for a walk

♦ **Waren ausführen** to export goods

**ausführlich** ADJECTIVE, ADVERB
[1] detailed ◇ *ein ausführlicher Bericht* a detailed report
[2] in detail ◇ *Sie hat mir ausführlich erzählt, wie es in den Ferien war.* She told me in detail what her holidays were like.

**ausfüllen** VERB (PERFECT **hat ausgefüllt**)
to fill in ◇ *Füllt bitte die Lücken im Text aus.* Please fill in the gaps in the text.
◇ *Hast du den Antrag schon ausgefüllt?* Have you filled in the application form yet?
♦ **Mein Beruf füllt mich nicht aus.** My job doesn't satisfy me.

die **Ausgabe** NOUN
[1] expenditure ◇ *Wir hatten in der letzten Zeit viele Ausgaben.* We've had a lot of expenditure recently.
[2] edition ◇ *Sie hat eine sehr alte Ausgabe von Goethes Werken.* She's got a very old edition of Goethe's works.
[3] issue ◇ *Ich habe das in der letzten Ausgabe meines Computermagazins gelesen.* I read it in the last issue of my computer magazine.

der **Ausgang** NOUN (PL die **Ausgänge**)
[1] exit ◇ *Ich warte dann am Ausgang auf euch.* I'll wait for you at the exit, then.
♦ **"Kein Ausgang"** "No exit"
[2] ending ◇ *Der Film hat einen sehr traurigen Ausgang.* The film has a very sad ending.
[3] result ◇ *Welchen Ausgang hatte das Spiel?* What was the result of the match?

**ausgeben** VERB (PRESENT **gibt aus,** IMPERFECT **gab aus,** PERFECT **hat ausgegeben**)
[1] to spend ◇ *Wir haben auf dem Volksfest fünfzig Mark ausgegeben.* We spent fifty marks at the fair.
[2] to distribute ◇ *Du musst dich da vorn anstellen, da werden die Karten ausgegeben.* You have to queue at the front there: that's where the tickets are being distributed.
♦ **einen ausgeben** to stand a round ◇ *Ich habe heute Geburtstag, darum gebe ich einen aus.* It's my birthday today, so I'm standing a round.
♦ **sich für jemanden ausgeben** to pass oneself off as somebody ◇ *Sie hat sich für meine Schwester ausgegeben.* She passed herself off as my sister.
♦ **sich als etwas ausgeben** to pretend to be something ◇ *Er hat sich als Computerfachmann ausgegeben.* He pretended to be a computer expert.

**ausgebucht** ADJECTIVE
fully booked

**ausgehen** VERB (IMPERFECT **ging aus,** PERFECT **ist ausgegangen**)

**1** to go out ◊ *Sollen wir heute Abend ausgehen?* Shall we go out this evening? ◊ *Fritz will mit dir ausgehen.* Fritz wants to go out with you. ◊ *Plötzlich ging das Licht aus.* Suddenly the light went out.

**2** to run out ◊ *Wir sollten tanken, bevor das Benzin ausgeht.* We ought to fill up before we run out of petrol.

♦ **Mir ging das Benzin aus.** I ran out of petrol.

♦ **Wie ist das Spiel ausgegangen?** How did the game end?

♦ **schlecht ausgehen** to turn out badly

♦ **wir können davon ausgehen, dass ...** we can assume that ...

**ausgelassen** ADJECTIVE
exuberant

**ausgenommen** CONJUNCTION
except ◊ *Alle kamen, ausgenommen Günter.* Everyone came except Günter.

♦ **Anwesende sind ausgenommen.** Present company excepted.

**ausgerechnet** ADVERB

♦ **ausgerechnet heute** today of all days

♦ **ausgerechnet du** you of all people

**ausgeschlossen** ADJECTIVE
impossible ◊ *Ich halte das für ausgeschlossen.* I think that's impossible.

**ausgezeichnet** ADJECTIVE, ADVERB

**1** excellent ◊ *Werner ist ein ausgezeichneter Koch.* Werner's an excellent cook.

**2** excellently ◊ *Sie hat es ausgezeichnet gemacht.* She did it excellently.

**ausgiebig** ADJECTIVE
substantial ◊ *Das Frühstück war sehr ausgiebig.* Breakfast was very substantial.

♦ **ausgiebig schlafen** to have a good sleep

♦ **sich ausgiebig erholen** to have a good long rest

**aushalten** VERB (PRESENT **hält aus,** IMPERFECT **hielt aus,** PERFECT **hat ausgehalten**)

♦ **Ich halte diese Hitze nicht aus!** I can't stand this heat.

♦ **Wie hast du es in dieser Stadt nur ausgehalten?** How could you stand living in this town?

♦ **Das ist nicht zum Aushalten.** It's unbearable.

sich **auskennen** VERB (IMPERFECT **kannte sich aus,** PERFECT **hat sich ausgekannt**)

**1** to know about ◊ *Sie kennt sich mit Kindern gut aus.* She knows a lot about children.

**2** to know one's way around ◊ *Er kennt sich in Stuttgart aus.* He knows his way around Stuttgart.

**auskommen** VERB (IMPERFECT **kam aus,** PERFECT **ist ausgekommen**)

♦ **mit jemandem auskommen** to get on with somebody ◊ *Ich komme mit meinen Eltern gut aus.* I get on well with my parents.

♦ **mit etwas auskommen** to manage on something ◊ *Ich muss mit fünfzig Mark in der Woche auskommen.* I have to manage on fifty marks a week.

die **Auskunft** NOUN (PL die **Auskünfte**)

**1** information ◊ *Nähere Auskunft erhalten Sie unter der folgenden Nummer.* For further information ring the following number.

**2** information office ◊ *Fragen Sie bei der Auskunft, wann der nächste Zug nach Bremen geht.* Ask at the information office when the next train leaves for Bremen.

♦ **Telefonauskunft** directory inquiries ◊ *Ruf doch die Auskunft an!* Ring directory inquiries.

**auslachen** VERB (PERFECT **hat ausgelacht**)
to laugh at ◊ *Sie hat mich nur ausgelacht.* She just laughed at me.

**ausladen** VERB (PRESENT **lädt aus,** IMPERFECT **lud aus,** PERFECT **hat ausgeladen**)
to unload ◊ *Wir müssen noch das Auto ausladen.* We still have to unload the car.

♦ **jemanden ausladen** to tell somebody not to come

das **Ausland** NOUN

♦ **im Ausland** abroad ◊ *Er lebt im Ausland.* He lives abroad.

♦ **ins Ausland** abroad ◊ *Nach dem Examen möchte sie ins Ausland gehen.* After the exams she wants to go abroad.

der **Ausländer** NOUN (PL die **Ausländer**)
foreigner ◊ *Ihr Mann ist Ausländer.* Her husband's a foreigner.

die **Ausländerin** NOUN
foreigner ◊ *Seine Frau ist Ausländerin.* His wife's a foreigner.

**ausländisch** ADJECTIVE
foreign

das **Auslandsgespräch** NOUN (PL die **Auslandsgespräche**)
international call

**auslassen** VERB (PRESENT **lässt aus,** IMPERFECT **ließ aus,** PERFECT **hat ausgelassen**)

**1** to leave out ◊ *Die nächste Übung können wir auslassen.* We can leave out the next exercise.

♦ **Ich lasse heute das Mittagessen aus.** I'm skipping lunch today.

**2** to leave off ◊ *Heute lass ich den Fernseher aus.* I'm leaving the television off today. ◊ *Bei der Hitze kannst du die Jacke auslassen.* You can leave your jacket off in this heat.

♦ **seine Wut an jemandem auslassen** to take one's anger out on somebody

**ausleeren** VERB (PERFECT **hat ausgeleert**)
to empty

**ausleihen** VERB (IMPERFECT **lieh aus,** PERFECT **hat ausgeliehen**)

**A**

to lend ◊ *Kannst du mir dein Moped ausleihen?* Can you lend me your moped?

♦ **sich etwas ausleihen** to borrow something ◊ *Ich habe mir das Wörterbuch meines Bruders ausgeliehen.* I've borrowed my brother's dictionary.

**ausloggen** VERB (PERFECT **hat ausgeloggt**)
to log off (*computer*)

**ausmachen** VERB (PERFECT **hat ausgemacht**)
[1] to turn off ◊ *Mach bitte das Radio aus, die Musik stört mich.* Please turn the radio off. The music's disturbing me.

♦ **das Licht ausmachen** to switch off the light

[2] to put out ◊ *Du solltest deine Zigarette ausmachen, bevor du hineingehst.* You should put your cigarette out before you go in.

[3] to arrange ◊ *Habt ihr schon einen Termin für das Fest ausgemacht?* Have you arranged a date for the party yet? ◊ *Ich habe mit ihr ausgemacht, dass wir uns um fünf Uhr treffen.* I've arranged to meet her at five.

[4] to settle ◊ *Macht das unter euch aus.* Settle the matter between you.

[5] to mind ◊ *Es macht mir nichts aus, wenn ich allein gehen muss.* I don't mind having to go alone. ◊ *Macht es Ihnen etwas aus, wenn ...?* Would you mind if ...?

die **Ausnahme** NOUN
exception

**ausnahmsweise** ADVERB
for once

**ausnützen** VERB (PERFECT **hat ausgenützt**)
to use

**auspacken** VERB (PERFECT **hat ausgepackt**)
to unpack

**ausprobieren** VERB (PERFECT **hat ausprobiert**)
to try out

der **Auspuff** NOUN (PL die **Auspuffe**)
exhaust

der **Auspufftopf** NOUN (PL die **Auspufftöpfe**)
silencer

**ausrechnen** VERB (PERFECT **hat ausgerechnet**)
to calculate

die **Ausrede** NOUN
excuse

**ausreichend** ADJECTIVE
[1] sufficient ◊ *ausreichend Geld* sufficient money
[2] adequate

ℹ *German marks range from one (**sehr gut**) to six (**ungenügend**).*

die **Ausreise** NOUN
departure

♦ **bei der Ausreise** when leaving the country

**ausrichten** VERB (PERFECT **hat ausgerichtet**)
[1] to tell ◊ *Ich werde es ihm ausrichten.* I'll tell him.

♦ **Richte bitte an deine Eltern schöne Grüße aus.** Please give my regards to your parents.

[2] to gear to ◊ *Wir müssen unser Veranstaltungsangebot mehr auf Jugendliche ausrichten.* We must gear our events more to young people.

**ausrufen** VERB (IMPERFECT **rief aus**, PERFECT **hat ausgerufen**)
to cry out

♦ **jemanden ausrufen lassen** to page somebody

das **Ausrufezeichen** NOUN (PL die **Ausrufezeichen**)
exclamation mark

sich **ausruhen** VERB (PERFECT **hat sich ausgeruht**)
to rest

**ausrüsten** VERB (PERFECT **hat ausgerüstet**)
to equip

die **Ausrüstung** NOUN
equipment

**ausschalten** VERB (PERFECT **hat ausgeschaltet**)
to switch off

**ausschlafen** VERB (PRESENT **schläft aus**, IMPERFECT **schlief aus**, PERFECT **hat ausgeschlafen**)
to have a good sleep

♦ **Morgen kann ich ausschlafen.** I can have a lie-in tomorrow.

♦ **Ich bin nicht ausgeschlafen.** I didn't get enough sleep.

**ausschließlich** ADVERB, PREPOSITION
[1] exclusively ◊ *Der Schulhof ist ausschließlich für Schüler dieser Schule.* The school yard is exclusively for pupils of this school.

[2] except ◊ *Wir haben jeden Tag geöffnet ausschließlich Sonntag.* We're open every day except Sunday.

**ausschneiden** VERB (IMPERFECT **schnitt aus**, PERFECT **hat ausgeschnitten**)
to cut out

der **Ausschuss** NOUN (GEN des **Ausschusses**, PL die **Ausschüsse**)
committee

**aussehen** VERB (PRESENT **sieht aus**, IMPERFECT **sah aus**, PERFECT **hat ausgesehen**)

see also **das Aussehen** NOUN

to look ◊ *Sie sieht sehr hübsch aus.* She looks very pretty. ◊ *Wie siehst du denn aus?* What do you look like! ◊ *Es sieht nach Regen aus.* It looks like rain. ◊ *Es sieht schlecht aus.* Things look bad.

das **Aussehen** NOUN

see also **aussehen** VERB

appearance

**aussein** VERB *see* **aus**

**außen** ADVERB
on the outside ◇ *Außen ist es rot.* It's red on the outside.

das **Außenministerium** NOUN (PL die **Außenministerien**)
foreign office

die **Außenpolitik** NOUN
foreign policy

der **Außenseiter** NOUN (PL die **Außenseiter**)
outsider

**außer** PREPOSITION, CONJUNCTION
The preposition **außer** takes the dative.
[1] apart from ◇ *Außer dir haben das alle verstanden.* Everyone has understood apart from you. ◇ *Wer war noch da außer Horst?* Apart from Horst, who was there?
◆ **außer Haus** out ◇ *Er ist heute den ganzen Tag außer Haus.* He's out all day today.
◆ **außer Landes** abroad
◆ **außer Gefahr** out of danger
◆ **außer Betrieb** out of order
◆ **außer sich sein** to be beside oneself ◇ *Sie war außer sich vor Wut.* She was beside herself with rage.
[2] if ... not ◇ *Wir machen morgen ein Picknick, außer es regnet.* We're having a picnic tomorrow if it doesn't rain.
◆ **nicht ... außer** not ... unless ◇ *Wir können sie nicht mitnehmen, außer sie ist schon reisefertig.* We can't take her with us unless she's all packed and ready to go.

**außerdem** CONJUNCTION
in addition

**äußere** ADJECTIVE
[1] outer ◇ *Sie bildeten einen äußeren und einen inneren Kreis.* They formed an outer and an inner circle.
[2] external ◇ *Nur zur äußeren Anwendung.* For external use only.
◆ **Der äußere Eindruck trügt manchmal.** Appearances are sometimes deceptive.

**außergewöhnlich** ADJECTIVE
unusual

**außerhalb** PREPOSITION, ADVERB
The preposition **außerhalb** takes the genitive.
[1] outside ◇ *Es liegt außerhalb der Stadt.* It's outside the town.
[2] out of town ◇ *Sie wohnt nicht in Ulm, sondern ziemlich weit außerhalb.* She doesn't live in Ulm, but quite a way out of town.
◆ **außerhalb der Saison** out of season

**äußern** VERB
to express ◇ *Sie hat den Wunsch geäußert, allein in die Ferien fahren zu dürfen.* She's expressed the wish to be allowed to go on holiday alone.
◆ **eine Meinung äußern** to give an opinion ◇ *Willst du nicht auch deine Meinung äußern?* Don't you want to give your opinion, too?

◆ **sich äußern** to comment ◇ *Sie wollte sich zu dem Vorwurf nicht äußern.* She didn't wish to comment on the accusation.

**außerordentlich** ADJECTIVE, ADVERB
exceptional ◇ *Sie hat eine außerordentliche Begabung.* She's exceptionally gifted.
◆ **Sie ist außerordentlich intelligent.** She's exceptionally intelligent.

**äußerst** ADVERB
see also **äußerste** ADJECTIVE
extremely

**äußerste** ADJECTIVE
see also **äußerst** ADVERB
utmost ◇ *Diese Sache ist von äußerster Wichtigkeit.* This matter is of the utmost importance.
◆ **Tausend Mark sind der äußerste Preis, den ich für den Computer bezahlen kann.** One thousand marks is the most I can pay for the computer.

die **Äußerung** NOUN
remark

die **Aussicht** NOUN
[1] view ◇ *Vom Hotel aus hat man eine schöne Aussicht aufs Meer.* You have a wonderful view of the sea from the hotel.
[2] prospect ◇ *Die Aussicht auf diese Stelle hat ihr neuen Mut gegeben.* The prospect of this job gave her new hope.
◆ **Das sind ja schöne Aussichten!** What a prospect!
◆ **etwas in Aussicht haben** to have the prospect of something ◇ *Sie hat eine Stelle bei Collins in Aussicht.* She has the prospect of a job with Collins.

**ausspannen** VERB (PERFECT **hat ausgespannt**)
to relax

die **Aussprache** NOUN
[1] pronunciation ◇ *Die Aussprache der Wörter ist mit phonetischen Zeichen angegeben.* The pronunciation of the words is shown by phonetic symbols.
[2] frank discussion ◇ *Ich hatte gestern eine lange Aussprache mit ihm.* I had a long, frank discussion with him yesterday.

**aussprechen** VERB (PRESENT **spricht aus**, IMPERFECT **sprach aus**, PERFECT **hat ausgesprochen**)
to pronounce ◇ *Wie spricht man dieses Wort aus?* How do you pronounce this word?
◆ **sich mit jemandem aussprechen** to talk things out with somebody ◇ *Meinst du nicht, wir sollten uns einmal aussprechen?* Don't you think we ought to talk things out?
◆ **sich gegen etwas aussprechen** to speak out against something ◇ *Die Mehrheit hat sich gegen eine Klassenfahrt nach*

*Helgoland ausgesprochen.* The majority spoke out against a school trip to Heligoland.

♦ **sich für etwas aussprechen** to speak out in favour of something ◊ *Die Lehrer haben sich für eine Verlängerung der Pausenzeiten ausgesprochen.* The teachers spoke out in favour of longer breaks.

♦ **Lass ihn doch aussprechen!** Let him finish.

**aussteigen** VERB (IMPERFECT **stieg aus**, PERFECT **ist ausgestiegen**)
to get off ◊ *Ich sah, wie sie aus der Straßenbahn ausstieg.* I saw her get off the tram.

**ausstellen** VERB (PERFECT **hat ausgestellt**)
[1] to exhibit ◊ *Im Museum werden zurzeit Bilder von Chagall ausgestellt.* Pictures by Chagall are currently being exhibited in the museum.
[2] to be on display ◊ *Im Schaufenster war exotisches Obst ausgestellt.* Exotic fruit was on display in the window.
[3] to switch off ◊ *Die Heizung wird im Mai ausgestellt.* The heating's switched off in May.
[4] to write ◊ *Die Lehrerin hat ihm ein gutes Zeugnis ausgestellt.* The teacher wrote him a good report.
[5] to issue ◊ *Auf welchem Amt werden Pässe ausgestellt?* Which office issues passports?

die **Ausstellung** NOUN
exhibition

**aussterben** VERB (PRESENT **stirbt aus**, IMPERFECT **starb aus**, PERFECT **ist ausgestorben**)
to die out

der **Ausstieg** NOUN
[1] exit ◊ *Der Ausstieg ist hinten.* The exit is at the back.
[2] abandonment ◊ *der Ausstieg aus der Atomenergie* abandonment of nuclear energy

**ausstreichen** VERB (IMPERFECT **strich aus**, PERFECT **hat ausgestrichen**)
to cross out

**aussuchen** VERB (PERFECT **hat ausgesucht**)
to choose ◊ *Such dir ein Eis aus.* Choose yourself an ice cream.

der **Austausch** NOUN (GEN des **Austausches**)
exchange ◊ *ein Schüleraustausch* a school exchange

**austauschen** VERB (PERFECT **hat ausgetauscht**)
[1] to replace ◊ *Ich habe die Festplatte ausgetauscht.* I've replaced the hard disk. ◊ *Wir müssen die Winterreifen gegen die Sommerreifen austauschen.* We'll have to replace our winter tyres with summer tyres.

[2] to substitute ◊ *Der Mittelstürmer wurde in der zweiten Halbzeit ausgetauscht.* The centre-forward was substituted in the second half.
♦ **Unsere Schule tauscht jedes Jahr Schüler mit einer Schule aus Cardiff aus.** Every year, our school has a student exchange with a school in Cardiff.
♦ **Wir tauschen seit ein paar Jahren Briefe aus.** We've been writing to each other for a few years.

**austeilen** VERB (PERFECT **hat ausgeteilt**)
to give out

die **Auster** NOUN
oyster

**austragen** VERB (PRESENT **trägt aus**, IMPERFECT **trug aus**, PERFECT **hat ausgetragen**)
[1] to deliver ◊ *Morgens trägt er immer die Post aus.* In the morning he always delivers the post.
[2] to hold ◊ *Der Wettkampf wird im Olympiastadion ausgetragen.* The competition will be held in the Olympic stadium.
♦ **Sie will das Kind austragen.** She wants to have the baby.

**Australien** NEUT NOUN
Australia
♦ **aus Australien** from Australia
♦ **in Australien** in Australia
♦ **nach Australien** to Australia

der **Australier** NOUN (PL die **Australier**)
Australian

die **Australierin** NOUN
Australian

**australisch** ADJECTIVE
Australian

**austreten** VERB (PRESENT **tritt aus**, IMPERFECT **trat aus**, PERFECT **ist ausgetreten**)
♦ **aus etwas austreten** to leave something ◊ *Sie ist aus dem Verein ausgetreten.* She's left the club.
♦ **Ich muss mal austreten.** I need to go to the loo.

**austrinken** VERB (IMPERFECT **trank aus**, PERFECT **hat ausgetrunken**)
to drink up ◊ *Er trank aus und ging.* He drank up and left.
♦ **Lass mich noch schnell meinen Saft austrinken.** Let me just quickly finish my juice.

der **Ausverkauf** NOUN (PL die **Ausverkäufe**)
clearance sale

**ausverkauft** ADJECTIVE
[1] sold out ◊ *Die Vorstellung ist leider ausverkauft.* The performance is sold out, I'm afraid.
[2] full ◊ *Das Kino war ausverkauft.* The cinema was full.

die **Auswahl** NOUN
selection ◊ *Sie haben eine große Auswahl an Schuhen.* They have a large selection of shoes.

**auswählen** VERB (PERFECT **hat ausgewählt**)
to select

**auswandern** VERB (PERFECT **ist ausgewandert**)
to emigrate ◊ *Sie sind nach Australien ausgewandert.* They emigrated to Australia.

**auswärts** ADVERB
[1] in another town ◊ *Sie wohnt in Calw, arbeitet aber auswärts.* She lives in Calw but works in another town.
[2] away ◊ *Unsere Mannschaft spielt nächste Woche auswärts.* Our team's playing away next week.
♦ **auswärts essen** to eat out

das **Auswärtsspiel** NOUN (PL die **Auswärtsspiele**)
away game

der **Ausweg** NOUN (PL die **Auswege**)
way out

**ausweichend** ADJECTIVE
evasive

der **Ausweis** NOUN (PL die **Ausweise**)
[1] identity card ◊ *Der Polizist wollte meinen Ausweis sehen.* The policeman wanted to see my identity card.
[2] card ◊ *Wenn du Schüler bist und deinen Ausweis zeigst, bekommst du Ermäßigung.* If you're a student and show them your card, you get a reduction.

**auswendig** ADVERB
by heart ◊ *etwas auswendig lernen* to learn something by heart

**auswerten** VERB (PERFECT **hat ausgewertet**)
to evaluate

die **Auswertung** NOUN
evaluation

**ausziehen** VERB (IMPERFECT **zog aus**, PERFECT **hat/ist ausgezogen**)
*For the perfect tense use **haben** when the verb has an object and **sein** when there is no object.*
[1] to take off ◊ *Sie hat ihren Mantel nicht ausgezogen.* She didn't take off her coat.
[2] to undress ◊ *Kannst du bitte die Kinder ausziehen und ins Bett bringen?* Can you undress the children and put them to bed, please?
♦ **sich ausziehen** to undress ◊ *Haben die Kinder sich schon ausgezogen?* Have the children undressed yet?
[3] to pull out ◊ *Der Zahnarzt hat mir zwei Zähne ausgezogen.* The dentist pulled out two of my teeth.
[4] to move out ◊ *Meine Nachbarn sind letzte Woche ausgezogen.* My neighbours moved out last week.

der **Auszubildende** NOUN (GEN des/der
die **Auszubildenden**, PL die **Auszubildenden**)
trainee

das **Auto** NOUN (PL die **Autos**)
car
♦ **Auto fahren** to drive

die **Autobahn** NOUN
motorway

das **Autobahndreieck** NOUN (PL die **Autobahndreiecke**)
motorway junction

das **Autobahnkreuz** NOUN (GEN des **Autobahnkreuzes**, PL die **Autobahnkreuze**)
motorway intersection

der **Autobus** NOUN (GEN des **Autobusses**, PL die **Autobusse**)
bus

der **Autofahrer** NOUN (PL die **Autofahrer**)
motorist

das **Autogramm** NOUN (PL die **Autogramme**)
autograph

das **Autokennzeichen** NOUN (PL die **Autokennzeichen**)
registration number

der **Automat** NOUN (GEN des **Automaten**, PL die **Automaten**)
machine

**automatisch** ADJECTIVE
automatic ◊ *Die Türen schließen automatisch.* The doors close automatically.

der **Autor** NOUN (PL die **Autoren**)
author

das **Autoradio** NOUN (PL die **Autoradios**)
car radio

das **Autorennen** NOUN (PL die **Autorennen**)
motor racing

die **Autorin** NOUN
author

**autoritär** ADJECTIVE
authoritarian

die **Autorität** NOUN
authority

der **Autostopp** NOUN
♦ **per Autostopp fahren** to hitchhike

das **Autotelefon** NOUN (PL die **Autotelefone**)
car phone

der **Autounfall** NOUN (PL die **Autounfälle**)
car accident

die **Autowäsche** NOUN
car wash

die **Axt** NOUN (PL die **Äxte**)
axe

# B

das **Baby** NOUN (PL die **Babys**)
baby
**babysitten** VERB (PERFECT **hat gebabysittet**)
to babysit
der **Babysitter** NOUN (PL die **Babysitter**)
babysitter
die **Babysitterin** NOUN
babysitter
der **Bach** NOUN (PL die **Bäche**)
stream
die **Backe** NOUN
cheek
**backen** VERB (PRESENT **bäckt**, IMPERFECT **backte**
or **buk**, PERFECT **hat gebacken**)
to bake
der **Bäcker** NOUN (PL die **Bäcker**)
baker ◊ *beim Bäcker* at the baker's ◊ *zum Bäcker* to the baker's
die **Bäckerei** NOUN
baker's
der **Backofen** NOUN (PL die **Backöfen**)
oven
das **Bad** NOUN (PL die **Bäder**)
bath
♦ **ein Bad im Meer** a swim in the sea
der **Badeanzug** NOUN (PL die **Badeanzüge**)
bathing suit
die **Badehose** NOUN
swimming trunks
die **Bademütze** NOUN
bathing cap
**baden** VERB
to have a bath
♦ **jemanden baden** to bath somebody
◊ *Das Baby muss noch gebadet werden.* The baby still has to be bathed.
♦ **sich baden** to have a bath
**Baden-Württemberg** NEUT NOUN
Baden-Württemberg

> ❶ **Baden-Württemberg** is one of the 16 *Länder*. Its capital is Stuttgart. Baden-Württemberg is home to the cuckoo clock and to Mercedes-Benz and Porsche.

der **Badeort** NOUN
spa
das **Badetuch** NOUN (PL die **Badetücher**)
bath towel
die **Badewanne** NOUN
bath (*tub*)
das **Badezimmer** NOUN (PL die **Badezimmer**)
bathroom
das **Badminton** NOUN (GEN des **Badminton**)
badminton
die **Bahn** NOUN (PL die **Bahnen**)

1 railway ◊ *Er arbeitet bei der Bahn.* He works for the railway.
♦ **Wir sind mit der Bahn gefahren.** We went by rail.
2 tram
3 lane ◊ *Die Schwimmerin auf Bahn drei liegt in Führung.* The swimmer in lane three is in the lead.
♦ **auf die schiefe Bahn geraten** to go off the rails
die **Bahnfahrt** NOUN
railway journey
der **Bahnhof** NOUN (PL die **Bahnhöfe**)
station ◊ *auf dem Bahnhof* at the station
die **Bahnhofshalle** NOUN
station concourse
der **Bahnsteig** NOUN (PL die **Bahnsteige**)
platform
der **Bahnübergang** NOUN (PL die **Bahnübergänge**)
level crossing
**bald** ADVERB
1 soon ◊ *Es wird bald Frühling.* It'll soon be spring.
♦ **Bis bald!** See you later.
2 almost ◊ *Ich hätte bald was gesagt.* I almost said something.
♦ **Wird's bald!** Get a move on!
der **Balkan** NOUN
Balkans
♦ **auf dem Balkan** in the Balkans
der **Balken** NOUN (PL die **Balken**)
beam
der **Balkon** NOUN (PL die **Balkons** or **Balkone**)
balcony
der **Ball** NOUN (PL die **Bälle**)
ball ◊ *Die Kinder spielen mit dem Ball.* The children are playing with the ball.
◊ *Mit wem kommst du zum Ball?* Who are you going to the ball with?
das **Ballett** NOUN (PL die **Ballette**)
ballet
der **Ballon** NOUN (PL die **Ballons** or **Ballone**)
balloon
der **Bambus** NOUN (GEN des **Bambusses**, PL die **Bambusse**)
bamboo
die **Banane** NOUN
banana
der **Band** NOUN (PL die **Bände**)
*see also* **die Band** NOUN, **das Band** NOUN
volume ◊ *ein Lexikon in fünf Bänden* an encyclopaedia in five volumes
die **Band** NOUN (PL die **Bands**)
*see also* **der Band** NOUN, **das Band** NOUN
band ◊ *Er spielt Gitarre in einer Band.* He plays the guitar in a band.
das **Band** NOUN (PL die **Bänder**)

☞

der **Band** NOUN, die **Band** NOUN

⊡1⊡ ribbon ◊ *Sie hatte ein rotes Band im Haar.* She had a red ribbon in her hair.

⊡2⊡ production line ◊ *Mein Vater arbeitet am Band.* My father works on the production line.

⊡3⊡ tape ◊ *Ich habe diesen Song auf Band.* I've got this song on tape.

♦ **etwas auf Band aufnehmen** to tape something

♦ **am laufenden Band** nonstop

**band** VERB *see* **binden**

die **Bank (1)** NOUN (PL die **Bänke**)

bench ◊ *Sie saß auf einer Bank im Park.* She was sitting on a park bench.

die **Bank (2)** NOUN (PL die **Banken**)

bank ◊ *Ich muss Geld von der Bank holen.* I'll have to get money from the bank.

der **Bankkonto** NOUN (PL die **Bankkonten**)

bank account

die **Bankleitzahl** NOUN

bank sort code

die **Banknote** NOUN

banknote

**bankrott** ADJECTIVE

bankrupt ◊ *Die Firma ist bankrott.* The firm is bankrupt.

♦ **Bankrott machen** to go bankrupt

die **Bar** NOUN (PL die **Bars**)

see also **bar** ADJECTIVE

bar

**bar** ADJECTIVE

see also **die Bar** NOUN

♦ **bares Geld** cash

♦ **etwas bar bezahlen** to pay cash for something

der **Bär** NOUN (GEN des **Bären**, PL die **Bären**)

bear

**barfuß** ADJECTIVE

barefoot

das **Bargeld** NOUN

cash

der **Barren** NOUN (PL die **Barren**)

parallel bars

der **Bart** NOUN (PL die **Bärte**)

beard

**bärtig** ADJECTIVE

bearded

**Basel** NEUT NOUN

Basle

♦ **nach Basel** to Basle

die **Basis** NOUN (PL die **Basen**)

basis

der **Bass** NOUN (GEN des **Basses**, PL die **Bässe**)

bass

**basteln** VERB

to make things ◊ *Ich bastle gern.* I like making things.

♦ **etwas basteln** to make something ◊ *Ich habe einen Untersetzer gebastelt.* I've made a coaster.

der **Bastler** NOUN (PL die **Bastler**)

do-it-yourselfer

♦ **Er ist ein guter Bastler.** He is good at making things.

**bat** VERB *see* **bitten**

die **Batterie** NOUN

battery

der **Bau** NOUN (PL die **Bauten**)

⊡1⊡ construction ◊ *Das Haus ist noch im Bau befindlich.* The house is still under construction.

⊡2⊡ building ◊ *In New York gibt es viele beeindruckende Bauten.* There are many impressive buildings in New York.

⊡3⊡ building site ◊ *In den Ferien arbeitet er auf dem Bau.* He works on a building site in the holidays.

der **Bauarbeiter** NOUN (PL die **Bauarbeiter**)

building worker

der **Bauch** NOUN (PL die **Bäuche**)

stomach ◊ *Mir tut der Bauch weh.* My stomach's sore.

der **Bauchnabel** NOUN (PL die **Bauchnabel**)

belly button

die **Bauchschmerzen** MASC PL NOUN

stomachache

**bauen** VERB

to build ◊ *Meine Eltern haben das Haus gebaut, in dem wir wohnen.* My parents built the house we live in.

der **Bauer** NOUN (GEN des **Bauern**, PL die **Bauern**)

⊡1⊡ farmer ◊ *Friedas Vater ist Bauer.* Frieda's father is a farmer.

⊡2⊡ pawn ◊ *Sie zog mit dem Bauer.* She moved the pawn.

die **Bäuerin** NOUN

⊡1⊡ farmer ◊ *Sie möchte Bäuerin werden.* She would like to be a farmer.

⊡2⊡ farmer's wife ◊ *Die Bäuerin melkt die Kühe, während der Bauer aufs Feld fährt.* The farmer's wife milks the cows while the farmer drives out to the fields.

der **Bauernhof** NOUN (PL die **Bauernhöfe**)

farm

**baufällig** ADJECTIVE

dilapidated

der **Baum** NOUN (PL die **Bäume**)

tree

die **Baumwolle** NOUN

cotton ◊ *eine Tischdecke aus Baumwolle* a cotton tablecloth

die **Baustelle** NOUN

building site

die **Bauten** PL NOUN *see* **Bau**

der **Bauunternehmer** NOUN (PL die **Bauunternehmer**)

building contractor

der **Bayer** NOUN (GEN des **Bayern**, PL die **Bayern**)

Bavarian

die **Bayerin** NOUN

Bavarian

**Bayern** NEUT NOUN

Bavaria

> **❶ Bayern** is one of the 16 **Länder**. Its capital is München (Munich). Bavaria has the longest political tradition of any of the Länder, and since 1945 has developed into an important industrial region.

**bayrisch** ADJECTIVE
Bavarian

**beabsichtigen** VERB (PERFECT **hat beabsichtigt**)
to intend ◊ *Ich beabsichtige, ins Ausland zu fahren.* I intend to go abroad.

**beachten** VERB (PERFECT **hat beachtet**)
[1] to pay attention to ◊ *Beachte ihn nicht!* Don't pay any attention to him. ◊ *Du solltest den Hinweis auf der Packung beachten.* You should pay attention to the instructions on the packet.
[2] to obey ◊ *Man muss die Verkehrsregeln beachten.* You have to obey the traffic regulations.
[3] to observe ◊ *Sie hat die Vorfahrt nicht beachtet.* She didn't observe the right of way.

**beachtlich** ADJECTIVE
considerable

der **Beamte** NOUN (GEN des **Beamten,** PL die **Beamten**)
[1] official ◊ *Der Beamte stempelte meinen Pass ab.* The official stamped my passport.
[2] civil servant

> **❶** In Germany, traditionally all public employees are civil servants. They enjoy many privileges.

◊ *Deutsche Lehrer sind Beamte.* German teachers are civil servants.

die **Beamtin** NOUN
civil servant ◊ *Meine Mutter ist Beamtin.* My mother's a civil servant.

**beängstigend** ADJECTIVE, ADVERB
alarming
♦ **Sie ist beängstigend schnell gefahren.** She drove alarmingly fast.

**beanspruchen** VERB (PERFECT **hat beansprucht**)
[1] to claim ◊ *Bei fünf Kindern können Sie Kindergeld beanspruchen.* You can claim child benefit if you have five children.
[2] to take up ◊ *Die Kinder beanspruchen meine ganze Zeit und Kraft.* The children take up all my time and energy.
♦ **jemanden beanspruchen** to take up somebody's time ◊ *Ich möchte Sie nicht länger beanspruchen.* I don't want to take up any more of your time.

[3] to take advantage of ◊ *Wir haben eure Gastfreundschaft lange genug beansprucht.* We've taken advantage of your hospitality for long enough.

**beantragen** VERB (PERFECT **hat beantragt**)
to apply for

**beantworten** VERB (PERFECT **hat beantwortet**)
to answer

**bearbeiten** VERB (PERFECT **hat bearbeitet**)
[1] to deal with ◊ *Welches Thema hat sie in ihrer Diplomarbeit bearbeitet?* What subject did she deal with in her dissertation?
[2] to process ◊ *Wir haben Ihren Antrag noch nicht bearbeitet.* We haven't processed your application yet.
[3] to treat ◊ *Sie hat den Fleck mit Fleckenmittel bearbeitet.* She treated the stain with stain remover.
♦ **jemanden bearbeiten** to work on somebody ◊ *Ich werde meine Mutter bearbeiten, dass sie mich gehen lässt.* I'll work on my mother and get her to let me go.

der **Becher** NOUN (PL die **Becher**)
[1] mug ◊ *Auf ihrem Schreibtisch stand ein Becher mit Kaffee.* There was a mug of coffee on her desk.
[2] carton
[3] tub

das **Becken** NOUN (PL die **Becken**)
[1] sink ◊ *Er ließ Wasser ins Becken laufen.* He ran water into the sink.
[2] pool
♦ **Sie hat ein breites Becken.** She has broad hips.

sich **bedanken** VERB (PERFECT **hat sich bedankt**)
to say thank you ◊ *Hast du dich auch bedankt?* Did you say thank you?
♦ **Ich bedanke mich für Ihre Gastfreundschaft.** Thank you for your hospitality.
♦ **sich bei jemandem bedanken** to say thank you to somebody

der **Bedarf** NOUN
demand ◊ *je nach Bedarf* according to demand
♦ **bei Bedarf** if necessary
♦ **Bedarf an etwas haben** to be in need of something ◊ *Wir haben Bedarf an Aushilfskräften.* We're in need of temporary workers.

**bedauerlich** ADJECTIVE
regrettable

**bedauern** VERB (PERFECT **hat bedauert**)
[1] to be sorry for ◊ *Wir bedauern es sehr, dass wir nicht kommen können.* We're very sorry that we can't come.
♦ **Ich bedaure!** I'm sorry!
♦ **Ich bedaure kein Wort.** I don't regret a single word!

2 to pity ◊ *Ich bedaure dich wirklich!* I really pity you!

**bedeckt** ADJECTIVE

1 covered ◊ *Die Erde war mit Laub bedeckt.* The ground was covered with leaves.

2 overcast ◊ *Heute ist es bedeckt.* It's overcast today.

die **Bedenken** NEUT PL NOUN

doubts ◊ *Ich habe Bedenken, ob das klappt.* I have my doubts as to whether it'll work.

♦ **Hast du keine Bedenken, wenn du deine Eltern so anlügst?** Don't you feel bad about lying to your parents like that?

**bedenklich** ADJECTIVE

1 dubious ◊ *Das sind sehr bedenkliche Methoden.* These are very dubious methods.

2 dangerous ◊ *Die Lage ist bedenklich.* The situation is dangerous.

♦ **Ihr Gesundheitszustand ist bedenklich.** Her state of health is giving cause for concern.

**bedeuten** VERB (PERFECT **hat bedeutet**)

to mean ◊ *Was bedeutet dieser Ausdruck?* What does this expression mean? ◊ *Was hat das zu bedeuten?* What's that supposed to mean? ◊ *Er bedeutet mir sehr viel.* He means a lot to me.

**bedeutend** ADJECTIVE

1 important ◊ *Er ist ein bedeutender Wissenschaftler.* He's an important scientist.

2 considerable ◊ *Sie haben eine bedeutende Summe dafür bezahlt.* They paid a considerable sum for it.

♦ **bedeutend besser** considerably better

♦ **bedeutend schlechter** considerably worse

die **Bedeutung** NOUN

1 meaning ◊ *die Bedeutung eines Worts* the meaning of a word

2 importance ◊ *eine Erfindung von großer Bedeutung* an invention of great importance

**bedienen** VERB (PERFECT **hat bedient**)

1 to serve ◊ *Wir wurden sehr schnell bedient.* We were served very quickly.

2 to operate ◊ *Er bedient die Druckmaschine.* He operates the printing press.

♦ **Kannst du einen Computer bedienen?** Can you use a computer?

♦ **sich bedienen** to help oneself ◊ *Bitte bedien dich!* Please help yourself.

die **Bedienung** NOUN

1 service ◊ *In diesem Geschäft ist die Bedienung schlecht.* The service is very poor in this shop.

2 waiter
waitress

◊ *Wir haben bei der Bedienung ein Bier bestellt.* We ordered a beer from the waitress.

3 shop assistant ◊ *Die Bedienung im Kaufhaus war äußerst unfreundlich.* The shop assistant in the department store was extremely unfriendly.

4 service charge ◊ *Die Bedienung ist im Preis enthalten.* The service charge is included in the price.

die **Bedingung** NOUN

condition ◊ *unter der Bedingung, dass ...* on condition that ...

**bedrohen** VERB (PERFECT **hat bedroht**)

to threaten

das **Bedürfnis** NOUN (GEN des **Bedürfnisses,** PL die **Bedürfnisse**)

need

das **Beefsteak** NOUN (PL die **Beefsteaks**)

steak

♦ **deutsches Beefsteak** hamburger

sich **beeilen** VERB (PERFECT **hat sich beeilt**)

to hurry

**beeindrucken** VERB (PERFECT **hat beeindruckt**)

to impress

**beeindruckend** ADJECTIVE

impressive

**beeinflussen** VERB (PRESENT **beeinflusst,** IMPERFECT **beeinflusste,** PERFECT **hat beeinflusst**)

to influence

**beenden** VERB (PERFECT **hat beendet**)

to end

die **Beerdigung** NOUN

funeral

die **Beere** NOUN

1 berry

2 grape

das **Beet** NOUN (PL die **Beete**)

bed ◊ *ein Blumenbeet* a flowerbed

sich **befassen** VERB (PERFECT **hat sich befasst**)

♦ **sich mit etwas befassen** to deal with something

der **Befehl** NOUN (PL die **Befehle**)

command

**befehlen** VERB (PRESENT **befiehlt,** IMPERFECT **befahl,** PERFECT **hat befohlen**)

1 to order ◊ *Der General hat den Rückzug befohlen.* The general ordered his men to retreat.

2 to give orders ◊ *Du hast hier nicht zu befehlen!* You're not the one who gives the orders here!

♦ **jemandem etwas befehlen** to order somebody to do something

**befestigen** VERB (PERFECT **hat befestigt**)

to fix ◊ *Die Regalbretter sind mit Schrauben an der Wand befestigt.* The shelves are fixed to the wall with screws.

sich **befinden** VERB (IMPERFECT **befand sich,** PERFECT **hat sich befunden**)

**to be** ◊ *Er befindet sich zur Zeit im Ausland.* He's abroad at the moment.

**befolgen** VERB (PERFECT **hat befolgt**)
to obey

**befördern** VERB (PERFECT **hat befördert**)
[1] to carry ◊ *Die städtischen Busse befördern täglich viele Menschen.* The municipal buses carry many people every day.
[2] to promote ◊ *Sie ist zur Abteilungsleiterin befördert worden.* She's been promoted to head of department.

die **Beförderung** NOUN
[1] transport ◊ *Das Rote Kreuz übernimmt die Beförderung der Hilfsgüter.* The Red Cross undertakes the transport of emergency supplies.
[2] promotion ◊ *Bei einer Beförderung bekommt man auch mehr Geld.* Promotion also means more money.

**befragen** VERB (PERFECT **hat befragt**)
to question

**befreien** VERB (PERFECT **hat befreit**)
[1] to set free ◊ *Die Geiseln sind noch nicht befreit.* The hostages haven't been set free yet.
[2] to exempt ◊ *Sie ist vom Sportunterricht befreit.* She's exempt from PE lessons.

**befreundet** ADJECTIVE
♦ **mit jemandem befreundet sein** to be friends with somebody ◊ *Ich bin mit Petra seit Jahren befreundet.* I've been friends with Petra for years.

**befriedigen** VERB (PERFECT **hat befriedigt**)
to satisfy

**befriedigend** ADJECTIVE
satisfactory

> ⓘ German marks range from one (**sehr gut**) to six (**ungenügend**).

**befristet** ADJECTIVE
limited

**befürchten** VERB (PERFECT **hat befürchtet**)
to fear

**befürworten** VERB (PERFECT **hat befürwortet**)
to support

**begabt** ADJECTIVE
talented

die **Begabung** NOUN
talent

**begann** VERB *see* **beginnen**

**begegnen** VERB (PERFECT **ist begegnet**)
♦ **jemandem begegnen** to meet somebody ◊ *Ich bin ihr heute schon einmal begegnet.* I've met her once today already. ◊ *Wir sind uns das erste Mal in London begegnet.* The first time we met was in London. ◊ *Eine solche Frechheit*

*ist mir noch nie begegnet.* I've never met such cheek.

die **Begegnung** NOUN
meeting

**begehen** VERB (IMPERFECT **beging**, PERFECT **hat begangen**)
to commit ◊ *Er hat einen Mord begangen.* He committed a murder.

**begehren** VERB (PERFECT **hat begehrt**)
to desire

**begehrt** ADJECTIVE
[1] in demand
[2] eligible

**begeistern** VERB (PERFECT **hat begeistert**)
to thrill ◊ *Der Film hat mich begeistert.* I was thrilled with the film.
♦ **sich für etwas begeistern** to get enthusiastic about something

**begeistert** ADJECTIVE
enthusiastic

**begießen** VERB (IMPERFECT **begoss**, PERFECT **hat begossen**)
to water ◊ *Sie begoss ihre Rosen.* She watered her roses.
♦ **das muss begossen werden!** that calls for a drink!

der **Beginn** NOUN
beginning ◊ *zu Beginn* at the beginning

**beginnen** VERB (IMPERFECT **begann**, PERFECT hat **begonnen**)
to start

**begleiten** VERB (PERFECT **hat begleitet**)
to accompany ◊ *Er hat mich zum Ball begleitet.* He accompanied me to the ball.

**beglückwünschen** VERB (PERFECT **hat beglückwünscht**)
to congratulate ◊ *Alle meine Freunde haben mich zur bestandenen Prüfung beglückwünscht.* All my friends congratulated me on passing the exam.

**begonnen** VERB *see* **beginnen**

**begraben** VERB (PRESENT **begräbt**, IMPERFECT **begrub**, PERFECT **hat begraben**)
to bury

**begreifen** VERB (IMPERFECT **begriff**, PERFECT **hat begriffen**)
to understand

der **Begriff** NOUN (PL die **Begriffe**)
term ◊ *Das ist ein Begriff aus der Architektur.* That is an architectural term.
♦ **im Begriff sein, etwas zu tun** to be about to do something ◊ *Ich war im Begriff zu gehen.* I was about to go.
♦ **schwer von Begriff** slow on the uptake
♦ **sich einen Begriff von etwas machen** to imagine something ◊ *Du machst dir keinen Begriff, wie schwierig das war.* You can't imagine how difficult it was.

**begriffsstutzig** ADJECTIVE
dense

**begründen** VERB (PERFECT **hat begründet**)

to justify

die **Begründung** NOUN
justification

**begrüßen** VERB (PERFECT **hat begrüßt**)
to welcome ◊ *Ich begrüße diese
Änderung sehr.* I very much welcome
this change.
♦ **Wir wurden sehr herzlich begrüßt.** We
received a very warm welcome.

die **Begrüßung** NOUN
welcome

**behaglich** ADJECTIVE
cosy

**behalten** VERB (PRESENT **behält,** IMPERFECT
**behielt,** PERFECT **hat behalten**)
[1] to keep ◊ *Kann ich das Buch noch ein
paar Tage behalten?* Can I keep the book
for another couple of days?
[2] to remember ◊ *Ich kann mir ihren
Namen nie behalten.* I can never
remember her name.

der **Behälter** NOUN (PL die **Behälter**)
container

**behandeln** VERB (PERFECT **hat behandelt**)
[1] to treat ◊ *Wir wurden sehr freundlich
behandelt.* We were treated in a very
friendly manner. ◊ *Die Wunde muss
behandelt werden.* The wound will have
to be treated. ◊ *Welcher Arzt behandelt
Sie?* Which doctor is treating you?
[2] to deal with ◊ *Der Film behandelt das
Thema Jugendkriminalität.* The film
deals with the subject of juvenile
delinquency.
♦ **Das Passiv haben wir in Englisch noch
nicht behandelt.** We haven't done the
passive in English yet.

die **Behandlung** NOUN
treatment

**behaupten** VERB (PERFECT **hat behauptet**)
to claim

**beherrschen** VERB (PERFECT **hat beherrscht**)
[1] to master ◊ *Ich beherrsche diese
Technik noch nicht.* I haven't mastered
this technique yet.
[2] to control ◊ *Er konnte seine Wut nicht
mehr beherrschen.* He couldn't control
his anger any longer.
♦ **sich beherrschen** to control oneself

**behilflich** ADJECTIVE
helpful
♦ **jemandem bei etwas behilflich sein** to
help somebody with something

**behindern** VERB (PERFECT **hat behindert**)
to hinder

**behindert** ADJECTIVE
disabled

der **Behinderte** NOUN (GEN des/der
die **Behinderten,** PL die **Behinderten**)
disabled person
♦ **die Behinderten** the disabled

die **Behinderung** NOUN

[1] obstruction ◊ *Das Fahrzeug stellt eine
Behinderung des Verkehrs dar.* The
vehicle is an obstruction to traffic.
[2] handicap ◊ *Sie hat gelernt, mit ihrer
Behinderung zu leben.* She's learned to
live with her handicap.

die **Behörde** NOUN
authorities

**bei** PREPOSITION
*The preposition **bei** takes the dative.*
[1] near ◊ *Unser Haus ist beim Bahnhof.*
Our house is near the station. ◊ *bei
München* near Munich
[2] at ◊ *Felix ist zur Zeit bei seiner
Großmutter.* Felix is at his grandmother's
at the moment. ◊ *Wenn man bei fremden
Leuten zu Besuch ist ...* When you're at
other people's houses ... ◊ *beim Friseur*
at the hairdresser's ◊ *bei Nacht* at night
♦ **bei uns** at our place
♦ **bei uns in Deutschland** in Germany
♦ **bei seinen Eltern wohnen** to live with
one's parents
♦ **Ich habe kein Geld bei mir.** I don't have
any money on me.
♦ **Ich habe zur Zeit meine Mutter bei mir.**
My mother's staying with me at the
moment.
♦ **Wenn du bei mir bist, habe ich keine
Angst.** When you're with me, I'm not
afraid.
♦ **bei einer Firma arbeiten** to work for a
firm ◊ *Sie arbeitet bei der Post.* She
works for the post office.
♦ **beim Militär** in the army
[3] on ◊ *bei meiner Ankunft* on my arrival
◊ *bei der Abreise* on departure
[4] during ◊ *beim Abendessen* during
dinner
♦ **Bei der Arbeit höre ich gern Musik.** I like
listening to music when I'm working.
♦ **beim Fahren** while driving
♦ **bei solcher Hitze** in such heat
♦ **bei Nebel** in fog
♦ **bei Regen** if it rains

**beibringen** VERB (IMPERFECT **brachte bei,**
PERFECT **hat beigebracht**)
♦ **jemandem etwas beibringen** to teach
somebody something ◊ *Sie hat mir
Schwimmen beigebracht.* She taught me
to swim.

die **Beichte** NOUN
confession

**beichten** VERB
♦ **etwas beichten** to confess something
◊ *Ich muss dir beichten, dass ich dein
Fahrrad benutzt habe.* I have to confess
that I used your bike.

**beide** ADJECTIVE, PRONOUN
*see also **beides** PRONOUN*
both ◊ *Ich habe beide Bücher gelesen.*
I've read both books. ◊ *Ich will beide.* I

want both of them. ◊ *jeder der beiden* both of them
- ◆ **Meine Eltern haben das beide verboten.** Both my parents have forbidden it.
- ◆ **meine beiden Brüder** both my brothers
- ◆ **die ersten beiden** the first two
- ◆ **wir beide** we two
- ◆ **einer von beiden** one of the two

**beides** PRONOUN

see also **beide** ADJECTIVE

both ◊ *Ich möchte beides.* I want both of them. ◊ *Beides ist schön.* Both of them are lovely.
- ◆ **alles beides** both of them

**beieinander** ADVERB
together

der **Beifahrer** NOUN (PL die **Beifahrer**)
passenger

der **Beifall** NOUN
applause
- ◆ **Beifall spenden** to applaud

**beige** ADJECTIVE
beige

das **Beil** NOUN (PL die **Beile**)
axe

die **Beilage** NOUN
1 supplement ◊ *eine Beilage zur Samstagszeitung* a supplement in Saturday's paper
2 side dish
- ◆ **Wir hatten Lamm und als Beilage Pommes frites und Brokkoli.** We had lamb with chips and broccoli.

**beilegen** VERB (PERFECT **hat beigelegt**)
1 to enclose ◊ *Ich lege einen Scheck bei.* I enclose a cheque.
2 to settle ◊ *Der Streit war schnell beigelegt.* The argument was quickly settled.

das **Beileid** NOUN
sympathy ◊ *Wir haben ihr unser Beileid ausgesprochen.* We offered her our sympathy.
- ◆ **herzliches Beileid** deepest sympathy

**beiliegend** ADVERB
enclosed

**beim** = **bei dem**

das **Bein** NOUN (PL die **Beine**)
leg

**beinahe** ADVERB
almost

der **Beinbruch** NOUN (PL die **Beinbrüche**)
broken leg ◊ *Sie wurde mit einem Beinbruch ins Krankenhaus eingeliefert.* She was taken to hospital with a broken leg.

**beisammen** ADVERB
together

das **Beisammensein** NOUN
get-together

**beiseite** ADVERB

to one side ◊ *Sie schob ihren Teller beiseite.* She pushed her plate to one side.
- ◆ **etwas beiseite legen** to put something by
- ◆ **etwas beiseite lassen** to leave something ◊ *Diese Frage sollten wir im Moment beiseite lassen.* We should leave this question for the moment.
- ◆ **etwas beiseite schaffen** to put something by ◊ *Er hat sehr viel Geld beiseite geschafft.* He's put a lot of money by.

das **Beispiel** NOUN (PL die **Beispiele**)
example
- ◆ **sich an jemandem ein Beispiel nehmen** to take a leaf out of somebody's book ◊ *Du solltest dir an deinem Bruder ein Beispiel nehmen.* You should take a leaf out of your brother's book.
- ◆ **zum Beispiel** for example

**beispielsweise** ADVERB
for example

**beißen** VERB (IMPERFECT **biss**, PERFECT **hat gebissen**)
1 to bite ◊ *Mein Hund beißt nicht.* My dog doesn't bite. ◊ *Sie biss in den Apfel.* She bit into the apple.
2 to burn ◊ *Der Rauch beißt mich in den Augen.* The smoke's burning my eyes.
- ◆ **sich beißen** to clash ◊ *Rosa beißt sich mit Orange.* Pink clashes with orange.

der **Beitrag** NOUN (PL die **Beiträge**)
1 contribution ◊ *einen Beitrag zu etwas leisten* to make a contribution to something
- ◆ **Er schreibt Beiträge für die Zeitung.** He writes articles for the newspaper.
2 membership fee ◊ *Der Beitrag für den Klub wird am Monatsanfang fällig.* Membership fees for the club are due at the beginning of the month.
3 premium ◊ *die Beiträge zur Krankenversicherung* the health insurance premiums

**beitragen** VERB (PRESENT **trägt bei**, IMPERFECT **trug bei**, PERFECT **hat beigetragen**)
- ◆ **zu etwas beitragen** to contribute to something ◊ *Er trägt selten etwas zum Unterricht bei.* He seldom contributes anything to the lesson.

**beitreten** VERB (PRESENT **tritt bei**, IMPERFECT **trat bei**, PERFECT **ist beigetreten**)
to join ◊ *einem Verein beitreten* to join a club

**bekämpfen** VERB (PERFECT **hat bekämpft**)
to fight ◊ *ein Feuer bekämpfen* to fight a fire
- ◆ **sich bekämpfen** to fight ◊ *Diese beiden Parteien bekämpfen sich seit Jahren.* These two parties have been fighting for years.

**bekannt** ADJECTIVE

**B**

☞

1 well-known ◊ *Sie ist eine bekannte Schauspielerin.* She's a well-known actress.

2 familiar ◊ *Bekannte Wörter brauche ich nicht nachzuschlagen.* I don't have to look up familiar words.

♦ **Sie kommt mir bekannt vor.** She seems familiar.

♦ **Das kommt mir bekannt vor.** That sounds familiar.

♦ **mit jemandem bekannt sein** to know somebody ◊ *Wir sind seit Jahren mit den Bauers bekannt.* We've known the Bauers for years.

♦ **für etwas bekannt sein** to be known for something ◊ *Sie ist für ihren Witz bekannt.* She's known for her humour.

♦ **Das ist mir bekannt.** I know that.

♦ **etwas bekannt geben** to announce something publicly

♦ **etwas bekannt machen** to announce something

der **Bekannte** NOUN (GEN des/der **Bekannten**, PL
die die **Bekannten**)

1 friend ◊ *Ein Bekannter von mir hat mir das erzählt.* A friend of mine told me.

2 acquaintance ◊ *Sie hat viele Bekannte, aber wenig Freunde.* She has a lot of acquaintances but few friends.

**bekanntgeben** VERB *see* **bekannt**

**bekanntlich** ADVERB
as you know ◊ *Rauchen macht bekanntlich süchtig.* As you know, smoking is addictive.

**bekanntmachen** VERB *see* **bekannt**

sich **beklagen** VERB (PERFECT **hat sich beklagt**)
to complain ◊ *Die Schüler haben sich darüber beklagt, dass sie Hausaufgaben aufbekommen haben.* The pupils complained about being given homework.

die **Bekleidung** NOUN
clothing

**bekommen** VERB (IMPERFECT **bekam**, PERFECT **hat bekommen**)

1 to get ◊ *Was hast du zum Geburtstag bekommen?* What did you get for your birthday? ◊ *Sie hat in Englisch eine schlechte Note bekommen.* She got bad marks in English, ◊ *Wir haben nichts zu essen bekommen.* We didn't get anything to eat.

♦ **Hunger bekommen** to feel hungry

♦ **Durst bekommen** to feel thirsty

♦ **Angst bekommen** to become afraid

♦ **ein Kind bekommen** to have a baby ◊ *Unsere Deutschlehrerin bekommt ein Kind.* Our German teacher's having a baby.

2 to catch ◊ *Ich habe den letzten Bus gerade noch bekommen.* I just caught the last bus.

♦ **Das fette Essen ist ihm nicht bekommen.** The fatty food didn't agree with him.

♦ **Was bekommen Sie?** What would you like?

♦ **Bekommen Sie schon?** Are you being served?

♦ **Was bekommen Sie dafür?** How much do I owe you?

*Be careful!* **bekommen** *does not mean to become.*

**belasten** VERB (PERFECT **hat belastet**)

1 to burden ◊ *Ich möchte dich nicht mit meinen Problemen belasten.* I don't want to burden you with my problems.

2 to load ◊ *Der Aufzug darf mit maximal zehn Personen belastet werden.* The lift's maximum load is ten people.

♦ **Unsere Umwelt ist mit zu vielen Schadstoffen belastet.** Too many harmful substances pollute our environment.

3 to debit ◊ *Wir werden Ihr Konto mit diesem Betrag belasten.* We will debit this amount from your account.

4 to incriminate ◊ *Die Zeugin hat den Angeklagten belastet.* The witness incriminated the accused.

**belästigen** VERB (PERFECT **hat belästigt**)
to pester

♦ **jemanden sexuell belästigen** to sexually harass somebody

die **Belastung** NOUN

1 burden ◊ *Kinder sind eine große Belastung.* Children are a great burden.

2 strain ◊ *Die Hitze stellt eine Belastung des Kreislaufs dar.* The heat puts a strain on the circulation.

♦ **die Belastung unserer Umwelt mit Schadstoffen** the pollution of our environment by harmful substances

**belegen** VERB (PERFECT **hat belegt**)
to register for ◊ *Ich habe einen Volkshochschulkurs für Spanisch belegt.* I've registered for an adult education course in Spanish.

♦ **Ist der Platz belegt?** Is this seat taken?

♦ **Das Hotel ist belegt.** The hotel's full.

♦ **den ersten Platz belegen** to come first

♦ **Womit soll ich dein Brot belegen?** What shall I put on your sandwich?

**belegt** ADJECTIVE

♦ **ein belegtes Brot** an open sandwich

♦ **Es ist belegt.** It's engaged. ◊ *Die Nummer ist belegt.* The number's engaged.

**beleidigen** VERB (PERFECT **hat beleidigt**)
to insult

die **Beleidigung** NOUN
insult

**Belgien** NEUT NOUN
Belgium

♦ **aus Belgien** from Belgium

♦ **in Belgien** in Belgium
♦ **nach Belgien** to Belgium

der **Belgier** NOUN (PL die **Belgier**)
Belgian

die **Belgierin** NOUN
Belgian

**belgisch** ADJECTIVE
Belgian

die **Belichtung** NOUN
exposure

der **Belichtungsmesser** NOUN (PL die **Belichtungsmesser**)
exposure meter

**beliebig** ADJECTIVE, ADVERB
[1] any you like ◊ *in beliebiger Reihenfolge* in any order you like ◊ *eine beliebige Anzahl* any number you like ◊ *Du kannst jeden beliebigen Schüler unserer Klasse fragen.* You can ask any pupil you like in our class.
[2] as you like ◊ *beliebig oft* as often as you like ◊ *beliebig viel* as much as you like ◊ *beliebig viele* as many as you like

**beliebt** ADJECTIVE
popular ◊ *sich bei jemandem beliebt machen* to make oneself popular with somebody

die **Beliebtheit** NOUN
popularity

**bellen** VERB
to bark

**belohnen** VERB (PERFECT **hat belohnt**)
to reward

die **Belohnung** NOUN
reward ◊ *zur Belohnung* as a reward

**belügen** VERB (IMPERFECT **belog**, PERFECT **hat belogen**)
to lie to

**belustigen** VERB (PERFECT **hat belustigt**)
to amuse

**bemerken** VERB (PERFECT **hat bemerkt**)
to notice ◊ *Ich habe keine Änderung bemerkt.* I haven't noticed any change.

die **Bemerkung** NOUN
remark

**bemitleiden** VERB (PERFECT **hat bemitleidet**)
to pity

sich **bemühen** VERB (PERFECT **hat sich bemüht**)
to make an effort ◊ *Er hat sich bemüht, höflich zu bleiben.* He made an effort to remain polite.
♦ **Bemühen Sie sich nicht, ich finde schon allein hinaus.** Don't trouble yourself, I'll show myself out.
♦ **Er hat sich sehr um seine Gäste bemüht.** He went to a lot of trouble for his guests.
♦ **Rudi muss sich um eine neue Arbeit bemühen.** Rudi's got to try and find a new job.
♦ **Ich werde mich bemühen!** I'll do my best!

**benachrichtigen** VERB (PERFECT **hat benachrichtigt**)
to inform

die **Benachrichtigung** NOUN
notification

**benachteiligt** ADJECTIVE
disadvantaged

sich **benehmen** VERB (PRESENT **benimmt sich**, IMPERFECT **benahm sich**, PERFECT **hat sich benommen**)
| see also **das Benehmen** NOUN |
to behave ◊ *sich anständig benehmen* to behave properly ◊ *Sie haben sich furchtbar benommen.* They behaved terribly. ◊ *Benimm dich!* Behave yourself!

das **Benehmen** NOUN
| see also **sich benehmen** VERB |
behaviour

**beneiden** VERB (PERFECT **hat beneidet**)
to envy
♦ **jemanden um etwas beneiden** to envy somebody something ◊ *Ich beneide dich um deine schöne Wohnung.* I envy you your lovely flat.
♦ **Er ist nicht zu beneiden.** I don't envy him.

**beneidenswert** ADJECTIVE
enviable
♦ **Sie ist beneidenswert reich.** She's enviably rich.

**benoten** VERB (PERFECT **hat benotet**)
to mark

**benutzen** VERB (PERFECT **hat benutzt**)
to use

der **Benutzer** NOUN (PL die **Benutzer**)
user

**benutzerfreundlich** ADJECTIVE
user-friendly

die **Benutzung** NOUN
use

das **Benzin** NOUN
petrol

der **Benzinkanister** NOUN (PL die **Benzinkanister**)
petrol can

**beobachten** VERB (PERFECT **hat beobachtet**)
to observe

**bequem** ADJECTIVE
[1] comfortable ◊ *ein bequemer Stuhl* a comfortable chair
♦ **eine bequeme Ausrede** a convenient excuse
[2] lazy ◊ *Er ist zu bequem, sich selbst etwas zu kochen.* He's too lazy to cook himself something.

**beraten** VERB (PRESENT **berät**, IMPERFECT **beriet**, PERFECT **hat beraten**)
[1] to give advice ◊ *Der Mann vom Arbeitsamt hat mich gut beraten.* The man at the job centre gave me good advice.

B

♦ **Lassen Sie sich von Ihrem Arzt beraten.** Consult your doctor.

[2] to discuss ◊ *Wir müssen das weitere Vorgehen beraten.* We have to discuss further action.

♦ **gut beraten sein** to be well advised
♦ **schlecht beraten sein** to be ill advised

**berauben** VERB (PERFECT **hat beraubt**)
to rob

**berechnen** VERB (PERFECT **hat berechnet**)
to charge ◊ *Was berechnen Sie für eine Beratung?* What do you charge for a consultation?

der **Bereich** NOUN (PL die **Bereiche**)
[1] field ◊ *In diesem Bereich kennt sie sich sehr gut aus.* She's very knowledgable in this field.

♦ **Er ist für den Bereich Kundendienst zuständig.** He's responsible for after-sales service.

[2] area ◊ *im Bereich der Innenstadt* in the city centre area

**bereit** ADJECTIVE
ready ◊ *Wir sind bereit abzufahren.* We're ready to leave. ◊ *Das Essen ist bereit.* Dinner's ready.

♦ **bereit sein, etwas zu tun** to be prepared to do something ◊ *Ich bin nicht bereit, noch länger zu warten.* I'm not prepared to wait any longer.

♦ **etwas bereit haben** to have something ready ◊ *Sie hat immer eine Ausrede bereit.* She always has an excuse ready.

**bereiten** VERB (PERFECT **hat bereitet**)
to cause ◊ *Das hat mir einige Schwierigkeiten bereitet.* That caused me some problems.

♦ **Die Kinder bereiten mir sehr viel Freude.** The children give me a great deal of pleasure.

**bereits** ADVERB
already

**bereuen** VERB (PERFECT **hat bereut**)
to regret

der **Berg** NOUN (PL die **Berge**)
[1] mountain ◊ *Im Winter fahren wir in die Berge zum Skifahren.* In winter we go skiing in the mountains.

[2] hill ◊ *Hinter unserem Haus ist ein kleiner Berg.* There's a small hill behind our house.

der **Bergarbeiter** NOUN (PL die **Bergarbeiter**)
miner

die **Bergbahn** NOUN (PL die **Bergbahnen**)
mountain railway

der **Bergbau** NOUN
mining

das **Bergsteigen** NOUN
mountaineering ◊ *Bergsteigen ist ihr Hobby.* Her hobby's mountaineering. ◊ *Sie ist beim Bergsteigen verunglückt.* She had a mountaineering accident.

der **Bergsteiger** NOUN (PL die **Bergsteiger**)
mountaineer

die **Bergwacht** NOUN
mountain rescue service

das **Bergwerk** NOUN (PL die **Bergwerke**)
mine

der **Bericht** NOUN (PL die **Berichte**)
report

**berichten** VERB (PERFECT **hat berichtet**)
to report ◊ *Die Zeitungen haben nichts über diesen Zwischenfall berichtet.* The newspapers didn't report anything about this incident.

**Berlin** NEUT NOUN
Berlin

> ❶ *Berlin* is one of the 16 *Länder*. It is a "city-state" like Bremen and Hamburg. From 1963 to 1989 it was divided by the Berlin Wall. Now it is again the German capital.

**berücksichtigen** VERB (PERFECT **hat berücksichtigt**)
to bear in mind

der **Beruf** NOUN (PL die **Berufe**)
occupation ◊ *Welchen Beruf hat dein Vater?* What's your father's occupation?

♦ **Sie ist Lehrerin von Beruf.** She's a teacher by profession.

**beruflich** ADJECTIVE
professional

♦ **beruflich unterwegs sein** to be away on business

der **Berufsberater** NOUN (PL die **Berufsberater**)
careers adviser

das **Berufspraktikum** NOUN (GEN des **Berufspraktikums**, PL die **Berufspraktika**)
work experience ◊ *Sie absolviert gerade ihr Berufspraktikum.* She's doing work experience.

die **Berufsschule** NOUN
technical college

**berufstätig** ADJECTIVE
working ◊ *Seit wann ist deine Mutter wieder berufstätig?* When did your mother start working again?

der **Berufsverkehr** NOUN
rush-hour traffic

**beruhigen** VERB (PERFECT **hat beruhigt**)
to calm down ◊ *Dem Lehrer gelang es nicht, die Klasse zu beruhigen.* The teacher didn't manage to calm the class down.

♦ **sich beruhigen** to calm down ◊ *Die Lage hat sich beruhigt.* Things have calmed down.

♦ **Beruhige dich doch!** Calm down!

das **Beruhigungsmittel** NOUN (PL die **Beruhigungsmittel**)
tranquillizer

**berühmt** ADJECTIVE
famous

**B**

**berühren** VERB (PERFECT **hat berührt**)
[1] to touch ◊ *Er berührte meinen Arm.*
He touched my arm.
[2] to affect ◊ *Die Armut der Menschen hat mich sehr berührt.* The poverty of the people affected me deeply.
[3] to touch on ◊ *Ich kann diese Frage heute nur berühren.* I can only touch on this question today.
♦ **sich berühren** to touch ◊ *Die beiden Drähte berührten sich.* The two wires touched.

die **Berührung** NOUN
contact ◊ *mit etwas in Berührung kommen* to come into contact with something

**beschädigen** VERB (PERFECT **hat beschädigt**)
to damage

**beschaffen** VERB (PERFECT **hat beschafft**)
to get ◊ *Ich muss mir ein Visum beschaffen.* I have to get a visa.
◊ *Können Sie mir nicht einen Job beschaffen?* Can't you get me a job?

**beschäftigen** VERB (PERFECT **hat beschäftigt**)
[1] to occupy ◊ *Kannst du nicht irgendwie die Kinder beschäftigen?* Can't you occupy the children somehow?
◊ *Diese Frage beschäftigt mich seit langem.* This question has been occupying me for a long time.
[2] to employ ◊ *Unsere Firma beschäftigt zweihundert Leute.* Our company employs two hundred people.
♦ **sich beschäftigen** to occupy oneself ◊ *Sebastian hat Mühe, sich allein zu beschäftigen.* Sebastian has difficulty occupying himself.
♦ **Kannst du dich mit den Kindern beschäftigen?** Can you keep the children occupied?
♦ **Der Artikel beschäftigt sich mit Jugendarbeitslosigkeit.** The article deals with youth unemployment.

**beschäftigt** ADJECTIVE
busy

die **Beschäftigung** NOUN
work ◊ *Er sucht eine Beschäftigung.* He's looking for work.
♦ **Sie ist zur Zeit ohne Beschäftigung.** She is unemployed at the moment.

der **Bescheid** NOUN (PL die **Bescheide**)
information ◊ *Ich warte auf den Bescheid des Konsulats.* I'm waiting for information from the consulate.
♦ **Bescheid wissen** to know ◊ *Weiß deine Mutter Bescheid, dass du hier bist?* Does your mother know that you're here? ◊ *Ich weiß Bescheid.* I know.
♦ **über etwas Bescheid wissen** to know a lot about something ◊ *Sie weiß über Grammatik gut Bescheid.* She knows a lot about grammar.

♦ **jemandem Bescheid sagen** to let somebody know

**bescheiden** ADJECTIVE
modest

die **Bescheinigung** NOUN
certificate ◊ *Du brauchst eine Bescheinigung über die Teilnahme am Kurs.* You need a certificate showing that you attended the course. ◊ *eine Bescheinigung des Arztes* a doctor's certificate

**beschenken** VERB (PERFECT **hat beschenkt**)
♦ **jemanden mit etwas beschenken** to give somebody something as a present
♦ **beschenkt werden** to receive a present ◊ *Wir sind reichlich beschenkt worden.* We received lots of presents.

die **Bescherung** NOUN
giving out of Christmas presents
♦ **Da haben wir die Bescherung!** What did I tell you!

**beschimpfen** VERB (PERFECT **hat beschimpft**)
to swear at

**beschleunigen** VERB (PERFECT **hat beschleunigt**)
[1] to increase ◊ *Wir müssen das Arbeitstempo beschleunigen.* We have to increase our work rate.
[2] to accelerate ◊ *Das Auto vor mir beschleunigte.* The car in front of me accelerated.

**beschließen** VERB (IMPERFECT **beschloss**, PERFECT **hat beschlossen**)
to decide ◊ *Wir haben beschlossen, nach Spanien zu fahren.* We decided to go to Spain.

der **Beschluss** NOUN (GEN des **Beschlusses**, PL die **Beschlüsse**)
decision

**beschränken** VERB (PERFECT **hat beschränkt**)
to limit ◊ *Wir müssen unsere Ausgaben beschränken.* We have to limit our spending.
♦ **sich auf etwas beschränken** to restrict oneself to something ◊ *Ich werde mich auf ein paar Worte beschränken.* I'll restrict myself to a few words.

**beschränkt** ADJECTIVE
[1] limited ◊ *Diese Regel hat nur beschränkte Gültigkeit.* This regulation only has limited validity.
[2] stupid ◊ *Wie kann man nur so beschränkt sein?* How can anyone be so stupid?

**beschreiben** VERB (IMPERFECT **beschrieb**, PERFECT **hat beschrieben**)
to describe ◊ *Können Sie den Täter beschreiben?* Can you describe the culprit?

die **Beschreibung** NOUN
description

**beschützen** VERB (PERFECT **hat beschützt**)

☞

to protect ◇ *Ich möchte euch vor diesen Gefahren beschützen.* I want to protect you from these dangers.

die **Beschwerde** NOUN
complaint ◇ *Wenn Sie eine Beschwerde haben, dann wenden Sie sich an den Geschäftsführer.* If you have a complaint, then please contact the manager.
♦ **Beschwerden** trouble ◇ *Mein Knie macht mir immer noch Beschwerden.* My knee's still giving me trouble.

sich **beschweren** VERB (PERFECT **hat beschwert**)
to complain ◇ *Deine Lehrerin hat sich über dich beschwert.* Your teacher has complained about you.

**beschwipst** ADJECTIVE
tipsy

**beseitigen** VERB (PERFECT **hat beseitigt**)
to remove

der **Besen** NOUN (PL die **Besen**)
broom

**besetzen** VERB (PERFECT **hat besetzt**)
[1] to occupy ◇ *Napoleons Truppen haben weite Teile Deutschlands besetzt.* Napoleon's troops occupied large areas of Germany.
♦ **Studenten haben dieses Haus besetzt.** Students are squatting in this house.
[2] to keep ◇ *Kannst du den Platz bitte für mich besetzen?* Can you keep this seat for me?
[3] to fill ◇ *Der Posten soll mit einer Frau besetzt werden.* The position is to be filled by a woman. ◇ *Die Stelle ist noch nicht besetzt.* The position hasn't been filled yet.

**besetzt** ADJECTIVE
[1] full ◇ *Der Zug war voll besetzt.* The train was full.
[2] engaged ◇ *Es ist besetzt.* It's engaged.
[3] taken ◇ *Ist der Platz hier besetzt?* Is this seat taken?

das **Besetztzeichen** NOUN (PL die **Besetztzeichen**)
engaged tone

**besichtigen** VERB (PERFECT **hat besichtigt**)
to visit

die **Besichtigung** NOUN
visit

**besitzen** VERB (IMPERFECT **besaß**, PERFECT **hat besessen**)
[1] to own ◇ *Sie besitzen ein Haus am Meer.* They own a house by the seaside.
[2] to have ◇ *Sie besitzt das Talent, sich mit allen zu zerstreiten.* She has the talent of quarrelling with everyone.

der **Besitzer** NOUN (PL die **Besitzer**)
owner

**besoffen** ADJECTIVE
plastered

**besondere** ADJECTIVE
special ◇ *Das sind besondere Umstände.* Those are special circumstances.

♦ **keine besonderen Kennzeichen** no distinguishing features

die **Besonderheit** NOUN
peculiarity

**besonders** ADVERB
particularly ◇ *Es hat mir nicht besonders gefallen.* I didn't particularly like it.

**besorgen** VERB (PERFECT **hat besorgt**)
to get ◇ *Kannst du mir nicht einen Ferienjob besorgen?* Can't you get me a holiday job? ◇ *Soll ich dir ein Taxi besorgen?* Shall I get you a taxi? ◇ *Ich muss Milch und Eier besorgen.* I'll have to get milk and eggs.

**besorgt** ADJECTIVE
worried ◇ *Sie ist sehr besorgt um dich.* She's very worried about you.

**besprechen** VERB (PRESENT **bespricht**, IMPERFECT **besprach**, PERFECT **hat besprochen**)
to discuss ◇ *Das muss ich mit deiner Mutter besprechen.* I'll have to discuss it with your mother.

die **Besprechung** NOUN
[1] meeting ◇ *Frau Airlie ist in einer Besprechung.* Ms Airlie is in a meeting.
[2] review ◇ *Hast du die Besprechung dieses Films gelesen?* Have you read the review of this film?

**besser** ADJECTIVE, ADVERB
better ◇ *eine bessere Note* a better mark ◇ *Du gehst jetzt besser nach Hause.* You'd better go home now.
♦ **Es geht ihm besser.** He's feeling better.
♦ **je schneller, desto besser** the quicker the better

sich **bessern** VERB
to improve ◇ *Das Wetter hat sich gebessert.* The weather's improved.

die **Besserung** NOUN
improvement
♦ **Gute Besserung!** Get well soon!

der **Bestandteil** NOUN (PL die **Bestandteile**)
[1] component ◇ *Hier werden die einzelnen Bestandteile der Maschine zusammengesetzt.* The individual components of the machine are assembled here.
[2] ingredient ◇ *Die Bestandteile sind in Gramm angegeben.* The ingredients are given in grams.
♦ **sich in seine Bestandteile auflösen** to fall to pieces

**bestätigen** VERB (PERFECT **hat bestätigt**)
to confirm ◇ *Ich kann bestätigen, dass sie die Wahrheit gesagt hat.* I can confirm that she told the truth.
♦ **Hiermit bestätigen wir den Erhalt Ihres Briefes.** We hereby acknowledge receipt of your letter.
♦ **sich bestätigen** to prove to be true ◇ *Mein Verdacht hat sich bestätigt.* My suspicion proved to be true.

**beste** ADJECTIVE

**B**

best ◊ *Sie ist die beste Schülerin der Klasse.* She's the best pupil in the class.
- **So ist es am besten.** It's best that way.
- **Am besten gehst du gleich.** You'd better go at once.
- **jemanden zum Besten haben** to pull somebody's leg
- **einen Witz zum Besten geben** to tell a joke
- **Es ist nur zu deinem Besten.** It's for your own good.

**bestechen** VERB (PRESENT **besticht**, IMPERFECT **bestach**, PERFECT **hat bestochen**)
to bribe

die **Bestechung** NOUN
bribery

das **Besteck** NOUN (PL die **Bestecke**)
cutlery

**bestehen** VERB (IMPERFECT **bestand**, PERFECT **hat bestanden**)

1 to be ◊ *Es besteht die Möglichkeit, einen Sprachkurs zu belegen.* There's the chance of registering for a language course. ◊ *Es besteht keine Hoffnung mehr, sie jemals wiederzusehen.* There's no more hope of ever seeing her again.

2 to exist ◊ *Die Firma besteht seit hundert Jahren.* The firm has existed for a hundred years.
- **etwas bestehen** to pass something ◊ *Ich hoffe, dass ich die Prüfung bestehe.* I hope I pass the exam.
- **Sie hat in Mathe mit "gut" bestanden.** She got a "B" in maths.
- **auf etwas bestehen** to insist on something ◊ *Wir bestehen auf sofortiger Bezahlung.* We insist on immediate payment.
- **bestehen aus** to consist of ◊ *Eine Fußballmannschaft besteht aus elf Spielern.* A football team consists of eleven players.

**bestehlen** VERB (PRESENT **bestiehlt**, IMPERFECT **bestahl**, PERFECT **hat bestohlen**)
- **jemanden bestehlen** to rob somebody

**bestellen** VERB (PERFECT **hat bestellt**)

1 to order ◊ *Ich habe im Versandhaus ein Kleid bestellt.* I've ordered a dress from a mail-order company. ◊ *Haben Sie schon bestellt?* Have you ordered yet? ◊ *Wir sollten ein Taxi bestellen.* We should order a taxi.

2 to reserve ◊ *Ich habe einen Tisch beim Chinesen bestellt.* I've reserved a table at the Chinese restaurant.

3 to send for ◊ *Der Direktor hat mich zu sich bestellt.* The headmaster sent for me.
- **Bestell deiner Mutter schöne Grüße.** Give my regards to your mother.
- **Soll ich ihr etwas von dir bestellen?** Shall I give her a message from you?

- **Ich soll dir von Martin bestellen, dass er nicht mitkommen kann.** Martin says to tell you that he can't come.

die **Bestellung** NOUN
order
- **auf Bestellung** to order

**bestenfalls** ADVERB
at best

**bestens** ADVERB
very well ◊ *Die Geschäfte gehen bestens.* Business is going very well.

**bestimmen** VERB (PERFECT **hat bestimmt**)
to decide ◊ *Du kannst bestimmen, wer mitkommen soll.* You can decide who's coming. ◊ *Wer bestimmt hier, was gemacht werden muss?* Who decides what has to be done?
- **Du hast hier nichts zu bestimmen!** You're not the one who decides here!
- **für jemanden bestimmt sein** to be meant for somebody ◊ *Diese Bemerkung war für mich bestimmt.* This comment was meant for me.
- **Das Geschenk ist für meine Freundin bestimmt.** The present's for my girlfriend.
- **für etwas bestimmt sein** to be intended for something ◊ *Dieses Geld ist für die Anschaffung von Computern bestimmt.* This money's intended for the purchase of computers.

**bestimmt** ADJECTIVE, ADVERB

1 certain ◊ *Wir treffen uns immer zu einer bestimmten Zeit.* We always meet at a certain time. ◊ *Die Teilnehmer sollten eine bestimmte Anzahl nicht überschreiten.* The participants shouldn't exceed a certain number.

2 particular ◊ *Ich suche ein ganz bestimmtes Buch.* I'm looking for a particular book.
- **Suchen Sie etwas Bestimmtes?** Are you looking for something in particular?
- **der bestimmte Artikel** the definite article
- **Ich habe ihn bestimmt gesehen.** I'm sure I've seen him.
- **Das hat er bestimmt nicht so gemeint.** I'm sure that's not how he meant it.
- **Hast du auch bestimmt keine Hausaufgaben auf?** Are you sure you don't have any homework?
- **Das hat sie bestimmt vergessen.** She's bound to have forgotten.

die **Bestimmung** NOUN
regulation ◊ *neue Sicherheitsbestimmungen* new safety regulations

**bestrafen** VERB (PERFECT **hat bestraft**)
to punish

die **Bestrahlung** NOUN
radiotherapy

der **Besuch** NOUN (PL die **Besuche**)

☞

[1] visit ◊ *Deutschland bereitet sich auf den Besuch der Königin vor.* Germany's preparing for the Queen's visit. ◊ *bei unserem Besuch in London* during our visit to London
◆ **Der Schulbesuch ist Pflicht.** School attendance is compulsory.
[2] visitor ◊ *Ist euer Besuch noch da?* Is your visitor still there?
◆ **bei jemandem einen Besuch machen** to pay somebody a visit
◆ **Besuch haben** to have visitors
◆ **bei jemandem zu Besuch sein** to be visiting somebody
◆ **zu Besuch kommen** to be visiting ◊ *Nächste Woche kommt Onja zu Besuch.* Onja's visiting us next week.
**besuchen** VERB (PERFECT **hat besucht**)
[1] to visit ◊ *Hast du schon das Planetarium besucht?* Have you visited the planetarium yet?
◆ **Besuch uns mal wieder!** Come again!
[2] to attend ◊ *Sie besucht das Gymnasium.* She attends grammar school.
◆ **Der Vortrag war sehr gut besucht.** The lecture was very well-attended.
◆ **Wir haben ein Konzert besucht.** We went to a concert.
der **Besucher** NOUN (PL die **Besucher**)
visitor
**betätigen** VERB (PERFECT **hat betätigt**)
◆ **die Hupe betätigen** to sound the horn
◆ **einen Schalter betätigen** to press a switch
◆ **die Bremse betätigen** to apply the brakes
◆ **Du solltest dich sportlich betätigen.** You should do some sport.
◆ **Mein Vater betätigt sich politisch.** My father's involved in politics.
**betäuben** VERB (PERFECT **hat betäubt**)
[1] to stun ◊ *Der Schlag hat ihn betäubt.* The blow stunned him.
[2] to anaesthetize ◊ *Der Patient muss betäubt werden.* The patient has to be anaesthetized.
das **Betäubungsmittel** NOUN (PL die **Betäubungsmittel**)
anaesthetic
die **Bete** NOUN
◆ **Rote Bete** beetroot
**beteiligen** VERB (PERFECT **hat beteiligt**)
◆ **sich an etwas beteiligen** to take part in something ◊ *Franz beteiligte sich nicht an der Diskussion.* Franz didn't take part in the discussion.
◆ **Kann ich mich an eurem Spiel beteiligen?** Can I join in your game?
◆ **Ich habe mich mit zehn Mark an seinem Geschenk beteiligt.** I gave ten marks towards his present.
◆ **Alle werden am Gewinn beteiligt.** Everyone will share in the winnings.

**beten** VERB
to pray
der **Beton** NOUN (PL die **Betons**)
concrete
**betonen** VERB (PERFECT **hat betont**)
to stress
die **Betonung** NOUN
stress ◊ *Wo liegt die Betonung bei diesem Wort?* Where's the stress in this word?
**beträchtlich** ADJECTIVE, ADVERB
[1] considerable ◊ *eine beträchtliche Summe* a considerable amount
[2] considerably ◊ *Es hat beträchtlich länger gedauert.* It took considerably longer.
der **Betrag** NOUN (PL die **Beträge**)
amount
**betragen** VERB (PRESENT **beträgt**, IMPERFECT **betrug**, PERFECT **hat betragen**)
see also **das Betragen** NOUN
to come to ◊ *Die Reparatur betrug zweihundert Mark.* The repair came to two hundred marks.
◆ **sich betragen** to behave ◊ *Ich hoffe, die Kinder haben sich ordentlich betragen.* I hope the children behaved well.
das **Betragen** NOUN
see also **betragen** VERB
behaviour ◊ *Ich werde mich über dein schlechtes Betragen beschweren.* I'm going to complain about your bad behaviour.
**betreffen** VERB (PRESENT **betrifft**, IMPERFECT **betraf**, PERFECT **hat betroffen**)
to concern
◆ **was mich betrifft** as far as I'm concerned
**betreten** VERB (PRESENT **betritt**, IMPERFECT **betrat**, PERFECT **hat betreten**)
to enter ◊ *Sie klopfte, bevor sie das Zimmer betrat.* She knocked before entering the room.
◆ **"Betreten verboten"** "Keep out"
der **Betrieb** NOUN (PL die **Betriebe**)
[1] firm ◊ *Unser Betrieb beschäftigt dreihundert Menschen.* Our firm employs three hundred people.
[2] operation ◊ *Die Maschine ist jetzt in Betrieb.* The machine is now in operation.
◆ **In der Stadt war heute viel Betrieb.** It was really busy in town today.
◆ **außer Betrieb sein** to be out of order ◊ *Der Fahrstuhl ist außer Betrieb.* The lift's out of order.
die **Betriebsferien** PL NOUN
company holidays
der **Betriebsleiter** NOUN (PL die **Betriebsleiter**)
manager
sich **betrinken** VERB (IMPERFECT **betrank sich**, PERFECT **hat sich betrunken**)
to get drunk
**betroffen** ADJECTIVE

**B**

full of concern ◊ *Sie machte ein betroffenes Gesicht.* Her face was full of concern.
- ♦ **Wir sind über diese Nachricht zutiefst betroffen.** We are deeply affected by the news.
- ♦ **von etwas betroffen sein** to be affected by something

**betrügen** VERB (IMPERFECT **betrog**, PERFECT **hat betrogen**)
- [1] to cheat ◊ *Der Händler hat dich betrogen.* The dealer's cheated you.
- [2] to defraud ◊ *Er hat seinen Arbeitgeber um Millionen betrogen.* He defrauded his employer of millions.
- ♦ **Hast du deine Freundin schon mal betrogen?** Have you ever been unfaithful to your girlfriend?

**betrunken** ADJECTIVE
drunk

das **Bett** NOUN (PL die **Betten**)
bed ◊ *ins Bett gehen* to go to bed ◊ *das Bett machen* to make the bed

der **Bettbezug** NOUN (PL die **Bettbezüge**)
duvet cover

die **Bettdecke** NOUN
blanket

**betteln** VERB
to beg

das **Bettlaken** NOUN (PL die **Bettlaken**)
sheet

der **Bettler** NOUN (PL die **Bettler**)
beggar

das **Betttuch** NOUN (PL die **Betttücher**)
sheet

die **Bettwäsche** NOUN
bed linen

das **Bettzeug** NOUN
bedding

**beugen** VERB
to bend ◊ *Ich kann den Arm nicht beugen.* I can't bend my arm.
- ♦ **sich beugen** to bow ◊ *Ich beuge mich der Mehrheit.* I bow to the majority.
- ♦ **Sie beugte sich über das Bett des Kindes.** She bent over the child's bed.

die **Beule** NOUN
- [1] bump ◊ *eine Beule am Kopf* a bump on the head
- [2] dent ◊ *Das Auto hat eine Beule.* The car has a dent in it.

**beunruhigen** VERB (PERFECT **hat beunruhigt**)
to alarm

**beurteilen** VERB (PERFECT **hat beurteilt**)
to judge ◊ *Ich beurteile die Leute nicht nach ihrem Aussehen.* I don't judge people on their appearance.

der **Beutel** NOUN (PL die **Beutel**)
- [1] bag ◊ *Sie tat die Einkäufe in den Beutel.* She put the shopping in the bag.
- [2] purse ◊ *Er nahm einen Zehnmarkschein aus dem Beutel.* He took a ten-mark note from the purse.

die **Bevölkerung** NOUN
population

**bevor** CONJUNCTION
before ◊ *Sie war gegangen, bevor ich es ihr sagen konnte.* She left before I could tell her.

**bevorstehen** VERB (IMPERFECT **stand bevor**, PERFECT **hat bevorgestanden**)
to be imminent ◊ *Die Prüfung steht bevor.* The exam's imminent.
- ♦ **jemandem bevorstehen** to be in store for somebody ◊ *Da steht uns ja einiger Ärger bevor.* There's trouble in store for us.

**bevorzugen** VERB (PERFECT **hat bevorzugt**)
to prefer

sich **bewähren** VERB (PERFECT **hat sich bewährt**)
to prove oneself ◊ *Er hat sich als mein Freund bewährt.* He proved himself to be my friend. ◊ *Diese Methode hat sich bewährt.* This method has proved itself.

**bewährt** ADJECTIVE
tried and tested ◊ *Das ist eine bewährte Methode.* That's a tried and tested method.
- ♦ **Sie ist eine bewährte Mitarbeiterin.** She's a reliable colleague.

**bewegen** VERB (PERFECT **hat bewegt**)
to move
- ♦ **sich bewegen** to move
- ♦ **jemanden zu etwas bewegen** to persuade somebody to do something

**beweglich** ADJECTIVE
- [1] movable ◊ *Die Puppe hat bewegliche Beine.* The doll has movable legs.
- [2] agile ◊ *Sie ist trotz ihres Alters noch sehr beweglich.* She's still very agile despite her age.

**bewegt** ADJECTIVE
- [1] eventful ◊ *Sie hatte ein bewegtes Leben.* She had an eventful life.
- [2] touched ◊ *Wir waren von seinen Worten sehr bewegt.* We were very touched by his words.

die **Bewegung** NOUN
- [1] movement ◊ *Mir fällt jede Bewegung schwer.* Every movement is difficult for me.
- [2] motion ◊ *Er setzte das Fahrzeug in Bewegung.* He set the vehicle in motion.
- [3] exercise ◊ *Du brauchst mehr Bewegung.* You need more exercise.

der **Beweis** NOUN (PL die **Beweise**)
- [1] proof ◊ *Die Polizei hat keine Beweise.* The police don't have any proof.
- [2] sign ◊ *als Beweis meiner Freundschaft* as a sign of my friendship

**beweisen** VERB (IMPERFECT **bewies**, PERFECT **hat bewiesen**)

☞

[1] to prove ◊ *Ich kann nicht beweisen, dass sie das gesagt hat.* I can't prove that she said it. ◊ *Die Polizei kann nichts beweisen.* The police can't prove anything.

[2] to show ◊ *Er hat sehr viel Mut bewiesen.* He showed great courage.

sich **bewerben** VERB (PRESENT **bewirbt sich,** IMPERFECT **bewarb sich,** PERFECT **hat sich beworben)**
to apply ◊ *Es haben sich dreißig Kandidaten beworben.* Thirty candidates have applied. ◊ *Sie hat sich bei Siemens um einen Ausbildungsplatz beworben.* She applied to Siemens for an apprenticeship.

der **Bewerber** NOUN (PL die **Bewerber)**
applicant

die **Bewerbung** NOUN
application

das **Bewerbungsformular** NOUN (PL die **Bewerbungsformulare)**
application form

das **Bewerbungsgespräch** NOUN (PL die **Bewerbungsgespräche)**
job interview

**bewerten** VERB (PERFECT **hat bewertet)**
to assess ◊ *Der Lehrer hat unsere Aufsätze zu bewerten.* The teacher has to assess our essays.

**bewirken** VERB (PERFECT **hat bewirkt)**
to bring about ◊ *Dieses Medikament wird eine schnelle Besserung bewirken.* This medicine will bring about a rapid improvement.
◆ **Meine Bitte hat nichts bewirkt.** My request didn't achieve anything.
◆ **Ich konnte bei ihm nichts bewirken.** I couldn't get anywhere with him.

**bewohnen** VERB (PERFECT **hat bewohnt)**
to live in ◊ *Das Haus wird von drei Familien bewohnt.* Three families live in the house.

der **Bewohner** NOUN (PL die **Bewohner)**
[1] inhabitant ◊ *die Bewohner des Landes* the inhabitants of the country
[2] resident ◊ *die Bewohner des Hauses* the residents of the house

**bewölkt** ADJECTIVE
cloudy

die **Bewölkung** NOUN
clouds

**bewundern** VERB (PERFECT **hat bewundert)**
to admire

die **Bewunderung** NOUN
admiration

**bewusst** ADJECTIVE
[1] conscious ◊ *umweltbewusst* environmentally conscious
[2] deliberate ◊ *Das war eine bewusste Beleidigung.* That was a deliberate insult.
◆ **Er hat ganz bewusst gelogen.** He lied quite deliberately.

◆ **sich einer Sache bewusst sein** to be aware of something ◊ *Ich bin mir der Konsequenzen bewusst.* I'm aware of the consequences.
◆ **Ihr wurde plötzlich bewusst, welche Folgen das haben könnte.** She suddenly realized the consequences this could have.

**bewusstlos** ADJECTIVE
unconscious
◆ **bewusstlos werden** to lose consciousness

die **Bewusstlosigkeit** NOUN
unconsciousness

das **Bewusstsein** NOUN
consciousness
◆ **bei Bewusstsein** conscious

**bezahlen** VERB (PERFECT **hat bezahlt)**
to pay ◊ *Er bezahlte die Rechnung.* He paid the bill.

die **Bezahlung** NOUN
payment

**bezeichnen** VERB (PERFECT **hat bezeichnet)**
[1] to mark ◊ *Bezeichnen Sie die Stelle mit einem Kreuz.* Mark the spot with a cross.
[2] to call ◊ *Sie hat mich als Lügnerin bezeichnet.* She called me a liar.

**bezeichnend** ADJECTIVE
typical ◊ *Das ist bezeichnend für sie!* That's typical of her!

**beziehen** VERB (IMPERFECT **bezog,** PERFECT **hat bezogen)**
[1] to cover ◊ *Sie beschloss, alle Kissen zu beziehen.* She decided to cover all the cushions.
◆ **das Bett beziehen** to change the bed
[2] to move into ◊ *Wann könnt ihr euer neues Haus beziehen?* When can you move into your new house?
[3] to get ◊ *Wir beziehen unsere Kartoffeln direkt vom Bauern.* We get our potatoes straight from the farm. ◊ *Sie beziehen Arbeitslosenhilfe.* They get unemployment benefit.
[4] to subscribe to ◊ *Ich beziehe eine Tageszeitung.* I subscribe to a daily newspaper.
◆ **sich beziehen** to cloud over ◊ *Der Himmel bezieht sich.* It's clouding over.
◆ **sich auf etwas beziehen** to refer to something ◊ *Sein Beispiel bezog sich auf das Tierreich.* His example referred to the animal kingdom.

die **Beziehung** NOUN
[1] relationship ◊ *Er hat eine Beziehung mit einer verheirateten Frau.* He has a relationship with a married woman.
[2] relations ◊ *unsere Beziehungen zu dieser Firma* our relations with this company ◊ *diplomatische Beziehungen* diplomatic relations

**B**

[3] connection ◊ *Es besteht eine Beziehung zwischen den beiden Straftaten.* There's a connection between the two crimes.
♦ **in dieser Beziehung** in this respect
♦ **Beziehungen haben** to have contacts ◊ *Er kann bestimmt etwas für dich tun, er hat Beziehungen.* I'm sure he can do something for you, he has contacts.
♦ **eine Beziehung zu etwas haben** to be able to relate to something ◊ *Ich habe keine Beziehung zu moderner Kunst.* I can't relate to modern art.

der **Bezirk** NOUN (PL die **Bezirke**)
district

der **Bezug** NOUN (PL die **Bezüge**)
cover ◊ *Das Sofa hatte einen bunten Bezug.* The sofa had a brightly-coloured cover.
♦ **Zu dieser Musik habe ich keinen Bezug.** I can't relate to this kind of music.
♦ **in Bezug auf** regarding ◊ *in Bezug auf Kinder* regarding children
♦ **Bezug nehmen auf** to refer to ◊ *Sie hat in ihrer Rede mehrfach Bezug auf ihren Vorredner genommen.* In her speech she referred several times to the previous speaker.

**bezüglich** PREPOSITION
*The preposition bezüglich takes the genitive.*
with reference to ◊ *Bezüglich Ihrer Anfrage können wir Ihnen mitteilen ...* With reference to your inquiry we can inform you that ...

**bezweifeln** VERB (PERFECT hat **bezweifelt**)
to doubt ◊ *Ich bezweifle das.* I doubt it.

der **BH** NOUN (PL die **BHs**) (= *Büstenhalter*)
bra

**Bhf.** ABBREVIATION (= *Bahnhof*)
station

die **Bibel** NOUN
Bible

die **Bibliothek** NOUN (PL die **Bibliotheken**)
library

**biegen** VERB (IMPERFECT bog, PERFECT hat gebogen)
to bend ◊ *Sie bog den Draht zur Seite.* She bent the wire to one side.
♦ **Ein Auto bog um die Kurve.** A car came round the corner.
♦ **Du musst an der Ampel rechts in die Seitenstraße biegen.** You'll have to turn right into the side street at the traffic lights.
♦ **sich biegen** to bend ◊ *Die Bäume bogen sich im Wind.* The trees were bending in the wind.

die **Biene** NOUN
bee

der **Bienenstich** NOUN (PL die **Bienenstiche**)
[1] bee sting
[2] cream-filled cake

das **Bier** NOUN (PL die **Biere** or **Bier**)
beer ◊ *Zwei Bier, bitte!* Two beers, please!

die **Bierhalle** NOUN
beer hall

der **Bierkeller** NOUN (PL die **Bierkeller**)
beer cellar

das **Bierzelt** NOUN
beer tent

**bieten** VERB (IMPERFECT bot, PERFECT hat geboten)
[1] to offer ◊ *Dieser Job bietet mir die Möglichkeit, meine Englischkenntnisse anzuwenden.* This job offers me the chance to use my knowledge of English.
[2] to bid ◊ *Sie hat zweihundert Mark für den Stuhl geboten.* She bid two hundred marks for the chair. ◊ *Wer bietet mehr?* Any more bids?
♦ **Ich will ins Ausland, sobald sich die Gelegenheit bietet.** I want to go abroad as soon as the opportunity arises.
♦ **sich etwas bieten lassen** to put up with something ◊ *Eine solche Frechheit lasse ich mir nicht bieten.* I won't put up with such cheek.

der **Bikini** NOUN (PL die **Bikinis**)
bikini

das **Bild** NOUN (PL die **Bilder**)
[1] picture ◊ *ein Bild von Picasso* a picture by Picasso
♦ **ein Bild der Verwüstung** a scene of destruction
[2] photo ◊ *Hast du ein Bild von deinem Freund?* Have you got a photo of your boyfriend?

**bilden** VERB
[1] to form ◊ *Bildet einen Kreis.* Form a circle. ◊ *Wie wird der Plural dieses Worts gebildet?* How do you form the plural of this word?
[2] to set up ◊ *Sie haben einen Ausschuss gebildet.* They set up a committee.
♦ **sich eine Meinung bilden** to form an opinion ◊ *In dieser Frage habe ich mir noch keine Meinung gebildet.* I haven't formed an opinion on this question yet.
♦ **Reisen bildet.** Travel broadens the mind.
♦ **sich bilden (1)** to form ◊ *Am Himmel bildeten sich dunkle Wolken.* Dark clouds formed in the sky.
♦ **sich bilden (2)** to educate oneself ◊ *Sie macht Kurse, um sich zu bilden.* She attends courses in order to educate herself.

der **Bildschirm** NOUN (PL die **Bildschirme**)
screen

der **Bildschirmschoner** NOUN (PL die **Bildschirmschoner**)
screen saver

die **Bildung** NOUN

☞

**1** education ◇ *Sie hat eine gute Bildung.* She has a good education.

**2** formation ◇ *Die Bildung des Plurals im Englischen ist ziemlich regelmäßig.* The formation of the plural in English is quite regular. ◇ *die Bildung der Regierung* the formation of the government

**billig** ADJECTIVE
cheap

die **Binde** NOUN
**1** bandage ◇ *eine elastische Binde* an elastic bandage

**2** sanitary towel ◇ *Sie benützt lieber Binden als Tampons.* She prefers sanitary towels to tampons.

**binden** VERB (IMPERFECT **band,** PERFECT **hat gebunden)**
to tie ◇ *Die Tomaten werden an einen Stock gebunden.* The tomatoes are tied to a cane. ◇ *Sie band die Haare zu einem Pferdeschwanz.* She tied her hair back into a ponytail.

♦ **ein Buch binden** to bind a book
♦ **sich binden** to get involved ◇ *Sie möchte sich in ihrem Alter noch nicht binden.* She doesn't want to get involved at her age.

der **Bindestrich** NOUN (PL die **Bindestriche)**
hyphen

der **Bindfaden** NOUN (PL die **Bindfäden)**
string

die **Bindung** NOUN
**1** tie ◇ *Meine emotionale Bindung an meine Eltern ...* My emotional ties to my parents ...

**2** bindings ◇ *Bei einem Sturz müsste die Bindung aufgehen.* When you fall the bindings should come open.

die **Biologie** NOUN
biology

**biologisch** ADJECTIVE
biological

die **Birke** NOUN
birch

die **Birne** NOUN
**1** pear ◇ *Zum Nachtisch gab es Birnen mit Schokoladensoße.* There were pears with chocolate sauce for dessert.

**2** bulb ◇ *Die Lampe funktioniert nicht, weil die Birne kaputt ist.* The lamp isn't working because the bulb's gone.

**bis** PREPOSITION, CONJUNCTION

*The preposition **bis** takes the accusative.*

**1** until ◇ *Sie bleibt bis Ende August in England.* She's staying in England until the end of August. ◇ *Du hast bis Montag Zeit.* You have until Monday. ◇ *bis es dunkel wird* until it gets dark

♦ **bis auf weiteres** until further notice

**2** by ◇ *Das Referat muss bis nächsten Montag fertig sein.* The assignment must be finished by next Monday.

♦ **bis in die Nacht** into the night
♦ **bis bald** see you later
♦ **bis gleich** see you soon
**3** as far as ◇ *Ich fahre bis Köln.* I'm going as far as Cologne.
♦ **bis hierher** this far
♦ **von ... bis ...** from ... to ... ◇ *von Köln bis Bonn* from Cologne to Bonn ◇ *von Anfang Mai bis Ende Juni* from the beginning of May to the end of June
**4** up to ◇ *Kinder bis drei fahren umsonst.* Children up to three travel free. ◇ *bis zu dreißig Grad* up to thirty degrees
♦ **zehn bis zwanzig** ten to twenty
♦ **bis zu** up to ◇ *Ich kann bis zu drei Personen mitnehmen.* I can take up to three people.
♦ **bis auf** apart from ◇ *Bis auf Jan sind alle mitgekommen.* Everybody came along apart from Jan.

**bisher** ADVERB
up to now

**bisherig** ADJECTIVE
previous

der **Biss** NOUN (GEN des **Bisses,** PL die **Bisse)**
bite

**biss** VERB see **beißen**

**bisschen** ADJECTIVE, ADVERB
bit ◇ *ein bisschen* a bit

**bissig** ADJECTIVE
**1** vicious
♦ **Vorsicht, bissiger Hund!** Beware of the dog!
**2** cutting ◇ *Er machte eine bissige Bemerkung.* He made a cutting remark.

**bist** VERB see **sein**

das **Bit** NOUN (PL die **Bits)**
bit ◇ *Bits und Bytes* bits and bytes

die **Bitte** NOUN

see also **bitte** EXCLAMATION

request ◇ *Ich habe eine Bitte.* I have a request. ◇ *auf seine Bitte hin* at his request

**bitte** EXCLAMATION

see also **die Bitte** NOUN

**1** please ◇ *Kann ich bitte noch etwas Saft haben?* Can I have some more juice, please? ◇ *Könnten Sie mir bitte sagen, wie ich zum Bahnhof komme?* Could you please tell me how to get to the station?
♦ **Wie bitte?** Pardon?
♦ **Hier bitte!** Here you are.
♦ **Bitte warten.** Please hold the line. (*phone*)
**2** don't mention it ◇ *Vielen Dank für die Hilfe! – Bitte!* Many thanks for your help! – Don't mention it!
♦ **Bitte schön!** It was a pleasure.
♦ **Bitte sehr!** You're welcome.
♦ **Darf ich? – Aber bitte!** May I? – Please do.

**bitten** VERB (IMPERFECT **bat,** PERFECT **hat gebeten)**

◆ **jemanden um etwas bitten** to ask somebody for something

**bitter** ADJECTIVE
   bitter

**blamieren** VERB (PERFECT **hat blamiert**)
◆ **sich blamieren** to make a fool of oneself
◆ **jemanden blamieren** to let somebody down

die **Blase** NOUN
   [1] bubble ◊ *Die Blase platzte.* The bubble burst.
   [2] blister ◊ *Ich habe Blasen an den Füßen.* I've got blisters on my feet.
   [3] bladder ◊ *Sie hat eine schwache Blase.* She has a weak bladder.

**blasen** VERB (PRESENT **bläst**, IMPERFECT **blies**, PERFECT **hat geblasen**)
   to blow

das **Blasinstrument** NOUN (PL die **Blasinstrumente**)
   wind instrument

die **Blaskapelle** NOUN
   brass band

die **Blasmusik** NOUN
   brass band music

**blass** ADJECTIVE
   pale ◊ *Als sie das hörte, wurde sie blass.* When she heard that, she turned pale.

das **Blatt** NOUN (PL die **Blätter**)
   [1] leaf ◊ *Im Herbst fallen die Blätter von den Bäumen.* In autumn, the leaves fall from the trees.
   [2] sheet ◊ *ein Blatt Papier* a sheet of paper
   [3] newspaper ◊ *In welchem Blatt hast du die Anzeige aufgegeben?* Which newspaper did you place the advertisement in?

**blau** ADJECTIVE
   [1] blue ◊ *Er hat blaue Augen.* He has blue eyes.
   [2] sloshed ◊ *Gestern Abend warst du ganz schön blau.* You were absolutely sloshed yesterday evening.
◆ **ein blaues Auge** a black eye
◆ **ein blauer Fleck** a bruise
◆ **eine Fahrt ins Blaue** a mystery tour

das **Blech** NOUN (PL die **Bleche**)
   [1] sheet metal
   [2] baking tray

das **Blei** NOUN
   lead

**bleiben** VERB (IMPERFECT **blieb**, PERFECT **ist geblieben**)
   [1] to stay ◊ *Wie lange bleiben Sie hier?* How long are you staying here? ◊ *Hoffentlich bleibt das Wetter schön.* I hope the weather will stay fine.
◆ **bei etwas bleiben** to stick to something ◊ *Ich bleibe bei meiner Meinung.* I'm sticking to my opinion.

   [2] to be left ◊ *Vom Kuchen war nur noch ein Stück für mich geblieben.* There was only one piece of cake left for me.
◆ **Es bleibt abzuwarten, was passiert.** We'll have to wait and see what happens.
◆ **Bleibt es bei morgen zehn Uhr?** Is ten o'clock tomorrow morning still on?
◆ **Wo bleibt sie denn?** Where's she got to?

**bleich** ADJECTIVE
   pale ◊ *Als er das hörte, wurde er bleich.* When he heard that, he turned pale.

**bleifrei** ADJECTIVE
   unleaded

der **Bleistift** NOUN (PL die **Bleistifte**)
   pencil

der **Bleistiftspitzer** NOUN (PL die **Bleistiftspitzer**)
   pencil sharpener

**blenden** VERB
   to blind ◊ *Das entgegenkommende Auto hat mich geblendet.* The approaching car blinded me.

**blendend** ADJECTIVE
   marvellous
◆ **Du siehst blendend aus.** You look marvellous.
◆ **sich blendend amüsieren** to have a wonderful time
◆ **Mir geht's blendend.** I'm feeling great.

der **Blick** NOUN (PL die **Blicke**)
   [1] glance ◊ *Ich habe mit einem Blick gesehen, dass das nicht gut gehen kann.* I saw at a glance that it couldn't work.
◆ **Er warf einen Blick auf die Uhr.** He glanced at the clock.
   [2] look ◊ *Sie warf mir einen verzweifelten Blick zu.* She gave me a desperate look.
   [3] view ◊ *Das Zimmer hat einen herrlichen Blick auf die Berge.* The room has a wonderful view of the mountains.
◆ **auf den ersten Blick** at first glance

**blicken** VERB
   to look ◊ *Sie blickte zur Seite.* She looked to one side.
◆ **sich blicken lassen** to show one's face ◊ *Er hat sich hier nie wieder blicken lassen.* He's never shown his face here again.
◆ **Das lässt tief blicken!** That's very revealing!

**blieb** VERB *see* **bleiben**

**blind** ADJECTIVE
   [1] blind ◊ *Er ist auf einem Auge blind.* He's blind in one eye.
   [2] tarnished ◊ *Der Spiegel war blind geworden.* The mirror had become tarnished.
◆ **ein blinder Passagier** a stowaway

der **Blinddarm** NOUN (PL die **Blinddärme**)
   appendix ◊ *Er wurde am Blinddarm operiert.* He had his appendix out.

**B**

die **Blinddarmentzündung** NOUN
   appendicitis
**blinzeln** VERB
   to blink
der **Blitz** NOUN (PL die **Blitze**)
   lightning ◊ *Der Blitz schlug in den Baum ein.* The tree was struck by lightning.
**blitzen** VERB
   ◆**Es blitzt.** There's a flash of lightning.
das **Blitzlicht** NOUN (PL die **Blitzlichter**)
   flashlight
der **Block** NOUN (PL die **Blöcke**)
   [1] block ◊ *Unsere Nachbarn aus dem nächsten Block haben uns gestern besucht.* Our neighbours from the next block visited us yesterday.
   [2] pad ◊ *Er riss ein Blatt vom Block und fing an zu schreiben.* He tore a sheet from the pad and began to write.
die **Blockflöte** NOUN
   recorder
**blöd** ADJECTIVE
   stupid ◊ *Du bist blöd!* You're stupid!
   ◆**blöd fragen** to ask stupid questions ◊ *Wer blöd fragt, bekommt auch eine blöde Antwort.* If you ask a stupid question, then you get a stupid answer.
der **Blödsinn** NOUN
   nonsense
**blond** ADJECTIVE
   [1] blond ◊ *Er hat blonde Haare.* He has blond hair.
   [2] blonde ◊ *Meine Schwester ist blond.* My sister's blonde. ◊ *Sie hat ihre Haare blond gefärbt.* She dyed her hair blonde.
**bloß** ADVERB, ADJECTIVE
   only ◊ *Er hat bloß einen Fehler gemacht.* He only made one mistake. ◊ *Wenn das bloß schon fertig wäre!* If only it was finished. ◊ *Das Konzert war ganz nett, bloß ein bisschen laut.* The concert was quite nice, only a little loud.
   ◆**Lass das bloß!** Don't do that!
   ◆**Wie ist das bloß passiert?** How on earth did that happen?
   ◆**Wo ist er bloß?** Where's he got to?
   ◆**mit bloßem Auge** with the naked eye
   ◆**der bloße Gedanke** the very thought
   ◆**bloßer Neid** sheer envy
**blühen** VERB
   to be in bloom ◊ *Zurzeit blüht der Flieder.* The lilac's in bloom at the moment.
die **Blume** NOUN
   flower ◊ *Sie hat mir einen Strauß Blumen mitgebracht.* She brought me a bunch of flowers.
das **Blumenbeet** NOUN (PL die **Blumenbeete**)
   flowerbed
der **Blumenkohl** NOUN (PL die **Blumenkohle**)
   cauliflower
die **Bluse** NOUN
   blouse
das **Blut** NOUN
   blood
der **Blutdruck** NOUN
   blood pressure
die **Blüte** NOUN
   blossom
**bluten** VERB
   to bleed ◊ *Meine Nase blutet.* My nose is bleeding.
die **Blutprobe** NOUN
   blood test
der **Blutspender** NOUN (PL die **Blutspender**)
   blood donor
die **Blutvergiftung** NOUN
   blood poisoning
der **Bock** NOUN
   ◆**Bock haben, etwas zu tun** to fancy doing something ◊ *Hast du Bock, mit ins Kino zu kommen?* Do you feel like coming to the cinema? ◊ *Ich habe heute überhaupt keinen Bock auf die Schule.* I don't fancy school today at all.
die **Bockwurst** NOUN (PL die **Bockwürste**)
   frankfurter
der **Boden** NOUN (PL die **Böden**)
   [1] soil ◊ *Der Boden ist in dieser Gegend sehr fruchtbar.* The soil in this area is very fertile. ◊ *auf deutschem Boden* on German soil
   [2] floor ◊ *Wir haben auf dem Boden gesessen.* We sat on the floor.
   [3] bottom ◊ *Das Schiff sank auf den Boden des Meers.* The ship sank to the bottom of the sea. ◊ *Das Fass hat einen hölzernen Boden.* The barrel has a wooden bottom.
   [4] attic ◊ *Wir haben die alten Möbel auf den Boden gebracht.* We put the old furniture into the attic.
die **Bodenschätze** MASC PL NOUN
   mineral resources
der **Bodensee** NOUN
   Lake Constance ◊ *eine Stadt am Bodensee* a town on Lake Constance
die **Bohne** NOUN
   bean
**bohren** VERB
   to bore ◊ *Sie bohrte ein Loch in das Brett.* She bored a hole in the shelf.
   ◆**Der Zahnarzt musste nicht bohren.** The dentist didn't have to drill.
   ◆**nach etwas bohren** to drill for something ◊ *In der Nordsee wird nach Erdöl gebohrt.* They're drilling for oil in the North Sea.
   ◆**in der Nase bohren** to pick one's nose
der **Bohrer** NOUN (PL die **Bohrer**)
   drill
die **Bohrinsel** NOUN
   oil rig
die **Bohrmaschine** NOUN

drill

der **Bohrturm** NOUN (PL die **Bohrtürme**)
derrick

die **Bombe** NOUN
bomb

der **Bonbon** NOUN (PL die **Bonbons**)
sweet

das **Boot** NOUN (PL die **Boote**)
boat

der **Bord** NOUN
> see also **das Bord** NOUN
♦ **an Bord** on board

das **Bord** NOUN (PL die **Borde**)
> see also **der Bord** NOUN

shelf ◊ *Er brachte über dem Schreibtisch ein Bord für seine Bücher an.* He put up a shelf over his desk for his books.

**borgen** VERB
to borrow ◊ *Das gehört nicht mir, das habe ich mir geborgt.* That doesn't belong to me, I borrowed it.
♦ **jemandem etwas borgen** to lend somebody something ◊ *Meine Schwester hat mir ihr Rennrad geborgt.* My sister lent me her racing bike.

die **Börse** NOUN
[1] purse ◊ *Sie nahm zehn Mark aus ihrer Börse.* She took ten marks out of her purse.
[2] stock exchange ◊ *Diese Aktien werden an der Börse gehandelt.* These shares are traded on the stock exchange.

**böse** ADJECTIVE
[1] bad ◊ *Er ist ein böser Mensch.* He's a bad man. ◊ *Die Kinder waren böse.* The children were bad. ◊ *Sie hat eine böse Erkältung.* She has a bad cold.
♦ **Er hat sich böse verletzt.** He's injured himself badly.
[2] angry ◊ *Ich habe ihm einen bösen Brief geschrieben.* I wrote him an angry letter.
♦ **böse werden** to get angry ◊ *Wenn du das noch einmal tust, werde ich böse.* If you do that again, I'll get angry.
♦ **auf jemanden böse sein** to be angry with somebody ◊ *Ich bin böse auf Martin, weil er nicht gekommen ist.* I'm angry with Martin because he didn't come.
♦ **Bist du mir noch böse?** Are you still angry with me?
♦ **Das war eine böse Überraschung.** That was a nasty shock.
♦ **Mit ihm sieht es böse aus.** It doesn't look too good for him.

**Bosnien** NEUT NOUN
Bosnia

**Bosnien-Herzegowina** NEUT NOUN
Bosnia-Herzegovina

**bot** VERB *see* **bieten**

die **Botschaft** NOUN

[1] message ◊ *Kannst du ihm eine Botschaft übermitteln?* Can you give him a message?
[2] embassy ◊ *Sie müssen das Visum auf der Botschaft beantragen.* You have to apply to the embassy for a visa.

**boxen** VERB
to box

der **Boxer** NOUN (PL die **Boxer**)
boxer

**brach** VERB *see* **brechen**

**brachte** VERB *see* **bringen**

der **Brand** NOUN (PL die **Brände**)
fire

**Brandenburg** NEUT NOUN
Brandenburg

> ℹ️ **Brandenburg** is one of the 16 **Länder**. Its capital is Potsdam, which is famous as Frederick the Great's residence. Agriculture and forestry are still important parts of the economy.

**Brasilien** NEUT NOUN
Brazil
♦ **aus Brasilien** from Brazil
♦ **nach Brasilien** to Brazil

**braten** VERB (PRESENT **brät**, IMPERFECT **briet**, PERFECT **hat gebraten**)
> see also **der Braten** NOUN
[1] to roast ◊ *Wir haben das Hähnchen im Backofen gebraten.* We roasted the chicken in the oven.
[2] to fry ◊ *Sie briet die Kartoffeln in der Pfanne.* She fried the potatoes in the frying pan.

der **Braten** NOUN (PL die **Braten**)
> see also **braten** VERB
roast

das **Brathähnchen** NOUN (PL die **Brathähnchen**)
roast chicken

die **Bratkartoffeln** FEM PL NOUN
fried potatoes

die **Bratpfanne** NOUN
frying pan

die **Bratwurst** NOUN (PL die **Bratwürste**)
fried sausage

der **Brauch** NOUN (PL die **Bräuche**)
custom

**brauchbar** ADJECTIVE
[1] usable ◊ *Dieses alte Gerät ist nicht mehr brauchbar.* The old appliance is no longer usable.
[2] capable ◊ *Sie ist eine sehr brauchbare Mitarbeiterin.* She's a very capable colleague.

**brauchen** VERB
[1] to need ◊ *Wir brauchen noch Brot und Butter.* We still need bread and butter. ◊ *Dazu brauche ich mindestens zwei Tage.* I'll need at least two days.

B

⟨2⟩ to have to ◊ *Du brauchst heute nicht kommen.* You don't have to come today. ◊ *Du brauchst nur Bescheid zu sagen, dann helfe ich dir.* You only have to let me know and I'll help you.

♦ **Das kann ich gut brauchen.** I could really do with that.

die **Brauerei** NOUN
brewery

**braun** ADJECTIVE
⟨1⟩ brown ◊ *Sie hat braune Haare und braune Augen.* She has brown hair and brown eyes.
⟨2⟩ tanned ◊ *Wir kamen ganz braun aus den Ferien zurück.* We came back all tanned from our holidays.

die **Braut** NOUN (PL die **Bräute**)
bride

der **Bräutigam** NOUN (PL die **Bräutigame**)
bridegroom

das **Brautpaar** NOUN (PL die **Brautpaare**)
bride and groom

**brav** ADJECTIVE
good ◊ *Die Kinder waren brav.* The children were good.
*Be careful! **brav** does not mean **brave**.*

**bravo!** EXCLAMATION
well done!

die **BRD** NOUN (= *Bundesrepublik Deutschland*)
Federal Republic of Germany

**brechen** VERB (PRESENT **bricht**, IMPERFECT **brach**, PERFECT **hat/ist gebrochen**)
*For the perfect tense use **haben** when the verb has an object and **sein** when there is no object. Use **haben** for to vomit.*
⟨1⟩ to break ◊ *Der Zweig ist gebrochen.* The branch broke. ◊ *Ich habe den Stock in zwei Teile gebrochen.* I broke the stick in two. ◊ *Ich habe mir den rechten Arm gebrochen.* I've broken my right arm. ◊ *Sie hat ihr Versprechen gebrochen.* She broke her promise. ◊ *einen Rekord brechen* to break a record
⟨2⟩ to vomit ◊ *Ihm wurde schlecht, und er musste brechen.* He felt ill and had to vomit.

**breit** ADJECTIVE
wide ◊ *Das Brett ist fünfzehn Zentimeter breit.* The plank is fifteen centimetres wide.

die **Breite** NOUN
width ◊ *die Breite des Tisches* the width of the table

**Bremen** NEUT NOUN
Bremen

ⓘ *The "Free Hanseatic City of Bremen" is one of the 16 **Länder**. It is a "city-state" like Berlin and Hamburg, and is made up of the cities Bremen and Bremerhaven.*

die **Bremse** NOUN
⟨1⟩ brake ◊ *Sie trat auf die Bremsen.* She stepped on the brakes.
⟨2⟩ horsefly ◊ *Wir sind von Bremsen gestochen worden.* We were bitten by horseflies.

**bremsen** VERB
to brake ◊ *Als er das Kind sah, bremste er.* When he saw the child, he braked.

♦ **Sie versuchte, das Auto zu bremsen.** She tried to stop the car.

♦ **Wenn sie erst einmal angefangen hat, dann ist sie nicht mehr zu bremsen.** Once she's started, there's no stopping her.

das **Bremslicht** NOUN (PL die **Bremslichter**)
brake light

das **Bremspedal** NOUN (PL die **Bremspedale**)
brake pedal

**brennen** VERB (IMPERFECT **brannte**, PERFECT **hat gebrannt**)
to burn ◊ *Das Holz ist zu nass, es brennt nicht.* The wood's too wet, it won't burn. ◊ *Im Wohnzimmer brennt Licht.* There's a light burning in the living room. ◊ *Der Schnaps brennt auf der Zunge.* The schnapps burns your tongue. ◊ *ein Loch in etwas brennen* to burn a hole in something

♦ **Das Haus brannte.** The house was on fire.

♦ **sich brennen** to burn oneself ◊ *Ich habe mich an der heißen Platte gebrannt.* I've burned myself on the hot plate.

♦ **darauf brennen, etwas zu tun** to be dying to do something ◊ *Ich brenne darauf, deinen Freund kennenzulernen.* I'm dying to meet your boyfriend.

die **Brennnessel** NOUN
stinging nettle

der **Brennstoff** NOUN (PL die **Brennstoffe**)
fuel

das **Brett** NOUN (PL die **Bretter**)
⟨1⟩ board ◊ *Die Hütte bestand aus ein paar zusammengenagelten Brettern.* The hut consisted of a few boards nailed together. ◊ *Sie stellte die Schachfiguren aufs Brett.* She set the chessmen on the board.
⟨2⟩ shelf ◊ *Die Gewürze stehen auf einem Brett über dem Herd.* The spices are on a shelf above the cooker.

♦ **das schwarze Brett** the notice board

♦ **Ich hatte ein Brett vor dem Kopf.** My mind went blank.

die **Brezel** NOUN
pretzel

**bricht** VERB see **brechen**

der **Brief** NOUN (PL die **Briefe**)
letter

der **Brieffreund** NOUN (PL die **Brieffreunde**)
pen friend
die **Brieffreundin** NOUN
pen friend
die **Brieffreundschaft** NOUN
◆**Ich habe eine Brieffreundschaft mit ihm.**
He's my pen friend.
der **Briefkasten** NOUN (PL die **Briefkästen**)
[1] letterbox
[2] postbox
die **Briefmarke** NOUN
stamp
die **Brieftasche** NOUN
wallet
der **Briefträger** NOUN (PL die **Briefträger**)
postman ◇ *Günter ist Briefträger.*
Günter's a postman.
die **Briefträgerin** NOUN
postwoman ◇ *Meine Tante ist
Briefträgerin.* My aunt's a
postwoman.
der **Briefumschlag** NOUN (PL die
**Briefumschläge**)
envelope
der **Briefwechsel** NOUN (PL die **Briefwechsel**)
correspondence
**briet** VERB *see* **braten**
die **Brille** NOUN
[1] glasses ◇ *Lesley trägt eine Brille.*
Lesley wears glasses. ◇ *eine Brille* a pair
of glasses
[2] goggles ◇ *Beim Schweißen sollte
man eine Brille tragen.* You should wear
goggles when welding.
[3] toilet seat ◇ *Ich hasse es, wenn
Männer die Brille oben lassen.* I hate it
when men leave the seat up.
**bringen** VERB (IMPERFECT **brachte**, PERFECT **hat
gebracht**)
[1] to bring ◇ *Unsere Gäste haben uns
einen schönen Blumenstrauß gebracht.*
Our guests have brought us a lovely
bunch of flowers. ◇ *Kann ich meine
Schwester mit zur Party bringen?* Can I
bring my sister to the party?
[2] to take ◇ *Meine Freunde haben mich
zum Flughafen gebracht.* My friends took
me to the airport. ◇ *jemanden nach
Hause bringen* to take somebody
home
[3] to bring in ◇ *Diese Anlage bringt fünf
Prozent Zinsen.* This investment brings in
five per cent interest.
[4] to publish ◇ *Alle Zeitungen brachten
diese Geschichte auf der ersten Seite.* All
the newspapers published this story on
the first page.
[5] to be on ◇ *Sieh mal in der Zeitung
nach, was das Theater bringt.* Look
in the paper to see what's on at the
theatre.
◆**jemanden zu etwas bringen** to make
somebody do something ◇ *Sie hat mich*

*zum Lachen gebracht.* She made me
laugh. ◇ *Du bringst mich noch zur
Verzweiflung.* You make me despair.
◆**jemanden dazu bringen, etwas zu tun** to
get somebody to do something ◇ *Wie
hast du deine Eltern dazu gebracht, dass
sie das erlaubt haben?* How did you get
your parents to let you do that?
◆**es über sich bringen, etwas zu tun** to
bring oneself to do something ◇ *Ich habe
es nicht über mich gebracht, ihr das zu
sagen.* I couldn't bring myself to tell her.
◆**Der Betrüger hat die alte Frau um ihre
ganzen Ersparnisse gebracht.** The
swindler cheated the old lady out of all
her savings.
◆**jemanden auf eine Idee bringen** to give
somebody an idea
◆**jemanden in Gefahr bringen** to put
somebody in danger
◆**Unser Computer bringt's nicht.** Our
computer's rubbish.
◆**Das bringt nichts!** That's no use!
der **Brite** NOUN (GEN des **Briten**, PL die **Briten**)
Briton
◆**die Briten** the British
die **Britin** NOUN
Briton
**britisch** ADJECTIVE
British
die **Brokkoli** PL NOUN
broccoli
die **Brombeere** NOUN
blackberry
die **Broschüre** NOUN
brochure
das **Brot** NOUN (PL die **Brote**)
[1] bread ◇ *Haben wir noch Brot im
Haus?* Do we still have some bread in the
house?
[2] loaf ◇ *Kannst du für die Party drei
Brote holen?* Can you get three loaves
for the party?
das **Brötchen** NOUN (PL die **Brötchen**)
roll
**browsen** VERB (PERFECT **hat gebrowst**)
to browse
der **Browser** NOUN (PL die **Browser**)
web browser
der **Bruch** NOUN (PL die **Brüche**)
[1] fracture ◇ *Sie wurde mit einem Bruch
ins Krankenhaus eingeliefert.* She was
taken to hospital with a fracture.
◆**zu Bruch gehen** to get broken ◇ *Die
ganzen Teller sind zu Bruch gegangen.*
All the plates got broken.
[2] hernia ◇ *Trag das nicht allein, du
hebst dir sonst einen Bruch!* Don't carry
that on your own, you'll give yourself a
hernia!
[3] fraction ◇ *Das Rechnen mit Brüchen
haben wir noch nicht gelernt.* We haven't
learned fractions yet.

die **Brücke** NOUN
bridge

der **Bruder** NOUN (PL die **Brüder**)
brother

der **Brühwürfel** NOUN (PL die **Brühwürfel**)
stock cube

**brüllen** VERB
to roar ◊ *Der Löwe brüllte.* The lion roared.
♦ **Er brüllte vor Schmerz.** He screamed with pain.

**brummen** VERB
1 to growl ◊ *Der Bär brummte.* The bear growled.
2 to buzz ◊ *Eine dicke Fliege brummte durchs Zimmer.* A huge fly buzzed around the room.
♦ **etwas brummen** to mumble something ◊ *Er hat irgendetwas Unfreundliches gebrummt.* He mumbled something unfriendly.

der **Brunnen** NOUN (PL die **Brunnen**)
1 fountain ◊ *Am Marktplatz steht ein Brunnen.* There's a fountain in the market square.
2 well ◊ *Die Burgbewohner bekamen ihr Wasser aus diesem Brunnen.* The inhabitants of the castle got their water from this well.

die **Brust** NOUN (PL die **Brüste**)
breast ◊ *Sie hat kleine Brüste.* She has small breasts.

der **Brustkasten** NOUN
chest

das **Brustschwimmen** NOUN
breaststroke

**brutal** ADJECTIVE
brutal

die **Brutalität** NOUN
brutality

**brutto** ADVERB
gross

das **BSE** NOUN
BSE (= bovine spongiform encephalopathy) ◊ *Nicht alle Kühe haben BSE.* Not all cows have got BSE.

das **Buch** NOUN (PL die **Bücher**)
book

die **Buche** NOUN
beech tree

**buchen** VERB
to book ◊ *Wir haben eine Reise nach Kreta gebucht.* We've booked a trip to Crete.

die **Bücherei** NOUN
library

das **Bücherregal** NOUN (PL die **Bücherregale**)
bookcase

der **Buchhalter** NOUN (PL die **Buchhalter**)
accountant

die **Buchhandlung** NOUN
bookshop

der **Buchladen** NOUN (PL die **Buchläden**)
bookshop

die **Büchse** NOUN
tin ◊ *Sie bewahrt den Tee in einer Büchse auf.* She keeps her tea in a tin.

der **Büchsenöffner** NOUN (PL die **Büchsenöffner**)
tin opener

der **Buchstabe** NOUN (GEN des **Buchstabens,** PL die **Buchstaben**)
letter of the alphabet

**buchstabieren** VERB (PERFECT **hat buchstabiert**)
to spell

**buchstäblich** ADVERB
literally ◊ *Sie kam buchstäblich in der letzten Minute.* She arrived at literally the last minute.

sich **bücken** VERB
to bend down

die **Bude** NOUN
stall ◊ *die Buden auf dem Jahrmarkt* the stalls at the fair
♦ **Kommt ihr noch mit auf meine Bude?** Do you want to come back to my place?

das **Büfett** NOUN (PL die **Büfetts**)
sideboard
♦ **kaltes Büfett** cold buffet

der **Bügel** NOUN (PL die **Bügel**)
hanger

das **Bügeleisen** NOUN (PL die **Bügeleisen**)
iron ◊ *Ich habe mir die Hand am Bügeleisen verbrannt.* I burnt my hand on the iron.

**bügeln** VERB
to iron

die **Bühne** NOUN
stage ◊ *auf der Bühne stehen* to be on stage

**buk** VERB *see* **backen**

**Bulgarien** NEUT NOUN
Bulgaria
♦ **aus Bulgarien** from Bulgaria
♦ **nach Bulgarien** to Bulgaria

der **Bummel** NOUN (PL die **Bummel**)
1 stroll ◊ *Wir machten einen Bummel an der Donau entlang.* We went for a stroll along the Danube.
2 window-shopping ◊ *Bei meinem Bummel durch die Innenstadt habe ich eine tolle Hose gesehen.* I saw a fantastic pair of trousers while I was window-shopping in the city centre.

**bummeln** VERB

*Use* **sein** *to form the perfect tense for* **to stroll** *and* **haben** *for* **to dawdle**.

1 to stroll ◊ *Wir sind durch die Stadt gebummelt.* We strolled through the town.
2 to dawdle ◊ *Heute hast du auf dem Heimweg aber gebummelt.* You've really been dawdling on your way home today.

**B**

der **Bund** NOUN (PL die **Bünde**)
   [1] association ◊ *Die Bauern schlossen sich zu einem Bund zusammen.* The farmers formed an association.
   ♦ **Bund und Länder** the Federal Government and the Länder
   [2] waistband ◊ *Die Hose ist am Bund zu eng.* The trousers are too tight at the waistband.

**Bundes-** PREFIX
   Federal

der **Bundesbürger** NOUN (PL die **Bundesbürger**)
   German citizen

der **Bundeskanzler** NOUN (PL die **Bundeskanzler**)
   Federal Chancellor

das **Bundesland** NOUN (PL die **Bundesländer**)
   state

die **Bundesliga** NOUN
   Premier League

> ⓘ The **Bundesliga** was founded in 1963, and consists of 18 teams. At the end of the season, play-offs between the bottom 3 clubs of the **Bundesliga** and the top 3 of the **zweite Bundesliga** decide who is relegated and who promoted.

der **Bundespräsident** NOUN (GEN des **Bundespräsidenten**, PL die **Bundespräsidenten**)
   Federal President

der **Bundesrat** NOUN
   upper chamber of the German Parliament

> ⓘ The **Bundesrat** is not directly elected, but is made up of representatives of the 16 **Länder**. In many cases, **Bundesrat** approval is required before laws (particularly amendments to the constitution) can be passed.

die **Bundesregierung** NOUN
   Federal government

die **Bundesrepublik** NOUN
   Federal Republic ◊ *die Bundesrepublik Deutschland* the Federal Republic of Germany

die **Bundesstraße** NOUN
   federal road

der **Bundestag** NOUN
   German Parliament

> ⓘ The **Bundestag** is the German parliamentary assembly, elected every four years.

die **Bundeswehr** NOUN
   German Armed Forces

> ⓘ The **Bundeswehr** is based on conscription for men, but there are also career servicemen. The basic period of military service is 10 months.

der **Bungalow** NOUN (GEN des **Bungalows**, PL die **Bungalows**)
   bungalow

**bunt** ADJECTIVE
   [1] brightly-coloured ◊ *Sie hatte ein buntes Kleid an.* She was wearing a brightly-coloured dress.
   [2] mixed ◊ *Unsere Klasse ist ein buntes Häufchen.* Our class is a mixed bunch.
   ♦ **Mir wird es zu bunt.** It's getting too much for me.

der **Buntstift** NOUN (PL die **Buntstifte**)
   coloured pencil

die **Burg** NOUN (PL die **Burgen**)
   castle

der **Bürger** NOUN (PL die **Bürger**)
   citizen

**bürgerlich** ADJECTIVE
   [1] civil ◊ *bürgerliche Rechte* civil rights
   [2] middle-class ◊ *eine gute bürgerliche Familie* a good middle-class family

der **Bürgermeister** NOUN (PL die **Bürgermeister**)
   mayor

der **Bürgersteig** NOUN (PL die **Bürgersteige**)
   pavement

das **Büro** NOUN (PL die **Büros**)
   office

die **Büroklammer** NOUN
   paper clip

die **Bürste** NOUN
   brush

**bürsten** VERB (PERFECT **hat gebürstet**)
   to brush

der **Bus** NOUN (GEN des **Busses**, PL die **Busse**)
   bus ◊ *mit dem Bus fahren* to go by bus

der **Busbahnhof** NOUN (PL die **Busbahnhöfe**)
   bus station

der **Busch** NOUN (PL die **Büsche**)
   bush

der **Busen** NOUN (PL die **Busen**)
   bosom

der **Busfahrer** NOUN (PL die **Busfahrer**)
   bus driver

die **Bushaltestelle** NOUN
   bus stop

die **Buslinie** NOUN
   bus route

das **Bußgeld** NOUN (PL die **Bußgelder**)
   fine

der **Büstenhalter** NOUN (PL die **Büstenhalter**)
   bra

die **Butter** NOUN
   butter

das **Butterbrot** NOUN (PL die **Butterbrote**)
   bread and butter

# C

**ca.** ABBREVIATION (= *circa*)
approx.

das **Café** NOUN (PL die **Cafés**)
café ◊ *Sonntags gehen wir immer ins Café.* On Sundays we always go to a café.

die **Cafeteria** NOUN (PL die **Cafeterias**)
cafeteria

**campen** VERB
to camp

das **Camping** NOUN
camping

der **Campingkocher** NOUN (PL die **Campingkocher**)
camping stove

der **Campingplatz** NOUN (GEN des **Campingplatzes**, PL die **Campingplätze**)
campsite

die **CD** NOUN (PL die **CDs**)
CD

die **CD-ROM** NOUN (PL die **CD-ROMs**)
CD-ROM

der **CD-Spieler** NOUN (PL die **CD-Spieler**)
CD player

das **Cello** NOUN (PL die **Cellos** or **Celli**)
cello ◊ *Ich spiele Cello.* I play the cello.

der **Cent** NOUN (PL die **Cents**)
cent

der **Champignon** NOUN (PL die **Champignons**)
button mushroom

die **Chance** NOUN
chance

das **Chaos** NOUN (GEN des **Chaos**)
chaos

**chaotisch** ADJECTIVE
chaotic

der **Charakter** NOUN (PL die **Charakter**)
character

**charmant** ADJECTIVE
charming

der **Charterflug** NOUN (PL die **Charterflüge**)
charter flight

der **Chatroom** NOUN (PL die **Chatrooms**)
chat room

der **Chauvinist** NOUN (GEN des **Chauvinisten**, PL die **Chauvinisten**)
chauvinist
♦ **männlicher Chauvinist** male chauvinist pig

der **Chef** NOUN (PL die **Chefs**)
[1] head ◊ *Er ist Chef einer großen Firma.* He's the head of a large company.
[2] boss ◊ *Da muss ich den Chef fragen.* I'll have to ask my boss.

die **Chefin** NOUN
boss

die **Chemie** NOUN
chemistry

der **Chemiker** NOUN (PL die **Chemiker**)
industrial chemist

**chemisch** ADJECTIVE
chemical
♦ **chemische Reinigung** dry cleaning

der **Chicorée** NOUN
chicory

**Chile** NEUT NOUN
Chile
♦ **aus Chile** from Chile
♦ **nach Chile** to Chile

**China** NEUT NOUN
China
♦ **aus China** from China
♦ **nach China** to China

der **Chinese** NOUN (GEN des **Chinesen**, PL die **Chinesen**)
Chinese
♦ **die Chinesen** the Chinese

die **Chinesin** NOUN
Chinese

**chinesisch** ADJECTIVE
Chinese

die **Chips** PL NOUN
crisps
*Be careful! The German word **Chips** does not mean **chips**.*

der **Chirurg** NOUN (GEN des **Chirurgen**, PL die **Chirurgen**)
surgeon

die **Chirurgie** NOUN
surgery

das **Chlor** NOUN
chlorine

der **Chor** NOUN (PL die **Chöre**)
choir ◊ *Sie singt im Chor.* She sings in a choir.

der **Christ** NOUN (GEN des **Christen**, PL die **Christen**)
Christian ◊ *Er ist Christ.* He's a Christian.

die **Christin** NOUN
Christian ◊ *Sie ist Christin.* She's a Christian.

**christlich** ADJECTIVE
Christian

**circa** ADVERB
approximately

**cm** ABBREVIATION (= *Zentimeter*)
cm

die **Cola** NOUN (PL die **Colas**)
Coke ®

der **Computer** NOUN (PL die **Computer**)
computer

die **Computeranlage** NOUN
computer system

das **Computerspiel** NOUN (PL die **Computerspiele**)

computer game
**cool** ADJECTIVE
  cool
der **Cousin** NOUN (PL die **Cousins**)
  cousin
die **Cousine** NOUN
  cousin
die **Creme** NOUN (PL die **Cremes**)
  [1] cream ◊ *eine Handcreme* a hand
cream
  [2] polish ◊ *Hast du schwarze*

*Schuhcreme?* Do you have any black
shoe polish?
  [3] mousse ◊ *eine Zitronencreme* a
lemon mousse
der **Curry** NOUN
  curry powder
die **Currywurst** NOUN (PL die **Currywürste**)
  curried sausage
der **Cursor** NOUN (PL die **Cursors**)
  cursor

**C**

# D

**da** ADVERB, CONJUNCTION

[1] there ◇ *Da ist es schön.* It's beautiful there.
- **da draußen** out there
- **Da haben wir Glück gehabt.** We were lucky there.
- **da sein** to be there

[2] here ◇ *Da liegt meine Brille ja.* Here are my glasses. ◇ *Da bin ich.* Here I am.
- **Ist noch Milch da?** Is there any milk left?
- **Da kann man nichts machen.** It can't be helped.

[3] since ◇ *Da du gerade hier bist ...* Since you're here ...

**dabehalten** VERB (PRESENT **behält da,** IMPERFECT **behielt da,** PERFECT **hat dabehalten**)
to keep

**dabei** ADVERB
- **nahe dabei** close by ◇ *Er stand nahe dabei, als die Bombe explodierte.* When the bomb exploded he was standing close by.
- **Sie hatten ihren Hund dabei.** They had their dog with them.
- **Was ist schon dabei?** What of it?
- **es ist doch nichts dabei, wenn ...** it doesn't matter if ...
- **Bleiben wir dabei.** Let's leave it at that.
- **Es bleibt dabei.** That's settled.
- **dabei sein** to be there ◇ *Ich bin dabei gewesen.* I was there.
- **Er war gerade dabei, zu gehen.** He was just about to leave.
- **Er hat es doch gemacht, dabei hatte ich ihn ausdrücklich gewarnt.** He did it even though I expressly warned him.

das **Dach** NOUN (PL die **Dächer**)
roof

der **Dachboden** NOUN (PL die **Dachböden**)
attic

**dachte** VERB *see* **denken**

der **Dackel** NOUN (PL die **Dackel**)
dachshund

**dadurch** ADVERB, CONJUNCTION

[1] through it ◇ *Er muss dadurch gekrochen sein.* He must have crawled through it.

[2] that's why ◇ *Dadurch habe ich mich verspätet.* That's why I was late.

[3] as a result ◇ *Der Zug hatte Verspätung, dadurch haben wir unseren Anschluss verpasst.* The train was late, and as a result we missed our connection.
- **dadurch, dass** because ◇ *Dadurch, dass sie kein Englisch kann ...* Because she doesn't speak any English ...

**dafür** ADVERB

[1] for it ◇ *Was hast du dafür bezahlt?* How much did you pay for it? ◇ *Was bekomme ich dafür?* What will I get for it?
- **Er ist bekannt dafür.** He's well-known for that.

[2] instead ◇ *Wenn du nicht mit ins Schwimmbad kannst, dann komm dafür doch mit ins Kino.* If you can't come with us to the swimming pool, then come along to the cinema instead.
- **Er kann nichts dafür.** He can't help it.

**dagegen** ADVERB, CONJUNCTION

[1] against it ◇ *Was hast du dagegen?* What have you got against it? ◇ *Ich war dagegen.* I was against it.
- **Ich habe nichts dagegen.** I don't mind.
- **Dagegen kann man nichts tun.** You can't do anything about it.

[2] into it ◇ *Er sah den Baum nicht und rannte dagegen.* He didn't see the tree and ran into it.

[3] for it ◇ *Das ist jetzt mein Ball, ich habe meine Murmeln dagegen getauscht.* This is my ball now – I swapped my marbles for it.

[4] by comparison ◇ *Dagegen ist unser Haus klein.* Our house is small by comparison.

[5] however ◇ *Sie wollte gehen, er dagegen wollte bleiben.* She wanted to leave, however he wanted to stay.

**daheim** ADVERB
at home

**daher** ADVERB, CONJUNCTION

[1] from there ◇ *Daher komme ich gerade.* I've just come from there.

[2] that's where ◇ *Das war ein schwerer Unfall; daher hat er sein kaputtes Bein.* It was a serious accident – that's where he got his bad leg.

[3] that's why ◇ *Sie war krank und konnte daher nicht mitkommen.* She was ill, and that's why she couldn't come.

**dahin** ADVERB
there ◇ *Dahin gehe ich jetzt.* I'm going there now.

**dahinten** ADVERB
over there

**dahinter** ADVERB
behind it ◇ *Er versteckte sich dahinter.* He hid behind it.
- **dahinter kommen** to find out ◇ *Meine Mutter ist dahinter gekommen, dass ich gestern nicht bei dir war.* My mother has found out that I wasn't at your place yesterday.

**damals** ADVERB
in those days

die **Dame** NOUN
- 1 lady
- 2 (chess, cards)
  queen
- 3 draughts ◊ *Dame ist mein Lieblingsspiel.* Draughts is my favourite game.

**damit** ADVERB, CONJUNCTION
- 1 with it ◊ *Wisch damit den Tisch ab.* Wipe the table with it.
- 2 by that ◊ *Was meint er damit?* What does he mean by that?
- ♦ **Was willst du damit sagen?** What are you getting at?
- ♦ **Genug damit!** That's enough of that!
- ♦ **Damit eilt es nicht.** There's no hurry.
- 3 so that ◊ *Ich sage dir das, damit du das weißt.* I'm telling you so that you know.

der **Dampf** NOUN
- steam

der **Dampfer** NOUN (PL die **Dampfer**)
- steamer ◊ *mit dem Dampfer fahren* to go by steamer
- ♦ **Du bist auf dem falschen Dampfer.** You've got the wrong idea.

**danach** ADVERB
- 1 afterwards ◊ *Ich habe etwas getrunken, und danach fühlte ich mich besser.* I had something to drink and afterwards felt much better.
- 2 accordingly ◊ *Verhalte dich bitte danach.* Please behave accordingly.

der **Däne** NOUN (GEN des **Dänen**, PL die **Dänen**)
- Dane

**daneben** ADVERB
- 1 beside it ◊ *Sein Stuhl stand daneben.* His chair was beside it.
- 2 by comparison ◊ *Er ist sehr klug, daneben wirkt sie ziemlich dumm.* He's very clever, and she seems rather stupid by comparison.

sich **danebenbenehmen** VERB (PRESENT **benimmt sich daneben,** IMPERFECT **benahm sich daneben,** PERFECT **hat sich danebenbenommen**)
- to misbehave

**Dänemark** NEUT NOUN
- Denmark
- ♦ **aus Dänemark** from Denmark
- ♦ **nach Dänemark** to Denmark

die **Dänin** NOUN
- Dane

**dänisch** ADJECTIVE
- Danish

der **Dank** NOUN
- | see also **dank** PREPOSITION |
- thanks ◊ *Unser Dank gilt vor allem Herrn Morris.* Our thanks to Mr Morris in particular.
- ♦ **Vielen Dank!** Many thanks.

**dank** PREPOSITION
- | see also **der Dank** NOUN |

*dank takes the genitive or dative.*
- thanks to ◊ *Dank meiner Schwester habe ich noch rechtzeitig davon erfahren.* Thanks to my sister I found out about it in time.

**dankbar** ADJECTIVE
- grateful ◊ *Ich bin dir sehr dankbar.* I'm very grateful to you.
- ♦ **eine dankbare Aufgabe** a rewarding task

**danke** EXCLAMATION
- thank you
- ♦ **Danke sehr!** Thank you.
- ♦ **Danke schön!** Thank you very much.
- ♦ **Nein, danke!** No, thanks.

**danken** VERB
- to thank ◊ *Ich möchte dir dafür danken.* I'd like to thank you for that.
- ♦ **nichts zu danken!** don't mention it!

**dann** ADVERB
- then
- ♦ **dann und wann** now and then

**daran** ADVERB
- on it ◊ *ein Päckchen mit einem Zettel daran* a parcel with a label on it
- ♦ **Ich habe nicht daran gedacht.** I didn't think of that.
- ♦ **Er ist daran gestorben.** He died of it.
- ♦ **Es liegt daran, dass ...** This is because ...
- ♦ **das Beste daran** the best thing about it
- ♦ **Ich war nahe daran, zu gehen.** I was on the point of going.

**darauf** ADVERB
- 1 on it ◊ *Nimm einen Untersetzer und stelle den Topf darauf.* Take a mat and put the pan on it.
- 2 afterwards ◊ *kurz darauf* shortly afterwards
- ♦ **die Tage darauf** the following days
- ♦ **am Tag darauf** the next day
- ♦ **Er ging darauf zu.** He walked towards it.
- ♦ **es kommt ganz darauf an, ob ...** it all depends whether ...

**daraus** ADVERB
- out of it ◊ *Sie nahm einen Keks daraus.* She took a biscuit out of it.
- ♦ **Was ist daraus geworden?** What became of it?
- ♦ **daraus geht hervor, dass ...** this means that ...

**darf** VERB see **dürfen**

**darin** ADVERB
- in it ◊ *eine Dose mit Keksen darin* a tin with biscuits in it
- ♦ **Darin sehe ich kein Problem.** I don't see any problem there.

der **Darm** NOUN (PL die **Därme**)
- intestine

**darstellen** VERB (PERFECT **hat dargestellt**)
- 1 to portray ◊ *etwas in einem günstigen Licht darstellen* to portray something in a good light

**D**

☞

2 to describe ◊ *So wie er es dargestellt hat, war alles ihre Schuld.* The way he described it, it was all her fault.

**darüber** ADVERB

1 over it ◊ *ein Tisch mit einer Lampe darüber* a table with a light over it ◊ *Da war eine Brücke, wir sind aber nicht darüber gefahren.* There was a bridge, but we didn't drive over it.

2 about it ◊ *Wir haben darüber gesprochen.* We talked about it. ◊ *Denk mal darüber nach.* Think about it.

3 more ◊ *Sie verdient fünftausend oder vielleicht sogar darüber.* She earns five thousand or maybe even more.

**darum** ADVERB, CONJUNCTION

1 round it ◊ *Sie machte ein rotes Band darum.* She put a red ribbon round it.

♦ **es geht darum, dass** ... the important thing is to ...

♦ **er würde viel darum geben, wenn** ... he would give a lot to ...

2 that's why ◊ *Darum bin ich nicht gekommen.* That's why I didn't come.

♦ **Ich tue es darum, weil** ... I'm doing it because ...

**darunter** ADVERB

1 under it ◊ *Der Topf ist heiß, leg einen Untersetzer darunter.* The pot's hot, put a mat under it.

♦ **ein Stockwerk darunter** one floor below

♦ **viele Jungen und zwei Mädchen darunter** a lot of boys and two girls

2 less ◊ *Er verdient nur zweitausend Mark oder vielleicht sogar darunter.* He earns only two thousand marks or maybe even less.

♦ **Was verstehst du darunter?** What do you understand by that?

**das** ARTICLE, PRONOUN

*das is the definite neuter article.*

1 the ◊ *das Auto* the car

♦ **das Leben** life

♦ **Er hat sich das Knie verletzt.** He's hurt his knee.

2 who ◊ *das Kind, das dir das gesagt hat* the child who told you

♦ **das Kind, das du gesehen hast** the child you saw

3 which ◊ *das Fahrrad, das du da siehst* the bike which you can see over there

♦ **das mit dem roten Sattel** the one with the red saddle

4 that ◊ *Das habe ich nicht gehört.* I didn't hear that.

♦ **das da** that one

**dasein** VERB *see* **da**

**dass** CONJUNCTION

that ◊ *Ich bin böse, dass er nicht gekommen ist.* I'm annoyed that he didn't come. ◊ *Ich weiß, dass du besser in Mathe bist als ich.* I know you're better at maths than me.

**dasselbe** PRONOUN

the same ◊ *dasselbe Kind* the same child

**dastehen** VERB (IMPERFECT **stand da,** PERFECT **hat dagestanden)**

to stand there

die **Datei** NOUN

file

die **Daten** NEUT PL NOUN

data

die **Datenbank** NOUN (PL die **Datenbanken)**

data base

die **Datenverarbeitung** NOUN

data processing

der **Dativ** NOUN (PL die **Dative)**

dative

das **Datum** NOUN (PL die **Daten)**

date

die **Dauer** NOUN

1 duration ◊ *für die Dauer meines Aufenthalts* for the duration of my stay

2 length ◊ *die Dauer einer Reise* the length of a journey ◊ *die Dauer eines Anrufs* the length of a call

♦ **von Dauer sein** to be permanent

♦ **Ihr Glück war nur kurzer Dauer.** Their happiness was only short-lived.

♦ **auf die Dauer (1)** in the long run ◊ *Auf die Dauer wird ihm das langweilig werden.* He'll get bored with it in the long run.

♦ **auf die Dauer (2)** indefinitely ◊ *Auf die Dauer geht das aber nicht.* That can't go on indefinitely.

die **Dauerkarte** NOUN

season ticket

**dauern** VERB

to last ◊ *Der Krieg hat zehn Jahre gedauert.* The war lasted ten years.

♦ **lange dauern** to take a long time ◊ *Das hat lange gedauert.* That took a long time. ◊ *Es hat sehr lang gedauert, bis er* ... It took him a long time to ...

♦ **Wie lange dauert das denn noch?** How much longer is this going to take?

**dauernd** ADJECTIVE, ADVERB

constant ◊ *Ich konnte sein dauerndes Stöhnen nicht ertragen.* I couldn't stand his constant moaning.

♦ **Musst du mich dauernd stören?** Do you have to constantly interrupt me?

die **Dauerwelle** NOUN

perm

der **Daumen** NOUN (PL die **Daumen)**

thumb

♦ **Ich drücke dir die Daumen.** I'll keep my fingers crossed for you.

**davon** ADVERB

1 of them ◊ *Sie nahm zwei davon.* She took two of them.

♦ **Sie nahm hundert Gramm davon.** She took a hundred grams.

2 away ◊ *Er lief davon.* He ran away.

**D**

[3] from it ◊ *Sie hat den Knopf davon abgetrennt.* She removed the button from it.

♦ **Sie bekommt Kopfschmerzen davon.** It gives her a headache.

♦ **davon abgesehen** apart from that

♦ **davon sprechen** to talk about it

♦ **Sie weiß nichts davon.** She doesn't know anything about it.

♦ **Was habe ich davon?** What's the point?

♦ **Das kommt davon!** That's what you get.

**davonkommen** VERB (IMPERFECT **kam davon,** PERFECT **ist davongekommen**)
to escape ◊ *Wir sind noch einmal davongekommen.* We've had a lucky escape.

**davor** ADVERB
[1] in front of it ◊ *Ich stellte mich davor.* I stood in front of it.
[2] first ◊ *Du solltest davor aber noch zum Friseur.* You ought to go to the hairdresser's first.

♦ **Ich habe dich davor gewarnt.** I warned you about it.

**dazu** ADVERB
with it ◊ *Was sollen wir dazu trinken?* What shall we drink with it?

♦ **ein Beispiel dazu** an example of this

♦ **seine Gedanken dazu** his thoughts on this

♦ **Möchtest du dich dazu äußern?** Do you wish to comment on it?

♦ **dazu fähig sein** to be capable of it

♦ **und dazu noch** and in addition

**dazwischen** ADVERB
[1] in between ◊ *Wir können dazwischen ja eine Pause machen.* We can have a break in between.
[2] between them ◊ *Siehst du die beiden Pfosten, stell dich dazwischen.* You see the two posts? Go and stand between them. ◊ *der Unterschied dazwischen* the difference between them

**dazwischenkommen** VERB (IMPERFECT **kam dazwischen,** PERFECT **ist dazwischengekommen**)

♦ **Es ist etwas dazwischengekommen.** Something's cropped up.

**DB** ABBREVIATION (= *Deutsche Bahn*)
German railways

die **DDR** NOUN (GEN die **DDR**)
(= *Deutsche Demokratische Republik*)
GDR ◊ *die ehemalige DDR* the former GDR

die **Decke** NOUN
[1] ceiling ◊ *Wir haben die Decke des Kinderzimmers gestrichen.* We've painted the ceiling of the children's room.
[2] blanket ◊ *eine Wolldecke* a woollen blanket

♦ **eine Tischdecke** a tablecloth

der **Deckel** NOUN (PL die **Deckel**)

lid

**decken** VERB
to cover ◊ *Er deckte die Hand über seine Augen.* He covered his eyes with his hand.

♦ **den Tisch decken** to lay the table

**dehnen** VERB
to stretch

♦ **Er dehnte sich und gähnte.** He stretched and yawned.

**dein** ADJECTIVE
[1] your ◊ *Dein Englischlehrer ist nett.* Your English teacher's nice. ◊ *Hat deine Mutter das erlaubt?* Did your mother let you? ◊ *Ist das dein Buch?* Is that your book? ◊ *Wo sind deine Eltern?* Where are your parents?
[2] yours ◊ *Der Bleistift hier, ist das deiner?* Is this pencil yours? ◊ *Meine Mutter heißt Ulla, wie heißt deine?* My mother's called Ulla, what's yours called? ◊ *Mein Fahrrad ist kaputt, kann ich deins benutzen?* My bike's broken, can I use yours? ◊ *Meine Noten waren nicht gut, wie waren deine?* My marks weren't good, what were yours like?

**deinetwegen** ADVERB
[1] for your sake ◊ *Ich habe deinetwegen darauf verzichtet.* I did without for your sake.
[2] on your account ◊ *Er hat sich deinetwegen aufgeregt.* He got upset on your account.

die **Deklination** NOUN
declension

**deklinieren** VERB (PERFECT **hat dekliniert**)
to decline

der **Delphin** NOUN (PL die **Delphine**)
dolphin

**dem** ARTICLE
*dem is the dative of der and das.*
the ◊ *auf dem Tisch* on the table

♦ **Gib es dem Mann.** Give it to the man.

♦ **der Mann, dem ich es gegeben habe** the man I gave it to

**demnächst** ADVERB
shortly

die **Demokratie** NOUN
democracy

**demokratisch** ADJECTIVE
democratic

die **Demonstration** NOUN
demonstration

**demonstrieren** VERB (PERFECT **hat demonstriert**)
to demonstrate

**den** ARTICLE
*den is the accusative of der.*
the ◊ *Ich sehe den Mann.* I can see the man. ◊ *durch den Wald* through the wood

♦ **Er hat sich den Fuß verletzt.** He's hurt his foot.

+ **der Mann, den ich gesehen habe** the man I saw

**denen** PRONOUN

*denen is the dative of die (plural).*

[1] whom
+ **die Leute, denen ich die Bücher gegeben habe** the people I gave the books to
+ **die Leute, denen ich helfen wollte** the people I wanted to help

[2] which ◇ *Probleme, denen wir nicht gewachsen sind* problems which we can't cope with

**denkbar** ADJECTIVE
conceivable

**denken** VERB (IMPERFECT **dachte,** PERFECT **hat gedacht**)
to think

das **Denkmal** NOUN (PL die **Denkmäler**)
monument

**denn** CONJUNCTION, ADVERB

[1] because ◇ *Ich habe sie nicht gesehen, denn sie war schon weg.* I didn't see her because she had already left.

[2] than ◇ *besser denn je* better than ever
+ **es sei denn ...** unless ...
+ **Warum denn?** But why?

**dennoch** CONJUNCTION
nevertheless

**deprimiert** ADJECTIVE
depressed

**der** ARTICLE, PRONOUN

*der is the definite masculine article and genitive and dative of die.*

[1] the ◇ *der Mann* the man
+ **der Tod** death
+ **das Auto der Frau** the woman's car
+ **Gib es der Frau.** Give it to the woman.

[2] who ◇ *der, der dir das gesagt hat* the person who told you that
+ **die Frau, der ich es gegeben habe** the woman I gave it to

[3] which ◇ *der Computer, der mir gehört* the computer which belongs to me
+ **der mit der Brille** the one with glasses
+ **der da** that one

**derselbe** PRONOUN
the same ◇ *derselbe Mann* the same man

**deshalb** ADVERB
that's why

**dessen** PRONOUN

*dessen is the genitive of der and das.*

whose ◇ *mein Freund, dessen Schwester krank ist* my friend whose sister is ill

**desto** ADVERB
all the ◇ *desto besser* all the better
+ **je ... desto ...** the ... the ... ◇ *Je mehr er sagte, desto wütender wurde sie.* The more he said, the angrier she became. ◇ *je eher, desto besser* the earlier the better

**deswegen** CONJUNCTION

that's why ◇ *Hat er deswegen so geschimpft?* Is that why he was so mad?
+ **Es ist spät, deswegen gehen wir jetzt.** It's late, so we're leaving.
+ **Ich sage das deswegen, weil das alle wissen müssen.** The reason I'm saying this is that everybody should know.

**deutlich** ADJECTIVE, ADVERB

[1] clear ◇ *mit klarer Stimme* in a clear voice

[2] clearly ◇ *Drück dich bitte deutlicher aus.* Please speak more clearly.
+ **ein deutlicher Unterschied** a distinct difference

das **Deutsch** NOUN (GEN des **Deutschen**)
see also **deutsch** ADJECTIVE
German ◇ *Er lernt Deutsch in der Schule.* He's learning German at school.
+ **auf Deutsch** in German

**deutsch** ADJECTIVE
see also **das Deutsch** NOUN
German

der **Deutsche** NOUN (GEN des/der **Deutschen,** PL
die die **Deutschen**)
German
+ **Ich bin Deutscher.** I'm German.

**Deutschland** NEUT NOUN
Germany
+ **aus Deutschland** from Germany
+ **in Deutschland** in Germany
+ **nach Deutschland** to Germany

der **Dezember** NOUN (GEN des **Dezember** or **Dezembers,** PL die **Dezember**)
December ◇ *im Dezember* in December ◇ *am vierten Dezember* on the fourth of December ◇ *Ulm, den 5. Dezember 2003* Ulm, 5 December 2003 ◇ *Heute ist der sechste Dezember.* Today is the sixth of December.

das **Dezimalsystem** NOUN
decimal system

**DGB** ABBREVIATION (= *Deutscher Gewerkschaftsbund*)
German trade union federation

**d. h.** ABBREVIATION (= *das heißt*)
i.e.

das **Dia** NOUN (PL die **Dias**)
slide

**diagonal** ADJECTIVE
diagonal

der **Dialekt** NOUN (PL die **Dialekte**)
dialect

der **Diamant** NOUN (GEN des **Diamanten,** PL die **Diamanten**)
diamond

die **Diät** NOUN
diet ◇ *Sie muss Diät halten.* She has to stick to a strict diet.

**dich** PRONOUN

[1] you ◇ *Ich habe dich gesehen.* I saw you.

2 yourself ◊ *Sieh dich mal im Spiegel an.* Look at yourself in the mirror.

**dicht** ADJECTIVE, ADVERB

1 dense ◊ *dichte Wälder* dense woods

2 thick ◊ *dichter Nebel* thick fog

3 watertight ◊ *Ist der Behälter dicht?* Is the container watertight?

♦ **Die Gasleitung war nicht dicht.** There was a leak in the gas pipe.

♦ **dichter Verkehr** heavy traffic

♦ **dicht an** close to ◊ *Geh nicht zu dicht ans Feuer.* Don't go too close to the fire.

der **Dichter** NOUN (PL die **Dichter**)

poet

**dick** ADJECTIVE

1 thick ◊ *Das Brett ist drei Zentimeter dick.* The plank's three centimetres thick.

2 fat ◊ *Ich bin zu dick.* I'm too fat.

der **Dickkopf** NOUN (PL die **Dickköpfe**)

♦ **einen Dickkopf haben** to be stubborn

die **Dickmilch** NOUN

soured milk

**die** ARTICLE, PRONOUN

*die is the definite feminine article and the definite article plural.*

1 the ◊ *die Frau* the woman ◊ *die Kinder* the children

♦ **die Liebe** love

♦ **Er hat sich die Hand verletzt.** He's hurt his hand.

2 who ◊ *die, die dir das gesagt hat* the person who told you that

♦ **die Frau, die du gesehen hast** the woman you saw

3 which ◊ *die Uhr, die mir gehört* the watch which belongs to me

♦ **die mit der Brille** the one with glasses

♦ **die da** that one

der **Dieb** NOUN (PL die **Diebe**)

thief

der **Diebstahl** NOUN (PL die **Diebstähle**)

theft

die **Diele** NOUN

hall ◊ *Sie stand vor dem Spiegel in der Diele.* She stood in front of the mirror in the hall.

**dienen** VERB (PERFECT **hat gedient**)

to serve ◊ *Es dient einem guten Zweck.* It serves a useful purpose.

♦ **womit kann ich Ihnen dienen?** what can I do for you?

der **Dienst** NOUN (PL die **Dienste**)

service

♦ **Dienst haben** to be on duty

der **Dienstag** NOUN (PL die **Dienstage**)

Tuesday ◊ *am Dienstag* on Tuesday

**dienstags** ADVERB

on Tuesdays

**dies** PRONOUN

1 this ◊ *Dies ist unser Haus.* This is our house.

2 these ◊ *Dies sind meine Bücher.* These are my books.

**diese** PRONOUN

1 this ◊ *Dieses Kleid gefällt mir besonders gut.* I particularly like this dress.

2 these ◊ *diese Bücher* these books

3 this one ◊ *Ich möchte diesen hier.* I'd like this one.

4 these ones ◊ *Ich suche ein Paar Sandalen, kann ich diese anprobieren?* I'm looking for a pair of sandals, can I try these ones on?

der **Diesel** NOUN

diesel

**dieselbe** PRONOUN

the same ◊ *dieselbe Frau* the same woman

**diesmal** ADVERB

this time

**digital** ADJECTIVE

digital ◊ *die digitale Revolution* the digital revolution

das **Digitalfernsehen** NOUN

digital television

das **Diktat** NOUN (PL die **Diktate**)

dictation

**diktieren** VERB (PERFECT **hat diktiert**)

to dictate

das **Ding** NOUN (PL die **Dinge**)

thing

das **Diplom** NOUN (PL die **Diplome**)

diploma

die **Diplomatie** NOUN

diplomacy

**diplomatisch** ADJECTIVE

diplomatic

**dir** PRONOUN

*dir is the dative of du.*

1 you ◊ *Ich habe es dir doch gesagt.* I told you so.

2 to you ◊ *Ich habe es dir gestern gegeben.* I gave it to you yesterday.

**direkt** ADJECTIVE

direct ◊ *Der Flug geht direkt.* It's a direct flight.

der **Direktor** NOUN (PL die **Direktoren**)

1 director ◊ *der Direktor der Firma* the director of the company

2 headmaster ◊ *Mein Bruder musste gestern zum Direktor.* My brother was sent to the headmaster yesterday.

die **Direktübertragung** NOUN

live broadcast

der **Dirigent** NOUN (GEN des **Dirigenten**, PL die **Dirigenten**)

conductor (*of orchestra*)

**dirigieren** VERB (PERFECT **hat dirigiert**)

to conduct ◊ *Wer dirigiert das Orchester?* Who's conducting the orchestra?

die **Diskette** NOUN

diskette

die **Disko** NOUN (PL die **Diskos**)

disco
die **Diskothek** NOUN
disco
die **Diskussion** NOUN
discussion
♦ **zur Diskussion stehen** to be under discussion
das **Diskuswerfen** NOUN
throwing the discus
**diskutieren** VERB (PERFECT **hat diskutiert**)
to discuss ◊ *Wir haben über Politik diskutiert.* We discussed politics.
**DJH** ABBREVIATION (= *Deutsches Jugendherbergswerk*)
German Youth Hostel Association
**DM** ABBREVIATION (= *Deutsche Mark*)
Deutschmark
die **D-Mark** NOUN (PL die **D-Mark**)
Deutschmark
**doch** ADVERB, CONJUNCTION
1 after all ◊ *Sie ist doch noch gekommen.* She came after all.
2 anyway ◊ *Du machst ja doch, was du willst.* You do what you want anyway.
3 but ◊ *Ich habe ihn eingeladen, doch er hatte keine Lust.* I invited him, but he didn't feel like it. ◊ *Sie ist doch noch so jung.* But she's still so young.
4 yes
*doch is used to contradict a negative statement.*
◊ *Du magst doch keine Süßigkeiten. – Doch!* You don't like sweets. – Yes I do.
◊ *Er ist sicher kein Österreicher. – Doch.* I'm sure he's not an Austrian. – Yes he is.
◊ *Das ist nicht wahr. – Doch!* That's not true. – Yes it is!
♦ **Komm doch.** Do come.
♦ **Lass ihn doch.** Just leave him.
der **Doktor** NOUN (PL die **Doktoren**)
doctor ◊ *Er ist Doktor der Philosophie.* He's a doctor of philosophy.
das **Dokument** NOUN
document
der **Dokumentarfilm** NOUN (PL die **Dokumentarfilme**)
documentary
die **Dokumentation** NOUN
documentation
**dolmetschen** VERB
to interpret
der **Dolmetscher** NOUN (PL die **Dolmetscher**)
interpreter
der **Dom** NOUN (PL die **Dome**)
cathedral
die **Donau** NOUN
Danube
der **Donner** NOUN (PL die **Donner**)
thunder
**donnern** VERB
to thunder ◊ *Es donnerte.* It was thundering.

der **Donnerstag** NOUN (PL die **Donnerstage**)
Thursday ◊ *am Donnerstag* on Thursday
**donnerstags** ADVERB
on Thursdays
**doof** ADJECTIVE
thick
das **Doppelbett** NOUN (PL die **Doppelbetten**)
double bed
die **Doppelfenster** NEUT PL NOUN
double glazing
das **Doppelhaus** NOUN (GEN des **Doppelhauses**, PL die **Doppelhäuser**)
semidetached house
der **Doppelpunkt** NOUN (PL die **Doppelpunkte**)
colon
die **Doppelstunde** NOUN
double period
**doppelt** ADJECTIVE
1 double ◊ *die doppelte Menge* double the amount
2 twice the ◊ *der doppelte Preis* twice the price ◊ *die doppelte Geschwindigkeit* twice the speed
♦ **doppelt so viel** twice as much
♦ **in doppelter Ausführung** in duplicate
das **Doppelzimmer** NOUN (PL die **Doppelzimmer**)
double room
das **Dorf** NOUN (PL die **Dörfer**)
village
**dort** ADVERB
there
♦ **dort drüben** over there
**dorther** ADVERB
from there
**dorthin** ADVERB
there ◊ *Wir gehen jetzt dorthin.* We're going there now.
die **Dose** NOUN
tin
der **Dosenöffner** NOUN (PL die **Dosenöffner**)
tin opener
der **Dotter** NOUN (PL die **Dotter**)
yolk
der **Drache** NOUN (GEN des **Drachen**, PL die **Drachen**)
dragon ◊ *Ein Drache bewacht den Schatz.* A dragon guards the treasure.
der **Drachen** NOUN (PL die **Drachen**)
kite ◊ *Wir haben Drachen fliegen lassen.* We've been flying our kites.
das **Drachenfliegen** NOUN
hang-gliding ◊ *Er ist beim Drachenfliegen verunglückt.* He had a hang-gliding accident.
der **Draht** NOUN (PL die **Drähte**)
wire
♦ **auf Draht sein** to be on the ball
das **Drama** NOUN (PL die **Dramen**)
drama
**dran** ADVERB
♦ **Jetzt bin ich dran!** It's my turn now.

**D**

◆ **Wer ist dran?** Whose turn is it?
◆ **gut dran sein** to be well-off
◆ **schlecht dran sein** to be in a bad way
**drauf** ADVERB *see* **darauf**
**draußen** ADVERB
    outside
der **Dreck** NOUN
    dirt
**dreckig** ADJECTIVE
    dirty ◊ *Mach deine Kleider nicht dreckig.*
    Don't get your clothes dirty.
**drehen** VERB
    to turn ◊ *Dreh mal deinen Kopf zur Seite.*
    Turn your head to one side.
◆ **eine Zigarette drehen** to roll a cigarette
◆ **einen Film drehen** to shoot a film
◆ **sich drehen** to turn
◆ **es dreht sich um ...** it's about ...
**drei** NUMBER
    | *see also* **die Drei** NOUN |
    three
die **Drei** NOUN
    | *see also* **drei** NUMBER |
    ⒈ three
    ⒉ satisfactory

> ⓘ German marks range from one (**sehr gut**) to six (**ungenügend**).

das **Dreieck** NOUN (PL die **Dreiecke**)
    triangle
**dreieckig** ADJECTIVE
    triangular
**dreihundert** NUMBER
    three hundred
**dreimal** ADVERB
    three times
**dreißig** NUMBER
    thirty
**dreiviertel** NUMBER
    three-quarters
die **Dreiviertelstunde** NOUN
    three-quarters of an hour ◊ *Eine Dreiviertelstunde war vergangen.* Three-quarters of an hour had passed.
**dreizehn** NUMBER
    thirteen
**drin** ADVERB *see* **darin**
**dringend** ADJECTIVE
    urgent
**drinnen** ADVERB
    inside
**dritte** ADJECTIVE
    third ◊ *Sie nahm beim dritten Klingeln ab.* She answered on the third ring. ◊ *Er kam als Dritter.* He was the third to arrive.
◆ **die Dritte Welt** the Third World
◆ **das Dritte Reich** the Third Reich
das **Drittel** NOUN (PL die **Drittel**)
    third
**drittens** ADVERB

    thirdly
die **Droge** NOUN
    drug
**drogenabhängig** ADJECTIVE
    addicted to drugs
die **Drogerie** NOUN
    chemist's shop,
der **Drogist** NOUN (GEN des **Drogisten**, PL die **Drogisten**)
    pharmacist
die **Drogistin** NOUN
    pharmacist
**drohen** VERB
    to threaten ◊ *jemandem drohen* to threaten somebody
**drüben** ADVERB
    over there
der **Druck** NOUN (PL die **Drucke**)
    ⒈ pressure ◊ *Der Behälter muss viel Druck aushalten.* The container has to withstand a lot of pressure.
◆ **jemanden unter Druck setzen** to put pressure on somebody
    ⒉ printing ◊ *der Druck eines Buches* the printing of a book
    ⒊ print ◊ *An der Wand hingen Drucke.* There were prints on the wall.
**drücken** VERB
    ⒈ to press ◊ *Er drückte auf den Knopf.* He pressed the button.
◆ **Sie drückte ihm die Hand.** She squeezed his hand.
    ⒉ to pinch ◊ *Meine Schuhe drücken.* My shoes pinch.
◆ **sich vor etwas drücken** to get out of something ◊ *Du willst dich bloß wieder vor dem Abwasch drücken.* You just want to get out of washing up again.
der **Drucker** NOUN (PL die **Drucker**)
    printer
der **Druckknopf** NOUN (PL die **Druckknöpfe**)
    press stud
die **Drucksache** NOUN
    printed matter
die **Druckschrift** NOUN
    block letters
die **Drüse** NOUN
    gland
der **Dschungel** NOUN (PL die **Dschungel**)
    jungle
**DTP** ABBREVIATION (= *Desktoppublishing*)
    DTP
**du** PRONOUN
    you ◊ *Hast du das gesehen?* Did you see that?
◆ **du sagen** to use the "du" form of address

> ⓘ The familiar form of address **du** (plural **ihr**) is used when addressing family members, friends, children under 16 and pets.

sich **ducken** VERB
  to duck
der **Dudelsack** NOUN (PL die **Dudelsäcke**)
  bagpipes ◊ *Er spielt Dudelsack.* He
  plays the bagpipes. ◊ *Sein Dudelsack
  liegt auf dem Tisch.* His bagpipes are on
  the table.
der **Duft** NOUN (PL die **Düfte**)
  scent
  **duften** VERB
  to smell ◊ *Hier duftet es nach Kaffee.* It
  smells of coffee here.
  **dumm** ADJECTIVE
  1 stupid ◊ *Das ist die dümmste
  Ausrede, die ich je gehört habe.*
  That's the stupidest excuse I've ever
  heard.
  2 bad ◊ *Es ist wirklich zu dumm, dass
  du nicht gekommen bist.* It's really too
  bad that you didn't come.
  ♦ **der Dumme sein** to draw the short straw
  **dummerweise** ADVERB
  stupidly
die **Dummheit** NOUN
  1 stupidity ◊ *Deine Dummheit ist
  wirklich grenzenlos.* Your stupidity really
  knows no bounds.
  2 stupid mistake ◊ *Es war eine
  Dummheit, ihr das zu erzählen.* It was a
  stupid mistake telling her that.
  ♦ **Dummheiten machen** to do
  something stupid ◊ *Macht bloß keine
  Dummheiten!* Don't do anything
  stupid.
der **Dummkopf** NOUN (PL die **Dummköpfe**)
  idiot
der **Dünger** NOUN (PL die **Dünger**)
  fertilizer
  **dunkel** ADJECTIVE
  dark ◊ *Im Zimmer war es dunkel.* It was
  dark in the room.
  ♦ **eine dunkle Stimme** a deep voice
  ♦ **eine dunkle Ahnung** a vague idea
  ♦ **dunkle Gestalten** sinister figures
  ♦ **dunkle Geschäfte** shady dealings
  ♦ **im Dunkeln tappen** to grope about in the
  dark
  ♦ **ein Dunkles** a dark beer
die **Dunkelheit** NOUN
  dark ◊ *Er hat Angst vor der Dunkelheit.*
  He's afraid of the dark.
  **dünn** ADJECTIVE
  thin
der **Dunst** NOUN (PL die **Dünste**)
  haze
  **durch** PREPOSITION, ADVERB
  *The preposition **durch** takes the
  accusative.*
  1 through ◊ *durch den Wald* through
  the wood ◊ *Ich habe die Stelle durch
  meinen Onkel bekommen.* I got the job
  through my uncle. ◊ *durch seine
  Bemühungen* through his efforts

  2 throughout ◊ *die ganze Nacht durch*
  throughout the night ◊ *den Sommer
  durch* throughout the summer
  3 owing to ◊ *Durch die Verspätung
  haben wir den Anschluss verpasst.*
  Owing to the delay we missed our
  connection.
  ♦ **Tod durch Herzschlag** death from a heart
  attack
  ♦ **durch die Post** by post
  ♦ **durch und durch** completely ◊ *Wir waren
  durch und durch nass.* We were
  completely soaked.
**durcharbeiten** VERB (PERFECT **hat
durchgearbeitet**)
  to work without a break
**durchblättern** VERB (PERFECT **hat
durchgeblättert**)
  to leaf through
der **Durchblick** NOUN (PL die **Durchblicke**)
  ♦ **Der hat den Durchblick.** He knows what's
  what.
**durchblicken** VERB (PERFECT **hat
durchgeblickt**)
  to understand
  ♦ **Bei Computern blickt Tobias durch.**
  Tobias knows his stuff with
  computers.
  ♦ **etwas durchblicken lassen** to hint at
  something
**durchdrehen** VERB (PERFECT **ist
durchgedreht**)
  to crack up
**durcheinander** ADVERB
  *see also das Durcheinander NOUN*
  1 in a mess ◊ *Warum ist dein Zimmer
  so durcheinander?* Why is your room in
  such a mess?
  2 confused ◊ *Ich war völlig
  durcheinander.* I was completely
  confused.
  ♦ **Du bringst mich ganz durcheinander.**
  You completely confuse me.
  ♦ **alles durcheinander trinken** to mix one's
  drinks
das **Durcheinander** NOUN
  *see also durcheinander ADVERB*
  1 mess ◊ *In ihrem Zimmer war ein
  völliges Durcheinander.* Her room was in
  a complete mess.
  2 confusion ◊ *Im Durcheinander des
  Aufbruchs habe ich das ganz vergessen.*
  In the confusion of leaving I completely
  forgot it.
**durchfahren** VERB (PRESENT **fährt durch,**
IMPERFECT **fuhr durch,** PERFECT **ist
durchgefahren**)
  1 to drive through ◊ *Wir sind durch
  einen Tunnel durchgefahren.* We drove
  through a tunnel.
  2 to drive without a break ◊ *Wir sind
  die ganze Nacht durchgefahren.* We
  drove all night without a break.

◆ **Der Zug fährt bis Hamburg durch.** The train runs direct to Hamburg.

die **Durchfahrt** NOUN (PL die **Durchfahrten**)
way through ◊ *auf unserer Durchfahrt durch Frankreich* on our way through France
◆ **"Durchfahrt verboten"** "no through road"

der **Durchfall** NOUN
diarrhoea

**durchfallen** VERB (PRESENT **fällt durch,** IMPERFECT **fiel durch,** PERFECT **ist durchgefallen**)
[1] to fall through ◊ *Die Münze ist durch dieses Gitter durchgefallen.* The coin fell through this grating.
[2] to fail ◊ *Sie ist in der Prüfung durchgefallen.* She failed the exam.

**durchführen** VERB (PERFECT **hat durchgeführt**)
to carry out

der **Durchgang** NOUN (PL die **Durchgänge**)
passageway ◊ *Zwischen den Häusern ist ein schmaler Durchgang.* There's a narrow passageway between the houses.

der **Durchgangsverkehr** NOUN
through traffic

**durchgehen** VERB (IMPERFECT **ging durch,** PERFECT **ist durchgegangen**)
[1] to go through ◊ *durch einen Tunnel durchgehen* to go through a tunnel
[2] to break loose ◊ *Das Pferd ist durchgegangen.* The horse has broken loose.
◆ **jemandem etwas durchgehen lassen** to let somebody get away with something
◆ **ein durchgehender Zug** a through train

**durchkommen** VERB (IMPERFECT **kam durch,** PERFECT **ist durchgekommen**)
[1] to get through ◊ *Obwohl die Öffnung sehr schmal war, sind wir durchgekommen.* Although the opening was very narrow, we got through.
[2] to pass ◊ *Es war knapp, aber ich bin durchgekommen.* It was a close shave, but I passed.
[3] to pull through ◊ *Er war schwer verletzt, ist aber durchgekommen.* He was seriously injured, but he pulled through.

**durchlassen** VERB (PRESENT **lässt durch,** IMPERFECT **ließ durch,** PERFECT **hat durchgelassen**)
to let through ◊ *Der Ordner wollte uns nicht durchlassen.* The steward didn't want to let us through.
◆ **Der Behälter lässt Wasser durch.** The container isn't watertight.

**durchlesen** VERB (PRESENT **liest durch,** IMPERFECT **las durch,** PERFECT **hat durchgelesen**)
to read through

**durchmachen** VERB (PERFECT **hat durchgemacht**)
to go through ◊ *Sie hat viel durchgemacht in ihrem Leben.* She's been through a lot in her life.
◆ **die Nacht durchmachen** to make a night of it

der **Durchmesser** NOUN (PL die **Durchmesser**)
diameter

**durchnehmen** VERB (PRESENT **nimmt durch,** IMPERFECT **nahm durch,** PERFECT **hat durchgenommen**)
to do ◊ *Wir nehmen gerade Shakespeare durch.* We're doing Shakespeare just now.

die **Durchreise** NOUN
journey through ◊ *die Durchreise durch die Schweiz* the journey through Switzerland
◆ **Ich bin nur auf der Durchreise.** I'm just passing through.

**durchs** = **durch das**

der **Durchschnitt** NOUN
average ◊ *Mein Notendurchschnitt liegt bei zwei.* My average mark is a "B".
◊ *über dem Durchschnitt* above average
◊ *unter dem Durchschnitt* below average
◊ *im Durchschnitt* on average

**durchschnittlich** ADJECTIVE, ADVERB
[1] average ◊ *Ich habe durchschnittliche Noten.* My marks are average.
[2] on average ◊ *Durchschnittlich brauche ich eine Stunde für die Hausaufgaben.* On average, my homework takes me an hour.

**durchsehen** VERB (PRESENT **sieht durch,** IMPERFECT **sah durch,** PERFECT **hat durchgesehen**)
to look through

**durchsetzen** VERB (PERFECT **hat durchgesetzt**)
◆ **sich durchsetzen** to assert oneself ◊ *Er kann sich nicht durchsetzen.* He doesn't know how to assert himself.
◆ **Du solltest dich mehr durchsetzen.** You should be more assertive.
◆ **Sie muss immer ihren Willen durchsetzen.** She always has to have her own way.
◆ **seinen Kopf durchsetzen** to get one's way

**durchsichtig** ADJECTIVE
transparent

**durchsprechen** VERB (PRESENT **spricht durch,** IMPERFECT **sprach durch,** PERFECT **hat durchgesprochen**)
to talk over

**durchsuchen** VERB (PERFECT **hat durchsucht**)
to search

**dürfen** VERB (PRESENT **darf,** IMPERFECT **durfte,** PERFECT **hat gedurft** or **dürfen**)
to be allowed to ◊ *Ich darf das.* I'm allowed to do that. ◊ *Er darf das nicht.* He's not allowed to do that. ◊ *Ich habe*

**D**

☞

*leider nicht gedurft.* Unfortunately, I wasn't allowed.

♦ **Darf ich?** May I?

♦ **Darf ich ins Kino?** Can I go to the cinema?

> *The past participle **dürfen** is used when **dürfen** is a modal auxiliary.*

♦ **etwas tun dürfen** to be allowed to do something ◊ *Die Kinder haben gestern länger aufbleiben dürfen.* The children were allowed to stay up late yesterday.

♦ **Es darf geraucht werden.** You may smoke.

♦ **darf nicht** must not ◊ *Das darf nicht geschehen.* That must not happen.

♦ **Da darf sie sich nicht wundern.** That shouldn't surprise her.

♦ **Das darf nicht wahr sein!** I don't believe it!

♦ **Darf ich Sie bitten, das zu tun?** Could I ask you to do that?

♦ **Was darf es sein?** What can I do for you?

♦ **Das dürfen Sie mir glauben.** You can take my word for it.

♦ **Das dürfte genug sein.** That should be enough.

♦ **Es dürfte Ihnen bekannt sein, dass ...** As you will probably know ...

die **Dürre** NOUN
drought ◊ *In Äthiopien hat es eine Dürre gegeben.* There was a drought in Ethiopia.

der **Durst** NOUN
thirst

♦ **Durst haben** to be thirsty

**durstig** ADJECTIVE
thirsty

die **Dusche** NOUN
shower

**duschen** VERB
to have a shower

♦ **sich duschen** to have a shower

das **Düsenflugzeug** NOUN (PL die **Düsenflugzeuge**)
jet (*plane*)

**düster** ADJECTIVE
1 dark ◊ *Hier drin ist es so düster.* It's so dark in here.
2 gloomy

das **Dutzend** NOUN (PL die **Dutzende** or **Dutzend**)
dozen ◊ *zwei Dutzend Bücher* two dozen books

**duzen** VERB
to address sb as "du"

> ℹ *The familiar form of address **du** (plural **ihr**) is used when addressing family members, friends, children under 16 and pets.*

**dynamisch** ADJECTIVE
dynamic

der **D-Zug** NOUN (PL die **D-Züge**)
through train

# E

die **Ebbe** NOUN
> low tide ◊ *bei Ebbe* at low tide

**eben** ADJECTIVE, ADVERB
> [1] flat ◊ *eine ebene Fläche* a flat surface
> [2] just ◊ *Er ist eben erst gegangen.* He's just gone.
> [3] exactly ◊ *Eben, das sage ich ja.* That's exactly what I'm saying.
> ♦ **eben deswegen** that's precisely why

die **Ebene** NOUN
> [1] plain ◊ *Wir sahen auf die Ebene hinunter.* We looked down onto the plain.
> [2] level ◊ *Das muss auf höherer Ebene entschieden werden.* That has to be decided at a higher level.

**ebenfalls** ADVERB
> likewise

**ebenso** ADVERB
> just as ◊ *Sie ist ebenso groß wie ihr Bruder.* She's just as tall as her brother.

das **Echo** NOUN (PL die **Echos**)
> echo

**echt** ADJECTIVE, ADVERB
> [1] real ◊ *echtes Gold* real gold
> ♦ **Der Geldschein ist nicht echt.** That banknote's a fake.
> [2] really ◊ *Die Party war echt gut.* The party was really good.
> ♦ **Echt?** Really?

die **Ecke** NOUN
> corner ◊ *um die Ecke* round the corner

der **Edelstein** NOUN (PL die **Edelsteine**)
> precious stone

die **EDV** NOUN (= *elektronische Datenverarbeitung*)
> electronic data processing

die **EG** NOUN (= *Europäische Gemeinschaft*)
> EC

**egal** ADJECTIVE
> all the same ◊ *Das ist mir egal.* It's all the same to me.
> ♦ **Das ist egal.** That makes no difference.
> ♦ **Egal, ob er das gesagt hat oder nicht.** It doesn't matter whether he said it or not.

**egoistisch** ADJECTIVE
> selfish

die **Ehe** NOUN
> see also **ehe** CONJUNCTION
> marriage

**ehe** CONJUNCTION
> see also **die Ehe** NOUN
> before ◊ *Ehe ich es vergesse, ...* Before I forget, ...

die **Ehefrau** NOUN
> wife

**ehemalig** ADJECTIVE
> former

der **Ehemann** NOUN (PL die **Ehemänner**)
> husband

das **Ehepaar** NOUN (PL die **Ehepaare**)
> married couple

**eher** ADVERB
> sooner ◊ *Das hättest du eher sagen müssen.* You should have said that sooner.
> ♦ **Das kommt schon eher der Wahrheit nahe.** That's more like the truth.

die **Ehre** NOUN
> honour

**ehrgeizig** ADJECTIVE
> ambitious

**ehrlich** ADJECTIVE
> honest

die **Ehrlichkeit** NOUN
> honesty

das **Ei** NOUN (PL die **Eier**)
> egg

die **Eiche** NOUN
> oak

das **Eichhörnchen** NOUN (PL die **Eichhörnchen**)
> squirrel

der **Eid** NOUN (PL die **Eide**)
> oath ◊ *einen Eid schwören* to swear an oath

die **Eidechse** NOUN
> lizard

der **Eierbecher** NOUN (PL die **Eierbecher**)
> egg cup

der **Eifer** NOUN
> enthusiasm

die **Eifersucht** NOUN
> jealousy

**eifersüchtig** ADJECTIVE
> jealous ◊ *Er ist eifersüchtig auf seine Schwester.* He's jealous of his sister.

**eifrig** ADJECTIVE
> eager

das **Eigelb** NOUN (PL die **Eigelb**)
> egg yolk

**eigen** ADJECTIVE
> own ◊ *meine eigene Meinung* my own opinion

die **Eigenart** NOUN
> peculiarity ◊ *Wir haben alle unsere Eigenarten.* We all have our own peculiarities.

**eigenartig** ADJECTIVE
> peculiar

die **Eigenschaft** NOUN
> quality

**eigensinnig** ADJECTIVE
> obstinate

**eigentlich** ADJECTIVE, ADVERB

☞

[1] actual ◊ *Er ist der eigentliche Besitzer.* He's the actual owner.

[2] actually ◊ *Eigentlich wollte ich heute nicht weggehen.* Actually I didn't want to go out today.

♦ **Eigentlich nicht.** Not really.

das **Eigentum** NOUN
property

der **Eigentümer** NOUN (PL die **Eigentümer**)
owner

sich **eignen** VERB
to be suited ◊ *Er eignet sich nicht für diese Stelle.* He's not suited to this position.

**eilen** VERB
to be urgent ◊ *Das eilt nicht.* It's not urgent.

**eilig** ADJECTIVE
urgent ◊ *Ich muss zuerst die eiligen Dinge erledigen.* I'll have to do the urgent things first.

♦ **es eilig haben** to be in a hurry

der **Eilzug** NOUN (PL die **Eilzüge**)
fast stopping train

der **Eimer** NOUN (PL die **Eimer**)
bucket

**ein** NUMBER, ARTICLE

see also **eins** NUMBER, **die Eins** NOUN

[1] one ◊ *Es war nur ein Kind da.* There was only one child there. ◊ *Ich möchte nur einen.* I only want one.

[2] somebody ◊ *Wenn einer dir das sagt, glaube es nicht.* If somebody tells you that, don't believe it.

[3] you ◊ *Da kann einem die Lust vergehen.* It's enough to put you off.

[4] a ◊ *ein Mann* a man ◊ *eine Frau* a woman ◊ *ein Kind* a child
an ◊ *ein Ei* an egg ◊ *eine Stunde* an hour

**einander** PRONOUN
each other

**einatmen** VERB (PERFECT **hat eingeatmet**)
to breathe in

die **Einbahnstraße** NOUN
one-way street

**einbiegen** VERB (IMPERFECT **bog ein**, PERFECT **ist eingebogen**)
to turn ◊ *Er ist in die zweite Seitenstraße eingebogen.* He turned down the second side street.

**einbilden** VERB (PERFECT **hat eingebildet**)
♦ **sich etwas einbilden** to imagine something ◊ *Das bildest du dir nur ein.* You're imagining it.

**einbrechen** VERB (PRESENT **bricht ein**, IMPERFECT **brach ein**, PERFECT **ist eingebrochen**)
to break in ◊ *Bei ihnen wurde eingebrochen.* Their house has been broken into. ◊ *Er ist in das Haus eingebrochen.* He broke into the house.

der **Einbrecher** NOUN (PL die **Einbrecher**)
burglar

der **Einbruch** NOUN (PL die **Einbrüche**)
break-in ◊ *In dieser Gegend gibt es häufiger Einbrüche.* There are a lot of break-ins in this area.

♦ **bei Einbruch der Nacht** at nightfall
♦ **vor Einbruch der Nacht** before nightfall

**eincremen** VERB (PERFECT **hat eingecremt**)
to put cream on

**eindeutig** ADJECTIVE
clear ◊ *eine eindeutige Antwort geben* to give a clear answer

der **Eindruck** NOUN (PL die **Eindrücke**)
impression

**eindrucksvoll** ADJECTIVE
impressive

**eine** see **ein**

**eineinhalb** NUMBER
one and a half

**einer** see **ein**

**einerseits** ADVERB
on the one hand ◊ *Einerseits ..., andererseits ...* On the one hand ..., on the other hand ...

**eines** see **ein**

**einfach** ADJECTIVE, ADVERB

[1] easy ◊ *Das war eine einfache Frage.* That was an easy question. ◊ *Das ist nicht einfach.* That isn't easy.

[2] simple ◊ *aus dem einfachen Grund ...* for the simple reason ... ◊ *Sie leben in sehr einfachen Verhältnissen.* They live very simple lives.

[3] single ◊ *eine einfache Fahrkarte* a single ticket

[4] simply ◊ *Ich will das einfach nicht.* I simply don't want it. ◊ *Er wollte einfach nicht begreifen.* He simply didn't want to understand.

die **Einfachheit** NOUN
simplicity

die **Einfahrt** NOUN
entrance

der **Einfall** NOUN (PL die **Einfälle**)
idea ◊ *Das war so ein Einfall von mir.* It was just an idea. ◊ *Du hast manchmal Einfälle!* You do come up with strange ideas sometimes!

**einfallen** VERB (PRESENT **fällt ein**, IMPERFECT **fiel ein**, PERFECT **ist eingefallen**)
♦ **jemandem einfallen** to occur to somebody ◊ *Mir ist das Wort nicht eingefallen.* The word didn't occur to me.
♦ **Das fällt mir gar nicht ein.** I wouldn't dream of it.
♦ **sich etwas einfallen lassen** to come up with a good idea ◊ *Meine Freunde haben sich zu meinem Geburtstag etwas Tolles einfallen lassen.* My friends came up with a really great idea for my birthday.

**E**

♦ **Lass dir was einfallen.** See if you can think of something.

das **Einfamilienhaus** NOUN (GEN des **Einfamilienhauses**, PL die **Einfamilienhäuser**)
detached family house

**einfarbig** ADJECTIVE
plain

der **Einfluss** NOUN (GEN des **Einflusses**, PL die **Einflüsse**)
influence ◊ *Er hat einen schlechten Einfluss auf dich.* He has a bad influence on you.

**einfrieren** VERB (IMPERFECT **fror ein**, PERFECT **hat/ist eingefroren**)
*For the perfect tense use* **haben** *when the verb has an object and* **sein** *when there is no object.*
to freeze ◊ *Wir haben die Reste eingefroren.* We've frozen the left-overs. ◊ *Die Leitung ist eingefroren.* The pipe has frozen.

die **Einfuhr** NOUN
import

die **Eingabe** NOUN
input ◊ *die Eingabe von Daten* data input

der **Eingang** NOUN (PL die **Eingänge**)
entrance

**eingeben** VERB (PRESENT **gibt ein**, IMPERFECT **gab ein**, PERFECT **hat eingegeben**)
to enter ◊ *Beate hat den Text in den Computer eingegeben.* Beate entered the text into the computer.

**eingebildet** ADJECTIVE
conceited ◊ *Sie ist furchtbar eingebildet.* She's terribly conceited.
♦ **Ihre Krankheit ist nur eingebildet.** Her illness is all in the imagination.

der **Eingeborene** NOUN (GEN des/der **Eingeborenen**, PL die **Eingeborenen**)
native

**eingehen** VERB (IMPERFECT **ging ein**, PERFECT **ist eingegangen**)
[1] to die ◊ *Mir ist schon wieder eine Pflanze eingegangen.* Another of my plants has died.
[2] to shrink ◊ *Der Pulli ist in der Wäsche eingegangen.* The pullover shrank in the wash.
♦ **auf etwas eingehen** to comment on something ◊ *Er ist auf meinen Vorschlag nicht eingegangen.* He didn't comment on my suggestion.

**eingenommen** ADJECTIVE
♦ **eingenommen von** taken with ◊ *Ich war sofort von dem Plan eingenommen.* I was immediately taken with the plan.
♦ **Du bist ja ziemlich von dir eingenommen.** You really fancy yourself.

**eingeschrieben** ADJECTIVE
registered ◊ *ein eingeschriebener Brief* a registered letter

**eingestellt** ADJECTIVE

♦ **auf etwas eingestellt sein** to be prepared for something ◊ *Ich war nicht auf Ihren Besuch eingestellt.* I wasn't prepared for your visit.

**eingießen** VERB (IMPERFECT **goss ein**, PERFECT **hat eingegossen**)
to pour ◊ *Darf ich Ihnen noch Kaffee eingießen?* Can I pour you some more coffee?

sich **eingewöhnen** VERB (PERFECT **hat sich eingewöhnt**)
♦ **sich eingewöhnen in** to settle down in ◊ *Sie hat sich gut in der neuen Schule eingewöhnt.* She's settled down very well in her new school.

**eingreifen** VERB (IMPERFECT **griff ein**, PERFECT **hat eingegriffen**)
to intervene

**einheimisch** ADJECTIVE
native

der/die **Einheimische** NOUN (GEN des/der **Einheimischen**, PL die **Einheimischen**)
local ◊ *Wir sollten einen Einheimischen fragen.* We should ask a local.

**einholen** VERB (PERFECT **hat eingeholt**)
[1] to catch up with ◊ *Wir werden euch sicher bald einholen.* We'll soon catch up with you.
[2] to make up ◊ *Wir haben die Verspätung nicht mehr eingeholt.* We didn't make up the delay.

**einhundert** NUMBER
a hundred

**einig** ADJECTIVE
♦ **sich einig sein** to be in agreement
♦ **einig werden** to reach an agreement

**einige** ADJECTIVE, PRONOUN
[1] some ◊ *einige Bücher* some books ◊ *einige von uns* some of us
♦ **einiges** quite a lot of things ◊ *Wir haben einiges gesehen.* We saw quite a lot of things.
[2] several ◊ *Wir sind dort einige Tage geblieben.* We stayed there several days. ◊ *Bei dem Konzert sind einige früher gegangen.* Several people left the concert early.

sich **einigen** VERB
to agree ◊ *Wir haben uns auf diesen Termin geeinigt.* We agreed on this date.

**einigermaßen** ADVERB
[1] somewhat ◊ *Ich war einigermaßen erstaunt.* I was somewhat surprised.
[2] reasonably ◊ *Diesmal hast du dich wenigstens einigermaßen angestrengt.* At least this time you've tried reasonably hard. ◊ *Das Wetter war einigermaßen trocken.* The weather was reasonably dry.

die **Einigung** NOUN
agreement

der **Einkauf** NOUN (PL die **Einkäufe**)
purchase

◆ **Einkäufe machen** to go shopping
**einkaufen** VERB (PERFECT **hat eingekauft**)
  1 to buy ◊ *Wir müssen Brot einkaufen.*
  We'll have to buy bread.
  2 to shop ◊ *Wir kaufen meist samstags
  ein.* We usually shop on Saturdays.
◆ **einkaufen gehen** to go shopping
der **Einkaufsbummel** NOUN (PL die
  **Einkaufsbummel**)
  shopping spree
die **Einkaufsliste** NOUN
  shopping list
die **Einkaufspassage** NOUN
  shopping arcade
der **Einkaufswagen** NOUN (PL die
  **Einkaufswagen**)
  shopping trolley
das **Einkaufszentrum** NOUN (PL die
  **Einkaufszentren**)
  shopping centre
der **Einkaufszettel** NOUN (PL die
  **Einkaufszettel**)
  shopping list
**einklammern** VERB (PERFECT **hat
  eingeklammert**)
  to put in brackets
das **Einkommen** NOUN (PL die **Einkommen**)
  income
**einladen** VERB (PRESENT **lädt ein**, IMPERFECT **lud
  ein**, PERFECT **hat eingeladen**)
  1 to invite ◊ *Sie hat mich zu ihrer Party
  eingeladen.* She's invited me to her
  party.
◆ **jemanden ins Kino einladen** to take
  somebody to the cinema
◆ **Ich lade dich ein.** I'll treat you.
  2 to load ◊ *Kannst du bitte die Koffer
  ins Auto einladen?* Can you load the
  cases into the car, please?
die **Einladung** NOUN
  invitation
**einlaufen** VERB (PRESENT **läuft ein**, IMPERFECT
  **lief ein**, PERFECT **ist eingelaufen**)
  1 to come in ◊ *Das Schiff läuft in den
  Hafen ein.* The ship is coming into the
  harbour.
  2 to shrink ◊ *Mein Pullover ist
  eingelaufen.* My jumper has shrunk.
sich **einleben** VERB (PERFECT **hat sich eingelebt**)
  to settle down ◊ *Wir haben uns in
  unserer neuen Schule gut eingelebt.*
  We've settled down well in our new
  school.
die **Einleitung** NOUN
  introduction
**einleuchten** VERB (PERFECT **hat
  eingeleuchtet**)
◆ **jemandem einleuchten** to make sense to
  somebody ◊ *Das leuchtet mir nicht ein.*
  That doesn't make sense to me.
**einleuchtend** ADJECTIVE
  clear

**einloggen** VERB (PERFECT **hat eingeloggt**)
  to log on (*computer*)
**einlösen** VERB
  to cash ◊ *Kann ich diesen Scheck
  einlösen?* Can I cash this cheque?
◆ **ein Versprechen einlösen** to keep a
  promise
**einmal** ADVERB
  1 once ◊ *Wenn du das erst einmal
  begriffen hast ...* Once you've understood
  it ...
◆ **Es war einmal ...** Once upon a time there
  was ...
◆ **noch einmal** once more
◆ **auf einmal** all at once ◊ *Auf einmal
  waren alle weg.* All at once they were all
  gone.
  2 one day ◊ *Das wirst du schon einmal
  begreifen.* You'll understand it one day.
◆ **Nehmen wir einmal an: ...** Let's just
  suppose: ...
◆ **nicht einmal** not even
**einmalig** ADJECTIVE
  1 unique ◊ *Das ist eine einmalige
  Gelegenheit.* This is a unique
  opportunity.
  2 single ◊ *Das erfordert nur eine
  einmalige Überprüfung.* That requires
  only a single check.
  3 fantastic ◊ *Das war eine einmalige
  Party.* That was a fantastic party.
sich **einmischen** VERB (PERFECT **hat sich
  eingemischt**)
  to interfere ◊ *Ich will mich nicht in deine
  Angelegenheiten einmischen.* I don't
  want to interfere in your affairs.
sich **einordnen** VERB (PERFECT **hat sich
  eingeordnet**)
  1 to fit in ◊ *Du musst lernen, dich
  einzuordnen.* You'll have to learn to fit in.
  2 to get into lane ◊ *Du musst dich in
  die linke Spur einordnen.* You'll have to
  get into the left-hand lane.
**einpacken** VERB (PERFECT **hat eingepackt**)
  to pack ◊ *Hast du deine Zahnbürste
  eingepackt?* Have you packed your
  toothbrush?
**einplanen** VERB (PERFECT **hat eingeplant**)
  to plan for
**einprägen** VERB (PERFECT **hat eingeprägt**)
◆ **sich etwas einprägen** to memorize
  something ◊ *Diesen Namen kann ich mir
  leicht einprägen.* I can easily memorize
  this name.
**einreiben** VERB (IMPERFECT **rieb ein**, PERFECT **hat
  eingerieben**)
  to rub in ◊ *Sie rieb sich das Gesicht mit
  Creme ein.* She rubbed cream into her
  face.
**einreichen** VERB (PERFECT **hat eingereicht**)
  to hand in
die **Einreise** NOUN
  entry

♦ **bei der Einreise** when entering the country

**einreisen** VERB (PERFECT **ist eingereist**)
♦ **in ein Land einreisen** to enter a country

**einrichten** VERB (PERFECT **hat eingerichtet**)
[1] to furnish ◊ *Sie haben ihr Haus antik eingerichtet.* They've furnished their house with antiques.
[2] to set up ◊ *Die Stadt hat eine Beratungsstelle eingerichtet.* The town has set up an advice bureau.
[3] to manage ◊ *Komm früher, wenn du es einrichten kannst.* Come earlier if you can manage.
♦ **sich auf etwas einrichten** to prepare for something ◊ *Wir hatten uns auf mehr Besucher eingerichtet.* We had prepared for more visitors.

die **Einrichtung** NOUN
[1] furnishings ◊ *Die moderne Einrichtung gefiel mir gut.* I liked the modern furnishings.
[2] facility ◊ *städtische Einrichtungen* municipal facilities

**einrosten** VERB (PERFECT **ist eingerostet**)
to get rusty

die **Eins** NOUN (PL die **Einsen**)
*see also* **eins** NUMBER
[1] one
[2] very good

ⓘ *German marks range from one (**sehr gut**) to six (**ungenügend**).*

**eins** NUMBER
*see also* **die Eins** NOUN, **ein** NUMBER, ARTICLE
one ◊ *Ich habe nur eins bekommen.* I only got one.
♦ **Es ist mir alles eins.** It's all the same to me.

**einsam** ADJECTIVE
[1] lonely ◊ *Ich fühle mich einsam.* I'm feeling lonely.
[2] remote ◊ *eine einsame Gegend* a remote area

**einsammeln** VERB (PERFECT **hat eingesammelt**)
to collect

**einschalten** VERB (PERFECT **hat eingeschaltet**)
to switch on ◊ *Schalt mal das Radio ein.* Switch the radio on.

**einschl.** ABBREVIATION (= *einschließlich*)
incl.

**einschlafen** VERB (PRESENT **schläft ein,** IMPERFECT **schlief ein,** PERFECT **ist eingeschlafen**)
to fall asleep

**einschließen** VERB (IMPERFECT **schloss ein,** PERFECT **hat eingeschlossen**)
[1] to lock in ◊ *Sie hat mich im Badezimmer eingeschlossen.* She locked me in the bathroom.

[2] to lock away ◊ *Du solltest die Wertsachen einschließen.* You should lock away the valuables.
[3] to include ◊ *Der Preis schließt die Verpflegung ein.* The price includes all meals.
♦ **sich einschließen** to lock oneself in ◊ *Sie hat sich in ihrem Zimmer eingeschlossen.* She locked herself in her room.

**einschließlich** ADVERB, PREPOSITION
*The preposition **einschließlich** takes the genitive.*
[1] inclusive ◊ *Wir sind vom zehnten bis einschließlich fünfzehnten Juni weg.* We're away from the tenth to the fifteenth of June inclusive.
[2] including ◊ *Das macht zwölf Mark einschließlich Bedienung.* That's twelve marks including service.

**einschränken** VERB (PERFECT **hat eingeschränkt**)
[1] to restrict ◊ *Dadurch wurde unsere Freiheit eingeschränkt.* This restricted our freedom.
[2] to reduce ◊ *Wir müssen die Kosten einschränken.* We'll have to reduce costs.
♦ **sich einschränken** to cut down

sich **einschreiben** VERB (IMPERFECT **schrieb sich ein,** PERFECT **hat sich eingeschrieben**)
*see also* **das Einschreiben** NOUN
to register ◊ *Hast du dich für den Kurs eingeschrieben?* Have you registered for the course?
♦ **sich an der Universität einschreiben** to enrol at university

das **Einschreiben** NOUN (PL die **Einschreiben**)
*see also* **einschreiben** VERB
recorded delivery

**einschüchtern** VERB (PERFECT **hat eingeschüchtert**)
to intimidate

**einsehen** VERB (PRESENT **sieht ein,** IMPERFECT **sah ein,** PERFECT **hat eingesehen**)
to see ◊ *Siehst du das nicht ein?* Don't you see that?

**einseitig** ADJECTIVE
one-sided

**einsenden** VERB (IMPERFECT **sendete ein** or **sandte ein,** PERFECT **hat eingesendet** or **hat eingesandt**)
to send in

**einsetzen** VERB (PERFECT **hat eingesetzt**)
[1] to put in ◊ *Setzt das richtige Wort ein.* Put in the correct word.
[2] to bet ◊ *Wie viel Geld hast du eingesetzt?* How much money did you bet?
[3] to use ◊ *An den Schulen werden immer mehr Computer eingesetzt.* More and more computers are being used in schools.

E

☞

4 to set in ◊ *Wenn der Winter einsetzt ...* When winter sets in ...

♦ **sich einsetzen** to work hard ◊ *Du solltest dich in der Schule etwas mehr einsetzen.* You should work harder at school.

♦ **sich für jemanden einsetzen** to support somebody

die **Einsicht** NOUN

♦ **zu der Einsicht kommen, dass ...** to come to the conclusion that ...

**einsilbig** ADJECTIVE

1 monosyllabic ◊ *ein einsilbiges Wort* a monosyllabic word

2 uncommunicative ◊ *Er war sehr einsilbig.* He was very uncommunicative.

**einsperren** VERB (PERFECT **hat eingesperrt**) to lock up

**einsprachig** ADJECTIVE monolingual

der **Einspruch** NOUN (PL die **Einsprüche**) objection

**einstecken** VERB (PERFECT **hat eingesteckt**)

1 to insert ◊ *Du musst zuerst eine Münze einstecken.* You have to insert a coin first.

♦ **einen Brief einstecken** to post a letter

♦ **ein Gerät einstecken** to plug in an appliance

2 to take ◊ *Hast du genügend Geld eingesteckt?* Have you taken enough money?

**einsteigen** VERB (IMPERFECT **stieg ein,** PERFECT **ist eingestiegen**)

1 to get on ◊ *Wir sind in den Bus eingestiegen.* We got on the bus.

♦ **Bitte einsteigen!** All aboard!

2 to climb in ◊ *Wir sind durchs Kellerfenster ins Haus eingestiegen.* We climbed into the house through the cellar window.

**einstellen** VERB (PERFECT **hat eingestellt**)

1 to adjust ◊ *den Spiegel einstellen* to adjust the mirror

♦ **eine Kamera einstellen** to focus a camera

2 to tune in to ◊ *Welchen Sender hast du da eingestellt?* Which station have you tuned in to?

3 to stop ◊ *Sie haben die Produktion eingestellt.* They've stopped production.

4 to employ ◊ *Sie wurde als Sekretärin eingestellt.* She was employed as a secretary.

♦ **sich auf etwas einstellen** to prepare oneself for something ◊ *Stell dich besser auf eine lange Warterei ein.* You'd better prepare yourself for a long wait.

die **Einstellung** NOUN attitude ◊ *Ich mag deine Einstellung nicht.* I don't like your attitude.

der **Einstieg** NOUN entrance ◊ *Der Einstieg ist vorn.* The entrance is at the front.

**einstimmen** VERB (PERFECT **hat eingestimmt**)

to join in ◊ *Alle stimmten in das Lied ein.* Everyone joined in the singing.

♦ **sich auf etwas einstimmen** to get oneself in the right mood for something

**eintägig** ADJECTIVE one-day

**eintausend** NUMBER a thousand

**eintönig** ADJECTIVE monotonous

der **Eintopf** NOUN (PL die **Eintöpfe**) stew

der **Eintrag** NOUN (PL die **Einträge**) entry ◊ *ein Eintrag im Wörterbuch* a dictionary entry

**eintragen** VERB (PRESENT **trägt ein,** IMPERFECT **trug ein,** PERFECT **hat eingetragen**) to write ◊ *Tragt die Vokabeln in euer Heft ein.* Write the vocabulary in your exercise book.

♦ **sich eintragen** to put one's name down ◊ *Hast du dich schon in die Liste eingetragen?* Have you put your name down on the list yet?

**einträglich** ADJECTIVE profitable

**eintreffen** VERB (PRESENT **trifft ein,** IMPERFECT **traf ein,** PERFECT **ist eingetroffen**)

1 to arrive ◊ *Sobald die Gäste eintreffen ...* As soon as the guests arrive ...

2 to come true ◊ *Die Prophezeiung ist tatsächlich eingetroffen.* The prophecy actually came true.

**eintreten** VERB (PRESENT **tritt ein,** IMPERFECT **trat ein,** PERFECT **ist eingetreten**)

♦ **eintreten in (1)** to enter ◊ *Er ist ins Zimmer eingetreten.* He entered the room.

♦ **eintreten in (2)** to join ◊ *Wann bist du in den Tennisclub eingetreten?* When did you join the tennis club?

♦ **Es ist eine Verzögerung eingetreten.** There has been a delay.

der **Eintritt** NOUN (PL die **Eintritte**) admission ◊ *Wie viel kostet der Eintritt?* How much does the admission cost?

♦ **"Eintritt frei"** "Admission free"

das **Eintrittsgeld** NOUN (PL die **Eintrittsgelder**) admission charge

die **Eintrittskarte** NOUN admission ticket

der **Eintrittspreis** NOUN (PL die **Eintrittspreise**) admission charge

**einverstanden** ADJECTIVE

♦ **einverstanden sein** to agree ◊ *Bist du mit dem Vorschlag einverstanden?* Do you agree to the suggestion?

♦ **Einverstanden!** Okay!

der **Einwanderer** NOUN (PL die **Einwanderer**) immigrant

**einwandern** VERB (PERFECT **ist eingewandert**)
to immigrate

die **Einwegflasche** NOUN
nonreturnable bottle

die **Einwegspritze** NOUN
disposable syringe

**einweihen** VERB (PERFECT **hat eingeweiht**)
to open ◊ *Morgen wird die neue Brücke eingeweiht.* The new bridge is being opened tomorrow.
♦ **jemanden in etwas einweihen** to initiate somebody into something ◊ *Wir haben die Neue in unseren Klub eingeweiht.* We've initiated the newcomer into our club.
♦ **Willst du mich nicht in dein Geheimnis einweihen?** Won't you let me in on your secret?

**einwerfen** VERB (PRESENT **wirft ein**, IMPERFECT **warf ein**, PERFECT **hat eingeworfen**)
to smash ◊ *Ich habe eine Scheibe eingeworfen.* I've smashed a pane.
♦ **einen Brief einwerfen** to post a letter
♦ **Geld einwerfen** to insert money

der **Einwohner** NOUN (PL die **Einwohner**)
inhabitant

das **Einwohnermeldeamt** NOUN (PL die **Einwohnermeldeämter**)
registration office

> ℹ *Anyone moving to a new address in Germany is required by law to register (**sich anmelden**) at the residents' registration office (**Einwohnermeldeamt**).*

der **Einwurf** NOUN (PL die **Einwürfe**)
1 slot ◊ *Sie steckte den Brief in den Einwurf.* She put the letter through the slot.
2 throw-in (*sport*) ◊ *Der Schiedsrichter gab einen Einwurf.* The referee gave a throw-in.

die **Einzahl** NOUN
singular

**einzahlen** VERB (PERFECT **hat eingezahlt**)
to pay

das **Einzelbett** NOUN (PL die **Einzelbetten**)
single bed

der **Einzelfahrschein** NOUN (PL die **Einzelfahrscheine**)
single ticket

die **Einzelheit** NOUN
detail

das **Einzelkind** NOUN (PL die **Einzelkinder**)
only child

**einzeln** ADJECTIVE, ADVERB
1 single ◊ *Jeder einzelne Schüler wurde befragt.* Every single pupil was asked.
2 odd ◊ *Ich habe ein paar einzelne Socken.* I've got a couple of odd socks.

3 one at a time ◊ *Bitte einzeln eintreten.* Please come in one at a time.
♦ **einzeln angeben** to specify
♦ **der Einzelne** the individual
♦ **ins Einzelne gehen** to go into details

das **Einzelteil** NOUN (PL die **Einzelteile**)
component

das **Einzelzimmer** NOUN (PL die **Einzelzimmer**)
single room

**einziehen** VERB (IMPERFECT **zog ein**, PERFECT **ist/hat eingezogen**)
*For the perfect tense use **haben** when the verb has an object and **sein** when there is no object.*
1 to retract
♦ **den Kopf einziehen** to duck one's head
2 to collect
3 to move in ◊ *Wann sind die neuen Nachbarn eingezogen?* When did the new neighbours move in?

**einzig** ADJECTIVE
only ◊ *Er ist unser einziges Kind.* He's our only child.
♦ **das Einzige** the only thing
♦ **der Einzige** the only one

**einzigartig** ADJECTIVE
unique

das **Eis** NOUN (PL die **Eis**)
1 ice ◊ *Es war Eis auf dem See.* There was ice on the lake.
2 ice cream ◊ *Möchtest du ein Eis?* Would you like an ice cream?

der **Eisbär** NOUN (GEN des **Eisbären**, PL die **Eisbären**)
polar bear

der **Eisbecher** NOUN (PL die **Eisbecher**)
sundae

der **Eisberg** NOUN (PL die **Eisberge**)
iceberg

die **Eisdiele** NOUN *
ice-cream parlour

das **Eisen** NOUN (PL die **Eisen**)
iron ◊ *Die Brücke ist aus Eisen.* The bridge is made of iron.

die **Eisenbahn** NOUN
railway

**eisern** ADJECTIVE
iron ◊ *eine eiserne Stange* an iron rod
♦ **die eiserne Reserve** emergency reserves

das **Eishockey** NOUN
ice hockey

**eisig** ADJECTIVE
icy

**eiskalt** ADJECTIVE
1 ice-cold ◊ *ein eiskaltes Getränk* an ice-cold drink
2 icy cold ◊ *In diesem Zimmer ist es eiskalt.* This room's icy cold.

der **Eiswürfel** NOUN (PL die **Eiswürfel**)
ice cube

der **Eiszapfen** NOUN (PL die **Eiszapfen**)
icicle

E

**eitel** ADJECTIVE
vain

der **Eiter** NOUN
pus

das **Eiweiß** NOUN (PL die **Eiweiße**)
[1] egg white ◊ *Das Eiweiß zu Schnee schlagen.* Whisk the egg whites until stiff.
[2] protein ◊ *eine eiweißreiche Diät* a diet rich in protein

der **Ekel** NOUN
disgust

**ekelhaft** ADJECTIVE
disgusting

sich **ekeln** VERB
to disgust
♦ **sich vor etwas ekeln** to find something disgusting ◊ *Ich ekle mich vor diesem Dreck.* I find this dirt disgusting.

der **Elch** NOUN (PL die **Elche**)
elk

der **Elefant** NOUN (GEN des **Elefanten**, PL die **Elefanten**)
elephant

**elegant** ADJECTIVE
elegant

der **Elektriker** NOUN (PL die **Elektriker**)
electrician

**elektrisch** ADJECTIVE
electric

die **Elektrizität** NOUN
electricity

das **Elektrogerät** NOUN
electrical appliance

der **Elektroherd** NOUN (PL die **Elektroherde**)
electric cooker

die **Elektronik** NOUN
electronics ◊ *Er studiert Elektronik.* He's studying electronics. ◊ *Die Elektronik am Auto ist kaputt.* There's something wrong with the electronics in the car.

**elektronisch** ADJECTIVE
electronic ◊ *elektronische Post* electronic mail ◊ *elektronischer Briefkasten* electronic mailbox

der **Elektrorasierer** NOUN (PL die **Elektrorasierer**)
electric razor

das **Element** NOUN (PL die **Elemente**)
element

das **Elend** NOUN
see also **elend** ADJECTIVE
misery

**elend** ADJECTIVE
see also **das Elend** NOUN
miserable ◊ *Ich fühle mich so elend.* I feel so miserable.

**elf** NUMBER
eleven ◊ *Sie ist elf.* She's eleven.

der **Elfmeter** NOUN (PL die **Elfmeter**)
penalty ◊ *einen Elfmeter schießen* to take a penalty

der **Ellbogen** NOUN (PL die **Ellbogen**)
elbow

die **Eltern** PL NOUN
parents

der **Elternteil** NOUN (PL die **Elternteile**)
parent ◊ *beide Elternteile* both parents

die **E-Mail** NOUN (PL die **E-Mails**)
e-mail ◊ *Meine E-Mail-Adresse ist ...* My e-mail address is ...

das **Emoticon** NOUN (PL die **Emoticons**)
smiley

der **Empfang** NOUN (PL die **Empfänge**)
[1] reception ◊ *Wart ihr auch bei dem Empfang?* Were you at the reception too?
[2] receipt ◊ *Bitte bestätigen Sie den Empfang der Ware.* Please acknowledge receipt of the goods.
♦ **in Empfang nehmen** to receive

**empfangen** VERB (PRESENT **empfängt**, IMPERFECT **empfing**, PERFECT **hat empfangen**)
to receive

der **Empfänger** NOUN (PL die **Empfänger**)
receiver

**empfänglich** ADJECTIVE
susceptible ◊ *Sie ist für Schmeicheleien sehr empfänglich.* She's very susceptible to flattery.

die **Empfängnisverhütung** NOUN
contraception

die **Empfangsbestätigung** NOUN
acknowledgement

die **Empfangsdame** NOUN
receptionist

**empfehlen** VERB (PRESENT **empfiehlt**, IMPERFECT **empfahl**, PERFECT **hat empfohlen**)
to recommend ◊ *Dieses Restaurant ist zu empfehlen.* This restaurant is to be recommended.

**empfinden** VERB (IMPERFECT **empfand**, PERFECT **hat empfunden**)
to feel ◊ *Ich empfinde nichts für sie.* I don't feel anything for her.

**empfindlich** ADJECTIVE
[1] sensitive ◊ *Er ist ein sehr empfindlicher Mensch.* He's very sensitive.
[2] touchy ◊ *Sie ist schrecklich empfindlich.* She's terribly touchy.

**empfohlen** VERB see **empfehlen**

das **Ende** NOUN (PL die **Enden**)
end
♦ **am Ende (1)** at the end ◊ *am Ende des Zuges* at the end of the train
♦ **am Ende (2)** in the end ◊ *Am Ende ist er dann doch mitgekommen.* He came in the end.
♦ **zu Ende gehen** to come to an end
♦ **zu Ende sein** to be finished
♦ **Ende Dezember** at the end of December

**enden** VERB
to end

**endgültig** ADJECTIVE
definite
die **Endivie** NOUN
endive
**endlich** ADVERB
finally ◊ *Ich bin endlich fertig.* I've finally finished. ◊ *Hast du das endlich begriffen?* Have you finally understood it?
♦ **Endlich!** At last!
♦ **Komm endlich!** Come on!
**endlos** ADJECTIVE
endless
das **Endspiel** NOUN (PL die **Endspiele**)
final
die **Endstation** NOUN
terminus
die **Endung** NOUN
ending
die **Energie** NOUN
energy ◊ *seine ganze Energie für etwas einsetzen* to devote all one's energies to something
**energisch** ADJECTIVE
energetic
**eng** ADJECTIVE
[1] narrow ◊ *ein enger Durchgang* a narrow passageway
[2] tight ◊ *Die Hose ist mir zu eng.* The trousers are too tight for me.
[3] close ◊ *Wir sind eng befreundet.* We are close friends.
die **Enge** NOUN
narrowness
♦ **jemanden in die Enge treiben** to drive somebody into a corner
der **Engel** NOUN (PL die **Engel**)
angel
**England** NEUT NOUN
England
♦ **aus England** from England
♦ **in England** in England
♦ **nach England** to England
der **Engländer** NOUN (PL die **Engländer**)
Englishman
♦ **Er ist Engländer.** He's English.
♦ **die Engländer** the English
die **Engländerin** NOUN
Englishwoman
♦ **Sie ist Engländerin.** She's English.
das **Englisch** NOUN (GEN des **Englischen**)
see also **englisch** ADJECTIVE
English ◊ *Er lernt Englisch in der Schule.* He's learning English at school.
**englisch** ADJECTIVE
English
der **Engpass** NOUN (GEN des **Engpasses**, PL die **Engpässe**)
bottleneck
der **Enkel** NOUN (PL die **Enkel**)
grandson
♦ **alle ihre Enkel** all her grandchildren
die **Enkelin** NOUN
granddaughter
das **Enkelkind** NOUN (PL die **Enkelkinder**)
grandchild
**enorm** ADJECTIVE
enormous ◊ *Er verdient enorm viel Geld.* He earns an enormous amount of money.
**entdecken** VERB (PERFECT **hat entdeckt**)
to discover
die **Ente** NOUN
duck
**entfernen** VERB (PERFECT **hat entfernt**)
to remove
**entfernt** ADJECTIVE
distant ◊ *ein entfernter Verwandter* a distant relative
♦ **weit entfernt** far away
♦ **weit davon entfernt sein, etwas zu tun** to be far from doing something
♦ **nicht im Entferntesten** not in the slightest
die **Entfernung** NOUN
distance
**entführen** VERB (PERFECT **hat entführt**)
to kidnap
**entgegen** PREPOSITION
*entgegen takes the dative.*
contrary to ◊ *entgegen meinen Anweisungen* contrary to my instructions
**entgegengesetzt** ADJECTIVE
[1] opposite ◊ *die entgegengesetzte Richtung* the opposite direction
[2] opposing ◊ *Er vertrat die entgegengesetzte Meinung.* He represented the opposing view.
**entgegenkommen** VERB (IMPERFECT **kam entgegen**, PERFECT **ist entgegengekommen**)
[1] to come towards ◊ *Uns kam ein Lastwagen entgegen.* A lorry came towards us.
[2] to meet half way ◊ *Ich werde Ihnen entgegenkommen, sagen wir zwanzig Mark.* I'll meet you half way, let's say twenty marks.
**entgegenkommend** ADJECTIVE
obliging
**entgehen** VERB (IMPERFECT **entging**, PERFECT **ist entgangen**)
♦ **jemandem entgehen** to escape somebody's attention ◊ *Dieser Fehler ist mir entgangen.* That mistake escaped my attention.
♦ **sich etwas entgehen lassen** to miss something ◊ *Das Konzert will ich mir nicht entgehen lassen.* I'm not going to miss the concert.
**enthalten** VERB (PRESENT **enthält**, IMPERFECT **enthielt**, PERFECT **hat enthalten**)
to contain ◊ *Dieses Fass enthält radioaktiven Müll.* This drum contains radioactive waste.

♦ **sich enthalten** to abstain ◊ *Sie hat sich bei der Abstimmung enthalten.* She abstained from voting.

**entkommen** VERB (IMPERFECT **entkam**, PERFECT **ist entkommen**)
to escape

**entlang** PREPOSITION

*entlang takes the accusative or the dative.*

along ◊ *Entlang der Mauer wuchs Efeu.* Ivy was growing along the wall. ◊ *Wir gingen den Fluss entlang.* We walked along the river.

**entlassen** VERB (PRESENT **entlässt**, IMPERFECT **entließ**, PERFECT **hat entlassen**)
[1] to release ◊ *Er wurde aus dem Gefängnis entlassen.* He was released from prison.
[2] to make redundant ◊ *500 Arbeiter mussten entlassen werden.* 500 workers had to be made redundant.

**entmutigen** VERB (PERFECT **hat entmutigt**)
to discourage

**entrüstet** ADJECTIVE
outraged

**entschädigen** VERB (PERFECT **hat entschädigt**)
to compensate ◊ *jemanden für etwas entschädigen* to compensate somebody for something

**entscheiden** VERB (IMPERFECT **entschied**, PERFECT **hat entschieden**)
to decide
♦ **sich entscheiden** to make up one's mind

**entscheidend** ADJECTIVE
decisive

die **Entscheidung** NOUN
decision

**entschieden** ADJECTIVE
[1] decided ◊ *Es ist entschieden, wir fahren nach Rom.* It's been decided that we're going to Rome.
[2] resolute ◊ *ein sehr entschiedener Mensch* a very resolute person

sich **entschließen** VERB (IMPERFECT **entschloss sich**, PERFECT **hat sich entschlossen**)
to decide

**entschlossen** ADJECTIVE
determined

der **Entschluss** NOUN (GEN des **Entschlusses**, PL die **Entschlüsse**)
decision

**entschuldigen** VERB (PERFECT **hat entschuldigt**)
[1] to excuse ◊ *Entschuldige bitte die Verspätung.* Please excuse the delay.
[2] to apologize ◊ *Du solltest dich besser bei ihm entschuldigen.* You'd better apologize to him.

die **Entschuldigung** NOUN

[1] apology ◊ *Hat er deine Entschuldigung angenommen?* Did he accept your apology?
♦ **jemanden um Entschuldigung bitten** to apologize to somebody
[2] excuse ◊ *Krankheit ist keine Entschuldigung.* Illness is no excuse.
♦ **Mein Vater hat mir eine Entschuldigung geschrieben.** My father wrote me a note for the teacher.
♦ **Entschuldigung!** Sorry.
♦ **Entschuldigung ...** Excuse me ...
◊ *Entschuldigung, können Sie mir sagen, wie spät es ist?* Excuse me, could you tell me what time it is?

**entsetzlich** ADJECTIVE
dreadful

**entsetzt** ADJECTIVE, ADVERB
horrified

die **Entsorgung** NOUN
waste disposal

sich **entspannen** VERB (PERFECT **hat sich entspannt**)
[1] to relax ◊ *Entspann dich!* Relax!
[2] to ease ◊ *Die Lage hat sich entspannt.* The situation has eased.

**entsprechen** VERB (PRESENT **entspricht**, IMPERFECT **entsprach**, PERFECT **hat entsprochen**)
to meet ◊ *Sie hat den Anforderungen nicht entsprochen.* She didn't meet the requirements.
♦ **Dieses Gerät entspricht nicht den Normen.** This appliance doesn't comply with the standards.

**entsprechend** ADJECTIVE, ADVERB
[1] appropriate ◊ *Die entsprechende Antwort ankreuzen.* Tick the appropriate answer.
[2] accordingly ◊ *Benimm dich entsprechend.* Behave accordingly.

**enttäuschen** VERB (PERFECT **hat enttäuscht**)
to disappoint

**enttäuschend** ADJECTIVE
disappointing

die **Enttäuschung** NOUN
disappointment

**entweder** CONJUNCTION
either
♦ **entweder ... oder ...** either ... or ...

**entwerten** VERB
to cancel ◊ *Du musst die Fahrkarte erst entwerten.* You have to cancel your ticket first.

der **Entwerter** NOUN (PL die **Entwerter**)
ticket stamping machine

> ℹ *When you travel by train or tram (and sometimes by bus) you have to stamp your ticket in an **Entwerter**. The machines are either on the platforms or inside the vehicles.*

**entwickeln** VERB (PERFECT **hat entwickelt**)
[1] to develop ◊ *Fähigkeiten entwickeln*
to develop skills ◊ *einen Film entwickeln*
to develop a film
[2] to show ◊ *Sie hat eine enorme
Energie entwickelt.* She showed terrific
energy.
♦ **sich entwickeln** to develop ◊ *Das
Geschäft entwickelt sich gut.* The
business is developing well.
♦ **Sie hat sich zu einem hübschen
Mädchen entwickelt.** She's turned into a
pretty girl.

die **Entwicklung** NOUN
development

die **Entwicklungshilfe** NOUN
development aid

das **Entwicklungsland** NOUN (PL die
**Entwicklungsländer**)
developing country

**entwürdigend** ADJECTIVE
degrading

**entzückend** ADJECTIVE
delightful

sich **entzünden** VERB (PERFECT **hat sich
entzündet**)
to become inflamed ◊ *Die Wunde hat
sich entzündet.* The wound has become
inflamed.

die **Entzündung** NOUN
inflammation

**entzwei** ADVERB
broken ◊ *Die Vase ist entzwei.* The vase
is broken.

der **Enzian** NOUN (PL die **Enziane**)
gentian

**er** PRONOUN
[1] he ◊ *Er ist größer als ich.* He's taller
than me.
[2] it ◊ *Schöner Ring, ist er neu?* Lovely
ring, is it new?
[3] him ◊ *Er ist es.* It's him. ◊ *Er war es
nicht, ich war's.* It wasn't him, it was me.

**erben** VERB
to inherit

**erblich** ADJECTIVE
hereditary

**erbrechen** VERB (PRESENT **erbricht**, IMPERFECT
**erbrach**, PERFECT **hat erbrochen**)
to vomit

die **Erbschaft** NOUN
inheritance

die **Erbse** NOUN
pea

das **Erdbeben** NOUN (PL die **Erdbeben**)
earthquake

die **Erdbeere** NOUN
strawberry

die **Erde** NOUN
earth
♦ **zu ebener Erde** at ground level
♦ **auf der ganzen Erde** all over the world

das **Erdgas** NOUN (GEN des **Erdgases**)
natural gas

das **Erdgeschoss** NOUN (GEN des
**Erdgeschosses**, PL die **Erdgeschosse**)
ground floor ◊ *im Erdgeschoss* on the
ground floor

die **Erdkunde** NOUN
geography

die **Erdnuss** NOUN (PL die **Erdnüsse**)
peanut

das **Erdöl** NOUN
mineral oil

sich **ereignen** VERB (PERFECT **hat sich ereignet**)
to happen

das **Ereignis** NOUN (GEN des **Ereignisses**, PL die
**Ereignisse**)
event

**erfahren** VERB (PRESENT **erfährt**, IMPERFECT
**erfuhr**, PERFECT **hat erfahren**)
see also **erfahren** ADJECTIVE
[1] to hear ◊ *Ich habe erfahren, dass du
heiraten willst.* I've heard that you want
to get married.
[2] to experience ◊ *Sie hat im Leben viel
Gutes erfahren.* She's experienced a lot
of good things in her life.

**erfahren** ADJECTIVE
see also **erfahren** VERB
experienced ◊ *Er ist ein erfahrener
Lehrer.* He's an experienced teacher.

die **Erfahrung** NOUN
experience

**erfassen** VERB (PERFECT **hat erfasst**)
[1] to understand ◊ *Ich habe den Text
noch nicht erfasst.* I haven't understood
the text yet.
[2] to register ◊ *Alle Aidsfälle
werden erfasst.* All AIDS cases are
registered.

**erfinden** VERB (IMPERFECT **erfand**, PERFECT **hat
erfunden**)
to invent

der **Erfinder** NOUN (PL die **Erfinder**)
inventor

**erfinderisch** ADJECTIVE
inventive

die **Erfindung** NOUN
invention

der **Erfolg** NOUN (PL die **Erfolge**)
success
♦ **Erfolg versprechend** promising
♦ **Viel Erfolg!** Good luck!

**erfolglos** ADJECTIVE
unsuccessful

**erfolgreich** ADJECTIVE
successful

**erforderlich** ADJECTIVE
necessary

**erfreulicherweise** ADVERB
happily

**erfreut** ADJECTIVE

**E**

☞

pleased ◊ *Über mein gutes Zeugnis war ich sehr erfreut.* I was very pleased with my good report.

**erfrieren** VERB (IMPERFECT **erfror,** PERFECT **ist erfroren)**
to freeze to death ◊ *Er ist erfroren.* He froze to death.
♦ **Die Pflanze ist erfroren.** The plant was killed by frost.
♦ **Er hat sich bei der Bergtour einen Zeh erfroren.** He got a frostbitten toe on his mountaineering trip.

die **Erfrischung** NOUN
refreshment

der **Erfrischungsstand** NOUN (PL die **Erfrischungsstände)**
refreshment stand

**erfüllen** VERB (PERFECT **hat erfüllt)**
to fulfil ◊ *Er hat ihr den Wunsch erfüllt.* He fulfilled her wish.
♦ **sich erfüllen** to come true ◊ *Die Prophezeiung hat sich erfüllt.* The prophecy came true.

**ergänzen** VERB (PERFECT **hat ergänzt)**
to complete ◊ *Ergänzt den Satz.* Complete the sentence.
♦ **sich ergänzen** to complement one another

das **Ergebnis** NOUN (GEN des **Ergebnisses,** PL die **Ergebnisse)**
result

die **Ergonomie** NOUN
ergonomics

**ergreifen** VERB (IMPERFECT **ergriff,** PERFECT **hat ergriffen)**
[1] to seize ◊ *Er ergriff meine Hand.* He seized my hand. ◊ *die Gelegenheit ergreifen* to seize the opportunity
♦ **einen Beruf ergreifen** to take up a profession
♦ **Maßnahmen gegen etwas ergreifen** to take measures against something
[2] to move ◊ *Ihr Schicksal hat uns sehr ergriffen.* Her fate moved us deeply.

**ergreifend** ADJECTIVE
moving

**ergriffen** ADJECTIVE
deeply moved

**erhalten** VERB (PRESENT **erhält,** IMPERFECT **erhielt,** PERFECT **hat erhalten)**
[1] to receive ◊ *Sie hat den ersten Preis erhalten.* She received first prize.
[2] to preserve ◊ *Das Gebäude sollte erhalten werden.* The building should be preserved.
♦ **gut erhalten** in good condition

**erhältlich** ADJECTIVE
obtainable

**erheitern** VERB (PERFECT **hat erheitert)**
to amuse

**erhitzen** VERB (PERFECT **hat erhitzt)**
to heat

sich **erholen** VERB (PERFECT **hat sich erholt)**
[1] to recover ◊ *Der Patient muss sich nach der Operation erholen.* The patient needs to recover after the operation.
[2] to have a rest ◊ *Wir haben uns in den Ferien gut erholt.* We had a good rest when we were on holiday.

**erholsam** ADJECTIVE
restful

die **Erholung** NOUN
rest ◊ *Wir fahren zur Erholung ans Meer.* We're going to the sea for a rest.

**erinnern** VERB (PERFECT **hat erinnert)**
♦ **erinnern an** to remind of ◊ *Du erinnerst mich an meine Schwester.* You remind me of my sister. ◊ *Erinnere mich bitte daran, dass wir noch Butter kaufen müssen.* Remind me that we still have to buy butter.
♦ **sich erinnern** to remember ◊ *Ich kann mich nicht erinnern.* I can't remember. ◊ *Erinnerst du dich noch an unser Abenteuer in Erlangen?* Can you still remember our adventure in Erlangen?

die **Erinnerung** NOUN
[1] memory ◊ *Wir haben Erinnerungen ausgetauscht.* We swapped memories.
[2] souvenir ◊ *eine Erinnerung an meinen Russlandaufenthalt* a souvenir of my stay in Russia

**erkältet** ADJECTIVE
♦ **erkältet sein** to have a cold

die **Erkältung** NOUN
cold

**erkennbar** ADJECTIVE
recognizable

**erkennen** VERB (IMPERFECT **erkannte,** PERFECT **hat erkannt)**
[1] to recognize ◊ *Ich hätte dich fast nicht erkannt.* I would hardly have recognized you.
[2] to see ◊ *Jetzt erkenne ich, dass das ein Fehler war.* I see now that it was a mistake.

**erklären** VERB (PERFECT **hat erklärt)**
to explain

die **Erklärung** NOUN
explanation
♦ **eine Liebeserklärung** a declaration of love

sich **erkundigen** VERB (PERFECT **hat sich erkundigt)**
♦ **sich erkundigen nach** to inquire about ◊ *Wir sollten uns nach den Abfahrtszeiten erkundigen.* We should inquire about departure times.
♦ **Er hat sich nach dir erkundigt.** He was asking about you.

**erlauben** VERB (PERFECT **hat erlaubt)**
♦ **jemandem etwas erlauben** to allow somebody to do something ◊ *Mein Vater hat mir erlaubt auszugehen.* My father allowed me to go out.

♦ **sich etwas erlauben** to allow oneself something ◊ *Ich erlaube mir jetzt ein Bier.* Now I'm going to allow myself a beer.

♦ **Was erlaubst du dir denn eigentlich?** How dare you!

die **Erlaubnis** NOUN (PL die **Erlaubnisse**)
permission

**erleben** VERB (PERFECT **hat erlebt**)
[1] to experience ◊ *Eine solche Frechheit habe ich selten erlebt.* I've seldom experienced such cheek.

♦ **Wir haben in den Ferien viel Schönes erlebt.** We had a lovely time on holiday.

♦ **Sie hat viel Schlimmes erlebt.** She's had a lot of bad experiences.

[2] to live through ◊ *Mein Opa hat den Zweiten Weltkrieg erlebt.* My grandpa lived through the Second World War.

[3] to live to see ◊ *Ich möchte die Geburt deines Kindes noch erleben.* I would like to live to see the birth of your child.

das **Erlebnis** NOUN (GEN des **Erlebnisses**, PL die **Erlebnisse**)
experience

**erledigen** VERB (PERFECT **hat erledigt**)
[1] to see to ◊ *Ich habe heute noch viel zu erledigen.* I've a lot to see to today.

♦ **Hast du deine Hausaufgaben schon erledigt?** Have you done your homework already?

[2] to wear out ◊ *Die Wanderung hat mich ziemlich erledigt.* The hike's really worn me out.

die **Erleichterung** NOUN
relief ◊ *Das war eine Erleichterung!* That was a relief!

der **Erlös** NOUN (GEN des **Erlöses**, PL die **Erlöse**)
proceeds ◊ *Der Erlös kommt Kindern in Rumänien zugute.* The proceeds will go to children in Romania.

**erlösen** VERB (PERFECT **hat erlöst**)
to save ◊ *Sie erlöste ihn aus einer gefährlichen Lage.* She saved him from a dangerous situation.

die **Ermahnung** NOUN
admonition

**ermäßigen** VERB (PERFECT **hat ermäßigt**)
to reduce

die **Ermäßigung** NOUN
reduction

**ermöglichen** VERB (PERFECT **hat ermöglicht**)
♦ **jemandem etwas ermöglichen** to make something possible for somebody

**ermorden** VERB (PERFECT **hat ermordet**)
to murder

**ermüdend** ADJECTIVE
tiring

**ermutigen** VERB (PERFECT **hat ermutigt**)
to encourage

**ernähren** VERB (PERFECT **hat ernährt**)

to support ◊ *Er hat eine Familie zu ernähren.* He has a family to support.

♦ **sich von etwas ernähren** to live on something ◊ *Sie ernähren sich hauptsächlich von Reis.* They live mainly on rice.

♦ **Du ernährst dich ungesund.** Your diet's unhealthy.

**ernennen** VERB (IMPERFECT **ernannte**, PERFECT **hat ernannt**)
to appoint

**erneuern** VERB (PERFECT **hat erneuert**)
to renew

**ernst** ADJECTIVE
see also **der Ernst** NOUN
serious

der **Ernst** NOUN
see also **ernst** ADJECTIVE
seriousness

♦ **Das ist mein Ernst.** I'm quite serious.

♦ **im Ernst** in earnest

**ernsthaft** ADJECTIVE
serious ◊ *ein ernsthaftes Gespräch* a serious talk ◊ *Glaubst du das ernsthaft?* Do you seriously believe that?

**ernstlich** ADJECTIVE, ADVERB
serious

♦ **ernstlich besorgt** seriously concerned

die **Ernte** NOUN
harvest

**ernten** VERB
to harvest ◊ *Es ist Zeit, die Kirschen zu ernten.* It's time to harvest the cherries.

♦ **Lob ernten** to earn praise

**erobern** VERB (PERFECT **hat erobert**)
to conquer

die **Eroberung** NOUN
conquest

**erotisch** ADJECTIVE
erotic

**erpressen** VERB (PERFECT **hat erpresst**)
[1] to blackmail ◊ *Du willst mich wohl erpressen?* Are you trying to blackmail me?

[2] to extort ◊ *Er hat von ihm Geld erpresst.* He extorted money from him.

**erraten** VERB (PRESENT **errät**, IMPERFECT **erriet**, PERFECT **hat erraten**)
to guess

die **Erregung** NOUN
excitement

**erreichen** VERB (PERFECT **hat erreicht**)
[1] to reach ◊ *Wir haben Hamburg am späten Nachmittag erreicht.* We reached Hamburg in the late afternoon.

[2] to catch ◊ *Wir haben den Zug nicht mehr erreicht.* We didn't manage to catch the train.

[3] to achieve ◊ *seinen Zweck erreichen* to achieve one's purpose ◊ *Was willst du damit erreichen?* What do you aim to achieve by this?

E

♦ **So erreichst du bei mir gar nichts.** You won't get anywhere with me by doing that.

der **Ersatzreifen** NOUN (PL die **Ersatzreifen**)
spare tyre

das **Ersatzteil** NOUN (PL die **Ersatzteile**)
spare part

**erschaffen** VERB (IMPERFECT **erschuf,** PERFECT **hat erschaffen**)
to create

**erscheinen** VERB (IMPERFECT **erschien,** PERFECT **ist erschienen**)
to appear

**erschießen** VERB (IMPERFECT **erschoss,** PERFECT **hat erschossen**)
to shoot dead

**erschöpft** ADJECTIVE
exhausted

die **Erschöpfung** NOUN
exhaustion

**erschrecken (1)** VERB (PERFECT **hat erschreckt**)
to frighten ◊ *Hast du mich erschreckt!* You really frightened me!

**erschrecken (2)** VERB (PRESENT **erschrickt,** IMPERFECT **erschrak,** PERFECT **ist erschrocken**)
to be frightened ◊ *Ich bin furchtbar erschrocken, als plötzlich das Licht ausging.* I was terribly frightened when the light suddenly went out.

♦ **Erschrick nicht, wenn du ihn siehst.** Don't be shocked when you see him.

**erschreckend** ADJECTIVE
alarming

**erschrocken** ADJECTIVE
frightened

**ersetzen** VERB (PERFECT **hat ersetzt**)
to replace ◊ *Du musst die Vase ersetzen.* You'll have to replace that vase.

♦ **jemandem die Unkosten ersetzen** to pay somebody's expenses

die **Ersparnisse** FEM PL NOUN
savings

**erst** ADVERB
[1] first ◊ *Erst will ich wissen, was das kostet.* First I want to know what it costs. ◊ *Mach erst mal die Arbeit fertig.* Finish your work first.

♦ **Wenn du das erst mal hinter dir hast, ...** Once you've got that behind you, ...
[2] only ◊ *Das ist erst gestern passiert.* That happened only yesterday. ◊ *Er ist gerade erst angekommen.* He's only just arrived.

♦ **erst als** not until ◊ *Er hat es erst gemacht, als ich es ihm befohlen habe.* He didn't do it until I told him.

♦ **erst morgen** not until tomorrow

♦ **erst um 5 Uhr** not until 5 o'clock

♦ **Wir fahren erst später.** We're not going until later.

**erstaunlich** ADJECTIVE
astonishing

**erstaunt** ADJECTIVE
astonished

**erstbeste** ADJECTIVE
first that comes along ◊ *Du kannst doch nicht den erstbesten Mann heiraten.* But you can't marry the first man that comes along.

**erste** ADJECTIVE
first ◊ *Ich habe gerade mein erstes Auto gekauft.* I've just bought my first car. ◊ *Er kam als Erster.* He was the first to arrive.

♦ **erste Hilfe** first aid

**erstechen** VERB (PRESENT **ersticht,** IMPERFECT **erstach,** PERFECT **hat erstochen**)
to stab to death

**erstens** ADVERB
firstly

**ersticken** VERB (PERFECT **ist erstickt**)
to suffocate ◊ *Ich bin fast erstickt.* I almost suffocated.

♦ **Er versuchte, die Flammen zu ersticken.** He tried to smother the flames.

♦ **in Arbeit ersticken** to be snowed under with work

**erstklassig** ADJECTIVE
first-class

**erstmals** ADVERB
for the first time

**ertragen** VERB (PRESENT **erträgt,** IMPERFECT **ertrug,** PERFECT **hat ertragen**)
to stand ◊ *Ich kann die Schmerzen kaum ertragen.* I can hardly stand the pain. ◊ *Sie erträgt es nicht, wenn man ihr widerspricht.* She can't stand being contradicted.

**erträglich** ADJECTIVE
bearable

**ertrinken** VERB (IMPERFECT **ertrank,** PERFECT **ist ertrunken**)
to drown

**erwachsen** ADJECTIVE
grown-up

der **Erwachsene** NOUN (GEN des/der
die **Erwachsenen,** PL die **Erwachsenen**)
adult ◊ *Erwachsene können das nicht verstehen.* Adults can't understand that.

die **Erwachsenenbildung** NOUN
adult education

**erwähnen** VERB (PERFECT **hat erwähnt**)
to mention

**erwarten** VERB (PERFECT **hat erwartet**)
to expect ◊ *Er erwartet zu viel von uns.* He's expecting too much of us.

♦ **Wir können es kaum erwarten, dass die Ferien beginnen.** We can hardly wait for the holidays to begin.

**erwartungsgemäß** ADVERB
as expected

**erweisen** VERB (IMPERFECT **erwies,** PERFECT **hat erwiesen**)

♦ **sich erweisen als** to prove to be ◊ *Er erwies sich als guter Schüler.* He proved to be a good pupil.

**erwerben** VERB (PRESENT **erwirbt**, IMPERFECT **erwarb**, PERFECT **hat erworben**)
to acquire

das **Erz** NOUN (GEN des **Erzes**, PL die **Erze**)
ore

**erzählen** VERB (PERFECT **hat erzählt**)
to tell

die **Erzählung** NOUN
story

**erzeugen** VERB (PERFECT **hat erzeugt**)
to produce ◊ *In dieser Gegend wird Wein erzeugt.* Wine is produced in this region.
♦ **Strom erzeugen** to generate electricity

das **Erzeugnis** NOUN (GEN des **Erzeugnisses**, PL die **Erzeugnisse**)
produce ◊ *ausländische Erzeugnisse* foreign produce

**erziehen** VERB (IMPERFECT **erzog**, PERFECT **hat erzogen**)
to bring up ◊ *Sie hat fünf Kinder erzogen.* She brought up five children. ◊ *Sie sollte ihre Kinder zu etwas mehr Höflichkeit erziehen.* She should bring her children up to be more polite.

die **Erziehung** NOUN
education

der **Erziehungsberechtigte** NOUN (GEN des/
die der **Erziehungsberechtigten**, PL die **Erziehungsberechtigten**)
parent or guardian ◊ *Du brauchst dafür die Unterschrift eines Erziehungsberechtigten.* You need the signature of your parent or guardian for this.

**es** PRONOUN
it ◊ *Es ist rot.* It's red. ◊ *Ich habe es nicht gesehen.* I didn't see it. ◊ *Es schneit.* It's snowing.

der **Esel** NOUN (PL die **Esel**)
donkey

der **Eskimo** NOUN (PL die **Eskimos**)
Eskimo

**essbar** ADJECTIVE
edible

**essen** VERB (PRESENT **isst**, IMPERFECT **aß**, PERFECT **hat gegessen**)
see also **das Essen** NOUN
to eat

das **Essen** NOUN (PL die **Essen**)
see also **essen** VERB
[1] meal ◊ *Komm doch am Freitag zum Essen.* Why don't you come for a meal on Friday?.
[2] food ◊ *Das Essen war lecker.* The food was delicious.

der **Essig** NOUN (PL die **Essige**)
vinegar

die **Essiggurke** NOUN
gherkin

die **Esskastanie** NOUN
sweet chestnut

das **Esszimmer** NOUN (PL die **Esszimmer**)
dining room

die **Etage** NOUN
floor ◊ *Wir wohnen in der dritten Etage.* We live on the third floor.

die **Etagenbetten** NEUT PL NOUN
bunk beds

das **Etikett** NOUN (PL die **Etikette** or **Etiketten**)
label ◊ *Lies mal, was auf dem Etikett steht.* Read what's on the label.

**etliche** PL PRONOUN
quite a few ◊ *etliche Leute* quite a few people

das **Etui** NOUN (PL die **Etuis**)
case ◊ *ein Brillenetui* a glasses case

**etwa** ADVERB
[1] about ◊ *Es waren etwa zwanzig.* There were about twenty.
[2] for instance ◊ *Leute wie etwa Jochen wissen das eben nicht.* People like Jochen, for instance, just don't know that.
♦ **Soll das etwa heißen, dass du nicht mitkommst?** Is that supposed to mean that you're not coming?
♦ **Hat er das etwa wirklich gesagt?** Did he really say that?
♦ **Du willst doch nicht etwa schon gehen.** You're not going already, are you?

**etwaig** ADJECTIVE
possible

**etwas** PRONOUN, ADVERB
[1] something ◊ *Wir sollten ihr etwas schenken.* We should give her something.
[2] anything ◊ *Hast du nicht etwas gehört?* Haven't you heard anything?
[3] a little ◊ *Wir sollten uns etwas ausruhen.* We should have a little rest. ◊ *Nur etwas Milch bitte.* Just a little milk, please.

die **EU** NOUN (= *Europäische Union*)
EU (= European Union)

**euch** PRONOUN
**euch** is the accusative and dative of **ihr**.
[1] you ◊ *Ich habe euch gesehen.* I saw you. ◊ *Ich komme mit euch.* I'll come with you.
[2] yourselves ◊ *Seht euch mal im Spiegel an.* Look at yourselves in the mirror.
[3] to you ◊ *Sie hat es euch gegeben.* She gave it to you.

**euer** PRONOUN, ADJECTIVE
[1] your ◊ *Euer Deutschlehrer ist nett.* Your German teacher is nice. ◊ *Wenn das eure Mutter erlaubt.* If your mother lets you. ◊ *Ist das euer Haus?* Is that your house? ◊ *Wir haben eure Bücher mitgebracht.* We've brought your books.

E

☞

2 yours ◊ *Das ist nicht unser Computer, das ist eurer.* That's not our computer, that's yours. ◊ *Unsere Mutter heißt Ulla, wie heißt eure?* Our mother's called Ulla, what's yours called? ◊ *Wenn es in unserem Haus nicht geht, feiern wir in eurem.* If it's not OK in our house, then we'll celebrate in yours. ◊ *Wir holen unsere Karten, sollen wir eure mitbringen?* We're picking up our tickets, shall we get yours too?

die **Eule** NOUN
owl

**eure** *see* **euer**

**eures** *see* **euer**

**euretwegen** ADVERB
1 for your sakes ◊ *Wir sind euretwegen nicht in Urlaub gefahren.* We didn't go on holiday for your sakes.
2 on your account ◊ *Er hat sich euretwegen aufgeregt.* He got upset on your account.

der **Euro** NOUN (PL die **Euros**)
euro ◊ *Das kostet fünf Euro.* It costs five euros.

**Europa** NEUT NOUN
Europe
♦ **aus Europa** from Europe
♦ **in Europa** in Europe
♦ **nach Europa** to Europe

der **Europäer** NOUN (PL die **Europäer**)
European

die **Europäerin** NOUN
European

**europäisch** ADJECTIVE
European

der **Euroscheck** NOUN (PL die **Euroschecks**)
Eurocheque

**e. V.** ABBREVIATION (= *eingetragener Verein*)
registered society

**evangelisch** ADJECTIVE
Protestant

**eventuell** ADVERB, ADJECTIVE
perhaps ◊ *Eventuell komme ich später nach.* Perhaps I'll come on later.
♦ **Eventuelle Fragen wird mein Kollege gerne beantworten.** My colleague will be pleased to answer any questions you may have.

Be careful! **eventuell** does not mean **eventual.**

**ewig** ADJECTIVE
eternal

die **Ewigkeit** NOUN
eternity

das **Examen** NOUN (PL die **Examen**)
exam

das **Exemplar** NOUN (PL die **Exemplare**)
1 copy ◊ *Von dem Buch habe ich zwei Exemplare.* I've got two copies of the book.
2 specimen ◊ *Er hat ein ganz seltenes Exemplar gefangen.* He caught a very rare specimen.

**explodieren** VERB (PERFECT **ist explodiert**)
to explode

die **Explosion** NOUN
explosion

der **Export** NOUN (PL die **Exporte**)
export

**exportieren** VERB (PERFECT **hat exportiert**)
to export

**extra** ADVERB, ADJECTIVE
see also **das Extra** NOUN
1 separately ◊ *Schicke die Diskette lieber extra.* It'd be better to send the diskette separately.
2 specially ◊ *Das wurde extra für sie angefertigt.* That was made specially for her. ◊ *Ich bin extra wegen dir gekommen.* I came specially because of you.
3 on purpose ◊ *Das hat er extra gemacht.* He did that on purpose.
4 extra ◊ *Ich habe das extra schnell gemacht.* I did it extra quickly. ◊ *Das sind extra starke Pfefferminzbonbons.* These are extra strong peppermints.
5 another ◊ *Stell noch einen extra Teller auf den Tisch.* Put another plate on the table.

das **Extra** NOUN (PL die **Extras**)
see also **extra** ADVERB
extra ◊ *ein Auto mit vielen Extras* a car with lots of extras

**extrem** ADJECTIVE
extreme

# F

**fabelhaft** ADJECTIVE
  fabulous
die **Fabrik** NOUN
  factory
  *Be careful!* **Fabrik** *does not mean* **fabric**.
der **Fabrikarbeiter** NOUN (PL die
  **Fabrikarbeiter**)
  factory worker
die **Fabrikarbeiterin** NOUN
  factory worker
das **Fach** NOUN (PL die **Fächer**)
  [1] shelf ◊ *Das ist mein Fach im Schrank.*
  This is my shelf in the cupboard.
  [2] pigeonhole ◊ *Jeder Lehrer hat im
  Lehrerzimmer ein Fach.* Every teacher
  has a pigeonhole in the staff room.
  [3] subject ◊ *In welchem Fach bist du am
  besten?* What subject are you best at?
der **Facharzt** NOUN (GEN des **Facharztes**, PL die
  **Fachärzte**)
  specialist (*doctor*)
die **Fachärztin** NOUN
  specialist (*doctor*)
der **Fachausdruck** NOUN (PL die
  **Fachausdrücke**)
  technical term
die **Fachfrau** NOUN
  expert
die **Fachhochschule** NOUN
  college
die **Fachschule** NOUN
  technical college
der **Fachmann** NOUN (PL die **Fachleute**)
  expert
das **Fachwerkhaus** NOUN (GEN des
  **Fachwerkhauses**, PL die **Fachwerkhäuser**)
  half-timbered house
die **Fackel** NOUN
  torch
der **Faden** NOUN (PL die **Fäden**)
  thread
**fähig** ADJECTIVE
  capable ◊ *Sie ist eine sehr fähige
  Lehrerin.* She's a very capable teacher.
  ◆ **fähig sein, etwas zu tun** to be capable of
  doing something ◊ *Bist du fähig, diesen
  Text zu übersetzen?* Are you capable of
  translating this text?
die **Fähigkeit** NOUN
  ability
die **Fahne** NOUN
  flag
  ◆ **eine Fahne haben** to stink of booze
der **Fahrausweis** NOUN (GEN des
  **Fahrausweises**, PL die **Fahrausweise**)
  ticket ◊ *Die Fahrausweise, bitte.* Tickets,
  please.
die **Fahrbahn** NOUN

  carriageway
die **Fähre** NOUN
  ferry
**fahren** VERB (PRESENT **fährt,** IMPERFECT **fuhr,**
  PERFECT **ist/hat gefahren**)
  *For the perfect tense use* **haben** *when
  the verb has an object and* **sein** *when
  there is no object.*
  [1] to drive ◊ *Er hat mich nach Hause
  gefahren.* He drove me home. ◊ *Er ist
  sehr schnell gefahren.* He drove very
  fast.
  ◆ **ein Rennen fahren** to drive in a race
  [2] to go ◊ *Der Intercity fährt stündlich.*
  The Intercity train goes every hour.
  [3] to leave ◊ *Wann seid ihr gefahren?*
  When did you leave?
  [4] to sail ◊ *Das Schiff fährt nach
  Amerika.* The ship's sailing to America.
  ◊ *Wir sind mit dem Schiff nach Amerika
  gefahren.* We sailed to America.
  ◆ **Rad fahren** to cycle ◊ *Früher bin ich viel
  Rad gefahren.* I used to cycle a lot.
  ◆ **mit dem Auto fahren** to go by car
  ◆ **mit dem Zug fahren** to go by train ◊ *Seid
  ihr mit dem Zug gefahren?* Did you go by
  train?
  ◆ **Sie fuhr mit der Hand über sein Haar.**
  She ran her hand through his hair.
der **Fahrer** NOUN (PL die **Fahrer**)
  driver
die **Fahrerflucht** NOUN
  hit-and-run accident
die **Fahrerin** NOUN
  driver
der **Fahrgast** NOUN (PL die **Fahrgäste**)
  passenger
das **Fahrgeld** NOUN (PL die **Fahrgelder**)
  fare ◊ *Bitte das Fahrgeld abgezählt
  bereithalten.* Please have exact fare
  ready.
die **Fahrkarte** NOUN
  ticket ◊ *Die Fahrkarten, bitte.* Tickets,
  please.
die **Fahrkartenausgabe** NOUN
  ticket office
der **Fahrkartenautomat** NOUN (GEN des
  **Fahrkartenautomaten**, PL die
  **Fahrkartenautomaten**)
  ticket machine
der **Fahrkartenschalter** NOUN (PL die
  **Fahrkartenschalter**)
  ticket office
**fahrlässig** ADJECTIVE
  negligent
der **Fahrlehrer** NOUN (PL die **Fahrlehrer**)
  driving instructor
der **Fahrplan** NOUN (PL die **Fahrpläne**)

☞

timetable
**fahrplanmäßig** ADJECTIVE
scheduled
der **Fahrpreis** NOUN (GEN des **Fahrpreises**, PL die **Fahrpreise**)
fare
die **Fahrprüfung** NOUN
driving test
das **Fahrrad** NOUN (PL die **Fahrräder**)
bicycle
der **Fahrradweg** NOUN (PL die **Fahrradwege**)
cycle lane
der **Fahrschein** NOUN (PL die **Fahrscheine**)
ticket ◊ *Die Fahrscheine, bitte.* Tickets, please.
der **Fahrscheinentwerter** NOUN (PL die **Fahrscheinentwerter**)
ticket stamping machine

> ⓘ *When you travel by train or tram (and sometimes by bus) you have to stamp your ticket in a* **Fahrscheinentwerter***. The machines are either on the platforms or inside the vehicles.*

die **Fahrschule** NOUN
driving school
der **Fahrstuhl** NOUN (PL die **Fahrstühle**)
lift
die **Fahrt** NOUN
[1] journey ◊ *Die Fahrt nach Hamburg war lang.* It was a long journey to Hamburg.
[2] trip ◊ *Am Wochenende haben wir eine Fahrt in den Schwarzwald gemacht.* We went on a trip to the Black Forest at the weekend.
♦ **Gute Fahrt!** Have a good journey.
die **Fahrtkosten** PL NOUN
travelling expenses
das **Fahrzeug** NOUN (PL die **Fahrzeuge**)
vehicle
der **Fahrzeugbrief** NOUN (PL die **Fahrzeugbriefe**)
log book
**fair** ADJECTIVE
fair ◊ *Das ist nicht fair!* That's not fair!
der **Faktor** NOUN (PL die **Faktoren**)
factor
die **Fakultät** NOUN
faculty
der **Falke** NOUN (GEN des **Falken**, PL die **Falken**)
falcon
der **Fall** NOUN (PL die **Fälle**)
case ◊ *Die Polizei untersucht den Fall.* The police are investigating the case. ◊ *In diesem Fall mache ich eine Ausnahme.* I'll make an exception in this case.
◊ *Welcher Fall steht nach "außer"?* Which case does "außer" take?

♦ **auf jeden Fall** definitely ◊ *Ich komme auf jeden Fall.* I'll definitely come.
♦ **für alle Fälle** just in case ◊ *Nimm für alle Fälle einen Schirm mit.* Take an umbrella, just in case.
♦ **Auf keinen Fall!** No way!
die **Falle** NOUN
trap
**fallen** VERB (PRESENT **fällt**, IMPERFECT **fiel**, PERFECT **ist gefallen**)
to fall
♦ **etwas fallen lassen (1)** to drop something ◊ *Lass es nicht fallen!* Don't drop it!
♦ **etwas fallen lassen (2)** to abandon something ◊ *Wir haben die Idee, in Frankreich Ferien zu machen, wieder fallen lassen.* We've abandoned the idea of spending our holidays in France.
♦ **eine Bemerkung fallen lassen** to make a remark
**fällen** VERB
♦ **einen Baum fällen** to fell a tree
♦ **ein Urteil fällen** to pronounce judgement
**fallenlassen** VERB see **fallen**
**fällig** ADJECTIVE
due
**falls** ADVERB
if
der **Fallschirm** NOUN (PL die **Fallschirme**)
parachute
**falsch** ADJECTIVE
[1] wrong ◊ *Die Antwort war falsch.* The answer was wrong.
♦ **jemanden falsch verstehen** to get somebody wrong
[2] false ◊ *falsche Zähne* false teeth
**fälschen** VERB
to forge
**fälschlicherweise** ADVERB
mistakenly
die **Fälschung** NOUN
forgery
die **Falte** NOUN
[1] fold ◊ *eine Falte im Papier* a fold in the paper
[2] crease ◊ *Die Hose ist voller Falten.* The trousers are all creased.
[3] wrinkle ◊ *Ihr Gesicht ist voller Falten.* Her face is all wrinkled.
[4] pleat ◊ *eine Rockfalte* a pleat in a skirt
**falten** VERB
to fold
**faltig** ADJECTIVE
[1] wrinkled ◊ *Er hat ein faltiges Gesicht.* He's got a wrinkled face.
[2] creased ◊ *Deine Hose ist ganz faltig.* Your trousers are all creased.
**familiär** ADJECTIVE
familiar

die **Familie** NOUN
family
der **Familienname** NOUN (GEN des **Familiennamens,** PL die **Familiennamen**)
surname
der **Familienstand** NOUN (PL die **Familienstände**)
marital status
der **Fan** NOUN (PL die **Fans**)
fan ◊ *Sie ist ein Fan von Sting.* She's a Sting fan.
**fand** VERB *see* **finden**
**fangen** VERB (PRESENT **fängt,** IMPERFECT **fing,** PERFECT **hat gefangen**)
to catch
die **Fantasie** NOUN
imagination
**fantasielos** ADJECTIVE
unimaginative
**fantasieren** VERB (PERFECT **hat fantasiert**)
to fantasize ◊ *Er fantasierte von einem Lottogewinn.* He fantasized about a win on the lottery.
**fantasievoll** ADJECTIVE
imaginative
**fantastisch** ADJECTIVE
fantastic
die **Farbe** NOUN
⑴ colour ◊ *Rosa ist Beates Lieblingsfarbe.* Pink is Beate's favourite colour.
⑵ paint ◊ *Hast du Farben, ich möchte was malen?* I'd like to do some painting, have you got any paints?
**farbecht** ADJECTIVE
colourfast
**färben** VERB
to dye ◊ *Sie hat ihre Haare gefärbt.* She's dyed her hair.
**farbenblind** ADJECTIVE
colour-blind
das **Farbfernsehen** NOUN
colour television
der **Farbfilm** NOUN (PL die **Farbfilme**)
colour film
das **Farbfoto** NOUN (PL die **Farbfotos**)
colour photograph
**farbig** ADJECTIVE
coloured
**farblos** ADJECTIVE
colourless
der **Farbstift** NOUN (PL die **Farbstifte**)
coloured pencil
der **Farbstoff** NOUN (PL die **Farbstoffe**)
dye
der **Farbton** NOUN (PL die **Farbtöne**)
shade
der **Fasan** NOUN (PL die **Fasane** *or* **Fasanen**)
pheasant
der **Fasching** NOUN (PL die **Faschinge**)
carnival

> *ⓘ The German carnival season lasts from 11 November to Shrove Tuesday but most events, fancy-dress processions and parties take place in the week leading up to Ash Wednesday.*

der **Faschingsdienstag** NOUN
Shrove Tuesday
die **Faser** NOUN
fibre
das **Fass** NOUN (GEN des **Fasses,** PL die **Fässer**)
barrel ◊ *ein Weinfass* a wine barrel
◆ **Bier vom Fass** draught beer
**fassen** VERB (PERFECT **hat gefasst**)
⑴ to grasp ◊ *Er fasste mich am Arm.* He grasped my arm.
⑵ to hold ◊ *Der Behälter fasst zwanzig Liter.* The container holds twenty litres.
⑶ to understand ◊ *Ich kann es nicht fassen, dass du das noch immer nicht gemacht hast.* I can't understand why you still haven't done it.
◆ **nicht zu fassen** unbelievable
◆ **sich fassen** to calm down
die **Fassung** NOUN
⑴ composure ◊ *Sie hat die Fassung verloren.* She lost her composure.
◆ **jemanden aus der Fassung bringen** to upset somebody
⑵ version ◊ *der Text in einer neuen Fassung* the text in a new version
**fassungslos** ADJECTIVE
speechless
**fast** ADVERB
almost
> *Be careful! The German word **fast** does not mean **fast**.*
**fasten** VERB
to fast
die **Fastenzeit** NOUN
Lent
das **Fastfood** NOUN (PL die **Fastfoods**)
fast food
die **Fastnacht** NOUN
carnival

> *ⓘ The German carnival season lasts from 11 November to Shrove Tuesday but most events, fancy-dress processions and parties take place in the week leading up to Ash Wednesday.*

**faul** ADJECTIVE
⑴ rotten ◊ *Der Apfel ist faul.* The apple's rotten.
⑵ lazy ◊ *Er ist der faulste Schüler.* He's our laziest pupil.
◆ **eine faule Ausrede** a lame excuse
◆ **Daran ist etwas faul.** There's something fishy about it.
**faulen** VERB
to rot

**F**

**faulenzen** VERB
to laze about

die **Faust** NOUN (PL die **Fäuste**)
fist
♦ **auf eigene Faust** off one's own bat

das **Fax** NOUN (GEN des **Faxes**, PL die **Faxe**)
fax

**faxen** VERB
to fax ◊ *jemandem etwas faxen* to fax
something to somebody

das **Faxgerät** NOUN (PL die **Faxgeräte**)
fax machine

die **Faxnummer** NOUN
fax number

der **FCKW** NOUN (= *Fluorchlorkohlenwasserstoff*)
CFC (= chlorofluorocarbon)

der **Februar** NOUN (GEN des **Februar** or **Februars**,
PL die **Februare**)
February ◊ *im Februar* in February ◊ *am
dritten Februar* on the third of February
◊ *Bonn, den 3. Februar 2005* Bonn, 3
February 2005 ◊ *Heute ist der zweite
Februar.* Today is the second of
February.

**fechten** VERB (PRESENT **ficht**, IMPERFECT **focht**,
PERFECT **hat gefochten**)
to fence

die **Feder** NOUN
[1] feather ◊ *Er hatte eine Feder am Hut.*
He had a feather in his hat.
[2] spring ◊ *Die Federn des Betts sind
ausgeleiert.* The bed springs have worn
out.

der **Federball** NOUN (PL die **Federbälle**)
shuttlecock

das **Federbett** NOUN (PL die **Federbetten**)
continental quilt

die **Federung** NOUN
suspension (*in car*)

die **Fee** NOUN
fairy

**fegen** VERB
to sweep

**fehl** ADJECTIVE
♦ **fehl am Platz** out of place

**fehlen** VERB
[1] to be absent ◊ *Er hat gestern in der
Schule gefehlt.* He was absent from
school yesterday.
[2] to be missing ◊ *Da fehlt ein Knopf.*
There's a button missing.
♦ **Wer fehlt?** Is anyone missing?
♦ **Mir fehlt das nötige Geld.** I haven't got
the money.
♦ **Du fehlst mir.** I miss you.
♦ **Was fehlt ihm?** What's wrong with him?

der **Fehler** NOUN (PL die **Fehler**)
[1] mistake ◊ *Wie viele Fehler hast du
gemacht?* How many mistakes did you
make?

[2] fault ◊ *Sein einziger Fehler ist, dass er
den Mund nicht halten kann.* His only
fault is that he can't keep his mouth shut.

die **Feier** NOUN
celebration

der **Feierabend** NOUN (PL die **Feierabende**)
clocking-off time
♦ **Feierabend machen** to clock off
♦ **Wann hat dein Vater Feierabend?** When
does your father finish work?
♦ **Schönen Feierabend!** Have a nice
evening.

**feierlich** ADJECTIVE
solemn

die **Feierlichkeit** NOUN
festivity (PL

**feiern** VERB
to celebrate

der **Feiertag** NOUN (PL die **Feiertage**)
holiday ◊ *ein öffentlicher Feiertag* a
public holiday

**feige** ADJECTIVE
see also **die Feige** NOUN
cowardly

die **Feige** NOUN
see also **feige** ADJECTIVE
fig

der **Feigling** NOUN (PL die **Feiglinge**)
coward

die **Feile** NOUN
file ◊ *eine Nagelfeile* a nailfile

**feilschen** VERB
to haggle

**fein** ADJECTIVE
[1] fine ◊ *feiner Sand* fine sand
[2] refined ◊ *feine Leute* refined people
♦ **Fein!** Great!

der **Feind** NOUN (PL die **Feinde**)
enemy

**feindlich** ADJECTIVE
hostile

die **Feindschaft** NOUN
hostility

das **Feld** NOUN (PL die **Felder**)
[1] field ◊ *Auf diesem Feld wächst Hafer.*
There are oats growing in this field.
[2] pitch ◊ *ein Fußballfeld* a football pitch
[3] square ◊ *Er rückte mit seinem Bauern
ein Feld vor.* He moved his pawn forward
one square.

der **Fels** NOUN (GEN des **Felsen**, PL die **Felsen**)
rock
♦ **die weißen Felsen von Dover** the white
cliffs of Dover

**feminin** ADJECTIVE
feminine

das **Fenster** NOUN (PL die **Fenster**)
window

der **Fensterladen** NOUN (PL die **Fensterläden**)
shutter

die **Fensterscheibe** NOUN
windowpane

die **Ferien** PL NOUN
   holidays
   ♦ **Ferien haben** to be on holiday
der **Ferienjob** NOUN (PL die **Ferienjobs**)
   holiday job
der **Ferienkurs** NOUN (GEN des **Ferienkurses,** PL
   die **Ferienkurse**)
   vacation course
das **Ferienlager** NOUN (PL die **Ferienlager**)
   holiday camp
   **fern** ADJECTIVE, ADVERB
   distant ◊ *in ferner Zukunft* in the distant
   future
   ♦ **fern von hier** a long way from here
   ♦ **der Ferne Osten** the Far East
die **Fernbedienung** NOUN
   remote control
das **Ferngespräch** NOUN (PL die
   **Ferngespräche**)
   long-distance call
das **Fernglas** NOUN (GEN des **Fernglases,** PL die
   **Ferngläser**)
   binoculars ◊ *ein Fernglas* a pair of
   binoculars
der **Fernsehapparat** NOUN (PL die
   **Fernsehapparate**)
   television set
das **Fernsehen** NOUN
   | see also **fernsehen** VERB |
   television ◊ *im Fernsehen* on television
   **fernsehen** VERB (PRESENT **sieht fern,** IMPERFECT
   **sah fern,** PERFECT **hat ferngesehen**)
   | see also **das Fernsehen** NOUN |
   to watch television
der **Fernseher** NOUN (PL die **Fernseher**)
   television set
der **Fernsehfilm** NOUN (PL die **Fernsehfilme**)
   TV film
die **Fernsehsendung** NOUN
   TV programme
die **Fernsehserie** NOUN
   TV series
der **Fernsprecher** NOUN (PL die **Fernsprecher**)
   telephone
die **Fernsteuerung** NOUN
   remote control
die **Ferse** NOUN
   heel ◊ *Ich habe eine Blase an der Ferse.*
   I've got a blister on my heel.
   **fertig** ADJECTIVE
   [1] ready ◊ *Das Essen ist fertig.* Dinner's
   ready.
   [2] finished ◊ *Der Aufsatz ist fertig.* The
   essay's finished. ◊ *Bist du mit deinen
   Hausaufgaben fertig?* Have you finished
   your homework?
   ♦ **es fertig bringen, etwas zu tun** to bring
   oneself to do something ◊ *Ich bringe es
   nicht fertig, ihr das zu sagen.* I can't bring
   myself to tell her.
   ♦ **etwas fertig machen** to finish something
   ◊ *Ich muss noch die Matheaufgaben*

*fertig machen.* I've just got to finish my
maths homework.
   ♦ **jemanden fertig machen (1)** to wear
   somebody out ◊ *Die Radtour hat mich
   fertig gemacht.* The cycling trip wore me
   out.
   ♦ **jemanden fertig machen (2)** to tear
   somebody off a strip ◊ *Meine
   Englischlehrerin hat mich heute fertig
   gemacht.* My English teacher tore me off
   a strip today.
   ♦ **sich fertig machen** to get ready
das **Fertiggericht** NOUN (PL die **Fertiggerichte**)
   ready meal
   **fertigmachen** VERB see **fertig**
   **fesselnd** ADJECTIVE
   captivating
das **Fest** NOUN (PL die **Feste**)
   | see also **fest** ADJECTIVE |
   [1] party ◊ *Fritz macht am Samstag ein
   Fest.* Fritz is having a party on Saturday.
   [2] festival ◊ *das Backnanger Straßenfest*
   the Backnang Street Festival
   ♦ **Frohes Fest!** Happy Christmas!
   **fest** ADJECTIVE, ADVERB
   | see also **das Fest** NOUN |
   firm ◊ *Er hielt sie mit festem Griff.* He
   had a firm grip of her. ◊ *Er hat einen
   festen Händedruck.* He has a firm
   handshake.
   ♦ **ein festes Einkommen** a regular income
   ♦ **fest schlafen** to sleep soundly
   ♦ **feste Nahrung** solids
   **festbinden** VERB (IMPERFECT **band fest,** PERFECT
   **hat festgebunden**)
   to tie ◊ *Sie hat ihren Hund am Baum
   festgebunden.* She tied her dog to the
   tree.
   **festhalten** VERB (PRESENT **hält fest,** IMPERFECT
   **hielt fest,** PERFECT **hat festgehalten**)
   to keep hold of ◊ *Du musst das Steuer
   festhalten.* You must keep hold of the
   wheel.
   ♦ **sich festhalten an** to hold on to ◊ *Sie
   hielt sich am Geländer fest.* She held on
   to the banister.
   **festigen** VERB
   to strengthen
die **Festigkeit** NOUN
   strength
das **Festland** NOUN
   mainland
   **festlegen** VERB (PERFECT **hat festgelegt**)
   to fix ◊ *einen Termin festlegen* to fix a
   date
   ♦ **sich festlegen** to commit oneself
   **festlich** ADJECTIVE
   festive
   **festmachen** VERB (PERFECT **hat festgemacht**)
   [1] to fix ◊ *Habt ihr den Termin schon
   festgemacht?* Have you fixed the date
   yet?

**F**

☞

2 to moor ◊ *Wir haben das Boot im Hafen festgemacht.* We moored the boat in the harbour.

die **Festnahme** NOUN
arrest

**festnehmen** VERB (PRESENT **nimmt fest,** IMPERFECT **nahm fest,** PERFECT **hat festgenommen)**
to arrest

die **Festplatte** NOUN
hard disk

die **Festspiele** NEUT PL NOUN
festival

**feststehen** VERB (IMPERFECT **stand fest,** PERFECT **hat festgestanden)**
to be certain ◊ *So viel steht fest: ...* This much is certain: ...

**feststellen** VERB (PERFECT **hat festgestellt)**
1 to establish ◊ *Wir konnten nicht feststellen, wer das geschrieben hatte.* We couldn't establish who'd written it.
2 to see ◊ *Ich stelle fest, dass du schon wieder nicht aufgepasst hast.* I see that you haven't been paying attention again.
◆ **Wir haben da einen Fehler festgestellt.** We've detected an error.

der **Festtag** NOUN
special day

das **Fett** NOUN (PL die **Fette)**

see also **fett** ADJECTIVE

fat

**fett** ADJECTIVE

see also **das Fett** NOUN

fat ◊ *Er ist zu fett.* He's too fat.
◆ **fettes Essen** greasy food
◆ **fette Schrift** bold type

**fettarm** ADJECTIVE
low-fat

**fettig** ADJECTIVE
greasy

der **Fetzen** NOUN (PL die **Fetzen)**
scrap ◊ *ein Fetzen Papier* a scrap of paper

**feucht** ADJECTIVE
1 damp ◊ *etwas mit einem feuchten Tuch abwischen* to wipe something with a damp cloth
2 humid ◊ *Das Klima ist sehr feucht.* The climate's very humid.

die **Feuchtigkeit** NOUN
1 moisture ◊ *Salz zieht Feuchtigkeit an.* Salt attracts moisture.
2 humidity ◊ *hohe Luftfeuchtigkeit* high humidity

das **Feuer** NOUN (PL die **Feuer)**
fire
◆ **Haben Sie Feuer?** Have you got a light?

der **Feuerlöscher** NOUN (PL die **Feuerlöscher)**
fire extinguisher

die **Feuerwehr** NOUN (PL die **Feuerwehren)**
fire brigade

das **Feuerwehrauto** NOUN (PL die **Feuerwehrautos)**
fire engine

der **Feuerwehrmann** NOUN (PL die **Feuerwehrleute** or **Feuerwehrmänner)**
fireman

das **Feuerwerk** NOUN (PL die **Feuerwerke)**
fireworks ◊ *Wir waren beim Feuerwerk.* We went to the fireworks.

das **Feuerzeug** NOUN (PL die **Feuerzeuge)**
lighter

das **Fieber** NOUN (PL die **Fieber)**
1 fever ◊ *Das Fieber wird sich in ein paar Tagen senken.* The fever will pass in a couple of days.
2 temperature ◊ *Hast du Fieber?* Have you got a temperature?

**fiel** VERB *see* **fallen**

**fies** ADJECTIVE
nasty

die **Figur** NOUN
figure ◊ *Sie hat eine gute Figur.* She's got a good figure.
◆ **eine Schachfigur** a chessman

die **Filiale** NOUN
branch

der **Film** NOUN (PL die **Filme)**
film

**filmen** VERB
to film

die **Filmkomödie** NOUN
comedy film

der **Filter** NOUN (PL die **Filter)**
filter

die **Filterzigarette** NOUN
tipped cigarette

der **Filzstift** NOUN (PL die **Filzstifte)**
felt-tip pen

das **Finanzamt** NOUN (PL die **Finanzämter)**
Inland Revenue Office

**finanziell** ADJECTIVE
financial

**finanzieren** VERB (PERFECT **hat finanziert)**
to finance

**finden** VERB (IMPERFECT **fand,** PERFECT **hat gefunden)**
1 to find ◊ *Hast du deinen Radiergummi gefunden?* Have you found your rubber?
2 to think ◊ *Ich finde, er sieht gut aus.* I think he's good-looking. ◊ *Ich finde sie nicht attraktiv.* I don't think she's attractive.
◆ **Ich finde nichts dabei, wenn ...** I don't see what's wrong with ... ◊ *Ich finde nichts dabei, wenn man mal einen Tag faulenzt.* I don't see what's wrong with lazing about for one day.
◆ **Das wird sich finden.** Things will work out.

**fing** VERB *see* **fangen**

der **Finger** NOUN (PL die **Finger)**
finger

der **Fingerabdruck** NOUN (PL die **Fingerabdrücke**)
fingerprint
♦ **genetische Fingerabdrücke** genetic fingerprinting

der **Fingernagel** NOUN (PL die **Fingernägel**)
fingernail

der **Finne** NOUN (GEN des **Finnen**, PL die **Finnen**)
Finn

die **Finnin** NOUN
Finn

**finnisch** ADJECTIVE
Finnish

**Finnland** NEUT NOUN
Finland
♦ **aus Finnland** from Finland
♦ **nach Finnland** to Finland

**finster** ADJECTIVE
[1] dark ◊ *Hier ist es aber finster.* It's dark in here.
[2] sinister ◊ *finstere Gestalten* sinister figures
♦ **ein finsteres Gesicht** a grim face

die **Finsternis** NOUN
darkness

die **Firma** NOUN (PL die **Firmen**)
firm

der **Fisch** NOUN (PL die **Fische**)
fish ◊ *Ich habe fünf Fische.* I've got five fish.
♦ **Fische** Pisces ◊ *Adelheid ist Fisch.* Adelheid's Pisces.

**fischen** VERB
to fish ◊ *Sonntags geht Alex immer fischen.* Alex always goes fishing on Sundays.

der **Fischer** NOUN (PL die **Fischer**)
fisherman

die **Fischerei** NOUN
fishing

der **Fischhändler** NOUN (PL die **Fischhändler**)
fishmonger

**fit** ADJECTIVE
fit ◊ *Ich halte mich mit Schwimmen fit.* I keep fit by swimming.

das **Fitnesszentrum** NOUN (PL die **Fitnesszentren**)
fitness centre

**fix** ADJECTIVE
♦ **fix und fertig (1)** finished ◊ *Alles war fix und fertig.* Everything was finished.
♦ **fix und fertig (2)** all in ◊ *Ich bin fix und fertig.* I'm all in.

der **Fixer** NOUN (PL die **Fixer**)
junkie

**flach** ADJECTIVE
[1] flat ◊ *Norddeutschland ist flach.* North Germany's flat.
[2] shallow ◊ *Ich brauche eine flache Schale.* I need a shallow bowl.

die **Fläche** NOUN

area ◊ *eine Fläche von hundert Quadratkilometern* an area of a hundred square kilometres

das **Flachland** NOUN
lowland

**flackern** VERB
to flicker

die **Flagge** NOUN
flag

die **Flamme** NOUN
flame

die **Flasche** NOUN
bottle ◊ *eine Flasche Mineralwasser* a bottle of mineral water

der **Flaschenöffner** NOUN (PL die **Flaschenöffner**)
bottle-opener

**flauschig** ADJECTIVE
fluffy

der **Fleck** NOUN (PL die **Flecke**)
[1] stain ◊ *Der Wein hat einen Fleck auf dem Teppich gemacht.* The wine left a stain on the carpet.
[2] spot ◊ *Das ist ein hübscher Fleck.* This is a beautiful spot.

das **Fleckenmittel** NOUN (PL die **Fleckenmittel**)
stain remover

**fleckig** ADJECTIVE
[1] spotted ◊ *Ein Dalmatiner hat ein fleckiges Fell.* A Dalmatian has a spotted coat.
[2] stained ◊ *Die Tischdecke ist ganz fleckig.* The tablecloth's all stained.

die **Fledermaus** NOUN (PL die **Fledermäuse**)
bat

das **Fleisch** NOUN
meat ◊ *Ich esse kein Fleisch.* I don't eat meat.

die **Fleischbrühe** NOUN
meat stock

der **Fleischer** NOUN (PL die **Fleischer**)
butcher

die **Fleischerei** NOUN
butcher's

der **Fleiß** NOUN (GEN des **Fleißes**)
hard work ◊ *Mit etwas Fleiß könntest du deine Noten verbessern.* With a bit of hard work you could improve your marks.

**fleißig** ADJECTIVE
hard-working ◊ *Silke ist eine fleißige Schülerin.* Silke's a hard-working pupil.
♦ **Ich war heute schon fleißig.** I've already done quite a bit of work today.

**flexibel** ADJECTIVE
flexible

**flicken** VERB
to mend

die **Fliege** NOUN
[1] fly ◊ *Er tut keiner Fliege etwas zuleide.* He wouldn't hurt a fly.

**F**

☞

2 bow tie ◊ *Er trug eine Fliege.* He was wearing a bow tie.

**fliegen** VERB (IMPERFECT **flog**, PERFECT **ist geflogen**)
to fly

**fliehen** VERB (IMPERFECT **floh**, PERFECT **ist geflohen**)
to flee

die **Fliese** NOUN
tile

das **Fließband** NOUN (PL die **Fließbänder**)
assembly line

**fließen** VERB (IMPERFECT **floss**, PERFECT **ist geflossen**)
to flow

**fließend** ADJECTIVE, ADVERB
1 running ◊ *fließendes Wasser* running water
2 fluent ◊ *Sie spricht fließend Englisch.* She is fluent in English.

**flink** ADJECTIVE
nimble

die **Flitterwochen** FEM PL NOUN
honeymoon

**flitzen** VERB (PERFECT **ist geflitzt**)
to dash

die **Flocke** NOUN
flake ◊ *eine Schneeflocke* a snowflake

**flog** VERB see **fliegen**

der **Floh** NOUN (PL die **Flöhe**)
flea

der **Flohmarkt** NOUN (PL die **Flohmärkte**)
flea market

die **Floskel** NOUN
set phrase

**floss** VERB see **fließen**

die **Flosse** NOUN
1 fin ◊ *die Flosse eines Hais* a shark's fin
2 flipper ◊ *Er hat seine Flossen mit ins Schwimmbad genommen.* He took his flippers with him to the swimming baths.

die **Flöte** NOUN
1 flute ◊ *Cordula spielt Flöte.* Cordula plays the flute.
2 recorder ◊ *Phil spielt Flöte.* Phil plays the recorder.

**fluchen** VERB
to curse

**flüchtig** ADJECTIVE
at large ◊ *Der Einbrecher ist noch flüchtig.* The burglar's still at large.
♦ **jemanden nur flüchtig kennen** to know somebody only superficially

der **Flüchtling** NOUN (PL die **Flüchtlinge**)
refugee

der **Flug** NOUN (PL die **Flüge**)
flight ◊ *Der Flug nach Atlanta ist verspätet.* The flight to Atlanta's been delayed.

das **Flugblatt** NOUN (PL die **Flugblätter**)
leaflet

der **Flügel** NOUN (PL die **Flügel**)

1 wing ◊ *die Flügel des Adlers* the eagle's wings
2 grand piano

der **Fluggast** NOUN (PL die **Fluggäste**)
airline passenger

die **Fluggesellschaft** NOUN
airline

der **Flughafen** NOUN (PL die **Flughäfen**)
airport

der **Fluglotse** NOUN (GEN des **Fluglotsen**, PL die **Fluglotsen**)
air traffic controller

der **Flugplan** NOUN (PL die **Flugpläne**)
flight schedule

der **Flugplatz** NOUN (GEN des **Flugplatzes**, PL die **Flugplätze**)
1 airport ◊ *Wir bringen dich zum Flugplatz.* We'll take you to the airport.
2 airfield ◊ *Dieser Flugplatz ist nur für Privatflugzeuge.* This airfield is only for private planes.

der **Flugschein** NOUN (PL die **Flugscheine**)
plane ticket

das **Flugticket** NOUN (PL die **Flugtickets**)
plane ticket

das **Flugzeug** NOUN (PL die **Flugzeuge**)
aeroplane

die **Flugzeugentführung** NOUN
hijacking

das **Fluor** NOUN
fluorine

der **Flur** NOUN (PL die **Flure**)
corridor
Be careful! *Flur* does not mean *floor*.

der **Fluss** NOUN (GEN des **Flusses**, PL die **Flüsse**)
river

das **Flüsschen** NOUN (PL die **Flüsschen**)
little river

**flüssig** ADJECTIVE
liquid

die **Flüssigkeit** NOUN
liquid

das **Flussufer** NOUN (PL die **Flussufer**)
river bank ◊ *am Flussufer* on the river bank

**flüstern** VERB
to whisper

die **Flut** NOUN (PL die **Fluten**)
1 flood ◊ *Wir haben eine Flut von Briefen bekommen.* We received a flood of letters.
2 high tide ◊ *Das Schiff läuft bei Flut aus.* The ship sails at high tide.

das **Flutlicht** NOUN (PL die **Flutlichter**)
floodlight

der **Föhn** NOUN (PL die **Föhne**)
1 foehn wind ◊ *Heute ist Föhn.* There's a foehn wind blowing today.

*ℹ The foehn wind is a dry, warm wind usually found to the north of the Alps.*

2 hair dryer
**föhnen** VERB
    to blow-dry
die **Folge** NOUN
    1 result ◊ *Er starb an den Folgen des Unfalls.* He died as a result of the accident.
    ♦ **etwas zur Folge haben** to result in something ◊ *Deine Faulheit wird schlechte Noten zur Folge haben.* Your laziness will result in bad marks.
    ♦ **Folgen haben** to have consequences ◊ *Das wird schlimme Folgen haben.* That'll have serious consequences.
    2 episode ◊ *Hast du die letzte Folge der "Lindenstraße" gesehen?* Did you see the latest episode of "Lindenstraße"?
    ♦ **ein Roman in Folgen** a serialized novel
**folgen** VERB (PERFECT **ist gefolgt**)
    to follow ◊ *Uns ist ein grünes Auto gefolgt.* We were followed by a green car. ◊ *Folgen Sie dem Wagen da.* Follow that car.
    ♦ **Ich konnte ihm nicht folgen.** I couldn't follow what he was saying.
    ♦ **Meine Kinder folgen nicht immer.** My children don't always do what they're told.
**folgend** ADJECTIVE
    following
die **Folgerung** NOUN
    conclusion
**folglich** ADVERB
    consequently
**folgsam** ADJECTIVE
    obedient
die **Folie** NOUN
    foil
**foltern** VERB
    to torture
der **Fön** Ⓡ NOUN (PL die **Föne**)
    hair dryer
**fordern** VERB
    to demand
die **Forderung** NOUN
    demand
die **Forelle** NOUN
    trout ◊ *drei Forellen* three trout
die **Form** NOUN
    1 shape ◊ *Das Auto hat eine elegante Form.* The car has an elegant shape.
    2 mould ◊ *Das Metall wird in eine Form gegossen.* The metal is poured into a mould.
    3 baking tin
das **Format** NOUN (PL die **Formate**)
    format
**formatieren** VERB (PERFECT **hat formatiert**)
    to format
die **Formel** NOUN

formula
**formen** VERB
    to form
**förmlich** ADJECTIVE
    formal
das **Formular** NOUN (PL die **Formulare**)
    form ◊ *ein Formular ausfüllen* to fill in a form
**formulieren** VERB (PERFECT **hat formuliert**)
    to formulate
der **Forscher** NOUN (PL die **Forscher**)
    1 research scientist ◊ *Die Forscher haben noch keinen Impfstoff gegen Aids entwickelt.* Research scientists have still not developed an AIDS vaccine.
    2 explorer ◊ *Eine Gruppe von Forschern ist im Amazonasgebiet verschollen.* A group of explorers is missing in the Amazon region.
die **Forschung** NOUN
    research
**fort** ADVERB
    gone ◊ *Mein Geldbeutel ist fort.* My purse is gone.
    ♦ **und so fort** and so on
    ♦ **in einem fort** on and on
    ♦ **Fort mit dir!** Away with you!
sich **fortbewegen** VERB (PERFECT **hat sich fortbewegt**)
    to move
**fortbleiben** VERB (IMPERFECT **blieb fort**, PERFECT **ist fortgeblieben**)
    to stay away
**fortfahren** VERB (PRESENT **fährt fort**, IMPERFECT **fuhr fort**, PERFECT **ist fortgefahren**)
    1 to leave ◊ *Sie sind gestern fortgefahren.* They left yesterday.
    2 to continue ◊ *Er fuhr in seiner Rede fort.* He continued with his speech.
**fortgeschritten** ADJECTIVE
    advanced
der **Fortschritt** NOUN (PL die **Fortschritte**)
    progress ◊ *Fortschritte machen* to make progress
**fortschrittlich** ADJECTIVE
    progressive
**fortsetzen** VERB (PERFECT **hat fortgesetzt**)
    to continue
die **Fortsetzung** NOUN
    1 continuation ◊ *die Fortsetzung des Krieges* the continuation of the war
    2 sequel ◊ *Hast du die Fortsetzung gelesen?* Have you read the sequel?
    ♦ **Morgen kommt die Fortsetzung des Krimis.** The detective story will be continued tomorrow.
    ♦ **Fortsetzung folgt** to be continued
das **Foto** NOUN (PL die **Fotos**)
    photo
der **Fotoapparat** NOUN (PL die **Fotoapparate**)
    camera

F

der **Fotograf** NOUN (GEN des **Fotografen,** PL die **Fotografen)**
  photographer
  *Be careful! Fotograf does not mean photograph.*

die **Fotografie** NOUN
  [1] photography ◊ *Die Fotografie ist sein Hobby.* His hobby is photography.
  [2] photograph ◊ *Ich habe eine Fotografie davon gesehen.* I've seen a photograph of it.

**fotografieren** VERB (PERFECT **hat fotografiert)**
  [1] to take a photo of ◊ *Kannst du uns mal fotografieren?* Can you take a photo of us?
  [2] to take photographs ◊ *Ich fotografiere in den Ferien nie.* I never take photographs on holiday.

die **Fotokopie** NOUN
  photocopy

**Fr.** ABBREVIATION (= *Frau*)
  [1] Mrs
  [2] Ms

die **Fracht** NOUN
  freight ◊ *Frachtkosten* freight charges

die **Frage** NOUN
  question ◊ *Könntest du bitte meine Frage beantworten?* Could you please answer my question?
  ◆ **etwas in Frage stellen** to question something
  ◆ **jemandem eine Frage stellen** to ask somebody a question
  ◆ **nicht in Frage kommen** to be out of the question

der **Fragebogen** NOUN (PL die **Fragebogen)**
  questionnaire

**fragen** VERB
  to ask ◊ *Kann ich dich was fragen?* Can I ask you something?

das **Fragezeichen** NOUN (PL die **Fragezeichen)**
  question mark

**fraglich** ADJECTIVE
  doubtful ◊ *Es ist sehr fraglich, ob wir kommen können.* It's very doubtful whether we can come.

der **Franc** NOUN (GEN des **Franc,** PL die **Francs)**
  franc ◊ *Er bezahlte 500 Franc.* He paid 500 francs.

der **Franken** NOUN (PL die **Franken)**
  franc ◊ *Er bezahlte 50 Franken.* He paid 50 francs.
  ◆ **der Schweizer Franken** the Swiss franc

**frankieren** VERB (PERFECT **hat frankiert)**
  ◆ **einen Brief frankieren** to put a stamp on a letter
  ◆ **ein frankierter Briefumschlag** a stamped self-addressed envelope

**Frankreich** NEUT NOUN
  France
  ◆ **aus Frankreich** from France
  ◆ **in Frankreich** in France

  ◆ **nach Frankreich** to France

der **Franzose** NOUN (GEN des **Franzosen,** PL die **Franzosen)**
  Frenchman
  ◆ **Er ist Franzose.** He's French.
  ◆ **die Franzosen** the French

die **Französin** NOUN
  Frenchwoman
  ◆ **Sie ist Französin.** She's French.

das **Französisch** NOUN (GEN des **Französischen)**
  | *see also* **französisch** ADJECTIVE |
  French ◊ *Er lernt Französisch in der Schule.* He's learning French at school.

**französisch** ADJECTIVE
  | *see also* **das Französisch** NOUN |
  French

**fraß** VERB *see* **fressen**

die **Frau** NOUN
  [1] woman ◊ *Sie ist eine nette Frau.* She's a nice woman.
  [2] wife ◊ *Herr Arnold ist mit seiner Frau gekommen.* Mr Arnold came with his wife.
  ◆ **Sehr geehrte Frau Braun (1)** Dear Mrs Braun
  ◆ **Sehr geehrte Frau Braun (2)** Dear Ms Braun

  > ❶ *Generally Frau is used to address all women whether married or not.*

  ◆ **Frau Doktor** Doctor

der **Frauenarzt** NOUN (GEN des **Frauenarztes,** PL die **Frauenärzte)**
  gynaecologist

die **Frauenbewegung** NOUN
  women's movement

das **Fräulein** NOUN (PL die **Fräulein)**
  [1] young lady ◊ *Würde das Fräulein vielleicht ihr Zimmer aufräumen?* Would the young lady perhaps tidy up her room?
  [2] Miss ◊ *Liebes Fräulein Dümmler* Dear Miss Dümmler

  > ❶ *Fräulein is hardly ever used nowadays and Frau is used instead to address all women whether married or not.*

**frech** ADJECTIVE
  cheeky

die **Frechheit** NOUN
  cheek

**frei** ADJECTIVE
  free
  ◆ **Ist der Platz hier frei?** Is this seat taken?
  ◆ **Wir haben im Momente keine freien Stellen.** We haven't got any vacancies at the moment.
  ◆ **ein freier Mitarbeiter** a freelancer
  ◆ **im Freien** in the open air

das **Freibad** NOUN (PL die **Freibäder)**

open-air swimming pool ◊ *Im Sommer gehe ich gern ins Freibad.* I like going to the open-air swimming pool in the summer.

**freibekommen** VERB (IMPERFECT **bekam frei,** PERFECT **hat freibekommen**)
- ♦ **jemanden freibekommen** to get somebody released
- ♦ **einen Tag freibekommen** to get a day off

**freigebig** ADJECTIVE
generous

**freihalten** VERB (PRESENT **hält frei,** IMPERFECT **hielt frei,** PERFECT **hat freigehalten**)
to keep free ◊ *Soll ich einen Platz für dich freihalten?* Shall I keep a seat for you?
- ♦ **"Einfahrt freihalten"** "Keep clear"

die **Freiheit** NOUN
- [1] freedom
- [2] liberty ◊ *sich Freiheiten herausnehmen* to take liberties

**freilassen** VERB (PRESENT **lässt frei,** IMPERFECT **ließ frei,** PERFECT **hat freigelassen**)
to free

**freinehmen** VERB (PRESENT **nimmt frei,** IMPERFECT **nahm frei,** PERFECT **hat freigenommen**)
- ♦ **sich einen Tag freinehmen** to take a day off ◊ *Ich werde mir morgen einen Tag freinehmen.* I'm taking the day off tomorrow.

der **Freitag** NOUN (PL die **Freitage**)
Friday ◊ *am Freitag* on Friday

**freitags** ADVERB
on Fridays

**freiwillig** ADJECTIVE
voluntary

die **Freizeit** NOUN
spare time ◊ *Was machst du in deiner Freizeit?* What do you do in your spare time?

die **Freizeitbeschäftigung** NOUN
leisure activity

der **Freizeitpark** NOUN (PL die **Freizeitparks**)
amusement park

das **Freizeitzentrum** NOUN (PL die **Freizeitzentren**)
leisure centre

**fremd** ADJECTIVE
- [1] strange ◊ *eine fremde Umgebung* strange surroundings
- [2] foreign ◊ *fremde Länder und Sprachen* foreign countries and languages
- ♦ **Ich bin in London fremd.** I'm a stranger to London.

der **Fremdenverkehr** NOUN
tourism

das **Fremdenzimmer** NOUN (PL die **Fremdenzimmer**)
guest room

die **Fremdsprache** NOUN

foreign language

das **Fremdwort** NOUN (PL die **Fremdwörter**)
foreign word

**fressen** VERB (PRESENT **frisst,** IMPERFECT **fraß,** PERFECT **hat gefressen**)
to eat
- ♦ **Er frisst wie ein Schwein.** He eats like a pig.

die **Freude** NOUN
- [1] joy ◊ *Welche Freude!* What joy!
- [2] delight ◊ *Zu meiner Freude hatten wir gestern keine Schule.* To my delight we didn't have any school yesterday.
- ♦ **Ich wollte dir eine Freude machen.** I wanted to make you happy.

**freuen** VERB
- ♦ **sich freuen** to be glad ◊ *Ich freue mich, dass du gekommen bist.* I'm glad you've come.
- ♦ **Freust du dich denn gar nicht?** Aren't you pleased at all?
- ♦ **sich auf etwas freuen** to look forward to something ◊ *Wir freuen uns darauf, euch zu sehen.* We're looking forward to seeing you.
- ♦ **sich über etwas freuen** to be pleased with something ◊ *Sie hat sich sehr über das Geschenk gefreut.* She was very pleased with the present.
- ♦ **Dein Brief hat mich sehr gefreut.** Your letter made me very happy.

der **Freund** NOUN (PL die **Freunde**)
- [1] friend ◊ *Alle meine Freunde waren da.* All my friends were there.
- [2] boyfriend ◊ *Hast du einen Freund?* Have you got a boyfriend?

die **Freundin** NOUN
- [1] friend ◊ *Wiltrud kommt mit ihrer Freundin.* Wiltrud's coming with her friend.
- [2] girlfriend ◊ *Tobias hat keine Freundin.* Tobias hasn't got a girlfriend.

**freundlich** ADJECTIVE
- [1] friendly ◊ *ein freundliches Lächeln* a friendly smile
- [2] kind ◊ *Das ist sehr freundlich von Ihnen.* That's very kind of you.

**freundlicherweise** ADVERB
kindly ◊ *Er hat uns freundlicherweise geholfen.* He kindly helped us.

die **Freundlichkeit** NOUN
friendliness

die **Freundschaft** NOUN
friendship

der **Frieden** NOUN (PL die **Frieden**)
peace
- ♦ **im Frieden** in peacetime

der **Friedhof** NOUN (PL die **Friedhöfe**)
cemetery

**friedlich** ADJECTIVE
peaceful

**frieren** VERB (IMPERFECT **fror,** PERFECT **hat gefroren**)

**F**

☞

to freeze ◊ *Ich friere.* I'm freezing.
♦ **Letzte Nacht hat es gefroren.** It was frosty last night.

die **Frikadelle** NOUN
rissole

**frisch** ADJECTIVE
fresh ◊ *frische Milch* fresh milk ◊ *ein frischer Wind* a fresh wind
♦ **Frisch gestrichen!** Wet paint!
♦ **sich frisch machen** to freshen oneself up

der **Friseur** NOUN (PL die **Friseure**)
hairdresser

die **Friseuse** NOUN
hairdresser

**frisieren** VERB (PERFECT **hat frisiert**)
♦ **jemanden frisieren** to do somebody's hair
♦ **sich frisieren** to do one's hair

**frisst** VERB *see* **fressen**

die **Frist** NOUN
deadline ◊ *eine Frist einhalten* to meet a deadline

die **Frisur** NOUN
hairdo

**Frl.** ABBREVIATION (= *Fräulein*)
Miss

**froh** ADJECTIVE
happy ◊ *frohe Gesichter* happy faces
♦ **Ich bin froh, dass ...** I'm glad that ...

**fröhlich** ADJECTIVE
cheerful

die **Fröhlichkeit** NOUN
cheerfulness

**fromm** ADJECTIVE
devout

der **Fronleichnam** NOUN
Corpus Christi ◊ *an Fronleichnam* on Corpus Christi

> ❶ *Fronleichnam is the second Thursday after Whitsun and is a public holiday in predominantly Catholic areas.*

**fror** VERB *see* **frieren**

der **Frosch** NOUN (PL die **Frösche**)
frog

der **Frost** NOUN (PL die **Fröste**)
frost ◊ *ein strenger Frost* a hard frost

**frösteln** VERB
to shiver

das **Frottee** NOUN (GEN des **Frottees**)
towelling

das **Frottiertuch** NOUN (PL die **Frottiertücher**)
towel

die **Frucht** NOUN (PL die **Früchte**)
fruit

**fruchtbar** ADJECTIVE
[1] fruitful ◊ *ein fruchtbares Gespräch* a fruitful conversation
[2] fertile ◊ *fruchtbarer Boden* fertile soil

der **Fruchtsaft** NOUN (PL die **Fruchtsäfte**)
fruit juice

**früh** ADJECTIVE, ADVERB
early ◊ *Komm lieber etwas früher.* It's better if you come a bit earlier.
♦ **heute früh** this morning

**früher** ADJECTIVE, ADVERB
[1] former ◊ *eine frühere Schülerin unserer Schule* a former pupil of our school
[2] once ◊ *Hier stand früher ein Haus.* A house once stood here.
♦ **Früher war das anders.** That used to be different.

**frühestens** ADVERB
at the earliest

das **Frühjahr** NOUN (PL die **Frühjahre**)
spring ◊ *im Frühjahr* in spring

der **Frühling** NOUN (PL die **Frühlinge**)
spring ◊ *im Frühling* in spring

das **Frühstück** NOUN
breakfast

**frühstücken** VERB
to have breakfast

**frustrieren** VERB (PERFECT **hat frustriert**)
to frustrate

der **Fuchs** NOUN (GEN des **Fuchses**, PL die **Füchse**)
fox

**fügen** VERB
to join ◊ *Er fügte ein Teil an ein anderes.* He joined one piece to another.
♦ **sich fügen** to be obedient

**fühlen** VERB
to feel ◊ *Fühl mal, wie weich das ist.* Feel how soft it is. ◊ *Ich fühle mich wohl.* I feel fine.

**fuhr** VERB *see* **fahren**

**führen** VERB
[1] to lead ◊ *Sie führte uns nach draußen.* She led us outside.
♦ **ein Geschäft führen** to run a business
[2] to be winning ◊ *Welche Mannschaft führt?* Which team's winning?

der **Führer** NOUN (PL die **Führer**)
[1] leader ◊ *der Parteiführer* the party leader
[2] guide ◊ *Unser Führer zeigte uns alle Sehenswürdigkeiten.* Our guide showed us all the sights.
[3] guidebook ◊ *Hast du einen Führer von Rom?* Have you got a guidebook of Rome?

der **Führerschein** NOUN (PL die **Führerscheine**)
driving licence
♦ **Wann hast du deinen Führerschein gemacht?** When did you sit your driving test?

die **Führung** NOUN
[1] lead ◊ *Unsere Mannschaft liegt in Führung.* Our team is in the lead.
[2] management ◊ *Das Geschäft hat unter neuer Führung wieder eröffnet.*

The business has reopened under new management.
**3** guided tour ◊ *Führungen durchs Museum finden stündlich statt.* There are guided tours of the museum every hour.

**füllen** VERB
**1** to fill ◊ *Sie füllte das Glas bis zum Rand.* She filled the glass to the brim.
**2** to stuff ◊ *Heute gibt es gefüllte Paprika.* We're having stuffed peppers today.

der **Füller** NOUN (PL die **Füller**)
fountain pen

der **Füllfederhalter** NOUN (PL die **Füllfederhalter**)
fountain pen

die **Füllung** NOUN
filling

das **Fundament** NOUN (PL die **Fundamente**)
foundations

das **Fundbüro** NOUN (PL die **Fundbüros**)
lost property office

**fundiert** ADJECTIVE
sound ◊ *fundierte Englischkenntnisse* a sound knowledge of English

**fünf** NUMBER
see also **die Fünf** NOUN
five

die **Fünf** NOUN
see also **fünf** NUMBER
**1** five
**2** poor

> 🛈 *German marks range from one (**sehr gut**) to six (**ungenügend**).*

**fünfhundert** NUMBER
five hundred

**fünfte** ADJECTIVE
fifth ◊ *Ich erkläre dir das jetzt zum fünften Mal.* This is the fifth time I've explained this to you. ◊ *Er kam als Fünfter.* He was the fifth to arrive.

**fünfzehn** NUMBER
fifteen

**fünfzig** NUMBER
fifty

der **Funke** NOUN (GEN des **Funkens**, PL die **Funken**)
spark

**funkeln** VERB
to sparkle

das **Funkgerät** NOUN (PL die **Funkgeräte**)
radio set

die **Funktion** NOUN
function

**funktionieren** VERB (PERFECT **hat funktioniert**)
to work

die **Funktionstaste** NOUN
function key

**für** PREPOSITION
*The preposition **für** takes the accusative.*
for ◊ *Das ist für dich.* This is for you.
♦ **was für** what kind of ◊ *Was für ein Fahrrad hast du?* What kind of bike have you got?
♦ **das Für und Wider** the pros and cons

die **Furcht** NOUN
fear

**furchtbar** ADJECTIVE
terrible

sich **fürchten** VERB
to be afraid ◊ *Ich fürchte mich vor diesem Mann.* I'm afraid of that man.

**fürchterlich** ADJECTIVE
awful

**füreinander** ADVERB
for each other

**fürs** = **für das**

der **Fuß** NOUN (GEN des **Fußes**, PL die **Füße**)
**1** foot ◊ *Mir tun die Füße weh.* My feet hurt.
**2** leg ◊ *Der Tisch hat vier Füße.* The table's got four legs.
♦ **zu Fuß** on foot

der **Fußball** NOUN (PL die **Fußbälle**)
football

der **Fußballplatz** NOUN (GEN des **Fußballplatzes**, PL die **Fußballplätze**)
football pitch

das **Fußballspiel** NOUN (PL die **Fußballspiele**)
football match

der **Fußballspieler** NOUN (PL die **Fußballspieler**)
footballer

der **Fußboden** NOUN (PL die **Fußböden**)
floor

der **Fußgänger** NOUN (PL die **Fußgänger**)
pedestrian

die **Fußgängerzone** NOUN
pedestrian precinct

das **Fußgelenk** NOUN (PL die **Fußgelenke**)
ankle

der **Fußweg** NOUN (PL die **Fußwege**)
footpath

das **Futter** NOUN (PL die **Futter**)
**1** feed ◊ *BSE entstand durch verseuchtes Futter.* BSE was the result of contaminated feed.
♦ **Hast du Futter für die Katze gekauft?** Have you bought cat food?
**2** lining ◊ *Der Mantel hat ein Futter aus Pelz.* The coat has a fur lining.

**füttern** VERB
**1** to feed ◊ *Kannst du bitte das Baby füttern?* Can you feed the baby, please?
**2** to line ◊ *Der Mantel ist gefüttert.* The coat's lined.

das **Futur** NOUN (PL die **Future**)
future

**F**

# G

**g** ABBREVIATION (= *Gramm*)
g
**gab** VERB *see* **geben**
die **Gabel** NOUN
fork
**gähnen** VERB
to yawn
die **Galerie** NOUN
gallery
**gammeln** VERB
to bum around
der **Gang** NOUN (PL die **Gänge**)
⊡ corridor ◊ *Häng deinen Mantel im Gang auf.* Hang your coat up in the corridor.
⊡ aisle ◊ *Ich hätte gern einen Platz am Gang.* I'd like an aisle seat.
⊡ gear ◊ *Mein Fahrrad hat zehn Gänge.* My bike has ten gears.
⊡ course ◊ *Das war erst der zweite Gang, und ich bin schon satt.* That was only that second course and I'm full already.
♦ **etwas in Gang bringen** to get something off the ground ◊ *Sie hat das Projekt in Gang gebracht.* She got the project off the ground.
die **Gans** NOUN (PL die **Gänse**)
goose
das **Gänseblümchen** NOUN (PL die **Gänseblümchen**)
daisy
die **Gänsehaut** NOUN
goose pimples
**ganz** ADJECTIVE, ADVERB
⊡ whole ◊ *die ganze Welt* the whole world ◊ *ganz Europa* the whole of Europe
♦ **sein ganzes Geld** all his money
⊡ quite ◊ *ganz gut* quite good
♦ **ganz und gar nicht** not at all
♦ **Es sieht ganz so aus.** It really looks like it.
**ganztags** ADVERB
full time ◊ *ganztags arbeiten* to work full time
die **Ganztagsschule** NOUN
all-day school
die **Ganztagsstelle** NOUN
full-time job
**gar** ADJECTIVE, ADVERB
done ◊ *Die Kartoffeln sind gar.* The potatoes are done.
♦ **gar nicht** not at all ◊ *Sie hat sich gar nicht gefreut.* She was not at all pleased. ◊ *gar nicht schlecht* not bad at all
♦ **gar nichts** nothing at all ◊ *Ich habe gar nichts zu tun.* I have nothing at all to do.

♦ **Ich habe gar nichts verstanden.** I didn't understand anything at all.
♦ **gar niemand** nobody at all
die **Garage** NOUN
garage (*for parking*)
**garantieren** VERB (PERFECT **hat garantiert**)
to guarantee
♦ **Er kommt garantiert.** He's sure to come.
die **Garderobe** NOUN
cloakroom ◊ *Ich habe meinen Mantel an der Garderobe abgegeben.* I left my coat in the cloakroom.
die **Gardine** NOUN
curtain ◊ *die Gardinen zuziehen* to shut the curtains
der **Garten** NOUN (PL die **Gärten**)
garden
das **Gas** NOUN (GEN des **Gases**, PL die **Gase**)
gas ◊ *Wir kochen mit Gas.* We cook with gas.
♦ **Gas geben** to accelerate
der **Gasherd** NOUN (PL die **Gasherde**)
gas cooker
das **Gaspedal** NOUN (PL die **Gaspedale**)
accelerator
die **Gasse** NOUN
lane ◊ *die schmalen Gassen der Altstadt* the narrow lanes of the old town
der **Gast** NOUN (PL die **Gäste**)
guest ◊ *Wir haben Gäste aus England.* We've got guests from England.
♦ **bei jemandem zu Gast sein** to be somebody's guest
das **Gästehaus** NOUN (GEN des **Gästehauses**, PL die **Gästehäuser**)
guest house
**gastfreundlich** ADJECTIVE
hospitable
die **Gastfreundschaft** NOUN
hospitality
der **Gastgeber** NOUN (PL die **Gastgeber**)
host
die **Gastgeberin** NOUN
hostess
das **Gasthaus** NOUN (GEN des **Gasthauses**, PL die **Gasthäuser**)
inn
der **Gasthof** NOUN (PL die **Gasthöfe**)
inn
die **Gaststätte** NOUN
pub

> ⓘ *In Germany there's practically no difference between pubs and restaurants. You can eat or drink in a **Gaststätte**, families are welcome and the opening hours are flexible.*

**geb.** ABBREVIATION (= *geboren*)
1 born ◊ *Peter Schmitz, geb. 1965* Peter Schmitz, born 1965
2 née ◊ *Frau Dümmler, geb. Schnorr* Mrs Dümmler, née Schnorr

das **Gebäck** NOUN (PL die **Gebäcke**)
pastry ◊ *Kuchen und Gebäck* cakes and pastries

**gebären** VERB (PRESENT **gebiert**, IMPERFECT **gebar**, PERFECT **hat geboren**)
to give birth to

das **Gebäude** NOUN (PL die **Gebäude**)
building

**geben** VERB (PRESENT **gibt**, IMPERFECT **gab**, PERFECT **hat gegeben**)
to give ◊ *Gib ihm bitte das Geld.* Please give him the money. ◊ *Kannst du dieses Buch bitte deiner Mutter geben.* Could you give this book to your mother, please.
♦ **Karten geben** to deal
♦ **es gibt** there is ◊ *Hier gibt es ein schönes Freibad.* There's a lovely open-air pool here. ◊ *In Stuttgart gibt es viele Parks.* There are many parks in Stuttgart. ◊ *Wenn wir zu spät kommen, gibt es Ärger.* There will be trouble if we arrive late.
♦ **Was gibt's?** What's up?
♦ **Was gibt es im Kino?** What's on at the cinema?
♦ **sich geschlagen geben** to admit defeat
♦ **Das wird sich schon geben.** That'll sort itself out.

das **Gebet** NOUN (PL die **Gebete**)
prayer

**gebeten** VERB *see* **bitten**

das **Gebiet** NOUN (PL die **Gebiete**)
1 area ◊ *ein bewaldetes Gebiet* a wooded area
2 field ◊ *Er ist Experte auf diesem Gebiet.* He's an expert in this field.

**gebildet** ADJECTIVE
cultured

das **Gebirge** NOUN (PL die **Gebirge**)
mountain chain ◊ *Die Alpen sind ein großes Gebirge.* The Alps are a large mountain chain.
♦ **ins Gebirge fahren** to go to the mountains

das **Gebiss** NOUN (GEN des **Gebisses**, PL die **Gebisse**)
1 teeth ◊ *Sie hat ein gesundes Gebiss.* She's got healthy teeth.
2 dentures ◊ *Opas Gebiss lag auf dem Tisch.* Grandpa's dentures were lying on the table.

**gebissen** VERB *see* **beißen**

**geblieben** VERB *see* **bleiben**

**geboren** VERB *see* **gebären**

**geboren** ADJECTIVE

1 born ◊ *Wann bist du geboren?* When were you born?
2 née ◊ *Frau Dümmler, geborene Schnorr* Mrs Dümmler, née Schnorr

**geborgen** ADJECTIVE
safe ◊ *Ich fühle mich bei dir geborgen.* I feel safe with you.

**geboten** VERB *see* **bieten**

**gebracht** VERB *see* **bringen**

**gebraten** ADJECTIVE
fried

der **Gebrauch** NOUN (PL die **Gebräuche**)
use ◊ *Der Gebrauch dieses Geräts ist sehr einfach.* This machine is very easy to use.
♦ **Sitten und Gebräuche** customs and traditions

**gebrauchen** VERB (PERFECT **hat gebraucht**)
to use

die **Gebrauchsanweisung** NOUN
directions for use ◊ *Wo ist die Gebrauchsanweisung?* Where are the directions for use?

**gebraucht** ADJECTIVE
used

der **Gebrauchtwagen** NOUN (PL die **Gebrauchtwagen**)
second-hand car

**gebrochen** VERB *see* **brechen**

die **Gebühr** NOUN
fee

die **Gebühreneinheit** NOUN
unit (*telephone*)

**gebührenfrei** ADJECTIVE
free of charge
♦ **ein gebührenfreier Anruf** Freefone ® call

**gebührenpflichtig** ADJECTIVE
subject to a charge
♦ **eine gebührenpflichtige Verwarnung** a fine

**gebunden** VERB *see* **binden**

die **Geburt** NOUN
birth ◊ *bei der Geburt* at the birth

**gebürtig** ADJECTIVE
native of ◊ *ein gebürtiger Schweizer* a native of Switzerland

das **Geburtsdatum** NOUN (PL die **Geburtsdaten**)
date of birth

der **Geburtsort** NOUN (PL die **Geburtsorte**)
birthplace

der **Geburtstag** NOUN (PL die **Geburtstage**)
birthday ◊ *Herzlichen Glückwunsch zum Geburtstag!* Happy Birthday!

das **Gebüsch** NOUN (PL die **Gebüsche**)
bushes

**gedacht** VERB *see* **denken**

das **Gedächtnis** NOUN (GEN des **Gedächtnisses**, PL die **Gedächtnisse**)
memory ◊ *Ich habe ein schlechtes Gedächtnis.* I've got a bad memory.

**G**

der **Gedanke** NOUN (GEN des **Gedankens,** PL die **Gedanken**)
thought
♦ **sich über etwas Gedanken machen** to think about something ◊ *Ich habe mir Gedanken über das gemacht, was du gesagt hast.* I've thought about what you said.

der **Gedankenstrich** NOUN (PL die **Gedankenstriche**)
dash

das **Gedeck** NOUN (PL die **Gedecke**)
1 cover ◊ *ein Gedeck für drei Personen* covers for three people
2 set menu ◊ *Sie bestellte ein Gedeck.* She ordered the set menu.

**gedeihen** VERB (IMPERFECT **gedieh,** PERFECT **ist gediehen**)
to thrive

das **Gedenken** NOUN
♦ **zum Gedenken an jemanden** in memory of somebody

das **Gedicht** NOUN (PL die **Gedichte**)
poem

das **Gedränge** NOUN
crush ◊ *Vor der Kinokasse herrschte großes Gedränge.* There was a huge crush at the cinema box office.

die **Geduld** NOUN
patience

sich **gedulden** VERB (PERFECT **hat sich geduldet**)
to be patient

**geduldig** ADJECTIVE
patient

**gedurft** VERB see **dürfen**

**geehrt** ADJECTIVE
♦ **Sehr geehrter Herr Butterfeld** Dear Mr Butterfeld

**geeignet** ADJECTIVE
suitable

die **Gefahr** NOUN
danger ◊ *in Gefahr schweben* to be in danger
♦ **Gefahr laufen, etwas zu tun** to run the risk of doing something
♦ **auf eigene Gefahr** at one's own risk

**gefährden** VERB (PERFECT **hat gefährdet**)
to endanger

**gefährlich** ADJECTIVE
dangerous

das **Gefälle** NOUN (PL die **Gefälle**)
gradient

**gefallen (1)** VERB see **fallen**

**gefallen (2)** VERB (PRESENT **gefällt,** IMPERFECT **gefiel,** PERFECT **hat gefallen**)
see also **der Gefallen** NOUN
♦ **Es gefällt mir.** I like it.
♦ **Das Geschenk hat ihr gefallen.** She liked the present.
♦ **Er gefällt mir.** I like him.
♦ **Das gefällt mir an ihm.** That's one thing I like about him.

♦ **sich etwas gefallen lassen** to put up with something ◊ *Eine solche Frechheit lasse ich mir nicht gefallen.* I'm not putting up with cheek like that.

der **Gefallen** NOUN (PL die **Gefallen**)
see also **gefallen** VERB
favour ◊ *Könntest du mir einen Gefallen tun?* Could you do me a favour?

**gefangen** VERB see **fangen**
♦ **jemanden gefangen nehmen** to take somebody prisoner

der **Gefangene** NOUN (GEN des/der
die **Gefangenen,** PL die **Gefangenen**)
prisoner ◊ *Ein Gefangener ist geflohen.* A prisoner has escaped.

**gefangennehmen** VERB see **gefangen**

die **Gefangenschaft** NOUN
captivity

das **Gefängnis** NOUN (GEN des **Gefängnisses,** PL die **Gefängnisse**)
prison

die **Gefängnisstrafe** NOUN
prison sentence

das **Gefäß** NOUN (GEN des **Gefäßes,** PL die **Gefäße**)
container

**gefasst** ADJECTIVE
composed ◊ *Sie war sehr gefasst.* She was very composed.
♦ **auf etwas gefasst sein** to be prepared for something ◊ *Ich war schon aufs Schlimmste gefasst.* I was prepared for the worst.

**geflogen** VERB see **fliegen**

**geflossen** VERB see **fließen**

das **Geflügel** NOUN
poultry

**gefragt** ADJECTIVE
in demand ◊ *Er ist ein sehr gefragter Künstler.* He's an artist very much in demand. ◊ *Handwerker sind sehr gefragt.* Tradesmen are in great demand.

**gefräßig** ADJECTIVE
greedy

das **Gefrierfach** NOUN (PL die **Gefrierfächer**)
icebox

**gefriergetrocknet** ADJECTIVE
freeze-dried

die **Gefriertruhe** NOUN
deep-freeze

**gefroren** ADJECTIVE
frozen

das **Gefühl** NOUN (PL die **Gefühle**)
feeling ◊ *Sie hat ein Gefühl für Kunst.* She's got a feeling for art.
♦ **etwas im Gefühl haben** to have a feel for something

**gefühlsmäßig** ADJECTIVE
instinctive

**gefüllt** ADJECTIVE
stuffed ◊ *gefüllte Auberginen* stuffed aubergines

**gefunden** VERB *see* **finden**

**gegangen** VERB *see* **gehen**

**gegeben** VERB *see* **geben**

**gegen** PREPOSITION

*The preposition **gegen** takes the accusative.*

[1] against ◊ *Ich bin gegen diese Idee.* I'm against this idea. ◊ *nichts gegen jemanden haben* to have nothing against somebody

♦ **ein Mittel gegen Schnupfen** something for colds

♦ **Maske gegen Botha** Maske versus Botha

[2] towards ◊ *gegen Osten* towards the east ◊ *gegen Abend* towards evening

♦ **gegen einen Baum fahren** to drive into a tree

[3] round about ◊ *gegen drei Uhr* round about three o'clock

die **Gegend** NOUN

area ◊ *die Gegend um Ulm* the area around Ulm

das **Gegenmittel** NOUN (PL die **Gegenmittel**)

antidote

der **Gegensatz** NOUN (GEN des **Gegensatzes**, PL die **Gegensätze**)

contrast

♦ **Im Gegensatz zu mir ist er gut in Mathe.** Unlike me, he's good at maths.

**gegenseitig** ADJECTIVE

mutual ◊ *gegenseitiges Vertrauen* mutual trust

♦ **sich gegenseitig helfen** to help each other

der **Gegenstand** NOUN (PL die **Gegenstände**)

object

das **Gegenteil** NOUN

opposite ◊ *Das ist das Gegenteil von schön.* That's the opposite of lovely.

♦ **im Gegenteil** on the contrary

**gegenüber** PREPOSITION, ADVERB

*The preposition **gegenüber** takes the dative.*

[1] opposite ◊ *Die Apotheke ist gegenüber.* The chemist's is opposite. ◊ *Er saß mir gegenüber.* He sat opposite me.

[2] towards ◊ *Sie waren mir gegenüber sehr freundlich.* They were very friendly towards me.

der **Gegenverkehr** NOUN

oncoming traffic

die **Gegenwart** NOUN

present ◊ *in der Gegenwart leben* to live in the present

**gegessen** VERB *see* **essen**

der **Gegner** NOUN (PL die **Gegner**)

opponent

**gegrillt** ADJECTIVE

grilled

das **Gehackte** NOUN (GEN des **Gehackten**)

mince ◊ *Ein Kilo Gehacktes, bitte.* A kilo of mince, please.

das **Gehalt** NOUN (PL die **Gehälter**)

salary ◊ *Er verdient ein gutes Gehalt.* He earns a good salary.

**gehässig** ADJECTIVE

spiteful

**geheim** ADJECTIVE

secret

♦ **geheim halten** to keep secret

das **Geheimnis** NOUN (GEN des **Geheimnisses**, PL die **Geheimnisse**)

[1] secret ◊ *Kannst du ein Geheimnis behalten?* Can you keep a secret?

[2] mystery ◊ *die Geheimnisse der Erde* the Earth's mysteries

**geheimnisvoll** ADJECTIVE

mysterious

die **Geheimnummer** NOUN

ex-directory number

♦ **Wir haben eine Geheimnummer.** We're ex-directory.

**gehemmt** ADJECTIVE

inhibited

**gehen** VERB (IMPERFECT **ging**, PERFECT **ist gegangen**)

[1] to go ◊ *Wir gehen jetzt.* We're going now. ◊ *schwimmen gehen* to go swimming

[2] to walk ◊ *Sollen wir gehen oder den Bus nehmen?* Shall we walk or go by bus?

♦ **Wie geht es dir?** How are you?

♦ **Wie geht's?** How are things?

♦ **Mir geht's gut.** I'm fine.

♦ **Ihm geht's gut.** He's fine.

♦ **Es geht.** Not bad.

♦ **Geht das?** Is that possible?

♦ **Geht's noch?** Can you manage?

♦ **Das geht nicht.** That's not on.

♦ **um etwas gehen** to be about something ◊ *In dem Film geht es um einen Bankraub.* The film's about a bank robbery.

♦ **Hier geht es um sehr viel Geld.** There's a lot of money at stake here.

der **Gehilfe** NOUN (GEN des **Gehilfen**, PL die **Gehilfen**)

assistant

das **Gehirn** NOUN (PL die **Gehirne**)

brain

die **Gehirnerschütterung** NOUN

concussion

**gehoben** VERB *see* **heben**

**geholfen** VERB *see* **helfen**

**gehorchen** VERB (PERFECT **hat gehorcht**)

to obey ◊ *Du solltest deinem Vater gehorchen.* You should obey your father. ◊ *Ein Hund sollte lernen zu gehorchen.* A dog should learn to obey.

**gehören** VERB (PERFECT **hat gehört**)

G

☞

♦ **jemandem gehören** to belong to somebody ◊ *Dieses Buch gehört mir.* This book belongs to me.

♦ **Das gehört sich einfach nicht.** That just isn't done.

**gehorsam** ADJECTIVE

see also **der Gehorsam** NOUN

obedient

der **Gehorsam** NOUN

see also **gehorsam** ADJECTIVE

obedience

der **Gehsteig** NOUN (PL die **Gehsteige**)

pavement

der **Gehweg** NOUN (PL die **Gehwege**)

pavement

der **Geier** NOUN (PL die **Geier**)

vulture

die **Geige** NOUN

violin ◊ *Wiltrud spielt Geige.* Wiltrud plays the violin.

**geil** ADJECTIVE

[1] horny ◊ *Wenn er das sieht, wird er geil.* When he sees that, he'll get horny.

[2] cool ◊ *Das war eine geile Party.* That was a cool party. ◊ *ein geiler Song* a cool song

die **Geisel** NOUN

hostage

der **Geist** NOUN (PL die **Geister**)

[1] ghost

[2] mind ◊ *Er hat einen regen Geist.* He has a lively mind.

♦ **Seine Rede sprühte vor Geist.** His speech was very witty.

**geistesabwesend** ADJECTIVE

absent-minded

**geisteskrank** ADJECTIVE

mentally ill

die **Geisteskrankheit** NOUN

mental illness

**geistig** ADJECTIVE

intellectual ◊ *ihre geistigen Fähigkeiten* her intellectual capabilities

♦ **geistige Getränke** alcoholic drinks

♦ **geistig behindert** mentally handicapped

der **Geiz** NOUN (GEN des **Geizes**)

meanness

der **Geizhals** NOUN (GEN des **Geizhalses**, PL die **Geizhälse**)

miser

**geizig** ADJECTIVE

mean

**gekannt** VERB *see* **kennen**

**geknickt** ADJECTIVE

dejected ◊ *Er war total geknickt.* He was completely dejected.

**gekonnt** VERB *see* **können**

**gekonnt** ADJECTIVE

skilful

das **Gekritzel** NOUN

scrawl

das **Gel** NOUN (PL die **Gele**)

gel

das **Gelächter** NOUN

laughter

**geladen** VERB *see* **laden**

**geladen** ADJECTIVE

[1] loaded ◊ *eine geladene Waffe* a loaded weapon

♦ **geladene Gäste** invited guests

[2] live ◊ *Vorsicht, der Zaun ist geladen.* Careful, the fence is live.

♦ **geladen sein** to be furious ◊ *Meine Mutter war geladen.* My mother was furious.

**gelähmt** ADJECTIVE

paralysed

das **Gelände** NOUN (PL die **Gelände**)

[1] grounds ◊ *auf dem Gelände der Schule* on the school grounds

[2] terrain ◊ *unwegsames Gelände* difficult terrain

♦ **Wir sind mit dem Mountainbike durchs Gelände gefahren.** We cycled cross-country on our mountain bikes.

♦ **ein Baugelände** a building site

**gelangweilt** ADJECTIVE

bored

**gelassen** VERB *see* **lassen**

**gelassen** ADJECTIVE

calm ◊ *Sie blieb gelassen.* She remained calm.

**geläufig** ADJECTIVE

common ◊ *ein geläufiger Begriff* a common term

♦ **Das ist mir nicht geläufig.** I'm not familiar with that.

**gelaunt** ADJECTIVE

♦ **gut gelaunt** in a good mood

♦ **schlecht gelaunt** in a bad mood

♦ **Wie ist er gelaunt?** What sort of mood's he in?

**gelb** ADJECTIVE

[1] yellow

[2] amber ◊ *Die Ampel war gelb.* The traffic lights were at amber.

die **Gelbsucht** NOUN

jaundice

das **Geld** NOUN (PL die **Gelder**)

money

♦ **etwas zu Geld machen** to sell something off

der **Geldautomat** NOUN (GEN des **Geldautomaten**, PL die **Geldautomaten**)

cash dispenser

der **Geldbeutel** NOUN (PL die **Geldbeutel**)

purse

der **Geldschein** NOUN (PL die **Geldscheine**)

banknote

die **Geldstrafe** NOUN

fine

das **Geldstück** NOUN (PL die **Geldstücke**)

coin

die **Geldtasche** NOUN

wallet

der **Geldwechsel** NOUN
changing of money ◇ *Beim Geldwechsel muss man eine Gebühr bezahlen.* There is a charge for changing money.
♦ **"Geldwechsel"** "bureau de change"

**gelegen** VERB *see* **liegen**

die **Gelegenheit** NOUN
[1] opportunity ◇ *Sobald ich eine Gelegenheit bekomme ...* As soon as I get an opportunity ... ◇ *bei jeder Gelegenheit* at every opportunity
[2] occasion ◇ *Bei dieser Gelegenheit trug sie das blaue Kostüm.* On this occasion she wore her blue suit.

**gelegentlich** ADVERB
[1] occasionally ◇ *Gelegentlich gehe ich ganz gern ins Kino.* I occasionally like going to the cinema.
[2] some time or other ◇ *Ich werde mich gelegentlich darum kümmern.* I'll do it some time or other.

das **Gelenk** NOUN (PL die **Gelenke**)
joint (*in body*)

**gelenkig** ADJECTIVE
supple

**gelernt** ADJECTIVE
skilled

**geliehen** VERB *see* **leihen**

**gelingen** VERB (IMPERFECT **gelang**, PERFECT **ist gelungen**)
to succeed ◇ *Sein Plan ist ihm nicht gelungen.* His plan didn't succeed.
♦ **Es ist mir gelungen, ihn zu überzeugen.** I succeeded in convincing him.
♦ **Der Kuchen ist gelungen.** The cake turned out well.

**gelten** VERB (PRESENT **gilt**, IMPERFECT **galt**, PERFECT **hat gegolten**)
to be valid ◇ *Dein Ausweis gilt nicht mehr.* Your passport is no longer valid.
♦ **es gilt, etwas zu tun** it's necessary to do something ◇ *Es gilt, sich zu entscheiden.* It's necessary to make a decision.
♦ **jemandem gelten** to be aimed at somebody ◇ *Diese Bemerkung hat dir gegolten.* This comment was aimed at you.
♦ **etwas gelten lassen** to accept something
♦ **Was gilt die Wette?** What do you bet?

**gelungen** VERB *see* **gelingen**

**gelungen** ADJECTIVE
successful

das **Gemälde** NOUN (PL die **Gemälde**)
painting ◇ *ein Gemälde von Rembrandt* a painting by Rembrandt

**gemein** ADJECTIVE
mean ◇ *Das war gemein!* That was mean!
♦ **etwas gemein haben mit** to have something in common with ◇ *Mit solchen Leuten habe ich nichts gemein.* I don't have anything in common with people like that.

**gemeinsam** ADJECTIVE, ADVERB
[1] joint ◇ *gemeinsame Anstrengungen* joint efforts
♦ **ein gemeinsames Abendessen** dinner together
[2] together ◇ *Wir sind gemeinsam zum Lehrer gegangen.* We went together to the teacher.
♦ **etwas gemeinsam haben** to have something in common ◇ *Wir haben viel gemeinsam.* We've a lot in common.

**gemischt** ADJECTIVE
mixed

**gemocht** VERB *see* **mögen**

das **Gemüse** NOUN (PL die **Gemüse**)
vegetables ◇ *Gemüse ist gesund.* Vegetables are healthy.

**gemusst** VERB *see* **müssen**

**gemustert** ADJECTIVE
patterned

das **Gemüt** NOUN (PL die **Gemüter**)
nature ◇ *Sie hat ein fröhliches Gemüt.* She has a happy nature.
♦ **die Gemüter erregen** to arouse strong feelings

**gemütlich** ADJECTIVE
[1] cosy ◇ *eine gemütliche Wohnung* a cosy flat
♦ **ein gemütlicher Abend** a pleasant evening
[2] good-natured ◇ *Sie ist ein gemütlicher Mensch.* She's good-natured.

das **Gen** NOUN (PL die **Gene**)
gene

**genannt** VERB *see* **nennen**

**genau** ADJECTIVE, ADVERB
[1] exact ◇ *Ich brauche genaue Zahlen.* I need exact figures.
♦ **Diese Übersetzung ist nicht sehr genau.** This translation isn't very accurate.
[2] exactly ◇ *Genau das habe ich auch gesagt.* That's exactly what I said. ◇ *Sie hatte genau dasselbe Kleid an.* She was wearing exactly the same dress. ◇ *Das ist genau anders herum.* That's exactly the opposite.
♦ **etwas genau nehmen** to take something seriously
♦ **genau genommen** strictly speaking

die **Genauigkeit** NOUN
accuracy

**genauso** ADVERB
♦ **genauso gut** just as good

**genehmigen** VERB (PERFECT **hat genehmigt**)
to approve
♦ **sich etwas genehmigen** to treat oneself to something ◇ *Ich werde mir jetzt ein Eis genehmigen.* I'm going to treat myself to an ice cream.

G

die **Genehmigung** NOUN
    [1] permission ◇ *Für den Umbau brauchen wir eine Genehmigung.* We need permission for the conversion.
    [2] permit ◇ *Hier ist meine Genehmigung.* Here's my permit.

die **Generation** NOUN
    generation

**Genf** NEUT NOUN
    Geneva
  ◆ **der Genfer See** Lake Geneva

**genial** ADJECTIVE
    brilliant

das **Genick** NOUN (PL die **Genicke**)
    back of the neck
  ◆ **Ich hätte mir fast das Genick gebrochen.** I nearly broke my neck.

das **Genie** NOUN (PL die **Genies**)
    genius

**genießbar** ADJECTIVE
    [1] edible ◇ *Das Essen war nicht genießbar.* The meal wasn't edible.
    [2] drinkable ◇ *Probier mal, ob der Tee genießbar ist.* Try the tea and see if it's drinkable.

**genießen** VERB (IMPERFECT **genoss**, PERFECT **hat genossen**)
    to enjoy ◇ *Wir haben die Ferien genossen.* We enjoyed our holidays.

**genmanipuliert** ADJECTIVE
    genetically modified ◇ *genmanipulierte Lebensmittel* genetically modified food

**genommen** VERB *see* **nehmen**

die **Gentechnologie** NOUN
    genetic engineering

**genug** ADJECTIVE
    enough ◇ *Wir haben genug Geld.* We've got enough money. ◇ *gut genug* good enough

**genügen** VERB (PERFECT **hat genügt**)
    to be enough ◇ *Das genügt noch nicht.* That isn't enough.
  ◆ **jemandem genügen** to be enough for somebody ◇ *Genügt dir das eine Stück?* Is one piece enough for you?

**genügend** ADJECTIVE
    sufficient

der **Genuss** NOUN (GEN des **Genusses**, PL die **Genüsse**)
    [1] pleasure ◇ *Es war ein Genuss!* That was sheer pleasure!
    [2] consumption ◇ *der Genuss von Alkohol* the consumption of alcohol
  ◆ **in den Genuss von etwas kommen** to receive the benefit of something

**genüsslich** ADVERB
    with relish

**geöffnet** ADJECTIVE
    open

die **Geografie** NOUN
    geography

die **Geometrie** NOUN
    geometry

das **Gepäck** NOUN
    luggage

die **Gepäckannahme** NOUN
    luggage office

die **Gepäckaufbewahrung** NOUN
    left-luggage office

die **Gepäckausgabe** NOUN
    baggage reclaim

**gepflegt** ADJECTIVE
    [1] well-groomed ◇ *gepflegte Hände* well-groomed hands
    [2] well-kept ◇ *ein gepflegter Park* a well-kept park

**gerade** ADJECTIVE, ADVERB
    [1] straight ◇ *eine gerade Strecke* a straight stretch
    [2] upright ◇ *eine gerade Haltung* an upright posture
  ◆ **eine gerade Zahl** an even number
    [3] just ◇ *Du kommst gerade richtig.* You've come just at the right time. ◇ *Das ist es ja gerade!* That's just it! ◇ *Er wollte gerade aufstehen.* He was just about to get up.
  ◆ **gerade erst** only just ◇ *Ich bin gerade erst gekommen.* I've only just arrived.
  ◆ **gerade noch** only just ◇ *Das geht gerade noch.* That's only just OK.
  ◆ **gerade deshalb** that's exactly why
  ◆ **gerade du** you of all people ◇ *Warum gerade ich?* Why me of all people?
  ◆ **nicht gerade** not exactly ◇ *Das war nicht gerade nett.* That wasn't exactly nice.

**geradeaus** ADVERB
    straight ahead

**gerannt** VERB *see* **rennen**

das **Gerät** NOUN (PL die **Geräte**)
    [1] gadget ◇ *ein Gerät zum Papierschneiden* a gadget for cutting paper
    [2] appliance ◇ *ein Haushaltsgerät* a household appliance
    [3] tool ◇ *ein Gartengerät* a garden tool
    [4] apparatus ◇ *Wir haben heute an den Geräten geturnt.* We did gymnastics on the apparatus today.
    [5] equipment ◇ *Geräte zum Angeln* fishing equipment

**geraten** VERB (PRESENT **gerät**, IMPERFECT **geriet**, PERFECT **ist geraten**)
    [1] to thrive ◇ *Hier geraten die Pflanzen.* Plants thrive here.
    [2] to turn out ◇ *Ihre Kinder sind alle gut geraten.* All their children have turned out well. ◇ *Der Kuchen ist mir nicht geraten.* The cake hasn't turned out well.
  ◆ **in etwas geraten** to get into something ◇ *Wir sind in den Stau geraten.* We got into a traffic jam.
  ◆ **in Angst geraten** to get frightened
  ◆ **nach jemandem geraten** to take after somebody

**geräuchert → Geschirr**

**geräuchert** ADJECTIVE
smoked

das **Geräusch** NOUN (PL die **Geräusche**)
sound

**gerecht** ADJECTIVE
fair ◊ *Das ist nicht gerecht!* That's not fair!

die **Gerechtigkeit** NOUN
justice

das **Gerede** NOUN
gossip ◊ *Das ist alles nur Gerede.* That's all just gossip.

**geregelt** ADJECTIVE
1 steady ◊ *eine geregelte Arbeit* a steady job
2 regular ◊ *geregelte Mahlzeiten* regular meals

**gereizt** ADJECTIVE
irritable

das **Gericht** NOUN (PL die **Gerichte**)
1 court ◊ *Wir sehen uns vor Gericht.* I'll see you in court.
2 dish ◊ *ein leckeres Gericht* a tasty dish
♦ **das Jüngste Gericht** the Last Judgement

**gerieben** VERB see **reiben**

**gering** ADJECTIVE
1 small ◊ *eine geringe Menge* a small amount
2 low ◊ *geringe Beteiligung* low participation
♦ **eine geringe Zeit** a short time

**geringschätzig** ADJECTIVE
disparaging

**geringste** ADJECTIVE
least ◊ *Das ist meine geringste Sorge.* That's the least of my worries.

**geritten** VERB see **reiten**

**gern** ADVERB
gladly ◊ *Das habe ich gern getan.* I did it gladly.
♦ **gern haben** to like ◊ *Ich habe sie sehr gern.* I like her a lot.
♦ **gern mögen** to like ◊ *Ich mag diese Art von Musik gern.* I like this kind of music.
♦ **etwas gern tun** to like doing something ◊ *Ich schwimme gern.* I like swimming.
♦ **Ich hätte gern ...** I'd like ... ◊ *Ich hätte gern ein Zitroneneis.* I'd like a lemon ice cream.
♦ **Er möchte jetzt gern nach Hause.** He'd like to go home now.
♦ **Ja, gern!** Yes, please.
♦ **Gern geschehen!** It's a pleasure.

**gerochen** VERB see **riechen**

die **Gerste** NOUN
barley

der **Geruch** NOUN (PL die **Gerüche**)
smell

das **Gerücht** NOUN (PL die **Gerüchte**)
rumour

das **Gerümpel** NOUN
junk

**gesalzen** VERB see **salzen**

**gesalzen** ADJECTIVE
♦ **gesalzene Preise** hefty prices

**gesamt** ADJECTIVE
whole ◊ *die gesamte Klasse* the whole class
♦ **die gesamten Kosten** the total cost
♦ **gesamte Werke** complete works
♦ **im Gesamten** all in all

die **Gesamtschule** NOUN
comprehensive school

> ❶ *Gesamtschulen* are the exception rather than the rule in Germany.

**gesandt** VERB see **senden**

das **Geschäft** NOUN (PL die **Geschäfte**)
1 shop ◊ *In welchem Geschäft hast du das gekauft?* Which shop did you buy that in?
2 business ◊ *Die Geschäfte gehen gut.* Business is good.
3 deal ◊ *Ich schlage dir ein Geschäft vor.* I'll make a deal with you. ◊ *Das war ein gutes Geschäft.* That was a good deal.

die **Geschäftsfrau** NOUN
businesswoman

der **Geschäftsmann** NOUN (PL die **Geschäftsmänner**)
businessman

die **Geschäftszeiten** FEM PL NOUN
business hours

**geschehen** VERB (PRESENT **geschieht**, IMPERFECT **geschah**, PERFECT **ist geschehen**)
to happen ◊ *Was ist geschehen?* What's happened? ◊ *Was ist mit ihm geschehen?* What's happened to him?

**gescheit** ADJECTIVE
clever

das **Geschenk** NOUN (PL die **Geschenke**)
present

die **Geschichte** NOUN
1 story ◊ *eine lustige Geschichte* a funny story
2 history ◊ *die deutsche Geschichte* German history
3 business ◊ *die Geschichte mit dem verschwundenen Pass* the business of the missing passport

**geschichtlich** ADJECTIVE
historical

**geschickt** ADJECTIVE
skilful

**geschieden** VERB see **scheiden**

**geschieden** ADJECTIVE
divorced

**geschienen** VERB see **scheinen**

das **Geschirr** NOUN
crockery ◊ *In welchem Schrank steht das Geschirr?* What cupboard is the crockery kept in?

**G**

☞

♦ **das Geschirr spülen** to do the dishes

die **Geschirrspülmaschine** NOUN
dishwasher

das **Geschirrtuch** NOUN (PL die **Geschirrtücher**)
dish cloth

das **Geschlecht** NOUN (PL die **Geschlechter**)
[1] sex ◊ *ein Kind weiblichen Geschlechts*
a child of the female sex
[2] gender ◊ *Welches Geschlecht hat*
*dieses Substantiv?* What gender is this
noun?

die **Geschlechtskrankheit** NOUN
sexually transmitted disease

der **Geschlechtsverkehr** NOUN
sexual intercourse

**geschlossen** VERB *see* **schließen**

**geschlossen** ADJECTIVE
shut
♦ **"Geschlossen"** "Closed"

der **Geschmack** NOUN (PL die **Geschmäcke**)
taste ◊ *Das ist nicht nach meinem*
*Geschmack.* This is not to my taste.
♦ **Geschmack an etwas finden** to come to
like something ◊ *Sie hat inzwischen*
*Geschmack an dieser Art von Sport*
*gefunden.* In the meantime she's come
to like this kind of sport.

**geschmacklos** ADJECTIVE
[1] tasteless ◊ *Die Suppe war ziemlich*
*geschmacklos.* The soup was pretty
tasteless.
[2] in bad taste ◊ *Das war ein*
*geschmackloser Witz.* That joke was in
bad taste.

**geschmackvoll** ADJECTIVE
tasteful

**geschnitten** VERB *see* **schneiden**

**geschossen** VERB *see* **schießen**

**geschrieben** VERB *see* **schreiben**

**geschrien** VERB *see* **schreien**

**geschützt** ADJECTIVE
protected

das **Geschwafel** NOUN
silly talk

das **Geschwätz** NOUN
chatter

**geschwätzig** ADJECTIVE
talkative

die **Geschwindigkeit** NOUN
speed

die **Geschwindigkeitsbeschränkung** NOUN
speed limit

die **Geschwindigkeitskontrolle** NOUN
speed check

die **Geschwister** PL NOUN
brothers and sisters

**geschwommen** VERB *see* **schwimmen**

das **Geschwür** NOUN (PL die **Geschwüre**)
ulcer

**gesellig** ADJECTIVE
sociable

die **Gesellschaft** NOUN
[1] society ◊ *die Gesellschaft verändern*
to change society
[2] company
♦ **jemandem Gesellschaft leisten** to keep
somebody company

**gesessen** VERB *see* **sitzen**

das **Gesetz** NOUN (GEN des **Gesetzes,** PL die
**Gesetze**)
law

**gesetzlich** ADJECTIVE
legal
♦ **gesetzlicher Feiertag** public holiday

das **Gesicht** NOUN (PL die **Gesichter**)
face

der **Gesichtsausdruck** NOUN
expression

**gespannt** ADJECTIVE
[1] strained ◊ *Die Lage in Nordirland ist*
*gespannt.* The situation in Northern
Ireland is strained.
[2] eager ◊ *gespannte Zuhörer* eager
listeners
♦ **Ich bin gespannt, ob ...** I wonder
whether ...
♦ **auf etwas gespannt sein** to look forward
to something ◊ *Ich bin auf das Fest*
*gespannt.* I'm looking forward to the
party.

das **Gespenst** NOUN (PL die **Gespenster**)
ghost

**gesperrt** ADJECTIVE
closed off

das **Gespräch** NOUN (PL die **Gespräche**)
[1] conversation ◊ *ein langes Gespräch* a
long conversation
[2] call ◊ *Frau Morris, ein Gespräch für*
*Sie.* Mrs Morris, there's a call for you.

**gesprächig** ADJECTIVE
talkative

**gesprochen** VERB *see* **sprechen**

**gesprungen** VERB *see* **springen**

die **Gestalt** NOUN
[1] shape ◊ *die Gestalt der Skulptur* the
shape of the sculpture
♦ **Gestalt annehmen** to take shape ◊ *Mein*
*Referat nimmt langsam Gestalt an.* My
assignment is slowly taking shape.
[2] figure ◊ *Ich konnte eine dunkle*
*Gestalt im Garten erkennen.* I could see a
dark figure in the garden.
♦ **in Gestalt von** in the form of

**gestalten** VERB (PERFECT **hat gestaltet**)
to lay out ◊ *Wer hat euren Garten*
*gestaltet?* Who laid out your garden?
♦ **Wie gestaltest du deine Freizeit?** How do
you spend your spare time?

**gestanden** VERB *see* **stehen**

das **Geständnis** NOUN (GEN des **Geständnisses,**
PL die **Geständnisse**)
confession

der **Gestank** NOUN
stench

**gestatten** VERB (PERFECT **hat/ist gestattet**)
to allow
◆ **Gestatten Sie?** May I?
**gestattet** ADJECTIVE
permitted ◊ *Das ist nicht gestattet.* That is not permitted.
die **Geste** NOUN
gesture
**gestehen** VERB (IMPERFECT **gestand,** PERFECT **hat gestanden**)
to confess
das **Gestein** NOUN (PL die **Gesteine**)
rock ◊ *vulkanisches Gestein* volcanic rock
das **Gestell** NOUN (PL die **Gestelle**)
[1] frame ◊ *ein Brillengestell* spectacle frames
[2] rack ◊ *ein Gestell für Weinflaschen* a wine rack
**gestern** ADVERB
yesterday
◆ **gestern Abend** yesterday evening
◆ **gestern Morgen** yesterday morning
**gestohlen** VERB see **stehlen**
**gestorben** VERB see **sterben**
**gestört** ADJECTIVE
disturbed
**gestreift** ADJECTIVE
striped
**gesund** ADJECTIVE
healthy
◆ **wieder gesund werden** to get better
die **Gesundheit** NOUN
health
◆ **Gesundheit!** Bless you!
**gesundheitlich** ADJECTIVE, ADVERB
health ◊ *gesundheitliche Probleme* health problems
◆ **Wie geht es Ihnen gesundheitlich?** How's your health?
**gesungen** VERB see **singen**
**getan** VERB see **tun**
das **Getränk** NOUN (PL die **Getränke**)
drink
die **Getränkekarte** NOUN
wine list
der **Getränkemarkt** NOUN (PL die **Getränkemärkte**)
drinks cash-and-carry
sich **getrauen** VERB (PERFECT **hat sich getraut**)
to dare ◊ *Sie hat sich nicht getraut hineinzugehen.* She didn't dare go in.
das **Getreide** NOUN (PL die **Getreide**)
cereals
**getrennt** ADJECTIVE
separate
das **Getriebe** NOUN (PL die **Getriebe**)
gearbox
**getrieben** VERB see **treiben**
**getroffen** VERB see **treffen**
**getrunken** VERB see **trinken**
**geübt** ADJECTIVE

experienced
**gewachsen** VERB see **wachsen**
**gewachsen** ADJECTIVE
◆ **jemandem gewachsen sein** to be a match for somebody ◊ *Er war seinem Gegner gewachsen.* He was a match for his opponent.
◆ **Sie ist den Kindern nicht gewachsen.** She can't cope with the children.
◆ **einer Sache gewachsen sein** to be up to something ◊ *Meinst du, du bist dieser Aufgabe gewachsen?* Do you think you're up to this job?
**gewagt** ADJECTIVE
risky
die **Gewalt** NOUN
[1] force ◊ *die Gewalt des Aufpralls* the force of the impact
[2] power ◊ *die staatliche Gewalt* the power of the state
[3] violence ◊ *Gewalt gegen Kinder* violence against children
◆ **mit aller Gewalt** with all one's might
**gewaltig** ADJECTIVE
tremendous ◊ *eine gewaltige Menge* a tremendous amount ◊ *Sie hat sich gewaltig angestrengt.* She tried tremendously hard.
◆ **ein gewaltiger Irrtum** a huge mistake
**gewalttätig** ADJECTIVE
violent
**gewann** VERB see **gewinnen**
das **Gewässer** NOUN (PL die **Gewässer**)
waters
das **Gewebe** NOUN (PL die **Gewebe**)
[1] fabric ◊ *ein feines Gewebe* a fine fabric
[2] tissue ◊ *Die Gewebeprobe hat ergeben, dass alles in Ordnung ist.* The tissue samples showed that there's nothing wrong.
das **Gewehr** NOUN (PL die **Gewehre**)
gun
die **Gewerkschaft** NOUN
trade union

> ❶ *Unions in Germany are mainly organized within the **Deutscher Gewerkschaftsbund (DGB)**.*

**gewesen** VERB see **sein**
das **Gewicht** NOUN (PL die **Gewichte**)
weight ◊ *das Gewicht meines Koffers* the weight of my case
**gewieft** ADJECTIVE
shrewd
der **Gewinn** NOUN (PL die **Gewinne**)
profit ◊ *Wir haben dieses Jahr einen Gewinn gemacht.* We've made a profit this year. ◊ *etwas mit Gewinn verkaufen* to sell something at a profit

**G**

**gewinnen** VERB (IMPERFECT **gewann,** PERFECT **hat gewonnen**)

to win ◊ *Sie hat den ersten Preis gewonnen.* She won first prize. ◊ *Er hat im Lotto gewonnen.* He had a win on the lottery.

♦ **an etwas gewinnen** to gain in something ◊ *Durch das neue Kunstmuseum hat die Stadt an Beliebtheit gewonnen.* As a result of the new art gallery the town has gained in popularity.

der **Gewinner** NOUN (PL die **Gewinner**)
winner

**gewiss** ADJECTIVE, ADVERB
certain ◊ *Zwischen den beiden besteht eine gewisse Ähnlichkeit.* There's a certain similarity between them.

♦ **Eine gewisse Frau Böttcher hat angerufen.** A Mrs Böttcher called.

♦ **Das weiß ich ganz gewiss.** I'm certain about that.

♦ **Das hat sie gewiss vergessen.** She must have forgotten.

das **Gewissen** NOUN (PL die **Gewissen**)
conscience

**gewissenhaft** ADJECTIVE
conscientious

**gewissermaßen** ADVERB
more or less

die **Gewissheit** NOUN
certainty

das **Gewitter** NOUN (PL die **Gewitter**)
thunderstorm

**gewöhnen** VERB (PERFECT **hat gewöhnt**)

♦ **sich an etwas gewöhnen** to get used to something ◊ *Ich muss mich erst an die neue Rechtschreibung gewöhnen.* I have to get used to the new spelling rules.

♦ **jemanden an etwas gewöhnen** to teach somebody something ◊ *Der Klassenlehrer hat versucht, seine Klasse an Disziplin zu gewöhnen.* The form teacher tried to teach his class discipline.

die **Gewohnheit** NOUN
habit ◊ *Es ist so eine Gewohnheit von mir, morgens Kaffee zu trinken.* I drink coffee in the morning. It's a habit of mine.

♦ **aus Gewohnheit** from habit

♦ **zur Gewohnheit werden** to become a habit

**gewöhnlich** ADJECTIVE

[1] usual ◊ *Ich bin heute früh zu der gewöhnlichen Zeit aufgestanden.* I got up at my usual time this morning. ◊ *Ich stehe gewöhnlich um sieben Uhr auf.* I usually get up at seven o'clock.

[2] ordinary ◊ *Das sind ganz gewöhnliche Leute.* They're quite ordinary people.

♦ **wie gewöhnlich** as usual

**gewohnt** ADJECTIVE

usual ◊ *Mir fehlt die gewohnte Umgebung.* I miss my usual surroundings.

♦ **etwas gewohnt sein** to be used to something ◊ *Ich bin es nicht gewohnt, dass man mir widerspricht.* I'm not used to being contradicted.

**gewonnen** VERB see **gewinnen**

**geworden** VERB see **werden**

**geworfen** VERB see **werfen**

das **Gewürz** NOUN (GEN des **Gewürzes,** PL die **Gewürze**)
spice

**gewusst** VERB see **wissen**

die **Gezeiten** PL NOUN
tides

**gezogen** VERB see **ziehen**

**gezwungen** VERB see **zwingen**

**gibt** VERB see **geben**

die **Gier** NOUN
greed

**gierig** ADJECTIVE
greedy ◊ *gierig nach Geld* greedy for money

**gießen** VERB (IMPERFECT **goss,** PERFECT **hat gegossen**)
to pour ◊ *Sie goss mir Wein ins Glas.* She poured wine into my glass.

♦ **die Blumen gießen** to water the flowers

♦ **Es gießt in Strömen.** It's pouring.

die **Gießkanne** NOUN
watering can

das **Gift** NOUN (PL die **Gifte**)
poison

*Be careful! The German word **Gift** does not mean **gift**.*

**giftig** ADJECTIVE
poisonous ◊ *eine giftige Pflanze* a poisonous plant

der **Giftmüll** NOUN
toxic waste

**ging** VERB see **gehen**

der **Gipfel** NOUN (PL die **Gipfel**)

[1] peak ◊ *die schneebedeckten Gipfel* the snow-covered peaks

[2] height ◊ *Das ist der Gipfel der Unverschämtheit.* That's the height of impudence.

der **Gips** NOUN (GEN des **Gipses,** PL die **Gipse**)
plaster ◊ *Ich muss die Risse mit Gips zuschmieren.* I'll have to fill in the cracks with plaster. ◊ *Sie hatte den rechten Arm in Gips.* Her right arm was in plaster.

der **Gipsverband** NOUN (PL die **Gipsverbände**)
plaster cast

die **Giraffe** NOUN
giraffe

das **Girokonto** NOUN (PL die **Girokonten**)
current account

die **Gitarre** NOUN
guitar ◊ *Ich spiele Gitarre.* I play the guitar.

**glänzen** VERB
to shine ◊ *Ihr Gesicht glänzte vor Freude.* Her face shone with joy.
♦ **Du hast in der Mathearbeit nicht gerade geglänzt.** You didn't exactly do brilliantly in your maths test.

**glänzend** ADJECTIVE
[1] shining ◊ *ein glänzendes Metall* shining metal
[2] brilliant ◊ *Das war eine glänzende Leistung.* That was a brilliant achievement.

das **Glas** NOUN (GEN des **Glases**, PL die **Gläser**)
glass

die **Glasscheibe** NOUN
pane

**glatt** ADJECTIVE
[1] smooth ◊ *Der Tisch hat eine glatte Oberfläche.* The table has a smooth surface.
[2] slippery ◊ *Pass auf, die Straßen sind glatt.* Be careful, the streets are slippery.
♦ **eine glatte Absage** a flat refusal
♦ **eine glatte Lüge** a downright lie
♦ **Das habe ich glatt vergessen.** It completely slipped my mind.

das **Glatteis** NOUN (GEN des **Glatteises**)
black ice ◊ *Bei Glatteis sollte man vorsichtig fahren.* When there's black ice, you have to drive carefully.

die **Glatze** NOUN
♦ **Er hat eine Glatze.** He's bald.
♦ **eine Glatze bekommen** to go bald

**glauben** VERB
[1] to believe ◊ *Ich habe kein Wort geglaubt.* I didn't believe a word.
[2] to think ◊ *Ich glaube, wir sind hier nicht willkommen.* I don't think we're welcome here.
♦ **jemandem glauben** to believe somebody ◊ *Ich glaube dir.* I believe you.
♦ **an etwas glauben** to believe in something ◊ *Glaubst du an ein Leben nach dem Tod?* Do you believe in life after death?

**glaubwürdig** ADJECTIVE
[1] credible ◊ *Das ist keine besonders glaubwürdige Geschichte.* That story's not particularly credible.
[2] trustworthy ◊ *Er ist ein glaubwürdiger Mensch.* He's a trustworthy person.

**gleich** ADJECTIVE, ADVERB
[1] same ◊ *Wir haben das gleiche Problem.* We have the same problem.
[2] identical ◊ *Bei einem Würfel sind alle Seiten gleich.* All the sides of a cube are identical.
[3] the same ◊ *Ich behandle alle meine Kinder gleich.* I treat all my children the same. ◊ *Sie waren genau gleich angezogen.* They were dressed exactly the same.
♦ **gleich groß** the same size

[4] equal ◊ *Wir wollen für die gleiche Arbeit auch die gleiche Bezahlung.* We want equal pay for equal work.
[5] straight away ◊ *Ich werde ihn gleich anrufen.* I'll call him straight away.
♦ **Ich bin gleich fertig.** I'll be ready in a minute.
♦ **Es ist mir gleich.** It's all the same to me.
♦ **Zwei mal zwei gleich vier.** Two times two equals four.
♦ **gleich nach** right after ◊ *Wir sind gleich nach dem Mittagessen abgefahren.* We left right after lunch.
♦ **gleich neben** right next to ◊ *Wir wohnen gleich neben der Schule.* We live right next to the school.

**gleichaltrig** ADJECTIVE
of the same age ◊ *gleichaltrige Schüler* pupils of the same age ◊ *Sie sind gleichaltrig.* They're the same age.

**gleichartig** ADJECTIVE
similar

**gleichbedeutend** ADJECTIVE
synonymous

die **Gleichberechtigung** NOUN
equal rights ◊ *die Gleichberechtigung der Frau* equal rights for women

**gleichen** VERB (IMPERFECT **glich**, PERFECT **hat geglichen**)
♦ **jemandem gleichen** to be like somebody ◊ *Du gleichst deinem Vater.* You're like your father.
♦ **einer Sache gleichen** to be like something ◊ *Unser Haus gleicht eurem.* Our house is like yours.
♦ **sich gleichen** to be alike

**gleichfalls** ADVERB
♦ **Danke gleichfalls!** The same to you.

das **Gleichgewicht** NOUN
balance

**gleichgültig** ADJECTIVE
[1] indifferent ◊ *Er zeigte sich ihr gegenüber ziemlich gleichgültig.* He seemed to be quite indifferent to her.
[2] not important ◊ *Es ist doch gleichgültig, wie wir das machen.* It's not important how we do it.

die **Gleichung** NOUN
equation

**gleichzeitig** ADVERB
at the same time ◊ *Ich kann doch nicht drei Dinge gleichzeitig tun.* I can't do three things at the same time.

das **Gleis** NOUN (GEN des **Gleises**, PL die **Gleise**)
[1] line ◊ *die Straßenbahngleise* the tram lines
[2] platform ◊ *Achtung auf Gleis drei.* Attention on platform three.

der **Gletscher** NOUN (PL die **Gletscher**)
glacier

**gliedern** VERB

**G**

to structure ◊ *Du musst deinen Aufsatz besser gliedern.* You must structure your essay better.

die **Gliederung** NOUN
structure ◊ *Die Gliederung meines Aufsatzes habe ich schon.* I've already worked out the structure of my essay.

**glimpflich** ADJECTIVE
♦ **glimpflich davonkommen** to get off lightly

**glitzern** VERB
1 to glitter ◊ *Das Wasser glitzerte in der Sonne.* The water glittered in the sun.
2 to twinkle ◊ *Die Sterne glitzerten.* The stars twinkled.

die **Glocke** NOUN
bell
♦ **etwas an die große Glocke hängen** to shout something from the rooftops

**glotzen** VERB
to gawp

das **Glück** NOUN
1 luck ◊ *Ein vierblättriges Kleeblatt bringt Glück.* A four-leaf clover brings good luck.
♦ **Glück haben** to be lucky ◊ *Ich habe viel Glück gehabt.* I was very lucky.
♦ **Viel Glück!** Good luck!
♦ **zum Glück** fortunately
2 happiness ◊ *Sie strahlte vor Glück.* She was beaming with happiness.

**glücklich** ADJECTIVE
1 happy ◊ *Ich bin sehr glücklich mit ihm.* I'm very happy with him. ◊ *Das waren glückliche Tage.* Those were happy days.
2 lucky ◊ *Das war ein glücklicher Zufall.* That was a lucky coincidence.

**glücklicherweise** ADVERB
fortunately

der **Glückwunsch** NOUN (PL die **Glückwünsche**)
congratulations ◊ *Herzlichen Glückwunsch zur bestandenen Prüfung.* Congratulations on passing your exam.
♦ **Herzlichen Glückwunsch zum Geburtstag.** Happy Birthday.

die **Glühbirne** NOUN
light bulb

**GmbH** ABBREVIATION (= *Gesellschaft mit beschränkter Haftung*)
limited company

das **Gold** NOUN
gold

**golden** ADJECTIVE
golden

der **Goldfisch** NOUN (PL die **Goldfische**)
goldfish ◊ *Ich habe zwei Goldfische.* I've got two goldfish.

der **Golf** NOUN (PL die **Golfe**)
see also **das Golf** NOUN
gulf ◊ *der Persische Golf* the Persian Gulf

das **Golf** NOUN
see also **der Golf** NOUN
golf ◊ *Mein Vater spielt Golf.* My father plays golf.

der **Golfplatz** NOUN (GEN des **Golfplatzes**, PL die **Golfplätze**)
golf course

der **Golfschläger** NOUN (PL die **Golfschläger**)
golf club ◊ *ein Satz Golfschläger* a set of golf clubs

der **Golfstrom** NOUN
the Gulf Stream

**gönnen** VERB
♦ **Sie gönnt mir offensichtlich meinen Erfolg nicht.** She obviously begrudges me my success.
♦ **sich etwas gönnen** to treat oneself to something ◊ *Ich werde mir ein Stück Kuchen gönnen.* I'm going to treat myself to a piece of cake.

der **Gott** NOUN (PL die **Götter**)
god
♦ **Mein Gott!** For heaven's sake! ◊ *Mein Gott, wie kann man nur so dumm sein!* For heaven's sake, how can you be so stupid!
♦ **Um Gottes willen!** For heaven's sake! ◊ *Um Gottes willen, tu das bloß nicht!* For heaven's sake don't do that!
♦ **Grüß Gott!** Hello!
♦ **Gott sei Dank!** Thank God!

die **Göttin** NOUN
goddess

**göttlich** ADJECTIVE
divine

das **Grab** NOUN (PL die **Gräber**)
grave

**graben** VERB (PRESENT **gräbt**, IMPERFECT **grub**, PERFECT **hat gegraben**)
see also **der Graben** NOUN
to dig

der **Graben** NOUN (PL die **Gräben**)
see also **graben** VERB
ditch

der **Grad** NOUN (PL die **Grad**)
degree ◊ *dreißig Grad im Schatten* thirty degrees in the shade

die **Grafikkarte** NOUN
graphics card ◊ *Welche Grafikkarte hast du in deinem PC?* What graphics card do you have in your PC?

**grafisch** ADJEKTIV
graphic

das **Gramm** NOUN (PL die **Gramme** or **Gramm**)
gram ◊ *hundert Gramm Käse* a hundred grams of cheese

die **Grammatik** NOUN
grammar

**graphisch** ADJECTIVE see **grafisch**

das **Gras** NOUN (GEN des **Grases**, PL die **Gräser**)
grass

**grässlich** ADJECTIVE

horrible

die **Gräte** NOUN
bone ◊ *Dieser Fisch hat zu viele Gräten.* This fish has too many bones in it.

**gratis** ADVERB
free of charge

**gratulieren** VERB (PERFECT **hat gratuliert**)
♦ **jemandem gratulieren** to congratulate somebody ◊ *Wir gratulierten ihr zum bestandenen Examen.* We congratulated her on passing her exam.
♦ **Gratuliere!** Congratulations!

**grau** ADJECTIVE
grey

das **Graubrot** NOUN (PL die **Graubrote**)
brown bread

der **Gräuel** NOUN (PL die **Gräuel**)
horror ◊ *die Gräuel des Bürgerkriegs* the horrors of civil war
♦ **Rote Bete sind mir ein Gräuel.** I loathe beetroot.

**grauen** VERB
♦ **Mir graut vor dem Mathetest.** I'm dreading the maths test.

**grauenhaft** ADJECTIVE
horrible

**grauhaarig** ADJECTIVE
grey-haired

**grausam** ADJECTIVE
cruel

die **Grausamkeit** NOUN
cruelty

**greifen** VERB (IMPERFECT **griff**, PERFECT **hat gegriffen**)
♦ **nach etwas greifen** to reach for something ◊ *Er griff nach meiner Hand.* He reached for my hand.
♦ **um sich greifen** to spread ◊ *Das Feuer griff schnell um sich.* The fire spread quickly.

**grell** ADJECTIVE
harsh ◊ *eine grelle Farbe* a harsh colour
♦ **ein greller Schrei** a piercing scream

die **Grenze** NOUN
[1] border ◊ *Wir sind an der Grenze nach Frankreich kontrolliert worden.* Our papers were checked at the French border.
[2] boundary ◊ *Der Zaun ist die Grenze zum Grundstück des Nachbarn.* The fence marks the boundary with our neighbour's property.
[3] limit ◊ *die Grenzen des guten Geschmacks* the limits of good taste

**grenzen** VERB
♦ **an etwas grenzen** to border on something ◊ *Unser Grundstück grenzt an das von Schmidts.* Our property borders on the Schmidt's.
♦ **Das grenzt an Wahnsinn.** It verges on madness.

**grenzenlos** ADJECTIVE
boundless

der **Greuel** NOUN see **Gräuel**

der **Grieche** NOUN (GEN des **Griechen**, PL die **Griechen**)
Greek

**Griechenland** NEUT NOUN
Greece
♦ **aus Griechenland** from Greece
♦ **nach Griechenland** to Greece

die **Griechin** NOUN
Greek

**griechisch** ADJECTIVE
Greek

**griesgrämig** ADJECTIVE
grumpy

der **Grieß** NOUN (GEN des **Grießes**)
semolina

der **Griff** NOUN (PL die **Griffe**)
[1] handle ◊ *Halte dich da an dem Griff fest.* Hold on to the handle.
[2] hold ◊ *Ich habe Judogriffe geübt.* I've been practising judo holds.

**griffbereit** ADJECTIVE
handy ◊ *etwas griffbereit halten* to keep something handy

der **Grill** NOUN (PL die **Grills**)
grill

**grillen** VERB
[1] to grill ◊ *gegrillter Fisch* grilled fish
[2] to have a barbecue ◊ *Wir wollen am Sonntag grillen.* We'd like to have a barbecue on Sunday.

**grinsen** VERB
to grin

die **Grippe** NOUN
flu

**grob** ADJECTIVE
[1] coarse ◊ *grober Sand* coarse sand
[2] rough ◊ *Sei nicht so grob zu deiner Schwester.* Don't be so rough with your sister.
[3] serious ◊ *ein grober Fehler* a serious mistake

der **Groschen** NOUN (PL die **Groschen**)
10-pfennig piece

**groß** ADJECTIVE, ADVERB
[1] big ◊ *Das war mein größter Fehler.* That was my biggest mistake. ◊ *Sie haben ein großes Haus.* They have a big house.
[2] tall ◊ *Mein Bruder ist viel größer als ich.* My brother is much taller than me. ◊ *Wie groß bist du?* How tall are you?
[3] great ◊ *Das war eine große Leistung.* That was a great achievement. ◊ *Er war ein großer Politiker.* He was a great politician.
♦ **großen Hunger haben** to be very hungry
♦ **die großen Ferien** the summer holidays
♦ **Er hat sich nicht groß angestrengt.** He didn't try very hard.

**G**

☞

♦ **Was soll ich da groß sagen?** What is there to say?

♦ **im Großen und Ganzen** on the whole

**großartig** ADJECTIVE
splendid

**Großbritannien** NEUT NOUN
Great Britain

♦ **aus Großbritannien** from Great Britain

♦ **in Großbritannien** in Great Britain

♦ **nach Großbritannien** to Great Britain

die **Größe** NOUN
1 size ◊ *Welche Schuhgröße hast du?* What size shoes do you take?
2 height ◊ *Im Pass steht bei den Angaben zur Person auch die Größe.* Your height's also included in your passport under personal details.

die **Großeltern** PL NOUN
grandparents

**großenteils** ADVERB
mostly

die **Großmutter** NOUN (PL die **Großmütter**)
grandmother

**großschreiben** VERB (IMPERFECT **schrieb groß**, PERFECT **hat großgeschrieben**)
to write in capitals

die **Großstadt** NOUN (PL die **Großstädte**)
city

**größtenteils** ADVERB
for the most part

der **Großvater** NOUN (PL die **Großväter**)
grandfather

**großzügig** ADJECTIVE, ADVERB
generous ◊ *Meine Eltern sind sehr großzügig.* My parents are very generous. ◊ *Sie hat großzügig darauf verzichtet.* She generously did without.

das **Grübchen** NOUN (PL die **Grübchen**)
dimple

**grün** ADJECTIVE
green ◊ *Die Ampel ist grün.* The traffic lights are at green.

der **Grund** NOUN (PL die **Gründe**)
1 reason ◊ *Nenn mir einen Grund, warum wir das nicht so machen können.* Give me one reason why we can't do it like this.

♦ **Aus welchem Grund ist er so böse?** Why is he so angry?
2 ground ◊ *Das Haus ist auf felsigem Grund gebaut.* The house is built on rocky ground.
3 bottom ◊ *Das Schiff sank auf den Grund des Meeres.* The ship sank to the bottom of the sea.

♦ **im Grunde genommen** basically

♦ **auf Grund** see **aufgrund**

♦ **zu Grunde** see **zugrunde**

**gründen** VERB
to found ◊ *Wir haben einen Fanklub gegründet.* We've founded a fan club.

**gründlich** ADJECTIVE, ADVERB

thorough ◊ *eine gründliche Vorbereitung zur Prüfung* thorough preparation for the exam ◊ *Wir haben das Haus gründlich geputzt.* We cleaned the house thoroughly.

♦ **Ich habe mich gründlich geirrt.** I was completely wrong.

der **Grundsatz** NOUN (GEN des **Grundsatzes**, PL die **Grundsätze**)
principle

**grundsätzlich** ADJECTIVE, ADVERB
1 fundamental ◊ *Es bleibt die grundsätzliche Frage, ob das erlaubt werden soll.* The fundamental question remains: should it be allowed?
2 basically ◊ *Grundsätzlich bin ich ja dafür, aber ...* Basically I'm in favour, but ...
3 on principle ◊ *Ich bin grundsätzlich gegen die Prügelstrafe.* I'm against corporal punishment on principle.

die **Grundschule** NOUN
primary school

die **Grünen** PL NOUN
the Greens

der **Grünstreifen** NOUN (PL die **Grünstreifen**)
central reservation

**grunzen** VERB
to grunt

die **Gruppe** NOUN
group

der **Gruselfilm** NOUN (PL die **Gruselfilme**)
horror film

**gruselig** ADJECTIVE
creepy

der **Gruß** NOUN (GEN des **Grußes**, PL die **Grüße**)
greeting

♦ **viele Grüße** best wishes

♦ **mit freundlichen Grüßen** yours sincerely

♦ **Grüße an** regards to ◊ *Grüße an deine Eltern.* Regards to your parents.

**grüßen** VERB
to say hello ◊ *Sie hat mich nicht gegrüßt.* She didn't say hello to me.

♦ **Grüß Lorna von mir.** Give Lorna my regards.

♦ **Lorna lässt dich grüßen.** Lorna sends her regards.

**gucken** VERB
to look

der **Gulasch** NOUN (PL die **Gulaschs**)
goulash

die **Gulaschsuppe** NOUN
goulash soup

**gültig** ADJECTIVE
valid

das **Gummi** NOUN (PL die **Gummis**)
*You can also say der Gummi.*
rubber ◊ *Die Reifen sind aus Gummi.* The tyres are made of rubber.

das **Gummiband** NOUN (PL die **Gummibänder**)

elastic band ◊ *Sie machte ein Gummiband um das Geschenk.* She put an elastic band round the present.

das **Gummibärchen** NOUN (PL die **Gummibärchen**)
jelly bear

**günstig** ADJECTIVE
convenient ◊ *Morgen wäre günstig.* Tomorrow would be convenient.
♦ **eine günstige Gelegenheit** a favourable opportunity
♦ **Das habe ich günstig bekommen.** It was a bargain.

die **Gurgel** NOUN
throat

**gurgeln** VERB
to gargle ◊ *Ich habe Halsschmerzen und brauche etwas zum Gurgeln.* I've got a sore throat and need something to gargle with.

die **Gurke** NOUN
cucumber ◊ *Sie mag Gurkensalat nicht.* She doesn't like cucumber salad.
♦ **saure Gurke** gherkin

der **Gurt** NOUN (PL die **Gurte**)
belt

der **Gürtel** NOUN (PL die **Gürtel**)
belt

**gut** ADJECTIVE, ADVERB
1 good ◊ *Ich habe gute Noten bekommen.* I got good marks. ◊ *Sie ist ein guter Mensch.* She's a good person. ◊ *Das ist ein guter Witz.* That's a good joke.
♦ **In Englisch habe ich "gut".** I got a B in English.

> ❶ German marks range from one (**sehr gut**) to six (**ungenügend**).

♦ **Alles Gute!** All the best.
♦ **also gut** all right then ◊ *Also gut, ich komme.* All right then, I'll come.
2 well ◊ *Sie hat das gut gemacht.* She did it well. ◊ *Ich kenne ihn gut.* I know him well.
♦ **gut schmecken** to taste good
♦ **gut drei Stunden** a good three hours
♦ **das kann gut sein** that may well be
♦ **Gut, aber ...** OK, but ...
♦ **Lass es gut sein.** That'll do.
♦ **Es ist zum Glück gut gegangen.** Fortunately it came off.
♦ **Mir geht's gut.** I'm fine.
♦ **gut gemeint** well-meant ◊ *ein gut gemeinter Rat* a well-meant piece of advice
♦ **jemandem gut tun** to do somebody good ◊ *Die Pause hat mir gut getan.* The break did me good.

die **Güter** NEUT PL NOUN
goods

**gutgehen** VERB *see* gut

**gutgemeint** ADJECTIVE *see* gut

das **Guthaben** NOUN (PL die **Guthaben**)
credit

**gütig** ADJECTIVE
kind

**gutmütig** ADJECTIVE
good-natured

der **Gutschein** NOUN (PL die **Gutscheine**)
voucher

**guttun** VERB *see* gut

das **Gymnasium** NOUN (PL die **Gymnasien**)
grammar school

die **Gymnastik** NOUN
keep-fit ◊ *Ich mache einmal in der Woche Gymnastik.* I do keep-fit once a week.

**G**

das **Haar** NOUN (PL die **Haare**)
hair ◇ *Sie hat dunkle Haare.* She's got dark hair.
♦ **um ein Haar** nearly

die **Haarbürste** NOUN
hairbrush

das **Haarwaschmittel** NOUN (PL die **Haarwaschmittel**)
shampoo

**haben** VERB (PRESENT **hat**, IMPERFECT **hatte**, PERFECT **hat gehabt**)
to have ◇ *Ich habe einen neuen Pulli.* I've got a new pullover. ◇ *Sie hat ihn nicht gesehen.* She hasn't seen him.
♦ **Marek hat heute Geburtstag.** It's Marek's birthday today.
♦ **Wir haben zur Zeit Ferien.** We're on holiday at the moment.
♦ **Welches Datum haben wir heute?** What's the date today?
♦ **Hunger haben** to be hungry
♦ **Angst haben** to be afraid
♦ **Woher hast du das?** Where did you get that from?
♦ **Was hast du denn?** What's the matter with you?
♦ **Ich hätte gern ...** I would like ...

das **Hackfleisch** NOUN
mince

der **Hafen** NOUN (PL die **Häfen**)
harbour

die **Hafenstadt** NOUN (PL die **Hafenstädte**)
port

der **Hafer** NOUN
oats

die **Haferflocken** FEM PL NOUN
porridge oats

**haftbar** ADJECTIVE
responsible ◇ *Eltern sind für ihre Kinder haftbar.* Parents are responsible for their children.

**haften** VERB
to stick ◇ *Der Klebstreifen haftet nicht.* The adhesive tape isn't sticking.
♦ **haften für** to be responsible for

die **Haftpflichtversicherung** NOUN
third party insurance

der **Hagel** NOUN
hail

**hageln** VERB
♦ **Es hagelt.** It's hailing.

der **Hahn** NOUN (PL die **Hähne**)
1 cock ◇ *Der Hahn krähte.* The cock crowed.
2 tap ◇ *Der Hahn tropft.* The tap's dripping.

das **Hähnchen** NOUN (PL die **Hähnchen**)
chicken ◇ *Heute gibt es Hähnchen.* We're having chicken today.

der **Hai** NOUN (PL die **Haie**)
shark

der **Haken** NOUN (PL die **Haken**)
1 hook ◇ *Häng deinen Anorak an den Haken.* Hang your anorak up on the hook.
2 catch ◇ *Die Sache hat einen Haken.* There's a catch.

**halb** ADJECTIVE
half ◇ *ein halber Kuchen* half a cake ◇ *eine halbe Stunde* half an hour
♦ **halb eins** half past twelve

**halbieren** VERB (PERFECT **hat halbiert**)
to halve

das **Halbjahr** NOUN (PL die **Halbjahre**)
six months

**halbjährlich** ADJECTIVE
half-yearly

die **Halbpension** NOUN
half board

**halbtags** ADVERB
♦ **halbtags arbeiten** to work part-time

die **Halbtagsarbeit** NOUN
part-time job

die **Halbtagsschule** NOUN
half-time school

**half** VERB *see* **helfen**

die **Hälfte** NOUN
half

die **Halle** NOUN
hall ◇ *eine Messehalle* an exhibition hall

das **Hallenbad** NOUN (PL die **Hallenbäder**)
indoor swimming pool

**hallo** EXCLAMATION
hello!

der **Hals** NOUN (GEN des **Halses**, PL die **Hälse**)
1 neck ◇ *Ich habe einen steifen Hals.* I've got a stiff neck.
2 throat ◇ *Mir tut der Hals weh.* My throat's sore.
♦ **Hals über Kopf** in a rush

die **Halskette** NOUN
necklace

die **Halsschmerzen** MASC PL NOUN
sore throat ◇ *Ich habe Halsschmerzen.* I've got a sore throat.

das **Halstuch** NOUN (PL die **Halstücher**)
scarf

**halt** EXCLAMATION
stop!
♦ **Halt machen** to stop

**haltbar** ADJECTIVE
durable ◇ *Das ist ein sehr haltbares Material.* That's a very durable material.
♦ **Butter ist nur begrenzt haltbar.** Butter only keeps for a limited time.

♦ **"Mindestens haltbar bis ..."** "Best before ..."

**halten** VERB (PRESENT **hält**, IMPERFECT **hielt**, PERFECT **hat gehalten**)
[1] to hold ◊ *Er hielt sie an der Hand.* He held her by the hand. ◊ *Kannst du das mal halten?* Can you hold that for a moment?
[2] to keep ◊ *Obst hält nicht lange.* Fruit doesn't keep long.
♦ **Ihre Freundschaft hat lange gehalten.** Their friendship has lasted a long time.
[3] to stop ◊ *Der Bus hielt vor dem Rathaus.* The bus stopped in front of the town hall.
♦ **halten für** to regard as ◊ *Man hält ihn für den besten Chirurgen in Deutschland.* He's regarded as being the best surgeon in Germany.
♦ **Ich habe sie für deine Mutter gehalten.** I took her for your mother.
♦ **halten von** to think of ◊ *Sie hält viel von dir.* She thinks a lot of you. ◊ *Ich halte nichts von dieser Methode.* I don't think much of this method.
♦ **sich rechts halten** to keep to the right

die **Haltestelle** NOUN
stop ◊ *die Haltestelle der Straßenbahn* the tram stop

**haltmachen** VERB *see* **halt**

die **Haltung** NOUN
[1] posture ◊ *Er hat eine aufrechte Haltung.* He has an upright posture.
[2] attitude ◊ *Ich bewundere deine Haltung in dieser Frage.* I admire your attitude in this issue.

**Hamburg** NEUT NOUN
Hamburg

> ⓘ The "Free Hanseatic City of Hamburg" is one of the 16 **Länder**. It is a "city-state" like Bremen and Berlin, and is Germany's principal seaport.

der **Hammer** NOUN (PL die **Hämmer**)
hammer

der **Hamster** NOUN (PL die **Hamster**)
hamster

**hamstern** VERB
to hoard

die **Hand** NOUN (PL die **Hände**)
hand

die **Handarbeit** NOUN
[1] manual work ◊ *Handarbeit macht ihm mehr Spaß als geistige Arbeit.* He enjoys manual work more than intellectual work.
[2] needlework ◊ *In Handarbeit hat sie eine Zwei.* She got a B in needlework.

der **Handball** NOUN
handball

die **Handbremse** NOUN
handbrake

das **Handbuch** NOUN (PL die **Handbücher**)
manual

der **Händedruck** NOUN
handshake

der **Handel** NOUN
[1] trade ◊ *der Handel mit Osteuropa* trade with Eastern Europe
♦ **Dieses Gerät ist überall im Handel erhältlich.** This appliance is available in all shops and retail outlets.
[2] deal ◊ *Wir haben einen Handel abgeschlossen.* We have concluded a deal.

**handeln** VERB
[1] to act ◊ *Wir müssen schnell handeln.* We'll have to act quickly.
[2] to trade ◊ *Er handelt mit Gebrauchtwaren.* He trades in second-hand goods.
♦ **mit jemandem handeln** to bargain with somebody ◊ *Ich habe versucht, mit ihm zu handeln, aber er wollte es mir nicht billiger geben.* I tried to bargain with him but he didn't want to give it to me any cheaper.
♦ **es handelt sich um ...** it's about ... ◊ *Sie wollte mir nicht sagen, worum es sich handelt.* She didn't want to tell me what it was about.
♦ **Hier handelt es sich um einen besonders schweren Fall von Allergie.** This is a particularly bad case of allergy.
♦ **handeln von** to be about ◊ *Die Geschichte handelt von einer kranken Frau.* The story's about a sick woman.

die **Handelsschule** NOUN
business school

das **Handgepäck** NOUN
hand luggage

der **Händler** NOUN (PL die **Händler**)
dealer ◊ *Ich habe meinen Computerhändler danach gefragt.* I asked my computer dealer about it.

**handlich** ADJECTIVE
handy

die **Handlung** NOUN
[1] act ◊ *Das war eine unüberlegte Handlung.* That was a rash act.
[2] plot ◊ *Ich habe die Handlung des Buches nicht genau verstanden.* I didn't really understand the plot of the book.
[3] shop ◊ *eine Eisenwarenhandlung* an ironmonger's shop

die **Handschrift** NOUN
handwriting

der **Handschuh** NOUN (PL die **Handschuhe**)
glove

die **Handtasche** NOUN
handbag

das **Handtuch** NOUN (PL die **Handtücher**)
towel

das **Handy** NOUN (PL die **Handys**)
mobile phone

**H**

**der Hang** NOUN (PL die **Hänge**)
slope

**hängen (1)** VERB (IMPERFECT **hängte,** PERFECT **hat gehängt**)
[1] to hang ◊ *Sie hat die Wäsche auf die Leine gehängt.* She hung her washing on the line.
[2] to hang ◊ *Sie hängten den Verbrecher.* They hanged the criminal.

**hängen (2)** VERB (IMPERFECT **hing,** PERFECT **hat gehangen**)
to hang ◊ *An der Wand hing ein Bild von Picasso.* A painting by Picasso was hanging on the wall.
♦ **hängen an** to be attached to ◊ *Sie hat sehr an ihrem Vater gehangen.* She was very attached to her father.

**Hannover** NEUT NOUN
Hanover

**das Hansaplast** ® NOUN
Elastoplast ®

**hänseln** VERB
to tease

**die Hansestadt** NOUN (PL die **Hansestädte**)
Hanseatic town

> ❶ The **Hanse** (Hanseatic League) was a powerful association of cities which dominated Baltic trade in the Middle Ages. Even today, Bremen, Hamburg, Lübeck, Rostock and Wismar still call themselves **Hansestädte**.

**harmlos** ADJECTIVE
harmless

**harmonisch** ADJECTIVE
harmonious

**hart** ADJECTIVE
hard ◊ *hart wie Stein* as hard as stone ◊ *Wir haben hart gearbeitet.* We worked hard. ◊ *Diese Kritik hat sie hart getroffen.* This criticism hit her hard.
♦ **harte Worte** harsh words
♦ **Das ist hart.** That's tough.
♦ **ein hart gekochtes Ei** a hard-boiled egg

**hartnäckig** ADJECTIVE
stubborn

**das Haschisch** NOUN (GEN des **Haschisch**)
hashish

**der Hase** NOUN (GEN des **Hasen,** PL die **Hasen**)
hare

**die Haselnuss** NOUN (PL die **Haselnüsse**)
hazelnut

**der Hass** NOUN (GEN des **Hasses**)
hatred

**hassen** VERB (PERFECT **hat gehasst**)
to hate

**hässlich** ADJECTIVE
[1] ugly ◊ *Sie ist das hässlichste Mädchen der Klasse.* She's the ugliest girl in the class.
[2] nasty ◊ *Es ist hässlich, so etwas zu sagen.* It's nasty to say things like that.

**hast** VERB *see* **haben**

**hastig** ADJECTIVE
hasty

**hat, hatte** VERB *see* **haben**

**der Haufen** NOUN (PL die **Haufen**)
heap ◊ *In ihrem Schlafzimmer lag ein Haufen schmutziger Wäsche.* There was a heap of dirty washing lying in her bedroom.
♦ **ein Haufen** ... heaps of ... ◊ *Ich habe einen Haufen Fehler gemacht.* I've made heaps of mistakes. ◊ *Er hat einen Haufen Geld dafür bezahlt.* He paid heaps of money for it. ◊ *ein Haufen Leute* heaps of people

**häufen** VERB
♦ **sich häufen** to accumulate ◊ *Der Müll häufte sich in den Straßen.* The rubbish accumulated in the streets.
♦ **Die Fälle von Asthma häufen sich.** Cases of asthma are on the increase.

**haufenweise** ADVERB
[1] heaps of ◊ *Dort gibt es haufenweise Ameisen.* There are heaps of ants there. ◊ *Wiltrud hat haufenweise CDs.* Wiltrud has heaps of CDs.
[2] in droves ◊ *Sie sind haufenweise angekommen.* They came in droves.

**häufig** ADJECTIVE, ADVERB
[1] frequent ◊ *sein häufiges Fehlen* his frequent absences
[2] frequently ◊ *Er fehlt häufig.* He is frequently absent.

**der Hauptbahnhof** NOUN (PL die **Hauptbahnhöfe**)
main station

**hauptberuflich** ADVERB
full-time ◊ *Er ist hauptberuflich als Gärtner tätig.* He's employed full-time as a gardener.

**das Hauptfach** NOUN (PL die **Hauptfächer**)
main subject

**das Hauptgericht** NOUN (PL die **Hauptgerichte**)
main course

**die Hauptsache** NOUN
main thing
♦ **Hauptsache, du bist gesund.** The main thing is that you're healthy.

**die Hauptsaison** NOUN (PL die **Hauptsaisons**)
high season

**die Hauptschule** NOUN
secondary school

**die Hauptstadt** NOUN (PL die **Hauptstädte**)
capital ◊ *Berlin ist die Hauptstadt von Deutschland.* Berlin's the capital of Germany.

**die Hauptstraße** NOUN
main street

**die Hauptverkehrszeit** NOUN
rush hour

das **Hauptwort** NOUN (PL die **Hauptwörter**)
noun

das **Haus** NOUN (GEN des **Hauses**, PL die **Häuser**)
house
♦ **nach Hause** home ◊ *Ich muss jetzt nach Hause.* I'll have to go home now.
♦ **zu Hause** at home

die **Hausarbeit** NOUN
1 housework ◊ *Am Wochenende hilft mein Vater bei der Hausarbeit.* My father helps with the housework at the weekend.
2 homework ◊ *Wir haben eine Hausarbeit zum Thema Umweltverschmutzung auf.* We've got homework on the subject of pollution.

der **Hausarzt** NOUN (GEN des **Hausarztes**, PL die **Hausärzte**)
family doctor

die **Hausaufgaben** FEM PL NOUN
homework ◊ *Heute waren die Hausaufgaben nicht schwierig.* Our homework wasn't difficult today.

die **Hausfrau** NOUN
housewife

der **Haushalt** NOUN (PL die **Haushalte**)
1 household ◊ *den Haushalt führen* to run the household
2 budget ◊ *der Haushalt für 2002* the 2002 budget

der **Hausmeister** NOUN (PL die **Hausmeister**)
caretaker

die **Hausnummer** NOUN
house number

der **Hausschlüssel** NOUN (PL die **Hausschlüssel**)
front-door key

der **Hausschuh** NOUN (PL die **Hausschuhe**)
slipper

das **Haustier** NOUN (PL die **Haustiere**)
pet

die **Haustür** NOUN
front door

die **Hauswirtschaft** NOUN
home economics

die **Hauswirtschaftslehre** NOUN
home economics

die **Haut** NOUN (PL die **Häute**)
skin

die **Hautcreme** NOUN (PL die **Hautcremes**)
skin cream

**Hbf.** ABBREVIATION (= *Hauptbahnhof*)
central station

der **Hebel** NOUN (PL die **Hebel**)
lever

**heben** VERB (IMPERFECT **hob**, PERFECT **hat gehoben**)
to lift

die **Hecke** NOUN
hedge

die **Hefe** NOUN
yeast

das **Heft** NOUN (PL die **Hefte**)
1 exercise book ◊ *Schreibt die Verbesserung in euer Heft.* Write the correction in your exercise books.
2 issue ◊ *Hast du noch das letzte Heft von "Geo"?* Have you got the latest issue of "Geo"?

die **Heftklammer** NOUN
paper clip

das **Heftpflaster** NOUN (PL die **Heftpflaster**)
sticking plaster

die **Heftzwecke** NOUN
drawing pin

die **Heide** NOUN
moor ◊ *Wir haben einen Spaziergang durch die Heide gemacht.* We went for a walk over the moor.
♦ **die Lüneburger Heide** Lüneburg Heath

das **Heidekraut** NOUN
heather

die **Heidelbeere** NOUN
blueberry

**heilbar** ADJECTIVE
curable

**heilen** VERB (PERFECT **hat/ist geheilt**)
*For the perfect tense use **haben** when the verb has an object and **sein** when there is no object.*
1 to cure ◊ *Viele Arten von Krebs kann man heilen.* Many kinds of cancer can be cured.
2 to heal ◊ *Die Wunde ist schnell geheilt.* The wound healed quickly.

**heilig** ADJECTIVE
holy

der **Heiligabend** NOUN (PL die **Heiligabende**)
Christmas Eve

der **Heilige** NOUN (GEN des/der **Heiligen**, PL die
die **Heiligen**)
saint ◊ *Er ist auch kein Heiliger.* He's no saint.

das **Heilmittel** NOUN (PL die **Heilmittel**)
remedy

das **Heim** NOUN (PL die **Heime**)
*see also **heim** ADVERB*
home ◊ *ein Heim für Kinder mit Lernschwierigkeiten* a home for children with learning difficulties

**heim** ADVERB
*see also **das Heim** NOUN*
home ◊ *Ich muss jetzt heim.* I'll have to go home now.

die **Heimat** NOUN
homeland ◊ *Deutschland ist meine Heimat.* Germany's my homeland.

**heimatlos** ADJECTIVE
homeless

die **Heimfahrt** NOUN
journey home

**heimgehen** VERB (IMPERFECT **ging heim**, PERFECT **ist heimgegangen**)
to go home

**heimkehren** VERB (PERFECT **ist heimgekehrt**)
to return home

**heimlich** ADJECTIVE
secret ◊ *Er hat das heimlich gemacht.* He did it secretly.

die **Heimreise** NOUN
journey home

das **Heimspiel** NOUN (PL die **Heimspiele**)
home game

der **Heimweg** NOUN (PL die **Heimwege**)
way home

das **Heimweh** NOUN
homesickness

**heimzahlen** VERB (PERFECT **hat heimgezahlt**)
♦ **jemandem etwas heimzahlen** to pay somebody back for something

die **Heirat** NOUN
marriage

**heiraten** VERB
to get married ◊ *Sie heiraten morgen.* They're getting married tomorrow.
♦ **jemanden heiraten** to marry somebody

**heiser** ADJECTIVE
hoarse

die **Heiserkeit** NOUN
hoarseness

**heiß** ADJECTIVE
hot ◊ *Mir ist heiß.* I'm hot. ◊ *heiße Schokolade* hot chocolate

**heißen** VERB (IMPERFECT **hieß**, PERFECT **hat geheißen**)
1 to be called ◊ *Er heißt Marek.* He's called Marek.
2 to mean ◊ *Das heißt, dass wir morgen früh aufstehen müssen.* That means that we'll have to get up early tomorrow.
♦ **es heißt ...** it is said ...
♦ **das heißt** that is to say

**heiter** ADJECTIVE
1 cheerful ◊ *Ich war in heiterer Laune.* I was in a cheerful mood.
2 bright ◊ *Das Wetter wird heiter bis bewölkt.* The weather will be cloudy with bright spells.

**heizen** VERB
to heat

der **Heizkörper** NOUN (PL die **Heizkörper**)
radiator

die **Heizung** NOUN
heating

**hektisch** ADJECTIVE
hectic

der **Held** NOUN (GEN des **Helden**, PL die **Helden**)
hero

die **Heldin** NOUN
heroine

**helfen** VERB (PRESENT **hilft**, IMPERFECT **half**, PERFECT **hat geholfen**)
to help ◊ *Kann ich dir helfen?* Can I help you? ◊ *Die Tablette hat geholfen.* The pill helped.

♦ **jemandem bei etwas helfen** to help somebody with something
♦ **sich zu helfen wissen** to be resourceful ◊ *Er weiß sich zu helfen.* He's very resourceful.
♦ **Es hilft nichts, du musst ...** It's no use, you'll have to ...

**hell** ADJECTIVE
bright ◊ *Hier ist es schön hell.* It's nice and bright here.
♦ **Sie hat einen hellen Teint.** She has a clear complexion.
♦ **eine helle Farbe** a light colour
♦ **ein Helles** a light beer

**hellblau** ADJECTIVE
light blue

**hellblond** ADJECTIVE
ash-blond

der **Helm** NOUN (PL die **Helme**)
helmet

das **Hemd** NOUN (PL die **Hemden**)
shirt
♦ **ein Unterhemd** a vest

die **Hemmung** NOUN
inhibition ◊ *Er hat furchtbare Hemmungen.* He has terrible inhibitions.

der **Henkel** NOUN (PL die **Henkel**)
handle ◊ *ein Eimer ohne Henkel* a bucket without a handle

die **Henne** NOUN
hen

**her** ADVERB
ago ◊ *Das ist fünf Jahre her.* That was five years ago.
♦ **von ... her** from ... ◊ *von England her* from England ◊ *von weit her* from a long way away
♦ **Wo bist du her?** Where do you come from?
♦ **Komm her zu mir.** Come here.
♦ **Her damit!** Hand it over!
♦ **Wo hat er das her?** Where did he get that from?

**herab** ADVERB
down

**herabhängen** VERB (IMPERFECT **hing herab**, PERFECT **hat herabgehangen**)
to hang down

**herablassen** VERB (PRESENT **lässt herab**, IMPERFECT **ließ herab**, PERFECT **hat herabgelassen**)
to lower ◊ *die Rollläden herablassen* to lower the blinds
♦ **sich herablassen, etwas zu tun** to condescend to do something

**herablassend** ADJECTIVE
condescending

**heran** ADVERB
♦ **Näher heran!** Come closer!

**heranfahren** VERB (PRESENT **fährt heran**, IMPERFECT **fuhr heran**, PERFECT **ist herangefahren**) to drive up ◊ *Kannst du noch etwas näher an die Garage heranfahren?* Can you drive closer up to the garage?

**herauf** ADVERB
up ◊ *Komm hier herauf.* Come up here.

**heraus** ADVERB
out

**herausbekommen** VERB (IMPERFECT **bekam heraus,** PERFECT **hat herausbekommen**)
⬜1 to get out ◊ *Ich habe den Fleck nicht herausbekommen.* I didn't get the stain out.
⬜2 to find out ◊ *Ich muss herausbekommen, warum er das gemacht hat.* I'll have to find out why he did it.

**herausfordern** VERB (PERFECT **hat herausgefordert**)
to challenge

**herauskommen** VERB (IMPERFECT **kam heraus,** PERFECT **ist herausgekommen**)
to come out ◊ *Die Maus ist aus ihrem Loch herausgekommen.* The mouse came out of its hole.
◆ **Dabei kommt nichts heraus.** Nothing will come of it.

**herausnehmen** VERB (PRESENT **nimmt heraus,** IMPERFECT **nahm heraus,** PERFECT **hat herausgenommen**)
to take out ◊ *Sie hat das Lesezeichen aus dem Buch herausgenommen.* She took the bookmark out of the book.
◆ **sich etwas herausnehmen** to take liberties ◊ *Du nimmst dir wirklich etwas zu viel heraus.* You really do take far too many liberties.

**herausrücken** VERB (PERFECT **hat/ist herausgerückt**)
*For the perfect tense use **haben** when the verb has an object and **sein** when there is no object.*
to fork out ◊ *Er wollte kein Geld herausrücken.* He didn't want to fork out any money.
◆ **mit etwas herausrücken** to come out with something ◊ *Endlich ist er mit der Wahrheit herausgerückt.* He finally came out with the truth.

sich **herausstellen** VERB (PERFECT **hat sich herausgestellt**)
to turn out ◊ *Es stellte sich heraus, dass ...* It turned out that ...

**herausziehen** VERB (IMPERFECT **zog heraus,** PERFECT **hat herausgezogen**)
to pull out

**herb** ADJECTIVE
bitter ◊ *eine herbe Enttäuschung* a bitter disappointment ◊ *ein herber Geschmack* a bitter taste

**herbei** ADVERB
over ◊ *Alle eilten herbei.* Everyone hurried over.

die **Herbergseltern** PL NOUN

wardens (*in youth hostel*)

die **Herbergsmutter** NOUN (PL die **Herbergsmütter**)
warden (*in youth hostel*)

der **Herbergsvater** NOUN (PL die **Herbergsväter**)
warden (*in youth hostel*)

**herbringen** VERB (IMPERFECT **brachte her,** PERFECT **hat hergebracht**)
to bring here

der **Herbst** NOUN (PL die **Herbste**)
autumn ◊ *im Herbst* in autumn

die **Herbstferien** PL NOUN
autumn holidays

**herbstlich** ADJECTIVE
autumnal

der **Herd** NOUN (PL die **Herde**)
cooker ◊ *ein Herd mit vier Platten* a cooker with four rings

die **Herde** NOUN
herd ◊ *eine Herde Kühe* a herd of cows
◆ **eine Schafherde** a flock of sheep

**herein** ADVERB
in ◊ *Noch mehr Menschen drängten herein.* Even more people pushed their way in. ◊ *Das Wasser strömte herein.* The water poured in.
◆ **Herein!** Come in!

**hereinbitten** VERB (IMPERFECT **bat herein,** PERFECT **hat hereingebeten**)
to ask in

**hereinfallen** VERB (PRESENT **fällt herein,** IMPERFECT **fiel herein,** PERFECT **ist hereingefallen**)
◆ **auf etwas hereinfallen** to fall for something ◊ *Auf einen solch plumpen Trick falle ich nicht herein.* I'm not falling for an obvious trick like that. ◊ *Sie ist auf einen Betrüger hereingefallen.* She fell for a swindler.

**hereinkommen** VERB (IMPERFECT **kam herein,** PERFECT **ist hereingekommen**)
to come in

**hereinlassen** VERB (PRESENT **lässt herein,** IMPERFECT **ließ herein,** PERFECT **hat hereingelassen**)
to let in

**hereinlegen** VERB (PERFECT **hat hereingelegt**)
◆ **jemanden hereinlegen** to take somebody for a ride ◊ *Er will dich bloß hereinlegen.* He's just trying to take you for a ride.

**hergeben** VERB (PRESENT **gibt her,** IMPERFECT **gab her,** PERFECT **hat hergegeben**)
to hand over ◊ *Gib das Buch her!* Hand over the book!
◆ **sich zu etwas hergeben** to lend one's name to something

**hergehen** VERB (IMPERFECT **ging her,** PERFECT **ist hergegangen**)
◆ **hinter jemandem hergehen** to follow somebody

☞

♦ **Es geht hoch her.** There are a lot of goings-on.

**herhören** VERB (PERFECT **hat hergehört**)
to listen ◊ *Alle mal herhören!* Listen everybody!

der **Hering** NOUN (PL die **Heringe**)
herring

**herkommen** VERB (IMPERFECT **kam her**, PERFECT **ist hergekommen**)
to come ◊ *Komm mal her!* Come here!

die **Herkunft** NOUN (PL die **Herkünfte**)
origin

das **Heroin** NOUN
heroin

der **Herr** NOUN (GEN des **Herrn**, PL die **Herren**)
[1] gentleman ◊ *Er ist ein feiner Herr.* He's a fine gentleman.
[2] Lord ◊ *Herr, gib uns Frieden!* Lord, give us peace.
♦ **Herr Mosbacher** Mr Mosbacher
♦ **Mein Herr!** Sir!
♦ **Meine Herren!** Gentlemen!

**herrlich** ADJECTIVE
marvellous

**herrschen** VERB
[1] to reign ◊ *Wann hat Karl der Große geherrscht?* When did Charlemagne reign?
[2] to be ◊ *Hier herrschen ja schöne Zustände.* This is a fine state of affairs. ◊ *Es herrscht noch Ungewissheit, wann das gemacht werden soll.* It's still uncertain when it's to be done.

**herstellen** VERB (PERFECT **hat hergestellt**)
to manufacture

der **Hersteller** NOUN (PL die **Hersteller**)
manufacturer

die **Herstellung** NOUN
manufacture

**herüber** ADVERB
[1] over here ◊ *Er kam langsam zu uns herüber.* He came slowly over to us.
[2] across ◊ *Sie versuchte, zu uns herüberzuschwimmen.* She tried to swim across to us.

**herum** ADVERB
round ◊ *Mach ein rotes Band herum.* Tie a red band round it.
♦ **um etwas herum** round something ◊ *Sie gingen ums Haus herum.* They went round the house.

**herumführen** VERB (PERFECT **hat herumgeführt**)
to show around

**herumgehen** VERB (IMPERFECT **ging herum**, PERFECT **ist herumgegangen**)
to walk about ◊ *Wir sind ein paar Stunden in der Stadt herumgegangen.* We walked about the town for a couple of hours.

♦ **um etwas herumgehen** to walk round something ◊ *Sie ging um den Tisch herum.* She walked round the table.

**herumkommen** VERB (IMPERFECT **kam herum**, PERFECT **ist herumgekommen**)
to come round ◊ *Ich sah sie um die Kurve herumkommen.* I saw her coming round the corner.
♦ **Sie ist schon viel herumgekommen.** She's seen a lot of the world.

sich **herumsprechen** VERB (PRESENT **spricht sich herum**, IMPERFECT **sprach sich herum**, PERFECT **hat sich herumgesprochen**)
to get around

**herunter** ADVERB
down

**heruntergekommen** ADJECTIVE
run-down

**herunterkommen** VERB (IMPERFECT **kam herunter**, PERFECT **ist heruntergekommen**)
[1] to come down ◊ *Sie ist zu uns heruntergekommen.* She came down to us.
[2] to become run-down ◊ *Das Haus ist in den letzten Jahren ziemlich heruntergekommen.* The house has become rather run-down in the past few years.

**herunterladen** VERB (PRESENT **lädt herunter**, IMPERFECT **lud herunter**, PERFECT **hat heruntergeladen**)
to download (*computer*) ◊ *eine Datei herunterladen* to download a file

**hervorbringen** VERB (IMPERFECT **brachte hervor**, PERFECT **hat hervorgebracht**)
to produce

**hervorragend** ADJECTIVE
excellent

**hervorrufen** VERB (IMPERFECT **rief hervor**, PERFECT **hat hervorgerufen**)
to cause

das **Herz** NOUN (GEN des **Herzens**, PL die **Herzen**)
[1] heart ◊ *Es bricht mir fast das Herz.* It almost breaks my heart.
[2] hearts ◊ *Herz ist Trumpf.* Hearts is trumps.

der **Herzinfarkt** NOUN (PL die **Herzinfarkte**)
heart attack

**herzlich** ADJECTIVE
warm ◊ *ein herzlicher Empfang* a warm welcome ◊ *Wir wurden herzlich begrüßt.* We were warmly welcomed.
♦ **Herzlich willkommen in Bamberg.** Welcome to Bamberg.
♦ **Herzlichen Glückwunsch!** Congratulations.
♦ **Herzliche Grüße.** Best wishes.

**herzlos** ADJECTIVE
heartless

der **Herzschlag** NOUN (PL die **Herzschläge**)
[1] heartbeat ◊ *bei jedem Herzschlag* with every heartbeat

2 heart attack ◊ *Er hat einen Herzschlag bekommen.* He had a heart attack.

**Hessen** NEUT NOUN
Hesse

> ❶ *Hessen* is one of the 16 *Länder. Its capital is Wiesbaden, yet its biggest city is Frankfurt am Main, which is Germany's principal financial centre and home to the Bundesbank.*

das **Heu** NOUN
hay
♦ **Geld wie Heu** stacks of money

**heulen** VERB
1 to howl ◊ *Die Wölfe heulten.* The wolves were howling.
2 to cry ◊ *Jetzt fang nicht gleich an zu heulen.* Now don't start crying.

der **Heuschnupfen** NOUN
hay fever ◊ *Sie leidet an Heuschnupfen.* She suffers from hay fever.

**heute** ADVERB
today
♦ **heute Abend** this evening
♦ **heute Morgen** this morning
♦ **heute früh** this morning

**heutig** ADJECTIVE
today's ◊ *die heutige Jugend* today's youth

**heutzutage** ADVERB
nowadays

die **Hexe** NOUN
witch

**hexen** VERB
♦ **Ich kann doch nicht hexen.** I can't work miracles.

der **Hexenschuss** NOUN (GEN des **Hexenschusses**)
lumbago

**hielt** VERB see **halten**

**hier** ADVERB
here ◊ *hier drinnen* in here
♦ **Hier spricht Lisa.** This is Lisa.
♦ **hier bleiben** to stay here

**hierher** ADVERB
here

**hiesig** ADJECTIVE
local ◊ *die hiesige Bevölkerung* the local population

**hieß** VERB see **heißen**

die **Hilfe** NOUN
help
♦ **erste Hilfe** first aid
♦ **Hilfe!** Help!

das **Hilfemenü** NOUN (PL die **Hilfemenüs**)
help menu

**hilflos** ADJECTIVE
helpless

**hilfreich** ADJECTIVE
helpful

**hilfsbereit** ADJECTIVE
ready to help

**hilft** VERB see **helfen**

die **Himbeere** NOUN
raspberry

der **Himmel** NOUN (PL die **Himmel**)
1 sky ◊ *ein wolkenloser Himmel* a cloudless sky
2 heaven ◊ *in den Himmel kommen* to go to heaven

**himmelblau** ADJECTIVE
sky-blue

die **Himmelsrichtung** NOUN
♦ **die vier Himmelsrichtungen** the four points of the compass

**himmlisch** ADJECTIVE
heavenly

**hin** ADVERB
♦ **hin und zurück** there and back
♦ **hin und her** to and fro
♦ **Wo ist er hin?** Where has he gone?
♦ **Geld hin, Geld her** money or no money
♦ **auf meine Bitte hin** at my request

**hinab** ADVERB
down

**hinauf** ADVERB
up

**hinaufsteigen** VERB (IMPERFECT **stieg hinauf**, PERFECT **ist hinaufgestiegen**)
to climb ◊ *Wir sind auf den Berg hinaufgestiegen.* We climbed up the mountain.

**hinaus** ADVERB
out

**hinausgehen** VERB (IMPERFECT **ging hinaus**, PERFECT **ist hinausgegangen**)
to go out ◊ *Sie ist kurz hinausgegangen.* She's gone out for a minute.
♦ **über etwas hinausgehen** to exceed something ◊ *Das geht weit über meine Erwartungen hinaus.* That far exceeds my expectations.

**hinausschieben** VERB (IMPERFECT **schob hinaus**, PERFECT **hat hinausgeschoben**)
to put off ◊ *Sie haben die Entscheidung hinausgeschoben.* They put the decision off.

**hinauswerfen** VERB (PRESENT **wirft hinaus**, IMPERFECT **warf hinaus**, PERFECT **hat hinausgeworfen**)
to throw out

**hindern** VERB
♦ **jemanden an etwas hindern** to prevent somebody from doing something ◊ *Ich konnte ihn nicht am Weggehen hindern.* I couldn't prevent him from going.

das **Hindernis** NOUN (GEN des **Hindernisses**, PL die **Hindernisse**)
obstacle

**hinein** ADVERB
in ◊ *Hinein mit dir!* In you go!

**hineingehen** VERB (IMPERFECT **ging hinein**, PERFECT **ist hineingegangen**)

**H**

☞

to go in ◊ *Geh doch hinein.* Go in.
♦ **hineingehen in** to go into ◊ *Sie traute sich nicht, ins Zimmer hineinzugehen.* She didn't dare go into the room.
♦ **Meinst du, der Koffer geht noch in den Kofferraum hinein?** Do you think there's still room for the case in the boot?

**hineinpassen** VERB (PERFECT **hat hineingepasst**)
to fit ◊ *Der Schlüssel passt nicht hinein.* The key doesn't fit.
♦ **hineinpassen in** to fit into ◊ *Dein Koffer passt gerade noch in den Kofferraum hinein.* Your case just fits into the boot.

die **Hinfahrt** NOUN
outward journey

**hinfallen** VERB (PRESENT **fällt hin,** IMPERFECT **fiel hin,** PERFECT **ist hingefallen**)
to fall ◊ *Sie stolperte und fiel hin.* She stumbled and fell.

der **Hinflug** NOUN (PL die **Hinflüge**)
outward flight

**hinhalten** VERB (PRESENT **hält hin,** IMPERFECT **hielt hin,** PERFECT **hat hingehalten**)
to hold out ◊ *Sie hielt ihren Teller hin.* She held out her plate.
♦ **jemanden hinhalten** to put somebody off

**hinken** VERB
to limp

**hinlegen** VERB (PERFECT **hat hingelegt**)
to put down ◊ *Leg das Buch dort drüben hin.* Put the book down over there.
♦ **sich hinlegen** to lie down

**hinnehmen** VERB (PRESENT **nimmt hin,** IMPERFECT **nahm hin,** PERFECT **hat hingenommen**)
to put up with ◊ *Das kann ich nicht länger hinnehmen.* I can't put up with this any longer.

die **Hinreise** NOUN
outward journey

sich **hinsetzen** VERB (PERFECT **hat sich hingesetzt**)
to sit down

**hinstellen** VERB (PERFECT **hat hingestellt**)
to put ◊ *Wo soll ich die Vase hinstellen?* Where shall I put the vase?
♦ **Er stellte sich vor den Lehrer hin.** He went and stood in front of the teacher.

**hinten** ADVERB
at the back ◊ *Er sitzt ganz hinten.* He sits at the very back.

**hinter** PREPOSITION

*Use the accusative to express movement or a change of place. Use the dative when there is no change of place.*

[1] behind ◊ *Stell dich hinter deine Schwester.* Stand behind your sister.
◊ *Ich saß hinter ihr.* I was sitting behind her.
[2] after ◊ *Wir hatten kurz hinter Köln eine Panne.* We broke down just after Cologne.

**hintere** ADJECTIVE

back ◊ *die hinteren Reihen* the back rows
♦ **der hintere Reifen** the rear tyre

**hintereinander** ADVERB
one after the other
♦ **dreimal hintereinander** three times in a row

der **Hintergrund** NOUN (PL die **Hintergründe**)
background

**hinterher** ADVERB
afterwards

der **Hintern** NOUN (GEN des **Hintern,** PL die **Hintern**)
bottom

das **Hinterrad** NOUN (PL die **Hinterräder**)
back wheel

**hinüber** ADVERB
over

**hinübergehen** VERB (IMPERFECT **ging hinüber,** PERFECT **ist hinübergegangen**)
to go over

**hinunter** ADVERB
down

**hinunterschlucken** VERB (PERFECT **hat hinuntergeschluckt**)
to swallow

der **Hinweg** NOUN (PL die **Hinwege**)
way there ◊ *auf dem Hinweg* on the way there

der **Hinweis** NOUN (GEN des **Hinweises,** PL die **Hinweise**)
[1] hint ◊ *Er hat mir nicht den kleinsten Hinweis gegeben, wie ich das machen soll.* He didn't give me the slightest hint as to how I was supposed to do it.
[2] instruction ◊ *Hinweise zur Bedienung* operating instructions

**hinweisen** VERB (IMPERFECT **wies hin,** PERFECT **hat hingewiesen**)
♦ **jemanden auf etwas hinweisen** to point something out to somebody

**hinzufügen** VERB (PERFECT **hat hinzugefügt**)
to add

das **Hirn** NOUN (PL die **Hirne**)
brain

der **Hirsch** NOUN (PL die **Hirsche**)
stag

**historisch** ADJECTIVE
historic

die **Hitparade** NOUN
charts

die **Hitze** NOUN
heat

**hitzefrei** ADJECTIVE
♦ **hitzefrei haben** to have time off school because of excessively hot weather

**ⓘ** *If the temperature reaches 28°C - 30°C at 10 a.m., then German children are sent home early and any afternoon lessons are cancelled.*

die **Hitzewelle** NOUN

heat wave

der **Hitzschlag** NOUN (PL die **Hitzschläge**)
heatstroke

das **Hobby** NOUN (PL die **Hobbys**)
hobby

das **Hoch** NOUN (PL die **Hochs**)
> see also **hoch** ADJECTIVE
[1] cheer ◊ *Ein Hoch auf die Gastgeber!*
Three cheers for the hosts!
[2] area of high pressure ◊ *ein Hoch über dem Atlantik* an area of high pressure over the Atlantic

**hoch** ADJECTIVE
> see also **das Hoch** NOUN
high ◊ *zehn Meter hoch* ten metres high
> *Before a noun or after an article, use* ***hohe***.
◊ *ein hoher Zaun* a high fence
♦ **Das ist mir zu hoch.** That's above my head.
♦ **hoch begabt** extremely talented

**hochachtungsvoll** ADVERB
yours faithfully

das **Hochdeutsch** NOUN (GEN des **Hochdeutschen**)
High German

der **Hochdruck** NOUN
high pressure

das **Hochgebirge** NOUN (PL die **Hochgebirge**)
high mountains

das **Hochhaus** NOUN (GEN des **Hochhauses**, PL die **Hochhäuser**)
multistorey building

**hochheben** VERB (IMPERFECT **hob hoch**, PERFECT **hat hochgehoben**)
to lift up

**hochnäsig** ADJECTIVE
stuck-up

die **Hochsaison** NOUN (PL die **Hochsaisons**)
high season

die **Hochschule** NOUN
[1] college
[2] university

die **Hochschulreife** NOUN
♦ **Sie hat die Hochschulreife.** She's got her A-levels.

der **Hochsommer** NOUN (PL die **Hochsommer**)
high summer

der **Hochsprung** NOUN (PL die **Hochsprünge**)
high jump

**höchst** ADVERB
extremely

**höchste** ADJECTIVE
highest ◊ *Die Zugspitze ist der höchste Berg Deutschlands.* The Zugspitze is the highest mountain in Germany.

**höchstens** ADVERB
at most

die **Höchstgeschwindigkeit** NOUN
maximum speed

die **Höchsttemperatur** NOUN
maximum temperature

**höchstwahrscheinlich** ADVERB
most probably

die **Hochzeit** NOUN
wedding

der **Hochzeitstag** NOUN (PL die **Hochzeitstage**)
[1] wedding day ◊ *An ihrem Hochzeitstag trug sie ein wunderschönes Kleid.* She wore a beautiful dress on her wedding day.
[2] wedding anniversary ◊ *Morgen ist ihr zehnter Hochzeitstag.* It's their tenth wedding anniversary tomorrow.

der **Hocker** NOUN (PL die **Hocker**)
stool

der **Hof** NOUN (PL die **Höfe**)
[1] yard ◊ *Die Kinder spielen im Hof.* The children are playing in the yard.
[2] farm ◊ *Dieser Bauer hat den größten Hof im Dorf.* This farmer has the largest farm in the village.

**hoffen** VERB
to hope ◊ *Ich hoffe, er kommt noch.* I hope he's coming.
♦ **auf etwas hoffen** to hope for something ◊ *Wir hoffen auf besseres Wetter.* We're hoping for better weather.

**hoffentlich** ADVERB
hopefully ◊ *Hoffentlich kommt er bald.* Hopefully he'll come soon. ◊ *Das passiert hoffentlich nie wieder.* Hopefully that won't happen again.
♦ **Hoffentlich nicht.** I hope not.

die **Hoffnung** NOUN
hope

**hoffnungslos** ADJECTIVE
hopeless

**hoffnungsvoll** ADJECTIVE
hopeful

**höflich** ADJECTIVE
polite

die **Höflichkeit** NOUN
politeness

**hohe** ADJECTIVE
> ***hohe*** *is the form of* ***hoch*** *used before a noun.*
high ◊ *ein hoher Zaun* a high fence

die **Höhe** NOUN
height

der **Höhepunkt** NOUN (PL die **Höhepunkte**)
climax ◊ *der Höhepunkt des Abends* the climax of the evening

**höher** ADJECTIVE, ADVERB
higher

**hohl** ADJECTIVE
hollow

die **Höhle** NOUN
cave

**holen** VERB
to get ◊ *Ich hole ihn.* I'll get him.

**H**

◆ **jemanden holen lassen** to send for somebody

**Holland** NEUT NOUN
Holland
◆ **aus Holland** from Holland
◆ **in Holland** in Holland
◆ **nach Holland** to Holland

der **Holländer** NOUN (PL die **Holländer**)
Dutchman
◆ **Er ist Holländer.** He's Dutch.
◆ **die Holländer** the Dutch

die **Holländerin** NOUN
Dutchwoman
◆ **Sie ist Holländerin.** She's Dutch.

**holländisch** ADJECTIVE
Dutch

die **Hölle** NOUN
hell

das **Holz** NOUN (GEN des **Holzes**, PL die **Hölzer**)
wood

die **Holzkohle** NOUN
charcoal

die **Homepage** NOUN
home page

**homosexuell** ADJECTIVE
homosexual

der **Honig** NOUN (PL die **Honige**)
honey

die **Honigmelone** NOUN
honeydew melon

der **Hopfen** NOUN (PL die **Hopfen**)
hops

**hörbar** ADJECTIVE
audible

**horchen** VERB
[1] to listen ◇ *Er horchte auf das kleinste Geräusch.* He listened for the slightest noise.
[2] to eavesdrop ◇ *Du hast an der Tür gehorcht!* You've been eavesdropping at the door!

**hören** VERB
to hear ◇ *Ich höre dich nicht.* I can't hear you.
◆ **Musik hören** to listen to music
◆ **Radio hören** to listen to the radio

der **Hörer** NOUN (PL die **Hörer**)
receiver ◇ *Sie hat einfach den Hörer aufgelegt.* She simply put down the receiver.

der **Horizont** NOUN (PL die **Horizonte**)
horizon ◇ *am Horizont* on the horizon

**horizontal** ADJECTIVE
horizontal

das **Horn** NOUN (PL die **Hörner**)
horn

der **Horror** NOUN
horror

der **Horrorfilm** NOUN (PL die **Horrorfilme**)
horror film

der **Horrorroman** NOUN (PL die **Horrorromane**)
horror novel

die **Hose** NOUN
trousers ◇ *eine Hose* a pair of trousers
*Be careful! The German word **Hose** does not mean **hose**.*

der **Hosenanzug** NOUN (PL die **Hosenanzüge**)
trouser suit

die **Hosentasche** NOUN
trouser pocket

der **Hosenträger** NOUN (PL die **Hosenträger**)
braces

das **Hotel** NOUN (PL die **Hotels**)
hotel

**Hr.** ABBREVIATION (= *Herr*)
Mr

**hübsch** ADJECTIVE
pretty

der **Hubschrauber** NOUN (PL die **Hubschrauber**)
helicopter

das **Hufeisen** NOUN (PL die **Hufeisen**)
horseshoe

die **Hüfte** NOUN
hip

der **Hügel** NOUN (PL die **Hügel**)
hill

**hügelig** ADJECTIVE
hilly

das **Huhn** NOUN (PL die **Hühner**)
chicken ◇ *Huhn mit Reis* chicken with rice

die **Hummel** NOUN
bumblebee

der **Hummer** NOUN (PL die **Hummer**)
lobster

der **Humor** NOUN
humour
◆ **Humor haben** to have a sense of humour

**humorvoll** ADJECTIVE
humorous

der **Hund** NOUN (PL die **Hunde**)
dog

die **Hundehütte** NOUN
kennel

**hundemüde** ADJECTIVE
dog-tired

**hundert** NUMBER
a hundred

der **Hunger** NOUN
hunger
◆ **Hunger haben** to be hungry

**hungrig** ADJECTIVE
hungry

die **Hupe** NOUN
horn ◇ *auf die Hupe drücken* to sound the horn

**hupen** VERB
to sound the horn

**hüpfen** VERB (PERFECT **ist gehüpft**)
to hop

der **Hürdenlauf** NOUN (PL die **Hürdenläufe**)
hurdles

der **Husten** NOUN

> see also **husten** VERB

cough ◊ *Sie hat Husten.* She has a
cough.

**husten** VERB

> see also **der Husten** NOUN

to cough

das **Hustenbonbon** NOUN (PL die
**Hustenbonbons**)

cough drop

der **Hustensaft** NOUN (PL die **Hustensäfte**)

cough mixture

der **Hut** NOUN (PL die **Hüte**)

> see also **die Hut** NOUN

hat

die **Hut** NOUN

> see also **der Hut** NOUN

◆ **auf der Hut sein** to be on one's guard

**hüten** VERB

to look after ◊ *Silke hütet heute Abend*
*unsere Kinder.* Silke's looking after our
children this evening.

◆ **ein Geheimnis hüten** to keep a secret

◆ **sich hüten, etwas zu tun** to take care not
to do something ◊ *Ich werde mich hüten,*
*ihr das zu sagen.* I'll take care not to say
that to her.

◆ **sich hüten vor** to be on one's guard
against ◊ *Hüte dich vor ihm, er lügt.* Be
on your guard against him, he's a liar.

die **Hütte** NOUN

hut

**hygienisch** ADJECTIVE

hygienic

**hypnotisieren** VERB (PERFECT **hat**
**hypnotisiert**)

to hypnotize

**hysterisch** ADJECTIVE

hysterical ◊ *Sie wurde hysterisch.* She
became hysterical.

**H**

# I

**IC** ABBREVIATION (= *Intercityzug*)
  Intercity train
**ICE** ABBREVIATION (= *Intercityexpress*)
  Intercity Express train
**ich** PRONOUN
  I ◊ *Ich weiß nicht.* I don't know.
  ◆ **Ich bin's!** It's me!
das **Icon** NOUN (PL die **Icons**)
  icon (*computer*) ◊ *ein Icon anklicken* to
  click on an icon
das **Ideal** NOUN (PL die **Ideale**)
  see also **ideal** ADJECTIVE
  ideal
**ideal** ADJECTIVE
  see also **das Ideal** NOUN
  ideal
die **Idee** NOUN
  idea
**identifizieren** VERB (PERFECT **hat**
  **identifiziert**)
  to identify
**identisch** ADJECTIVE
  identical
die **Ideologie** NOUN
  ideology
**ideologisch** ADJECTIVE
  ideological
der **Idiot** NOUN (GEN des **Idioten**, PL die **Idioten**)
  idiot
**idiotisch** ADJECTIVE
  idiotic
der **Igel** NOUN (PL die **Igel**)
  hedgehog
**ihm** PRONOUN
  *ihm is the dative of er and es.*
  **1** him ◊ *Kannst du ihm sagen, wie spät
  es ist?* Can you tell him what the time is?
  **2** to him ◊ *Gib es ihm!* Give it to him.
  **3** it ◊ *Das Meerschweinchen hat Hunger,
  gib ihm was zu essen.* The guinea pig's
  hungry, give it something to eat.
**ihn** PRONOUN
  *ihn is the accusative of er.*
  him ◊ *Ich habe ihn gesehen.* I saw him.
**ihnen** PRONOUN
  see also **Ihnen** PRONOUN
  *ihnen is the dative of sie (plural).*
  **1** them ◊ *Ich sage es ihnen.* I'll tell them.
  **2** to them ◊ *Gib es ihnen.* Give it to
  them.
**Ihnen** PRONOUN
  see also **ihnen** PRONOUN
  *Ihnen is the dative of Sie.*
  **1** you ◊ *Darf ich Ihnen etwas zu trinken
  anbieten?* May I offer you something to
  drink?
  **2** to you ◊ *Darf ich Ihnen das geben?*
  May I give this to you?

**ihr** PRONOUN
  see also **Ihr** ADJECTIVE, **ihr** ADJECTIVE
  **1** you ◊ *Habt ihr das gesehen?* Did you
  see that?

  *❶ The familiar form of address **ihr** is
  used when addressing family
  members, friends, children under 16
  and pets.*

  ◊ *Ihr seid es.* It's you.
  *ihr is also the dative of **sie** (singular).*
  **2** her ◊ *Kannst du ihr das bitte
  ausrichten?* Can you please tell her?
  ◆ **Er steht neben ihr.** He's standing beside
  her.
  **3** to her ◊ *Gib es ihr.* Give it to her.
**ihr** ADJECTIVE
  see also **Ihr** ADJECTIVE, **ihr** PRONOUN
  **1** her ◊ *Ihr Vater ist nett.* Her father's
  nice. ◊ *Ihre Mutter hat mir das gesagt.*
  Her mother told me. ◊ *Das ist ihr
  Fahrrad.* That's her bike. ◊ *Ihre Eltern
  sind prima.* Her parents are great.
  **2** hers ◊ *Das ist nicht ihr Füller, ihrer ist
  schwarz.* That's not her pen, hers is
  black. ◊ *Meine Mutter heißt Ulla, ihre
  auch.* My mother's called Ulla, so is hers.
  ◊ *Mein Fahrrad war kaputt, also habe ich
  ihres genommen.* My bike was broken,
  so I took hers. ◊ *Seine Noten sind
  schlecht, ihre sind viel besser.* His marks
  are bad, hers are much better.
  **3** their ◊ *Das ist ihr Lehrer.* That's their
  teacher. ◊ *Ihre Englischlehrerin ist netter
  als unsere.* Their English teacher's nicer
  than ours. ◊ *Ihr Haus liegt gleich neben
  unserem.* Their house is right next door
  to ours. ◊ *die Bäume und ihre Blätter* the
  trees and their leaves
  **4** theirs ◊ *Das ist nicht ihr Lehrer, ihrer
  heißt Herr Schulz.* That's not their
  teacher, theirs is called Mr Schulz.
  ◊ *Unsere Schule macht einen
  Wandertag, ihre nicht.* Our school is
  going rambling, theirs isn't. ◊ *Das ist
  nicht ihr Haus, ihres ist in der
  Hauptstraße.* That's not their house,
  theirs is on the main road. ◊ *Unsere
  Lehrer sind streng, ihre sind viel netter.*
  Our teachers are strict, theirs are much
  nicer.
**Ihr** ADJECTIVE
  see also **ihr** ADJECTIVE, **ihr** PRONOUN
  **1** your ◊ *Ihr Vater ist nett.* Your father's
  nice. ◊ *Ihre Mutter hat mir das gesagt.*
  Your mother told me. ◊ *Ist das Ihr
  Fahrrad?* Is that your bike? ◊ *Leben Ihre
  Eltern noch?* Are your parents still alive?

2 yours ◊ *Das ist nicht Ihr Füller, Ihrer ist hier.* That's not your pen, yours is here. ◊ *Meine Mutter heißt Ulla, wie heißt Ihre?* My mother's called Ulla, what's yours called? ◊ *Mein Fahrrad ist kaputt, kann ich Ihres nehmen?* My bike's broken, can I take yours? ◊ *Unsere Kinder sind nicht so artig wie Ihre.* Our children aren't as well-behaved as yours.

**ihretwegen** ADVERB

see also **Ihretwegen**

*ihretwegen refers to **sie** (singular or plural).*

1 for her sake ◊ *Ich habe ihretwegen auf den Urlaub verzichtet.* I went without a holiday for her sake.

2 on her account ◊ *Er hat sich ihretwegen furchtbar aufgeregt.* He got terribly upset on her account.

3 as far as she's concerned ◊ *Sie sagt, dass du ihretwegen ruhig gehen kannst.* She says that as far as she's concerned you can go.

4 for their sake ◊ *Wir haben ihretwegen auf den Urlaub verzichtet.* We went without a holiday for their sake.

5 on their account ◊ *Er hat sich ihretwegen furchtbar aufgeregt.* He got terribly upset on their account.

6 as far as they're concerned ◊ *Sie sagen, dass du ihretwegen ruhig gehen kannst.* They say that as far as they're concerned you can go.

**Ihretwegen** ADVERB

see also **ihretwegen**

*Ihretwegen refers to **Sie**.*

1 for your sake ◊ *Ich habe Ihretwegen auf den Urlaub verzichtet.* I went without a holiday for your sake.

2 on your account ◊ *Er hat sich Ihretwegen furchtbar aufgeregt.* He got terribly upset on your account.

die **Illustrierte** NOUN (GEN der **Illustrierten**)
  magazine

**im** = **in dem**

der **Imbiss** NOUN (GEN des **Imbisses,** PL die **Imbisse**)
  snack

die **Imbisshalle** NOUN
  snack bar

der **Imbissstand** NOUN (PL die **Imbissstände**)
  hot-dog stand

die **Imbissstube** NOUN
  snack bar

**immatrikulieren** VERB (PERFECT **hat immatrikuliert**)
  to register (*at university*)

**immer** ADVERB
  always ◊ *Du kommst immer zu spät.* You're always late.
  ♦ **immer wieder** again and again
  ♦ **immer noch** still
  ♦ **immer noch nicht** still not

♦ **für immer** forever
♦ **immer wenn ich ...** every time I ...
♦ **immer schöner** more and more beautiful
♦ **immer trauriger** sadder and sadder
♦ **wer auch immer** whoever
♦ **was auch immer** whatever

**immerhin** ADVERB
  at least

das **Imperfekt** NOUN (PL die **Imperfekte**)
  imperfect

**impfen** VERB
  to vaccinate ◊ *jemanden gegen etwas impfen* to vaccinate somebody against something

der **Impfstoff** NOUN (PL die **Impfstoffe**)
  vaccine

die **Impfung** NOUN
  vaccination

**imponieren** VERB (PERFECT **hat imponiert**)
  to impress ◊ *jemandem imponieren* to impress somebody

der **Import** NOUN (PL die **Importe**)
  import

**importieren** VERB (PERFECT **hat importiert**)
  to import

**improvisieren** VERB (PERFECT **hat improvisiert**)
  to improvise

**imstande** ADJECTIVE
♦ **imstande sein, etwas zu tun** to be able to do something

**in** PREPOSITION

*Use the accusative to express movement or a change of place. Use the dative when there is no change of place.*

1 in ◊ *Es ist im Schrank.* It's in the cupboard. ◊ *Sie ist in der Stadt.* She's in town. ◊ *Sie wurde rot im Gesicht.* She went red in the face.

2 into ◊ *Lege es in diese Schublade.* Put it into this drawer. ◊ *Sie geht in die Stadt.* She's going into town.

♦ **in der Schule sein** to be at school
♦ **in die Schule gehen** to go to school
♦ **in diesem Jahr** this year
♦ **heute in zwei Wochen** two weeks today
♦ **bis ins zwanzigste Jahrhundert** into the twentieth century
♦ **in sein** to be in ◊ *Inline-Skates sind jetzt in.* In-line skates are in at the moment.

**inbegriffen** ADVERB
  included

der **Inder** NOUN (PL die **Inder**)
  Indian

die **Inderin** NOUN
  Indian

der **Indianer** NOUN (PL die **Indianer**)
  Native American

die **Indianerin** NOUN
  Native American

**indianisch** ADJECTIVE
  Native American

das **Indien** NOUN
India
♦ **aus Indien** from India
♦ **nach Indien** to India

**indisch** ADJECTIVE
Indian

**indiskutabel** ADJECTIVE
out of the question

die **Industrie** NOUN
industry

das **Industriegebiet** NOUN (PL die **Industriegebiete**)
industrial area

die **Industriestadt** NOUN (PL die **Industriestädte**)
industrial town

der **Infarkt** NOUN (PL die **Infarkte**)
coronary

die **Infektion** NOUN
infection

der **Infinitiv** NOUN (PL die **Infinitive**)
infinitive

**infizieren** VERB (PERFECT **hat infiziert**)
to infect ◊ *Sie hat ihren Bruder infiziert.* She infected her brother.
♦ **sich bei jemandem infizieren** to catch something from somebody

die **Inflation** NOUN
inflation

**infolge** PREPOSITION
*The preposition **infolge** takes the genitive.*
as a result of

**infolgedessen** ADVERB
consequently

die **Informatik** NOUN
computer science

der **Informatiker** NOUN (PL die **Informatiker**)
computer scientist

die **Information** NOUN
information ◊ *Weitere Informationen lassen wir Ihnen zukommen.* We will send you further information.

das **Informationsbüro** NOUN (PL die **Informationsbüros**)
information bureau

**informieren** VERB (PERFECT **hat informiert**)
to inform
♦ **sich über etwas informieren** to find out about something ◊ *Ich werde mich über die Bedingungen informieren.* I'll find out about the terms.
♦ **sich über jemanden informieren** to make enquiries about somebody ◊ *Ich habe mich über ihn informiert.* I've made enquiries about him.

der **Ingenieur** NOUN (PL die **Ingenieure**)
engineer

die **Ingenieurschule** NOUN
school of engineering

der **Ingwer** NOUN
ginger

der **Inhaber** NOUN (PL die **Inhaber**)
owner ◊ *Wir müssen den Inhaber des Hauses fragen, ob das geht.* We'll have to ask the owner of the house if it's all right.
♦ **der Inhaber einer Lizenz** the licence holder

der **Inhalt** NOUN (PL die **Inhalte**)
[1] contents ◊ *Der Inhalt der Flasche war grün.* The contents of the bottle were green.
[2] content ◊ *Fasse den Inhalt dieser Geschichte zusammen.* Summarize the content of this story.
[3] volume ◊ *Berechne den Inhalt des Würfels.* Calculate the volume of the cube.

die **Inhaltsangabe** NOUN
summary

das **Inhaltsverzeichnis** NOUN (GEN des **Inhaltsverzeichnisses**, PL die **Inhaltsverzeichnisse**)
table of contents

**inkl.** ABBREVIATION (= *inklusive*)
incl.

**inklusive** PREPOSITION, ADVERB
*The preposition **inklusive** takes the genitive.*
[1] inclusive of ◊ *ein Computer inklusive Bildschirm* a computer inclusive of monitor
[2] included ◊ *Die Bedienung ist inklusive.* Service is included.

das **Inland** NOUN
♦ **im In- und Ausland** at home and abroad

**innen** ADVERB
inside

der **Innenminister** NOUN (PL die **Innenminister**)
Home Secretary

die **Innenpolitik** NOUN
domestic policy

**innenpolitisch** ADJECTIVE
internal

die **Innenstadt** NOUN (PL die **Innenstädte**)
town centre

**innere** ADJECTIVE
internal ◊ *innere Blutungen* internal bleeding ◊ *die inneren Angelegenheiten des Landes* the internal matters of the country

die **Innereien** FEM PL NOUN
innards

**innerhalb** ADVERB, PREPOSITION
*The preposition **innerhalb** takes the genitive.*
[1] within ◊ *innerhalb von zwei Tagen* within two days
♦ **Ich schaffe das nicht innerhalb der gesetzten Frist.** I won't manage that by the deadline.
[2] during ◊ *Der Bus fährt nur innerhalb der Woche, nicht an Wochenenden.* The

bus only runs during the week, not at the weekend.

**inoffiziell** ADJECTIVE
unofficial

**ins** = **in das**

**insbesondere** ADVERB
particularly

die **Inschrift** NOUN
inscription

das **Insekt** NOUN (PL die **Insekten**)
insect

der **Insektenstich** NOUN (PL die **Insektenstiche**)
insect bite

die **Insel** NOUN
island

**insgesamt** ADVERB
in all ◊ *Er hat insgesamt drei Fahrräder.*
He has three bikes in all. ◊ *Insgesamt waren dreihundert Leute gekommen.* In all, three hundred people came.

der **Instinkt** NOUN (PL die **Instinkte**)
instinct

**instinktiv** ADJECTIVE
instinctive

das **Instrument** NOUN (PL die **Instrumente**)
instrument

**intellektuell** ADJECTIVE
intellectual

**intelligent** ADJECTIVE
intelligent

die **Intelligenz** NOUN
intelligence

**intensiv** ADJECTIVE
intensive

der **Intercityexpress** NOUN (GEN des **Intercityexpresses**, PL die **Intercityexpresse**)
Intercity Express train

der **Intercityzug** NOUN (PL die **Intercityzüge**)
Intercity train

**interessant** ADJECTIVE
interesting

das **Interesse** NOUN (PL die **Interessen**)
interest
 ◆ **Interesse haben an** to be interested in
 ◊ *Hast du Interesse an einem gebrauchten Notebook?* Are you interested in a used notebook?
 ◊ *Manfred scheint Interesse an dir zu haben.* Manfred seems to be interested in you.

**interessieren** VERB (PERFECT **hat interessiert**)
to interest ◊ *Es interessiert mich, was du in den Ferien erlebt hast.* I'm interested to know what you did in your holidays.
 ◆ **sich interessieren für** to be interested in
 ◊ *Ich interessiere mich für Kunst.* I'm interested in art.

das **Internat** NOUN (PL die **Internate**)
boarding school

**international** ADJECTIVE

international

das **Internet** NOUN
Internet

der **Internet-Anbieter** NOUN (PL die **Internet-Anbieter**)
Internet Service Provider

der **Internetbenutzer** NOUN (PL die **Internetbenutzer**)
Internet user

das **Internet-Café** NOUN (PL die **Internet-Cafés**)
Internet café

**interpretieren** VERB (PERFECT **hat interpretiert**)
to interpret

**intransitiv** ADJECTIVE
intransitive

**inwiefern** ADVERB
how far ◊ *Ich weiß nicht, inwiefern das stimmt.* I don't know how far that's right.

**inzwischen** ADVERB
meanwhile

der **Irak** NOUN
Iraq
 ◆ **aus dem Irak** from Iraq
 ◆ **im Irak** in Iraq
 ◆ **in den Irak** to Iraq

**irakisch** ADJECTIVE
Iraqi

der **Iran** NOUN
Iran
 ◆ **aus dem Iran** from Iran
 ◆ **im Iran** in Iran
 ◆ **in den Iran** to Iran

**iranisch** ADJECTIVE
Iranian

der **Ire** NOUN (GEN des **Iren**, PL die **Iren**)
Irishman
 ◆ **die Iren** the Irish

**irgend** ADVERB
at all ◊ *Komm, wenn es irgend geht.*
Come if it's at all possible.

**irgendein** ADJECTIVE
 [1] some ◊ *Irgendein Mann hat mir das gesagt.* Some man told me. ◊ *Irgendeine Ausrede wird dir schon einfallen.* You'll think of some excuse.
 ◆ **Bring mir irgendein Getränk mit.** Bring me something to drink.
 ◆ **Welchen Kuli willst du? – Irgendeinen.**
Which pen do you want? – Any one.
 [2] any ◊ *Ich will nicht irgendeinen Computer.* I don't just want any computer. ◊ *Gibt es nicht irgendeine Möglichkeit?* Isn't there any chance?

**irgendetwas** PRONOUN
 [1] something ◊ *irgendetwas Schönes* something nice
 [2] anything ◊ *Hast du irgendetwas gehört?* Did you hear anything?

**irgendjemand** PRONOUN

**I**

☞

1 somebody ◊ *Das hat mir irgendjemand gesagt.* Somebody told me.

2 anybody ◊ *Hast du irgendjemanden gesehen?* Did you see anybody?

**irgendwann** ADVERB
sometime

**irgendwas** PRONOMEN

1 something ◊ *Er murmelte irgendwas.* He murmured something.

2 anything ◊ *Was soll ich anziehen? – Irgendwas.* What shall I wear? – Anything.

**irgendwie** ADVERB
somehow

**irgendwo** ADVERB
somewhere

**irgendwohin** ADVERB
somewhere ◊ *Ich habe das irgendwohin gelegt.* I've put it somewhere.
◆ **Stell es irgendwohin.** Put it anywhere.

die **Irin** NOUN
Irishwoman

**irisch** ADJECTIVE
Irish

**Irland** NEUT NOUN
Ireland
◆ **aus Irland** from Ireland
◆ **in Irland** in Ireland
◆ **nach Irland** to Ireland

die **Ironie** NOUN
irony

**ironisch** ADJECTIVE
ironic ◊ *Das war ironisch gemeint.* That was meant to be ironic.

**irre** ADJECTIVE, ADVERB

1 mad ◊ *Wer ist denn auf diese irre Idee gekommen?* Who thought up this mad idea?

2 fantastic ◊ *Das war ein irres Konzert.* That was a fantastic concert.

3 incredibly ◊ *Er ist irre schnell gefahren.* He drove incredibly fast. ◊ *Die Party war irre gut.* The party was incredibly good.

**irreführen** VERB (PERFECT **hat irregeführt**)
to mislead

**irren** VERB

*Use **haben** to form the perfect tense for **to be mistaken** but **sein** for **to wander about**.*

◆ **sich irren** to be mistaken ◊ *Du hast dich geirrt.* You were mistaken. to wander about ◊ *Sie ist durch die Straßen geirrt.* She wandered about the streets.

**irrsinnig** ADJECTIVE, ADVERB

1 crazy ◊ *Das ist doch eine irrsinnige Idee.* That's a crazy idea.

2 incredibly ◊ *Er ist irrsinnig schnell gefahren.* He drove incredibly fast.

der **Irrtum** NOUN (PL die **Irrtümer**)
mistake

der **Islam** NOUN
Islam

**Island** NEUT NOUN
Iceland
◆ **nach Island** to Iceland

**Israel** NEUT NOUN
Israel
◆ **aus Israel** from Israel
◆ **nach Israel** to Israel

der **Israeli** NOUN (PL die **Israelis**)
die Israeli ◊ *Sie ist mit einem Israeli verheiratet.* He is married to an Israeli.

**israelisch** ADJECTIVE
Israeli

**isst** VERB see **essen**

**ist** VERB see **sein**

**Italien** NEUT NOUN
Italy
◆ **aus Italien** from Italy
◆ **in Italien** in Italy
◆ **nach Italien** to Italy

der **Italiener** NOUN (PL die **Italiener**)
Italian

die **Italienerin** NOUN
Italian

**italienisch** ADJECTIVE
Italian

# J

**ja** ADVERB
1 yes ◊ *Hast du das gesehen? – Ja.* Did you see that? – Yes, I did.
♦ **Ich glaube ja.** I think so.
2 really? ◊ *Ich habe mir ein neues Auto gekauft. – Ach ja?* I've bought a new car. – Really?
♦ **Ich habe gekündigt. – Ja?** I've quit. – Have you?
♦ **Du kommst, ja?** You're coming, aren't you?
♦ **Sei ja vorsichtig!** Do be careful.
♦ **Sie wissen ja, dass ...** As you know, ...
♦ **Tu das ja nicht!** Don't you dare do that!
♦ **Ich habe es ja gewusst.** I just knew it.
♦ **ja, also ...** well ... ◊ *Ja, also wenn ihr alle geht, dann gehe ich mit.* Well, if you're all going, then I'm going too.

**die Jacht** NOUN
yacht

**die Jacke** NOUN
1 jacket ◊ *Sie trug einen blauen Rock und eine schwarze Jacke.* She was wearing a blue skirt and a black jacket.
2 cardigan ◊ *Wenn es dir kalt ist, solltest du eine Jacke anziehen.* If you're cold, you should put on a cardigan.

**das Jackett** NOUN (PL die **Jacketts**)
jacket

**die Jagd** NOUN (PL die **Jagden**)
1 hunt ◊ *Er fiel während der Jagd vom Pferd.* He fell off his horse during the hunt.
2 hunting ◊ *Alan geht oft zur Jagd.* Alan often goes hunting.

**jagen** VERB

> Use **haben** to form the perfect tense for **to hunt** or **to chase** but **sein** for **to race**.

1 to hunt ◊ *Sonntags geht er jagen.* He goes hunting on Sundays. ◊ *Er hat in Afrika Löwen gejagt.* He hunted lions in Africa. ◊ *Meine Katze jagt Mäuse.* My cat hunts mice.
2 to chase ◊ *Die Polizei hat die Bankräuber gejagt, aber nicht eingeholt.* The police chased the bank robbers but didn't catch them.
3 to race ◊ *Wir sind mit ihr ins Krankenhaus gejagt.* We raced with her to the hospital.
♦ **Damit kann man mich jagen.** I can't stand that.

**das Jahr** NOUN (PL die **Jahre**)
year ◊ *Ich bin vierzehn Jahre alt.* I'm fourteen years old.
♦ **die neunziger Jahre** the nineties

**jahrelang** ADVERB
for years

**die Jahreszeit** NOUN
season
♦ **zu jeder Jahreszeit** throughout the year ◊ *Man bekommt inzwischen zu jeder Jahreszeit Erdbeeren.* You can now get strawberries throughout the year.

**der Jahrgang** NOUN (PL die **Jahrgänge**)
♦ **Sie ist mein Jahrgang.** She was born in the same year as me.
♦ **Welcher Jahrgang bist du?** In which year were you born?

**das Jahrhundert** NOUN (PL die **Jahrhunderte**)
century

**jährlich** ADJECTIVE, ADVERB
yearly

**der Jahrmarkt** NOUN (PL die **Jahrmärkte**)
funfair

**das Jahrtausend** NOUN (PL die **Jahrtausende**)
millennium

**jähzornig** ADJECTIVE
hot-tempered

**die Jalousie** NOUN
Venetian blind

**der Jammer** NOUN
misery
♦ **Es ist ein Jammer, dass ...** It's a crying shame that ...

**jämmerlich** ADJECTIVE
pitiful ◊ *ein jämmerliches Miauen* a pitiful miaowing
♦ **jämmerlich weinen** to cry bitterly

**jammern** VERB
to whine ◊ *Hör auf zu jammern!* Stop whining.

**der Januar** NOUN (GEN des **Januar** or **Januars,** PL die **Januare**)
January ◊ *im Januar* in January ◊ *am dritten Januar* on the third of January ◊ *Ulm, den 3. Januar 2005* Ulm, 3 January 2005 ◊ *Heute ist der dritte Januar.* Today is the third of January.

**Japan** NEUT NOUN
Japan
♦ **aus Japan** from Japan
♦ **nach Japan** to Japan

**der Japaner** NOUN (PL die **Japaner**)
Japanese

**die Japanerin** NOUN
Japanese

**japanisch** ADJECTIVE
Japanese

**jaulen** VERB
to howl

**jawohl** ADVERB
yes

**je** ADVERB, CONJUNCTION
1 ever ◊ *Warst du je in Italien?* Have you ever been to Italy? ◊ *Hast du so was je*

*gesehen?* Did you ever see anything like it?

2 each ◊ *Wir haben je zwei Stück bekommen.* We got two pieces each. ◊ *Sie zahlten je drei Mark.* They paid three marks each.

♦ **je nach** depending on ◊ *Je nach Größe sind sie verschieden teuer.* Prices vary depending on size.

♦ **je nachdem** it depends ◊ *Wir kommen vielleicht etwas später, je nachdem, wie lange wir unterwegs sind.* We'll perhaps be a little late, it depends how long we take to get there.

♦ **je nachdem, ob** ... depending on whether ... ◊ *Wir kommen vielleicht mit den Kindern, je nachdem ob sie Lust haben.* We'll come with the children depending on whether they feel like it or not.

♦ **je ... umso ...** the ... the ... ◊ *Je schneller er fuhr, umso mehr Angst hatte sie.* The faster he drove, the more frightened she was.

♦ **je eher, desto besser** the sooner the better

♦ **besser denn je** better than ever

♦ **Es geht mir besser denn je.** Things have never been better.

die **Jeans** NOUN (PL die **Jeans**)
  jeans
  ♦ **eine Jeans** a pair of jeans ◊ *Ich habe mir eine neue Jeans gekauft.* I've bought myself a new pair of jeans.

**jede** ADJECTIVE, PRONOUN
  1 every ◊ *Jeder Schüler bekommt ein Zeugnis.* Every pupil receives a report. ◊ *Ich besuche sie jede Woche.* I visit her every week. ◊ *Er gab jedem Mädchen ein Bonbon.* He gave every girl a sweet.
  ♦ **jeder** everybody ◊ *Jeder weiß, dass das nicht erlaubt ist.* Everybody knows that that's not allowed.
  2 each ◊ *Jeder von euch bekommt ein Stück.* Each of you will get a piece. ◊ *Jede seiner Freundinnen war anders.* Each of his girlfriends was different.
  ♦ **Jedes der Kinder hat mir etwas geschenkt.** Each child gave me something.

**jedenfalls** ADVERB
  in any case

**jedermann** PRONOUN
  everyone

**jederzeit** ADVERB
  at any time

**jedesmal** ADVERB
  every time

**jedoch** ADVERB
  however

**jemals** ADVERB
  ever

**jemand** PRONOUN

1 somebody ◊ *Jemand hat mir gesagt, dass du krank bist.* Somebody told me that you were ill.
2 anybody ◊ *War jemand zu Hause?* Was anybody at home?

**jene** PRONOUN
  1 that ◊ *in jener Zeit* at that time
  2 those ◊ *in jenen Tagen* in those days

**jetzt** ADVERB
  now ◊ *Sie ist jetzt in der Schweiz.* She's in Switzerland now.

**jeweils** ADVERB
  ♦ **jeweils zwei zusammen** two at a time
  ♦ **zu jeweils fünf Mark** at five marks each

der **Job** NOUN (PL die **Jobs**)
  job

das **Jod** NOUN
  iodine

**jodeln** VERB
  to yodel

**joggen** VERB
  *Use **haben** for the perfect tense when you describe the activity and **sein** when you describe the motion.*
  to jog ◊ *Früher habe ich oft gejoggt.* I used to jog a lot. ◊ *Wir sind durch den Wald gejoggt.* We jogged through the woods.

das **Jogging** NOUN
  jogging

der **Jogginganzug** NOUN (PL die **Jogginganzüge**)
  tracksuit

der **Joghurt** NOUN (PL die **Joghurts**)
  yogurt

der **Jogurt** NOUN (PL die **Jogurts**)
  see **Joghurt**

die **Johannisbeere** NOUN
  redcurrant ◊ *Johannisbeeren sind mir zu sauer.* Redcurrants are too sour for me.
  ♦ **Schwarze Johannisbeere** blackcurrant

der **Journalist** NOUN (GEN des **Journalisten,** PL die **Journalisten**)
  journalist

**jubeln** VERB
  to rejoice

das **Jubiläum** NOUN (PL die **Jubiläen**)
  anniversary ◊ *Nächstes Jahr feiert unsere Schule ihr zwanzigjähriges Jubiläum.* Our school's celebrating its twentieth anniversary next year.

**jucken** VERB
  to be itchy ◊ *Meine Nase juckt.* My nose is itchy.
  ♦ **Es juckt mich am Arm.** My arm's itchy.
  ♦ **Das juckt mich.** That's itchy.

der **Jude** NOUN (GEN des **Juden,** PL die **Juden**)
  Jew

die **Jüdin** NOUN
  Jew

**jüdisch** ADJECTIVE
  Jewish

die **Jugend** NOUN
>    youth ◊ *In meiner Jugend habe ich*
>    *Fußball gespielt.* I used to play football in
>    my youth. ◊ *die Jugend von heute* the
>    youth of today

die **Jugendherberge** NOUN
>    youth hostel

der **Jugendklub** NOUN (PL die **Jugendklubs**)
>    youth club

**jugendlich** ADJECTIVE
>    youthful ◊ *Er hat ein jugendliches*
>    *Gesicht.* He has a youthful face. ◊ *Sie*
>    *sieht sehr jugendlich aus.* She looks very
>    youthful.

der **Jugendliche** NOUN (GEN des/der
die **Jugendlichen**, PL die **Jugendlichen**)
>    teenager ◊ *Ich habe einen Jugendlichen*
>    *dabei beobachtet, wie er die Wand*
>    *besprüht hat.* I watched a teenager spray
>    the wall.

das **Jugendzentrum** NOUN (PL die
**Jugendzentren**)
>    youth centre

**Jugoslawien** NEUT NOUN
>    Yugoslavia ◊ *das frühere Jugoslawien*
>    the former Yugoslavia

**jugoslawisch** ADJECTIVE
>    Yugoslavian

der **Juli** NOUN (GEN des **Juli** or **Julis**, PL die **Julis**)
>    July ◊ *im Juli* in July ◊ *am dritten Juli* on
>    the third of July ◊ *Ulm, den 3. Juli 2004*
>    Ulm, 3 July 2004 ◊ *Heute ist der dritte*
>    *Juli.* Today is the third of July.

**jung** ADJECTIVE
>    young ◊ *Er ist drei Jahre jünger als ich.*
>    He's three years younger than me.

der **Junge** NOUN (GEN des **Jungen**, PL die
**Jungen**)
>    ⃞ *see also* **das Junge** NOUN
>    boy ◊ *In unserer Klasse gibt es zehn*
>    *Jungen und fünfzehn Mädchen.* There
>    are ten boys and fifteen girls in our class.

das **Junge** NOUN (GEN des **Jungen**, PL die
**Jungen**)
>    ⃞ *see also* **der Junge** NOUN
>    young animal
>    ✦ **eine Löwin mit ihren Jungen** a lioness
>    with her young

die **Jungfrau** NOUN
>    [1] virgin
>    [2] Virgo ◊ *Veronika ist Jungfrau.*
>    Veronika's Virgo.

**jüngste** ADJECTIVE
>    [1] youngest ◊ *Er ist der jüngste Schüler*
>    *der Klasse.* He's the youngest pupil in the
>    class.
>    [2] latest ◊ *die jüngsten Entwicklungen*
>    the latest developments

der **Juni** NOUN (GEN des **Juni** or **Junis**, PL die
**Junis**)
>    June ◊ *im Juni* in June ◊ *am fünfzehnten*
>    *Juni* on the fifteenth of June ◊ *Ulm, den*
>    *3. Juni 2001* Ulm, 3 June 2001 ◊ *Heute ist*
>    *der dritte Juni.* Today is the third of
>    June.

der **Juwelier** NOUN (PL die **Juweliere**)
>    jeweller

der **Jux** NOUN
>    laugh ◊ *Das war ein Jux!* That was a
>    laugh! ◊ *Wir haben das aus Jux*
>    *gemacht.* We did it for a laugh.

**J**

# K

das **Kabel** NOUN (PL die **Kabel**)
  1 wire ◊ *Das Kabel des Telefons ist zu kurz.* The telephone wire is too short.
  2 cable ◊ *Das Kabel der Seilbahn muss regelmäßig überprüft werden.* The cable on the cable car has to be checked regularly.

der **Kabelanschluss** NOUN (GEN des **Kabelanschlusses,** PL die **Kabelanschlüsse**)
  cable connection

das **Kabelfernsehen** NOUN
  cable television

die **Kabine** NOUN
  1 cabin ◊ *Wir hatten zu zweit eine Kabine auf dem Schiff.* The two of us shared a cabin on the ship.
  2 cubicle ◊ *Sie können das Kleid dort hinten in der Kabine anprobieren.* You can try the dress on in the cubicle over there.

der **Käfer** NOUN (PL die **Käfer**)
  beetle

der **Kaffee** NOUN (PL die **Kaffees** *or* **Kaffee**)
  coffee ◊ *Herr Ober, zwei Kaffee bitte.* Two coffees please, waiter.

die **Kaffeekanne** NOUN
  coffeepot

die **Kaffeepause** NOUN
  coffee break ◊ *Wir machten Kaffeepause.* We had a coffee break.

der **Käfig** NOUN (PL die **Käfige**)
  cage

**kahl** ADJECTIVE
  bald ◊ *sein kahler Kopf* his bald head
  ♦ **die kahlen Bäume im Winter** the bare trees in winter
  ♦ **kahl geschoren** shaven

der **Kai** NOUN (PL die **Kais**)
  quay

der **Kaiser** NOUN (PL die **Kaiser**)
  emperor

der **Kakao** NOUN (PL die **Kakaos** *or* **Kakao**)
  cocoa ◊ *Herr Ober, zwei Kakao bitte.* Two cups of cocoa please, waiter.

das **Kalb** NOUN (PL die **Kälber**)
  calf (*animal*)

das **Kalbfleisch** NOUN
  veal

der **Kalender** NOUN (PL die **Kalender**)
  1 calendar ◊ *An der Wand hing ein Kalender mit Bildern von Picasso.* A calendar with pictures by Picasso was hanging on the wall.
  2 diary ◊ *Sie holte ihren Kalender aus der Tasche.* She got her diary out of her bag.

der **Kalk** NOUN
  1 lime (*stone*)

  2 calcium ◊ *Ein Mangel an Kalk kann zu schlechten Zähnen führen.* A lack of calcium can lead to bad teeth.

die **Kalorie** NOUN
  calorie

**kalorienarm** ADJECTIVE
  low in calories

**kalt** ADJECTIVE
  cold ◊ *Heute ist es kälter als gestern.* It's colder today than yesterday.
  ♦ **Mir ist kalt.** I'm cold.
  ♦ **etwas kalt stellen** to chill something ◊ *Du solltest den Weißwein kalt stellen.* You should chill the white wine.

die **Kälte** NOUN
  1 cold ◊ *Bei dieser Kälte gehe ich nicht raus.* I'm not going out in this cold.
  2 coldness ◊ *Die Kälte des Wassers hat uns vom Baden abgehalten.* The coldness of the water stopped us from bathing.

**kam** VERB *see* **kommen**

das **Kamel** NOUN (PL die **Kamele**)
  camel

die **Kamera** NOUN (PL die **Kameras**)
  camera

der **Kamerad** NOUN (GEN des **Kameraden,** PL die **Kameraden**)
  friend

der **Kamillentee** NOUN (PL die **Kamillentees**)
  camomile tea

der **Kamin** NOUN (PL die **Kamine**)
  open fire
  ♦ **Wir saßen am Kamin.** We sat by the fire.

der **Kamm** NOUN (PL die **Kämme**)
  comb

**kämmen** VERB
  to comb ◊ *Sie kann es nicht leiden, wenn man sie kämmt.* She can't stand having her hair combed. ◊ *Ich muss meiner kleinen Schwester die Haare kämmen.* I have to comb my little sister's hair.
  ♦ **sich kämmen** to comb one's hair

der **Kampf** NOUN (PL die **Kämpfe**)
  1 fight ◊ *der Kampf zwischen Tyson und Bruno* the fight between Tyson and Bruno
  2 contest ◊ *Dieses Jahr findet der Kampf um den Pokal in Großbritannien statt.* The contest for the cup is taking place in Great Britain this year.
  3 struggle ◊ *Ich habe die Prüfung geschafft, aber es war ein Kampf.* I passed the exam but it was a struggle.

**kämpfen** VERB
  to fight

**Kanada** NEUT NOUN

Canada
- **aus Kanada** from Canada
- **in Kanada** in Canada
- **nach Kanada** to Canada

der **Kanadier** NOUN (PL die **Kanadier**)
Canadian

die **Kanadierin** NOUN
Canadian

**kanadisch** ADJECTIVE
Canadian

der **Kanal** NOUN (PL die **Kanäle**)
[1] canal ◊ *Diese beiden Flüsse sind durch einen Kanal verbunden.* These two rivers are connected by a canal.
[2] drain

die **Kanalinseln** FEM PL NOUN
Channel Islands

der **Kanaltunnel** NOUN (PL die **Kanaltunnel**)
Channel Tunnel

der **Kanarienvogel** NOUN (PL die **Kanarienvögel**)
canary

**kanarisch** ADJECTIVE
- **die Kanarischen Inseln** the Canaries

der **Kandidat** NOUN (GEN des **Kandidaten**, PL die **Kandidaten**)
candidate

das **Känguru** NOUN (PL die **Kängurus**)
kangaroo

das **Kaninchen** NOUN (PL die **Kaninchen**)
rabbit

der **Kanister** NOUN (PL die **Kanister**)
can ◊ *ein Benzinkanister* a petrol can

**kann** VERB see **können**

das **Kännchen** NOUN (PL die **Kännchen**)
pot ◊ *ein Kännchen Kaffee* a pot of coffee
- **ein Kännchen mit Milch** a jug of milk

die **Kanne** NOUN
[1] pot (*for coffee*)
[2] churn (*for milk*)
[3] watering can

die **Kante** NOUN
edge

die **Kantine** NOUN
canteen ◊ *Mittags isst sie in der Kantine.* She eats in the canteen at lunchtime.

das **Kanu** NOUN (PL die **Kanus**)
canoe
- **Kanu fahren** to go canoeing

der **Kanzler** NOUN (PL die **Kanzler**)
chancellor

die **Kapelle** NOUN
[1] chapel ◊ *Auf dem Berg stand eine Kapelle.* There was a chapel on the mountain.
[2] band ◊ *Die Kapelle spielte einen Walzer.* The band was playing a waltz.

**kapieren** VERB (PERFECT **hat kapiert**)
to understand ◊ *Ich habe heute in Mathe nichts kapiert.* I didn't understand anything in maths today. ◊ *Hast du das*

*endlich kapiert?* Have you finally understood?
- **Sie hat den Witz nicht kapiert.** She didn't get the joke.

das **Kapital** NOUN
capital (*money*)

der **Kapitän** NOUN (PL die **Kapitäne**)
captain

das **Kapitel** NOUN (PL die **Kapitel**)
chapter

die **Kappe** NOUN
cap

**kaputt** ADJECTIVE
[1] broken ◊ *Mein Computer ist kaputt.* My computer's broken.
- **Am Auto ist etwas kaputt.** There's something wrong with the car.
[2] knackered ◊ *Ich bin von der Wanderung total kaputt.* I'm completely knackered after the walk.

**kaputtgehen** VERB (IMPERFECT **ging kaputt**, PERFECT **ist kaputtgegangen**)
[1] to break ◊ *Mein Computer ist gestern kaputtgegangen.* My computer broke yesterday.
[2] (*material*)
to wear out
[3] (*plant*)
to die
[4] (*relationship*)
to break up

**kaputtmachen** VERB (PERFECT **hat kaputtgemacht**)
[1] to break ◊ *Mach mir bloß mein Fahrrad nicht kaputt!* Don't you dare break my bike! ◊ *Sie hat den Teller kaputtgemacht.* She's broken the plate.
[2] to wear out ◊ *Die viele Arbeit macht mich noch kaputt.* All this work is wearing me out.
- **sich kaputtmachen** to wear oneself out ◊ *Du solltest mal Ferien machen, du machst dich ja kaputt.* You should take a holiday, you're wearing yourself out.

die **Kapuze** NOUN
hood ◊ *ein Anorak mit Kapuze* an anorak with a hood

der **Karfreitag** NOUN
Good Friday

die **Karibik** NOUN
the Caribbean ◊ *Wir fahren in die Karibik.* We're going to the Caribbean. ◊ *Wir machen in der Karibik Ferien.* We're spending our holidays in the Caribbean.

**karibisch** ADJECTIVE
- **die Karibischen Inseln** the Caribbean Islands

**kariert** ADJECTIVE
[1] checked ◊ *Sie hatte ein kariertes Kleid an.* She was wearing a checked dress.
[2] squared ◊ *Für Mathe brauchst du ein Heft mit kariertem Papier.* You need an

**K**

☞

exercise book with squared paper for maths.

die **Karies** NOUN
tooth decay ◊ *Sie hat Karies.* She has tooth decay.

der **Karneval** NOUN (PL die **Karnevale** or **Karnevals**)
carnival

> ❶ *The German carnival season lasts from 11 November to Shrove Tuesday but most events, fancy-dress processions and parties take place in the week leading up to Ash Wednesday.*

das **Karo** NOUN (PL die **Karos**)
[1] square ◊ *Das Muster bestand aus kleinen Karos.* The pattern was made up of little squares.
[2] diamonds ◊ *Karo ist Trumpf.* Diamonds is trumps.

die **Karotte** NOUN
carrot

die **Karriere** NOUN
career
♦ **Karriere machen** to get on ◊ *Es ist schwer für Frauen, in der Politik Karriere zu machen.* It's hard for women to get on in politics.

die **Karte** NOUN
[1] card ◊ *Sie hat uns aus dem Urlaub eine Karte geschickt.* She sent us a card from her holiday. ◊ *Ich weiß nicht, welche Karte ich ausspielen soll.* I don't know which card I should play.
♦ **die gelbe Karte** the yellow card
♦ **die rote Karte** the red card
[2] map ◊ *Sieh mal auf der Karte nach, wie weit wir noch fahren müssen.* Look on the map to see how far we still have to go.
[3] menu ◊ *Der Ober brachte uns die Karte.* The waiter brought us the menu.
[4] ticket ◊ *Kannst du Karten fürs Konzert besorgen?* Can you get us tickets for the concert? ◊ *Ich fahre morgen nach Bonn, die Karte habe ich schon gekauft.* I'm going to Bonn tomorrow, I've already bought my ticket.
♦ **alles auf eine Karte setzen** to put all one's eggs in one basket

das **Kartenspiel** NOUN (PL die **Kartenspiele**)
[1] card game ◊ *Ich habe ein neues Kartenspiel gelernt.* I've learned a new card game.
[2] pack of cards ◊ *Hast du ein Kartenspiel da?* Have you got a pack of cards?

die **Kartoffel** NOUN
potato

der **Kartoffelbrei** NOUN
mashed potatoes

der **Kartoffelsalat** NOUN (PL die **Kartoffelsalate**)
potato salad

der **Karton** NOUN (PL die **Kartons**)
[1] cardboard ◊ *Wir haben das Bild auf Karton aufgezogen.* We mounted the picture on cardboard.
[2] cardboard box ◊ *Sie packte die Bücher in einen Karton.* She packed the books in a cardboard box.

das **Karussell** NOUN (PL die **Karussells**)
roundabout ◊ *Ich möchte Karussell fahren.* I'd like to go on the roundabout.

der **Käse** NOUN (PL die **Käse**)
cheese

der **Käsekuchen** NOUN (PL die **Käsekuchen**)
cheesecake

die **Kaserne** NOUN
barracks ◊ *In unserer Nähe gibt es eine Kaserne.* There's a barracks near us.

die **Kasse** NOUN
[1] till ◊ *Die meisten Geschäfte haben elektronische Kassen.* Most shops have an electronic till.
[2] checkout ◊ *Es war nur eine von fünf Kassen besetzt.* Only one of the five checkouts was open.
♦ **an der Kasse** at the checkout
[3] box office ◊ *Sie können Ihre Karten telefonisch vorbestellen und an der Kasse abholen.* You may order your tickets in advance and collect them from the box office.
[4] ticket office ◊ *Karten fürs Fußballspiel bekommen Sie auch an der Kasse des Stadions.* You can also get tickets for the football match at the ticket office in the stadium.
[5] cash box ◊ *Alle Barbeträge bewahren wir in dieser Kasse auf.* We keep all the cash in this cash box.
[6] health insurance ◊ *Bei welcher Kasse sind Sie versichert?* What health insurance have you got?

> ❶ *In Germany one can choose between different health insurance schemes. There is no "National Health Service".*

♦ **gut bei Kasse sein** to be in the money

der **Kassenzettel** NOUN (PL die **Kassenzettel**)
receipt

die **Kassette** NOUN
[1] tape ◊ *Diesen Song habe ich auf Kassette.* I've got this song on tape. ◊ *eine Videokassette* a video tape
[2] small box ◊ *Sie bewahrt ihren Schmuck in einer Kassette auf.* She keeps her jewellery in a small box.

der **Kassettenrekorder** NOUN (PL die **Kassettenrekorder**)
tape recorder

**kassieren** VERB (PERFECT **hat kassiert**)
to take ◊ *Die Polizei hat seinen Führerschein kassiert.* The police took his driving licence.
♦ **Der Parkwächter hat sechs Mark Parkgebühren kassiert.** The park attendant charged us six marks to park the car.
♦ **Darf ich kassieren?** Would you like to pay now?

der **Kassierer** NOUN (PL die **Kassierer**)
cashier

die **Kastanie** NOUN
[1] chestnut
[2] chestnut tree

der **Kasten** NOUN (PL die **Kästen**)
[1] box ◊ *Er warf den Brief in den Kasten.* He put the letter in the box.
[2] case ◊ *Sie legte die Geige zurück in den Kasten.* She put the violin back in its case.
♦ **ein Kasten Bier** a crate of beer

der **Katalog** NOUN (PL die **Kataloge**)
catalogue

der **Katalysator** NOUN (PL die **Katalysatoren**)
catalytic converter ◊ *ein Auto mit Katalysator* a car with catalytic converter

**katastrophal** ADJECTIVE, ADVERB
catastrophic
♦ **katastrophal schlecht** appallingly bad

die **Katastrophe** NOUN
disaster

die **Kategorie** NOUN
category

der **Kater** NOUN (PL die **Kater**)
[1] tomcat ◊ *Wir haben einen Kater und eine Katze.* We have a tomcat and a female cat.
[2] hangover ◊ *Nach der Party hatte ich einen furchtbaren Kater.* I had a terrible hangover after the party.

die **Kathedrale** NOUN
cathedral

**katholisch** ADJECTIVE
Catholic

das **Kätzchen** NOUN (PL die **Kätzchen**)
kitten

die **Katze** NOUN
cat
♦ **für die Katz** for nothing

**kauen** VERB
to chew

der **Kauf** NOUN (PL die **Käufe**)
purchase ◊ *der Kauf eines Autos* the purchase of a car
♦ **ein guter Kauf** a bargain

**kaufen** VERB
to buy

der **Käufer** NOUN (PL die **Käufer**)
buyer

die **Kauffrau** NOUN
businesswoman

das **Kaufhaus** NOUN (GEN des **Kaufhauses**, PL die **Kaufhäuser**)
department store

der **Kaufmann** NOUN (PL die **Kaufleute**)
[1] businessman ◊ *ein erfolgreicher Kaufmann* a successful businessman
[2] grocer ◊ *zum Kaufmann gehen* to go to the grocer's

der **Kaugummi** NOUN (PL die **Kaugummis**)
chewing gum

**kaum** ADVERB
hardly ◊ *Ich habe kaum geschlafen.* I hardly slept.

der **Kegel** NOUN (PL die **Kegel**)
[1] skittle
[2] cone ◊ *die Form eines Kegels haben* to be shaped like a cone

die **Kegelbahn** NOUN
skittle alley

**kegeln** VERB
to play skittles

die **Kehle** NOUN
throat

der **Keil** NOUN (PL die **Keile**)
wedge

der **Keim** NOUN (PL die **Keime**)
[1] shoot ◊ *Eine Woche nach der Aussaat zeigen sich die ersten Keime.* The first shoots appear a week after sowing.
[2] germ ◊ *Das Mittel tötete die Keime ab.* The medicine killed the germs.
♦ **etwas im Keim ersticken** to nip something in the bud

**kein** ADJECTIVE, PRONOUN
*When combined with a noun, **kein** is used for masculine and neuter nouns, **keine** for feminine and plural nouns. On its own **keiner** is used for masculine, **keine** for feminine and plural, and **keines** or **keins** for neuter.*
[1] not ... any ◊ *Ich habe keine Geschwister.* I don't have any brothers or sisters. ◊ *Ich will keinen Streit.* I don't want any quarrelling. ◊ *Er zeigt kein Interesse an Computern.* He doesn't show any interest in computers. ◊ *Er behauptet, hier gäbe es Mäuse, ich habe aber noch keine gesehen.* He claims that there are mice here but I haven't seen any. ◊ *Von den Autos hat mir keines gefallen.* I didn't like any of the cars.
[2] no ◊ *Kein Tier könnte in diesem Klima überleben.* No animal could survive in this climate.
♦ **"Kein Zutritt"** "No entry"
♦ **Ich habe keine Lust.** I don't feel like it.
♦ **Ich habe keinen Hunger.** I'm not hungry.
[3] nobody ◊ *Alle waren eingeladen, es ist aber keiner gekommen.* Everybody was invited but nobody came.
♦ **Ich kenne hier keinen.** I don't know anybody here.

**K**

☞

◆ **Warum hat er eine Einladung bekommen und ich keine?** Why did he get an invitation and not me?

**keinerlei** ADJECTIVE
no ... whatsoever ◊ *Ich habe damit keinerlei Probleme.* I don't have any problems with it whatsoever.

**keinesfalls** ADVERB
on no account

**keineswegs** ADVERB
by no means

der **Keks** NOUN (PL die **Kekse**)
biscuit

der **Keller** NOUN (PL die **Keller**)
cellar

der **Kellner** NOUN (PL die **Kellner**)
waiter

die **Kellnerin** NOUN
waitress

**kennen** VERB (IMPERFECT **kannte**, PERFECT **hat gekannt**)
to know ◊ *Ich kenne ihn nicht.* I don't know him. ◊ *Ich kenne London gut.* I know London well.

◆ **kennen lernen (1)** to meet ◊ *Sie hat ihren Freund bei einem Fußballspiel kennen gelernt.* She met her boyfriend at a football match.

◆ **kennen lernen (2)** to get to know ◊ *Ich würde ihn gern besser kennen lernen.* I'd like to get to know him better.

◆ **sich kennen lernen (1)** to meet ◊ *Wir haben uns auf einer Party kennen gelernt.* We met at a party.

◆ **sich kennen lernen (2)** to get to know each other ◊ *Wir haben uns im Laufe der Zeit immer besser kennen gelernt.* We got to know each other better and better as time went on.

die **Kenntnis** NOUN (PL die **Kenntnisse**)
knowledge ◊ *Deutschkenntnisse wären von Vorteil.* Knowledge of German would be an advantage.

◆ **etwas zur Kenntnis nehmen** to note something

◆ **jemanden in Kenntnis setzen** to inform somebody

das **Kennzeichen** NOUN (PL die **Kennzeichen**)
mark ◊ *unveränderliche Kennzeichen* distinguishing marks

◆ **das Auto mit dem Kennzeichen S-MJ 2714** the car with the registration S-MJ 2714

der **Kerl** NOUN (PL die **Kerle**)
bloke

◆ **Sie ist ein netter Kerl.** She's a good sort.

der **Kern** NOUN (PL die **Kerne**)
1 pip ◊ *Klementinen haben keine Kerne.* Clementines don't have any pips.
2 stone ◊ *der Kern der Kirsche* the cherry stone
3 kernel (*of nut*)
4 nucleus

5 core ◊ *der Reaktorkern* the reactor core

◆ **Wir sollten zum Kern des Problems kommen.** We should get to the heart of the problem.

die **Kernenergie** NOUN
nuclear energy

**kerngesund** ADJECTIVE
fit as a fiddle

das **Kernkraftwerk** NOUN (PL die **Kernkraftwerke**)
nuclear power station

die **Kernwaffen** FEM PL NOUN
nuclear weapons

die **Kerze** NOUN
1 candle ◊ *Sie zündete eine Kerze an.* She lit a candle.
2 plug ◊ *Bei der Inspektion werden die Kerzen erneuert.* The plugs are changed while the car is being serviced.

die **Kette** NOUN
chain

**keuchen** VERB
to pant

der **Keuchhusten** NOUN
whooping cough ◊ *Meine Schwester hat Keuchhusten.* My sister has whooping cough.

die **Keule** NOUN
1 club ◊ *Er schlug ihm mit einer Keule über den Kopf.* He hit him over the head with a club.
2 leg ◊ *Beim Hähnchen mag ich am liebsten die Keule.* My favourite part of a chicken is the leg.

**kg** ABBREVIATION (= *Kilogramm*)
kg

**kichern** VERB
to giggle

der **Kiefer** NOUN (PL die **Kiefer**)
see also **die Kiefer** NOUN
jaw

die **Kiefer** NOUN
see also **der Kiefer** NOUN
pine tree

der **Kies** NOUN
gravel

das **Kilo** NOUN (PL die **Kilos** or **Kilo**)
kilo ◊ *Ich muss ein paar Kilos loswerden.* I need to lose a couple of kilos. ◊ *Ich hätte gern zwei Kilo Tomaten.* Can I have two kilos of tomatoes. ◊ *Ich wiege fünfzig Kilo.* I weigh eight stone.

das **Kilogramm** NOUN (PL die **Kilogramme** or **Kilogramm**)
kilogram ◊ *zwei Kilogramm Äpfel* two kilograms of apples

der **Kilometer** NOUN (PL die **Kilometer**)
kilometre ◊ *mit achtzig Kilometern pro Stunde* at fifty miles per hour

das **Kind** NOUN (PL die **Kinder**)
child

◆ **von Kind auf** from childhood

◆ **ein Kind bekommen** to have a baby

der **Kindergarten** NOUN (PL die **Kindergärten**)
kindergarten

die **Kindergärtnerin** NOUN
kindergarten teacher

das **Kindergeld** NOUN
child benefit

die **Kinderkrippe** NOUN
crèche

die **Kinderlähmung** NOUN
polio ◊ *Sie hatte als Kind Kinderlähmung.* She had polio as a child.

**kinderleicht** ADJECTIVE
child's play ◊ *Es war kinderleicht.* It was child's play.

das **Kindermädchen** NOUN (PL die **Kindermädchen**)
nanny

der **Kinderpfleger** NOUN (PL die **Kinderpfleger**)
paediatric nurse

die **Kinderpflegerin** NOUN
paediatric nurse

die **Kindertagesstätte** NOUN
day nursery

der **Kinderwagen** NOUN (PL die **Kinderwagen**)
pram

die **Kindheit** NOUN
childhood

**kindisch** ADJECTIVE
childish

◆ **sich kindisch benehmen** to behave childishly

**kindlich** ADJECTIVE
childlike

das **Kinn** NOUN (PL die **Kinne**)
chin

das **Kino** NOUN (PL die **Kinos**)
cinema ◊ *ins Kino gehen* to go to the cinema

der **Kiosk** NOUN (PL die **Kioske**)
kiosk

die **Kirche** NOUN
church

die **Kirchweih** NOUN
funfair

die **Kirmes** NOUN (PL die **Kirmessen**)
funfair

die **Kirsche** NOUN
cherry

das **Kissen** NOUN (PL die **Kissen**)
1 cushion ◊ *Auf dem Sofa lagen bunte Kissen.* There were brightly-coloured cushions on the sofa.
2 pillow ◊ *Er schläft ohne Kissen.* He sleeps without a pillow.

**kitschig** ADJECTIVE
kitschy

**kitzeln** VERB
to tickle

**kitzlig** ADJECTIVE

**ticklish** ◊ *Ich bin kitzlig an den Füßen.* My feet are ticklish. ◊ *Das ist eine ganz kitzlige Angelegenheit.* That's a very ticklish matter.

die **Kiwi** NOUN (PL die **Kiwis**)
kiwi fruit

**klagen** VERB
1 to wail ◊ *"Hätte ich doch nur auf dich gehört", klagte er.* "If only I had listened to you", he wailed.

◆ **über jemanden klagen** to complain about somebody ◊ *Sie klagt dauernd über ihre Kinder.* She's constantly complaining about her children.

◆ **Sie klagt in letzter Zeit oft über Kopfschmerzen.** She's been complaining of headaches a lot recently.

2 to sue ◊ *Wir werden gegen ihn klagen.* We're going to sue him.

◆ **Sie hat mir ihr Leid geklagt.** She poured out her sorrows to me.

die **Klammer** NOUN (PL die **Klammern**)
1 bracket ◊ *Sie schrieb in Klammern eine Erklärung dazu.* She wrote an explanation in brackets.
2 peg (*clothes peg*)
3 brace (*for teeth*) ◊ *Viele Kinder müssen eine Klammer tragen.* Many children have to wear a brace.

die **Klamotten** PL NOUN
stuff ◊ *Pack deine Klamotten!* Get your stuff!

der **Klang** NOUN (PL die **Klänge**)
sound

die **Klappe** NOUN
1 flap ◊ *Über dem Briefkasten ist eine Klappe.* There's a flap over the letterbox.
2 valve ◊ *Die Klappe an seinem Herzen hat ein Loch.* His heart valve has a hole in it.
3 trap ◊ *Er soll die Klappe halten.* He should keep his trap shut.

◆ **Sie hat eine große Klappe.** She's got a big mouth.

**klappen** VERB
to work ◊ *Das kann ja nicht klappen.* That won't work. ◊ *Das Experiment hat geklappt.* The experiment worked.

◆ **etwas klappen** to tip something ◊ *Sie klappte den Sitz nach oben.* She tipped up the seat. ◊ *Er klappte den Deckel der Kiste nach hinten.* He tipped the lid of the chest back.

**klappern** VERB
to rattle

der **Klappstuhl** NOUN (PL die **Klappstühle**)
folding chair

der **Klapptisch** NOUN (PL die **Klapptische**)
folding table

**klar** ADJECTIVE
clear ◊ *Das Wasser ist sehr klar.* The water is very clear. ◊ *Ich brauche einen*

**K**

☞

*klaren Kopf.* I need a clear head. ◊ *eine klare Antwort* a clear answer

◆ **Mir ist nicht klar, was er eigentlich will.** I'm not clear about what he really wants.

◆ **sich über etwas im Klaren sein** to be clear about something ◊ *Bist du dir über die Konsequenzen im Klaren?* Are you clear about the consequences?

◆ **Na klar!** Of course!

**klären** VERB

[1] to clarify ◊ *Wir sollten diese Frage klären.* We should clarify this matter.

◆ **Ich muss zuerst mit meinen Eltern klären, ob das geht.** I'll have to ask my parents if it's OK.

◆ **Die Polizei hat diesen Fall nie geklärt.** The police have never solved this case.

[2] to purify ◊ *In dieser Anlage wird das Abwasser geklärt.* The sewage is purified in this plant.

◆ **sich klären** to clear itself up ◊ *Dieses Problem hat sich inzwischen geklärt.* The problem has cleared itself up in the meantime.

**die Klarheit** NOUN

[1] clarity

◆ **Wir brauchen in dieser Sache Klarheit.** This matter must be clarified.

[2] clearness ◊ *die Klarheit des Wassers* the clearness of the water

**die Klarinette** NOUN

clarinet ◊ *Oliver spielt Klarinette.* Oliver plays the clarinet.

**klarstellen** VERB (PERFECT **hat klargestellt**)

to make clear ◊ *Ich möchte doch mal klarstellen, dass ich das nie gesagt habe.* I would like to make it quite clear that I never said that.

**die Klasse** NOUN

see also **klasse** ADJECTIVE

class ◊ *Wir sind in der ersten Klasse gefahren.* We travelled first class. ◊ *Unsere Klasse fährt nach England.* Our class is going to England.

◆ **große Klasse sein** to be great ◊ *Unser Sportlehrer ist große Klasse.* Our sports teacher's really great.

**klasse** ADJECTIVE

see also **die Klasse** NOUN

smashing ◊ *Er ist ein klasse Lehrer.* He's a smashing teacher.

**die Klassenarbeit** NOUN

test

> 🛈 The **Klassenarbeit** is the main form of assessment in German schools. Over the school year, German pupils write between 6 and 8 **Klassenarbeiten**, usually 45 minutes long, in their core subjects (generally maths, German and English).

◊ *Wir schreiben morgen in Englisch eine Klassenarbeit.* We've got a written English test tomorrow.

**das Klassenbuch** NOUN (PL **die Klassenbücher**)

class register

**die Klassenfahrt** NOUN (PL **die Klassenfahrten**)

class trip

**der Klassenkamerad** NOUN (GEN des **Klassenkameraden**, PL die **Klassenkameraden**)

classmate

**die Klassenkameradin** NOUN

classmate

**der Klassenlehrer** NOUN (PL die **Klassenlehrer**)

class teacher

**die Klassenlehrerin** NOUN

class teacher

**der Klassensprecher** NOUN (PL die **Klassensprecher**)

class representative

**die Klassensprecherin** NOUN

class representative

**das Klassenzimmer** NOUN (PL die **Klassenzimmer**)

classroom

**klassisch** ADJECTIVE

classical

**der Klatsch** NOUN (GEN des **Klatsches**)

gossip ◊ *Hast du schon den neuesten Klatsch gehört?* Have you heard the latest gossip?

**klatschen** VERB

[1] to clap ◊ *Die Zuschauer klatschten.* The audience clapped.

[2] to gossip ◊ *Über das Königshaus wird viel geklatscht.* There's a lot of gossip about the royal family.

[3] to batter ◊ *Der Regen klatschte gegen die Scheiben.* The rain battered against the panes.

◆ **jemandem Beifall klatschen** to applaud somebody

**klauen** VERB (PERFECT **hat geklaut**)

to pinch

**das Klavier** NOUN

piano ◊ *Bettina spielt Klavier.* Bettina plays the piano.

**kleben** VERB

to stick ◊ *Ich habe die zerbrochene Vase wieder geklebt.* I've stuck the broken vase together again.

◆ **etwas an etwas kleben** to stick something on something ◊ *Sie hat das Bild der Gruppe an ihre Wand geklebt.* She stuck the picture of the band on her wall.

◆ **an etwas kleben** to stick to something ◊ *An der Windschutzscheibe klebten lauter tote Insekten.* There were lots of dead insects stuck to the windscreen.

◆ **Das klebt nicht.** It doesn't stick.

◆ **jemandem eine kleben** to thump somebody
**klebrig** ADJECTIVE
  sticky
der **Klebstoff** NOUN (PL die **Klebstoffe**)
  glue
der **Klebstreifen** NOUN (PL die **Klebstreifen**)
  adhesive tape
der **Klecks** NOUN (PL die **Kleckse**)
  stain
der **Klee** NOUN
  clover
das **Kleid** NOUN (PL die **Kleider**)
  dress ◊ *Sie trug ein rotes Kleid.* She was wearing a red dress.
◆ **Kleider** clothes ◊ *Er räumte seine Kleider auf.* He put his clothes away.
der **Kleiderbügel** NOUN (PL die **Kleiderbügel**)
  coat hanger
der **Kleiderschrank** NOUN (PL die **Kleiderschränke**)
  wardrobe
die **Kleidung** NOUN
  clothing
das **Kleidungsstück** NOUN (PL die **Kleidungsstücke**)
  garment
**klein** ADJECTIVE
  small ◊ *ein kleines Kind* a small child ◊ *ein kleiner Betrag* a small amount
◆ **als ich klein war** when I was little
das **Kleingeld** NOUN
  small change
der **Klempner** NOUN (PL die **Klempner**)
  plumber
**klettern** VERB (PERFECT **ist geklettert**)
  to climb
**klicken** VERB
  to click (*computer*) ◊ *mit der Maus klicken* to click on the mouse
das **Klima** NOUN (PL die **Klimas**)
  climate
die **Klimaanlage** NOUN
  air conditioning
die **Klingel** NOUN
  bell
**klingeln** VERB
  to ring
◆ **Es klingelte.** The doorbell rang.
**klingen** VERB (IMPERFECT **klang**, PERFECT **hat geklungen**)
  to sound ◊ *Das Klavier klingt verstimmt.* The piano sounds out of tune. ◊ *Der Vorschlag klingt gut.* The suggestion sounds good. ◊ *Du klingst deprimiert.* You sound depressed.
die **Klinik** NOUN
  clinic
die **Klinke** NOUN
  handle (*of door*)
die **Klippe** NOUN
  cliff

das **Klo** NOUN (PL die **Klos**)
  loo
der **Klon** NOUN (PL die **Klone**)
  clone
**klonen** VERB
  to clone ◊ *ein geklontes Schaf* a cloned sheep
**klopfen** VERB
  [1] to knock ◊ *Sie klopfte an die Tür.* She knocked on the door.
◆ **Es klopft.** There's somebody knocking on the door.
  [2] to pound ◊ *Mein Herz klopfte vor Aufregung.* My heart was pounding with excitement.
◆ **jemandem auf die Schulter klopfen** to tap somebody on the shoulder
das **Kloster** NOUN (PL die **Klöster**)
  [1] monastery
  [2] convent
der **Klub** NOUN (PL die **Klubs**)
  club (*association*)
**klug** ADJECTIVE
  intelligent
◆ **Es wäre klüger gewesen, nichts zu sagen.** It would have been more sensible not to say anything.
die **Klugheit** NOUN
  intelligence
**km** ABBREVIATION (= *Kilometer*)
  km
**knabbern** VERB
  to nibble ◊ *Sie knabberte an einem Keks.* She nibbled a biscuit.
das **Knäckebrot** NOUN
  crispbread
**knacken** VERB
  to crack ◊ *Nüsse knacken* to crack nuts ◊ *einen Code knacken* to crack a code
◆ **ein Auto knacken** to break into a car
der **Knall** NOUN (PL die **Knalle**)
  bang ◊ *Die Tür schlug mit einem Knall zu.* The door closed with a bang.
**knapp** ADJECTIVE
  [1] tight ◊ *Sie hatte einen sehr knappen Pulli an.* She was wearing a very tight pullover.
  [2] scarce ◊ *Benzin ist knapp.* Petrol is scarce.
◆ **knapp bei Kasse** short of money
◆ **Wenn das Taschengeld knapp wird, geht sie immer zu ihren Großeltern.** When her pocket money runs out she always goes to her grandparents.
  [3] just ◊ *Sie ist knapp fünfzehn Jahre alt.* She has just turned fifteen.
◆ **eine knappe Stunde** just under an hour
◆ **knapp unter** just under ◊ *Das kostet knapp unter tausend Mark.* That costs just under a thousand marks.
◆ **Wir haben knapp verloren.** We only just lost.

**K**

**kneifen** VERB (IMPERFECT **kniff**, PERFECT **hat gekniffen**)

[1] to pinch ◊ *Er hat mich in den Arm gekniffen.* He pinched my arm.

[2] to back out ◊ *Als er springen sollte, hat er gekniffen.* When it was his turn to jump, he backed out.

die **Kneipe** NOUN
pub

das **Knie** NOUN (PL die **Knie**)
knee

der **Kniestrumpf** NOUN (PL die **Kniestrümpfe**)
knee-length sock

**knipsen** VERB (PERFECT **hat geknipst**)

[1] to take a snap ◊ *Die Touristen knipsten den Eiffelturm.* The tourists took snaps of the Eiffel Tower.

[2] to punch ◊ *Der Schaffner knipste die Fahrkarten.* The ticket collector punched the tickets.

der **Knoblauch** NOUN
garlic

die **Knoblauchzehe** NOUN
clove of garlic

der **Knöchel** NOUN (PL die **Knöchel**)

[1] knuckle ◊ *Ich habe mir die Knöchel an der rechten Hand geschürft.* I've scraped the knuckles of my right hand.

[2] ankle ◊ *Bei dem Sprung habe ich mir den Knöchel verstaucht.* I sprained my ankle when I jumped.

der **Knochen** NOUN (PL die **Knochen**)
bone

der **Knödel** NOUN (PL die **Knödel**)
dumpling

der **Knopf** NOUN (PL die **Knöpfe**)
button

der **Knoten** NOUN (PL die **Knoten**)

[1] knot ◊ *Sie machte einen Knoten in die Schnur.* She tied a knot in the string.

[2] bun ◊ *Sie trug das Haar in einem Knoten.* She wore her hair in a bun.

[3] lump ◊ *Sie hat einen Knoten in der Brust entdeckt.* She noticed a lump in her breast.

der **Knüppel** NOUN (PL die **Knüppel**)

[1] cudgel ◊ *Die Robbenbabys werden mit Knüppel erschlagen.* The baby seals are beaten with cudgels.

[2] truncheon ◊ *Die Polizisten gingen mit Knüppeln gegen die Demonstranten vor.* The police used truncheons against the demonstrators.

[3] joystick (*aeroplane*)

der **Koch** NOUN (PL die **Köche**)
cook

**kochen** VERB

[1] to cook ◊ *Was kochst du heute?* What are you cooking today?

♦ **Sie kann gut kochen.** She's a good cook.

♦ **Ich koche gern.** I like cooking.

[2] to boil ◊ *Das Wasser kocht.* The water's boiling.

der **Kocher** NOUN (PL die **Kocher**)
cooker

die **Köchin** NOUN
cook

der **Kochtopf** NOUN (PL die **Kochtöpfe**)
saucepan

der **Koffer** NOUN (PL die **Koffer**)
suitcase

der **Kofferkuli** NOUN (PL die **Kofferkulis**)
luggage trolley

der **Kofferraum** NOUN (PL die **Kofferräume**)
boot (*of car*)

der **Kohl** NOUN
cabbage

die **Kohle** NOUN

[1] coal ◊ *Wir heizen mit Kohle.* We use coal for heating.

[2] charcoal ◊ *Wir brauchen noch Kohle zum Grillen.* We need charcoal for the barbecue.

[3] dough (*money*)

♦ **Ich habe keine Kohle.** I'm broke.

das **Kohlenfeuer** NOUN (PL die **Kohlenfeuer**)
coal fire

der **Kohlenherd** NOUN (PL die **Kohlenherde**)
coal-burning stove

das **Kohlenhydrat** NOUN (PL die **Kohlenhydrate**)
carbohydrate

die **Kohlensäure** NOUN
carbon dioxide

♦ **Mineralwasser mit Kohlensäure** sparkling mineral water

die **Kokosnuss** NOUN (PL die **Kokosnüsse**)
coconut

der **Kollege** NOUN (GEN des **Kollegen,** PL die **Kollegen**)
colleague

die **Kollegin** NOUN
colleague

**Köln** NEUT NOUN
Cologne

♦ **nach Köln** to Cologne

das **Kölnischwasser** NOUN
eau de Cologne

der **Komfort** NOUN
luxury ◊ *ein Auto mit allem Komfort* a luxury car

der **Komiker** NOUN (PL die **Komiker**)
comedian

**komisch** ADJECTIVE
funny ◊ *ein komischer Film* a funny film ◊ *ein komisches Gefühl* a funny feeling

das **Komma** NOUN (PL die **Kommas**)
comma

♦ **zwei Komma drei (2,3)** two point three (2.3)

**kommen** VERB (IMPERFECT **kam**, PERFECT **ist gekommen**)

[1] to come ◊ *Wann ist der Brief gekommen?* When did the letter come?

◊ *Kommst du auch zur Party?* Are you coming to the party too?

◆ **Komm gut nach Hause!** Safe journey home.

[2] to get ◊ *Wie komme ich zum Bahnhof?* How do I get to the station?

◆ **unter ein Auto kommen** to be run over by a car

[3] to appear ◊ *Es wird Frühling, die Schneeglöckchen kommen schon.* Spring is coming, the snowdrops are appearing.

◆ **Bei Felix kommen jetzt die zweiten Zähne.** Felix's second teeth are coming through.

[4] to go ◊ *Er ist gestern ins Krankenhaus gekommen.* He went into hospital yesterday. ◊ *Das kommt in den Schrank.* That goes in the cupboard.

◆ **Mit sechs kommt man in die Schule.** You start school at six.

◆ **Wer kommt zuerst?** Who's first?

◆ **Jetzt kommst du an die Reihe.** It's your turn now.

◆ **kommenden Sonntag** next Sunday

◆ **kommen lassen** to send for ◊ *Ich habe mir den Katalog kommen lassen.* I've sent for the catalogue. ◊ *Der Direktor hat ihn kommen lassen.* The headmaster sent for him.

◆ **auf etwas kommen** to think of something ◊ *Darauf bin ich nicht gekommen.* I didn't think of that.

◆ **Wie kommst du auf die Idee?** What gave you that idea?

◆ **Ich komme nicht auf seinen Namen.** His name escapes me.

◆ **Er kommt aus Bayern.** He comes from Bavaria. ◊ *Kiwis kommen aus Neuseeland.* Kiwi fruit come from New Zealand.

◆ **Sie ist durchs Abitur gekommen.** She got through her Abitur.

◆ **ums Leben kommen** to lose one's life ◊ *Sie ist bei einem Unfall ums Leben gekommen.* She lost her life in an accident.

◆ **Das kommt davon!** That's what you get!

◆ **zu sich kommen** to come round ◊ *Die Patientin ist noch nicht wieder zu sich gekommen.* The patient hasn't come round again yet.

◆ **zu etwas kommen (1)** to get something ◊ *Wie bist du zu dem Computer gekommen?* How did you get the computer?

◆ **zu etwas kommen (2)** to get round to something ◊ *Ich mache das, sobald ich dazu komme.* I'll do it as soon as I get round to it.

die **Kommode** NOUN
    chest of drawers

der **Kommunismus** NOUN (GEN des **Kommunismus**)
    communism

die **Komödie** NOUN
    comedy

**kompatibel** ADJECTIVE
    compatible

**kompetent** ADJECTIVE
    competent

das **Kompliment** NOUN (PL die **Komplimente**)
    compliment ◊ *Er hat ihr zu ihrem Kuchen ein Kompliment gemacht.* He complimented her on her cake.

**kompliziert** ADJECTIVE
    complicated

der **Komponist** NOUN (GEN des **Komponisten,** PL die **Komponisten**)
    composer

das **Kompott** NOUN (PL die **Kompotte**)
    compote

der **Konditor** NOUN (PL die **Konditoren**)
    pastry cook

die **Konditorei** NOUN
    cake shop

das **Kondom** NOUN (PL die **Kondome**)
    condom

die **Konfektion** NOUN
    ready-to-wear clothing

der **Konflikt** NOUN (PL die **Konflikte**)
    conflict

der **König** NOUN (PL die **Könige**)
    king

die **Königin** NOUN
    queen

**königlich** ADJECTIVE
    royal

das **Königreich** NOUN (PL die **Königreiche**)
    kingdom

◆ **das Vereinigte Königreich** the United Kingdom

die **Konjugation** NOUN
    conjugation

**konjugieren** VERB (PERFECT **hat konjugiert**)
    to conjugate

die **Konjunktion** NOUN
    conjunction

der **Konjunktiv** NOUN (PL die **Konjunktive**)
    subjunctive

die **Konkurrenz** NOUN
    [1] competition ◊ *Auf diesem Sektor ist die Konkurrenz groß.* Competition is keen in this sector.
    [2] competitors ◊ *Sie ist zur Konkurrenz gegangen.* She's gone over to our competitors.

**können** VERB (PRESENT **kann,** IMPERFECT **konnte,** PERFECT **hat gekonnt** or **können**)
    see also **das Können** NOUN

*The past participle **können** is used when **können** is a modal auxiliary.*

[1] can ◊ *Kannst du schwimmen?* Can you swim? ◊ *Sie hat nicht früher kommen können.* She couldn't come earlier.

K

☞

◆ **Morgen werde ich nicht kommen können.** I won't be able to come tomorrow.

◆ **Ich kann nicht ...** I can't ...

◆ **Ich kann nicht mehr. (1)** I can't go on. ◊ *Ich mache jetzt Schluss, ich kann nicht mehr.* I'll have to stop now, I can't go on.

◆ **Ich kann nicht mehr. (2)** I'm full up. ◊ *Willst du noch ein Stück Kuchen? – Nein danke, ich kann nicht mehr.* Would you like another piece of cake? – No thanks, I'm full up.

[2] **may** ◊ *Kann ich gehen?* May I go? ◊ *Sie könnten Recht haben.* You may be right.

◆ **es kann sein, dass ...** it may be that ... ◊ *Es kann sein, dass ich etwas später komme.* It may be that I'll come a little later.

◆ **Am Wochenende durften sie ins Kino.** They were allowed to go to the cinema at the weekend.

◆ **Kann ich mit?** Can I come with you?

◆ **Ich kann nichts dafür.** It's not my fault.

◆ **Das kann sein.** That's possible.

[3] **to know** ◊ *Er kann viele Geschichtszahlen.* He knows a lot of historical dates.

◆ **Können Sie Deutsch?** Can you speak German?

◆ **Sie kann keine Mathematik.** She can't do mathematics.

das **Können** NOUN
   *see also* **können**
   ability ◊ *Sie hat ihr Können bewiesen.* She has proved her ability.

**konnte** VERB *see* **können**

**konservativ** ADJECTIVE
   conservative

die **Konserve** NOUN
   tinned food

die **Konservenbüchse** NOUN
   tin

der **Konsonant** NOUN (GEN des **Konsonanten**, PL die **Konsonanten**)
   consonant

der **Kontakt** NOUN (PL die **Kontakte**)
   contact

die **Kontaktlinsen** FEM PL NOUN
   contact lenses

der **Kontinent** NOUN (PL die **Kontinente**)
   continent

das **Konto** NOUN (PL die **Konten**)
   account ◊ *Geld auf ein Konto einzahlen* to pay money into an account

die **Kontrolle** NOUN
   control ◊ *die Passkontrolle* passport control ◊ *Sie hat die Kontrolle über das Fahrzeug verloren.* She lost control of the vehicle. ◊ *etwas unter Kontrolle haben* to have something under control

der **Kontrolleur** NOUN (PL die **Kontrolleure**)
   inspector

**kontrollieren** VERB (PERFECT **hat kontrolliert**)
   to check ◊ *Kann ich bitte Ihre Fahrkarten kontrollieren?* May I check your tickets please?

sich **konzentrieren** VERB (PERFECT **hat sich konzentriert**)
   to concentrate ◊ *Ich kann mich nicht konzentrieren.* I can't concentrate.

das **Konzert** NOUN (PL die **Konzerte**)
   [1] concert ◊ *Wir waren gestern Abend im Konzert.* We were at a concert yesterday evening.
   [2] concerto ◊ *ein Konzert für Klavier und Violine* a concerto for piano and violin

der **Kopf** NOUN (PL die **Köpfe**)
   head

der **Kopfhörer** NOUN (PL die **Kopfhörer**)
   headphones

das **Kopfkissen** NOUN (PL die **Kopfkissen**)
   pillow

der **Kopfsalat** NOUN (PL die **Kopfsalate**)
   lettuce

die **Kopfschmerzen** MASC PL NOUN
   headache ◊ *Ich habe Kopfschmerzen.* I've got a headache.

die **Kopie** NOUN
   copy

**kopieren** VERB (PERFECT **hat kopiert**)
   to copy

◆ **kopieren und einfügen** to copy and paste

das **Kopiergerät** NOUN (PL die **Kopiergeräte**)
   photocopier

der **Korb** NOUN (PL die **Körbe**)
   basket

◆ **jemandem einen Korb geben** to turn somebody down

der **Korken** NOUN (PL die **Korken**)
   cork

der **Korkenzieher** NOUN (PL die **Korkenzieher**)
   corkscrew

das **Korn** NOUN (PL die **Körner**)
   corn

der **Körper** NOUN (PL die **Körper**)
   body

**körperbehindert** ADJECTIVE
   disabled

der **Körperteil** NOUN (PL die **Körperteile**)
   part of the body

die **Korrektur** NOUN
   correction ◊ *Wir müssen die Korrektur ins gleiche Heft wie die Arbeit schreiben.* We have to write the corrections in the same exercise book as the test. ◊ *Der Text war voller Korrekturen.* The text was full of corrections.

◆ **Die Mathelehrerin ist noch nicht fertig mit den Korrekturen.** The maths teacher hasn't finished her marking yet.

**korrigieren** VERB (PERFECT **hat korrigiert**)
   to correct

die **Kosmetik** NOUN
   cosmetics

**kosmetisch** ADJECTIVE
cosmetic

die **Kost** NOUN
1 food ◊ *Sie ernährt sich von gesunder Kost.* She eats healthy food.
2 board ◊ *Für Kost und Unterkunft ist gesorgt.* Board and lodging will be provided.

**kostbar** ADJECTIVE
precious ◊ *Du vergeudest meine kostbare Zeit.* You're wasting my precious time.

die **Kosten** PL NOUN
see also **kosten** VERB
1 costs ◊ *die Kosten tragen* to bear the costs
2 expense ◊ *Bei vielen Kindern hat man auch viele Kosten.* Lots of children mean a lot of expense.
♦ **auf jemandes Kosten** at somebody's expense ◊ *Sie ist auf Kosten der Firma zu der Konferenz gefahren.* She went to the conference at the company's expense.

**kosten** VERB
see also **die Kosten** NOUN
1 to cost ◊ *Mein Fahrrad hat zweitausend Mark gekostet.* My bike cost two thousand marks.
♦ **Was kostet ...?** How much is ...?
2 to taste ◊ *Willst du die Soße mal kosten?* Would you like to taste the sauce? ◊ *Koste mal, ob das schmeckt.* Taste it and see if it's good.

**kostenlos** ADJECTIVE
free of charge

**köstlich** ADJECTIVE
1 hilarious ◊ *Das war ein köstlicher Film.* That was a hilarious film. ◊ *ein köstlicher Witz* a hilarious joke
2 delicious (*food*)
♦ **sich köstlich amüsieren** to have a marvellous time

das **Kostüm** NOUN (PL die **Kostüme**)
costume
♦ **ein Damenkostüm** a ladies' suit

das **Kotelett** NOUN (PL die **Koteletts**)
chop

**krabbeln** VERB (PERFECT **ist gekrabbelt**)
to crawl

der **Krach** NOUN
1 crash ◊ *Die Vase fiel mit einem lauten Krach zu Boden.* The vase fell on the ground with a loud crash.
2 noise ◊ *Unsere Nachbarn machen viel Krach.* Our neighbours make a lot of noise.
3 row ◊ *Sie hat Krach mit ihrem Freund.* She had a row with her boyfriend.

die **Kraft** NOUN (PL die **Kräfte**)
strength ◊ *Samson hat seine Kraft verloren.* Samson lost his strength.
♦ **Er hat viel Kraft.** He's very strong.
♦ **mit aller Kraft** with all one's might

♦ **Kinder kosten viel Kraft.** Children require a lot of energy.
♦ **Sie scheint magische Kräfte zu haben.** She seems to have magic powers.
♦ **Das Gesetz tritt am ersten August in Kraft.** The law comes into effect on the first of August.

das **Kraftfahrzeug** NOUN (PL die **Kraftfahrzeuge**)
motor vehicle

**kräftig** ADJECTIVE, ADVERB
1 strong ◊ *Er ist ein kräftiger Junge.* He is a strong boy.
2 hard ◊ *ein kräftiger Schlag* a hard blow ◊ *kräftig schütteln* to shake hard
♦ **kräftig üben** to practise a lot ◊ *Wenn du kräftig übst, dann schaffst du es.* If you practise a lot, you'll do it.

das **Kraftwerk** NOUN (PL die **Kraftwerke**)
power station

der **Kragen** NOUN (PL die **Kragen**)
collar

die **Kralle** NOUN
1 claw ◊ *die Krallen der Katze* the cat's claws
2 talon ◊ *die Krallen des Vogels* the bird's talons

der **Kram** NOUN
stuff ◊ *Ich habe den ganzen Kram weggeworfen.* I threw all the stuff away.
♦ **Mach doch deinen Kram allein!** Do it yourself!
♦ **Das passt mir nicht in den Kram.** It doesn't suit me.

**krank** ADJECTIVE
ill ◊ *Ich bin krank.* I'm ill. ◊ *Ich habe eine kranke Mutter.* My mother's ill.

das **Krankenhaus** NOUN (GEN des **Krankenhauses**, PL die **Krankenhäuser**)
hospital

die **Krankenkasse** NOUN
health insurance

> ❶ In Germany one can choose between different health insurance schemes. There is no "National Health Service".

der **Krankenpfleger** NOUN (PL die **Krankenpfleger**)
male nurse

der **Krankenschein** NOUN (PL die **Krankenscheine**)
health insurance card

die **Krankenschwester** NOUN
nurse

die **Krankenversicherung** NOUN
health insurance

der **Krankenwagen** NOUN (PL die **Krankenwagen**)
ambulance

die **Krankheit** NOUN
illness

**K**

# krankschreiben → Küche

**krankschreiben** VERB (IMPERFECT **schrieb krank**, PERFECT **hat krankgeschrieben**)
♦ **jemanden krankschreiben** to give somebody a sick note ◊ *Der Arzt hat ihn für eine Woche krankgeschrieben.* The doctor gave him a sick note for a week.

**kratzen** VERB
to scratch
♦ **sich kratzen** to scratch oneself

**kraus** ADJECTIVE
frizzy ◊ *Sie hat krause Haare.* She has frizzy hair.

das **Kraut** NOUN (PL die **Kräuter**)
[1] herb ◊ *eine Salatsoße mit frischen Kräutern* a salad dressing with fresh herbs
[2] sauerkraut ◊ *Heute gibt es Würstchen mit Kraut.* We're having sausages and sauerkraut today.

die **Krawatte** NOUN
tie

**kreativ** ADJECTIVE
creative

der **Krebs** NOUN (GEN des **Krebses**, PL die **Krebse**)
[1] crab ◊ *Krebse bewegen sich seitlich voran.* Crabs move sideways.
[2] cancer ◊ *Sie ist an Krebs gestorben.* She died of cancer.
[3] Cancer
♦ **Beate ist Krebs.** Beate's Cancer.

der **Kredit** NOUN (PL die **Kredite**)
credit ◊ *auf Kredit* on credit

die **Kreditkarte** NOUN
credit card

die **Kreide** NOUN
chalk

der **Kreis** NOUN (GEN des **Kreises**, PL die **Kreise**)
[1] circle ◊ *Stellt euch im Kreis auf.* Form a circle. ◊ *mein Freundeskreis* my circle of friends
[2] district ◊ *Blaubeuren liegt im Kreis Ulm.* Blaubeuren is in the district of Ulm.
♦ **im Kreis gehen** to go round in circles

**kreischen** VERB
to shriek ◊ *Sie kreischte laut.* She shrieked loudly.

der **Kreislauf** NOUN
circulation ◊ *Sie hat einen labilen Kreislauf.* She has bad circulation.

der **Kreisverkehr** NOUN (PL die **Kreisverkehre**)
roundabout

das **Kreuz** NOUN (GEN des **Kreuzes**, PL die **Kreuze**)
[1] cross ◊ *Sie markierte die Stelle mit einem Kreuz.* She marked the place with a cross.
♦ **Mir tut das Kreuz weh.** My back's sore.
[2] clubs ◊ *Kreuz ist Trumpf.* Clubs is trumps.

die **Kreuzung** NOUN
[1] crossroads ◊ *An der Kreuzung fährst du links.* You go left at the crossroads.
[2] cross ◊ *Das ist eine Kreuzung zwischen Pferd und Esel.* It's a cross between a horse and a donkey.

das **Kreuzworträtsel** NOUN (PL die **Kreuzworträtsel**)
crossword puzzle

**kriechen** VERB (IMPERFECT **kroch**, PERFECT **ist gekrochen**)
[1] to crawl ◊ *Das Baby kroch zur Tür.* The baby crawled towards the door. ◊ *Der Verkehr kriecht.* The traffic is crawling.
[2] to grovel ◊ *Er kriecht vor seinem Chef.* He's grovelling to his boss.

der **Krieg** NOUN (PL die **Kriege**)
war

**kriegen** VERB
to get ◊ *Ich kriege einen Schnupfen.* I'm getting a cold.
♦ **Sie kriegt ein Kind.** She's going to have a baby.

der **Krimi** NOUN (PL die **Krimis**)
thriller

der **Kriminalfilm** NOUN (PL die **Kriminalfilme**)
crime thriller

der **Kriminalroman** NOUN (PL die **Kriminalromane**)
detective story

**kriminell** ADJECTIVE
criminal

die **Krise** NOUN
crisis

**kritisch** ADJECTIVE
critical

**kritisieren** VERB (PERFECT **hat kritisiert**)
to criticize

**Kroatien** NEUT NOUN
Croatia
♦ **aus Kroatien** from Croatia
♦ **nach Kroatien** to Croatia

das **Krokodil** NOUN (PL die **Krokodile**)
crocodile

die **Krone** NOUN
crown

die **Kröte** NOUN
toad

der **Krug** NOUN (PL die **Krüge**)
[1] jug ◊ *Sie stellte einen Krug Saft auf den Tisch.* She put a jug of juice on the table.
[2] beer mug ◊ *Er trinkt sein Bier immer aus einem Krug.* He always drinks his beer out of a beer mug.

**krumm** ADJECTIVE
♦ **ein krummer Rücken** a humped back
♦ **Mach nicht so einen krummen Rücken.** Don't slouch.
♦ **Sitz nicht so krumm.** Sit up straight.

die **Küche** NOUN
[1] kitchen
[2] cooking ◊ *die französische Küche* French cooking

der **Kuchen** NOUN (PL die **Kuchen**)
  [1] cake ◊ *ein Marmorkuchen* a marble cake
  [2] flan ◊ *ein Obstkuchen* a fruit flan
der **Kuckuck** NOUN (PL die **Kuckucke**)
  cuckoo
die **Kuckucksuhr** NOUN
  cuckoo clock
die **Kugel** NOUN
  [1] bullet ◊ *Er wurde von einer Kugel getroffen.* He was hit by a bullet.
  [2] ball ◊ *Die Wahrsagerin hat eine Kugel aus Glas.* The fortune teller has a crystal ball.
der **Kugelschreiber** NOUN (PL die **Kugelschreiber**)
  Biro ®
die **Kuh** NOUN (PL die **Kühe**)
  cow
  **kühl** ADJECTIVE
  cool ◊ *Abends wurde es kühl.* In the evenings it got cool.
der **Kühler** NOUN (PL die **Kühler**)
  radiator (*in car*)
der **Kühlschrank** NOUN (PL die **Kühlschränke**)
  fridge
die **Kühltruhe** NOUN
  freezer
  **kühn** ADJECTIVE
  bold
der **Kuli** NOUN (PL die **Kulis**)
  Biro ®
die **Kultur** NOUN
  [1] culture
  ◆ **Kultur haben** to be cultured
  [2] civilization ◊ *die abendländische Kultur* Western civilization
der **Kulturbeutel** NOUN (PL die **Kulturbeutel**)
  toilet bag
  **kulturell** ADJECTIVE
  cultural
der **Kümmel** NOUN (PL die **Kümmel**)
  caraway seed
der **Kummer** NOUN
  sorrow
  ◆ **Hast du Kummer?** Have you got problems?
  **kümmern** VERB
  to concern ◊ *Was kümmert mich seine Kritik?* Why should his criticism concern me?
  ◆ **Das kümmert mich nicht.** That doesn't worry me.
  ◆ **sich um jemanden kümmern** to look after somebody
  ◆ **sich um etwas kümmern** to see to something ◊ *Kannst du dich um meine Pflanzen kümmern?* Can you see to my plants? ◊ *Ich kümmere mich darum, dass das gemacht wird.* I'll see to it that it's done.

  ◆ **Sie kümmert sich nicht um das Gerede der Leute.** She doesn't care about what people say.
der **Kunde** NOUN (GEN des **Kunden,** PL die **Kunden**)
  customer
  **kündigen** VERB
  [1] to hand in one's notice ◊ *Die Arbeit gefällt mir nicht, ich werde kündigen.* I don't like the job, I'm going to hand in my notice.
  ◆ **die Stellung kündigen** to hand in one's notice
  ◆ **Der Chef hat ihr gekündigt.** The boss gave her her notice.
  ◆ **die Wohnung kündigen** to give notice on one's flat
  [2] to cancel ◊ *Ich habe mein Abonnement gekündigt.* I've cancelled my subscription.
die **Kündigung** NOUN
  notice ◊ *Er reichte seine Kündigung ein.* He handed in his notice.
die **Kundin** NOUN
  customer
die **Kundschaft** NOUN
  customers
die **Kunst** NOUN (PL die **Künste**)
  [1] art ◊ *Sie interessiert sich für Kunst.* She's interested in art.
  [2] knack ◊ *Er beherrscht die Kunst, andere zu überzeugen.* He's got the knack of persuading others.
  ◆ **Das ist doch keine Kunst.** It's easy.
die **Kunstfaser** NOUN
  man-made fibre
der **Künstler** NOUN (PL die **Künstler**)
  artist
die **Künstlerin** NOUN
  artist
  **künstlerisch** ADJECTIVE
  artistic ◊ *künstlerisch begabt sein* to have artistic talents
  **künstlich** ADJECTIVE
  artificial
der **Kunststoff** NOUN (PL die **Kunststoffe**)
  synthetic material
das **Kunststück** NOUN (PL die **Kunststücke**)
  trick
das **Kunstwerk** NOUN (PL die **Kunstwerke**)
  work of art
das **Kupfer** NOUN
  copper (*metal*)
die **Kupplung** NOUN
  clutch ◊ *Bei Automatikwagen gibt es keine Kupplung.* Automatic cars don't have a clutch.
die **Kur** NOUN
  health cure ◊ *eine Kur machen* to take a health cure
der **Kürbis** NOUN (GEN des **Kürbisses,** PL die **Kürbisse**)

**K**

☞

pumpkin

der **Kurort** NOUN (PL die **Kurorte**)
   health resort

der **Kurs** NOUN (GEN des **Kurses**, PL die **Kurse**)
   [1] course ◊ *Ich mache einen Kurs, um Spanisch zu lernen.* I'm doing a course to learn Spanish.
   [2] rate ◊ *Wie ist der Kurs des Pfunds?* What's the rate for the pound?

die **Kurve** NOUN
   [1] bend ◊ *Ein Auto bog um die Kurve.* A car came round the bend.
   [2] curve ◊ *die Kurve eines Schaubilds* the curve on a graph

**kurz** ADJECTIVE
   short ◊ *Sie hat kurze Haare.* She has short hair. ◊ *Wir fahren über Feuerbach, das ist kürzer.* We'll go via Feuerbach, it's shorter. ◊ *Sie hat eine kurze Rede gehalten.* She made a short speech.
   ◆ **kurz gesagt** in short
   ◆ **zu kurz kommen** to come off badly
   ◆ **den Kürzeren ziehen** to get the worst of it

die **Kurzarbeit** NOUN
   short-time work

die **Kürze** NOUN
   shortness

**kürzen** VERB
   [1] to shorten ◊ *Du solltest den Aufsatz etwas kürzen.* You should shorten your essay a little.
   [2] to cut ◊ *Mein Vater hat mir das Taschengeld gekürzt.* My father has cut my pocket money.

die **Kurzgeschichte** NOUN
   short story

**kürzlich** ADVERB
   recently

**kurzsichtig** ADJECTIVE
   short-sighted

die **Kusine** NOUN
   cousin

der **Kuss** NOUN (GEN des **Kusses**, PL die **Küsse**)
   kiss

**küssen** VERB
   to kiss ◊ *Sie hat mich geküsst.* She kissed me.
   ◆ **sich küssen** to kiss ◊ *Sie küssten sich.* They kissed.

die **Küste** NOUN
   coast

# L

**l** ABBREVIATION (= *Liter*)
  l

das **Labor** NOUN (PL die **Labore** *or* **Labors**)
  lab

**lächeln** VERB
  | *see also* das **Lächeln** NOUN |
  to smile

das **Lächeln** NOUN
  | *see also* **lächeln** VERB |
  smile

**lachen** VERB
  to laugh

**lächerlich** ADJECTIVE
  ridiculous

der **Lachs** NOUN (GEN des **Lachses**, PL die **Lachse**)
  salmon ◊ *drei Lachse* three salmon

der **Lack** NOUN (PL die **Lacke**)
  [1] varnish ◊ *Er hat das Holz mit Lack behandelt.* He treated the wood with varnish.
  [2] paint ◊ *Der Lack an meinem Auto ist stumpf geworden.* The paint on my car has become dull.

**lackieren** VERB (PERFECT **hat lackiert**)
  [1] to varnish ◊ *Ich lackiere mir die Nägel.* I'm varnishing my nails.
  [2] to spray ◊ *Das Auto muss lackiert werden.* The car has to be sprayed.

der **Laden** NOUN (PL die **Läden**)
  | *see also* **laden** VERB |
  [1] shop ◊ *In welchem Laden hast du das gekauft?* Which shop did you buy it in?
  [2] shutter ◊ *Im Sommer machen wir tagsüber die Läden zu.* In summer we close the shutters during the day.

**laden** VERB (PRESENT **lädt**, IMPERFECT **lud**, PERFECT **hat geladen**)
  | *see also* der **Laden** NOUN |
  [1] to load ◊ *Wir haben das Gepäck ins Auto geladen.* We loaded the luggage into the car. ◊ *Das Programm wird geladen.* The program is being loaded. ◊ *eine Waffe laden* to load a weapon
  ◆ **eine Batterie laden** to charge a battery
  [2] to summon ◊ *Ich wurde als Zeugin geladen.* I was summoned as a witness.

die **Ladung** NOUN
  [1] cargo ◊ *Das Flugzeug hatte zu viel Ladung an Bord.* The plane had too much cargo on board.
  [2] loading ◊ *Ein Arbeiter ist bei der Ladung des Schiffes verunglückt.* A worker was injured while loading the ship.
  [3] summons ◊ *Wenn Sie eine Ladung als Zeuge bekommen, müssen Sie erscheinen.* If you receive a summons to appear as a witness, you have to attend.

[4] charge ◊ *eine Ladung Dynamit* a charge of dynamite

die **Lage** NOUN
  [1] situation ◊ *Die politische Lage auf dem Balkan ist brisant.* The political situation in the Balkans is explosive.
  [2] layer ◊ *Die Torte bestand aus mehreren Lagen.* The gateau was made up of several layers.
  ◆ **in der Lage sein, etwas zu tun** to be in a position to do something

das **Lager** NOUN (PL die **Lager**)
  [1] camp ◊ *Er fährt im Sommer in ein Lager der Pfadfinder.* He's going to a scout camp in the summer.
  [2] warehouse ◊ *Die Fabrik hat ein eigenes Lager.* The factory has its own warehouse.
  [3] stockroom ◊ *Die Verkäuferin hat im Lager nachgesehen.* The sales assistant looked in the stockroom.

**lagern** VERB
  [1] to store ◊ *kühl lagern* to store in a cool place ◊ *trocken lagern* to store in a dry place
  [2] to lay down ◊ *Der Verletzte sollte auf der Seite gelagert werden.* The injured person should be laid down on his side.
  [3] to camp ◊ *Die Indianer lagerten am Fluss.* The Indians camped by the river.

**lahm** ADJECTIVE
  [1] lame ◊ *Das Pferd ist lahm.* The horse is lame.
  [2] slow ◊ *Er ist furchtbar lahm.* He is terribly slow.

**lähmen** VERB
  to paralyse

die **Lähmung** NOUN
  paralysis

der **Laib** NOUN (PL die **Laibe**)
  loaf

der **Laie** NOUN (GEN des **Laien,** PL die **Laien**)
  layman

das **Laken** NOUN (PL die **Laken**)
  sheet (*on bed*)

die **Lakritze** NOUN
  liquorice

das **Lamm** NOUN (PL die **Lämmer**)
  lamb

das **Lammfleisch** NOUN
  lamb (*meat*)

die **Lampe** NOUN
  lamp

das **Lampenfieber** NOUN
  stage fright

das **Land** NOUN (PL die **Länder**)
  [1] country ◊ *Italien ist ein schönes Land.* Italy is a beautiful country. ◊ *Am*

☞

*Wochenende fahren wir aufs Land.* We're going to the country at the weekend.

♦ **auf dem Land** in the country

♦ **an Land** on land ◊ *Wenn wir wieder an Land sind ...* When we're on land again ...

[2] state ◊ *Die Bundesrepublik besteht aus sechzehn Ländern.* The Federal Republic consists of sixteen states.

der **Landarbeiter** NOUN (PL die **Landarbeiter**)
farm worker

die **Landarbeiterin** NOUN
farm worker

die **Landebahn** NOUN
runway

**landen** VERB (PERFECT **ist gelandet**)
to land

die **Landeskunde** NOUN
regional and cultural studies

die **Landkarte** NOUN
map

der **Landkreis** NOUN (GEN des **Landkreises**, PL die **Landkreise**)
administrative district

> ❶ *The German administrative hierarchy starts with the **Stadt/Gemeinde** (town/community), and continues via the **Landkreis** (administrative district) and **Land** (federal state) to the **Bund** (federation).*

**ländlich** ADJECTIVE
rural

die **Landschaft** NOUN
[1] countryside ◊ *Die toskanische Landschaft ist sehr schön.* The Tuscan countryside is very beautiful.
[2] landscape ◊ *Turner hat viele Landschaften gemalt.* Turner painted many landscapes.

die **Landstraße** NOUN
country road

die **Landung** NOUN
landing ◊ *Das Flugzeug verunglückte bei der Landung.* The plane crashed on landing.

der **Landwirt** NOUN (PL die **Landwirte**)
farmer

die **Landwirtschaft** NOUN
agriculture

**lang** ADJECTIVE
[1] long ◊ *Sie hat lange Haare.* She has long hair. ◊ *Das war eine lange Rede.* That was a long speech. ◊ *Sie war länger als erwartet weg.* She was away longer than expected. ◊ *Es wird nicht lang dauern.* It won't take long.
[2] tall ◊ *Mathis ist der Längste in unserer Klasse.* Mathis is the tallest in our class.

**langatmig** ADJECTIVE
long-winded

**lange** ADVERB

for a long time ◊ *Sie war lange krank.* She was ill for a long time.

♦ **lange dauern** to last a long time

♦ **lange brauchen** to take a long time

die **Länge** NOUN
length ◊ *Sie hat die Länge und Breite des Zimmers ausgemessen.* She measured the length and breadth of the room. ◊ *die Länge eines Films* the length of a film

**langen** VERB
to have enough ◊ *Meinst du das Geld langt?* Do you think we have enough money?

♦ **Das Fleisch hat nicht für alle gelangt.** There wasn't enough meat to go round.

♦ **Es langt mir.** I've had enough.

♦ **nach etwas langen** to reach for something ◊ *Er langte nach dem Apfel.* He reached for the apple.

die **Langeweile** NOUN
boredom

**langfristig** ADJECTIVE, ADVERB
long-term ◊ *eine langfristige Besserung* a long-term improvement ◊ *Wir müssen langfristig planen.* We have to plan long-term.

der **Langlauf** NOUN
cross-country skiing ◊ *Sie macht gern Langlauf.* She likes to go cross-country skiing.

**länglich** ADJECTIVE
longish

**langsam** ADJECTIVE, ADVERB
[1] slow
[2] slowly ◊ *langsam fahren* to drive slowly

♦ **Das wird langsam langweilig.** This is getting boring.

die **Langsamkeit** NOUN
slowness

der **Langschläfer** NOUN (PL die **Langschläfer**)
late riser

die **Langspielplatte** NOUN
LP

**längst** ADVERB

♦ **Das ist längst fertig.** That was finished a long time ago.

♦ **Das weiß ich längst.** I've known that for a long time.

♦ **Er ist längst nicht so gescheit wie seine Schwester.** He's far from being as bright as his sister.

**längste** ADJECTIVE
longest ◊ *der längste Tag des Jahres* the longest day of the year

**langweilen** VERB
to bore ◊ *Langweile ich dich?* Am I boring you?

♦ **sich langweilen** to be bored

**langweilig** ADJECTIVE
boring

**langwierig** ADJECTIVE
lengthy

der **Lappen** NOUN (PL die **Lappen**)
rag ◊ *mit einem feuchten Lappen* with a
damp rag

der **Laptop** NOUN (PL die **Laptops**)
laptop

der **Lärm** NOUN
noise

der **Laser** NOUN (PL die **Laser**)
laser

**lassen** VERB (PRESENT **lässt**, IMPERFECT **ließ**,
PERFECT **gelassen** or **lassen**)
*The past participle lassen is used when
lassen is a modal auxiliary.*
[1] to stop ◊ *Du solltest das Rauchen
lassen.* You should stop smoking. ◊ *Er
kann das Trinken nicht lassen.* He can't
stop drinking. ◊ *Sie kann's nicht lassen.*
She won't stop doing it.
♦ **Lass das!** Stop that!
[2] to leave ◊ *Kann ich die Kinder hier
lassen?* Can I leave the children here?
◊ *jemanden allein lassen* to leave
somebody alone ◊ *Wir haben das Auto
zu Hause gelassen.* We left the car at
home. ◊ *etwas lassen, wie es ist* to leave
something as it is
♦ **Lassen wir das!** Let's leave it.
♦ **Lass mal, ich mache das schon.** Leave it,
I'll do it.
♦ **Lass mich!** Leave me alone.
♦ **jemanden irgendwohin lassen** to let
somebody go somewhere ◊ *Sie lässt die
Katze nicht ins Schlafzimmer.* She
doesn't let the cat into the bedroom.
◊ *jemanden ins Haus lassen* to let
somebody into the house
♦ **etwas machen lassen** to have something
done ◊ *Ich habe mir den Katalog
schicken lassen.* I had the catalogue sent
to me. ◊ *Sie hat sich die Haare schneiden
lassen.* She had her hair cut.
♦ **jemanden etwas tun lassen** to let
somebody do something ◊ *Sie hat uns
nicht ins Kino gehen lassen.* She didn't
let us go to the cinema.
♦ **jemanden etwas wissen lassen** to let
somebody know something
♦ **jemanden warten lassen** to keep
somebody waiting
♦ **Das lässt sich machen.** That can be
done.
♦ **Lass uns gehen.** Let's go.

**lässig** ADJECTIVE
casual

die **Last** NOUN
load ◊ *Er stöhnte unter der schweren
Last.* He groaned under the heavy load.
♦ **jemandem zur Last fallen** to be a burden
to somebody

**lästern** VERB

to make nasty remarks ◊ *Lästert ihr
schon wieder über eure Lehrerin?* Are
you making nasty remarks about your
teacher again?

**lästig** ADJECTIVE
tiresome

der **Lastwagen** NOUN (PL die **Lastwagen**)
lorry

das **Latein** NOUN
Latin

**Lateinamerika** NEUT NOUN
Latin America

die **Laterne** NOUN
[1] lantern ◊ *Die Kinder trugen Laternen.*
The children carried lanterns.
[2] streetlamp ◊ *Vor unserem Haus steht
eine Laterne.* There's a streetlamp in
front of our house.

der **Lauch** NOUN (PL die **Lauche**)
leek

der **Lauf** NOUN (PL die **Läufe**)
[1] run ◊ *Er machte einen Lauf durch den
Wald.* He went for a run through the
forest.
[2] race ◊ *Sie hat den Lauf über
vierhundert Meter gewonnen.* She won
the four-hundred-metre race.
[3] course ◊ *der Lauf des Flusses* the
course of the river
[4] barrel ◊ *Er richtete den Lauf seiner
Pistole auf mich.* He aimed the barrel of
his pistol at me.
♦ **im Laufe der Woche** in the course of the
week
♦ **einer Sache ihren Lauf lassen** to let
something take its course

die **Laufbahn** NOUN
career

**laufen** VERB (PRESENT **läuft**, IMPERFECT **lief**,
PERFECT **ist gelaufen**)
[1] to run ◊ *Sie liefen so schnell sie
konnten.* They ran as fast as they could.
◊ *Er läuft Marathon.* He runs marathons.
[2] to walk ◊ *Wir mussten nach Hause
laufen.* We had to walk home.

**laufend** ADJECTIVE, ADVERB
[1] running ◊ *bei laufendem Motor* with
the engine running
[2] current ◊ *die laufenden Ausgaben*
current expenses
♦ **auf dem Laufenden sein** to be up to date
♦ **auf dem Laufenden halten** to keep up to
date
[3] always ◊ *Musst du mich laufend
stören?* Do you always have to interrupt
me?

der **Läufer** NOUN (PL die **Läufer**)
[1] runner ◊ *Die Läufer standen am Start.*
The runners were at the start. ◊ *Im Flur
liegt ein roter Läufer.* There's a red
runner in the hall.
[2] bishop ◊ *Sie zog mit dem Läufer.* She
moved her bishop.

**L**

die **Läuferin** NOUN
runner

die **Laufmasche** NOUN
ladder (*in tights*)

das **Laufwerk** NOUN (PL die **Laufwerke**)
disk drive ◊ *Die Diskette in Laufwerk A einlegen.* Put the diskette in disk drive A.

die **Laune** NOUN
mood ◊ *Was hat sie für eine Laune?* What kind of mood is she in? ◊ *Ich habe gute Laune.* I'm in a good mood.
♦ **Ich bin deine Launen leid.** I'm fed up with your bad moods.
♦ **Sie ist aus einer Laune heraus nach Italien gefahren.** She took it into her head to go off to Italy.

**launisch** ADJECTIVE
[1] temperamental ◊ *Sie ist ein sehr launischer Mensch.* She's very temperamental.
[2] bad-tempered ◊ *Er war heute schrecklich launisch.* He was terribly bad-tempered today.

die **Laus** NOUN (PL die **Läuse**)
louse

**laut** ADJECTIVE, ADVERB, PREPOSITION
see also **der Laut** NOUN
[1] loud ◊ *Ich mag laute Musik nicht.* I don't like loud music.
♦ **Hier ist es schrecklich laut.** It's terribly noisy here.
[2] loudly ◊ *Sie schrie so laut sie konnte.* She screamed as loudly as she could.
♦ **laut lesen** to read aloud
[3] according to ◊ *Laut unserem Vertrag ...* According to our contract ...

der **Laut** NOUN (PL die **Laute**)
see also **laut** ADJECTIVE
sound

**lauten** VERB
[1] to go ◊ *Wie lautet die zweite Strophe des Lieds?* How does the second verse of the song go?
[2] to be ◊ *Das Urteil lautete auf zehn Jahre Gefängnis.* The sentence was ten years' imprisonment.

**läuten** VERB
to ring ◊ *Die Glocken läuten.* The bells are ringing. ◊ *Ich habe geläutet, es hat aber niemand aufgemacht.* I rang but nobody answered.

**lauter** ADVERB
nothing but ◊ *Sie hat lauter Lügen erzählt.* She told nothing but lies.

die **Lautschrift** NOUN
phonetics

der **Lautsprecher** NOUN (PL die **Lautsprecher**)
loudspeaker

die **Lautstärke** NOUN
volume

**lauwarm** ADJECTIVE
lukewarm

die **Lawine** NOUN
avalanche

das **Leben** NOUN (PL die **Leben**)
see also **leben** VERB
life
♦ **ums Leben kommen** to lose one's life ◊ *Er ist bei einem Unfall ums Leben gekommen.* He lost his life in an accident.

**leben** VERB
see also **das Leben** NOUN
to live

**lebend** ADJECTIVE
living

**lebendig** ADJECTIVE
[1] alive ◊ *Er konnte lebendig aus den Trümmern geborgen werden.* He was rescued from the ruins alive.
[2] lively ◊ *Sie ist ein sehr lebendiges Kind.* She's a very lively child.

die **Lebensgefahr** NOUN
mortal danger ◊ *Die Geiseln waren in Lebensgefahr.* The hostages were in mortal danger.
♦ **"Lebensgefahr!"** "danger!"

**lebensgefährlich** ADJECTIVE
[1] dangerous ◊ *eine lebensgefährliche Kurve* a dangerous corner
[2] critical ◊ *eine lebensgefährliche Krankheit* a critical illness
♦ **lebensgefährlich verletzt** critically injured

die **Lebenshaltungskosten** PL NOUN
cost of living

**lebenslänglich** ADJECTIVE
for life
♦ **Er hat eine lebenslängliche Gefängnisstrafe bekommen.** He received a life sentence.

der **Lebenslauf** NOUN (PL die **Lebensläufe**)
CV (= curriculum vitae)

die **Lebensmittel** NEUT PL NOUN
food

das **Lebensmittelgeschäft** NOUN (PL die **Lebensmittelgeschäfte**)
grocer's shop

die **Lebensmittelvergiftung** NOUN
food poisoning

der **Lebensstandard** NOUN
standard of living

der **Lebensunterhalt** NOUN
livelihood

die **Lebensversicherung** NOUN
life insurance

die **Leber** NOUN
liver

der **Leberfleck** NOUN (PL die **Leberflecke**)
mole (*on skin*)

die **Leberwurst** NOUN (PL die **Leberwürste**)
liver sausage

das **Lebewesen** NOUN (PL die **Lebewesen**)
creature

**lebhaft** ADJECTIVE
  lively
der **Lebkuchen** NOUN (PL die **Lebkuchen**)
  gingerbread
**lecken** VERB
  [1] to leak ◊ *Der Behälter leckt.* The
  container's leaking.
  [2] to lick ◊ *Die Katze leckte sich das Fell.*
  The cat licked its fur. ◊ *Sie leckte am Eis.*
  She licked her ice.
**lecker** ADJECTIVE
  delicious ◊ *lecker schmecken* to taste
  delicious
das **Leder** NOUN (PL die **Leder**)
  leather
die **Lederhose** NOUN
  leather trousers

> ❶ *Lederhosen* are the traditional dress
> in South Germany and Austria.

**ledig** ADJECTIVE
  single ◊ *"Familienstand: ledig"* "Marital
  status: single"
**leer** ADJECTIVE
  empty ◊ *eine leere Flasche* an empty
  bottle ◊ *leere Drohungen* empty threats
  ◆ **ein leeres Blatt Papier** a blank sheet of
  paper
  ◆ **ein leerer Blick** a vacant expression
  ◆ **leer machen** to empty
die **Leere** NOUN
  emptiness
**leeren** VERB
  to empty
die **Leerung** NOUN
  [1] emptying ◊ *Die Leerung der*
  *Mülltonnen erfolgt freitags.* The dustbins
  are emptied on Fridays.
  [2] collection *(from postbox)* ◊ *"Nächste*
  *Leerung: 18 Uhr"* "Next collection: 6
  p.m."
**legal** ADJECTIVE
  legal
**legen** VERB
  [1] to put ◊ *Sie legte das Kind ins Bett.*
  She put the child to bed. ◊ *Leg das*
  *Besteck in die Schublade.* Put the cutlery
  in the drawer. ◊ *Er legte das Buch aus*
  *der Hand.* He put the book down.
  [2] to lay ◊ *Sie legten den Verletzten auf*
  *eine Decke.* They laid the injured man on
  a blanket. ◊ *Sie legte ihren Mantel über*
  *den Stuhl.* She laid her coat over the
  chair. ◊ *ein Ei legen* to lay an egg
  ◆ **sich legen (1)** to lie down ◊ *Sie legte sich*
  *auf das Sofa.* She lay down on the sofa.
  ◊ *Ich lege mich ins Bett.* I'm going to lie
  down. ◊ *Wir legten uns an den Strand.*
  We lay down on the beach.
  ◆ **sich legen (2)** to drop ◊ *Der Wind hat*
  *sich gelegt.* The wind has dropped.

◆ **Das wird sich legen.** That will sort itself
  out.
die **Lehne** NOUN
  [1] arm ◊ *Sie saß auf der Lehne des*
  *Sofas.* She sat on the arm of the sofa.
  [2] back ◊ *Der Sessel hat eine hohe*
  *Lehne.* The chair has a high back.
**lehnen** VERB
  to lean
der **Lehnstuhl** NOUN (PL die **Lehnstühle**)
  armchair
die **Lehre** NOUN
  [1] apprenticeship ◊ *bei jemandem in die*
  *Lehre gehen* to serve one's
  apprenticeship with somebody
  [2] lesson ◊ *Lass dir das eine Lehre sein!*
  Let that be a lesson to you!
**lehren** VERB (PERFECT **hat gelehrt**)
  to teach
der **Lehrer** NOUN (PL die **Lehrer**)
  teacher
die **Lehrerin** NOUN
  teacher
das **Lehrerzimmer** NOUN (PL die
  **Lehrerzimmer**)
  staff room
das **Lehrjahr** NOUN (PL die **Lehrjahre**)
  year as an apprentice
der **Lehrling** NOUN (PL die **Lehrlinge**)
  apprentice
der **Lehrplan** NOUN (PL die **Lehrpläne**)
  syllabus
die **Lehrstelle** NOUN
  apprenticeship
die **Leiche** NOUN
  corpse
**leicht** ADJECTIVE
  [1] light ◊ *leichtes Gepäck* light luggage
  [2] easy ◊ *Die Klassenarbeit war leicht.*
  The class test was easy.
  ◆ **jemandem leicht fallen** to be easy for
  somebody
  ◆ **es sich leicht machen** to make things
  easy for oneself ◊ *Du machst es dir*
  *wirklich zu leicht.* You really make things
  too easy for yourself.
die **Leichtathletik** NOUN
  athletics
**leichtfallen** VERB *see* **leicht**
**leichtmachen** VERB *see* **leicht**
der **Leichtsinn** NOUN
  carelessness
**leichtsinnig** ADJECTIVE
  careless
das **Leid** NOUN
  > *see also* **leid** ADJECTIVE

  sorrow
  ◆ **Es tut mir Leid.** I'm sorry.
  ◆ **Er tut mir Leid.** I'm sorry for him.
  ◆ **zu Leide** *see* **zuleide**
**leid** ADJECTIVE
  > *see also* **das Leid** NOUN

**L**

☞

## leiden → lenken

◆ **etwas leid sein** to be tired of something ◇ *Ich bin deine ewigen Klagen leid.* I'm tired of your constant complaining.

**leiden** VERB (IMPERFECT **litt**, PERFECT **hat gelitten**)
to suffer ◇ *Sie leidet an Asthma.* She suffers from asthma. ◇ *Wir leiden unter der Hitze.* We're suffering from the heat.

◆ **jemanden gut leiden können** to like somebody

◆ **Ich kann ihn nicht leiden.** I can't stand him.

**leider** ADVERB
unfortunately ◇ *Ich kann leider nicht kommen.* Unfortunately I can't come.

◆ **Ja, leider.** Yes, I'm afraid so.

◆ **Leider nicht.** I'm afraid not. ◇ *Er hat mir leider nicht geholfen.* I'm afraid he didn't help me.

**leihen** VERB (IMPERFECT **lieh**, PERFECT **hat geliehen**)
to lend ◇ *Kannst du mir fünfzig Mark leihen?* Can you lend me fifty marks?

◆ **sich etwas leihen** to borrow something ◇ *Das ist nicht mein Fahrrad, ich habe es mir von meiner Schwester geliehen.* That's not my bike, I've borrowed it from my sister.

**der Leim** NOUN (PL die **Leime**)
glue

**die Leine** NOUN
[1] line ◇ *Sie hängte die Wäsche auf die Leine.* She hung the washing on the line.
[2] lead ◇ *Hunde müssen an der Leine geführt werden.* Dogs must be kept on a lead.

**das Leinen** NOUN (PL die **Leinen**)
linen

**leise** ADJECTIVE, ADVERB
[1] quiet ◇ *Seid bitte leise.* Please be quiet.
[2] quietly ◇ *Sie sprach mit leiser Stimme.* She spoke quietly. ◇ *Sie kam ganz leise ins Zimmer.* She came into the room very quietly.

**leisten** VERB
[1] to do ◇ *Du hast gute Arbeit geleistet.* You've done a good job.
[2] to achieve ◇ *Sie hat viel geleistet im Leben.* She's achieved a lot in her life.

◆ **jemandem Gesellschaft leisten** to keep somebody company

◆ **sich etwas leisten** to treat oneself to something ◇ *Ich leiste mir heute einen freien Tag.* I'm going to treat myself to a day off today.

◆ **sich etwas leisten können** to be able to afford something ◇ *Ich kann mir keinen neuen Computer leisten.* I can't afford a new computer. ◇ *Ich kann es mir nicht leisten, schon wieder zu spät zu kommen.* I can't afford to be late again.

**die Leistung** NOUN

[1] performance ◇ *Sie haben die Leistung des Motors verbessert.* They've improved the performance of the engine.

◆ **schulische Leistungen** school results

[2] achievement ◇ *eine sportliche Leistung* a sporting achievement ◇ *Das war wirklich eine Leistung!* That really was an achievement.

**leiten** VERB
[1] to direct ◇ *Das Wasser wird durch Rohre geleitet.* The water is directed through pipes.
[2] to lead ◇ *eine Partei leiten* to lead a party
[3] to run ◇ *Wer leitet diese Firma?* Who runs this company?
[4] to chair ◇ *Wer hat die Versammlung geleitet?* Who chaired the meeting?

◆ **Metall leitet Strom besonders gut.** Metal is a good conductor of electricity.

**der Leiter** NOUN (PL die **Leiter**)
> see also **die Leiter** NOUN
head ◇ *der Leiter des Museums* the head of the museum

**die Leiter** NOUN
> see also **der Leiter** NOUN
ladder ◇ *eine Leiter hinaufklettern* to climb a ladder

**die Leitung** NOUN
[1] management ◇ *Ihr wurde die Leitung der Abteilung übertragen.* She was entrusted with the management of the department.

◆ **Wer hatte bei der Diskussion die Leitung?** Who chaired the discussion?
[2] direction ◇ *der Jugendchor unter Leitung von ...* the youth choir under the direction of ...
[3] pipe ◇ *In unserer Straße werden neue Leitungen für Wasser und Gas verlegt.* They're laying new water and gas pipes in our road.
[4] cable ◇ *Die Leitung steht unter Strom.* The cable is live.
[5] line ◇ *Alle Leitungen waren besetzt.* All the lines were busy.

◆ **eine lange Leitung haben** to be slow on the uptake

**die Lektion** NOUN
lesson

**die Lektüre** NOUN
[1] reading ◇ *Stör sie nicht bei der Lektüre.* Don't disturb her while she's reading.
[2] reading matter ◇ *Das ist die richtige Lektüre für die Ferien.* That's the right reading matter for the holidays.
[3] set text ◇ *Welche Lektüre habt ihr dieses Jahr in Englisch?* What are your set texts in English this year?
*Be careful!* **Lektüre** *does not mean* **lecture***.*

**lenken** VERB

to steer ◊ *ein Fahrzeug lenken* to steer a car
♦ **Sie lenkte das Gespräch auf ein anderes Thema.** She led the conversation round to another subject.

das **Lenkrad** NOUN (PL die **Lenkräder**)
steering wheel

die **Lenkstange** NOUN
handlebars

**lernen** VERB
to learn

das **Lesebuch** NOUN (PL die **Lesebücher**)
reading book

**lesen** VERB (PRESENT **liest**, IMPERFECT **las**, PERFECT **hat gelesen**)
to read

**leserlich** ADJECTIVE
legible ◊ *eine leserliche Handschrift* legible handwriting ◊ *leserlich schreiben* to write legibly

das **Lesezeichen** NOUN (PL die **Lesezeichen**)
bookmark

**letzte** ADJECTIVE
[1] last ◊ *In der letzten Arbeit habe ich eine Zwei geschrieben.* I got a "B" in the last test. ◊ *Ich habe noch einen letzten Wunsch.* I have one last wish. ◊ *letzte Woche* last week
♦ **als Letzter** last ◊ *Franz kam als Letzter.* Franz arrived last.
♦ **zum letzten Mal** for the last time
[2] latest ◊ *Laut letzten Informationen kam es zu schweren Unruhen.* According to latest reports there were serious riots.

**letztens** ADVERB
lately

**leuchten** VERB
to shine ◊ *jemandem ins Gesicht leuchten* to shine a light in somebody's face

der **Leuchter** NOUN (PL die **Leuchter**)
candlestick

der **Leuchtstift** NOUN (PL die **Leuchtstifte**)
highlighter

der **Leuchtturm** NOUN (PL die **Leuchttürme**)
lighthouse

die **Leute** PL NOUN
people

das **Lexikon** NOUN (PL die **Lexika**)
encyclopedia

das **Licht** NOUN (PL die **Lichter**)
light

das **Lichtjahr** NOUN (PL die **Lichtjahre**)
light year

der **Lichtschalter** NOUN (PL die **Lichtschalter**)
light switch

das **Lid** NOUN (PL die **Lider**)
eyelid

der **Lidschatten** NOUN (PL die **Lidschatten**)
eyeshadow

**lieb** ADJECTIVE
dear ◊ *Liebe Bettina* Dear Bettina ◊ *Lieber Herr Schlüter* Dear Mr Schlüter
♦ **Das ist lieb von dir.** That's nice of you.
♦ **jemanden lieb haben** to be fond of somebody

die **Liebe** NOUN
love

**lieben** VERB
to love

**liebenswürdig** ADJECTIVE
kind

die **Liebenswürdigkeit** NOUN
kindness

**lieber** ADVERB
rather ◊ *Ich hätte jetzt lieber einen Kaffee.* I'd rather have a coffee just now. ◊ *Ich gehe lieber nicht.* I'd rather not go.
♦ **Lass das lieber!** I'd leave that if I were you.
♦ **Ich sage lieber nichts.** I'd better not say anything.
♦ **etwas lieber haben** to prefer something ◊ *Was hast du lieber, Mathe oder Chemie?* What do you prefer, maths or chemistry?

der **Liebesbrief** NOUN (PL die **Liebesbriefe**)
love letter

die **Liebesgeschichte** NOUN
love story

der **Liebeskummer** NOUN
♦ **Liebeskummer haben** to be lovesick

der **Liebesroman** NOUN (PL die **Liebesromane**)
romantic novel

**liebevoll** ADJECTIVE
loving

**liebhaben** VERB *see* **lieb**

der **Liebling** NOUN (PL die **Lieblinge**)
darling

**Lieblings-** PREFIX
favourite ◊ *Was ist dein Lieblingsfach?* What's your favourite subject?

**liebste** ADJECTIVE
favourite ◊ *Der Winter ist meine liebste Jahreszeit.* Winter is my favourite season.
♦ **am liebsten** best ◊ *Am liebsten lese ich Kriminalromane.* I like detective stories best.

das **Lied** NOUN (PL die **Lieder**)
song

**lief** VERB *see* **laufen**

**liefern** VERB
[1] to deliver ◊ *Wir liefern die Möbel ins Haus.* We deliver the furniture to your door.
[2] to supply ◊ *Das Kraftwerk liefert den Strom für die ganze Gegend.* The power station supplies electricity to the whole area.
♦ **den Beweis liefern** to produce proof

der **Lieferwagen** NOUN (PL die **Lieferwagen**)
van

**L**

**liegen** VERB (IMPERFECT **lag,** PERFECT **hat gelegen)**

  **1** to lie ◊ *Sie lag auf dem Bett.* She lay on the bed. ◊ *Wir haben den ganzen Tag am Strand gelegen.* We lay on the beach all day. ◊ *Auf meinem Schreibtisch liegt eine Menge Papier.* There's a lot of paper lying on my desk.

  ♦ **Es lag viel Schnee.** There was a lot of snow.

  **2** to be ◊ *Unser Haus liegt sehr zentral.* Our house is very central. ◊ *Ulm liegt an der Donau.* Ulm is on the Danube.

  ♦ **nach Süden liegen** to face south

  ♦ **Mir liegt viel daran.** It matters a lot to me.

  ♦ **Mir liegt nichts daran.** It doesn't matter to me.

  ♦ **Es liegt bei dir, ob** ... It's up to you whether ...

  ♦ **Sprachen liegen mir nicht.** Languages are not my thing.

  ♦ **Woran liegt es?** How come?

  ♦ **Das liegt am Wetter.** It's because of the weather.

  ♦ **liegen bleiben (1)** to lie in ◊ *Morgen ist Sonntag, da kann ich liegen bleiben.* It's Sunday tomorrow, so I can lie in.

  ♦ **liegen bleiben (2)** not to get up ◊ *Der verletzte Spieler blieb liegen.* The injured player didn't get up.

  ♦ **liegen bleiben (3)** to be left behind ◊ *Der Schirm ist liegen geblieben.* The umbrella's been left behind.

  ♦ **Unser Auto ist liegen geblieben.** Our car has broken down.

  ♦ **etwas liegen lassen** to leave something ◊ *Ich muss diese Arbeit liegen lassen.* I'll have to leave this job. ◊ *Ich habe meinen Schirm liegen lassen.* I've left my umbrella.

der **Liegestuhl** NOUN (PL die **Liegestühle**)
  deck chair

der **Liegewagen** NOUN (PL die **Liegewagen**)
  couchette

der **Lift** NOUN (PL die **Lifte** or **Lifts**)
  lift (*elevator*)

die **Liga** NOUN (PL die **Ligen**)
  league

**lila** ADJECTIVE
  purple ◊ *Sie hatte einen lila Hut auf.* She was wearing a purple hat.

die **Limo** NOUN (PL die **Limos**)
  lemonade

die **Limonade** NOUN
  lemonade

die **Limone** NOUN
  lime

das **Lineal** NOUN (PL die **Lineale**)
  ruler ◊ *einen Strich mit dem Lineal ziehen* to draw a line with a ruler

die **Linie** NOUN
  line

die **Linke** NOUN (GEN der **Linken**)
  see also **linke** ADJECTIVE

  **1** left ◊ *Zu Ihrer Linken sehen Sie das Rathaus.* On your left you'll see the town hall.

  **2** left hand ◊ *Er schlug mit der Linken zu.* He hit it out with his left hand.

**linke** ADJECTIVE
  see also **die Linke** NOUN, **links** ADVERB
  left ◊ *In Großbritannien fährt man auf der linken Seite.* In Great Britain they drive on the left. ◊ *Mein linkes Auge tut weh.* My left eye's hurting. ◊ *Er hat sich den linken Arm gebrochen.* He broke his left arm.

**links** ADVERB
  see also **linke** ADJECTIVE
  left ◊ *links abbiegen* to turn left

  ♦ **links fahren** to drive on the left

  ♦ **links überholen** to overtake on the left

  ♦ **Er schreibt mit links.** He writes with his left hand.

  ♦ **Links sehen Sie das Rathaus.** On the left you'll see the town hall.

  ♦ **links von der Kirche** to the left of the church

  ♦ **links von mir** on my left

  ♦ **links wählen** to vote for a left-wing party

  ♦ **etwas mit links machen** to do something easily

der **Linkshänder** NOUN (PL die **Linkshänder**)
  ♦ **Er ist Linkshänder.** He's left-handed.

die **Linkshänderin** NOUN
  ♦ **Sie ist Linkshänderin.** She's left-handed.

die **Linkskurve** NOUN
  left-hand bend

der **Linksverkehr** NOUN
  driving on the left
  ♦ **In Großbritannien ist Linksverkehr.** They drive on the left in Britain.

die **Linse** NOUN
  **1** lentil ◊ *Linsensuppe* lentil soup
  **2** lens ◊ *die Linse der Kamera* the camera lens

die **Lippe** NOUN
  lip

der **Lippenstift** NOUN (PL die **Lippenstifte**)
  lipstick

**lispeln** VERB
  to lisp

die **Liste** NOUN
  list

der **Liter** NOUN (PL die **Liter**)
  *You can also say das Liter.*
  litre

die **Literatur** NOUN
  literature

**live** ADVERB
  live

die **Lizenz** NOUN
  licence

der **Lkw** NOUN (GEN des **Lkw** or **Lkws**, PL die **Lkws**) (= *Lastkraftwagen*)
lorry

das **Lob** NOUN
praise
**loben** VERB
to praise

das **Loch** NOUN (PL die **Löcher**)
hole

die **Locke** NOUN
curl
♦ **Sie hat Locken.** She has curly hair.

der **Lockenwickler** NOUN (PL die **Lockenwickler**)
curler

**locker** ADJECTIVE
[1] loose ◊ *ein lockerer Zahn* a loose tooth
[2] relaxed ◊ *eine lockere Atmosphäre* a relaxed atmosphere

**lockerlassen** VERB (PRESENT **lässt locker**, IMPERFECT **ließ locker**, PERFECT **hat lockergelassen**)
♦ **nicht lockerlassen** not to let up ◊ *Er ließ nicht locker mit seinen Fragen.* He didn't let up with his questions.

**lockig** ADJECTIVE
curly

der **Löffel** NOUN (PL die **Löffel**)
spoon
♦ **ein Löffel Zucker** a spoonful of sugar

die **Logik** NOUN
logic
**logisch** ADJECTIVE
logical

der **Lohn** NOUN (PL die **Löhne**)
[1] wages ◊ *Freitags wird der Lohn ausbezahlt.* The wages are paid on Fridays.
[2] reward ◊ *Das ist jetzt der Lohn für meine Mühe!* That's the reward for my efforts.

**lohnen** VERB
♦ **Das lohnt sich.** It's worth it.

**lohnend** ADJECTIVE
worthwhile

die **Lohnsteuer** NOUN
income tax

das **Lokal** NOUN (PL die **Lokale**)
pub

die **Lokomotive** NOUN
locomotive

das **Lorbeerblatt** NOUN (PL die **Lorbeerblätter**)
bay leaf

das **Los** NOUN (GEN des **Loses**, PL die **Lose**)
see also **los** ADJECTIVE
lottery ticket ◊ *Mein Los hat gewonnen.* My lottery ticket has won.

**los** ADJECTIVE
see also **das Los** NOUN
loose ◊ *Die Schraube ist los.* The screw's loose.

♦ **Dort ist viel los.** There's a lot going on there.
♦ **Dort ist nichts los.** There's nothing going on there.
♦ **Was ist los?** What's the matter?
♦ **Den Schirm bist du los.** You've lost that umbrella for good.
♦ **Los!** Go on!

**losbinden** VERB (IMPERFECT **band los**, PERFECT **hat losgebunden**)
to untie

**löschen** VERB
to put out ◊ *ein Feuer löschen* to put out a fire ◊ *das Licht löschen* to put out the light
♦ **den Durst löschen** to quench one's thirst
♦ **eine Datei löschen** to delete a file
♦ **ein Tonband löschen** to erase a tape

die **Löschtaste** NOUN
delete key

**lose** ADJECTIVE
loose ◊ *lose Blätter* loose sheets ◊ *etwas lose verkaufen* to sell something loose
♦ **ein loses Mundwerk** a big mouth

**lösen** VERB
[1] to solve ◊ *ein Rätsel lösen* to solve a puzzle ◊ *ein Problem lösen* to solve a problem
[2] to loosen ◊ *Kannst du diesen Knoten lösen?* Can you loosen the knot?
♦ **etwas von etwas lösen** to remove something from something ◊ *Sie löste das Etikett vom Glas.* She removed the label from the jar.
♦ **sich lösen (1)** to come loose ◊ *Eine Schraube hatte sich gelöst.* A screw had come loose.
♦ **sich lösen (2)** to dissolve ◊ *Die Tablette löst sich in Wasser.* The pill dissolves in water.
♦ **sich lösen (3)** to resolve itself ◊ *Das Problem hat sich inzwischen gelöst.* The problem has resolved itself in the meantime.
♦ **eine Fahrkarte lösen** to buy a ticket

**losfahren** VERB (PRESENT **fährt los**, IMPERFECT **fuhr los**, PERFECT **ist losgefahren**)
to leave

**losgehen** VERB (IMPERFECT **ging los**, PERFECT **ist losgegangen**)
[1] to set out ◊ *Wir sollten so langsam losgehen.* It's time we were setting out.
[2] to start ◊ *Wann geht der Film los?* When does the film start?
♦ **auf jemanden losgehen** to go for somebody ◊ *Er ging mit einem Messer auf sie los.* He went for her with a knife.

**loslassen** VERB (PRESENT **lässt los**, IMPERFECT **ließ los**, PERFECT **hat losgelassen**)
to let go of

**loslaufen** VERB (PRESENT **läuft los**, IMPERFECT **lief los**, PERFECT **ist losgelaufen**)
to run off

**L**

**löslich** ADJECTIVE
soluble

die **Lösung** NOUN
solution ◊ *Weißt du die Lösung des Rätsels?* Do you know the solution to the puzzle?

**loswerden** VERB (PRESENT **wird los,** IMPERFECT **wurde los,** PERFECT **ist losgeworden**)
to get rid of

das **Lotto** NOUN (PL die **Lottos**)
National Lottery

die **Lottozahlen** FEM PL NOUN
winning lottery numbers

der **Löwe** NOUN (GEN des **Löwen,** PL die **Löwen**)
1 lion
2 Leo ◊ *Manfred ist Löwe.* Manfred's Leo.

die **Lücke** NOUN
gap

die **Luft** NOUN (PL die **Lüfte**)
air ◊ *Ich brauche frische Luft.* I need some fresh air.
♦ **in der Luft liegen** to be in the air
♦ **jemanden wie Luft behandeln** to ignore somebody

der **Luftballon** NOUN (PL die **Luftballons** *or* **Luftballone**)
balloon

der **Luftdruck** NOUN
atmospheric pressure

das **Luftkissenboot** NOUN (PL die **Luftkissenboote**)
hovercraft

die **Luftlinie** NOUN
♦ **in der Luftlinie** as the crow flies

die **Luftmatratze** NOUN
air bed

die **Luftpost** NOUN
airmail ◊ *per Luftpost* by airmail

die **Luftverschmutzung** NOUN
air pollution

die **Lüge** NOUN
lie

**lügen** VERB (IMPERFECT **log,** PERFECT **hat gelogen**)
to lie ◊ *Ich müsste lügen, wenn ...* I would be lying if ...
♦ **Er lügt ständig.** He's always telling lies.

der **Lügner** NOUN (PL die **Lügner**)
liar

der **Lumpen** NOUN (PL die **Lumpen**)
rag ◊ *in Lumpen herumlaufen* to go around in rags

die **Lunge** NOUN
lung

die **Lungenentzündung** NOUN
pneumonia

die **Lupe** NOUN
magnifying glass
♦ **unter die Lupe nehmen** to scrutinize

die **Lust** NOUN
♦ **Lust haben, etwas zu tun** to feel like doing something ◊ *Hast du Lust, ins Kino zu gehen?* Do you feel like going to the cinema?
♦ **keine Lust haben, etwas zu tun** not to feel like doing something ◊ *Sie hatte keine Lust, mit auf die Party zu kommen.* She didn't feel like coming to the party.
♦ **Lust auf etwas haben** to feel like something ◊ *Ich habe Lust auf eine kalte Limonade.* I feel like some cold lemonade.

**lustig** ADJECTIVE
funny ◊ *eine lustige Geschichte* a funny story

**lutschen** VERB
to suck ◊ *am Daumen lutschen* to suck one's thumb

der **Lutscher** NOUN (PL die **Lutscher**)
lollipop

**Luxemburg** NEUT NOUN
Luxembourg
♦ **aus Luxemburg** from Luxembourg
♦ **nach Luxemburg** to Luxembourg

der **Luxus** NOUN (GEN des **Luxus**)
luxury

# M

**m** ABBREVIATION (= *Meter*)
　**m**

**machbar** ADJECTIVE
　feasible

**machen** VERB
　⑴ to do ◊ *Hausaufgaben machen* to do
　one's homework ◊ *etwas sorgfältig
　machen* to do something carefully ◊ *Was
　machst du heute Nachmittag?* What are
　you doing this afternoon? ◊ *Lass mal, ich
　mach das schon.* Leave it, I'll do it.
　◆ **eine Prüfung machen** to sit an exam
　◆ **den Führerschein machen** to take driving
　lessons
　⑵ to make ◊ *aus Holz gemacht* made of
　wood ◊ *Kaffee machen* to make coffee
　◊ *einen Fehler machen* to make a
　mistake ◊ *Krach machen* to make a
　noise ◊ *Das macht müde.* It makes you
　tired.
　◆ **Schluss machen** to finish
　◆ **ein Foto machen** to take a photo
　◆ **das Radio leiser machen** to turn the
　radio down
　⑶ to cause ◊ *Das hat mir viel Mühe
　gemacht.* This caused me a lot of trouble.
　◊ *Ich möchte Ihnen keine
　Schwierigkeiten machen.* I don't want to
　cause you any difficulties.
　◆ **viel Arbeit machen** to cause a lot of work
　◆ **Das macht die Kälte.** It's the cold that
　does that.
　⑷ to be ◊ *Drei und fünf macht acht.*
　Three and five is eight. ◊ *Was macht
　das?* How much is that? ◊ *Das macht drei
　Mark.* That's three marks.
　◆ **Was macht die Arbeit?** How's the work
　going?
　◆ **Was macht dein Bruder?** How's your
　brother doing?
　◆ **Das macht nichts.** That doesn't matter.
　◆ **Die Kälte macht mir nichts.** I don't mind
　the cold.
　◆ **sich machen** to come on ◊ *Eine Zwei in
　Physik, du machst dich!* A "B" in physics,
　you're coming on.
　◆ **sich verständlich machen** to make
　oneself understood
　◆ **sich nichts aus etwas machen** not to be
　very keen on something ◊ *Ich mache mir
　nichts aus Süßigkeiten.* I'm not very keen
　on sweets.
　◆ **Mach's gut!** Take care!
　◆ **Mach schon!** Come on!

die **Macht** NOUN (PL die **Mächte**)
　power

das **Mädchen** NOUN (PL die **Mädchen**)
　girl

der **Mädchenname** NOUN (GEN des
　**Mädchennamens,** PL die **Mädchennamen**)
　maiden name

**mag** VERB *see* **mögen**

das **Magazin** NOUN
　magazine ◊ *Ich habe das in einem
　Magazin gelesen.* I read it in a magazine.

der **Magen** NOUN (PL die **Magen** *or* **Mägen**)
　stomach

die **Magenschmerzen** MASC PL NOUN
　stomachache ◊ *Ich habe
　Magenschmerzen.* I've got a
　stomachache.

die **Magenverstimmung** NOUN
　stomach upset

**mager** ADJECTIVE
　⑴ lean ◊ *mageres Fleisch* lean meat
　⑵ thin ◊ *Sie ist furchtbar mager.* She's
　terribly thin.

der **Magnet** NOUN (GEN des **Magnets** *or*
　**Magneten,** PL die **Magneten**)
　magnet

**magnetisch** ADJECTIVE
　magnetic

**mähen** VERB
　to mow

**mahlen** VERB (PERFECT **hat gemahlen**)
　to grind

die **Mahlzeit** NOUN
　meal ◊ *Wir essen drei Mahlzeiten am
　Tag.* We eat three meals a day.

der **Mai** NOUN (GEN des **Mai** *or* **Mais,** PL die **Maie**)
　May ◊ *im Mai* in May ◊ *am sechsten Mai*
　on 6 May ◊ *Ulm, den 6. Mai 2006* Ulm, 6
　May 2006 ◊ *Heute ist der sechste Mai.*
　Today is the sixth of May.
　◆ **der Erste Mai** May Day

das **Maiglöckchen** NOUN (PL die **Maiglöckchen**)
　lily of the valley

der **Maikäfer** NOUN (PL die **Maikäfer**)
　cockchafer

**mailen** VERB (PERFECT **hat gemailt**)
　to e-mail ◊ *Hast du es gemailt?* Did you
　e-mail it?

die **Mailingliste** NOUN (PL die **Mailinglisten**)
　mailing list

der **Mais** NOUN (GEN des **Maises**)
　maize

die **Majonäse** NOUN
　mayonnaise

der **Majoran** NOUN
　marjoram

das **Mal** NOUN (PL die **Male**)
　*see also* **mal** ADVERB
　⑴ time ◊ *das fünfte Mal* the fifth time
　◊ *zum ersten Mal* for the first time ◊ *Wie
　viele Male hast du es versucht?* How
　many times have you tried?

[2] mark ◊ *Sie hat ein rotes Mal im Gesicht.* She has a red mark on her face.

**mal** ADVERB

see also **das Mal** NOUN

times ◊ *zwei mal fünf* two times five ◊ *Wir haben sechsmal geklingelt.* We rang six times.

♦ **Warst du schon mal in Paris?** Have you ever been to Paris?

♦ **Wir möchten auch mal nach England fahren.** We'd like to go to England sometime.

**malen** VERB
to paint

der **Maler** NOUN (PL die **Maler**)
painter

**malerisch** ADJECTIVE
picturesque

das **Mallorca** NOUN
Majorca

♦ **nach Mallorca** to Majorca

**malnehmen** VERB (PRESENT **nimmt mal,** IMPERFECT **nahm mal,** PERFECT **hat malgenommen**)
to multiply

das **Malz** NOUN (GEN des **Malzes**)
malt

die **Mama** NOUN (PL die **Mamas**)
mum

die **Mami** NOUN (PL die **Mamis**)
mummy

**man** PRONOUN
you ◊ *Man kann nie wissen.* You never know. ◊ *Wie schreibt man das?* How do you spell that?

♦ **man sagt, ...** they say ...
♦ **Man hat mir gesagt ...** I was told that ...

der **Manager** NOUN (PL die **Manager**)
manager

**manche** PRONOUN
some ◊ *Manche Bücher sind langweilig.* Some books are boring. ◊ *Manche Schüler meinen wohl, man müsste keine Hausaufgaben machen.* Some pupils seem to think they don't have to do any homework.

**manchmal** ADVERB
sometimes

die **Mandarine** NOUN
mandarin orange

die **Mandel** NOUN
[1] almond ◊ *ein Kuchen mit Nüssen und Mandeln* a cake with nuts and almonds
[2] tonsil ◊ *Sie hat entzündete Mandeln.* Her tonsils are inflamed.

die **Mandelentzündung** NOUN
tonsillitis

der **Mangel** NOUN (PL die **Mängel**)
[1] lack ◊ *Schlafmangel* lack of sleep
[2] shortage ◊ *Der Mangel an Arbeitsplätzen führt zu immer größerer*

Arbeitslosigkeit. The shortage of jobs is causing rising unemployment.
[3] fault ◊ *Das Gerät weist mehrere Mängel auf.* The appliance has several faults.

**mangelhaft** ADJECTIVE
[1] poor ◊ *Wegen seiner schlechten Grammatikkenntnisse hat er mangelhaft bekommen.* He got a poor mark because of his bad grammar.

> ❶ German marks range from one (**sehr gut**) to six (**ungenügend**).

[2] faulty ◊ *Mangelhafte Waren kann man zurückgehen lassen.* You can return faulty goods.

**mangels** PREPOSITION

*The preposition **mangels** takes the genitive.*

for lack of ◊ *Er wurde mangels Beweisen freigesprochen.* He was acquitted for lack of evidence.

die **Manieren** PL NOUN
manners ◊ *Sie hat keine Manieren.* She doesn't have any manners.

der **Mann** NOUN (PL die **Männer**)
[1] man ◊ *Es war ein Mann am Telefon.* There was a man on the phone.
[2] husband ◊ *Frau Maier kam mit ihrem Mann.* Mrs Maier came with her husband.

♦ **seinen Mann stehen** to hold one's own
♦ **Alle Mann an Deck!** All hands on deck!

**männlich** ADJECTIVE
[1] male ◊ *meine männlichen Kollegen* my male colleagues

♦ **Eine männliche Person wurde am Tatort gesehen.** A man was seen at the scene of the crime.

[2] masculine ◊ *ein männliches Substantiv* a masculine noun

die **Mannschaft** NOUN
[1] team ◊ *die deutsche Mannschaft* the German team
[2] crew ◊ *der Kapitän und seine Mannschaft* the captain and his crew

der **Mantel** NOUN (PL die **Mäntel**)
coat ◊ *Er hatte einen Mantel an.* He was wearing a coat.

die **Mappe** NOUN
[1] briefcase
[2] folder

*Be careful!* **Mappe** *does not mean map.*

das **Märchen** NOUN (PL die **Märchen**)
fairy tale

die **Margarine** NOUN
margarine

der **Marienkäfer** NOUN (PL die **Marienkäfer**)
ladybird

die **Marine** NOUN
navy ◊ *Er ist bei der Marine.* He's in the navy.

die **Marionette** NOUN
puppet

die **Mark** NOUN (PL die **Mark**)
mark ◊ *Das kostet fünf Mark.* It costs five marks.

die **Marke** NOUN
[1] brand ◊ *Für diese Marke sieht man in letzter Zeit viel Werbung.* There's been a lot of advertising for this brand recently.
[2] make ◊ *Welche Marke fährt dein Vater?* What make of car does your father drive?
[3] voucher
♦ **eine Briefmarke** a postage stamp

die **Markenkleidung** NOUN
brand-name clothing

die **Markenware** NOUN
branded goods

**markieren** VERB (PERFECT **hat markiert**)
to mark ◊ *Sie hat die Stelle mit Leuchtstift markiert.* She marked the place with a highlighter.

das **Markstück** NOUN (PL die **Markstücke**)
one-mark piece

der **Markt** NOUN (PL die **Märkte**)
market

der **Marktplatz** NOUN (GEN des **Marktplatzes**, PL die **Marktplätze**)
market place

die **Marmelade** NOUN
jam ◊ *Erdbeermarmelade* strawberry jam
♦ **Orangenmarmelade** marmalade

der **Marmor** NOUN (PL die **Marmore**)
marble

der **März** NOUN (GEN des **März** or **Märzes**, PL die **Märze**)
March ◊ *im März* in March ◊ *am dritten März* on the third of March ◊ *Ulm, den 3. März 2001* Ulm, 3 March 2001 ◊ *Heute ist der dritte März.* Today is the third of March.

das **Marzipan** NOUN (PL die **Marzipane**)
marzipan

die **Masche** NOUN
[1] mesh ◊ *Das Netz hatte feine Maschen.* The net had a very fine mesh.
[2] stitch
♦ **Das ist die neueste Masche.** That's the latest thing.

die **Maschine** NOUN
[1] machine ◊ *Werkzeug wird heutzutage von Maschinen hergestellt.* Nowadays tools are manufactured by machines. ◊ *Kannst du die schmutzige Wäsche bitte in die Maschine tun?* Can you put the dirty washing in the machine?
[2] engine ◊ *Dieses Motorrad hat eine starke Maschine.* This motorbike has a powerful engine.
[3] typewriter ◊ *Sie hat ihr Referat mit der Maschine geschrieben.* She typed her assignment.

[4] plane

das **Maschinengewehr** NOUN (PL die **Maschinengewehre**)
machine gun

die **Masern** PL NOUN
measles ◊ *Masern sind bei Erwachsenen ziemlich gefährlich.* Measles is quite dangerous for adults.

die **Maske** NOUN
mask

sich **maskieren** VERB (PERFECT **hat sich maskiert**)
[1] to disguise oneself ◊ *Die Täter hatten sich maskiert.* The culprits had disguised themselves.
[2] to dress up ◊ *Als was wirst du dich maskieren?* What are you dressing up as?
♦ **Die Bankräuber waren maskiert.** The bank robbers were masked.

das **Maß** NOUN (GEN des **Maßes**, PL die **Maße**)
see also **die Maß** NOUN
[1] measure ◊ *In Deutschland werden metrische Maße verwendet.* Metric measures are used in Germany.
♦ **Wie sind die Maße des Zimmers?** What are the measurements of the room?
[2] extent ◊ *Sie war zu einem hohen Maß selbst schuld.* To a large extent she had only herself to blame.
♦ **Maß halten** to show moderation

die **Maß** NOUN (PL die **Maß**)
see also **das Maß** NOUN
litre of beer

die **Massage** NOUN
massage

die **Masse** NOUN
mass

**massenhaft** ADJECTIVE
masses of ◊ *Du hast massenhaft Fehler gemacht.* You've made masses of mistakes.

die **Massenmedien** NEUT PL NOUN
mass media

**maßhalten** VERB see **Maß**

**massieren** VERB (PERFECT **hat massiert**)
to massage ◊ *Kannst du mir bitte den Rücken massieren?* Can you massage my back, please?

**mäßig** ADJECTIVE
moderate

der **Maßkrug** NOUN (PL die **Maßkrüge**)
tankard

die **Maßnahme** NOUN
step ◊ *Maßnahmen ergreifen* to take steps

der **Maßstab** NOUN (PL die **Maßstäbe**)
[1] standard ◊ *Dieses Gerät setzt neue Maßstäbe.* This appliance sets new standards.
[2] scale ◊ *In welchem Maßstab ist diese Karte?* What's the scale of this map?

der **Mast** NOUN (PL die **Maste** or **Masten**)

**M**

☞

1 mast ◊ *Am Mast hing die britische Fahne.* The Union Jack was hanging from the mast.

2 pylon ◊ *Neben unserem Garten steht ein Hochspannungsmast.* There's a high-tension pylon beside our garden.

das **Material** NOUN (PL die **Materialien**)
material ◊ *Aus welchem Material ist das gemacht?* What material is it made of? ◊ *Ich sammle Material für mein Referat.* I'm collecting material for my assignment.

**materialistisch** ADJECTIVE
materialistic
♦ **materialistisch eingestellt sein** to be materialistic

die **Mathe** NOUN
maths

die **Mathematik** NOUN
mathematics ◊ *Mathematik ist mein Lieblingsfach.* Mathematics is my favourite subject.

**mathematisch** ADJECTIVE
mathematical

der **Matjeshering** NOUN (PL die **Matjesheringe**)
young herring

die **Matratze** NOUN
mattress

der **Matrose** NOUN (GEN des **Matrosen,** PL die **Matrosen**)
sailor

der **Matsch** NOUN
1 mud ◊ *Deine Schuhe sind voller Matsch.* Your shoes are covered in mud.
2 slush

**matschig** ADJECTIVE
1 muddy ◊ *Nach dem Regen war der Weg sehr matschig.* The path was very muddy after the rain.
2 slushy ◊ *Bei matschigem Schnee macht das Skifahren keinen Spaß.* Skiing isn't fun when the snow is slushy.

**matt** ADJECTIVE
1 weak ◊ *Bei der Hitze fühle ich mich so matt.* I feel so weak in this heat.
2 dull ◊ *Ihre Augen waren ganz matt.* Her eyes were really dull.
3 matt ◊ *Möchten Sie die Abzüge Hochglanz oder matt?* Would you like the prints glossy or matt?
4 mate ◊ *Schach und matt* checkmate

die **Matte** NOUN
mat

die **Mauer** NOUN
wall

das **Maul** NOUN (PL die **Mäuler**)
mouth ◊ *Die Katze hatte einen Vogel im Maul.* The cat had a bird in its mouth.
♦ **Halt's Maul!** Shut your face!

der **Maulkorb** NOUN (PL die **Maulkörbe**)
muzzle

der **Maulwurf** NOUN (PL die **Maulwürfe**)
mole

der **Maurer** NOUN (PL die **Maurer**)
bricklayer

die **Maus** NOUN (PL die **Mäuse**)
mouse ◊ *Sie hat Angst vor Mäusen.* She's afraid of mice. ◊ *Du musst zweimal mit der Maus klicken.* You have to click the mouse twice.

die **Mausefalle** NOUN
mousetrap

der **Mausklick** NOUN (PL die **Mausklicks**)
mouse click
♦ **per Mausklick** by clicking the mouse

**maximal** ADJECTIVE, ADVERB
1 maximum ◊ *der maximale Betrag* the maximum amount
2 at most ◊ *Wir können maximal eine Woche wegfahren.* We can go away for a week at most.

die **Mayonnaise** NOUN
mayonnaise

der **Mechaniker** NOUN (PL die **Mechaniker**)
mechanic

**mechanisch** ADJECTIVE, ADVERB
mechanical ◊ *Das Gerät hat einen mechanischen Schaden.* The appliance has a mechanical fault.
♦ **etwas mechanisch tun** to do something mechanically

der **Mechanismus** NOUN (GEN des **Mechanismus,** PL die **Mechanismen**)
mechanism

**meckern** VERB
to moan ◊ *Müsst ihr über alles meckern?* Do you have to moan about everything?

das **Mecklenburg-Vorpommern** NOUN
Mecklenburg-Western Pomerania

> ⓘ *Mecklenburg-Vorpommern is one of the 16 **Länder**. Its capital is Schwerin. It is Germany's most rural and thinly populated **Land**, and is becoming increasingly popular with tourists.*

die **Medaille** NOUN
medal

die **Medien** PL NOUN
media

das **Medikament** NOUN (PL die **Medikamente**)
drug ◊ *verschreibungspflichtige Medikamente* prescribed drugs

die **Medizin** NOUN
medicine

**medizinisch** ADJECTIVE
medical

das **Meer** NOUN (PL die **Meere**)
sea ◊ *Wir wohnen am Meer.* We live by the sea.

der **Meeresspiegel** NOUN
sea level

der **Meerrettich** NOUN
horseradish

das **Meerschweinchen** NOUN (PL die
**Meerschweinchen**)
  guinea pig

das **Mehl** NOUN (PL die **Mehle**)
  flour

**mehr** ADJECTIVE, ADVERB
  more

**mehrdeutig** ADJECTIVE
  ambiguous

**mehrere** ADJECTIVE
  several

**mehreres** PRONOUN
  several things

**mehrfach** ADJECTIVE, ADVERB
  [1] many ◊ *Das Gerät hat mehrfache
  Verwendungsmöglichkeiten.* This gadget
  has many uses.
  [2] repeated ◊ *Es ist mir erst nach
  mehrfachen Versuchen gelungen.* I only
  managed after repeated attempts. ◊ *Ich
  habe mehrfach versucht, dich zu
  erreichen.* I've tried repeatedly to get
  hold of you.

die **Mehrfahrtenkarte** NOUN
  multi-journey ticket

die **Mehrheit** NOUN
  majority

**mehrmalig** ADJECTIVE
  repeated

**mehrmals** ADVERB
  repeatedly

die **Mehrwertsteuer** NOUN
  value added tax

die **Mehrzahl** NOUN
  [1] majority ◊ *Die Mehrzahl der Schüler
  besitzt einen Computer.* The majority of
  pupils have a computer.
  [2] plural ◊ *Wie heißt die Mehrzahl von
  "woman"?* What's the plural of "woman"?

**meiden** VERB (IMPERFECT **mied**, PERFECT **hat
  gemieden**)
  to avoid

die **Meile** NOUN
  mile

**mein** ADJECTIVE, PRONOUN
  [1] my ◊ *Mein Englischlehrer ist nett.* My
  English teacher's nice. ◊ *Meine Mutter
  erlaubt es nicht.* My mother won't allow
  it. ◊ *Ich finde mein Buch nicht.* I can't find
  my book. ◊ *Meine Eltern sind Klasse.* My
  parents are great.
  [2] mine ◊ *Das ist nicht mein Füller,
  meiner ist blau.* That's not my pen,
  mine's blue. ◊ *Seine Mutter heißt Anne,
  meine auch.* His mother's called Anne,
  so's mine. ◊ *Wenn dein Fahrrad kaputt
  ist, kannst du meins nehmen.* If your
  bike's broken you can use mine. ◊ *Sie
  hat schlechte Noten, aber meine sind
  auch nicht besser.* Her marks are bad but
  mine aren't any better.

**meinen** VERB
  [1] to think ◊ *Ich meine, wir sollten jetzt
  gehen.* I think we should go now. ◊ *Was
  meint deine Mutter zu deinem Freund?*
  What does your mother think about your
  boyfriend? ◊ *Sollen wir sie zur Party
  einladen, was meinst du?* Should we
  invite her to the party, what do you
  think?
  [2] to say ◊ *Unser Lehrer meint, wir
  sollten am Wochenende keine Aufgaben
  machen.* Our teacher says that we
  shouldn't do any homework at the
  weekend.
  [3] to mean ◊ *Was meint er mit diesem
  Wort?* What does he mean by this word?
  ◊ *Ich verstehe nicht, was du meinst.* I
  don't understand what you mean. ◊ *So
  habe ich das nicht gemeint.* I didn't mean
  it like that.
  ◆ **Das will ich meinen!** I should think so.

**meinetwegen** ADVERB
  [1] for my sake ◊ *Ihr müsst meinetwegen
  nicht auf euren Urlaub verzichten.* You
  don't have to do without your holiday for
  my sake.
  [2] on my account ◊ *Hat er sich
  meinetwegen so aufgeregt?* Did he get
  so upset on my account?
  [3] as far as I'm concerned
  ◊ *Meinetwegen kannst du gehen.* As far
  as I'm concerned you can go.
  ◆ **Kann ich das machen? – Meinetwegen.**
  Can I do that? – I don't mind.

die **Meinung** NOUN
  opinion ◊ *Er hat mich nach meiner
  Meinung zu diesem Punkt gefragt.* He
  asked for my opinion on this subject.
  ◆ **meiner Meinung nach** in my opinion
  ◊ *Meiner Meinung nach sollten Kinder
  nicht so viel fernsehen.* In my opinion
  children shouldn't watch so much
  television.
  ◆ **Ganz meine Meinung!** I quite agree.
  ◆ **jemandem die Meinung sagen** to give
  somebody a piece of one's mind
  *Be careful! **Meinung** does not mean
  **meaning**.*

die **Meinungsumfrage** NOUN
  opinion poll

**meist** ADVERB
  usually ◊ *Samstags bin ich meist zu
  Hause.* I'm usually at home on
  Saturdays.

**meiste** ADJECTIVE
  most ◊ *Die meisten Bücher habe ich
  schon gelesen.* I've already read most of
  the books. ◊ *Hast du die Bücher alle
  gelesen? – Ja, die meisten.* Have you
  read all the books? – Yes, most of them.
  ◊ *Die meisten meinen, das sei einfach.*
  Most people think it's easy. ◊ *Die
  meisten von euch kennen dieses Wort
  sicher.* Most of you must know this word.

**M**

☞

◆ **am meisten (1)** most ◊ *Darüber hat sie sich am meisten aufgeregt.* This upset her most.

◆ **am meisten (2)** the most ◊ *Er hat am meisten gewonnen.* He won the most.

**meistens** ADVERB
usually ◊ *Samstags bin ich meistens zu Hause.* I'm usually at home on Saturdays.

der **Meister** NOUN (PL die **Meister**)
1 champion ◊ *Er ist deutscher Meister im Ringen.* He's the German wrestling champion.
2 master craftsman ◊ *Der Meister bildet Lehrlinge aus.* The master craftsman trains apprentices.

die **Meisterschaft** NOUN
championship ◊ *Wer hat die Meisterschaft gewonnen?* Who won the championship?

**melden** VERB (PERFECT **hat gemeldet**)
to report ◊ *Er meldete den Diebstahl bei der Polizei.* He reported the theft to the police.
◆ **sich melden (1)** to answer (*phone*) ◊ *Es meldet sich niemand.* There's no answer.
◆ **sich melden (2)** to put one's hand up (*in school*)
◆ **sich polizeilich melden** to register with the police

die **Melodie** NOUN
tune

die **Melone** NOUN
1 melon
2 bowler hat ◊ *Er trug eine Melone.* He was wearing a bowler hat.

die **Menge** NOUN
1 quantity ◊ *etwas in großen Mengen bestellen* to order a large quantity of something
2 crowd ◊ *Ich habe ihn in der Menge verloren.* I lost him in the crowd.
◆ **eine Menge** a lot of ◊ *Du hast eine Menge Fehler gemacht.* You've made a lot of mistakes. ◊ *Hast du CDs? – Ja, eine Menge.* Have you got any CDs? – Yes, lots.

der **Mensch** NOUN (GEN des **Menschen**, PL die **Menschen**)
human being ◊ *Es heißt, dass sich der Mensch durch die Sprache vom Tier unterscheidet.* It's said that what distinguishes human beings from animals is language.
◆ **Wie viele Menschen sind schon glücklich?** How many people are happy?
◆ **kein Mensch** nobody

der **Menschenverstand** NOUN
◆ **gesunder Menschenverstand** common sense

die **Menschheit** NOUN
mankind

**menschlich** ADJECTIVE
human

die **Mentalität** NOUN
mentality

das **Menü** NOUN (PL die **Menüs**)
set meal

**merken** VERB
to notice ◊ *Hat sie gemerkt, dass ich gefehlt habe?* Did she notice that I wasn't there? ◊ *Ich habe den Fehler nicht gemerkt.* I didn't notice the mistake.
◆ **sich etwas merken** to remember something ◊ *Dieses Wort kann ich mir nie merken.* I can never remember that word.
◆ **Das werd' ich mir merken!** I won't forget that in a hurry!

**merkwürdig** ADJECTIVE
odd
◆ **sich merkwürdig benehmen** to behave strangely

die **Messe** NOUN
1 fair ◊ *Auf der Messe wurden die neuesten Modelle gezeigt.* The latest models were shown at the fair.
2 mass ◊ *Sie geht jeden Sonntag zur Messe.* She goes to mass every Sunday.

**messen** VERB (PRESENT **misst**, IMPERFECT **maß**, PERFECT **hat gemessen**)
to measure ◊ *Hast du die Länge gemessen?* Have you measured the length?
◆ **bei jemandem Fieber messen** to take somebody's temperature
◆ **Mit ihm kannst du dich nicht messen.** You're no match for him.

das **Messer** NOUN (PL die **Messer**)
knife

das **Messgerät** NOUN (PL die **Messgeräte**)
gauge

das **Messing** NOUN
brass

das **Metall** NOUN (PL die **Metalle**)
metal

der **Meter** NOUN (PL die **Meter**)
metre

das **Metermaß** NOUN (GEN des **Metermaßes**, PL die **Metermaße**)
tape measure

die **Methode** NOUN
method

der **Metzger** NOUN (PL die **Metzger**)
butcher ◊ *Er ist Metzger.* He's a butcher. ◊ *beim Metzger* at the butcher's

die **Metzgerei** NOUN
butcher's

**miauen** VERB
to miaow

**mich** PRONOUN
*mich is the accusative of ich.*
1 me ◊ *Er hat mich zu seiner Party eingeladen.* He's invited me to his party.

⚁ myself ◊ *Ich sehe mich im Spiegel.* I can see myself in the mirror.

die **Miene** NOUN
look
♦ **eine finstere Miene machen** to look grim

**mies** ADJECTIVE
lousy ◊ *Mir geht's mies.* I feel lousy.

die **Miete** NOUN
rent
♦ **zur Miete wohnen** to live in rented accommodation

**mieten** VERB
⚀ to rent

> ⓘ It is far more usual to live in rented accommodation in Germany than it is in Britain. Flats are mainly rented unfurnished.

◊ *Wir haben eine Ferienwohnung gemietet.* We've rented a holiday flat. ⚁ to hire ◊ *Man kann am Flughafen ein Auto mieten.* You can hire a car at the airport.

das **Mietshaus** NOUN (GEN des **Mietshauses**, PL die **Mietshäuser**)
block of rented flats

der **Mietvertrag** NOUN (PL die **Mietverträge**)
lease

der **Mietwagen** NOUN (PL die **Mietwagen**)
rental car

das **Mikrofon** NOUN (PL die **Mikrofone**)
microphone

das **Mikroskop** NOUN (PL die **Mikroskope**)
microscope

die **Mikrowelle** NOUN
microwave

der **Mikrowellenherd** NOUN (PL die **Mikrowellenherde**)
microwave oven

die **Milch** NOUN
milk

**mild** ADJECTIVE
⚀ mild ◊ *eine milde Seife* a mild soap ◊ *mildes Wetter* mild weather
⚁ lenient ◊ *ein mildes Urteil* a lenient sentence ◊ *ein milder Richter* a lenient judge

das **Militär** NOUN
army ◊ *zum Militär gehen* to join the army

**militärisch** ADJECTIVE
military

die **Milliarde** NOUN
billion

der **Millimeter** NOUN (PL die **Millimeter**)
millimetre

die **Million** NOUN
million

der **Millionär** NOUN (PL die **Millionäre**)
millionaire ◊ *Er ist Millionär.* He's a millionaire.

die **Minderheit** NOUN
minority ◊ *in der Minderheit sein* to be in the minority

**minderjährig** ADJECTIVE
underage ◊ *Sie ist noch minderjährig.* She's still underage.

der die **Minderjährige** NOUN (GEN des/der **Minderjährigen**, PL die **Minderjährigen**)
minor ◊ *Minderjährige dürfen keinen Alkohol kaufen.* Minors are not allowed to buy alcohol.

**minderwertig** ADJECTIVE
inferior

das **Mindestalter** NOUN
minimum age

**mindeste** ADJECTIVE
♦ **das Mindeste** the least ◊ *Das ist das Mindeste, was du tun kannst.* That's the least you can do.
♦ **nicht im Mindesten** not in the least ◊ *Sie war nicht im Mindesten überrascht.* She wasn't in the least surprised.
♦ **zum Mindesten** at least ◊ *Zum Mindesten hättest du ja anrufen können.* You could at least have phoned.

**mindestens** ADVERB
at least

das **Mineral** NOUN (PL die **Minerale** or **Mineralien**)
mineral

das **Mineralwasser** NOUN (PL die **Mineralwasser**)
mineral water

das **Minirock** NOUN (PL die **Miniröcke**)
miniskirt

der **Minister** NOUN (PL die **Minister**)
minister (*in government*)

das **Ministerium** NOUN (PL die **Ministerien**)
ministry

**minus** ADVERB
minus

die **Minute** NOUN
minute

**mir** PRONOUN

> *mir is the dative of ich.*

⚀ me ◊ *Kannst du mir sagen, wie spät es ist?* Can you tell me the time?
⚁ to me ◊ *Gib es mir!* Give it to me.
♦ **mir nichts, dir nichts** just like that ◊ *Sie war mir nichts, dir nichts verschwunden.* She disappeared just like that.

**mischen** VERB
to mix

die **Mischung** NOUN
mixture

**miserabel** ADJECTIVE
dreadful ◊ *Mir geht's miserabel.* I feel dreadful.

**missbilligen** VERB (PERFECT **hat missbilligt**)
to disapprove of

der **Missbrauch** NOUN
abuse

**M**

der **Misserfolg** NOUN (PL die **Misserfolge**)
failure

**misshandeln** VERB (PERFECT **hat misshandelt**)
to ill-treat

**missmutig** ADJECTIVE
sullen

**misstrauen** VERB (PERFECT **hat misstraut**)
*see also* **das Misstrauen** NOUN
♦ **jemandem misstrauen** to mistrust somebody

das **Misstrauen** NOUN
*see also* **misstrauen** VERB
suspicion

**misstrauisch** ADJECTIVE
suspicious

das **Missverständnis** NOUN (GEN des **Missverständnisses**, PL die **Missverständnisse**)
misunderstanding

**missverstehen** VERB (IMPERFECT **missverstand**, PERFECT **hat missverstanden**)
to misunderstand

der **Mist** NOUN
[1] manure ◊ *Im Frühling werden die Felder mit Mist gedüngt.* The fields are fertilized with manure in the spring.
[2] rubbish ◊ *Warum isst du so einen Mist?* Why do you eat such rubbish? ◊ *Heute kommt wieder nur Mist im Fernsehen.* There's nothing but rubbish on TV again today. ◊ *Du redest Mist.* You're talking rubbish.
♦ **Mist!** Blast!
*Be careful! The German word **Mist** does not mean **mist**.*

die **Mistel** NOUN
mistletoe

**mit** PREPOSITION, ADVERB
*The preposition **mit** takes the dative.*
[1] with ◊ *Er ist mit seiner Freundin gekommen.* He came with his girlfriend. ◊ *mit Filzstift geschrieben* written with a felt-tip pen
[2] by ◊ *mit dem Auto* by car ◊ *mit der Bahn* by train ◊ *mit dem Bus* by bus
♦ **mit zehn Jahren** at the age of ten
♦ **Sie ist mit die Beste in ihrer Klasse.** She is one of the best in her class.
♦ **Wollen Sie mit?** Do you want to come along?

der **Mitarbeiter** NOUN (PL die **Mitarbeiter**)
[1] colleague ◊ *meine Mitarbeiter und ich* my colleagues and I
[2] collaborator ◊ *die Mitarbeiter an diesem Projekt* the collaborators on this project
[3] employee ◊ *Die Firma hat 500 Mitarbeiter.* The company has 500 employees.

**mitbringen** VERB (IMPERFECT **brachte mit**, PERFECT **hat mitgebracht**)
to bring along ◊ *Kann ich meine Freundin mitbringen?* Can I bring my girlfriend along?
♦ **Wir haben Tante Anita ein Geschenk mitgebracht.** We took a present for Aunt Anita.

**miteinander** ADVERB
with each another

der **Mitesser** NOUN (PL die **Mitesser**)
blackhead

**mitfahren** VERB (PRESENT **fährt mit**, IMPERFECT **fuhr mit**, PERFECT **ist mitgefahren**)
♦ **Wir fahren nach Berlin. Willst du mitfahren?** We're going to Berlin. Do you want to come too?
♦ **Die Klasse fährt nach England, aber ich fahre nicht mit.** The class are going to England but I'm not going with them.
♦ **Willst du mit uns im Auto mitfahren?** Do you want a lift in our car?

**mitgeben** VERB (PRESENT **gibt mit**, IMPERFECT **gab mit**, PERFECT **hat mitgegeben**)
to give

das **Mitglied** NOUN (PL die **Mitglieder**)
member

die **Mitgliedschaft** NOUN
membership

**mithelfen** VERB (PRESENT **hilft mit**, IMPERFECT **half mit**, PERFECT **hat mitgeholfen**)
to help

**mitkommen** VERB (IMPERFECT **kam mit**, PERFECT **ist mitgekommen**)
[1] to come along ◊ *Willst du nicht mitkommen?* Wouldn't you like to come along?
[2] to keep up ◊ *In Mathe komme ich nicht mit.* I can't keep up in maths.

das **Mitleid** NOUN
[1] sympathy
♦ **Ich habe wirklich Mitleid mit dir.** I really sympathize with you.
[2] pity ◊ *Er kennt kein Mitleid.* He knows no pity.

**mitmachen** VERB (PERFECT **hat mitgemacht**)
to join in

**mitnehmen** VERB (PRESENT **nimmt mit**, IMPERFECT **nahm mit**, PERFECT **hat mitgenommen**)
[1] to take ◊ *Kannst du den Brief zur Post mitnehmen?* Can you take the letter to the post office? ◊ *Ich habe meine Freundin zur Party mitgenommen.* I took my girlfriend to the party.
♦ **Die Polizei ist gekommen und hat ihn mitgenommen.** The police came and took him away.
♦ **zum Mitnehmen** to take away
[2] to affect ◊ *Die Scheidung ihrer Eltern hat sie sehr mitgenommen.* Her parents' divorce really affected her.

der **Mitschüler** NOUN (PL die **Mitschüler**)
schoolmate

die **Mitschülerin** NOUN

schoolmate

**mitspielen** VERB
to join in ◊ *Willst du nicht mitspielen?*
Don't you want to join in?
♦ **Wer hat bei dem Match mitgespielt?**
Who played in the match?

der **Mittag** NOUN (PL die **Mittage**)
midday ◊ *gegen Mittag* around midday
♦ **zu Mittag essen** to have lunch
♦ **heute Mittag** at lunchtime
♦ **morgen Mittag** tomorrow lunchtime
♦ **gestern Mittag** yesterday lunchtime

das **Mittagessen** NOUN (PL die **Mittagessen**)
lunch

**mittags** ADVERB
at lunchtime

die **Mittagspause** NOUN
lunch break

die **Mitte** NOUN
middle

**mitteilen** VERB
♦ **jemandem etwas mitteilen** to inform
somebody of something

die **Mitteilung** NOUN
communication

das **Mittel** NOUN (PL die **Mittel**)
means ◊ *Wir werden jedes Mittel
einsetzen, um die Genehmigung zu
bekommen.* We will use every means to
gain approval. ◊ *ein Mittel zum Zweck* a
means to an end ◊ *Sie griff zu ziemlich
unfairen Mitteln.* She used rather unfair
means.
♦ **ein Mittel gegen Husten** something for a
cough
♦ **ein Mittel gegen Flecken** a stain remover
♦ **öffentliche Mittel** public funds

das **Mittelalter** NOUN
Middle Ages ◊ *im Mittelalter* in the
Middle Ages

**Mitteleuropa** NEUT NOUN
Central Europe

**mittelgroß** ADJECTIVE
[1] medium-sized ◊ *Bremen ist eine
mittelgroße Stadt.* Bremen is a medium-
sized city.
[2] of medium height ◊ *Christine ist
mittelgroß.* Christine is of medium
height.

**mittelmäßig** ADJECTIVE
mediocre

das **Mittelmeer** NOUN
the Mediterranean

der **Mittelpunkt** NOUN (PL die **Mittelpunkte**)
centre

der **Mittelstürmer** NOUN (PL die **Mittelstürmer**)
centre-forward

die **Mittelwelle** NOUN
medium wave

**mitten** ADVERB
in the middle ◊ *mitten auf der Straße* in
the middle of the street ◊ *mitten am Tag*

in the middle of the day ◊ *mitten in der
Nacht* in the middle of the night

die **Mitternacht** NOUN
midnight ◊ *um Mitternacht* at midnight

**mittlere** ADJECTIVE
[1] middle ◊ *Das mittlere von den
Fahrrädern ist meins.* The bike in the
middle is mine. ◊ *Der mittlere Teil des
Buches ist langweilig.* The middle section
of the book is boring.
[2] average ◊ *Die mittleren Temperaturen
liegen bei zwanzig Grad.* The average
temperature is twenty degrees.
♦ **mittleren Alters** middle-aged ◊ *eine Frau
mittleren Alters* a middle-aged woman
♦ **mittlere Reife** O-levels

**mittlerweile** ADVERB
meanwhile

der **Mittwoch** NOUN (PL die **Mittwoche**)
Wednesday ◊ *am Mittwoch* on
Wednesday

**mittwochs** ADVERB
on Wednesdays

der **Mixer** NOUN (PL die **Mixer**)
mixer (*kitchen appliance*)

das **Mobbing** NOUN
workplace bullying

die **Möbel** NEUT PL NOUN
furniture

das **Möbelstück** NOUN (PL die **Möbelstücke**)
piece of furniture

der **Möbelwagen** NOUN (PL die **Möbelwagen**)
removal van

das **Mobiltelefon** NOUN (PL die **Mobiltelefone**)
mobile phone

**möblieren** VERB (PERFECT **hat möbliert**)
to furnish ◊ *Sie hat ihre Wohnung sehr
geschmackvoll möbliert.* She has
furnished her flat very tastefully.
♦ **möbliert wohnen** to live in furnished
accommodation

**möchte** VERB *see* **mögen**

die **Mode** NOUN
fashion

das **Modell** NOUN (PL die **Modelle**)
model

**modern** ADJECTIVE
modern

**modernisieren** VERB (PERFECT **hat
modernisiert**)
to modernize

**modisch** ADJECTIVE
fashionable ◊ *Jane trägt sehr modische
Kleidung.* Jane wears very fashionable
clothes.

das **Mofa** NOUN (PL die **Mofas**)
small moped

**mogeln** VERB
to cheat

**mögen** VERB (PRESENT **mag,** IMPERFECT **mochte,**
PERFECT **hat gemocht** *or* **mögen**)

**M**

☞

*The past participle mögen is used when mögen is a modal auxiliary.*
to like ◊ *Ich mag Süßes.* I like sweet things. ◊ *Ich habe sie noch nie gemocht.* I've never liked her.
◆ **Ich möchte ...** I'd like ... ◊ *Ich möchte ein Erdbeereis.* I'd like a strawberry ice cream. ◊ *Er möchte in die Stadt.* He'd like to go into town. ◊ *Möchtest du ...?* Would you like ...?
◆ **Ich möchte nicht, dass du ...** I wouldn't like you to ... ◊ *Ich möchte nicht, dass du dich übergangen fühlst.* I wouldn't like you to feel you were being ignored.
◆ **Ich mag nicht mehr.** I've had enough.
◆ **etwas tun mögen** to like to do something ◊ *Magst du noch mit zu mir kommen?* Would you like to come back to my place? ◊ *Möchtest du etwas essen?* Would you like something to eat?
◆ **etwas nicht tun mögen** not to want to do something ◊ *Sie mag nicht bleiben.* She doesn't want to stay. ◊ *Ich möchte nicht, dass du so spät nach Hause kommst.* I don't want you coming home so late.

**möglich** ADJECTIVE
possible ◊ *Das ist gar nicht möglich!* That's not possible. ◊ *so viel wie möglich* as much as possible

**möglicherweise** ADVERB
possibly

die **Möglichkeit** NOUN
possibility
◆ **nach Möglichkeit** if possible

**möglichst** ADVERB
as ... as possible ◊ *Komm möglichst bald.* Come as soon as possible.

die **Möhre** NOUN
carrot

der **Moment** NOUN (PL die **Momente**)
moment ◊ *Wir müssen den richtigen Moment abwarten.* We have to wait for the right moment.
◆ **im Moment** at the moment
◆ **Moment mal!** Just a moment.

**momentan** ADJECTIVE, ADVERB
[1] momentary ◊ *Das ist nur eine momentane Schwäche.* It's only a momentary weakness.
[2] at the moment ◊ *Ich bin momentan sehr beschäftigt.* I'm very busy at the moment.

die **Monarchie** NOUN
monarchy

der **Monat** NOUN (PL die **Monate**)
month

**monatelang** ADVERB
for months

**monatlich** ADJECTIVE, ADVERB
monthly

die **Monatskarte** NOUN
monthly ticket

der **Mond** NOUN (PL die **Monde**)
moon

der **Monitor** NOUN (PL die **Monitore**)
monitor

der **Montag** NOUN (PL die **Montage**)
Monday ◊ *am Montag* on Monday

**montags** ADVERB
on Mondays

das **Moor** NOUN (PL die **Moore**)
moor

das **Moped** NOUN (PL die **Mopeds**)
moped

die **Moral** NOUN
[1] morals ◊ *Sie hat keine Moral.* She hasn't any morals.
[2] moral ◊ *Und die Moral der Geschichte ist: ...* And the moral of the story is: ...

**moralisch** ADJECTIVE
moral

der **Mord** NOUN (PL die **Morde**)
murder

der **Mörder** NOUN (PL die **Mörder**)
murderer
*Be careful! Mörder does not mean murder.*

die **Mörderin** NOUN
murderer

**morgen** ADVERB
see also der Morgen NOUN
tomorrow
◆ **morgen früh** tomorrow morning
◆ **Bis morgen!** See you tomorrow!

der **Morgen** NOUN (PL die **Morgen**)
see also morgen ADVERB
morning ◊ *Wir haben den ganzen Morgen Unterricht.* We've got lessons all morning.
◆ **Guten Morgen!** Good morning.

**morgens** ADVERB
in the morning ◊ *Morgens bin ich immer müde.* I'm always tired in the morning.
◆ **von morgens bis abends** from morning to night

**morgig** ADJECTIVE
tomorrow's ◊ *das morgige Fest* tomorrow's party
◆ **der morgige Tag** tomorrow

die **Mosel** NOUN
Moselle

das **Motiv** NOUN (PL die **Motive**)
motive ◊ *Was war sein Motiv?* What was his motive?

die **Motivation** NOUN
motivation

**motivieren** VERB (PERFECT **hat motiviert**)
to motivate

der **Motor** NOUN (PL die **Motoren**)
[1] engine ◊ *Das Auto hat einen starken Motor.* The car has a powerful engine.
[2] motor ◊ *ein Außenbordmotor* an outboard motor

das **Motorboot** NOUN (PL die **Motorboote**)

motorboat
das **Motorrad** NOUN (PL die **Motorräder**)
motorcycle
der **Motorroller** NOUN (PL die **Motorroller**)
scooter
die **Möwe** NOUN
seagull
die **Mücke** NOUN
midge
der **Mückenstich** NOUN (PL die **Mückenstiche**)
midge bite
**müde** ADJECTIVE
tired ◊ *Ich bin sehr müde.* I'm very tired.
die **Müdigkeit** NOUN
tiredness
die **Mühe** NOUN
trouble ◊ *Das macht gar keine Mühe.*
That's no trouble.
♦ **mit Müh und Not** with great difficulty
♦ **sich Mühe geben** to go to a lot of trouble
◊ *Die Gastgeberin hat sich viele Mühe
gegeben.* The hostess went to a lot of
trouble.
♦ **Du solltest dir in Englisch mehr Mühe
geben.** You should try harder in English.
die **Mühle** NOUN
mill ◊ *In dieser Mühle wird Korn
gemahlen.* Corn is ground in this mill.
◊ *Hast du eine Mühle, um den Kaffee zu
mahlen?* Do you have a coffee mill?
der **Müll** NOUN
refuse
die **Müllabfuhr** NOUN
**1** disposal of rubbish ◊ *Die Gebühren
für die Müllabfuhr sollen erhöht werden.*
The charges for the disposal of rubbish
are to be increased.
**2** dustmen ◊ *Morgen kommt die
Müllabfuhr.* The dustmen come
tomorrow.
der **Mülleimer** NOUN (PL die **Mülleimer**)
rubbish bin
die **Mülltonne** NOUN
dustbin
die **Müllverbrennungsanlage** NOUN
waste incineration plant
**multiplizieren** VERB (PERFECT **hat
multipliziert**)
to multiply
der **Mumps** NOUN (GEN des **Mumps**)
mumps ◊ *Mumps ist sehr unangenehm.*
Mumps is very unpleasant.
**München** NEUT NOUN
Munich
♦ **nach München** to Munich
der **Mund** NOUN (PL die **Münder**)
mouth
♦ **Halt den Mund!** Shut up!
der **Mundgeruch** NOUN
bad breath ◊ *Sie hat Mundgeruch.* She
has bad breath.
die **Mundharmonika** NOUN

mouth organ
**mündlich** ADJECTIVE
oral ◊ *eine mündliche Prüfung* an oral
exam
die **Munition** NOUN
ammunition
das **Münster** NOUN (PL die **Münster**)
cathedral
**munter** ADJECTIVE
lively
die **Münze** NOUN
coin
der **Münzfernsprecher** NOUN (PL die
**Münzfernsprecher**)
payphone
**murmeln** VERB
to mumble ◊ *Er murmelte irgendwas
vor sich hin.* He mumbled something.
**mürrisch** ADJECTIVE
sullen
die **Muschel** NOUN
**1** mussel ◊ *Ich esse gern Muscheln.* I
like mussels.
**2** shell ◊ *Wir haben am Strand
Muscheln gesammelt.* We collected
shells on the beach.
**3** receiver ◊ *Du musst in die Muschel
sprechen.* You have to speak into the
receiver.
das **Museum** NOUN (PL die **Museen**)
museum
die **Musik** NOUN
music
**musikalisch** ADJECTIVE
musical ◊ *musikalisch begabt sein* to be
musically gifted
die **Musikbox** NOUN
jukebox
der **Musiker** NOUN (PL die **Musiker**)
musician
das **Musikinstrument** NOUN (PL die
**Musikinstrumente**)
musical instrument
**musizieren** VERB (PERFECT **hat musiziert**)
to make music
der **Muskat** NOUN (PL die **Muskate**)
nutmeg
der **Muskel** NOUN (PL die **Muskeln**)
muscle
das **Müsli** NOUN (PL die **Müsli**)
muesli
**müssen** VERB (PRESENT **muss,** IMPERFECT
**musste,** PERFECT **hat gemusst** or **müssen**)
*The past participle **müssen** is used when
**müssen** is a modal auxiliary.*
must ◊ *Ich muss es tun.* I must do it. ◊ *Er
hat gehen müssen.* He had to go.
♦ **Ich musste es tun.** I had to do it.
♦ **Er muss es nicht tun.** He doesn't have to
do it.
♦ **Muss ich?** Do I have to?
♦ **Muss das sein?** Is that really necessary?

**M**

☞

◆ **Das hättest du nicht tun müssen.** You needn't have done that.

◆ **Es muss nicht wahr sein.** It needn't be true.

◆ **Sie hätten ihn fragen müssen.** You should have asked him.

◆ **Es muss geregnet haben.** It must have rained.

◆ **Ich muss mal.** I need the loo.

das **Muster** NOUN (PL die **Muster**)

⓵ pattern ◇ *ein Kleid mit einem geometrischen Muster* a dress with a geometric pattern

⓶ sample ◇ *Lass dir von dem Stoff doch ein Muster geben.* Ask them to give you a sample of the material.

der **Mut** NOUN

courage

◆ **Nur Mut!** Cheer up!

◆ **jemandem Mut machen** to encourage somebody

◆ **zu Mute** *see* **zumute**

**mutig** ADJECTIVE

courageous

die **Mutter (1)** NOUN (PL die **Mütter**)

mother ◇ *Meine Mutter erlaubt das nicht.* My mother doesn't allow that.

die **Mutter (2)** NOUN (PL die **Muttern**)

nut ◇ *Hast du die Mutter zu dieser Schraube gesehen?* Have you seen the nut for this bolt?

die **Muttersprache** NOUN

mother tongue

der **Muttertag** NOUN (PL die **Muttertage**)

Mother's Day

die **Mutti** NOUN (PL die **Muttis**)

mummy

die **Mütze** NOUN

cap

**MwSt** ABBREVIATION (= *Mehrwertsteuer*)

VAT (= value added tax)

# N

**na** EXCLAMATION

well ◊ *Na, kommst du mit?* Well, are you coming?
- **Na gut.** Okay then.
- **Na ja, ...** Well, ...

der **Nabel** NOUN (PL die **Nabel**)

navel

**nach** PREPOSITION, ADVERB

*The preposition nach takes the dative.*

[1] to ◊ *nach Berlin* to Berlin ◊ *nach Italien* to Italy
- **nach Süden** south
- **nach links** left
- **nach rechts** right
- **nach oben** up
- **nach hinten** back

[2] after ◊ *Ich fange nach Weihnachten damit an.* I'll start on it after Christmas. ◊ *die nächste Straße nach der Kreuzung* the first street after the crossroads ◊ *einer nach dem anderen* one after the other ◊ *Nach Ihnen!* After you!
- **Ihm nach!** After him!
- **zehn nach drei** ten past three

[3] according to ◊ *Nach unserer Englischlehrerin wird das so geschrieben.* According to our English teacher, that's how it's spelt.
- **nach und nach** little by little
- **nach wie vor** still

**nachahmen** VERB (PERFECT **hat nachgeahmt**)

to imitate

der **Nachbar** NOUN (GEN des **Nachbarn**, PL die **Nachbarn**)

neighbour

die **Nachbarin** NOUN

neighbour

die **Nachbarschaft** NOUN

neighbourhood

**nachdem** CONJUNCTION

[1] after ◊ *Nachdem er gegangen war, haben wir Witze erzählt.* After he left we told jokes.

[2] since ◊ *Nachdem du sowieso zur Post gehst, könntest du mein Päckchen aufgeben?* Since you're going to the post office anyway, could you post my parcel?
- **je nachdem** it depends ◊ *Du kommst doch auch mit? – Je nachdem.* You're coming along too, aren't you? – It depends.
- **je nachdem, ob** depending on whether ◊ *Wir kommen mit dem Rad oder dem Auto, je nachdem, ob es regnet oder nicht.* We'll be coming by bike or by car, depending on whether it rains or not.

**nachdenken** VERB (IMPERFECT **dachte nach**, PERFECT **hat nachgedacht**)

- **nachdenken über** to think about ◊ *Ich habe über deine Frage nachgedacht.* I've been thinking about your question.

**nachdenklich** ADJECTIVE

pensive

**nacheinander** ADVERB

one after the other

**nachgeben** VERB (PRESENT **gibt nach**, IMPERFECT **gab nach**, PERFECT **hat nachgegeben**)

[1] to give way ◊ *Das Brett hat nachgegeben.* The plank gave way.

[2] to give in ◊ *Ich werde nicht nachgeben.* I won't give in.

**nachgehen** VERB (IMPERFECT **ging nach**, PERFECT **ist nachgegangen**)

- **jemandem nachgehen** to follow somebody
- **einer Sache nachgehen** to look into something ◊ *Wir werden Ihrer Beschwerde nachgehen.* We will look into your complaint.
- **Die Uhr geht nach.** The clock is slow.

**nachgiebig** ADJECTIVE

indulgent

**nachher** ADVERB

afterwards

die **Nachhilfestunde** NOUN

private lesson

der **Nachhilfeunterricht** NOUN

extra tuition

**nachholen** VERB (PERFECT **hat nachgeholt**)

[1] to catch up on ◊ *Weil er gefehlt hat, muss er jetzt viel nachholen.* As he was absent, he's got a lot to catch up on.

[2] to make up for ◊ *Wir konnten meinen Geburtstag nicht feiern, werden das aber nachholen.* We weren't able to celebrate my birthday, but we'll make up for it.
- **eine Prüfung nachholen** to do an exam at a later date

**nachkommen** VERB (IMPERFECT **kam nach**, PERFECT **ist nachgekommen**)

to come later ◊ *Wir gehen schon mal, du kannst ja später nachkommen.* We'll go on and you can come later.
- **einer Verpflichtung nachkommen** to fulfil an obligation

**nachlassen** VERB (PRESENT **lässt nach**, IMPERFECT **ließ nach**, PERFECT **hat nachgelassen**)

[1] to deteriorate ◊ *Seine Leistungen haben merklich nachgelassen.* His marks have deteriorated considerably.
- **Ihr Gedächtnis lässt nach.** Her memory is going.
- **Er hat nachgelassen.** He's got worse.

☞

2 to ease off ◊ *Die Schmerzen haben nachgelassen.* The pain has eased off.

3 to die down ◊ *sobald der Sturm nachlässt* as soon as the storm dies down

♦ **Der Händler hat mir zwanzig Mark nachgelassen.** The salesman gave me twenty marks off.

**nachlässig** ADJECTIVE
careless

♦ **etwas nachlässig machen** to do something carelessly ◊ *Sie macht ihre Hausaufgaben ziemlich nachlässig.* She does her homework pretty carelessly.

**nachlaufen** VERB (PRESENT **läuft nach,** IMPERFECT **lief nach,** PERFECT **ist nachgelaufen**)

♦ **jemandem nachlaufen** to run after somebody ◊ *Sie hat ihren Schirm vergessen, lauf ihr schnell nach.* She's forgotten her umbrella. Quick, run after her.

to chase ◊ *Er läuft allen Mädchen nach.* He chases all the girls.

**nachmachen** VERB (PERFECT **hat nachgemacht**)

1 to copy ◊ *Macht alle meine Bewegungen nach.* Copy all my movements.

2 to imitate ◊ *Sie kann unsere Mathelehrerin gut nachmachen.* She's good at imitating our maths teacher.

3 to forge ◊ *ein Gemälde nachmachen* to forge a painting

♦ **Das ist nicht echt, sondern nachgemacht.** This isn't genuine, it's a fake.

der **Nachmittag** NOUN (PL die **Nachmittage**)
afternoon ◊ *am Nachmittag* in the afternoon

♦ **heute Nachmittag** this afternoon

**nachmittags** ADVERB
in the afternoon

der **Nachname** NOUN (GEN des **Nachnamens,** PL die **Nachnamen**)
surname ◊ *Wie heißt du mit Nachnamen?* What's your surname?

**nachprüfen** VERB (PERFECT **hat nachgeprüft**)
to check ◊ *nachprüfen, ob* to check whether

die **Nachricht** NOUN

1 news ◊ *Wir haben noch keine Nachricht von ihr.* We still haven't had any news of her.

♦ **die Nachrichten** the news ◊ *Was kommt in den Nachrichten?* What's on the news?

2 message ◊ *Kannst du ihm eine Nachricht von mir übermitteln?* Can you give him a message from me?

**nachschicken** VERB (PERFECT **hat nachgeschickt**)
to forward

**nachschlagen** VERB (PRESENT **schlägt nach,** IMPERFECT **schlug nach,** PERFECT **hat nachgeschlagen**)

to look up (*in dictionary*)

**nachsehen** VERB (PRESENT **sieht nach,** IMPERFECT **sah nach,** PERFECT **hat nachgesehen**)

to check ◊ *Sieh mal nach, ob noch genügend Brot da ist.* Check whether we've still got enough bread. ◊ *Ich habe im Wörterbuch nachgesehen.* I've checked in the dictionary. ◊ *Mein Vater sieht immer meine Englischaufgaben nach.* My father always checks my English homework.

♦ **jemandem etwas nachsehen** to forgive somebody something ◊ *Den kleinen Fehler sollten wir ihm nachsehen.* We ought to forgive him this little mistake.

♦ **das Nachsehen haben** to come off worst

**nachsenden** VERB (IMPERFECT **sendete** *or* **sandte nach,** PERFECT **hat nachgesendet** *or* **nachgesandt**)

to send on ◊ *Ich habe ihr den Brief nachgesendet.* I've sent the letter on to her.

**nachsichtig** ADJECTIVE
lenient

**nachsitzen** VERB (IMPERFECT **saß nach,** PERFECT **hat nachgesessen**)

♦ **nachsitzen müssen** to be kept in ◊ *Er musste nachsitzen, weil er seine Hausaufgaben vergessen hatte.* He was kept in because he had forgotten to do his homework.

die **Nachspeise** NOUN
pudding ◊ *Was gibt's als Nachspeise?* What's for pudding?

**nachsprechen** VERB (PRESENT **spricht nach,** IMPERFECT **sprach nach,** PERFECT **hat nachgesprochen**)

♦ **jemandem nachsprechen** to repeat after somebody ◊ *Ich sage es vor, und ihr sprecht nach.* I'll say it, and you repeat after me. ◊ *Sie spricht ihrem Vater alles nach.* She repeats everything her father says.

**nächste** ADJECTIVE
see also **nahe, näher**

1 next ◊ *Wir nehmen den nächsten Zug.* We'll take the next train. ◊ *Beim nächsten Mal passt du besser auf.* Be more careful next time. ◊ *nächstes Jahr* next year

♦ **als Nächstes** next ◊ *Was machen wir als Nächstes?* What'll we do next?

♦ **Der Nächste bitte!** Next, please!

2 nearest ◊ *Wo ist hier die nächste Post?* Where's the nearest post office?

♦ **Das ist der nächste Weg.** That's the shortest way.

die **Nacht** NOUN (PL die **Nächte**)
night

♦ **Gute Nacht!** Good night.

der **Nachteil** NOUN (PL die **Nachteile**)
disadvantage

das **Nachthemd** NOUN (PL die **Nachthemden**)
nightshirt

die **Nachtigall** NOUN
nightingale

der **Nachtisch** NOUN
pudding ◊ *Was gibt's zum Nachtisch?*
What's for pudding?

der **Nachtklub** NOUN (PL die **Nachtklubs**)
night club

das **Nachtleben** NOUN
nightlife

**nächtlich** ADJECTIVE
nightly

**nachträglich** ADJECTIVE, ADVERB
[1] subsequent ◊ *eine nachträgliche
Korrektur* a subsequent correction
♦ **nachträgliche Glückwünsche** belated
best wishes
[2] later ◊ *Nachträglich habe ich
eingesehen, dass das ein Fehler war.* I
later realized that it was a mistake.

die **Nachtruhe** NOUN
sleep ◊ *Ich brauche meine Nachtruhe.* I
need my sleep.

**nachts** ADVERB
at night

der **Nacken** NOUN (PL die **Nacken**)
nape of the neck

**nackt** ADJECTIVE
naked ◊ *Er war nackt.* He was naked.
♦ **nackte Arme** bare arms
♦ **nackte Tatsachen** plain facts

die **Nadel** NOUN
[1] needle ◊ *Ich brauche Nadel und
Faden.* I need a needle and thread.
[2] pin ◊ *Ich habe mich an der Nadel des
Ansteckers gestochen.* I've pricked
myself on the pin of my badge.

der **Nagel** NOUN (PL die **Nägel**)
nail

die **Nagelbürste** NOUN
nailbrush

die **Nagelfeile** NOUN
nailfile

der **Nagellack** NOUN (PL die **Nagellacke**)
nail varnish

**nagelneu** ADJECTIVE
brand-new

die **Nagelschere** NOUN
nail scissors ◊ *eine Nagelschere* a pair
of nail scissors

**nagen** VERB
to gnaw ◊ *an etwas nagen* to gnaw on
something

das **Nagetier** NOUN (PL die **Nagetiere**)
rodent

**nahe** ADJECTIVE, ADVERB, PREPOSITION
see also **näher, nächste**
[1] near ◊ *in der nahen Zukunft* in the
near future
♦ **nahe bei** near ◊ *nahe bei der Kirche* near
the church

[2] close ◊ *Der Bahnhof ist ganz nah.* The
station's quite close. ◊ *nahe Verwandte*
close relatives ◊ *nahe Freunde* close
friends ◊ *Unser Haus ist nahe der
Universität.* Our house is close to the
university. ◊ *den Tränen nahe* close to
tears
♦ **mit jemandem nah verwandt sein** to be
closely related to somebody
♦ **der Nahe Osten** the Middle East
♦ **Die Prüfungen rücken näher.** The exams
are getting closer.
♦ **nahe daran sein, etwas zu tun** to be
close to doing something ◊ *Ich war nahe
daran aufzugeben.* I was close to giving
up.
♦ **jemandem etwas nahe legen** to suggest
something to somebody
♦ **nahe liegend** obvious

die **Nähe** NOUN
♦ **in der Nähe** near ◊ *Unsere Schule liegt in
der Nähe des Bahnhofs.* Our school is
near the station. ◊ *Ich wohne in der Nähe
von Rostock.* I live near Rostock.
♦ **aus der Nähe** close up ◊ *wenn man das
aus der Nähe betrachtet* if you look at it
close up

**nahelegen** VERB see **nahe**

**naheliegend** ADJECTIVE see **nahe**

**nähen** VERB
to sew

**näher** ADJECTIVE, ADVERB
see also **nahe, nächste**
[1] nearer ◊ *Die Straßenbahnhaltestelle
ist näher als die Bushaltestelle.* The tram
stop is nearer than the bus stop.
[2] more detailed ◊ *Nähere Auskünfte
erteilt Ihnen unser Informationsdienst.*
Our information service will give you
more detailed information.
♦ **Näheres** details ◊ *Ich wüsste gern
Näheres.* I'd like to have more details.
♦ **näher kommen** to get closer

sich **nähern** VERB
to get closer ◊ *Wir näherten uns dem
Bahnhof.* We were approaching the
station.

**nahezu** ADVERB
nearly

**nahm** VERB see **nehmen**

die **Nähmaschine** NOUN
sewing machine

die **Nähnadel** NOUN
needle

**nahrhaft** ADJECTIVE
nourishing

die **Nahrung** NOUN
food ◊ *feste Nahrung* solid food

das **Nahrungsmittel** NOUN (PL die
**Nahrungsmittel**)
foodstuffs

die **Naht** NOUN (PL die **Nähte**)

N

☞

seam ◊ *Die Hose ist an der Naht geplatzt.* The trousers have split along the seam.

der **Nahverkehr** NOUN
local traffic

der **Nahverkehrszug** NOUN (PL die **Nahverkehrszüge**)
local train

der **Name** NOUN (GEN des **Namens,** PL die **Namen**)
name ◊ *Mein Name ist ...* My name is ...
♦ **im Namen von** on behalf of

der **Namenstag** NOUN (PL die **Namenstage**)
name day

**nämlich** ADVERB
[1] you see ◊ *Sie ist nämlich meine beste Freundin.* You see, she's my best friend.
[2] that is to say ◊ *Nächstes Jahr, nämlich im März ...* Next year, that is to say in March ...
♦ **Ich kann nicht kommen, ich bin nämlich krank.** I can't come, I'm ill.

**nannte** VERB *see* **nennen**

**nanu** EXCLAMATION
well, well!

die **Narbe** NOUN
scar

die **Narkose** NOUN
anaesthetic

**naschen** VERB
♦ **Sie nascht gern.** She's got a sweet tooth.
♦ **Wer hat von der Torte genascht?** Who's been at the cake?

die **Nase** NOUN
nose ◊ *Meine Nase blutet.* My nose is bleeding.

das **Nasenbluten** NOUN
nosebleed ◊ *Ich hatte Nasenbluten.* I had a nosebleed.

**nass** ADJECTIVE
wet ◊ *Nach dem Regen war die Wäsche noch nässer.* After the rain, the washing was even wetter.

die **Nässe** NOUN
wetness

die **Nation** NOUN
nation

die **Nationalhymne** NOUN
national anthem

die **Nationalität** NOUN
nationality

die **Natur** NOUN
[1] country ◊ *Wir gehen gern in der Natur spazieren.* We like to go for a walk in the country.
[2] constitution ◊ *Sie hat eine robuste Natur.* She's got a strong constitution.

**natürlich** ADJECTIVE, ADVERB
[1] natural ◊ *Das ist ihre natürliche Haarfarbe.* That's her natural hair colour.
[2] of course ◊ *Wir kommen natürlich.* Of course we'll come. ◊ *Sie hat das*

natürlich wieder vergessen. She's forgotten it again, of course. ◊ *Ja, natürlich!* Yes, of course.

das **Naturschutzgebiet** NOUN (PL die **Naturschutzgebiete**)
nature reserve

der **Naturschutzpark** NOUN (PL die **Naturschutzparks**)
national park

die **Naturwissenschaft** NOUN
natural science

der **Naturwissenschaftler** NOUN (PL die **Naturwissenschaftler**)
scientist

der **Nazi** NOUN (PL die **Nazis**)
Nazi ◊ *Sie ist ein Nazi.* She's a Nazi.

der **Nebel** NOUN (PL die **Nebel**)
[1] mist
[2] fog

**nebelig** ADJECTIVE
[1] misty
[2] foggy

**neben** PREPOSITION
*Use the accusative to express movement or a change of place. Use the dative when there is no change of place.*
[1] next to ◊ *Dein Rad steht neben meinem.* Your bike's next to mine. ◊ *Stell dein Rad neben meines.* Put your bike next to mine.
[2] apart from
*neben takes the dative in this sense.*
◊ *Neben den Sehenswürdigkeiten haben wir uns auch ein Theaterstück angesehen.* Apart from the sights, we also saw a play.

**nebenan** ADVERB
next door

**nebenbei** ADVERB
[1] at the same time ◊ *Ich kann nicht Hausaufgaben machen und nebenbei fernsehen.* I can't do my homework and watch TV at the same time.
[2] on the side ◊ *Sie hat nebenbei noch einen anderen Job.* She has another job on the side.
♦ **Sie sagte ganz nebenbei, dass sie nicht mitkommen wollte.** She mentioned quite casually that she didn't want to come along.
♦ **Nebenbei bemerkt, ...** Incidentally, ...

**nebenberuflich** ADVERB
as a second job ◊ *Er ist nebenberuflich als Gärtner tätig.* He has a second job as a gardener.

**nebeneinander** ADVERB
side by side

das **Nebenfach** NOUN (PL die **Nebenfächer**)
subsidiary subject

der **Nebenfluss** NOUN (GEN des **Nebenflusses,** PL die **Nebenflüsse**)
tributary

**nebenher** ADVERB
[1] on the side ◊ *Er verdient nebenher noch Geld durch Zeitungaustragen.* He also earns money on the side doing a paper round.
[2] at the same time ◊ *Sie bügelt und sieht nebenher fern.* She does the ironing and watches TV at the same time.
[3] alongside ◊ *Wir sind mit dem Rad gefahren, der Hund lief nebenher.* We rode our bikes and the dog ran alongside.

die **Nebenstraße** NOUN
side street

**neblig** ADJECTIVE
[1] misty
[2] foggy

**nee** ADVERB
no

der **Neffe** NOUN (GEN des **Neffen**, PL die **Neffen**)
nephew

**negativ** ADJECTIVE
see also **das Negativ** NOUN
negative ◊ *HIV-negativ* HIV-negative

das **Negativ** NOUN (PL die **Negative**)
see also **negativ** ADJECTIVE
negative ◊ *Kann ich von den Bildern das Negativ haben?* Can I have the negatives of these pictures?

**nehmen** VERB (PRESENT **nimmt**, IMPERFECT **nahm**, PERFECT **hat genommen**)
to take ◊ *Sie nahm eine Mark aus dem Geldbeutel.* She took a mark out of her purse. ◊ *Wir nehmen besser den Bus in die Stadt.* We'd better take the bus into town. ◊ *Hast du deine Medizin genommen?* Have you taken your medicine? ◊ *Nimm ihn nicht ernst!* Don't take him seriously.
♦ **Ich nehme ein Erdbeereis.** I'll have a strawberry ice cream.
♦ **Nimm dir doch bitte!** Please help yourself.
♦ **Wir haben eine Kleinigkeit zu uns genommen.** We had a bite to eat.

der **Neid** NOUN
envy

**neidisch** ADJECTIVE
envious ◊ *Sie ist neidisch auf ihren Bruder.* She's envious of her brother.

**nein** ADVERB
no ◊ *Hast du das gesehen? – Nein.* Did you see that? – No, I didn't.
♦ **Ich glaube nein.** I don't think so.

die **Nektarine** NOUN
nectarine

die **Nelke** NOUN
[1] carnation ◊ *Er brachte mir einen Strauß Nelken.* He brought me a bunch of carnations.
[2] clove ◊ *Zum Glühwein braucht man Nelken.* You need cloves to make mulled wine.

**nennen** VERB (IMPERFECT **nannte**, PERFECT **hat genannt**)
[1] to call ◊ *Sie haben ihren Sohn Manfred genannt.* They called their son Manfred. ◊ *Die Band nennt sich "Die Zerstörer".* The band call themselves "The Destroyers". ◊ *Wie nennt man ...?* What do you call ...?
[2] to name ◊ *Kannst du mir einen Fluss in England nennen?* Can you name a river in England?

das **Neonlicht** NOUN
neon light

die **Neonröhre** NOUN
strip light

der **Nerv** NOUN (PL die **Nerven**)
nerve
♦ **jemandem auf die Nerven gehen** to get on somebody's nerves

die **Nervensäge** NOUN
pain in the neck

der **Nervenzusammenbruch** NOUN (PL die **Nervenzusammenbrüche**)
nervous breakdown

**nervös** ADJECTIVE
nervous

die **Nervosität** NOUN
nervousness

das **Nest** NOUN (PL die **Nester**)
[1] nest ◊ *Der Vogel hat ein Nest gebaut.* The bird has built a nest.
[2] dump ◊ *Wiblingen ist ein Nest.* Wiblingen is a dump.

**nett** ADJECTIVE
[1] lovely ◊ *Vielen Dank für den netten Abend.* Thanks for a lovely evening.
[2] nice ◊ *Wir haben uns nett unterhalten.* We had a nice talk.
[3] kind ◊ *Wären Sie vielleicht so nett, mir zu helfen?* Would you be so kind as to help me? ◊ *Das war sehr nett von dir.* That was very kind of you.
♦ **Er war ganz nett frech.** He was pretty damn cheeky.

**netto** ADVERB
net ◊ *Sie verdient dreitausend Mark netto.* She earns three thousand marks net.

das **Netz** NOUN (GEN des **Netzes**, PL die **Netze**)
[1] net ◊ *Die Fischer werfen ihre Netze aus.* The fishers cast their nets. ◊ *Der Ball ging ins Netz.* The ball went into the net.
[2] string bag ◊ *Sie packte die Einkäufe ins Netz.* She packed her shopping into a string bag.
[3] network ◊ *ein weit verzweigtes Netz an Rohren* an extensive network of pipes ◊ *einen Computer ans Netz anschließen* to connect a computer to the network

**N**

**neu** ADJECTIVE
new ◊ *Ist der Pulli neu?* Is that pullover new? ◊ *Sie hat einen neuen Freund.* She's got a new boyfriend. ◊ *Ich bin neu hier.* I'm new here.
♦ **neue Sprachen** modern languages
♦ **neueste** latest ◊ *die neuesten Nachrichten* the latest news
♦ **seit neuestem** recently
♦ **neu schreiben** to rewrite
♦ **Das ist mir neu!** That's news to me.

**neuartig** ADJECTIVE
new kind of ◊ *ein neuartiges Wörterbuch* a new kind of dictionary

die **Neugier** NOUN
curiosity

**neugierig** ADJECTIVE
curious

die **Neuheit** NOUN
[1] new product ◊ *Auf der Messe werden alle Neuheiten vorgestellt.* All new products are presented at the trade fair.
[2] newness ◊ *Ich muss mich erst auf die Neuheit dieser Situation einstellen.* I've still got to get used to the newness of the situation.

die **Neuigkeit** NOUN
news ◊ *Gibt es irgendwelche Neuigkeiten?* Is there any news?

das **Neujahr** NOUN
New Year

der **Neujahrstag** NOUN (PL die **Neujahrstage**)
New Year's Day

**neulich** ADVERB
the other day

**neun** NUMBER
nine

**neunte** ADJECTIVE
ninth ◊ *Heute ist der neunte Juni.* Today is the ninth of June.

**neunzehn** NUMBER
nineteen

**neunzig** NUMBER
ninety

**neurotisch** ADJECTIVE
neurotic

**Neuseeland** NEUT NOUN
New Zealand
♦ **aus Neuseeland** from New Zealand
♦ **nach Neuseeland** to New Zealand

der **Neuseeländer** NOUN (PL die **Neuseeländer**)
New Zealander

die **Neuseeländerin** NOUN
New Zealander

**neutral** ADJECTIVE
neutral

das **Neutrum** NOUN (PL die **Neutra** or **Neutren**)
neuter

**nicht** ADVERB
not ◊ *Ich bin nicht müde.* I'm not tired. ◊ *Er ist es nicht.* It's not him.
♦ **Er raucht nicht. (1)** He isn't smoking.

♦ **Er raucht nicht. (2)** He doesn't smoke.
♦ **Ich kann das nicht – Ich auch nicht.** I can't do it – Neither can I.
♦ **Es regnet nicht mehr.** It's not raining any more.
♦ **Nicht!** Don't!
♦ **Nicht berühren!** Do not touch!
♦ **Du bist müde, nicht wahr?** You're tired, aren't you?
♦ **Das ist schön, nicht wahr?** It's nice, isn't it?
♦ **Was du nicht sagst!** You don't say!

die **Nichte** NOUN
niece

der **Nichtraucher** NOUN (PL die **Nichtraucher**)
nonsmoker

**nichts** PRONOUN
nothing ◊ *nichts zu verzollen* nothing to declare ◊ *nichts Neues* nothing new
♦ **Ich habe nichts gesagt.** I didn't say anything.
♦ **Nichts ist so wie früher.** Things aren't what they used to be.
♦ **Das macht nichts.** It doesn't matter.
♦ **für nichts und wieder nichts** for nothing

der **Nichtschwimmer** NOUN (PL die **Nichtschwimmer**)
nonswimmer

**nicken** VERB
to nod

**nie** ADVERB
never ◊ *Das habe ich nie gesagt.* I never said that. ◊ *Das werde ich nie vergessen.* I'll never forget that. ◊ *Das habe ich noch nie gehört.* I've never heard that. ◊ *Ich war noch nie in Indien.* I've never been to India.
♦ **nie wieder** never again ◊ *Tu das nie wieder.* Don't ever do that again.
♦ **nie mehr** never again ◊ *Sie hat nie mehr geschrieben.* She never wrote to me again.
♦ **nie und nimmer** no way ◊ *Das kann nie und nimmer stimmen.* There's no way that can be right.

**nieder** ADJECTIVE, ADVERB
[1] low ◊ *ein niederer Rang* a low rank
♦ **ein niederer Beamter** a low-ranking government officer
[2] base ◊ *niedere Instinkte* base instincts
♦ **Nieder mit ...!** Down with ...! ◊ *Nieder mit dem Diktator!* Down with the dictator!

**niedergeschlagen** ADJECTIVE
dejected

die **Niederlage** NOUN
defeat

die **Niederlande** NEUT PL NOUN
the Netherlands
♦ **aus den Niederlanden** from the Netherlands
♦ **in den Niederlanden** in the Netherlands
♦ **in die Niederlande** to the Netherlands

der **Niederländer** NOUN (PL die **Niederländer**)
Dutchman
♦ **Er ist Niederländer.** He's Dutch.

die **Niederländerin** NOUN
Dutchwoman
♦ **Sie ist Niederländerin.** She's Dutch.

**niederländisch** ADJECTIVE
Dutch

**Niedersachsen** NEUT NOUN
Lower Saxony

> ❶ *Niedersachsen is one of the 16 Länder. Its capital is Hannover. Its most important industries are mining and car manufacturing (Volkswagen). The Hannover Industrial Fair is the largest in the world.*

der **Niederschlag** NOUN (PL die **Niederschläge**)
precipitation
♦ **heftige Niederschläge** heavy rain
♦ **radioaktiver Niederschlag** radioactive fallout

**niedlich** ADJECTIVE
sweet ◊ *niedlich aussehen* to look sweet

**niedrig** ADJECTIVE
[1] low ◊ *Die Decke ist sehr niedrig.* The ceiling is very low. ◊ *niedrige Temperaturen* low temperatures
[2] shallow ◊ *Hier ist der Fluss niedriger.* The river is shallower here.
[3] base ◊ *niedrige Motive* base motives

**niemals** ADVERB
never

**niemand** PRONOUN
[1] nobody ◊ *Niemand hat mir Bescheid gesagt.* Nobody told me.
[2] not ... anybody ◊ *Ich habe niemanden gesehen.* I haven't seen anybody. ◊ *Sie hat mit niemandem darüber gesprochen.* She hasn't mentioned it to anybody.

die **Niere** NOUN
kidney

**nieseln** VERB
to drizzle

**niesen** VERB
to sneeze

die **Niete** NOUN
[1] stud ◊ *Jeans mit Nieten* jeans with studs
[2] blank ◊ *Ich habe eine Niete gezogen.* I've drawn a blank.
♦ **In Mathe ist er eine Niete.** He's useless at maths.

das **Nikotin** NOUN
nicotine

**nimmt** VERB see **nehmen**

**nirgends** ADVERB
[1] nowhere ◊ *Nirgends sonst gibt es so schöne Blumen.* Nowhere else will you find such beautiful flowers.
[2] not ... anywhere ◊ *Hier gibt es nirgends ein Schwimmbad.* There isn't a

swimming pool anywhere here. ◊ *Ich habe ihn nirgends gesehen.* I haven't seen him anywhere.

**nirgendwo** ADVERB see **nirgends**

das **Niveau** NOUN (PL die **Niveaus**)
level

**noch** ADVERB, CONJUNCTION
still ◊ *Ich habe noch Hunger.* I'm still hungry. ◊ *Das kann noch passieren.* That might still happen.
♦ **Bleib doch noch ein bisschen!** Stay a bit longer.
♦ **Das wirst du noch lernen.** You'll learn.
♦ **Er wird noch kommen.** He'll come.
♦ **heute noch** today
♦ **noch am selben Tag** the very same day
♦ **noch vor einer Woche** only a week ago
♦ **noch im neunzehnten Jahrhundert** as late as the nineteenth century
♦ **Wer noch?** Who else? ◊ *Wer war noch da?* Who else was there?
♦ **Was noch?** What else? ◊ *Was will er noch?* What else does he want?
♦ **noch nicht** not yet ◊ *Ich bin noch nicht fertig.* I haven't finished yet.
♦ **noch nie** never ◊ *Ich war noch nie in Leeds.* I've never been to Leeds.
♦ **immer noch** still ◊ *Du bist ja immer noch da!* How come you're still here? ◊ *Das Haus ist immer noch nicht fertig.* The house still isn't finished.
♦ **noch einmal** again
♦ **noch dreimal** three more times
♦ **noch einer** another one
♦ **noch größer** even bigger
♦ **Das ist noch besser.** That's better still.
♦ **Geld noch und noch** loads of money
♦ **weder ... noch ...** neither ... nor ...

**nochmals** ADVERB
again

der **Nominativ** NOUN (PL die **Nominative**)
nominative

**Nordamerika** NEUT NOUN
North America

der **Norden** NOUN
north

**Nordirland** NEUT NOUN
Northern Ireland
♦ **aus Nordirland** from Northern Ireland
♦ **in Nordirland** in Northern Ireland
♦ **nach Nordirland** to Northern Ireland

**nördlich** ADJECTIVE, PREPOSITION, ADVERB
northerly ◊ *Wir fuhren in nördlicher Richtung.* We drove in a northerly direction.
♦ **nördlich einer Sache** to the north of something ◊ *Das Kraftwerk liegt nördlich der Stadt.* The power station is to the north of the city.
♦ **nördlich von** north of ◊ *Düsseldorf liegt nördlich von Köln.* Düsseldorf is north of Cologne.

der **Nordosten** NOUN

**N**

☞

northeast

der **Nordpol** NOUN
North Pole ◇ *am Nordpol* at the North Pole

**Nordrhein-Westfalen** NEUT NOUN
North Rhine-Westphalia

> ❶ **Nordrhein-Westfalen** *is one of the 16 Länder. Its capital is Düsseldorf. It is Germany's most densely populated state, and includes the Ruhr district.*

die **Nordsee** NOUN
North Sea ◇ *Wir fahren an die Nordsee.* We're going to the North Sea. ◇ *Wir waren an der Nordsee.* We've been to the North Sea.

der **Nordwesten** NOUN
northwest

**nörgeln** VERB
to moan ◇ *Er hat immer etwas zu nörgeln.* He always finds something to moan about.

die **Norm** NOUN
standard ◇ *Für die meisten technischen Geräte gibt es Normen.* There are set standards for most technical equipment.

**normal** ADJECTIVE
normal

das **Normalbenzin** NOUN
regular petrol

> ❶ *The type of petrol generally used in Germany is unleaded.*

**normalerweise** ADVERB
normally

**Norwegen** NEUT NOUN
Norway
◆ **aus Norwegen** from Norway
◆ **nach Norwegen** to Norway

der **Norweger** NOUN (PL die **Norweger**)
Norwegian

die **Norwegerin** NOUN
Norwegian

**norwegisch** ADJECTIVE
Norwegian

die **Not** NOUN
◆ **zur Not** if necessary ◇ *Zur Not kannst du ja später nachkommen.* You can join us later if necessary.

der **Notausgang** NOUN (PL die **Notausgänge**)
emergency exit

die **Notbremse** NOUN
emergency brake

der **Notdienst** NOUN (PL die **Notdienste**)
emergency service

**notdürftig** ADJECTIVE
makeshift ◇ *eine notdürftige Reparatur* a makeshift repair

die **Note** NOUN

[1] mark ◇ *Max hat gute Noten.* Max has got good marks.
[2] note ◇ *Welche Note hast du eben gespielt?* What note did you just play?

der **Notfall** NOUN (PL die **Notfälle**)
emergency

**notfalls** ADVERB
if need be

**notieren** VERB (PERFECT **hat notiert**)
to note down

**nötig** ADJECTIVE
necessary ◇ *wenn nötig* if necessary
◆ **etwas nötig haben** to need something

die **Notiz** NOUN
[1] note ◇ *Sein Kalender ist voller Notizen.* His diary is full of notes.
[2] item ◇ *Das stand heute in einer kleinen Notiz in der Zeitung.* There was a short item on it in the newspaper today.
◆ **Notiz nehmen von** to take notice of ◇ *Er hat von mir keine Notiz genommen.* He didn't take any notice of me.

der **Notizblock** NOUN (PL die **Notizblöcke**)
notepad

das **Notizbuch** NOUN (PL die **Notizbücher**)
notebook

**notlanden** VERB (PERFECT **ist notgelandet**)
to make an emergency landing

der **Notruf** NOUN (PL die **Notrufe**)
emergency call

die **Notrufsäule** NOUN
emergency telephone

**notwendig** ADJECTIVE
necessary

der **November** NOUN (GEN des **November** or **Novembers**, PL die **November**)
November ◇ *im November* in November ◇ *am neunten November* on the ninth of November ◇ *Freiburg, den 9. November 2000* Freiburg, 9 November 2000 ◇ *Heute ist der neunte November.* Today is the ninth of November.

**Nr.** ABBREVIATION (= *Nummer*)
No.

der **Nu** NOUN
◆ **im Nu** in an instant

**nüchtern** ADJECTIVE
[1] sober ◇ *Nach drei Gläsern Wein bist du nicht mehr nüchtern.* After three glasses of wine you aren't sober any more. ◇ *nüchterne Tatsachen* sober facts
[2] with an empty stomach ◇ *Kommen Sie nüchtern ins Krankenhaus.* Come to the hospital with an empty stomach.
◆ **auf nüchternen Magen** on an empty stomach
◆ **Wenn ich mir die Lage nüchtern betrachte ...** When I look at the situation in a matter-of-fact way ...

die **Nudel** NOUN
noodle ◇ *Es waren Nudeln in der Suppe.* There were noodles in the soup.

◆**Nudeln** pasta ◊ *Nudeln sind meine Lieblingsspeise.* Pasta is my favourite food.

die **Null** NOUN

[see also **null** NUMBER]

[1] zero ◊ *Du musst zuerst eine Null wählen.* You have to dial zero first.

[2] nonentity ◊ *Er ist doch eine völlige Null.* He's a complete nonentity.

**null** NUMBER

[see also **die Null** NOUN]

[1] nil ◊ *Sie haben eins zu null gespielt.* They won one nil.

[2] no ◊ *Ich hatte null Fehler.* I had no mistakes.

◆**null Uhr** midnight

◆**null und nichtig** null and void

**numerieren** VERB *see* **nummerieren**

die **Nummer** NOUN

[1] number ◊ *Ich kann seine Nummer auswendig.* I know his number by heart.

[2] size ◊ *Die Schuhe sind eine Nummer zu groß.* These shoes are a size too big.

**nummerieren** VERB (PERFECT **hat nummeriert**)

to number

das **Nummernschild** NOUN (PL die **Nummernschilder**)

number plate

**nun** ADVERB, EXCLAMATION

[1] now ◊ *von nun an* from now on

[2] well ◊ *Nun, was gibt's Neues?* Well, what's new?

◆**Das ist nun mal so.** That's the way it is.

**nur** ADVERB

only ◊ *Das hat nur zwanzig Mark gekostet.* It only cost twenty marks. ◊ *Es sind nur fünf Leute da gewesen.* There were only five people there.

◆**Wo bleibt er nur?** Where on earth can he be?

◆**Was hat sie nur?** What on earth's wrong with her?

die **Nuss** NOUN (PL die **Nüsse**)

nut

der **Nutzen** NOUN

[see also **nutzen** VERB]

◆**von Nutzen** useful ◊ *Sprachkenntnisse sind immer von Nutzen.* It's always useful to know a foreign language.

◆**Das ist bestimmt zu deinem Nutzen.** It's for your own good.

**nutzen** VERB

[see also **der Nutzen** NOUN]

to help ◊ *Sprachkenntnisse können dir im Ausland viel nutzen.* Knowing a language can help you a lot abroad.

◆**etwas nutzen** to make use of something ◊ *Du solltest die Zeit nutzen.* You ought to make use of the time.

◆**Das nutzt ja doch nichts.** That's pointless.

◆**Es nutzt alles nichts, wir müssen ...** There's no getting around it, we'll have to ...

**nützen** VERB *see* **nutzen**

**nützlich** ADJECTIVE

useful ◊ *sich nützlich machen* to make oneself useful

**nutzlos** ADJECTIVE

useless

**N**

# O

**o. Ä.** ABBREVIATION (= *oder Ähnliche*)
  or similar

die **Oase** NOUN
  oasis

**ob** CONJUNCTION
  [1] whether ◊ *Ich weiß nicht, ob ich kommen kann.* I don't know whether I can come.
  [2] if ◊ *Sie fragt, ob du auch kommst.* She wants to know if you're coming too.
  ◆ **Ob das wohl wahr ist?** Can that be true?
  ◆ **Und ob!** You bet!

**obdachlos** ADJECTIVE
  homeless

**oben** ADVERB
  on top ◊ *oben auf dem Schrank* on top of the cupboard
  ◆ **oben auf dem Berg** up on the mountain
  ◆ **Die Schlafzimmer sind oben.** The bedrooms are upstairs.
  ◆ **nach oben** up ◊ *Der Fahrstuhl fährt nach oben.* The lift is going up. ◊ *Ich gehe nach oben in mein Zimmer.* I'm going up to my room.
  ◆ **von oben** down ◊ *Der Fahrstuhl kommt von oben.* The lift is going down. ◊ *Bringst du mir von oben die Bettwäsche mit?* Bring the bed clothes down with you.
  ◆ **oben ohne** topless
  ◆ **jemanden von oben bis unten ansehen** to look somebody up and down
  ◆ **Befehl von oben** orders from above

der **Ober** NOUN (PL die **Ober**)
  waiter
  ◆ **Herr Ober!** Waiter!

**obere** ADJECTIVE
  see also **oberste** ADJECTIVE
  upper ◊ *die oberen Stockwerke* the upper floors
  ◆ **Nimm das obere Buch.** Take the book from the top of the pile.
  ◆ **die oberen Klassen** the senior classes

die **Oberfläche** NOUN
  surface

**oberflächlich** ADJECTIVE
  superficial ◊ *Er ist sehr oberflächlich in seiner Arbeit.* His work is very superficial.
  ◆ **jemanden nur oberflächlich kennen** to know somebody only slightly

das **Obergeschoss** NOUN (GEN des **Obergeschosses**, PL die **Obergeschosse**)
  upper storey

das **Oberhaus** NOUN (GEN des **Oberhauses**)
  upper chamber

der **Oberschenkel** NOUN (PL die **Oberschenkel**)
  thigh

die **Oberschule** NOUN
  grammar school

**oberste** ADJECTIVE
  see also **obere** ADJECTIVE
  topmost ◊ *Das Buch steht auf dem obersten Regalbrett.* The book is on the topmost shelf.
  ◆ **Sie ist in der obersten Klasse.** She's in the top class.

die **Oberstufe** NOUN
  upper school

das **Oberteil** NOUN (PL die **Oberteile**)
  upper part

die **Oberweite** NOUN
  bust measurement

**obgleich** CONJUNCTION
  although ◊ *Obgleich sie müde war, blieb sie lange auf.* Although she was tired, she stayed up late.

das **Objekt** NOUN (PL die **Objekte**)
  object

das **Objektiv** NOUN (PL die **Objektive**)
  see also **objektiv** ADJECTIVE
  lens (*of camera*)

**objektiv** ADJECTIVE
  see also **das Objektiv** NOUN
  objective

das **Obst** NOUN
  fruit

der **Obstbaum** NOUN (PL die **Obstbäume**)
  fruit tree

der **Obstkuchen** NOUN (PL die **Obstkuchen**)
  fruit tart

der **Obstsalat** NOUN (PL die **Obstsalate**)
  fruit salad

**obwohl** CONJUNCTION
  although ◊ *Obwohl sie müde war, blieb sie lange auf.* Although she was tired, she stayed up late.

der **Ochse** NOUN (GEN des **Ochsen**, PL die **Ochsen**)
  ox

**öde** ADJECTIVE
  dull ◊ *eine öde Landschaft* a dull landscape
  ◆ **Diese Arbeit ist echt öde.** This job's really the pits.

**oder** CONJUNCTION
  or ◊ *entweder ich oder du* either me or you
  ◆ **Das stimmt, oder?** That's right, isn't it?

der **Ofen** NOUN (PL die **Öfen**)
  [1] oven ◊ *Der Kuchen ist im Ofen.* The cake's in the oven.
  [2] heater
  ◆ **Mach bitte den Ofen an, mir ist kalt.** Put the fire on, I'm cold.

**offen** ADJECTIVE

open ◊ *Das Fenster ist offen.* The window's open. ◊ *Die Banken sind bis sechzehn Uhr offen.* The banks are open until four o'clock. ◊ *Sie ist ein sehr offener Mensch.* She's a very open person.
- ◆ **offen gesagt** to be honest
- ◆ **Ich gebe dir eine offene Antwort.** I'll be frank with you.
- ◆ **eine offene Stelle** a vacancy
- ◆ **offen bleiben (1)** to stay open ◊ *Soll das Fenster offen bleiben?* Is the window supposed to stay open?
- ◆ **offen bleiben (2)** to remain open ◊ *Diese Möglichkeit bleibt uns noch offen.* This option remains open to us.

**offensichtlich** ADJECTIVE, ADVERB
- [1] obvious ◊ *ein offensichtlicher Fehler* an obvious mistake
- [2] obviously ◊ *Er ist offensichtlich nicht zufrieden.* He's obviously dissatisfied.

**öffentlich** ADJECTIVE
public
- ◆ **öffentliche Verkehrsmittel** public transport

die **Öffentlichkeit** NOUN
public ◊ *Die Öffentlichkeit wurde nicht informiert.* The public were not informed.
- ◆ **in aller Öffentlichkeit** in public

**offiziell** ADJECTIVE
official

der **Offizier** NOUN (PL die **Offiziere**)
officer

**öffnen** VERB
to open ◊ *jemandem die Tür öffnen* to open the door for somebody

der **Öffner** NOUN (PL die **Öffner**)
opener

die **Öffnung** NOUN
opening

die **Öffnungszeiten** FEM PL NOUN
opening times

**oft** ADVERB
> see also **öfter** ADVERB

often ◊ *Wie oft warst du schon in London?* How often have you been to London?

**öfter** ADVERB
> see also **oft** ADVERB

more often ◊ *Ich würde dich gern öfter besuchen.* I would like to visit you more often.
- ◆ **Sie war in letzter Zeit öfter krank.** She's been ill a lot recently.

**öfters** ADVERB
often

**oh** EXCLAMATION
oh ◊ *Oh, das wusste ich nicht.* Oh, I didn't know that.

**ohne** PREPOSITION, CONJUNCTION
> *The preposition **ohne** takes the accusative.*

without ◊ *Ich fahre ohne meine Eltern in Ferien.* I'm going on holiday without my parents. ◊ *Ich habe das ohne Wörterbuch übersetzt.* I translated it without a dictionary.
- ◆ **Das ist nicht ohne.** It's not half bad.
- ◆ **ohne weiteres** easily ◊ *Das ist ohne weiteres in einer Woche zu schaffen.* That can easily be done in a week.
- ◆ **Du kannst doch nicht so ohne weiteres gehen.** You can't just leave.
- ◆ **ohne etwas zu tun** without doing something ◊ *Sie ist gegangen, ohne Bescheid zu sagen.* She left without telling anyone. ◊ *ohne zu fragen* without asking

die **Ohnmacht** NOUN
- ◆ **in Ohnmacht fallen** to faint

**ohnmächtig** ADJECTIVE
- ◆ **ohnmächtig werden** to faint
- ◆ **Sie ist ohnmächtig.** She's fainted.

das **Ohr** NOUN (PL die **Ohren**)
ear
- ◆ **Er hat sehr gute Ohren.** His hearing is very good.

die **Ohrenschmerzen** MASC PL NOUN
earache ◊ *Sie hat Ohrenschmerzen.* She's got earache.

die **Ohrfeige** NOUN
slap across the face

**ohrfeigen** VERB
- ◆ **jemanden ohrfeigen** to slap somebody across the face

der **Ohrring** NOUN (PL die **Ohrringe**)
earring

**oje** EXCLAMATION
oh dear!

**ökologisch** ADJECTIVE
ecological

der **Oktober** NOUN (GEN des **Oktober** or **Oktobers**, PL die **Oktober**)
October ◊ *im Oktober* in October ◊ *am dritten Oktober* on the third of October ◊ *Ulm, den 3. Oktober 2010* Ulm, 3 October 2010. ◊ *Heute ist der dritte Oktober.* Today is the third of October.

das **Oktoberfest** NOUN (PL die **Oktoberfeste**)
Munich beer festival

das **Öl** NOUN (PL die **Öle**)
oil

die **Ölfarbe** NOUN
oil paint

die **Ölheizung** NOUN
oil-fired central heating

**ölig** ADJECTIVE
oily

**oliv** ADJECTIVE
olive-green

die **Olive** NOUN
olive

der **Ölmessstab** NOUN (PL die **Ölmessstäbe**)
dipstick

O

die **Ölsardine** NOUN
sardine

der **Ölwechsel** NOUN (PL die **Ölwechsel**)
oil change

die **Olympiade** NOUN
Olympic Games

der **Olympiasieger** NOUN (PL die **Olympiasieger**)
Olympic champion

die **Olympiasiegerin** NOUN
Olympic champion

**olympisch** ADJECTIVE
Olympic

das **Ölzeug** NOUN
oilskins

die **Oma** NOUN (PL die **Omas**)
granny

das **Omelett** NOUN (PL die **Omeletts**)
omelette

die **Omi** NOUN (PL die **Omis**)
granny

der **Onkel** NOUN (PL die **Onkel**)
uncle

**online** ADVERB
on line

der **Opa** NOUN (PL die **Opas**)
grandpa

die **Oper** NOUN
1 opera ◊ *eine Oper von Verdi* an opera by Verdi
2 opera house ◊ *die Mailänder Oper* the Milan opera house

die **Operation** NOUN
operation

der **Operationssaal** NOUN (PL die **Operationssäle**)
operating theatre

die **Operette** NOUN
operetta

**operieren** VERB (PERFECT **hat operiert**)
to operate on ◊ *jemanden operieren* to operate on somebody
♦ **Sie muss operiert werden.** She has to have an operation.
♦ **Sie wurde am Auge operiert.** She had an eye operation.

das **Opfer** NOUN (PL die **Opfer**)
1 sacrifice ◊ *Das war ein großes Opfer für ihn.* It was a great sacrifice for him.
2 victim ◊ *Der Unfall hat viele Opfer gefordert.* The accident claimed a lot of victims.

der **Opi** NOUN (PL die **Opis**)
grandpa

die **Opposition** NOUN
opposition

die **Optik** NOUN
optics

der **Optiker** NOUN (PL die **Optiker**)
optician

**optimal** ADJECTIVE, ADVERB

optimum ◊ *Das ist die optimale Lösung.* That's the optimum solution.
♦ **Sie hat das optimal gelöst.** She solved it in the best possible way.
♦ **Wir haben den Platz optimal genutzt.** We made the best possible use of the space available.

der **Optimismus** NOUN (GEN des **Optimismus**)
optimism

der **Optimist** NOUN (GEN des **Optimisten,** PL die **Optimisten**)
optimist

**optimistisch** ADJECTIVE
optimistic

die **Orange** NOUN
see also **orange** ADJECTIVE
orange

**orange** ADJECTIVE
see also **die Orange** NOUN
orange

der **Orangensaft** NOUN (PL die **Orangensäfte**)
orange juice

das **Orchester** NOUN (PL die **Orchester**)
orchestra

**ordentlich** ADJECTIVE, ADVERB
1 tidy ◊ *Seine Wohnung ist sehr ordentlich.* His flat's very tidy. ◊ *Ich bin ein ordentlicher Mensch.* I'm a tidy person.
2 decent ◊ *Das sind ordentliche Leute.* They're decent people. ◊ *eine ordentliche Portion* a decent portion
♦ **Ich brauche jetzt etwas Ordentliches zu essen.** Now I need a decent meal.
3 respectable ◊ *Das ist eine ordentliche Leistung.* That's a respectable achievement.
4 neatly ◊ *Du solltest ordentlicher schreiben.* You should write more neatly.
5 properly ◊ *Kannst du dich nicht ordentlich benehmen?* Can't you behave properly?
♦ **Es hat ordentlich geschneit.** There's been a fair bit of snow.
♦ **Sie haben ihn ordentlich verprügelt.** They beat him up good and proper.

**ordinär** ADJECTIVE
vulgar
♦ **sich ordinär ausdrücken** to use vulgar expressions

**ordnen** VERB
to put in order

der **Ordner** NOUN (PL die **Ordner**)
file
♦ **Diese Unterlagen hefte ich in einem Ordner ab.** I'll file these documents away.

die **Ordnung** NOUN
order ◊ *Ruhe und Ordnung* law and order
♦ **Auf meinem Schreibtisch herrscht Ordnung.** On my desk, everything is in its place.
♦ **Sie liebt Ordnung.** She likes everything to be in its place.

♦ **Das hat schon alles seine Ordnung.**
Everything is as it should be.

♦ **Ordnung machen** to tidy up ◊ *Du solltest in deinem Zimmer Ordnung machen.* You should tidy up your room.

♦ **Mit meinem Auto ist etwas nicht in Ordnung.** Something's wrong with my car.

♦ **etwas wieder in Ordnung bringen** to repair something ◊ *Er hat das defekte Gerät wieder in Ordnung gebracht.* He repaired the faulty appliance.

♦ **Ich muss meine Wohnung in Ordnung bringen.** I'll have to tidy up my flat.

♦ **Ist alles in Ordnung?** Is everything okay?

♦ **In Ordnung!** Okay!

das **Organ** NOUN (PL die **Organe**)
organ ◊ *die inneren Organe* internal organs

die **Organisation** NOUN
organization

**organisch** ADJECTIVE
organic

**organisieren** VERB (PERFECT **hat organisiert**)
to organize ◊ *Wer hat das Fest organisiert?* Who organized the party?

die **Orgel** NOUN
organ ◊ *Sie spielt Orgel.* She plays the organ.

der **Orient** NOUN
Orient

**orientalisch** ADJECTIVE
oriental

sich **orientieren** VERB (PERFECT **hat sich orientiert**)
⬜1 to find one's way around ◊ *Ich brauche einen Stadtplan, um mich besser orientieren zu können.* I need a city map to be able to find my way around better.
⬜2 to find out ◊ *Ich muss mich orientieren, wie das gehandhabt wird.* I'll have to find out what the procedure is.

die **Orientierung** NOUN
⬜1 bearings ◊ *Wir haben die Orientierung verloren.* We've lost our bearings.
⬜2 information ◊ *Diese Broschüre ist zu Ihrer Orientierung.* This brochure is for your information.

das **Original** NOUN (PL die **Originale**)
original

**originell** ADJECTIVE
original

der **Orkan** NOUN (PL die **Orkane**)
hurricane

der **Ort** NOUN (PL die **Orte**)
place
♦ **an Ort und Stelle** on the spot

die **Orthografie** NOUN
spelling

**örtlich** ADJECTIVE
local

das **Ortsgespräch** NOUN (PL die **Ortsgespräche**)
local phone call

der **Osten** NOUN
east

das **Osterei** NOUN (PL die **Ostereier**)
Easter egg

die **Osterferien** PL NOUN
Easter holidays

der **Osterhase** NOUN (GEN des **Osterhasen,** PL die **Osterhasen**)
Easter bunny

der **Ostermontag** NOUN (PL die **Ostermontage**)
Easter Monday

das **Ostern** NOUN (PL die **Ostern**)
Easter ◊ *an Ostern* at Easter

das **Österreich** NOUN
Austria

> ⓘ *Austria borders on Germany, the Czech Republic, Slovakia, Hungary, Slovenia, Italy and Switzerland. Its capital is Vienna and its currency the Schilling.*

♦ **aus Österreich** from Austria
♦ **in Österreich** in Austria
♦ **nach Österreich** to Austria

der **Österreicher** NOUN (PL die **Österreicher**)
Austrian

die **Österreicherin** NOUN
Austrian

**österreichisch** ADJECTIVE
Austrian

> ⓘ *People in Austria speak a dialect of German.*

**östlich** ADJECTIVE, PREPOSITION, ADVERB
easterly ◊ *in östlicher Richtung* in an easterly direction
♦ **östlich einer Sache** to the east of something ◊ *Das Kraftwerk liegt östlich der Stadt.* The power station is to the east of the city.
♦ **östlich von** east of ◊ *Jena liegt östlich von Erfurt.* Jena is east of Erfurt.

die **Ostsee** NOUN
Baltic ◊ *Wir fahren an die Ostsee.* We're going to the Baltic. ◊ *Wir waren an der Ostsee.* We've been to the Baltic.

**oval** ADJECTIVE
oval

der **Ozean** NOUN (PL die **Ozeane**)
ocean

das **Ozon** NOUN
ozone

das **Ozonloch** NOUN (PL die **Ozonlöcher**)
ozone hole

die **Ozonschicht** NOUN
ozone layer

**O**

# P

das **Paar** NOUN (PL die **Paare**)
  ⓵ pair ◇ *Ich habe ein Paar Schuhe
  gekauft.* I've bought a pair of shoes.
  ⓶ couple ◇ *Sie sind ein sehr glückliches
  Paar.* They're a very happy couple.
  ◆ **ein paar** a few
**paarmal** ADVERB
  ◆ **ein paarmal** a few times
**paarweise** ADVERB
  in pairs ◇ *Sie hängt die Socken
  paarweise auf die Leine.* She's hanging
  out the socks in pairs. ◇ *Stellt euch bitte
  paarweise auf.* Line up in pairs, please.
das **Päckchen** NOUN (PL die **Päckchen**)
  ⓵ small parcel ◇ *Wie viel kostet ein
  Päckchen ins Ausland?* How much does
  it cost to post a small parcel abroad?
  ⓶ packet ◇ *Sie raucht ein Päckchen pro
  Tag.* She smokes a packet a day.
**packen** VERB
  ⓵ to pack ◇ *Hast du deinen Koffer schon
  gepackt?* Have you already packed your
  suitcase?
  ⓶ to grasp ◇ *Sie packte mich am Arm.*
  She grasped my arm.
  ◆ **Er hat die Prüfung nicht gepackt.** He
  didn't manage to get through the exam.
das **Packpapier** NOUN
  brown paper
die **Packung** NOUN
  packet ◇ *eine Packung Tee* a packet of
  tea ◇ *eine Packung Zigaretten* a packet of
  cigarettes
  ◆ **eine Packung Pralinen** a box of
  chocolates
**pädagogisch** ADJECTIVE
  educational
das **Paket** NOUN (PL die **Pakete**)
  ⓵ packet ◇ *Ich habe ein Paket
  Waschpulver gekauft.* I bought a packet
  of washing powder.
  ⓶ parcel ◇ *Die Gebühren für Pakete
  stehen in dieser Liste.* Parcel rates are in
  this list.
die **Paketannahme** NOUN
  parcels office
der **Palast** NOUN (PL die **Paläste**)
  palace
die **Palme** NOUN
  palm tree
die **Pampelmuse** NOUN
  grapefruit
die **Panik** NOUN
  panic
**panisch** ADJECTIVE
  ◆ **panische Angst vor etwas haben** to be
  terrified of something
  ◆ **panisch reagieren** to panic

die **Panne** NOUN
  ⓵ breakdown ◇ *Wir hatten eine Panne
  auf der Autobahn.* We had a breakdown
  on the motorway.
  ⓶ slip ◇ *Mir ist da eine kleine Panne
  passiert.* I made a slight slip.
der **Panzer** NOUN (PL die **Panzer**)
  ⓵ tank ◇ *Die Armee setzte Panzer ein.*
  The army used tanks.
  ⓶ shell ◇ *der Panzer einer Schildkröte* a
  tortoise's shell
der **Papa** NOUN (PL die **Papas**)
  daddy
der **Papagei** NOUN (PL die **Papageien**)
  parrot
das **Papier** NOUN (PL die **Papiere**)
  paper
der **Papierkorb** NOUN (PL die **Papierkörbe**)
  wastepaper basket
die **Papiertüte** NOUN
  paper bag
die **Pappe** NOUN
  cardboard
der **Paprika** NOUN (PL die **Paprikas**)
  ⓵ paprika ◇ *Ich habe das Hähnchen mit
  Paprika gewürzt.* I've seasoned the
  chicken with paprika.
  ⓶ pepper ◇ *Heute gibt es gefüllte
  Paprikas.* We're having stuffed peppers
  today.
der **Papst** NOUN (PL die **Päpste**)
  pope
die **Parabolantenne** NOUN
  satellite dish
das **Paradies** NOUN (GEN des **Paradieses**, PL die
  **Paradiese**)
  paradise
**parallel** ADJECTIVE
  parallel
die **Parallele** NOUN
  parallel
das **Pärchen** NOUN (PL die **Pärchen**)
  couple ◇ *Auf der Parkbank saß ein
  Pärchen.* There was a couple sitting on
  the bench in the park.
das **Parfüm** NOUN (PL die **Parfüms** or **Parfüme**)
  perfume
der **Pariser** NOUN (PL die **Pariser**)
  ⓵ Parisian
  ⓶ condom ◇ *Auf den meisten Toiletten
  gibt es Automaten mit Parisern.* Most
  toilets have condom machines.
die **Pariserin** NOUN
  Parisian
der **Park** NOUN (PL die **Parks**)
  park
die **Parkanlage** NOUN
  park

**parken** VERB
to park

das **Parkett** NOUN (PL die **Parkette** or **Parketts**)
stalls (*theatre*)

das **Parkhaus** NOUN (GEN des **Parkhauses**, PL die **Parkhäuser**)
multistorey car park

die **Parklücke** NOUN
parking space

der **Parkplatz** NOUN (GEN des **Parkplatzes**, PL die **Parkplätze**)
car park

die **Parkscheibe** NOUN
parking disc

der **Parkschein** NOUN
car-park ticket

die **Parkuhr** NOUN
parking meter

das **Parkverbot** NOUN (PL die **Parkverbote**)
 ◆ **Hier ist Parkverbot.** You're not allowed to park here.

das **Parlament** NOUN (PL die **Parlamente**)
parliament

die **Parole** NOUN
 [1] motto ◊ *"Morgenstund hat Gold im Mund" ist seine Parole.* His motto is: "The early bird catches the worm".
 [2] slogan ◊ *ausländerfeindliche Parolen* racist slogans

die **Partei** NOUN
party (*political*)
 ◆ **Partei für jemanden ergreifen** to take somebody's side

**parteiisch** ADJECTIVE
biased

das **Parterre** NOUN (PL die **Parterres**)
 [1] ground floor ◊ *Wir wohnen im Parterre.* We live on the ground floor.
 [2] stalls (*theatre*)

die **Partie** NOUN
 [1] area ◊ *Die Creme auf die Augenpartie auftragen.* Apply the cream to the area around the eyes.
 [2] game ◊ *eine Partie Schach* a game of chess
 ◆ **mit von der Partie sein** to join in

das **Partizip** NOUN (PL die **Partizipien**)
participle

der **Partner** NOUN (PL die **Partner**)
partner

die **Partnerin** NOUN
partner

die **Partnerstadt** NOUN (PL die **Partnerstädte**)
twin town

die **Party** NOUN (PL die **Partys**)
party ◊ *eine Party veranstalten* to have a party

der **Pass** NOUN (GEN des **Passes**, PL die **Pässe**)
 [1] passport ◊ *Für Indien brauchst du einen Pass.* You need a passport for India.

 [2] pass ◊ *Im Winter ist der Pass gesperrt.* The pass is closed in winter.

die **Passage** NOUN
passage
 ◆ **eine Einkaufspassage** a shopping arcade

der **Passagier** NOUN (PL die **Passagiere**)
passenger

**passen** VERB
 [1] to fit ◊ *Die Hose passt nicht.* The trousers don't fit. ◊ *Es ist zu groß und passt nicht in meinen Koffer.* It's too big and doesn't fit in my suitcase.
 [2] to suit ◊ *Passt dir Dienstag?* Does Tuesday suit you? ◊ *Dieser Termin passt mir nicht.* That date doesn't suit me.
 ◆ **Es passt mir nicht, dass du so frech bist.** I don't like you being so cheeky.
 ◆ **zu etwas passen** to go with something ◊ *Der Rock passt nicht zu deiner Bluse.* The skirt doesn't go with your blouse.
 ◆ **zu jemandem passen** to be right for somebody ◊ *Er passt nicht zu dir.* He's not right for you.
 [3] to pass ◊ *Auf die Frage muss ich passen.* I'll have to pass on that question.

**passend** ADJECTIVE
 [1] matching ◊ *Ich muss jetzt dazu passende Schuhe kaufen.* I now must buy some matching shoes.
 ◆ **Ich suche zu dem Rock noch eine passende Bluse.** I'm looking for a blouse to match this skirt.
 [2] appropriate ◊ *Sie hat ein paar passende Worte gesprochen.* She said a few appropriate words.
 [3] convenient ◊ *Das ist nicht die passende Gelegenheit.* This isn't a convenient time.

**passieren** VERB (PERFECT **ist passiert**)
to happen ◊ *Was ist passiert?* What happened? ◊ *Mir ist etwas Lustiges passiert.* Something funny happened to me.

das **Passiv** NOUN (PL die **Passive**)
  see also **passiv** ADJECTIVE
passive

**passiv** ADJECTIVE, ADVERB
  see also **das Passiv** NOUN
passive ◊ *passives Rauchen* passive smoking ◊ *passiv zusehen* to watch passively

das **Passivrauchen** NOUN
passive smoking

die **Passkontrolle** NOUN
passport control

das **Passwort** NOUN (PL die **Passwörter**)
password

die **Paste** NOUN
paste

die **Pastete** NOUN
pie (*savoury*)

der **Pate** NOUN (GEN des **Paten**, PL die **Paten**)
godfather

**P**

das **Patenkind** NOUN (PL die **Patenkinder**)
godchild

das **Patent** NOUN (PL die **Patente**)
patent

die **Patentante** NOUN
godmother

der **Patient** NOUN (GEN des **Patienten**, PL die **Patienten**)
patient

die **Patientin** NOUN
patient

die **Patin** NOUN
godmother

die **Patrone** NOUN
cartridge

**patschnass** ADJECTIVE
soaking wet

die **Pauke** NOUN
kettledrum ◊ *Er spielt Pauke.* He plays the kettledrum.
♦ **auf die Pauke hauen** to live it up

**pauken** VERB
1 to swot ◊ *Vor der Arbeit habe ich ziemlich gepaukt.* I swotted quite a lot before the test.
2 to swot up ◊ *Ich muss Vokabeln pauken.* I have to swot up my vocabulary.

die **Pauschalreise** NOUN
package tour

die **Pause** NOUN
1 break ◊ *eine Pause machen* to have a break ◊ *die große Pause* the long break
2 interval ◊ *In der Pause haben wir über das Stück gesprochen.* We talked about the play during the interval.

der **Pazifik** NOUN
Pacific

der **PC** NOUN (GEN des **PCs**, PL die **PCs**)
PC

das **Pech** NOUN
bad luck ◊ *Das war Pech!* That was bad luck.
♦ **Pech haben** to be unlucky
♦ **Pech!** Hard luck!

das **Pedal** NOUN (PL die **Pedale**)
pedal

der **Pegel** NOUN (PL die **Pegel**)
water level

**peinlich** ADJECTIVE
1 embarrassing ◊ *eine peinliche Frage* an embarrassing question
2 awkward ◊ *eine peinliche Angelegenheit* an awkward situation
♦ **Das ist mir aber peinlich.** I'm dreadfully sorry.
♦ **peinlich genau** painstakingly ◊ *Sie hat das peinlich genau überprüft.* She checked it painstakingly.

die **Peitsche** NOUN
whip

die **Pelle** NOUN
skin

die **Pellkartoffeln** FEM PL NOUN
potatoes boiled in their skins

der **Pelz** NOUN (GEN des **Pelzes**, PL die **Pelze**)
fur

das **Pendel** NOUN (PL die **Pendel**)
pendulum

**pendeln** VERB (PERFECT **ist gependelt**)
to commute ◊ *Er pendelt zwischen Tübingen und Stuttgart.* He commutes between Tübingen and Stuttgart.
♦ **Der Bus pendelt zwischen Bahnhof und Flughafen.** A shuttle bus runs between the station and the airport.

der **Pendelverkehr** NOUN
1 shuttle service ◊ *Die Fluggesellschaft hat einen Pendelverkehr zwischen Köln und Berlin eingerichtet.* The airline set up a shuttle service between Cologne and Berlin.
2 commuter traffic ◊ *Zwischen Tübingen und Stuttgart besteht ein reger Pendelverkehr.* There is heavy commuter traffic between Tübingen and Stuttgart.

der **Pendler** NOUN (PL die **Pendler**)
commuter

**penetrant** ADJECTIVE
1 overpowering ◊ *ein penetranter Geruch* an overpowering smell
2 pushy ◊ *ein penetranter Vertreter* a pushy salesman
♦ **penetrant werden** to get aggressive

der **Penis** NOUN (GEN des **Penis**, PL die **Penisse**)
penis

**pennen** VERB
to kip ◊ *Ich habe auf dem Fußboden gepennt.* I kipped on the floor.
♦ **Was macht er? – Er pennt.** What's he doing? – He's having a kip.

der **Penner** NOUN (PL die **Penner**)
dosser

die **Pension** NOUN
1 pension ◊ *Er bezieht eine ordentliche Pension.* He gets a decent pension.
♦ **in Pension gehen** to retire
2 guesthouse ◊ *Wir haben in einer Pension übernachtet.* We stayed overnight in a guesthouse.

**pensioniert** ADJECTIVE
retired

das **Perfekt** NOUN (PL die **Perfekte**)
see also **perfekt** ADJECTIVE
perfect

**perfekt** ADJECTIVE
see also **das Perfekt** NOUN
perfect ◊ *ein perfektes Alibi* a perfect alibi ◊ *perfekt passen* to fit perfectly

die **Periode** NOUN
period

die **Perle** NOUN
pearl

**perplex** ADJECTIVE

dumbfounded

die **Person** NOUN
person
♦ **ich für meine Person** ... personally I ...

das **Personal** NOUN
staff ◊ *das Hotelpersonal* the hotel staff

der **Personalausweis** NOUN (GEN des
**Personalausweises,** PL die
**Personalausweise**)
identity card

der **Personalchef** NOUN (PL die **Personalchefs**)
personnel manager

der **Personalcomputer** NOUN (PL die
**Personalcomputer**)
personal computer

die **Personalien** FEM PL NOUN
particulars

das **Personalpronomen** NOUN (PL die
**Personalpronomen**)
personal pronoun

der **Personenzug** NOUN (PL die **Personenzüge**)
passenger train

**persönlich** ADJECTIVE, ADVERB
[1] personal ◊ *das persönliche Fürwort*
the personal pronoun ◊ *eine persönliche
Beleidigung* a personal insult
◊ *persönlich werden* to get personal
[2] in person ◊ *persönlich erscheinen* to
appear in person
[3] personally ◊ *jemanden persönlich
kennen* to know somebody personally
◊ *Das war nicht persönlich gemeint.* It
wasn't meant personally.

die **Persönlichkeit** NOUN
personality

die **Perücke** NOUN
wig

der **Pessimismus** NOUN (GEN des **Pessimismus**)
pessimism

der **Pessimist** NOUN (GEN des **Pessimisten,** PL
die **Pessimisten**)
pessimist

**pessimistisch** ADJECTIVE
pessimistic

die **Pest** NOUN
plague
♦ **jemanden wie die Pest hassen** to loathe
somebody

die **Petersilie** NOUN
parsley

das **Petroleum** NOUN
paraffin

**Pf** ABBREVIATION (= *Pfennig*)
pfennig

der **Pfad** NOUN (PL die **Pfade**)
path

der **Pfadfinder** NOUN (PL die **Pfadfinder**)
boy scout

die **Pfadfinderin** NOUN
girl guide

das **Pfand** NOUN (PL die **Pfänder**)

[1] deposit ◊ *Auf der Flasche ist ein Pfand
von dreißig Pfennig.* There's a deposit of
thirty pfennigs on the bottle.
[2] forfeit ◊ *Wer die Frage nicht
beantworten kann, muss ein Pfand
geben.* Anyone who cannot answer the
question must pay a forfeit.

die **Pfandflasche** NOUN
returnable bottle

die **Pfanne** NOUN
frying pan

der **Pfannkuchen** NOUN (PL die **Pfannkuchen**)
pancake

der **Pfarrer** NOUN (PL die **Pfarrer**)
parish priest

der **Pfau** NOUN (PL die **Pfauen**)
peacock

**Pfd.** ABBREVIATION (= *Pfund*)
pound (*weight*)

der **Pfeffer** NOUN (PL die **Pfeffer**)
pepper

das **Pfefferkorn** NOUN (PL die **Pfefferkörner**)
peppercorn

der **Pfefferkuchen** NOUN (PL die **Pfefferkuchen**)
gingerbread

das **Pfefferminzbonbon** NOUN (PL die
**Pfefferminzbonbons**)
peppermint

die **Pfefferminze** NOUN
mint

die **Pfeffermühle** NOUN
pepper mill

die **Pfeife** NOUN
[1] whistle
[2] pipe ◊ *Mein Bruder raucht Pfeife.* My
brother smokes a pipe.

**pfeifen** VERB (IMPERFECT **pfiff,** PERFECT **hat
gepfiffen**)
to whistle

der **Pfeil** NOUN (PL die **Pfeile**)
arrow

der **Pfennig** NOUN (PL die **Pfennige** or **Pfennig**)
pfennig
*There are 100 **Pfennige** in a **Mark**.*
◊ *Eine Kopie kostet dreißig Pfennig.* One
copy costs thirty pfennigs.

das **Pferd** NOUN (PL die **Pferde**)
horse

das **Pferderennen** NOUN (PL die **Pferderennen**)
[1] race meeting ◊ *Er geht regelmäßig zu
Pferderennen.* He regularly goes to race
meetings.
[2] horse-racing ◊ *Ich interessiere mich
nicht für Pferderennen.* I'm not interested
in horse-racing.

der **Pferdeschwanz** NOUN (GEN des
**Pferdeschwanzes,** PL die **Pferdeschwänze**)
ponytail

der **Pferdestall** NOUN (PL die **Pferdeställe**)
stable

das **Pfingsten** NOUN (GEN des **Pfingsten,** PL die
**Pfingsten**)

**P**

☞

Whitsun ◊ *an Pfingsten* at Whitsun

der **Pfirsich** NOUN (PL die **Pfirsiche**)
peach

die **Pflanze** NOUN
plant
**pflanzen** VERB
to plant

das **Pflaster** NOUN (PL die **Pflaster**)
[1] plaster ◊ *Sie klebte ein Pflaster auf die Wunde.* She put a plaster on the cut.
[2] paving stones ◊ *Jemand hatte das Pflaster in der Fußgängerzone bemalt.* Somebody had been painting on the paving stones in the pedestrian precinct.

die **Pflaume** NOUN
plum

die **Pflege** NOUN
[1] care ◊ *Diese Pflanze braucht nicht viel Pflege.* This plant doesn't need much care. ◊ *ein Mittel zur Pflege von Leder* a leather-care product
[2] nursing ◊ *Ein krankes Baby braucht viel Pflege.* A sick baby needs a lot of nursing.
♦ **ein Kind in Pflege geben** to have a child fostered

die **Pflegeeltern** PL NOUN
foster parents

das **Pflegekind** NOUN (PL die **Pflegekinder**)
foster child

**pflegeleicht** ADJECTIVE
easy-care ◊ *ein pflegeleichter Stoff* an easy-care fabric
♦ **ein pflegeleichter Mensch** an uncomplicated person

**pflegen** VERB
[1] to nurse ◊ *Sie pflegt ihre kranke Mutter.* She's nursing her sick mother.
[2] to look after ◊ *Briten pflegen ihren Rasen.* The British look after their lawns.
♦ **Womit pflegst du dein Gesicht?** How do you care for your face?
♦ **gepflegte Hände** well-cared-for hands
♦ **gepflegt aussehen** to look well-groomed

der **Pfleger** NOUN (PL die **Pfleger**)
male nurse

die **Pflicht** NOUN
duty ◊ *Es ist deine Pflicht, dich darum zu kümmern.* It's your duty to take care of it.

**pflichtbewusst** ADJECTIVE
conscientious

das **Pflichtfach** NOUN (PL die **Pflichtfächer**)
compulsory subject

**pflücken** VERB
to pick ◊ *Wir haben Himbeeren gepflückt.* We picked raspberries. ◊ *einen Strauß pflücken* to pick a bunch of flowers

die **Pforte** NOUN
gate

der **Pförtner** NOUN (PL die **Pförtner**)
doorman

der **Pfosten** NOUN (PL die **Pfosten**)
post ◊ *Der Ball traf den Pfosten.* The ball hit the post.

die **Pfote** NOUN
paw ◊ *Der Hund hat schmutzige Pfoten.* The dog's paws are dirty.

**pfui** EXCLAMATION
ugh!

das **Pfund** NOUN (PL die **Pfunde** or **Pfund**)
pound ◊ *drei Pfund Äpfel* three pounds of apples ◊ *dreißig britische Pfund* thirty pounds sterling

**pfuschen** VERB
to be sloppy
♦ **Die Handwerker haben gepfuscht.** The craftmen produced sloppy work.
♦ **jemandem ins Handwerk pfuschen** to stick one's nose into somebody's business

die **Pfütze** NOUN
puddle

die **Phantasie** NOUN *see* **Fantasie**
**phantasieren** VERB *see* **fantasieren**
**phantastisch** ADJECTIVE *see* **fantastisch**

die **Philosophie** NOUN
philosophy
**philosophisch** ADJECTIVE
philosophical

**phlegmatisch** ADJECTIVE
lethargic

die **Phonetik** NOUN
phonetics ◊ *Die Phonetik steht in eckigen Klammern.* Phonetics are given in square brackets.
**phonetisch** ADJECTIVE
phonetic

das **Photo** NOUN *see* **Foto**

die **Physik** NOUN
physics ◊ *Physik ist mein Lieblingsfach.* Physics is my favourite subject.

der **Physiker** NOUN (PL die **Physiker**)
physicist
**physisch** ADJECTIVE
physical

der **Pickel** NOUN (PL die **Pickel**)
[1] pimple ◊ *Du hast einen Pickel auf der Nase.* You've got a pimple on your nose.
[2] pickaxe ◊ *Die Arbeiter haben den Straßenbelag mit Pickeln aufgeschlagen.* The workers broke up the road surface with pickaxes.
[3] ice axe ◊ *Die Bergsteiger hatten Seile und Pickel dabei.* The mountaineers had ropes and ice axes with them.
**pickelig** ADJECTIVE
spotty

das **Picknick** NOUN (PL die **Picknicks**)
picnic ◊ *Picknick machen* to have a picnic

der **Piepser** NOUN (PL die **Piepser**)
bleeper

das **Piercing** NOUN (PL die **Piercings**)

① body piercing
② body jewellery

as **Pik** NOUN (PL die **Pik**)
spades ◇ *Pik ist Trumpf.* Spades is
trumps.

**pikant** ADJECTIVE
spicy

die **Pille** NOUN
pill ◇ *Sie nimmt die Pille.* She's on the
pill.

der **Pilot** NOUN (GEN des **Piloten**, PL die **Piloten**)
pilot

das **Pils** NOUN (GEN des **Pils**, PL die **Pils**)
Pilsner lager

der **Pilz** NOUN (GEN des **Pilzes**, PL die **Pilze**)
① mushroom ◇ *eine Soße mit Pilzen* a
mushroom sauce
② toadstool ◇ *Der Fliegenpilz ist giftig.*
The fly agaric is a toadstool.

**pinkeln** VERB
to pee

die **Pinnwand** NOUN (PL die **Pinnwände**)
noticeboard

der **Pinsel** NOUN (PL die **Pinsel**)
paintbrush

die **Pinzette** NOUN
tweezers ◇ *eine Pinzette* a pair of
tweezers

der **Pirat** NOUN (GEN des **Piraten**, PL die **Piraten**)
pirate

die **Piste** NOUN
① run ◇ *Wir sind die blaue Piste
runtergefahren.* We skied down the blue
run.
② runway ◇ *Das Flugzeug stand auf der
Piste und wartete auf die Starterlaubnis.*
The plane stood on the runway waiting
for clearance for takeoff.

die **Pistole** NOUN
pistol

die **Pizza** NOUN (PL die **Pizzas**)
pizza

der **Pkw** NOUN (GEN des **Pkw** or **Pkws**, PL die
**Pkws**) (= *Personenkraftwagen*)
car

**plagen** VERB
to bother ◇ *Was plagt dich denn?* What's
bothering you?
♦ **Mich plagen Zahnschmerzen.** I've got
dreadful toothache.
♦ **Sie muss sich in der Schule ziemlich
plagen.** She finds school hard going.
♦ **Mit diesem Problem plage ich mich
schon seit einiger Zeit.** I've been
wrestling with this problem for some
time now.

das **Plakat** NOUN (PL die **Plakate**)
poster

der **Plan** NOUN (PL die **Pläne**)
① plan ◇ *Unser Plan war, vor ihm da zu
sein.* Our plan was to arrive before him.

② map ◇ *Hast du einen Plan von
München?* Have you got a map of
Munich?

**planen** VERB
to plan ◇ *Wir planen unseren nächsten
Urlaub.* We're planning our next holiday.
♦ **einen Mord planen** to plot a murder

der **Planet** NOUN (GEN des **Planeten**, PL die
**Planeten**)
planet

**planmäßig** ADJECTIVE
① according to plan ◇ *Alles verlief
planmäßig.* Everything went according to
plan.
② scheduled ◇ *planmäßige Ankunft*
scheduled arrival
♦ **Die Maschine ist planmäßig gelandet.**
The plane landed on time.

das **Plastik** NOUN
see also **die Plastik** NOUN
plastic ◇ *Die meisten Spielzeuge sind
heute aus Plastik.* Most toys these days
are made of plastic.

die **Plastik** NOUN
see also **das Plastik** NOUN
sculpture

der **Plastikbeutel** NOUN (PL die **Plastikbeutel**)
plastic bag

die **Plastiktüte** NOUN
plastic bag

**platt** ADJECTIVE
flat ◇ *ein platter Reifen* a flat tyre
◇ *plattes Land* flat country
♦ **etwas platt drücken** to flatten something
♦ **Ich bin platt!** I'm flabbergasted!

**plattdeutsch** ADJECTIVE
low German

die **Platte** NOUN
① plate ◇ *Sie stellte den Topf auf die
Platte.* She put the saucepan on the
plate.
♦ **eine Platte mit Käseaufschnitt** a platter
of assorted cheeses
♦ **Die Platte des Tisches war zerkratzt.** The
tabletop was scratched.
♦ **ein Loch mit einer Platte aus Holz
abdecken** to cover a hole with a wooden
board
② record ◇ *Sie hat alle Platten der
Beatles.* She's got all the Beatles'
records.

der **Plattenspieler** NOUN (PL die **Plattenspieler**)
record player

der **Plattfuß** NOUN (GEN des **Plattfußes**, PL die
**Plattfüße**)
flat foot
♦ **Sie hat Plattfüße.** She's flat-footed.

der **Platz** NOUN (GEN des **Platzes**, PL die **Plätze**)
① place ◇ *Das ist ein schöner Platz zum
Zelten.* That's a good place to pitch a
tent. ◇ *Das Buch steht nicht an seinem
Platz.* The book isn't in its place. ◇ *der
erste Platz* the first place

**P**

☞

2 seat ◊ *Wir hatten Plätze in der ersten Reihe.* We had seats in the front row.
◊ *Ist hier noch ein Platz frei?* Are all these seats taken?
♦ **Platz nehmen** to take a seat
3 room ◊ *Das Sofa braucht zu viel Platz.* The sofa takes up too much room.
◊ *jemandem Platz machen* to make room for somebody
4 square ◊ *Auf dem Platz vor der Kirche ist zweimal die Woche Markt.* There's a market twice a week on the square in front of the church.
5 playing field
♦ **Der Schiedsrichter schickte ihn vom Platz.** The referee sent him off.

das **Plätzchen** NOUN (PL die **Plätzchen**)
1 spot ◊ *ein hübsches Plätzchen* a beautiful spot
2 biscuit ◊ *Zum Kaffee gab es Plätzchen.* There were biscuits with the coffee.

**platzen** VERB (PERFECT **ist geplatzt**)
1 to burst ◊ *Der Luftballon ist geplatzt.* The balloon has burst.
2 to explode ◊ *In der Innenstadt ist gestern eine Bombe geplatzt.* A bomb exploded in the town centre yesterday.
♦ **vor Wut platzen** to be livid

die **Platzkarte** NOUN
seat reservation

**plaudern** VERB
to chat

die **Pleite** NOUN
see also **pleite** ADJECTIVE
1 bankruptcy ◊ *die Pleite einer Firma* the bankruptcy of a company
♦ **Pleite machen** to go bust
2 flop ◊ *Die Veranstaltung war eine Pleite.* The event was a flop.

**pleite** ADJECTIVE
see also **die Pleite** NOUN
broke ◊ *Ich bin total pleite.* I'm stony-broke.

die **Plombe** NOUN
filling ◊ *Ich habe noch keine einzige Plombe.* I still haven't got a single filling.

**plombieren** VERB (PERFECT **hat plombiert**)
to fill ◊ *Ein Zahn muss plombiert werden.* One tooth will have to be filled.

**plötzlich** ADJECTIVE, ADVERB
1 sudden ◊ *ihr plötzliches Erscheinen* her sudden appearance
2 suddenly ◊ *Sie war plötzlich weg.* Suddenly she was gone.

**plump** ADJECTIVE
clumsy ◊ *plumpe Bewegungen* clumsy movements
♦ **ein plumper Körper** a shapeless body
♦ **eine plumpe Lüge** a blatant lie

der **Plural** NOUN (PL die **Plurale**)
plural

das **Plus** NOUN (GEN des **Plus**)
see also **plus** ADVERB
1 plus ◊ *Steht vor der Zahl ein Plus oder ein Minus?* Is there a plus or a minus in front of the figure?
2 profit ◊ *Die Firma hat dieses Jahr ein Plus gemacht.* The company has made a profit this year.
3 advantage ◊ *Sprachkenntnisse sind immer ein Plus.* Language skills are always an advantage.

**plus** ADVERB
see also **das Plus** NOUN
plus

das **Plutonium** NOUN
plutonium

**PLZ** ABBREVIATION (= *Postleitzahl*)
postcode

der **Po** NOUN (PL die **Pos**)
bum

der **Pokal** NOUN (PL die **Pokale**)
1 cup ◊ *Welche Mannschaft hat den Pokal gewonnen?* Which team won the cup?
2 goblet ◊ *Sie tranken Wein aus Pokalen.* They drank wine out of goblets.

das **Pokalspiel** NOUN (PL die **Pokalspiele**)
cup tie

der **Pol** NOUN (PL die **Pole**)
pole ◊ *am Pol* at the Pole

der **Pole** NOUN (GEN des **Polen**, PL die **Polen**)
Pole
♦ **Er ist Pole.** He's Polish.

**Polen** NEUT NOUN
Poland
♦ **aus Polen** from Poland
♦ **nach Polen** to Poland

die **Police** NOUN
insurance policy

**polieren** VERB (PERFECT **hat poliert**)
to polish

die **Polin** NOUN
Pole
♦ **Sie ist Polin.** She's Polish.

die **Politik** NOUN
1 politics ◊ *Politik interessiert mich nicht.* Politics doesn't interest me.
2 policy ◊ *die Politik Großbritanniens in Bezug auf BSE* Great Britain's policy on BSE

der **Politiker** NOUN (PL die **Politiker**)
politician

**politisch** ADJECTIVE
political

die **Polizei** NOUN
police
Note that **Polizei** is used with a singular verb and **police** with a plural verb.
◊ *Die Polizei ist noch nicht da.* The police haven't arrived yet.

der **Polizeibeamte** NOUN (GEN des **Polizeibeamten**, PL die **Polizeibeamten**) police officer ◇ *Wir wurden von einem Polizeibeamten angehalten.* We were stopped by a police officer.

die **Polizeibeamtin** NOUN
police officer ◇ *Sie ist Polizeibeamtin.* She's a police officer.

**polizeilich** ADJECTIVE
◆**Er wird polizeilich gesucht.** The police are looking for him.

das **Polizeirevier** NOUN (PL die **Polizeireviere**)
police station

die **Polizeistunde** NOUN
closing time (*of bars*)

die **Polizeiwache** NOUN
police station

der **Polizist** NOUN (GEN des **Polizisten**, PL die **Polizisten**)
policeman ◇ *Dietmar ist Polizist.* Dietmar's a policeman.

die **Polizistin** NOUN
policewoman ◇ *Ursula ist Polizistin.* Ursula's a policewoman.

der **Pollen** NOUN (PL die **Pollen**)
pollen

**polnisch** ADJECTIVE
Polish

die **Polypen** PL NOUN
adenoids ◇ *Ihm wurden die Polypen entfernt.* He had his adenoids removed.

die **Pommes** PL NOUN
chips ◇ *Pommes mit Majonäse* chips with mayonnaise

die **Pommes frites** PL NOUN
chips ◇ *Würstchen mit Pommes frites* sausages and chips

**pompös** ADJECTIVE
ostentatious

das **Pony** NOUN (PL die **Ponys**)
see also **der Pony** NOUN
pony ◇ *Wir sind auf Ponys geritten.* We rode ponies.

der **Pony** NOUN (PL die **Ponys**)
see also **das Pony** NOUN
fringe ◇ *Sie trägt einen Pony.* She's got a fringe.

der **Pop** NOUN
pop

die **Popmusik** NOUN
pop music

**poppig** ADJECTIVE
bright ◇ *poppige Farben* bright colours

der **Popstar** NOUN (PL die **Popstars**)
pop star

die **Pore** NOUN
pore

die **Pornografie** NOUN
pornography

**porös** ADJECTIVE
porous

der **Porree** NOUN (PL die **Porrees**)
leek

das **Portemonnaie** NOUN (PL die **Portemonnaies**)
purse

der **Portier** NOUN (PL die **Portiers**)
porter

die **Portion** NOUN
portion ◇ *eine große Portion* a big portion ◇ *Zwei Portionen Pommes frites, bitte.* Two portions of chips, please.
◆**Dazu gehört eine ordentliche Portion Mut.** You need quite a bit of courage for that.

das **Portmonee** NOUN (PL die **Portmonees**)
purse

das **Porto** NOUN (PL die **Portos**)
postage

**Portugal** NEUT NOUN
Portugal
◆**aus Portugal** from Portugal
◆**nach Portugal** to Portugal

der **Portugiese** NOUN (GEN des **Portugiesen**, PL die **Portugiesen**)
Portuguese

die **Portugiesin** NOUN
Portuguese

**portugiesisch** ADJECTIVE
Portuguese

das **Porzellan** NOUN
[1] porcelain ◇ *eine Figur aus Porzellan* a porcelain figurine
[2] china ◇ *Das Porzellan habe ich von meiner Oma geerbt.* I inherited the china from my grandma.

die **Posaune** NOUN
trombone ◇ *Franz spielt Posaune.* Franz plays the trombone.

**positiv** ADJECTIVE
positive ◇ *HIV-positiv* HIV-positive

das **Possessivpronomen** NOUN (PL die **Possessivpronomen**)
possessive pronoun

die **Post** NOUN
[1] post office ◇ *Bring bitte das Päckchen zur Post.* Please take the parcel to the post office.
[2] mail ◇ *Ist Post für mich gekommen?* Was there any mail for me?

das **Postamt** NOUN (PL die **Postämter**)
post office

die **Postanweisung** NOUN
postal order

der **Posten** NOUN (PL die **Posten**)
[1] post ◇ *Sie hat einen guten Posten als Chefsekretärin.* She's got a good post as a director's secretary.
[2] sentry ◇ *Die Armee hat vor dem Gebäude Posten aufgestellt.* The army posted sentries in front of the building.
[3] item ◇ *Dieser Posten ist nicht auf der Preisliste aufgeführt.* This item doesn't appear on the price list.

das **Poster** NOUN (PL die **Poster**)

**P**

poster

das **Postfach** NOUN (PL die **Postfächer**)
post office box

die **Postkarte** NOUN
postcard

**postlagernd** ADVERB
poste restante

die **Postleitzahl** NOUN
postcode

**postwendend** ADVERB
by return of post

das **Postwertzeichen** NOUN (PL die **Postwertzeichen**)
postage stamp

die **Pracht** NOUN
splendour

**prächtig** ADJECTIVE, ADVERB
[1] magnificent ◊ *ein prächtiges Haus* a magnificent house
[2] marvellous ◊ *Wir haben uns prächtig amüsiert.* We had a marvellous time.

**prachtvoll** ADJECTIVE
splendid

das **Prädikat** NOUN (PL die **Prädikate**)
predicate ◊ *Subjekt und Prädikat eines Satzes* subject and predicate of a sentence

**prahlen** VERB
to brag

der **Praktikant** NOUN (GEN des **Praktikanten**, PL die **Praktikanten**)
trainee

die **Praktikantin** NOUN
trainee

das **Praktikum** NOUN (GEN des **Praktikums**, PL die **Praktika**)
practical training ◊ *Sie absolviert ihr Praktikum.* She's doing her practical training.

**praktisch** ADJECTIVE
[1] practical ◊ *ein praktischer Mensch* a practical person
[2] handy ◊ *ein praktisches Gerät* a handy gadget
♦ **praktischer Arzt** general practitioner
♦ **praktisch begabt sein** to be good with one's hands

die **Praline** NOUN
chocolate

die **Präposition** NOUN
preposition

das **Präsens** NOUN (GEN des **Präsens**)
present tense

das **Präservativ** NOUN (PL die **Präservative**)
condom

der **Präsident** NOUN (GEN des **Präsidenten**, PL die **Präsidenten**)
president

die **Praxis** NOUN (PL die **Praxen**)
[1] practical experience ◊ *Ihr fehlt die Praxis.* She lacks practical experience.

♦ **etwas in die Praxis umsetzen** to put something into practice
[2] surgery ◊ *Kommen Sie zur Behandlung in die Praxis.* Come to the surgery for treatment.
[3] practice ◊ *Mein Anwalt hat seine eigene Praxis aufgemacht.* My solicitor has opened his own practice.

die **Predigt** NOUN
sermon

der **Preis** NOUN (GEN des **Preises**, PL die **Preise**)
[1] price ◊ *Die Preise für Computer sind gefallen.* Computer prices have fallen.
[2] prize ◊ *Ihr Hund hat einen Preis gewonnen.* Her dog's won a prize.
♦ **um keinen Preis** not at any price

die **Preiselbeere** NOUN
cranberry

**preisgünstig** ADJECTIVE
inexpensive

die **Preislage** NOUN
price range

das **Preisschild** NOUN (PL die **Preisschilder**)
price tag

der **Preisträger** NOUN (PL die **Preisträger**)
prizewinner

**preiswert** ADJECTIVE
inexpensive

die **Prellung** NOUN
bruise

der **Premierminister** NOUN (PL die **Premierminister**)
prime minister

die **Presse** NOUN
press

**pressen** VERB
to press

der **Priester** NOUN (PL die **Priester**)
priest

**prima** ADJECTIVE
super ◊ *ein prima Hotel* a super hotel

der **Prinz** NOUN (GEN des **Prinzen**, PL die **Prinzen**)
prince

die **Prinzessin** NOUN
princess

das **Prinzip** NOUN (PL die **Prinzipien**)
principle
♦ **aus Prinzip** as a matter of principle

**privat** ADJECTIVE
private

der **Privatpatient** NOUN (GEN des **Privatpatienten**, PL die **Privatpatienten**)
private patient

die **Privatschule** NOUN
fee-paying school

das **Privileg** NOUN (PL die **Privilegien**)
privilege

**pro** PREPOSITION
*The preposition **pro** takes the accusative.*
per ◊ *zwei Mark pro Person* two marks per person
♦ **einmal pro Woche** once a week

die **Probe** NOUN

[1] test ◊ *Wir müssen eine Probe machen, ob er geeignet ist.* We need to do a test to see if he's suitable.

[2] sample ◊ *Die Probe wird im Labor untersucht.* The sample's being examined in the laboratory.

[3] rehearsal ◊ *die letzte Probe vor der Aufführung* the final rehearsal before the performance

♦ **jemanden auf die Probe stellen** to test somebody

**probieren** VERB (PERFECT **hat probiert**)

to try ◊ *Probier mal eine andere Methode.* Try a different method. ◊ *Willst du mal von dem Käse probieren?* Would you like to try some of the cheese?

das **Problem** NOUN (PL die **Probleme**)

problem ◊ *Kein Problem!* No problem.

das **Produkt** NOUN (PL die **Produkte**)

product

die **Produktion** NOUN

[1] production ◊ *die Produktion von Luxusautos* the production of luxury cars

[2] output ◊ *Wir müssen unsere Produktion erhöhen.* We must increase our output.

**produzieren** VERB (PERFECT **hat produziert**)

to produce

der **Professor** NOUN (PL die **Professoren**)

professor

der **Profi** NOUN (PL die **Profis**)

pro ◊ *Er spielt wie ein Profi.* He plays like a pro.

der **Profit** NOUN (PL die **Profite**)

profit

**profitieren** VERB (PERFECT **hat profitiert**)

♦ **von etwas profitieren** to profit from something

das **Programm** NOUN (PL die **Programme**)

[1] programme ◊ *das Programm des heutigen Abends* this evening's programme

[2] program ◊ *Für die Kalkulation arbeite ich mit einem anderen Programm.* I've got a different program for spreadsheets.

**programmieren** VERB (PERFECT **hat programmiert**)

to program

der **Programmierer** NOUN (PL die **Programmierer**)

programmer

das **Projekt** NOUN (PL die **Projekte**)

project

das **Promille** NOUN (PL die **Promille**)

alcohol level ◊ *Er hatte drei Promille.* He had an alcohol level of three hundred milligrams in a hundred millilitres of blood.

das **Pronomen** NOUN (PL die **Pronomen**)

pronoun

der **Prophet** NOUN (GEN des **Propheten,** PL die **Propheten**)

prophet

die **Proportion** NOUN

proportion

die **Prosa** NOUN

prose

**prosit** EXCLAMATION

cheers!

♦ **Prosit Neujahr!** Happy New Year!

der **Prospekt** NOUN (PL die **Prospekte**)

brochure

Be careful! **Prospekt** does not mean **prospect**.

**prost** EXCLAMATION

cheers!

die **Prostituierte** NOUN (GEN der **Prostituierten**)

prostitute

die **Prostitution** NOUN

prostitution

das **Protein** NOUN (PL die **Proteine**)

protein

der **Protest** NOUN (PL die **Proteste**)

protest

**protestantisch** ADJECTIVE

Protestant

**protestieren** VERB (PERFECT **hat protestiert**)

to protest

das **Protokoll** NOUN (PL die **Protokolle**)

[1] minutes ◊ *Wer schreibt das Protokoll der heutigen Besprechung?* Who is taking the minutes of today's meeting?

[2] statement ◊ *Der Zeuge muss das polizeiliche Protokoll unterschreiben.* The witness must sign the statement he made to the police.

**protzen** VERB

to show off

**protzig** ADJECTIVE

showy ◊ *ein protziges Auto* a showy car

der **Proviant** NOUN (PL die **Proviante**)

provisions

**provisorisch** ADJECTIVE

provisional

**provozieren** VERB (PERFECT **hat provoziert**)

to provoke

das **Prozent** NOUN (PL die **Prozente**)

per cent ◊ *zehn Prozent* ten per cent

der **Prozess** NOUN (GEN des **Prozesses,** PL die **Prozesse**)

trial ◊ *der Prozess gegen die Terroristen* the trial of the terrorists

♦ **einen Prozess gewinnen** to win a case

**prüde** ADJECTIVE

prudish

**prüfen** VERB

[1] to test ◊ *Wir werden morgen in Chemie geprüft.* We're having a chemistry test tomorrow.

[2] to check ◊ *Vor der Reise sollte man den Ölstand prüfen.* You should check the oil before your journey.

**P**

der **Prüfer** NOUN (PL die **Prüfer**)
examiner

die **Prüfung** NOUN
[1] examination ◊ *Sie hat die Prüfung bestanden.* She's passed the examination.
[2] check ◊ *Bei der Prüfung der Bremsen haben wir einen Defekt festgestellt.* During a check on the brakes we found a fault.

der **Prügel** NOUN (PL die **Prügel**)
stick ◊ *Er schlug ihn mit einem Prügel.* He hit him with a stick.
♦ **Prügel bekommen** to get a hiding

die **Prügelei** NOUN
fight

**prügeln** VERB
to beat ◊ *Eltern sollten ihre Kinder nicht prügeln.* Parents shouldn't beat their children.
♦ **sich prügeln** to fight ◊ *Ich will mich nicht mit dir prügeln.* I don't want to fight you.

die **Prügelstrafe** NOUN
corporal punishment

**psychisch** ADJECTIVE
psychological

der **Psychologe** NOUN (GEN des **Psychologen**, PL die **Psychologen**)
psychologist ◊ *Ihr Vater ist Psychologe.* Her father is a psychologist.

die **Psychologie** NOUN
psychology

**psychologisch** ADJECTIVE
psychological

der **Psychotherapeut** NOUN (GEN des **Psychotherapeuten**, PL die **Psychotherapeuten**)
psychotherapist ◊ *Herr Müller ist Psychotherapeut.* Mr Müller is a psychotherapist.

die **Pubertät** NOUN
puberty ◊ *während der Pubertät* during puberty

das **Publikum** NOUN
audience

der **Pudding** NOUN (PL die **Puddinge** or **Puddings**)
blancmange

der **Puder** NOUN (PL die **Puder**)
powder

der **Puffer** NOUN (PL die **Puffer**)
buffer

der **Pulli** NOUN (PL die **Pullis**)
pullover

der **Pullover** NOUN (PL die **Pullover**)
pullover

der **Puls** NOUN (GEN des **Pulses**, PL die **Pulse**)
pulse
♦ **jemandem den Puls fühlen** to take somebody's pulse

das **Pult** NOUN (PL die **Pulte**)
desk

das **Pulver** NOUN (PL die **Pulver**)
powder

der **Pulverschnee** NOUN
powder snow

die **Pumpe** NOUN
pump

**pumpen** VERB
[1] to pump ◊ *Das Öl wird durch die Pipeline gepumpt.* The oil's pumped along the pipeline.
[2] to lend ◊ *Kannst du mir mal deinen Walkman pumpen?* Can you lend me your Walkman?
[3] to borrow ◊ *Ich habe mir das Rad meiner Schwester gepumpt.* I've borrowed my sister's bike.

der **Punkt** NOUN (PL die **Punkte**)
[1] full stop ◊ *Am Satzende steht ein Punkt.* A full stop goes at the end of a sentence.
[2] point ◊ *In diesem Punkt gebe ich dir Recht.* On this point I agree with you.
[3] dot ◊ *Das Schiff war nur noch ein kleiner Punkt am Horizont.* The ship was only a small dot on the horizon.

**pünktlich** ADJECTIVE, ADVERB
[1] punctual ◊ *Sie ist nicht sehr pünktlich.* She's not very punctual.
[2] on time ◊ *Der Zug kam pünktlich an.* The train arrived on time.

die **Pünktlichkeit** NOUN
punctuality

die **Puppe** NOUN
doll

**pur** ADJECTIVE
pure ◊ *Das ist pures Gold.* That's pure gold. ◊ *Das ist doch der pure Wahnsinn.* But that's pure madness.
♦ **Whisky pur** neat whisky

die **Pute** NOUN
turkey

der **Puter** NOUN (PL die **Puter**)
turkey

**putzen** VERB
[1] to clean ◊ *Sie putzt jeden Samstag das Haus.* She cleans the house every Saturday.
[2] to wipe ◊ *Putz dir die Schuhe, bevor du reinkommst.* Wipe your shoes before you come in.
♦ **sich die Nase putzen** to blow one's nose
♦ **sich die Zähne putzen** to brush one's teeth

die **Putzfrau** NOUN
cleaner

der **Putzmann** NOUN (PL die **Putzmänner**)
cleaner

das **Puzzle** NOUN (PL die **Puzzles**)
jigsaw

der **Pyjama** NOUN (PL die **Pyjamas**)
pyjamas ◊ *ein Pyjama* a pair of pyjamas

die **Pyramide** NOUN
pyramid

# Q

**qm** ABBREVIATION (= *Quadratmeter*)
m²

das **Quadrat** NOUN (PL die **Quadrate**)
square

**quadratisch** ADJECTIVE
square

der **Quadratmeter** NOUN (PL die
**Quadratmeter**)
square metre ◊ *eine Wohnung von
achtzig Quadratmetern* a flat of eighty
square metres

**quaken** VERB
1 to croak (*frog*)
2 to quack (*duck*)

die **Qual** NOUN
1 agony ◊ *Treppensteigen ist für sie
eine Qual.* Climbing the stairs is agony
for her.
2 anguish ◊ *Die Qualen, die ich bei
dieser Prüfung ausgestanden habe ...*
The anguish I went through in that
exam ...

**quälen** VERB
to treat cruelly ◊ *Tiere quälen* to treat
animals cruelly
♦ **sich quälen (1)** to struggle ◊ *Sie quälte
sich die Treppe hinauf.* She struggled up
the steps.
♦ **sich quälen (2)** to torment oneself ◊ *Quäl
dich nicht so!* Don't torment yourself like
that.
♦ **Er muss sich in der Schule ziemlich
quälen.** School's quite a trial for him.

die **Qualifikation** NOUN (PL die
**Qualifikationen**)
qualification

sich **qualifizieren** VERB (PERFECT **hat sich
qualifiziert**)
to qualify ◊ *Sie hat sich für die
Weltmeisterschaft qualifiziert.* She
qualified for the world championships.

**qualifiziert** ADJECTIVE
qualified

die **Qualität** NOUN
quality

die **Qualle** NOUN
jellyfish ◊ *zwei Quallen* two jellyfish

der **Qualm** NOUN
thick smoke

**qualmen** VERB
to smoke ◊ *Der Schornstein qualmt.* The
chimney is smoking.

die **Quantität** NOUN
quantity

der **Quark** NOUN
quark

der **Quarz** NOUN (GEN des **Quarzes**)
quartz

**quasseln** VERB
to natter

der **Quatsch** NOUN
rubbish ◊ *Erzähl keinen Quatsch.* Don't
talk rubbish.
♦ **Quatsch machen** to fool around
♦ **Mach keinen Quatsch!** Don't be
foolish!

**quatschen** VERB
to natter

die **Quelle** NOUN
1 spring ◊ *heiße Quellen* hot springs
2 source ◊ *aus zuverlässiger Quelle*
from a reliable source

**quer** ADVERB
1 diagonally ◊ *Die Streifen auf dem
Stoff verlaufen quer.* The stripes run
diagonally across the material.
♦ **quer auf dem Bett** across the bed
2 at right angles ◊ *Die Mannstraße
verläuft quer zur Müllerstraße.* Mann
Street runs at right angles to Müller
Street.

die **Querflöte** NOUN
flute ◊ *Cordula spielt Querflöte.* Cordula
plays the flute.

**querschnittsgelähmt** ADJECTIVE
paraplegic

die **Querstraße** NOUN
♦ **eine Straße mit vielen Querstraßen** a
road with a lot of side streets off it
♦ **Biegen Sie an der zweiten Querstraße
links ab.** Take the second street on the
left.

**quetschen** VERB
1 to squash ◊ *Pass auf, dass die
Tomaten nicht gequetscht werden.* Mind
the tomatoes don't get squashed.
2 to cram ◊ *Sie quetschte das Kleid
noch in ihren Koffer.* She crammed the
dress into her case.
♦ **Ich habe mir den Finger in der Tür
gequetscht.** I trapped my finger in the
door.

die **Quetschung** NOUN
bruise

**quietschen** VERB
to squeak

**quitt** ADJECTIVE
quits ◊ *Jetzt sind wir quitt.* We're quits
now.

die **Quittung** NOUN
receipt ◊ *Brauchen Sie eine Quittung?*
Do you need a receipt?

# R

der **Rabatt** NOUN (PL die **Rabatte**)
  discount
die **Rache** NOUN
  revenge
der **Rachen** NOUN (PL die **Rachen**)
  throat
  **rächen** VERB
  ◆ **etwas rächen** to avenge something
  ◆ **sich rächen** to take revenge
  ◆ **Das wird sich rächen.** You'll pay for that.
das **Rad** NOUN (PL die **Räder**)
  [1] wheel
  [2] bike ◊ *Wir sind mit dem Rad gekommen.* We came by bike.
  ◆ **Rad fahren** to cycle
der **Radar** NOUN (PL die **Radare**)
  *You can also say das Radar.*
  radar
die **Radarfalle** NOUN
  speed trap
die **Radarkontrolle** NOUN
  radar-controlled speed check
  **radebrechen** VERB
  ◆ **Deutsch radebrechen** to speak broken German
  **radeln** VERB (PERFECT **ist geradelt**)
  to cycle ◊ *Wir sind an den Bodensee geradelt.* We cycled to Lake Constance.
  **radfahren** VERB *see* **Rad**
der **Radfahrer** NOUN (PL die **Radfahrer**)
  cyclist
der **Radfahrweg** NOUN (PL die **Radfahrwege**)
  cycle track
der **Radiergummi** NOUN (PL die **Radiergummis**)
  rubber
das **Radieschen** NOUN (PL die **Radieschen**)
  radish
das **Radio** NOUN (PL die **Radios**)
  radio
  **radioaktiv** ADJECTIVE
  radioactive
die **Radioaktivität** NOUN
  radioactivity
das **Radrennen** NOUN (PL die **Radrennen**)
  [1] cycle race ◊ *Er hat an dem Radrennen teilgenommen.* He took part in the cycle race.
  [2] cycle racing ◊ *Sie begeistert sich für Radrennen.* She's a cycle racing fan.
der **Radsport** NOUN
  cycling
der **Rahm** NOUN
  cream
der **Rahmen** NOUN (PL die **Rahmen**)
  frame ◊ *der Rahmen eines Bildes* the frame of a picture
  ◆ **im Rahmen des Möglichen** within the bounds of possibility
die **Rakete** NOUN
  rocket
der **Rand** NOUN (PL die **Ränder**)
  [1] edge ◊ *Er stand am Rand des Schwimmbeckens.* He stood on the edge of the swimming pool.
  [2] rim ◊ *der Rand der Tasse* the rim of the cup
  ◆ **eine Brille mit Goldrand** a pair of gold-rimmed glasses
  [3] margin ◊ *Lass an der Seite des Blattes einen Rand.* Leave a margin at the edge of the page.
  [4] ring ◊ *In der Badewanne waren dunkle Ränder.* There were dark rings in the bath tub.
  [5] verge ◊ *Die Firma steht am Rand des Bankrotts.* The company's on the verge of bankruptcy.
  ◆ **außer Rand und Band** out of control
  **randalieren** VERB (PERFECT **hat randaliert**)
  to go on the rampage
der **Rang** NOUN (PL die **Ränge**)
  [1] rank (*military*) ◊ *Er steht im Rang eines Hauptmanns.* He has the rank of captain.
  ◆ **ein Mann ohne Rang und Namen** a man without any standing
  [2] circle (*theatre*) ◊ *erster Rang* dress circle ◊ *zweiter Rang* upper circle
  **ranzig** ADJECTIVE
  rancid
der **Rappen** NOUN (PL die **Rappen**)
  rappen ◊ *Der Schweizer Franken hat hundert Rappen.* There're one hundred rappen in a Swiss franc.

  ⓘ *In the French-speaking part of Switzerland you talk about* **Centime** *rather than* **Rappen.**

  **rasch** ADJECTIVE, ADVERB
  quick ◊ *Das war rasch gemacht.* That was quickly done.
  ◆ **Ich gehe noch rasch beim Bäcker vorbei.** I'll just pop round to the baker's.
der **Rasen** NOUN (PL die **Rasen**)
  *see also* **rasen** VERB
  lawn
  **rasen** VERB (PERFECT **ist gerast**)
  *see also* **der Rasen** NOUN
  to race ◊ *Wir sind durch die engen Straßen gerast.* We raced along the narrow streets.
der **Rasenmäher** NOUN (PL die **Rasenmäher**)
  lawnmower

der **Rasierapparat** NOUN (PL die
  **Rasierapparate**)
  shaver
die **Rasiercreme** NOUN (PL die **Rasiercremes**)
  shaving cream
  **rasieren** VERB (PERFECT **hat rasiert**)
  to shave
  ♦ **sich rasieren** to shave
die **Rasierklinge** NOUN
  razor blade
das **Rasiermesser** NOUN (PL die **Rasiermesser**)
  razor
das **Rasierwasser** NOUN (PL die **Rasierwasser**)
  shaving lotion
die **Rasse** NOUN
  ⒈ race ◊ *Rassenunruhen* race riots
  ⒉ breed ◊ *Welche Rasse ist Ihr Hund?*
  What breed is your dog?
der **Rassenhass** NOUN (GEN des **Rassenhasses**)
  racial hatred
die **Rassentrennung** NOUN
  racial segregation
der **Rassismus** NOUN (GEN des **Rassismus**)
  racism
die **Rast** NOUN
  rest
  ♦ **Rast machen** to stop for a break
  **rasten** VERB
  to rest
das **Rasthaus** NOUN (PL die **Rasthäuser**)
  services (*motorway*)
der **Rasthof** NOUN (PL die **Rasthöfe**)
  services (*motorway*)
der **Rastplatz** NOUN (GEN des **Rastplatzes**, PL die
  **Rastplätze**)
  lay-by
die **Raststätte** NOUN
  service area
die **Rasur** NOUN
  shaving
der **Rat** NOUN (PL die **Ratschläge**)
  advice ◊ *Ich habe viele Ratschläge
  bekommen.* I've been given a lot of
  advice.
  ♦ **ein Rat** a piece of advice
  ♦ **jemanden zu Rate ziehen** to consult
  somebody
  ♦ **Ich weiß keinen Rat.** I don't know what
  to do.
die **Rate** NOUN
  instalment
  **raten** VERB (PRESENT **rät**, IMPERFECT **riet**, PERFECT
  **hat geraten**)
  to guess ◊ *Rat mal, wie alt ich bin.*
  Guess how old I am.
  ♦ **jemandem raten** to advise somebody
  ◊ *Sie hat mir geraten, einen Arzt
  aufzusuchen.* She advised me to see a
  doctor.
das **Rathaus** NOUN (GEN des **Rathauses**, PL die
  **Rathäuser**)
  town hall

die **Ration** NOUN
  ration
  **rationalisieren** VERB (PERFECT **hat
  rationalisiert**)
  to rationalize
  **rationell** ADJECTIVE
  efficient
  **ratlos** ADJECTIVE
  at a loss ◊ *Ich bin ratlos, was ich tun soll.*
  I'm at a loss as to what to do.
  ♦ **Sie sah mich ratlos an.** She gave me a
  helpless look.
der **Ratschlag** NOUN (PL die **Ratschläge**)
  piece of advice ◊ *Ich habe viele
  Ratschläge bekommen.* I've been given a
  lot of advice.
das **Rätsel** NOUN (PL die **Rätsel**)
  ⒈ puzzle ◊ *Sie löst gern Rätsel.* She likes
  solving puzzles.
  ⒉ mystery ◊ *Das ist mir ein Rätsel.* It's a
  mystery to me.
  **rätselhaft** ADJECTIVE
  mysterious
  ♦ **Es ist mir rätselhaft ...** It's a mystery to
  me ...
der **Ratskeller** NOUN (PL die **Ratskeller**)
  town-hall restaurant
die **Ratte** NOUN
  rat
  **rau** ADJECTIVE
  ⒈ rough ◊ *raue Haut* rough skin
  ⒉ husky ◊ *eine raue Stimme* a husky
  voice
  ⒊ sore ◊ *ein rauer Hals* a sore throat
  ⒋ harsh ◊ *raues Wetter* harsh weather
  ◊ *ein rauer Wind* a harsh wind
  ♦ **Hier herrschen raue Sitten.** People here
  have rough-and-ready ways.
der **Raub** NOUN
  robbery
das **Raubtier** NOUN (PL die **Raubtiere**)
  predator
der **Rauch** NOUN
  smoke
  **rauchen** VERB
  to smoke ◊ *Er raucht Pfeife.* He smokes a
  pipe.
  ♦ **"Rauchen verboten"** "No smoking"
der **Raucher** NOUN (PL die **Raucher**)
  smoker
das **Raucherabteil** NOUN (PL die
  **Raucherabteile**)
  smoking compartment
  **räuchern** VERB
  to smoke ◊ *Fisch räuchern* to smoke fish
das **Rauchfleisch** NOUN
  smoked meat
  **rauh** ADJECTIVE *see* **rau**
der **Raum** NOUN (PL die **Räume**)
  ⒈ space ◊ *Sie haben eine Rakete in den
  Raum geschossen.* They launched a

**R**

☞

rocket into space. ◊ *Raum und Zeit* space and time

**2** room ◊ *Eine Wohnung mit vier Räumen ist nicht groß genug für uns.* A four-roomed flat isn't big enough for us. ◊ *Dieses Gerät braucht wenig Raum.* This appliance doesn't take up much room.

**3** area ◊ *Im Raum Stuttgart kommt es morgen zu Gewittern.* There will be thunderstorms in the Stuttgart area tomorrow.

**räumen** VERB

**1** to clear ◊ *Im Winter müssen die Bürgersteige von Schnee geräumt werden.* The pavements have to be cleared of snow in winter. ◊ *Die Polizei hat das besetzte Haus geräumt.* The police cleared the squat.

**2** to move away from ◊ *Die Polizei forderte die Schaulustigen auf, die Unfallstelle zu räumen.* The police ordered the onlookers to move away from the scene of the accident.

**3** to vacate ◊ *Bitte räumen Sie Ihr Zimmer bis spätestens zehn Uhr.* Please vacate your room by ten o'clock at the latest.

**4** to clear away ◊ *Könnt ihr bitte das Geschirr vom Tisch räumen?* Could you clear away the dishes, please?

**5** to put away ◊ *Räum bitte deine Spielsachen in den Schrank.* Please put your toys away in the cupboard.

die **Raumfähre** NOUN
space shuttle

die **Raumfahrt** NOUN
space travel

der **Rauminhalt** NOUN (PL die **Rauminhalte**)
volume

**räumlich** ADJECTIVE
spatial

die **Räumlichkeiten** FEM PL NOUN
premises

das **Raumschiff** NOUN (PL die **Raumschiffe**)
spaceship

der **Rausch** NOUN (PL die **Räusche**)
♦ **einen Rausch haben** to be drunk
♦ **seinen Rausch ausschlafen** to sleep it off

das **Rauschgift** NOUN (PL die **Rauschgifte**)
drug

der **Rauschgiftsüchtige** NOUN (GEN des/der
die **Rauschgiftsüchtigen**, PL die
**Rauschgiftsüchtigen**)
drug addict ◊ *Gestern wurde ein Rauschgiftsüchtiger tot aufgefunden.* A drug addict was found dead yesterday.

sich **räuspern** VERB
to clear one's throat

**reagieren** VERB (PERFECT **hat reagiert**)
**1** to react ◊ *Wie hat sie auf diesen Vorwurf reagiert?* How did she react to the allegation?

**2** to respond ◊ *Die Bremsen haben nicht reagiert.* The brakes didn't respond.

die **Reaktion** NOUN
reaction

**reaktionär** ADJECTIVE
reactionary

der **Reaktor** NOUN (PL die **Reaktoren**)
reactor

**realisieren** VERB (PERFECT **hat realisiert**)
**1** to fulfil ◊ *Er hat seine Träume realisiert.* He's fulfilled his dreams.

**2** carry out ◊ *Wir sollten diese Pläne realisieren.* We ought to carry out these plans.

**3** realize ◊ *Sie hat gar nicht realisiert, dass er schon längst weg war.* She simply didn't realize that he had long since left.

**realistisch** ADJECTIVE
realistic

die **Realschule** NOUN
secondary school

> ❶ Pupils enter **Realschule** at the age of about ten, and leave after six years. It is not as academically oriented as the **Gymnasium**.

der **Rechen** NOUN (PL die **Rechen**)
rake

das **Rechnen** NOUN
| see also **rechnen** VERB |
arithmetic ◊ *Bettina ist gut im Rechnen.* Bettina's good at arithmetic.

**rechnen** VERB
| see also **das Rechnen** NOUN |
to work out ◊ *Lass mich rechnen, wie viel das wird.* Let me work out how much that's going to be.

♦ **Bettina kann gut rechnen.** Bettina's good at arithmetic.

♦ **Klinsmann wird zu den besten Fußballspielern gerechnet.** Klinsmann is regarded as one of the best footballers.

♦ **Man rechnet Mexico City zu den Megastädten.** Mexico City is classed as one of the metropolises.

♦ **rechnen mit (1)** to reckon with ◊ *Mit wie vielen Besuchern können wir rechnen?* How many visitors can we reckon with?

♦ **rechnen mit (2)** to reckon on ◊ *Mit dieser Reaktion hatte ich nicht gerechnet.* I hadn't reckoned on this reaction.

♦ **rechnen auf** to count on ◊ *Wir rechnen auf deine Unterstützung.* We're counting on your support.

der **Rechner** NOUN (PL die **Rechner**)
**1** calculator ◊ *Ich habe das mit meinem Rechner nachgerechnet.* I've checked it with my calculator.

**2** computer ◊ *Er hat sich für seinen Rechner einen neuen Prozessor gekauft.* He's bought a new CPU for his computer.

die **Rechnung** NOUN
> ⚊1⚊ calculations ◊ *Meine Rechnung ergibt, dass wir noch zweihundert Mark haben.* According to my calculations, we still have two hundred marks left.
> ⚊2⚊ invoice ◊ *Die Rechnung liegt der Sendung bei.* The invoice is enclosed.

das **Recht** NOUN (PL die **Rechte**)
> *see also* **recht** ADJECTIVE, ADVERB
> ⚊1⚊ right ◊ *Es ist mein Recht, das zu erfahren.* It's my right to know that. ◊ *Ich habe ein Recht auf eine Erklärung.* I've got a right to an explanation.
> ◆ **im Recht sein** to be in the right ◊ *Obwohl er im Recht war, hat er nachgegeben.* Although he was in the right, he gave in.
> ◆ **Recht haben** to be right ◊ *Wer hat nun Recht?* Who's right? ◊ *Sie will immer Recht haben.* She always has to be right.
> ◆ **jemandem Recht geben** to agree with somebody ◊ *Ich muss dir Recht geben, das war nicht nett.* I have to agree with you – that wasn't nice.
> ◆ **etwas mit Recht tun** to be right to do something ◊ *Sie hat sich mit Recht beschwert.* She was right to complain.
> ⚊2⚊ law ◊ *Sie wurde nach deutschem Recht zu zehn Jahren Gefängnis verurteilt.* She was sentenced under German law to ten years' imprisonment.
> ◆ **Recht sprechen** to administer justice

**recht** ADJECTIVE, ADVERB
> *see also* **das Recht** NOUN, **rechte** ADJECTIVE, **rechts** ADVERB
> ⚊1⚊ right ◊ *Es war nicht recht, dass du sie belogen hast.* It wasn't right of you to lie to her. ◊ *Dies ist nicht der rechte Moment, um darüber zu sprechen.* This isn't the right moment to talk about it.
> ◆ **Wenn ich dich recht verstehe ...** If I understand you correctly ...
> ◆ **Das geschieht dir recht!** Serves you right!
> ⚊2⚊ quite ◊ *Das scheint recht einfach.* It seems quite simple.
> ◆ **jemandem recht sein** to be all right with somebody ◊ *Wenn es deiner Mutter recht ist, übernachte ich gern bei euch.* If it's all right with your mother, I'd like to stay the night at your place.
> ◆ **Das ist mir recht.** That suits me.
> ◆ **es jemandem recht machen** to please somebody ◊ *Dir kann man es auch nie recht machen!* There's no pleasing you.
> ◆ **Jetzt erst recht!** Now more than ever.

die **Rechte** NOUN (GEN der **Rechten**)
> *see also* **rechte** ADJECTIVE, **das Rechte** NOUN
> ⚊1⚊ right ◊ *Zu Ihrer Rechten sehen Sie das Rathaus.* On your right you'll see the town hall.
> ⚊2⚊ right hand ◊ *Er schlug mit der Rechten zu.* He hit out with his right hand.

⚊3⚊ right-wing ◊ *eine Partei der Rechten* a right-wing party

**rechte** ADJECTIVE
> *see also* **recht** ADJECTIVE, **die Rechte** NOUN, **das Rechte** NOUN, **rechts** ADVERB
> right ◊ *In Deutschland fährt man auf der rechten Seite.* They drive on the right in Germany. ◊ *Mein rechtes Auge tut weh.* My right eye's hurting. ◊ *Er hat sich den rechten Arm gebrochen.* He broke his right arm.

das **Rechte** NOUN (GEN des **Rechten**)
> *see also* **die Rechte** NOUN, **rechte** ADJECTIVE
> right thing ◊ *Pass auf, dass du das Rechte sagst.* Make sure you say the right thing.
> ◆ **etwas Rechtes** something proper ◊ *Du solltest etwas Rechtes lernen.* You ought to learn something proper.
> ◆ **nichts Rechtes** nothing decent ◊ *Ich habe den ganzen Tag noch nichts Rechtes gegessen.* I haven't had anything decent to eat all day.

**rechteckig** ADJECTIVE
> rectangular

**rechtfertigen** VERB
> to justify ◊ *Wie kannst du dein Verhalten rechtfertigen?* How can you justify your behaviour?
> ◆ **sich rechtfertigen** to justify oneself

**rechtmäßig** ADJECTIVE
> lawful

**rechts** ADVERB
> *see also* **rechte** ADJECTIVE
> right ◊ *rechts abbiegen* to turn right
> ◆ **rechts überholen** to overtake on the right
> ◆ **Er schreibt mit rechts.** He writes with his right hand.
> ◆ **Rechts sehen Sie das Rathaus.** On the right you'll see the town hall.
> ◆ **rechts von der Kirche** to the right of the church
> ◆ **rechts von mir** on my right
> ◆ **rechts wählen** to vote for a right-wing party

der **Rechtsanwalt** NOUN (PL die **Rechtsanwälte**)
> lawyer

die **Rechtsanwältin** NOUN
> lawyer

die **Rechtschreibung** NOUN
> spelling

der **Rechtshänder** NOUN (PL die **Rechtshänder**)
> ◆ **Er ist Rechtshänder.** He's right-handed.

die **Rechtshänderin** NOUN
> ◆ **Sie ist Rechtshänderin.** She's right-handed.

die **Rechtskurve** NOUN
> right-hand bend

der **Rechtsverkehr** NOUN
> driving on the right
> ◆ **In Deutschland ist Rechtsverkehr.** They drive on the right in Germany.

**R**

**rechtwinklig** ADJECTIVE
  right-angled
**rechtzeitig** ADJECTIVE, ADVERB
  in time ◊ *Ich bitte um rechtzeitige Benachrichtigung.* Please let me know in time. ◊ *Wir sind rechtzeitig angekommen.* We arrived in time.
**recyceln** VERB (PERFECT **hat recycelt**)
  to recycle
das **Recycling** NOUN
  recycling
der **Redakteur** NOUN (PL die **Redakteure**)
  editor
die **Redaktion** NOUN
  ⊡ editing ◊ *die Redaktion eines Buches* the editing of a book
  ⊡ editorial staff ◊ *Die Redaktion hat das Manuskript abgelehnt.* The editorial staff rejected the manuscript.
  ⊡ editorial office ◊ *Er arbeitet in unserer Redaktion.* He works in our editorial office.
die **Rede** NOUN
  speech ◊ *Er hat eine witzige Rede gehalten.* He made an amusing speech.
  ✦ **jemanden zur Rede stellen** to take somebody to task
**reden** VERB
  ⊡ to talk ◊ *Wir haben über das Wetter geredet.* We talked about the weather. ◊ *Du redest Unsinn.* You're talking nonsense.
  ⊡ to speak ◊ *Ich werde mit deiner Mutter reden.* I'll speak to your mother. ◊ *Ich rede nicht gern vor so vielen Menschen.* I don't like speaking in front of so many people. ◊ *Der Präsident redet zum Volk.* The President's speaking to the country.
  ⊡ to say ◊ *Was reden die Leute über uns?* What are people saying about us?
die **Redewendung** NOUN
  expression
der **Redner** NOUN (PL die **Redner**)
  speaker
**reduzieren** VERB (PERFECT **hat reduziert**)
  to reduce
das **Referat** NOUN (PL die **Referate**)
  ⊡ assignment ◊ *Ich muss in Geografie ein Referat schreiben.* I have to write an assignment in geography.
  ⊡ paper ◊ *Sie hat ein Referat über Shakespeare gehalten.* She gave a paper on Shakespeare.
  ⊡ section ◊ *Er ist Leiter des Referats Umweltschutz.* He's head of the environmental protection section.
der **Reflex** NOUN (GEN des **Reflexes**, PL die **Reflexe**)
  reflex
**reflexiv** ADJECTIVE
  reflexive
die **Reform** NOUN
  reform
das **Regal** NOUN (PL die **Regale**)
  ⊡ bookcase ◊ *In ihrem Regal stehen viele Krimis.* There are a lot of detective stories in her bookcase.
  ⊡ rack ◊ *ein Regal für Weinflaschen* a wine rack
  ⊡ shelf ◊ *Auf dem Regal standen Kräuter.* There were herbs on the shelf.
die **Regel** NOUN
  ⊡ rule ◊ *Keine Regel ohne Ausnahme.* The exception proves the rule.
  ⊡ period ◊ *Meine Regel ist ausgeblieben.* I've missed a period.
**regelmäßig** ADJECTIVE, ADVERB
  regular ◊ *in regelmäßigen Abständen* at regular intervals ◊ *Die Busse verkehren regelmäßig.* The buses run regularly.
die **Regelmäßigkeit** NOUN
  regularity
**regeln** VERB
  ⊡ to direct ◊ *Ein Polizist regelte den Verkehr.* A policeman was directing the traffic.
  ⊡ to control ◊ *die Lautstärke regeln* to control the volume
  ⊡ to settle ◊ *Ich habe da noch eine Sache mit ihm zu regeln.* I've still got something to settle with him.
  ⊡ to arrange ◊ *Wir haben das so geregelt, dass er abwäscht und ich putze.* We've arranged things so that he washes the dishes and I do the cleaning.
  ✦ **sich von selbst regeln** to take care of itself
der **Regen** NOUN (PL die **Regen**)
  rain
der **Regenbogen** NOUN (PL die **Regenbogen**)
  rainbow
der **Regenmantel** NOUN (PL die **Regenmäntel**)
  raincoat
der **Regenschauer** NOUN (PL die **Regenschauer**)
  shower
der **Regenschirm** NOUN (PL die **Regenschirme**)
  umbrella
der **Regenwurm** NOUN (PL die **Regenwürmer**)
  earthworm
**regieren** VERB (PERFECT **hat regiert**)
  ⊡ to govern ◊ *Wer regiert zur Zeit Russland?* Who governs Russia nowadays?
  ⊡ to reign ◊ *Wann hat Elisabeth die Erste regiert?* When did Elizabeth the First reign?
die **Regierung** NOUN
  ⊡ government ◊ *die deutsche Regierung* the German government
  ⊡ reign ◊ *England unter der Regierung von Elisabeth der Zweiten* England during the reign of Elizabeth the Second
**regnen** VERB
  to rain ◊ *Es regnet.* It's raining.

**regnerisch** ADJECTIVE
rainy

das **Reh** NOUN (PL die **Rehe**)
deer

**reiben** VERB (IMPERFECT **rieb,** PERFECT **hat gerieben**)
[1] to rub ◊ *Warum reibst du dir die Augen?* Why are you rubbing your eyes?
[2] to grate ◊ *Er rieb Käse über die Kartoffeln.* He grated cheese over the potatoes.

die **Reibung** NOUN
friction

das **Reich** NOUN (PL die **Reiche**)
see also **reich** ADJECTIVE
[1] empire ◊ *Das Reich Hadrians erstreckte sich bis Schottland.* Hadrian's empire reached as far as Scotland.
[2] kingdom ◊ *das Reich der Tiere* the animal kingdom
♦ **das Dritte Reich** the Third Reich

**reich** ADJECTIVE
see also **das Reich** NOUN
rich

**reichen** VERB
[1] to be enough ◊ *Der Kuchen wird nicht für alle reichen.* There won't be enough cake for everybody.
[2] to give ◊ *Sie reichte mir die Hand.* She gave me her hand.
♦ **jemandem etwas reichen** to pass somebody something ◊ *Kannst du mir bitte die Butter reichen?* Can you pass me the butter, please?
♦ **Nur ein Salat reicht ihm nicht.** A salad won't be enough for him.
♦ **Das Gehalt reicht ihr nicht, sie will mehr.** She can't get by on her salary, she wants more.
♦ **Mir reicht's!** I've had enough.
♦ **Unser Garten reicht bis zum Fluss.** Our garden goes right down to the river.

**reif** ADJECTIVE
[1] ripe ◊ *Die Äpfel sind noch nicht reif.* The apples aren't ripe yet.
[2] mature ◊ *Für sein Alter ist er schon sehr reif.* He's very mature for his age.

der **Reifen** NOUN (PL die **Reifen**)
[1] tyre ◊ *Mir ist ein Reifen geplatzt.* I've got a burst tyre.
[2] hoop ◊ *ein Hula-Hoop-Reifen* a hula hoop

der **Reifendruck** NOUN
tyre pressure

die **Reifenpanne** NOUN
puncture

die **Reihe** NOUN
row ◊ *Stellt euch in einer Reihe auf.* Stand in a row. ◊ *Wir saßen in der zweiten Reihe.* We sat in the second row.
♦ **Eine ganze Reihe von Menschen ist abergläubisch.** A whole lot of people are superstitious.

♦ **der Reihe nach** in turn
♦ **Er ist an der Reihe.** It's his turn.
♦ **an die Reihe kommen** to have one's turn

die **Reihenfolge** NOUN
order ◊ *alphabetische Reihenfolge* alphabetical order

das **Reihenhaus** NOUN (GEN des **Reihenhauses,** PL die **Reihenhäuser**)
terraced house

**rein** ADJECTIVE, ADVERB
[1] pure ◊ *Das ist reines Gold.* That's pure gold. ◊ *reine Seide* pure silk
[2] clean ◊ *Damit wird die Wäsche rein.* This will get the washing clean. ◊ *reine Luft* clean air ◊ *reine Haut* clear skin
[3] sheer ◊ *Das ist der reine Wahnsinn.* That's sheer madness. ◊ *Das ist das reinste Vergnügen.* It's sheer pleasure.
[4] purely ◊ *Rein technisch ist das machbar.* From a purely technical point of view it's feasible.
♦ **rein gar nichts** absolutely nothing
♦ **etwas ins Reine schreiben** to make a fair copy of something
♦ **etwas ins Reine bringen** to clear something up
[5] in ◊ *Deckel auf und rein mit dem Müll.* Off with the lid and in with the rubbish. ◊ *Los rein mit dir, Zeit fürs Bett!* Come on, in you come, it's time for bed.

der **Reinfall** NOUN (PL die **Reinfälle**)
let-down

die **Reinheit** NOUN
purity ◊ *die Reinheit des Biers* the purity of beer
♦ **Für die Reinheit Ihrer Wäsche ...** To get your washing really clean ...

**reinigen** VERB
to clean

die **Reinigung** NOUN
[1] cleaning ◊ *ein Mittel zur Reinigung der Polster* an cleaning agent for upholstery
[2] cleaner's ◊ *Bring bitte meine Hose in die Reinigung.* Please take my trousers to the cleaner's.
♦ **chemische Reinigung (1)** dry cleaning ◊ *Bei diesem Stoff empfehlen wir eine chemische Reinigung.* We recommend dry cleaning for this material.
♦ **chemische Reinigung (2)** dry cleaner's ◊ *Im Einkaufszentrum gibt es auch eine chemische Reinigung.* There's also a dry cleaner's in the shopping mall.

der **Reis** NOUN (GEN des **Reises**)
rice

die **Reise** NOUN
journey ◊ *Auf meiner letzten Reise durch Ägypten habe ich viel gesehen.* I saw a lot on my last journey through Egypt.
♦ **Reisen** travels ◊ *Auf seinen Reisen hat er viel erlebt.* He has experienced a lot on his travels.

**R**

☞

♦ **Gute Reise!** Have a good journey.

das **Reiseandenken** NOUN (PL die **Reiseandenken**)
souvenir

das **Reisebüro** NOUN (PL die **Reisebüros**)
travel agency

der **Reisebus** NOUN (GEN des **Reisebusses**, PL die **Reisebusse**)
coach

der **Reiseführer** NOUN (PL die **Reiseführer**)
[1] guidebook ◊ *Ich habe einen Reiseführer für Griechenland gekauft.* I've bought a guidebook to Greece.
[2] travel guide ◊ *Unser Reiseführer hat uns alles erklärt.* Our travel guide explained everything to us.

der **Reiseleiter** NOUN (PL die **Reiseleiter**)
courier

**reisen** VERB (PERFECT **ist gereist**)
to travel ◊ *Ich reise gern.* I like travelling.
♦ **reisen nach** to go to ◊ *In den Sommerferien wollen wir nach Griechenland reisen.* We want to go to Greece in the summer holidays.

der **Reisende** NOUN (GEN des/der **Reisenden**, PL
die die **Reisenden**)
traveller ◊ *Ein Reisender hatte sich verirrt.* A traveller has got lost.

der **Reisepass** NOUN (GEN des **Reisepasses**, PL die **Reisepässe**)
passport

der **Reisecheck** NOUN (PL die **Reiseschecks**)
traveller's cheque

das **Reiseziel** NOUN (PL die **Reiseziele**)
destination

**reißen** VERB (IMPERFECT **riss**, PERFECT **hat/ist gerissen**)

*Use **haben** to form the perfect tense. Use **sein** to form the perfect tense for **to break**.*

[1] to tear ◊ *Er riss ihren Brief in tausend Stücke.* He tore her letter into a thousand pieces. ◊ *Sie riss sich die Kleider vom Leib.* She tore her clothes off.
[2] to break ◊ *Das Seil ist gerissen.* The rope has broken.
[3] to snatch ◊ *Er hat mir den Geldbeutel aus der Hand gerissen.* He snatched my purse from my hand.
[4] to drag ◊ *Sie hat ihn zu Boden gerissen.* She dragged him to the floor.
[5] to wrench ◊ *Er riss das Steuer nach links.* He wrenched the steering wheel to the left.
[6] to tug ◊ *Er riss an der Leine.* He tugged on the rope.
♦ **Witze reißen** to crack jokes
♦ **etwas an sich reißen** to seize something ◊ *Er hat versucht, die Macht an sich zu reißen.* He tried to seize power.
♦ **Ich habe das Kind in letzter Minute an mich gerissen.** I pulled the child towards me in the nick of time.

♦ **sich um etwas reißen** to scramble for something ◊ *Die Kinder haben sich um die Luftballons gerissen.* The children scrambled for the balloons.

der **Reißnagel** NOUN (PL die **Reißnägel**)
drawing pin

der **Reißverschluss** NOUN (GEN des **Reißverschlusses**, PL die **Reißverschlüsse**)
zip

**reiten** VERB (IMPERFECT **ritt**, PERFECT **ist geritten**)
to ride

der **Reiter** NOUN (PL die **Reiter**)
rider

die **Reitschule** NOUN
riding school

der **Reiz** NOUN (GEN des **Reizes**, PL die **Reize**)
[1] charm ◊ *der Reiz dieser Stadt* the charm of this town ◊ *Er war von ihren Reizen ganz begeistert.* He was quite taken with her charms.
[2] appeal ◊ *der Reiz der Großstadt* appeal of the big city

**reizbar** ADJECTIVE
irritable

**reizen** VERB
[1] to appeal to ◊ *Diese Arbeit reizt mich sehr.* The work greatly appeals to me. ◊ *Es würde mich reizen, mal nach Kreta zu fahren.* The idea of going to Crete appeals to me.
[2] to annoy ◊ *Du musst den Hund nicht reizen.* Don't annoy the dog.
[3] to irritate ◊ *Der Rauch reizt die Augen.* Smoke irritates the eyes.

**reizend** ADJECTIVE
charming

**reizvoll** ADJECTIVE
attractive

die **Reklame** NOUN
[1] advertising ◊ *Im Fernsehen gibt es viel zu viel Reklame.* There's far too much advertising on television.
[2] advertisement ◊ *zehn Seiten Reklame* ten pages of advertisements

der **Rekord** NOUN (PL die **Rekorde**)
record ◊ *Der Rekord liegt bei zehn Metern.* The record is ten metres. ◊ *einen neuen Rekord aufstellen* to set a new record

der **Rektor** NOUN (PL die **Rektoren**)
[1] headteacher ◊ *Der Rektor ist bei uns für die Stundenpläne zuständig.* At our school, the headteacher's in charge of timetables.
[2] vice-chancellor ◊ *Zu Semesterbeginn hält der Rektor eine Rede.* At the beginning of term the vice-chancellor gives a speech.

das **Rektorat** NOUN (PL die **Rektorate**)
headteacher's office ◊ *Franz, du sollst aufs Rektorat kommen.* Franz, you're to go to the headteacher's office.

**relativ** ADVERB
relatively ◊ *Das ist relativ einfach.* That's relatively easy.

**relaxt** ADJECTIVE
relaxed

die **Religion** NOUN
religion

die **Religionslehre** NOUN
religious education

**religiös** ADJECTIVE
religious

das **Rendezvous** NOUN (GEN des **Rendezvous**, PL die **Rendezvous**)
date ◊ *Sie hatte gestern Abend ein Rendezvous mit Michael.* She had a date with Michael last night.

das **Rennen** NOUN (PL die **Rennen**)
> see also **rennen** VERB

race ◊ *ein Pferderennen* a horse race ◊ *ein Autorennen* a motor race

**rennen** VERB (IMPERFECT **rannte**, PERFECT **ist gerannt**)
> see also **das Rennen** NOUN

to run

der **Rennfahrer** NOUN (PL die **Rennfahrer**)
racing driver

das **Rennpferd** NOUN (PL die **Rennpferde**)
racehorse

der **Rennwagen** NOUN (PL die **Rennwagen**)
racing car

**renovieren** VERB (PERFECT **hat renoviert**)
to renovate

**rentabel** ADJECTIVE
[1] lucrative ◊ *eine rentable Arbeit* a lucrative job
[2] profitable ◊ *Das wäre nicht rentabel.* That wouldn't be profitable.

die **Rentabilität** NOUN
profitability

die **Rente** NOUN
pension
♦ **in Rente gehen** to retire
*Be careful! Rente does not mean rent.*

sich **rentieren** VERB (PERFECT **hat sich rentiert**)
to be profitable ◊ *Das Geschäft rentiert sich nicht mehr.* The business is no longer profitable.
♦ **Das hat sich rentiert.** That was worthwhile.

der **Rentner** NOUN (PL die **Rentner**)
pensioner

die **Reparatur** NOUN
repair

die **Reparaturwerkstatt** NOUN (PL die **Reparaturwerkstätten**)
garage (*repair shop*)

**reparieren** VERB (PERFECT **hat repariert**)
to repair

die **Reportage** NOUN
[1] report ◊ *Ich habe eine Reportage über die Zustände in Rumänien gelesen.* I read a report about conditions in Romania.
[2] live commentary ◊ *Hast du im Radio die Reportage des Europapokalspiels gehört?* Did you hear the live commentary on the European cup game on the radio?

der **Reporter** NOUN (PL die **Reporter**)
reporter

das **Reptil** NOUN (PL die **Reptilien**)
reptile

die **Republik** NOUN
republic

**republikanisch** ADJECTIVE
republican

das **Reservat** NOUN (PL die **Reservate**)
reservation

die **Reserve** NOUN
reserve

das **Reserverad** NOUN (PL die **Reserveräder**)
spare wheel

**reservieren** VERB (PERFECT **hat reserviert**)
to reserve ◊ *Ich habe einen Tisch für heute Abend reservieren lassen.* I've reserved a table for this evening.

die **Reservierung** NOUN
reservation

der **Respekt** NOUN
respect

**respektieren** VERB (PERFECT **hat respektiert**)
to respect

**respektlos** ADJECTIVE
disrespectful

**respektvoll** ADJECTIVE
respectful

der **Rest** NOUN (PL die **Reste**)
[1] rest ◊ *Den Rest bezahle ich später.* I'll pay the rest later. ◊ *Die meisten sind früher gegangen, der Rest hat noch lange gefeiert.* Most left early, but the rest carried on celebrating for a long time.
[2] left-over ◊ *Heute gab's die Reste von gestern.* Today we had yesterday's left-overs.
♦ **die Reste** the remains ◊ *Das sind die Reste der alten Stadtmauer.* These are the remains of the old town walls.

das **Restaurant** NOUN (PL die **Restaurants**)
restaurant

**restaurieren** VERB (PERFECT **hat restauriert**)
to restore

**restlich** ADJECTIVE
remaining

das **Resultat** NOUN (PL die **Resultate**)
result

**retten** VERB
to rescue

der **Rettich** NOUN (PL die **Rettiche**)
radish

die **Rettung** NOUN
[1] rescue ◊ *Alle zeigten bei der Rettung großen Mut.* They all showed great courage during the rescue.

**R**

☞

2 salvation ◊ *Das war meine Rettung.*
That was my salvation.

3 hope ◊ *seine letzte Rettung* his last
hope

das **Rettungsboot** NOUN (PL die
**Rettungsboote**)
lifeboat

der **Rettungsdienst** NOUN (PL die
**Rettungsdienste**)
rescue service

der **Rettungsring** NOUN (PL die **Rettungsringe**)
lifebelt

der **Rettungswagen** NOUN (PL die
**Rettungswagen**)
ambulance

die **Reue** NOUN
remorse ◊ *Der Täter zeigt keine Reue.*
The culprit doesn't show any remorse.

das **Revier** NOUN (PL die **Reviere**)
1 police station ◊ *Der Polizist nahm ihn
mit aufs Revier.* The policeman took him
to the police station.
2 territory ◊ *Das männliche Tier
verteidigt sein Revier.* The male animal
defends his territory.

die **Revolution** NOUN
revolution ◊ *die Revolution von 1789* the
revolution of 1789

der **Revolver** NOUN (PL die **Revolver**)
revolver

das **Rezept** NOUN (PL die **Rezepte**)
1 recipe ◊ *Kannst du mir mal das
Rezept von deinem Käsekuchen geben?*
Can you give me your cheesecake
recipe?
2 prescription ◊ *Dieses Medikament
bekommt man nur auf Rezept.* You
can only get this medicine on
prescription.

die **Rezeption** NOUN
reception

**rezeptpflichtig** ADJECTIVE
available only on prescription
♦ **rezeptpflichtige Medikamente**
prescribed drugs

das **R-Gespräch** NOUN (PL die **R-Gespräche**)
reverse charge call

der **Rhabarber** NOUN
rhubarb

der **Rhein** NOUN
Rhine

ⓘ *The Rhine is 1320 km long and the
entire 865 km which flows through
Germany is navigable, making it an
important inland waterway. It flows
past such important cities as Karlsruhe,
Mannheim, Ludwigshafen, Mainz,
Cologne, Düsseldorf and Duisburg.*

**Rheinland-Pfalz** NEUT NOUN
Rhineland-Palatinate

ⓘ *Rheinland-Pfalz is one of the 16
Länder. Its capital is Mainz. It is home
to the BASF chemicals giant and to
Germany's biggest television network,
ZDF (Channel 2).*

das **Rheuma** NOUN
rheumatism ◊ *Meine Oma hat Rheuma.*
My granny's got rheumatism.

der **Rhythmus** NOUN (GEN des **Rhythmus**, PL die
**Rhythmen**)
rhythm

**richten** VERB
1 to point ◊ *Er richtete das Fernrohr
zum Himmel.* He pointed the telescope at
the sky.
♦ **eine Waffe auf jemanden richten** to aim
a weapon at somebody
2 to prepare ◊ *Er hatte das Mittagessen
schon gerichtet.* He had already prepared
lunch.
♦ **etwas an jemanden richten** to address
something to somebody ◊ *Der Brief war
an meine Eltern gerichtet.* The letter was
addressed to my parents.
♦ **Ich richte mich ganz nach dir.** I'll do
whatever you want.
♦ **sich nach etwas richten (1)** to conform to
something ◊ *Auch du solltest dich
danach richten, wie wir das hier machen.*
You should conform to our way of doing
things.
♦ **sich nach etwas richten (2)** to be
determined by something ◊ *Das Angebot
richtet sich nach der Nachfrage.* Supply
is determined by demand.

der **Richter** NOUN (PL die **Richter**)
judge

**richtig** ADJECTIVE, ADVERB
1 right ◊ *Wir müssen den richtigen
Zeitpunkt abwarten.* We must wait for
the right moment. ◊ *Es war nicht richtig
von dir, ihn zu belügen.* It wasn't right of
you to lie to him.
♦ **Bin ich hier richtig?** Have I come to the
right place?
♦ **der Richtige** the right person
♦ **das Richtige** the right thing
2 correctly ◊ *Du hast das nicht richtig
geschrieben.* You haven't written that
correctly.
3 proper ◊ *Ich will ein richtiges
Motorrad und kein Moped.* I want a
proper motorbike, not a moped.
4 really ◊ *Wir waren richtig froh, als es
vorbei war.* We were really glad when it
was over.

die **Richtung** NOUN
direction ◊ *Wir gehen in die falsche
Richtung.* We are going in the wrong
direction. ◊ *in östlicher Richtung* in an
easterly direction

**rieb** VERB *see* **reiben**

**riechen** VERB (IMPERFECT **roch**, PERFECT **hat gerochen**)
to smell ◊ *Ich rieche Gas.* I can smell gas. ◊ *Das riecht gut.* That smells good. ◊ *Ich kann nichts riechen.* I can't smell anything.
♦ **an etwas riechen** to smell something ◊ *Sie roch an der Rose.* She smelled the rose.
♦ **nach etwas riechen** to smell of something ◊ *Hier riecht es nach Benzin.* It smells of petrol here.
♦ **Ich kann ihn nicht riechen.** I can't stand him.

**rief** VERB *see* **rufen**

der **Riegel** NOUN (PL die **Riegel**)
[1] bolt ◊ *Sie schob den Riegel vor die Tür.* She bolted the door.
[2] bar ◊ *Für unterwegs haben wir einen Schokoriegel mitgenommen.* We've brought a bar of chocolate to eat on the way.

der **Riese** NOUN (GEN des **Riesen,** PL die **Riesen**)
giant

der **Riesenerfolg** NOUN (PL die **Riesenerfolge**)
enormous success

**riesengroß** ADJECTIVE
gigantic

das **Riesenrad** NOUN (PL die **Riesenräder**)
big wheel ◊ *mit dem Riesenrad fahren* to go on the big wheel

**riesig** ADJECTIVE
huge

**riet** VERB *see* **raten**

die **Rille** NOUN
groove

das **Rind** NOUN (PL die **Rinder**)
[1] (*male*)
ox
[2] (*female*)
cow
♦ **Rinder** cattle ◊ *Seine Rinder sind im Sommer auf der Weide.* His cattle spend the summer on the meadow.
[3] beef ◊ *Wir essen kaum noch Rind.* We hardly eat beef any more.

die **Rinde** NOUN
[1] rind ◊ *Er schnitt die Rinde vom Käse ab.* He cut the rind off the cheese.
[2] crust ◊ *frisches Brot mit knuspriger Rinde* fresh crusty bread
[3] bark ◊ *Er ritzte ihren Namen in die Rinde einer Eiche.* He carved her name into the bark of an oak tree.

das **Rindfleisch** NOUN
beef

der **Ring** NOUN (PL die **Ringe**)
ring

das **Ringbuch** NOUN (PL die **Ringbücher**)
ring binder

das **Ringen** NOUN
wrestling ◊ *Ringen ist sein Hobby.* His hobby is wrestling.

der **Ringkampf** NOUN (PL die **Ringkämpfe**)
wrestling bout

der **Ringrichter** NOUN (PL die **Ringrichter**)
referee

**ringsum** ADVERB
all around ◊ *Wir sahen ringsum Menschen.* We saw people all around. ◊ *Er blickte ringsum.* He looked all around.

die **Rippe** NOUN
rib

das **Risiko** NOUN (PL die **Risiken**)
risk

**riskant** ADJECTIVE
risky

**riskieren** VERB (PERFECT **hat riskiert**)
to risk

der **Riss** NOUN (GEN des **Risses,** PL die **Risse**)
[1] crack ◊ *Die Maus verschwand durch einen Riss in der Mauer.* The mouse disappeared into a crack in the wall. ◊ *Der trockene Boden war voller Risse.* The dry soil was full of cracks.
[2] tear ◊ *Er hatte einen Riss in der Hose.* There was a tear in his trousers.

**rissig** ADJECTIVE
[1] cracked ◊ *Von der Trockenheit ist die Erde rissig geworden.* The soil is cracked as a result of the drought.
[2] chapped ◊ *Vom vielen Waschen hat sie ganz rissige Hände.* Her hands are all chapped from doing so much washing.

**ritt** VERB *see* **reiten**

der **Ritter** NOUN (PL die **Ritter**)
knight

der **Rivale** NOUN (GEN des **Rivalen,** PL die **Rivalen**)
rival

die **Robbe** NOUN
seal ◊ *ein Robbenbaby* a seal pup

der **Roboter** NOUN (PL die **Roboter**)
robot

**roch** VERB *see* **riechen**

der **Rock** NOUN (PL die **Röcke**)
skirt

der **Roggen** NOUN
rye

**roh** ADJECTIVE
[1] raw ◊ *rohes Fleisch* raw meat ◊ *Karotten esse ich am liebsten roh.* I like carrots best raw.
[2] callous ◊ *Sei nicht so roh.* Don't be so callous.
[3] rough ◊ *Er hat sie ziemlich roh mit sich gezogen.* He dragged her off pretty roughly.

das **Rohr** NOUN (PL die **Rohre**)
[1] pipe ◊ *Das Abwasser wird durch Rohre in die Kanalisation geleitet.* Sewage is fed into the sewer via pipes.

**R**

☞

2 cane ◊ *ein Stuhl aus Rohr* a cane chair
3 reeds ◊ *In dem Teich wuchs Rohr.* Reeds were growing in the pond.

der **Rohstoff** NOUN (PL die **Rohstoffe**)
raw material

der **Rolladen** NOUN *see* **Rollladen**

das **Rollbrett** NOUN (PL die **Rollbretter**)
skateboard

die **Rolle** NOUN
1 role ◊ *Der Schauspieler hat die Rolle des Königs gut gespielt.* The actor was good in the role of the king. ◊ *Die Rolle der Frau hat sich geändert.* The role of women has changed.
2 castor ◊ *ein Stuhl mit Rollen* a chair with castors
3 roll ◊ *eine Rolle Toilettenpapier* a roll of toilet paper
4 reel ◊ *Sie hat den Faden von der Rolle abgewickelt.* She unwound the thread from the reel.
♦ **keine Rolle spielen** not to matter ◊ *Das Wetter spielt keine Rolle.* The weather doesn't matter.
♦ **eine wichtige Rolle spielen bei** to play a major role in ◊ *Er hat bei der Planung des Abschlussfestes eine wichtige Rolle gespielt.* He played a major role in organizing the end-of-term party.

**rollen** VERB (PERFECT **hat/ist gerollt**)
*For the perfect tense use **haben** when the verb has an object and **sein** when there is no object.*
to roll ◊ *Sie haben den Stein den Berg hinuntergerollt.* They rolled the stone down the hill. ◊ *Der Ball ist direkt vor ein Auto gerollt.* The ball rolled right in front of a car.

der **Roller** NOUN (PL die **Roller**)
scooter

der **Rollkragen** NOUN (PL die **Rollkragen**)
polo neck

der **Rollladen** NOUN (PL die **Rollläden**)
shutter

der **Rollschuh** NOUN (PL die **Rollschuhe**)
roller skate

der **Rollstuhl** NOUN (PL die **Rollstühle**)
wheelchair

die **Rolltreppe** NOUN
escalator

**Rom** NEUT NOUN
Rome
♦ **nach Rom** to Rome

der **Roman** NOUN (PL die **Romane**)
novel

**romantisch** ADJECTIVE
romantic

**römisch** ADJECTIVE
Roman

**röntgen** VERB
to X-ray

**rosa** ADJECTIVE

pink ◊ *Sie hatte ein rosa Kleid an.* She was wearing a pink dress.

die **Rose** NOUN
rose

der **Rosenkohl** NOUN
Brussels sprouts ◊ *Rosenkohl ist mein Lieblingsgemüse.* Brussels sprouts are my favourite vegetable.

der **Rosenmontag** NOUN (PL die **Rosenmontage**)
Monday before Shrove Tuesday

> ℹ **Rosenmontag** *is an important day in the carnival festivities. Cities such as Cologne, Düsseldorf and Mainz traditionally have long processions with carnival floats on* **Rosenmontag**.

die **Rosine** NOUN
raisin

der **Rosmarin** NOUN
rosemary

die **Rosskastanie** NOUN
horse chestnut

der **Rost** NOUN (PL die **Roste**)
rust ◊ *An diesem Auto ist viel Rost.* This car has a lot of rust on it.
♦ **ein Bratrost** a grill

**rosten** VERB (PERFECT **ist gerostet**)
to rust

**rösten** VERB
1 to roast ◊ *geröstete Erdnüsse* roasted peanuts
2 to toast ◊ *Brot rösten* to toast bread
3 to grill ◊ *Würstchen auf dem Grill rösten* to grill sausages

**rostig** ADJECTIVE
rusty

**rot** ADJECTIVE
red ◊ *Sein Gesicht wurde immer röter.* His face got redder and redder.
♦ **in den roten Zahlen** in the red
♦ **das Rote Meer** the Red Sea

die **Röteln** PL NOUN
German measles ◊ *Röteln sind für schwangere Frauen gefährlich.* German measles is dangerous for pregnant women.

**rothaarig** ADJECTIVE
red-haired

der **Rotkohl** NOUN
red cabbage

der **Rotwein** NOUN (PL die **Rotweine**)
red wine

die **Roulade** NOUN
beef olive

die **Route** NOUN
route

der **Rowdy** NOUN (PL die **Rowdys**)
hooligan

die **Rübe** NOUN

beet ◊ *Der Bauer füttert die Kühe mit Rüben.* The farmer feeds his cows on beet.
◆ **Gelbe Rübe** carrot
◆ **Rote Rübe** beetroot
**rüber** ADVERB
over ◊ *Komm hier rüber, da siehst du besser.* Come over here, you'll get a better view. ◊ *Ich geh mal zu den Nachbarn rüber.* I'm just going over to our neighbours.
der **Rücken** NOUN (PL die **Rücken**)
| see also **rücken** VERB |
back ◊ *Er schläft auf dem Rücken.* He sleeps on his back.
**rücken** VERB (PERFECT **ist/hat gerückt**)
| see also **der Rücken** NOUN |
*For the perfect tense use **haben** when the verb has an object and **sein** when there is no object.*
[1] to move over ◊ *Rück mal ein bisschen.* Move over a bit.
[2] to shift ◊ *Sie rückten den Schrank zur Seite.* They shifted the cupboard to one side.
das **Rückenmark** NOUN
spinal cord
die **Rückenschmerzen** PL NOUN
backache
das **Rückenschwimmen** NOUN
backstroke
die **Rückfahrkarte** NOUN
return ticket
die **Rückfahrt** NOUN
return journey
der **Rückflug** NOUN (PL die **Rückflüge**)
return flight
die **Rückgabe** NOUN
return
**rückgängig** ADJECTIVE
◆ **etwas rückgängig machen** to cancel something
das **Rückgrat** NOUN (PL die **Rückgrate**)
spine
die **Rückkehr** NOUN
return ◊ *bei unserer Rückkehr* on our return
das **Rücklicht** NOUN (PL die **Rücklichter**)
rear light
die **Rückreise** NOUN
return journey
der **Rucksack** NOUN (PL die **Rucksäcke**)
rucksack
die **Rücksicht** NOUN
consideration
◆ **auf jemanden Rücksicht nehmen** to show consideration for somebody ◊ *Du solltest mehr Rücksicht auf deine Mitschüler nehmen.* You should show more consideration for your fellow pupils.
**rücksichtslos** ADJECTIVE

inconsiderate
◆ **ein rücksichtsloser Fahrer** a reckless driver
**rücksichtsvoll** ADJECTIVE
considerate
der **Rücksitz** NOUN (PL die **Rücksitze**)
back seat ◊ *Dieser Sportwagen hat keine Rücksitze.* This sports car has no back seats.
◆ **Kinder sollten auf dem Rücksitz mitfahren.** Children should travel in the back.
der **Rückspiegel** NOUN (PL die **Rückspiegel**)
rear-view mirror
das **Rückspiel** NOUN (PL die **Rückspiele**)
return match
der **Rücktritt** NOUN (PL die **Rücktritte**)
resignation
**rückwärts** ADVERB
backwards ◊ *rückwärts zählen* to count backwards
◆ **rückwärts fahren** to reverse ◊ *Er fuhr rückwärts in die Garage.* He reversed into the garage.
der **Rückwärtsgang** NOUN (PL die **Rückwärtsgänge**)
reverse gear
der **Rückweg** NOUN (PL die **Rückwege**)
way back
das **Ruder** NOUN (PL die **Ruder**)
[1] oar ◊ *ein Boot mit zwei Rudern* a boat with two oars
[2] rudder ◊ *Der Steuermann steht am Ruder.* The helmsman stands at the rudder.
das **Ruderboot** NOUN (PL die **Ruderboote**)
rowing boat
**rudern** VERB (PERFECT **hat/ist gerudert**)
*Use **haben** for the perfect tense when you describe the activity and **sein** when you describe the motion.*
to row ◊ *Zuerst hat er gerudert, dann sie.* First he rowed, then she did. ◊ *Wir sind über den See gerudert.* We rowed across the lake.
der **Ruf** NOUN (PL die **Rufe**)
[1] shout ◊ *Wir hörten seine Rufe.* We heard his shouts.
[2] reputation ◊ *Das schadet seinem Ruf.* This will damage his reputation.
**rufen** VERB (IMPERFECT **rief**, PERFECT **hat gerufen**)
[1] to call out ◊ *Ich habe gerufen, es hat mich aber niemand gehört.* I called out, but nobody heard me.
◆ **Der Patient rief nach der Schwester.** The patient called for the nurse.
[2] to call ◊ *Wir sollten den Arzt rufen.* We ought to call the doctor. ◊ *Sie hat mir ein Taxi gerufen.* She called me a taxi.
[3] to shout ◊ *Sie rief um Hilfe.* She shouted for help.
die **Rufnummer** NOUN
telephone number

**R**

die **Ruhe** NOUN

> ⃞1 rest ◊ *Nach den anstrengenden Tagen brauche ich etwas Ruhe.* After the strain of the last few days I need a rest.
>
> ⃞2 peace ◊ *Jetzt kann ich in Ruhe arbeiten.* Now I can work in peace.
>
> ⃞3 peace and quiet ◊ *Die Kinder sind weg, ich genieße die Ruhe.* The children are out and I'm enjoying the peace and quiet.
>
> ✦ **in aller Ruhe** calmly
>
> ✦ **jemanden aus der Ruhe bringen** to unsettle somebody ◊ *Dieser Anruf hat mich aus der Ruhe gebracht.* The phone call unsettled me.
>
> ⃞4 silence ◊ *Ich bitte um etwas mehr Ruhe.* I would ask you for a bit more silence.
>
> ✦ **Ruhe!** Silence!
>
> ✦ **jemanden in Ruhe lassen** to leave somebody alone ◊ *Lass endlich deine Schwester in Ruhe.* Will you leave your sister alone!
>
> ✦ **sich zur Ruhe setzen** to retire

der **Ruhestand** NOUN

> retirement
>
> ✦ **Mein Vater ist im Ruhestand.** My father has retired.

die **Ruhestörung** NOUN

> breach of the peace

der **Ruhetag** NOUN

> day off ◊ *einen Ruhetag einlegen* to have a day off
>
> ✦ **"Mittwochs Ruhetag"** "closed on Wednesdays"

**ruhig** ADJECTIVE, ADVERB

> ⃞1 quiet ◊ *Im Haus war alles ruhig.* The house was completely quiet. ◊ *Die Kinder haben ruhig gespielt.* The children played quietly. ◊ *Seid endlich ruhig!* Will you be quiet!
>
> ⃞2 still ◊ *Bleib ruhig stehen, dann tut dir der Hund nichts.* If you keep still the dog won't hurt you.
>
> ✦ **eine ruhige Hand** a steady hand
>
> ⃞3 calm ◊ *Wie kannst du so ruhig bleiben?* How can you stay so calm? ◊ *Ich bin ganz ruhig in die Prüfung gegangen.* I went quite calmly into the exam.
>
> ✦ **ein ruhiges Gewissen** a clear conscience
>
> ✦ **Kommen Sie ruhig herein!** Come on in.

der **Ruhm** NOUN

> fame

das **Rührei** NOUN (PL die **Rühreier**)

> scrambled eggs

**rühren** VERB

> ⃞1 to stir ◊ *Sie rührte mit dem Löffel in der Soße.* She stirred the sauce with the spoon.
>
> ⃞2 to move ◊ *Ich kann meine Beine nicht rühren.* I can't move my legs.

> ✦ **sich rühren** to move ◊ *Sie hatte so Angst, dass sie sich nicht rührte.* She was so afraid that she didn't move.
>
> ✦ **jemanden rühren** to move somebody ◊ *Die Armut der Kinder hat uns gerührt.* The children's poverty moved us.
>
> ✦ **rühren an (1)** to touch ◊ *Rühr nicht an den Draht, da ist Strom drauf.* Don't touch the wire, it's live.
>
> ✦ **rühren an (2)** to bring up ◊ *An dieses Thema solltest du nicht rühren.* You shouldn't bring this subject up.

**rührend** ADJECTIVE

> touching ◊ *eine rührende Geschichte* a touching story ◊ *Er ist rührend naiv.* He's touchingly naive.

die **Ruine** NOUN

> ruin

**ruinieren** VERB (PERFECT **hat ruiniert**)

> to ruin

**rülpsen** VERB

> to belch

der **Rumäne** NOUN (GEN des **Rumänen**, PL die **Rumänen**)

> Romanian

**Rumänien** NEUT NOUN

> Romania
>
> ✦ **aus Rumänien** from Romania
>
> ✦ **nach Rumänien** to Romania

die **Rumänin** NOUN

> Romanian

**rumänisch** ADJECTIVE

> Romanian

der **Rummel** NOUN

> ⃞1 hullabaloo ◊ *Das war vielleicht ein Rummel in der Stadt.* There was quite a hullabaloo in town.
>
> ⃞2 fair ◊ *Wir sind auf dem Rummel Karussell gefahren.* We went on a roundabout at the fair.

der **Rummelplatz** NOUN (GEN des **Rummelplatzes**, PL die **Rummelplätze**)

> fairground

**rund** ADJECTIVE, ADVERB

> ⃞1 round ◊ *Sie hat ein rundes Gesicht.* She's got a round face.
>
> ⃞2 about ◊ *Das kostet rund hundert Mark.* It costs about a hundred marks.
>
> ✦ **rund um etwas** around something

die **Runde** NOUN

> ⃞1 lap ◊ *Das Auto fuhr ein paar Runden.* The car drove a few laps.
>
> ⃞2 round ◊ *Diese Runde zahle ich.* I'll get this round.

---

> ❶ It isn't usual to buy rounds in Germany. Normally people just order what they want from the waiter, and pay when they leave. You can, however, buy a round (**eine Runde schmeißen**) if you're feeling generous.

3 lap ◊ *Er liegt in der letzten Runde in Führung.* He's in the lead on the last lap.

4 party ◊ *Wir waren eine fröhliche Runde.* We were a merry party.

die **Rundfahrt** NOUN
round trip

der **Rundfunk** NOUN
broadcasting
♦ **im Rundfunk** on the radio

**runter** ADVERB
1 off ◊ *Runter vom Tisch!* Get off the table!
2 down ◊ *Dann ging's den Berg runter.* Then off we went down the mountain.

**runterladen** VERB (PRESENT **lädt runter,** IMPERFECT **lud runter,** PERFECT **hat runtergeladen)**
to download (*computer*) ◊ *eine Datei runterladen* to download a file

der **Ruß** NOUN (GEN des **Rußes**)
soot

der **Russe** NOUN (GEN des **Russen,** PL die **Russen**)
Russian

der **Rüssel** NOUN (PL die **Rüssel**)
1 snout ◊ *der Rüssel eines Schweins* a pig's snout
2 trunk ◊ *der Rüssel eines Elefanten* an elephant's trunk

**rußig** ADJECTIVE

sooty

die **Russin** NOUN
Russian

**russisch** ADJECTIVE
Russian

**Russland** NEUT NOUN
Russia
♦ **aus Russland** from Russia
♦ **nach Russland** to Russia

die **Rüstung** NOUN
1 suit of armour ◊ *In der Burg standen ein paar rostige Rüstungen.* There were a couple of rusty suits of armour in the castle.
2 armaments ◊ *Es wird viel Geld für Rüstung ausgegeben.* A lot of money is spent on armaments.

die **Rutschbahn** NOUN
slide

**rutschen** VERB (PERFECT **ist gerutscht**)
1 to slip ◊ *Sie ist auf dem Eis gerutscht und hingefallen.* She slipped and fell on the ice. ◊ *Der Teller ist mir aus der Hand gerutscht.* The plate slipped out of my hand.
2 to move over ◊ *Rutsch mal ein bisschen!* Move over a bit.

**rutschig** ADJECTIVE
slippery

**R**

# S

der **Saal** NOUN (PL die **Säle**)
 hall
das **Saarland** NOUN
 Saarland

> ⓘ The **Saarland** is one of the 16
> **Länder**. Its capital is Saarbrücken.
> While its coal and steel industries have
> been in crisis, it still has flourishing
> ceramics and glass industries.

die **Sache** NOUN
 [1] thing ◇ Räum bitte deine Sachen weg.
 Please put your things away. ◇ Pack
 warme Sachen ein. Pack warm things.
 [2] matter ◇ Wir sollten diese Sache
 ausdiskutieren. We should discuss this
 matter fully. ◇ Die Polizei wird dieser
 Sache nachgehen. The police will
 investigate this affair.
 [3] job ◇ Es ist deine Sache, dich darum
 zu kümmern. It's your job to see to it.
 ✦ **Mach keine Sachen!** Don't be silly!
 ✦ **Was machst du denn für Sachen?** The
 things you do!
 ✦ **zur Sache** to the point ◇ Komm endlich
 zur Sache! Get to the point!

**sachlich** ADJECTIVE
 [1] objective ◇ ein sehr sachlicher Bericht
 a very objective report ◇ Du solltest
 sachlich bleiben. You should remain
 objective.
 [2] factual ◇ Was er sagt, ist sachlich
 falsch. What he says is factually
 inaccurate.

**sächlich** ADJECTIVE
 neuter
**Sachsen** NEUT NOUN
 Saxony

> ⓘ **Sachsen** is one of the 16 **Länder**. Its
> capital is Dresden. Its largest city,
> Leipzig, is famous for its industrial fair
> and was one of the main centres of the
> peaceful revolt against the DDR
> regime.

**Sachsen-Anhalt** NEUT NOUN
 Saxony-Anhalt

> ⓘ **Sachsen-Anhalt** is one of the 16
> **Länder**. Its capital is Magdeburg. It has
> a rich cultural past: Martin Luther and
> Georg Friedrich Händel were born
> here, and the Bauhaus school of
> architecture was situated in Dessau.

**sächsisch** ADJECTIVE
 Saxon

**sachte** ADVERB
 softly
der **Sack** NOUN (PL die **Säcke**)
 sack
die **Sackgasse** NOUN
 cul-de-sac
der **Saft** NOUN (PL die **Säfte**)
 juice
**saftig** ADJECTIVE
 juicy
die **Säge** NOUN
 saw
**sagen** VERB
 [1] to say ◇ Ich kann noch nicht sagen, ob
 ich komme. I can't say yet if I'll come.
 ◇ Habe ich etwas Falsches gesagt? Have I
 said something wrong? ◇ Wie sagt man
 "danke" auf Japanisch? How do you say
 "thank you" in Japanese? ◇ Was sagst du
 zu meinem Vorschlag? What do you say
 to my suggestion? ◇ Sie sagt, sie habe
 das nicht gewusst. She says that she
 didn't know that.
 ✦ **Man sagt, dass ...** It's said that ...
 [2] to tell ◇ Kannst du ihm bitte sagen, er
 soll seine Eltern anrufen. Can you tell
 him to call his parents. ◇ Ich werde es ihr
 sagen. I'll tell her. ◇ Sag ihm, er solle das
 nicht tun. Tell him he shouldn't do it.
 ◇ sagen Sie ihm, dass ... tell him that ...
 ✦ **etwas zu jemandem sagen** to call
 somebody something ◇ Die Kinder sagen
 Onja zu mir. The children call me Onja.
 ✦ **zu sagen haben** to have a say ◇ Du hast
 hier nichts zu sagen. You don't have a
 say in this matter.
 ✦ **Es hat nichts zu sagen, dass er sich noch
 nicht gemeldet hat.** The fact that he
 hasn't called doesn't mean anything.

**sägen** VERB
 to saw
**sagenhaft** ADJECTIVE
 [1] legendary ◇ der sagenhafte König
 Artus the legendary King Arthur
 [2] terrific ◇ Das war ein sagenhaftes
 Glück. That was terrific luck.

**sah** VERB see **sehen**
die **Sahne** NOUN
 cream
die **Saison** NOUN (PL die **Saisons**)
 season
die **Saite** NOUN
 string
das **Saiteninstrument** NOUN (PL die
 **Saiteninstrumente**)
 stringed instrument
der **Sakko** NOUN (PL die **Sakkos**)
 jacket

der **Salat** NOUN (PL die **Salate**)
    **1** salad ◊ *Es gab verschiedene Salate.*
There were various salads.
    **2** lettuce ◊ *Am liebsten mag ich grünen Salat.* I like lettuce best.

die **Salatsoße** NOUN
    salad dressing

die **Salbe** NOUN
    ointment

der **Salbei** NOUN (GEN des **Salbeis**)
    sage

das **Salz** NOUN (GEN des **Salzes**)
    salt

**salzen** VERB (PERFECT **hat gesalzen**)
    to salt

**salzig** ADJECTIVE
    salty

die **Salzkartoffeln** FEM PL NOUN
    boiled potatoes

die **Salzstange** NOUN
    pretzel stick

das **Salzwasser** NOUN
    salt water

der **Samen** NOUN (PL die **Samen**)
    seed ◊ *Hast du die Blumensamen schon ausgesät?* Have you sown the flower seeds yet?

**sammeln** VERB
    **1** to collect ◊ *Er sammelt Briefmarken.* He collects stamps. ◊ *Sie sammeln für ein Waisenhaus.* They're collecting for an orphanage. ◊ *Altpapier wird gesammelt und wieder verwertet.* Waste paper is collected and recycled.
    **2** to gather ◊ *Wir haben Pilze gesammelt.* We gathered mushrooms.

die **Sammlung** NOUN
    collection

der **Samstag** NOUN (PL die **Samstage**)
    Saturday ◊ *am Samstag* on Saturday

**samstags** ADVERB
    on Saturdays

der **Samt** NOUN (PL die **Samte**)
    see also **samt** PREPOSITION
    velvet

**samt** PREPOSITION
    see also **der Samt** NOUN
    *The preposition* **samt** *takes the dative.*
    with ◊ *Sie kamen samt Kindern und Hund.* They came with their children and dog.

der **Sand** NOUN
    sand

die **Sandale** NOUN
    sandal

die **Sandburg** NOUN
    sand castle

**sandig** ADJECTIVE
    sandy

der **Sandkasten** NOUN (PL die **Sandkästen**)
    sandpit

der **Sandstein** NOUN (PL die **Sandsteine**)

    sandstone

**sandstrahlen** VERB
    to sandblast ◊ *Die Gebäude wurden alle gesandstrahlt.* All the buildings were sandblasted.

der **Sandstrand** NOUN (PL die **Sandstrände**)
    sandy beach

**sandte** VERB *see* **senden**

**sanft** ADJECTIVE
    gentle ◊ *etwas sanft berühren* to touch something gently

**sang** VERB *see* **singen**

der **Sänger** NOUN (PL die **Sänger**)
    singer

die **Sängerin** NOUN
    singer

die **Sardelle** NOUN
    anchovy

die **Sardine** NOUN
    sardine

der **Sarg** NOUN (PL die **Särge**)
    coffin

der **Sarkasmus** NOUN (GEN des **Sarkasmus,** PL die **Sarkasmen**)
    sarcasm

**saß** VERB *see* **sitzen**

der **Satellit** NOUN (GEN des **Satelliten,** PL die **Satelliten**)
    satellite

das **Satellitenfernsehen** NOUN
    satellite television

**satt** ADJECTIVE
    full ◊ *Ich bin satt.* I'm full.
    ♦ **Wir sind nicht satt geworden.** We didn't get enough to eat.
    ♦ **sich satt essen** to eat one's fill
    ♦ **satt machen** to be filling
    ♦ **satte Farben** rich colours ◊ *ein sattes Rot* a rich red
    ♦ **jemanden satt sein** to be fed up with somebody
    ♦ **etwas satt haben** to be fed up with something

der **Sattel** NOUN (PL die **Sättel**)
    saddle

der **Satz** NOUN (GEN des **Satzes,** PL die **Sätze**)
    **1** sentence ◊ *Bitte antworte mit einem ganzen Satz.* Please answer in a complete sentence.
    ♦ **ein Nebensatz** a subordinate clause
    ♦ **ein Adverbialsatz** an adverbial clause
    **2** theorem ◊ *der Satz des Pythagoras* Pythagoras' theorem
    **3** set ◊ *Becker hat den ersten Satz verloren.* Becker lost the first set. ◊ *ein Satz Schraubenschlüssel* a set of screwdrivers
    **4** rate ◊ *Die Krankenversicherung hat ihre Sätze erhöht.* The health insurance has increased its rates.

das **Satzzeichen** NOUN (PL die **Satzzeichen**)
    punctuation mark

**S**

**sauber** ADJECTIVE
[1] clean ◊ *Die Wäsche ist nicht sauber geworden.* The washing hasn't come up clean.
[2] fine ◊ *Du bist mir ein sauberer Freund!* You're a fine friend!
♦ **sauber machen** to clean

die **Sauberkeit** NOUN
cleanness

die **Sauce** NOUN
sauce

**sauer** ADJECTIVE
[1] sour ◊ *Der Apfel ist sauer.* The apple is sour. ◊ *Die Milch ist sauer geworden.* The milk has turned sour.
[2] acid ◊ *saurer Regen* acid rain
[3] cross ◊ *Ich bin sauer auf meine Freundin.* I'm cross with my girlfriend.

der **Sauerbraten** NOUN (PL die **Sauerbraten**)
marinated beef

die **Sauerei** NOUN
[1] scandal ◊ *Es ist eine Sauerei, dass wir länger arbeiten müssen.* It's a scandal that we have to work longer hours.
[2] mess ◊ *Wer hat denn die Sauerei im Bad gemacht?* Who made the mess in the bathroom?
[3] obscenity ◊ *Über solche Sauereien kann ich nicht lachen.* I can't laugh at such obscenities.

das **Sauerkraut** NOUN
sauerkraut (*pickled cabbage*)

der **Sauerstoff** NOUN
oxygen

**saufen** VERB (PRESENT **säuft**, IMPERFECT **soff**, PERFECT **hat gesoffen**)
to booze

**saugen** VERB (IMPERFECT **saugte** or **sog**, PERFECT **hat gesaugt** or **gesogen**)
to suck

das **Säugetier** NOUN (PL die **Säugetiere**)
mammal

der **Säugling** NOUN (PL die **Säuglinge**)
infant

die **Säule** NOUN
column

die **Sauna** NOUN (PL die **Saunas**)
sauna

die **Säure** NOUN
acid ◊ *Die Säure hat den Stein zerfressen.* The acid has eaten away at the stone.

das **Saxofon** NOUN (PL die **Saxofone**)
*see* **Saxophon**

das **Saxophon** NOUN (PL die **Saxophone**)
saxophone ◊ *Er spielt Saxophon.* He plays the saxophone.

die **S-Bahn** NOUN
suburban railway

die **SB-Tankstelle** NOUN
self-service petrol station

das **Schach** NOUN
chess ◊ *Ich kann kein Schach spielen.* I can't play chess.

das **Schachbrett** NOUN (PL die **Schachbretter**)
chessboard

die **Schachfigur** NOUN
chessman

die **Schachtel** NOUN
box

**schade** ADJECTIVE, EXCLAMATION
a pity ◊ *Es ist schade um das gute Essen.* It's a pity to waste good food. ◊ *Das ist aber schade.* That's a pity.
♦ **Wie schade!** What a pity! ◊ *Wie schade, dass du nicht mitkommen kannst.* What a pity you can't come.
♦ **für etwas zu schade sein** to be too good for something ◊ *Diese Decke ist doch zu schade für ein Picknick.* This blanket is too good for a picnic.
♦ **sich zu schade sein für etwas** to consider oneself too good for something ◊ *Du bist dir für so eine Arbeit wohl zu schade?* So you consider yourself too good for a job like that?

der **Schädel** NOUN (PL die **Schädel**)
skull

der **Schaden** NOUN (PL die **Schäden**)
  *see also* **schaden** VERB
[1] damage ◊ *Der Schaden an seinem Auto war nicht so groß.* The damage to his car wasn't too bad.
[2] injury ◊ *Sie hat den Unfall ohne Schaden überstanden.* She came out of the accident without injury.
[3] disadvantage ◊ *Es soll dein Schaden nicht sein.* It won't be to your disadvantage.

**schaden** VERB
  *see also* **der Schaden** NOUN
♦ **jemandem schaden** to harm somebody ◊ *Ich habe den Eindruck, dass sie mir schaden will.* I've got the feeling that she wants to harm me.
♦ **einer Sache schaden** to damage something ◊ *Das hat unserem Ruf geschadet.* That's damaged our reputation.
♦ **es kann nicht schaden ...** it can't do any harm ... ◊ *Es kann nicht schaden, wenn du die Vokabeln noch einmal wiederholst.* It can't do any harm for you to go over the vocabulary once more.

der **Schadenersatz** NOUN (GEN des **Schadenersatzes**)
compensation

**schädigen** VERB (PERFECT **hat geschädigt**)
to damage

**schädlich** ADJECTIVE
harmful ◊ *Rauchen ist schädlich.* Smoking is harmful. ◊ *Alkohol ist für die Leber schädlich.* Alcohol is harmful to your liver.

der **Schadstoff** NOUN (PL die **Schadstoffe**)
harmful substance

das **Schaf** NOUN (PL die **Schafe**)
sheep (PL ◊ *zehn Schafe* ten sheep

der **Schäferhund** NOUN (PL die **Schäferhunde**)
Alsatian

**schaffen (1)** VERB (IMPERFECT **schuf,** PERFECT
**hat geschaffen)**
to create ◊ *Die Regierung will neue
Arbeitsplätze schaffen.* The government
wants to create new jobs.

**schaffen (2)** VERB (IMPERFECT **schaffte,** PERFECT
**hat geschafft)**
to manage ◊ *Die Übersetzung schaffe
ich heute noch.* I'll manage that
translation today. ◊ *Er schafft das nicht
allein.* He won't manage to do that on his
own.
♦ **Wir haben den Zug gerade noch
geschafft.** We just managed to catch the
train.
♦ **eine Prüfung schaffen** to pass an exam
♦ **Ich bin geschafft!** I'm shattered!

der **Schal** NOUN (PL die **Schale** *or* **Schals**)
scarf

die **Schale** NOUN
[1] skin ◊ *eine Bananenschale* a banana
skin
[2] peel ◊ *die Kartoffelschalen* the potato
peel ◊ *eine Zitronenschale* lemon peel
[3] shell ◊ *Die Nussschalen nicht in den
Kompost werfen.* Don't throw the
nutshells onto the compost heap. ◊ *Diese
Eier haben sehr dünne Schalen.* These
eggs have very thin shells.
[4] bowl ◊ *Auf dem Tisch stand eine
Schale mit Obst.* There was a bowl of
fruit on the table.

**schälen** VERB
[1] to peel ◊ *einen Apfel schälen* to peel
an apple
[2] to shell ◊ *Nüsse schälen* to shell nuts
♦ **sich schälen** to peel ◊ *Ich schäle mich auf
der Nase.* My nose is peeling.

der **Schall** NOUN
sound

der **Schalldämpfer** NOUN (PL die
**Schalldämpfer**)
silencer

die **Schallmauer** NOUN
sound barrier

die **Schallplatte** NOUN
record

**schalten** VERB
[1] to switch ◊ *den Herd auf "aus"
schalten* to switch the cooker to "off"
[2] to change gear ◊ *Du solltest schalten.*
You should change gear.
♦ **in den vierten Gang schalten** to change
into fourth
[3] to catch on ◊ *Ich habe zu spät
geschaltet.* I caught on too late.

der **Schalter** NOUN (PL die **Schalter**)

[1] counter ◊ *Zahlen Sie bitte am Schalter
dort drüben.* Please pay at the counter
over there.
[2] switch ◊ *Wo ist der Lichtschalter?*
Where is the light switch?

das **Schaltjahr** NOUN (PL die **Schaltjahre**)
leap year

sich **schämen** VERB
to be ashamed ◊ *sich einer Sache
schämen* to be ashamed of something

die **Schande** NOUN
disgrace

**scharf** ADJECTIVE
[1] sharp ◊ *ein scharfes Messer* a sharp
knife ◊ *eine scharfe Kurve* a sharp corner
♦ **ein scharfer Wind** a biting wind
[2] hot ◊ *Indisches Essen ist schärfer als
deutsches.* Indian food is hotter than
German food.
♦ **scharfe Munition** live ammunition
♦ **scharf schießen** to shoot with live
ammunition
♦ **scharf nachdenken** to think hard
♦ **auf etwas scharf sein** to be mad about
something ◊ *Er ist ganz scharf auf
Gummibärchen.* He is mad about jelly
bears.
♦ **auf jemanden scharf sein** to fancy
somebody ◊ *Ich glaube, Manfred ist
scharf auf dich.* I think Manfred fancies
you.

der **Schaschlik** NOUN (PL die **Schaschliks**)
*You can also say das Schaschlik.*
kebab

der **Schatten** NOUN (PL die **Schatten**)
shadow
♦ **Wir saßen im Schatten.** We sat in the
shade.

**schattig** ADJECTIVE
shady

der **Schatz** NOUN (GEN des **Schatzes,** PL die
**Schätze**)
[1] treasure ◊ *der Schatz der Piraten* the
pirates' treasure
[2] darling ◊ *Du bist ein Schatz!* You're a
darling! ◊ *Mein Schatz.* My darling.

das **Schätzchen** NOUN (PL die **Schätzchen**)
darling

**schätzen** VERB
[1] to guess ◊ *Schätz mal, wie viel das
gekostet hat.* Guess how much that cost.
♦ **Man kann sein Alter schlecht schätzen.**
It's difficult to tell how old he is.
[2] to value ◊ *Ich werde die alte Uhr
schätzen lassen.* I'm going to have the
old clock valued.
[3] to appreciate ◊ *Ich schätze deine Hilfe
sehr.* I really appreciate your help.

das **Schaubild** NOUN (PL die **Schaubilder**)
diagram

**schauen** VERB
to look ◊ *Schau mal an die Tafel.* Look at
the board.

**S**

der **Schauer** NOUN (PL die **Schauer**)

[1] shower ◊ *Für morgen sind Schauer angesagt.* Showers are forecast for tomorrow.

[2] shudder ◊ *Ein Schauer überlief sie.* A shudder ran through her body.

die **Schaufel** NOUN

shovel

das **Schaufenster** NOUN (PL die **Schaufenster**)

shop window

der **Schaufensterbummel** NOUN (PL die **Schaufensterbummel**)

window shopping

die **Schaukel** NOUN

swing

**schaukeln** VERB

to swing

der **Schaumgummi** NOUN

foam rubber

das **Schauspiel** NOUN

play (*theatre*)

der **Schauspieler** NOUN (PL die **Schauspieler**)

actor

die **Schauspielerin** NOUN

actress

der **Scheck** NOUN (PL die **Schecks**)

cheque

das **Scheckbuch** NOUN (PL die **Scheckbücher**)

chequebook

das **Scheckheft** NOUN (PL die **Scheckhefte**)

cheque book

die **Scheckkarte** NOUN

cheque card

die **Scheibe** NOUN

slice ◊ *Sie belegte das Brot mit mehreren Scheiben Wurst.* She put several slices of cold meat on the bread.

der **Scheibenwischer** NOUN (PL die **Scheibenwischer**)

windscreen wiper

**scheiden** VERB (IMPERFECT **schied**, PERFECT **hat geschieden**)

♦ **sich scheiden lassen** to get a divorce

♦ **geschieden sein** to be divorced

die **Scheidung** NOUN

divorce

der **Schein** NOUN (PL die **Scheine**)

[1] light ◊ *beim Schein einer Kerze* by the light of a candle

[2] appearance ◊ *Der Schein trügt.* Appearances are deceptive.

[3] note ◊ *Er hat in großen Scheinen bezahlt.* He paid in large notes.

[4] certificate ◊ *Am Ende des Semesters bekommt man einen Schein.* You get a certificate at the end of the semester.

♦ **etwas zum Schein tun** to pretend to do something ◊ *Er ging zum Schein auf den Vorschlag ein.* He pretended to go along with the suggestion.

**scheinbar** ADVERB

apparently

**scheinen** VERB (IMPERFECT **schien**, PERFECT **hat geschienen**)

[1] to shine ◊ *Die Sonne scheint.* The sun is shining.

[2] to seem ◊ *Sie scheint glücklich zu sein.* She seems to be happy.

der **Scheinwerfer** NOUN (PL die **Scheinwerfer**)

[1] headlamp ◊ *Die Scheinwerfer des entgegenkommenden Autos haben mich geblendet.* The headlamps of the approaching car blinded me.

[2] floodlight ◊ *Die Scheinwerfer beleuchteten das Stadion.* The floodlights lit the stadium.

[3] spotlight ◊ *Das Gemälde wird von einem Scheinwerfer angestrahlt.* The painting is lit up by a spotlight.

die **Scheiße** NOUN

shit

**scheitern** VERB (PERFECT **ist gescheitert**)

to fail

der **Schenkel** NOUN (PL die **Schenkel**)

thigh

**schenken** VERB

[1] to give ◊ *Was haben dir deine Eltern zum Geburtstag geschenkt?* What did your parents give you for your birthday? ◊ *Das habe ich geschenkt bekommen.* I was given it as a present.

[2] to pour ◊ *Sie schenkte ihm noch etwas Rotwein ins Glas.* She poured some more red wine into his glass.

♦ **sich etwas schenken** to skip something ◊ *Die Geigenstunde werde ich mir heute schenken.* I'm going to skip my violin lesson today.

♦ **Das ist geschenkt! (1)** That's a giveaway!

♦ **Das ist geschenkt! (2)** That's worthless!

die **Scherbe** NOUN

piece ◊ *eine Glasscherbe* a piece of glass

die **Schere** NOUN

[1] scissors ◊ *eine Schere* a pair of scissors

[2] shears ◊ *Wo ist die Schere, um die Hecke zu schneiden?* Where are the shears for cutting the hedge?

**scheren (1)** VERB (IMPERFECT **schor**, PERFECT **hat geschoren**)

♦ **Schafe scheren** to shear sheep

**scheren (2)** VERB (IMPERFECT **scherte**, PERFECT **hat geschert**)

to bother ◊ *Es schert mich wenig, was die Leute sagen.* It doesn't really bother me what people say.

♦ **sich um etwas scheren** to care about something ◊ *Sie schert sich nicht um die Spielregeln.* She doesn't care about the rules.

♦ **Scher dich um deine eigenen Angelegenheiten.** Mind your own business!

♦ **Scher dich zum Teufel!** Go to hell!

der **Scherz** NOUN (GEN des **Scherzes**, PL die **Scherze**)
joke ◊ *Das war doch nur ein Scherz!* It was only a joke.
♦ **zum Scherz** for fun

**scheußlich** ADJECTIVE
dreadful ◊ *Das Wetter war scheußlich.* The weather was dreadful.
♦ **Das tut scheußlich weh.** It hurts dreadfully.

der **Schi** NOUN (PL die **Schi** or **Schier**)
ski

die **Schicht** NOUN
[1] layer ◊ *Auf dem Weg lag eine Schicht Sand.* There was a layer of sand on the path.
[2] class ◊ *soziale Schichten* social classes
[3] shift ◊ *Mein Vater arbeitet Schicht.* My father works shifts.

**schick** ADJECTIVE
stylish ◊ *ein schicker Hosenanzug* a stylish trouser suit
♦ **schick angezogen** stylishly dressed

**schicken** VERB
to send ◊ *Ich habe ihr ein Päckchen geschickt.* I've sent her a parcel. ◊ *Sie hat ihren Sohn zum Bäcker geschickt.* She sent her son to the baker's.

das **Schicksal** NOUN
fate

**schieben** VERB (IMPERFECT **schob**, PERFECT **hat geschoben**)
to push ◊ *Wir mussten das Auto schieben.* We had to push the car. ◊ *Könnt ihr mal schieben?* Could you lot push?
♦ **die Schuld auf jemanden schieben** to put the blame on somebody

der **Schiedsrichter** NOUN (PL die **Schiedsrichter**)
[1] referee ◊ *Der Schiedsrichter pfiff das Spiel an.* The referee blew the whistle to start the game.
[2] umpire ◊ *Bei einem Tennisspiel sagt der Schiedsrichter den Spielstand an.* In a tennis match the umpire gives the score.

**schief** ADJECTIVE, ADVERB
crooked ◊ *Die Wände des Hauses sind schief.* The walls of the house are crooked.
♦ **Das Bild hängt schief.** The picture isn't hanging straight.
♦ **der Schiefe Turm von Pisa** the Leaning Tower of Pisa
♦ **ein schiefer Blick** a funny look
♦ **Er hatte seinen Hut schief aufgesetzt.** He was wearing his hat at an angle.
♦ **schief gehen** to go wrong

**schielen** VERB
to squint

**schien** VERB see **scheinen**

die **Schiene** NOUN
[1] rail ◊ *Die Schienen sind verrostet.* The rails have rusted.
[2] splint ◊ *Sie hatte den Arm in einer Schiene.* She had her arm in a splint.

**schießen** VERB (IMPERFECT **schoss**, PERFECT **hat geschossen**)
[1] to shoot ◊ *Nicht schießen!* Don't shoot! ◊ *Er hat ein Kaninchen geschossen.* He shot a rabbit. ◊ *Er hat auf einen Polizisten geschossen.* He shot at a policeman.
[2] to kick ◊ *Sie schoss den Ball ins Tor.* She kicked the ball into the goal.

das **Schiff** NOUN (PL die **Schiffe**)
ship

die **Schifffahrt** NOUN
shipping

der **Schikoree** NOUN
chicory

das **Schild** NOUN (PL die **Schilder**)
sign ◊ *Das ist eine Einbahnstraße, hast du das Schild nicht gesehen?* This is a one-way street, didn't you see the sign?
♦ **ein Namensschild** a nameplate

die **Schildkröte** NOUN
[1] tortoise
[2] turtle

der **Schilling** NOUN (PL die **Schillinge** or **Schilling**)
schilling ◊ *Das kostet hundert Schilling.* It costs a hundred schillings. ◊ *Ich muss noch Schillinge besorgen.* I still have to get some schillings.

der **Schimmel** NOUN (PL die **Schimmel**)
[1] mould ◊ *Auf dem Käse ist Schimmel.* There's mould on the cheese.
[2] white horse ◊ *Sie ritt auf einem Schimmel.* She rode a white horse.

**schimmelig** ADJECTIVE
mouldy

**schimmeln** VERB
to go mouldy

der **Schimpanse** NOUN (GEN des **Schimpansen**, PL die **Schimpansen**)
chimpanzee

**schimpfen** VERB
to scold ◊ *Hat deine Mutter geschimpft?* Did your mother scold you?
♦ **auf jemanden schimpfen** to curse somebody ◊ *Schüler schimpfen gern auf ihre Lehrer.* Pupils like cursing their teachers.
♦ **über etwas schimpfen** to complain about something ◊ *Meine Kinder schimpfen über zu viel Hausaufgaben.* My children complain about having too much homework.

das **Schimpfwort** NOUN (PL die **Schimpfwörter**)
term of abuse

der **Schinken** NOUN (PL die **Schinken**)
ham

**S**

der **Schirm** NOUN (PL die **Schirme**)
umbrella ◊ *Nimm einen Schirm mit!*
Take an umbrella!
- **der Sonnenschirm** the sunshade
- **eine Mütze mit Schirm** a peaked cap

die **Schlacht** NOUN
battle

**schlachten** VERB
to slaughter

der **Schlachter** NOUN (PL die **Schlachter**)
butcher

das **Schlachtfeld** NOUN (PL die **Schlachtfelder**)
battlefield

der **Schlachthof** NOUN (PL die **Schlachthöfe**)
slaughterhouse

der **Schlaf** NOUN
sleep

der **Schlafanzug** NOUN (PL die **Schlafanzüge**)
pyjamas ◊ *ein Schlafanzug* a pair of
pyjamas

**schlafen** VERB (PRESENT **schläft**, IMPERFECT
**schlief**, PERFECT **hat geschlafen**)
to sleep ◊ *Hast du gut geschlafen?* Did
you sleep well? ◊ *Schlaf gut!* Sleep well.
- **schlafen gehen** to go to bed

**schlaff** ADJECTIVE
[1] drained ◊ *Ich bin total schlaff.* I'm
drained.
- **Bei der Hitze bin ich so schlaff.** The heat
really takes it out of me.
[2] exhausted ◊ *Nach der Gartenarbeit
war ich total schlaff.* I was completely
exhausted after working in the garden.
[3] slack ◊ *Das Seil ist zu schlaff.* The
rope is too slack.

**schlaflos** ADJECTIVE
sleepless

der **Schlafraum** NOUN (PL die **Schlafräume**)
dormitory

der **Schlafsaal** NOUN (PL die **Schlafsäle**)
dormitory

der **Schlafsack** NOUN (PL die **Schlafsäcke**)
sleeping bag

die **Schlaftablette** NOUN
sleeping pill

der **Schlafwagen** NOUN (PL die **Schlafwagen**)
sleeping car

das **Schlafzimmer** NOUN (PL die **Schlafzimmer**)
bedroom

der **Schlag** NOUN (PL die **Schläge**)
[1] blow ◊ *ein Schlag auf den Kopf* a
blow to the head ◊ *Ich bin durchgefallen,
das ist ein Schlag.* I've failed, that's a
blow.
[2] stroke ◊ *Mein Opa hat einen Schlag
gehabt und ist gelähmt.* My granddad's
had a stroke and he's now paralysed.
[3] shock ◊ *Fass nicht an den Draht, sonst
bekommst du einen Schlag.* Don't touch
that wire, otherwise you'll get a shock.
- **Er hat von seinem Vater Schläge
bekommen.** His father gave him a hiding.

- **mit einem Schlag** all at once

**schlagen** VERB (PRESENT **schlägt**, IMPERFECT
**schlug**, PERFECT **hat geschlagen**)
[1] to beat ◊ *Meine Eltern haben mich
noch nie geschlagen.* My parents have
never beaten me. ◊ *England hat Holland
vier zu eins geschlagen.* England beat
Holland four one. ◊ *Ihr Herz schlug
schneller.* Her heart beat faster.
- **Sahne schlagen** to whip cream
[2] to hit ◊ *Er schlug mit dem Hammer
auf den Nagel.* He hit the nail with the
hammer. ◊ *Sie schlug mit der Faust auf
den Tisch.* She hit the table with her fist.
- **Er schlägt den Nagel in die Wand.** He
hammers the nail into the wall.
- **Die Uhr schlägt zehn.** The clock strikes
ten.
- **Es hat eben zehn geschlagen.** It's just
struck ten.
- **nach jemandem schlagen** to take after
somebody ◊ *Sie schlägt nach ihrer
Mutter.* She takes after her mother.
- **sich gut schlagen** to do well ◊ *Er hat sich
in der Prüfung gut geschlagen.* He did
well in the exam.

der **Schlager** NOUN (PL die **Schlager**)
hit

der **Schläger** NOUN (PL die **Schläger**)
[1] thug ◊ *Franz ist ein Schläger.* Franz is
a thug.
[2] bat ◊ *Baseball und Tischtennis spielt
man mit einem Schläger.* You play
baseball and table tennis with a bat.
[3] racket ◊ *Für Tennis, Federball und
Squash braucht man einen Schläger.*
You need a racket for tennis, badminton
and squash.
- **ein Golfschläger** a golf club
- **ein Hockeyschläger** a hockey stick

die **Schlägerei** NOUN
fight

**schlagfertig** ADJECTIVE
quick-witted

die **Schlagsahne** NOUN
whipped cream

die **Schlagzeile** NOUN
headline

das **Schlagzeug** NOUN (PL die **Schlagzeuge**)
drums ◊ *Er spielt Schlagzeug.* He plays
the drums. ◊ *Am Schlagzeug: Freddy
Braun.* On drums: Freddy Braun.

der **Schlagzeuger** NOUN (PL die **Schlagzeuger**)
drummer

der **Schlamm** NOUN
mud

**schlampen** VERB
to be sloppy
- **Bei den Hausaufgaben hast du
geschlampt.** Your homework's sloppy.

die **Schlamperei** NOUN

[1] untidiness ◊ *Deine Schlamperei regt mich auf.* Your untidiness gets on my nerves.

[2] sloppy work ◊ *So eine Schlamperei kannst du doch nicht abgeben.* You can't possibly hand in such sloppy work.

**schlampig** ADJECTIVE
sloppy

die **Schlange** NOUN

[1] snake ◊ *eine giftige Schlange* a poisonous snake

[2] queue ◊ *Vor dem Kino stand eine lange Schlange.* There was a long queue outside the cinema.

◆ **Schlange stehen** to queue ◊ *Wir mussten für die Karten Schlange stehen.* We had to queue for the tickets.

**schlank** ADJECTIVE
slim ◊ *Sie ist sehr schlank.* She's very slim.

die **Schlankheitskur** NOUN
diet ◊ *eine Schlankheitskur machen* to be on a diet

**schlapp** ADJECTIVE
worn out ◊ *Ich fühle mich schlapp.* I feel worn out.

**schlau** ADJECTIVE
cunning

der **Schlauch** NOUN (PL die **Schläuche**)

[1] hose ◊ *Er hat den Garten mit dem Schlauch gespritzt.* He watered the garden with the hose.

[2] inner tube ◊ *Ich brauche einen neuen Schlauch für mein Fahrrad.* I need a new inner tube for my bike.

das **Schlauchboot** NOUN (PL die **Schlauchboote**)
rubber dinghy

**schlecht** ADJECTIVE, ADVERB

[1] bad ◊ *Er ist in Mathe schlecht.* He is bad at maths. ◊ *Meine Augen werden immer schlechter.* My eyes are getting worse.

◆ **ein schlechtes Gewissen** a guilty conscience

◆ **Die Milch ist schlecht geworden.** The milk's turned.

[2] badly ◊ *Ich habe schlecht geschlafen.* I slept badly.

◆ **schlecht gelaunt** in a bad mood

◆ **Mir ist schlecht.** I feel sick.

◆ **ein schlecht bezahlter Job** a poorly paid job

◆ **Ihm geht es schlecht.** He's in a bad way.

◆ **jemanden schlecht machen** to run somebody down ◊ *Du solltest ihn nicht dauernd schlecht machen.* You shouldn't constantly run him down.

**schleichen** VERB (IMPERFECT **schlich**, PERFECT **ist geschlichen**)
to creep

die **Schleife** NOUN

[1] loop ◊ *Der Fluss macht eine Schleife.* The river makes a loop.

[2] bow ◊ *Sie hatte eine Schleife im Haar.* She had a bow in her hair.

**Schleswig-Holstein** NEUT NOUN
Schleswig-Holstein

> ⓘ **Schleswig-Holstein** is one of the 16 **Länder**. Its capital is Kiel. It is Germany's northernmost state, bordered by the North Sea and the Baltic, and by Denmark in the north.

die **Schleuder** NOUN

[1] catapult ◊ *Er hat mit seiner Schleuder ein Fenster getroffen.* He hit a window with his catapult.

[2] spin-dryer ◊ *Tu die nassen Sachen in die Schleuder.* Put your wet things in the spin-dryer.

**schleudern** VERB (PERFECT **hat/ist geschleudert**)

*For the perfect tense use **haben** when the verb has an object and **sein** when there is no object.*

[1] to hurl ◊ *Sie hat das Buch in die Ecke geschleudert.* She hurled the book into the corner.

[2] to spin ◊ *Du solltest die nasse Wäsche schleudern.* You should spin the wet washing.

[3] to skid ◊ *Das Auto ist geschleudert.* The car skidded.

**schlief** VERB see **schlafen**

**schließen** VERB (IMPERFECT **schloss**, PERFECT **hat geschlossen**)
to shut ◊ *Schließ bitte das Fenster.* Please shut the window. ◊ *Wann schließen die Geschäfte?* When do the shops shut? ◊ *Sie hatte die Augen geschlossen.* She had her eyes shut. ◊ *Der Betrieb wurde geschlossen.* The company was shut down.

◆ **mit jemandem Freundschaft schließen** to make friends with somebody

◆ **etwas aus etwas schließen** to gather something from something ◊ *Aus dem, was er sagte, schließe ich, dass er nicht mitkommen will.* I gather from what he said that he doesn't want to come.

◆ **Schließ bitte nicht von dir auf andere.** Don't judge others by your own standards.

**schließlich** ADVERB
finally

◆ **schließlich doch** after all

**schlimm** ADJECTIVE
bad

**schlimmer** ADJECTIVE
worse

**schlimmste** ADJECTIVE
worst ◊ *mein schlimmster Feind* my worst enemy

**S**

**schlimmstenfalls** ADVERB
at the worst

der **Schlips** NOUN
tie (*necktie*)

der **Schlitten** NOUN (PL die **Schlitten**)
sledge ◊ *Im Winter sind wir viel Schlitten gefahren.* We went sledging a lot in the winter.

das **Schlittenfahren** NOUN
sledging

der **Schlittschuh** NOUN (PL die **Schlittschuhe**)
skate
♦ **Schlittschuh laufen** to skate

der **Schlitz** NOUN (GEN des **Schlitzes**, PL die **Schlitze**)
[1] slit ◊ *Der Rock hat hinten einen Schlitz.* The skirt has a slit at the back.
[2] slot ◊ *Du musst das Markstück in den Schlitz werfen.* You have to put the mark in the slot.
[3] flies ◊ *Der Schlitz an deiner Hose ist auf.* Your flies are open.

das **Schloss** NOUN (GEN des **Schlosses**, PL die **Schlösser**)
[1] lock ◊ *Sie steckte den Schlüssel ins Schloss.* She put the key in the lock.
[2] clasp ◊ *Kannst du mir bitte das Schloss an meiner Kette aufmachen?* Can you please open the clasp of my necklace?
[3] chateau ◊ *das Schloss in Versailles* the chateau of Versailles

**schloss** VERB see **schließen**

**schluchzen** VERB
to sob

der **Schluckauf** NOUN
hiccups ◊ *Er hatte einen Schluckauf.* He had hiccups.

**schlucken** VERB
to swallow

**schludern** VERB
to do sloppy work

**schlug** VERB see **schlagen**

der **Schluss** NOUN (GEN des **Schlusses**, PL die **Schlüsse**)
[1] end ◊ *am Schluss des Jahres* at the end of the year
♦ **Das Buch hat einen traurigen Schluss.** The book has a sad ending.
[2] conclusion ◊ *Ich habe meine Schlüsse gezogen.* I've drawn my conclusions.
♦ **zum Schluss** finally ◊ *Zum Schluss haben wir noch ein Lied gesungen.* Finally we sang a song.
♦ **Schluss machen** to finish ◊ *Wir sollten langsam Schluss machen.* We should be finishing now.
♦ **mit jemandem Schluss machen** to finish with somebody ◊ *Warum hast du mit Manfred Schluss gemacht?* Why did you finish with Manfred?

der **Schlüssel** NOUN (PL die **Schlüssel**)

key ◊ *Wo ist mein Fahrradschlüssel?* Where's the key for my bike? ◊ *der Schlüssel zum Erfolg* the key to success

das **Schlüsselbein** NOUN (PL die **Schlüsselbeine**)
collar bone

der **Schlüsselbund** NOUN (PL die **Schlüsselbunde**)
bunch of keys

der **Schlüsselring** NOUN (PL die **Schlüsselringe**)
keyring

der **Schlussverkauf** NOUN
sales ◊ *Dieses Kleid habe ich im Schlussverkauf bekommen.* I got this dress in the sales.

**schmal** ADJECTIVE
narrow ◊ *ein schmaler Durchgang* a narrow passageway
♦ **Sie hat ein schmales Gesicht.** She has a thin face.
♦ **Du bist schmäler geworden.** You've lost weight.
*Be careful!* **schmal** *does not mean* **small**.

**schmatzen** VERB
to eat noisily

**schmecken** VERB
to taste ◊ *Wie schmeckt eine Mango?* What does a mango taste like? ◊ *Das schmeckt gut.* That tastes good.
♦ **Es schmeckt ihm.** He likes it.

**schmeicheln** VERB
♦ **jemandem schmeicheln** to flatter somebody

**schmeißen** VERB (IMPERFECT **schmiss**, PERFECT **hat geschmissen**)
to throw

**schmelzen** VERB (PRESENT **schmilzt**, IMPERFECT **schmolz**, PERFECT **hat/ist geschmolzen**)
*For the perfect tense use* **haben** *when the verb has an object and* **sein** *when there is no object.*
to melt ◊ *Sie haben Schnee geschmolzen.* They melted snow. ◊ *Das Eis ist geschmolzen.* The ice has melted.

der **Schmerz** NOUN (GEN des **Schmerzes**, PL die **Schmerzen**)
[1] pain ◊ *ein stechender Schmerz in der Seite* a stabbing pain in the side
[2] grief ◊ *Sie verbarg ihren Schmerz über diesen Verlust.* She hid her grief over her loss.

**schmerzen** VERB (PERFECT **hat geschmerzt**)
to hurt

das **Schmerzmittel** NOUN (PL die **Schmerzmittel**)
painkiller

die **Schmerztablette** NOUN
painkiller

der **Schmetterling** NOUN (PL die **Schmetterlinge**)
butterfly

die **Schminke** NOUN
make-up
**schminken** VERB
to make up ◊ *Hast du dir die Augen geschminkt?* Have you made up your eyes?
♦ **Ich schminke mich selten.** I seldom use make-up.
**schmollen** VERB
to sulk
der **Schmuck** NOUN
1 jewellery ◊ *Sie trägt selten Schmuck.* She seldom wears jewellery.
2 decoration ◊ *bunte Kugeln als Schmuck für den Weihnachtsbaum* bright baubles as Christmas tree decorations
**schmücken** VERB
to decorate
**schmuggeln** VERB
to smuggle
**schmusen** VERB
to cuddle ◊ *Sie hat mit Felix geschmust.* She cuddled Felix.
der **Schmutz** NOUN (GEN des **Schmutzes**)
dirt
**schmutzig** ADJECTIVE
dirty
der **Schnabel** NOUN (PL die **Schnäbel**)
beak ◊ *Der Schnabel der Amsel ist gelb.* The blackbird's beak is yellow.
die **Schnalle** NOUN
buckle
der **Schnaps** NOUN (GEN des **Schnapses**, PL die **Schnäpse**)
schnapps
**schnarchen** VERB
to snore
**schnaufen** VERB
to puff
die **Schnauze** NOUN
1 nose ◊ *Der Hund hat eine kalte Schnauze.* The dog has a cold nose.
2 gob ◊ *Halt die Schnauze!* Shut your gob!
♦ **die Schnauze von etwas voll haben** to be fed up to the back teeth of something
sich **schnäuzen** VERB
to blow one's nose
die **Schnecke** NOUN
snail
♦ **eine Nacktschnecke** a slug
der **Schnee** NOUN
snow ◊ *Heute Nacht ist viel Schnee gefallen.* A lot of snow fell last night.
der **Schneeball** NOUN (PL die **Schneebälle**)
snowball
der **Schneemann** NOUN (PL die **Schneemänner**)
snowman
der **Schneepflug** NOUN (PL die **Schneepflüge**)
snowplough

**schneiden** VERB (IMPERFECT **schnitt**, PERFECT **hat geschnitten**)
to cut ◊ *Kannst du bitte Brot schneiden?* Can you cut some bread, please?
◊ *jemandem die Haare schneiden* to cut somebody's hair ◊ *Du solltest dir die Haare schneiden lassen.* You should have your hair cut.
♦ **sich schneiden (1)** to cut oneself ◊ *Ich habe mich geschnitten.* I've cut myself.
◊ *Ich habe mir in den Finger geschnitten.* I've cut my finger.
♦ **sich schneiden (2)** to intersect ◊ *Die beiden Geraden schneiden sich.* The two straight lines intersect.
**schneien** VERB
♦ **Es schneit.** It's snowing.
**schnell** ADJECTIVE, ADVERB
1 fast ◊ *Sie hat ein schnelles Auto.* She has a fast car. ◊ *Sie ist schnell gefahren.* She drove fast.
2 quickly ◊ *Ich rief schnell einen Krankenwagen.* I quickly phoned for an ambulance.
♦ **Ich gehe noch schnell bei meiner Freundin vorbei.** I'm just popping in to my girlfriend's.
die **Schnelligkeit** NOUN
speed
der **Schnellimbiss** NOUN (GEN des **Schnellimbisses**, PL die **Schnellimbisse**)
snack bar
**schnellstens** ADVERB
as quickly as possible
der **Schnellzug** NOUN (PL die **Schnellzüge**)
express train
sich **schneuzen** VERB *see* **schnäuzen**
der **Schnitt** NOUN (PL die **Schnitte**)
1 cut ◊ *Der Schnitt blutet.* The cut's bleeding. ◊ *Das Kleid hat einen eleganten Schnitt.* The dress has an elegant cut.
2 average ◊ *Ich habe im Zeugnis einen Schnitt von drei.* I've got an average of C in my report.
3 pattern ◊ *Hast du zu dem Rock einen Schnitt?* Have you got a pattern for this skirt?
**schnitt** VERB *see* **schneiden**
der **Schnittlauch** NOUN
chive
die **Schnittstelle** NOUN
interface
die **Schnittwunde** NOUN
cut
das **Schnitzel** NOUN (PL die **Schnitzel**)
escalope ◊ *Ich bestelle mir ein Schnitzel.* I'm going to order an escalope.
**schnitzen** VERB
to carve
der **Schnorchel** NOUN (PL die **Schnorchel**)
snorkel

**S**

**schnüffeln** VERB
to sniff

der **Schnuller** NOUN (PL die **Schnuller**)
dummy ◇ *Das Baby saugte am Schnuller.* The baby sucked the dummy.

der **Schnupfen** NOUN (PL die **Schnupfen**)
cold ◇ *Meine Schwester hat Schnupfen.* My sister has a cold.

die **Schnur** NOUN (PL die **Schnüre**)
[1] string ◇ *Du solltest eine Schnur um das Päckchen machen.* You should put string round the parcel.
[2] flex ◇ *Die Schnur von der Lampe ist zu kurz.* The flex of the lamp is too short.

der **Schnurrbart** NOUN (PL die **Schnurrbärte**)
moustache

**schnurren** VERB
to purr

der **Schnürsenkel** NOUN (PL die **Schnürsenkel**)
shoelace

der **Schock** NOUN (PL die **Schocks**)
shock

**schockieren** VERB (PERFECT **hat schockiert**)
to shock

die **Schokolade** NOUN
chocolate ◇ *eine heiße Schokolade* a hot chocolate

**schon** ADVERB
already ◇ *Ich bin schon fertig.* I've already finished.
◆ **Ist er schon da?** Is he there yet?
◆ **Warst du schon einmal da?** Have you ever been there?
◆ **Ich war schon einmal da.** I've been there before.
◆ **Das war schon immer so.** That's always been the case.
◆ **Hast du schon gehört?** Have you heard?
◆ **schon oft** often
◆ **schon der Gedanke** the very thought
◆ **Du wirst schon sehen.** You'll see.
◆ **Das wird schon noch gut.** That'll be OK.
◆ **ja schon, aber ...** yes, but ...
◆ **schon möglich** possible
◆ **Schon gut!** OK!
◆ **Du weißt schon.** You know.
◆ **Komm schon!** Come on!

**schön** ADJECTIVE
[1] beautiful ◇ *Sie haben ein schönes Haus.* They have a beautiful house.
[2] nice ◇ *Es waren schöne Ferien.* The holidays were nice. ◇ *Schönes Wochenende!* Have a nice weekend.
◆ **Schöne Grüße an deine Eltern!** Regards to your parents.
◆ **Sie ist ganz schön frech.** She's pretty damn cheeky.
◆ **na schön** very well ◇ *Na schön, dann geht halt spielen.* Very well then, go and play.

**schonend** ADJECTIVE, ADVERB
gentle ◇ *jemandem etwas schonend beibringen* to break something gently to somebody

die **Schönheit** NOUN
beauty

sich **schönmachen** VERB (PERFECT **hat sich schöngemacht**)
to make oneself look nice

**schöpfen** VERB
to ladle ◇ *Sie schöpfte Suppe in die Teller.* She ladled soup into the plates.
◆ **Luft schöpfen** to get some air

die **Schöpfung** NOUN
creation

der **Schornstein** NOUN (PL die **Schornsteine**)
chimney

**schoss** VERB *see* **schießen**

der **Schotte** NOUN (GEN des **Schotten**, PL die **Schotten**)
Scot
◆ **Er ist Schotte.** He's Scottish.

die **Schottin** NOUN
Scot
◆ **Sie ist Schottin.** She's Scottish.

**schottisch** ADJECTIVE
Scottish

**Schottland** NEUT NOUN
Scotland
◆ **aus Schottland** from Scotland
◆ **in Schottland** in Scotland
◆ **nach Schottland** to Scotland

**schräg** ADJECTIVE
sloping ◇ *Das Haus hat ein schräges Dach.* The house has a sloping roof.
◆ **etwas schräg stellen** to put something at an angle
◆ **schräg gegenüber** diagonally opposite

der **Schrägstrich** NOUN (PL die **Schrägstriche**)
slash

der **Schrank** NOUN (PL die **Schränke**)
[1] cupboard ◇ *Der Besen ist im Schrank in der Küche.* The broom's in the cupboard in the kitchen.
[2] wardrobe ◇ *Ich räume meine Kleider in den Schrank.* I'll put my clothes away in the wardrobe.

die **Schranke** NOUN
barrier

die **Schrankwand** NOUN (PL die **Schrankwände**)
wall unit

die **Schraube** NOUN
[1] screw
[2] bolt

der **Schraubenschlüssel** NOUN (PL die **Schraubenschlüssel**)
spanner

der **Schraubenzieher** NOUN (PL die **Schraubenzieher**)
screwdriver

der **Schreck** NOUN

fright ◊ *Ich habe einen furchtbaren Schreck bekommen.* I got a terrible fright.

**schreckhaft** ADJECTIVE
jumpy

**schrecklich** ADJECTIVE, ADVERB
[1] terrible ◊ *Das Wetter war schrecklich schlecht.* The weather was terrible.
[2] terribly ◊ *Das tut schrecklich weh.* It hurts terribly. ◊ *Es tut mir schrecklich Leid.* I'm terribly sorry.

der **Schrei** NOUN (PL die **Schreie**)
[1] scream ◊ *Als sie die Spinne sah, stieß sie einen Schrei aus.* When she saw the spider she let out a scream.
[2] shout ◊ *Wir hörten einen Schrei um Hilfe.* We heard a shout for help.

der **Schreibblock** NOUN (PL die **Schreibblöcke**)
writing pad

**schreiben** VERB (IMPERFECT **schrieb,** PERFECT **hat geschrieben**)
[1] to write ◊ *Ich habe ihr einen Brief geschrieben.* I've written her a letter.
♦ **Wir schreiben morgen eine Arbeit in Englisch.** We've got a written English test tomorrow.
♦ **Wir sollten uns schreiben.** We should write to each other.
[2] to spell ◊ *Wie schreibt man seinen Namen?* How do you spell his name?

die **Schreibmaschine** NOUN
typewriter

das **Schreibpapier** NOUN
notepaper

der **Schreibtisch** NOUN (PL die **Schreibtische**)
desk

die **Schreibwaren** FEM PL NOUN
stationery

das **Schreibwarengeschäft** NOUN (PL die **Schreibwarengeschäfte**)
stationery shop

das **Schreibzeug** NOUN
writing materials

**schreien** VERB (IMPERFECT **schrie,** PERFECT **hat geschrien**)
[1] to scream ◊ *Sie schrie vor Schmerzen.* She screamed with pain.
[2] to shout ◊ *Wir haben geschrien, du hast uns aber nicht gehört.* We shouted but you didn't hear us.

der **Schreiner** NOUN (PL die **Schreiner**)
joiner

**schrieb** VERB see **schreiben**

die **Schrift** NOUN
[1] writing ◊ *Sie hat eine schöne Schrift.* She has lovely writing.
[2] font ◊ *Welche Schrift soll ich für das Dokument nehmen?* Which font should I use for the document?

**schriftlich** ADJECTIVE, ADVERB
written ◊ *eine schriftliche Entschuldigung* a written apology

♦ **etwas schriftlich festhalten** to put something in writing

der **Schriftsteller** NOUN (PL die **Schriftsteller**)
writer

**schrill** ADJECTIVE
shrill

der **Schritt** NOUN (PL die **Schritte**)
[1] step ◊ *Er machte einen vorsichtigen Schritt nach vorn.* He took a careful step forward.
[2] walk ◊ *Ich habe dich an deinem Schritt erkannt.* I recognized you by your walk.
[3] pace ◊ *Sie ging mit schnellen Schritten nach Hause.* She walked home at a brisk pace.
♦ **Schritt fahren** to drive at walking pace

der **Schrott** NOUN
scrap metal

**schrumpfen** VERB (PERFECT **ist geschrumpft**)
[1] to shrink ◊ *Der Pulli ist in der Wäsche geschrumpft.* The pullover shrank in the wash.
[2] to shrivel ◊ *Die Äpfel sind geschrumpft.* The apples have shrivelled.

die **Schublade** NOUN
drawer

**schüchtern** ADJECTIVE
shy

der **Schuh** NOUN (PL die **Schuhe**)
shoe

die **Schuhcreme** NOUN (PL die **Schuhcremes**)
shoe polish

die **Schuhgröße** NOUN
shoe size ◊ *Welche Schuhgröße hast du?* What shoe size are you?

die **Schularbeiten** FEM PL NOUN
homework ◊ *Hast du deine Schularbeiten schon gemacht?* Have you done your homework?

die **Schulaufgaben** FEM PL NOUN
homework ◊ *Heute haben wir keine Schulaufgaben bekommen.* We didn't get any homework today.

das **Schulbuch** NOUN (PL die **Schulbücher**)
school book

die **Schuld** NOUN
see also **schuld** ADJECTIVE
[1] guilt ◊ *Seine Schuld konnte nicht bewiesen werden.* His guilt couldn't be proved.
[2] fault ◊ *Es war deine Schuld, dass wir zu spät kamen.* It was your fault that we arrived late.
♦ **jemandem Schuld geben** to blame somebody

**schuld** ADJECTIVE
see also **die Schuld** NOUN
♦ **an etwas schuld sein** to be to blame for something ◊ *Du bist an der Verspätung schuld.* You are to blame for the delay.

S

☞

♦ **Sie ist schuld, dass wir eine Strafarbeit bekommen haben.** It's her fault that we got lines.

♦ **Er ist schuld.** It's his fault.

die **Schulden** PL NOUN

see also **schulden** VERB

debt ◊ *Ich muss noch meine Schulden bei dir bezahlen.* I still have to pay off my debts to you. ◊ *Staatsschulden* national debt

**schulden** VERB

see also **die Schulden** NOUN

to owe ◊ *Was schulde ich dir?* How much do I owe you?

**schuldig** ADJECTIVE

guilty ◊ *Meinst du, dass die Angeklagte schuldig ist?* Do you think that the accused is guilty?

♦ **jemandem etwas schuldig sein** to owe somebody something ◊ *Was bin ich dir schuldig?* How much do I owe you?

♦ **Er ist mir noch immer eine Antwort schuldig.** He still hasn't given me an answer.

der **Schuldirektor** NOUN (PL die **Schuldirektoren**)

headmaster

die **Schuldirektorin** NOUN

headmistress

die **Schule** NOUN

school ◊ *in der Schule* at school

der **Schüler** NOUN (PL die **Schüler**)

pupil

die **Schülerin** NOUN

pupil

die **Schülervertretung** NOUN

pupil representation

die **Schulferien** PL NOUN

school holidays

**schulfrei** ADJECTIVE

♦ **ein schulfreier Tag** a holiday

♦ **Sonntag ist schulfrei.** Sunday isn't a school day.

der **Schulhof** NOUN (PL die **Schulhöfe**)

playground

das **Schuljahr** NOUN (PL die **Schuljahre**)

school year

die **Schulmappe** NOUN

school bag

**schulpflichtig** ADJECTIVE

of school age

die **Schulstunde** NOUN

period

der **Schultag** NOUN (PL die **Schultage**)

♦ **mein erster Schultag** my first day at school

die **Schultasche** NOUN

school bag

die **Schulter** NOUN

shoulder

die **Schulverwaltung** NOUN

school administration

das **Schulzeugnis** NOUN (GEN des **Schulzeugnisses**, PL die **Schulzeugnisse**)

school report

**schummeln** VERB

to cheat ◊ *Du schummelst!* You're cheating!

die **Schuppe** NOUN

scale ◊ *Der Fisch hat glänzende Schuppen.* The fish has shiny scales.

♦ **Schuppen** dandruff ◊ *ein Haarwaschmittel gegen Schuppen* an anti-dandruff shampoo

die **Schürze** NOUN

apron

der **Schuss** NOUN (GEN des **Schusses**, PL die **Schüsse**)

shot ◊ *Wir hörten einen Schuss.* We heard a shot.

die **Schüssel** NOUN

bowl

die **Schusswaffe** NOUN

firearm

der **Schuster** NOUN (PL die **Schuster**)

cobbler

der **Schutt** NOUN

rubble ◊ *Der Schutt von der Baustelle wird morgen weggebracht.* The rubble from the building site will be removed tomorrow.

♦ **Schutt abladen verboten!** No dumping!

der **Schuttabladeplatz** NOUN (GEN des **Schuttabladeplatzes**, PL die **Schuttabladeplätze**)

refuse dump

**schütteln** VERB

to shake

♦ **sich schütteln** to shake oneself

**schütten** VERB

[1] to pour ◊ *Soll ich dir Saft ins Glas schütten?* Shall I pour you some juice?

[2] to spill ◊ *Pass auf, dass du den Kaffee nicht auf die Tischdecke schüttest.* Be careful that you don't spill coffee on the tablecloth.

♦ **Es schüttet.** It's pouring down.

der **Schutz** NOUN (GEN des **Schutzes**)

[1] protection ◊ *Zum Schutz gegen die Sonne solltest du dich eincremen.* You should put some cream on to protect against the sun.

[2] shelter ◊ *Sie suchten Schutz in der Berghütte.* They took shelter in a mountain hut.

♦ **jemanden in Schutz nehmen** to stand up for somebody

der **Schütze** NOUN (GEN des **Schützen**, PL die **Schützen**)

[1] marksman ◊ *Er ist ein guter Schütze.* He's a good marksman.

[2] Sagittarius ◊ *Martin ist Schütze.* Martin's Sagittarius.

**schützen** VERB

to protect ◊ *Die Pflanzen sollten vor zu großer Hitze geschützt werden.* The plants should be protected from too much heat. ◊ *Diese Creme schützt die Haut gegen Sonnenbrand.* This cream protects the skin from sunburn.

♦ **sich gegen etwas schützen** to protect oneself from something ◊ *Schützen Sie sich gegen Sonnenbrand.* Protect yourself from sunburn.

**schwach** ADJECTIVE
weak ◊ *Ihre Stimme wurde immer schwächer.* Her voice became weaker and weaker.

♦ **Das war eine schwache Leistung!** That wasn't very good.

die **Schwäche** NOUN
weakness

der **Schwächling** NOUN (PL die **Schwächlinge**)
weakling

der **Schwachsinn** NOUN
balderdash

**schwachsinnig** ADJECTIVE
idiotic ◊ *So eine schwachsinnige Idee!* What an idiotic idea!

der **Schwager** NOUN (PL die **Schwäger**)
brother-in-law

die **Schwägerin** NOUN
sister-in-law

der **Schwamm** NOUN (PL die **Schwämme**)
sponge

**schwamm** VERB *see* **schwimmen**

**schwanger** ADJECTIVE
pregnant ◊ *Sie ist im dritten Monat schwanger.* She's three months pregnant.

**schwanken** VERB
[1] to sway ◊ *Das Schiff schwankte.* The ship swayed.
[2] to stagger ◊ *Er schwankte und fiel dann um.* He staggered and fell down.
[3] to fluctuate ◊ *Die Temperaturen schwanken.* Temperatures are fluctuating. ◊ *Der Kurs des Pfunds schwankt.* The exchange rate of the pound is fluctuating.

der **Schwanz** NOUN (GEN des **Schwanzes**, PL die **Schwänze**)
tail

**schwänzen** VERB
to skive off ◊ *Ich habe heute die Turnstunde geschwänzt.* I skived off PE today.

der **Schwarm** NOUN (PL die **Schwärme**)
swarm ◊ *ein Schwarm Fliegen* a swarm of flies

♦ **Er ist mein Schwarm.** I have a crush on him.

**schwärmen** VERB (PERFECT **hat/ist geschwärmt**)

*Use **sein** to form the perfect tense for **to swarm**.*

to swarm ◊ *Die Bienen sind aus dem Bienenstock geschwärmt.* The bees swarmed out of the hive.

♦ **schwärmen für** to have a crush on ◊ *Sie schwärmt für ihren Mathelehrer.* She has a crush on her maths teacher.

♦ **schwärmen von** to rave about ◊ *Er hat von dem Konzert geschwärmt.* He raved about the concert.

**schwarz** ADJECTIVE
black ◊ *Der Himmel wurde immer schwärzer.* The sky turned blacker and blacker.

♦ **schwarz sehen** to look on the black side of things ◊ *Sieh doch nicht immer so schwarz.* Don't always look on the black side of things.

♦ **schwarzes Brett** notice board

♦ **ins Schwarze treffen** to hit the bull's eye

das **Schwarzbrot** NOUN (PL die **Schwarzbrote**)
brown rye bread

der **Schwarze** NOUN (GEN des/der **Schwarzen**, PL
die die **Schwarzen**)
black

**schwarzfahren** VERB (PRESENT **fährt schwarz**, IMPERFECT **fuhr schwarz**, PERFECT **ist schwarzgefahren**)

♦ **Sie fährt in der Straßenbahn immer schwarz.** She never pays her tram fare.

**schwarzsehen** VERB *see* **schwarz**

der **Schwarzwald** NOUN
Black Forest

**schwarzweiß** ADJECTIVE
black and white

**schwätzen** VERB
to chatter

der **Schwätzer** NOUN (PL die **Schwätzer**)
windbag

der **Schwede** NOUN (GEN des **Schweden**, PL die **Schweden**)
Swede

♦ **Er ist Schwede.** He's Swedish.

**Schweden** NEUT NOUN
Sweden

♦ **aus Schweden** from Sweden
♦ **nach Schweden** to Sweden

die **Schwedin** NOUN
Swede

**schwedisch** ADJECTIVE
Swedish

der **Schwefel** NOUN
sulphur

**schweigen** VERB (IMPERFECT **schwieg**, PERFECT **hat geschwiegen**)
[1] to be silent ◊ *Die Kinder finden es schwierig, mehr als fünf Minuten lang zu schweigen.* The children find it difficult to be silent for more than five minutes.
[2] to stop talking ◊ *Sag ihm, er soll schweigen.* Tell him to stop talking.

das **Schwein** NOUN (PL die **Schweine**)
pig

**S**

☞

♦ **Schwein haben** to be really lucky ◊ *Da hatten wir ja noch mal Schwein.* We were really lucky there.

der **Schweinebraten** NOUN (PL die **Schweinebraten**)
roast pork

das **Schweinefleisch** NOUN
pork

die **Schweinerei** NOUN
[1] scandal ◊ *Es ist eine Schweinerei, dass wir länger arbeiten müssen.* It's a scandal that we have to work longer hours.
[2] mess ◊ *Wer hat denn die Schweinerei im Bad gemacht?* Who made the mess in the bathroom?
[3] obscenity ◊ *Über solche Schweinereien kann ich nicht lachen.* I can't laugh at such obscenities.

der **Schweiß** NOUN (GEN des **Schweißes**)
sweat

die **Schweiz** NOUN
Switzerland

> *i Switzerland is bordered by Germany, Austria, Liechstenstein, Italy and France. Its capital is Berne and its currency the Franken. Roughly 60% of the population (mainly in the North and East) speak a German dialect. French, Italian and Rhaeto-Romanic are also spoken.*

♦ **aus der Schweiz** from Switzerland
♦ **in der Schweiz** in Switzerland
♦ **in die Schweiz** to Switzerland

der **Schweizer** NOUN (PL die **Schweizer**)
Swiss ◊ *die Schweizer* the Swiss

die **Schweizerin** NOUN
Swiss

**schweizerisch** ADJECTIVE
Swiss

die **Schwellung** NOUN
swelling

**schwer** ADJECTIVE, ADVERB
[1] heavy ◊ *Ich habe einen schweren Koffer.* I have a heavy suitcase. ◊ *Er hat eine schwere Erkältung.* He has a heavy cold.
♦ **Ich habe einen schweren Kopf.** I've got a headache.
[2] difficult ◊ *Die Mathearbeit war schwer.* The maths test was difficult.
♦ **Sie ist schwer in Ordnung.** She's a great person.
♦ **Er ist schwer verletzt.** He's badly injured.
♦ **jemandem schwer fallen** to be difficult for somebody ◊ *Das dürfte dir nicht schwer fallen.* That shouldn't be too difficult for you.

das **Schwert** NOUN (PL die **Schwerter**)
sword

die **Schwester** NOUN
[1] sister ◊ *Meine Schwester ist jünger als ich.* My sister's younger than me.
[2] nurse ◊ *Die Schwester hat mir eine Schmerztablette gegeben.* The nurse gave me a painkiller.

die **Schwiegereltern** PL NOUN
parents-in-law

die **Schwiegermutter** NOUN (PL die **Schwiegermütter**)
mother-in-law

der **Schwiegersohn** NOUN (PL die **Schwiegersöhne**)
son-in-law

die **Schwiegertochter** NOUN (PL die **Schwiegertöchter**)
daughter-in-law

der **Schwiegervater** NOUN (PL die **Schwiegerväter**)
father-in-law

**schwierig** ADJECTIVE
difficult

die **Schwierigkeit** NOUN
difficulty

das **Schwimmbad** NOUN (PL die **Schwimmbäder**)
swimming pool

das **Schwimmbecken** NOUN (PL die **Schwimmbecken**)
swimming pool

**schwimmen** VERB (IMPERFECT **schwamm**, PERFECT **ist geschwommen**)
[1] to swim ◊ *Er kann nicht schwimmen.* He can't swim.
[2] to float ◊ *Auf dem Fluss schwammen Äste.* Branches were floating on the river.
[3] to flounder ◊ *Bei der Prüfung bin ich ganz schön geschwommen.* I really floundered in the exam.

die **Schwimmweste** NOUN
life jacket

der **Schwindel** NOUN
[1] dizzy spell ◊ *Bei hohem Fieber muss man auch mit Schwindel rechnen.* If you have a high temperature, you can also expect to have dizzy spells.
[2] fraud ◊ *Der Schwindel wurde entdeckt.* The fraud was discovered.

**schwindelfrei** ADJECTIVE
♦ **schwindelfrei sein** to have a good head for heights ◊ *Ich bin nicht schwindelfrei.* I don't have a good head for heights.

**schwindeln** VERB
to fib

**schwindlig** ADJECTIVE
dizzy
♦ **Mir ist schwindlig.** I feel dizzy.

der **Schwips** NOUN (GEN des **Schwipses**, PL die **Schwipse**)
♦ **einen Schwips haben** to be tipsy

**schwitzen** VERB
to sweat

**schwören** VERB (IMPERFECT **schwor**, PERFECT **hat geschworen**)
to swear

**schwul** ADJECTIVE
gay

**schwül** ADJECTIVE
close

der **Schwule** NOUN (GEN des/der **Schwulen**, PL
die   die **Schwulen**)
gay ◊ *Ich habe nichts gegen Schwule.* I
have nothing against gays.

der **Schwung** NOUN (PL die **Schwünge**)
swing ◊ *Sie setzte das Pendel in
Schwung.* She started the pendulum
swinging.
◆ **Der Party fehlte irgendwie der Schwung.**
The party never really got going.
◆ **Ein heißes Bad wird mich wieder in
Schwung bringen.** A hot bath will get me
going again.

**sechs** NUMBER
> see also **die Sechs** NOUN

six

die **Sechs** NOUN
> see also **sechs** NUMBER

1 six
2 unsatisfactory

> ℹ️ German marks range from one (**sehr
> gut**) to six (**ungenügend**).

**sechshundert** NUMBER
six hundred

**sechste** ADJECTIVE
sixth ◊ *Er kam als Sechster.* He was the
sixth to arrive.

das **Sechstel** NOUN (PL die **Sechstel**)
sixth

**sechzehn** NUMBER
sixteen

**sechzig** NUMBER
sixty

die **See** NOUN
> see also **der See** NOUN

sea ◊ *auf See* at sea
◆ **Wir fahren im Sommer an die See.** We're
going to the seaside in the summer.

der **See** NOUN (PL die **Seen**)
> see also **die See** NOUN

lake ◊ *der Genfer See* Lake Geneva

der **Seehund** NOUN (PL die **Seehunde**)
seal

**seekrank** ADJECTIVE
seasick

der **Seelachs** NOUN (GEN des **Seelachses,** PL die
**Seelachse**)
rock salmon

die **Seele** NOUN
soul

**seelenruhig** ADVERB
calmly

der **Seeräuber** NOUN (PL die **Seeräuber**)
pirate

das **Segel** NOUN (PL die **Segel**)
sail

das **Segelboot** NOUN (PL die **Segelboote**)
yacht

das **Segelfliegen** NOUN
gliding

das **Segelflugzeug** NOUN (PL die
**Segelflugzeuge**)
glider

**segeln** VERB (PERFECT **ist gesegelt**)
to sail

das **Segelschiff** NOUN (PL die **Segelschiffe**)
sailing ship

der **Segen** NOUN (PL die **Segen**)
blessing

**sehen** VERB (PRESENT **sieht**, IMPERFECT **sah**,
PERFECT **hat gesehen**)
1 to see ◊ *Hast du den Film schon
gesehen?* Have you seen the film yet?
◆ **siehe Seite fünf** see page five
2 to look ◊ *Sieh mal an die Tafel.* Look
at the board.
◆ **schlecht sehen** to have bad eyesight
◊ *Sie sieht schlecht.* She has bad
eyesight.
◆ **mal sehen, ob ...** let's see if ... ◊ *Mal
sehen, ob Post für mich gekommen ist.*
Let's see if there's any post for me.
◆ **Kommst du mit? – Mal sehen.** Are you
coming? – I'll see.

**sehenswert** ADJECTIVE
worth seeing

die **Sehenswürdigkeiten** FEM PL NOUN
sights

sich **sehnen** VERB
◆ **sich sehnen nach** to long for

die **Sehnsucht** NOUN (PL die **Sehnsüchte**)
longing

**sehnsüchtig** ADJECTIVE
longing

**sehr** ADVERB
1 very ◊ *Das ist sehr schön.* That's very
nice.
◆ **sehr gut** very good

> ℹ️ German marks range from one (**sehr
> gut**) to six (**ungenügend**).

2 a lot ◊ *Sie hat sehr geweint.* She cried
a lot.
◆ **zu sehr** too much
◆ **Sehr geehrter Herr Ahlers** Dear Mr
Ahlers

die **Seide** NOUN
silk

die **Seife** NOUN
soap

die **Seifenoper** NOUN
soap opera

das **Seil** NOUN (PL die **Seile**)

**S**

☞

**[1]** rope ◊ *Sie hatten ihn mit einem Seil gefesselt.* They had tied him up with a rope.

**[2]** cable ◊ *das Seil des Skilifts* the cable of the ski lift

die **Seilbahn** NOUN
cable car

**sein** VERB (PRESENT **ist**, IMPERFECT **war**, PERFECT **ist gewesen**)

see also **sein** ADJECTIVE

to be ◊ *Ich bin müde.* I'm tired. ◊ *Du bist doof.* You're stupid. ◊ *Er ist reich.* He's rich. ◊ *Sie ist Lehrerin.* She's a teacher. ◊ *Es ist kalt.* It's cold. ◊ *Wir sind Schüler am Gymnasium.* We're pupils at the grammar school. ◊ *Ihr seid spät dran.* You're late. ◊ *Sie sind vom Zirkus.* They're from the circus. ◊ *Wir waren dort.* We were there. ◊ *Wir sind im Schwimmbad gewesen.* We've been to the swimming pool. ◊ *Seien Sie nicht böse.* Don't be angry.

♦ **Das wäre gut.** That would be a good thing.

♦ **Wenn ich Sie wäre ...** If I were you ...

♦ **Das wär's.** That's it.

♦ **Morgen bin ich in Rom.** Tomorrow I'll be in Rome.

♦ **Waren Sie mal in Rom?** Have you ever been to Rome?

♦ **Mir ist kalt.** I'm cold.

♦ **Was ist?** What's the matter?

♦ **Ist was?** Is something the matter?

♦ **es sei denn, dass ...** unless ...

♦ **wie dem auch sei** be that as it may

♦ **Wie wäre es mit ...?** How about ...?

♦ **Lass das sein!** Stop that!

**sein** ADJECTIVE

see also **sein** VERB

**[1]** his ◊ *Sein Deutschlehrer ist nett.* His German teacher's nice. ◊ *Seine Mutter erlaubt das nicht.* His mother doesn't allow it. ◊ *Das ist sein Buch.* That's his book. ◊ *Seine Eltern sind klasse.* His parents are great. ◊ *Das ist nicht mein Füller, das ist seiner.* That's not my pen, it's his. ◊ *Meine Mutter heißt Anne, seine auch.* My mother's called Anne, so is his. ◊ *Mein Fahrrad war kaputt, also habe ich seins genommen.* My bike was broken, so I took his. ◊ *Ich habe schlechte Noten, aber seine sind nicht besser.* My marks are bad, but his aren't much better.

**[2]** its ◊ *Der Fuchs kam aus seiner Höhle.* The fox came out of its lair. ◊ *Jedes Buch hat seinen Platz.* Each book has its place.

**seiner** PRONOUN

*seiner* is the genitive of *er*.

of him ◊ *Wir gedenken seiner.* We're thinking of him.

**seinetwegen** ADVERB

**[1]** for his sake ◊ *Ihr müsst seinetwegen nicht auf euren Urlaub verzichten.* You don't have to do without your holiday for his sake.

**[2]** on his account ◊ *Hat sie sich seinetwegen so aufgeregt?* Did she get so upset on his account?

**[3]** as far as he's concerned ◊ *Er sagt, dass du seinetwegen gehen kannst.* He says that as far as he's concerned you can go.

**seit** PREPOSITION, CONJUNCTION

*The preposition **seit** takes the dative.*

since ◊ *Seit er verheiratet ist, spielt er nicht mehr Fußball.* He's stopped playing football since he got married. ◊ *Seit letztem Jahr habe ich nichts mehr von ihm gehört.* I haven't heard anything from him since last year.

♦ **Er ist seit einer Woche hier.** He's been here for a week.

♦ **seit langem** for a long time

**seitdem** ADVERB, CONJUNCTION

since ◊ *Seitdem sie im Gymnasium ist, hat sie kaum mehr Zeit.* Since she's been going to grammar school, she's hardly had any time.

♦ **Ich habe seitdem nichts mehr von ihr gehört.** I haven't heard from her since then.

die **Seite** NOUN

**[1]** side ◊ *Die rechte Seite des Autos war beschädigt.* The right side of the car was damaged.

**[2]** page ◊ *Das steht auf Seite fünfzig.* It's on page fifty.

das **Seitenstechen** NOUN

stitch ◊ *Ich habe Seitenstechen.* I've got a stitch.

der **Sekretär** NOUN
secretary

das **Sekretariat** NOUN (PL die **Sekretariate**)
secretary's office

die **Sekretärin** NOUN
secretary

der **Sekt** NOUN (PL die **Sekte**)
sparkling wine

die **Sekunde** NOUN
second ◊ *zehn Sekunden* ten seconds

**selber** PRONOUN = **selbst**

**selbst** PRONOUN, ADVERB

**[1]** on one's own ◊ *Das Kind kann sich selbst anziehen.* The child can get dressed on her own. ◊ *Ich werde schon selbst eine Lösung finden.* I'll find a solution on my own.

♦ **ich selbst** I myself

♦ **er selbst** he himself

♦ **wir selbst** we ourselves

♦ **Sie ist die Liebenswürdigkeit selbst.** She's kindness itself.

♦ **Er braut sein Bier selbst.** He brews his own beer.

♦ **Wie geht's? – Gut, und selbst?** How are things? – Fine, and yourself?

♦ **von selbst** by itself ◊ *Die Bombe ist von selbst losgegangen.* The bomb went off by itself.

⸤2⸥ even ◊ *Selbst meine Mutter findet Oasis gut.* Even my mother likes Oasis.

♦ **selbst wenn** even if ◊ *Du musst das machen, selbst wenn du keine Lust hast.* You have to do it even if you don't feel like it.

**selbständig** ADJECTIVE
independent ◊ *Du solltest langsam selbständiger werden.* It's about time you started to become more independent. ◊ *ein selbständiger Staat* an independent country

♦ **Kannst du das nicht selbständig entscheiden?** Can't you decide on your own?

♦ **sich selbständig machen** to become self-employed

♦ **Sie hat sich als Übersetzerin selbständig gemacht.** She set herself up as a self-employed translator.

die **Selbstbedienung** NOUN
self-service

**selbstbewusst** ADJECTIVE
self-confident

der **Selbstmord** NOUN (PL die **Selbstmorde**)
suicide ◊ *Selbstmord begehen* to commit suicide

**selbstsicher** ADJECTIVE
self-assured

**selbstständig** ADJECTIVE *see* **selbständig**

**selbstsüchtig** ADJECTIVE
selfish

die **Selbstverpflegung** NOUN
self-catering

**selbstverständlich** ADJECTIVE, ADVERB
⸤1⸥ obvious ◊ *Das ist für mich durchaus nicht selbstverständlich.* It's not at all obvious to me.

♦ **Es ist doch selbstverständlich, dass man da hilft.** It goes without saying that you should help.

♦ **Ich halte das für selbstverständlich.** I take that for granted.

⸤2⸥ of course ◊ *Ich habe mich selbstverständlich sofort bedankt.* Of course I said thank you immediately. ◊ *Kommt er mit? – Selbstverständlich.* Is he coming? – Of course. ◊ *Ich habe selbstverständlich nicht unterschrieben.* Of course I didn't sign.

das **Selbstvertrauen** NOUN
self-confidence

**selig** ADJECTIVE
blissful ◊ *Er hatte ein seliges Lächeln auf dem Gesicht.* He had a blissful smile on his face.

♦ **Sie war selig, als sie ihn sah.** She was overjoyed to see him.

der **Sellerie** NOUN
celeriac

**selten** ADJECTIVE, ADVERB
⸤1⸥ rare ◊ *eine seltene Pflanze* a rare plant
⸤2⸥ rarely ◊ *Wir gehen selten ins Kino.* We rarely go to the cinema.

**seltsam** ADJECTIVE
curious

das **Semester** NOUN (PL die **Semester**)
semester

das **Semikolon** NOUN (PL die **Semikolons** or **Semikola**)
semicolon

das **Seminar** NOUN (PL die **Seminare**)
seminar ◊ *Ich mache dieses Semester ein Seminar über Steinbeck.* I'm doing a seminar on Steinbeck this semester.

die **Semmel** NOUN
roll

die **Sendefolge** NOUN
series

**senden** VERB (IMPERFECT **sendete** or **sandte**, PERFECT **hat gesendet** or **gesandt**)
⸤1⸥ to send ◊ *Bitte senden Sie mir Ihren neuesten Katalog.* Please send me your latest catalogue.
⸤2⸥ to broadcast ◊ *Der Spielfilm wird im dritten Programm gesendet.* The film will be broadcast on Channel three. ◊ *Wir senden bis Mitternacht.* We broadcast until midnight.

die **Sendereihe** NOUN
series

die **Sendung** NOUN
⸤1⸥ transmission ◊ *Während der Sendung darf das Studio nicht betreten werden.* Nobody's allowed to enter the studio during transmission.
⸤2⸥ programme ◊ *Kennst du die Sendung "Tiere im Zoo"?* Do you know the programme "Animals in the Zoo"?
⸤3⸥ consignment ◊ *Für Sie ist eine Sendung mit Mustern angekommen.* A consignment of samples has arrived for you.

der **Senf** NOUN (PL die **Senfe**)
mustard

der **Senior** NOUN (PL die **Senioren**)
senior citizen

die **Sensation** NOUN
sensation

**sensibel** ADJECTIVE
sensitive ◊ *Sie ist ein sehr sensibler Mensch.* She's a very sensitive person.
*Be careful! **sensibel** does not mean **sensible**.*

**sentimental** ADJECTIVE
sentimental ◊ *Nun werd nicht sentimental!* Now don't get sentimental.

der **September** NOUN
September ◊ *im September* in September ◊ *am elften September* on

**S**

☞

the eleventh of September ◊ *Ulm, den 11. September 2003* Ulm, 11 September 2003 ◊ *Heute ist der elfte September.* Today is the eleventh of September.

die **Serie** NOUN
series

**seriös** ADJECTIVE
respectable
> Be careful! **seriös** does not mean **serious.**

der **Server** NOUN (PL die **Server**)
server

das **Service** NOUN (GEN des **Service** or **Services**, PL die **Service**)
> see also **der Service** NOUN

set ◊ *Sie hat ein hübsches Teeservice aus Porzellan.* She has a lovely china tea set.

der **Service** NOUN (GEN des **Service**, PL die **Services**)
> see also **das Service** NOUN

service ◊ *In dem Hotel ist der Service ausgezeichnet.* The service in the hotel is excellent.

die **Serviette** NOUN
serviette

**servus** EXCLAMATION
[1] hello!
[2] goodbye!

der **Sessel** NOUN (PL die **Sessel**)
armchair

der **Sessellift** NOUN (PL die **Sessellifte**)
chairlift

**setzen** VERB
to put ◊ *Sie setzte das Kind auf den Stuhl.* She put the child on the chair. ◊ *Er setzte das Glas an den Mund.* He put the glass to his lips. ◊ *Hast du meinen Namen auf die Liste gesetzt?* Have you put my name on the list?
◆ **ein Komma setzen** to put a comma
◆ **jemandem eine Frist setzen** to set somebody a deadline
◆ **sich setzen (1)** to settle ◊ *Der Kaffeesatz hat sich gesetzt.* The coffee grounds have settled.
◆ **sich setzen (2)** to sit down ◊ *Setz dich doch!* Do sit down! ◊ *Er setzte sich aufs Sofa.* He sat down on the sofa.
◆ **Sie setzte sich aufs Fahrrad.** She got on her bike.
◆ **auf etwas setzen** to bet on something ◊ *Er hat hundert Mark auf die Nummer zwei gesetzt.* He bet a hundred marks on number two.

die **Seuche** NOUN
epidemic

**seufzen** VERB
to sigh

der **Sex** NOUN (GEN des **Sex** or **Sexes**)
sex

**sexuell** ADJECTIVE
sexual

das **Shampoo** NOUN (PL die **Shampoos**)
shampoo

**Sibirien** NEUT NOUN
Siberia

**sibirisch** ADJECTIVE
Siberian

**sich** PRONOUN
[1] himself ◊ *Er redet mit sich selbst.* He's talking to himself.
herself
◊ *Sie spricht nicht gern über sich selbst.* She doesn't like to talk about herself. ◊ *Sie hat sich einen Pullover gekauft.* She bought herself a jumper.
itself
◊ *Das Boot hat sich wieder aufgerichtet.* The boat righted itself.
[2] themselves ◊ *Meine Eltern haben sich ein neues Auto gekauft.* My parents have bought themselves a new car. ◊ *Sie bleiben gern unter sich.* They keep themselves to themselves.
[3] each other ◊ *Sie lieben sich.* They love each other.
◆ **Sie wäscht sich.** She's washing herself.
◆ **Sie wäscht sich die Haare.** She's washing her hair.
◆ **Er schneidet sich die Nägel.** He's cutting his nails.
◆ **Man fragt sich, ob ...** One wonders whether ...
◆ **Sie wiederholen sich.** You're repeating yourself.
◆ **Haben Sie Ihren Ausweis bei sich?** Do you have your pass on you?
◆ **Er hat nichts bei sich.** He's got nothing on him.
◆ **Dieses Auto fährt sich gut.** This car drives well.
◆ **Dieser Artikel verkauft sich gut.** This article sells well.
◆ **Hier sitzt es sich gut.** This is a good place to sit.

**sicher** ADJECTIVE, ADVERB
[1] safe ◊ *Das ist ein sehr sicheres Auto.* It's a very safe car.
[2] certain ◊ *Der Termin ist noch nicht sicher.* The date isn't certain yet.
◆ **Ich bin nicht sicher.** I'm not sure.
[3] reliable ◊ *eine sichere Methode* a reliable method
◆ **vor jemandem sicher sein** to be safe from somebody ◊ *In einer Großstadt ist man vor Taschendieben nicht sicher.* You're never safe from pickpockets in a city.
◆ **vor etwas sicher sein** to be safe from something ◊ *Bei ihr ist man vor Überraschungen nie sicher.* With her you're never safe from surprises.
[4] definitely ◊ *Sie kommt sicher nicht mehr.* She's definitely not coming anymore.

♦ **Er weiß das sicher schon.** I'm sure he knows that already.

♦ **sicher nicht** surely not

♦ **Aber sicher!** Of course!

die **Sicherheit** NOUN

safety ◊ *Tragen Sie einen Helm zu Ihrer eigenen Sicherheit.* Wear a helmet for your own safety. ◊ *Diese Maßnahmen dienen der Sicherheit der Fluggäste.* These measures are for passenger safety.

♦ **Hier sind wir in Sicherheit.** We're safe here.

♦ **Ich kann nicht mit Sicherheit sagen, ob ich komme.** I can't say for sure if I'll come.

der **Sicherheitsgurt** NOUN (PL die **Sicherheitsgurte**)

seat belt

**sicherlich** ADVERB

certainly

**sichern** VERB

to secure ◊ *Maßnahmen, die Arbeitsplätze sichern* measures to secure jobs

♦ **Daten sichern** to back up data ◊ *Die Daten werden stündlich auf Band gesichert.* The data are backed up onto tape every hour.

♦ **jemandem etwas sichern** to secure something for somebody ◊ *Ich habe dir einen guten Platz gesichert.* I've secured a good place for you.

die **Sicherung** NOUN

1 securing ◊ *Maßnahmen zur Sicherung der Arbeitsplätze* measures for securing jobs

2 fuse ◊ *Die Sicherung ist durchgebrannt.* The fuse has blown.

die **Sicherungskopie** NOUN

backup copy

die **Sicht** NOUN

view ◊ *Wir hatten eine gute Sicht auf die Berge.* We had a good view of the mountains. ◊ *Du versperrst mir die Sicht.* You're blocking my view.

♦ **auf lange Sicht** on a long-term basis

♦ **aus jemandes Sicht** as somebody sees it ◊ *Aus meiner Sicht ist das zu schaffen.* As I see it, it can be done.

**sichtbar** ADJECTIVE

visible

**Sie** PRONOUN

see also **sie** PRONOUN

you

ℹ️ *The formal form of address **Sie** (singular and plural) is used when addressing people you don't know or your superiors. Teachers say **Sie** to children over the age of 16.*

◊ *Möchten Sie mitkommen?* Would you like to come? ◊ *Ich kenne Sie.* I know you.

**sie** PRONOUN

see also **Sie** PRONOUN

1 she ◊ *Sie ist sehr hübsch.* She's very pretty.

2 it ◊ *Schöne Tasche, ist sie neu?* Lovely bag, is it new? ◊ *Kann ich deine Tasche haben, oder brauchst du sie noch?* Can I have your bag or do you need it?

3 her ◊ *Ich kenne sie nicht.* I don't know her.

4 they ◊ *Sie sind alle gekommen.* They all came.

5 them ◊ *Ich habe sie alle eingeladen.* I've invited all of them.

das **Sieb** NOUN (PL die **Siebe**)

1 sieve ◊ *Wir sollten da Mehl durch ein Sieb schütten.* We should rub the flour through a sieve.

2 strainer ◊ *Hast du ein Teesieb?* Have you got a tea strainer?

**sieben** NUMBER

seven

**siebenhundert** NUMBER

seven hundred

**siebte** ADJECTIVE

seventh ◊ *Er kam als Siebter.* He was the seventh to arrive.

**siebzehn** NUMBER

seventeen

**siebzig** NUMBER

seventy

die **Siedlung** NOUN

1 settlement ◊ *eine indianische Siedlung* an Indian settlement

2 estate ◊ *Sie wohnt in unserer Siedlung.* She lives on our estate.

der **Sieg** NOUN (PL die **Siege**)

victory

**siegen** VERB

to win ◊ *Welche Mannschaft hat gesiegt?* Which team won?

der **Sieger** NOUN (PL die **Sieger**)

winner ◊ *Brasilien war 1994 Sieger der Fußballweltmeisterschaft.* Brazil was the winner of the 1994 World Cup.

**siehe** VERB *see* **sehen**

**siezen** VERB

to address as "Sie"

ℹ️ *The formal form of address **Sie** (singular and plural) is used when addressing people you don't know or your superiors. Teachers say **Sie** to children over the age of 16.*

die **Silbe** NOUN

syllable

das **Silber** NOUN

silver

**S**

das **Silvester** NOUN (PL die **Silvester**)
New Year's Eve
**singen** VERB (IMPERFECT **sang**, PERFECT **hat gesungen**)
to sing
der **Singular** NOUN (PL die **Singulare**)
singular
**sinken** VERB (IMPERFECT **sank**, PERFECT **ist gesunken**)
[1] to sink ◊ *Das Schiff ist gesunken.* The ship has sunk.
[2] to fall ◊ *Die Preise für Computer sind gesunken.* The prices of computers have fallen.
der **Sinn** NOUN (PL die **Sinne**)
[1] sense ◊ *die fünf Sinne* the five senses
[2] meaning ◊ *Ich verstehe den Sinn dieses Satzes nicht.* I don't understand the meaning of this sentence. ◊ *Was ist der Sinn des Lebens?* What's the meaning of life?
♦ **Sinn für etwas haben** to have a sense of something ◊ *Sie hat viel Sinn für Humor.* She has a great sense of humour.
♦ **jemandem in den Sinn kommen** to come to somebody ◊ *Die Idee kam mir plötzlich in den Sinn.* The idea suddenly came to me.
♦ **Es hat keinen Sinn.** There's no point.
**sinnlos** ADJECTIVE
[1] pointless ◊ *Es ist sinnlos, das zu tun.* It's pointless doing that.
[2] meaningless ◊ *Er hat sinnloses Zeug geredet.* He talked meaningless rubbish.
**sinnvoll** ADJECTIVE
sensible ◊ *Das wäre eine sinnvolle Änderung.* That would be a sensible change.
die **Situation** NOUN
situation
der **Sitz** NOUN (GEN des **Sitzes**, PL die **Sitze**)
seat
**sitzen** VERB (IMPERFECT **saß**, PERFECT **hat gesessen**)
to sit ◊ *Er saß auf dem Stuhl.* He was sitting on the chair.
♦ **sitzen bleiben (1)** to remain seated ◊ *Bleiben Sie sitzen.* Please remain seated.
♦ **sitzen bleiben (2)** to have to repeat a year

> ⓘ *In Germany, pupils do not automatically move up (***werden versetzt***) to the next class at the end of the school year. If their performance is not good enough, they have to repeat the school year. This is known as* **sitzen bleiben***.*

◊ *Ich habe Angst, dass ich dieses Jahr sitzen bleibe.* I'm worried that I'll have to repeat this year.

♦ **Diese Hose sitzt.** These trousers fit well.
die **Sitzgelegenheit** NOUN
place to sit down
der **Sitzplatz** NOUN (GEN des **Sitzplatzes**, PL die **Sitzplätze**)
seat
die **Sitzung** NOUN
meeting
der **Skandal** NOUN (PL die **Skandale**)
scandal
**Skandinavien** NEUT NOUN
Scandinavia
♦ **aus Skandinavien** from Scandinavia
♦ **nach Skandinavien** to Scandinavia
**skandinavisch** ADJECTIVE
Scandinavian
das **Skelett** NOUN (PL die **Skelette**)
skeleton
der **Ski** NOUN (PL die **Ski** or **Skier**)
ski
♦ **Ski fahren** to ski
der **Skifahrer** NOUN (PL die **Skifahrer**)
skier
das **Skilaufen** NOUN
skiing
der **Skilehrer** NOUN (PL die **Skilehrer**)
ski instructor
der **Skilift** NOUN (PL die **Skilifte** or **Skilifts**)
ski lift
der **Skistock** NOUN (PL die **Skistöcke**)
ski pole
der **Skorpion** NOUN (PL die **Skorpione**)
[1] scorpion
[2] Scorpio ◊ *Sie ist Skorpion.* She's Scorpio.
der **Slip** NOUN (PL die **Slips**)
pants ◊ *ein Slip* a pair of pants
die **Slowakei** NOUN
Slovakia
♦ **aus der Slowakei** from Slovakia
♦ **in die Slowakei** to Slovakia
der **Smoking** NOUN (PL die **Smokings**)
dinner jacket
**SMV** ABBREVIATION (= *Schülermitverwaltung*)
school council
**SO** ADVERB, CONJUNCTION, EXCLAMATION
[1] so ◊ *Ich hatte mich so darauf gefreut.* I was so looking forward to it. ◊ *so schön* so nice ◊ *zwanzig oder so* twenty or so
♦ **so groß wie ...** as big as ...
♦ **das hat ihn so geärgert, dass ...** that annoyed him so much that ...
♦ **so einer wie ich** somebody like me
[2] like that ◊ *Mach es nicht so.* Don't do it like that.
♦ **... oder so was** ... or something like that
♦ **Na so was!** Well, well!
♦ **und so weiter** and so on
♦ **Ich habe es so bekommen.** I got it for nothing.
♦ **so dass** so that

♦**So?** Really?

♦**So, das wär's.** So, that's it then.

**sobald** CONJUNCTION
as soon as

das **Söckchen** NOUN (PL die **Söckchen**)
ankle sock

die **Socke** NOUN
sock

**sodass** CONJUNCTION
so that

das **Sofa** NOUN (PL die **Sofas**)
sofa

**sofort** ADVERB
immediately

die **Software** NOUN
software

**sogar** ADVERB
even

**sogleich** ADVERB
straight away

die **Sohle** NOUN
sole

der **Sohn** NOUN (PL die **Söhne**)
son

**solch** PRONOUN
such ◊ *Sie ist solch eine nette Frau.*
She's such a nice lady.

♦**ein solcher** a ... like that ◊ *Ein solcher Fehler sollte nicht passieren.* A mistake like that shouldn't happen. ◊ *Eine solche Wohnung würde mir auch gefallen.* I'd like a flat like that. ◊ *Ein solches Mountainbike hätte ich auch gern.* I'd also really like to have a mountain bike like that.

♦**Solche Fehler solltest du nicht mehr machen.** You shouldn't be making mistakes like that any more.

♦**eine solche Frechheit** such a cheek

der **Soldat** NOUN (GEN des **Soldaten**, PL die **Soldaten**)
soldier

**solide** ADJECTIVE
[1] solid ◊ *Dieser Tisch ist aus solidem Holz.* This table is of solid wood.

♦**Sie hat solide Grammatikkenntnisse.** Her grammar is sound.

[2] respectable ◊ *Wir führen ein solides Leben.* We lead a respectable life. ◊ *Er ist solide geworden.* He's become respectable.

**sollen** VERB (IMPERFECT **sollte**, PERFECT **hat gesollt** *or* **sollen**)

*The past participle **sollen** is used when **sollen** is a modal auxiliary.*

[1] to be supposed to ◊ *Ich soll um fünf Uhr dort sein.* I'm supposed to be there at five o'clock. ◊ *Was soll das heißen?* What's that supposed to mean? ◊ *Morgen soll es schön werden.* It's supposed to be nice tomorrow.

[2] to have to ◊ *Du sollst sofort nach Hause.* You have to go home immediately. ◊ *Sie sagt, du sollst nach Hause kommen.* She says that you have to come home.

♦**Sag ihm, er soll warten.** Tell him he's to wait.

[3] should ◊ *Ich sollte meine Hausaufgaben machen.* I should do my homework. ◊ *Du hättest nicht gehen sollen.* You shouldn't have gone. ◊ *Was soll ich machen?* What should I do? ◊ *sollte das passieren, ...* if that should happen ...

♦**Sie soll verheiratet sein.** She's said to be married.

♦**man sollte glauben, dass ...** you would think that ...

♦**Soll ich dir helfen?** Shall I help you?

♦**Soll ich?** Shall I?

♦**Ich hätte eigentlich nicht gesollt.** I really shouldn't have.

♦**Was soll das?** What's all this?

♦**Das sollst du nicht.** You shouldn't do that.

♦**Was soll's?** What the hell!

der **Sommer** NOUN (PL die **Sommer**)
summer ◊ *im Sommer* in summer

die **Sommerferien** PL NOUN
summer holidays

**sommerlich** ADJECTIVE
[1] summery ◊ *ein sommerliches Kleid* a summery dress
[2] summer ◊ *sommerliche Kleidung* summer clothes ◊ *sommerliches Wetter* summer weather

der **Sommerschlussverkauf** NOUN (PL die **Sommerschlussverkäufe**)
summer sale

die **Sommersprossen** FEM PL NOUN
freckles

das **Sonderangebot** NOUN (PL die **Sonderangebote**)
special offer

**sonderbar** ADJECTIVE
strange

die **Sonderfahrt** NOUN
special trip

**sondern** CONJUNCTION
but

♦**nicht nur ..., sondern auch** not only ..., but also

der **Sonderpreis** NOUN
special price

der **Sonnabend** NOUN (PL die **Sonnabende**)
Saturday ◊ *am Sonnabend* on Saturday

**sonnabends** ADVERB
on Saturdays

die **Sonne** NOUN
sun

sich **sonnen** VERB
to sun oneself

**S**

der **Sonnenbrand** NOUN (PL die **Sonnenbrände**)
sunburn

die **Sonnenbräune** NOUN
suntan

die **Sonnenbrille** NOUN
sunglasses ◊ *Sie trug eine Sonnenbrille.* She was wearing sunglasses.

die **Sonnencreme** NOUN (PL die **Sonnencremes**)
suntan lotion

die **Sonnenenergie** NOUN
solar power

die **Sonnenmilch** NOUN
suntan lotion

das **Sonnenöl** NOUN (PL die **Sonnenöle**)
suntan oil

der **Sonnenschein** NOUN
sunshine

der **Sonnenschirm** NOUN (PL die **Sonnenschirme**)
sunshade

der **Sonnenstich** NOUN
sunstroke

**sonnig** ADJECTIVE
sunny

der **Sonntag** NOUN (PL die **Sonntage**)
Sunday ◊ *am Sonntag* on Sunday

**sonntags** ADVERB
on Sundays

**sonst** ADVERB, CONJUNCTION
[1] normally ◊ *Was ist mit dir? Du bist doch sonst nicht so still.* What's wrong with you? You're not normally so quiet. ◊ *Die Kinder sind sonst eigentlich artiger.* The children normally behave better.
[2] else ◊ *Wer sonst?* Who else? ◊ *Was sonst?* What else? ◊ *Sonst war niemand da.* Nobody else was there. ◊ *sonst nichts* nothing else
♦ **sonst noch** else ◊ *Was hast du sonst noch bekommen?* What else did you get?
♦ **Haben Sie sonst noch einen Wunsch?** Would you like anything else?
♦ **Sonst noch etwas?** Anything else?
[3] otherwise ◊ *Ich habe etwas Kopfschmerzen, aber sonst geht's mir gut.* I've got a headache, otherwise I feel fine. ◊ *Geh besser nach Hause, sonst macht sich deine Mutter Sorgen.* You'd better go home otherwise your mother will be worried.

**sonstig** ADJECTIVE
other

**sonstwo** ADVERB
somewhere else

**sooft** CONJUNCTION
whenever

die **Sorge** NOUN
worry
♦ **Ich mache mir Sorgen.** I'm worried.

**sorgen** VERB

♦ **für jemanden sorgen** to look after somebody
♦ **für etwas sorgen** to see to something
♦ **sich um jemanden sorgen** to worry about somebody

**sorgfältig** ADJECTIVE
careful

die **Sorte** NOUN
[1] sort ◊ *Welche Sorte Äpfel ist das?* What sort of apple is that?
[2] brand ◊ *Welche Sorte Waschmittel verwenden Sie?* What brand of detergent do you use?

**sortieren** VERB (PERFECT **hat sortiert**)
to sort out

die **Soße** NOUN
[1] sauce ◊ *Eis mit Himbeersoße* ice cream with raspberry sauce
[2] gravy ◊ *Schweinebraten mit Soße* roast pork with gravy
[3] dressing ◊ *Salat mit einer Joghurtsoße* salad with a yoghurt dressing

das **Souvenir** NOUN (PL die **Souvenirs**)
souvenir

**soviel** ADVERB *see* **viel**

**soviel** CONJUNCTION
as far as
♦ **soviel ich weiß** as far as I know

**soweit** ADVERB *see* **weit**

**soweit** CONJUNCTION
as far as ◊ *Soweit ich weiß, kann er nicht kommen.* As far as I know, he can't come.

**sowenig** ADVERB *see* **wenig**

**sowie** CONJUNCTION
as soon as ◊ *Ich rufe an, sowie ich Bescheid weiß.* I'll phone as soon as I know.

**sowieso** ADVERB
anyway

**sowohl** CONJUNCTION
♦ **sowohl ... als auch** both ... and

**sozial** ADJECTIVE
social

der **Sozialdemokrat** NOUN (GEN des **Sozialdemokraten**, PL die **Sozialdemokraten**)
social democrat

die **Sozialhilfe** NOUN
social security ◊ *Sozialhilfe bekommen* to be on social security

die **Sozialkunde** NOUN
social studies

die **Sozialversicherung** NOUN
social security

die **Sozialwissenschaften** PL NOUN
social sciences

**sozusagen** ADVERB
so to speak

die **Spalte** NOUN

**1** crack ◊ *Durch die Trockenheit hatten sich tiefe Spalten gebildet.* Deep cracks had formed as a result of the dry spell.

**2** column ◊ *Der Text ist in zwei Spalten gedruckt.* The text is printed in two columns.

**spalten** VERB
to split

**Spanien** NEUT NOUN
Spain
♦ **aus Spanien** from Spain
♦ **in Spanien** in Spain
♦ **nach Spanien** to Spain

der **Spanier** NOUN (PL die **Spanier**)
Spaniard
♦ **Er ist Spanier.** He's Spanish.
♦ **die Spanier** the Spanish

die **Spanierin** NOUN
Spaniard
♦ **Sie ist Spanierin.** She's Spanish.

das **Spanisch** NOUN (GEN des **Spanischen**)
see also **spanisch** ADJECTIVE
Spanish ◊ *Er lernt Spanisch in der Schule.* He's learning Spanish at school.

**spanisch** ADJECTIVE
Spanish

**spannend** ADJECTIVE
exciting

die **Spannung** NOUN
**1** suspense ◊ *ein Film voller Spannung* a film full of suspense
♦ **Sie erwartet die Prüfungsergebnisse mit Spannung.** She can't wait for the exam results.
**2** tension ◊ *Das führte zu Spannungen zwischen den beiden Ländern.* That caused tension between the two countries.

das **Sparbuch** NOUN (PL die **Sparbücher**)
savings book

die **Sparbüchse** NOUN
money box

**sparen** VERB
to save ◊ *Wir müssen sparen.* We have to save. ◊ *Sie hat hundert Mark gespart.* She's saved a hundred marks. ◊ *Energie sparen* to save energy ◊ *Er spart für ein Mountainbike.* He's saving for a mountain bike.
♦ **sich etwas sparen (1)** not to bother with something ◊ *Den Film kannst du dir sparen.* Don't bother with that film.
♦ **sich etwas sparen (2)** to keep something to oneself ◊ *Spar dir deine Bemerkungen.* You can keep your remarks to yourself.
♦ **mit etwas sparen** to be sparing with something
♦ **an etwas sparen** to economize on something ◊ *Sie spart in letzter Zeit am Essen.* She's been economizing on food recently.

**Be careful! sparen does not mean to spare.**

der **Spargel** NOUN
asparagus

die **Sparkasse** NOUN
savings bank

**sparsam** ADJECTIVE
**1** economical ◊ *ein sparsames Auto* an economical car ◊ *Wir sollten mit den Rohstoffen sparsam umgehen.* We should be economical with raw materials.
**2** thrifty ◊ *Sie ist sehr sparsam.* She's very thrifty.

das **Sparschwein** NOUN (PL die **Sparschweine**)
piggy bank

der **Spaß** NOUN (GEN des **Spaßes**, PL die **Späße**)
fun ◊ *Wir hatten in den Ferien viel Spaß.* We had great fun in the holidays.
♦ **Sie versteht keinen Spaß.** She has no sense of humour.
♦ **Skifahren macht mir Spaß.** I like skiing.
♦ **zum Spaß** for fun ◊ *Ich mache den Kurs nur zum Spaß.* I'm only doing the course for fun.
♦ **Ich habe das doch nur zum Spaß gesagt.** I only said it as a joke.
♦ **Viel Spaß!** Have fun!

**spät** ADJECTIVE, ADVERB
late ◊ *Es wird spät.* It's getting late.
♦ **Wir kamen zu spät.** We were late.
♦ **Wie spät ist es?** What's the time?

**später** ADJECTIVE, ADVERB
later
♦ **Bis später!** See you later!

**spätestens** ADVERB
at the latest

der **Spatz** NOUN (GEN des **Spatzen**, PL die **Spatzen**)
sparrow

**spazieren** VERB
♦ **spazieren fahren** to go for a drive
♦ **spazieren gehen** to go for a walk

der **Spaziergang** NOUN (PL die **Spaziergänge**)
walk ◊ *einen Spaziergang machen* to go for a walk

der **Speck** NOUN
bacon

das **Speerwerfen** NOUN
throwing the javelin

der **Speicher** NOUN (PL die **Speicher**)
**1** loft ◊ *Die alten Möbel sind auf dem Speicher.* The old furniture's in the loft.
**2** storehouse ◊ *Die alten Speicher am Hafen wurden zu Wohnungen umgebaut.* The old storehouses at the harbour were converted into flats.
**3** memory ◊ *Ich will den Speicher meines Computers erweitern.* I want to expand the memory of my computer.

**speichern** VERB (PERFECT **hat gespeichert**)
**1** to store ◊ *Energie speichern* to store energy

**S**

☞

2 to save ◇ *eine Datei speichern* to save a file

das **Speiseeis** NOUN
ice cream

die **Speisekarte** NOUN
menu ◇ *Könnte ich bitte die Speisekarte haben?* Could I have the menu please?

der **Speisesaal** NOUN
dining room

der **Speisewagen** NOUN (PL die **Speisewagen**)
dining car

die **Spende** NOUN
donation

**spenden** VERB
to donate ◇ *Ich habe zehn Mark gespendet.* I've donated ten marks.
♦**Bitte spenden Sie für die Flüchtlinge.** Please give a donation for the refugees.
♦**Blut spenden** to give blood
  *Be careful! spenden does not mean to spend.*

der **Spender** NOUN (PL die **Spender**)
donor

**spendieren** VERB (PERFECT **hat spendiert**)
♦**jemandem etwas spendieren** to stand somebody something ◇ *Mutti hat uns ein Eis spendiert.* Mum stood us all an ice cream.

die **Sperre** NOUN
1 barrier ◇ *Vor dem Eingang befand sich eine Sperre.* There was a barrier in front of the entrance.
2 ban ◇ *Er erhielt eine Sperre von drei Monaten.* He got a three-month ban.

**sperren** VERB (PERFECT **hat gesperrt**)
1 to close ◇ *Die Polizei hat die Straße gesperrt.* The police closed the road.
2 to obstruct ◇ *Es ist verboten, gegnerische Spieler zu sperren.* Obstructing the opposition is not allowed.
3 to lock ◇ *Diese Dateien sind gesperrt.* These files are locked.

die **Spezialität** NOUN
speciality

der **Spiegel** NOUN (PL die **Spiegel**)
mirror ◇ *Er sah in den Spiegel.* He looked in the mirror.

das **Spiegelbild** NOUN (PL die **Spiegelbilder**)
reflection

das **Spiegelei** NOUN (PL die **Spiegeleier**)
fried egg

das **Spiel** NOUN (PL die **Spiele**)
1 game ◇ *Sollen wir ein Spiel spielen?* Shall we play a game? ◇ *Hast du das Spiel England gegen Deutschland gesehen?* Did you see the England-Germany game? ◇ *Sie hat das erste Spiel des zweiten Satzes verloren.* She lost the first game of the second set.
2 pack ◇ *Hast du ein Spiel Karten?* Do you have a pack of cards?
♦**ein Theaterspiel** a play

**spielen** VERB
to play ◇ *Die Kinder spielen im Garten.* The children are playing in the garden. ◇ *Wollen wir Tennis spielen?* Shall we play tennis? ◇ *Wer spielt den Hamlet?* Who's playing Hamlet? ◇ *Wir haben um Geld gespielt.* We played for money.

**spielend** ADVERB
easily

der **Spieler** NOUN (PL die **Spieler**)
1 player ◇ *Wir brauchen noch einen dritten Spieler.* We still need a third player.
2 gambler ◇ *Er ist ein leidenschaftlicher Spieler.* He's a passionate gambler.

das **Spielfeld** NOUN (PL die **Spielfelder**)
pitch

der **Spielfilm** NOUN (PL die **Spielfilme**)
feature film

der **Spielplatz** NOUN (GEN des **Spielplatzes**, PL die **Spielplätze**)
playground

die **Spielregel** NOUN
rule ◇ *Ich erkläre euch die Spielregeln.* I'll explain the rules of the game to you.

die **Spielsachen** FEM PL NOUN
toys

der **Spielverderber** NOUN (PL die **Spielverderber**)
spoilsport

das **Spielzeug** NOUN (PL die **Spielzeuge**)
toy

das **Spielzimmer** NOUN (PL die **Spielzimmer**)
playroom

der **Spinat** NOUN
spinach

die **Spinne** NOUN
spider

**spinnen** VERB (IMPERFECT **spann**, PERFECT **hat gesponnen**)
1 to spin ◇ *Wolle spinnen* to spin wool
2 to be crazy ◇ *Du spinnst wohl!* You're crazy!

die **Spionage** NOUN
espionage

**spionieren** VERB (PERFECT **hat spioniert**)
to spy

**spitz** ADJECTIVE
pointed
♦**ein spitzer Winkel** an acute angle
♦**eine spitze Zunge** a sharp tongue
♦**eine spitze Bemerkung** a caustic remark

die **Spitze** NOUN
1 point ◇ *Die Spitze des Bleistifts ist abgebrochen.* The point of the pencil has broken off.
2 peak ◇ *Die Spitzen der Berge waren schneebedeckt.* The peaks of the mountains were covered with snow.
3 top ◇ *Welche Mannschaft liegt an der Spitze?* Which team is top?

**4** lace ◊ *An ihrem Kleid war ein Kragen aus Spitze.* Her dress had a lace collar.
♦ **Das war Spitze!** That was great!

**spitzen** VERB
to sharpen

der **Spitzer** NOUN (PL die **Spitzer**)
pencil sharpener

der **Spitzname** NOUN (GEN des **Spitznamens,** PL die **Spitznamen**)
nickname

der **Splitter** NOUN (PL die **Splitter**)
splinter

**sponsern** VERB
to sponsor

der **Sport** NOUN
sport

die **Sportart** NOUN
sport ◊ *verschiedene Sportarten* various sports

der **Sportler** NOUN (PL die **Sportler**)
sportsman

die **Sportlerin** NOUN
sportswoman

**sportlich** ADJECTIVE
sporty ◊ *Bettina ist sehr sportlich.* Bettina is very sporty.

der **Sportplatz** NOUN (GEN des **Sportplatzes,** PL die **Sportplätze**)
sports field

der **Sportschuh** NOUN (PL die **Sportschuhe**)
trainer

der **Sportverein** NOUN (PL die **Sportvereine**)
sports club

das **Sportzentrum** NOUN (PL die **Sportzentren**)
sports centre

**spotten** VERB
♦ **spotten über** to ridicule ◊ *Ich kann es nicht leiden, wenn man über mich spottet.* I can't stand being ridiculed.

**sprach** VERB *see* **sprechen**

die **Sprache** NOUN
language

der **Sprachführer** NOUN (PL die **Sprachführer**)
phrase book

das **Sprachlabor** NOUN (PL die **Sprachlabors** or **Sprachlabore**)
language laboratory

**sprachlich** ADJECTIVE
linguistic

**sprachlos** ADJECTIVE
speechless

**sprang** VERB *see* **springen**

**sprechen** VERB (PRESENT **spricht,** IMPERFECT **sprach,** PERFECT **hat gesprochen**)
**1** to talk ◊ *Seid bitte ruhig, wenn ich spreche.* Please be quiet, I'm talking.
◊ *Du sprichst so leise.* You talk so quietly. ◊ *Wir haben von dir gesprochen.* We were talking about you.
**2** to say ◊ *Sie hat kein Wort gesprochen.* She didn't say a word.

**3** to speak ◊ *Ich spreche Italienisch ziemlich schlecht.* I speak Italian pretty badly.
♦ **jemanden sprechen** to speak to somebody ◊ *Der Direktor will dich sprechen.* The headmaster wants to speak to you.
♦ **mit jemandem über etwas sprechen** to speak to somebody about something
♦ **Das spricht für ihn.** That's a point in his favour.

die **Sprechstunde** NOUN
surgery (*doctor's*)

**spricht** VERB *see* **sprechen**

das **Sprichwort** NOUN (PL die **Sprichwörter**)
proverb

**springen** VERB (IMPERFECT **sprang,** PERFECT **ist gesprungen**)
**1** to jump ◊ *Er sprang über den Zaun.* He jumped over the fence.
**2** to crack ◊ *Das Glas ist gesprungen.* The glass has cracked.

die **Spritze** NOUN
**1** syringe ◊ *Die Spritze muss steril sein.* The syringe has to be sterile.
**2** injection ◊ *Der Arzt hat mir eine Spritze gegeben.* The doctor gave me an injection.
**3** nozzle ◊ *Die Spritze am Gartenschlauch ist nicht dicht.* The nozzle on the garden hose leaks.

**spritzen** VERB (PERFECT **hat/ist gespritzt**)
*Use* **haben** *to form the perfect tense. Use* **sein** *to form the perfect tense for* **to spurt out.**
**1** to spray ◊ *Er hat sein Fahrrad grün gespritzt.* He's sprayed his bike green.
♦ **den Garten spritzen** to water the garden
♦ **jemanden nass spritzen** to splash somebody
♦ **Als er durch die Pfütze fuhr, hat es gespritzt.** When he drove through the puddle, the water splashed up.
**2** to spurt out ◊ *Das Wasser ist nach allen Seiten gespritzt.* The water spurted out all over the place. ◊ *Das Blut spritzte aus der Wunde.* The blood spurted out of the wound.

der **Sprudel** NOUN (PL die **Sprudel**)
mineral water
♦ **süßer Sprudel** lemonade

**sprühen** VERB (PERFECT **hat/ist gesprüht**)
*For the perfect tense use* **haben** *when the verb has an object and* **sein** *when there is no object. Use* **haben** *to form the perfect tense for* **to sparkle.**
**1** to spray ◊ *Sie hat Haarspray auf ihre Haare gesprüht.* She sprayed her hair with hairspray.
**2** to fly ◊ *In alle Richtungen sind Funken gesprüht.* Sparks flew in all directions.

**S**

☞

3 to sparkle ◊ *Er hat gestern Abend vor Witz gesprüht.* He was sparkling with humour yesterday evening.

der **Sprung** NOUN (PL die **Sprünge**)
1 jump ◊ *Das war ein weiter Sprung.* That was a long jump.
2 crack ◊ *Die Tasse hat einen Sprung.* There is a crack in the cup.

das **Sprungbrett** NOUN (PL die **Sprungbretter**)
springboard

die **Spucke** NOUN
spit

**spucken** VERB
to spit

das **Spülbecken** NOUN (PL die **Spülbecken**)
kitchen sink

die **Spüle** NOUN
kitchen sink

**spülen** VERB
1 to rinse ◊ *Wollsachen muss man gut spülen.* Woollens have to be rinsed well.
2 to wash up ◊ *Wenn du spülst, dann trockne ich ab.* If you wash up I'll dry.

die **Spülmaschine** NOUN
dishwasher

das **Spülmittel** NOUN (PL die **Spülmittel**)
washing-up liquid

die **Spur** NOUN
1 track ◊ *Wir sahen Spuren im Sand.* We saw tracks in the sand. ◊ *Das Band hat eine Spur für Bilder und eine andere für den Ton.* The tape has one track for pictures and another for sound.
2 lane ◊ *Der Fahrer vor mir hat plötzlich die Spur gewechselt.* The driver in front of me suddenly changed lane.
3 trace ◊ *Auf ihrem Gesicht sah man die Spuren der Anstrengung.* You could see the traces of strain on her face.
4 trail ◊ *Die Polizei verfolgte seine Spur.* The police followed his trail.
◆ **Das Essen war eine Spur zu scharf.** The meal was a touch too spicy.

**spüren** VERB
to feel

der **Staat** NOUN (PL die **Staaten**)
state
◆ **die Vereinigten Staaten von Amerika** the United States of America

**staatlich** ADJECTIVE
1 state ◊ *staatliche Fördermittel* state subsidies ◊ *ein staatliche Schule* a state school
2 state-run ◊ *eine staatliche Einrichtung* a state-run organization

die **Staatsangehörigkeit** NOUN
nationality

**stabil** ADJECTIVE
1 stable ◊ *Die Lage ist stabil.* The situation is stable.
2 sturdy ◊ *stabile Möbel* sturdy furniture

der **Stachel** NOUN (PL die **Stacheln**)
1 spike ◊ *Ich habe mir die Hose an einem Stachel aufgerissen.* I've torn my trousers on a spike.
2 spine ◊ *Ein Igel hat Stacheln.* A hedgehog has spines. ◊ *Dieser Kaktus hat lange Stacheln.* This cactus has long spines.
3 sting ◊ *Ich habe versucht, den Stachel der Biene herauszuziehen.* I tried to take the bee sting out.

die **Stachelbeere** NOUN
gooseberry

der **Stacheldraht** NOUN (PL die **Stacheldrähte**)
barbed wire

das **Stadion** NOUN (PL die **Stadien**)
stadium

die **Stadt** NOUN (PL die **Städte**)
town

der **Stadtbummel** NOUN (PL die **Stadtbummel**)
stroll through the town

**städtisch** ADJECTIVE
municipal

der **Stadtkreis** NOUN (PL die **Stadtkreise**)
town borough

die **Stadtmitte** NOUN
town centre

der **Stadtplan** NOUN (PL die **Stadtpläne**)
street map

der **Stadtrand** NOUN (PL die **Stadtränder**)
outskirts

die **Stadtrundfahrt** NOUN
tour of the city

der **Stadtteil** NOUN (PL die **Stadtteile**)
part of town

das **Stadtwappen** NOUN (PL die **Stadtwappen**)
municipal coat of arms

das **Stadtzentrum** NOUN (PL die **Stadtzentren**)
city centre

der **Staffellauf** NOUN (PL die **Staffelläufe**)
relay race

der **Stahl** NOUN
steel

**stahl** VERB see **stehlen**

der **Stall** NOUN (PL die **Ställe**)
stable ◊ *Die Pferde sind im Stall.* The horses are in the stable.
◆ **ein Hühnerstall** a henhouse

der **Stamm** NOUN (PL die **Stämme**)
1 trunk ◊ *Der Baum hat einen dicken Stamm.* The tree has a thick trunk.
2 tribe ◊ *Er gehört zum Stamm der Bantus.* He belongs to the Bantu tribe.
3 stem ◊ *Die Endung wird an den Stamm des Verbs angehängt.* The ending's added to the stem of the verb.

**stammen** VERB
◆ **stammen aus** to come from

der **Stammgast** NOUN (PL die **Stammgäste**)
regular customer

der **Stammtisch** NOUN (PL die **Stammtische**)
table for the regulars

*i* *In Germany it is usual for a group of friends to reserve a table in the same pub or restaurant for the same time each week.*

der **Stand** NOUN (PL die **Stände**)
  [1] state ◊ *Was ist der Stand der Dinge?* What's the state of affairs?
  [2] score ◊ *Sie sind beim Stand von eins zu eins in die Pause.* The score was one all at half-time.
  [3] stand ◊ *An welchen Stand hast du den Luftballon gekauft?* Which stand did you buy the balloon at?
  [4] level ◊ *Prüf mal den Ölstand.* Check the oil level.
  ◆ **zu Stande** *see* **zustande**
  **stand** VERB *see* **stehen**
  **ständig** ADJECTIVE
  constant ◊ *Musst du ständig stören?* Do you constantly have to interrupt?

der **Standort** NOUN (PL die **Standorte**)
  location

der **Stapel** NOUN (PL die **Stapel**)
  pile
  **starb** VERB *see* **sterben**
  **stark** ADJECTIVE
  [1] strong ◊ *Mein Bruder ist stärker als du.* My brother's stronger than you.
  [2] heavy ◊ *starke Regenfälle* heavy rain
  ◆ **starke Kopfschmerzen** a splitting headache
  [3] great ◊ *Das war stark!* That was great!

der **Start** NOUN (PL die **Starts**)
  [1] start ◊ *Es waren über hundert Läufer am Start.* There were over a hundred runners at the start.
  [2] takeoff ◊ *Die Maschine war bereit zum Start.* The machine was ready for takeoff.
  **starten** VERB
  [1] to start ◊ *Wann startet das Rennen?* When does the race start?
  [2] to take off ◊ *Das Flugzeug startet gleich.* The plane is about to take off.

die **Station** NOUN
  [1] station ◊ *An welcher Station müssen wir aussteigen?* Which station do we have to get off at?
  [2] hospital ward ◊ *Der Patient wurde auf eine andere Station verlegt.* The patient's been moved to another ward.
  **statt** CONJUNCTION, PREPOSITION
  *The preposition* **statt** *takes the genitive or the dative.*
  instead of ◊ *Statt nach Hause zu gehen, sind wir noch in die Disko.* Instead of going home, we went to the disco. ◊ *Sie kam statt ihres Bruders.* She came instead of her brother.
  **stattfinden** VERB (IMPERFECT **fand statt**, PERFECT **hat stattgefunden**)
  to take place

der **Stau** NOUN (PL die **Staus**)
  traffic
  jam ◊ *Wir sind im Stau stecken geblieben.* We were stuck in a traffic jam.

der **Staub** NOUN
  dust
  ◆ **Staub wischen** to dust
  **staubig** ADJECTIVE
  dusty
  **staubsaugen** VERB (PERFECT **hat staubgesaugt**)
  to hoover

der **Staubsauger** NOUN (PL die **Staubsauger**)
  vacuum cleaner
  **staunen** VERB
  to be astonished

die **Stauung** NOUN
  congestion
  **Std.** ABBREVIATION (= **Stunde**)
  hr.

das **Steak** NOUN (PL die **Steaks**)
  steak
  **stechen** VERB (PRESENT **sticht**, IMPERFECT **stach**, PERFECT **hat gestochen**)
  [1] to prick ◊ *Ich habe mich mit der Nadel gestochen.* I've pricked myself with the needle.
  [2] to sting ◊ *Mich hat eine Biene gestochen.* A bee stung me.
  [3] to bite ◊ *Reibe dich ein, damit du nicht gestochen wirst.* Rub something on so that you won't be bitten.
  [4] to take ◊ *Sie hat meine Dame mit dem König gestochen.* She took my queen with her king.

die **Steckdose** NOUN
  socket
  **stecken** VERB
  [1] to put ◊ *Sie steckte ihren Geldbeutel in die Tasche.* She put her purse in her bag.
  [2] to insert ◊ *Stecken Sie die Münze in den Schlitz.* Insert the coin into the slot.
  [3] to stick ◊ *Steck deinen Finger nicht in das Loch!* Don't stick your finger in the hole.
  [4] to pin ◊ *Ich steckte das Abzeichen an meine Jacke.* I pinned the badge onto my jacket.
  [5] to be stuck ◊ *Wir stecken im Stau.* We are stuck in a traffic jam.
  ◆ **Wo steckt sie nur?** Where on earth is she?

der **Stecker** NOUN (PL die **Stecker**)
  plug

die **Stecknadel** NOUN
  pin
  **stehen** VERB (IMPERFECT **stand**, PERFECT **hat gestanden**)
  [1] to stand ◊ *Es war so voll, dass wir stehen mussten.* It was so full that we had to stand.

**S**

☞

2 to be ◊ *Vor unserem Haus steht eine Kastanie.* There's a chestnut tree in front of our house.

3 to say ◊ *In der Zeitung steht, dass das Wetter besser wird.* It says in the newspaper that the weather will improve.

♦ **zum Stehen kommen** to come to a halt ◊ *Der Verkehr kam zum Stehen.* The traffic came to a halt.

♦ **Es steht schlecht um ihn.** Things are bad for him.

♦ **jemandem stehen** to suit somebody ◊ *Blau steht dir gut.* Blue suits you.

♦ **Wie steht's? (1)** How are things?

♦ **Wie steht's? (2)** What's the score?

♦ **stehen bleiben** to stop ◊ *Meine Uhr ist stehen geblieben.* My watch has stopped.

die **Stehlampe** NOUN
standard lamp

**stehlen** VERB (PRESENT **stiehlt**, IMPERFECT **stahl**, PERFECT **hat gestohlen**)
to steal

**steif** ADJECTIVE
stiff

**steigen** VERB (IMPERFECT **stieg**, PERFECT **ist gestiegen**)
1 to rise ◊ *Der Ballon stieg zum Himmel.* The balloon rose into the sky.
2 to climb ◊ *Sie ist auf die Leiter gestiegen.* She climbed up the ladder.

♦ **in etwas steigen** to get into something ◊ *Er stieg ins Auto.* He got into the car.

♦ **Sie stieg in den Zug.** She got on the train.

♦ **auf etwas steigen** to get on something ◊ *Sie stieg aufs Fahrrad.* She got on her bike.

die **Steigung** NOUN
incline

**steil** ADJECTIVE
steep

der **Stein** NOUN (PL die **Steine**)
stone

der **Steinbock** NOUN (PL die **Steinböcke**)
Capricorn ◊ *Er ist Steinbock.* He's Capricorn.

**steinig** ADJECTIVE
stony

die **Stelle** NOUN
1 place ◊ *Ich habe mir die Stelle im Buch angestrichen.* I've marked the place in the book.

♦ **an dieser Stelle** here
2 job ◊ *Ich suche eine neue Stelle.* I'm looking for a new job.
3 office ◊ *Bei welcher Stelle kann man einen Pass bekommen?* In which office can you get a passport?

♦ **An deiner Stelle würde ich das nicht tun.** I wouldn't do it if I were you.

**stellen** VERB

1 to put ◊ *Ich habe die Vase auf den Tisch gestellt.* I put the vase on the table.
2 to set ◊ *Stell deine Uhr nach meiner.* Set your watch by mine.
3 to supply ◊ *Die Lehrbücher werden gestellt.* The course books will be supplied.

♦ **sich irgendwohin stellen** to stand somewhere ◊ *Stellt euch bitte an die Wand.* Please stand against the wall.

♦ **sich stellen** to give oneself up ◊ *Der Dieb hat sich gestellt.* The thief gave himself up.

♦ **sich dumm stellen** to pretend to be stupid

die **Stellenanzeige** NOUN
job advertisement

die **Stellung** NOUN
position ◊ *In welcher Stellung schläfst du?* Which position do you sleep in? ◊ *Er hat eine gute Stellung.* He has a good position.

♦ **zu etwas Stellung nehmen** to comment on something

der **Stellvertreter** NOUN (PL die **Stellvertreter**)
deputy

der **Stempel** NOUN (PL die **Stempel**)
stamp

**stempeln** VERB
to stamp

♦ **jemanden zum Sündenbock stempeln** to make somebody a scapegoat

die **Steppdecke** NOUN
quilt

die **Sterbehilfe** NOUN
euthanasia

**sterben** VERB (PRESENT **stirbt**, IMPERFECT **starb**, PERFECT **ist gestorben**)
to die

die **Stereoanlage** NOUN
stereo

der **Stern** NOUN (PL die **Sterne**)
star ◊ *die Sterne am Himmel* the stars in the sky

das **Sternzeichen** NOUN (PL die **Sternzeichen**)
star sign ◊ *Was ist dein Sternzeichen?* What star sign are you?

das **Steuer** NOUN (PL die **Steuer**)
| see also **die Steuer** NOUN |
wheel ◊ *Wer saß am Steuer?* Who was at the wheel?

die **Steuer** NOUN
| see also **das Steuer** NOUN |
tax ◊ *Wir müssen viel Steuern bezahlen.* We have to pay a lot of tax.

das **Steuerrad** NOUN (PL die **Steuerräder**)
steering wheel

der **Steward** NOUN (PL die **Stewards**)
steward

die **Stewardess** NOUN (PL die **Stewardessen**)
stewardess

der **Stich** NOUN (PL die **Stiche**)

⬚1⬚ <u>bite</u> ◊ *Das Mittel schützt vor Stichen.*
This gives protection from bites. ◊ *ein
Mückenstich* a midge bite
◆ **ein Bienenstich** a bee sting
⬚2⬚ <u>stab</u> ◊ *Er tötete sie mit zwölf Stichen.*
He killed her by stabbing her twelve
times.
⬚3⬚ <u>stitch</u> ◊ *Sie hat den Aufhänger mit ein
paar Stichen angenäht.* She sewed on
the loop with a couple of stitches. ◊ *Die
Wunde wurde mit drei Stichen genäht.*
Three stitches were put in the wound.
⬚4⬚ <u>trick</u> ◊ *Ich habe beim letzten Spiel
keinen Stich gemacht.* I didn't win any
tricks in the last game.
⬚5⬚ <u>engraving</u> ◊ *ein Kupferstich* a copper
engraving
◆ **jemanden im Stich lassen** to leave
somebody in the lurch
**sticken** VERB
to embroider
der **Stickstoff** NOUN
nitrogen
der **Stiefel** NOUN (PL die **Stiefel**)
boot
das **Stiefkind** NOUN (PL die **Stiefkinder**)
stepchild
die **Stiefmutter** NOUN (PL die **Stiefmütter**)
stepmother
der **Stiefvater** NOUN (PL die **Stiefväter**)
stepfather
**stiehlt** VERB *see* **stehlen**
der **Stiel** NOUN (PL die **Stiele**)
⬚1⬚ <u>handle</u> ◊ *der Stiel des Besens* the
broom handle
⬚2⬚ <u>stem</u> ◊ *Er hat den Stiel der Tulpe
abgeknickt.* He snapped the stem off the
tulip.
der **Stier** NOUN (PL die **Stiere**)
⬚1⬚ <u>bull</u> ◊ *Der Stier wurde getötet.* The
bull was killed.
⬚2⬚ <u>Taurus</u> ◊ *Brigitte ist Stier.* Brigitte's
Taurus.
der **Stift** NOUN (PL die **Stifte**)
⬚1⬚ <u>peg</u> ◊ *Das Brett wird mit Stiften an der
Wand befestigt.* The board is fixed to the
wall with pegs.
⬚2⬚ <u>crayon</u> ◊ *Sebastian hat lauter bunte
Stifte bekommen.* Sebastian got lots of
coloured crayons.
⬚3⬚ <u>pencil</u> ◊ *Schreib lieber mit Kuli als mit
einem Stift.* I'd rather you wrote with a
Biro than a pencil.
**stiften** VERB
◆ **Sie hat eine Runde Eis gestiftet.** She
bought us all an ice cream.
◆ **Unruhe stiften** to cause trouble
der **Stil** NOUN (PL die **Stile**)
style
**still** ADJECTIVE
quiet ◊ *Seid mal still.* Be quiet.
◆ **Sie stand ganz still.** She stood quite still.
die **Stille** NOUN

quietness
◆ **in aller Stille** quietly
**stillhalten** VERB (PRESENT **hält still,** IMPERFECT
**hielt still,** PERFECT **hat stillgehalten**)
to keep still
**stillschweigend** ADVERB
tacitly
die **Stimme** NOUN
⬚1⬚ <u>voice</u> ◊ *Er hat eine laute Stimme.* He
has a loud voice.
⬚2⬚ <u>vote</u> ◊ *Er bekam nur zwanzig
Stimmen.* He only got twenty votes.
◆ **Wem hast du deine Stimme gegeben?**
Who did you vote for?
**stimmen** VERB
to be right ◊ *Die Übersetzung stimmt
nicht.* The translation isn't right. ◊ *Das
stimmt nicht!* That's not right!
◆ **ein Instrument stimmen** to tune an
instrument
◆ **stimmen für** to vote for
◆ **stimmen gegen** to vote against
◆ **Stimmt so!** Keep the change.
die **Stimmung** NOUN
mood
**stinken** VERB (IMPERFECT **stank,** PERFECT **hat
gestunken**)
to stink
das **Stipendium** NOUN (PL die **Stipendien**)
grant
**stirbt** VERB *see* **sterben**
die **Stirn** NOUN
forehead
der **Stock (1)** NOUN (PL die **Stöcke**)
stick ◊ *Er hat ihn mit einem Stock
geschlagen.* He hit him with a stick.
der **Stock (2)** NOUN (PL die **Stock** *or*
**Stockwerke**)
floor ◊ *Wir wohnen im dritten Stock.* We
live on the third floor.
der **Stoff** NOUN (PL die **Stoffe**)
⬚1⬚ <u>fabric</u> ◊ *Das ist ein hübscher Stoff.*
That's a pretty fabric.
⬚2⬚ <u>material</u> ◊ *Ich sammle Stoff für mein
Referat.* I'm collecting material for my
assignment.
**stöhnen** VERB
to groan
**stolpern** VERB (PERFECT **ist gestolpert**)
⬚1⬚ <u>to stumble</u> ◊ *Er ist gestolpert und
gefallen.* He stumbled and fell.
⬚2⬚ <u>to trip</u> ◊ *Er ist über einen Stein
gestolpert.* He tripped over a stone.
**stolz** ADJECTIVE
proud ◊ *Ich bin stolz auf dich.* I'm proud
of you.
der **Stöpsel** NOUN (PL die **Stöpsel**)
plug
**stören** VERB
to disturb ◊ *Störe ich?* Am I disturbing
you? ◊ *Ich will nicht länger stören.* I
won't disturb you any longer.

**S**

◆ **Stört es dich, wenn ich rauche?** Do you mind if I smoke?

◆ **Das stört meine Konzentration.** That's stopping me from concentrating.

◆ **Die Leitung war gestört.** It was a bad line.

◆ **sich an etwas stören** to worry about something ◊ *Stör dich nicht an der Schrift, der Inhalt ist wichtig.* Don't worry about the writing, it's the content that counts.

**störend** ADJECTIVE
disturbing

die **Störung** NOUN
1 interruption ◊ *Diese dauernden Störungen regen mich auf.* These constant interruptions are getting on my nerves.
2 interference ◊ *Es war eine Störung beim Bild.* There was interference to the picture.

**stoßen** VERB (PRESENT **stößt**, IMPERFECT **stieß**, PERFECT **hat gestoßen**)

◆ **den Kopf an etwas stoßen** to bump one's head on something ◊ *Ich habe mir an der niedrigen Decke den Kopf gestoßen.* I bumped my head on the low ceiling.

◆ **sich stoßen** to bump oneself ◊ *Sie hat einen blauen Fleck, wo sie sich gestoßen hat.* She has a bruise where she bumped herself.

◆ **sich an etwas stoßen** to take exception to something ◊ *Sie hat sich an seinem schlechten Benehmen gestoßen.* She took exception to his bad behaviour.

◆ **an etwas stoßen** to bump into something ◊ *Pass auf, dass du nicht an die Statue stößt.* Watch out that you don't bump into the statue.

◆ **auf etwas stoßen** to come across ◊ *Heute bin ich auf dem Flohmarkt auf ein tolles Buch gestoßen.* I came across a great book at the flea market today.

**stottern** VERB
to stutter

**Str.** ABBREVIATION (= *Straße*)
St

die **Strafarbeit** NOUN
lines ◊ *Ich habe eine Strafarbeit bekommen.* I got lines.

die **Strafe** NOUN
1 punishment ◊ *Zur Strafe müsst ihr länger bleiben.* You'll be kept in after school as a punishment.
◆ **eine Gefängnisstrafe** a prison sentence
2 fine ◊ *Er musste eine Strafe von dreißig Mark bezahlen.* He had to pay a thirty mark fine.

der **Strahl** NOUN (PL die **Strahlen**)
1 ray ◊ *radioaktive Strahlen* radioactive rays ◊ *ein Sonnenstrahl* a ray of sunlight
◆ **ein Lichtstrahl** a beam of light

2 jet ◊ *ein Wasserstrahl* a jet of water

**strahlen** VERB
1 to shine ◊ *Die Sterne strahlten hell.* The stars shone brightly.
2 to beam ◊ *Sie strahlte, als sie das hörte.* She beamed when she heard that.

die **Strahlung** NOUN
radiation

der **Strand** NOUN (PL die **Strände**)
1 beach ◊ *Wir haben den ganzen Tag am Strand gelegen.* We lay on the beach all day.
2 shore ◊ *Das wurde an den Strand gespült.* That was washed up on the shore.

die **Strapaze** NOUN
strain

**strapazieren** VERB (PERFECT **hat strapaziert**)
1 to be hard on ◊ *Du hast heute deinen Computer ganz schön strapaziert.* You've been really hard on your computer today.
2 to wear out ◊ *Die Wanderung hat uns ziemlich strapaziert.* The walk has really worn us out.

die **Straße** NOUN
1 street ◊ *In welcher Straße wohnt Eva?* Which street does Eva live in?
2 road ◊ *Wir sind die Straße entlang der Küste gefahren.* We drove along the coast road.

die **Straßenbahn** NOUN
tram

der **Strauß** NOUN (GEN des **Straußes**, PL die **Sträuße**)
bunch of flowers ◊ *Wir haben unserer Gastgeberin einen Strauß mitgebracht.* We brought our hostess a bunch of flowers.

der **Streber** NOUN (PL die **Streber**)
swot

die **Strecke** NOUN
1 distance ◊ *Wir haben diese Strecke an einem Tag zurückgelegt.* We covered this distance in one day. ◊ *Bis zu ihm ist es noch eine ziemliche Strecke.* It's still quite a distance to his place.
2 line ◊ *Auf der Strecke zwischen Stuttgart und Ulm gab es ein Zugunglück.* There's been a train accident on the Stuttgart to Ulm line.

der **Streich** NOUN (PL die **Streiche**)
trick ◊ *Sie haben dem Lehrer einen Streich gespielt.* They played a trick on the teacher.

**streicheln** VERB
to stroke

**streichen** VERB (IMPERFECT **strich**, PERFECT **hat gestrichen**)
1 to stroke ◊ *Sie strich über seine Haare.* She stroked his hair.
2 to spread ◊ *Sie strich Honig aufs Brot.* She spread honey on the bread.

◆**Butter aufs Brot streichen** to butter bread

[3] to paint ◊ *Ich muss dringend mein Zimmer streichen.* I really must paint my room.

[4] to delete ◊ *Den zweiten Satz kannst du streichen.* You can delete the second sentence.

[5] to cancel ◊ *Der Direktor hat den Schulausflug gestrichen.* The headmaster has cancelled the school trip.

das **Streichholz** NOUN (GEN des **Streichholzes**, PL die **Streichhölzer**)
match

der **Streifen** NOUN (PL die **Streifen**)
strip

der **Streifenwagen** NOUN (PL die **Streifenwagen**)
patrol car

der **Streik** NOUN (PL die **Streiks**)
strike
**streiken** VERB
to go on strike
◆**Sie streiken.** They're on strike.

der **Streit** NOUN (PL die **Streite**)
argument

sich **streiten** VERB (IMPERFECT **stritt**, PERFECT **hat gestritten**)
to argue ◊ *Sie streiten sich ständig.* They argue constantly.
◆**Darüber lässt sich streiten.** That's debatable.

**streng** ADJECTIVE
[1] strict ◊ *Meine Eltern sind furchtbar streng.* My parents are terribly strict.
[2] severe ◊ *Es war ein strenger Winter.* It was a severe winter. ◊ *Das wird streng bestraft.* That will be severely punished.
[3] sharp ◊ *Wo kommt der strenge Geruch her?* Where's that sharp smell coming from?

der **Stress** NOUN (GEN des **Stresses**)
stress
◆**Ich bin im Stress!** I'm stressed out.
**stressen** VERB (PRESENT **stresst**, IMPERFECT **stresste**, PERFECT **hat gestresst**)
to put under stress
**stressig** ADJECTIVE
stressful

der **Strich** NOUN (PL die **Striche**)
[1] line ◊ *Mach einen Strich unter die Spalte.* Draw a line under the column.
[2] stroke ◊ *Mit ein paar Strichen zeichnete er ein Haus.* He drew a house with a couple of strokes.
◆**auf den Strich gehen** to be on the game

der **Strichkode** NOUN (PL die **Strichkodes**)
bar code

der **Strichpunkt** NOUN (PL die **Strichpunkte**)
semicolon

der **Strick** NOUN (PL die **Stricke**)
rope

**stricken** VERB
to knit

das **Stroh** NOUN
straw

der **Strohhalm** NOUN (PL die **Strohhalme**)
drinking straw

der **Strom** NOUN (PL die **Ströme**)
current ◊ *der Wechselstrom* alternating current
◆**Vorsicht, auf dem Draht ist Strom.** Be careful, the wire is live.
◆**Sie haben den Strom abgeschaltet.** They've cut off the electricity.
◆**Ein Strom von Zuschauern kam aus dem Stadion.** A stream of spectators was coming out of the stadium.

die **Strömung** NOUN
current

der **Strumpf** NOUN (PL die **Strümpfe**)
stocking

die **Strumpfhose** NOUN
tights ◊ *eine Strumpfhose* a pair of tights

das **Stück** NOUN (PL die **Stücke**)
[1] piece ◊ *Sie schnitt ein Stück Käse ab.* She cut off a piece of cheese.
[2] play ◊ *Wir haben ein Stück von Brecht angesehen.* We saw a play by Brecht.

das **Stückchen** NOUN (PL die **Stückchen**)
little piece

der **Student** NOUN (GEN des **Studenten**, PL die **Studenten**)
student

die **Studentin** NOUN
student

**studieren** VERB (PERFECT **hat studiert**)
to study ◊ *Mein Bruder studiert Physik.* My brother's studying physics.

das **Studium** NOUN (PL die **Studien**)
studies

die **Stufe** NOUN
[1] step ◊ *Vorsicht, Stufe!* Mind the step!
[2] stage ◊ *Er hat bereits eine fortgeschrittene Stufe erreicht.* He's already reached an advanced stage. ◊ *eine Entwicklungsstufe* a stage of development

der **Stuhl** NOUN (PL die **Stühle**)
chair

**stumm** ADJECTIVE
[1] silent ◊ *Sie blieb stumm.* She remained silent.
[2] dumb ◊ *Sie ist von Geburt an stumm.* She's been dumb from birth.

**stumpf** ADJECTIVE
blunt ◊ *Er wurde mit einem stumpfen Gegenstand am Kopf getroffen.* He was hit on the head with a blunt object.
◆**ein stumpfer Winkel** an obtuse angle

**stumpfsinnig** ADJECTIVE
mindless

die **Stunde** NOUN

**S**

☞

[1] hour ◊ *Ich komme in einer Stunde.* I'll come in an hour.

[2] lesson ◊ *Was haben wir in der letzten Stunde behandelt?* What did we do in the last lesson?

der **Stundenplan** NOUN (PL die **Stundenpläne**)
timetable

**stündlich** ADJECTIVE
hourly ◊ *stündlich verkehren* to run hourly

**stur** ADJECTIVE
obstinate

der **Sturm** NOUN (PL die **Stürme**)
storm

**stürmen** VERB (PERFECT **ist/hat gestürmt**)
*Use **sein** to form the perfect tense for **to storm (out)**. Use **haben** to form the perfect tense for all other meanings.*
to storm ◊ *Er ist aus dem Zimmer gestürmt.* He stormed out of the room. ◊ *Die Polizei hat das Gebäude gestürmt.* The police stormed the building.
♦ *Es stürmt.* There's a gale blowing.

**stürmisch** ADJECTIVE
stormy

der **Sturz** NOUN (GEN des **Sturzes**, PL die **Stürze**)
[1] fall ◊ *Bei dem Sturz hat sie sich das Bein gebrochen.* She broke her leg in the fall.
[2] overthrow ◊ *Alle freuten sich über den Sturz des Diktators.* Everybody was pleased about the overthrow of the dictator.

**stürzen** VERB (PERFECT **hat/ist gestürzt**)
*Use **sein** to form the perfect tense. Use **haben** to form the perfect tense for **to overthrow** and for **sich stürzen**.*
[1] to fall ◊ *Sie ist vom Pferd gestürzt.* She fell off a horse.
♦ *Das Flugzeug ist ins Meer gestürzt.* The plane crashed into the sea.
[2] to rush ◊ *Er kam ins Zimmer gestürzt.* He rushed into the room.
[3] to overthrow ◊ *Die Regierung wurde gestürzt.* The government has been overthrown.
♦ *sich stürzen* to plunge ◊ *Sie stürzte sich ins Wasser.* She plunged into the water.
♦ *Er hat sich vom Fernsehturm gestürzt.* He threw himself off the television tower.

der **Sturzhelm** NOUN (PL die **Sturzhelme**)
crash helmet

die **Stütze** NOUN
support

das **Styropor** ® NOUN
polystyrene

das **Subjekt** NOUN (PL die **Subjekte**)
subject

das **Substantiv** NOUN (PL die **Substantive**)
noun

**subtrahieren** VERB (PERFECT **hat subtrahiert**)
to subtract

die **Subvention** NOUN
subsidy

die **Suche** NOUN
search

**suchen** VERB
to look for ◊ *Ich suche meinen Radiergummi.* I'm looking for my rubber. ◊ *Wir haben gesucht, es aber nicht gefunden.* We looked for it but couldn't find it.
♦ *Er wird von der Polizei gesucht.* The police are looking for him.
♦ *nach etwas suchen* to look for something ◊ *Wonach suchst du?* What are you looking for?

die **Suchmaschine** NOUN
search engine (*Internet*)

**süchtig** ADJECTIVE
addicted ◊ *heroinsüchtig* addicted to heroin

der **Süchtige** NOUN (GEN des/der **Süchtigen**, PL
die die **Süchtigen**)
addict ◊ *Ein Süchtiger hat uns erzählt, wie er süchtig geworden ist.* An addict told us how he became addicted.

**Südafrika** NEUT NOUN
South Africa
♦ *aus Südafrika* from South Africa
♦ *nach Südafrika* to South Africa

**Südamerika** NEUT NOUN
South America
♦ *aus Südamerika* from South America
♦ *nach Südamerika* to South America

der **Süden** NOUN
south

**südlich** ADJECTIVE, PREPOSITION, ADVERB
southerly ◊ *in südlicher Richtung* in a southerly direction
♦ *südlich einer Sache* to the south of something ◊ *Das Kraftwerk liegt südlich der Stadt.* The power station's to south of the city.
♦ *südlich von* south of ◊ *Das liegt südlich von Rom.* It is south of Rome.

der **Südosten** NOUN
southeast

der **Südpol** NOUN
South Pole ◊ *am Südpol* at the South Pole

der **Südwesten** NOUN
southwest

die **Summe** NOUN
total

**summen** VERB
[1] to buzz ◊ *Die Bienen summten.* The bees were buzzing.
[2] to hum ◊ *Sie summte vor sich hin.* She was humming. ◊ *Er hat ein Lied gesummt.* He hummed a song.

der **Sumpf** NOUN (PL die **Sümpfe**)
swamp

die **Sünde** NOUN

sin

das **Super** NOUN
four star ◊ *Ich tanke Super.* My car takes four star.

das **Superbenzin** NOUN
four-star petrol

der **Superlativ** NOUN (PL die **Superlative**)
superlative

der **Supermarkt** NOUN (PL die **Supermärkte**)
supermarket

die **Suppe** NOUN
soup

das **Surfbrett** NOUN (PL die **Surfbretter**)
surfboard

**surfen** VERB (PERFECT **hat gesurft**)
to surf
♦ **im Internet surfen** to surf the Net

**süß** ADJECTIVE
sweet

die **Süßigkeit** NOUN
sweet ◊ *Sie isst gern Süßigkeiten.* She likes eating sweets.

der **Süßstoff** NOUN (PL die **Süßstoffe**)
sweetener

die **Süßwaren** PL NOUN
confectionery

der **Süßwarenladen** NOUN (PL die **Süßwarenläden**)
sweetshop

das **Süßwasser** NOUN
fresh water

das **Symbol** NOUN (PL die **Symbole**)
symbol

**symmetrisch** ADJECTIVE
symmetrical

die **Sympathie** NOUN
fondness ◊ *Ihre Sympathie für ihn ist offensichtlich.* Her fondness for him is obvious.

**sympathisch** ADJECTIVE
likeable ◊ *Er ist ein sympathischer Mensch.* He's a likeable person.
♦ **Er ist mir sympathisch.** I like him.
*Be careful!* **sympathisch** *does not mean* **sympathetic***.*

die **Synagoge** NOUN
synagogue

**synchronisieren** VERB (PERFECT **hat synchronisiert**)
to dub ◊ *ein synchronisierter Film* a dubbed film

das **Synonym** NOUN (PL die **Synonyme**)
synonym

**synthetisch** ADJECTIVE
synthetic

das **System** NOUN (PL die **Systeme**)
system

**systematisch** ADJECTIVE
systematic

die **Szene** NOUN
scene

**S**

# T

der **Tabak** NOUN (PL die **Tabake**)
tobacco

die **Tabelle** NOUN
table

die **Tabellenkalkulation** NOUN
spreadsheet

das **Tablett** NOUN (PL die **Tablette**)
tray

die **Tablette** NOUN
tablet

der **Tachometer** NOUN (PL die **Tachometer**)
speedometer

**tadellos** ADJECTIVE
faultless

die **Tafel** NOUN
blackboard ◊ *Der Lehrer schrieb das Wort an die Tafel.* The teacher wrote the word on the blackboard.
♦ **eine Tafel Schokolade** a bar of chocolate

der **Tag** NOUN (PL die **Tage**)
[1] day ◊ *Ich war den ganzen Tag weg.* I was away all day.
[2] daylight ◊ *Wir möchten noch bei Tag ankommen.* We want to arrive in daylight.
♦ **an den Tag kommen** to come to light
♦ **Guten Tag!** Hello!

das **Tageblatt** NOUN (PL die **Tageblätter**)
daily newspaper

das **Tagebuch** NOUN (PL die **Tagebücher**)
diary ◊ *ein Tagebuch führen* to keep a diary

**tagelang** ADVERB
for days

der **Tagesanbruch** NOUN
dawn ◊ *bei Tagesanbruch* at dawn

das **Tagesgericht** NOUN (PL die **Tagesgerichte**)
dish of the day

die **Tageskarte** NOUN
[1] menu of the day
[2] day ticket

das **Tageslicht** NOUN
daylight

der **Tageslichtprojektor** NOUN (PL die **Tageslichtprojektoren**)
overhead projector

die **Tagesschau** NOUN
TV news

die **Tageszeit** NOUN
time of day

die **Tageszeitung** NOUN
daily paper

**täglich** ADJECTIVE, ADVERB
daily

**tagsüber** ADVERB
during the day

die **Taille** NOUN
waist

der **Takt** NOUN (PL die **Takte**)
tact ◊ *Sie behandelte die Sache mit viel Takt.* She showed great tact in dealing with the matter.
♦ **Er hat überhaupt keinen Takt.** He's completely tactless.
♦ **den Takt angeben** to keep time ◊ *Der Lehrer gab den Takt an.* The teacher kept time.
♦ **im Stundentakt** at hourly intervals

die **Taktik** NOUN
tactics ◊ *Das ist die falsche Taktik.* Those are the wrong tactics.

**taktisch** ADJECTIVE
tactical ◊ *Das war taktisch unklug.* That was a tactical mistake.

**taktlos** ADJECTIVE
tactless

**taktvoll** ADJECTIVE
tactful

das **Tal** NOUN (PL die **Täler**)
valley

das **Talent** NOUN (PL die **Talente**)
talent

**talentiert** ADJECTIVE
talented

der **Tampon** NOUN (PL die **Tampons**)
tampon

der **Tank** NOUN (PL die **Tanks**)
tank

**tanken** VERB
to get petrol ◊ *Wir müssen noch tanken.* We still have to get petrol.

die **Tankstelle** NOUN
petrol station

der **Tankwart** NOUN (PL die **Tankwarte**)
petrol pump attendant

die **Tanne** NOUN
fir

der **Tannenzapfen** NOUN (PL die **Tannenzapfen**)
fir cone

die **Tante** NOUN
aunt

der **Tanz** NOUN (GEN des **Tanzes**, PL die **Tänze**)
dance

**tanzen** VERB
to dance

die **Tanzschule** NOUN
dancing school

> ⓘ It is very common for German boys and girls to go to a **Tanzschule** when they are about 14.

die **Tapete** NOUN
wallpaper

**tapezieren** VERB (PERFECT **hat tapeziert**)

to wallpaper

**tapfer** ADJECTIVE
brave

die **Tapferkeit** NOUN
bravery

die **Tasche** NOUN
[1] pocket ◊ *Er hatte die Hände in der Hosentasche.* He had his hands in his trouser pockets.
[2] bag ◊ *Sie kann ihre Tasche nicht finden.* She can't find her bag.

das **Taschenbuch** NOUN (PL die **Taschenbücher**)
paperback

der **Taschendieb** NOUN
pickpocket

das **Taschengeld** NOUN (PL die **Taschengelder**)
pocket money

die **Taschenlampe** NOUN
torch

das **Taschenmesser** NOUN (PL die **Taschenmesser**)
penknife

der **Taschenrechner** NOUN (PL die **Taschenrechner**)
pocket calculator

das **Taschentuch** NOUN (PL die **Taschentücher**)
handkerchief

die **Tasse** NOUN
cup ◊ *eine Tasse Tee* a cup of tea

die **Tastatur** NOUN
keyboard

die **Taste** NOUN
[1] button ◊ *Welche Taste muss ich drücken, um die Waschmaschine anzustellen?* What button do I have to press to start the washing machine?
[2] key ◊ *Bei der Schreibmaschine und der Computertastatur gibt es eine Hochstelltaste.* There's a shift key on the typewriter and the computer keyboard.

die **Tat** NOUN (PL die **Taten**)
deed ◊ *Das war eine tapfere Tat.* That was a brave deed. ◊ *eine gute Tat* a good deed
◆ **Der Beschuldigte hat die Tat gestanden.** The accused confessed to the crime.
◆ **in der Tat** indeed

**tat** VERB *see* **tun**

der **Täter** NOUN (PL die **Täter**)
culprit

**tätig** ADJECTIVE
◆ **tätig sein** to work ◊ *Er ist als Journalist tätig.* He works as a journalist.

die **Tätigkeit** NOUN
[1] activity ◊ *kriminelle Tätigkeiten* criminal activities
[2] occupation ◊ *Welche Tätigkeit übt dein Vater aus?* What's your father's occupation?

**tätowieren** VERB (PERFECT **hat tätowiert**)
to tattoo

die **Tatsache** NOUN
fact

**tatsächlich** ADJECTIVE, ADVERB
[1] actual ◊ *Der tatsächliche Grund war ein anderer als der, den sie angegeben hatte.* The actual reason was different from the one she gave.
[2] really ◊ *Das hat sie tatsächlich gesagt.* She really did say that. ◊ *Er ist tatsächlich rechtzeitig gekommen.* He really has come in time.

**taub** ADJECTIVE
deaf ◊ *Sie ist auf dem rechten Ohr taub.* She's deaf in her right ear.

die **Taube** NOUN
[1] pigeon ◊ *die Tauben auf dem Marktplatz* the pigeons in the market square
[2] dove ◊ *die Friedenstaube* the dove of peace

die **Taubheit** NOUN
deafness

**taubstumm** ADJECTIVE
deaf-mute

**tauchen** VERB (PERFECT **hat/ist getaucht**)
*Use **haben** for the perfect tense when you describe the activity and **sein** when you describe the motion.*
[1] to dip ◊ *Sie hat ihren Zeh ins Wasser getaucht.* She dipped her toe into the water.
[2] to dive ◊ *Als Kind habe ich viel getaucht.* I used to dive a lot as a child. ◊ *Er ist nach dem versunkenen Schatz getaucht.* He dived in search of the sunken treasure.

der **Taucheranzug** NOUN (PL die **Taucheranzüge**)
diving suit

**tauen** VERB
◆ **Es taut.** It's thawing.

die **Taufe** NOUN
christening

**taufen** VERB
to christen

**taugen** VERB
◆ **nichts taugen** to be no good ◊ *Das Programm taugt nichts.* The program's no good.

**tauschen** VERB
to exchange

**täuschen** VERB
[1] to deceive ◊ *Du hast mich bewusst getäuscht.* You deliberately deceived me.
[2] to be deceptive ◊ *Der äußere Anschein täuscht oft.* Appearances are often deceptive.
◆ **sich täuschen** to be wrong

die **Täuschung** NOUN
deception
◆ **eine optische Täuschung** an optical illusion

**T**

**tausend** NUMBER
thousand

das **Taxi** NOUN (GEN des **Taxis**, PL die **Taxis**)
taxi

der **Taxifahrer** NOUN (PL die **Taxifahrer**)
taxi driver

der **Taxistand** NOUN (PL die **Taxistände**)
taxi rank

die **Technik** NOUN
[1] technology ◊ *hochentwickelte
Technik* advanced technology
♦ **die Gentechnik** genetic engineering
[2] technique ◊ *Sie beherrscht diese
Technik des Hochsprungs noch nicht.*
She hasn't mastered this high-jump
technique yet.

der **Techniker** NOUN (PL die **Techniker**)
technician
**technisch** ADJECTIVE
technical

die **Technologie** NOUN
technology

der **TEE** NOUN (= *Trans-Europa-Express*)
Trans-Europe Express

der **Tee** NOUN (PL die **Tees**)
tea ◊ *Tee mit Milch und Zucker* tea with
milk and sugar ◊ *Tee mit Zitrone* lemon
tea
♦ **der Kamillentee** camomile tea

der **Teebeutel** NOUN (PL die **Teebeutel**)
tea bag

die **Teekanne** NOUN
teapot

der **Teelöffel** NOUN (PL die **Teelöffel**)
teaspoon
♦ **ein Teelöffel Zucker** a teaspoonful of
sugar

der **Teer** NOUN
tar

das **Teesieb** NOUN (PL die **Teesiebe**)
tea strainer

der **Teich** NOUN (PL die **Teiche**)
pond

der **Teig** NOUN (PL die **Teige**)
dough

die **Teigwaren** FEM PL NOUN
pasta

der **Teil** NOUN (PL die **Teile**)
*You can also say das Teil.*
[1] part ◊ *der erste Teil des Buches* the
first part of the book
♦ **das Ersatzteil** the spare part
[2] share ◊ *Ich möchte meinen Teil am
Gewinn.* I would like my share of the
profit.
[3] component part ◊ *Er hat das Fahrrad
in seine Teile zerlegt.* He dismantled the
bike into its component parts.
♦ **Sie waren zum Teil beschädigt.** Some of
them were damaged.

**teilen** VERB
to divide

♦ **mit jemandem teilen** to share with
somebody

**teilnehmen** VERB (PRESENT **nimmt teil,**
IMPERFECT **nahm teil,** PERFECT **hat
teilgenommen**)
♦ **an etwas teilnehmen** to take part in
something ◊ *Du solltest am Wettbewerb
teilnehmen!* You ought to take part in the
competition.

der **Teilnehmer** NOUN (PL die **Teilnehmer**)
participant

**teils** ADVERB
partly

**teilweise** ADVERB
in parts ◊ *Das Buch war teilweise sehr
spannend.* The book was thrilling in
parts.
♦ **Sie waren teilweise beschädigt.** Some of
them were damaged.

die **Teilzeitarbeit** NOUN
part-time work

der **Teilzeitjob** NOUN (PL die **Teilzeitjobs**)
part-time job

der **Teint** NOUN (PL die **Teints**)
complexion

die **Telearbeit** NOUN
teleworking

das **Telefax** NOUN (GEN des **Telefax,** PL die
**Telefaxe**)
fax

das **Telefon** NOUN (PL die **Telefone**)
telephone

der **Telefonanruf** NOUN (PL die **Telefonanrufe**)
telephone call

das **Telefonat** NOUN (PL die **Telefonate**)
phone call

das **Telefonbuch** NOUN (PL die **Telefonbücher**)
phone book

das **Telefonhäuschen** NOUN (PL die
**Telefonhäuschen**)
telephone box

der **Telefonhörer** NOUN (PL die **Telefonhörer**)
receiver ◊ *Er nahm den Telefonhörer ab.*
He picked up the receiver.

**telefonieren** VERB (PERFECT **hat telefoniert**)
to telephone
♦ **Ich habe gestern mit ihr telefoniert.** I
talked to her on the phone yesterday.

**telefonisch** ADJECTIVE
telephone ◊ *eine telefonische Nachricht*
a telephone message
♦ **Sie können mich telefonisch erreichen.**
You can contact me by phone.

die **Telefonkarte** NOUN
phonecard

die **Telefonnummer** NOUN
telephone number

die **Telefonzelle** NOUN
telephone box

das **Telegramm** NOUN (PL die **Telegramme**)
telegram

das **Teleobjektiv** NOUN (PL die **Teleobjektive**)

telephoto lens

das **Teleskop** NOUN (PL die **Teleskope**)
telescope

der **Teller** NOUN (PL die **Teller**)
plate

das **Temperament** NOUN (PL die **Temperamente**)
♦ **Sie hat das Stück mit Temperament gespielt.** She gave a lively rendition of the piece.
♦ **Sie hat ein ziemlich lebhaftes Temperament.** She's quite a vivacious person.

**temperamentvoll** ADJECTIVE
vivacious

die **Temperatur** NOUN
temperature

das **Tempo** NOUN (PL die **Tempos**)
[1] speed ◊ *Er ist mit einem irren Tempo gefahren.* He drove at breakneck speed.
[2] rate ◊ *Wir müssen unser Arbeitstempo steigern.* We must increase our work rate.

**tendieren** VERB (PERFECT **hat tendiert**)
♦ **zu etwas tendieren** to tend towards something

das **Tennis** NOUN (GEN des **Tennis**)
tennis

der **Tennisplatz** NOUN (GEN des **Tennisplatzes**, PL die **Tennisplätze**)
tennis court

der **Tennisschläger** NOUN (PL die **Tennisschläger**)
tennis racket

der **Tennisspieler** NOUN (PL die **Tennisspieler**)
tennis player

der **Teppich** NOUN (PL die **Teppiche**)
carpet

der **Teppichboden** NOUN (PL die **Teppichböden**)
wall-to-wall carpet

der **Termin** NOUN (PL die **Termine**)
[1] date ◊ *Habt ihr schon einen Termin ausgemacht?* Have you already arranged a date?
[2] deadline ◊ *Ich muss den Aufsatz bis zu dem Termin fertig haben.* I must have the essay finished by that deadline.
[3] appointment ◊ *Ich habe einen Termin beim Zahnarzt.* I've got an appointment with the dentist.

der **Terminkalender** NOUN (PL die **Terminkalender**)
appointments diary

die **Terrasse** NOUN
terrace

der **Terror** NOUN
terror

der **Terrorismus** NOUN (GEN des **Terrorismus**)
terrorism

der **Terrorist** NOUN (GEN des **Terroristen**, PL die **Terroristen**)

terrorist

der **Tesafilm** ® NOUN
Sellotape ®

der **Test** NOUN (PL die **Tests**)
test

das **Testament** NOUN (PL die **Testamente**)
will ◊ *sein Testament machen* to make one's will

**testen** VERB
to test

**teuer** ADJECTIVE
expensive

der **Teufel** NOUN (PL die **Teufel**)
devil

der **Text** NOUN (PL die **Texte**)
[1] text ◊ *Lest den Text auf Seite zehn.* Read the text on page ten.
[2] lyrics ◊ *Kannst du mir den Text von dem Song übersetzen?* Can you translate the lyrics of the song for me?

die **Textilien** FEM PL NOUN
textiles

die **Textverarbeitung** NOUN
word processing

das **Textverarbeitungssystem** NOUN (PL die **Textverarbeitungssysteme**)
word processor

das **Theater** NOUN (PL die **Theater**)
[1] theatre ◊ *Wir gehen ins Theater.* We're going to the theatre.
♦ **Theater spielen** to act
[2] fuss ◊ *Mach nicht so ein Theater!* Don't make such a fuss.

das **Theaterstück** NOUN (PL die **Theaterstücke**)
play

die **Theke** NOUN
[1] bar ◊ *Er stand an der Theke und trank ein Bier.* He stood at the bar drinking a beer.
[2] counter ◊ *Das bekommen Sie an der Käsetheke.* You'll get that at the cheese counter.

das **Thema** NOUN (PL die **Themen**)
subject

die **Themse** NOUN
Thames

**theoretisch** ADJECTIVE
theoretical ◊ *Rein theoretisch betrachtet ist das richtig.* From a purely theoretical point of view, that's correct.

die **Theorie** NOUN
theory

die **Therapie** NOUN
therapy

das **Thermometer** NOUN (PL die **Thermometer**)
thermometer

die **Thermosflasche** NOUN
Thermos ®

die **These** NOUN
thesis

der **Thron** NOUN (PL die **Throne**)
throne

**T**

der **Thunfisch** NOUN (PL die **Thunfische**)
tuna

das **Thüringen** NOUN
Thuringia

> ℹ️ *Thüringen is one of the 16 Länder.*
> *Its capital is Erfurt. With its extensive*
> *forests, it is sometimes called*
> *"Germany's green heartland". It is not*
> *only rural, however: the Zeiss precision*
> *engineering company is based in Jena.*

der **Thymian** NOUN (PL die **Thymiane**)
thyme

**ticken** VERB
to tick ◊ *Die Uhr tickte.* The clock was
ticking.
♦ **Du tickst ja nicht richtig!** You're off your
rocker!

das **Tief** NOUN (PL die **Tiefs**)
see also **tief** ADJECTIVE
depression ◊ *ein Tief über*
*Norddeutschland* a depression over
North Germany

**tief** ADJECTIVE
see also **das Tief** NOUN
[1] deep ◊ *Wie tief ist das Wasser?* How
deep's the water?
[2] low (*neckline, price, note*) ◊ *ein tief*
*ausgeschnittenes Kleid* a low-cut dress

der **Tiefdruck** NOUN
low pressure

die **Tiefe** NOUN
depth

die **Tiefgarage** NOUN
underground garage

**tiefgekühlt** ADJECTIVE
frozen

die **Tiefkühlkost** NOUN
frozen food

die **Tiefkühltruhe** NOUN
freezer

die **Tiefsttemperatur** NOUN
minimum temperature

das **Tier** NOUN (PL die **Tiere**)
animal

der **Tierarzt** NOUN (GEN des **Tierarztes,** PL die
**Tierärzte**)
vet

der **Tiergarten** NOUN (PL die **Tiergärten**)
zoo

**tierisch** ADJECTIVE
animal ◊ *tierische Fette* animal fats
♦ **Du hast dich tierisch benommen.** You
behaved terribly.

der **Tierkreis** NOUN (GEN des **Tierkreises**)
zodiac

die **Tierquälerei** NOUN
cruelty to animals

der **Tiger** NOUN (PL die **Tiger**)
tiger

die **Tinte** NOUN
ink

der **Tintenfisch** NOUN (PL die **Tintenfische**)
squid

der **Tipp** NOUN (PL die **Tipps**)
tip

**tippen** VERB
[1] to tap ◊ *Sie tippte leicht an die Statue.*
She lightly tapped the statue.
[2] to type ◊ *Tippst du dein Referat?* Are
you typing your assignment?
♦ **Mein Freund tippt im Lotto.** My friend
plays the lottery.
♦ **Auf wen tippst du bei den Wahlen?**
Who're you tipping to win the elections?

der **Tippfehler** NOUN (PL die **Tippfehler**)
typing error

**Tirol** NEUT NOUN
Tyrol

der **Tiroler** NOUN (PL die **Tiroler**)
Tyrolean

die **Tirolerin** NOUN
Tyrolean

der **Tisch** NOUN (PL die **Tische**)
table ◊ *bei Tisch* at table

die **Tischdecke** NOUN
tablecloth

der **Tischler** NOUN (PL die **Tischler**)
joiner

das **Tischtennis** NOUN
table tennis

das **Tischtuch** NOUN (PL die **Tischtücher**)
tablecloth

der **Titel** NOUN (PL die **Titel**)
title

der **Toast** NOUN (PL die **Toasts**)
toast

das **Toastbrot** NOUN (PL die **Toastbrote**)
bread for toasting

der **Toaster** NOUN (PL die **Toaster**)
toaster

**toben** VERB
[1] to rage ◊ *Der Sturm tobte die ganze*
*Nacht.* The storm raged all night long.
♦ **Wenn er das erfährt, wird er toben.** If he
finds out he'll go mad.
[2] to romp about ◊ *Die Kinder toben im*
*Garten.* The children are romping about
in the garden.

die **Tochter** NOUN (PL die **Töchter**)
daughter

der **Tod** NOUN (PL die **Tode**)
death

**todernst** ADJECTIVE, ADVERB
grave ◊ *ein todernstes Gesicht* a grave
face
♦ **Er hat das todernst gesagt.** He said it in
deadly earnest.

die **Todesstrafe** NOUN
death penalty

**todkrank** ADJECTIVE
critically ill

**tödlich** ADJECTIVE

deadly ◊ *eine tödliche Waffe* a deadly weapon

♦ **ein tödlicher Unfall** a fatal accident

**todmüde** ADJECTIVE
exhausted

**todschick** ADJECTIVE
smart

die **Toilette** NOUN
toilet

das **Toilettenpapier** NOUN
toilet paper

**tolerant** ADJECTIVE
tolerant

**toll** ADJECTIVE
terrific

die **Tollwut** NOUN
rabies

die **Tomate** NOUN
tomato

das **Tomatenmark** NOUN
tomato purée

der **Ton** NOUN (PL die **Töne**)

1 sound ◊ *Es war kein Ton zu hören.* Not a sound could be heard.

2 note ◊ *Mit welchen Ton fängt das Lied an?* What note does the song start on?

3 tone of voice ◊ *Sein Ton gefiel mir nicht.* I didn't like his tone of voice.

4 shade ◊ *Pastelltöne sind in.* Pastel shades are in.

5 stress ◊ *Bei Substantiven liegt der Ton meist auf der ersten Silbe.* Nouns are usually stressed on the first syllable.

das **Tonband** NOUN (PL die **Tonbänder**)
tape

das **Tonbandgerät** NOUN (PL die **Tonbandgeräte**)
tape recorder

die **Tonne** NOUN
ton ◊ *Es wiegt drei Tonnen.* It weighs three tons.

der **Topf** NOUN (PL die **Töpfe**)
pot

das **Tor** NOUN (PL die **Tore**)

1 gate ◊ *Das Tor war offen.* The gate was open.

2 goal ◊ *Wer hat das zweite Tor geschossen?* Who scored the second goal?

der **Torf** NOUN
peat

die **Torte** NOUN

1 gateau

2 flan

der **Torwart** NOUN (PL die **Torwarte**)
goalkeeper

**tot** ADJECTIVE
dead

♦ **Er war sofort tot.** He was killed instantly.

**total** ADJECTIVE, ADVERB

1 complete ◊ *Das ist doch der totale Wahnsinn.* But that's complete madness.

2 completely ◊ *Das ist total verrückt.* That's completely mad.

**totalitär** ADJECTIVE
totalitarian

der **Totalschaden** NOUN (PL die **Totalschäden**)
complete write-off

der **Tote** NOUN (GEN des/der **Toten**, PL die **Toten**)
die dead body ◊ *Auf der Straße lag ein Toter.* There was a dead body lying in the road.

♦ **die Toten begraben** to bury the dead

**töten** VERB
to kill

sich **totlachen** VERB (PERFECT **hat sich totgelacht**)
to laugh one's head off

die **Tour** NOUN (PL die **Touren**)
trip ◊ *auf Tour gehen* to go on a trip

♦ **auf vollen Touren** at full speed

der **Tourismus** NOUN (GEN des **Tourismus**)
tourism

der **Tourist** NOUN (GEN des **Touristen**, PL die **Touristen**)
tourist

die **Touristenklasse** NOUN
tourist class

die **Tournee** NOUN
tour ◊ *Bon Jovi auf Tournee* Bon Jovi on tour ◊ *auf Tournee gehen* to go on tour

die **Tracht** NOUN
traditional costume ◊ *Im Schwarzwald tragen die Frauen noch Tracht.* Women still wear traditional costume in the Black Forest.

♦ **eine Tracht Prügel** a sound beating

die **Tradition** NOUN
tradition

**traditionell** ADJECTIVE
traditional

**traf** VERB *see* **treffen**

**tragbar** ADJECTIVE
portable ◊ *ein tragbarer Fernseher* a portable TV

**träge** ADJECTIVE
sluggish

**tragen** VERB (PRESENT **trägt**, IMPERFECT **trug**, PERFECT **hat getragen**)

1 to carry ◊ *Kannst du meinen Koffer tragen?* Can you carry my case?

2 to bear ◊ *die Verantwortung tragen* to bear responsibility

3 (clothes, glasses)
to wear ◊ *Sie trug ein weißes Kleid und eine Sonnenbrille.* She was wearing a white dress and sunglasses.

♦ **Ich trag's mit Fassung.** I'll just have to grin and bear it.

die **Tragetasche** NOUN
carrier bag

die **Trägheit** NOUN
laziness

**tragisch** ADJECTIVE
tragic

**T**

die **Tragödie** NOUN
tragedy

der **Trainer** NOUN (PL die **Trainer**)
coach

**trainieren** VERB (PERFECT **hat trainiert**)
[1] to train ◊ *Sie trainiert täglich für den Wettkampf.* She trains for the competition every day.
[2] to coach ◊ *Wer trainiert diese Tennisspielerin?* Who coaches this tennis player?
[3] to practise ◊ *Diese Übung muss ich noch mehr trainieren.* I need to practise this exercise more.

das **Training** NOUN (PL die **Trainings**)
training

der **Trainingsanzug** NOUN (PL die **Trainingsanzüge**)
track suit

**trampen** VERB
to hitchhike

der **Tramper** NOUN (PL die **Tramper**)
hitchhiker

die **Tramperin** NOUN
hitchhiker

die **Träne** NOUN
tear ◊ *in Tränen ausbrechen* to burst into tears

das **Tränengas** NOUN (GEN des **Tränengases**)
tear gas

**trank** VERB *see* **trinken**

die **Transplantation** NOUN
transplant ◊ *eine Herztransplantation* a heart transplant
♦ **eine Hauttransplantation** a skin graft

der **Transport** NOUN (PL die **Transporte**)
transport

**transportieren** VERB (PERFECT **hat transportiert**)
to transport

das **Transportmittel** NOUN (PL die **Transportmittel**)
means of transport

die **Traube** NOUN
grape

der **Traubenzucker** NOUN (PL die **Traubenzucker**)
glucose

**trauen** VERB
♦ **jemandem trauen** to trust somebody
♦ **sich trauen** to dare ◊ *Ich wette, du traust dich nicht!* I bet you don't dare.

der **Traum** NOUN (PL die **Träume**)
dream

**träumen** VERB
to dream ◊ *Ich habe von dir geträumt.* I dreamt about you.

**traumhaft** ADJECTIVE
wonderful ◊ *Es waren traumhafte Ferien.* It was a wonderful holiday.

**traurig** ADJECTIVE
sad

die **Traurigkeit** NOUN
sadness

das **Treffen** NOUN (PL die **Treffen**)
*see also* **treffen** VERB
meeting

**treffen** VERB (PRESENT **trifft**, IMPERFECT **traf**, PERFECT **hat getroffen**)
*see also* das **Treffen** NOUN
[1] to hit ◊ *Er hat die Zielscheibe getroffen.* He hit the target. ◊ *Sie wurde am Kopf getroffen.* She was hit on the head.
♦ **Du hast nicht getroffen.** You missed.
[2] to meet ◊ *Ich habe ihn gestern im Supermarkt getroffen.* I met him yesterday in the supermarket. ◊ *Wir sind in London auf ihn getroffen.* We met him in London.
♦ **sich treffen** to meet ◊ *Wir treffen uns am Bahnhof.* We'll meet at the station. ◊ *Sie treffen sich einmal in der Woche.* They meet once a week.
[3] to affect ◊ *Die Bemerkung hat sie sehr getroffen.* The remark affected her deeply.
♦ **eine Entscheidung treffen** to make a decision
♦ **Maßnahmen treffen** to take steps
♦ **es traf sich, dass ...** it so happened that ...
♦ **Das trifft sich gut!** How very convenient!

**treffend** ADJECTIVE
pertinent

der **Treffer** NOUN (PL die **Treffer**)
[1] hit ◊ *Das Schiff musste einen Volltreffer hinnehmen.* The ship took a direct hit.
[2] goal ◊ *Klinsmann hat einen Treffer erzielt.* Klinsmann scored a goal. ◊ *Ich hatte vier Treffer im Lotto.* I got four numbers in the lottery.

der **Treffpunkt** NOUN (PL die **Treffpunkte**)
meeting place

**treiben** VERB (IMPERFECT **trieb**, PERFECT **hat/ist getrieben**)

Use **haben** to form the perfect tense. Use **sein** to form the perfect tense for **to drift**.

[1] to drive ◊ *Sie trieben die Kühe auf das Feld.* They drove the cows into the field.
♦ **Sport treiben** to do sport
♦ **Unsinn treiben** to fool around
♦ **jemanden zu etwas treiben** to drive somebody to something ◊ *Du treibst mich zur Verzweiflung.* You drive me to despair.
♦ **Sie hat uns zur Eile getrieben.** She made us hurry up.
[2] to drift ◊ *Das Schiff ist aufs Meer getrieben.* The ship drifted out to sea.

das **Treibhaus** NOUN (GEN des **Treibhauses**, PL die **Treibhäuser**)
greenhouse

der **Treibhauseffekt** NOUN

greenhouse effect

der **Treibstoff** NOUN (PL die **Treibstoffe**)
fuel

**trennen** VERB
1 to separate ◊ *Er hat die beiden Raufbolde getrennt.* He separated the two ruffians.
2 to make a distinction between ◊ *Diese beiden Begriffe muss man sauber trennen.* You have to make a clear distinction between these two concepts.
3 to hyphenate ◊ *Wie wird dieses Wort getrennt?* Where do you hyphenate this word?
♦ **sich trennen** to separate ◊ *Die beiden haben sich getrennt.* The two of them have separated.
♦ **Du solltest dich von ihm trennen.** You ought to leave him.
♦ **sich von etwas trennen** to part with something ◊ *Ich trenne mich ungern von dem Buch.* I'm loath to part with this book.

die **Trennung** NOUN
separation

die **Treppe** NOUN
stairs

das **Treppenhaus** NOUN (GEN des **Treppenhauses**, PL die **Treppenhäuser**)
staircase

**treten** VERB (PRESENT **tritt**, IMPERFECT **trat**, PERFECT **hat/ist getreten**)

*For the perfect tense use **haben** when the verb has an object and **sein** when there is no object.*

1 to step ◊ *Sie ist in die Pfütze getreten.* She stepped in the puddle. ◊ *Er trat auf die Bremse.* He stepped on the brakes. ◊ *Er trat ans Mikrophon.* He stepped up to the microphone.
♦ **mit jemandem in Verbindung treten** to get in touch with somebody
♦ **in Erscheinung treten** to appear
♦ **Mir sind die Tränen in die Augen getreten.** Tears came to my eyes.
2 to kick ◊ *Sie hat mich getreten.* She kicked me.
3 to tread ◊ *Er ist mir auf den Fuß getreten.* He trod on my foot.
♦ **Sie trat nach dem Hund.** She kicked the dog.

**treu** ADJECTIVE
faithful ◊ *Bist du mir auch treu gewesen?* Have you been faithful to me?

die **Treue** NOUN
faithfulness

die **Tribüne** NOUN
1 grandstand ◊ *Die Fans auf der Tribüne pfiffen.* The fans on the grandstand whistled.

2 platform ◊ *Der Redner stand auf einer Tribüne.* The speaker stood on a platform.

der **Trichter** NOUN (PL die **Trichter**)
1 funnel ◊ *Sie hat das Öl mit einem Trichter in die Flasche gefüllt.* She used a funnel to fill the bottle with oil.
2 crater ◊ *Das Gelände war von Bombentrichtern übersät.* The area was pitted with bomb craters.

der **Trick** NOUN (PL die **Tricks**)
trick ◊ *Das war ein fauler Trick.* That was a dirty tricks.

der **Trickfilm** NOUN (PL die **Trickfilme**)
cartoon

**trieb** VERB *see* **treiben**

**trifft** VERB *see* **treffen**

das **Trimester** NOUN (PL die **Trimester**)
term (*university*)

der **Trimm-dich-Pfad** NOUN (PL die **Trimm-dich-Pfade**)
keep-fit trail

sich **trimmen** VERB (PERFECT **hat getrimmt**)
to keep fit

**trinkbar** ADJECTIVE
drinkable

**trinken** VERB (IMPERFECT **trank**, PERFECT **hat getrunken**)
to drink
♦ **Ich habe zu viel getrunken.** I've had too much to drink.

das **Trinkgeld** NOUN (PL die **Trinkgelder**)
tip ◊ *Er gab dem Taxifahrer ein großzügiges Trinkgeld.* He gave the taxi driver a generous tip.

die **Trinkhalle** NOUN
refreshment kiosk

das **Trinkwasser** NOUN (PL die **Trinkwässer**)
drinking water

**trocken** ADJECTIVE
dry

**trocknen** VERB
to dry

der **Trödel** NOUN
junk

der **Trödelmarkt** NOUN (PL die **Trödelmärkte**)
flea market

**trödeln** VERB
to dawdle

die **Trommel** NOUN
drum ◊ *Er spielt Trommel.* He plays the drums.

das **Trommelfell** NOUN (PL die **Trommelfelle**)
eardrum

**trommeln** VERB
to drum

die **Trompete** NOUN
trumpet ◊ *Sie spielt Trompete.* She plays the trumpet.

der **Trompeter** NOUN (PL die **Trompeter**)
trumpeter

die **Tropen** PL NOUN

**T**

☞

tropics

der **Tropfen** NOUN (PL die **Tropfen**)
drop

**tropisch** ADJECTIVE
tropical

der **Trost** NOUN
consolation

**trösten** VERB
to console

**trostlos** ADJECTIVE
bleak ◊ *eine trostlose Landschaft* a bleak
landscape

der **Trostpreis** NOUN (GEN des **Trostpreises**, PL
die **Trostpreise**)
consolation prize

der **Trottel** NOUN (PL die **Trottel**)
prat

der **Trotz** NOUN (GEN des **Trotzes**)
see also **trotz** PREPOSITION
defiance ◊ *ihm zum Trotz* in defiance of
him
♦ **etwas aus Trotz tun** to do something
defiantly

**trotz** PREPOSITION
see also **der Trotz** NOUN
*The preposition* **trotz** *takes the dative or
genitive.*
in spite of

**trotzdem** ADVERB
all the same ◊ *Ich gehe trotzdem.* I'm
going all the same.

**trotzig** ADJECTIVE
defiant

**trüb** ADJECTIVE
[1] dull ◊ *Es war ein trüber Tag.* It was a
dull day.
[2] cloudy ◊ *Das Wasser war trüb.* The
water was cloudy.
[3] gloomy ◊ *Die Zukunftsaussichten sind
ziemlich trüb.* Prospects for the future are
pretty gloomy.

der **Trubel** NOUN
hurly-burly

der **Trübsinn** NOUN
gloom

**trübsinnig** ADJECTIVE
gloomy

**trug** VERB see **tragen**

**trügen** VERB (IMPERFECT **trog**, PERFECT **hat
getrogen**)
to be deceptive ◊ *Der Schein trügt.*
Appearances are deceptive.

der **Trugschluss** NOUN (GEN des **Trugschlusses**,
PL die **Trugschlüsse**)
false conclusion

die **Trümmer** PL NOUN
[1] wreckage ◊ *die Trümmer des
Flugzeugs* the wreckage of the aeroplane
[2] ruins ◊ *Nach dem Bombenangriff war
die Stadt voller Trümmer.* After the air
raid the town was in ruins.

der **Trumpf** NOUN (PL die **Trümpfe**)

**trump** ◊ *Herz ist Trumpf.* Hearts is
trumps.

die **Trunkenheit** NOUN
drunkenness
♦ **Trunkenheit am Steuer** drink-driving

die **Truppen** FEM PL NOUN
troops

der **Truthahn** NOUN (PL die **Truthähne**)
turkey

der **Tscheche** NOUN (GEN des **Tschechen**, PL die
**Tschechen**)
Czech

die **Tschechin** NOUN
Czech

**tschechisch** ADJECTIVE
Czech

**tschüs** EXCLAMATION
cheerio!

das **T-Shirt** NOUN (PL die **T-Shirts**)
T-shirt

die **Tube** NOUN
tube ◊ *eine Tube Zahnpasta* a tube of
toothpaste

das **Tuch** NOUN (PL die **Tücher**)
[1] cloth ◊ *Mit welchem Tuch soll ich
abstauben?* Which cloth should I use for
dusting?
[2] towel ◊ *Nimm dir ein großes Tuch ins
Schwimmbad mit.* Take a large towel
with you to the swimming baths.
[3] scarf ◊ *Sie hatte ein seidenes Tuch
um den Hals.* She wore a silk scarf
around her neck.

**tüchtig** ADJECTIVE
competent ◊ *Er ist ein sehr tüchtiger
Mensch.* He's a very competent person.
♦ **Er nahm einen tüchtigen Schluck aus
der Flasche.** He took a hefty swig from
the bottle.

die **Tugend** NOUN
virtue

die **Tulpe** NOUN
tulip

der **Tumor** NOUN (PL die **Tumore**)
tumour

**tun** VERB (IMPERFECT **tat**, PERFECT **hat getan**)
[1] to do ◊ *Was sollen wir jetzt tun?* What
shall we do now? ◊ *Er hat den ganzen
Tag nichts getan.* He hasn't done
anything all day. ◊ *Kann ich etwas für
dich tun?* Can I do anything for you?
◊ *Was kann ich für Sie tun?* What can I
do for you?
[2] to put ◊ *Sie tat die Teller in den
Schrank.* She put the plates in the
cupboard.
[3] to act ◊ *Tu nicht so unschuldig!* Don't
act so innocent.
[4] to pretend ◊ *Sie tat, als ob sie
schliefe.* She pretended to be sleeping.
◊ *Er ist nicht krank, er tut nur so.* He isn't
ill, he's only pretending.

◆**Der Hund tut dir bestimmt nichts.** The dog won't hurt you.

◆**Hoffentlich hast du dir bei dem Sturz nichts getan.** I hope you didn't hurt yourself when you fell.

◆**Es tut sich viel.** A lot's happening.

◆**Ein belegtes Brot tut es auch.** A sandwich will do.

◆**mit etwas zu tun haben** to have something to do with something ◊ *Seine Laune hat etwas mit seiner Krankheit zu tun.* His mood has something to do with his illness.

◆**Mit ihm will ich nichts zu tun haben.** I won't have anything to do with him.

◆**Das tut nichts zur Sache.** That's neither here nor there.

der **Tunfisch** NOUN (PL die **Tunfische**)
   tuna

der **Tunnel** NOUN (PL die **Tunnel**)
   tunnel

der **Tupfen** NOUN (PL die **Tupfen**)
   dot

die **Tür** NOUN
   door

der **Türke** NOUN (GEN des **Türken**, PL die **Türken**)
   Turk

die **Türkei** NOUN
   Turkey
◆**aus der Türkei** from Turkey
◆**in der Türkei** in Turkey
◆**in die Türkei** to Turkey

die **Türkin** NOUN
   Turk

**türkis** ADJECTIVE
   turquoise

**türkisch** ADJECTIVE
   Turkish

der **Turm** NOUN (PL die **Türme**)
   [1] tower ◊ *die Türme der Burg* the castle towers
   [2] steeple ◊ *Das Ulmer Münster hat den höchsten Kirchturm der Welt.* Ulm Cathedral has the world's highest steeple.
   [3] rook ◊ *Er machte einen Zug mit dem*

*Turm.* He moved his rook.

das **Turnen** NOUN
   | see also **turnen** VERB |
   [1] gymnastics ◊ *Die Russinnen sind im Turnen gut.* The Russian women are good at gymnastics.
   [2] physical education ◊ *Wir haben in der vierten Stunde Turnen.* We have PE in the fourth period.

**turnen** VERB
   | see also **das Turnen** NOUN |
   [1] to do gymnastics ◊ *Sie turnt nicht gern.* She doesn't like doing gymnastics.
   [2] to perform ◊ *Sie hat die Kür hervorragend geturnt.* She performed the free programme brilliantly.

die **Turnhalle** NOUN
   gym

die **Turnhose** NOUN
   gym shorts ◊ *eine Turnhose* a pair of gym shorts

das **Turnier** NOUN (PL die **Turniere**)
   tournament

der **Turnschuh** NOUN (PL die **Turnschuhe**)
   trainer ◊ *ein Paar Turnschuhe* a pair of trainers

der **Turnverein** NOUN (PL die **Turnvereine**)
   sports club

das **Turnzeug** NOUN
   gym things ◊ *Wo ist mein Turnzeug?* Where are my gym things?

die **Tüte** NOUN
   bag

der **TÜV** NOUN (PL die **TÜVs**)
   (= *Technischer Überwachungsverein*)
   MOT ◊ *Mein Auto ist nicht durch den TÜV gekommen.* My car failed its MOT.

der **Typ** NOUN (PL die **Typen**)
   [1] type ◊ *Er ist ein athletischer Typ.* He's an athletic type.
   [2] bloke ◊ *der Typ da drüben* the bloke over there

**typisch** ADJECTIVE
   typical ◊ *typisch für* typical of

**T**

# U

die **U-Bahn** NOUN
underground ◊ *mit der U-Bahn fahren* to
travel by underground

die **U-Bahn-Station** NOUN
underground station

**übel** ADJECTIVE
bad ◊ *ein übler Geruch* a bad smell
◊ *eine üble Lage* a bad situation ◊ *Nicht
übel!* Not bad.
♦ **jemandem ist übel** somebody feels sick
♦ **Sie hat dir die Bemerkung übel
genommen.** She was offended by your
remark.

die **Übelkeit** NOUN
nausea

**übelnehmen** VERB *see* **übel**

**üben** VERB
to practise

**über** PREPOSITION, ADVERB
*Use the accusative to express movement
or a change of place. Use the dative
when there is no change of place.*
[1] over ◊ *Über dem Tisch hängt eine
Lampe.* There's a lamp hanging over the
table. ◊ *Sie legten ein Brett über das
Loch.* They put a board over the hole.
◊ *Flugzeuge dürfen nicht über dieses
Gebiet fliegen.* Planes are not allowed to
fly over this area. ◊ *Über Weihnachten
bin ich zu Hause.* I'm at home over
Christmas. ◊ *Wir fahren über die
Feiertage zu meinen Eltern.* We're going
to my parents over the holidays. ◊ *Kinder
über zwölf Jahren* children over twelve
years of age ◊ *Das hat über hundert
Mark gekostet.* It cost over a hundred
marks.
♦ **Das Flugzeug flog hoch über der Stadt.**
The plane flew high above the town.
♦ **Ich bin den ganzen Tag über zu Hause.**
I'm at home all day long.
♦ **zwei Grad über Null** two degrees above
zero
♦ **ein Scheck über zweihundert Mark** a
cheque for two hundred marks
[2] across ◊ *Er ging quer über das Feld.*
He went across the field.
[3] via ◊ *nach Köln über Aachen* to
Cologne via Aachen ◊ *über Satellit* via
satellite
[4] about ◊ *Wir haben über das Wetter
geredet.* We talked about the weather.
◊ *ein Buch über ...* a book about ...
[5] through ◊ *Ich habe den Job über
einen Freund bekommen.* I got the job
through a friend.
♦ **über jemanden lachen** to laugh at
somebody

♦ **Sie liebt ihn über alles.** She loves him
more than anything.
♦ **über und über** over and over
♦ **über kurz oder lang** sooner or later
♦ **etwas über haben** to be fed up with
something ◊ *Ich habe Kartoffeln langsam
über.* I'm getting fed up with potatoes.

**überall** ADVERB
everywhere

sich **überanstrengen** VERB (PERFECT **hat sich
überanstrengt)**
to overexert oneself

**überaus** ADVERB
exceedingly

**überbieten** VERB (IMPERFECT **überbot**, PERFECT
**hat überboten)**
to outbid ◊ *Er bot zweitausend Mark,
aber wir haben ihn überboten.* He bid
two thousand marks but we outbid him.
♦ **einen Rekord überbieten** to break a
record
♦ **sich überbieten** to excel oneself

der **Überblick** NOUN (PL die **Überblicke)**
[1] view ◊ *Von hier aus hat man einen
guten
Überblick über das Gelände.* You can get
a good view of the area from here.
[2] overview ◊ *ein Überblick über die
unregelmäßigen Verben* an overview of
irregular verbs
[3] overall impression ◊ *Ich muss mir
erst mal einen Überblick verschaffen.* I
have to get an overall impression first.
♦ **den Überblick verlieren** to lose track of
things
♦ **Sie hat den Überblick über ihre Arbeit
verloren.** She has no idea where she is
with her work.

**überdenken** VERB (IMPERFECT **überdachte,**
PERFECT **hat überdacht)**
to think over

der **Überdruss** NOUN (GEN des **Überdrusses)**
♦ **bis zum Überdruss** ad nauseam

**übereifrig** ADJECTIVE
overeager

**übereinander** ADVERB
one on top of the other ◊ *Sie legte die
Bücher übereinander.* She put one book
on top of the other.
♦ **übereinander sprechen** to talk about
each other

**überempfindlich** ADJECTIVE
hypersensitive

**überfahren** VERB (PRESENT **überfährt,**
IMPERFECT **überfuhr**, PERFECT **hat überfahren)**
to run over ◊ *Die Katze wurde von
einem Auto überfahren.* The cat was run
over by a car.

die **Überfahrt** NOUN
  crossing
der **Überfall** NOUN (PL die **Überfälle**)
  [1] raid ◇ *ein Banküberfall* a bank raid
  ◇ *ein Überfall auf ein fremdes Land* a
  raid on a foreign country
  [2] assault ◇ *Er wurde das Opfer eines
  Überfalls.* He was the victim of an
  assault.
  **überfallen** VERB (PRESENT **überfällt**, IMPERFECT
  **überfiel**, PERFECT **hat überfallen**)
  [1] to attack ◇ *Sie ist im Park überfallen
  worden.* She was attacked in the park.
  ◆ **eine Bank überfallen** to raid a bank
  [2] to descend on ◇ *Am Wochenende hat
  mich meine Freundin mit ihren Eltern
  überfallen.* My girlfriend and her parents
  descended on me at the weekend.
  **überfällig** ADJECTIVE
  overdue
  **überfliegen** VERB (IMPERFECT **überflog**, PERFECT
  **hat überflogen**)
  [1] to fly over ◇ *Flugzeuge dürfen
  Wohngebiete nicht überfliegen.* Planes
  are not allowed to fly over residential
  areas.
  [2] to skim through ◇ *Ich habe das Buch
  nur überflogen.* I only skimmed through
  the book.
  **überflüssig** ADJECTIVE
  superfluous
  **überfordern** VERB (PERFECT **hat überfordert**)
  to ask too much of ◇ *Unser Mathelehrer
  überfordert uns.* Our maths teacher asks
  too much of us.
  ◆ **Du solltest dich nicht überfordern.** You
  shouldn't overtax yourself.
  **überfüllt** ADJECTIVE
  [1] overcrowded ◇ *Die Gefängnisse sind
  völlig überfüllt.* The prisons are
  completely overcrowded.
  ◆ **Die Straßen waren überfüllt.** The streets
  were crowded with people.
  [2] oversubscribed ◇ *Der Computerkurs
  ist überfüllt.* The computer course is
  oversubscribed.
der **Übergang** NOUN (PL die **Übergänge**)
  [1] crossing ◇ *ein Fußgängerübergang* a
  pedestrian crossing
  [2] transition ◇ *der Übergang vom
  Sommer zum Herbst* the transition from
  summer to autumn
  **übergeben** VERB (PRESENT **übergibt**, IMPERFECT
  **übergab**, PERFECT **hat übergeben**)
  to hand over ◇ *Sie hat uns die Schlüssel
  übergeben.* She handed the keys over to
  us.
  ◆ **sich übergeben** to be sick
  **überglücklich** ADJECTIVE
  overjoyed
  **überhaupt** ADVERB
  [1] at all ◇ *Kannst du überhaupt Auto
  fahren?* Can you drive a car at all? ◇ *Hast*

*du überhaupt zugehört?* Have you been
listening at all? ◇ *Ich habe überhaupt
keine Lust.* I don't feel like it at all.
  [2] in general ◇ *Die Engländer sind
  überhaupt sehr höflich.* In general the
  English are very polite.
  ◆ **überhaupt nicht** not at all ◇ *Der Film hat
  mir überhaupt nicht gefallen.* I didn't like
  the film at all.
  ◆ **überhaupt nichts** nothing at all ◇ *Was
  hat er gesagt? – Überhaupt nichts.* What
  did he say? – Nothing at all.
  ◆ **Er hat überhaupt nichts gesagt.** He
  didn't say anything at all.
  **überheblich** ADJECTIVE
  arrogant
  **überholen** VERB (PERFECT **hat überholt**)
  [1] to overtake ◇ *Er hat rechts überholt.*
  He overtook on the right.
  [2] to check over ◇ *Ich muss mein
  Fahrrad überholen.* I have to check my
  bike over.
  **überholt** ADJECTIVE
  out-of-date
das **Überholverbot** NOUN (PL die
  **Überholverbote**)
  restriction on overtaking
  **überhören** VERB (PERFECT **hat überhört**)
  [1] not to hear ◇ *Sie hat das Klingeln
  überhört.* She didn't hear the bell.
  [2] to ignore ◇ *Deine Frechheit überhöre
  ich.* I shall ignore your cheek.
  **überlassen** VERB (PRESENT **überlässt**, IMPERFECT
  **überließ**, PERFECT **hat überlassen**)
  ◆ **jemandem etwas überlassen** to leave
  something up to somebody ◇ *Ich
  überlasse es dir, wann du das machst.* I'll
  leave it up to you when you do it.
  **überlasten** VERB (PERFECT **hat überlastet**)
  to overload ◇ *Der Aufzug war überlastet.*
  The lift was overloaded.
  ◆ **Ich fühle mich überlastet.** I feel
  overworked.
  **überleben** VERB (PERFECT **hat überlebt**)
  to survive
  **überlegen** VERB (PERFECT **hat überlegt**)
  | see also **überlegen** ADJECTIVE |
  to think about ◇ *Ich muss mir deinen
  Vorschlag überlegen.* I'll have to think
  about your suggestion. ◇ *Überleg doch
  mal.* Think about it.
  **überlegen** ADJECTIVE
  | see also **überlegen** VERB |
  better ◇ *Er ist ihr in Englisch überlegen.*
  He's better at English than she is.
  ◆ **Unsere Mannschaft hat überlegen
  gewonnen.** Our team won convincingly.
die **Überlegung** NOUN
  consideration
die **Überlieferung** NOUN
  tradition
  **überlisten** VERB (PERFECT **hat überlistet**)

**U**

☞

to outwit

**überm** = **über dem**

**übermäßig** ADJECTIVE
excessive

**übermorgen** ADVERB
the day after tomorrow

**übernächste** ADJECTIVE
next but one
◆ **An der übernächsten Haltestelle muss ich aussteigen.** I need to get off at the next stop but one.

**übernachten** VERB (PERFECT **hat übernachtet**)
◆ **bei jemandem übernachten** to spend the night at somebody's house

die **Übernachtung** NOUN
overnight stay
◆ **Übernachtung mit Frühstück** bed and breakfast

**übernehmen** VERB (PRESENT **übernimmt**, IMPERFECT **übernahm**, PERFECT **hat übernommen**)
to take over ◊ *Er hat das Geschäft seines Vaters übernommen.* He's taken over his father's business. ◊ *Er hat das Amt des Klassensprechers übernommen.* He took over as class representative.
◆ **sich übernehmen** to take on too much

**überprüfen** VERB (PERFECT **hat überprüft**)
to check

**überqueren** VERB (PERFECT **hat überquert**)
to cross

**überraschen** VERB (PERFECT **hat überrascht**)
to surprise

**überrascht** ADJECTIVE
surprised

die **Überraschung** NOUN
surprise

**überreden** VERB (PERFECT **hat überredet**)
to persuade ◊ *Kannst du sie nicht überreden mitzukommen?* Can't you persuade her to come?

**übers** = **über das**

das **Überschallflugzeug** NOUN (PL die **Überschallflugzeuge**)
supersonic jet

**überschätzen** VERB (PERFECT **hat überschätzt**)
to overestimate

**überschlagen** VERB (PRESENT **überschlägt**, IMPERFECT **überschlug**, PERFECT **hat überschlagen**)
to estimate ◊ *Wir sollten die Kosten für das Fest überschlagen.* We should estimate how much the party will cost.
◆ **eine Seite überschlagen** to miss a page
◆ **Das Auto hat sich überschlagen.** The car rolled over.

**überschnappen** VERB (PERFECT **ist übergeschnappt**)
to flip one's lid ◊ *Du bist wohl übergeschnappt!* You've flipped your lid!

die **Überschrift** NOUN
heading

der **Überschuss** NOUN (GEN des **Überschusses**, PL die **Überschüsse**)
◆ **ein Überschuss an** a surplus of

**überschüssig** ADJECTIVE
surplus

**überschütten** VERB (PERFECT **hat überschüttet**)
◆ **jemanden mit etwas überschütten** to shower somebody with something ◊ *Sie haben uns mit Geschenken überschüttet.* They showered us with presents.

die **Überschwemmung** NOUN
flood

**übersehen** VERB (PRESENT **übersieht**, IMPERFECT **übersah**, PERFECT **hat übersehen**)
1 to overlook ◊ *Sie hat ein paar Fehler übersehen.* She overlooked a couple of mistakes.
2 to see ◊ *Wir können die Folgen noch nicht übersehen.* We can't see the consequences yet.

**übersetzen** VERB (PERFECT **hat übersetzt**)
to translate ◊ *Übersetzt den Text ins Englische.* Translate the text into English.

der **Übersetzer** NOUN (PL die **Übersetzer**)
translator

die **Übersetzerin** NOUN
translator

die **Übersetzung** NOUN
translation ◊ *Das war eine schwierige Übersetzung.* That was a difficult translation.

die **Übersicht** NOUN
1 view ◊ *Von hier aus hat man eine gute Übersicht.* You get a good view from here.
2 overview ◊ *eine Übersicht über die unregelmäßigen Verben* an overview of irregular verbs

**übersichtlich** ADJECTIVE
clear ◊ *Die Tabelle ist nicht besonders übersichtlich.* The table isn't particularly clear. ◊ *etwas übersichtlich gestalten* to arrange something clearly
◆ **ein übersichtliches Gelände** open country

**überspringen** VERB (IMPERFECT **übersprang**, PERFECT **hat übersprungen**)
1 to jump over ◊ *Er hat die Hürde übersprungen.* He jumped over the hurdle.
2 to skip ◊ *Das nächste Kapitel können wir überspringen.* We can skip the next chapter.

**überstehen** VERB (IMPERFECT **überstand**, PERFECT **hat überstanden**)
1 to get over ◊ *Wir haben das Schlimmste überstanden.* We've got over the worst.

2 **to survive** ◊ *Die Pflanze hat den Winter nicht überstanden.* The plant didn't survive the winter.

**übersteigen** VERB (IMPERFECT **überstieg,** PERFECT **hat überstiegen)**
to exceed ◊ *Das übersteigt unsere Erwartungen.* That exceeds our expectations.

**überstimmen** VERB (PERFECT **hat überstimmt)**
to outvote

die **Überstunden** FEM PL NOUN
overtime ◊ *Er macht viele Überstunden.* He does a lot of overtime.

**überstürzen** VERB (PERFECT **hat überstürzt)**
to rush ◊ *Du solltest nichts überstürzen.* You shouldn't rush into things.
♦ **sich überstürzen** to follow one another in rapid succession ◊ *Die Ereignisse überstürzten sich.* One event followed another in rapid succession.

**überstürzt** ADJECTIVE
rash ◊ *eine überstürzte Entscheidung* a rash decision
♦ **Sie sind überstürzt abgereist.** They left in a rush.

**übertragen** VERB (PRESENT **überträgt,** IMPERFECT **übertrug,** PERFECT **hat übertragen)**
*see also* **übertragen** ADJECTIVE
1 **to broadcast** ◊ *Wir übertragen das Spiel live.* We're broadcasting the game live.
2 **to copy** ◊ *Sie hat den Text in ihr Heft übertragen.* She copied the text into her exercise book.
♦ **eine Krankheit übertragen** to transmit an illness
♦ **Sie hat mir diese Aufgabe übertragen.** She has assigned this task to me.
♦ **sich übertragen auf** to spread to ◊ *Ihre Nervosität hat sich auf die Kinder übertragen.* Her nervousness spread to the children.

**übertragen** ADJECTIVE
*see also* **übertragen** VERB
figurative ◊ *die übertragene Bedeutung eines Wortes* the figurative meaning of a word

**übertreffen** VERB (PRESENT **übertrifft,** IMPERFECT **übertraf,** PERFECT **hat übertroffen)**
to surpass

**übertreiben** VERB (IMPERFECT **übertrieb,** PERFECT **hat übertrieben)**
to exaggerate

die **Übertreibung** NOUN
exaggeration

**übertrieben** ADJECTIVE
excessive

**überwachen** VERB (PERFECT **hat überwacht)**
1 **to supervise** ◊ *Wer soll die Kinder überwachen?* Who will supervise the children?

2 **to keep under surveillance** ◊ *Die Polizei überwacht ihn.* The police are keeping him under surveillance.

**überwältigend** ADJECTIVE
overwhelming

**überweisen** VERB (IMPERFECT **überwies,** PERFECT **hat überwiesen)**
to transfer

**überwinden** VERB (IMPERFECT **überwand,** PERFECT **hat überwunden)**
to overcome ◊ *Jetzt haben wir alle Schwierigkeiten überwunden.* Now we've overcome all difficulties.
♦ **sich überwinden** to force oneself ◊ *Ich musste mich überwinden, das zu essen.* I had to force myself to eat it.

**überzeugen** VERB (PERFECT **hat überzeugt)**
to convince

**überzeugend** ADJECTIVE
convincing

die **Überzeugung** NOUN
conviction ◊ *Er sagte es ohne große Überzeugung.* He said it without much conviction.

**üblich** ADJECTIVE
usual

das **U-Boot** NOUN (PL die **U-Boote)**
submarine

**übrig** ADJECTIVE
remaining ◊ *Die übrigen Gäste sind auch bald gegangen.* The remaining guests left soon afterwards.
♦ **Ist noch Kuchen übrig?** Is there any cake left?
♦ **für jemanden etwas übrig haben** to be fond of somebody
♦ **die übrigen** the others
♦ **das Übrige** the rest
♦ **im Übrigen** besides
♦ **übrig bleiben** to be left
♦ **übrig lassen** to leave ◊ *Habt ihr uns etwas Kuchen übriggelassen?* Have you left us any cake?

**übrigens** ADVERB
by the way ◊ *Übrigens, du schuldest mir noch zehn Mark.* By the way, you still owe me ten marks.

**übriglassen** VERB *see* **übrig**

die **Übung** NOUN
1 **practice** ◊ *Mir fehlt die Übung.* I need more practice.
♦ **Übung macht den Meister.** Practice makes perfect.
2 **exercise** ◊ *Bitte macht jetzt Übung dreizehn.* Please do exercise thirteen now. ◊ *eine Turnübung* a gym exercise

das **Ufer** NOUN (PL die **Ufer)**
1 **bank** ◊ *Wir saßen am Ufer des Rheins.* We sat on the bank of the Rhine.
2 **shore** ◊ *Treibholz, das ans Ufer gespült wurde* driftwood which was washed up onto the shore

**U**

die **Uhr** NOUN
 1 clock ◊ *Die Uhr am Bahnhof sollte richtig gehen.* The station clock should be right.
 2 watch ◊ *Er sah auf seine Uhr.* He looked at his watch.
 ◆ **Wie viel Uhr ist es?** What time is it?
 ◆ **ein Uhr** one o'clock
 ◆ **zwanzig Uhr** eight o'clock in the evening
 ◆ **um fünf Uhr** at five o'clock

der **Uhrzeiger** NOUN (PL die **Uhrzeiger**)
 hand

der **Uhrzeigersinn** NOUN
 ◆ **im Uhrzeigersinn** clockwise
 ◆ **entgegen dem Uhrzeigersinn** anticlockwise

die **Uhrzeit** NOUN
 time

**ulkig** ADJECTIVE
 funny

der **Ultraschall** NOUN
 ultrasound

**um** PREPOSITION, CONJUNCTION, ADVERB
 *see also* **umso** CONJUNCTION
 *The preposition um takes the accusative.*
 1 round ◊ *Sie legte sich einen Schal um den Hals.* She wrapped a scarf round her neck. ◊ *Wir sind um die Stadt herumgefahren.* We drove round the town.
 ◆ **um Weihnachten** around Christmas
 2 at ◊ *um acht Uhr* at eight o'clock
 3 by ◊ *etwas um vier Zentimeter kürzen* to shorten something by four centimetres
 ◆ **um zehn Prozent teurer** ten per cent more expensive
 ◆ **um vieles besser** better by far
 ◆ **der Kampf um den Titel** the battle for the title
 ◆ **um Geld spielen** to play for money
 ◆ **um ... willen** for the sake of ...
 *um ... willen takes the genitive.*
 ◊ *um deinetwillen* for your sake ◊ *um meiner Mutter willen* for my mother's sake
 ◆ **um ... zu** in order to ...
 *um ... zu is used with the infinitive.*
 ◊ *Ich gehe in die Schule, um etwas zu lernen.* I go to school in order to learn something.
 ◆ **zu klug, um zu ...** too clever to ...
 4 about ◊ *um die dreißig Leute* about thirty people
 ◆ **Die zwei Stunden sind um.** The two hours are up.

**umarmen** VERB (PERFECT **hat umarmt**)
 to hug ◊ *Sie umarmten sich.* They hugged.

**umblättern** VERB (PERFECT **hat umgeblättert**)
 to turn over

**umbringen** VERB (IMPERFECT **brachte um**, PERFECT **hat umgebracht**)
 to kill

**umdrehen** VERB (PERFECT **hat umgedreht**)
 to turn round ◊ *Dreh das Bild mal um.* Turn the picture round.
 ◆ **sich umdrehen** to turn round

**umfallen** VERB (PRESENT **fällt um**, IMPERFECT **fiel um**, PERFECT **ist umgefallen**)
 to fall down

der **Umfang** NOUN
 1 extent ◊ *Der Umfang der Arbeiten war am Anfang nicht absehbar.* The extent of the work couldn't be seen at the beginning.
 2 circumference ◊ *Berechnet den Umfang des Kreises.* Calculate the circumference of the circle.

die **Umfrage** NOUN
 poll

der **Umgang** NOUN
 ◆ **Solche Leute sind kein Umgang für dich.** You shouldn't go about with people like that.
 ◆ **Sie ist erfahren im Umgang mit Kindern.** She's very experienced in dealing with children.
 ◆ **Für Schüler ist der Umgang mit dem Computer selbstverständlich geworden.** It's become a matter of course for pupils to work with computers.

**umgänglich** ADJECTIVE
 sociable

die **Umgangsformen** FEM PL NOUN
 manners

die **Umgangssprache** NOUN
 colloquial language

**umgeben** VERB (PRESENT **umgibt**, IMPERFECT **umgab**, PERFECT **hat umgeben**)
 to surround

die **Umgebung** NOUN
 1 surroundings ◊ *ein Haus in schöner Umgebung* a house in beautiful surroundings
 2 environment ◊ *Diese Pflanze wächst am besten in sonniger Umgebung.* This plant grows best in a sunny environment.

**umgehen** (1) VERB (IMPERFECT **ging um**, PERFECT **ist umgegangen**)
 *Note that here the stress is on um.*
 ◆ **mit jemandem grob umgehen** to treat somebody roughly
 ◆ **mit Geld sparsam umgehen** to be careful with one's money
 ◆ **Sie kann nicht gut mit Geld umgehen.** She's not very good with money.

**umgehen** (2) VERB (IMPERFECT **umging**, PERFECT **hat umgangen**)
 *Note that here the stress is on gehen.*
 to avoid ◊ *Dieses Problem sollten wir besser umgehen.* It would be better if we could avoid this problem.

**umgehend** ADJECTIVE
 immediate

die **Umgehungsstraße** NOUN
bypass

**umgekehrt** ADJECTIVE, ADVERB
1 reverse ◊ *in umgekehrter Reihenfolge* in reverse order
♦ **Es war nicht so, es war genau umgekehrt.** It wasn't like that, it was exactly the opposite.
2 the other way around ◊ *Du musst das Bild umgekehrt hängen.* You'll have to hang the picture the other way round. ◊ *Mach das doch umgekehrt, und fang hiermit an.* Do it the other way round and start here.
♦ **... und umgekehrt ...** and vice versa

**umhauen** VERB (PERFECT **hat umgehauen**)
1 to bowl over ◊ *Die Neuigkeit wird dich umhauen.* The news will bowl you over.
2 to fell ◊ *Sie haben die alte Eiche umgehauen.* They've felled the old oak tree.

**umherziehen** VERB (IMPERFECT **zog umher,** PERFECT **ist umhergezogen**)
to wander from place to place

sich **umhören** VERB (PERFECT **hat sich umgehört**)
to ask around

**umkehren** VERB (PERFECT **hat/ist umgekehrt**)
*For the perfect tense use **haben** when the verb has an object and **sein** when there is no object.*
1 to turn back ◊ *Wir sind auf halbem Weg umgekehrt.* We turned back halfway.
2 to turn round ◊ *Warum hast du das Bild umgekehrt?* Why did you turn the picture round?
3 to turn inside out ◊ *Sie hat ihre Tasche umgekehrt, den Schlüssel aber nicht gefunden.* She turned her bag inside out but couldn't find the key.
4 to turn upside down ◊ *Kehr mal den Eimer um, dann kann ich mich draufstellen.* Turn the bucket upside down so that I can stand on it.

**umkippen** VERB (PERFECT **hat/ist umgekippt**)
*For the perfect tense use **haben** when the verb has an object and **sein** when there is no object.*
1 to tip over ◊ *Der Stuhl ist umgekippt.* The chair tipped over.
2 to overturn ◊ *Sie haben das Boot umgekippt.* They overturned the boat.
3 to keel over ◊ *Wenn ich Blut sehe, kippe ich immer um.* I keel over whenever I see blood.

die **Umkleidekabine** NOUN
changing cubicle

der **Umkleideraum** NOUN (PL die **Umkleideräume**)
changing room

**umkommen** VERB (IMPERFECT **kam um,** PERFECT **ist umgekommen**)
to be killed ◊ *Alle Passagiere sind umgekommen.* All the passengers were killed.

der **Umkreis** NOUN (GEN des **Umkreises,** PL die **Umkreise**)
neighbourhood
♦ **im Umkreis von** within a radius of

die **Umlage** NOUN
♦ **Wir haben eine Umlage gemacht.** We shared the costs.

der **Umlaut** NOUN (PL die **Umlaute**)
umlaut

**umlegen** VERB (PERFECT **hat umgelegt**)
1 to put on ◊ *Du solltest dir eine Jacke umlegen.* You should put on a jacket.
♦ **die Kosten für etwas umlegen** to divide the cost of something
2 to bump off ◊ *Er ist von der Mafia umgelegt worden.* He was bumped off by the Mafia.

**umleiten** VERB (PERFECT **hat umgeleitet**)
to divert

die **Umleitung** NOUN
diversion

**umrechnen** VERB (PERFECT **hat umgerechnet**)
to convert

die **Umrechnung** NOUN
conversion

der **Umrechnungskurs** NOUN (GEN des **Umrechnungskurses,** PL die **Umrechnungskurse**)
rate of exchange

der **Umriss** NOUN (GEN des **Umrisses,** PL die **Umrisse**)
outline

**umrühren** VERB (PERFECT **hat umgerührt**)
to stir

**ums** = um das

der **Umsatz** NOUN (GEN des **Umsatzes,** PL die **Umsätze**)
turnover

**umschalten** VERB (PERFECT **hat umgeschaltet**)
to switch ◊ *Schalt bitte ins zweite Programm um.* Please switch over to Channel two.
♦ **Die Ampel hat auf Gelb umgeschaltet.** The traffic lights changed to amber.
♦ **Wir schalten um ins Studio.** We'll now go back to the studio.

sich **umschauen** VERB (PERFECT **hat sich umgeschaut**)
to look round

der **Umschlag** NOUN (PL die **Umschläge**)
1 cover ◊ *Alle meine Mathehefte haben einen schwarzen Umschlag.* All my maths exercise books have a black cover.
2 jacket ◊ *Ich habe den Umschlag von dem Wörterbuch abgemacht.* I took the jacket off the dictionary.

U

☞

③ envelope ◊ *Sie steckte den Brief in den Umschlag.* She put the letter in the envelope.

④ compress ◊ *Bei Fieber helfen kalte Umschläge.* Cold compresses help if you have a temperature.

die **Umschweife** MASC PL NOUN
♦ **ohne Umschweife** without beating about the bush

sich **umsehen** VERB (PRESENT **sieht sich um,** IMPERFECT **sah sich um,** PERFECT **hat sich umgesehen**)
to look around ◊ *Als sie Schritte hörte, sah sie sich um.* When she heard steps, she looked around.
♦ **sich nach etwas umsehen** to look for something ◊ *Ich sehe mich zurzeit nach einer neuen Wohnung um.* I'm looking for a new flat at the moment.

**umso** CONJUNCTION
so much ◊ *umso besser* so much the better ◊ *umso schlimmer* so much the worse
♦ **Je mehr ich höre, umso weniger verstehe ich.** The more I hear the less I understand.

**umsonst** ADVERB
① in vain ◊ *Wir haben umsonst gewartet.* We waited in vain.
② for nothing ◊ *Wir sind umsonst ins Museum gekommen.* We got into the museum for nothing.
♦ **Diese Broschüre gibt es umsonst.** This brochure is free of charge.

der **Umstand** NOUN (PL die **Umstände**)
circumstance ◊ *unter keinen Umständen* under no circumstances
♦ **Wenn es keine Umstände macht.** If it's no trouble.
♦ **unter Umständen** possibly
♦ **in anderen Umständen sein** to be pregnant

**umständlich** ADJECTIVE
① complicated ◊ *Das ist aber umständlich, wie du das machst.* The way you do it is complicated.
② long-winded ◊ *eine umständliche Erklärung* a long-winded explanation
♦ **Werner ist ziemlich umständlich.** Werner makes life difficult for himself.

**umsteigen** VERB (IMPERFECT **stieg um,** PERFECT **ist umgestiegen**)
to change ◊ *Wir müssen in München umsteigen.* We have to change in Munich.

**umstellen (1)** VERB (PERFECT **hat umgestellt**)
*Note that here the stress is on **um**.*
to move ◊ *Ich werde meinen Schreibtisch umstellen.* I'm going to move my desk.
♦ **Wann wurde in Großbritannien auf metrische Maße umgestellt?** When did Great Britain go over to the metric system?

♦ **sich umstellen** to adapt ◊ *Jetzt, wo das Baby da ist, müssen wir uns umstellen.* Now that the baby's here we have to adapt.

**umstellen (2)** VERB (PERFECT **hat umstellt**)
*Note that here the stress is on **stellen**.*
to surround ◊ *Die Polizei hat das Haus umstellt.* The police have surrounded the house.

**umstritten** ADJECTIVE
controversial ◊ *ein umstrittenes Thema* a controversial subject

der **Umtausch** NOUN
exchange

**umtauschen** VERB (PERFECT **hat umgetauscht**)
to exchange

der **Umweg** NOUN (PL die **Umwege**)
detour ◊ *Wir haben einen Umweg gemacht.* We made a detour.

die **Umwelt** NOUN
environment

**umweltfeindlich** ADJECTIVE
ecologically harmful

**umweltfreundlich** ADJECTIVE
environment-friendly

der **Umweltschützer** NOUN (PL die **Umweltschützer**)
environmentalist

die **Umweltverschmutzung** NOUN
environmental pollution

**umwerfen** VERB (PRESENT **wirft um,** IMPERFECT **warf um,** PERFECT **hat umgeworfen**)
to knock over ◊ *Wer hat den Stuhl umgeworfen?* Who knocked the chair over?
♦ **Diese Nachricht hat mich umgeworfen.** The news really threw me.

**umwerfend** ADJECTIVE
fantastic

**umziehen** VERB (IMPERFECT **zog um,** PERFECT **hat/ist umgezogen**)
*Use **haben** to form the perfect tense. Use **sein** to form the perfect tense for **to move**.*
① to change ◊ *Ich habe Carolin heute schon zweimal umgezogen.* I've already changed Carolin's clothes twice today.
♦ **sich umziehen** to get changed ◊ *Wenn ich mich umgezogen habe, können wir gehen.* We can go when I've got changed.
② to move ◊ *Mein Freund ist nach Bremen umgezogen.* My friend's moved to Bremen.

der **Umzug** NOUN (PL die **Umzüge**)
① move ◊ *Alle meine Freunde haben beim Umzug geholfen.* All my friends helped with the move.
② procession ◊ *Zu Karneval finden überall Umzüge statt.* There are processions everywhere during the Carnival.

**unabhängig** ADJECTIVE
independent

die **Unabhängigkeit** NOUN
independence

**unangebracht** ADJECTIVE
uncalled-for

**unangenehm** ADJECTIVE
unpleasant

die **Unannehmlichkeiten** FEM PL NOUN
trouble ◊ *Das gibt Unannehmlichkeiten mit dem Klassenlehrer.* That'll cause trouble with the class teacher.

**unanständig** ADJECTIVE
improper

**unartig** ADJECTIVE
naughty

**unaufmerksam** ADJECTIVE
inattentive

**unausgeglichen** ADJECTIVE
moody

**unausstehlich** ADJECTIVE
intolerable

**unbeabsichtigt** ADJECTIVE
unintentional

**unbedeutend** ADJECTIVE
unimportant

**unbedingt** ADJECTIVE, ADVERB
[1] unconditional ◊ *Ich verlange unbedingten Gehorsam.* I demand unconditional obedience.
[2] really ◊ *Er wollte unbedingt nach Hause.* He really wanted to go home. ◊ *Den Film musst du dir unbedingt ansehen.* You really have to see that film.

**unbefriedigend** ADJECTIVE
unsatisfactory

**unbefriedigt** ADJECTIVE
unsatisfied

**unbegreiflich** ADJECTIVE
inconceivable

**unbehaglich** ADJECTIVE
uncomfortable ◊ *Mir war's unbehaglich.* I felt uncomfortable. ◊ *Der Stuhl ist unbehaglich.* The chair is uncomfortable.
♦ **ein unbehagliches Gefühl** an uneasy feeling

**unbekannt** ADJECTIVE
unknown

**unbeliebt** ADJECTIVE
unpopular

**unbequem** ADJECTIVE
uncomfortable ◊ *Das Bett ist unbequem.* The bed's uncomfortable.
♦ **Er ist ein sehr unbequemer Mensch.** He's a very awkward person.

**unbesetzt** ADJECTIVE
vacant

**unbestimmt** ADJECTIVE
[1] indefinite ◊ *der unbestimmte Artikel* the indefinite article

[2] uncertain ◊ *Es ist noch unbestimmt, wann wir Ferien machen.* It's still uncertain when we're going on holiday.

**unbewusst** ADJECTIVE
unconscious

**und** CONJUNCTION
and
♦ **und so weiter** and so on
♦ **Na und?** So what?

**undankbar** ADJECTIVE
ungrateful

**undeutlich** ADJECTIVE
indistinct

**uneben** ADJECTIVE
uneven

**unehrlich** ADJECTIVE
dishonest

**unempfindlich** ADJECTIVE
practical ◊ *Wir brauchen für das Sofa einen unempfindlichen Bezug.* We need a practical cover for the sofa.
♦ **Ich bin gegen Kälte unempfindlich.** I don't feel the cold.

**unendlich** ADJECTIVE
infinite

**unentschieden** ADJECTIVE
undecided
♦ **unentschieden enden** to end in a draw

**unerfahren** ADJECTIVE
inexperienced

**unerfreulich** ADJECTIVE
unpleasant

**unerträglich** ADJECTIVE
unbearable ◊ *Die Schmerzen sind unerträglich.* The pain's unbearable.

**unerwünscht** ADJECTIVE
undesirable

**unfähig** ADJECTIVE
incapable ◊ *zu etwas unfähig sein* to be incapable of something

**unfair** ADJECTIVE
unfair

der **Unfall** NOUN (PL die **Unfälle**)
accident

**unfreundlich** ADJECTIVE
unfriendly

die **Unfreundlichkeit** NOUN
unfriendliness

der **Unfug** NOUN
[1] mischief ◊ *Die Kinder machen dauernd Unfug.* The children are always getting up to mischief.
[2] nonsense ◊ *Red nicht so einen Unfug.* Don't talk such nonsense.

der **Ungar** NOUN (GEN des **Ungarn**, PL die **Ungarn**)
Hungarian

die **Ungarin** NOUN
Hungarian

**ungarisch** ADJECTIVE
Hungarian

**Ungarn** NEUT NOUN

**U**

☞

Hungary
- **aus Ungarn** from Hungary
- **nach Ungarn** to Hungary

**ungebildet** ADJECTIVE
uneducated

die **Ungeduld** NOUN
impatience

**ungeduldig** ADJECTIVE
impatient

**ungeeignet** ADJECTIVE
unsuitable

**ungefähr** ADJECTIVE
approximate ◊ *Kannst du mir eine ungefähre Zeit nennen?* Can you give me an approximate time? ◊ *um ungefähr zwei Uhr* at approximately two o'clock

**ungefährlich** ADJECTIVE
harmless

das **Ungeheuer** NOUN (PL die **Ungeheuer**)
see also **ungeheuer** ADJECTIVE, ADVERB
monster ◊ *das Ungeheuer von Loch Ness* the Loch Ness monster

**ungeheuer** ADJECTIVE, ADVERB
see also **das Ungeheuer** NOUN
[1] huge ◊ *eine ungeheure Menge* a huge amount
[2] extremely ◊ *Das war ungeheuer nett von dir.* That was extremely nice of you.

**ungehörig** ADJECTIVE
impertinent

der **Ungehorsam** NOUN
see also **ungehorsam** ADJECTIVE
disobedience

**ungehorsam** ADJECTIVE
see also **der Ungehorsam** NOUN
disobedient

**ungeklärt** ADJECTIVE
unsolved ◊ *ein ungeklärtes Rätsel* an unsolved puzzle

**ungelegen** ADJECTIVE
inconvenient ◊ *Ich hoffe, ich komme nicht ungelegen.* I hope I haven't come at an inconvenient time.

**ungelernt** ADJECTIVE
unskilled ◊ *ein ungelernter Arbeiter* an unskilled worker

**ungemütlich** ADJECTIVE
[1] uncomfortable ◊ *ein ungemütlicher Stuhl* an uncomfortable chair
[2] disagreeable ◊ *Jetzt wird er ungemütlich.* Now he's going to get disagreeable.

**ungenau** ADJECTIVE
inaccurate

**ungenießbar** ADJECTIVE
[1] inedible ◊ *Das Essen war ungenießbar.* The food was inedible.
[2] undrinkable ◊ *Diese Limonade ist ungenießbar.* This lemonade's undrinkable.

[3] unbearable ◊ *Du bist heute aber ungenießbar.* You're really unbearable today.

**ungenügend** ADJECTIVE
[1] insufficient ◊ *eine ungenügende Menge* an insufficient amount
[2] unsatisfactory

❶ German marks range from one (**sehr gut**) to six (**ungenügend**).

**ungepflegt** ADJECTIVE
- **ein ungepflegter Garten** a neglected garden
- **ungepflegte Hände** uncared-for hands

**ungerade** ADJECTIVE
- **eine ungerade Zahl** an odd number

**ungerecht** ADJECTIVE
unjust

die **Ungerechtigkeit** NOUN
injustice

**ungern** ADVERB
reluctantly

**ungeschickt** ADJECTIVE
clumsy

**ungestört** ADJECTIVE
undisturbed

**ungesund** ADJECTIVE
unhealthy

**ungewiss** ADJECTIVE
uncertain

die **Ungewissheit** NOUN
uncertainty

**ungewöhnlich** ADJECTIVE
unusual

**ungewohnt** ADJECTIVE
unaccustomed

das **Ungeziefer** NOUN
vermin

**ungezogen** ADJECTIVE
rude

**ungezwungen** ADJECTIVE
natural

**unglaublich** ADJECTIVE
incredible

das **Unglück** NOUN (PL die **Unglücke**)
[1] accident ◊ *Er ist bei einem Unglück ums Leben gekommen.* He lost his life in an accident.
[2] misfortune ◊ *Lass sie in ihrem Unglück nicht allein.* Don't leave her alone in her misfortune.
- **Eine schwarze Katze bringt Unglück.** A black cat means bad luck.

**unglücklich** ADJECTIVE
[1] unhappy ◊ *Sie ist furchtbar unglücklich.* She's terribly unhappy.
[2] unfortunate ◊ *ein unglücklicher Zufall* an unfortunate coincidence ◊ *eine unglückliche Formulierung* an unfortunate choice of words

♦ **Sie ist unglücklich gefallen.** She fell awkwardly.

**unglücklicherweise** ADVERB
unfortunately

**ungültig** ADJECTIVE
invalid

**ungünstig** ADJECTIVE
unfavourable

**unheilbar** ADJECTIVE
incurable

**unheimlich** ADJECTIVE, ADVERB
  1 weird ◊ *Das war ein unheimliches Geräusch.* That was a weird noise.
♦ **Mir wird's etwas unheimlich.** I'm getting a bit scared.
  2 incredibly ◊ *Das hat mich unheimlich gefreut.* I was incredibly pleased about it.

**unhöflich** ADJECTIVE
impolite

die **Uni** NOUN (PL die **Unis**)
uni

die **Uniform** NOUN
uniform

**uninteressant** ADJECTIVE
uninteresting

die **Universität** NOUN
university

die **Unkenntnis** NOUN
ignorance

**unklar** ADJECTIVE
unclear
♦ **über etwas im Unklaren sein** to be unclear about something ◊ *Ich bin mir über mein Berufsziel noch im Unklaren.* I'm still unclear about what I want to do.
♦ **jemanden über etwas im Unklaren lassen** to leave somebody in the dark about something

**unklug** ADJECTIVE
unwise

die **Unkosten** PL NOUN
expenses

**unleserlich** ADJECTIVE
illegible

**unlogisch** ADJECTIVE
illogical

**unlösbar** ADJECTIVE
insoluble ◊ *ein unlösbares Problem* an insoluble problem

**unmissverständlich** ADJECTIVE
unmistakeable

**unmittelbar** ADJECTIVE
immediate

**unmöglich** ADJECTIVE
impossible

die **Unmöglichkeit** NOUN
impossibility

**unmoralisch** ADJECTIVE
immoral

**unnötig** ADJECTIVE
unnecessary

**unordentlich** ADJECTIVE
untidy

die **Unordnung** NOUN
disorder

**unparteilsch** ADJECTIVE
impartial

**unpassend** ADJECTIVE
  1 inappropriate ◊ *unpassende Kleidung* inappropriate clothes
  2 inopportune ◊ *zu einer unpassenden Zeit* at an inopportune time

**unpersönlich** ADJECTIVE
impersonal ◊ *das unpersönliche Fürwort* the impersonal pronoun

**unpraktisch** ADJECTIVE
unpractical

**unpünktlich** ADJECTIVE
♦ **Sie ist immer unpünktlich.** She's always late.

das **Unrecht** NOUN
  see also **unrecht** ADJECTIVE
wrong ◊ *ein großes Unrecht* a great wrong
♦ **zu Unrecht** wrongly
♦ **Unrecht haben** to be wrong

**unrecht** ADJECTIVE
  see also **das Unrecht** NOUN
wrong ◊ *Du tust ihr unrecht.* You are wronging her.

**unregelmäßig** ADJECTIVE
irregular ◊ *ein unregelmäßiges Verb* an irregular verb

**unreif** ADJECTIVE
  1 not ripe ◊ *Der Apfel ist noch unreif.* The apple's not ripe yet.
  2 immature ◊ *Elisabeth ist noch furchtbar unreif.* Elisabeth's still terribly immature.

**unrichtig** ADJECTIVE
incorrect

die **Unruhe** NOUN
unrest

der **Unruhestifter** NOUN (PL die **Unruhestifter**)
troublemaker

**unruhig** ADJECTIVE
restless

**uns** PRONOUN
  ***uns** is the accusative and dative of **wir**.*
  1 us ◊ *Sie haben uns eingeladen.* They've invited us.
  2 to us ◊ *Sie haben es uns gegeben.* They gave it to us.
  3 ourselves ◊ *Wir fragen uns, ob das sein muss.* We're asking ourselves whether that is necessary.
  4 each other ◊ *Wir lieben uns.* We love each other.

**unschlagbar** ADJECTIVE
invincible

die **Unschuld** NOUN
innocence

**unschuldig** ADJECTIVE
innocent

**U**

**unselbstständig** ADJECTIVE
dependent

**unser** ADJECTIVE
1 our ◊ *Unser Deutschlehrer ist nett.* Our German teacher's nice. ◊ *Unsere Mathelehrerin ist streng.* Our maths teacher's strict. ◊ *Unser Haus ist ganz in der Nähe der Schule.* Our house is very near the school. ◊ *Unsere Lehrer sind prima.* Our teachers are great.
2 ours ◊ *Das ist nicht euer Lehrer, das ist unserer.* He's not your teacher, he's ours. ◊ *Seine Note war besser als unsere.* His mark was better than ours. ◊ *Wenn du kein Wörterbuch hast, kannst du unseres mitbenutzen.* If you don't have a dictionary, you can use ours. ◊ *Deine Eltern sind netter als unsere.* Your parents are nicer than ours.

**unseretwegen** ADVERB
1 for our sake ◊ *Ihr braucht unseretwegen nicht zu warten.* You needn't wait for our sake.
2 on our account ◊ *Hat sie sich unseretwegen so aufgeregt?* Did she get so upset on our account?
3 as far as we're concerned ◊ *Unseretwegen kann man das gern anders machen.* As far as we're concerned you're welcome to do it differently.

**unsicher** ADJECTIVE
1 uncertain ◊ *Es ist unsicher, ob wir kommen können.* It's uncertain whether we can come.
2 insecure ◊ *Elisabeth ist sehr unsicher.* Elisabeth's very insecure.

**unsichtbar** ADJECTIVE
invisible

der **Unsinn** NOUN
nonsense ◊ *Unsinn erzählen* to talk nonsense
◆ **Unsinn machen** to do silly things

**unsportlich** ADJECTIVE
not sporty ◊ *Tobias ist ziemlich unsportlich.* Tobias is not at all sporty.
◆ **unsportliches Verhalten** unsportsmanlike behaviour

**unsre** = **unsere**

**unsympathisch** ADJECTIVE
unpleasant ◊ *ein unsympathischer Mensch* an unpleasant person
◆ **Er ist mir unsympathisch.** I don't like him.

**unten** ADVERB
1 at the bottom ◊ *Das beste Buch lag unten auf dem Stapel.* The best book was at the bottom of the pile.
2 downstairs ◊ *Mutter ist unten in der Küche.* Mother's downstairs in the kitchen.
3 at the bottom ◊ *Er stand unten an der Treppe.* He was standing at the bottom

of the stairs. ◊ *unten am Berg* at the bottom of the mountain
◆ **nach unten** down

**unter** PREPOSITION
1 under
*Use the accusative to express movement or a change of place. Use the dative when there is no change of place.*
◊ *Die Katze lag unter dem Tisch.* The cat lay under the table. ◊ *Der Ball rollte unter den Tisch.* The ball rolled under the table. ◊ *unter achtzehn Jahren* under eighteen years of age
◆ **Die Temperaturen sanken unter Null.** The temperatures dropped below zero degrees.
2 among ◊ *Unter den Büchern war auch ein Atlas.* There was also an atlas among the books.
◆ **Sie waren unter sich.** They were by themselves.
◆ **einer unter ihnen** one of them
◆ **unter anderem** among other things

das **Unterbewusstsein** NOUN
subconscious

**unterbrechen** VERB (PRESENT **unterbricht,** IMPERFECT **unterbrach,** PERFECT **hat unterbrochen**)
to interrupt

die **Unterbrechung** NOUN
interruption

**unterdrücken** VERB (PERFECT **hat unterdrückt**)
to suppress ◊ *Sie unterdrückte ein Lächeln.* She suppressed a smile.
◆ **Menschen unterdrücken** to oppress people

**untere** ADJECTIVE
lower ◊ *die unteren Stockwerke* the lower floors

die **Unterführung** NOUN
underpass

**untergehen** VERB (IMPERFECT **ging unter,** PERFECT **ist untergegangen**)
1 to sink
2 to set ◊ *sobald die Sonne untergegangen ist ...* as soon as the sun has set ...
◆ **Die Welt geht unter.** The world's coming to an end.
◆ **Seine Rede ging im Lärm unter.** His speech was drowned out by the noise.

das **Untergeschoss** NOUN
basement

**unterhalb** PREPOSITION
*The preposition **unterhalb** takes the genitive.*
below ◊ *Ihr Haus befindet sich unterhalb der Kirche.* Her house is below the church.

**unterhalten** VERB (PRESENT **unterhält,** IMPERFECT **unterhielt,** PERFECT **hat unterhalten**)

1 to entertain ◊ *Sie hat uns den ganzen Abend mit lustigen Geschichten unterhalten.* She entertained us with funny stories all evening.

2 to run ◊ *Das Schwimmbad wird von der Stadt unterhalten.* The swimming pool is run by the town council.

♦ **sich unterhalten** to talk ◊ *Wir haben uns über dich unterhalten.* We talked about you.

**unterhaltsam** ADJECTIVE
entertaining

die **Unterhaltung** NOUN
1 talk ◊ *Es war eine sehr aufschlussreiche Unterhaltung.* It was a very informative talk.
2 entertainment ◊ *Zur Unterhaltung der Gäste spielt die örtliche Musikkapelle.* Entertainment will be provided by the local brass band.

das **Unterhemd** NOUN (PL die **Unterhemden**)
vest

die **Unterhose** NOUN
underpants ◊ *eine Unterhose* a pair of underpants

die **Unterkunft** NOUN (PL die **Unterkünfte**)
accommodation

der **Untermieter** NOUN (PL die **Untermieter**)
lodger

das **Unternehmen** NOUN (PL die **Unternehmen**)
see also **unternehmen** VERB
enterprise

**unternehmen** VERB (PRESENT **unternimmt**, IMPERFECT **unternahm**, PERFECT **hat unternommen**)
see also **das Unternehmen** NOUN
♦ **Was sollen wir heute unternehmen?** What shall we do today?

der **Unternehmer** NOUN (PL die **Unternehmer**)
entrepreneur

**unternehmungslustig** ADJECTIVE
enterprising

der **Unterricht** NOUN
lessons ◊ *Nachmittags haben wir selten Unterricht.* We seldom have lessons in the afternoon.

**unterrichten** VERB (PERFECT **hat unterrichtet**)
1 to teach ◊ *Sie unterrichtet Englisch.* She teaches English.
♦ **Wer unterrichtet euch in Sport?** Who do you have for sport?
2 to inform ◊ *Wir müssen deine Eltern davon unterrichten.* We'll have to inform your parents.

das **Unterrichtsfach** NOUN (PL die **Unterrichtsfächer**)
subject

der **Unterrock** NOUN (PL die **Unterröcke**)
underskirt

**untersagt** ADJECTIVE
forbidden

**unterschätzen** VERB (PERFECT **hat unterschätzt**)
to underestimate

**unterscheiden** VERB (IMPERFECT **unterschied**, PERFECT **hat unterschieden**)
to distinguish ◊ *Man muss zwischen Sachlichkeit und Unfreundlichkeit unterscheiden.* You have to distinguish between objectivity and unfriendliness.
♦ **sich unterscheiden** to differ

der **Unterschied** NOUN (PL die **Unterschiede**)
difference
♦ **im Unterschied zu** as distinct from

**unterschiedlich** ADJECTIVE
different ◊ *Sie haben sehr unterschiedliche Begabungen.* They have very different talents. ◊ *Sie sind unterschiedlich groß.* They're different sizes.
♦ **Das Wetter war sehr unterschiedlich.** The weather was mixed.

**unterschreiben** VERB (IMPERFECT **unterschrieb**, PERFECT **hat unterschrieben**)
to sign ◊ *Du musst das Zeugnis unterschreiben lassen.* You have to have the report signed.

die **Unterschrift** NOUN
signature

**unterste** ADJECTIVE
bottom ◊ *Es ist im untersten Fach.* It's on the bottom shelf.
♦ **Sie ist in der untersten Klasse.** She's in the first form.

sich **unterstellen (1)** VERB (PERFECT **hat sich untergestellt**)
*Note that here the stress is on* **unter**.
to take shelter ◊ *Es hat so stark geregnet, dass wir uns unterstellen mussten.* It was raining so heavily that we had to take shelter.

**unterstellen (2)** VERB (PERFECT **hat unterstellt**)
*Note that here the stress is on* **stellen**.
to imply ◊ *Willst du mir vielleicht unterstellen, dass ich das absichtlich getan habe?* Are you perhaps implying that I did it on purpose?

**unterstreichen** VERB (IMPERFECT **unterstrich**, PERFECT **hat unterstrichen**)
to underline

die **Unterstufe** NOUN
lower school

**unterstützen** VERB (PERFECT **hat unterstützt**)
to support

die **Unterstützung** NOUN
support

**untersuchen** VERB (PERFECT **hat untersucht**)
to examine

die **Untersuchung** NOUN
examination

die **Untertasse** NOUN
saucer ◊ *eine fliegende Untertasse* a flying saucer

das **Unterteil** NOUN (PL die **Unterteile**)
  lower part
**unterteilen** VERB (PERFECT **hat unterteilt**)
  to divide up
der **Untertitel** NOUN (PL die **Untertitel**)
  subtitle
die **Unterwäsche** NOUN
  underwear
**unterwegs** ADVERB
  on the way
**untreu** ADJECTIVE
  unfaithful
**untrinkbar** ADJECTIVE
  undrinkable
**untröstlich** ADJECTIVE
  inconsolable
**unübersichtlich** ADJECTIVE
  unclear
**ununterbrochen** ADJECTIVE
  uninterrupted
**unveränderlich** ADJECTIVE
  unchangeable
**unverantwortlich** ADJECTIVE
  irresponsible
**unverbesserlich** ADJECTIVE
  incorrigible
**unverbleit** ADJECTIVE
  unleaded ◊ *Ich fahre unverbleit.* I use
  unleaded.
**unvergesslich** ADJECTIVE
  unforgettable
**unvermeidlich** ADJECTIVE
  unavoidable
**unvernünftig** ADJECTIVE
  foolish
**unverschämt** ADJECTIVE
  impudent
die **Unverschämtheit** NOUN
  impudence
**unverständlich** ADJECTIVE
  unintelligible
  ◆ **Es ist mir unverständlich, wie ...** I just
  don't understand how ...
**unverzeihlich** ADJECTIVE
  unpardonable
**unvollkommen** ADJECTIVE
  imperfect
**unvollständig** ADJECTIVE
  incomplete
**unvorbereitet** ADJECTIVE
  unprepared
**unvoreingenommen** ADJECTIVE
  unbiased
**unvorsichtig** ADJECTIVE
  careless
**unvorstellbar** ADJECTIVE
  inconceivable
**unwahr** ADJECTIVE
  untrue
**unwahrscheinlich** ADJECTIVE, ADVERB
  [1] unlikely ◊ *eine unwahrscheinliche*

*Geschichte* an unlikely story
  [2] incredibly ◊ *Ich habe mich*
  *unwahrscheinlich gefreut.* I was
  incredibly pleased.
**unwichtig** ADJECTIVE
  unimportant
**unwirksam** ADJECTIVE
  ineffective
**unzählig** ADJECTIVE
  countless
**unzerbrechlich** ADJECTIVE
  unbreakable
**unzertrennlich** ADJECTIVE
  inseparable
**unzufrieden** ADJECTIVE
  dissatisfied
**unzutreffend** ADJECTIVE
  incorrect
**uralt** ADJECTIVE
  ancient
der **Ureinwohner** NOUN (PL die **Ureinwohner**)
  original inhabitant
der **Urin** NOUN (PL die **Urine**)
  urine
die **Urkunde** NOUN
  certificate
der **Urlaub** NOUN (PL die **Urlaube**)
  holiday ◊ *Wir fahren morgen in Urlaub.*
  We're going on holiday tomorrow.
die **Ursache** NOUN
  cause
  ◆ **Keine Ursache!** That's all right.
**ursprünglich** ADJECTIVE, ADVERB
  [1] original ◊ *Wir mussten unsere*
  *ursprünglichen Pläne aufgeben.* We had
  to abandon our original plans.
  [2] originally ◊ *Ursprünglich wollten wir*
  *nach Griechenland fahren.* We originally
  wanted to go to Greece.
das **Urteil** NOUN (PL die **Urteile**)
  [1] opinion ◊ *Wie lautet dein Urteil?*
  What's your opinion?
  [2] sentence ◊ *Die Richter haben das*
  *Urteil noch nicht verkündet.* The judges
  haven't passed sentence yet.
**urteilen** VERB
  to judge
der **Urwald** NOUN (PL die **Urwälder**)
  jungle
die **Urzeit** NOUN
  prehistoric times
die **USA** PL NOUN
  USA
  ◆ **aus den USA** from the USA
  ◆ **in den USA** in the USA
  ◆ **nach den USA** to the USA
**usw.** ABBREVIATION (= *und so weiter*)
  etc
**utopisch** ADJECTIVE
  utopian

# V

**vage** ADJECTIVE
vague

der **Vampir** NOUN (PL die **Vampire**)
vampire

die **Vanille** NOUN
vanilla

die **Vase** NOUN
vase

der **Vater** NOUN (PL die **Väter**)
father

**väterlich** ADJECTIVE
fatherly

das **Vaterunser** NOUN (PL die **Vaterunser**)
Lord's prayer

der **Vati** NOUN (PL die **Vatis**)
daddy

der **Vegetarier** NOUN (PL die **Vegetarier**)
vegetarian

die **Vegetarierin** NOUN
vegetarian

**vegetarisch** ADJECTIVE
vegetarian

das **Veilchen** NOUN (PL die **Veilchen**)
violet

die **Vene** NOUN
vein

das **Ventil** NOUN (PL die **Ventile**)
valve

der **Ventilator** NOUN (PL die **Ventilatoren**)
fan

**verabreden** VERB (PERFECT **hat verabredet**)
to arrange ◊ *Wir sollten Zeit und Ort des Treffens verabreden.* We ought to arrange when and where to meet.
◆ **sich mit jemandem verabreden** to arrange to meet somebody
◆ **mit jemandem verabredet sein** to have arranged to meet somebody ◊ *Ich bin mit meiner Mutter verabredet.* I've arranged to meet my mother.
◆ **Ich bin heute Abend mit meiner Freundin verabredet.** I'm seeing my girlfriend tonight.

die **Verabredung** NOUN
date
◆ **Ich habe um fünf eine Verabredung mit meiner Mutter.** I'm meeting my mother at five.

**verabschieden** VERB (PERFECT **hat verabschieden**)
to say goodbye to ◊ *Wir verabschiedeten unsere Gäste.* We said goodbye to our guests.
◆ **sich verabschieden** to take one's leave

**verallgemeinern** VERB (PERFECT **hat verallgemeinert**)
to generalize

**veralten** VERB (PERFECT **ist veraltet**)
to become obsolete

**veränderlich** ADJECTIVE
changeable

**verändern** VERB (PERFECT **hat verändert**)
to change
◆ **sich verändern** to change ◊ *Sie hat sich in den letzten beiden Monaten verändert.* She's changed in the last couple of months.

die **Veränderung** NOUN
change

die **Veranlagung** NOUN
disposition ◊ *eine nervöse Veranlagung* a nervous disposition

**veranlassen** VERB (PERFECT **hat veranlasst**)
◆ **etwas veranlassen** to have something done
◆ **Was hat dich veranlasst, so zu reagieren?** What made you react like that?
◆ **sich veranlasst sehen, etwas zu tun** to be prompted to do something

**veranschaulichen** VERB (PERFECT **hat veranschaulicht**)
to illustrate

**veranstalten** VERB (PERFECT **hat veranstaltet**)
to organize

der **Veranstalter** NOUN (PL die **Veranstalter**)
organizer

die **Veranstaltung** NOUN
event

**verantworten** VERB (PERFECT **hat verantwortet**)
to take responsibility for ◊ *Wenn das nicht klappt, hast du das zu verantworten.* If it doesn't work, you'll have to take responsibility for it.
◆ **Das kann ich nicht verantworten.** I couldn't possibly allow that.

**verantwortlich** ADJECTIVE
responsible

die **Verantwortung** NOUN
responsibility

**verantwortungsbewusst** ADJECTIVE
responsible

**verantwortungslos** ADJECTIVE
irresponsible

**verarbeiten** VERB (PERFECT **hat verarbeitet**)
[1] to process ◊ *In diesem Werk wird Metall verarbeitet.* Metal is processed in this factory.
◆ **etwas zu etwas verarbeiten** to make something into something ◊ *Der Plastikmüll wird zu Parkbänken verarbeitet.* Plastic waste is made into park benches.

☞

2 to digest ◊ *Ich muss die Reiseeindrücke erst noch verarbeiten.* I still have to digest my impressions from the journey.

**verärgern** VERB (PERFECT **hat verärgert**)
to annoy

das **Verb** NOUN (PL die **Verben**)
verb

der **Verband** NOUN (PL die **Verbände**)
1 dressing
◆ **Die Schwester hat ihm einen Verband angelegt.** The nurse dressed his wound.
2 association ◊ *Die Bauern haben sich zu einem Verband zusammengeschlossen.* The farmers have formed an association.

der **Verbandskasten** NOUN (PL die **Verbandskästen**)
first-aid box

das **Verbandszeug** NOUN
first-aid kit

**verbergen** VERB (PRESENT **verbirgt**, IMPERFECT **verbarg**, PERFECT **hat verborgen**)
to hide
◆ **sich vor jemandem verbergen** to hide from somebody

**verbessern** VERB (PERFECT **hat verbessert**)
1 to improve ◊ *Ich konnte meine Noten verbessern.* I was able to improve my marks.
2 to correct ◊ *Meine Mutter hat meine Hausaufgaben verbessert.* My mother corrected my homework.
◆ **sich verbessern** to improve ◊ *In Mathe habe ich mich verbessert.* I've improved in maths.

die **Verbesserung** NOUN
1 improvement ◊ *eine Verbesserung seiner Leistungen* an improvement in his work
2 correction ◊ *Schreibt bitte die Verbesserung ins Heft.* Please write the correction in your exercise book.

**verbiegen** VERB (IMPERFECT **verbog**, PERFECT **hat verbogen**)
to bend

**verbieten** VERB (IMPERFECT **verbot**, PERFECT **hat verboten**)
to forbid ◊ *Meine Mutter hat mir verboten, mit Frank auszugehen.* My mother forbade me to go out with Frank.

**verbinden** VERB (IMPERFECT **verband**, PERFECT **hat verbunden**)
1 to combine ◊ *Ich habe das Nützliche mit dem Angenehmen verbunden.* I was able to combine business with pleasure.
2 to bandage ◊ *Die Wunde muss verbunden werden.* The wound has to be bandaged.
◆ **jemandem die Augen verbinden** to blindfold somebody

3 to connect ◊ *Ein Kanal verbindet die beiden Flüsse.* A canal connects the two rivers.
4 to put through ◊ *Können Sie mich bitte mit Frau Karl verbinden?* Can you put me through to Mrs Karl, please? ◊ *Ich verbinde!* I'm putting you through.
◆ **Sie sind falsch verbunden.** You've got the wrong number.

**verbindlich** ADJECTIVE
1 definite ◊ *Ich hätte gern eine verbindliche Antwort.* I'd like a definite answer.
2 obliging ◊ *Die Verkäuferin war äußerst verbindlich.* The shop assistant was extremely obliging.

die **Verbindung** NOUN (PL die **Verbindungen**)
1 connection ◊ *Es gibt eine direkte Verbindungen nach München.* There is a direct connection to Munich.
2 communication ◊ *eine telefonische Verbindung* a telephone communication
◆ **eine chemische Verbindung** a compound

**verbleit** ADJECTIVE
leaded

**verblüffen** VERB (PERFECT **hat verblüfft**)
to amaze

die **Verblüffung** NOUN
amazement

**verbluten** VERB (PERFECT **ist verblutet**)
to bleed to death

**verborgen** ADJECTIVE
hidden

das **Verbot** NOUN (PL die **Verbote**)
ban ◊ *Die Regierung verhängte ein Verbot für Rindfleischimporte aus England.* The government imposed a ban on beef imports from England.

**verboten** ADJECTIVE
forbidden
◆ **Rauchen verboten!** No smoking

der **Verbrauch** NOUN
consumption

**verbrauchen** VERB (PERFECT **hat verbraucht**)
to use up ◊ *Das Gerät verbraucht viel Strom.* The machine uses up a lot of electricity.

der **Verbraucher** NOUN (PL die **Verbraucher**)
consumer

der **Verbrauchermarkt** NOUN (PL die **Verbrauchermärkte**)
hypermarket

das **Verbrechen** NOUN (PL die **Verbrechen**)
crime

der **Verbrecher** NOUN (PL die **Verbrecher**)
criminal

**verbreiten** VERB (PERFECT **hat verbreitet**)
1 to spread ◊ *eine Krankheit verbreiten* to spread a disease
2 to broadcast ◊ *eine Nachricht verbreiten* to broadcast a message

◆ **sich verbreiten** to spread ◊ *Die Seuche hat sich inzwischen im ganzen Land verbreitet.* The epidemic has since spread all over the country. ◊ *Die Nachricht von seinem Tod hat sich schnell verbreitet.* The news of his death spread quickly.

**verbrennen** VERB (IMPERFECT **verbrannte,** PERFECT **hat verbrannt)**
  [1] to burn ◊ *In dieser Anlage wird Müll verbrannt.* Waste is burnt in this plant.
  [2] to cremate ◊ *Sie möchte nach ihrem Tod verbrannt werden.* She'd like to be cremated when she dies.

**verbringen** VERB (IMPERFECT **verbrachte,** PERFECT **hat verbracht)**
  to spend ◊ *Wir haben das Wochenende im Schwarzwald verbracht.* We spent the weekend in the Black Forest.

**verbrühen** VERB (PERFECT **hat verbrüht)**
  to scald ◊ *Ich habe mir den Arm verbrüht.* I've scalded my arm.
◆ **sich verbrühen** to scald oneself ◊ *Pass auf, dass du dich nicht verbrühst.* Careful you don't scald yourself.

der **Verdacht** NOUN (PL die **Verdachte)**
  suspicion

**verdächtig** ADJECTIVE
  suspicious

**verdächtigen** VERB (PERFECT **hat verdächtigt)**
  to suspect

**verdammt** ADJECTIVE, ADVERB
  damned ◊ *Diese verdammten Fliegen!* These damned flies!
◆ **Verdammt noch mal!** Damn it all!
◆ **Verdammt!** Damn!

**verdampfen** VERB (PERFECT **ist verdampft)**
  to evaporate

**verdanken** VERB (PERFECT **hat verdankt)**
◆ **jemandem sein Leben verdanken** to owe one's life to somebody ◊ *Sie verdankt ihm ihr Leben.* She owes her life to him.

**verdauen** VERB (PERFECT **hat verdaut)**
  to digest

**verdaulich** ADJECTIVE
◆ **Das ist schwer verdaulich.** That's hard to digest.

die **Verdauung** NOUN
  digestion

**verderben** VERB (PRESENT **verdirbt,** IMPERFECT **verdarb,** PERFECT **hat/ist verdorben)**
  *Use **haben** to form the perfect tense. Use **sein** to form the perfect tense for **to go bad.***
  [1] to ruin ◊ *Du verdirbst dir bei dem schlechten Licht die Augen.* You'll ruin your eyes in this bad light. ◊ *Er hat mir den Urlaub verdorben.* He ruined my holiday.
  [2] to corrupt ◊ *Geld verdirbt den Menschen.* Money corrupts people.

◆ **es mit jemandem verderben** to get into somebody's bad books ◊ *Sie will es mit keinem verderben.* She doesn't want to get into anybody's bad books.
  [3] to go bad ◊ *Die Wurst ist verdorben.* The sausage has gone bad.

**verdienen** VERB (PERFECT **hat verdient)**
  [1] to earn ◊ *Wie viel verdient dein Vater?* How much does your father earn?
  [2] to deserve ◊ *Du hast die Strafe verdient.* You deserved the punishment.

**verdoppeln** VERB (PERFECT **hat verdoppelt)**
  to double

**verdreifachen** VERB (PERFECT **hat verdreifacht)**
  to treble

**verdünnen** VERB (PERFECT **hat verdünnt)**
  to dilute

**verdunsten** VERB (PERFECT **ist verdunstet)**
  to evaporate

**verdursten** VERB (PERFECT **ist verdurstet)**
  to die of thirst

**verdutzt** ADJECTIVE
  nonplussed

der **Verein** NOUN (PL die **Vereine)**
  club ◊ *ein Sportverein* a sports club

**vereinbar** ADJECTIVE
◆ **mit etwas vereinbar** compatible with something

**vereinbaren** VERB (PERFECT **hat vereinbart)**
  to agree on

die **Vereinbarung** NOUN
  agreement

**vereinen** VERB (PERFECT **hat vereint)**
  [1] to unite ◊ *Das geteilte Land wurde wieder vereint.* The divided country was reunited.
  [2] to reconcile ◊ *Ich kann das nicht mit meinem Gewissen vereinen.* I can't reconcile that with my conscience.
◆ **Mit vereinten Kräften schaffen wir das.** If we all pull together, we'll manage to do it.
◆ **die Vereinten Nationen** the United Nations

**vereinfachen** VERB (PERFECT **hat vereinfacht)**
  to simplify

**vereinigen** VERB (PERFECT **hat vereinigt)**
  to unite

**vereinzelt** ADJECTIVE
  isolated ◊ *vereinzelte Schauer* isolated showers

**vererben** VERB (PERFECT **hat vererbt)**
  to leave ◊ *Meine Oma hat mir all ihre Bücher vererbt.* My granny left me all her books.
◆ **sich vererben** to be hereditary ◊ *Krampfadern vererben sich.* Varicose veins are hereditary.

**verfahren** VERB (PRESENT **verfährt,** IMPERFECT **verfuhr,** PERFECT **hat/ist verfahren)**

**V**

☞

1 to proceed ◊ *Wie sollen wir verfahren?* How shall we proceed?

2 to use up ◊ *Wir haben 50 Liter Benzin verfahren.* We have used up 50 litres of petrol.

◆ **Wir haben uns verfahren.** We have lost our way.

das **Verfahren** NOUN (PL die **Verfahren**)

1 process ◊ *Das ist ein neuartiges Verfahren zum Recyceln von Plastik.* This is a new recycling process for plastic.

2 proceedings ◊ *ein Verfahren gegen jemanden einleiten* to bring proceedings against somebody

die **Verfassung** NOUN

1 constitution ◊ *Die Opposition hat eine Änderung der Verfassung beantragt.* The opposition's called for an amendment to the constitution.

2 state ◊ *Ich bin nicht in der Verfassung, da mitzumachen.* I'm in no state to join in.

**verfaulen** VERB (PERFECT **ist verfault**)
to rot

**verflixt** ADJECTIVE
damn

**verfolgen** VERB (PERFECT **hat verfolgt**)

1 to pursue ◊ *Die Polizei verfolgte die Täter.* The police pursued the culprits.

◆ **Die Hunde verfolgten ihre Fährte.** The dogs tracked them.

2 to persecute ◊ *In vielen Ländern werden Minderheiten verfolgt.* Minorities are persecuted in many countries.

die **Verfolgung** NOUN

1 hunt ◊ *Die Verfolgung der Täter war erfolgreich.* The hunt for the culprits had a successful outcome.

2 persecution ◊ *die Verfolgung von Minderheiten* the persecution of minorities

**verfügbar** ADJECTIVE
available

die **Verfügung** NOUN

◆ **etwas zur Verfügung haben** to have something at one's disposal ◊ *Nicht alle Schüler haben einen Computer zur Verfügung.* Not all pupils have a computer at their disposal.

◆ **Die Bibliothek steht allen Schülern zur Verfügung.** The library's open to all pupils.

◆ **Sollten Sie meine Hilfe brauchen, stehe ich Ihnen zur Verfügung.** If you should need my help, I will be at your service.

**verführen** VERB (PERFECT **hat verführt**)

1 to tempt ◊ *Verführ mich nicht, ich habe schon zwei Stück Kuchen gegessen.* Don't tempt me, I've already had two pieces of cake.

2 to seduce ◊ *Er hat versucht, sie zu verführen.* He tried to seduce her.

**vergammeln** VERB (PERFECT **ist vergammelt**)

to go off ◊ *Pfui, das Fleisch ist ja total vergammelt.* Ugh, the meat's gone right off.

◆ **etwas vergammeln lassen** to let something go ◊ *Wir haben den Garten ziemlich vergammeln lassen.* We've rather let the garden go.

die **Vergangenheit** NOUN
past ◊ *in der Vergangenheit* in the past

**vergasen** VERB (PERFECT **hat vergast**)
to gas

der **Vergaser** NOUN (PL die **Vergaser**)
carburettor

**vergaß** VERB *see* **vergessen**

**vergeben** VERB (PRESENT **vergibt**, IMPERFECT **vergab**, PERFECT **hat vergeben**)

to forgive ◊ *Kannst du mir noch einmal vergeben?* Can you forgive me one more time? ◊ *Diese Lüge werde ich dir nie vergeben.* I'll never forgive you for that lie.

◆ **vergeben sein** to be taken ◊ *Tut mir Leid, die Stelle ist schon vergeben.* Sorry, the job's already taken.

◆ **Er ist schon vergeben.** He's already spoken for.

**vergeblich** ADVERB, ADJECTIVE

in vain ◊ *Wir haben uns vergeblich bemüht.* We tried, but in vain. ◊ *All mein Reden war vergeblich.* All my words were in vain.

**vergehen** VERB (IMPERFECT **verging**, PERFECT **ist vergangen**)
to pass

◆ **Wie schnell die Zeit doch vergeht!** How time flies!

◆ **Mir ist der Appetit vergangen.** I've lost my appetite.

◆ **sich an jemandem vergehen** to indecently assault somebody ◊ *Er soll sich an kleinen Mädchen vergangen haben.* He's said to have indecently assaulted young girls.

**vergessen** VERB (PRESENT **vergisst**, IMPERFECT **vergaß**, PERFECT **hat vergessen**)
to forget ◊ *Ich habe seinen Namen vergessen.* I've forgotten his name.

◆ **Vergiss nicht, die Blumen zu gießen.** Remember to water the flowers.

**vergesslich** ADJECTIVE
forgetful

**vergeuden** VERB (PERFECT **hat vergeudet**)
to squander

**vergewaltigen** VERB (PERFECT **hat vergewaltigt**)
to rape ◊ *Er hat eine Frau vergewaltigt.* He raped a woman.

die **Vergewaltigung** NOUN
rape

sich **vergewissern** VERB (PERFECT **hat sich vergewissert**)
to make sure

**vergiften** VERB (PERFECT **hat vergiftet**)

to poison

die **Vergiftung** NOUN
poisoning

das **Vergissmeinnicht** NOUN (PL die **Vergissmeinnicht**)
forget-me-not

**vergisst** VERB see **vergessen**

der **Vergleich** NOUN (PL die **Vergleiche**)
comparison
♦ **im Vergleich zu** compared with

**vergleichen** VERB (IMPERFECT **verglich**, PERFECT **hat verglichen**)
to compare ◊ *Er hat mein Wörterbuch mit seinem verglichen.* He compared my dictionary with his. ◊ *Man kann doch Äpfel und Birnen nicht vergleichen.* You can't compare apples and pears.

das **Vergnügen** NOUN (PL die **Vergnügen**)
pleasure
♦ **Viel Vergnügen!** Have fun!

**vergnügt** ADJECTIVE
cheerful

**vergraben** VERB (PRESENT **vergräbt**, IMPERFECT **vergrub**, PERFECT **hat vergraben**)
to bury

**vergrößern** VERB (PERFECT **hat vergrößert**)
[1] to enlarge ◊ *Ich habe das Foto vergrößern lassen.* I had the photo enlarged.
[2] to extend ◊ *Wir wollen das Haus vergrößern.* We want to extend the house.
♦ **sich vergrößern** to grow larger ◊ *Die Klasse hat sich stark vergrößert.* The class has grown considerably larger.

die **Vergrößerung** NOUN
[1] enlargement ◊ *Kann man mit dem Kopierer auch Vergrößerungen machen?* Can you do enlargements with the copier as well?
[2] expansion ◊ *eine Vergrößerung der Firma* an expansion of the company

das **Vergrößerungsglas** NOUN (GEN des **Vergrößerungsglases**, PL die **Vergrößerungsgläser**)
magnifying glass

**verhaften** VERB (PERFECT **hat verhaftet**)
to arrest

das **Verhalten** NOUN
see also **verhalten** VERB
behaviour

sich **verhalten** VERB (PRESENT **verhält sich**, IMPERFECT **verhielt sich**, PERFECT **hat sich verhalten**)
see also das **Verhalten** NOUN
to behave ◊ *Er hat sich uns gegenüber sehr fair verhalten.* He behaved very fairly towards us.

das **Verhältnis** NOUN (GEN des **Verhältnisses**, PL die **Verhältnisse**)

[1] affair ◊ *Er hat ein Verhältnis mit einer verheirateten Frau.* He's having an affair with a married woman.
[2] proportion ◊ *Unser Gehalt steht in keinem Verhältnis zu unserer Leistung.* Our salary is not in proportion to our efforts.
♦ **Verhältnisse (1)** conditions ◊ *Wenn die Verhältnisse anders wären, könnten wir die Arbeit schneller beenden.* If conditions were different we could get the work finished sooner.
♦ **Verhältnisse (2)** background ◊ *Er kommt aus bescheidenen Verhältnissen.* He comes from a modest background.
♦ **über seine Verhältnisse leben** to live beyond one's means

**verhältnismäßig** ADVERB
relatively

**verhandeln** VERB (PERFECT **hat verhandelt**)
to negotiate ◊ *Sie verhandeln einen Waffenstillstand.* They're negotiating a ceasefire.
♦ **Mein Fall wird nächste Woche vor dem Arbeitsgericht verhandelt.** My case is being heard by the industrial tribunal next week.

die **Verhandlung** NOUN
[1] negotiation ◊ *die Friedensverhandlungen* peace negotiations ◊ *Wir sind mit der Firma noch in Verhandlung.* We're still involved in negotiations with the company.
[2] trial ◊ *Die Verhandlung gegen Klitt ist morgen.* Klitt's trial is tomorrow.
[3] hearing ◊ *die Verhandlung vor dem Arbeitsgericht* the hearing before the industrial tribunal

**verharmlosen** VERB (PERFECT **hat verharmlost**)
to play down

**verhauen** VERB (PERFECT **hat verhauen**)
to beat up

**verheerend** ADJECTIVE
devastating

**verheimlichen** VERB (PERFECT **hat verheimlicht**)
♦ **jemandem etwas verheimlichen** to keep something secret from somebody

**verheiratet** ADJECTIVE
married

**verhexen** VERB (PERFECT **hat verhext**)
♦ **Es ist wie verhext.** It's jinxed.

**verhindern** VERB (PERFECT **hat verhindert**)
to prevent
♦ **verhindert sein** to be unable to make it ◊ *Ich bin leider verhindert.* I'm afraid I can't make it.

**verhören** VERB (PERFECT **hat verhört**)
[1] to interrogate ◊ *Die Polizei hat ihn verhört.* The police interrogated him.
[2] to examine ◊ *Der Zeuge wurde verhört.* The witness was examined.

**V**

☞

♦ **sich verhören** to mishear ◇ *Ich muss mich wohl verhört haben.* I must have misheard.

**verhungern** VERB (PERFECT **ist verhungert**) to starve to death

das **Verhütungsmittel** NOUN (PL die **Verhütungsmittel**) contraceptive

sich **verirren** VERB (PERFECT **hat sich verirrt**) to get lost ◇ *Wir hatten uns im Nebel verirrt.* We lost our way in the fog.

der **Verkauf** NOUN (PL die **Verkäufe**) sale

**verkaufen** VERB (PERFECT **hat verkauft**) to sell

der **Verkäufer** NOUN (PL die **Verkäufer**) shop assistant ◇ *Der Verkäufer hat uns sehr gut beraten.* The shop assistant was extremely helpful.

die **Verkäuferin** NOUN shop assistant ◇ *Sie ist Verkäuferin in einer Modeboutique.* She's a shop assistant in a fashion boutique.

der **Verkehr** NOUN
1 traffic ◇ *Heute war viel Verkehr auf den Straßen.* There was heavy traffic on the roads today.
2 intercourse ◇ *Haben Sie mit der Frau Verkehr gehabt?* Did you have intercourse with this woman?

die **Verkehrsampel** NOUN traffic lights

das **Verkehrsamt** NOUN (PL die **Verkehrsämter**) tourist office

die **Verkehrsmeldung** NOUN traffic announcement

das **Verkehrsmittel** NOUN (PL die **Verkehrsmittel**) means of transport

das **Verkehrsnetz** NOUN (GEN des **Verkehrsnetzes**, PL die **Verkehrsnetze**) traffic network

das **Verkehrsschild** NOUN (PL die **Verkehrsschilder**) road sign

der **Verkehrsunfall** NOUN (PL die **Verkehrsunfälle**) traffic accident

das **Verkehrszeichen** NOUN (PL die **Verkehrszeichen**) traffic sign

**verkehrt** ADJECTIVE wrong ◇ *Das war die verkehrte Antwort.* That was the wrong answer.
♦ **verkehrt herum** back to front ◇ *Du hast deinen Pulli verkehrt herum an.* You've got your pullover on back to front.

sich **verkleiden** VERB (PERFECT **hat sich verkleidet**) to dress up ◇ *Sie verkleidete sich als Hexe.* She dressed up as a witch.

**verkleinern** VERB (PERFECT **hat verkleinert**) to reduce ◇ *Wir sollten den Zeilenabstand verkleinern.* We should reduce the line spacing.
♦ **sich verkleinern** to grow smaller ◇ *Die Klasse hat sich stark verkleinert.* The class has grown considerably smaller.

**verklemmt** ADJECTIVE inhibited

der **Verlag** NOUN (PL die **Verlage**) publisher

**verlangen** VERB (PERFECT **hat verlangt**) to ask for ◇ *Ich verlange etwas mehr Verständnis.* I'm asking for a bit more understanding. ◇ *Wie viel hat er dafür verlangt?* How much did he ask for it?
♦ **Er hat zehn Mark dafür verlangt.** He charged ten marks for it.
♦ **etwas von jemandem verlangen** to expect something of somebody ◇ *Unser Chemielehrer verlangt zu viel von uns.* Our chemistry teacher expects too much of us.

**verlängern** VERB (PERFECT **hat verlängert**)
1 to extend ◇ *Wir haben die Ferien um eine Woche verlängert.* We've extended our holiday by a week.
2 to lengthen ◇ *Wir müssen das Seil verlängern.* We'll have to lengthen the rope.

die **Verlängerungsschnur** NOUN (PL die **Verlängerungsschnüre**) extension cable

**verlassen** VERB (PRESENT **verlässt**, IMPERFECT **verließ**, PERFECT **hat verlassen**)
see also **verlassen** ADJECTIVE
to leave ◇ *Er hat seine Frau und Kinder verlassen.* He's left his wife and children.
♦ **Verlassen Sie sofort das Gebäude!** Get out of the building immediately.
♦ **sich verlassen auf** to depend on ◇ *Ich kann mich doch auf dich verlassen.* I hope I can depend on you.

**verlassen** ADJECTIVE
see also **verlassen** VERB
1 deserted ◇ *eine verlassene Gegend* a deserted area ◇ *die verlassene Ehefrau* the deserted wife
2 empty ◇ *ein verlassenes Haus* an empty house
♦ **Sie fühlte sich allein und verlassen.** She felt all alone.

sich **verlaufen** VERB (PRESENT **verläuft sich**, IMPERFECT **verlief sich**, PERFECT **hat sich verlaufen**)
1 to get lost ◇ *Wir haben uns im Wald verlaufen.* We got lost in the forest.
2 to disperse ◇ *Nach Ende der Veranstaltung verlief sich die Menge.* After the event the crowd dispersed.

**verlegen** ADJECTIVE embarrassed

**♦ nicht verlegen um** never at a loss for
◊ *Sie ist nie um eine Ausrede verlegen.*
She's never at a loss for an excuse.

der **Verleih** NOUN (PL die **Verleihe**)
hire
**♦ ein Fahrradverleih** a bicycle hire shop

**verleihen** VERB (IMPERFECT **verlieh**, PERFECT **hat verliehen**)
[1] to lend ◊ *Ich habe mein Wörterbuch an sie verliehen.* I've lent her my dictionary.
[2] to hire out ◊ *Ich suche jemanden, der Fahrräder verleiht.* I'm looking for somebody who hires out bikes.
[3] to award ◊ *Sie hat einen Preis verliehen bekommen.* She was awarded a prize.

**verleiten** VERB (PERFECT **hat verleitet**)
**♦ jemanden dazu verleiten, etwas zu tun** to tempt somebody into doing something

**verlernen** VERB (PERFECT **hat verlernt**)
to forget

**verletzen** VERB (PERFECT **hat verletzt**)
[1] to hurt ◊ *Deine Bemerkung hat mich verletzt.* Your remark hurt me.
[2] to injure ◊ *Sie ist schwer verletzt.* She's seriously injured.
**♦ ein Gesetz verletzen** to violate a law

der **Verletzte** NOUN (GEN des/der **Verletzten**, PL
die die **Verletzten**)
injured person ◊ *Auf der Straße lag ein Verletzter.* An injured person was lying in the street.

die **Verletzung** NOUN
injury
**♦ Er hatte schwere Verletzungen.** He was seriously injured.
**♦ Das ist eine Verletzung der Spielregeln.** That's against the rules of the game.

sich **verlieben** VERB (PERFECT **hat sich verliebt**)
**♦ sich in jemanden verlieben** to fall in love with somebody

**verliebt** ADJECTIVE
in love ◊ *Ich bin in Anke verliebt.* I'm in love with Anke.

**verlieren** VERB (IMPERFECT **verlor**, PERFECT **hat verloren**)
to lose

der **Verlierer** NOUN (PL die **Verlierer**)
loser

sich **verloben** VERB (PERFECT **hat sich verlobt**)
**♦ sich mit jemandem verloben** to get engaged to somebody

der **Verlobte** NOUN (GEN des **Verlobten**, PL die **Verlobten**)
see also die **Verlobte** NOUN
fiancé ◊ *Mathias ist mein Verlobter.* Mathias is my fiancé.

die **Verlobte** NOUN (GEN der **Verlobten**, PL die **Verlobten**)
see also der **Verlobte** NOUN

fiancée ◊ *Ingrid ist seine Verlobte.* Ingrid's his fiancée.

die **Verlobung** NOUN
engagement

**verlor, verloren** VERB see **verlieren**

**verloren** ADJECTIVE
lost ◊ *die verlorene Zeit wieder einholen* to make up for lost time
**♦ verlorene Eier** poached eggs
**♦ verloren gehen** to get lost

die **Verlosung** NOUN
raffle

der **Verlust** NOUN (PL die **Verluste**)
loss

**vermehren** VERB (PERFECT **hat vermehrt**)
increase ◊ *Die Firma hat ihren Umsatz vermehrt.* The company has increased its turnover.
**♦ sich vermehren** to reproduce ◊ *Wie vermehren sich Regenwürmer?* How do earthworms reproduce?

**vermeiden** VERB (IMPERFECT **vermied**, PERFECT **hat vermieden**)
to avoid

**vermieten** VERB (PERFECT **hat vermietet**)
[1] to let ◊ *"Zimmer zu vermieten"* "Rooms to let"
[2] to rent ◊ *Sie vermietet Zimmer.* She rents rooms.
[3] to hire out ◊ *Wir vermieten Boote und Fahrräder.* We hire out boats and bikes.

der **Vermieter** NOUN (PL die **Vermieter**)
landlord

die **Vermieterin** NOUN
landlady

**vermissen** VERB (PERFECT **hat vermisst**)
to miss ◊ *Ich habe dich vermisst.* I missed you.
**♦ Ich vermisse eines meiner Bücher.** One of my books is missing.

das **Vermögen** NOUN (PL die **Vermögen**)
wealth
**♦ ein Vermögen kosten** to cost a fortune

**vermuten** VERB (PERFECT **hat vermutet**)
[1] to guess ◊ *Ich kann nur vermuten, was er damit gemeint hat.* I can only guess what he meant by that.
**♦ Man vermutet, dass er im Ausland ist.** He is thought to be abroad.
[2] to suspect ◊ *Die Polizei vermutet, dass er der Täter ist.* The police suspect that he's the culprit.
[3] to suppose ◊ *Ich vermute, dass er das noch nicht weiß.* I don't suppose that he knows that yet.

**vermutlich** ADJECTIVE, ADVERB
[1] probable ◊ *die vermutliche Ursache* the probable cause
[2] probably ◊ *Sie ist vermutlich schon gegangen.* She has probably already left.

die **Vermutung** NOUN

**V**

1 supposition ◊ *Das legt die Vermutung nahe, dass sie schon gegangen ist.* It seems a likely supposition that she's already gone.

2 suspicion ◊ *Die Polizei hat eine Vermutung, wer der Täter gewesen sein könnte.* The police have a suspicion as to who the culprit could have been.

**vernachlässigen** VERB (PERFECT **hat vernachlässigt**)
to neglect

**vernichten** VERB (PERFECT **hat vernichtet**)
to destroy
♦ **Insekten vernichten** to exterminate insects
♦ **Unkraut vernichten** to eradicate weeds

**vernichtend** ADJECTIVE
crushing ◊ *Unsere Mannschaft wurde vernichtend geschlagen.* Our team suffered a crushing defeat.
♦ **ein vernichtender Blick** a withering look
♦ **eine vernichtende Kritik** a scathing review

die **Vernunft** NOUN
reason

**vernünftig** ADJECTIVE
reasonable ◊ *Sei doch vernünftig!* Be reasonable! ◊ *ein vernünftiger Preis* a reasonable price
♦ **etwas Vernünftiges essen** to eat something decent

**veröffentlichen** VERB (PERFECT **hat veröffentlicht**)
to publish

die **Verpackung** NOUN
packing

das **Verpackungsmaterial** NOUN (PL die **Verpackungsmaterialien**)
packaging

**verpassen** VERB (PERFECT **hat verpasst**)
to miss
♦ **jemandem eine Ohrfeige verpassen** to give somebody a clip round the ear

**verpflegen** VERB (PERFECT **hat verpflegt**)
to cater for ◊ *Die Flüchtlinge wurden vom Roten Kreuz verpflegt.* The Red Cross catered for the refugees.

die **Verpflegung** NOUN
food ◊ *Für Ihre Verpflegung wird gesorgt.* Food will be laid on. ◊ *Die Verpflegung im Schullandheim war gut.* The food at the school camp was good.

**verpflichten** VERB (PERFECT **hat verpflichtet**)
to sign ◊ *Der VfB will Köpke verpflichten.* VfB want to sign Köpke.
♦ **sich verpflichten, etwas zu tun** to promise to do something ◊ *Du hast dich verpflichtet, für die Musik zu sorgen.* You promised to organize the music.
♦ **Sie haben sich verpflichtet, für Ersatz zu sorgen.** You undertook to find a replacement.

♦ **verpflichtet sein, etwas zu tun** to be obliged to do something
♦ **Er ist zum Stillschweigen verpflichtet.** He's sworn to silence.
♦ **Das verpflichtet Sie zu nichts.** This doesn't commit you to anything.
♦ **jemandem zu Dank verpflichtet sein** to be obliged to somebody

**verprügeln** VERB (PERFECT **hat verprügelt**)
to beat up

**verraten** VERB (PRESENT **verrät**, IMPERFECT **verriet**, PERFECT **hat verraten**)
1 to betray ◊ *Er hat seine Mittäter verraten.* He betrayed his accomplices.
2 to report ◊ *Fritz hat uns beim Lehrer verraten.* Fritz reported us to the teacher.
3 to tell ◊ *Verrate mir doch, wer es war.* Tell me who it was. ◊ *Ich habe dieses Geheimnis niemandem verraten.* I haven't told anyone the secret.
♦ **sich verraten** to give oneself away

**verregnet** ADJECTIVE
rainy

**verreisen** VERB (PERFECT **ist verreist**)
to go away ◊ *Ich möchte diesen Sommer verreisen.* I'd like to go away this summer.
♦ **Wir wollen nach Israel verreisen.** We intend to go to Israel.

**verrenken** VERB (PERFECT **hat verrenkt**)
to sprain ◊ *Er hat sich den Knöchel verrenkt.* He sprained his ankle.

**verrosten** VERB (PERFECT **ist verrostet**)
to rust

**verrückt** ADJECTIVE
crazy

der **Verrückte** NOUN (GEN des/der **Verrückten**, PL
die die **Verrückten**)
maniac ◊ *Er ist gefahren wie ein Verrückter.* He drove like a maniac.

die **Verrücktheit** NOUN
madness

**verrufen** ADJECTIVE
disreputable

der **Vers** NOUN (GEN des **Verses**, PL die **Verse**)
verse

der **Versager** NOUN (PL die **Versager**)
failure

**versalzen** VERB (PERFECT **hat versalzen**)
to put too much salt in ◊ *Sie hat die Suppe versalzen.* She put too much salt in the soup.
♦ **Die Suppe ist versalzen.** There's too much salt in the soup.

**versammeln** VERB (PERFECT **hat versammelt**)
to assemble

die **Versammlung** NOUN
meeting

das **Versandhaus** NOUN (GEN des **Versandhauses**, PL die **Versandhäuser**)
mail-order firm

**versäumen** VERB (PERFECT **hat versäumt**)
to miss ◊ *Ich habe wegen Krankheit drei Stunden versäumt.* I missed three lessons due to illness.
♦ **es versäumen, etwas zu tun** to fail to do something ◊ *Sie hat es versäumt, sich rechtzeitig anzumelden.* She failed to register in time.
♦ **Sie sollten nicht versäumen, sich die Kathedrale anzusehen.** Don't miss a visit to the cathedral.

sich **verschätzen** VERB (PERFECT **hat sich verschätzt**)
to misjudge

**verschenken** VERB (PERFECT **hat verschenkt**)
to give away

**verschicken** VERB (PERFECT **hat verschickt**)
to send away

**verschieben** VERB (IMPERFECT **verschob**, PERFECT **hat verschoben**)
to postpone ◊ *Wir müssen das Fest verschieben.* We'll have to postpone the party.

**verschieden** ADJECTIVE
different ◊ *Die zwei Brüder sind sehr verschieden.* The two brothers are very different.
♦ **verschiedene** various ◊ *Wir haben verschiedene Sehenswürdigkeiten besichtigt.* We've seen various sights.
♦ **Sie sind verschieden groß.** They are different sizes.

**verschlafen** VERB (PRESENT **verschläft**, IMPERFECT **verschlief**, PERFECT **hat verschlafen**)
see also **verschlafen** ADJECTIVE
[1] to sleep in ◊ *Tut mir Leid, ich habe verschlafen.* Sorry, I slept in.
[2] to sleep through ◊ *Er hat den ganzen Vormittag verschlafen.* He slept through the whole morning.
[3] to forget ◊ *Ich habe deinen Geburtstag total verschlafen.* I completely forgot your birthday.

**verschlafen** ADJECTIVE
see also **verschlafen** VERB
sleepy ◊ *Sie sah mich mit einem verschlafenen Blick an.* She gave me a sleepy look. ◊ *ein verschlafenes kleines Dorf* a sleepy little village

**verschlechtern** VERB (PERFECT **hat verschlechtert**)
to make worse ◊ *Das verschlechtert die Lage.* That makes the situation worse.
♦ **Sie hat ihre Noten gewaltig verschlechtert.** Her marks have got considerably worse.
♦ **sich verschlechtern** to get worse ◊ *Die Lage hat sich verschlechtert.* The situation's got worse. ◊ *In Englisch habe ich mich verschlechtert.* My marks in English have got worse.

♦ **Sein Gesundheitszustand hat sich noch weiter verschlechtert.** His condition has deteriorated even further.

**verschleißen** VERB (IMPERFECT **verschliss**, PERFECT **hat verschlissen**)
to wear out ◊ *eine verschlissene Jacke* a worn-out jacket

**verschlimmern** VERB (PERFECT **hat verschlimmert**)
to make worse ◊ *Du verschlimmerst alles, wenn du weiter lügst.* You'll make everything worse if you go on lying.
♦ **sich verschlimmern** to get worse ◊ *Die Lage hat sich verschlimmert.* The situation's got worse.

**verschlucken** VERB (PERFECT **hat verschluckt**)
to swallow ◊ *Ich habe eine Gräte verschluckt.* I've swallowed a fish bone.
♦ **sich verschlucken** to choke ◊ *Ich habe mich an einer Erdnuss verschluckt.* I choked on a peanut.

der **Verschluss** NOUN (GEN des **Verschlusses**, PL die **Verschlüsse**)
[1] cap ◊ *Die Flasche hat einen kindersicheren Verschluss.* The bottle has a childproof cap.
[2] fastening ◊ *Kannst du mir den Verschluss an meinem Kleid aufmachen?* Can you undo the fastening of my dress?
[3] catch ◊ *der Verschluss der Tasche* the catch of the bag ◊ *der Verschluss an einer Halskette* the catch of a necklace

**verschmutzen** VERB (PERFECT **hat verschmutzt**)
to soil
♦ **Die Straße war stark verschmutzt.** The road was very dirty.
♦ **die Umwelt verschmutzen** to pollute the environment

**verschneit** ADJECTIVE
covered with snow
♦ **eine verschneite Straße** a snow-covered road

**verschonen** VERB (PERFECT **hat verschont**)
♦ **jemanden mit etwas verschonen** to spare somebody something ◊ *Sie verschonte mich mit den ganzen Einzelheiten.* She spared me all the details.

**verschreiben** VERB (IMPERFECT **verschrieb**, PERFECT **hat verschrieben**)
to prescribe ◊ *Der Arzt hat mir Antibiotika verschrieben.* The doctor prescribed me antibiotics.
♦ **sich verschreiben** to make a spelling mistake

**verschreibungspflichtig** ADJECTIVE
available on prescription only
♦ **verschreibungspflichtige Medikamente** prescribed drugs

**verschütten** VERB (PERFECT **hat verschüttet**)

**V**

☞

<u>to spill</u> ◊ *Sie hat den Kaffee verschüttet.*
She spilt the coffee.
◆ **verschüttet werden** to be buried ◊ *Bei dem Erdbeben wurden zahlreiche Menschen verschüttet.* Many people were buried in the earthquake.
**verschweigen** VERB (IMPERFECT **verschwieg**, PERFECT **hat verschwiegen**)
◆ **jemandem etwas verschweigen** to keep something from somebody
**verschwenden** VERB (PERFECT **hat verschwendet**)
<u>to waste</u> ◊ *Zeit verschwenden* to waste time
die **Verschwendung** NOUN
<u>waste</u>
**verschwinden** VERB (IMPERFECT **verschwand**, PERFECT **ist verschwunden**)
<u>to disappear</u>
**verschwitzt** ADJECTIVE
<u>sweaty</u>
**verschwommen** ADJECTIVE
<u>blurred</u>
das **Versehen** NOUN (PL die **Versehen**)
<u>oversight</u> ◊ *Das war ein Versehen.* It was an oversight.
◆ **aus Versehen** by mistake
**versehentlich** ADVERB
<u>by mistake</u>
**versenden** VERB (IMPERFECT **versendete** or **versandte**, PERFECT **hat versendet** or **versandt**)
<u>to dispatch</u>
**versessen** ADJECTIVE
◆ **auf etwas versessen sein** to be mad about something ◊ *Sie ist ganz versessen auf ihn.* She's mad about him.
**versetzen** VERB (PERFECT **hat versetzt**)
<u>to transfer</u> ◊ *Mein Vater wird nach Berlin versetzt.* My father's being transferred to Berlin.
◆ **jemanden in die nächste Klasse versetzen** to move somebody up into the next class

---

ⓘ *In Germany, pupils do not automatically move up (werden versetzt) to the next class at the end of the school year. If their performance is not good enough, they have to repeat the school year. This is known as sitzen bleiben.*

---

◆ **jemanden versetzen** to stand somebody up ◊ *Meine Freundin hat mich versetzt.* My girlfriend stood me up.
◆ **sich in jemandes Lage versetzen** to put oneself in somebody's shoes ◊ *Wenn du dich einmal in meine Lage versetzt ...* If you put yourself in my shoes ...
◆ **jemandem einen Schlag versetzen** to hit somebody

◆ **jemandem einen Tritt versetzen** to kick somebody
◆ **jemanden in gute Laune versetzen** to put somebody in a good mood
**verseuchen** VERB (PERFECT **hat verseucht**)
<u>to contaminate</u>
**versichern** VERB (PERFECT **hat versichert**)
① <u>to assure</u> ◊ *Er hat mir versichert, dass das stimmt.* He assured me that this is correct.
② <u>to insure</u> ◊ *Wir sind nicht gegen Diebstahl versichert.* We are not insured against theft.
die **Versicherung** NOUN
<u>insurance</u>
sich **versöhnen** VERB (PERFECT **hat sich versöhnt**)
<u>to make up</u> ◊ *Na, habt ihr euch wieder versöhnt?* Well, have you two made up again?
◆ **sich mit jemandem versöhnen** to make it up with somebody ◊ *Ich habe mich wieder mit ihm versöhnt.* I made it up with him again.
**versorgen** VERB (PERFECT **hat versorgt**)
<u>to supply</u> ◊ *Von hier aus wird die Stadt mit Elektrizität versorgt.* The town is supplied with electricity from here.
◆ **einen Kranken versorgen** to look after a patient
◆ **Wer versorgt die Blumen während der Ferien?** Who's watering the plants during the holidays?
◆ **eine Familie versorgen** to support a family
sich **verspäten** VERB (PERFECT **hat sich verspätet**)
<u>to be late</u>
**verspätet** ADJECTIVE
<u>late</u> ◊ *die verspätete Ankunft* the late arrival
◆ **der verspätete Flug** the delayed flight
◆ **verspätete Glückwünsche** belated best wishes
die **Verspätung** NOUN
<u>delay</u>
◆ **Verspätung haben** to be late
das **Versprechen** NOUN (PL die **Versprechen**)
⏎ *see also* **versprechen** VERB
<u>promise</u> ◊ *Sie hat ihr Versprechen gehalten.* She kept her promise.
**versprechen** VERB (PRESENT **verspricht**, IMPERFECT **versprach**, PERFECT **hat versprochen**)
⏎ *see also* **das Versprechen** NOUN
<u>to promise</u> ◊ *Du hast es versprochen.* You promised.
◆ **Ich habe mir von dem Kurs mehr versprochen.** I expected more from this course.
der **Verstand** NOUN
<u>mind</u>
◆ **den Verstand verlieren** to go out of one's mind

♦ **über jemandes Verstand gehen** to be beyond somebody

**verständigen** VERB (PERFECT **hat verständigt**)
to inform ◊ *Wir müssen ihre Eltern verständigen.* We must inform her parents.
♦ **sich verständigen** to communicate ◊ *Wir konnten uns auf Englisch verständigen.* We were able to communicate in English.
♦ **sich auf etwas verständigen** to agree on something ◊ *Wir haben uns auf folgendes Vorgehen verständigt.* We've agreed on the following plan of action.

**verständlich** ADJECTIVE
understandable
♦ **sich verständlich ausdrücken** to express oneself clearly

**verständnisvoll** ADJECTIVE
understanding ◊ *Meine Eltern sind sehr verständnisvoll.* My parents are very understanding.

**verstärken** VERB (PERFECT **hat verstärkt**)
to strengthen ◊ *Wir müssen den Karton verstärken.* We'll have to strengthen the box. ◊ *ein Team verstärken* to strengthen a team
♦ **den Ton verstärken** to amplify the sound
♦ **Das verstärkt die Schmerzen.** That makes the pain worse.

der **Verstärker** NOUN (PL die **Verstärker**)
amplifier

die **Verstärkung** NOUN
reinforcements ◊ *Wir brauchen Verstärkung.* We need reinforcements.

**verstauchen** VERB (PERFECT **hat verstaucht**)
to sprain ◊ *Ich habe mir den Knöchel verstaucht.* I've sprained my ankle.

das **Versteck** NOUN (PL die **Verstecke**)
hiding place

**verstecken** VERB (PERFECT **hat versteckt**)
to hide

**verstehen** VERB (IMPERFECT **verstand**, PERFECT **hat verstanden**)
to understand ◊ *Ich habe die Frage nicht verstanden.* I didn't understand the question. ◊ *Ich verstehe nicht.* I don't understand.
♦ **sich verstehen** to get on ◊ *Die beiden verstehen sich blendend.* The two of them get on marvellously.
♦ **Das versteht sich von selbst.** That goes without saying.

**verstellbar** ADJECTIVE
adjustable

**verstellen** VERB (PERFECT **hat verstellt**)
1 to adjust ◊ *Man kann die Höhe verstellen.* The height can be adjusted.
2 to reset ◊ *Wer hat die Uhr verstellt?* Who reset the clock?

3 to block ◊ *Der Ausgang war mit Kisten verstellt.* The exit was blocked by crates.
4 to disguise ◊ *Sie hat ihre Stimme verstellt.* She disguised her voice.
♦ **sich verstellen** to put on an act

**verstimmt** ADJECTIVE
1 out of tune ◊ *Meine Geige ist verstimmt.* My violin's out of tune.
2 cross ◊ *Worüber bist du denn so verstimmt?* What are you so cross about?
♦ **ein verstimmter Magen** an upset stomach

**verstopft** ADJECTIVE
1 blocked ◊ *ein verstopfter Abfluss* a blocked drain
2 constipated ◊ *Ich bin seit gestern verstopft.* I've been constipated since yesterday.

die **Verstopfung** NOUN
1 obstruction ◊ *eine Verstopfung im Rohr* an obstruction in the pipe
2 constipation ◊ *Ich habe Verstopfung.* I'm constipated.

**verstreuen** VERB (PERFECT **hat verstreut**)
to scatter

der **Versuch** NOUN (PL die **Versuche**)
1 attempt ◊ *Ich habe den Versuch gemacht, Spanisch zu lernen.* I made an attempt to learn Spanish. ◊ *Sie ist schon beim ersten Versuch gescheitert.* She failed at the very first attempt.
2 experiment ◊ *Versuche mit Tieren lehnen wir ab.* We disapprove of experiments with animals.

**versuchen** VERB (PERFECT **hat versucht**)
to try ◊ *Ich versuche zu kommen.* I'll try to come. ◊ *Willst du mal die Soße versuchen?* Would you like to try the sauce?
♦ **sich an etwas versuchen** to try one's hand at something ◊ *Ich habe mich am Töpfern versucht.* I tried my hand at pottery.

das **Versuchskaninchen** NOUN (PL die **Versuchskaninchen**)
guinea pig

**vertagen** VERB (PERFECT **hat vertagt**)
to adjourn

**vertauschen** VERB (PERFECT **hat vertauscht**)
1 to mix up ◊ *Die Babys wurden im Krankenhaus vertauscht.* They mixed the babies up at the hospital. ◊ *Er hat offensichtlich seinen Mantel mit meinem vertauscht.* He must have got his coat and mine mixed up.
2 to exchange ◊ *Er hat seinen Sportwagen mit einem Familienwagen vertauscht.* He exchanged his sports car for a family car.

**verteidigen** VERB (PERFECT **hat verteidigt**)
to defend

der **Verteidiger** NOUN (PL die **Verteidiger**)

[1] defender ◊ *Der Verteidiger wurde gefoult.* The defender was fouled.

[2] defence counsel ◊ *Wer ist der Verteidiger des Angeklagten?* Who's counsel for the defence?

**verteilen** VERB (PERFECT **hat verteilt**)

[1] to hand out ◊ *Sie verteilte die Hefte an die Schüler.* She handed the exercise books out to the pupils.

[2] to spread ◊ *Die Salbe sollte gleichmäßig auf der Haut verteilt werden.* The ointment should be spread evenly over the skin.

der **Vertrag** NOUN (PL die **Verträge**)

[1] contract ◊ *ein Arbeitsvertrag* a contract of employment

[2] treaty ◊ *ein Friedensvertrag* a peace treaty

**vertragen** VERB (PRESENT **verträgt**, IMPERFECT **vertrug**, PERFECT **hat vertragen**)

[1] to be able to stand ◊ *Ich vertrage die Hitze nicht.* I can't stand the heat.

[2] to tolerate ◊ *Ich kann eine solche Behandlung nicht vertragen.* I can't tolerate such treatment.

♦ **sich vertragen** to get along ◊ *Die beiden vertragen sich blendend.* The two of them get along marvellously.

♦ **sich wieder vertragen** to patch things up ◊ *Na, vertragt ihr euch wieder?* Well, have you patched things up again?

**verträglich** ADJECTIVE

[1] good-natured ◊ *ein verträglicher Mensch* a good-natured person

[2] easily digestible ◊ *Im Sommer sollte man nur leicht verträgliche Speisen zu sich nehmen.* In summer, you should only eat easily digestible food.

♦ **Das Medikament ist gut verträglich.** The drug has no side effects.

das **Vertrauen** NOUN

| *see also* **vertrauen** VERB |
|---|

trust ◊ *Vertrauen zu jemandem haben* to have trust in somebody

**vertrauen** VERB (PERFECT **hat vertraut**)

| *see also* **das Vertrauen** NOUN |
|---|

♦ **jemandem vertrauen** to trust somebody

♦ **vertrauen auf** to rely on ◊ *Ich vertraue auf dich.* I'm relying on you.

♦ **Ich vertraue auf mein Glück.** I'm trusting my luck.

**vertraulich** ADJECTIVE

[1] confidential ◊ *ein vertrauliches Gespräch* a confidential talk

[2] familiar ◊ *Ich verbiete mir diesen vertraulichen Ton.* I'll not have you talking to me in such familiar way.

**vertraut** ADJECTIVE

familiar ◊ *vertraute Gesichter* familiar faces

**vertreiben** VERB (IMPERFECT **vertrieb**, PERFECT **hat vertrieben**)

[1] to drive ◊ *Er hat uns von seinem Grundstück vertrieben.* He drove us off his land. ◊ *Während des Krieges wurden viele Menschen aus ihrer Heimat vertrieben.* Many people were driven from their homes during the war.

[2] to sell ◊ *Wir vertreiben Hardware und Software.* We sell hardware and software.

♦ **sich die Zeit vertreiben** to pass the time ◊ *Ich habe mir die Zeit mit Kreuzworträtseln vertrieben.* I passed the time doing crosswords.

**vertreten** VERB (PRESENT **vertritt**, IMPERFECT **vertrat**, PERFECT **hat vertreten**)

[1] to stand in for ◊ *Während ich in Urlaub bin, vertritt mich Frau Wengel.* While I'm on holiday, Mrs Wengel's standing in for me.

[2] to represent ◊ *Die Lobby vertritt die Interessen der Wirtschaft.* The lobby represents business interests.

♦ **eine Meinung vertreten** to hold an opinion

♦ **sich den Fuß vertreten** to twist one's ankle ◊ *Ich habe mir den Fuß vertreten.* I've twisted my ankle.

♦ **sich die Beine vertreten** to stretch one's legs ◊ *Ich will mir nur etwas die Beine vertreten.* I just want to stretch my legs a bit.

der **Vertreter** NOUN (PL die **Vertreter**)

sales representative ◊ *Er ist Vertreter für Collins.* He's a sales representative for Collins.

der **Vertrieb** NOUN (PL die **Vertriebe**)

[1] sale ◊ *Der Vertrieb von Raubkopien steht unter Strafe.* The sale of pirate copies is punishable by law.

[2] marketing department ◊ *Sie arbeitet im Vertrieb.* She works in the marketing department.

sich **vertun** VERB (IMPERFECT **vertat sich**, PERFECT **hat sich vertan**)

to make a mistake

**verübeln** VERB (PERFECT **hat verübelt**)

♦ **jemandem etwas verübeln** to be cross with somebody because of something

**verüben** VERB (PERFECT **hat verübt**)

to commit

**verunglücken** VERB (PERFECT **ist verunglückt**)

to have an accident ◊ *Sie sind mit dem Auto verunglückt.* They've had a car accident.

**verursachen** VERB (PERFECT **hat verursacht**)

to cause

**verurteilen** VERB (PERFECT **hat verurteilt**)

to condemn

**vervielfältigen** VERB (PERFECT **hat vervielfältigt**)

to copy

**vervollständigen** VERB (PERFECT **hat vervollständigt**)
<u>to complete</u>

sich **verwählen** VERB (PERFECT **hat sich verwählt**)
<u>to dial the wrong number</u>

die **Verwaltung** NOUN
<u>administration</u> ◊ *Er arbeitet in der Verwaltung.* He works in administration.

**verwandt** ADJECTIVE
♦ **mit jemandem verwandt sein** to be related to somebody

der **Verwandte** NOUN (GEN des/der
die **Verwandten**, PL die **Verwandten**)
<u>relative</u> ◊ *Ein Verwandter von mir ist gestern gestorben.* A relative of mine died yesterday.

die **Verwandtschaft** NOUN
<u>relations</u> ◊ *Die ganze Verwandtschaft war eingeladen.* All my relations were invited.

**verwechseln** VERB (PERFECT **hat verwechselt**)
[1] <u>to confuse</u> ◊ *Du darfst die beiden Begriffe nicht verwechseln.* You mustn't confuse the two ideas.
[2] <u>to mix up</u> ◊ *Sie haben offensichtlich die Mäntel verwechselt.* They must have got their coats mixed up.
♦ **verwechseln mit (1)** to confuse with ◊ *Ich verwechsle "akut" immer mit "aktuell".* I always confuse "akut" with "aktuell".
♦ **verwechseln mit (2)** to mistake for ◊ *Ich habe dich mit deiner Schwester verwechselt.* I mistook you for your sister.
♦ **Sie sind zum Verwechseln ähnlich.** They're the spitting image of each other.

die **Verwechslung** NOUN
<u>mix-up</u>

**verweigern** VERB (PERFECT **hat verweigert**)
♦ **jemandem etwas verweigern** to refuse somebody something ◊ *Sie verweigerte ihm das Besuchsrecht für die Kinder.* She refused him access to the children.
♦ **den Gehorsam verweigern** to refuse to obey
♦ **die Aussage verweigern** to refuse to testify

der **Verweis** NOUN (GEN des **Verweises**, PL die
**Verweise**)
<u>reprimand</u> ◊ *Er hat für sein Zuspätkommen einen schweren Verweis bekommen.* He was given a severe reprimand for being late.

**verwelken** VERB (PERFECT **ist verwelkt**)
<u>to fade</u>

**verwenden** VERB (IMPERFECT **verwendete** or
**verwandte**, PERFECT **hat verwendet** or
**verwandt**)
[1] <u>to use</u> ◊ *Verwenden Sie einen Computer?* Do you use a computer?
[2] (*effort, time, work*)

<u>to spend</u> ◊ *Ich habe auf diesen Aufsatz viel Zeit verwendet.* I spent a lot of time on this essay.

**verwerten** VERB (PERFECT **hat verwertet**)
<u>to utilize</u>

**verwesen** VERB (PERFECT **ist verwest**)
<u>to decay</u>

**verwickeln** VERB (PERFECT **hat verwickelt**)
♦ **sich verwickeln** to get tangled ◊ *Die Schnur hat sich verwickelt.* The line's got tangled.
♦ **jemanden in etwas verwickeln** to involve somebody in something ◊ *Ich möchte in diese Angelegenheit nicht verwickelt werden.* I don't want to get involved in this business.

**verwickelt** ADJECTIVE
<u>complicated</u> ◊ *Das ist eine ziemlich verwickelte Angelegenheit.* This is a pretty complicated matter.

**verwirren** VERB (PERFECT **hat verwirrt**)
[1] <u>to confuse</u> ◊ *Jetzt hast du mich total verwirrt.* Now you've completely confused me.
[2] <u>to tangle up</u> (*thread*) ◊ *Die Katze hat die Wolle verwirrt.* The cat's tangled the wool up.

**verwöhnen** VERB (PERFECT **hat verwöhnt**)
<u>to spoil</u>

**verwunden** VERB (PERFECT **hat verwundet**)
<u>to wound</u>

der **Verwundete** NOUN (GEN des/der
die **Verwundeten**, PL die **Verwundeten**)
<u>injured person</u> ◊ *Der Arzt versorgt gerade einen Verwundeten.* The doctor is just attending to an injured person.

die **Verwundung** NOUN
<u>injury</u>

sich **verzählen** VERB (PERFECT **hat sich verzählt**)
<u>to miscount</u>

das **Verzeichnis** NOUN (GEN des **Verzeichnisses**,
PL die **Verzeichnisse**)
<u>list</u> ◊ *Am Ende des Buches ist ein Verzeichnis aller Fachbegriffe.* At the end of the book there's a list of all the technical terms.
♦ **das Inhaltsverzeichnis** the table of contents
♦ **das Dateienverzeichnis** the file directory

**verzeihen** VERB (IMPERFECT **verzieh**, PERFECT
**hat verziehen**)
<u>to forgive</u> ◊ *jemandem etwas verzeihen* to forgive somebody for something

die **Verzeihung** NOUN
<u>forgiveness</u>
♦ **Verzeihung, ich wollte Sie nicht treten.** Sorry, I didn't mean to kick you.
♦ **Verzeihung, aber können Sie mir sagen, wie spät es ist?** Excuse me, could you tell me what time it is?

**verzichten** VERB (PERFECT **hat verzichtet**)
♦ **auf etwas verzichten (1)** to do without something ◊ *Ich werde heute wohl auf*

**V**

*meinen Mittagsschlaf verzichten müssen.* It looks like I'll have to do without my afternoon nap today. ◊ *Ich verzichte auf deine Hilfe.* I can do without your help.

♦ **auf etwas verzichten (2)** to forego something ◊ *Er hat auf eine Bezahlung verzichtet.* He forewent payment. ◊ *Ich verzichte nicht auf meine Rechte.* I won't forego my rights.

die **Verzierung** NOUN
decoration

**verzögern** VERB (PERFECT **hat verzögert**)
to delay

**verzollen** VERB (PERFECT **hat verzollt**)
to pay duty on ◊ *Den Whisky müssen Sie verzollen.* You have to pay duty on that whisky.

♦ **Haben Sie etwas zu verzollen?** Have you anything to declare?

die **Verzögerung** NOUN
delay

**verzweifeln** VERB (PERFECT **ist verzweifelt**)
to despair

**verzweifelt** ADJECTIVE
desperate

die **Verzweiflung** NOUN
despair

der **Vetter** NOUN (PL die **Vettern**)
cousin

das **Video** NOUN (PL die **Videos**)
video

das **Videogerät** NOUN (PL die **Videogeräte**)
video recorder

der **Videorekorder** NOUN (PL die **Videorekorder**)
video recorder

das **Vieh** NOUN
cattle ◊ *Das Vieh ist auf der Weide.* The cattle are out in the meadow.

**viel** ADJECTIVE, ADVERB
[1] a lot of ◊ *Sie haben viel Arbeit.* They've got a lot of work.
[2] much ◊ *Wir haben nicht viel Geld.* We haven't got much money. ◊ *Wir haben nicht viel gelernt.* We didn't learn much.

♦ **Vielen Dank!** Thank you very much.
[3] a lot ◊ *Wir haben viel gesehen.* We saw a lot.

♦ **viel zu wenig** far too little
♦ **Viel Glück!** Good luck.
♦ **so viel** so much ◊ *Sie hat so viel gelernt.* She's learned so much. ◊ *Rede nicht so viel.* Don't talk so much.
♦ **so viel wie** as much as ◊ *Sie hat so viel wie ich bekommen.* She got as much as I did. ◊ *so viel wie möglich* as much as possible
♦ **wie viel?** how much?
♦ **zu viel** too much
♦ **viel versprechend** promising

**viele** PL PRONOUN
[1] a lot of ◊ *Sie hat viele Bücher.* She's got a lot of books.

[2] many ◊ *Er hat nicht viele Fehler gemacht.* He didn't make many mistakes. ◊ *Viele Schüler mögen Chemie nicht.* Many pupils don't like chemistry.

♦ **Viele wissen das nicht.** A lot of people don't know that.

**vieles** PRONOUN
many things ◊ *Vieles war neu für mich.* Many things were new to me.

**vielleicht** ADVERB
perhaps

**vielmals** ADVERB
♦ **Danke vielmals!** Many thanks!

**vielseitig** ADJECTIVE
many-sided

**vielversprechend** ADJECTIVE *see* **viel**

**vier** NUMBER
*see also* **die Vier** NOUN
four

die **Vier** NOUN
*see also* **vier** NUMBER
[1] four
[2] adequate

*i* German marks range from one (**sehr gut**) to six (**ungenügend**).

das **Viereck** NOUN (PL die **Vierecke**)
[1] rectangle
[2] square

**viereckig** ADJECTIVE
[1] rectangular
[2] square

**vierte** ADJECTIVE
fourth ◊ *Sie hat erst beim vierten Klingeln abgenommen.* She didn't answer until the fourth ring. ◊ *Er kam als Vierter.* He was the fourth to arrive.

das **Viertel** NOUN (PL die **Viertel**)
quarter ◊ *Viertel vor zwei* quarter to two

das **Vierteljahr** NOUN (PL die **Vierteljahre**)
quarter

**vierteljährlich** ADJECTIVE
quarterly

**vierteln** VERB
[1] to divide by four ◊ *wenn man den Betrag viertelt ...* if you divide the amount by four ...
[2] to cut into quarters ◊ *Sie hat den Kuchen geviertelt.* She cut the cake into quarters.

die **Viertelnote** NOUN
crotchet

die **Viertelstunde** NOUN
quarter of an hour

**vierzehn** NUMBER
fourteen
♦ **in vierzehn Tagen** in a fortnight

**vierzehntägig** ADJECTIVE
fortnightly

**vierzig** NUMBER
forty

die **Villa** NOUN (PL die **Villen**)
  villa
**virtuell** ADJECTIVE
  virtual ◊ *die virtuelle Realität* virtual
  reality
der **Virus** NOUN (GEN des **Virus**, PL die **Viren**)
  virus ◊ *Er ist an einem Virus erkrankt.* He
  caught a virus. ◊ *Im Computersystem ist
  ein Virus.* There's a computer virus in the
  system.
die **Visen** PL NOUN *see* **Visum**
die **Visitenkarte** NOUN
  business card
das **Visum** NOUN (PL die **Visen**)
  visa
das **Vitamin** NOUN (PL die **Vitamine**)
  vitamin
der **Vogel** NOUN (PL die **Vögel**)
  bird
  ◆ **einen Vogel haben** to have a screw loose
  ◆ **jemandem den Vogel zeigen** to make a
  rude sign

> *ℹ In Germany you make a rude sign at
> somebody by tapping your forehead to
> show that you think they are stupid.*

die **Vokabel** NOUN
  word
das **Vokabular** NOUN (PL die **Vokabulare**)
  vocabulary
der **Vokal** NOUN (PL die **Vokale**)
  vowel
das **Volk** NOUN (PL die **Völker**)
  [1] people ◊ *das einfache Volk* the simple
  people
  [2] nation ◊ *das deutsche Volk* the
  German nation
das **Volksfest** NOUN (PL die **Volksfeste**)
  fair
die **Volkshochschule** NOUN
  adult education classes
die **Volkswirtschaft** NOUN
  economics
**voll** ADJECTIVE
  full
  ◆ **etwas voll machen** to fill something up
  ◆ **voll und ganz** completely
  ◆ **jemanden für voll nehmen** to take
  somebody seriously
  ◆ **voll tanken** to fill up
**vollends** ADVERB
  completely
**völlig** ADJECTIVE, ADVERB
  [1] complete ◊ *bis zur völligen
  Erschöpfung* to the point of complete
  exhaustion
  [2] completely ◊ *Das ist völlig
  unmöglich.* That's completely
  impossible. ◊ *Ich bin völlig deiner
  Meinung.* I completely agree with you.
**volljährig** ADJECTIVE

of age ◊ *volljährig werden* to come of
  age
**vollkommen** ADJECTIVE
  perfect ◊ *vollkommen richtig* perfectly
  right
  ◆ **vollkommen unmöglich** completely
  impossible
das **Vollkornbrot** NOUN (PL die **Vollkornbrote**)
  wholemeal bread
die **Vollmacht** NOUN
  power of attorney
der **Vollmond** NOUN
  full moon ◊ *bei Vollmond* at full moon
die **Vollpension** NOUN
  full board
**vollschlank** ADJECTIVE
  plump (*person*)
  ◆ **Mode für Vollschlanke** fashion for the
  fuller figure
**vollständig** ADJECTIVE
  complete
die **Vollwertkost** NOUN
  wholefood
**vom** = **von dem**
**von** PREPOSITION
  *von takes the dative.*
  [1] from ◊ *von Hamburg nach Kiel* from
  Hamburg to Kiel
  ◆ **Wir sind um fünf von Hamburg
  losgefahren.** We left Hamburg at five.
  ◆ **von ... bis** from ... to ◊ *von morgens bis
  abends* from morning to night
  ◆ **von ... an** from ... ◊ *Von Mai an wohnen
  wir in Regensburg.* We'll be living in
  Regensburg from May.
  ◆ **von ... aus** from ... ◊ *Ich habe es vom
  Fenster aus gesehen.* I saw it from my
  window.
  ◆ **etwas von sich aus tun** to do something
  of one's own accord ◊ *Du solltest das
  von dir aus machen.* You should do it of
  your own accord.
  ◆ **von mir aus** I don't mind ◊ *Von mir aus
  können wir gehen.* I don't mind if we go.
  ◆ **Von wo bist du?** Where are you from?
  ◆ **Von wann ist der Brief?** When's the
  letter from?
  [2] by ◊ *Ich bin von einem Hund gebissen
  worden.* I was bitten by a dog. ◊ *ein
  Gedicht von Schiller* a poem by Schiller
  ◆ **von etwas kommen** to be caused by
  something ◊ *Der Husten kommt vom
  Rauchen.* The cough is caused by
  smoking.
  [3] of ◊ *ein Freund von mir* a friend of
  mine ◊ *Wie nett von dir!* How nice of
  you!
  ◆ **jeweils zwei von zehn** two out of every
  ten
  [4] about ◊ *Er erzählte vom Urlaub.* He
  talked about his holiday.
  ◆ **Von wegen!** No way!
**voneinander** ADVERB

**V**

from each other

**vor** PREPOSITION, ADVERB

*Use the accusative to express movement or a change of place. Use the dative when there is no change of place.*

1 in front of ◊ *Er stand vor dem Spiegel.* He stood in front of the mirror. ◊ *Stell den Stuhl vor das Fenster.* Put the chair in front of the window.

2 before ◊ *Der Artikel steht vor dem Substantiv.* The article goes before the noun. ◊ *Bei Fragen stellt man das Verb vor das Substantiv.* In questions, put the verb before the noun. ◊ *Vor der Kirche links abbiegen.* Turn left just before you get to the church. ◊ *Du solltest vor der Prüfung mehr lernen.* You ought to study more before the exam. ◊ *Ich war vor ihm da.* I was there before him.

3 ago ◊ *vor zwei Tagen* two days ago ◊ *vor einem Jahr* a year ago

◆ **Es ist fünf vor vier.** It's five to four.

◆ **vor kurzem** a little while ago

4 with ◊ *vor Wut* with rage ◊ *vor Liebe* with love

◆ **vor Hunger sterben** to die of hunger

◆ **vor lauter Arbeit** because of work

◆ **vor allem** above all

◆ **vor und zurück** backwards and forwards

**vorankommen** VERB (IMPERFECT **kam voran,** PERFECT **ist vorangekommen**)
to make progress

**voraus** ADVERB
ahead ◊ *Fahr du schon mal voraus.* You go on ahead. ◊ *Er war seiner Zeit voraus.* He was ahead of his time.

◆ **im Voraus** in advance

**vorausgehen** VERB (IMPERFECT **ging voraus,** PERFECT **ist vorausgegangen**)
1 to go on ahead ◊ *Geht ihr voraus, ich komme nach.* Go on ahead, I'll catch up with you.
2 to precede ◊ *Der Schlägerei ging ein Streit voraus.* The fight was preceded by an argument.

**voraussetzen** VERB (PERFECT **hat vorausgesetzt**)
to assume ◊ *Ich setze voraus, dass du auch kommst.* I assume that you're coming too.

◆ **Gute Englischkenntnisse werden vorausgesetzt.** A good command of English is essential.

◆ **vorausgesetzt, dass ...** provided that ...

die **Voraussetzung** NOUN
prerequisite

◆ **unter der Voraussetzung, dass ...** provided that ...

**voraussichtlich** ADVERB
probably

**vorbei** ADVERB
past ◊ *Fahren Sie am Rathaus vorbei.* Drive past the town hall.

◆ **Ich sehe noch kurz bei ihr vorbei.** I'll just pop round to her place.

◆ **vorbei sein** to be over ◊ *Damit ist es nun vorbei.* That's all over now.

**vorbeigehen** VERB (IMPERFECT **ging vorbei,** PERFECT **ist vorbeigegangen**)
to go past ◊ *Er ging vorbei, ohne zu grüßen.* He went past without saying hello.

◆ **an etwas vorbeigehen** to go past something ◊ *Sie ist am Schaufenster vorbeigegangen, ohne es zu beachten.* She went past the shop window without looking at it.

◆ **bei jemandem vorbeigehen** to call in at somebody's ◊ *Kannst du beim Bäcker vorbeigehen?* Can you call in at the baker's? ◊ *Ich gehe noch schnell bei meiner Freundin vorbei.* I'm just going to call in at my girlfriend's.

**vorbeikommen** VERB (IMPERFECT **kam vorbei,** PERFECT **ist vorbeigekommen**)
◆ **bei jemandem vorbeikommen** to drop in on somebody

**vorbereiten** VERB (PERFECT **hat vorbereitet**)
to prepare

die **Vorbereitung** NOUN
preparation

**vorbeugen** VERB (PERFECT **hat vorgebeugt**)
◆ **sich vorbeugen** to lean forward
◆ **einer Sache vorbeugen** to prevent something ◊ *um einer Erkältung vorzubeugen* to prevent a cold

**vorbeugend** ADJECTIVE
preventive

die **Vorbeugung** NOUN
prevention ◊ *zur Vorbeugung gegen* for the prevention of

das **Vorbild** NOUN (PL die **Vorbilder**)
role model ◊ *Er ist mein Vorbild.* He's my role model.

◆ **sich jemanden zum Vorbild nehmen** to follow somebody's example ◊ *Du solltest dir deinen Bruder zum Vorbild nehmen.* You ought to follow your brother's example.

**vordere** ADJECTIVE
front ◊ *Das Haus hat einen vorderen und einen hinteren Eingang.* The house has a front door and a back door.

die **Vorderseite** NOUN
front

**vorderste** ADJECTIVE
front ◊ *die vorderste Reihe* the front row

◆ **Gebt das bitte an den vordersten Schüler durch.** Please pass it to the pupil at the front.

**voreilig** ADJECTIVE
hasty ◊ *Du solltest nicht voreilig urteilen.* You shouldn't make hasty judgements.

**voreingenommen** ADJECTIVE
biased

**vorenthalten** VERB (PRESENT **enthält vor,** IMPERFECT **enthielt vor,** PERFECT **hat vorenthalten**)
♦ **jemandem etwas vorenthalten** to withhold something from somebody

**vorerst** ADVERB
for the moment

die **Vorfahrt** NOUN
right of way
♦ **Vorfahrt achten!** Give way!

der **Vorfall** NOUN (PL die **Vorfälle**)
incident

**vorführen** VERB (PERFECT **hat vorgeführt**)
to show

der **Vorgänger** NOUN (PL die **Vorgänger**)
predecessor

das **Vorgehen** NOUN
see also **vorgehen** VERB
action

**vorgehen** VERB (IMPERFECT **ging vor,** PERFECT **ist vorgegangen**)
see also **das Vorgehen** NOUN
[1] to go on ahead ◊ *Geht ihr vor, ich komme nach.* Go on ahead, I'll catch up.
[2] to go up to ◊ *Sie ging ans Rednerpult vor.* She went up to the lectern.
[3] to proceed ◊ *Ich weiß nicht, wie wir vorgehen sollen.* I don't know how we should proceed.
♦ **Die Uhr geht vor.** The clock is fast.
♦ **Was geht hier vor?** What's going on here?

der **Vorgeschmack** NOUN
foretaste

**vorgestern** ADVERB
the day before yesterday

**vorhaben** VERB (PRESENT **hat vor,** IMPERFECT **hatte vor,** PERFECT **hat vorgehabt**)
to intend ◊ *Wir haben vor, nach Italien zu fahren.* We intend to go to Italy. ◊ *Was hast du vor?* What do you intend to do?
♦ **Ich habe heute viel vor.** I've got a lot planned for today.
♦ **Was hast du heute Abend vor?** What are you doing this evening?

der **Vorhang** NOUN (PL die **Vorhänge**)
curtain

**vorher** ADVERB
beforehand

die **Vorhersage** NOUN
forecast

**vorhersehbar** ADJECTIVE
predictable

**vorhersehen** VERB (PRESENT **sieht vorher,** IMPERFECT **sah vorher,** PERFECT **hat vorhergesehen**)
to foresee

**vorhin** ADVERB
just now

**vorig** ADJECTIVE
previous

**vorkommen** VERB (IMPERFECT **kam vor,** PERFECT **ist vorgekommen**)
[1] to happen ◊ *So ein Fehler sollte nicht vorkommen.* A mistake like that shouldn't happen.
♦ **jemandem vorkommen** to seem to somebody ◊ *Das kommt mir komisch vor.* That seems funny to me.
♦ **sich dumm vorkommen** to feel stupid ◊ *Ich kam mir dumm vor.* I felt stupid.
[2] to come out ◊ *Komm endlich hinter dem Schrank vor.* Come out from behind that cupboard, will you?

**vorläufig** ADJECTIVE
provisional

**vorlaut** ADJECTIVE
impertinent

**vorlesen** VERB (PRESENT **liest vor,** IMPERFECT **las vor,** PERFECT **hat vorgelesen**)
to read out

**vorletzte** ADJECTIVE
last but one ◊ *Ich wohne im vorletzten Haus.* My house is the last but one.

die **Vorliebe** NOUN
partiality
♦ **Sie hat eine Vorliebe für Krimis.** She's partial to detective stories.

der **Vormittag** NOUN (PL die **Vormittage**)
morning ◊ *am Vormittag* in the morning

**vormittags** ADVERB
in the morning

**vorn** ADVERB
in front ◊ *Der deutsche Schwimmer liegt vorn.* The German swimmer is in front.
♦ **nach vorn** to the front
♦ **von vorn anfangen** to start at the beginning

der **Vorname** NOUN (GEN des **Vornamens,** PL die **Vornamen**)
first name

**vornehm** ADJECTIVE
[1] distinguished ◊ *eine vornehme Familie* a distinguished family
[2] refined ◊ *sich vornehm ausdrücken* to use refined language ◊ *vornehme Manieren* refined manners
[3] posh ◊ *ein vornehmes Hotel* a posh hotel
[4] elegant ◊ *eine vornehme Dame* an elegant lady
♦ **Tu nicht so vornehm!** Don't put on airs and graces.

**vornehmen** VERB (PRESENT **nimmt vor,** IMPERFECT **nahm vor,** PERFECT **hat vorgenommen**)
♦ **sich etwas vornehmen** to resolve to do something

**vornherein** ADVERB
♦ **von vornherein** from the start

der **Vorort** NOUN (PL die **Vororte**)
suburb

der **Vorrat** NOUN (PL die **Vorräte**)

☞

stock ◊ *solange der Vorrat reicht* while stocks last

**vorrätig** ADJECTIVE
in stock

die **Vorrichtung** NOUN
device

der **Vorsatz** NOUN (GEN des **Vorsatzes**, PL die **Vorsätze**)
intention ◊ *Er hat lauter gute Vorsätze.* His intentions are all good.

der **Vorschlag** NOUN (PL die **Vorschläge**)
suggestion

**vorschlagen** VERB (PRESENT **schlägt vor**, IMPERFECT **schlug vor**, PERFECT **hat vorgeschlagen**)
to suggest

die **Vorschrift** NOUN
rule ◊ *Das ist gegen die Vorschriften.* It's against the rules.

die **Vorsicht** NOUN
caution
◆ **Vorsicht! (1)** Look out!
◆ **Vorsicht! (2)** Caution!
◆ **Vorsicht, Stufe!** Mind the step!

**vorsichtig** ADJECTIVE
careful

**vorsichtshalber** ADVERB
just in case

die **Vorsilbe** NOUN
prefix

die **Vorspeise** NOUN
starter

der **Vorsprung** NOUN (PL die **Vorsprünge**)
lead ◊ *Wir haben einen Vorsprung vor unseren Konkurrenten gewonnen.* We have gained a lead over our competitors.

die **Vorstadt** NOUN (PL die **Vorstädte**)
suburbs

**vorstellbar** ADJECTIVE
conceivable

**vorstellen** VERB (PERFECT **hat vorgestellt**)
◆ **sich etwas vorstellen** to imagine something ◊ *Stell dir mal vor, wir wären jetzt im Urlaub.* Imagine we were on holiday right now.
◆ **jemanden jemandem vorstellen** to introduce somebody to somebody ◊ *Darf ich Ihnen meinen Mann vorstellen?* May I introduce my husband to you?

die **Vorstellung** NOUN
[1] performance ◊ *Die Vorstellung endet gegen zehn Uhr.* The performance ends at about ten.
[2] idea ◊ *Hast du eine Vorstellung, wie wir das machen sollen?* Have you got any idea how we should do that?

das **Vorstellungsgespräch** NOUN (PL die **Vorstellungsgespräche**)
interview (*for job*)

**vortäuschen** VERB (PERFECT **hat vorgetäuscht**)
to feign

der **Vorteil** NOUN (PL die **Vorteile**)
advantage
◆ **im Vorteil sein** to have the advantage

der **Vortrag** NOUN (PL die **Vorträge**)
talk ◊ *einen Vortrag halten* to give a talk

**vorüber** ADVERB
over

**vorübergehend** ADJECTIVE
passing
◆ **Das Geschäft ist vorübergehend geschlossen.** The shop's temporarily closed.

das **Vorurteil** NOUN (PL die **Vorurteile**)
prejudice

der **Vorverkauf** NOUN (PL die **Vorverkäufe**)
advance booking

die **Vorwahl** NOUN
dialling code

die **Vorwahlnummer** NOUN
dialling code

der **Vorwand** NOUN (PL die **Vorwände**)
pretext

**vorwärts** ADVERB
forward

der **Vorwärtsgang** NOUN (PL die **Vorwärtsgänge**)
forward gear

**vorwegnehmen** VERB (PRESENT **nimmt vorweg**, IMPERFECT **nahm vorweg**, PERFECT **hat vorweggenommen**)
to anticipate

**vorwerfen** VERB (PRESENT **wirft vor**, IMPERFECT **warf vor**, PERFECT **hat vorgeworfen**)
◆ **jemandem etwas vorwerfen** to accuse somebody of something
◆ **sich nichts vorzuwerfen haben** to have nothing to reproach oneself for

**vorwiegend** ADVERB
predominantly

das **Vorwort** NOUN (PL die **Vorworte**)
preface

der **Vorwurf** NOUN (PL die **Vorwürfe**)
reproach
◆ **jemandem Vorwürfe machen** to reproach somebody
◆ **Ich mache mir solche Vorwürfe!** I blame myself.

**vorzeigen** VERB (PERFECT **hat vorgezeigt**)
to show

**vorziehen** VERB (IMPERFECT **zog vor**, PERFECT **hat vorgezogen**)
[1] to prefer ◊ *Was ziehst du vor: Kaffee oder Tee?* Do you prefer coffee or tea?
[2] to pull forward ◊ *Du solltest den Stuhl etwas vorziehen.* You should pull your chair forward a bit.

**vulgär** ADJECTIVE
vulgar ◊ *sich vulgär ausdrücken* to use vulgar language

der **Vulkan** NOUN (PL die **Vulkane**)
volcano

# W

die **Waage** NOUN
    [1] scales ◊ *Die Waage stimmt nicht genau.* The scales aren't accurate.
    [2] Libra ◊ *Ulla ist Waage.* Ulla's Libra.
**waagerecht** ADJECTIVE
    horizontal
**wach** ADJECTIVE
    ◆**wach sein** to be awake
die **Wache** NOUN
    guard ◊ *Wache stehen* to stand guard
das **Wachs** NOUN (GEN des **Wachses**, PL die **Wachse**)
    wax
**wachsen** VERB (PRESENT **wächst**, IMPERFECT **wuchs**, PERFECT **ist gewachsen**)
    to grow
das **Wachstum** NOUN
    growth
**wackelig** ADJECTIVE
    wobbly
die **Wade** NOUN
    calf ◊ *Ich habe mich an der Wade verletzt.* I've hurt my calf.
die **Waffe** NOUN
    weapon
die **Waffel** NOUN
    [1] waffle ◊ *Heute gab's zum Mittagessen Waffeln.* We had waffles for lunch today.
    [2] wafer ◊ *Willst du eine Waffel zu deinem Eis?* Would you like a wafer with your ice?
der **Wagen** NOUN (PL die **Wagen**)
    see also **wagen** VERB
    [1] car ◊ *Seid ihr mit dem Wagen da?* Did you come by car?
    [2] carriage ◊ *ein Eisenbahnwagen* a railway carriage
    ◆**ein Pferdewagen** a cart
**wagen** VERB
    see also **der Wagen** NOUN
    ◆**es wagen, etwas zu tun** to dare to do something
    ◆**sich irgendwohin wagen** to dare to go somewhere
der **Wagenheber** NOUN (PL die **Wagenheber**)
    jack (*for car*)
**waghalsig** ADJECTIVE
    foolhardy
die **Wahl** NOUN (PL die **Wahlen**)
    [1] choice ◊ *Du hast die Wahl.* It's your choice.
    [2] election ◊ *Wann sind die nächsten Wahlen?* When are the next elections?
**wählen** VERB
    [1] to choose ◊ *Du kannst wählen, entweder das rote oder das grüne.* You can choose, either the red one or the green one.

    [2] to vote ◊ *Wer wurde zum Klassensprecher gewählt?* Who was voted class representative?
    ◆**Wählt Kowalski!** Vote for Kowalski.
    ◆**Nächsten Sonntag wird gewählt.** There are elections next Sunday.
    [3] to dial ◊ *Sie wählte die Nummer ihrer Freundin.* She dialled her friend's number.
**wählerisch** ADJECTIVE
    particular
das **Wahlfach** NOUN (PL die **Wahlfächer**)
    optional subject
der **Wahnsinn** NOUN
    madness
**wahnsinnig** ADJECTIVE, ADVERB
    [1] mad ◊ *Wer hatte denn diese wahnsinnige Idee?* Whose mad idea was it?
    [2] incredibly ◊ *Das Kleid war wahnsinnig schön.* The dress was incredibly pretty. ◊ *Das tut wahnsinnig weh.* It's incredibly sore.
**wahr** ADJECTIVE
    true ◊ *eine wahre Geschichte* a true story
    ◆**Sie ist verheiratet, nicht wahr?** She's married, isn't she?
**während** PREPOSITION, CONJUNCTION
    *The preposition **während** takes the genitive.*
    [1] during ◊ *Was hast du während der Ferien gemacht?* What did you do during the holidays?
    [2] while ◊ *Sie sah fern, während sie ihre Hausaufgaben machte.* She was watching TV while she was doing her homework.
    [3] whereas ◊ *Er ist ganz nett, während seine Frau unhöflich ist.* He's quite nice, whereas his wife's impolite.
**wahrhaben** VERB
    ◆**etwas nicht wahrhaben wollen** to refuse to admit something
die **Wahrheit** NOUN
    truth
**wahrnehmen** VERB (PRESENT **nimmt wahr**, IMPERFECT **nahm wahr**, PERFECT **hat wahrgenommen**)
    to perceive
der **Wahrsager** NOUN (PL die **Wahrsager**)
    fortune teller
die **Wahrsagerin** NOUN
    fortune teller
**wahrscheinlich** ADJECTIVE, ADVERB
    [1] likely ◊ *Das ist nicht sehr wahrscheinlich.* That's not very likely.
    [2] probably ◊ *Er kommt wahrscheinlich nicht.* He's probably not coming.

die **Wahrscheinlichkeit** NOUN
probability ◊ *aller Wahrscheinlichkeit nach* in all probability

die **Währung** NOUN
currency

der **Wal** NOUN (PL die **Wale**)
whale

der **Wald** NOUN (PL die **Wälder**)
[1] wood ◊ *Hinter unserem Haus ist ein Wald.* There's a wood behind our house.
[2] forest ◊ *die Wälder Kanadas* the forests of Canada

**Wales** NEUT NOUN
Wales
♦ **aus Wales** from Wales
♦ **in Wales** in Wales
♦ **nach Wales** to Wales

der **Walfisch** NOUN (PL die **Walfische**)
whale

der **Waliser** NOUN (PL die **Waliser**)
Welshman
♦ **Er ist Waliser.** He's Welsh.
♦ **die Waliser** the Welsh

die **Waliserin** NOUN
Welshwoman
♦ **Sie ist Waliserin.** She's Welsh.

**walisisch** ADJECTIVE
Welsh

der **Walkman** ® NOUN (PL die **Walkmen** or **Walkmans**)
Walkman ®

die **Walnuss** NOUN (PL die **Walnüsse**)
walnut

die **Wand** NOUN (PL die **Wände**)
wall

der **Wanderer** NOUN (PL die **Wanderer**)
rambler

die **Wanderin** NOUN
rambler

**wandern** VERB (PERFECT **ist gewandert**)
to hike ◊ *Wir sind am Wochenende gewandert.* We went hiking at the weekend.

die **Wanderung** NOUN
hike

der **Wandschrank** NOUN (PL die **Wandschränke**)
wall cupboard

**wann** ADVERB
when

das **Wappen** NOUN (PL die **Wappen**)
coat of arms

**war** VERB see **sein**

die **Ware** NOUN
goods

das **Warenhaus** NOUN (GEN des **Warenhauses**, PL die **Warenhäuser**)
department store

**warf** VERB see **werfen**

**warm** ADJECTIVE
warm ◊ *Heute ist es wärmer als gestern.* It's warmer today than yesterday.

♦ **ein warmes Essen** a hot meal
♦ **Mir ist warm.** I'm warm.

die **Wärme** NOUN
warmth

die **Wärmflasche** NOUN
hot-water bottle

das **Warndreieck** NOUN (PL die **Warndreiecke**)
warning triangle

**warnen** VERB
to warn ◊ *jemanden vor etwas warnen* to warn somebody of something

die **Warnung** NOUN
warning

**warten** VERB
to wait ◊ *Ich habe eine Stunde gewartet.* I waited an hour.
♦ **warten auf** to wait for ◊ *Ich warte draußen auf dich.* I'll wait outside for you.
♦ **auf sich warten lassen** to take a long time

der **Warteraum** NOUN (PL die **Warteräume**)
waiting room

der **Wartesaal** NOUN (PL die **Wartesäle**)
waiting room (*in station*)

das **Wartezimmer** NOUN (PL die **Wartezimmer**)
waiting room

**warum** ADVERB
why

**was** PRONOUN
[1] what ◊ *Was hast du gesagt?* What did you say?
♦ **Was für ein ...** What kind of ... ◊ *Was für ein Fahrrad hast du?* What kind of bike do you have?
♦ **Was für eine Enttäuschung!** What a disappointment!
[2] something ◊ *Heute gibt's was Leckeres zum Mittagessen.* We're having something delicious for lunch today.

**waschbar** ADJECTIVE
washable

das **Waschbecken** NOUN (PL die **Waschbecken**)
washbasin

die **Wäsche** NOUN
washing ◊ *Wäsche waschen* to do the washing
♦ **Tu dein Hemd in die Wäsche.** Put your shirt in the wash.
♦ **die Bettwäsche** bed linen
♦ **die Unterwäsche** underwear

die **Wäscheklammer** NOUN
clothes peg

die **Wäscheleine** NOUN
washing line

**waschen** VERB (PRESENT **wäscht**, IMPERFECT **wusch**, PERFECT **hat gewaschen**)
to wash
♦ **sich waschen** to have a wash
♦ **sich die Hände waschen** to wash one's hands ◊ *Ich muss mir die Hände waschen.* I'll have to wash my hands.

der **Waschlappen** NOUN (PL die **Waschlappen**)
face cloth

die **Waschmaschine** NOUN
washing machine

das **Waschmittel** NOUN (PL die **Waschmittel**)
detergent

das **Waschpulver** NOUN (PL die **Waschpulver**)
washing powder

der **Waschraum** NOUN (PL die **Waschräume**)
washroom

der **Waschsalon** NOUN (PL die **Waschsalons**)
launderette

das **Wasser** NOUN (PL die **Wasser** or **Wässer**)
water

**wasserdicht** ADJECTIVE
waterproof

der **Wasserfall** NOUN (PL die **Wasserfälle**)
waterfall

die **Wasserfarbe** NOUN
watercolour

der **Wasserhahn** NOUN (PL die **Wasserhähne**)
tap

der **Wassermann** NOUN
Aquarius ◊ *Gerda ist Wassermann.*
Gerda's Aquarius.

die **Wassermelone** NOUN
water melon

der **Wasserstoff** NOUN
hydrogen

die **Watte** NOUN
cotton wool

das **WC** NOUN (PL die **WCs**)
WC

der **Webmaster** NOUN (PL die **Webmaster**)
webmaster

das **Web-Magazin** NOUN (PL die **Web-Magazine**)
webzine

die **Webseite** NOUN
web page

die **Website** NOUN (PL die **Websites**)
website

der **Wechsel** NOUN (PL die **Wechsel**)
change

der **Wechselkurs** NOUN (GEN des **Wechselkurses**, PL die **Wechselkurse**)
rate of exchange

**wechseln** VERB
[1] to change ◊ *Wir mussten einen Reifen wechseln.* We had to change a tyre.
◊ *Wie viel Geld wechselst du?* How much money are you changing?
◆ **Blicke wechseln** to exchange glances
[2] to have change ◊ *Können Sie wechseln?* Do you have any change?
◊ *Kannst du mir zehn Mark in Münzen wechseln?* Have you got change for ten marks?

die **Wechselstube** NOUN
bureau de change

**wecken** VERB
to wake up

der **Wecker** NOUN (PL die **Wecker**)
alarm clock

**weder** CONJUNCTION
neither
◆ **weder ... noch ...** neither ... nor ...

der **Weg** NOUN (PL die **Wege**)
| *see also* **weg** ADVERB |
[1] way ◊ *Es gibt sicher einen Weg, das zu reparieren.* There must be a way to repair it.
[2] path ◊ *Ein Weg führte zur Kapelle hinauf.* A path led up to the chapel.
[3] route ◊ *Welchen Weg habt ihr genommen?* Which route did you take?
◆ **sich auf den Weg machen** to be on one's way
◆ **jemandem aus dem Weg gehen** to keep out of somebody's way

**weg** ADVERB
| *see also* **der Weg** NOUN |
away ◊ *Geh weg!* Go away!
◆ **Weg da!** Out of the way!
◆ **Finger weg!** Hands off!
◆ **Er war schon weg.** He'd already left.

**wegbleiben** VERB (IMPERFECT **blieb weg**, PERFECT **ist weggeblieben**)
to stay away

**wegen** PREPOSITION
*The preposition **wegen** takes the dative or sometimes the genitive.*
because of ◊ *Wegen dir bin ich zu spät gekommen.* Because of you I arrived late.
◊ *Wegen des schlechten Wetters wurde die Veranstaltung abgesagt.* The event was cancelled because of the bad weather.

**weggehen** VERB (IMPERFECT **ging weg**, PERFECT **ist weggegangen**)
to go away

**weglassen** VERB (PRESENT **lässt weg**, IMPERFECT **ließ weg**, PERFECT **hat weggelassen**)
to leave out

**weglaufen** VERB (PRESENT **läuft weg**, IMPERFECT **lief weg**, PERFECT **ist weggelaufen**)
to run away

**weglegen** VERB (PERFECT **hat weggelegt**)
to put aside

**wegmachen** VERB (PERFECT **hat weggemacht**)
to get rid of ◊ *einen Fleck wegmachen* to get rid of a stain
◆ **die Satteltasche vom Fahrrad wegmachen** to take the saddlebag off the bike

**wegmüssen** VERB (PRESENT **muss weg**, IMPERFECT **musste weg**, PERFECT **hat weggemusst** or **wegmüssen**)
to have to go

**wegnehmen** VERB (PRESENT **nimmt weg**, IMPERFECT **nahm weg**, PERFECT **hat weggenommen**)
to take away

**W**

**wegtun** VERB (IMPERFECT **tat weg**, PERFECT **hat weggetan**)
to put away

der **Wegweiser** NOUN (PL die **Wegweiser**)
signpost

**wegwerfen** VERB (PRESENT **wirft weg**, IMPERFECT **warf weg**, PERFECT **hat weggeworfen**)
to throw away

das **Weh** NOUN (PL die **Wehe**)
ache

**weh** ADJECTIVE see **wehtun**

der **Wehrdienst** NOUN (PL die **Wehrdienste**)
military service

> ℹ️ Young men are generally conscripted into the **Wehrdienst** when they leave school. The basic period of military service is 10 months.

der **Wehrdienstverweigerer** NOUN (PL die **Wehrdienstverweigerer**)
conscientious objector

sich **wehren** VERB
to defend oneself

die **Wehrpflicht** NOUN
compulsory military service

**wehtun** VERB (IMPERFECT **tat weh**, PERFECT **hat wehgetan**)
1 to hurt ◊ Mein Bein tut weh. My leg hurts.
2 to be sore ◊ Mein Hals tut weh. My throat's sore.
♦ **sich wehtun** to hurt oneself ◊ Hast du dir wehgetan? Have you hurt yourself?
♦ **jemandem wehtun** to hurt somebody ◊ Ich möchte dir nicht wehtun, aber das war nicht sehr intelligent. I don't want to hurt you, but that really wasn't very clever.

das **Weibchen** NOUN (PL die **Weibchen**)
female

**weiblich** ADJECTIVE
feminine ◊ ein weibliches Substantiv a feminine noun

**weich** ADJECTIVE
soft ◊ ein weiches Bett a soft bed

sich **weigern** VERB
to refuse

das **Weihnachten** NOUN (GEN des **Weihnachten**)
Christmas ◊ an Weihnachten at Christmas
♦ **Frohe Weihnachten!** Merry Christmas.

die **Weihnachtsferien** PL NOUN
Christmas holidays

das **Weihnachtslied** NOUN (PL die **Weihnachtslieder**)
Christmas carol

der **Weihnachtsmann** NOUN (PL die **Weihnachtsmänner**)
Father Christmas

der **Weihnachtsmarkt** NOUN (PL die **Weihnachtsmärkte**)
Christmas fair

der **Weihnachtstag** NOUN (PL die **Weihnachtstage**)
♦ **der erste Weihnachtstag** Christmas Day
♦ **der zweite Weihnachtstag** Boxing Day

**weil** CONJUNCTION
because

die **Weile** NOUN
while ◊ Es wird eine Weile dauern. It'll take a while.

der **Wein** NOUN (PL die **Weine**)
wine

der **Weinberg** NOUN (PL die **Weinberge**)
vineyard

die **Weinbergschnecke** NOUN
snail

der **Weinbrand** NOUN (PL die **Weinbrände**)
brandy

**weinen** VERB
to cry
♦ **Das ist zum Weinen.** It's enough to make you cry.

das **Weinglas** NOUN (GEN des **Weinglases**, PL die **Weingläser**)
wine glass

die **Weinkarte** NOUN
wine list

der **Weinkeller** NOUN (PL die **Weinkeller**)
1 wine cellar
2 wine bar

die **Weinprobe** NOUN
wine tasting

die **Weinstube** NOUN
wine bar

die **Weintraube** NOUN
grape

die **Weise** NOUN
way ◊ Die Art und Weise, wie er uns behandelt hat. The way he treated us.
♦ **Es ist egal, auf welche Weise du das machst.** It doesn't matter how you do it.
♦ **auf diese Weise** in this way

die **Weisheit** NOUN
wisdom

der **Weisheitszahn** NOUN (PL die **Weisheitszähne**)
wisdom tooth

**weiß** VERB see **wissen**

**weiß** ADJECTIVE
white

das **Weißbrot** NOUN (PL die **Weißbrote**)
white bread

der **Weißwein** NOUN (PL die **Weißweine**)
white wine

**weit** ADJECTIVE, ADVERB
1 long ◊ Das ist eine weite Reise. That's a long journey. ◊ Das war sein weitester Wurf. That was his longest throw.
2 far ◊ Wie weit ist es ...? How far is it ...? ◊ Nach Berlin ist es weiter als nach

*München.* It's further to Berlin than to Munich.

[3] baggy ◊ *Sie hatte einen weiten Pulli an.* She was wearing a baggy pullover.
- **ein weiter Begriff** a broad idea
- **in weiter Ferne** in the far distance
- **Das geht zu weit.** That's going too far.
- **so weit sein** to be ready ◊ *Ich bin so weit.* I'm ready.
- **so weit wie möglich** as far as possible
- **Ich bin so weit zufrieden.** By and large I'm quite satisfied.

**weitaus** ADVERB
by far

**weiter** ADJECTIVE, ADVERB
further ◊ *Wenn du noch weitere Fragen hast ...* If you have any further questions ... ◊ *Alles Weitere besprechen wir morgen.* We can discuss any further details tomorrow.
- **ohne weiteres** just like that ◊ *Ich kann doch nicht so ohne weiteres gehen.* I can't go just like that.
- **Ich könnte das ohne weiteres tun.** I could do that no problem.
- **weiter nichts** nothing else
- **weiter niemand** nobody else

**weiterarbeiten** VERB (PERFECT **hat weitergearbeitet**)
to go on working

sich **weiterbilden** VERB (PERFECT **hat sich weitergebildet**)
to continue one's education

die **Weiterbildung** NOUN
further education

die **Weiterfahrt** NOUN
continuation of the journey

**weitergehen** VERB (IMPERFECT **ging weiter,** PERFECT **ist weitergegangen**)
to go on

**weiterhin** ADVERB
- **etwas weiterhin tun** to go on doing something

**weiterleiten** VERB (PERFECT **hat weitergeleitet**)
to pass on

**weitermachen** VERB (PERFECT **hat weitergemacht**)
to continue

der **Weitsprung** NOUN
long jump

der **Weizen** NOUN
wheat

**welche** PRONOUN
[1] which ◊ *Welcher Mann?* Which man?
◊ *Welche Frau?* Which woman?
◊ *Welches Mädchen?* Which girl?
◊ *Welcher von beiden?* Which of the two? ◊ *Welchen hast du genommen?* Which one did you take?
- **Welch eine Überraschung!** What a surprise!
- **Welche Freude!** What joy!

[2] some ◊ *Ich habe Kirschen, willst du welche?* I have some cherries, would you like some? ◊ *Ich habe welche.* I have some. ◊ *Bei den Programmen gibt es welche, die echt schwierig sind.* There are some programs that are really difficult. ◊ *Ich habe kein Geld dabei, wenn du welches hast, musst du zahlen.* I don't have any money, if you have some then you'll have to pay.
[3] any ◊ *Ich brauche Briefmarken, hast du welche?* I need stamps, have you got any? ◊ *Ich brauche Kleingeld, hast du welches?* I need change, have you got any?

die **Welle** NOUN
wave

die **Wellenlänge** NOUN
wavelength

die **Wellenlinie** NOUN
wavy line

der **Wellensittich** NOUN (PL die **Wellensittiche**)
budgie

die **Welt** NOUN
world

das **Weltall** NOUN
universe

**weltberühmt** ADJECTIVE
world-famous

der **Weltkrieg** NOUN (PL die **Weltkriege**)
world war

der **Weltmeister** NOUN (PL die **Weltmeister**)
world champion

der **Weltraum** NOUN
space

**wem** PRONOUN
*wem is the dative of wer.*
to whom
- **Wem hast du das Buch gegeben?** Who did you give the book to?
- **Mit wem bist du gekommen?** Who did you come with?

**wen** PRONOUN
*wen is the accusative of wer.*
whom
- **Wen hast du gesehen?** Who did you see?

**wenig** ADJECTIVE, ADVERB
little
- **so wenig wie** as little as ◊ *Er macht so wenig wie möglich.* He does as little as possible. ◊ *Ich habe so wenig Geld wie du.* I have as little money as you.
- **zu wenig** too little

**wenige** PL PRONOUN
few ◊ *Das wissen nur wenige.* Only a few people know that.

**weniger** ADJECTIVE, ADVERB
[1] less ◊ *Ich habe weniger Geld als du.* I have less money than you.
[2] fewer ◊ *Ich habe weniger Fehler gemacht.* I've made fewer mistakes.

W

☞

3 minus ◊ *Zehn weniger drei ist sieben.*
Ten minus three is seven.
♦ **Unser Geld wird immer weniger.** Our
money's running out.

**wenigste** ADJECTIVE
least ◊ *Das ist das wenigste, was ich tun
kann.* That's the least I can do.
♦ **am wenigsten** the least ◊ *Die Clowns
haben mir am wenigsten gefallen.* I liked
the clowns the least.

**wenigstens** ADVERB
at least

**wenn** CONJUNCTION
1 if ◊ *Wenn er anruft, sag mir Bescheid.*
If he calls, tell me.
♦ **selbst wenn ...** even if ...
♦ **wenn ich doch ...** if only I ...
2 when ◊ *Wenn ich nach Hause komme,
dusche ich erst mal.* When I get home,
the first thing I'm going to do is have a
shower.
♦ **immer wenn** whenever ◊ *Immer wenn
ich frage, lacht er nur.* Whenever I ask, he
just laughs.

**wer** PRONOUN
who
*Be careful! **wer** does not mean **where**.*

die **Werbeagentur** NOUN
advertising agency

das **Werbefernsehen** NOUN
commercial television

**werben** VERB (PRESENT **wirbt**, IMPERFECT **warb**,
PERFECT **hat geworben**)
to advertise ◊ *Im Fernsehen wird zu viel
geworben.* There's too much advertising
on TV.
♦ **Mitglieder werben** to recruit members

der **Werbespot** NOUN (PL die **Werbespots**)
commercial

die **Werbung** NOUN
advert ◊ *Hast du die Werbung für den
neuen Schokoriegel gesehen?* Have you
seen the advert for the new chocolate
bar? ◊ *Wenn Werbung kommt, schalte
ich um.* I switch over when the adverts
come on.
♦ **Er arbeitet in der Werbung.** He works in
advertising.
♦ **für etwas Werbung machen** to advertise
something

**werden** VERB (PRESENT **wird**, IMPERFECT **wurde**,
PERFECT **ist geworden** or bei Passiv **worden**)
1 to become ◊ *Sie ist Lehrerin
geworden.* She became a teacher. ◊ *Er
ist reich geworden.* He became rich.
◊ *Was ist aus ihm geworden?* What
became of him?
♦ **Erster werden** to come first
♦ **Was willst du einmal werden?** What do
you want to be?
♦ **rot werden** to turn red
♦ **Es ist gut geworden.** It turned out well.

♦ **Die Fotos sind gut geworden.** The
photos have come out well.
♦ **Es ist nichts geworden.** It came to
nothing.
♦ **Es wird Tag.** It's getting light.
♦ **Es wird Nacht.** It's getting dark.
♦ **Mir wird kalt.** I'm getting cold.
♦ **Mir wird schlecht.** I feel sick.
♦ **Das muss anders werden.** That'll have to
change.
2 will
*werden is used to form the future tense.*
◊ *Er wird es tun.* He'll do it.
♦ **Er wird das nicht tun.** He won't do it.
♦ **Es wird gleich regnen.** It's going to rain.
3 to be
*werden is used to form the passive.*
◊ *gebraucht werden* to be needed ◊ *Er ist
erschossen worden.* He's been shot.
◊ *Mir wurde gesagt, dass ...* I was told
that ...
*werden is used to form the conditional
tense.*
♦ **Ich würde ...** I would ...
♦ **Er würde gern ...** He'd like to ...
♦ **Ich würde lieber ...** I'd rather ...
♦ **Sie wird in der Küche sein.** She'll be in
the kitchen.

**werfen** VERB (PRESENT **wirft**, IMPERFECT **warf**,
PERFECT **hat geworfen**)
to throw

das **Werken** NOUN
handicrafts

die **Werkstatt** NOUN (PL die **Werkstätten**)
1 workshop ◊ *eine Werkstatt für
Behinderte* a workshop for the
handicapped
2 garage ◊ *Das Auto ist in der
Werkstatt.* The car's in the garage.

der **Werktag** NOUN (PL die **Werktage**)
working day

**werktags** ADVERB
on working days

das **Werkzeug** NOUN (PL die **Werkzeuge**)
tool

der **Wert** NOUN (PL die **Werte**)
see also **wert** ADJECTIVE
value
♦ **Wert legen auf** to attach importance to
◊ *Sie legt großen Wert auf rechtzeitiges
Erscheinen.* She attaches great
importance to punctuality.
♦ **Es hat doch keinen Wert.** There's no
point.

**wert** ADJECTIVE
see also **der Wert** NOUN
worth ◊ *Wie viel ist das Bild wert?* How
much is that picture worth? ◊ *Das ist
nichts wert.* It's not worth anything.
◊ *Das ist viel wert.* It's worth a lot.

**wertlos** ADJECTIVE
worthless

**wertvoll** ADJECTIVE

valuable

das **Wesen** NOUN (PL die **Wesen**)
manner ◊ *Er hat ein freundliches Wesen.*
He has a friendly manner.

**wesentlich** ADJECTIVE
significant

**weshalb** ADVERB
why

die **Wespe** NOUN
wasp

der **Wespenstich** NOUN (PL die **Wespenstiche**)
wasp sting

**wessen** PRONOUN
*wessen is the genitive of wer.*
whose

die **Weste** NOUN
waistcoat

der **Westen** NOUN
west

der **Western** NOUN (PL die **Western**)
western

**westlich** ADJECTIVE, PREPOSITION, ADVERB
westerly ◊ *in westlicher Richtung* in a
westerly direction
♦ **westlich einer Sache** to the west of
something ◊ *Das Kraftwerk liegt westlich
der Stadt.* The power station's to the
west of the city.
♦ **westlich von** west of ◊ *Essen liegt
westlich von Bochum.* Essen's west of
Bochum.

**weswegen** ADVERB
why

der **Wettbewerb** NOUN (PL die **Wettbewerbe**)
competition

die **Wette** NOUN
bet

**wetten** VERB
to bet ◊ *Ich wette, du fällst durchs
Examen.* I bet you fail the exam.

das **Wetter** NOUN
weather

der **Wetterbericht** NOUN (PL die
**Wetterberichte**)
weather report

die **Wetterlage** NOUN (PL die **Wetterlagen**)
weather situation

die **Wettervorhersage** NOUN
weather forecast

der **Wettkampf** NOUN (PL die **Wettkämpfe**)
contest

der **Wettlauf** NOUN (PL die **Wettläufe**)
race

**wichtig** ADJECTIVE
important

der **Widder** NOUN (PL die **Widder**)
1 ram
2 Aries ◊ *Horst ist Widder.* Horst's Aries.

**widerlich** ADJECTIVE
disgusting

**widerspenstig** ADJECTIVE
wilful

**widersprechen** VERB (PRESENT **widerspricht**,
IMPERFECT **widersprach**, PERFECT **hat
widersprochen**)
♦ **jemandem widersprechen** to contradict
somebody

der **Widerspruch** NOUN (PL die **Widersprüche**)
contradiction

der **Widerstand** NOUN (PL die **Widerstände**)
resistance

**widerwillig** ADJECTIVE
unwilling

**widmen** VERB
1 to dedicate ◊ *Er hat das Buch seiner
Mutter gewidmet.* He dedicated the book
to his mother.
2 to devote ◊ *Sie widmet ihrer Familie
viel Zeit.* She devotes a lot of time to her
family.
♦ **sich einer Sache widmen** to devote
oneself to something ◊ *Jetzt kann ich
mich meinen Hobbys widmen.* Now I can
devote myself to my hobbies.

**wie** ADVERB
how ◊ *Wie groß?* How big? ◊ *Wie
schnell?* How fast? ◊ *Wie schön!* How
lovely! ◊ *Und wie!* And how!
♦ **Wie wär's?** How about it?
♦ **Wie geht's dir?** How are you?
♦ **Wie ist er?** What's he like?
♦ **Wie gut du das kannst!** You're very
good at it.
♦ **Wie bitte? (1)** Pardon? ◊ *Wie bitte, was
haben Sie gesagt?* Pardon, what did you
say?
♦ **Wie bitte? (2)** What? ◊ *Wie bitte, du
willst zweitausend Mark von mir haben?*
What? You want me to give you two
thousand marks?
♦ **so schön wie ...** as beautiful as ...
♦ **wie ich schon sagte** as I said
♦ **wie du** like you
♦ **singen wie ein ...** to sing like a ...
♦ **wie zum Beispiel** such as

**wieder** ADVERB
again ◊ *wieder da sein* to be back again
◊ *Gehst du schon wieder?* Are you off
again?
♦ **wieder ein ...** another ... ◊ *wenn du
wieder einen Geldbeutel findest ...* if you
find another purse ...
♦ **wieder aufbereiten** to recycle
♦ **jemanden wieder erkennen** to recognize
somebody
♦ **wieder verwerten** to recycle

**wiederbekommen** VERB (IMPERFECT **bekam
wieder**, PERFECT **hat wiederbekommen**)
to get back

**wiedererkennen** VERB see **wieder**

**wiederholen** VERB (PERFECT **hat wiederholt**)
to repeat

die **Wiederholung** NOUN
1 repetition ◊ *Es darf keine
Wiederholung dieses Vorfalls geben.*

**W**

There must be no repetition of this incident.

$\boxed{2}$ repeat ◊ *Im Fernsehen kommen zu viele Wiederholungen.* There are too many repeats on TV.

das **Wiederhören** NOUN
◆ **Auf Wiederhören!** Goodbye. (*on telephone, radio*)

**wiedersehen** VERB (PRESENT **sieht wieder,** IMPERFECT **sah wieder,** PERFECT **hat wiedergesehen**)
to see again
◆ **Auf Wiedersehen!** Goodbye.

**wiedervereinigen** VERB (PERFECT **hat wiedervereinigt**)
to reunify ◊ *das wiedervereinigte Deutschland* reunified Germany

**wiederverwerten** VERB *see* **wieder**

die **Wiederverwertung** NOUN
recycling

die **Wiege** NOUN
cradle

**wiegen** VERB (IMPERFECT **wog,** PERFECT **hat gewogen**)
to weigh ◊ *Ich habe mich heute früh gewogen.* I weighed myself this morning.

**Wien** NEUT NOUN
Vienna

die **Wiese** NOUN
meadow

**wieso** ADVERB
why

**wie viel** ADJECTIVE
how much ◊ *Wie viel hat das gekostet?* How much did it cost?
◆ **wie viel Menschen** how many people

**wievielmal** ADVERB
how often

**wievielte** ADJECTIVE
◆ **Zum wievielten Mal?** How many times?
◆ **Den Wievielten haben wir?** What's the date?
◆ **Der wievielte Besucher war er?** How many visitors were there before him?

**wieweit** CONJUNCTION
to what extent

**wild** ADJECTIVE
wild

**wildfremd** ADJECTIVE
◆ **ein wildfremder Mensch** a complete stranger

das **Wildleder** NOUN (PL die **Wildleder**)
suede

**will** VERB *see* **wollen**

der **Wille** NOUN (GEN des **Willens,** PL die **Willen**)
will ◊ *Ich habe es aus freiem Willen getan.* I did it of my own free will.

**willkommen** ADJECTIVE
welcome ◊ *Herzlich willkommen!* Welcome!

◆ **jemanden willkommen heißen** to welcome somebody

**wimmeln** VERB
◆ **Es wimmelt von ...** It's teeming with ...

die **Wimper** NOUN
eyelash

die **Wimperntusche** NOUN
mascara

der **Wind** NOUN (PL die **Winde**)
wind

die **Windel** NOUN
nappy ◊ *Kannst du dem Baby die Windeln wechseln?* Can you change the baby's nappy?

die **Windenergie** NOUN
wind energy

**windig** ADJECTIVE
windy ◊ *Es ist windig.* It's windy.

die **Windmühle** NOUN
windmill

die **Windpocken** PL NOUN
chickenpox ◊ *Windpocken sind ansteckend.* Chickenpox is catching.

die **Windschutzscheibe** NOUN
windscreen

das **Windsurfen** NOUN
windsurfing

der **Winkel** NOUN (PL die **Winkel**)
$\boxed{1}$ angle ◊ *ein spitzer Winkel* an acute angle
$\boxed{2}$ corner ◊ *Ich habe jeden Winkel des Zimmers durchsucht.* I've searched every corner of the room.

**winken** VERB
to wave ◊ *jemandem winken* to wave to somebody

der **Winter** NOUN (PL die **Winter**)
winter ◊ *im Winter* in winter

**winzig** ADJECTIVE
tiny

**wir** PRONOUN
we ◊ *Wir kommen.* We're coming.
◆ **wir alle** all of us
◆ **Wir sind's.** It's us.

der **Wirbel** NOUN (PL die **Wirbel**)
$\boxed{1}$ vertebra ◊ *Sie hat sich einen Wirbel gebrochen.* She's broken a vertebra.
$\boxed{2}$ hubbub ◊ *der Wirbel vor Weihnachten* the hubbub before Christmas
$\boxed{3}$ stir ◊ *Das hat für einigen Wirbel gesorgt.* That caused quite a stir.

die **Wirbelsäule** NOUN
spine

**wird** VERB *see* **werden**

**wirft** VERB *see* **werfen**

**wirken** VERB
$\boxed{1}$ to have an effect ◊ *Die Tablette wirkt schon.* The pill's already having an effect.
$\boxed{2}$ to seem ◊ *Er wirkte traurig.* He seemed sad.

**wirklich** ADJECTIVE, ADVERB

[1] real ◊ *Er ist ein wirklicher Freund.* He's a real friend.

[2] really ◊ *Das ist wirklich passiert.* That really happened. ◊ *Ich weiß es wirklich nicht.* I really don't know.

die **Wirklichkeit** NOUN
reality

**wirksam** ADJECTIVE
effective

die **Wirkung** NOUN
effect ◊ *Wirkung auf etwas haben* to have an effect on something

**wirr** ADJECTIVE
confused

der **Wirrwarr** NOUN
chaos

der **Wirsing** NOUN
savoy cabbage

**wirst** VERB *see* **werden**

der **Wirt** NOUN (PL die **Wirte**)
landlord

die **Wirtin** NOUN
landlady

die **Wirtschaft** NOUN
[1] pub ◊ *Wir sind in einer Wirtschaft eingekehrt.* We stopped at a pub.
[2] economy ◊ *Die Wirtschaft leidet unter der Rezession.* The economy's suffering because of the recession.

**wirtschaftlich** ADJECTIVE
[1] economical ◊ *Die große Packung ist wirtschaftlicher.* The large packet's more economical.
[2] economic ◊ *ein wirtschaftlicher Aufschwung* an economic upswing

die **Wirtschaftslehre** NOUN
economics

das **Wirtshaus** NOUN (GEN des **Wirtshauses**, PL die **Wirtshäuser**)
inn

**wischen** VERB
to wipe

der **Wischlappen** NOUN (PL die **Wischlappen**)
cloth (for cleaning)

das **Wissen** NOUN
*see also* **wissen** VERB
knowledge

**wissen** VERB (PRESENT **weiß**, IMPERFECT **wusste**, PERFECT **hat gewusst**)
*see also* **das Wissen** NOUN
to know ◊ *Sie weiß sehr viel.* She knows a lot. ◊ *Weißt du, wie die Hauptstadt von Deutschland heißt?* Do you know what the capital of Germany is called? ◊ *Ich weiß es nicht.* I don't know.
♦ *Was weiß ich!* How should I know?

die **Wissenschaft** NOUN
science

der **Wissenschaftler** NOUN (PL die **Wissenschaftler**)
scientist

**wissenschaftlich** ADJECTIVE
scientific

die **Witwe** NOUN
widow ◊ *Sie ist Witwe.* She's a widow.

der **Witwer** NOUN (PL die **Witwer**)
widower ◊ *Er ist Witwer.* He's a widower.

der **Witz** NOUN (GEN des **Witzes**, PL die **Witze**)
joke ◊ *einen Witz erzählen* to tell a joke

der **Witzbold** NOUN (PL die **Witzbolde**)
joker

**witzig** ADJECTIVE
funny

**wo** ADVERB
where ◊ *Wo warst du?* Where were you?
*Be careful! wo does not mean who.*

**woanders** ADVERB
elsewhere

die **Woche** NOUN
week ◊ *nächste Woche* next week

das **Wochenende** NOUN (PL die **Wochenenden**)
weekend ◊ *am Wochenende* at the weekend

**wochenlang** ADJECTIVE, ADVERB
for weeks

der **Wochentag** NOUN (PL die **Wochentage**)
weekday

**wochentags** ADVERB
on weekdays

**wöchentlich** ADJECTIVE, ADVERB
weekly

**wofür** ADVERB
what ... for ◊ *Wofür brauchst du das Geld?* What do you need the money for?

**wog** VERB *see* **wiegen**

**woher** ADVERB
where ... from ◊ *Woher sind Sie?* Where do you come from?

**wohin** ADVERB
[1] where ... to ◊ *Wohin zieht ihr um?* Where are you moving to?
[2] where ◊ *Wohin gehst du?* Where are you going?

das **Wohl** NOUN
*see also* **wohl** ADVERB
benefit ◊ *zu eurem Wohl* for your benefit
♦ *Zum Wohl!* Cheers!

**wohl** ADVERB
*see also* **das Wohl** NOUN
probably ◊ *Das hat er wohl vergessen.* He's probably forgotten.
♦ *Es ist wohl gestohlen worden.* It must have been stolen.
♦ *Das ist doch wohl nicht dein Ernst!* Surely you're not being serious!
♦ *Das mag wohl sein.* That may well be.
♦ *Ob das wohl stimmt?* I wonder if that's true.
♦ *Er weiß das sehr wohl.* He knows that perfectly well.
♦ *sich wohl fühlen (1)* to be happy ◊ *Ich fühle mich in diesem Haus sehr wohl.* I'm very happy in this house.

**W**

♦ **sich wohl fühlen (2)** to feel well ◊ *Sie fühlte sich nicht wohl.* She didn't feel well.

♦ **Ich muss wohl oder übel hingehen.** I have to go whether I like it or not.

die **Wohltätigkeitsorganisation** NOUN
  charitable organization

**wohlweislich** ADVERB
  prudently

der **Wohnblock** NOUN (PL die **Wohnblocks**)
  block of flats

**wohnen** VERB
  to live ◊ *Ich wohne in Bremen.* I live in Bremen.

die **Wohngemeinschaft** NOUN
  ♦ **Ich wohne in einer Wohngemeinschaft.** I share a flat.

das **Wohnheim** NOUN (PL die **Wohnheime**)
  [1] home ◊ *ein Wohnheim für ältere Menschen* a home for senior citizens
  ♦ **ein Studentenwohnheim** a hall of residence
  [2] hostel

der **Wohnort** NOUN (PL die **Wohnorte**)
  place of residence

der **Wohnsitz** NOUN (GEN des **Wohnsitzes**, PL die **Wohnsitze**)
  place of residence

die **Wohnung** NOUN
  flat

der **Wohnwagen** NOUN (PL die **Wohnwagen**)
  caravan

das **Wohnzimmer** NOUN (PL die **Wohnzimmer**)
  living room

der **Wolf** NOUN (PL die **Wölfe**)
  wolf

die **Wolke** NOUN
  cloud

der **Wolkenkratzer** NOUN (PL die **Wolkenkratzer**)
  skyscraper

**wolkenlos** ADJECTIVE
  cloudless

**wolkig** ADJECTIVE
  cloudy

die **Wolle** NOUN
  wool

**wollen** VERB (PRESENT **will**, IMPERFECT **wollte**, PERFECT **hat gewollt** or **wollen**)
  *The past participle **wollen** is used when **wollen** is a modal auxiliary.*
  to want ◊ *Er hat nicht gewollt.* He didn't want to. ◊ *Er wollte das nicht.* He didn't want it. ◊ *Ich will nach Hause.* I want to go home.
  ♦ **Wenn du willst.** If you like.
  ♦ **etwas tun wollen** to want to do something ◊ *Er hat unbedingt gehen wollen.* He really wanted to go.
  ♦ **Ich wollte, ich wäre ...** I wish I were ...

**womit** ADVERB

[1] with which ◊ *Das ist der Gegenstand, womit er erschlagen wurde.* This is the instrument with which he was killed.
[2] what ... with ◊ *Womit hast du das repariert?* What did you repair it with?

**womöglich** ADVERB
  probably

**wonach** ADVERB
  [1] what ... for ◊ *Das war genau, wonach er gesucht hatte.* That was just what he had been looking for.
  [2] what ... by ◊ *Wonach sollen wir die Uhr stellen?* What shall we set the clock by?

**woran** ADVERB
  ♦ **das Paket, woran dieser Zettel hing** the parcel, the note was attached to
  ♦ **die Krankheit, woran sie gestorben ist** the illness she died of
  ♦ **Woran war dieser Zettel befestigt?** What was this note attached to?
  ♦ **Woran ist er gestorben?** What did he die of?

**worauf** ADVERB
  what ... on ◊ *Worauf soll ich den Computer stellen?* What shall I put the computer on?
  ♦ **der Tisch, worauf der Computer steht** the table the computer is on

**woraus** ADVERB
  ♦ **das Material, woraus es hergestellt ist** the material it is made of
  ♦ **das Leck, woraus Gas strömte** the hole gas was pouring out of
  ♦ **Woraus ist diese Statue?** What's the statue made of?
  ♦ **Woraus kamen die Schreie?** Where did the cries come from?

**worin** ADVERB
  what ... in ◊ *Worin war das versteckt?* What was it hidden in?
  ♦ **die Schublade, worin der Schlüssel ist** the drawer the key is in
  ♦ **Worin besteht der Unterschied?** What's the difference?

das **Wort** NOUN (PL die **Wörter** or **Worte**)
  word ◊ *Sie sprach ein paar bewegende Worte.* She said a few moving words. ◊ *Manche Wörter werden wie im Französischen ausgesprochen.* Some words are pronounced as in French.
  ♦ **jemanden beim Wort nehmen** to take somebody at his word ◊ *Ich nahm sie beim Wort.* I took her at her word.
  ♦ **mit anderen Worten** in other words

das **Wörterbuch** NOUN (PL die **Wörterbücher**)
  dictionary

**wörtlich** ADJECTIVE
  literal

der **Wortschatz** NOUN (GEN des **Wortschatzes**)
  vocabulary

das **Wortspiel** NOUN (PL die **Wortspiele**)
  pun

**worüber** ADVERB

♦ **das Thema, worüber wir reden** the subject we're talking about

♦ **der Tisch, worüber eine Lampe hing** the table a lamp was hanging over

♦ **Worüber habt ihr gesprochen?** What did you talk about?

**worunter** ADVERB

<u>what ... under</u> ◊ *Worunter hat sich die Katze verkrochen?* What did the cat crawl under?

♦ **der Tisch, worunter die Katze lag** the table the cat was lying under

**wovon** ADVERB

♦ **Das war es, wovon wir sprachen.** That was what we were talking about.

♦ **das Essen, wovon ihm schlecht wurde** the food which made him ill

♦ **Wovon habt ihr gesprochen?** What did you talk about?

♦ **Wovon ist ihm schlecht geworden?** What made him ill?

**wovor** ADVERB

♦ **das Haus, wovor du stehst** the house you're standing in front of

♦ **die Arbeit, wovor sie am meisten Angst hat** the test which she's most afraid of

♦ **Wovor hast du Angst?** What are you afraid of?

**wozu** ADVERB

[1] <u>why</u> ◊ *Wozu willst du das wissen?* Why do you want to know that?

[2] <u>what ... for</u> ◊ *Wozu dient dieser Schalter?* What's this switch for? ◊ *Wozu brauchst du einen Computer?* What do you need a computer for?

das **Wrack** NOUN (PL die **Wracks**)

<u>wreck</u>

der **Wucher** NOUN

♦ **Das ist Wucher!** That's daylight robbery!

**wund** ADJECTIVE

<u>sore</u> ◊ *Ich habe mir die Füße beim Einkaufen wund gelaufen.* My feet are sore from going round the shops.

die **Wunde** NOUN

<u>wound</u>

das **Wunder** NOUN (PL die **Wunder**)

<u>miracle</u>

♦ **es ist kein Wunder** it's no wonder

**wunderbar** ADJECTIVE

<u>wonderful</u>

**wundern** VERB

<u>to surprise</u> ◊ *Diese Frage hat mich sehr gewundert.* This question really surprised me.

♦ **sich wundern über** to be surprised at ◊ *Ich wundere mich immer wieder über ihr Wissen.* I'm always surprised at how much she knows. ◊ *Ich wundere mich, dass er noch nicht angerufen hat.* I'm surprised that he hasn't phoned yet.

♦ **Ich muss mich schon über dich wundern.** I must say you surprise me.

♦ **Es wundert mich, dass du das fragst.** I'm surprised you ask.

♦ **Er wird sich noch wundern!** He's in for a surprise!

**wunderschön** ADJECTIVE

<u>beautiful</u>

**wundervoll** ADJECTIVE

<u>wonderful</u>

der **Wunsch** NOUN (PL die **Wünsche**)

<u>wish</u>

**wünschen** VERB

<u>to wish</u> ◊ *Ich wünsche dir viel Erfolg!* I wish you every success.

♦ **sich etwas wünschen** to want something ◊ *Ich wünsche mir zum Geburtstag Inline-Skates.* I want in-line skates for my birthday.

**wurde** VERB *see* **werden**

der **Wurf** NOUN (PL die **Würfe**)

<u>throw</u>

der **Würfel** NOUN (PL die **Würfel**)

[1] <u>dice</u> ◊ *zwei Würfel* two dice ◊ *Wir haben Würfel gespielt.* We played dice.

[2] <u>cube</u> ◊ *Ein Würfel hat sechs gleich große Flächen.* A cube has six equal surfaces.

**würfeln** VERB

[1] <u>to throw a dice</u> ◊ *Ich bin dran mit Würfeln.* It's my turn to throw the dice.

[2] <u>to dice</u> ◊ *den Speck würfeln* to dice the bacon

der **Würfelzucker** NOUN

<u>lump sugar</u>

der **Wurm** NOUN (PL die **Würmer**)

<u>worm</u>

die **Wurst** NOUN (PL die **Würste**)

[1] <u>sausage</u> ◊ *Leberwurst* liver sausage

[2] <u>cold meat</u>

♦ **Das ist mir Wurst.** I don't give a toss.

das **Würstchen** NOUN (PL die **Würstchen**)

<u>sausage</u>

die **Würstchenbude** NOUN

<u>hot dog stand</u>

die **Würze** NOUN

<u>seasoning</u>

die **Wurzel** NOUN

<u>root</u>

**wusch** VERB *see* **waschen**

**wusste** VERB *see* **wissen**

die **Wüste** NOUN

<u>desert</u>

die **Wut** NOUN

<u>rage</u>

♦ **eine Wut haben** to be furious

der **Wutanfall** NOUN (PL die **Wutanfälle**)

<u>fit of rage</u>

**wütend** ADJECTIVE

<u>furious</u> ◊ *Ich bin wütend auf ihn.* I'm furious with him.

**WWW** ABBREVIATION (= *World Wide Web*)

<u>WWW</u>

♦ **eine WWW-Seite** a web page

**x-beliebig** ADJECTIVE
<u>any ... whatever</u> ◊ *Wähle eine x-
beliebige Zahl.* Choose any number
whatever.
**x-mal** ADVERB
<u>any number of times</u> ◊ *Ich habe es ihm*

*x-mal gesagt.* I've told him any number
of times.
das **Xylofon** NOUN (PL die **Xylofone**)
*see* **Xylophon**
das **Xylophon** NOUN (PL die **Xylophone**)
<u>xylophone</u>

das **Yoga** NOUN (GEN des **Yoga** *or* **Yogas**)
<u>yoga</u>
das **Ypsilon** NOUN (GEN des **Ypsilon** *or* **Ypsilons**,

PL die **Ypsilons**)
<u>the letter Y</u>

# Z

die **Zacke** NOUN
  peak ◊ *die Zacke einer Fieberkurve* the peak of a temperature chart
  ◆ **eine Bergzacke** a jagged peak
  ◆ **die Zacken der Gabel** the prongs of the fork
  ◆ **die Zacken des Kamms** the teeth of the comb

**zaghaft** ADJECTIVE
  timid

**zäh** ADJECTIVE
  ① tough ◊ *Das Steak ist zäh.* The steak's tough. ◊ *Ich bin zäh, ich halte es noch eine Weile aus.* I'm tough, I can stand it for a bit yet.
  ② slow-moving ◊ *Der Verkehr war zäh.* Traffic was slow-moving.

die **Zahl** NOUN
  number

**zahlen** VERB
  to pay ◊ *Wie viel hast du dafür gezahlt?* How much did you pay for it?
  ◆ **Zahlen bitte!** The bill, please!

**zählen** VERB
  to count ◊ *Ich zähle bis drei.* I'll count to three. ◊ *Ich habe die Hefte gezählt.* I've counted the exercise books.
  ◆ **zählen auf** to count on ◊ *Wir zählen auf dich.* We're counting on you.
  ◆ **zählen zu** to be one of ◊ *Er zählt zu den besseren Schülern.* He's one of the better pupils.

**zahlreich** ADJECTIVE
  numerous

die **Zahlung** NOUN
  payment

das **Zahlwort** NOUN (PL die **Zahlwörter**)
  numeral

**zahm** ADJECTIVE
  tame

der **Zahn** NOUN (PL die **Zähne**)
  tooth

der **Zahnarzt** NOUN (GEN des **Zahnarztes**, PL die **Zahnärzte**)
  dentist

die **Zahnbürste** NOUN
  toothbrush

die **Zahncreme** NOUN (PL die **Zahncremes**)
  toothpaste

das **Zahnfleisch** NOUN
  gums ◊ *Mein Zahnfleisch blutet.* My gums are bleeding.

die **Zahnpasta** NOUN (PL die **Zahnpasten**)
  toothpaste

die **Zahnschmerzen** MASC PL NOUN
  toothache

der **Zahnstein** NOUN
  tartar

der **Zahnstocher** NOUN (PL die **Zahnstocher**)
  toothpick

die **Zange** NOUN
  ① pliers ◊ *Ich brauche eine isolierte Zange.* I need a pair of insulated pliers.
  ② pincers ◊ *die Zangen eines Hummers* a lobster's pincers

**zappeln** VERB
  ① to wriggle ◊ *Der Fisch zappelt noch.* The fish is still wriggling.
  ② to fidget ◊ *Hör auf zu zappeln.* Stop fidgeting.

**zart** ADJECTIVE
  ① soft ◊ *zarte Haut* soft skin
  ② gentle ◊ *eine zarte Berührung* a gentle touch
  ③ delicate ◊ *zarte Farben* delicate colours ◊ *Sie ist ein sehr zartes Kind.* She's a very delicate child.
  ◆ **zartes Fleisch** tender meat

**zärtlich** ADJECTIVE
  loving ◊ *Mein Freund ist sehr zärtlich.* My boyfriend's very loving. ◊ *ein zärtlicher Kuss* a loving kiss ◊ *eine zärtliche Berührung* a loving touch

die **Zauberei** NOUN
  magic

der **Zaun** NOUN (PL die **Zäune**)
  fence

**z. B.** ABBREVIATION (= *zum Beispiel*)
  e.g.

das **ZDF** ABBREVIATION (= *Zweites Deutsches Fernsehen*)
  German TV channel

der **Zebrastreifen** NOUN (PL die **Zebrastreifen**)
  zebra crossing

die **Zehe** NOUN
  toe ◊ *die große Zehe* the big toe
  ◆ **eine Knoblauchzehe** a clove of garlic

**zehn** NUMBER
  ten

**zehnte** ADJECTIVE
  tenth

das **Zeichen** NOUN (PL die **Zeichen**)
  sign

der **Zeichentrickfilm** NOUN (PL die **Zeichentrickfilme**)
  animated cartoon

**zeichnen** VERB
  to draw ◊ *Marek kann gut zeichnen.* Marek's good at drawing. ◊ *Sie hat eine Maus gezeichnet.* She's drawn a mouse.

die **Zeichnung** NOUN
  drawing

der **Zeigefinger** NOUN (PL die **Zeigefinger**)
  index finger

**zeigen** VERB

1 to show ◊ *Sie hat mir ihre Fotos gezeigt.* She showed me her photos. ◊ *Zeig mal, was du da hast.* Show us what you've got there.

2 to point ◊ *Sie zeigte an die Tafel.* She pointed to the blackboard.

♦ **zeigen auf** to point at ◊ *Man zeigt nicht mit dem Finger auf Menschen.* Don't point at people.

♦ **es wird sich zeigen** time will tell ◊ *Es wird sich zeigen, ob er das kann.* Time will tell whether he can do it.

♦ **Es zeigte sich, dass ...** It turned out that ... ◊ *Es zeigte sich, dass der Text zu schwierig war.* It turned out that the text was too difficult.

der **Zeiger** NOUN (PL die **Zeiger**)
  1 hand ◊ *der große und der kleine Zeiger der Uhr* the big hand and the little hand of the clock
  2 pointer ◊ *der Zeiger der Waage* the pointer of the scales

die **Zeile** NOUN
  line ◊ *Ich schreibe ihr ein paar Zeilen.* I'm going to write her a few lines.

die **Zeit** NOUN
  1 time ◊ *Wir haben keine Zeit mehr.* We haven't got any more time. ◊ *Um welche Zeit seid ihr nach Hause gekommen?* What time did you get home?
  2 tense ◊ *die Zeiten der Vergangenheit* the past tenses

♦ **zur Zeit** at the moment

♦ **sich Zeit lassen** to take one's time ◊ *Da hast du dir aber viel Zeit gelassen.* You've been taking your time.

♦ **von Zeit zu Zeit** from time to time

♦ **Zeit raubend** time-consuming

  **zeitlich** ADJECTIVE
  chronological

die **Zeitlupe** NOUN
  slow motion ◊ *in Zeitlupe* in slow motion

  **zeitraubend** ADJECTIVE *see* **Zeit**

der **Zeitraum** NOUN (PL die **Zeiträume**)
  period ◊ *innerhalb dieses Zeitraums* within this period

die **Zeitschrift** NOUN
  magazine

die **Zeitung** NOUN
  newspaper

der **Zeitungskiosk** NOUN (PL die **Zeitungskioske**)
  newspaper kiosk

der **Zeitungsstand** NOUN (PL die **Zeitungsstände**)
  newspaper stand

die **Zeitverschwendung** NOUN
  waste of time ◊ *Das ist doch Zeitverschwendung!* That's just a waste of time.

das **Zeitwort** NOUN (PL die **Zeitwörter**)
  verb

die **Zelle** NOUN
  1 cell ◊ *Im Alter sterben die Zellen ab.* Cells die off in old age.
  2 call box ◊ *Ich rufe aus einer Zelle an.* I'm phoning from a call box.

das **Zelt** NOUN (PL die **Zelte**)
  tent

  **zelten** VERB
  to camp

der **Zeltplatz** NOUN (GEN des **Zeltplatzes**, PL die **Zeltplätze**)
  camp site

der **Zement** NOUN (PL die **Zemente**)
  cement

  **zensieren** VERB (PERFECT **hat zensiert**)
  1 to censor ◊ *Der Film wurde zensiert.* The film was censored.
  2 to give a mark ◊ *Wie hat deine Deutschlehrerin den Aufsatz zensiert?* What mark did your German teacher give you for your essay?

die **Zensur** NOUN
  mark ◊ *Ich habe durchweg gute Zensuren.* I've got good marks in everything.

der **Zentimeter** NOUN (PL die **Zentimeter**)
  centimetre

der **Zentner** NOUN (PL die **Zentner**)
  hundredweight ◊ *drei Zentner* three hundredweight

  **zentral** ADJECTIVE
  central

die **Zentrale** NOUN
  1 head office ◊ *Das Gerät müssen wir in der Zentrale anfordern.* We'll have to order the appliance from the head office.
  2 switchboard ◊ *Du musst dich über die Zentrale verbinden lassen.* You have to go through the switchboard.

die **Zentralheizung** NOUN
  central heating

das **Zentrum** NOUN (PL die **Zentren**)
  centre

  **zerbrechen** VERB (PRESENT **zerbricht**, IMPERFECT **zerbrach**, PERFECT **hat/ist zerbrochen**)
  *For the perfect tense use **haben** when the verb has an object and **sein** when there is no object.*
  to break ◊ *Sie hat den Teller zerbrochen.* She's broken the plate. ◊ *Der Teller ist zerbrochen.* The plate broke.

  **zerbrechlich** ADJECTIVE
  fragile

  **zerreißen** VERB (IMPERFECT **zerriss**, PERFECT **hat/ist zerrissen**)
  *For the perfect tense use **haben** when the verb has an object and **sein** when there is no object.*
  1 to tear to pieces ◊ *Sie hat seinen Brief zerrissen.* She tore his letter to pieces.

♦ **Sie hatte völlig zerrissene Kleider an.**
Her clothes were all tattered.
[2] to tear ◊ *Der Umschlag ist unterwegs zerrissen.* The envelope got torn in the post.

**zerren** VERB
to drag ◊ *Er zerrte sie in die Büsche.* He dragged her into the bushes.
♦ **zerren an** to tug at ◊ *Der Hund zerrte an der Leine.* The dog tugged at its leash.

**zerrissen** VERB *see* **zerreißen**

**zerschlagen** VERB (PRESENT **zerschlägt,** IMPERFECT **zerschlug,** PERFECT **hat zerschlagen**)
to smash ◊ *Sie haben alles Porzellan zerschlagen.* They smashed all the china.
♦ **sich zerschlagen** to fall through ◊ *Unsere Ferienpläne haben sich zerschlagen.* Our holiday plans have fallen through.

**zerschneiden** VERB (IMPERFECT **zerschnitt,** PERFECT **hat zerschnitten**)
to cut up

der **Zerstäuber** NOUN (PL die **Zerstäuber**)
atomizer

**zerstören** VERB (PRESENT **hat zerstört**)
to destroy

die **Zerstörung** NOUN
destruction

**zerstreuen** VERB (PERFECT **hat zerstreut**)
[1] to entertain ◊ *Er hat uns mit lustigen Geschichten zerstreut.* He entertained us with amusing stories.
[2] to scatter ◊ *Warum hast du die Blätter im ganzen Zimmer zerstreut?* Why have you scattered the papers all over the room? ◊ *Unsere Familie ist über ganz Deutschland zerstreut.* Our family's scattered all over Germany.
♦ **jemandes Angst zerstreuen** to allay somebody's fears

**zerstreut** ADJECTIVE
[1] absent-minded ◊ *Er ist furchtbar zerstreut.* He's terribly absent-minded.
[2] scattered ◊ *Sie sammelte die zerstreuten Seiten auf.* She picked up the scattered pages.

der **Zettel** NOUN (PL die **Zettel**)
[1] note ◊ *Auf dem Küchentisch liegt ein Zettel für dich.* There's a note on the kitchen table for you.
[2] piece of paper ◊ *Sie schrieb seine Telefonnummer auf einen Zettel.* She wrote his telephone number on a piece of paper.
[3] form ◊ *Wenn du dem Klub beitreten willst, musst du diesen Zettel ausfüllen.* If you want to join the club you'll have to fill in this form.

das **Zeug** NOUN
[1] stuff ◊ *Was ist das für ein Zeug?* What's this stuff? ◊ *mein Sportzeug* my sports stuff
[2] gear ◊ *mein Angelzeug* my fishing gear

♦ **dummes Zeug** nonsense ◊ *Das ist doch dummes Zeug.* That's just a lot of nonsense.
♦ **das Zeug haben zu** to have the makings of ◊ *Er hat das Zeug zum Lehrer.* He has the makings of a teacher.

der **Zeuge** NOUN (GEN des **Zeugen,** PL die **Zeugen**)
witness

die **Zeugin** NOUN
witness

das **Zeugnis** NOUN (GEN des **Zeugnisses,** PL die **Zeugnisse**)
report ◊ *Oliver hat ein sehr gutes Zeugnis.* Oliver's got a very good report.

die **Ziege** NOUN
goat

der **Ziegel** NOUN (PL die **Ziegel**)
[1] brick ◊ *eine Mauer aus Ziegeln* a brick wall
[2] tile ◊ *Deutsche Dächer sind meist mit roten Ziegeln gedeckt.* German roofs are usually covered with red tiles.

**ziehen** VERB (IMPERFECT **zog,** PERFECT **hat/ist gezogen**)
Use **sein** to form the perfect tense for **to move** (house) and **to roam**. Use **haben** for **to move** (in chess), **to draw** and **to pull**.
[1] to draw ◊ *Er hat eine Niete gezogen.* He drew a blank.
[2] to pull ◊ *Sie zog mich am Ärmel.* She pulled at my sleeve.
[3] to move ◊ *Sie sind nach Wuppertal gezogen.* They've moved to Wuppertal. ◊ *Er zog mit seinem Turm.* He moved his rook.
[4] to roam ◊ *Früher zogen die Zigeuner durchs Land.* In the old days, gypsies used to roam the countryside.
♦ **Es zieht.** There's a draught.
♦ **sich in die Länge ziehen** to be drawn out

das **Ziel** NOUN (PL die **Ziele**)
[1] destination ◊ *Unser heutiges Ziel ist Bonn.* Our destination today is Bonn.
[2] finishing line ◊ *Er ging als Erster durchs Ziel.* He was the first to cross the finishing line.
[3] target ◊ *Ulm war das Ziel eines Bombenangriffs.* Ulm was the target of an air raid.
[4] goal ◊ *Es ist nicht mein Ziel im Leben, reich zu werden.* Getting rich is not my goal in life.

**zielen** VERB
to aim ◊ *Er hat auf seine Beine gezielt.* He aimed at his legs.

die **Zielscheibe** NOUN
target ◊ *Er traf die Zielscheibe mit seinem ersten Schuss.* He hit the target with his first shot.

**ziemlich** ADJECTIVE, ADVERB

Z

☞

**1** quite ◊ *Das war eine ziemliche Katastrophe.* That was quite a disaster.

**2** fair ◊ *eine ziemliche Menge Fehler* a fair number of mistakes

**3** rather ◊ *Er war ziemlich sauer.* He was rather cross.

◆ **ziemlich viel** quite a bit ◊ *Wir haben ziemlich viel erledigt.* We've got through quite a bit.

sich **zieren** VERB
> to act coy

**zierlich** ADJECTIVE
> dainty

die **Ziffer** NOUN
> figure

**zig** ADJECTIVE
> umpteen

die **Zigarette** NOUN
> cigarette

der **Zigarettenautomat** NOUN (GEN des **Zigarettenautomaten**, PL die **Zigarettenautomaten**)
> cigarette machine

die **Zigarettenschachtel** NOUN
> cigarette packet

das **Zigarillo** NOUN (PL die **Zigarillos**)
> *You can also say der Zigarillo.*
> cigarillo

die **Zigarre** NOUN
> cigar

der **Zigeuner** NOUN (PL die **Zigeuner**)
> gipsy

die **Zigeunerin** NOUN
> gipsy

das **Zimmer** NOUN (PL die **Zimmer**)
> room

◆ **"Zimmer frei"** "Vacancies"

das **Zimmermädchen** NOUN (PL die **Zimmermädchen**)
> chambermaid

der **Zimmernachweis** NOUN (GEN des **Zimmernachweises**, PL die **Zimmernachweise**)
> accommodation office

der **Zimt** NOUN
> cinnamon

das **Zinn** NOUN

**1** tin ◊ *In Cornwall wurde früher Zinn abgebaut.* They used to mine tin in Cornwall.

**2** pewter ◊ *Mein Bruder sammelt Zinn.* My brother collects pewter.

der **Zins** NOUN (GEN des **Zinses**, PL die **Zinsen**)
> interest ◊ *acht Prozent Zinsen* eight per cent interest

das **Zip-Laufwerk** NOUN (PL die **Zip-Laufwerke**)
> zip drive

**zirka** ADVERB
> approximately

der **Zirkus** NOUN (GEN des **Zirkus**, PL die **Zirkusse**)
> circus

**zischen** VERB
> to hiss

das **Zitat** NOUN (PL die **Zitate**)
> quotation

**zitieren** VERB (PERFECT **hat zitiert**)
> to quote

die **Zitrone** NOUN
> lemon

die **Zitronenlimonade** NOUN
> lemonade

der **Zitronensaft** NOUN (PL die **Zitronensäfte**)
> lemon juice

**zittern** VERB
> to tremble ◊ *vor Angst zittern* to tremble with fear

◆ **Sie zitterte vor Kälte.** She was shivering.

der **Zivildienst** NOUN
> community service

> ⓘ *Instead of doing national service in the German armed forces, young men can opt to do community service as* **Zivildienstleistende** *or* **Zivis**, *for example with the Red Cross or in an old people's home.*

die **Zivilisation** NOUN
> civilization

**zögern** VERB
> to hesitate

der **Zoll** NOUN (PL die **Zölle**)

**1** customs ◊ *Wir mussten am Zoll lange warten.* We had to wait a long time at customs.

**2** duty ◊ *Darauf musst du Zoll bezahlen.* You have to pay duty on that.

der **Zollbeamte** NOUN (GEN des **Zollbeamten**, PL die **Zollbeamten**)
> customs official ◊ *Ein Zollbeamter hat unser Auto durchsucht.* A customs official searched our car.

**zollfrei** ADJECTIVE
> duty-free

die **Zollkontrolle** NOUN
> customs check

die **Zone** NOUN
> zone

der **Zoo** NOUN (PL die **Zoos**)
> zoo

**zoologisch** ADJECTIVE
> zoological

der **Zopf** NOUN (PL die **Zöpfe**)

**1** plait ◊ *Man stellt sich deutsche Mädchen immer mit zwei blonden Zöpfen vor.* You always imagine German girls as having two blonde plaits.

**2** pigtail ◊ *Sie hatte ihre Haare zu einem Zopf zusammengebunden.* She had put her hair into a pigtail.

der **Zorn** NOUN
> anger

**zornig** ADJECTIVE

**zu** PREPOSITION, CONJUNCTION, ADVERB

*The preposition* **zu** *takes the dative.*

1 to ◇ *zum Bahnhof gehen* to go to the station ◇ *zum Arzt gehen* to go to the doctor ◇ *zur Schule gehen* to go to school ◇ *zur Kirche gehen* to go to church ◇ *Genau das habe ich zu ihm gesagt.* That's exactly what I said to him. ◇ *Sollen wir zu euch gehen?* Shall we go to your place?

◆ **Sie sah zu ihm hin.** She looked towards him.

◆ **zum Fenster herein** through the window

◆ **zu meiner Linken** on my left

*zu is used with the infinitive.*

◇ *etwas zu essen* something to eat

◆ **um besser sehen zu können** in order to see better

◆ **ohne es zu wissen** without knowing it

2 at ◇ *zu Ostern* at Easter

◆ **zu Hause** at home

◆ **bis zum ersten Mai (1)** until the first of May ◇ *Das Sonderangebot gilt bis zum ersten Mai.* The special offer is valid until the first of May.

◆ **bis zum ersten Mai (2)** by the first of May ◇ *Bis zum ersten Mai muss mein Referat fertig sein.* My assignment has to be finished by the first of May.

◆ **zu meinem Geburtstag** for my birthday

◆ **zu meiner Zeit** in my time

3 with ◇ *Wein zum Essen trinken* to drink wine with one's meal

◆ **sich zu jemandem setzen** to sit down beside somebody

◆ **Setz dich doch zu uns.** Come and sit with us.

◆ **Anmerkungen zu etwas** notes on something

4 for ◇ *Wasser zum Waschen* water for washing

◆ **Papier zum Schreiben** paper to write on

◆ **zu etwas werden** to develop into something ◇ *Sie ist zu einer hübschen jungen Dame geworden.* She's developed into an attractive young lady.

◆ **jemanden zu etwas machen** to make somebody something ◇ *Sie haben mich zur Klassensprecherin gemacht.* They made me class representative.

◆ **drei zu zwei** three two ◇ *Unsere Mannschaft hat drei zu zwei gewonnen.* Our team won three two.

◆ **das Stück zu zwei Mark** at two marks each

◆ **zum ersten Mal** for the first time

◆ **zu meiner Freude** to my delight

◆ **zum Scherz** as a joke

◆ **zu Fuß** on foot

◆ **Es ist zum Weinen.** It's enough to make you cry.

5 too ◇ *zu schnell* too fast ◇ *zu sehr* too much

6 closed ◇ *Die Geschäfte haben zu.* The shops are closed.

◆ **zu sein** to be shut ◇ *Das Fenster war zu.* The window was shut.

**zuallererst** ADVERB
first of all

**zuallerletzt** ADVERB
last of all

das **Zubehör** NOUN (PL die **Zubehöre**)
accessories ◇ *Das Zubehör kostet extra.* You pay extra for the accessories.

**zubereiten** VERB (PERFECT **hat zubereitet**)
to prepare

**zubinden** VERB (IMPERFECT **band zu,** PERFECT **hat zugebunden**)
to tie up

**zubringen** VERB (IMPERFECT **brachte zu,** PERFECT **hat zugebracht**)
to spend ◇ *Ich habe viel Zeit bei ihnen zugebracht.* I spent a lot of time with them.

die **Zucchini** PL NOUN
courgette

**züchten** VERB
1 to breed ◇ *Er züchtet Tauben.* He breeds pigeons.
2 to grow ◇ *Mein Vater züchtet Rosen.* My father grows roses.

**zucken** VERB
1 to twitch ◇ *Seine Mundwinkel zuckten.* The corners of his mouth twitched.
2 to flash ◇ *Ein Blitz zuckte durch die Nacht.* Lightning flashed across the night sky.

◆ **mit den Schultern zucken** to shrug one's shoulders

der **Zucker** NOUN
1 sugar ◇ *Ich nehme keinen Zucker in den Tee.* I don't take sugar in my tea.
2 diabetes ◇ *Meine Tante hat Zucker.* My aunt's got diabetes.

der **Zuckerguss** NOUN (GEN des **Zuckergusses,** PL die **Zuckergüsse**)
icing

**zuckerkrank** ADJECTIVE
diabetic

die **Zuckerkrankheit** NOUN
diabetes

**zudecken** VERB (PERFECT **hat zugedeckt**)
1 to cover up ◇ *Man sollte das Loch zudecken.* They ought to cover up the hole.
2 to tuck up ◇ *Sie deckte die Kinder zu.* She tucked the children up.

**zueinander** ADVERB
1 to one another ◇ *Seid nett zueinander.* Be nice to one another.

◆ **Wir haben viel Vertrauen zueinander.** We trust each other.

Z

**2** together ◇ *Wir halten zueinander, egal, was kommt.* Whatever happens, we'll stick together.

**zuerst** ADVERB

**1** first ◇ *Was soll ich zuerst machen?* What shall I do first? ◇ *Er ist zuerst gekommen, dann kam seine Schwester.* He arrived first, then his sister.

**2** at first ◇ *Zuerst war sie noch etwas schüchtern.* At first, she was still a bit shy.

◆ **zuerst einmal** first of all ◇ *Wir sollten zuerst einmal klären, was das kostet.* First of all we ought to check how much it costs.

die **Zufahrt** NOUN

approach road

◆ **"keine Zufahrt"** "no access"

der **Zufall** NOUN (PL die **Zufälle**)

**1** chance ◇ *Wie es der Zufall so wollte ...* As chance would have it ...

◆ **durch Zufall** by chance ◇ *Ich habe es durch Zufall gefunden.* I found it by chance.

**2** coincidence ◇ *Es war schon ein Zufall, dass ich ihm in London begegnet bin.* It was quite a coincidence that I met him in London. ◇ *Was für ein glücklicher Zufall!* What a happy coincidence! ◇ *So ein Zufall!* What a coincidence!

**zufällig** ADJECTIVE, ADVERB

**1** chance ◇ *eine zufällige Begegnung* a chance meeting

**2** by chance ◇ *Ich habe das Restaurant ganz zufällig gefunden.* I found the restaurant quite by chance.

◆ **Ich habe zufällig Zeit.** I happen to have time.

**3** by any chance ◇ *Hast du zufällig mein Heft gesehen?* Have you seen my exercise book by any chance?

**zufrieden** ADJECTIVE

satisfied ◇ *Ich bin mit deinen Leistungen nicht zufrieden.* I'm not satisfied with your work. ◇ *Bist du jetzt zufrieden?* Are you satisfied now? ◇ *ein zufriedener Gesichtsausdruck* a satisfied expression

**zufrieren** VERB (IMPERFECT **fror zu,** PERFECT **ist zugefroren**)

to freeze over ◇ *Der See ist zugefroren.* The lake's frozen over.

der **Zug** NOUN (PL die **Züge**)

**1** train ◇ *Wir sind mit dem Zug gefahren.* We went by train.

**2** draught ◇ *Hier ist ein furchtbarer Zug.* There's a terrible draught in here.

**3** move ◇ *Du bist am Zug.* It's your move.

**4** gulp ◇ *Er trank das Glas auf einen Zug leer.* He emptied the glass in one gulp.

**5** trait ◇ *Sein Geiz ist ein unangenehmer Zug an ihm.* His meanness is an unpleasant trait.

◆ **etwas in vollen Zügen genießen** to enjoy something to the full

die **Zugabe** NOUN

**1** free gift ◇ *Beim Kauf von drei Packungen bekommen Sie einen Dosierlöffel als Zugabe.* Buy three packets and get a measuring spoon as a free gift.

**2** encore ◇ *Die Zuhörer brüllten: "Zugabe, Zugabe".* The audience roared: "encore, encore".

**zugeben** VERB (PRESENT **gibt zu,** IMPERFECT **gab zu,** PERFECT **hat zugegeben**)

to admit ◇ *Gib doch zu, dass du dich getäuscht hast.* Admit you were wrong. ◇ *Sie wollte ihren Irrtum nicht zugeben.* She didn't want to admit her mistake.

**zugehen** VERB (IMPERFECT **ging zu,** PERFECT **ist zugegangen**)

to shut ◇ *Die Tür geht nicht zu.* The door won't shut.

◆ **auf jemanden zugehen** to walk up to somebody ◇ *Sie ging auf den Mann zu und fragte ihn nach dem Weg.* She walked up to the man and asked him the way.

◆ **auf etwas zugehen** to walk towards something ◇ *Sie ging auf den Eingang zu, kehrte dann aber wieder um.* She walked towards the entrance but then turned back again.

◆ **Es geht dort seltsam zu.** There are strange goings-on there.

◆ **dem Ende zugehen** to be nearing the end

der **Zugführer** NOUN (PL die **Zugführer**)

chief guard (*on train*)

**zugig** ADJECTIVE

draughty

**zügig** ADJECTIVE

swift ◇ *eine zügige Entscheidung* a swift decision

**zugreifen** VERB (IMPERFECT **griff zu,** PERFECT **hat zugegriffen**)

**1** to help oneself ◇ *Greift ungeniert zu, es ist genügend Kuchen da!* Feel free to help yourselves, there's plenty of cake.

**2** to seize ◇ *Er sah das Seil und griff zu.* He saw the rope and seized it.

**3** to lend a hand ◇ *Du könntest ruhig ein bisschen zugreifen und mich nicht alles allein machen lassen.* You could at least lend a hand a bit instead of letting me do everything.

**zugrunde** ADVERB

◆ **elend zugrunde gehen** to come to a wretched end ◇ *Er fing an zu trinken und ging elend zugrunde.* He took to drink and came to a wretched end.

◆ **zugrunde richten** to destroy ◇ *Alkohol und Drogen haben sie zugrunde gerichtet.* Alcohol and drugs have destroyed her.

◆ **einer Sache etwas zugrunde legen** to base something on something ◊ *Diesem Film liegt ein Roman zugrunde.* This film is based on a novel.

**zugunsten** PREPOSITION

The preposition **zugunsten** takes the dative or the genitive.

in favour of ◊ *Das Gericht entschied zugunsten des Angeklagten.* The court decided in favour of the accused.

**zugute** ADVERB

◆ **jemandem zugute kommen** to stand somebody in good stead ◊ *Meine Englischkenntnisse sind mir im Urlaub zugute gekommen.* My knowledge of English stood me in good stead on holiday.

das **Zuhause** NOUN (GEN des **Zuhause**)
home

**zuhören** VERB (PERFECT **hat zugehört**)
to listen ◊ *Du hörst mir ja gar nicht zu.* You're not listening to me at all.

der **Zuhörer** NOUN (PL die **Zuhörer**)
listener

**zukommen** VERB (IMPERFECT **kam zu,** PERFECT **ist zugekommen**)

◆ **auf jemanden zukommen** to come up to somebody ◊ *Er kam auf uns zu und fragte uns, wie spät es ist.* He came up to us and asked what time it was.

◆ **jemandem etwas zukommen lassen** to give somebody something ◊ *Mein Onkel hat mir etwas Geld zukommen lassen.* My uncle gave me some money.

◆ **etwas auf sich zukommen lassen** to take something as it comes ◊ *Warum lässt du diese Sache nicht einfach auf dich zukommen?* Why don't you just take things as they come?

die **Zukunft** NOUN
future ◊ *in Zukunft* in the future

die **Zukunftspläne** PL NOUN
plans for the future

**zulassen** VERB (PRESENT **lässt zu,** IMPERFECT **ließ zu,** PERFECT **hat zugelassen**)

[1] to allow ◊ *Ich kann es nicht zulassen, dass du so spät noch fernsiehst.* I can't allow you to watch TV so late.

[2] to register ◊ *Hast du dein Moped schon zugelassen?* Have you registered your moped yet?

[3] to leave closed ◊ *Bitte lass das Fenster zu.* Please leave the window closed.

◆ **Lass den Brief zu.** Don't open the letter.

**zulässig** ADJECTIVE
permissible

**zuleide** ADVERB

◆ **jemandem etwas zuleide tun** to hurt somebody ◊ *Bitte tu ihr nichts zuleide.* Please don't hurt her.

**zuletzt** ADVERB

[1] last ◊ *Er wurde zuletzt in Begleitung einer Dame gesehen.* He was last seen in the company of a lady. ◊ *Wir sollten das zuletzt machen.* We should do that last.

[2] in the end ◊ *Zuletzt hat sie es dann doch verstanden.* In the end she understood.

**zuliebe** ADVERB

◆ **jemandem zuliebe** to please somebody ◊ *Er ist mir zuliebe zu Hause geblieben.* He stayed at home to please me.

**zum** = **zu dem**

**zumachen** VERB (PERFECT **hat zugemacht**)

[1] to shut ◊ *Mach bitte die Tür zu.* Please shut the door. ◊ *Wann machen die Geschäfte zu?* When do the shops shut?

[2] to fasten ◊ *Kannst du mal bitte mein Kleid zumachen?* Can you fasten my dress, please?

**zumindest** ADVERB
at least

**zumute** ADVERB

◆ **Wie ist ihm zumute?** How does he feel?

**zumuten** VERB (PERFECT **hat zugemutet**)

◆ **jemandem etwas zumuten** to ask something of somebody ◊ *Das kann ich ihm nicht zumuten.* I can't ask that of him.

die **Zumutung** NOUN

◆ **Das ist eine Zumutung!** That's asking too much.

**zunächst** ADVERB
first of all ◊ *Wir sollten zunächst diese Frage klären.* We ought to clear this issue up first of all.

◆ **zunächst einmal** to start with

**zunehmen** VERB (PRESENT **nimmt zu,** IMPERFECT **nahm zu,** PERFECT **hat zugenommen**)

[1] to increase ◊ *Der Lärm nahm zu.* The noise increased.

[2] to put on weight ◊ *Ich habe schon wieder zugenommen.* I've put on weight yet again.

◆ **Er hat fünf Kilo zugenommen.** He's put on five kilos.

die **Zuneigung** NOUN
affection

◆ **Ich empfinde große Zuneigung für ihn.** I'm very fond of him.

die **Zunge** NOUN
tongue

**zur** = **zu der**

**zurechnungsfähig** ADJECTIVE
compos mentis

sich **zurechtfinden** VERB (IMPERFECT **fand sich zurecht,** PERFECT **hat sich zurechtgefunden**)
to find one's way

**zurechtkommen** VERB (IMPERFECT **kam zurecht,** PERFECT **ist zurechtgekommen**)
to manage

**zurechtlegen** VERB (PERFECT **hat zurechtgelegt**)

Z

☞

to sort out ◊ *Ich habe die Sachen für die Ferien schon zurechtgelegt.* I've already sorted out my things for my holiday.

♦ **sich eine Ausrede zurechtlegen** to think up an excuse ◊ *Na, welche Ausrede hast du dir denn diesmal zurechtgelegt?* Well, what excuse have you thought up this time?

**zurück** ADVERB
back

**zurückbekommen** VERB (IMPERFECT **bekam zurück**, PERFECT **hat zurückbekommen**)
to get back

**zurückbringen** VERB (IMPERFECT **brachte zurück**, PERFECT **hat zurückgebracht**)
to bring back

**zurückerstatten** VERB (PERFECT **hat zurückerstattet**)
to refund

**zurückfahren** VERB (PRESENT **fährt zurück**, IMPERFECT **fuhr zurück**, PERFECT **ist/hat zurückgefahren**)

*For the perfect tense use **haben** when the verb has an object and **sein** when there is no object.*

to return ◊ *Wann fahrt ihr zurück?* When do you return?

♦ **jemanden zurückfahren** to drive somebody back ◊ *Sie hat mich nach Hause zurückgefahren.* She drove me back home.

**zurückgeben** VERB (PRESENT **gibt zurück**, IMPERFECT **gab zurück**, PERFECT **hat zurückgegeben**)
to give back ◊ *Gib mir bitte mein Buch zurück.* Please give me my book back.

**zurückgehen** VERB (IMPERFECT **ging zurück**, PERFECT **ist zurückgegangen**)
1 to go back ◊ *Wir sollten zurückgehen, bevor es zu spät wird.* We should go back before it gets too late.
2 to recede ◊ *Das Hochwasser ist zurückgegangen.* The floodwater receded.
3 to fall ◊ *Die Nachfrage geht zurück.* Demand is falling.

♦ **zurückgehen auf** to date back to ◊ *Die Gründung der Stadt Aachen geht auf Karl den Großen zurück.* The founding of the city of Aachen dates back to Charlemagne.

**zurückhaltend** ADJECTIVE
reserved ◊ *Er ist sehr zurückhaltend.* He is very reserved.

**zurückkehren** VERB (PERFECT **ist zurückgekehrt**)
to return

**zurückkommen** VERB (IMPERFECT **kam zurück**, PERFECT **ist zurückgekommen**)
to come back ◊ *Er kam nach dem Film zurück.* He came back after the film.
◊ *Darf ich auf das zurückkommen, was*

*Sie vorhin gesagt haben?* May I come back to what you were saying earlier?

♦ **Komm nicht zu spät zurück.** Don't be too late back.

**zurücklegen** VERB (PERFECT **hat zurückgelegt**)
1 to put back ◊ *Leg das Buch bitte an seinen Platz zurück.* Please put the book back in its place.
2 to put by ◊ *Wir haben für die Ferien etwas Geld zurückgelegt.* We've put some money by for the holidays.
3 to put aside ◊ *Können Sie mir diesen Pulli bitte zurücklegen?* Could you put this pullover aside for me, please?
4 to cover ◊ *Wir haben heute zweihundert Kilometer zurückgelegt.* We've covered two hundred kilometres today.

**zurücknehmen** VERB (PRESENT **nimmt zurück**, IMPERFECT **nahm zurück**, PERFECT **hat zurückgenommen**)
to take back

**zurückrufen** VERB (PERFECT **hat zurückgerufen**)
to call back ◊ *Können Sie mich morgen zurückrufen?* Can you call me back tomorrow?

**zurücktreten** VERB (PRESENT **tritt zurück**, IMPERFECT **trat zurück**, PERFECT **ist zurückgetreten**)
1 to step back ◊ *Treten Sie etwas zurück bitte!* Step back a bit, please.
2 to resign ◊ *Warum ist er zurückgetreten?* Why did he resign?

**zurückzahlen** VERB (PERFECT **hat zurückgezahlt**)
to repay ◊ *Du solltest endlich das geliehene Geld zurückzahlen.* It's high time you repaid the money you borrowed.

**zurückziehen** VERB (IMPERFECT **zog zurück**, PERFECT **hat zurückgezogen**)
to pull back ◊ *Sie zog die Hand zurück.* She pulled her hand back.

♦ **ein Angebot zurückziehen** to withdraw an offer
♦ **sich zurückziehen** to retire ◊ *Sie hat sich in ihr Zimmer zurückgezogen.* She has retired to her room. ◊ *Er hat sich aus dem öffentlichen Leben zurückgezogen.* He has retired from public life.

**zusagen** VERB (PERFECT **hat zugesagt**)
1 to promise ◊ *Er hat mir seine Hilfe zugesagt.* He promised to help me.
2 to accept an invitation ◊ *Die meisten Gäste haben zugesagt.* Most of the guests have accepted the invitation.

♦ **jemandem zusagen** to appeal to somebody ◊ *Das Konzert hat mir nicht zugesagt.* The concert didn't appeal to me.

**zusammen** ADVERB

together

**zusammenbleiben** VERB (IMPERFECT **blieb zusammen**, PERFECT **sind zusammengeblieben**)
to stay together

**zusammenbrechen** VERB (PRESENT **bricht zusammen**, IMPERFECT **brach zusammen**, PERFECT **ist zusammengebrochen**)
[1] to collapse ◊ *Das Gebäude ist zusammengebrochen.* The building collapsed.
[2] to break down ◊ *Als sie von seinem Tod erfuhr, ist sie zusammengebrochen.* When she heard of his death she broke down.

**zusammenfassen** VERB (PERFECT **hat zusammengefasst**)
to summarize ◊ *Sie fasste das Gesagte noch einmal kurz zusammen.* She briefly summarized once again what had been said.

die **Zusammenfassung** NOUN
summary

der **Zusammenhang** NOUN (PL die **Zusammenhänge**)
connection ◊ *Gibt es einen Zusammenhang zwischen diesen Ereignissen?* Is there a connection between these events?
♦ **im Zusammenhang mit** in connection with ◊ *Zwei Männer wurden im Zusammenhang mit dem Mord verhört.* Two men were questioned in connection with the murder.
♦ **aus dem Zusammenhang** out of context ◊ *Du hast mich aus dem Zusammenhang zitiert.* You've quoted me out of context.

**zusammenhängen** VERB (IMPERFECT **hing zusammen**, PERFECT **hat zusammengehangen**)
to be connected ◊ *Die beiden Ereignisse hängen miteinander zusammen.* The two events are connected.

**zusammenkommen** VERB (IMPERFECT **kam zusammen**, PERFECT **ist zusammengekommen**)
[1] to meet up ◊ *Früher sind wir öfter zusammengekommen.* We used to meet up more often.
[2] to come together ◊ *Es ist alles zusammengekommen.* Everything came together.

**zusammenlegen** VERB (PERFECT **hat zusammengelegt**)
[1] to fold ◊ *Sie legte die Wäsche zusammen.* She folded the washing.
[2] to merge ◊ *Die beiden Klassen sollen zusammengelegt werden.* The two classes are to be merged.
[3] to combine ◊ *Wir können unsere Geburtstagspartys doch zusammenlegen.* We can combine our birthday parties.
[4] to club together ◊ *Wir haben zusammengelegt und ihr eine CD gekauft.* We clubbed together and bought her a CD.

**zusammennehmen** VERB (PRESENT **nimmt zusammen**, IMPERFECT **nahm zusammen**, PERFECT **hat zusammengenommen**)
to summon up ◊ *Ich musste meinen ganzen Mut zusammennehmen.* I had to summon up all my courage.
♦ **alles zusammengenommen** all in all
♦ **sich zusammennehmen** to pull oneself together

**zusammenpassen** VERB (PERFECT **hat zusammengepasst**)
[1] to be well suited ◊ *Die beiden passen gut zusammen.* The two are well suited.
[2] to go together ◊ *Der Pulli und die Hose passen nicht zusammen.* The pullover and the trousers don't go together.

**zusammenschreiben** VERB (IMPERFECT **schrieb zusammen**, PERFECT **hat zusammengeschrieben**)
♦ **Schreibt man dieses Wort zusammen oder auseinander?** Is this written as one word or two?

das **Zusammensein** NOUN
get-together ◊ *ein gemütliches Zusammensein* a cosy get-together

**zusammenstellen** VERB (PERFECT **hat zusammengestellt**)
[1] to put together ◊ *Stellt alle Stühle zusammen.* Put all the chairs together.
[2] to compile ◊ *Ich habe eine Wunschliste zusammengestellt.* I've compiled a list of presents I'd like.

der **Zusammenstoß** NOUN (GEN des **Zusammenstoßes**, PL die **Zusammenstöße**)
collision

**zusammenstoßen** VERB (PRESENT **stößt zusammen**, IMPERFECT **stieß zusammen**, PERFECT **sind zusammengestoßen**)
to collide

**zusammenzählen** VERB (PERFECT **hat zusammengezählt**)
to add up

**zusätzlich** ADJECTIVE, ADVERB
[1] additional ◊ *Wir sollen eine zusätzliche Englischstunde bekommen.* We're to get an additional English lesson.
[2] in addition ◊ *Zusätzlich zu den Matheaufgaben muss ich noch Physik machen.* I still have some physics to do in addition to my maths homework.

**zuschauen** VERB (PERFECT **hat zugeschaut**)
to watch ◊ *Habt ihr beim Match zugeschaut?* Did you watch the match?

die **Zuschauer** MASC PL NOUN
audience ◊ *Die Zuschauer haben geklatscht.* The audience clapped.

**Z**

**zuschicken** VERB (PERFECT **hat zugeschickt**)
- **jemandem etwas zuschicken** to send somebody something ◊ *Wir werden Ihnen unseren Katalog zuschicken.* We'll send you our catalogue.

der **Zuschlag** NOUN (PL die **Zuschläge**)
surcharge ◊ *Für den ICE brauchst du einen Zuschlag.* You have to pay a surcharge if you go by Intercity Express.

**zuschlagpflichtig** ADJECTIVE
subject to a surcharge ◊ *Der ICE ist zuschlagpflichtig.* The Intercity Express is subject to a surcharge.

**zusehen** VERB (PRESENT **sieht zu**, IMPERFECT **sah zu**, PERFECT **hat zugesehen**)
to watch ◊ *Wir haben beim Match zugesehen.* We watched the match. ◊ *Er stand nur dabei und sah zu.* He just stood there watching.
- **jemandem zusehen** to watch somebody ◊ *Ich habe ihr dabei zugesehen, wie sie ihr Zimmer aufräumte.* I watched her tidy up her room.
- **zusehen, dass etwas gemacht wird** to make sure something is done ◊ *Sieh zu, dass die Kinder früh ins Bett kommen.* Make sure that the children go to bed early.

**zusenden** VERB (IMPERFECT **sendete** *or* **sandte zu**, PERFECT **hat zugesendet** *or* **zugesandt**)
to send ◊ *Wir werden Ihnen unseren Prospekt zusenden.* We'll send you our brochure.

der **Zustand** NOUN (PL die **Zustände**)
[1] state ◊ *Das Haus war in einem furchtbaren Zustand.* The house was in an awful state. ◊ *Das sind hier ja schreckliche Zustände.* This is a terrible state of affairs.
[2] condition ◊ *Das Auto ist noch in gutem Zustand.* The car's still in good condition.

**zustande** ADVERB
- **zustande bringen** to bring about
- **zustande kommen** to come about

**zuständig** ADJECTIVE
- **Dafür bin ich nicht zuständig.** That's not my responsibility.
- **der zuständige Beamte** the official in charge

**zustimmen** VERB (PERFECT **hat zugestimmt**)
to agree ◊ *Ich stimme dir zu.* I agree with you.

die **Zustimmung** NOUN
[1] consent ◊ *Du brauchst die Zustimmung deiner Eltern.* You need your parents' consent.
[2] approval ◊ *wenn das deine Zustimmung findet* if that meets with your approval

**zustoßen** VERB (PRESENT **stößt zu**, IMPERFECT **stieß zu**, PERFECT **ist zugestoßen**)
to happen ◊ *Ihm ist doch hoffentlich nichts zugestoßen.* Let's hope nothing's happened to him.

die **Zutaten** FEM PL NOUN
ingredients

**zutreffen** VERB (PRESENT **trifft zu**, IMPERFECT **traf zu**, PERFECT **hat zugetroffen**)
[1] to be true ◊ *Es trifft nicht zu, dass ich das Buch mitgenommen habe.* It's not true that I took the book with me.
[2] to apply ◊ *Diese Beschreibung trifft nicht auf sie zu.* This description doesn't apply to her.

**zutreffend** ADJECTIVE
- **Zutreffendes bitte unterstreichen.** Please underline where applicable.

**zuverlässig** ADJECTIVE
reliable

**zuversichtlich** ADJECTIVE
confident

**zuviel** ADVERB *see* **viel**

**zuvor** ADVERB
before ◊ *der Tag zuvor* the day before

**zuwenig** ADVERB *see* **wenig**

**zuwider** ADVERB
- **Spinnen sind mir zuwider.** I detest spiders.

**zuziehen** VERB (IMPERFECT **zog zu**, PERFECT **hat zugezogen**)
[1] to draw ◊ *Es wird dunkel, zieh bitte die Vorhänge zu.* It's getting dark, please draw the curtains.
[2] to call in ◊ *Wir sollten einen Fachmann zuziehen.* We should call in an expert.
- **sich etwas zuziehen** to catch something ◊ *Ich habe mir eine Erkältung zugezogen.* I've caught a cold.

**zuzüglich** PREPOSITION
*The preposition zuzüglich takes the genitive.*
plus ◊ *zweihundert Mark zuzüglich der Spesen* two hundred marks plus expenses

der **Zwang** NOUN (PL die **Zwänge**)
compulsion

**zwängen** VERB
to squeeze

**zwanglos** ADJECTIVE
informal ◊ *ein zwangloses Gespräch* an informal talk

**zwanzig** NUMBER
twenty

**zwar** ADVERB
although ◊ *Ich habe das zwar gesagt, aber es war nicht so gemeint.* Although I said it, it wasn't meant like that.
- **das ist zwar ..., aber ...** that may be ... but ... ◊ *Das ist zwar viel, aber mir reicht es nicht.* That may be a lot, but it's not enough for me.

◆ **Sie ist zwar klug, aber diesmal hat sie Unrecht.** She may be clever, but she's wrong this time.

◆ **und zwar am Sonntag** on Sunday to be precise

◆ **und zwar so schnell, dass ...** in fact, so quickly that ...

der **Zweck** NOUN (PL die **Zwecke**)

  ☐1 purpose ◊ *Was ist der Zweck Ihres Besuchs?* What's the purpose of your visit?

  ☐2 point ◊ *Was ist der Zweck dieser Übung?* What's the point of this exercise? ◊ *Es hat keinen Zweck.* There's no point.

**zwecklos** ADJECTIVE

  pointless

**zwei** NUMBER

  | see also **die Zwei** NOUN |

  two

die **Zwei** NOUN

  | see also **zwei** NUMBER |

  ☐1 two

  ☐2 good

> ❶ *German marks range from one (**sehr gut**) to six (**ungenügend**).*

**zweideutig** ADJECTIVE

  ☐1 ambiguous ◊ *Sie hat sich zweideutig ausgedrückt.* She expressed herself very ambiguously.

  ☐2 suggestive ◊ *Er macht immer so zweideutige Witze.* He's always making such suggestive jokes.

**zweierlei** ADJECTIVE

◆ **zweierlei Stoff** two different kinds of material

◆ **Das sind doch zweierlei Dinge.** They're two different things.

◆ **zweierlei Meinung** of differing opinions

**zweifach** ADJECTIVE, ADVERB

  ☐1 double ◊ *die zweifache Menge* double the quantity

  ☐2 twice ◊ *Der Brief war zweifach gefaltet.* The letter had been folded twice.

der **Zweifel** NOUN (PL die **Zweifel**)

  doubt ◊ *ohne Zweifel* without doubt

**zweifelhaft** ADJECTIVE

  ☐1 doubtful ◊ *Es ist noch zweifelhaft, ob wir kommen.* It's still doubtful whether we're coming.

  ☐2 dubious ◊ *eine zweifelhafte Lösung* a dubious solution

◆ **ein zweifelhaftes Kompliment** a backhanded compliment

**zweifellos** ADVERB

  doubtless

◆ **Sie hat sich zweifellos bemüht.** There's no doubt that she tried.

**zweifeln** VERB

◆ **an etwas zweifeln** to doubt something ◊ *Ich zweifle an der Richtigkeit dieser Aussage.* I doubt the truth of this statement.

◆ **zweifeln, ob** to doubt whether ◊ *Ich zweifle, ob wir das schaffen.* I doubt whether we'll make it.

der **Zweig** NOUN (PL die **Zweige**)

  branch

die **Zweigstelle** NOUN

  branch ◊ *Die nächste Zweigstelle ist in Villach.* The nearest branch is in Villach.

**zweihundert** NUMBER

  two hundred

**zweimal** ADVERB

  twice

**zweisprachig** ADJECTIVE

  bilingual

**zweispurig** ADJECTIVE

  two-lane

**zweit** ADVERB

◆ **zu zweit (1)** together ◊ *Wir fahren zu zweit in die Ferien.* We're going on holiday together.

◆ **zu zweit (2)** in twos ◊ *Stellt euch zu zweit auf.* Line up in twos.

**zweitbeste** ADJECTIVE

  second best

**zweite** ADJECTIVE

  second ◊ *Er kam als Zweiter.* He was the second to arrive.

**zweitens** ADVERB

  secondly

**zweitgrößte** ADJECTIVE

  second largest

**zweitklassig** ADJECTIVE

  inferior

**zweitletzte** ADJECTIVE

  last but one ◊ *Er ging als Zweitletzter durchs Ziel.* He was last but one to cross the finishing line.

der **Zwerg** NOUN (PL die **Zwerge**)

  dwarf

die **Zwetschge** NOUN

  damson

der **Zwieback** NOUN (PL die **Zwiebacke**)

  rusk

die **Zwiebel** NOUN

  onion ◊ *Sebastian mag keine Zwiebeln.* Sebastian doesn't like onions.

der **Zwilling** NOUN (PL die **Zwillinge**)

  twin ◊ *Diese Zwillinge sehen sich zum Verwechseln ähnlich.* The twins are the spitting image of each other.

◆ **Zwillinge** Gemini ◊ *Michael ist Zwilling.* Michael's Gemini.

**zwingen** VERB (IMPERFECT **zwang**, PERFECT **hat gezwungen**)

  to force

**zwinkern** VERB

**Z**

☞

to wink ◊ *Als sie das sagte, zwinkerte er wissend*. When she said that he winked knowingly.

**zwischen** PREPOSITION

*Use the accusative to express movement or a change of place. Use the dative when there is no change of place.*

between ◊ *Er stand zwischen den beiden Mädchen.* He was standing between the two girls. ◊ *Stell deinen Stuhl zwischen unsere.* Put your chair between ours.

das **Zwischending** NOUN

cross ◊ *Das ist ein Zwischending zwischen Schreibmaschine und Computer.* It's a cross between a typewriter and a computer.

**zwischendurch** ADVERB

in between ◊ *Wir haben zwischendurch eine Pause gemacht.* We had a break in between.

der **Zwischenfall** NOUN (PL die **Zwischenfälle**)

incident

die **Zwischenfrage** NOUN

question

die **Zwischenlandung** NOUN

stopover

**zwischenmenschlich** ADJECTIVE

interpersonal ◊ *zwischenmenschliche Beziehungen* interpersonal relationships

**zwitschern** VERB

to chirp

**zwölf** NUMBER

twelve

**Zypern** NEUT NOUN

Cyprus

◆ **aus Zypern** from Cyprus

◆ **nach Zypern** to Cyprus

# GERMAN IN ACTION

# PUZZLES AND WORDGAMES

The wordgames on the following pages have been designed to give you practic
in using your dictionary. Make sure you read the "Dictionary Skills" section at th
front of this book before you start. Don't worry, there are answers at the end o
the wordgames in case you get really stuck!

## WORDGAME 1

### ▶ CHOOSING THE RIGHT TRANSLATION ◀

Complete the crossword below by looking up the English words in the list and
finding the correct German translations. There is a slight catch, however! All the
English words have more than one German translation, but only one will fi
correctly into the crossword. Beside each English word we have given you a clue
telling you whether the correct translation is a noun, adjective, adverb or verb.

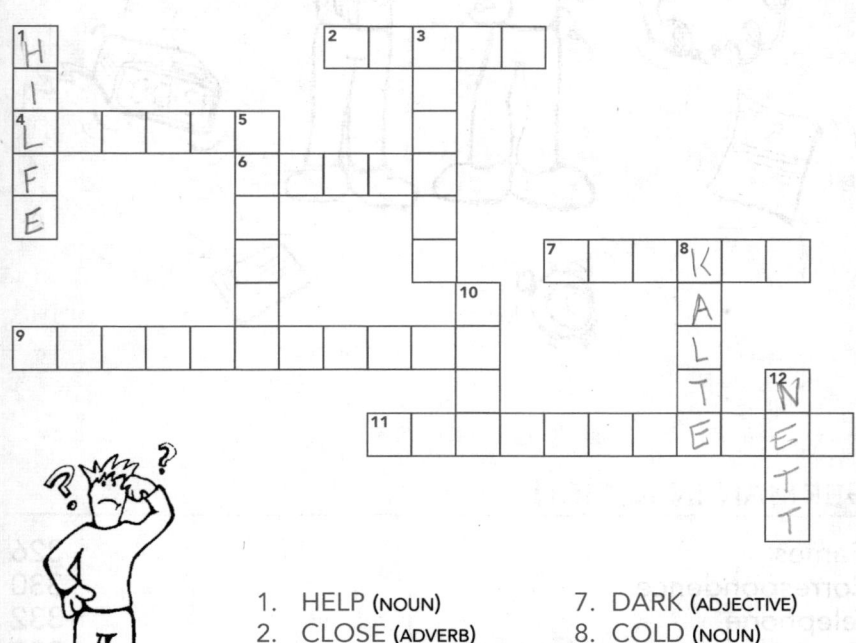

1. HELP (NOUN)
2. CLOSE (ADVERB)
3. ALONE (ADVERB)
4. LIGHT (ADJECTIVE)
5. KICK (VERB)
6. ROLL (NOUN)

7. DARK (ADJECTIVE)
8. COLD (NOUN)
9. ALTERNATIVE (NOUN)
10. EMPTY (ADJECTIVE)
11. DELAY (VERB)
12. KIND (ADJECTIVE)

# WORDGAME 2a + 2b

## ► NOUNS ◄

a. This list contains the singular form of some German nouns. Use your dictionary to find the plural form. Remember that the plural may appear separately, or it may be shown in the same entry as the singular form. Don't forget, if the plural form is regular, it won't be shown in the dictionary.

b. Use your dictionary to find the genitive of the following nouns. If it is irregular, the genitive form appears in brackets and in bold on the line below the singular form. Remember that if the genitive form is regular, it won't be shown in the dictionary.

| SINGULAR | PLURAL |
|---|---|
| das Haus | |
| der Garten | |
| das Pferd | |
| die Freundin | |
| das Abendessen | |
| das Abonnement | |
| die Frau | |
| der Gast | |
| die Fahrt | |
| der Mann | |

| SINGULAR | GENITIVE |
|---|---|
| der Arzt | |
| der Bär | |
| die Hose | |
| das Kind | |
| der Laden | |
| der Herr | |
| die Maus | |
| der August | |
| die Bluse | |
| der Astronaut | |

# WORDGAME 3

## ▶ VERB TENSES ◀

Use the German verb tables on pages 344 to 356 to help you fill in the blanks in the table below.

| INFINITIVE | PRESENT | IMPERFECT | PERFECT | FUTURE |
|---|---|---|---|---|
| machen | | | | du |
| gehen | | er | | |
| | ihr habt | | | |
| lesen | du | | | |
| fahren | | | wir | |
| beginnen | | | | ich |
| essen | er | | | |
| können | | | ich | |
| | | | sie hat geholfen | |
| schwimmen | | | er | |
| tun | | es | | |
| sprechen | | | | er |
| nehmen | | ich | | |
| wollen | ich | | | |
| | | wir standen | | |

# ▶ ANSWERS ◀

## WORDGAME 1

1. Hilfe
2. knapp
3. allein
4. leicht
5. treten
6. Rolle
7. dunkel
8. Kälte
9. Alternative
10. leer
11. verschieben
12. nett

## WORDGAME 2a

*Plural forms*
1. die Häuser
2. die Gärten
3. die Pferde
4. die Freundinnen
5. die Abendessen
6. die Abonnements
7. die Frauen
8. die Gäste
9. die Fahrten
10. die Männer

## WORDGAME 2b

*Genitive forms*
1. des Arztes
2. des Bären
3. der Hose
4. des Kinds *or*
   des Kindes
5. des Ladens
6. des Herrn
7. der Maus
8. des August *or*
   des Augustes
9. der Bluse
10. des Astronauten

## WORDGAME 3

1. du wirst machen
2. er ging
3. haben
4. du liest
5. wir sind gefahren
6. ich werde beginnen
7. er isst
8. ich habe gekonnt
9. helfen
10. er ist geschwommen
11. es tat
12. er wird sprechen
13. ich nahm
14. ich will
15. stehen

# CORRESPONDENCE

## ▶ LETTER

München, 15 Mai 2001

**Place & Date**

Liebe Oma und Opa!

Vielen Dank für die CDs, die ihr mir zum Geburtstag geschickt habt. Sie sind von zwei meiner Lieblingsgruppen, und ich höre sie mir sehr gerne an.

Ansonsten gibt es nicht viel Neues. Die meiste Zeit lerne ich für die Prüfungen, die in zwei Wochen beginnen. Ich hoffe, dass ich alle bestehe. Nur vor der Matheprüfung graut es mir, denn in Mathe bin ich gar nicht gut.

Mutti erzählte mir, dass ihr nächste Woche nach England in den Urlaub fahrt. Ich wünsche euch schöne und erholsame Tage dort.

Herzliche Grüße von eurer

Franziska

**Or:**
Viele liebe Grüße von ...
Alles Liebe, eure ...

## STARTING A PERSONAL LETTER

**Vielen Dank für deinen Brief ...**
**Ich habe mich sehr gefreut, von dir zu hören.**
**Es tut mir Leid, dass ich nicht früher geschrieben habe.**

*Thanks for your letter ...*
*It is lovely to hear from you.*
*Sorry I haven't written sooner.*

## ENDING A PERSONAL LETTER

**Bitte antworte bald!**
**Viele Grüße an ...**
**... lässt vielmals grüßen.**

*Write soon!*
*Give my love to ...*
*... sends his/her best wishes.*

# CORRESPONDENCE

## ► EMAIL

To give your email address to
someone in German, say:
**"claudia at n t online Punkt d e"**

---

| | **Neue Nachricht** |
|---|---|
| An: | claudia@nt-online.de |
| Von: | susan@comp.net |
| Betreff: | Konzert am 11.2. |
| cc: | gernhausen@intercom.de |
| bcc: | |

Anhang        Senden

---

Hallo alle zusammen!

Ich habe gerade das neue Album von "Rockstar" gekauft. Es ist
absolute Spitze. Ich habe noch zwei Karten extra bekommen,
für das Konzert, das "Rockstar" nächste Woche in Hamburg gibt.
Ich hoffe, ihr kommt beide mit.

Bis bald! Susan

---

| Neue Nachricht | New message |
|---|---|
| An | To |
| Von | From |
| Betreff | Subject |
| cc | cc |
| bcc | bcc |
| Anhang | Attachment |
| Senden | Send |

# TELEPHONE

## ▶ WHEN YOUR NUMBER ANSWERS

– **Guten Tag. Spreche ich mit Jenny?**
– Hello! Is that Jenny?

– **Könnte ich bitte mit Tom sprechen?**
– Could I speak to Tom, please?

– **Können Sie ihm bitte sagen, dass er mich anrufen soll.**
– Would you ask him to call me back?

## ▶ ANSWERING THE TELEPHONE

– **Guten Tag. Hier ist Susan.**　　　　– Hello! It's Susan speaking.

– **Am Apparat.**　　　　– Speaking.

– **Wer ist am Apparat, bitte?**　　　　– Who's speaking?

## ▶ WHEN THE SWITCHBOARD ANSWERS

– **Wer is am Apparat, bitte?**　　　　– Who shall I say is calling?

– **Ich verbinde Sie.**　　　　– I'm putting you through.

– **Bitte bleiben Sie am Apparat.**　　　　– Please hold.

– **Wollen Sie eine Nachricht hinterlassen?**　– Would you like to leave a message?

## ▶ DIFFICULTIES

– **Ich komme nicht durch.**
– I can't get through.

　　　　　　　– **Sie haben sich verwählt.**
　　　　　　　– I'm afraid you have the wrong number.

　　　　　　　– **Die Verbindung ist sehr schlecht.**
　　　　　　　– This is a very bad line.

　　　　　　　– **Ihr Telefon is kaputt.**
　　　　　　　– Their phone is out of order.

# NUMBERS

| | | | | | | |
|---|---|---|---|---|---|
| 1 | **eins** | 11 | **elf** | 21 | **einundzwanzig** |
| 2 | **zwei** | 12 | **zwölf** | 30 | **dreißig** |
| 3 | **drei** | 13 | **dreizehn** | 40 | **vierzig** |
| 4 | **vier** | 14 | **vierzehn** | 50 | **fünfzig** |
| 5 | **fünf** | 15 | **fünfzehn** | 60 | **sechzig** |
| 6 | **sechs** | 16 | **sechzehn** | 70 | **siebzig** |
| 7 | **sieben** | 17 | **siebzehn** | 80 | **achtzig** |
| 8 | **acht** | 18 | **achtzehn** | 90 | **neunzig** |
| 9 | **neun** | 19 | **neunzehn** | 100 | **hundert** |
| 10 | **zehn** | 20 | **zwanzig** | | |

| | | | |
|---|---|---|---|
| 101 | **hundert(und)eins** | 1,000 | **tausend** |
| 200 | **zweihundert** | 1,001 | **tausend(und)eins** |
| 201 | **zweihundert(und)eins** | 1,000,000 | **eine Million** |

## ▶ FRACTIONS etc

| | |
|---|---|
| 1/2 | **ein Halb** |
| 1/3 | **ein Drittel** |
| 1/4 | **ein Viertel** |
| 1/5 | **ein Fünftel** |
| 0.5 | **null Komma fünf (0,5)** |
| 3.4 | **drei Komma vier (3,4)** |
| 6.89 | **sechs Komma acht neun (6,89)** |
| 10% | **zehn Prozent** |
| 100% | **hundert Prozent** |

## ▶ EXAMPLES

| | |
|---|---|
| **auf Seite neunzehn** | on page nineteen |
| **im siebten Kapitel** | in chapter seven |
| **im Maßstab eins zu fünfundzwanzig** | on the scale of one to twenty-five |

# NUMBERS

| | | | |
|---|---|---|---|
| 1st | **erste (1.)** | 14th | **vierzehnte (14.)** |
| 2nd | **zweite (2.)** | 15th | **fünfzehnte (15.)** |
| 3rd | **dritte (3.)** | 16th | **sechzehnte (16.)** |
| 4th | **vierte (4.)** | 17th | **siebzehnte (17.)** |
| 5th | **fünfte (5.)** | 18th | **achtzehnte (18.)** |
| 6th | **sechste (6.)** | 19th | **neunzehnte (19.)** |
| 7th | **siebte (7.)** | 20th | **zwanzigste (20.)** |
| 8th | **achte (8.)** | 21st | **einundzwanzigste (21.)** |
| 9th | **neunte (9.)** | 30th | **dreißigste (30.)** |
| 10th | **zehnte (10.)** | 100th | **hundertste (100.)** |
| 11th | **elfte (11.)** | 101st | **hunderterste (101.)** |
| 12th | **zwölfte (12.)** | 1000th | **tausendste (1000.)** |
| 13th | **dreizehnte (13.)** | | |

**Horst war Erster**

▶ EXAMPLES

**er wohnt im fünften Stock**      he lives on the fifth floor
**er war Dritter**      he came in third
**ein Viertel des Kuchens**      a quarter of the cake

## ► WOCHENTAGE

**Montag**
**Dienstag**
**Mittwoch**
**Donnerstag**
**Freitag**
**Samstag**
**Sonntag**

### Wann?

**am Montag**
**montags**
**jeden Montag**
**letzten Dienstag**
**nächsten Freitag**
**Samstag in einer Woche**
**nächsten Samstag in zwei Wochen**

## ► DAYS OF THE WEEK

Monday
Tuesday
Wednesday
Thursday
Friday
Saturday
Sunday

### When?

on Monday
on Mondays
every Monday
last Tuesday
next Friday
a week on Saturday
two weeks on Saturday

## ► MONATE

**Januar**
**Februar**
**März**
**April**
**Mai**
**Juni**
**Juli**
**August**
**September**
**Oktober**
**November**
**Dezember**

### Wann?

**im Februar**
**am 1.** *or* **ersten Dezember 2001**
**zweitausendeins**

Was haben wir heute?
Heute ist...
**Montag, 26. Mai** *or*
  **Montag, der sechsundzwanzigste Mai**

## ► MONTHS OF THE YEAR

January
February
March
April
May
June
July
August
September
October
November
December

### When?

in February
on December 1st 2001
in two thousand and one

What day is it?
It's...
Monday, the 26th May *or*
  Monday, the twenty-sixth of May

# TIME

**Wie spät ist es?**

**Es ist...**

What time is it?
What's the time?
It's...

**Um wie viel Uhr?**  At what time?

**ein Uhr**

**zehn nach eins**

**Viertel nach eins**

**halb zwei**

**zwanzig vor zwei**

**Viertel vor zwei**

**um Mitternacht**

**um Mittag**

**um ein Uhr (nachmittags)**

**um acht Uhr (abends)**

*In Germany times are often given in the twenty-four hour clock.*

**um 11.15**
*or*
**elf Uhr fünfzehn**

**um 20.45**
*or*
**zwanzig Uhr fünfundvierzig**

## German ≠ English

### aktuell ≠ actual

| | | |
|---|---|---|
| ein **aktuelles** Thema | → | a **topical** issue |
| The film is based on **actual** events. | → | Der Film basiert auf **wirklichen** Begebenheiten. |

### also ≠ also

| | | |
|---|---|---|
| Was sollen wir **also** tun? | → | What shall we do, **then**? |
| My sister **also** came. | → | Meine Schwester ist **auch** gekommen. |

### Angel ≠ angel

| | | |
|---|---|---|
| Die **Angel** ist kaputt. | → | The **fishing rod** is broken. |
| She's an **angel**! | → | Sie ist ein **Engel**! |

### bekommen ≠ become

| | | |
|---|---|---|
| Was hast du zum Geburtstag **bekommen**? | → | What did you **get** for your birthday? |
| He wants to **become** a famous writer. | → | Er will ein berühmter Schriftsteller **werden**. |

### brav ≠ brave

| | | |
|---|---|---|
| Die Kinder waren **brav**. | → | The children were **good**. |
| Be **brave**! | → | Sei **mutig**! |

### Chips ≠ chips

| | | |
|---|---|---|
| Möchtet ihr **Chips**? | → | Would you like some **crisps**? |
| We bought some **chips**. | → | Wir haben **Pommes frites** gekauft. |

### eventuell ≠ eventual

| | | |
|---|---|---|
| **Eventuell** komme ich später nach. | → | **Perhaps** I'll come later. |
| **Eventually** he passed his driving test. | → | Er bestand **schließlich** die Fahrprüfung. |

## Fabrik ≠ fabric

Die **Fabrik** wird nächstes Jahr geschlossen. → The **factory** will be closed down next year.

400 metres of **fabric** → 400 Meter **Stoff**

## fast ≠ fast

Es ist **fast** Mitternacht. → It's **almost** midnight.

a **fast** car → ein **schnelles** Auto

## Flur ≠ floor

Der **Flur** muss sauber gemacht werden. → The **corridor** must be cleaned.

She is sitting on the **floor**. → Sie sitzt auf dem **Fußboden**.

## Fotograf ≠ photograph

Er ist **Fotograf**. → He is a **photographer**.

I took a **photograph**. → Ich habe ein **Foto** gemacht.

## Gift ≠ gift

Dieses **Gift** wirkt schnell. → This **poison** acts fast.

The necklace is a **gift** from my father. → Die Halskette ist ein **Geschenk** von meinem Vater.

## Hose ≠ hose

eine **Hose** → a **pair of trousers**

a garden **hose** → ein Garten**schlauch**

## Lektüre ≠ lecture

tör sie nicht bei der **Lektüre**. → Don't disturb her while she is **reading**.

e is giving a **lecture** at the art gallery. → Er hält einen **Vortrag** in der Kunstgalerie.

## Mappe ≠ map

Die Fotos sind in einer **Mappe**. → The photographs are in a **folder**.

road **map** → eine Straßen**karte**

## Meinung ≠ meaning

heiner **Meinung** nach → in my **opinion**

The **meaning** of this word is not clear. → Die **Bedeutung** dieses Wortes ist nicht klar.

## Mist ≠ mist

Du redest **Mist**. → You're talking **rubbish**.

horning **mist** → Morgen**nebel**

## Mörder ≠ murder

Er ist ein **Mörder**. → He's a **murderer**.

He has been charged with **murder**. → Er ist des **Mordes** angeklagt.

## Prospekt ≠ prospect

ein **Prospekt** mit Urlaubsreisen → a holiday **brochure**

t will improve my career **prospects**. → Das wird meine Berufs**aussichten** verbessern.

## Rente ≠ rent

Seine **Rente** reicht nicht aus. → His **pension** isn't enough.

I am behind with my **rent** this month. → Ich habe die **Miete** diesen Monat noch nicht bezahlt.

## schmal ≠ small

| | | |
|---|---|---|
| ein **schmaler** Durchgang | ⟶ | a **narrow** passageway |
| I have a **small** car. | ⟶ | Ich habe ein **kleines** Auto. |

## sensibel ≠ sensible

| | | |
|---|---|---|
| Sie ist ein sehr **sensibler** Mensch. | ⟶ | She's a very **sensitive** person. |
| Be **sensible**! | ⟶ | Sie **vernünftig**! |

## seriös ≠ serious

| | | |
|---|---|---|
| Er ist ein **seriöser** Geschäftsmann. | ⟶ | He is a **respectable** businessman. |
| Are you **serious**? | ⟶ | Ist das dein **Ernst**? |

## sparen ≠ spare

| | | |
|---|---|---|
| Wir müssen **sparen**. | ⟶ | We must **save**. |
| There's no room to **spare**. | ⟶ | Es ist kein Platz **übrig**. |

## sympathisch ≠ sympathetic

| | | |
|---|---|---|
| Er ist ein **sympatischer** Mensch. | ⟶ | He is a **likeable** person. |
| She is a **sympathetic** listener. | ⟶ | Sie hört **verständnisvoll** zu. |

## wer ≠ where

| | | |
|---|---|---|
| **Wer** ist das? | ⟶ | **Who** is that? |
| **Where** do you live? | ⟶ | **Wo** wohnst du? |

## wo ≠ who

| | | |
|---|---|---|
| **Wo** warst du? | ⟶ | **Where** were you? |
| **Who** said that? | ⟶ | **Wer** hat das gesagt? |

# GERMAN VERB TABLES

## CONTENTS

# GERMAN VERB TABLES

This section contains thirteen important German verbs that you need to learn. German verbs fall mainly into two categories – **regular** (weak) and **irregular** – and it is important to learn which verbs fall into which category.

At the top of each table you will find the infinitive, the imperative and the past participle, plus examples of how you might want to use the verb. The lower section of the tables shows you how to form six tenses of the verb:

| | |
|---|---|
| PRESENT | e.g. ich sage = **I say** *or* **I am saying** |
| IMPERFECT | e.g. ich sagte = **I was saying** *or* **I said** |
| PERFECT | e.g. ich habe gesagt = **I said** *or* **I have said** |
| FUTURE | e.g. ich werde sagen = **I will say** |
| CONDITIONAL | e.g. ich würde sagen = **I would say** |
| PRESENT SUBJUNCTIVE | e.g. ich sage = **I say** |

## ▶ REGULAR (WEAK) VERBS

German regular verbs follow a set pattern. Once you have learnt this pattern, you will be able to form *any* regular verb.

### HOW TO FORM A REGULAR VERB

i.  a) To form the present and imperfect tense, take the infinitive minus the last two letters.
     This is called the **stem** e.g. *machen* → **mach**
ii. Next add the appropriate **ending**. You need to ask yourself two questions:

   a) **Who** is doing the verb (ich, du, er *etc*)?
   b) **When** are they doing it (in the present, the past or the future)?

Look at the verb tables for **machen**. The endings can be tagged onto the stem of *any* regular verb.

## ▶ HABEN, SEIN AND WERDEN

**Haben** (to have) and **sein** (to be) are very important verbs which **must** be learnt. You use them to say "I have" *etc* or "I am" *etc*. The present tense of **haben** and **sein** are also used to form the **perfect tense**. In most cases, **haben** is used to form the perfect tense, but verbs of movement like **gehen** (to go) and **fahren** (to drive) use **sein** e.g. the German for "he has gone" is **er *ist* gegangen**, not **er *hat* gegangen**. You will have to learn which verbs use **sein**.

### HOW TO FORM THE PERFECT TENSE

a) Take the infinitive of a German verb e.g. **lachen**
b) Does it use **haben** or **sein** to form the perfect tense? **Lachen** uses **haben**
c) Take the present tense form of **haben** or **sein** that goes with the person who **did** the action e.g. **he** laughed – the German for "he" is **er**, so to form the perfect tense of **lachen** we use **er hat**

') Add the **past participle** – this is shown near the top of each verb table. If you want to form the past participle of *any* regular verb, simply take the infinitive of the verb, add **ge** to it, knock off the last two letters and add **t** e.g. **ge**lieb**t**, **ge**setz**t**. For a regular separable verb, add **ge** between the prefix and the stem, knock off the last two letters and add **t** e.g. ab**ge**hol**t**. In our example, **lachen** is a regular verb, so the past participle is ge + lach + t → **gelacht**.
) The German for "he laughed" is "**er hat gelacht**"

**Verden** (to become) is also used to form the **future tense**, and the conditional ense of **werden** is used in forming the **conditional tense** of *any* verb.

## HOW TO FORM THE FUTURE AND CONDITIONAL TENSES

) To form the future tense, take the present tense form of **werden** that goes with the person who **will do** the action e.g. **he** will speak – the German for "he" is **er**, so to form the future tense of **sprechen** we use **er wird**. To form the conditional tense – he would speak – take the conditional tense of **werden** for **er** – **er würde**
) Add the infinitive of the German verb e.g. **sprechen**
:) The German for "he will speak" is "**er wird sprechen**", and for "he would speak" is "**er würde sprechen**"

## ► IRREGULAR VERBS

Many German verbs are irregular and this means that you have to learn them individually. One type of irregular verb in German is the strong verb, which changes the vowel in the past tense and does not add **t** in the past participle e.g. **gehen - ging - gegangen**. There are tables showing different types of irregular verbs in this section, including several of the most important ones. When you are translating from German and meet an unfamiliar verb form, you may be able to guess from the context that it comes from one of these verbs, and you can use the verb table to check. The most common irregular verb parts are listed on the German side of the dictionary, so you could also look there.

## HOW TO USE THE VERB TABLES

You will find some useful example phrases at the top of each verb table, but if you can't find what you need to say or write in German there, use the verb table tself to help you. Imagine that you want to find the German for "he is going". Here's how to do it:

a) Look up **go** on the English-German side of the dictionary to find the German translation **gehen**
b) Turn to the verb table section of your dictionary and find **gehen**
c) When is he going? He is going **now**, so look for the heading *PRESENT*
d) Who is going? **He** is. The German for "he" is **er** so look for **er** under the *PRESENT* heading
e) The German for "he is going" is "**er geht**"

# GERMAN VERB TABLES

## ▶ machen

to do or to make

### IMPERATIVE

mach
macht
machen Sie

### EXAMPLE PHRASES

*Was* **machst** *du?* What are you doing?
*Ich* **habe** *die Betten* **gemacht**.
  I made the beds.
*Ich* **werde** *es morgen* **machen**.
  I'll do it tomorrow.

### PAST PARTICIPLE

gemacht

### PRESENT

| ich | mache |
|---|---|
| du | machst |
| er | macht |
| wir | machen |
| ihr | macht |
| sie | machen |

### PERFECT

| ich | habe gemacht |
|---|---|
| du | hast gemacht |
| er | hat gemacht |
| wir | haben gemacht |
| ihr | habt gemacht |
| sie | haben gemacht |

### FUTURE

| ich | werde machen |
|---|---|
| du | wirst machen |
| er | wird machen |
| wir | werden machen |
| ihr | werdet machen |
| sie | werden machen |

### IMPERFECT

| ich | machte |
|---|---|
| du | machtest |
| er | machte |
| wir | machten |
| ihr | machtet |
| sie | machten |

### CONDITIONAL

| ich | würde machen |
|---|---|
| du | würdest machen |
| er | würde machen |
| wir | würden machen |
| ihr | würdet machen |
| sie | würden machen |

### PRESENT SUBJUNCTIVE

| ich | mache |
|---|---|
| du | machest |
| er | mache |
| wir | machen |
| ihr | machet |
| sie | machen |

# GERMAN VERB TABLES

## ▶ wissen

to know

*EXAMPLE PHRASES*

*Ich* **weiß** *nicht.* I don't know.
*Er* **hat** *nichts davon* **gewusst.**
  He didn't know anything about it.
*Sie* **wussten**, *wo das Kino war.*
  They knew where the cinema was.

*IMPERATIVE*

wisse
wisset
wissen Sie

*PAST PARTICIPLE*

gewusst

---

*PRESENT*

| ich | weiß |
| du | weißt |
| er | weiß |
| wir | wissen |
| ihr | wisst |
| sie | wissen |

*PERFECT*

| ich | habe gewusst |
| du | hast gewusst |
| er | hat gewusst |
| wir | haben gewusst |
| ihr | habt gewusst |
| sie | haben gewusst |

*FUTURE*

| ich | werde wissen |
| du | wirst wissen |
| er | wird wissen |
| wir | werden wissen |
| ihr | werdet wissen |
| sie | werden wissen |

*IMPERFECT*

| ich | wusste |
| du | wusstest |
| er | wusste |
| wir | wussten |
| ihr | wusstet |
| sie | wussten |

*CONDITIONAL*

| ich | würde wissen |
| du | würdest wissen |
| er | würde wissen |
| wir | würden wissen |
| ihr | würdet wissen |
| sie | würden wissen |

*PRESENT SUBJUNCTIVE*

| ich | wisse |
| du | wissest |
| er | wisse |
| wir | wissen |
| ihr | wisset |
| sie | wissen |

# GERMAN VERB TABLES

## ► sich waschen

to wash (oneself)

*IMPERATIVE*

wasch dich
wascht euch
waschen Sie sich

*EXAMPLE PHRASES*

*Ich **habe mir** die Hände **gewaschen**.*
I washed my hands.
*Er **wäscht sich** jeden Tag.*
He washes every day.
*Die Katze **wusch sich** in der Sonne.*
The cat was washing itself in the
sunshine.

*PAST PARTICIPLE*

gewaschen

*PRESENT*

ich wasche mich
du wäschst dich
er wäscht sich
wir waschen uns
ihr wascht euch
sie waschen sich

*IMPERFECT*

ich wusch mich
du wuschest dich
er wusch sich
wir wuschen uns
ihr wuscht euch
sie wuschen sich

*PERFECT*

ich habe mich gewaschen
du hast dich gewaschen
er hat sich gewaschen
wir haben uns gewaschen
ihr habt euch gewaschen
sie haben sich gewaschen

*CONDITIONAL*

ich würde mich waschen
du würdest dich waschen
er würde sich waschen
wir würden uns waschen
ihr würdet euch waschen
sie würden sich waschen

*FUTURE*

ich werde mich waschen
du wirst dich waschen
er wird sich waschen
wir werden uns waschen
ihr werdet euch waschen
sie werden sich waschen

*PRESENT SUBJUNCTIVE*

ich wasche mich
du waschest dich
er wasche sich
wir waschen uns
ihr waschet euch
sie waschen sich

# GERMAN VERB TABLES

## ► aufstehen

to get up or to stand up

### EXAMPLE PHRASES

*Ich muss früh **aufstehen**.*
I have to get up early.
*Als er hereinkam, **stand** ich **auf**.*
I stood up when he entered.
*Die ganze Klasse **ist aufgestanden**.*
The whole class stood up.

### IMPERATIVE

steh auf
steht auf
stehen Sie auf

### PAST PARTICIPLE

aufgestanden

### PRESENT

| | |
|---|---|
| ich | stehe auf |
| du | stehst auf |
| er | steht auf |
| wir | stehen auf |
| ihr | steht auf |
| sie | stehen auf |

### IMPERFECT

| | |
|---|---|
| ich | stand auf |
| du | standst auf |
| er | stand auf |
| wir | standen auf |
| ihr | standet auf |
| sie | standen auf |

### PERFECT

| | |
|---|---|
| ich | bin aufgestanden |
| du | bist aufgestanden |
| er | ist aufgestanden |
| wir | sind aufgestanden |
| ihr | seid aufgestanden |
| sie | sind aufgestanden |

### CONDITIONAL

| | |
|---|---|
| ich | würde aufstehen |
| du | würdest aufstehen |
| er | würde aufstehen |
| wir | würden aufstehen |
| ihr | würdet aufstehen |
| sie | würden aufstehen |

### FUTURE

| | |
|---|---|
| ich | werde aufstehen |
| du | wirst aufstehen |
| er | wird aufstehen |
| wir | werden aufstehen |
| ihr | werdet aufstehen |
| sie | werden aufstehen |

### PRESENT SUBJUNCTIVE

| | |
|---|---|
| ich | stehe auf |
| du | stehest auf |
| er | stehe auf |
| wir | stehen auf |
| ihr | stehet auf |
| sie | stehen auf |

# GERMAN VERB TABLES

## ▶ können

can *or* to be able to

### EXAMPLE PHRASES

*Er* **kann** *gut schwimmen.* He can swim well.
*Sie* **konnte** *kein Wort Deutsch.* She couldn't speak a word of German.
**Kann** *ich gehen?* Can I go?

### PAST PARTICIPLE

gekonnt *or* können

### PRESENT

ich kann
du kannst
er kann
wir können
ihr könnt
sie können

### PERFECT

ich habe gekonnt
du hast gekonnt
er hat gekonnt
wir haben gekonnt
ihr habt gekonnt
sie haben gekonnt

### FUTURE

ich werde können
du wirst können
er wird können
wir werden können
ihr werdet können
sie werden können

### IMPERFECT

ich konnte
du konntest
er konnte
wir konnten
ihr konntet
sie konnten

### CONDITIONAL

ich könnte
du könntest
er könnte
wir könnten
ihr könntet
sie könnten

### PRESENT SUBJUNCTIVE

ich könne
du könnest
er könne
wir können
ihr könnet
sie können

# → müssen

*must or to have to*

*EXAMPLE PHRASES*

Ich **muss** *aufs Klo.* I must go to the loo.
*Wir* **müssen** *jeden Abend unsere Hausaufgaben machen.*
  We have to do our homework every night.
*Sie* **hat** *abwaschen* **müssen.** She had to wash up.

*PAST PARTICIPLE*

gemusst *or* müssen

---

*PRESENT*

| | |
|---|---|
| ich | muss |
| du | musst |
| er | muss |
| wir | müssen |
| ihr | müsst |
| sie | müssen |

*PERFECT*

| | |
|---|---|
| ich | habe gemusst |
| du | hast gemusst |
| er | hat gemusst |
| wir | haben gemusst |
| ihr | habt gemusst |
| sie | haben gemusst |

*FUTURE*

| | |
|---|---|
| ich | werde müssen |
| du | wirst müssen |
| er | wird müssen |
| wir | werden müssen |
| ihr | werdet müssen |
| sie | werden müssen |

*IMPERFECT*

| | |
|---|---|
| ich | musste |
| du | musstest |
| er | musste |
| wir | mussten |
| ihr | musstet |
| sie | mussten |

*CONDITIONAL*

| | |
|---|---|
| ich | müsste |
| du | müsstest |
| er | müsste |
| wir | müssten |
| ihr | müsstet |
| sie | müssten |

*PRESENT SUBJUNCTIVE*

| | |
|---|---|
| ich | müsse |
| du | müssest |
| er | müsse |
| wir | müssen |
| ihr | müsset |
| sie | müssen |

# GERMAN VERB TABLES

## ▶ fahren

to drive *or* to go

fahr
fahrt
fahren Sie

*EXAMPLE PHRASES*

*Sie **fahren** mit dem Bus in die Schule.*
They go to school by bus.
*Rechts **fahren**!* Drive on the right!
*Ich **bin** mit der Familie nach Spanien
**gefahren**.* I went to Spain with
my family.

*PAST PARTICIPLE*

gefahren

| *PRESENT* | *IMPERFECT* |
|---|---|
| ich fahre | ich fuhr |
| du fährst | du fuhrst |
| er fährt | er fuhr |
| wir fahren | wir fuhren |
| ihr fahrt | ihr fuhrt |
| sie fahren | sie fuhren |

| *PERFECT* | *CONDITIONAL* |
|---|---|
| ich bin gefahren | ich würde fahren |
| du bist gefahren | du würdest fahren |
| er ist gefahren | er würde fahren |
| wir sind gefahren | wir würden fahren |
| ihr seid gefahren | ihr würdet fahren |
| sie sind gefahren | sie würden fahren |

| *FUTURE* | *PRESENT SUBJUNCTIVE* |
|---|---|
| ich werde fahren | ich fahre |
| du wirst fahren | du fahrest |
| er wird fahren | er fahre |
| wir werden fahren | wir fahren |
| ihr werdet fahren | ihr fahret |
| sie werden fahren | sie fahren |

## gehen

to go

EXAMPLE PHRASES

Die Kinder **gingen** ins Haus.
The children went into the house.
Wie **geht** es dir? How are you?
Wir **sind** gestern schwimmen **gegangen**.
We went swimming yesterday.

IMPERATIVE

geh
geht
gehen Sie

PAST PARTICIPLE

gegangen

| PRESENT | | IMPERFECT *I went* | |
|---|---|---|---|
| ich | gehe | ich | ging |
| du | gehst | du | gingst |
| er | geht | er | ging |
| wir | gehen | wir | gingen |
| ihr | geht | ihr | gingt |
| sie | gehen | sie | gingen |

| PERFECT *I have gone* | | CONDITIONAL | |
|---|---|---|---|
| ich | bin gegangen | ich | würde gehen |
| du | bist gegangen | du | würdest gehen |
| er | ist gegangen | er | würde gehen |
| wir | sind gegangen | wir | würden gehen |
| ihr | seid gegangen | ihr | würdet gehen |
| sie | sind gegangen | sie | würden gehen |

| FUTURE | | PRESENT SUBJUNCTIVE | |
|---|---|---|---|
| ich | werde gehen | ich | gehe |
| du | wirst gehen | du | gehest |
| er | wird gehen | er | gehe |
| wir | werden gehen | wir | gehen |
| ihr | werdet gehen | ihr | gehet |
| sie | werden gehen | sie | gehen |

# GERMAN VERB TABLES

## ▶ kommen

to come

komm
kommt
kommen Sie

*EXAMPLE PHRASES*

*Er **kam** die Straße entlang.*
  He was coming along the street.
*Ich **komme** zu deiner Party.*
  I'm coming to your party.
*Woher **kommst** du?*
  Where do you come from?

*PAST PARTICIPLE*

gekommen

---

*PRESENT*

  ich komme
  du kommst
  er kommt
  wir kommen
  ihr kommt
  sie kommen

*PERFECT*

  ich bin gekommen
  du bist gekommen
  er ist gekommen
  wir sind gekommen
  ihr seid gekommen
  sie sind gekommen

*FUTURE*

  ich werde kommen
  du wirst kommen
  er wird kommen
  wir werden kommen
  ihr werdet kommen
  sie werden kommen

*IMPERFECT*

  ich kam
  du kamst
  er kam
  wir kamen
  ihr kamt
  sie kamen

*CONDITIONAL*

  ich würde kommen
  du würdest kommen
  er würde kommen
  wir würden kommen
  ihr würdet kommen
  sie würden kommen

*PRESENT SUBJUNCTIVE*

  ich komme
  du kommest
  er komme
  wir kommen
  ihr kommet
  sie kommen

## ➤ essen

o eat

*Ich* **esse** *kein Fleisch.* I don't eat meat.
*Wir* **haben** *nichts* **gegessen**.
 We haven't had anything to eat.
*Ich möchte was* **essen**.
 I'd like something to eat.

### IMPERATIVE

iss
esst
essen Sie

### PAST PARTICIPLE

gegessen

| PRESENT | | IMPERFECT | |
|---|---|---|---|
| ich | esse | ich | aß |
| du | isst | du | aßest |
| er | isst | er | aß |
| wir | essen | wir | aßen |
| ihr | esst | ihr | aßt |
| sie | essen | sie | aßen |

| PERFECT | | CONDITIONAL | |
|---|---|---|---|
| ich | habe gegessen | ich | würde essen |
| du | hast gegessen | du | würdest essen |
| er | hat gegessen | er | würde essen |
| wir | haben gegessen | wir | würden essen |
| ihr | habt gegessen | ihr | würdet essen |
| sie | haben gegessen | sie | würden essen |

| FUTURE | | PRESENT SUBJUNCTIVE | |
|---|---|---|---|
| ich | werde essen | ich | esse |
| du | wirst essen | du | essest |
| er | wird essen | er | esse |
| wir | werden essen | wir | essen |
| ihr | werdet essen | ihr | esset |
| sie | werden essen | sie | essen |

# GERMAN VERB TABLES

## ▶ haben

to have

### IMPERATIVE

hab
habt
haben Sie

### PAST PARTICIPLE

gehabt

### EXAMPLE PHRASES

**Hast** du eine Schwester?
 Have you got a sister?
Er **hatte** Hunger. He was hungry.
Ich **hätte** gern ein Eis.
 I'd like an ice cream.
Sie **hat** heute Geburtstag.
 It's her birthday today.

### PRESENT

ich habe
du hast
er hat
wir haben
ihr habt
sie haben

### PERFECT

ich habe gehabt
du hast gehabt
er hat gehabt
wir haben gehabt
ihr habt gehabt
sie haben gehabt

### FUTURE

ich werde haben
du wirst haben
er wird haben
wir werden haben
ihr werdet haben
sie werden haben

### IMPERFECT

ich hatte
du hattest
er hatte
wir hatten
ihr hattet
sie hatten

### CONDITIONAL

ich hätte
du hättest
er hätte
wir hätten
ihr hättet
sie hätten

### PRESENT SUBJUNCTIVE

ich habe
du habest
er habe
wir haben
ihr habet
sie haben

## sein

to be

Er **ist** zehn Jahre alt. He is ten years old.
Mir **ist** kalt. I'm cold.
Wir **waren** gestern im Theater.
We were at the theatre yesterday.
**Seid** ruhig! Be quiet!

*IMPERATIVE*

sei
seid
seien Sie

*PAST PARTICIPLE*

gewesen

| *PRESENT* | | | *IMPERFECT* | |
|---|---|---|---|---|
| ich | bin | | ich | war |
| du | bist | | du | warst |
| er | ist | | er | war |
| wir | sind | | wir | waren |
| ihr | seid | | ihr | wart |
| sie | sind | | sie | waren |

| *PERFECT* | | | *CONDITIONAL* | |
|---|---|---|---|---|
| ich | bin gewesen | | ich | wäre |
| du | bist gewesen | | du | wärst |
| er | ist gewesen | | er | wäre |
| wir | sind gewesen | | wir | wären |
| ihr | seid gewesen | | ihr | wärt |
| sie | sind gewesen | | sie | wären |

| *FUTURE* | | | *PRESENT SUBJUNCTIVE* | |
|---|---|---|---|---|
| ich | werde sein | | ich | sei |
| du | wirst sein | | du | seiest |
| er | wird sein | | er | sei |
| wir | werden sein | | wir | seien |
| ihr | werdet sein | | ihr | seiet |
| sie | werden sein | | sie | seien |

# GERMAN VERB TABLES

## ▶ werden

to become

*IMPERATIVE*

werde
werdet
werden Sie

*EXAMPLE PHRASES*

*Mir* **wird** *schlecht.* I feel ill.
*Ich will Lehrerin* **werden**.
 I want to be a teacher.
*Der Kuchen* **ist** *gut* **geworden**.
 The cake turned out well.

*PAST PARTICIPLE*

geworden

*PRESENT*

| ich | werde |
|---|---|
| du | wirst |
| er | wird |
| wir | werden |
| ihr | werdet |
| sie | werden |

*PERFECT*

| ich | bin geworden |
|---|---|
| du | bist geworden |
| er | ist geworden |
| wir | sind geworden |
| ihr | seid geworden |
| sie | sind geworden |

*FUTURE*

| ich | werde werden |
|---|---|
| du | wirst werden |
| er | wird werden |
| wir | werden werden |
| ihr | werdet werden |
| sie | werden werden |

*IMPERFECT*

| ich | wurde |
|---|---|
| du | wurdest |
| er | wurde |
| wir | wurden |
| ihr | wurdet |
| sie | wurden |

*CONDITIONAL*

| ich | würde werden |
|---|---|
| du | würdest werden |
| er | würde werden |
| wir | würden werden |
| ihr | würdet werden |
| sie | würden werden |

*PRESENT SUBJUNCTIVE*

| ich | werde |
|---|---|
| du | werdest |
| er | werde |
| wir | werden |
| ihr | werdet |
| sie | werden |

verbs which use 'sein'

| INFINITIVE | PRESENT INDICATIVE 2nd pers sing | ♦ 3rd pers sing | IMPERFECT INDICATIVE | PAST PARTICIPLE |
|---|---|---|---|---|
| backen | bäckst | ♦ bäckt | backte or buk | gebacken |
| befehlen | befiehlst | ♦ befiehlt | befahl | befohlen |
| beginnen | beginnst | ♦ beginnt | begann | begonnen |
| beißen | beißt | ♦ beißt | biss | gebissen |
| bewegen | bewegst | ♦ bewegt | bewog | bewogen |
| biegen | biegst | ♦ biegt | bog | gebogen |
| bieten | bietest | ♦ bietet | bot | geboten |
| binden | bindest | ♦ bindet | band | gebunden |
| bitten | bittest | ♦ bittet | bat | gebeten |
| blasen | bläst | ♦ bläst | blies | geblasen |
| bleiben* | bleibst | ♦ bleibt | blieb | geblieben |
| braten | brätst | ♦ brät | briet | gebraten |
| brechen* | brichst | ♦ bricht | brach | gebrochen |
| brennen | brennst | ♦ brennt | brannte | gebrannt |
| bringen | bringst | ♦ bringt | brachte | gebracht |
| denken | denkst | ♦ denkt | dachte | gedacht |
| dringen* | dringst | ♦ dringt | drang | gedrungen |
| dürfen | darfst | ♦ darf | durfte | gedurft |
| empfangen | empfängst | ♦ empfängt | empfing | empfangen |
| empfehlen | empfiehlst | ♦ empfiehlt | empfahl | empfohlen |
| erschrecken* | erschrickst | ♦ erschrickt | erschrak | erschrocken |
| essen | isst | ♦ isst | aß | gegessen |
| fahren* | fährst | ♦ fährt | fuhr | gefahren |
| fallen* | fällst | ♦ fällt | fiel | gefallen |
| fangen | fängst | ♦ fängt | fing | gefangen |
| fechten | fichtst | ♦ ficht | focht | gefochten |
| finden | findest | ♦ findet | fand | gefunden |
| flechten | flichtst | ♦ flicht | flocht | geflochten |
| fliegen* | fliegst | ♦ fliegt | flog | geflogen |
| fliehen* | fliehst | ♦ flieht | floh | geflohen |
| fließen* | fließt | ♦ fließt | floss | geflossen |
| fressen | frisst | ♦ frisst | fraß | gefressen |
| frieren | frierst | ♦ friert | fror | gefroren |
| gebären | gebierst | ♦ gebiert | gebar | geboren |
| geben | gibst | ♦ gibt | gab | gegeben |
| gedeihen* | gedeihst | ♦ gedeiht | gedieh | gediehen |
| gehen* | gehst | ♦ geht | ging | gegangen |
| gelingen* | - | ♦ gelingt | gelang | gelungen |
| gelten | giltst | ♦ gilt | galt | gegolten |

| INFINITIVE | PRESENT INDICATIVE 2nd pers sing ♦ 3rd pers sing | | IMPERFECT INDICATIVE | PAST PARTICIPLE |
|---|---|---|---|---|
| genießen | genießt | ♦ genießt | genoss | genossen |
| geraten* | gerätst | ♦ gerät | geriet | geraten |
| geschehen* | - | ♦ geschieht | geschah | geschehen |
| gewinnen | gewinnst | ♦ gewinnt | gewann | gewonnen |
| gießen | gießt | ♦ gießt | goss | gegossen |
| gleichen | gleichst | ♦ gleicht | glich | geglichen |
| gleiten* | gleitest | ♦ gleitet | glitt | geglitten |
| graben | gräbst | ♦ gräbt | grub | gegraben |
| greifen | greifst | ♦ greift | griff | gegriffen |
| haben | hast | ♦ hat | hatte | gehabt |
| halten | hältst | ♦ hält | hielt | gehalten |
| hängen | hängst | ♦ hängt | hing | gehangen |
| hauen | haust | ♦ haut | hieb | gehauen |
| heben | hebst | ♦ hebt | hob | gehoben |
| heißen | heißt | ♦ heißt | hieß | geheißen |
| helfen | hilfst | ♦ hilft | half | geholfen |
| kennen | kennst | ♦ kennt | kannte | gekannt |
| klingen | klingst | ♦ klingt | klang | geklungen |
| kneifen | kneifst | ♦ kneift | kniff | gekniffen |
| kommen* | kommst | ♦ kommt | kam | gekommen |
| können | kannst | ♦ kann | konnte | gekonnt |
| kriechen* | kriechst | ♦ kriecht | kroch | gekrochen |
| laden | lädst | ♦ lädt | lud | geladen |
| lassen | lässt | ♦ lässt | ließ | gelassen |
| laufen* | läufst | ♦ läuft | lief | gelaufen |
| leiden | leidest | ♦ leidet | litt | gelitten |
| leihen | leihst | ♦ leiht | lieh | geliehen |
| lesen | liest | ♦ liest | las | gelesen |
| liegen* | liegst | ♦ liegt | lag | gelegen |
| lügen | lügst | ♦ lügt | log | gelogen |
| mahlen | mahlst | ♦ mahlt | mahlte | gemahlen |
| meiden | meidest | ♦ meidet | mied | gemieden |
| messen | misst | ♦ misst | maß | gemessen |
| misslingen* | - | ♦ misslingt | misslang | misslungen |
| mögen | magst | ♦ mag | mochte | gemocht |
| müssen | musst | ♦ muss | musste | gemusst |
| nehmen | nimmst | ♦ nimmt | nahm | genommen |
| nennen | nennst | ♦ nennt | nannte | genannt |
| pfeifen | pfeifst | ♦ pfeift | pfiff | gepfiffen |
| raten | rätst | ♦ rät | riet | geraten |
| reiben | reibst | ♦ reibt | rieb | gerieben |
| reißen* | reißt | ♦ reißt | riss | gerissen |

| INFINITIVE | PRESENT INDICATIVE 2nd pers sing | ♦ 3rd pers sing | IMPERFECT INDICATIVE | PAST PARTICIPLE |
|---|---|---|---|---|
| **reiten*** | reitest | ♦ reitet | ritt | geritten |
| **rennen*** | rennst | ♦ rennt | rannte | gerannt |
| **riechen** | riechst | ♦ riecht | roch | gerochen |
| **ringen** | ringst | ♦ ringt | rang | gerungen |
| **rufen** | rufst | ♦ ruft | rief | gerufen |
| **salzen** | salzt | ♦ salzt | salzte | gesalzen |
| **saufen** | säufst | ♦ säuft | soff | gesoffen |
| **saugen** | saugst | ♦ saugt | sog | gesogen or gesaugt |
| **schaffen** | schaffst | ♦ schafft | schuf | geschaffen |
| **scheiden*** | scheidest | ♦ scheidet | schied | geschieden |
| **scheinen** | scheinst | ♦ scheint | schien | geschienen |
| **scheißen** | scheißt | ♦ scheißt | schiss | geschissen |
| **scheren** | scherst | ♦ schert | schor | geschoren |
| **schieben** | schiebst | ♦ schiebt | schob | geschoben |
| **schießen** | schießt | ♦ schießt | schoss | geschossen |
| **schlafen** | schläfst | ♦ schläft | schlief | geschlafen |
| **schlagen** | schlägst | ♦ schlägt | schlug | geschlagen |
| **schleichen*** | schleichst | ♦ scheicht | schlich | geschlichen |
| **schließen** | schließt | ♦ schließt | schloss | geschlossen |
| **schmeißen** | schmeißt | ♦ schmeißt | schmiss | geschmissen |
| **schmelzen*** | schmilzt | ♦ schmilzt | schmolz | geschmolzen |
| **schneiden** | schneidest | ♦ schneidet | schnitt | geschnitten |
| **schreiben** | schreibst | ♦ schreibt | schrieb | geschrieben |
| **schreien** | schreist | ♦ schreit | schrie | geschrien |
| **schweigen** | schweigst | ♦ schweigt | schwieg | geschwiegen |
| **schwimmen*** | schwimmst | ♦ schwimmt | schwamm | geschwommen |
| **schwingen** | schwingst | ♦ schwingt | schwang | geschwungen |
| **schwören** | schwörst | ♦ schwört | schwor | geschworen |
| **sehen** | siehst | ♦ sieht | sah | gesehen |
| **sein*** | bist | ♦ ist | war | gewesen |
| **senden** | sendest | ♦ sendet | sandte | gesandt |
| **singen** | singst | ♦ singt | sang | gesungen |
| **sinken*** | sinkst | ♦ sinkt | sank | gesunken |
| **sitzen*** | sitzt | ♦ sitzt | saß | gesessen |
| **sollen** | sollst | ♦ soll | sollte | gesollt |
| **speien** | speist | ♦ speit | spie | gespie(e)n |
| **spinnen** | spinnst | ♦ spinnt | spann | gesponnen |
| **sprechen** | sprichst | ♦ spricht | sprach | gesprochen |
| **springen*** | springst | ♦ springt | sprang | gesprungen |
| **stechen** | stichst | ♦ sticht | stach | gestochen |
| **stecken** | steckst | ♦ steckt | steckte or stak | gesteckt |
| **stehen** | stehst | ♦ steht | stand | gestanden |

| INFINITIVE | PRESENT INDICATIVE 2nd pers sing | ♦ 3rd pers sing | IMPERFECT INDICATIVE | PAST PARTICIPLE |
|---|---|---|---|---|
| **stehlen** | stiehlst | ♦ stiehlt | stahl | gestohlen |
| **steigen*** | steigst | ♦ steigt | stieg | gestiegen |
| **sterben*** | stirbst | ♦ stirbt | starb | gestorben |
| **stinken** | stinkst | ♦ stinkt | stank | gestunken |
| **stoßen** | stößt | ♦ stößt | stieß | gestoßen |
| **streichen** | streichst | ♦ streicht | strich | gestrichen |
| **streiten** | streitest | ♦ streitet | stritt | gestritten |
| **tragen** | trägst | ♦ trägt | trug | getragen |
| **treffen** | triffst | ♦ trifft | traf | getroffen |
| **treiben*** | treibst | ♦ treibt | trieb | getrieben |
| **treten*** | trittst | ♦ tritt | trat | getreten |
| **trinken** | trinkst | ♦ trinkt | trank | getrunken |
| **trügen** | trügst | ♦ trügt | trog | getrogen |
| **tun** | tust | ♦ tut | tat | getan |
| **verderben** | verdirbst | ♦ verdirbt | verdarb | verdorben |
| **vergessen** | vergisst | ♦ vergisst | vergaß | vergessen |
| **verlieren** | verlierst | ♦ verliert | verlor | verloren |
| **verschwinden** | verschwindest | ♦ verschwindet | verschwand | verschwunden |
| **verzeihen** | verzeihst | ♦ verzeiht | verzieh | verziehen |
| **wachsen*** | wächst | ♦ wächst | wuchs | gewachsen |
| **waschen** | wäschst | ♦ wäscht | wusch | gewaschen |
| **weisen** | weist | ♦ weist | wies | gewiesen |
| **werben** | wirbst | ♦ wirbt | warb | geworben |
| **werden*** | wirst | ♦ wird | wurde | geworden |
| **werfen** | wirfst | ♦ wirft | warf | geworfen |
| **wiegen** | wiegst | ♦ wiegt | wog | gewogen |
| **winden** | windest | ♦ windet | wand | gewunden |
| **wissen** | weißt | ♦ weiß | wusste | gewusst |
| **wollen** | willst | ♦ will | wollte | gewollt |
| **ziehen*** | ziehst | ♦ zieht | zog | gezogen |
| **zwingen** | zwingst | ♦ zwingt | zwang | gezwungen |

# ENGLISH ~ GERMAN

# A

**A** NOUN
die <u>Eins</u> (*school mark*) (PL die Einsen) ◊ *I got an A for my essay.* Ich habe für meinen Aufsatz eine Eins bekommen.

**a** ARTICLE
*In the nominative use **ein** for masculine and neuter nouns, **eine** for feminine nouns.*
1 <u>ein</u> ◊ *a man* ein Mann ◊ *I saw a man.* Ich habe einen Mann gesehen. ◊ *a child* ein Kind ◊ *an apple* ein Apfel
2 <u>eine</u> ◊ *a woman* eine Frau ◊ *He gave it to a woman.* Er hat es einer Frau gegeben.
*You do not translate **a** when you want to describe what somebody does for a living.*
◊ *He's a butcher.* Er ist Metzger. ◊ *She's a doctor.* Sie ist Ärztin.
♦ **once a week** einmal pro Woche
♦ **thirty kilometres an hour** dreißig Kilometer in der Stunde
♦ **thirty pence a kilo** dreißig Pence das Kilo
♦ **a hundred pounds** einhundert Pfund

**AA** NOUN (= *Automobile Association*)
der <u>ADAC</u>

to **abandon** VERB
1 (*place*)
<u>verlassen</u> (PRESENT verlässt, IMPERFECT verließ, PERFECT hat verlassen)
2 (*plan, idea*)
<u>aufgeben</u> (PRESENT gibt auf, IMPERFECT gab auf, PERFECT hat aufgegeben)

**abbey** NOUN
das <u>Kloster</u> (PL die Klöster)

**abbreviation** NOUN
die <u>Abkürzung</u>

**ability** NOUN
die <u>Fähigkeit</u>
♦ **to have the ability to do something** fähig sein, etwas zu tun

**able** ADJECTIVE
♦ **to be able to do something** etwas tun können

to **abolish** VERB
<u>abschaffen</u> (PERFECT hat abgeschafft)

**abortion** NOUN
die <u>Abtreibung</u>
♦ **She had an abortion.** Sie hat abgetrieben.

**about** PREPOSITION, ADVERB
1 <u>wegen</u> (*concerning*) ◊ *I'm phoning about tomorrow's meeting.* Ich rufe wegen des morgigen Treffens an.
2 <u>etwa</u> (*approximately*) ◊ *It takes about ten hours.* Es dauert etwa zehn Stunden.
◊ *about a hundred pounds* etwa hundert Pfund ◊ *at about eleven o'clock* um etwa elf Uhr
3 <u>in ... herum</u> (*around*) ◊ *to walk about the town* in der Stadt herumlaufen
4 <u>über</u> ◊ *a book about the London Underground* ein Buch über die Londoner U-Bahn
♦ **to be about to do something** gerade etwas tun wollen ◊ *I was about to go out.* Ich wollte gerade gehen.
♦ **to talk about something** über etwas reden ◊ *We talked about the weather.* Wir haben über das Wetter geredet.
♦ **What's the film about?** Wovon handelt der Film?
♦ **How about going to the cinema?** Wie wär's, wenn wir ins Kino gingen?

**above** PREPOSITION, ADVERB
<u>über</u> ◊ *above forty degrees* über vierzig Grad
*Use the accusative to express movement or a change of place. Use the dative when there is no change of place.*
◊ *He put his hands above his head.* Er hielt die Hände über den Kopf. ◊ *The lamp is hanging above the table.* Die Lampe hängt über dem Tisch.
♦ **the flat above** die Wohnung darüber
♦ **mentioned above** oben erwähnt
♦ **above all** vor allem

**abroad** ADVERB
1 <u>im Ausland</u> ◊ *She lives abroad.* Sie lebt im Ausland.
2 <u>ins Ausland</u> ◊ *to go abroad* ins Ausland gehen

**abrupt** ADJECTIVE
<u>brüsk</u> ◊ *He was a bit abrupt with me.* Er war etwas brüsk zu mir.

**abruptly** ADVERB
<u>plötzlich</u> ◊ *He got up abruptly.* Er stand plötzlich auf.

**absence** NOUN
die <u>Abwesenheit</u>

**absent** ADJECTIVE
<u>abwesend</u>

**absent-minded** ADJECTIVE
<u>zerstreut</u> ◊ *She's a bit absent-minded.* Sie ist etwas zerstreut.

**absolutely** ADVERB
1 <u>völlig</u> (*completely*) ◊ *Beate's absolutely right.* Beate hat völlig Recht.
2 <u>ganz sicher</u> ◊ *Do you think it's a good idea? – Absolutely!* Meinst du, das ist eine gute Idee? – Ganz sicher!

**absurd** ADJECTIVE
<u>absurd</u> ◊ *That's absurd!* Das ist absurd!

**abuse** NOUN
| see also **abuse** VERB |

☞

der <u>Missbrauch</u> (*of power, drugs*)
♦ **child abuse** die Kindesmisshandlung
♦ **to shout abuse at somebody** jemanden beschimpfen
to **abuse** VERB

> see also **abuse** NOUN

<u>missbrauchen</u> (PERFECT hat missbraucht)
◊ *to abuse drugs* Drogen missbrauchen
♦ **abused children** misshandelte Kinder
**abusive** ADJECTIVE
<u>beleidigend</u> ◊ *He became abusive.* Er wurde beleidigend.
**academic** ADJECTIVE
♦**the academic year** das Studienjahr
**academy** NOUN
die <u>Akademie</u> ◊ *a military academy* eine Militärakademie
to **accelerate** VERB
<u>beschleunigen</u> (PERFECT hat beschleunigt)
**accelerator** NOUN
das <u>Gaspedal</u> (PL die Gaspedale)
**accent** NOUN
der <u>Akzent</u> (PL die Akzente) ◊ *He's got a German accent.* Er hat einen deutschen Akzent.
to **accept** VERB
<u>annehmen</u> (PRESENT nimmt an, IMPERFECT nahm an, PERFECT hat angenommen)
**acceptable** ADJECTIVE
<u>annehmbar</u>
**access** NOUN
1 der <u>Zugang</u> ◊ *He has access to confidential information.* Er hat Zugang zu vertraulichen Informationen.
2 das <u>Besuchsrecht</u> ◊ *Her ex-husband has access to the children.* Ihr geschiedener Mann hat ein Besuchsrecht.
**accessible** ADJECTIVE
<u>erreichbar</u> ◊ *It's only accessible via a secret entrance.* Es ist nur durch einen Geheimeingang erreichbar.
**accessory** NOUN
♦**fashion accessories** die Modeartikel PL
**accident** NOUN
der <u>Unfall</u> (PL die Unfälle) ◊ *to have an accident* einen Unfall haben
♦ **by accident (1)** (*by mistake*) versehentlich ◊ *The burglar killed him by accident.* Der Einbrecher hat ihn versehentlich getötet.
♦ **by accident (2)** (*by chance*) zufällig ◊ *She met him by accident.* Sie ist ihm zufällig begegnet.
**accidental** ADJECTIVE
<u>zufällig</u>
to **accommodate** VERB
<u>unterbringen</u> (IMPERFECT brachte unter, PERFECT hat untergebracht)
♦ **The hotel can accommodate fifty people.** Das Hotel hat Platz für fünfzig Gäste.
**accommodation** NOUN
die <u>Unterkunft</u> (PL die Unterkünfte)
to **accompany** VERB

<u>begleiten</u> (PERFECT hat begleitet)
**accord** NOUN
♦**of his own accord** aus eigenem Antrieb ◊ *He left of his own accord.* Er ist aus eigenem Antrieb gegangen.
**accordingly** ADVERB
<u>entsprechend</u>
**according to** PREPOSITION
<u>laut</u> ◊ *According to him, everyone had gone.* Laut ihm waren alle weggegangen.
**accordion** NOUN
das <u>Akkordeon</u> (PL die Akkordeons)
**account** NOUN
1 das <u>Konto</u> (PL die Konten) ◊ *a bank account* ein Bankkonto
♦ **to do the accounts** die Buchführung machen
2 (*report*)
der <u>Bericht</u> (PL die Berichte)
♦ **He gave a detailed account of what happened.** Er berichtete genau, was passiert war.
♦ **to take something into account** etwas berücksichtigen
♦ **on account of** wegen ◊ *We couldn't go out on account of the bad weather.* Wir konnten wegen des schlechten Wetters nicht raus.
♦ **to account for** erklären ◊ *If she was ill, that would account for her poor results.* Wenn sie krank war, dann würde das ihre schlechten Resultate erklären.
**accountable** ADJECTIVE
♦**to be accountable to someone** jemandem gegenüber verantwortlich sein
**accountancy** NOUN
die <u>Buchführung</u>
**accountant** NOUN
1 (*bookkeeper*)
der <u>Buchhalter</u> (PL die Buchhalter)
die <u>Buchhalterin</u>
◊ *She's an accountant.* Sie ist Buchhalterin.
2 (*tax consultant*)
der <u>Steuerberater</u> (PL die Steuerberater)
die <u>Steuerberaterin</u>
**accuracy** NOUN
die <u>Genauigkeit</u>
**accurate** ADJECTIVE
<u>genau</u> ◊ *accurate information* genaue Information
**accurately** ADVERB
<u>genau</u>
**accusation** NOUN
der <u>Vorwurf</u> (PL die Vorwürfe)
to **accuse** VERB
♦**to accuse somebody of something (1)** jemanden einer Sache beschuldigen ◊ *She accused her husband of lying.* Sie beschuldigte ihren Mann, er würde lügen.

♦ **to accuse somebody of something** (2)
(*police*) jemanden einer Sache anklagen
◊ *The police are accusing her of murder.*
Die Polizei klagt sie wegen Mordes an.

**ace** NOUN
das Ass (GEN des Asses, PL die Asse) ◊ *the
ace of hearts* das Herzass

**ache** NOUN
see also **ache** VERB
der Schmerz (GEN des Schmerzes, PL die
Schmerzen) ◊ *I have an ache in my side.*
Ich habe Schmerzen in der Seite.

to **ache** VERB
see also **ache** NOUN
wehtun (IMPERFECT tat weh, PERFECT hat
wehgetan) ◊ *My leg's aching.* Mein Bein
tut weh.

to **achieve** VERB
[1] (*an aim*)
erreichen (PERFECT hat erreicht)
[2] (*victory*)
erringen (IMPERFECT errang, PERFECT hat
errungen)

**achievement** NOUN
die Leistung ◊ *That was quite an
achievement.* Das war eine Leistung.

**acid** NOUN
die Säure

**acid rain** NOUN
der saure Regen

**acne** NOUN
die Akne ◊ *She's got acne.* Sie hat Akne.

to **acquit** VERB
♦ **to be acquitted** freigesprochen werden
◊ *He was acquitted of murder.* Er wurde
von der Mordanklage freigesprochen.

**acre** NOUN
der Morgen (PL die Morgen)

**acrobat** NOUN
der Akrobat (GEN des Akrobaten, PL die
Akrobaten)
die Akrobatin
◊ *He's an acrobat.* Er ist Akrobat.

**across** PREPOSITION, ADVERB
über
*Use the accusative to express movement
or a change of place. Use the dative
when there is no change of place.*
◊ *the shop across the road* der Laden
über der Straße ◊ *to walk across the road*
über die Straße gehen
♦ **across from** (*opposite*) gegenüber +DAT
◊ *He sat down across from her.* Er setzte
sich ihr gegenüber.

to **act** VERB
see also **act** NOUN
[1] spielen (*in play, film*) ◊ *He acts really
well.* Er spielt wirklich gut. ◊ *She's acting
the part of Juliet.* Sie spielt die Rolle der
Julia.
[2] handeln (*take action*) ◊ *The police
acted quickly.* Die Polizei hat schnell
gehandelt.

♦ **She acts as his interpreter.** Sie übersetzt
für ihn.

**act** NOUN
see also **act** VERB
der Akt (*in play*) (PL die Akte) ◊ *in the first
act* im ersten Akt

**action** NOUN
die Handlung
♦ **The film was full of action.** In dem Film
gab es viel Action.
♦ **to take firm action against somebody**
hart gegen jemanden vorgehen

**active** ADJECTIVE
aktiv ◊ *He's a very active person.* Er ist
ein sehr aktiver Mensch. ◊ *an active
volcano* ein aktiver Vulkan

**activity** NOUN
die Tätigkeit
♦ **outdoor activities** die Betätigung im
Freien SING

**actor** NOUN
der Schauspieler (PL die Schauspieler)
◊ *Brad Pitt is a well-known actor.* Brad
Pitt ist ein bekannter Schauspieler.

**actress** NOUN
die Schauspielerin ◊ *Julia Roberts is a
well-known actress.* Julia Roberts ist eine
bekannte Schauspielerin.

**actual** ADJECTIVE
wirklich ◊ *The film is based on actual
events.* Der Film basiert auf wirklichen
Begebenheiten.
*Be careful not to translate actual by
aktuell.*

**actually** ADVERB
[1] wirklich (*really*) ◊ *Did it actually
happen?* Ist das wirklich passiert?
[2] eigentlich (*in fact*) ◊ *Actually, I don't
know him at all.* Eigentlich kenne ich ihn
überhaupt nicht.

**acupuncture** NOUN
die Akupunktur

**ad** NOUN
[1] die Anzeige (*in paper*)
[2] die Werbung (*on TV, radio*)

**AD** ABBREVIATION
n. Chr. (= nach Christus) ◊ *in 800 AD* im
Jahre 800 n. Chr.

to **adapt** VERB
bearbeiten (PERFECT hat bearbeitet) ◊ *His
novel was adapted for television.*
Sein Roman wurde fürs Fernsehen
bearbeitet.
♦ **to adapt to something** (*get used to*) sich
in etwas eingewöhnen ◊ *He adapted to
his new school very quickly.* Er hat sich
in der neuen Schule sehr schnell
eingewöhnt.

**adaptor** NOUN
der Adapter (PL die Adapter)

to **add** VERB

hinzufügen (PERFECT hat hinzugefügt) ◊ *Add two eggs to the mixture.* Fügen Sie dem Teig zwei Eier hinzu.

♦ **to add up** zusammenzählen ◊ *Add the figures up.* Zähle die Zahlen zusammen.

**addict** NOUN
(*drug addict*)
der Süchtige (GEN des Süchtigen, PL die Süchtigen)
die Süchtige (GEN der Süchtigen) ◊ *an addict (man)* ein Süchtiger

♦ **Martin's a football addict.** Martin ist ein Fußballnarr.

**addicted** ADJECTIVE
süchtig ◊ *She's addicted to heroin.* Sie ist heroinsüchtig. ◊ *She's addicted to soap operas.* Sie ist süchtig nach Seifenopern.

**addition** NOUN
♦ **in addition** außerdem ◊ *He's broken his leg and, in addition, he's caught a cold.* Er hat sich das Bein gebrochen, und außerdem hat er einen Schnupfen bekommen.

♦ **in addition to** zusätzlich zu ◊ *In addition to the price of the cassette, there's a charge for postage.* Zusätzlich zum Preis der Kassette wird eine Versandgebühr berechnet.

**address** NOUN
| see also **address** VERB |

die Adresse ◊ *What's your address?* Wie ist Ihre Adresse?

to **address** VERB
| see also **address** NOUN |

1 (*envelope, letter*)
adressieren (PERFECT hat adressiert)
2 (*speak to*)
sprechen zu (PRESENT spricht, IMPERFECT sprach, PERFECT hat gesprochen) ◊ *She addressed the audience.* Sie sprach zum Publikum.

**adjective** NOUN
das Adjektiv (PL die Adjektive)

to **adjust** VERB
einstellen (PERFECT hat eingestellt) ◊ *He adjusted the seat to the right height.* Er stellte den Stuhl auf die richtige Höhe ein.

♦ **to adjust to something** (*get used to*) sich in etwas eingewöhnen ◊ *He adjusted to his new school very quickly.* Er hat sich in der neuen Schule schnell eingewöhnt.

**adjustable** ADJECTIVE
verstellbar

**administration** NOUN
die Verwaltung

**admiral** NOUN
der Admiral (PL die Admirale)

to **admire** VERB
bewundern (PERFECT hat bewundert)

**admission** NOUN

der Eintritt ◊ *"admission free"* "Eintritt frei"

to **admit** VERB
zugeben (PRESENT gibt zu, IMPERFECT gab zu, PERFECT hat zugegeben) ◊ *I must admit that ...* Ich muss zugeben, dass ... ◊ *He admitted that he'd done it.* Er gab zu, dass er es getan hat.

**adolescence** NOUN
die Pubertät

**adolescent** NOUN
der Jugendliche (GEN des Jugendlichen, PL die Jugendlichen)
die Jugendliche (GEN der Jugendlichen) ◊ *an adolescent (male)* ein Jugendlicher

to **adopt** VERB
1 (*child*)
adoptieren (PERFECT hat adoptiert) ◊ *Phil was adopted.* Phil wurde adoptiert.
2 (*idea*)
übernehmen (PRESENT übernimmt, IMPERFECT übernahm, PERFECT hat übernommen) ◊ *The system of multiple choice questions has been adopted for many exams.* Das Multiple-Choice-System ist für viele Prüfungen übernommen worden.

**adopted** ADJECTIVE
adoptiert

♦ **an adopted son** ein Adoptivsohn

**adoption** NOUN
die Adoption

to **adore** VERB
bewundern (PERFECT hat bewundert)

**Adriatic Sea** NOUN
die Adria

**adult** NOUN
der Erwachsene (GEN des Erwachsenen, PL die Erwachsenen)
die Erwachsene (GEN der Erwachsenen) ◊ *an adult (man)* ein Erwachsener

♦ **adult education** die Erwachsenenbildung

to **advance** VERB
| see also **advance** NOUN |

1 (*move forward*)
vorrücken (PERFECT ist vorgerückt) ◊ *The troops are advancing.* Die Truppen rücken vor.
2 (*progress*)
Fortschritte machen ◊ *Technology has advanced a lot.* Die Technik hat große Fortschritte gemacht.

**advance** NOUN
| see also **advance** VERB |

♦ **in advance** vorher ◊ *They bought the tickets in advance.* Sie haben die Karten vorher gekauft.

**advance booking** NOUN
die Vorbestellung ◊ *Reductions are offered for advance booking.* Bei Vorbestellung gibt es Rabatt.

♦ **Advance booking is essential.** Es ist wichtig vorzubestellen.

**advanced** ADJECTIVE
fortgeschritten

**advantage** NOUN
der Vorteil (PL die Vorteile) ◊ *Going to university has many advantages.* Das Studium hat viele Vorteile.
♦ **to take advantage of something** etwas ausnützen ◊ *He took advantage of the good weather to go for a walk.* Er hat das schöne Wetter ausgenützt und einen Spaziergang gemacht.
♦ **to take advantage of somebody** jemanden ausnützen ◊ *The company was taking advantage of its employees.* Die Firma nützte ihre Angestellten aus.

**adventure** NOUN
das Abenteuer (PL die Abenteuer)

**adverb** NOUN
das Adverb (PL die Adverbien)

**advert** NOUN *see* **advertisement**

to **advertise** VERB
annoncieren (PERFECT hat annonciert) ◊ *Jobs are advertised in the paper.* Stellenangebote werden in der Zeitung annonciert.

**advertisement** NOUN
[1] die Anzeige (*in paper*)
[2] die Werbung (*on TV, radio*)

**advertising** NOUN
die Werbung ◊ *She works in advertising.* Sie ist in der Werbung tätig. ◊ *They've increased spending on advertising.* Sie geben mehr Geld für Werbung aus.

**advice** NOUN
der Rat ◊ *to give somebody advice* jemandem einen Rat geben
♦ **a piece of advice** ein Rat ◊ *He gave me a good piece of advice.* Er gab mir einen guten Rat.

to **advise** VERB
raten (PRESENT rät, IMPERFECT riet, PERFECT hat geraten) ◊ *He advised me to wait.* Er riet mir zu warten. ◊ *He advised me not to go there.* Er hat mir geraten, nicht dorthin zu gehen.

**aerial** NOUN
die Antenne

**aerobics** PL NOUN
das Aerobic ◊ *I'm going to aerobics tonight.* Ich mache heute Abend Aerobic.

**aeroplane** NOUN
das Flugzeug (PL die Flugzeuge)

**aerosol** NOUN
der Spray (PL die Sprays)

**affair** NOUN
[1] (*romantic*)
das Verhältnis (GEN des Verhältnisses, PL die Verhältnisse) ◊ *to have an affair with somebody* mit jemandem ein Verhältnis haben
[2] (*event*)

die Angelegenheit

to **affect** VERB
[1] (*influence*)
beeinflussen (PERFECT hat beeinflusst) ◊ *Does violence on television affect children's behaviour?* Beeinflusst Gewalt im Fernsehen das Verhalten von Kindern?
[2] (*have effect on*)
beeinträchtigen (PERFECT hat beeinträchtigt) ◊ *The bad weather has affected sales.* Das schlechte Wetter hat den Absatz beeinträchtigt.
♦ **It affects me deeply.** Es geht mir sehr nahe.

**affectionate** ADJECTIVE
liebevoll

to **afford** VERB
sich leisten ◊ *I can't afford a new pair of jeans.* Ich kann mir keine neue Jeans leisten. ◊ *We can't afford to go on holiday.* Wir können es uns nicht leisten, in Urlaub zu fahren.

**afraid** ADJECTIVE
♦ **to be afraid of something** vor etwas Angst haben ◊ *I'm afraid of spiders.* Ich habe Angst vor Spinnen.
♦ **I'm afraid I can't come.** ich kann leider nicht kommen.
♦ **I'm afraid so.** Ja, leider.
♦ **I'm afraid not.** Leider nicht.

**Africa** NOUN
Afrika NEUT
♦ **from Africa** aus Afrika
♦ **to Africa** nach Afrika

**African** ADJECTIVE
see also **African** NOUN
afrikanisch

**African** NOUN
see also **African** ADJECTIVE
der Afrikaner (PL die Afrikaner)
die Afrikanerin

**after** PREPOSITION, ADVERB, CONJUNCTION
nach +DAT ◊ *after dinner* nach dem Abendessen ◊ *He ran after me.* Er rannte mir nach.
♦ **soon after** kurz danach
♦ **after I'd had a rest** nachdem ich mich ausgeruht hatte
♦ **After having eaten I left.** Nachdem ich gegessen hatte, ging ich.
♦ **after all** schließlich

**afternoon** NOUN
der Nachmittag (PL die Nachmittage)
♦ **three o'clock in the afternoon** drei Uhr nachmittags
♦ **this afternoon** heute Nachmittag
♦ **on Saturday afternoon** Samstag Nachmittag

**afters** SING *or* PL NOUN
der Nachtisch SING (PL die Nachtische)

**aftershave** NOUN
das After-shave (PL die After-shaves)

**afterwards** ADVERB
<u>danach</u> ◊ *She left not long afterwards.*
Sie ging kurz danach.

**again** ADVERB
[1] <u>wieder</u> (*once more*) ◊ *They're friends
again.* Sie sind wieder Freunde.
[2] <u>noch einmal</u> (*one more time*) ◊ *Can
you tell me again?* Kannst du mir das
noch einmal sagen?
♦ **not ... again** nie mehr ◊ *I won't go there
again.* Dort gehe ich nie mehr hin.
♦ **Do it again!** Mach's noch mal!
♦ **Not again!** Nicht schon wieder!
♦ **again and again** immer wieder

**against** PREPOSITION
<u>gegen</u> ◊ *He leant against the wall.* Er
lehnte gegen die Wand. ◊ *I'm against
nuclear testing.* Ich bin gegen Atomtests.

**age** NOUN
das <u>Alter</u> (PL die Alter) ◊ *an age limit* eine
Altersgrenze
♦ **at the age of sixteen** mit sechzehn
♦ **I haven't been to the cinema for ages.**
Ich war schon ewig nicht mehr im Kino.

**aged** ADJECTIVE
♦ **aged ten** zehn Jahre alt

**agenda** NOUN
die <u>Tagesordnung</u>

**agent** NOUN
der <u>Agent</u> (GEN des Agenten, PL die
Agenten)
die <u>Agentin</u>
♦ **an estate agent** ein Immobilienmakler
♦ **a travel agent** ein Reisebüro

**aggressive** ADJECTIVE
<u>aggressiv</u>

**ago** ADVERB
♦ **two days ago** vor zwei Tagen
♦ **two years ago** vor zwei Jahren
♦ **not long ago** vor kurzem
♦ **How long ago did it happen?** Wie lange
ist das her?

**agony** NOUN
♦ **He was in agony.** Er hatte furchtbare
Schmerzen.

to **agree** VERB
♦ **to agree with somebody** jemandem
zustimmen ◊ *I agree with your sister.* Ich
stimme deiner Schwester zu.
♦ **to agree to do something** bereit sein,
etwas zu tun ◊ *He agreed to go and pick
her up.* Er war bereit, sie abzuholen.
♦ **to agree that ...** (*admit*) zugeben, dass ...
◊ *I agree that it's difficult.* Ich gebe zu,
dass das schwierig ist.
♦ **Garlic doesn't agree with me.** Ich
vertrage Knoblauch nicht.

**agreed** ADJECTIVE
<u>ausgemacht</u> ◊ *at the agreed time* zur
ausgemachten Zeit

**agreement** NOUN
die <u>Abmachung</u>

♦ **to be in agreement** übereinstimmen
◊ *Everybody was in agreement with Ray.*
Alle stimmten mit Ray überein.

**agricultural** ADJECTIVE
<u>landwirtschaftlich</u>

**agriculture** NOUN
die <u>Landwirtschaft</u>

**ahead** ADVERB
<u>voraus</u> ◊ *We sent him on ahead.* Wir
schickten ihn voraus.
♦ **The Germans are five points ahead.** Die
Deutschen führen mit fünf Punkten.
♦ **She looked straight ahead.** Sie sah
geradeaus.
♦ **ahead of time** vorzeitig
♦ **to plan ahead** vorausplanen
♦ **Go ahead!** Ja bitte!

**aid** NOUN
♦ **in aid of charity** für wohltätige Zwecke

**AIDS** NOUN
das <u>Aids</u> (GEN des Aids) ◊ *He died of
AIDS.* Er starb an Aids.

to **aim** VERB
see also **aim** NOUN
♦ **to aim at** zielen auf +ACC ◊ *He aimed a gun
at me.* Er zielte mit der Pistole auf mich.
♦ **The film is aimed at children.** Der Film ist
für Kinder gedacht.
♦ **to aim to do something** beabsichtigen,
etwas zu tun ◊ *Janice aimed to leave at
five o'clock.* Janice beabsichtigte, um
fünf Uhr zu gehen.

**aim** NOUN
see also **aim** VERB
das <u>Ziel</u> (PL die Ziele) ◊ *The aim of the
festival is to raise money.* Ziel des
Festivals ist, Geld aufzutreiben.

**air** NOUN
die <u>Luft</u> (PL die Lüfte)
♦ **to get some fresh air** frische Luft
schnappen
♦ **by air** mit dem Flugzeug ◊ *I prefer to
travel by air.* Ich reise lieber mit dem
Flugzeug.

**air-conditioned** ADJECTIVE
<u>mit Klimaanlage</u>

**air conditioning** NOUN
die <u>Klimaanlage</u>

**Air Force** NOUN
die <u>Luftwaffe</u>

**air hostess** NOUN
die <u>Stewardess</u> (PL die Stewardessen)
◊ *She's an air hostess.* Sie ist
Stewardess.

**airline** NOUN
die <u>Fluggesellschaft</u>

**airmail** NOUN
♦ **by airmail** mit Luftpost

**airplane** NOUN US
das <u>Flugzeug</u> (PL die Flugzeuge)

**airport** NOUN
der <u>Flughafen</u> (PL die Flughäfen)

**aisle** NOUN
 1 (*in church*)
 der Mittelgang (PL die Mittelgänge)
 2 (*in plane*)
 der Gang (PL die Gänge) ◊ *an aisle seat*
 ein Platz am Gang
**alarm** NOUN
 der Alarm (*warning*) (PL die Alarme)
 ♦ **a fire alarm** ein Feueralarm
**alarm clock** NOUN
 der Wecker (PL die Wecker)
**album** NOUN
 das Album (PL die Alben)
**alcohol** NOUN
 der Alkohol
**alcoholic** NOUN
 see also **alcoholic** ADJECTIVE
 der Alkoholiker (PL die Alkoholiker)
 die Akoholikerin
 ◊ *He's an alcoholic.* Er ist Alkoholiker.
**alcoholic** ADJECTIVE
 see also **alcoholic** NOUN
 alkoholisch ◊ *alcoholic drinks*
 alkoholische Getränke
**alert** ADJECTIVE
 1 aufgeweckt (*bright*) ◊ *He's a very alert
 baby.* Er ist ein sehr aufgewecktes Baby.
 2 wachsam (*paying attention*) ◊ *We must
 stay alert.* Wir müssen wachsam bleiben.
**A levels** PL NOUN
 das Abitur SING

> **ⓘ** *Germans take their **Abitur** at the age
> of 19. The students sit examinations in
> a variety of subjects to attain an overall
> grade. If you pass, you have the right
> to a place at university.*

**alike** ADVERB
 ♦ **to look alike** sich ähnlich sehen ◊ *The
 two sisters look alike.* Die beiden
 Schwestern sehen sich ähnlich.
**alive** ADJECTIVE
 am Leben
**all** ADJECTIVE, PRONOUN, ADVERB
 1 alle ◊ *all the books* alle Bücher
 ♦ **all the time** die ganze Zeit
 ♦ **all day** den ganzen Tag
 2 alles ◊ *He ate it all.* Er hat alles
 gegessen. ◊ *I ate all of it.* Ich habe alles
 gegessen.
 ♦ **All of us went.** Wir sind alle
 hingegangen.
 ♦ **after all** schließlich ◊ *After all, nobody
 can make us go.* Schließlich kann uns
 niemand zwingen hinzugehen.
 ♦ **all alone** ganz allein ◊ *She's all alone.* Sie
 ist ganz allein.
 ♦ **not at all** überhaupt nicht ◊ *I'm not tired
 at all.* Ich bin überhaupt nicht müde.
 ♦ **The score is five all.** Es steht fünf zu
 fünf.
**allergic** ADJECTIVE

**allergisch**
 ♦ **to be allergic to something** allergisch
 gegen etwas sein ◊ *I'm allergic to cats.*
 Ich bin allergisch gegen Katzen.
**allergy** NOUN
 die Allergie (PL die Allergien)
**alley** NOUN
 die Gasse
to **allow** VERB
 ♦ **to be allowed to do something** etwas
 tun dürfen ◊ *He's not allowed to go out
 at night.* Er darf abends nicht ausgehen.
 ♦ **to allow somebody to do something**
 jemandem erlauben, etwas zu tun ◊ *His
 mum allowed him to go out.* Seine
 Mama hat ihm erlaubt auszugehen.
**all right** ADVERB
 1 gut (*okay*) ◊ *Everything turned out all
 right.* Alles ist gut gegangen.
 ♦ **Are you all right?** Bist du in Ordnung?
 2 okay (*not bad*) ◊ *The film was all right.*
 Der Film war okay.
 3 einverstanden (*when agreeing*) ◊ *We'll
 talk about it later. – All right.* Wir reden
 später darüber. – Einverstanden.
 ♦ **Is that all right with you?** Ist das okay?
**almond** NOUN
 die Mandel (PL die Mandeln)
**almost** ADVERB
 fast ◊ *I've almost finished.* Ich bin fast
 fertig.
**alone** ADJECTIVE, ADVERB
 allein ◊ *She lives alone.* Sie lebt allein.
 ♦ **to leave somebody alone** jemanden in
 Ruhe lassen ◊ *Leave her alone!* Lass sie
 in Ruhe!
 ♦ **to leave something alone** etwas nicht
 anfassen ◊ *Leave my things alone!* Fass
 meine Sachen nicht an!
**along** PREPOSITION, ADVERB
 entlang ◊ *Chris was walking along the
 beach.* Chris ging am Strand entlang.
 ♦ **all along** die ganze Zeit ◊ *He was lying to
 me all along.* Er hat mich die ganze Zeit
 belogen.
**aloud** ADVERB
 laut ◊ *He read the poem aloud.* Er las das
 Gedicht vor.
**alphabet** NOUN
 das Alphabet (PL die Alphabete)
**Alps** PL NOUN
 die Alpen FEM PL
**already** ADVERB
 schon ◊ *Liz had already gone.* Liz war
 schon weg.
**also** ADVERB
 auch
 *Be careful not to translate **also** by the
 German word **also**.*
**altar** NOUN
 der Altar (PL die Altare)
to **alter** VERB
 verändern (PERFECT hat verändert)

**alternate** ADJECTIVE
♦ **on alternate days** abwechselnd jeden zweiten Tag
**alternative** NOUN
⊡ *see also* **alternative** ADJECTIVE
die Alternative ◊ *Fruit is a healthy alternative to chocolate.* Obst ist eine gesunde Alternative zu Schokolade.
♦ **You have no alternative.** Du hast keine andere Wahl.
♦ **There are several alternatives.** Es gibt mehrere Möglichkeiten.
**alternative** ADJECTIVE
⊡ *see also* **alternative** NOUN
andere ◊ *an alternative solution* eine andere Lösung ◊ *an alternative suggestion* ein anderer Vorschlag
♦ **alternative medicine** die alternative Medizin
**alternatively** ADVERB
♦ **Alternatively, we could just stay at home.** Wir könnten auch zu Hause bleiben.
**although** CONJUNCTION
obwohl ◊ *Although she was tired, she stayed up late.* Obwohl sie müde war, blieb sie lange auf.
**altogether** ADVERB
⬚1⬚ insgesamt (*in total*) ◊ *You owe me twenty pounds altogether.* Du schuldest mir insgesamt zwanzig Pfund.
⬚2⬚ ganz (*completely*) ◊ *I'm not altogether happy with your work.* Ich bin mit Ihrer Arbeit nicht ganz zufrieden.
**aluminium** NOUN (US **aluminum**)
das Aluminium
**always** ADVERB
immer ◊ *He's always moaning.* Er beklagt sich immer.
**am** VERB *see* **be**
**a.m.** ABBREVIATION
morgens ◊ *at four a.m.* um vier Uhr morgens
**amateur** NOUN
der Amateur (PL die Amateure)
die Amateurin
◊ *He's an amateur.* Er ist Amateur.
to **amaze** VERB
♦ **to be amazed** erstaunt sein ◊ *I was amazed that I managed to do it.* Ich war erstaunt, dass ich es geschafft habe.
**amazing** ADJECTIVE
⬚1⬚ erstaunlich (*surprising*) ◊ *That's amazing news!* Das sind erstaunliche Neuigkeiten!
⬚2⬚ ausgezeichnet (*excellent*) ◊ *Vivian's an amazing cook.* Vivian ist eine ausgezeichnete Köchin.
**ambassador** NOUN
der Botschafter (PL die Botschafter)
die Botschafterin
**amber** ADJECTIVE

♦ **an amber light** eine gelbe Ampel
**ambition** NOUN
der Ehrgeiz (GEN des Ehrgeizes)
**ambitious** ADJECTIVE
ehrgeizig ◊ *She's very ambitious.* Sie ist sehr ehrgeizig.
**ambulance** NOUN
der Krankenwagen (PL die Krankenwagen)
**amenities** PL NOUN
♦ **The hotel has very good amenities.** Das Hotel hat viel zu bieten.
**America** NOUN
Amerika NEUT
♦ **from America** aus Amerika
♦ **in America** in Amerika
♦ **to America** nach Amerika
**American** ADJECTIVE
⊡ *see also* **American** NOUN
amerikanisch ◊ *He's American.* Er ist Amerikaner. ◊ *She's American.* Sie ist Amerikanerin.
**American** NOUN
⊡ *see also* **American** ADJECTIVE
der Amerikaner (PL die Amerikaner)
die Amerikanerin
♦ **the Americans** die Amerikaner
**among** PREPOSITION
unter +DAT ◊ *I was among friends.* Ich war unter Freunden.
♦ **among other things** unter anderem
**amount** NOUN
⬚1⬚ der Betrag (PL die Beträge) ◊ *a large amount of money* ein großer Geldbetrag
⬚2⬚ die Menge ◊ *a huge amount of rice* eine enorme Menge Reis
**amp** NOUN
⬚1⬚ (*of electricity*)
das Ampère (GEN des Ampère, PL die Ampère)
⬚2⬚ (*for hi-fi*)
der Verstärker (PL die Verstärker)
**amplifier** NOUN
der Verstärker (*for hi-fi*) (PL die Verstärker)
to **amuse** VERB
belustigen (PERFECT hat belustigt)
♦ **He was most amused by the story.** Er fand die Geschichte sehr lustig.
**amusement** NOUN
das Vergnügen (*enjoyment*) (PL die Vergnügen)
♦ **amusement arcade** die Spielhalle
**amusement arcade** NOUN
die Spielhalle
**an** ARTICLE *see* **a**
to **analyse** VERB
analysieren (PERFECT hat analysiert)
**analysis** NOUN
die Analyse
to **analyze** VERB US
analysieren (PERFECT hat analysiert)

**A**

**ancestor** NOUN
der Vorfahr (GEN des Vorfahren, PL die Vorfahren)
die Vorfahrin

**anchor** NOUN
der Anker (PL die Anker)

**ancient** ADJECTIVE
alt ◊ *This is an ancient custom.* Das ist ein alter Brauch.
♦ **ancient Greece** das antike Griechenland
♦ **an ancient monument** ein historisches Denkmal

**and** CONJUNCTION
und ◊ *you and me* du und ich ◊ *Two and two are four.* Zwei und zwei gibt vier. ◊ *He talked and talked.* Er redete und redete.
♦ **Please try and come!** Versuche bitte zu kommen!
♦ **better and better** immer besser

**angel** NOUN
der Engel (PL die Engel)
*Be careful not to translate* **angel** *by the German word* **Angel***.*

**anger** NOUN
die Wut

**angle** NOUN
der Winkel (PL die Winkel)

**angler** NOUN
der Angler (PL die Angler)
die Anglerin

**angling** NOUN
das Angeln ◊ *His favourite hobby is angling.* Angeln ist sein Lieblingshobby.

**angry** ADJECTIVE
böse ◊ *Dad looks very angry.* Papa sieht sehr böse aus.
♦ **to be angry with somebody** mit jemandem böse sein ◊ *Mum's really angry with you.* Mama ist sehr böse mit dir.
♦ **to get angry** wütend werden

**animal** NOUN
das Tier (PL die Tiere)

**ankle** NOUN
der Fußknöchel (PL die Fußknöchel)

**anniversary** NOUN
der Jahrestag (PL die Jahrestage)
♦ **wedding anniversary** der Hochzeitstag

to **announce** VERB
ankündigen (PERFECT hat angekündigt)

**announcement** NOUN
die Ankündigung

to **annoy** VERB
ärgern ◊ *He's really annoying me.* Er ärgert mich echt.
♦ **to get annoyed** wütend werden ◊ *I saw that he was getting annoyed.* Ich sah, dass er wütend wurde.

**annoying** ADJECTIVE
ärgerlich ◊ *It's really annoying.* Es ist wirklich ärgerlich.

**annual** ADJECTIVE

jährlich ◊ *an annual meeting* ein jährliches Treffen

**anonymous** ADJECTIVE
anonym

**anorak** NOUN
der Anorak (PL die Anoraks)

**another** ADJECTIVE
*Use* **noch ein** *for masculine and neuter nouns,* **noch eine** *for feminine nouns.*
[1] noch ein ◊ *I bought another hat.* Ich habe noch einen Hut gekauft. ◊ *Would you like another piece of cake?* Möchtest du noch ein Stück Kuchen?
noch eine ◊ *Would you like another cup of tea?* Möchten Sie noch eine Tasse Tee?
*Use* **ein anderer** *for masculine,* **eine andere** *for feminine and* **ein anderes** *for neuter nouns.*
[2] (*different*)
ein anderer ◊ *Could you show me another hat?* Könnten Sie mir einen anderen Hut zeigen?
eine andere ◊ *My girlfriend goes to another school.* Meine Freundin besucht eine andere Schule.
ein anderes ◊ *Have you got another shirt?* Haben Sie noch ein anderes Hemd?
♦ **another time** ein andermal

to **answer** VERB
| see also **answer** NOUN |
beantworten (PERFECT hat beantwortet) ◊ *Can you answer my question?* Kannst du meine Frage beantworten?
♦ **to answer the phone** ans Telefon gehen
♦ **to answer the door** aufmachen ◊ *Can you answer the door, please?* Kannst du bitte aufmachen?

**answer** NOUN
| see also **answer** VERB |
[1] die Antwort (*to question*)
[2] die Lösung (*to problem*)

**answering machine** NOUN
der Anrufbeantworter (PL die Anrufbeantworter)

**ant** NOUN
die Ameise

to **antagonize** VERB
verärgern (PERFECT hat verärgert) ◊ *He didn't want to antagonize her.* Er wollte sie nicht verärgern.

**Antarctic** NOUN
die Antarktis

**anthem** NOUN
♦ **the national anthem** die Nationalhymne

**antibiotic** NOUN
das Antibiotikum (PL die Antibiotika)

**antidepressant** NOUN
das Antidepressivum (PL die Antidepressiva)

**antique** NOUN

☞

die Antiquität (*furniture*)

**antique shop** NOUN
der Antiquitätenladen (PL die Antiquitätenläden)

**antiseptic** NOUN
das Antiseptikum (PL die Antiseptika)

**any** ADJECTIVE, PRONOUN, ADVERB
*In most cases **any** is not translated.*
◊ *Would you like any bread?* Möchten Sie Brot? ◊ *Have you got any mineral water?* Haben Sie Mineralwasser?
*Use **kein** for **not any**.*
◊ *We haven't got any milk left.* Wir haben keine Milch mehr. ◊ *I haven't got any money.* Ich habe kein Geld. ◊ *I haven't got any books.* Ich habe keine Bücher. ◊ *Sorry, we haven't got any.* Tut mir Leid, wir haben keine.

♦ **any more (1)** (*additional*) noch etwas ◊ *Would you like any more coffee?* Möchten Sie noch etwas Kaffee?

♦ **any more (2)** (*no longer*) nicht mehr ◊ *I don't love him any more.* Ich liebe ihn nicht mehr.

**anybody** PRONOUN
1 jemand (*in question*) ◊ *Has anybody got a pen?* Hat jemand etwas zum Schreiben?
2 jeder (*no matter who*) ◊ *Anybody can learn to swim.* Jeder kann schwimmen lernen.
*Use **niemand** for **not ... anybody**.*
◊ *I can't see anybody.* Ich kann niemanden sehen.

**anyhow** ADVERB
sowieso ◊ *He doesn't want to go out and anyhow he's not allowed.* Er will nicht ausgehen, und er darf es sowieso auch nicht.

**anyone** PRONOUN
1 jemand (*in question*) ◊ *Has anyone got a pen?* Hat jemand etwas zum Schreiben?
2 jeder (*no matter who*) ◊ *Anyone can learn to swim.* Jeder kann schwimmen lernen.
*Use **niemand** for **not ... anyone**.*
◊ *I can't see anyone.* Ich kann niemanden sehen.

**anything** PRONOUN
1 etwas (*in question*) ◊ *Would you like anything to eat?* Möchtest du etwas zu essen?
2 alles (*no matter what*) ◊ *Anything could happen.* Alles könnte passieren.
*Use **nichts** for **not ... anything**.*
◊ *I can't hear anything.* Ich kann nichts hören.

**anyway** ADVERB
sowieso ◊ *He doesn't want to go out and anyway he's not allowed.* Er will nicht ausgehen, und er darf es sowieso auch nicht.

**anywhere** ADVERB
1 irgendwo (*in question*) ◊ *Have you seen my coat anywhere?* Hast du irgendwo meinen Mantel gesehen?
2 überall ◊ *You can buy stamps almost anywhere.* Man kann fast überall Briefmarken kaufen.
*Use **nirgends** for **not ... anywhere**.*
3 nirgends ◊ *I can't find it anywhere.* Ich kann es nirgends finden.

**apart** ADVERB
♦ **The two towns are ten kilometres apart.** Die zwei Städte liegen zehn Kilometer voneinander entfernt.

♦ **apart from** abgesehen von ◊ *Apart from that, everything's fine.* Davon abgesehen ist alles in Ordnung.

**apartment** NOUN
die Wohnung

to **apologize** VERB
sich entschuldigen (PERFECT hat sich entschuldigt) ◊ *He apologized for being late.* Er entschuldigte sich für sein Zuspätkommen.

♦ **I apologize!** Ich bitte um Entschuldigung!

**apology** NOUN
die Entschuldigung

**apostrophe** NOUN
der Apostroph (PL die Apostrophe)

**apparatus** NOUN
der Apparat (PL die Apparate)

**apparent** ADJECTIVE
offensichtlich

**apparently** ADVERB
offensichtlich

to **appeal** VERB
see also **appeal** NOUN
bitten (IMPERFECT bat, PERFECT hat gebeten) ◊ *They appealed for help.* Sie baten um Hilfe.

♦ **to appeal to somebody** (*attract*) jemanden reizen ◊ *Does that appeal to you?* Reizt dich das?

**appeal** NOUN
see also **appeal** VERB
der Aufruf (PL die Aufrufe)

to **appear** VERB
1 (*come into view*)
kommen (IMPERFECT kam, PERFECT ist gekommen) ◊ *The bus appeared around the corner.* Der Bus kam um die Ecke.
♦ **to appear on TV** im Fernsehen auftreten
2 (*seem*)
scheinen (IMPERFECT schien, PERFECT hat geschienen) ◊ *She appeared to be asleep.* Sie schien zu schlafen.

**appearance** NOUN
das Äußere (*looks*) (GEN des Äußeren) ◊ *She takes great care over her appearance.* Sie achtet sehr auf ihr Äußeres.

**appendicitis** NOUN
die Blinddarmentzündung

**A**

**appetite** NOUN
der Appetit

to **applaud** VERB
klatschen

**applause** NOUN
der Beifall

**apple** NOUN
der Apfel (PL die Äpfel)
♦ **an apple tree** ein Apfelbaum MASC

**applicant** NOUN
der Bewerber (PL die Bewerber)
die Bewerberin
◊ *There were a hundred applicants for the job.* Es gab hundert Bewerber für die Stelle.

**application** NOUN
♦ **a job application** eine Bewerbung

**application form** NOUN
[1] (*for job*)
das Bewerbungsformular (PL die Bewerbungsformulare)
[2] (*for university*)
das Anmeldeformular (PL die Anmeldeformulare)

to **apply** VERB
♦ **to apply for a job** sich für eine Stelle bewerben ◊ *She applied for the job as a secretary.* Sie bewarb sich für die Sekretärinnenstelle.
♦ **to apply to** (*be relevant*) zutreffen auf ◊ *This rule doesn't apply to me.* Diese Regel trifft auf mich nicht zu.

**appointment** NOUN
der Termin (PL die Termine) ◊ *I've got a dental appointment.* Ich habe einen Zahnarzttermin.

to **appreciate** VERB
zu schätzen wissen (PRESENT weiß zu schätzen, IMPERFECT wusste zu schätzen, PERFECT hat zu schätzen gewusst) ◊ *I really appreciate your help.* Ich weiß deine Hilfe wirklich zu schätzen.

**apprentice** NOUN
der Lehrling (PL die Lehrlinge)
*der Lehrling is also used for women.*
◊ *She is an apprentice.* Sie ist Lehrling.

to **approach** VERB
[1] (*get nearer to*)
sich nähern ◊ *He approached the house.* Er näherte sich dem Haus.
[2] (*tackle*)
angehen (IMPERFECT ging an, PERFECT hat angegangen) ◊ *to approach a problem* ein Problem angehen

**appropriate** ADJECTIVE
passend ◊ *That dress isn't very appropriate for an interview.* Dieses Kleid ist für ein Vorstellungsgespräch nicht sehr passend.

**approval** NOUN
die Zustimmung

to **approve** VERB
♦ **to approve of** gutheißen ◊ *I don't approve of his choice.* Ich heiße seine Wahl nicht gut.
♦ **They didn't approve of his girlfriend.** Sie hatten etwas gegen seine Freundin.

**approximate** ADJECTIVE
ungefähr

**apricot** NOUN
die Aprikose

**April** NOUN
der April ◊ *in April* im April
♦ **April Fool's Day** der erste April
♦ **April Fool!** April, April!

**apron** NOUN
die Schürze

**Aquarius** NOUN
der Wassermann ◊ *I'm Aquarius.* Ich bin Wassermann.

**Arab** ADJECTIVE
[see also **Arab** NOUN]
arabisch ◊ *the Arab countries* die arabischen Länder

**Arab** NOUN
[see also **Arab** ADJECTIVE]
der Araber (PL die Araber)
die Araberin

**Arabic** ADJECTIVE
arabisch

**arch** NOUN
der Bogen (PL die Bögen)

**archaeologist** NOUN (US **archeologist**)
der Archäologe (GEN des Archäologen, PL die Archäologen)
die Archäologin
◊ *She's an archaeologist.* Sie ist Archäologin.

**archaeology** NOUN
die Archäologie

**archbishop** NOUN
der Erzbischof (PL die Erzbischöfe)

**archeologist** NOUN US
der Archäologe (GEN des Archäologen, PL die Archäologen)
die Archäologin
◊ *She's an archaeologist.* Sie ist Archäologin.

**archeology** NOUN US
die Archäologie

**architect** NOUN
der Architekt (GEN des Architekten, PL die Architekten)
die Architektin
◊ *She's an architect.* Sie ist Architektin.

**architecture** NOUN
die Architektur

**Arctic** NOUN
die Arktis

**are** VERB *see* **be**

**area** NOUN
[1] die Gegend ◊ *She lives in the London area.* Sie lebt in der Gegend von London.

☞

[2] das Viertel (PL die Viertel) ◊ *My favourite area of London is Soho.* Soho ist mein Lieblingsviertel von London.

[3] die Fläche ◊ *The field has an area of one thousand square metres.* Das Feld hat eine Fläche von eintausend Quadratmetern.

**Argentina** NOUN
Argentinien NEUT
♦ **from Argentina** aus Argentinien
♦ **to Argentina** nach Argentinien

**Argentinian** ADJECTIVE
argentinisch

to **argue** VERB
streiten (IMPERFECT stritt, PERFECT hat gestritten) ◊ *They never stop arguing.* Sie streiten dauernd.

**argument** NOUN
der Streit (PL die Streite)
♦ **to have an argument** Streit haben ◊ *They had an argument.* Sie hatten Streit.

**Aries** NOUN
der Widder ◊ *I'm Aries.* Ich bin Widder.

**arm** NOUN
der Arm (PL die Arme)

**armchair** NOUN
der Sessel (PL die Sessel)

**armour** NOUN (US **armor**)
die Rüstung
♦ **a suit of armour** eine Rüstung

**army** NOUN
die Armee (PL die Armeen)

**around** PREPOSITION, ADVERB
[1] um ◊ *She wore a scarf around her neck.* Sie trug einen Schal um den Hals.
[2] etwa (*approximately*) ◊ *It costs around a hundred pounds.* Es kostet etwa einhundert Pfund.
[3] gegen (*date, time*) ◊ *Let's meet at around eight p.m.* Treffen wir uns gegen acht Uhr abends.
♦ **around here (1)** (*nearby*) hier in der Nähe ◊ *Is there a chemist's around here?* Gibt es hier in der Nähe eine Apotheke?
♦ **around here (2)** (*in this area*) hier in der Gegend ◊ *He lives around here.* Er wohnt hier in der Gegend.

to **arrange** VERB
♦ **to arrange to do something** verabreden, etwas zu tun ◊ *They arranged to go out together on Friday.* Sie haben verabredet, am Freitag zusammen auszugehen.
♦ **to arrange a meeting** ein Treffen ausmachen ◊ *Can we arrange a meeting?* Können wir ein Treffen ausmachen?
♦ **to arrange a party** eine Party vorbereiten

**arrangement** NOUN
der Plan (*plan*) (PL die Pläne)
♦ **They made arrangements to go out on Friday night.** Sie haben verabredet, am Freitagabend auszugehen.

to **arrest** VERB
| *see also* **arrest** NOUN |
verhaften (PERFECT hat verhaftet) ◊ *The police have arrested five people.* Die Polizei hat fünf Leute verhaftet.

**arrest** NOUN
| *see also* **arrest** VERB |
die Verhaftung
♦ **You're under arrest!** Sie sind verhaftet!

**arrival** NOUN
die Ankunft (PL die Ankünfte)

to **arrive** VERB
ankommen (IMPERFECT kam an, PERFECT ist angekommen) ◊ *I arrived at five o'clock.* Ich bin um fünf Uhr angekommen.

**arrogant** ADJECTIVE
arrogant

**arrow** NOUN
der Pfeil (PL die Pfeile)

**art** NOUN
die Kunst (PL die Künste)

**artery** NOUN
die Arterie

**art gallery** NOUN
die Kunstgalerie

**article** NOUN
der Artikel (PL die Artikel) ◊ *a newspaper article* ein Zeitungsartikel

**artificial** ADJECTIVE
künstlich

**artist** NOUN
der Künstler (PL die Künstler)
die Künstlerin
◊ *She's an artist.* Sie ist Künstlerin.

**artistic** ADJECTIVE
künstlerisch

**as** CONJUNCTION, ADVERB
[1] als (*while*) ◊ *He came in as I was leaving.* Er kam herein, als ich gehen wollte.
♦ **He works as a waiter in the holidays.** In den Ferien jobbt er als Kellner.
[2] da (*since*) ◊ *As it's Sunday, you can have a lie-in.* Da es Sonntag ist, kannst du ausschlafen.
♦ **as ... as so ...** so ◊ *Peter's as tall as Michael.* Peter ist so groß wie Michael. ◊ *Her coat cost twice as much as mine.* Ihr Mantel hat doppelt so viel wie meiner gekostet.
♦ **as much ... as** so viel ... wie ◊ *I haven't got as much money as you.* Ich habe nicht so viel Geld wie du.
♦ **as soon as possible** sobald wie möglich ◊ *I'll do it as soon as possible.* Ich tue es sobald wie möglich.
♦ **as from tomorrow** ab morgen ◊ *As from tomorrow, the shops will stay open until ten p.m.* Ab morgen haben die Geschäfte bis zehn Uhr abends auf.
♦ **as if** als ob
♦ **as though** als ob

Note that **als ob** is followed by the subjunctive.

◊ *She acted as though she hadn't seen me.* Sie tat so, als ob sie mich nicht sähe.

**asap** ABBREVIATION (= *as soon as possible*)
sobald wie möglich

**ash** NOUN
die Asche

**ashamed** ADJECTIVE
♦**to be ashamed** sich schämen ◊ *You should be ashamed of yourself!* Du solltest dich schämen!

**ashtray** NOUN
der Aschenbecher (PL die Aschenbecher)

**Asia** NOUN
Asien NEUT
♦**from Asia** aus Asien
♦**to Asia** nach Asien

**Asian** ADJECTIVE
| see also **Asian** NOUN |
asiatisch ◊ *He's Asian.* Er ist Asiate.
◊ *She's Asian.* Sie ist Asiatin.

**Asian** NOUN
| see also **Asian** ADJECTIVE |
der Asiate (GEN des Asiaten, PL die Asiaten)
die Asiatin

to **ask** VERB
[1] (*inquire, request*)
fragen ◊ *"Have you finished?" she asked.* "Bist du fertig?" fragte sie.
♦**to ask somebody something** jemanden etwas fragen ◊ *He asked her how old she was.* Er fragte sie, wie alt sie ist.
♦**to ask for something** um etwas bitten ◊ *He asked for a cup of tea.* Er bat um eine Tasse Tee.
♦**to ask somebody to do something** jemanden bitten, etwas zu tun ◊ *She asked him to do the shopping.* Sie bat ihn einzukaufen.
♦**to ask about something** sich nach etwas erkundigen ◊ *I asked about train times to Leeds.* Ich habe mich nach Zugverbindungen nach Leeds erkundigt.
♦**to ask somebody a question** jemanden etwas fragen
[2] (*invite*)
einladen (PRESENT lädt ein, IMPERFECT lud ein, PERFECT hat eingeladen) ◊ *Have you asked Matthew to the party?* Hast du Matthew zur Party eingeladen?
♦**He asked her out.** (*on a date*) Er hat sie um ein Rendezvous gebeten.

**asleep** ADJECTIVE
♦**to be asleep** schlafen ◊ *He's asleep.* Er schläft.
♦**to fall asleep** einschlafen ◊ *I fell asleep in front of the TV.* Ich bin beim Fernsehen eingeschlafen.

**asparagus** NOUN
der Spargel (PL die Spargel)

**aspect** NOUN

der Aspekt (PL die Aspekte)

**aspirin** NOUN
die Schmerztablette

**asset** NOUN
der Vorteil (PL die Vorteile) ◊ *Her experience will be an asset to the firm.* Ihre Erfahrung wird für die Firma von Vorteil sein.

**assignment** NOUN
das Referat (*in school*) (PL die Referate)

**assistance** NOUN
die Hilfe

**assistant** NOUN
[1] (*in shop*)
der Verkäufer (PL die Verkäufer)
die Verkäuferin
[2] (*helper*)
der Assistent (GEN des Assistenten, PL die Assistenten)
die Assistentin

**association** NOUN
der Verband (PL die Verbände)

**assortment** NOUN
[1] die Auswahl (*choice*) ◊ *a large assortment of cheeses* eine große Auswahl an Käse
[2] die Mischung (*mixture*) ◊ *an assortment of biscuits* eine Keksmischung

to **assume** VERB
annehmen (PRESENT nimmt an, IMPERFECT nahm an, PERFECT hat angenommen) ◊ *I assume she won't be coming.* Ich nehme an, dass sie nicht kommt.

to **assure** VERB
versichern (PERFECT hat versichert) ◊ *He assured me he was coming.* Er versicherte mir, dass er kommt.

**asthma** NOUN
das Asthma ◊ *I've got asthma.* Ich habe Asthma.

to **astonish** VERB
erstaunen (PERFECT hat erstaunt) ◊ *She was astonished.* Sie war erstaunt.

**astonishing** ADJECTIVE
erstaunlich

**astrology** NOUN
die Astrologie

**astronaut** NOUN
der Astronaut (GEN des Astronauten, PL die Astronauten)
die Astronautin

**astronomy** NOUN
die Astronomie

**asylum** NOUN
das Asyl ◊ *to ask for asylum* um Asyl bitten

**asylum-seeker** NOUN
der Asylbewerber (PL die Asylbewerber)
die Asylbewerberin

**at** PREPOSITION

**1** um ◊ *at four o'clock* um vier Uhr
**2** an ◊ *at Christmas* an Weihnachten
◊ *What are you doing at the weekend?*
Was machst du am Wochenende?
♦ **at night** nachts
**3** mit ◊ *at fifty kilometres per hour* mit
fünfzig Stundenkilometern
**4** in ◊ *at school* in der Schule ◊ *at the
office* im Büro
♦ **at home** zu Hause
♦ **two at a time** jeweils zwei
♦ **at the races** beim Pferderennen

**ate** VERB *see* **eat**

**Athens** NOUN
Athen NEUT
♦ **from Athens** aus Athen

**athlete** NOUN
der Athlet (GEN des Athleten, PL die
Athleten)
die Athletin

**athletic** ADJECTIVE
athletisch

**athletics** NOUN
die Leichtathletik ◊ *I like watching the
athletics on TV.* Ich sehe mir im
Fernsehen gern Leichtathletik an.

**Atlantic** NOUN
der Atlantik

**atlas** NOUN
der Atlas (GEN des Atlasses, PL die
Atlanten)

**atmosphere** NOUN
die Atmosphäre

**atom** NOUN
das Atom (PL die Atome)

**atomic** ADJECTIVE
♦ **an atomic bomb** eine Atombombe

to **attach** VERB
festbinden (IMPERFECT band fest, PERFECT hat
festgebunden) ◊ *They attached a rope to
the car.* Sie banden ein Seil am Auto fest.
♦ **Please find attached ...** Anbei erhalten
Sie ...

**attached** ADJECTIVE
♦ **to be attached to somebody** an
jemandem hängen ◊ *He's very attached
to his family.* Er hängt sehr an seiner
Familie.

to **attack** VERB
see also **attack** NOUN
angreifen (IMPERFECT griff an, PERFECT hat
angegriffen) ◊ *The dog attacked me.* Der
Hund hat mich angegriffen.

**attack** NOUN
see also **attack** VERB
der Angriff (PL die Angriffe)

**attempt** NOUN
see also **attempt** VERB
der Versuch (PL die Versuche) ◊ *She
gave up after several attempts.* Sie gab
nach mehreren Versuchen auf.

to **attempt** VERB

see also **attempt** NOUN
versuchen (PERFECT hat versucht)
♦ **to attempt to do something** versuchen,
etwas zu tun ◊ *I attempted to write a
song.* Ich habe versucht, ein Lied zu
schreiben.

to **attend** VERB
teilnehmen (PRESENT nimmt teil, IMPERFECT
nahm teil, PERFECT hat teilgenommen) ◊ *to
attend a meeting* an einem Treffen
teilnehmen

**attention** NOUN
die Aufmerksamkeit
♦ **to pay attention to something** auf etwas
achten ◊ *He didn't pay attention to what I
was saying.* Er hat nicht darauf geachtet,
was ich sagte.

**attic** NOUN
der Speicher (PL die Speicher)

**attitude** NOUN
die Einstellung ◊ *I really don't like your
attitude!* Mir gefällt deine Einstellung
nicht!

**attorney** NOUN US
der Rechtsanwalt (PL die Rechtsanwälte)
die Rechtsanwältin
◊ *My mother's an attorney.* Meine Mutter
ist Rechtsanwältin.

to **attract** VERB
anziehen (IMPERFECT zog an, PERFECT hat
angezogen) ◊ *The Lake District attracts
lots of tourists.* Der Lake District zieht
viele Touristen an.

**attraction** NOUN
die Attraktion ◊ *a tourist attraction* eine
Touristenattraktion

**attractive** ADJECTIVE
attraktiv ◊ *She's very attractive.* Sie ist
sehr attraktiv.

**aubergine** NOUN
die Aubergine

**auction** NOUN
die Auktion

**audience** NOUN
die Zuschauer MASC PL (*in theatre*) ◊ *The
audience laughed loudly.* Die Zuschauer
lachten laut.

**audition** NOUN
**1** (*of actor*)
die Vorsprechprobe
**2** (*of musician*)
das Vorspiel (PL die Vorspiele)

**August** NOUN
der August ◊ *in August* im August

**aunt** NOUN
die Tante ◊ *my aunt* meine Tante

**aunty** NOUN
die Tante ◊ *my aunty* meine Tante

**au pair** NOUN
das Au-pair-Mädchen (PL die Au-pair-
Mädchen) ◊ *She's an au pair.* Sie ist Au-
pair-Mädchen.

**Australia** NOUN
Australien NEUT
♦ **from Australia** aus Australien
♦ **in Australia** in Australien
♦ **to Australia** nach Australien

**Australian** ADJECTIVE
see also **Australian** NOUN
australisch ◊ *He's Australian.* Er ist
Australier. ◊ *She's Australian.* Sie ist
Australierin.

**Australian** NOUN
see also **Australian** ADJECTIVE
der Australier (PL die Australier)
die Australierin
♦ **the Australians** die Australier

**Austria** NOUN
Österreich NEUT
♦ **from Austria** aus Österreich
♦ **in Austria** in Österreich
♦ **to Austria** nach Österreich

**Austrian** ADJECTIVE
see also **Austrian** NOUN
österreichisch ◊ *He's Austrian.* Er ist
Österreicher. ◊ *She's Austrian.* Sie ist
Österreicherin.

**Austrian** NOUN
see also **Austrian** ADJECTIVE
der Österreicher (PL die Österreicher)
die Österreicherin
♦ **the Austrians** die Österreicher

**author** NOUN
der Autor (PL die Autoren)
die Autorin
◊ *She's a famous author.* Sie ist eine
berühmte Autorin.

**autobiography** NOUN
die Autobiografie

**autograph** NOUN
das Autogramm (PL die Autogramme)
◊ *May I have your autograph?* Kann ich
Ihr Autogramm haben?

**automatic** ADJECTIVE
automatisch ◊ *an automatic door* eine
automatische Tür

**automatically** ADVERB
automatisch

**autumn** NOUN
der Herbst (PL die Herbste) ◊ *in autumn*
im Herbst

**availability** NOUN
die Erhältlichkeit (*of goods*)
♦ **subject to availability** falls vorrätig

**available** ADJECTIVE
erhältlich ◊ *Free brochures are available
on request.* Auf Anfrage sind kostenlose
Prospekte erhältlich.
♦ **Is Mr Cooke available today?** Ist Herr
Cooke heute zu sprechen?

**avalanche** NOUN
die Lawine

**avenue** NOUN
die Allee

**average** NOUN

see also **average** ADJECTIVE
der Durchschnitt (PL die Durchschnitte)
◊ *on average* im Durchschnitt

**average** ADJECTIVE
see also **average** NOUN
durchschnittlich ◊ *the average price* der
durchschnittliche Preis

**avocado** NOUN
die Avocado (PL die Avocados)

to **avoid** VERB
[1] meiden (IMPERFECT mied, PERFECT hat
gemieden) ◊ *He avoids her when she's in
a bad mood.* Er meidet sie, wenn sie
schlechte Laune hat.
[2] vermeiden ◊ *You should avoid going
out on your own at night.* Du solltest
vermeiden, nachts allein auszugehen.

**awake** ADJECTIVE
♦ **to be awake** wach sein ◊ *Is she awake?*
Ist sie wach? ◊ *He was still awake.* Er war
noch wach.

**award** NOUN
der Preis (PL die Preise) ◊ *He's won an
award.* Er hat einen Preis bekommen.

**aware** ADJECTIVE
♦ **to be aware that...** sich bewusst sein,
dass...
♦ **to be aware of something** etw merken
◊ *We are aware of what is happening.*
Wir merken, was geschieht.
♦ **not that I am aware of** nicht dass ich
wüsste

**away** ADJECTIVE, ADVERB
weg (*not here*) ◊ *Felix is away today.* Felix
ist heute weg. ◊ *He's away for a week.* Er
ist eine Woche lang weg.
♦ **The town's two kilometres away.** Die
Stadt ist zwei Kilometer entfernt.
♦ **The coast is two hours away by car.** Zur
Küste sind es mit dem Auto zwei Stunden.
♦ **Go away!** Geh weg!

**away match** NOUN
das Auswärtsspiel (PL die
Auswärtsspiele) ◊ *Our team has an away
match this week.* Unsere Mannschaft hat
diese Woche ein Auswärtsspiel.

**awful** ADJECTIVE
schrecklich ◊ *That's awful!* Das ist
schrecklich!
♦ **an awful lot of ...** furchtbar viel ... ◊ *an
awful lot of work* furchtbar viel Arbeit

**awfully** ADVERB
furchtbar ◊ *I'm awfully sorry.* Es tut mir
furchtbar Leid.

**awkward** ADJECTIVE
[1] schwierig (*difficult*) ◊ *an awkward
situation* eine schwierige Situation
[2] unangenehm (*embarrassing*) ◊ *an
awkward question* eine unangenehme
Frage

**axe** NOUN
die Axt (PL die Äxte)

# B

**BA** ABBREVIATION (= *Bachelor of Arts*)
der Magister (PL die Magister)
♦ **She's got a BA in History.** Sie hat einen
Magistertitel in Geschichte.

**baby** NOUN
das Baby (PL die Babys)
**baby carriage** NOUN US
der Buggy (PL die Buggys)
to **babysit** VERB
babysitten ◊ *Veronika is babysitting for
her friend.* Veronika babysittet bei ihrer
Freundin.

**babysitter** NOUN
der Babysitter (PL die Babysitter)
die Babysitterin

**babysitting** NOUN
das Babysitten

**bachelor** NOUN
der Junggeselle (GEN des Junggesellen,
PL die Junggesellen) ◊ *He's a bachelor.* Er
ist Junggeselle.

**back** NOUN
see also **back** ADJECTIVE, VERB
1 (*of person, horse, book*)
der Rücken (PL die Rücken)
2 (*of page, house*)
die Rückseite ◊ *Write your name on the
back.* Schreiben Sie Ihren Namen auf die
Rückseite.
♦ **in the back of the car** hinten im Auto
♦ **at the back** hinten ◊ *He's sitting at the
back.* Er sitzt hinten.

**back** ADJECTIVE, ADVERB
see also **back** NOUN, VERB
hintere ◊ *the back wheel of my bike* das
hintere Rad meines Fahrrads
♦ **the back seat** der Rücksitz
♦ **the back door** die Hintertür
♦ **to get back** zurückkommen ◊ *What time
did you get back?* Wann bist du
zurückgekommen?
♦ **We went there by bus and walked back.**
Wir sind mit dem Bus hingefahren und
zu Fuß zurückgegangen.
♦ **He's not back yet.** Er ist noch nicht
zurück.
♦ **to call somebody back** jemanden
zurückrufen ◊ *I'll call back later.* Ich rufe
später zurück.

to **back** VERB
see also **back** NOUN, ADJECTIVE
♦ **to back somebody** für jemanden sein
◊ *I'm backing the Labour Party.* Ich bin
für die Labour-Party.
♦ **to back a horse** auf ein Pferd setzen ◊ *He
backed the wrong horse.* Er hat auf das
falsche Pferd gesetzt.

♦ **to back out** einen Rückzieher machen
◊ *They promised to help and then
backed out.* Sie haben versprochen zu
helfen, haben dann aber einen
Rückzieher gemacht.
♦ **to back somebody up** jemanden
unterstützen

**backache** NOUN
die Rückenschmerzen MASC PL ◊ *to have
backache* Rückenschmerzen haben

**backbone** NOUN
das Rückgrat (PL die Rückgrate)

to **backfire** VERB
schief gehen (*go wrong*) (IMPERFECT ging
schief, PERFECT ist schief gegangen)

**background** NOUN
der Hintergrund (PL die Hintergründe)
◊ *a house in the background* ein Haus im
Hintergrund ◊ *his family background*
sein familiärer Hintergrund
♦ **background noise** die
Hintergrundgeräusche NEUT PL

**backhand** NOUN
die Rückhand (PL die Rückhände)

**backing** NOUN
die Unterstützung (*support*)

**backpack** NOUN
der Rucksack (PL die Rucksäcke)

**backpacker** NOUN
der Wanderer (PL die Wanderer)
die Wanderin

**back pain** NOUN
die Rückenschmerzen MASC PL ◊ *to have
back pain* Rückenschmerzen haben

**backside** NOUN
der Hintern (GEN des Hintern, PL die
Hintern)

**backstroke** NOUN
das Rückenschwimmen

**backup** NOUN
die Unterstützung (*support*)
♦ **a backup file** eine Sicherungsdatei

**backwards** ADVERB
zurück ◊ *to take a step backwards* einen
Schritt zurück machen
♦ **to fall backwards** nach hinten fallen

**back yard** NOUN
der Hinterhof (PL die Hinterhöfe)

**bacon** NOUN
der Speck ◊ *bacon and eggs* Eier mit
Speck

**bad** ADJECTIVE
1 schlecht ◊ *a bad film* ein schlechter
Film ◊ *the bad weather* das schlechte
Wetter ◊ *to be in a bad mood* schlechte
Laune haben ◊ *not bad* nicht schlecht
◊ *That's not bad at all.* Das ist gar nicht
schlecht.

**B**

♦ **to be bad at something** in etwas schlecht sein ◊ *I'm really bad at maths.* In Mathe bin ich wirklich schlecht.
[2] schlimm (*serious*) ◊ *a bad accident* ein schlimmer Unfall
[3] böse (*naughty*) ◊ *You bad boy!* Du böser Junge!
♦ **to go bad** (*food*) schlecht werden
♦ **I feel bad about it.** Das tut mir echt Leid.

**badge** NOUN
[1] (*metal*)
der Button (PL die Buttons)
[2] (*sticker*)
der Aufkleber (PL die Aufkleber)

**badly** ADVERB
schlecht ◊ *badly paid* schlecht bezahlt
♦ **badly wounded** schwer verletzt
♦ **He's badly in need of some money.** Er braucht dringend Geld.

**badminton** NOUN
das Badminton ◊ *to play badminton* Badminton spielen

**bad-tempered** ADJECTIVE
♦ **to be bad-tempered (1)** (*by nature*) griesgrämig sein ◊ *He's a really bad-tempered person.* Er ist wirklich ein griesgrämiger Mensch.
♦ **to be bad-tempered (2)** (*temporarily*) schlechte Laune haben ◊ *He was really bad-tempered yesterday.* Er hatte gestern wirklich schlechte Laune.

to **baffle** VERB
verblüffen (PERFECT hat verblüfft) ◊ *She was baffled.* Sie war verblüfft.

**bag** NOUN
die Tasche
♦ **an old bag** (*person*) eine alte Schachtel

**baggage** NOUN
das Gepäck

**baggage reclaim** NOUN
die Gepäckausgabe

**baggy** ADJECTIVE
weit (*clothes*)

**bagpipes** PL NOUN
der Dudelsack (PL die Dudelsäcke) ◊ *Ed plays the bagpipes.* Ed spielt Dudelsack.

to **bake** VERB
backen (PRESENT bäckt, IMPERFECT backte, PERFECT hat gebacken) ◊ *to bake a cake* einen Kuchen backen

**baked beans** PL NOUN
die gebackenen Bohnen PL

**baker** NOUN
der Bäcker (PL die Bäcker)
die Bäckerin
◊ *He's a baker.* Er ist Bäcker.

**bakery** NOUN
die Bäckerei

**baking** ADJECTIVE
♦ **It's baking in here!** Hier ist es furchtbar heiß!

**balance** NOUN
see also **balance** VERB
das Gleichgewicht ◊ *to lose one's balance* das Gleichgewicht verlieren

to **balance** VERB
see also **balance** NOUN
balancieren (PERFECT ist balanciert) ◊ *I balanced on the window ledge.* Ich balancierte auf dem Fensterbrett.
♦ **The boxes were carefully balanced.** Die Kartons befanden sich genau im Gleichgewicht.

**balanced** ADJECTIVE
ausgewogen ◊ *a balanced diet* eine ausgewogene Ernährung

**balcony** NOUN
der Balkon (PL die Balkone)

**bald** ADJECTIVE
glatzköpfig
♦ **to be bald** eine Glatze haben

**ball** NOUN
der Ball (PL die Bälle)

**ballet** NOUN
das Ballett (PL die Ballette)
*Note that you pronounce the "tt" in German.*
◊ *We went to a ballet.* Wir sind ins Ballett gegangen. ◊ *ballet lessons* Ballettstunden

**ballet dancer** NOUN
der Balletttänzer (PL die Balletttänzer)
die Balletttänzerin

**ballet shoes** PL NOUN
die Ballettschuhe MASC PL

**balloon** NOUN
der Luftballon (*at parties*) (PL die Luftballone)
♦ **a hot-air balloon** ein Heißluftballon

**ballpoint pen** NOUN
der Kugelschreiber (PL die Kugelschreiber)

**ban** NOUN
see also **ban** VERB
das Verbot (PL die Verbote)

to **ban** VERB
see also **ban** NOUN
verbieten (IMPERFECT verbot, PERFECT hat verboten) ◊ *to ban somebody from doing something* jemandem verbieten, etwas zu tun
♦ **She was banned from driving.** Sie bekam Fahrverbot.

**banana** NOUN
die Banane ◊ *a banana skin* eine Bananenschale

**band** NOUN
[1] (*rock band*)
die Band (PL die Bands)
[2] (*brass band*)
die Kapelle

**bandage** NOUN
see also **bandage** VERB
der Verband (PL die Verbände)

to **bandage** VERB

> see also **bandage** NOUN

verbinden (IMPERFECT verband, PERFECT hat verbunden) ◊ *The nurse bandaged his arm*. Die Schwester verband ihm den Arm.

**Band-Aid** ® NOUN US
das Heftpflaster (PL die Heftpflaster)

**bandit** NOUN
der Bandit (GEN des Banditen, PL die Banditen)

**bang** NOUN

> see also **bang** VERB

1 der Knall (PL die Knalle) ◊ *I heard a loud bang*. Ich habe einen lauten Knall gehört.

2 der Schlag (PL die Schläge) ◊ *a bang on the head* ein Schlag auf den Kopf

◆ **Bang!** Peng!

to **bang** VERB

> see also **bang** NOUN

anschlagen (*part of body*) (PRESENT schlägt an, IMPERFECT schlug an, PERFECT hat angeschlagen) ◊ *I banged my head*. Ich habe mir den Kopf angeschlagen.

◆ **to bang the door** die Tür zuknallen

◆ **to bang on the door** gegen die Tür hämmern

**banger** NOUN
die Bratwurst (PL die Bratwürste)
◊ *bangers and mash* Bratwürste mit Kartoffelbrei

**bank** NOUN
1 (*financial*)
die Bank (PL die Banken)
2 (*of river, lake*)
das Ufer (PL die Ufer)

to **bank on** VERB
sich verlassen auf (PRESENT verlässt, IMPERFECT verließ, PERFECT hat verlassen) ◊ *I was banking on your coming today*. Ich hatte mich darauf verlassen, dass du heute kommst. ◊ *I wouldn't bank on it*. Ich würde mich nicht darauf verlassen.

**bank account** NOUN
das Bankkonto (PL die Bankkonten)

**banker** NOUN
der Banker (PL die Banker)
die Bankerin

**bank holiday** NOUN
der Feiertag (PL die Feiertage)

**banknote** NOUN
die Banknote

**bankrupt** ADJECTIVE
bankrott

**banned** ADJECTIVE
verboten

**bar** NOUN
1 (*pub*)
die Bar (PL die Bars)
2 (*counter*)
die Theke

◆ **a bar of chocolate** eine Tafel Schokolade

◆ **a bar of soap** ein Stück Seife

**barbaric** ADJECTIVE
barbarisch

**barbecue** NOUN
das Barbecue (PL die Barbecues)

◆ **We could have a barbecue this evening.** Wir könnten heute Abend grillen.

**barber** NOUN
der Herrenfriseur (PL die Herrenfriseure)

**bare** ADJECTIVE
nackt

**barefoot** ADJECTIVE, ADVERB
barfuß ◊ *The children go around barefoot*. Die Kinder laufen barfuß herum. ◊ *She was barefoot*. Sie war barfuß.

**barely** ADVERB
kaum ◊ *I could barely hear what she was saying*. Ich konnte kaum hören, was sie sagte.

**bargain** NOUN
das Schnäppchen (PL die Schnäppchen)
◊ *It was a bargain!* Das war ein Schnäppchen!

**barge** NOUN
der Kahn (PL die Kähne)

to **bark** VERB
bellen

**barmaid** NOUN
die Bardame ◊ *She's a barmaid*. Sie ist Bardame.

**barman** NOUN
der Barkeeper (PL die Barkeeper) ◊ *He's a barman*. Er ist Barkeeper.

**barn** NOUN
die Scheune

**barrel** NOUN
das Fass (GEN des Fasses, PL die Fässer)

**barrier** NOUN
die Schranke

**bartender** NOUN US
der Barkeeper (PL die Barkeeper)

**base** NOUN
1 (*basis*)
die Basis (PL die Basen) ◊ *a good base for a successful career* eine gute Basis für eine erfolgreiche Karriere
2 (*of lamp, mountain*)
der Fuß (GEN des Fußes, PL die Füße)
3 (*of container*)
der Boden (PL die Böden)
4 (*for paint, make-up*)
die Grundlage
5 (*military*)
der Stützpunkt (PL die Stützpunkte)

**baseball** NOUN
der Baseball ◊ *a baseball cap* eine Baseballmütze

**based** ADJECTIVE
◆ **based on** basierend auf +DAT

**basement** NOUN
das Untergeschoss (GEN des Untergeschosses, PL die Untergeschosse)

to **bash** VERB
| see also **bash** NOUN |

♦ **to bash something** auf etwas einschlagen ◊ *They tried to bash the door in.* Sie versuchten, die Tür einzuschlagen.

**bash** NOUN
| see also **bash** VERB |

♦ **I'll have a bash.** Ich versuch's mal.

**basic** ADJECTIVE
1 elementar (*knowledge, education*)
♦ **basic vocabulary** der Grundwortschatz
♦ **It's a basic model.** Es ist ein Grundmodell.
2 einfach ◊ *The accommodation is pretty basic.* Die Unterkunft ist sehr einfach.

**basically** ADVERB
eigentlich ◊ *Basically, I just don't like him.* Eigentlich mag ich ihn nicht.

**basics** PL NOUN
die Grundlagen FEM PL

**basil** NOUN
das Basilikum

**basin** NOUN
(*washbasin*)
das Waschbecken (PL die Waschbecken)

**basis** NOUN
♦ **on a daily basis** täglich
♦ **on a regular basis** regelmäßig

**basket** NOUN
der Korb (PL die Körbe)

**basketball** NOUN
der Basketball

**bass** NOUN
der Bass (GEN des Basses, PL die Bässe)
◊ *He plays bass.* Er spielt Bass. ◊ *He's a bass.* Er singt Bass.
♦ **a bass drum** eine Basstrommel
♦ **a bass guitar** eine Bassgitarre

**bassoon** NOUN
das Fagott (PL die Fagotte) ◊ *I play the bassoon.* Ich spiele Fagott.

**bastard** NOUN
der Scheißkerl *rude*
(PL die Scheißkerle) ◊ *You bastard!* Du Scheißkerl!

**bat** NOUN
1 (*for cricket, rounders, table tennis*)
der Schläger (PL die Schläger)
2 (*animal*)
die Fledermaus (PL die Fledermäuse)

**bath** NOUN
1 das Bad (PL die Bäder) ◊ *a hot bath* ein heißes Bad
♦ **to have a bath** baden
2 (*bathtub*)
die Badewanne ◊ *There's a spider in the bath.* In der Badewanne ist eine Spinne.

to **bathe** VERB
baden

**bathing suit** NOUN US

der Badeanzug (PL die Badeanzüge)

**bathroom** NOUN
das Badezimmer (PL die Badezimmer)

**baths** PL NOUN
das Schwimmbad (PL die Schwimmbäder)

**bath towel** NOUN
das Badetuch (PL die Badetücher)

**batter** NOUN
der Pfannkuchenteig

**battery** NOUN
die Batterie

**battle** NOUN
die Schlacht ◊ *the Battle of Hastings* die Schlacht von Hastings
♦ **It was a battle, but we managed in the end.** Es war ein Kampf, aber wir haben es schließlich geschafft.

**battleship** NOUN
das Schlachtschiff (PL die Schlachtschiffe)

**bay** NOUN
die Bucht

**BC** ABBREVIATION (= *before Christ*) v. Chr. (= vor Christus) ◊ *in 200 BC* im Jahre 200 v. Chr.

to **be** VERB
sein (PRESENT ist, IMPERFECT war, PERFECT ist gewesen) ◊ *I'm tired.* Ich bin müde.
◊ *You're late.* Du bist spät dran. ◊ *She's English.* Sie ist Engländerin. ◊ *It's cold.* Es ist kalt. ◊ *It's a nice day.* Es ist ein schöner Tag. ◊ *It's four o'clock.* Es ist vier Uhr. ◊ *I'm fourteen.* Ich bin vierzehn.
◊ *We are all happy.* Wir sind alle glücklich. ◊ *I've been ill.* Ich war krank.
◊ *I've never been to Dresden.* Ich war noch nie in Dresden.
♦ **to be beaten** geschlagen werden
*Questions like "isn't it?" don't exist in German.*
◊ *She's pretty, isn't she?* Sie ist hübsch, nicht wahr? ◊ *The film was good, wasn't it?* Der Film war gut, nicht wahr?
*You do not translate a when you want to describe somebody's occupation.*
◊ *She's a doctor.* Sie ist Ärztin. ◊ *He's a student.* Er ist Student. ◊ *He's a bachelor.* Er ist Junggeselle.
♦ **I'm cold.** Mir ist kalt.
♦ **I'm hungry.** Ich habe Hunger.

**beach** NOUN
der Strand (PL die Strände)

**bead** NOUN
die Perle

**beak** NOUN
der Schnabel (PL die Schnäbel)

**beam** NOUN
der Strahl (PL die Strahlen)

**beans** PL NOUN
1 die Bohnen FEM PL
2 die gebackenen Bohnen FEM PL (*baked beans*)

ⓘ *Few Germans eat baked beans and not many shops sell them.*

◇ **beans on toast** gebackene Bohnen in Tomatensoße auf Toast
♦ **broad beans** dicke Bohnen
♦ **green beans** grüne Bohnen
♦ **kidney beans** Kidneybohnen

**bean sprouts** PL NOUN
die Sojasprossen PL

**bear** NOUN
> see also **bear** VERB

der Bär (GEN des Bären, PL die Bären)
to **bear** VERB
> see also **bear** NOUN

ertragen (*endure*) (PRESENT erträgt, IMPERFECT ertrug, PERFECT hat ertragen) ◇ *I can't bear it.* Ich kann es nicht ertragen.
♦ **to bear up** sich halten
♦ **Bear up!** Kopf hoch!
♦ **If you would bear with me for a moment** ... Wenn Sie sich bitte einen Moment gedulden könnten ...

**beard** NOUN
der Bart (PL die Bärte) ◇ *He's got a beard.* Er hat einen Bart.
♦ **a man with a beard** ein bärtiger Mann

**bearded** ADJECTIVE
bärtig

**beat** NOUN
> see also **beat** VERB

der Rhythmus (GEN des Rhythmus, PL die Rhythmen)
to **beat** VERB
> see also **beat** NOUN

schlagen (PRESENT schlägt, IMPERFECT schlug, PERFECT hat geschlagen) ◇ *We beat them three nil.* Wir haben sie drei zu null geschlagen.
♦ **Beat it!** Hau ab! (*informal*)
♦ **to beat somebody up** (*informal*) jemanden zusammenschlagen

**beautiful** ADJECTIVE
schön

**beautifully** ADVERB
schön

**beauty** NOUN
die Schönheit

**beauty spot** NOUN
das schöne Fleckchen (PL die schönen Fleckchen)

**became** VERB *see* **become**

**because** CONJUNCTION
weil ◇ *I did it because* ... Ich habe es getan, weil ...
♦ **because of** wegen ◇ *because of the weather* wegen des Wetters

to **become** VERB
werden (PRESENT wird, IMPERFECT wurde, PERFECT ist geworden) ◇ *He became a*

*famous writer.* Er wurde ein berühmter Schriftsteller.
*Be careful not to translate* **to become** *by* **bekommen.**

**bed** NOUN
das Bett (PL die Betten) ◇ *in bed* im Bett
♦ **to go to bed** ins Bett gehen ◇ *to go to bed with somebody* mit jemandem ins Bett gehen

**bed and breakfast** NOUN
das Zimmer mit Frühstück (PL die Zimmer mit Frühstück) ◇ *How much is it for bed and breakfast?* Wie viel kostet das Zimmer mit Frühstück?
♦ **We stayed in a bed and breakfast.** Wir waren in einer Frühstückspension.

**bedclothes** PL NOUN
die Bettwäsche SING

**bedding** NOUN
das Bettzeug

**bedroom** NOUN
das Schlafzimmer (PL die Schlafzimmer)

**bedsit** NOUN
das möblierte Zimmer (GEN des möblierten Zimmers, PL die möblierten Zimmer)

**bedspread** NOUN
die Tagesdecke

**bedtime** NOUN
♦ **Ten o'clock is my usual bedtime.** Ich gehe normalerweise um zehn Uhr ins Bett.
♦ **Bedtime!** Ab ins Bett!

**bee** NOUN
die Biene

**beef** NOUN
das Rindfleisch
♦ **roast beef** das Roastbeef

**beefburger** NOUN
die Frikadelle

**been** VERB *see* **be**

**beer** NOUN
das Bier (PL die Biere *or* Bier)
*When ordering more than one beer use the plural form* **Bier.**
◇ *Two beers, please!* Zwei Bier bitte!

**beetle** NOUN
der Käfer (PL die Käfer)

**beetroot** NOUN
die Rote Bete

**before** PREPOSITION, CONJUNCTION, ADVERB
1 vor ◇ *before Tuesday* vor Dienstag
2 bevor ◇ *Before opening the packet, read the instructions.* Lesen Sie die Bedienungsanleitung, bevor Sie die Packung aufmachen. ◇ *I'll phone before I leave.* Ich rufe an, bevor ich gehe.
3 schon (*already*) ◇ *I've seen this film before.* Ich habe diesen Film schon gesehen. ◇ *Have you been to Scotland before?* Warst du schon einmal in Schottland?
♦ **the day before** am Tag davor

♦**the week before** die Woche davor
**beforehand** ADVERB
**vorher**
to **beg** VERB
  [1] (*for money*)
  **betteln**
  [2] **anflehen** (PERFECT hat angefleht) ◊ *He begged me to stop.* Er flehte mich an aufzuhören.
**began** VERB *see* **begin**
**beggar** NOUN
  der **Bettler** (PL die Bettler)
  die **Bettlerin**
to **begin** VERB
  **anfangen** (PRESENT fängt an, IMPERFECT fing an, PERFECT hat angefangen)
  ♦**to begin doing something** anfangen, etwas zu tun
**beginner** NOUN
  der **Anfänger** (PL die Anfänger)
  die **Anfängerin**
  ◊ *I'm just a beginner.* Ich bin noch Anfänger.
**beginning** NOUN
  der **Anfang** (PL die Anfänge) ◊ *in the beginning* am Anfang
**begun** VERB *see* **begin**
**behalf** NOUN
  ♦**on behalf of somebody** für jemanden ◊ *on her behalf* für sie
to **behave** VERB
  **sich benehmen** (PRESENT benimmt sich, IMPERFECT benahm sich, PERFECT hat sich benommen) ◊ *He behaved like an idiot.* Er hat sich wie ein Idiot benommen.
  ◊ *She behaved very badly.* Sie hat sich sehr schlecht benommen.
  ♦**to behave oneself** sich anständig benehmen ◊ *Did the children behave themselves?* Haben sich die Kinder anständig benommen?
  ♦**Behave!** Sei brav!
**behaviour** NOUN (US **behavior**)
  das **Benehmen**
**behind** PREPOSITION, ADVERB
  | *see also* **behind** NOUN |
  **hinter**
  *Use the accusative to express movement or a change of place. Use the dative when there is no change of place.*
  ◊ *the wall behind the television* die Wand hinter dem Fernseher ◊ *The book fell behind the television.* Das Buch fiel hinter den Fernseher.
  ♦**to be behind** (*late*) im Rückstand sein ◊ *I'm behind with my revision.* Ich bin mit dem Pauken im Rückstand.
**behind** NOUN
  | *see also* **behind** PREPOSITION, ADVERB |
  der **Hintern** (GEN des Hintern, PL die Hintern)
**beige** ADJECTIVE

**beige**
**Belgian** ADJECTIVE
  | *see also* **Belgian** NOUN |
  **belgisch**
  ♦**He's Belgian.** Er ist Belgier.
  ♦**She's Belgian.** Sie ist Belgierin.
**Belgian** NOUN
  | *see also* **Belgian** ADJECTIVE |
  der **Belgier** (PL die Belgier)
  die **Belgierin**
  ♦**the Belgians** die Belgier
**Belgium** NOUN
  **Belgien** NEUT
  ♦**from Belgium** aus Belgien
  ♦**in Belgium** in Belgien
  ♦**to Belgium** nach Belgien
to **believe** VERB
  **glauben** ◊ *I don't believe you.* Ich glaube dir nicht.
  ♦**to believe in something** an etwas glauben ◊ *Do you believe in ghosts?* Glaubst du an Gespenster? ◊ *to believe in God* an Gott glauben
**bell** NOUN
  [1] (*doorbell, in school*)
  die **Klingel**
  ♦**to ring the bell** klingeln
  ♦**When the bell rings the children go out into the playground.** Wenn es klingelt, gehen die Kinder auf den Schulhof.
  [2] (*in church*)
  die **Glocke**
  [3] das **Glöckchen** (PL die Glöckchen)
  ◊ *Our cat has a bell on its neck.* Unsere Katze hat ein Glöckchen um den Hals.
**belly** NOUN
  der **Bauch** (PL die Bäuche)
to **belong** VERB
  **gehören** (PERFECT hat gehört)
  ♦**to belong to somebody** jemandem gehören ◊ *Who does it belong to?* Wem gehört das? ◊ *That belongs to me.* Das gehört mir.
  ♦**Do you belong to any clubs?** Bist du Mitglied in irgendeinem Klub?
  ♦**Where does this belong?** Wo gehört das hin?
**belongings** PL NOUN
  die **Sachen** FEM PL
**below** PREPOSITION, ADVERB
  [1] **unterhalb** ◊ *below the castle* unterhalb der Burg
  [2] **unter**
  *Use the accusative to express movement or a change of place. Use the dative when there is no change of place.*
  ◊ *The bucket is below the sink.* Der Eimer ist unter der Spüle. ◊ *Put the cloth below the sink.* Leg das Tuch unter die Spüle.
  [3] **darunter** ◊ *on the floor below* im Stock darunter
  ♦**ten degrees below freezing** zehn Grad unter null

B

**belt** NOUN
der Gürtel (PL die Gürtel)
**beltway** NOUN US
die Umgehungsstraße
**bench** NOUN
1 (seat)
die Bank (PL die Bänke)
2 (for woodwork)
die Werkbank (PL die Werkbänke)
**bend** NOUN
see also **bend** VERB
1 die Kurve (in road)
2 die Biegung (in river)
to **bend** VERB
see also **bend** NOUN
1 (leg, arm)
beugen ◊ I can't bend my arm. Ich kann
den Arm nicht beugen.
♦ **to bend down** sich bücken
♦ **to bend over** sich nach vorne beugen
2 (object)
verbiegen (IMPERFECT verbog, PERFECT hat
verbogen) ◊ You've bent it. Du hast es
verbogen.
♦ **It bends easily.** Das lässt sich leicht
biegen.
♦ **"do not bend"** "nicht knicken"
**beneath** PREPOSITION
*Use the accusative to express movement
or a change of place. Use the dative
when there is no change of place.*
unter ◊ He placed his football boots
beneath the chair. Er stellte seine
Fußballschuhe unter den Stuhl. ◊ She
found his jumper beneath the bed. Sie
fand seinen Pullover unter dem Bett.
**benefit** NOUN
see also **benefit** VERB
der Vorteil (advantage) (PL die
Vorteile)
♦ **unemployment benefit** die
Arbeitslosenunterstützung
to **benefit** VERB
see also **benefit** NOUN
profitieren ◊ You'll benefit from that
experience. Du wirst von dieser
Erfahrung profitieren.
♦ **He benefited from the change.** Die
Veränderung hat ihm gut getan.
**bent** VERB see **bend**
**bent** ADJECTIVE
verbogen ◊ a bent fork eine verbogene
Gabel
**berserk** ADJECTIVE
♦ **to go berserk** durchdrehen ◊ She went
berserk. Sie hat durchgedreht.
**berth** NOUN
1 (on ship)
die Koje
2 (on train)
der Schlafwagenplatz (PL die
Schlafwagenplätze)
**beside** PREPOSITION

neben
*Use the accusative to express movement
or a change of place. Use the dative
when there is no change of place.*
◊ the lamp beside the television die
Lampe neben dem Fernseher ◊ Put that
chair beside the television. Stell den
Stuhl neben den Fernseher.
♦ **I was beside myself.** Ich war außer mir.
♦ **That's beside the point.** Das tut hier
nichts zur Sache.
**besides** ADVERB
außerdem ◊ Besides, it's too expensive.
Und außerdem ist es zu teuer.
**best** ADJECTIVE, ADVERB
1 beste ◊ He's the best player in the
team. Er ist der beste Spieler der
Mannschaft. ◊ Janet's the best at maths.
Janet ist in Mathe die Beste.
2 am besten ◊ Emma sings best. Emma
singt am besten.
♦ **to do one's best** sein Bestes tun ◊ It's not
perfect, but I did my best. Es ist nicht
vollkommen, aber ich habe mein Bestes
getan.
♦ **to make the best of it** das Beste daraus
machen ◊ We'll have to make the best of
it. Wir müssen das Beste daraus machen.
**best man** NOUN
der Trauzeuge (GEN des Trauzeugen, PL
die Trauzeugen)

❶ *There is no real equivalent in
Germany to **best man**. A **Trauzeuge** is
merely an official witness to the
wedding ceremony.*

**bet** NOUN
see also **bet** VERB
die Wette ◊ to make a bet eine Wette
machen
to **bet** VERB
see also **bet** NOUN
wetten
♦ **I bet you he won't come.** Wetten, dass er
nicht kommt.
♦ **I bet he forgot.** Wetten, dass er es
vergessen hat.
to **betray** VERB
verraten (PRESENT verrät, IMPERFECT verriet,
PERFECT hat verraten)
**better** ADJECTIVE, ADVERB
besser ◊ This one's better than that one.
Dieses hier ist besser als das da. ◊ a
better way to do it eine bessere Methode
◊ You'd better do it straight away. Das
machst du besser sofort. ◊ I'd better go
home. Ich gehe besser nach Hause.
◊ That's better! Das ist schon besser!
♦ **better still** noch besser ◊ Go and see her
tomorrow, or better still, go today. Geh
morgen zu ihr, oder noch besser, geh
heute.

**B**

◆**to get better (1)** (*improve*) besser werden
◇ *I hope the weather gets better soon.*
Ich hoffe, das Wetter wird bald besser.
◇ *My German is getting better.* Mein
Deutsch wird besser.
◆**to get better (2)** (*from illness*) sich
erholen
◆**I hope you get better soon.** Gute
Besserung!
◆**to feel better** sich besser fühlen ◇ *Are
you feeling better now?* Fühlst du dich
jetzt besser?
**betting shop** NOUN
das Wettbüro (PL die Wettbüros)

> ❶ There are very few betting shops in
> Germany and betting is far less popular
> than in the UK.

**between** PREPOSITION
> *Use the accusative to express movement
> or a change of place. Use the dative
> when there is no change of place.*
zwischen ◇ *The cathedral is between the
town hall and the river.* Der Dom liegt
zwischen dem Rathaus und dem Fluss.
◇ *He sat down between the two girls.* Er
setzte sich zwischen die beiden
Mädchen. ◇ *between fifteen and twenty
minutes* zwischen fünfzehn und zwanzig
Minuten
to **beware** VERB
◆**"Beware of the dog!"** "Vorsicht bissiger
Hund!"
to **bewilder** VERB
verwirren ◇ *She was bewildered.* Sie
war verwirrt.
**beyond** PREPOSITION
hinter ◇ *There was a lake beyond the
mountain.* Hinter dem Berg war ein See.
◆**beyond belief** nicht zu glauben
◆**beyond repair** nicht mehr zu reparieren
**biased** ADJECTIVE
voreingenommen
**Bible** NOUN
die Bibel
**bicycle** NOUN
das Fahrrad (PL die Fahrräder)
**bifocals** PL NOUN
die Bifokalbrille ◇ *a pair of bifocals* eine
Bifokalbrille
**big** ADJECTIVE
groß ◇ *a big house* ein großes Haus ◇ *a
bigger house* ein größeres Haus ◇ *my
big brother* mein großer Bruder ◇ *her big
sister* ihre große Schwester
◆**He's a big guy.** Er ist kräftig gebaut.
**bigheaded** ADJECTIVE
eingebildet
**bike** NOUN
das Fahrrad (PL die Fahrräder) ◇ *by bike*
mit dem Fahrrad
**bikini** NOUN

der Bikini (PL die Bikinis)
**bilingual** ADJECTIVE
zweisprachig
**bill** NOUN
⚊1⚊ die Rechnung ◇ *the gas bill* die
Gasrechnung
◆**Can we have the bill, please?** Können
wir bitte zahlen?
⚊2⚊ (*banknote*)
der Geldschein (PL die Geldscheine) ◇ *a
dollar bill* ein Dollarschein
**billiards** SING NOUN
das Billard ◇ *to play billiards* Billard
spielen
**billion** NOUN
die Milliarde
**bin** NOUN
⚊1⚊ (*indoors*)
der Abfalleimer (PL die Abfalleimer)
⚊2⚊ (*outside*)
der Mülleimer (PL die Mülleimer)
**bingo** NOUN
das Bingo
**binoculars** PL NOUN
das Fernglas (PL die Ferngläser) ◇ *a pair
of binoculars* ein Fernglas
**biochemistry** NOUN
die Biochemie
**biography** NOUN
die Biografie
**biology** NOUN
die Biologie
**bird** NOUN
der Vogel (PL die Vögel)
**bird-watching** NOUN
◆**My hobby's bird-watching.** Mein Hobby
ist das Beobachten von Vögeln.
**Biro** ® NOUN
der Kuli (PL die Kulis)
**birth** NOUN
die Geburt ◇ *date of birth* das
Geburtsdatum
**birth certificate** NOUN
die Geburtsurkunde
**birth control** NOUN
die Empfängnisverhütung ◇ *Before we
go on holiday, we'd better talk about
birth control.* Bevor wir in Urlaub fahren,
sollten wir uns über
Empfängnisverhütung unterhalten.
**birthday** NOUN
der Geburtstag (PL die Geburtstage)
◇ *When's your birthday?* Wann hast du
Geburtstag? ◇ *a birthday cake* ein
Geburtstagskuchen ◇ *I'm going to have a
birthday party.* Ich gebe eine
Geburtstagsparty.
**biscuit** NOUN
der Keks (PL die Kekse)
**bishop** NOUN
der Bischof (PL die Bischöfe)
**bit** VERB *see* **bite**

**bit** NOUN
das Stück (*piece*) (PL die Stücke) ◊ *Would you like another bit?* Möchtest du noch ein Stück? ◊ *a bit of cake* ein Stück Kuchen
◆ **a bit (1)** etwas ◊ *He's a bit mad.* Er ist etwas böse. ◊ *a bit too hot* etwas zu heiß
◆ **a bit (2)** ein bisschen ◊ *Wait a bit!* Warte ein bisschen! ◊ *Do you play football? – A bit.* Spielst du Fußball? – Ein bisschen.
◆ **a bit of** (*a little*) etwas ◊ *a bit of music* etwas Musik ◊ *It's a bit of a nuisance.* Das ist schon etwas ärgerlich.
◆ **to fall to bits** kaputtgehen
◆ **to take something to bits** etwas auseinander nehmen
◆ **bit by bit** nach und nach

**bitch** NOUN
[1] (*rude: person*)
das Miststück (PL die Miststücke)
[2] (*female dog*)
die Hündin

to **bite** VERB
| see also **bite** NOUN |
[1] (*person, dog*)
beißen (IMPERFECT biss, PERFECT hat gebissen)
[2] (*insect*)
stechen (PRESENT sticht, IMPERFECT stach, PERFECT hat gestochen) ◊ *I got bitten by mosquitoes.* Ich bin von Mücken gestochen worden.
◆ **to bite one's nails** an den Nägeln kauen

**bite** NOUN
| see also **bite** VERB |
[1] (*insect bite*)
der Stich (PL die Stiche)
[2] (*animal bite*)
der Biss (GEN des Bisses, PL die Bisse)
◆ **to have a bite to eat** eine Kleinigkeit essen

**bitter** ADJECTIVE
| see also **bitter** NOUN |
[1] bitter
[2] bitterkalt (*weather, wind*) ◊ *It's bitter today.* Heute ist es bitterkalt.

**bitter** NOUN
| see also **bitter** ADJECTIVE |
das dunkle Bier (PL die dunklen Biere)

> ❶ *German beers are completely different from British ones. There is no real equivalent to* **bitter**.

**black** ADJECTIVE
schwarz ◊ *a black jacket* eine schwarze Jacke
◆ **She's black.** Sie ist eine Schwarze.

**blackberry** NOUN
die Brombeere

**blackbird** NOUN
die Amsel

**blackboard** NOUN
die Tafel

**black coffee** NOUN
der schwarze Kaffee (PL die schwarzen Kaffees)

**blackcurrant** NOUN
die Schwarze Johannisbeere

**blackmail** NOUN
| see also **blackmail** VERB |
die Erpressung ◊ *That's blackmail!* Das ist Erpressung!

to **blackmail** VERB
| see also **blackmail** NOUN |
erpressen (PERFECT hat erpresst) ◊ *He blackmailed her.* Er erpresste sie.

**blackout** NOUN
der Stromausfall (*power cut*) (PL die Stromausfälle)
◆ **to have a blackout** (*faint*) ohnmächtig werden

**black pudding** NOUN
die Blutwurst (PL die Blutwürste)

**blacksmith** NOUN
der Schmied ◊ *He's a blacksmith.* Er ist Schmied.

**blade** NOUN
die Klinge

to **blame** VERB
◆ **Don't blame me!** Ich bin nicht schuld!
◆ **I blame him.** Ich gebe ihm die Schuld.
◆ **He blamed it on my sister.** Er gab meiner Schwester die Schuld.

**blank** ADJECTIVE
| see also **blank** NOUN |
[1] leer (*paper, page*)
[2] unbespielt (*cassette, video*)
◆ **My mind went blank.** Ich hatte ein Brett vor dem Kopf.

**blank** NOUN
| see also **blank** ADJECTIVE |
die Lücke ◊ *Fill in the blanks.* Füllt die Lücken aus.

**blank cheque** NOUN
der Blankoscheck (PL die Blankoschecks)

**blanket** NOUN
die Decke

**blast** NOUN
◆ **a bomb blast** eine Bombenexplosion

**blatant** ADJECTIVE
unverschämt ◊ *a blatant liar* ein unverschämter Lügner

**blaze** NOUN
das Feuer (PL die Feuer)

**blazer** NOUN
der Blazer (PL die Blazer)

**bleach** NOUN
das Bleichmittel (PL die Bleichmittel)

**bleached** ADJECTIVE
gebleicht ◊ *bleached hair* gebleichtes Haar

**bleak** ADJECTIVE
trostlos ◊ *The future looks bleak.* Die Zukunft sieht trostlos aus.

**B**

to **bleed** VERB
　bluten ◊ *My nose is bleeding.* Ich blute
　aus der Nase.
**bleeper** NOUN
　der Piepser (PL die Piepser)
**blender** NOUN
　der Mixer (PL die Mixer)
to **bless** VERB
　segnen (*religiously*)
　◆**Bless you!** (*after sneezing*) Gesundheit!
**blew** VERB *see* **blow**
**blind** ADJECTIVE
　see also **blind** NOUN
　blind
**blind** NOUN
　see also **blind** ADJECTIVE
　das Rollo (*fabric*) (PL die Rollos)
**blindfold** NOUN
　see also **blindfold** VERB
　die Augenbinde
to **blindfold** VERB
　see also **blindfold** NOUN
　◆**to blindfold somebody** jemandem die
　Augen verbinden
to **blink** VERB
　zwinkern
**bliss** NOUN
　◆**It was bliss!** Es war eine Wonne!
**blister** NOUN
　die Blase
**blizzard** NOUN
　der Schneesturm (PL die
　Schneestürme)
**blob** NOUN
　der Tropfen (PL die Tropfen) ◊ *a blob of
　glue* ein Tropfen Klebstoff
**block** NOUN
　see also **block** VERB
　der Block (PL die Blöcke) ◊ *He lives in our
　block.* Er lebt in unserem Block.
　◆**a block of flats** ein Wohnblock MASC
to **block** VERB
　see also **block** NOUN
　blockieren (PERFECT hat blockiert)
**blockage** NOUN
　die Verstopfung (*in pipe or tube*) ◊ *The
　tea leaves created a blockage in the pipe.*
　Die Teeblätter haben eine Verstopfung
　im Rohr verursacht.
**bloke** NOUN
　der Typ (*informal*) (PL die Typen)
**blonde** ADJECTIVE
　blond ◊ *She's got blonde hair.* Sie hat
　blondes Haar.
**blood** NOUN
　das Blut
**blood pressure** NOUN
　der Blutdruck
　◆**to have high blood pressure** zu hohen
　Blutdruck haben
**blood sports** PL NOUN
　der Blutsport

**blood test** NOUN
　die Blutuntersuchung
**bloody** ADJECTIVE
　◆**bloody difficult** verdammt schwer
　(*informal*)
　◆**that bloody television** der
　Scheißfernseher (*informal*)
　◆**Bloody hell!** Scheiße! (*informal*)
**blouse** NOUN
　die Bluse
**blow** NOUN
　see also **blow** VERB
　der Schlag (PL die Schläge)
to **blow** VERB
　see also **blow** NOUN
　1 (*person*)
　blasen (PRESENT bläst, IMPERFECT blies, PERFECT
　hat geblasen)
　2 (*wind*)
　wehen
　◆**to blow one's nose** sich die Nase
　putzen ◊ *Blow your nose!* Putz dir die
　Nase!
　◆**to blow a whistle** pfeifen
　◆**to blow out a candle** eine Kerze
　ausblasen
　◆**to blow up (1)** in die Luft jagen ◊ *The
　terrorists blew up a police station.* Die
　Terroristen haben ein Polizeirevier in die
　Luft gejagt.
　◆**to blow up (2)** aufblasen ◊ *to blow
　up a balloon* einen Luftballon
　aufblasen
　◆**The house blew up.** Das Haus flog in die
　Luft.
**blow-dry** NOUN
　das Föhnen
　◆**A cut and blow-dry, please.** Schneiden
　und Föhnen bitte.
**blown** VERB *see* **blow**
**blue** ADJECTIVE
　blau ◊ *a blue dress* ein blaues
　Kleid
　◆**a blue film** ein Pornofilm MASC
　◆**It came out of the blue.** Das kam aus
　heiterem Himmel.
**blues** PL NOUN
　der Blues (*music*) SING (GEN des Blues)
to **bluff** VERB
　see also **bluff** NOUN
　bluffen
**bluff** NOUN
　see also **bluff** VERB
　der Bluff (PL die Bluffs) ◊ *It's just a bluff.*
　Das ist ein Bluff.
**blunder** NOUN
　der Schnitzer (PL die Schnitzer)
**blunt** ADJECTIVE
　1 unverblümt (*person*)
　2 stumpf (*knife*)
to **blush** VERB
　rot werden (PRESENT wird rot, IMPERFECT
　wurde rot, PERFECT ist rot geworden)

**board** NOUN
1. das Brett (PL die Bretter)
2. (*blackboard*)
die Tafel ◊ *Write it on the board.* Schreib es an die Tafel.
3. (*noticeboard*)
das schwarze Brett (PL die schwarzen Bretter)
♦ **on board** an Bord
♦ **full board** die Vollpension

**boarder** NOUN
der Internatsschüler (PL die Internatsschüler)
die Internatsschülerin

**board game** NOUN
das Brettspiel (PL die Brettspiele)

**boarding card** NOUN
die Bordkarte

**boarding school** NOUN
das Internat (PL die Internate) ◊ *I go to boarding school.* Ich gehe in ein Internat.

to **boast** VERB
prahlen ◊ *to boast about something* mit etwas prahlen

**boat** NOUN
das Boot (PL die Boote)

**body** NOUN
der Körper (PL die Körper)

**bodybuilding** NOUN
das Bodybuilding ◊ *He does bodybuilding.* Er macht Bodybuilding.

**bodyguard** NOUN
der Leibwächter (PL die Leibwächter)

**bog** NOUN
das Moor (*marsh*) (PL die Moore)

**boil** NOUN
| see also **boil** VERB |
der Furunkel (PL die Furunkel)

to **boil** VERB
| see also **boil** NOUN |
kochen ◊ *to boil some water* Wasser kochen ◊ *to boil an egg* ein Ei kochen ◊ *The water's boiling.* Das Wasser kocht.
♦ **to boil over** überkochen ◊ *The milk boiled over.* Die Milch ist übergekocht.

**boiled** ADJECTIVE
♦ **a soft-boiled egg** ein weich gekochtes Ei NEUT
♦ **boiled potatoes** Salzkartoffeln FEM PL

**boiling** ADJECTIVE
♦ **It's boiling in here!** Hier ist eine Bruthitze!
♦ **boiling hot** brütend heiß ◊ *a boiling hot day* ein brütend heißer Tag

**bolt** NOUN
1. (*on door*)
der Riegel (PL die Riegel)
2. (*with nut*)
der Bolzen (PL die Bolzen)

**bomb** NOUN
| see also **bomb** VERB |
die Bombe

Note that you pronounce the second "b" in German.

to **bomb** VERB
| see also **bomb** NOUN |
bombardieren (PERFECT hat bombardiert)

**bomber** NOUN
der Bomber (PL die Bomber)

Note that you pronounce the second "b" in German.

**bombing** NOUN
der Bombenangriff (PL die Bombenangriffe)

**bond** NOUN
die Bindung (*between people*) ◊ *There is a strong bond between the two brothers.* Zwischen den beiden Brüdern besteht eine enge Bindung.

**bone** NOUN
1. (*of human, animal*)
der Knochen (PL die Knochen)
2. (*of fish*)
die Gräte

**bone dry** ADJECTIVE
knochentrocken

**bonfire** NOUN
das Feuer (PL die Feuer)

**bonnet** NOUN
die Motorhaube (*of car*)

**bonus** NOUN
1. (*extra payment*)
der Bonus (PL die Bonusse)
2. (*added advantage*)
der Vorteil

**book** NOUN
| see also **book** VERB |
das Buch (PL die Bücher)

to **book** VERB
| see also **book** NOUN |
buchen ◊ *We haven't booked.* Wir haben nicht gebucht.

**bookcase** NOUN
1. (*open*)
das Bücherregal (PL die Bücherregale)
2. (*with doors*)
der Bücherschrank (PL die Bücherschränke)

**booklet** NOUN
die Broschüre

**bookmark** NOUN
das Lesezeichen (PL die Lesezeichen)

**bookshelf** NOUN
das Bücherbrett (PL die Bücherbretter)
♦ **bookshelves** das Bücherregal SING

**bookshop** NOUN
die Buchhandlung

to **boost** VERB
Auftrieb geben (PRESENT gibt, IMPERFECT gab, PERFECT hat gegeben) ◊ *The win boosted the team's morale.* Der Sieg gab der Mannschaft moralischen Auftrieb.

**boot** NOUN
1. (*of car*)
der Kofferraum (PL die Kofferräume)

2 *(footwear)*
der Stiefel (PL die Stiefel)
♦**football boots** die Fußballschuhe MASC PL

**booze** NOUN
der Alkohol

**border** NOUN
die Grenze

**bore** VERB *see* **bear**

**bored** ADJECTIVE
♦**to be bored** sich langweilen
♦**I'm bored.** Ich langweile mich.
♦**She gets bored easily.** Ihr wird schnell
langweilig.

**boredom** NOUN
die Langeweile (GEN der Langenweile)

**boring** ADJECTIVE
langweilig

**born** ADJECTIVE
♦**to be born** geboren werden ◊ *I was born
in 1982.* Ich bin 1982 geboren.

**borne** VERB *see* **bear**

to **borrow** VERB
ausleihen (IMPERFECT lieh aus, PERFECT hat
ausgeliehen) ◊ *Can I borrow your pen?*
Kann ich deinen Schreiber ausleihen?
♦**to borrow something from somebody**
sich etwas von jemandem leihen ◊ *I
borrowed some money from a friend.* Ich
habe mir von einem Freund Geld
geliehen.

**Bosnia** NOUN
Bosnien NEUT
♦**from Bosnia** aus Bosnien
♦**to Bosnia** nach Bosnien

**Bosnian** ADJECTIVE
bosnisch

**boss** NOUN
der Chef (PL die Chefs)
die Chefin

to **boss around** VERB
♦**to boss somebody around** jemanden
herumkommandieren

**bossy** ADJECTIVE
herrisch

**both** ADJECTIVE, PRONOUN
beide ◊ *We both went.* Wir sind beide
gegangen. ◊ *Emma and Jane both went.*
Emma und Jane sind beide gegangen.
◊ *Both of your answers are wrong.* Beide
Antworten sind falsch. ◊ *Both of them
have left.* Beide sind gegangen. ◊ *Both of
us went.* Wir sind beide gegangen.
♦**both ... and** sowohl ... als auch ◊ *He
speaks both French and Italian.* Er spricht
sowohl Französisch als auch Italienisch.

**bother** NOUN
⸢ *see also* **bother** VERB ⸥
der Ärger ◊ *We had a spot of bother
with the car.* Wir hatten Ärger mit dem
Auto.
♦**No bother!** Kein Problem!

to **bother** VERB

⸢ *see also* **bother** NOUN ⸥
1 *(worry)*
beunruhigen (PERFECT hat beunruhigt) ◊ *Is
something bothering you?* Beunruhigt
dich etwas?
2 *(disturb)*
stören ◊ *I'm sorry to bother you.* Es tut
mir Leid, dass ich dich störe.
♦**no bother** kein Problem
♦**Don't bother!** Nicht nötig!
♦**to bother to do something** es für nötig
finden, etwas zu tun ◊ *He didn't bother to
tell me about it.* Er hat es nicht für nötig
gefunden, es mir zu sagen.

**bottle** NOUN
die Flasche

**bottle bank** NOUN
der Altglascontainer (PL die
Altglascontainer)

**bottle-opener** NOUN
der Flaschenöffner (PL die
Flaschenöffner)

**bottom** NOUN
⸢ *see also* **bottom** ADJECTIVE ⸥
1 *(of container, bag, sea)*
der Boden (PL die Böden)
2 *(buttocks)*
der Hintern (GEN des Hintern, PL die
Hintern)
3 *(of list)*
das Ende (PL die Enden)
♦**at the bottom of page two** unten auf
Seite zwei

**bottom** ADJECTIVE
⸢ *see also* **bottom** NOUN ⸥
unterste ◊ *the bottom shelf* das unterste
Regalbrett
♦**the bottom sheet** das Bettlaken

**bought** VERB *see* **buy**

to **bounce** VERB
hüpfen (PERFECT ist gehüpft)

**bouncer** NOUN
der Rausschmeißer (PL die
Rausschmeißer)

**bound** ADJECTIVE
♦**He's bound to say that.** Er muss das ja
sagen.
♦**She's bound to come.** Sie kommt
sicher.

**boundary** NOUN
die Grenze

**bow** NOUN
⸢ *see also* **bow** VERB ⸥
1 die Schleife *(knot)* ◊ *to tie a bow* eine
Schleife machen
2 der Bogen (PL die Bogen) ◊ *a bow and
arrow* ein Pfeil und Bogen

to **bow** VERB
⸢ *see also* **bow** NOUN ⸥
sich verneigen (PERFECT hat sich verneigt)

**bowels** PL NOUN
die Eingeweide NEUT PL

**bowl** NOUN

☞

see also **bowl** VERB

die Schale (*for soup, cereal*)

to **bowl** VERB

see also **bowl** NOUN

werfen (*in cricket*) (PRESENT wirft, IMPERFECT warf, PERFECT hat geworfen)

**bowler** NOUN

(*in cricket*)

der Werfer (PL die Werfer)

die Werferin

**bowling** NOUN

das Bowling

♦ **to go bowling** Bowling spielen

♦ **a bowling alley** eine Bowlingbahn

**bowls** SING NOUN

das Boccia (GEN des Boccia)

*The "cc" in Boccia is pronounced like "ch" in church.*

◊ *to play bowls* Boccia spielen

**bow tie** NOUN

die Fliege

**box** NOUN

die Schachtel ◊ *a box of matches* eine Schachtel Streichhölzer

♦ **a cardboard box** ein Karton MASC

**boxer** NOUN

der Boxer (PL die Boxer)

**boxer shorts** PL NOUN

die Boxershorts PL ◊ *He was wearing a pair of boxer shorts.* Er hatte Boxershorts an.

**boxing** NOUN

das Boxen

**Boxing Day** NOUN

der zweite Weihnachtsfeiertag

**boy** NOUN

der Junge (GEN des Jungen, PL die Jungen)

**boyfriend** NOUN

der Freund (PL die Freunde) ◊ *Have you got a boyfriend?* Hast du einen Freund?

**bra** NOUN

der BH (PL die BHs)

**brace** NOUN

die Zahnspange (*on teeth*) ◊ *She wears a brace.* Sie hat eine Zahnspange.

**bracelet** NOUN

das Armband (PL die Armbänder)

**brackets** PL NOUN

die Klammern FEM PL ◊ *in brackets* in Klammern

**brain** NOUN

das Gehirn (PL die Gehirne)

**brainy** ADJECTIVE

gescheit

**brake** NOUN

see also **brake** VERB

die Bremse

to **brake** VERB

see also **brake** NOUN

bremsen

**branch** NOUN

[1] (*of tree*)

der Zweig (PL die Zweige)

[2] (*of bank*)

die Filiale

**brand** NOUN

die Marke ◊ *a well-known brand of coffee* eine bekannte Kaffeemarke

**brand name** NOUN

der Markenname (GEN des Markennamens, PL die Markennamen)

**brand-new** ADJECTIVE

brandneu

**brandy** NOUN

der Weinbrand (PL die Weinbrände)

**brass** NOUN

das Messing (*metal*)

♦ **the brass section** die Blechbläser MASC PL

**brass band** NOUN

die Blaskapelle

**brat** NOUN

♦ **He's a spoiled brat.** Er ist ein verwöhnter Balg.

**brave** ADJECTIVE

mutig

*Be careful not to translate brave by brav.*

**Brazil** NOUN

Brasilien NEUT

♦ **from Brazil** aus Brasilien

♦ **to Brazil** nach Brasilien

**bread** NOUN

das Brot (PL die Brote) ◊ *bread and butter* Brot mit Butter

♦ **brown bread** das Graubrot

♦ **white bread** das Weißbrot

> ❶ *There is a huge variety of types of bread in Germany which can't simply be divided into brown and white.*

**break** NOUN

see also **break** VERB

die Pause (*rest*) ◊ *to take a break* eine Pause machen ◊ *during morning break* während der Vormittagspause

♦ **the Christmas break** die Weihnachtsfeiertage MASC PL

♦ **Give me a break!** Mach mal halblang!

to **break** VERB

see also **break** NOUN

[1] kaputtmachen (PERFECT hat kaputtgemacht) ◊ *Careful, you'll break something!* Vorsicht, du machst sonst was kaputt!

[2] (*record, law*)

brechen (PRESENT bricht, IMPERFECT brach, PERFECT hat gebrochen) ◊ *to break a promise* sein Versprechen brechen

♦ **to break one's leg** sich das Bein brechen ◊ *I broke my leg.* Ich habe mir das Bein gebrochen.

♦ **He broke his arm.** Er hat sich den Arm gebrochen.

**B**

**3** (*get broken*)
brechen ◊ *Careful, it'll break!* Vorsicht,
es bricht!

to **break down** VERB
eine Panne haben (PRESENT hat eine
Panne, IMPERFECT hatte eine Panne, PERFECT
hat eine Panne gehabt) ◊ *The car broke
down.* Das Auto hatte eine Panne.

to **break in** VERB
einbrechen (PRESENT bricht ein, IMPERFECT
brach ein, PERFECT hat eingebrochen)

to **break into** VERB
einbrechen in (PRESENT bricht ein, IMPERFECT
brach ein, PERFECT ist eingebrochen)
◊ *Thieves broke into the house.* Diebe
brachen in das Haus ein.

to **break off** VERB
abbrechen (PRESENT bricht ab, IMPERFECT
brach ab, PERFECT hat abgebrochen) ◊ *I
broke off a small piece.* Ich habe ein
kleines Stück abgebrochen.

to **break open** VERB
aufbrechen (*door, cupboard*) (PRESENT
bricht auf, IMPERFECT brach auf, PERFECT hat
aufgebrochen)

to **break out** VERB
ausbrechen (PRESENT bricht aus, IMPERFECT
brach aus, PERFECT ist ausgebrochen)
♦ **to break out in a rash** einen Ausschlag
bekommen

to **break up** VERB
**1** (*crowd*)
sich auflösen (PERFECT hat sich aufgelöst)
**2** (*meeting, party*)
zu Ende gehen (IMPERFECT ging zu Ende,
PERFECT ist zu Ende gegangen)
**3** (*couple*)
sich trennen
♦ **to break up a fight** eine Schlägerei
beenden
♦ **We break up next Wednesday.** Nächsten
Mittwoch ist der letzte Schultag.

**breakdown** NOUN
**1** (*in vehicle*)
die Panne ◊ *to have a breakdown* eine
Panne haben
**2** (*mental*)
der Nervenzusammenbruch (PL die
Nervenzusammenbrüche) ◊ *to have a
breakdown* einen
Nervenzusammenbruch haben

**breakdown van** NOUN
das Pannenfahrzeug (PL die
Pannenfahrzeuge)

**breakfast** NOUN
das Frühstück (PL die Frühstücke) ◊ *What
would you like for breakfast?* Was
möchtest du zum Frühstück?
♦ **to have breakfast** frühstücken

**break-in** NOUN
der Einbruch (PL die Einbrüche)

**breast** NOUN
die Brust (PL die Brüste)

♦ **chicken breast** die Hähnchenbrust

to **breast-feed** VERB
stillen

**breaststroke** NOUN
das Brustschwimmen

**breath** NOUN
der Atem
♦ **to have bad breath** Mundgeruch haben
♦ **to be out of breath** außer Atem sein
♦ **to get one's breath back** verschnaufen

to **breathe** VERB
atmen
♦ **to breathe in** einatmen
♦ **to breathe out** ausatmen

to **breed** VERB
see also **breed** NOUN
züchten ◊ *to breed dogs* Hunde züchten

**breed** NOUN
see also **breed** VERB
die Rasse

**breeze** NOUN
die Brise

**brewery** NOUN
die Brauerei

**bribe** NOUN
see also **bribe** VERB
die Bestechung

to **bribe** VERB
see also **bribe** NOUN
bestechen (PRESENT besticht, IMPERFECT
bestach, PERFECT hat bestochen)

**brick** NOUN
der Backstein (PL die Backsteine) ◊ *a
brick wall* eine Backsteinmauer

**bricklayer** NOUN
der Maurer (PL die Maurer)
die Maurerin

**bride** NOUN
die Braut (PL die Bräute)

**bridegroom** NOUN
der Bräutigam (PL die Bräutigame)

**bridesmaid** NOUN
die Brautjungfer

**bridge** NOUN
**1** die Brücke ◊ *a suspension bridge* eine
Hängebrücke
**2** das Bridge (GEN des Bridge) ◊ *to play
bridge* Bridge spielen

**brief** ADJECTIVE
kurz

**briefcase** NOUN
die Aktentasche

**briefly** ADVERB
kurz

**briefs** PL NOUN
die Unterhose ◊ *a pair of briefs* eine
Unterhose

**bright** ADJECTIVE
**1** hell (*light*)
**2** leuchtend (*colour*) ◊ *a brighter colour*
eine leuchtendere Farbe
♦ **bright blue** hellblau

☞

③ intelligent ◊ *He's not very bright.* Er ist nicht besonders intelligent.

**brilliant** ADJECTIVE
① prima (*wonderful*) ◊ *Brilliant!* Prima!
② glänzend (*clever*) ◊ *a brilliant scientist* ein glänzender Wissenschaftler

to **bring** VERB
① bringen (IMPERFECT brachte, PERFECT hat gebracht) ◊ *Could you bring me my trainers?* Könntest du mir meine Sportschuhe bringen?
② (*bring along*)
mitbringen ◊ *Bring warm clothes.* Bringt warme Kleidung mit! ◊ *Can I bring a friend?* Darf ich einen Freund mitbringen?
♦ **to bring about** herbeiführen
♦ **to bring back** zurückbringen
♦ **to bring forward** vorverlegen ◊ *The meeting was brought forward.* Die Sitzung wurde vorverlegt.
♦ **to bring up** aufziehen ◊ *She brought up five children on her own.* Sie hat fünf Kinder alleine aufgezogen.

**Britain** NOUN
Großbritannien NEUT
♦ **from Britain** aus Großbritannien
♦ **in Britain** in Großbritannien
♦ **to Britain** nach Großbritannien
♦ **Great Britain** Großbritannien

**British** ADJECTIVE
britisch
♦ **He's British.** Er ist Brite.
♦ **She's British.** Sie ist Britin.
♦ **the British** die Briten MASC PL
♦ **the British Isles** die Britischen Inseln

**Brittany** NOUN
die Bretagne
♦ **in Brittany** in der Bretagne

**broad** ADJECTIVE
breit (*wide*)
♦ **in broad daylight** am helllichten Tag

**broadcast** NOUN
| see also **broadcast** VERB |
die Sendung

to **broadcast** VERB
| see also **broadcast** NOUN |
senden ◊ *The interview was broadcast all over the world.* Das Interview wurde in der ganzen Welt gesendet.

**broad-minded** ADJECTIVE
tolerant

**broccoli** SING NOUN
die Brokkoli MASC PL ◊ *Broccoli is her favourite vegetable.* Ihr Lieblingsgemüse ist Brokkoli.

**brochure** NOUN
die Broschüre

to **broil** VERB US
grillen

**broke** VERB *see* **break**

**broke** ADJECTIVE

♦ **to be broke** (*without money*) pleite sein

**broken** VERB *see* **break**

**broken** ADJECTIVE
① kaputt ◊ *It's broken.* Es ist kaputt.
② gebrochen (*limb*) ◊ *He's got a broken arm.* Er hat einen gebrochenen Arm.

**bronchitis** NOUN
die Bronchitis

**bronze** NOUN
die Bronze ◊ *the bronze medal* die Bronzemedaille

**brooch** NOUN
die Brosche

**broom** NOUN
der Besen (PL die Besen)

**brother** NOUN
der Bruder (PL die Brüder) ◊ *my brother* mein Bruder ◊ *my big brother* mein großer Bruder

**brother-in-law** NOUN
der Schwager (PL die Schwäger)

**brought** VERB *see* **bring**

**brown** ADJECTIVE
braun
♦ **brown bread** das Graubrot

**Brownie** NOUN
der Wichtel (*Girl Guide*) (PL die Wichtel)

to **browse** VERB
browsen (*computer*) (PERFECT hat gebrowst)
♦ **to browse through a book** in einem Buch schmökern

**browser** NOUN
der Browser (*Internet*) (PL die Browser)

**bruise** NOUN
der blaue Fleck (PL die blauen Flecke)

**brush** NOUN
| see also **brush** VERB |
① die Bürste
② (*paintbrush*)
der Pinsel (PL die Pinsel)

to **brush** VERB
| see also **brush** NOUN |
bürsten
♦ **to brush one's hair** sich die Haare bürsten ◊ *I brushed my hair.* Ich habe mir die Haare gebürstet.
♦ **to brush one's teeth** die Zähne putzen ◊ *I brush my teeth every night.* Ich putze jeden Abend die Zähne.

**Brussels** NOUN
Brüssel NEUT ◊ *to Brussels* nach Brüssel

**Brussels sprouts** PL NOUN
der Rosenkohl SING ◊ *The Brussel sprouts were salty.* Der Rosenkohl war versalzen.

**brutal** ADJECTIVE
brutal

**BSc** ABBREVIATION (= *Bachelor of Science*)
der Magister (PL die Magister)
♦ **She's got a BSc in Chemistry.** Sie hat einen Magistertitel in Chemie.

**BSE** NOUN (= *bovine spongiform encephalopathy*)
das BSE

**bubble** NOUN
die Blase

**bubble bath** NOUN
das Schaumbad (PL die Schaumbäder)

**bubble gum** NOUN
der Bubblegum (PL die Bubblegums)

**bucket** NOUN
der Eimer (PL die Eimer)

**buckle** NOUN
die Schnalle (*on belt, watch, shoe*)

**Buddhism** NOUN
der Buddhismus (GEN des Buddhismus)
◊ *Buddhism is the main religion of Sri Lanka.* Der Buddhismus ist die Hauptreligion in Sri Lanka.

**Buddhist** ADJECTIVE
buddhistisch

**buddy** NOUN US
der Kumpel (PL die Kumpel)

**budget** NOUN
see also **budget** VERB
das Budget (PL die Budgets)

to **budget** VERB
see also **budget** NOUN
einplanen (PERFECT hat eingeplant) ◊ *They budgeted $10 million for advertising.* Sie planten 10 Millionen Dollar für Werbung ein.

**budgie** NOUN
der Wellensittich (PL die Wellensittiche)

**buffet** NOUN
das Büfett (PL die Büfetts)

**buffet car** NOUN
der Speisewagen (PL die Speisewagen)

**bug** NOUN
1 (*insect*)
die Wanze
♦ **There are many bugs there.** Dort gibt es viel Ungeziefer.
♦ **a stomach bug** eine Magen-Darm-Infektion
♦ **There's a bug going round.** Da geht etwas herum.
2 (*in computer*)
der Programmfehler (PL die Programmfehler)

**bugged** ADJECTIVE
verwanzt ◊ *The room was bugged.* Das Zimmer war verwanzt.

to **build** VERB
bauen ◊ *They're going to build houses here.* Hier werden Häuser gebaut.
♦ **to build up** (*increase*) zunehmen

**builder** NOUN
1 (*owner of firm*)
der Bauunternehmer (PL die Bauunternehmer)
die Bauunternehmerin
2 (*worker*)
der Bauarbeiter (PL die Bauarbeiter)
die Bauarbeiterin

**building** NOUN
das Gebäude (PL die Gebäude)

**built** VERB *see* **build**

**bulb** NOUN
die Glühbirne (*electric*)

**Bulgaria** NOUN
Bulgarien NEUT
♦ **from Bulgaria** aus Bulgarien
♦ **to Bulgaria** nach Bulgarien

**bull** NOUN
der Stier (PL die Stiere)

**bullet** NOUN
die Kugel

**bulletin board** NOUN
das schwarze Brett (*computer*) (PL die schwarzen Bretter)

**bullfighting** NOUN
der Stierkampf (PL die Stierkämpfe)

**bully** NOUN
see also **bully** VERB
♦ **He's a big bully.** Er tyrannisiert andere gern.

to **bully** VERB
see also **bully** NOUN
tyrannisieren (PERFECT hat tyrannisiert)

**bum** NOUN
der Po (*informal: bottom*) (PL die Pos)

**bum bag** NOUN
die Gürteltasche

**bump** NOUN
see also **bump** VERB
1 (*lump*)
die Beule
2 (*minor accident*)
der Zusammenstoß (GEN des Zusammenstoßes, PL die Zusammenstöße)
♦ **We had a bump.** Es hat gebumst.

to **bump** VERB
see also **bump** NOUN
♦ **to bump into something** gegen etwas laufen ◊ *She bumped into the wall.* Sie ist gegen die Wand gelaufen.
♦ **We bumped into his car.** Wir sind in sein Auto gefahren.
♦ **I bumped into the headteacher.** Ich bin zufällig dem Rektor begegnet.

**bumper** NOUN
die Stoßstange

**bumpy** ADJECTIVE
holperig

**bun** NOUN
das Brötchen (PL die Brötchen)

**bunch** NOUN
♦ **a bunch of flowers** ein Blumenstrauß MASC
♦ **a bunch of grapes** eine Traube
♦ **a bunch of keys** ein Schlüsselbund MASC

**bunches** PL NOUN
die Rattenschwänze MASC PL ◊ *She has her hair in bunches.* Sie hat Rattenschwänze.

**bungalow** NOUN
der Bungalow (PL die Bungalows)
**bunk** NOUN
1 das Bett (PL die Betten)
2 (*on ship*)
die Koje
**burger** NOUN
der Hamburger (PL die Hamburger)
**burglar** NOUN
der Einbrecher (PL die Einbrecher)
die Einbrecherin
to **burglarize** VERB US
einbrechen in +ACC (PRESENT bricht ein,
IMPERFECT brach ein, PERFECT ist
eingebrochen)
◆ **Her house was burglarized.** Bei ihr
wurde eingebrochen.
**burglary** NOUN
der Einbruch (PL die Einbrüche)
to **burgle** VERB
einbrechen in +ACC (PRESENT bricht ein,
IMPERFECT brach ein, PERFECT ist
eingebrochen)
◆ **Her house was burgled.** Bei ihr wurde
eingebrochen.
**burn** NOUN
see also **burn** VERB
die Verbrennung
to **burn** VERB
see also **burn** NOUN
1 (*rubbish, documents*)
verbrennen (IMPERFECT verbrannte, PERFECT
hat verbrannt)
2 (*food*)
anbrennen lassen (PRESENT lässt
anbrennen, IMPERFECT ließ anbrennen,
PERFECT hat anbrennen lassen) ◊ *I burned
the cake.* Ich habe den Kuchen
anbrennen lassen.
◆ **to burn oneself** sich verbrennen ◊ *I
burned myself on the oven door.* Ich
habe mich an der Ofentür verbrannt.
◆ **I've burned my hand.** Ich habe mir die
Hand verbrannt.
◆ **to burn down** abbrennen ◊ *The factory
burned down.* Die Fabrik ist abgebrannt.
to **burst** VERB
platzen (PERFECT ist geplatzt) ◊ *The balloon
burst.* Der Luftballon ist geplatzt.
◆ **to burst a balloon** einen Luftballon
platzen lassen
◆ **to burst out laughing** laut loslachen
◆ **to burst into flames** in Flammen
aufgehen
◆ **to burst into tears** in Tränen ausbrechen
to **bury** VERB
1 (*dead people, animals*)
begraben (PRESENT begräbt, IMPERFECT
begrub, PERFECT hat begraben) ◊ *We buried
my guinea pig in the garden.* Wir haben
mein Meerschweinchen im Garten
begraben.
2 (*things*)

vergraben ◊ *My dog buried a bone in
the flowerbed.* Mein Hund hat im
Blumenbeet einen Knochen vergraben.
**bus** NOUN
der Bus (GEN des Busses, PL die Busse)
◊ *the bus driver* der Busfahrer ◊ *a bus
stop* eine Bushaltestelle ◊ *the school bus*
der Schulbus
◆ **a bus pass** (*monthly*) eine Monatskarte
für den Bus

> ❶ Almost all German cities operate an
> integrated public transport system; you
> can buy a weekly **(Wochenkarte)**,
> monthly **(Monatskarte)** or yearly
> **(Jahreskarte)** pass which are valid for
> that period on all buses, trams and
> light railway vehicles in a particular
> zone.

◆ **a bus station** eine Bushaltestelle
◆ **a bus ticket** eine Busfahrkarte
**bush** NOUN
der Busch (PL die Büsche)
**business** NOUN
1 (*firm*)
die Firma (PL die Firmen) ◊ *He's got his
own business.* Er hat seine eigene
Firma.
2 (*commerce*)
das Geschäft (PL die Geschäfte) ◊ *a
business trip* eine Geschäftsreise
◆ **He's away on business.** Er ist
geschäftlich unterwegs.
◆ **It's none of my business.** Das geht mich
nichts an.
**businessman** NOUN
der Geschäftsmann (PL die
Geschäftsleute)
**businesswoman** NOUN
die Geschäftsfrau
**busker** NOUN
der Straßenmusikant (GEN des
Straßenmusikanten, PL die
Straßenmusikanten)
die Straßenmusikantin
**bus stop** NOUN
die Bushaltestelle
**bust** NOUN
der Busen (*chest*) (PL die Busen)
◆ **bust measurement** die Oberweite
**busy** ADJECTIVE
1 beschäftigt (*person*)
2 belebt (*shop, street*)
3 besetzt (*phone line*)
◆ **It's been a busy day.** Es war viel los
heute.
**busy signal** NOUN US
das Besetztzeichen (PL die
Besetztzeichen)
**but** CONJUNCTION

**B**

aber ◊ *I'd like to come, but I'm busy.* Ich würde gerne kommen, aber ich habe zu tun.

**butcher** NOUN
der <u>Metzger</u> (PL die Metzger)
die <u>Metzgerin</u>
◊ *He's a butcher.* Er ist Metzger.

**butcher's** NOUN
die <u>Metzgerei</u>

**butter** NOUN
die <u>Butter</u>

**butterfly** NOUN
der <u>Schmetterling</u> (PL die Schmetterlinge)

**buttocks** PL NOUN
der <u>Hintern</u> SING (GEN des Hintern, PL die Hintern)

**button** NOUN
der <u>Knopf</u> (PL die Knöpfe)

to **buy** VERB
| see also **buy** NOUN |
<u>kaufen</u> ◊ *He bought me an ice cream.* Er hat mir ein Eis gekauft.
♦ **to buy something from somebody** etwas von jemandem kaufen ◊ *I bought a watch from him.* Ich habe von ihm eine Uhr gekauft.

**buy** NOUN
| see also **buy** VERB |
der <u>Kauf</u> (PL die Käufe) ◊ *It was a good*

*buy.* Es war ein guter Kauf.

**by** PREPOSITION
[1] <u>von</u> ◊ *The thieves were caught by the police.* Die Diebe wurden von der Polizei erwischt. ◊ *a painting by Picasso* ein Gemälde von Picasso
[2] <u>mit</u> ◊ *by car* mit dem Auto ◊ *by train* mit dem Zug ◊ *by bus* mit dem Bus
[3] <u>bei</u> (*close to*) ◊ *Where's the bank? – It's by the post office.* Wo ist die Bank? – Sie ist bei der Post.
♦ **by day** bei Tag
♦ **by night** bei Nacht
[4] <u>bis</u> (*not later than*) ◊ *We have to be there by four o'clock.* Wir müssen bis vier Uhr dort sein.
♦ **by the time ...** bis ... ◊ *By the time I got there it was too late.* Bis ich dort war, war es zu spät.
♦ **That's fine by me.** Ist in Ordnung!
♦ **all by himself** ganz allein
♦ **all by herself** ganz allein
♦ **I did it all by myself.** Ich habe es ganz allein gemacht.
♦ **by the way** übrigens

**bye** EXCLAMATION
<u>tschüss</u>!

**bypass** NOUN
die <u>Umgehungsstraße</u> (*road*)

# C

cab NOUN
das Taxi (PL die Taxis)
cabbage NOUN
der Kohl
cabin NOUN
die Kabine (on ship)
cabinet NOUN
♦ a bathroom cabinet ein
Badezimmerschränkchen NEUT
♦ a drinks cabinet eine Bar
cable NOUN
das Kabel (PL die Kabel)
cable car NOUN
die Drahtseilbahn
cable television NOUN
das Kabelfernsehen
cactus NOUN
der Kaktus (GEN des Kaktus, PL die
Kakteen)
cadet NOUN
♦ a police cadet ein Polizeischüler MASC
♦ a cadet officer ein Offiziersanwärter MASC
café NOUN
die Imbissstube
cage NOUN
der Käfig (PL die Käfige)
cagoule NOUN
die Windjacke
cake NOUN
der Kuchen (PL die Kuchen)
to calculate VERB
rechnen
calculation NOUN
die Rechnung
calculator NOUN
der Taschenrechner (PL die
Taschenrechner)
calendar NOUN
der Kalender (PL die Kalender)
calf NOUN
1 (of cow)
das Kalb (PL die Kälber)
2 (of leg)
die Wade
call NOUN

see also **call** VERB

der Anruf (by phone) (PL die Anrufe)
◊ Thanks for your call. Danke für Ihren
Anruf.
♦ a phone call ein Telefongespräch NEUT
♦ to be on call (doctor) Bereitschaftsdienst
haben ◊ He's on call this evening. Er hat
heute Abend Bereitschaftsdienst.
to call VERB

see also **call** NOUN

1 (by phone)
anrufen (IMPERFECT rief an, PERFECT hat
angerufen) ◊ I'll tell him you called. Ich

sage ihm, dass du angerufen hast. ◊ This
is the number to call. Das ist die
Nummer, die du anrufen musst.
♦ to call back (phone again) zurückrufen
◊ I'll call back at six o'clock. Ich rufe um
sechs Uhr zurück.
2 (fetch)
rufen ◊ We called the police. Wir haben
die Polizei gerufen.
3 (by name)
nennen (IMPERFECT nannte, PERFECT hat
genannt) ◊ Everyone calls him Jimmy.
Alle nennen ihn Jimmy. ◊ He called me
an idiot. Er hat mich einen Idioten
genannt.
♦ to be called heißen ◊ He's called Fluffy.
Er heißt Fluffy. ◊ What's she called? Wie
heißt sie?
♦ to call somebody names jemanden
beschimpfen
♦ to call for abholen ◊ I'll call for you at
half past two. Ich hole dich um halb drei
ab.
♦ to call off absagen ◊ The match was
called off. Das Spiel wurde abgesagt.
call box NOUN
die Telefonzelle
call centre NOUN
das Callcenter (PL die Callcenters)
calm ADJECTIVE
ruhig
to calm down VERB
sich beruhigen (PERFECT hat sich beruhigt)
◊ Calm down! Beruhige dich!
Calor gas ® NOUN
das Butangas
calorie NOUN
die Kalorie
calves PL NOUN see calf
camcorder NOUN
der Camcorder (PL die Camcorder)
came VERB see come
camel NOUN
das Kamel (PL die Kamele)
camera NOUN
1 (for photos)
der Fotoapparat (PL die Fotoapparate)
2 (for filming, TV)
die Kamera (PL die Kameras)
cameraman NOUN
der Kameramann (PL die
Kameramänner)
to camp VERB

see also **camp** NOUN

zelten
camp NOUN

see also **camp** VERB

das Lager (PL die Lager)

♦ **a camp bed** eine Campingliege

**campaign** NOUN

see also **campaign** VERB

die Kampagne

to **campaign** VERB

see also **campaign** NOUN

sich einsetzen (PERFECT hat sich eingesetzt) ◊ *They are campaigning for a change in the law.* Sie setzen sich für eine Gesetzesänderung ein.

**camper** NOUN

☐1 (*person*)

der Camper (PL die Camper)

die Camperin

☐2 (*van*)

das Wohnmobil (PL die Wohnmobile)

**camping** NOUN

das Camping

♦ **to go camping** zelten ◊ *We went camping in Cornwall.* Wir waren in Cornwall zelten.

**camping gas** ℝ NOUN

das Campinggas

**campsite** NOUN

der Zeltplatz (PL die Zeltplätze)

**campus** NOUN

das Universitätsgelände (PL die Universitätsgelände)

**can** NOUN

see also **can** VERB

☐1 (*tin*)

die Dose ◊ *a can of sweetcorn* eine Dose Mais ◊ *a can of beer* eine Dose Bier

☐2 (*jerry can*)

der Kanister (PL die Kanister) ◊ *a can of petrol* ein Benzinkanister

**can** VERB

see also **can** NOUN

können (PRESENT kann, IMPERFECT konnte, PERFECT hat können) ◊ *I can't come.* Ich kann nicht kommen. ◊ *Can I help you?* Kann ich dir helfen? ◊ *You could hire a bike.* Du könntest dir ein Fahrrad mieten. ◊ *I couldn't sleep because of the noise.* Ich konnte wegen des Lärms nicht schlafen. ◊ *I can swim.* Ich kann schwimmen. ◊ *He can't drive.* Er kann nicht Auto fahren. ◊ *Can you speak German?* Können Sie Deutsch?

♦ **That can't be true!** Das darf nicht wahr sein!

♦ **You could be right.** Da könntest du Recht haben.

**Canada** NOUN

Kanada NEUT

♦ **from Canada** aus Kanada

♦ **in Canada** in Kanada

♦ **to Canada** nach Kanada

**Canadian** ADJECTIVE

see also **Canadian** NOUN

kanadisch ◊ *He's Canadian.* Er ist Kanadier. ◊ *She's Canadian.* Sie ist Kanadierin.

**Canadian** NOUN

see also **Canadian** ADJECTIVE

der Kanadier (PL die Kanadier)

die Kanadierin

**canal** NOUN

der Kanal (PL die Kanäle)

**Canaries** NOUN

♦ **the Canaries** die Kanarischen Inseln PL

**canary** NOUN

der Kanarienvogel (PL die Kanarienvögel)

to **cancel** VERB

☐1 absagen (PERFECT hat abgesagt) ◊ *The match was cancelled.* Das Spiel wurde abgesagt.

☐2 (*booking*)

stornieren (PERFECT hat storniert) ◊ *He cancelled his hotel booking.* Er hat seine Hotelreservierung storniert.

**cancellation** NOUN

die Absage

**cancer** NOUN

der Krebs (GEN des Krebses) ◊ *He's got cancer.* Er hat Krebs.

♦ **I'm Cancer.** Ich bin Krebs.

**candidate** NOUN

der Kandidat (GEN des Kandidaten, PL die Kandidaten)

die Kandidatin

**candle** NOUN

die Kerze

**candy** NOUN US

☐1 (*sweet*)

das Bonbon (PL die Bonbons)

☐2 (*sweets*)

die Süßigkeit

**candyfloss** NOUN

die Zuckerwatte

**cannabis** NOUN

das Cannabis (GEN des Cannabis)

**canned** ADJECTIVE

in Dosen (*food*) ◊ *canned beer* Bier in Dosen

**cannot** VERB see can

**canoe** NOUN

das Kanu (PL die Kanus)

**canoeing** NOUN

♦ **to go canoeing** Kanu fahren ◊ *We went canoeing.* Wir gingen Kanu fahren.

**can-opener** NOUN

der Dosenöffner (PL die Dosenöffner)

**can't** VERB see can

**canteen** NOUN

die Kantine

**canvas** NOUN

die Leinwand (PL die Leinwände)

**cap** NOUN

☐1 (*hat*)

die Mütze

☐2 (*of bottle, tube*)

der Verschluss (GEN des Verschlusses, PL die Verschlüsse)

**capable** ADJECTIVE
fähig
♦ **to be capable of doing something** etwas
tun können ◊ *She is capable of looking
after herself.* Sie kann auf sich selbst
aufpassen.

**capacity** NOUN
[1] die Fähigkeit ◊ *He has the capacity to
score a goal from almost any position.* Er
hat die Fähigkeit, aus fast jeder Position
ein Tor zu schießen.
[2] das Fassungsvermögen (*quantity*)
◊ *This tank has a capacity of fifty litres.*
Der Tank hat ein Fassungsvermögen von
fünfzig Litern.

**cape** NOUN
das Kap (PL die Kaps) ◊ *Cape Horn* Kap
Hoorn

**capital** NOUN
[1] die Hauptstadt (PL die Hauptstädte)
◊ *Cardiff is the capital of Wales.* Cardiff
ist die Hauptstadt von Wales.
[2] (*letter*)
der Großbuchstabe (GEN des
Großbuchstaben, PL die Großbuchstaben)
◊ *Write your address in capitals.* Schreib
deine Adresse in Großbuchstaben.

**capitalism** NOUN
der Kapitalismus (GEN des Kapitalismus)

**capital punishment** NOUN
die Todesstrafe

**Capricorn** NOUN
der Steinbock ◊ *I'm Capricorn.* Ich bin
Steinbock.

to **capsize** VERB
kentern (PERFECT ist gekentert)

**captain** NOUN
der Kapitän (PL die Kapitäne)
die Kapitänin
◊ *She's captain of the hockey team.* Sie
ist die Kapitänin der Hockeymannschaft.

**caption** NOUN
die Bildunterschrift

to **capture** VERB
[1] (*person*)
gefangen nehmen (PRESENT nimmt
gefangen, IMPERFECT nahm gefangen, PERFECT
hat gefangen genommen) ◊ *He was
captured by the enemy.* Er wurde vom
Feind gefangen genommen.
[2] (*animal*)
fangen (PRESENT fängt, IMPERFECT fing, PERFECT
hat gefangen) ◊ *They managed to
capture the lion.* Sie konnten den Löwen
fangen.

**car** NOUN
das Auto (PL die Autos)
♦ **to go by car** mit dem Auto fahren ◊ *We
went by car.* Wir sind mit dem Auto
gefahren.
♦ **a car crash** ein Autounfall MASC

**caramel** NOUN

das Karamellbonbon (*sweet*) (PL die
Karamellbonbons)

**caravan** NOUN
der Wohnwagen (PL die Wohnwagen)
◊ *a caravan site* ein Campingplatz für
Wohnwagen

**card** NOUN
die Karte
♦ **a card game** ein Kartenspiel NEUT

**cardboard** NOUN
der Karton (PL die Kartons)

**cardigan** NOUN
die Strickjacke

**card phone** NOUN
das Kartentelefon (PL die Kartentelefone)

**care** NOUN
┌─────────────────────┐
│ see also **care** VERB │
└─────────────────────┘
die Vorsicht
♦ **with care** vorsichtig
♦ **to take care of** aufpassen auf +ACC ◊ *I take
care of the children on Saturdays.* Ich
passe samstags auf die Kinder auf.
♦ **Take care!** (1) (*Be careful!*) Sei vorsichtig!
♦ **Take care!** (2) (*Look after yourself!*) Pass
auf dich auf!

to **care** VERB
┌─────────────────────┐
│ see also **care** NOUN │
└─────────────────────┘
♦ **to care about** achten auf +ACC ◊ *They care
about their image.* Sie achten auf ihr
Image.
♦ **I don't care!** Das ist mir egal! ◊ *She
doesn't care.* Das ist ihr egal.
♦ **to care for somebody** (*patients, old
people*) jemanden pflegen

**career** NOUN
die Karriere

**careful** ADJECTIVE
vorsichtig ◊ *Be careful!* Sei vorsichtig!

**carefully** ADVERB
[1] sorgsam ◊ *She carefully avoided the
subject.* Sie vermied das Thema
sorgsam.
[2] vorsichtig (*safely*) ◊ *Drive carefully!*
Fahr vorsichtig!
♦ **Think carefully!** Denk gut nach!

**careless** ADJECTIVE
[1] schluderig (*work*)
♦ **a careless mistake** ein Flüchtigkeitsfehler
MASC
[2] nachlässig (*person*) ◊ *She's very
careless.* Sie ist sehr nachlässig.
[3] unvorsichtig ◊ *a careless driver* ein
unvorsichtiger Fahrer

**caretaker** NOUN
der Hausmeister (PL die Hausmeister)
die Hausmeisterin

**car ferry** NOUN
die Autofähre

**cargo** NOUN
die Fracht

**car hire** NOUN
der Autoverleih (PL die Autoverleihe)

**Caribbean** ADJECTIVE

| see also **Caribbean** NOUN |
|---|

karibisch

**Caribbean** NOUN

| see also **Caribbean** ADJECTIVE |
|---|

**[1]** die Karibik (*islands*) ◊ *We're going to the Caribbean.* Wir fahren in die Karibik.
◊ *He's from the Caribbean.* Er kommt aus der Karibik.

**[2]** das Karibische Meer (*sea*)

**caring** ADJECTIVE
  liebevoll

♦ **the caring professions** die Pflegeberufe

**carnation** NOUN
  die Nelke

**carnival** NOUN
  der Karneval (PL die Karnevale)

**carol** NOUN
♦ **a Christmas carol** ein Weihnachtslied NEUT

**car park** NOUN
  der Parkplatz (PL die Parkplätze)

**carpenter** NOUN
  der Schreiner (PL die Schreiner)
  die Schreinerin
  ◊ *He's a carpenter.* Er ist Schreiner.

**carpentry** NOUN
  die Schreinerei

**carpet** NOUN
  der Teppich (PL die Teppiche) ◊ *a Persian carpet* ein Perserteppich

**car phone** NOUN
  das Autotelefon (PL die Autotelefone)

**carriage** NOUN
  der Eisenbahnwagen (PL die Eisenbahnwagen)

**carrier bag** NOUN
  die Tragetasche

**carrot** NOUN
  die Karotte

to **carry** VERB
  tragen (PRESENT trägt, IMPERFECT trug, PERFECT hat getragen) ◊ *He carried her bag.* Er trug ihre Tasche.

♦ **a plane carrying a hundred passengers** ein Flugzeug mit hundert Passagieren an Bord

♦ **to carry on** weitermachen ◊ *She carried on talking.* Sie redete weiter. ◊ *Carry on!* Mach weiter!

♦ **to carry out** (*orders*) ausführen

**carrycot** NOUN
  die Babytragetasche

**cart** NOUN
  der Karren (PL die Karren)

**carton** NOUN
  die Tüte (*of milk, juice*)

**cartoon** NOUN
  **[1]** (*film*)
  der Zeichentrickfilm (PL die Zeichentrickfilme)
  **[2]** (*in newspaper*)
  der Cartoon (PL die Cartoons)

♦ **a strip cartoon** ein Comic MASC

**cartridge** NOUN
  die Patrone

to **carve** VERB
  aufschneiden (*meat*) (IMPERFECT schnitt auf, PERFECT hat aufgeschnitten)

**case** NOUN
  **[1]** der Koffer (PL die Koffer) ◊ *I've packed my case.* Ich habe meinen Koffer gepackt.
  **[2]** der Fall (PL die Fälle) ◊ *in some cases* in manchen Fällen ◊ *Which case does "außer" take?* Welcher Fall steht nach "außer"?

♦ **in that case** in dem Fall ◊ *I don't want it. – In that case, I'll take it.* Ich will es nicht. – In dem Fall nehme ich es.

♦ **in case** für den Fall ◊ *in case it rains* für den Fall, dass es regnet

♦ **just in case** für alle Fälle ◊ *Take some money, just in case.* Nimm für alle Fälle Geld mit.

**cash** NOUN
  das Bargeld ◊ *I desperately need some cash.* Ich brauche dringend Bargeld.

♦ **in cash** in bar ◊ *two thousand pounds in cash* zweitausend Pfund in bar

♦ **to pay cash** bar bezahlen

♦ **I'm a bit short of cash.** Ich bin etwas knapp bei Kasse.

♦ **a cash card** eine Geldautomatenkarte

♦ **the cash desk** die Kasse

♦ **a cash dispenser** ein Geldautomat MASC

♦ **a cash register** eine Registrierkasse

**cashew nut** NOUN
  die Cashewnuss (PL die Cashewnüsse)

**cashier** NOUN
  der Kassierer (PL die Kassierer)
  die Kassiererin

**cashmere** NOUN
  der Kaschmir ◊ *a cashmere sweater* ein Kaschmirpullover

**casino** NOUN
  das Kasino (PL die Kasinos)

**casserole** NOUN
  der Schmortopf (PL die Schmortöpfe)

♦ **a casserole dish** eine Kasserolle

**cassette** NOUN
  die Kassette

♦ **cassette recorder** der Kassettenrekorder

♦ **cassette player** der Kassettenspieler

**cast** NOUN
  die Besetzung ◊ *After the play, we met the cast.* Nach dem Stück haben wir die Besetzung kennen gelernt.

**castle** NOUN
  die Burg

**casual** ADJECTIVE
  **[1]** leger ◊ *I prefer casual clothes.* Ich trage lieber legere Kleidung.
  **[2]** lässig ◊ *a casual attitude* eine lässige Haltung
  **[3]** beiläufig ◊ *It was just a casual remark.* Es war nur eine beiläufige Bemerkung.

**C**

**casually** ADVERB
♦**to dress casually** sich leger kleiden
**casualty** NOUN
die Unfallstation (*hospital department*)
**cat** NOUN
die Katze ◊ *Have you got a cat?* Hast du eine Katze?
**catalogue** NOUN
der Katalog (PL die Kataloge)
**catalytic converter** NOUN
der Katalysator (PL die Katalysatoren)
**catarrh** NOUN
der Katarrh (PL die Katarrhe)
**catastrophe** NOUN
die Katastrophe
to **catch** VERB
**1** fangen (PRESENT fängt, IMPERFECT fing, PERFECT hat gefangen) ◊ *My cat catches birds.* Meine Katze fängt Vögel.
♦**to catch a thief** einen Dieb fassen
♦**to catch somebody doing something** jemanden dabei erwischen, wie er etwas tut ◊ *If they catch you smoking ...* Wenn sie dich beim Rauchen erwischen ...
**2** (*bus, train*)
nehmen (PRESENT nimmt, IMPERFECT nahm, PERFECT hat genommen) ◊ *We caught the last bus.* Wir haben den letzten Bus genommen.
**3** (*hear*)
mitbekommen (IMPERFECT bekam mit, PERFECT hat mitbekommen) ◊ *I didn't catch his name.* Ich habe seinen Namen nicht mitbekommen.
♦**to catch up** aufholen ◊ *I've got a lot to catch up on.* Ich habe viel aufzuholen.
♦**to catch a cold** einen Schnupfen bekommen
**catching** ADJECTIVE
ansteckend ◊ *It's not catching.* Das ist nicht ansteckend.
**catering** NOUN
♦**Who did the catering?** Wer hat das Essen und die Getränke geliefert?
**cathedral** NOUN
die Kathedrale
**Catholic** ADJECTIVE
see also **Catholic** NOUN
katholisch
**Catholic** NOUN
see also **Catholic** ADJECTIVE
der Katholik (GEN des Katholiken, PL die Katholiken)
die Katholikin
♦**I'm a Catholic.** Ich bin katholisch.
**cattle** PL NOUN
das Vieh SING
**caught** VERB *see* **catch**
**cauliflower** NOUN
der Blumenkohl (PL die Blumenkohle)
**cause** NOUN
see also **cause** VERB

die Ursache ◊ *The cause of the fire was a short-circuit.* Ein Kurzschluss war die Ursache für das Feuer.
to **cause** VERB
see also **cause** NOUN
verursachen (PERFECT hat verursacht) ◊ *to cause an accident* einen Unfall verursachen
**cautious** ADJECTIVE
vorsichtig
**cautiously** ADVERB
vorsichtig
**cave** NOUN
die Höhle
**caviar** NOUN
der Kaviar
**CCTV** ABBREVIATION (= *closed-circuit television*)
die Videoüberwachung
**CD** NOUN
die CD (PL die CDs)
**CD player** NOUN
der CD-Spieler (PL die CD-Spieler)
**CD-ROM** NOUN
die CD-ROM (PL die CD-ROMs)
**ceasefire** NOUN
der Waffenstillstand (PL die Waffenstillstände)
**ceiling** NOUN
die Decke
to **celebrate** VERB
feiern (*birthday*)
**celebration** NOUN
die Feier
**celebrity** NOUN
die Berühmtheit
**celery** NOUN
der Stangensellerie (GEN des Stangensellerie, PL die Stangenselleries)
**cell** NOUN
die Zelle
**cellar** NOUN
der Keller (PL die Keller) ◊ *a wine cellar* ein Weinkeller
**cello** NOUN
das Cello (PL die Celli) ◊ *I play the cello.* Ich spiele Cello.
**cement** NOUN
der Zement
**cemetery** NOUN
der Friedhof (PL die Friedhöfe)
**cent** NOUN
der Cent (PL die Cents *or* Cent)
*When talking about amounts of money use the plural form **Cent**.*
◊ *twenty cents* zwanzig Cent
**centenary** NOUN
das hundertjährige Jubiläum (PL die hundertjährigen Jubiläen)
**center** NOUN US
das Zentrum (PL die Zentren) ◊ *a sports centre* ein Sportzentrum

**centigrade** ADJECTIVE
♦**twenty degrees centigrade** zwanzig Grad Celsius
**centimetre** NOUN (US **centimeter**)
der Zentimeter (PL die Zentimeter)
◊ *twenty centimetres* zwanzig Zentimeter
**central** ADJECTIVE
zentral
**central heating** NOUN
die Zentralheizung
**centre** NOUN
das Zentrum (PL die Zentren) ◊ *a sports centre* ein Sportzentrum
**century** NOUN
das Jahrhundert (PL die Jahrhunderte)
◊ *the twentieth century* das zwanzigste Jahrhundert ◊ *the twenty-first century* das einundzwanzigste Jahrhundert
**cereal** NOUN
die Getreideflocken FEM PL ◊ *I have cereal for breakfast.* Zum Frühstück esse ich Getreideflocken.
**ceremony** NOUN
die Zeremonie
**certain** ADJECTIVE
[1] sicher ◊ *I'm absolutely certain it was him.* Ich bin ganz sicher, dass er es war.
♦**I don't know for certain.** Ich bin mir nicht sicher.
♦**to make certain** sich vergewissern ◊ *I made certain the door was locked.* Ich habe mich vergewissert, dass die Tür abgeschlossen war.
[2] bestimmt ◊ *a certain person* eine bestimmte Person
**certainly** ADVERB
natürlich ◊ *I certainly expected something better.* Ich habe natürlich etwas Besseres erwartet.
♦**Certainly not!** Sicher nicht!
♦**Was it a surprise? – It certainly was!** War's eine Überraschung? – Und ob!
**certificate** NOUN
die Urkunde
**CFC** NOUN (= *chlorofluorocarbon*)
der FCKW (= Fluorchlorkohlenwasserstoff)
**chain** NOUN
die Kette
**chair** NOUN
[1] der Stuhl (PL die Stühle) ◊ *a table and four chairs* ein Tisch und vier Stühle
[2] (*armchair*)
der Sessel (PL die Sessel)
**chairlift** NOUN
der Sessellift (PL die Sessellifte)
**chairman** NOUN
der Vorsitzende (GEN des Vorsitzenden, PL die Vorsitzenden) ◊ *a chairman* ein Vorsitzender
**chalet** NOUN
das Ferienhaus (PL die Ferienhäuser)
**chalk** NOUN

die Kreide
**challenge** NOUN
see also **challenge** VERB
die Herausforderung
to **challenge** VERB
see also **challenge** NOUN
♦**She challenged me to a race.** Sie wollte mit mir um die Wette laufen.
**challenging** ADJECTIVE
anspruchsvoll ◊ *a challenging job* eine anspruchsvolle Arbeit
**chambermaid** NOUN
das Zimmermädchen (PL die Zimmermädchen)
**champagne** NOUN
der Champagner (PL die Champagner)
**champion** NOUN
der Meister (PL die Meister)
die Meisterin
**championship** NOUN
die Meisterschaft
**chance** NOUN
[1] die Chance ◊ *Do you think I've got any chance?* Meinst du, ich habe eine Chance? ◊ *Their chances of winning are very good.* Ihre Gewinnchancen sind sehr gut.
[2] die Möglichkeit ◊ *I'd like to have a chance to travel.* Ich hätte gern die Möglichkeit zu reisen.
♦**I'll write when I get the chance.** Ich schreibe, sobald ich dazu komme.
♦**by chance** zufällig ◊ *We met by chance.* Wir haben uns zufällig kennen gelernt.
♦**to take a chance** ein Risiko eingehen ◊ *I'm taking no chances!* Ich gehe kein Risiko ein!
♦**No chance!** Denkste!
**Chancellor of the Exchequer** NOUN
der Schatzkanzler (PL die Schatzkanzler)
**chandelier** NOUN
der Kronleuchter (PL die Kronleuchter)
to **change** VERB
see also **change** NOUN
[1] sich verändern (PERFECT hat sich verändert) ◊ *The town has changed a lot.* Die Stadt hat sich sehr verändert.
[2] (*money, job*)
wechseln ◊ *I'd like to change fifty pounds.* Ich würde gern fünfzig Pfund wechseln. ◊ *He wants to change his job.* Er möchte den Job wechseln.
♦**You have to change trains in Stuttgart.** Sie müssen in Stuttgart umsteigen.
♦**I'm going to change my shoes.** Ich ziehe andere Schuhe an.
♦**to change one's mind** es sich anders überlegen ◊ *I've changed my mind.* Ich habe es mir anders überlegt.
♦**to change gear** schalten
[3] sich umziehen (IMPERFECT zog sich um, PERFECT hat sich umgezogen) ◊ *She's*

☞

*changing to go out.* Sie zieht sich zum Ausgehen um.
♦ **to get changed** sich umziehen ◊ *I'm going to get changed.* Ich ziehe mich um.
4 (*swap*)
umtauschen (PERFECT hat umgetauscht) ◊ *Can I change this sweater? It's too small.* Kann ich diesen Pullover umtauschen? Er ist zu klein.

**change** NOUN
| see also **change** VERB |
1 die Änderung
♦ **There's been a change of plan.** Die Pläne haben sich geändert.
♦ **a change of clothes** Kleidung zum Wechseln
♦ **for a change** zur Abwechslung ◊ *Let's play tennis for a change.* Lass uns zur Abwechslung Tennis spielen.
2 das Kleingeld (*money*) ◊ *I haven't got any change.* Ich habe kein Kleingeld.

**changeable** ADJECTIVE
wechselhaft

**changing room** NOUN
der Umkleideraum (PL die Umkleideräume)

**channel** NOUN
das Programm (*TV*) (PL die Programme) ◊ *There's football on the other channel.* Im anderen Programm gibt es Fußball.
♦ **the English Channel** der Ärmelkanal
♦ **the Channel Islands** die Kanalinseln
♦ **the Channel Tunnel** der Kanaltunnel

**chaos** NOUN
das Chaos (GEN des Chaos)

**chap** NOUN
der Kerl (PL die Kerle) ◊ *He's a nice chap.* Er ist ein netter Kerl.

**chapel** NOUN
die Kapelle (*part of church*)

**chapter** NOUN
das Kapitel (PL die Kapitel)

**character** NOUN
1 der Charakter (PL die Charaktere) ◊ *Give me some idea of his character.* Beschreiben Sie mir seinen Charakter.
♦ **She's quite a character.** Sie ist ein Unikum.
2 (*in play, film*)
die Figur ◊ *the character played by Tom Cruise* die Figur, die Tom Cruise spielt

**characteristic** NOUN
das Merkmal (PL die Merkmale)

**charcoal** NOUN
die Holzkohle

**charge** NOUN
| see also **charge** VERB |
die Gebühr ◊ *Is there a charge for delivery?* Wird für die Zustellung eine Gebühr erhoben? ◊ *an extra charge* eine Extragebühr
♦ **free of charge** kostenlos

♦ **to reverse the charges** ein R-Gespräch führen ◊ *I'd like to reverse the charges.* Ich möchte gern ein R-Gespräch führen.
♦ **to be on a charge** angeklagt sein ◊ *He's on a charge of murder.* Er ist des Mordes angeklagt.
♦ **to be in charge** die Verantwortung haben ◊ *Mrs Munday was in charge of the group.* Mrs Munday hatte die Verantwortung für die Gruppe.

to **charge** VERB
| see also **charge** NOUN |
1 (*money*)
verlangen (PERFECT hat verlangt) ◊ *How much did he charge you?* Wie viel hat er verlangt? ◊ *They charge ten pounds an hour.* Sie verlangen zehn Pfund die Stunde.
2 (*with crime*)
anklagen (PERFECT hat angeklagt) ◊ *The police have charged him with murder.* Die Polizei hat ihn des Mordes angeklagt.

**charity** NOUN
die Wohlfahrt ◊ *She does a lot of work for charity.* Sie arbeitet viel für die Wohlfahrt.
♦ **He gave the money to charity.** Er hat das Geld für wohltätige Zwecke gespendet.

**charm** NOUN
der Charme
*Note that the "e" in **Charme** is silent.*
◊ *He's got a lot of charm.* Er hat viel Charme.

**charming** ADJECTIVE
bezaubernd

**chart** NOUN
die Grafik ◊ *The chart shows the rise of unemployment.* Die Grafik stellt den Anstieg der Arbeitslosigkeit dar.
♦ **the charts** die Hitparade SING ◊ *This album is number one in the charts.* Dieses Album ist auf Platz eins der Hitparade.

**charter flight** NOUN
der Charterflug (PL die Charterflüge)

to **chase** VERB
| see also **chase** NOUN |
verfolgen (PERFECT hat verfolgt)

**chase** NOUN
| see also **chase** VERB |
die Verfolgung
♦ **a car chase** eine Verfolgungsjagd im Auto

**chat** NOUN
das Schwätzchen (PL die Schwätzchen) ◊ *to have a chat* ein Schwätzchen halten

**chat room** NOUN
der Chatroom (PL die Chatrooms)

**chat show** NOUN
die Talkshow (PL die Talkshows)

**chauvinist** NOUN
♦ **male chauvinist** der Chauvi

**cheap** ADJECTIVE

billig ◇ *a cheap T-shirt* ein billiges T-Shirt
◇ *It's cheaper by bus.* Mit dem Bus ist es
billiger.

to **cheat** VERB
see also **cheat** NOUN
betrügen (IMPERFECT betrog, PERFECT hat
betrogen) ◇ *He cheated me.* Er hat mich
betrogen.
♦ **You're cheating!** (*in games, at school*) Du
schummelst!

**cheat** NOUN
see also **cheat** VERB
der Betrüger (PL die Betrüger)
die Betrügerin

**check** NOUN
see also **check** VERB
1 die Kontrolle ◇ *a security check* eine
Sicherheitskontrolle
2 US (*bill*)
die Rechnung
◇ *The waiter brought us the check.* Der
Kellner brachte uns die Rechnung.
3 US
der Scheck (PL die Schecks)
◇ *to write a check* einen Scheck
ausstellen

to **check** VERB
see also **check** NOUN
nachsehen (PRESENT sieht nach, IMPERFECT
sah nach, PERFECT hat nachgesehen) ◇ *I'll
check the time of the train.* Ich sehe die
Abfahrtszeiten des Zuges nach. ◇ *Could
you check the oil, please?* Könnten Sie
bitte das Öl nachsehen?
♦ **to check in** einchecken ◇ *What time do I
have to check in?* Wann muss ich
einchecken?
♦ **to check out** (*from hotel*) sich auschecken

**checked** ADJECTIVE
kariert ◇ *a checked shirt* ein kariertes
Hemd

**checkers** SING NOUN US
Dame FEM ◇ *Checkers is her favourite
game.* Dame ist ihr Lieblingsspiel.

**check-in** NOUN
der Check-in (PL die Check-ins)

**checking account** NOUN US
das Girokonto (PL die Girokonten)

**checkout** NOUN
die Kasse

**check-up** NOUN
der Check-up (PL die Check-ups)

**cheddar** NOUN
der Cheddar (PL die Cheddars)

**cheek** NOUN
1 die Wange ◇ *He kissed her on the
cheek.* Er küsste sie auf die Wange.
2 die Frechheit ◇ *What a cheek!* So eine
Frechheit!

**cheeky** ADJECTIVE
frech ◇ *Don't be cheeky!* Sei nicht so
frech! ◇ *a cheeky smile* ein freches
Lächeln

**cheer** NOUN
see also **cheer** VERB
der Hurraruf (PL die Hurrarufe)
♦ **to give a cheer** hurra rufen
♦ **Cheers! (1)** (*good health*) Prost!
♦ **Cheers! (2)** (*thanks*) Danke schön!

to **cheer** VERB
see also **cheer** NOUN
1 (*team*)
anfeuern (PERFECT hat angefeuert)
2 (*speaker*)
zujubeln (PERFECT hat zugejubelt) ◇ *The
speaker was cheered.* Dem Redner
wurde zugejubelt.
♦ **to cheer somebody up** jemanden
aufheitern ◇ *I was trying to cheer him up.*
Ich habe versucht, ihn aufzuheitern.
♦ **Cheer up!** Kopf hoch!

**cheerful** ADJECTIVE
fröhlich

**cheerio** EXCLAMATION
tschüs

**cheese** NOUN
der Käse (PL die Käse)

**chef** NOUN
der Küchenchef (PL die Küchenchefs)

**chemical** NOUN
die Chemikalie

**chemist** NOUN
1 (*pharmacist*)
der Apotheker (PL die Apotheker)
die Apothekerin
2 (*pharmacy*)
die Apotheke ◇ *You get it from the
chemist.* Du bekommst das in der
Apotheke.
3 (*shop selling toiletries*)
die Drogerie
4 (*scientist*)
der Chemiker (PL die Chemiker)
die Chemikerin

**chemistry** NOUN
die Chemie ◇ *the chemistry lab* das
Chemielabor

**cheque** NOUN
der Scheck (PL die Schecks) ◇ *to write a
cheque* einen Scheck ausstellen ◇ *to pay
by cheque* mit Scheck bezahlen

**chequebook** NOUN
das Scheckheft (PL die Scheckhefte)

---
ⓘ *German banks provide customers
with cheques in an envelope or wallet,
usually ten at a time, rather than
chequebooks.*
---

**cherry** NOUN
die Kirsche

**chess** NOUN
das Schach ◇ *to play chess* Schach
spielen

**chessboard** NOUN
das Schachbrett (PL die Schachbretter)

**C**

**chest** NOUN
die Brust (*of person*) (PL die Brüste)
♦ **his chest measurement** seine Oberweite
♦ **a chest of drawers** eine Kommode

**chestnut** NOUN
die Kastanie

to **chew** VERB
kauen

**chewing gum** NOUN
der Kaugummi (PL die Kaugummis)

**chick** NOUN
das Küken (PL die Küken) ◊ *a hen and her chicks* eine Henne mit ihren Küken

**chicken** NOUN
1 (*food*)
das Hähnchen (PL die Hähnchen) ◊ *I bought a chicken in the supermarket.* Ich habe im Supermarkt ein Hähnchen gekauft.
2 (*live*)
das Huhn (PL die Hühner) ◊ *My mother used to keep chickens.* Meine Mutter hat früher Hühner gehalten.

**chickenpox** SING NOUN
die Windpocken PL ◊ *My sister has chickenpox.* Meine Schwester hat Windpocken.

**chickpeas** PL NOUN
die Kichererbsen PL

**chief** NOUN
see also **chief** ADJECTIVE
der Chef (PL die Chefs) ◊ *the chief of security* der Sicherheitschef

**chief** ADJECTIVE
see also **chief** NOUN
hauptsächlich ◊ *His chief reason for resigning was the low pay.* Der hauptsächliche Grund für seine Kündigung war die geringe Bezahlung.

**child** NOUN
das Kind (PL die Kinder) ◊ *all the children* alle Kinder

**childish** ADJECTIVE
kindisch

**child minder** NOUN
die Tagesmutter (PL die Tagesmütter)

**children** PL NOUN *see* **child**

**Chile** NOUN
Chile NEUT
♦ **from Chile** aus Chile
♦ **to Chile** nach Chile

to **chill** VERB
kalt stellen ◊ *Put the wine in the fridge to chill.* Stell den Wein kalt.

**chilli** NOUN
der Chili (PL die Chilis)
♦ **chilli peppers** die Peperoni PL

**chilly** ADJECTIVE
kühl

**chimney** NOUN
der Schornstein (PL die Schornsteine)

**chin** NOUN
das Kinn (PL die Kinne)

**china** NOUN
das Porzellan ◊ *a china plate* ein Porzellanteller MASC

**China** NOUN
China NEUT
♦ **from China** aus China
♦ **to China** nach China

**Chinese** ADJECTIVE
see also **Chinese** NOUN
chinesisch ◊ *a Chinese restaurant* ein chinesisches Restaurant
♦ **a Chinese man** ein Chinese
♦ **a Chinese woman** eine Chinesin

**Chinese** NOUN
see also **Chinese** ADJECTIVE
das Chinesisch (*language*) (GEN des Chinesischen)
♦ **the Chinese** (*people*) die Chinesen

**chip** NOUN
der Chip (*in computer*) (PL die Chips)

**chips** PL NOUN
1 die Pommes frites FEM PL (*fried potatoes*) ◊ *We bought some chips.* Wir haben Pommes frites gekauft.
2 die Kartoffelchips MASC PL (*crisps*)
*Be caerful not to translate* **chips** *by the German word* **Chips**.

**chiropodist** NOUN
der Fußpfleger (PL die Fußpfleger)
die Fußpflegerin
◊ *He's a chiropodist.* Er ist Fußpfleger.

**chives** PL NOUN
der Schnittlauch

**chocolate** NOUN
die Schokolade ◊ *a chocolate cake* ein Schokoladenkuchen ◊ *hot chocolate* heiße Schokolade

**choice** NOUN
die Wahl ◊ *I had no choice.* Ich hatte keine andere Wahl.

**choir** NOUN
der Chor (PL die Chöre) ◊ *I sing in the school choir.* Ich singe im Schulchor.

to **choke** VERB
ersticken (PERFECT ist erstickt) ◊ *Help him, he's choking!* Helft ihm, er erstickt!

to **choose** VERB
auswählen (PERFECT hat ausgewählt)
◊ *She chose the red shirt.* Sie hat das rote Hemd ausgewählt.

to **chop** VERB
see also **chop** NOUN
klein hacken (PERFECT hat klein gehackt)
◊ *She chopped the onions.* Sie hackte die Zwiebeln klein.

**chop** NOUN
see also **chop** VERB
das Kotelett (PL die Koteletts) ◊ *a pork chop* ein Schweinekotelett

**chopsticks** PL NOUN

die <u>Stäbchen</u> NEUT PL
**chose** VERB *see* **choose**
**chosen** VERB *see* **choose**
**Christ** NOUN
　<u>Christus</u> (GEN Christi) ◊ *the birth of Christ*
　die Geburt Christi
**christening** NOUN
　die <u>Taufe</u>
**Christian** NOUN
　┌──────────────────────────────┐
　│ *see also* **Christian** ADJECTIVE │
　└──────────────────────────────┘
　der <u>Christ</u> (GEN des Christen, PL die
　Christen)
　die <u>Christin</u>
**Christian** ADJECTIVE
　┌──────────────────────────┐
　│ *see also* **Christian** NOUN │
　└──────────────────────────┘
　<u>christlich</u>
**Christian name** NOUN
　der <u>Vorname</u> (GEN des Vornamens, PL die
　Vornamen)
**Christmas** NOUN
　<u>Weihnachten</u> NEUT ◊ *Happy Christmas!*
　Fröhliche Weihnachten!
◆**Christmas Day** der erste
　Weihnachtsfeiertag
◆**Christmas Eve** Heiligabend

> ⓘ *Traditionally, in Germany gifts are*
> *exchanged on Christmas Eve.*

◊ *on Christmas Eve* an Heiligabend
◆**a Christmas tree** ein Weihnachtsbaum
　MASC
◆**a Christmas card** eine Weihnachtskarte

> ⓘ *Most Germans send very few*
> *Christmas cards.*

◆**Christmas dinner** das Weihnachtsessen

> ⓘ *Germans traditionally eat goose at*
> *Christmas rather than turkey.*

◆**Christmas pudding**

> ⓘ *Germans don't have any traditional*
> *dessert at Christmas. Most know what*
> ***Christmas pudding** is, but almost*
> *always refer to it as **Plumpudding**.*

to **chuck out** VERB
　<u>rauswerfen</u> (PRESENT wirft raus, IMPERFECT
　warf raus, PERFECT hat rausgeworfen)
　◊ *You'll need to chuck out some of these*
　*books.* Du musst ein paar von diesen
　Büchern rauswerfen.
**chunk** NOUN
　das <u>Stück</u> (PL die Stücke) ◊ *Cut the meat*
　*into chunks.* Schneiden Sie das Fleisch in
　Stücke.
**church** NOUN
　die <u>Kirche</u> ◊ *I don't go to church every*
　*Sunday.* Ich gehe nicht jeden Sonntag in
　die Kirche.

◆**the Church of England** die anglikanische
　Kirche
**cider** NOUN
　der <u>Apfelwein</u>
**cigar** NOUN
　die <u>Zigarre</u>
**cigarette** NOUN
　die <u>Zigarette</u>
**cigarette lighter** NOUN
　der <u>Zigarettenanzünder</u> (PL die
　Zigarettenanzünder)
**cinema** NOUN
　das <u>Kino</u> (PL die Kinos) ◊ *I'm going to the*
　*cinema this evening.* Ich gehe heute
　Abend ins Kino.
**cinnamon** NOUN
　der <u>Zimt</u>
**circle** NOUN
　der <u>Kreis</u> (PL die Kreise)
**circular** ADJECTIVE
　<u>rund</u>
**circulation** NOUN
　[1] der <u>Kreislauf</u> (*of blood*)
　[2] die <u>Auflage</u> (*of newspaper*)
**circumstances** PL NOUN
　die <u>Umstände</u> MASC PL
**circus** NOUN
　der <u>Zirkus</u> (GEN des Zirkus, PL die
　Zirkusse)
**citizen** NOUN
　der <u>Bürger</u> (PL die Bürger)
　die <u>Bürgerin</u>
◆**a German citizen** ein deutscher
　Staatsbürger
**city** NOUN
　die <u>Stadt</u> (PL die Städte)
◆**the city centre** die Innenstadt ◊ *It's in the*
　*city centre.* Es liegt in der Innenstadt.
◆**the City** die Londoner City
**city technology college** NOUN
　die <u>technische Fachschule</u>
**civilization** NOUN
　die <u>Zivilisation</u>
**civil servant** NOUN
　der <u>Beamte</u> (GEN des Beamten, PL die
　Beamten)
　die <u>Beamtin</u>

> ⓘ *In Germany most teachers are*
> ***Beamte**.*

◊ *He's a civil servant.* Er ist Beamter.
**civil war** NOUN
　der <u>Bürgerkrieg</u> (PL die Bürgerkriege)
to **claim** VERB
　┌──────────────────────────┐
　│ *see also* **claim** NOUN │
　└──────────────────────────┘
　[1] <u>behaupten</u> (PERFECT hat behauptet)
　◊ *He claims to have found the money.* Er
　behauptet, er habe das Geld gefunden.
　*Note the use of the subjunctive.*
　[2] (*receive*)

bekommen (IMPERFECT bekam, PERFECT hat bekommen) ◊ *She's claiming unemployment benefit.* Sie bekommt Arbeitslosenunterstützung.

◆**to claim on one's insurance** seine Versicherung in Anspruch nehmen ◊ *We claimed on our insurance.* Wir haben unsere Versicherung in Anspruch genommen.

**claim** NOUN

see also **claim** VERB

der Anspruch (*on insurance policy*) (PL die Ansprüche)

◆**to make a claim for damages** Schadenersatz beanspruchen

to **clap** VERB

klatschen (*applaud*) ◊ *The audience clapped.* Das Publikum klatschte.

◆**to clap one's hands** klatschen

**clarinet** NOUN

die Klarinette ◊ *I play the clarinet.* Ich spiele Klarinette.

to **clash** VERB

1 (*colours*)

sich beißen (IMPERFECT bissen sich, PERFECT haben sich gebissen) ◊ *These two colours clash.* Diese beiden Farben beißen sich.

2 (*events*)

sich überschneiden (IMPERFECT überschnitt sich, PERFECT hat sich überschnitten) ◊ *The concert clashes with Ann's party.* Das Konzert überschneidet sich mit Anns Party.

**clasp** NOUN

der Verschluss (*of necklace*) (GEN des Verschlusses, PL die Verschlüsse)

**class** NOUN

1 die Klasse (*group*) ◊ *We're in the same class.* Wir sind in derselben Klasse.

2 die Stunde (*lesson*) ◊ *I go to dancing classes.* Ich nehme Tanzstunden.

**classic** ADJECTIVE

see also **classic** NOUN

klassisch ◊ *a classic example* ein klassisches Beispiel

**classic** NOUN

see also **classic** ADJECTIVE

der Klassiker (*book, film*) (PL die Klassiker)

**classical** ADJECTIVE

klassisch ◊ *I like classical music.* Ich mag klassische Musik.

**classmate** NOUN

der Klassenkamerad (GEN des Klassenkameraden, PL die Klassenkameraden)
die Klassenkameradin

**classroom** NOUN

das Klassenzimmer (PL die Klassenzimmer)

**clause** NOUN

1 (*in legal document*)
die Klausel

2 (*in grammar*)
der Satz (GEN des Satzes, PL die Sätze)

**claw** NOUN

1 die Kralle (*of cat, dog*)

2 die Klaue (*of bird*)

3 die Schere (*of crab, lobster*)

**clean** ADJECTIVE

see also **clean** VERB

sauber ◊ *a clean shirt* ein sauberes Hemd

to **clean** VERB

see also **clean** ADJECTIVE

sauber machen (PERFECT hat sauber gemacht)

**cleaner** NOUN

der Putzmann (PL die Putzmänner)
die Putzfrau
◊ *She's a cleaner.* Sie ist Putzfrau.

**cleaner's** NOUN

die Reinigung

**cleaning lady** NOUN

die Putzfrau

**cleansing lotion** NOUN

die Reinigungslotion

**clear** ADJECTIVE

see also **clear** VERB

1 klar ◊ *It's clear you don't believe me.* Es ist klar, dass du mir nicht glaubst.

2 frei (*road, way*) ◊ *The road's clear now.* Die Straße ist jetzt frei.

to **clear** VERB

see also **clear** ADJECTIVE

1 räumen ◊ *The police are clearing the road after the accident.* Die Polizei räumt die Straße nach dem Unfall.

2 (*fog, mist*)

sich auflösen (PERFECT hat sich aufgelöst) ◊ *The mist soon cleared.* Der Nebel löste sich bald auf.

◆**to be cleared of a crime** von einem Verbrechen freigesprochen werden ◊ *She was cleared of murder.* Sie wurde von der Mordanklage freigesprochen.

◆**to clear the table** den Tisch abräumen ◊ *I'll clear the table.* Ich räume den Tisch ab.

◆**to clear up** aufräumen ◊ *Who's going to clear all this up?* Wer räumt das alles auf?

◆**I think it's going to clear up.** (*weather*) Ich glaube, es hellt sich auf.

**clearly** ADVERB

klar ◊ *She explained it very clearly.* Sie hat es sehr klar erklärt. ◊ *The English coast was clearly visible.* Die englische Küste war klar zu sehen.

◆**to speak clearly** deutlich sprechen

**clementine** NOUN

die Klementine

to **clench** VERB

◆**She clenched her fists.** Sie ballte die Fäuste.

**clerk** NOUN
der Büroangestellte (GEN des
Büroangestellten, PL die
Büroangestellten)
die Büroangestellte (GEN der
Büroangestellten) ◊ *She's a clerk.* Sie ist
Büroangestellte.

**clever** ADJECTIVE
[1] klug ◊ *She's very clever.* Sie ist sehr
klug.
[2] genial (*ingenious*) ◊ *a clever system*
ein geniales System ◊ *What a clever
idea!* Das ist eine geniale Idee!

to **click on** VERB
anklicken (*computer*) (PERFECT hat
angeklickt) ◊ *to click on an icon* ein Icon
anklicken
♦ **to click on the mouse** mit der Maus
klicken

**client** NOUN
der Klient (GEN des Klienten, PL die
Klienten)
die Klientin

**cliff** NOUN
die Klippe

**climate** NOUN
das Klima (PL die Klimas)

to **climb** VERB
[1] steigen auf +ACC
(IMPERFECT stieg, PERFECT ist gestiegen)
◊ *We're going to climb Snowdon.* Wir
steigen auf den Snowdon.
[2] (*stairs*)
hinaufgehen (IMPERFECT ging hinauf, PERFECT
ist hinaufgegangen) ◊ *I watched him
climb the stairs.* Ich sah ihn die Treppe
hinaufgehen.
♦ **She finds it difficult to climb the stairs.**
Das Treppensteigen fällt ihr schwer.

**climber** NOUN
der Kletterer (PL die Kletterer)
die Kletterin

**climbing** NOUN
das Klettern
♦ **to go climbing** klettern gehen ◊ *We're
going climbing in Scotland.* Wir gehen in
Schottland klettern.

**clingfilm** NOUN
die Frischhaltefolie

**clinic** NOUN
die Klinik

**cloakroom** NOUN
[1] die Garderobe (*for coats*)
[2] die Toilette (*toilet*)

**clock** NOUN
die Uhr
♦ **a grandfather clock** eine Standuhr
♦ **an alarm clock** ein Wecker MASC
♦ **a clock radio** ein Radiowecker MASC

**clockwork** NOUN
das Uhrwerk
♦ **to go like clockwork** wie am Schnürchen
gehen (*informal*)

**clog** NOUN
[1] (*modern*)
der Clog (PL die Clogs)
[2] (*traditional, made of wood*)
der Holzschuh (PL die Holzschuhe)

**clone** NOUN
⊟ *see also* **clone** VERB
der Klon (PL die Klone)

to **clone** VERB
⊟ *see also* **clone** NOUN
klonen ◊ *a cloned sheep* ein geklontes
Schaf

**close** ADJECTIVE, ADVERB
⊟ *see also* **close** VERB
[1] nahe (*near*) ◊ *close relations* nahe
Verwandte ◊ *I'm very close to my sister.*
Ich stehe meiner Schwester sehr nahe.
♦ **The shops are very close.** Die Geschäfte
sind ganz in der Nähe.
♦ **She's a close friend of mine.** Sie ist eine
gute Freundin von mir.
♦ **Come closer!** Komm näher!
♦ **close to** in der Nähe +GEN ◊ *The youth
hostel is close to the station.* Die
Jugendherberge ist in der Nähe des
Bahnhofs.
[2] knapp (*contest*) ◊ *It's going to be very
close.* Das wird sehr knapp.
[3] schwül (*weather*) ◊ *It's close this
afternoon.* Heute Nachmittag ist es
schwül.

to **close** VERB
⊟ *see also* **close** ADJECTIVE
schließen (IMPERFECT schloss, PERFECT hat
geschlossen) ◊ *What time does the pool
close?* Wann schließt das Schwimmbad?
◊ *The doors close automatically.* Die
Türen schließen automatisch.
♦ **Please close the door.** Bitte mach die Tür
zu.

**closed** ADJECTIVE
geschlossen ◊ *The bank's closed.* Die
Bank ist geschlossen.

**closely** ADVERB
genau (*look, examine*)

**cloth** NOUN
der Stoff (*material*) (PL die Stoffe)
♦ **a cloth** ein Lappen MASC ◊ *Wipe it with a
damp cloth.* Wischen Sie es mit einem
feuchten Lappen ab.

**clothes** PL NOUN
die Kleider NEUT PL ◊ *new clothes* neue
Kleider
♦ **a clothes line** eine Wäscheleine
♦ **a clothes peg** eine Wäscheklammer

**cloud** NOUN
die Wolke

**cloudy** ADJECTIVE
bewölkt

**clove** NOUN
♦ **a clove of garlic** eine Knoblauchzehe

**clown** NOUN
der Clown (PL die Clowns)

**club** NOUN
der Klub (PL die Klubs) ◊ *a tennis club* ein Tennisklub ◊ *the youth club* der Jugendklub
♦ **clubs** (*in cards*) Kreuz NEUT ◊ *the ace of clubs* das Kreuzass

to **club together** VERB
zusammenlegen (PERFECT hat zusammengelegt) ◊ *We clubbed together to buy her a present.* Wir haben zusammengelegt, um ein Geschenk für sie zu kaufen.

**clubbing** NOUN
♦ **to go clubbing** in Klubs gehen

**clue** NOUN
der Hinweis (PL die Hinweise) ◊ *an important clue* ein wichtiger Hinweis
♦ **I haven't a clue.** Ich habe keine Ahnung.

**clumsy** ADJECTIVE
tollpatschig ◊ *Toby is even clumsier than his sister.* Toby ist noch tollpatschiger als seine Schwester.

**clutch** NOUN
see also **clutch** VERB
die Kupplung (*of car*)

to **clutch** VERB
see also **clutch** NOUN
umklammern (PERFECT hat umklammert) ◊ *She clutched my arm and begged me not to go.* Sie umklammerte meinen Arm und flehte mich an, nicht zu gehen.

**clutter** NOUN
der Kram ◊ *There's so much clutter in here.* Hier liegt so viel Kram herum.

**coach** NOUN
1 der Reisebus (GEN des Reisebusses, PL die Reisebusse) ◊ *We went there by coach.* Wir sind mit dem Bus dorthin gefahren. ◊ *the coach station* der Busbahnhof ◊ *a coach trip* eine Busreise
2 (*trainer*)
der Trainer (PL die Trainer)
die Trainerin
◊ *the German coach* der deutsche Trainer

**coal** NOUN
die Kohle
♦ **a coal mine** eine Kohlezeche
♦ **a coal miner** ein Bergarbeiter MASC

**coarse** ADJECTIVE
1 grob ◊ *The bag was made of coarse black cloth.* Die Tasche war aus grobem schwarzem Stoff gemacht.
2 grobkörnig ◊ *The sand is very coarse on that beach.* Der Sand an diesem Strand ist sehr grobkörnig.

**coast** NOUN
die Küste ◊ *It's on the west coast of Scotland.* Es liegt an der Westküste Schottlands.

**coastguard** NOUN
die Küstenwache

**coat** NOUN
der Mantel (PL die Mäntel) ◊ *a warm coat* ein warmer Mantel
♦ **a coat of paint** ein Anstrich MASC

**coat hanger** NOUN
der Kleiderbügel (PL die Kleiderbügel)

**cobweb** NOUN
das Spinnennetz

**cocaine** NOUN
das Kokain

**cock** NOUN
der Hahn (*bird*) (PL die Hähne)

**cockerel** NOUN
der Hahn (PL die Hähne)

**cockney** NOUN
der Cockney (PL die Cockneys) ◊ *I'm a cockney.* Ich bin Cockney.

**cocoa** NOUN
der Kakao (PL die Kakaos *or* Kakao) ◊ *a cup of cocoa* eine Tasse Kakao
*When ordering more than one cup of cocoa use the plural form **Kakao**.*
◊ *Two cocoas, please.* Zwei Kakao bitte.

**coconut** NOUN
die Kokosnuss (PL die Kokosnüsse)

**cod** NOUN
der Kabeljau (PL die Kabeljaue)

**code** NOUN
der Code (PL die Codes)

**coffee** NOUN
der Kaffee (PL die Kaffees *or* Kaffee) ◊ *A cup of coffee, please.* Eine Tasse Kaffee, bitte.
*When ordering more than one coffee use the plural form **Kaffee**.*
◊ *Two coffees, please.* Zwei Kaffee bitte.

**coffeepot** NOUN
die Kaffeekanne

**coffee table** NOUN
der Couchtisch (PL die Couchtische)

**coffin** NOUN
der Sarg (PL die Särge)

**coin** NOUN
die Münze
♦ **a five-mark coin** ein Fünfmarkstück NEUT

**coincidence** NOUN
der Zufall (PL die Zufälle)

**coin phone** NOUN
das Münztelefon

**Coke** ® NOUN
die Cola (PL die Colas) ◊ *a can of Coke* ® eine Dose Cola

**colander** NOUN
der Seiher (PL die Seiher)

**cold** ADJECTIVE
see also **cold** NOUN
kalt ◊ *The water's cold.* Das Wasser ist kalt. ◊ *It's cold today.* Heute ist es kalt.
*When you talk about a person being **cold**, you use the impersonal construction.*
◊ *I'm cold.* Mir ist kalt. ◊ *Are you cold?* Ist dir kalt?

**cold** NOUN

> see also **cold** ADJECTIVE

[1] die <u>Kälte</u> ◊ *I can't stand the cold.* Ich kann Kälte nicht ausstehen.

[2] der <u>Schnupfen</u> (PL die Schnupfen) ◊ *to catch a cold* einen Schnupfen bekommen ◊ *to have a cold* einen Schnupfen haben ◊ *I've got a bad cold.* Ich habe einen üblen Schnupfen.

♦ **a cold sore** ein Fieberbläschen NEUT

**coleslaw** NOUN
der <u>Krautsalat</u> (PL die Krautsalate)

to **collapse** VERB
<u>zusammenbrechen</u> (PRESENT bricht zusammen, IMPERFECT brach zusammen, PERFECT ist zusammengebrochen) ◊ *He collapsed.* Er brach zusammen.

**collar** NOUN
[1] (*of coat, shirt*)
der <u>Kragen</u> (PL die Kragen)
[2] (*for animal*)
das <u>Halsband</u> (PL die Halsbänder)

**collarbone** NOUN
das <u>Schlüsselbein</u> (PL die Schlüsselbeine) ◊ *I broke my collarbone.* Ich habe mir das Schlüsselbein gebrochen.

**colleague** NOUN
der <u>Kollege</u> (GEN des Kollegen, PL die Kollegen)
die <u>Kollegin</u>

to **collect** VERB
[1] <u>einsammeln</u> (PERFECT hat eingesammelt) ◊ *The teacher collected the exercise books.* Der Lehrer hat die Hefte eingesammelt.
[2] <u>sammeln</u> ◊ *I collect stamps.* Ich sammle Briefmarken. ◊ *They're collecting for charity.* Sie sammeln für wohltätige Zwecke.
[3] (*come to fetch*)
<u>abholen</u> (PERFECT hat abgeholt) ◊ *Their mother collects them from school.* Ihre Mutter holt sie von der Schule ab.

**collect call** NOUN US
das <u>R-Gespräch</u> (PL die R-Gespräche)

**collection** NOUN
die <u>Sammlung</u> ◊ *my CD collection* meine CD-Sammlung ◊ *a collection for charity* eine Spendensammlung

**collector** NOUN
der <u>Sammler</u> (PL die Sammler)
die <u>Sammlerin</u>

**college** NOUN
die <u>Fachhochschule</u>

> ❶ A **Fachhochschule** is an institute of higher education for pupils aged over 18, which combines academic studies with work experience. It is oriented towards the needs of industry and commerce.

to **collide** VERB
<u>zusammenstoßen</u> (PRESENT stößt zusammen, IMPERFECT stieß zusammen, PERFECT ist zusammengestoßen)

**collie** NOUN
der <u>Collie</u> (PL die Collies)

**colliery** NOUN
die <u>Zeche</u>

**collision** NOUN
der <u>Zusammenstoß</u> (GEN des Zusammenstoßes, PL die Zusammenstöße)

**colon** NOUN
der <u>Doppelpunkt</u> (*punctuation mark*)

**colonel** NOUN
der <u>Oberst</u> (GEN des Obersten, PL die Obersten)

**colour** NOUN (US **color**)
die <u>Farbe</u> ◊ *What colour is it?* Welche Farbe hat es?

♦ **a colour film** (*for camera*) ein Farbfilm MASC

**colourful** ADJECTIVE (US **colorful**)
<u>farbig</u>

**colouring** NOUN (US **coloring**)
der <u>Farbstoff</u> (*for food*) (PL die Farbstoffe)

**comb** NOUN

> see also **comb** VERB

der <u>Kamm</u> (PL die Kämme)

to **comb** VERB

> see also **comb** NOUN

♦ **to comb one's hair** sich kämmen ◊ *You haven't combed your hair.* Du hast dich nicht gekämmt.

**combination** NOUN
die <u>Kombination</u>

to **combine** VERB
<u>vereinen</u> (PERFECT hat vereint) ◊ *The film combines humour with suspense.* Der Film vereint Humor und Spannung.

to **come** VERB
<u>kommen</u> (IMPERFECT kam, PERFECT ist gekommen) ◊ *I'm coming!* Ich komme! ◊ *The letter came this morning.* Der Brief kam heute früh. ◊ *Can I come too?* Kann ich mitkommen? ◊ *Some friends came to see us.* Einige Freunde sind zu Besuch gekommen. ◊ *I'll come with you.* Ich komme mit dir.

♦ **to come across** zufällig finden ◊ *I came across a dress that I hadn't worn for years.* Ich fand zufällig ein Kleid, das ich schon Jahre nicht mehr an hatte.

♦ **She comes across as a nice girl.** Sie scheint ein nettes Mädchen zu sein.

♦ **to come back** zurückkommen ◊ *Come back!* Komm zurück!

♦ **to come down (1)** (*person, lift*) herunterkommen

♦ **to come down (2)** (*prices*) fallen

☞

◆**to come from** kommen aus ◊ *I come from Germany.* Ich komme aus Deutschland. ◊ *Where do you come from?* Woher kommen Sie?

◆**to come in** hereinkommen ◊ *Come in!* Herein!

◆**Come on!** Na komm!

◆**to come out** herauskommen ◊ *when we came out of the cinema* als wir aus dem Kino kamen ◊ *It's just come out on video.* Es ist gerade als Video herausgekommen.

◆**None of my photos came out.** Meine Fotos sind alle nichts geworden.

◆**to come round** (*after faint, operation*) wieder zu sich kommen

◆**to come up** heraufkommen ◊ *Come up here!* Komm hier herauf!

◆**to come up to somebody** auf jemanden zukommen ◊ *She came up to me and kissed me.* Sie kam auf mich zu und küsste mich.

**comedian** NOUN
der Komiker (PL die Komiker)
die Komikerin

**comedy** NOUN
die Komödie

**comfortable** ADJECTIVE
bequem

◆**I'm very comfortable, thanks.** Danke, ich fühle mich sehr wohl.

**comic** NOUN
das Comicheft (*magazine*) (PL die Comichefte)

**comic strip** NOUN
der Comicstrip (PL die Comicstrips)

**coming** ADJECTIVE
kommend ◊ *in the coming months* in den kommenden Monaten

**comma** NOUN
das Komma (PL die Kommas)

**command** NOUN
der Befehl (PL die Befehle)

**comment** NOUN
see also **comment** VERB
der Kommentar (PL die Kommentare) ◊ *He made no comment.* Er gab keinen Kommentar ab. ◊ *No comment!* Kein Kommentar!

to **comment** VERB
see also **comment** NOUN

◆**to comment on something** eine Bemerkung zu etwas machen

**commentary** NOUN
der Kommentar (*on TV, radio*) (PL die Kommentare)

**commentator** NOUN
(*sports*)
der Sportreporter (PL die Sportreporter)
die Sportreporterin

**commercial** NOUN
der Werbespot (PL die Werbespots)

**commission** NOUN

die Provision

◆**Salesmen work on commission.** Verkäufer arbeiten auf Provisionsbasis.

to **commit** VERB

◆**to commit a crime** ein Verbrechen begehen

◆**to commit oneself** sich festlegen ◊ *I don't want to commit myself.* Ich will mich nicht festlegen.

◆**to commit suicide** Selbstmord begehen ◊ *He committed suicide.* Er beging Selbstmord.

**committee** NOUN
der Ausschuss (GEN des Ausschusses, PL die Ausschüsse)

**common** ADJECTIVE
see also **common** NOUN
gebräuchlich ◊ *"Smith" is a very common surname.* "Smith" ist ein sehr gebräuchlicher Nachname.

◆**in common** gemein ◊ *We've got a lot in common.* Wir haben viel gemein.

**common** NOUN
see also **common** ADJECTIVE
die Gemeindewiese ◊ *We went for a walk on the common.* Wir sind auf der Gemeindewiese spazieren gegangen.

**Commons** PL NOUN

◆**the House of Commons** das britische Unterhaus

**common sense** NOUN
der gesunde Menschenverstand ◊ *Use your common sense!* Benutze deinen gesunden Menschenverstand!

to **communicate** VERB
kommunizieren (PERFECT hat kommuniziert)

**communication** NOUN
die Kommunikation

**communion** NOUN
die Kommunion ◊ *my First Communion* meine Erstkommunion

**communism** NOUN
der Kommunismus (GEN des Kommunismus)

**communist** NOUN
see also **communist** ADJECTIVE
der Kommunist (GEN des Kommunisten, PL die Kommunisten)
die Kommunistin

**communist** ADJECTIVE
see also **communist** NOUN
kommunistisch

◆**the Communist Party** die Kommunistische Partei

**community** NOUN
die Gemeinschaft

◆**the local community** die Gemeinde

to **commute** VERB
pendeln (PERFECT ist gependelt) ◊ *She commutes between Liss and London.* Sie pendelt zwischen Liss und London.

**compact disc** NOUN
die <u>Compact Disc</u> (PL die Compact Discs)
♦ **compact disc player** der CD-Spieler
**companion** NOUN
der <u>Gefährte</u> (GEN des Gefährten, PL die Gefährten)
die <u>Gefährtin</u>
**company** NOUN
1 das <u>Unternehmen</u> (PL die Unternehmen) ◊ *He works for a big company.* Er arbeitet für ein großes Unternehmen.
2 die <u>Gesellschaft</u> ◊ *an insurance company* eine Versicherungsgesellschaft
♦ **a theatre company** ein Theaterensemble NEUT
♦ **to keep somebody company** jemandem Gesellschaft leisten ◊ *I'll keep you company.* Ich leiste dir Gesellschaft.
**comparatively** ADVERB
<u>relativ</u>
to **compare** VERB
<u>vergleichen</u> (IMPERFECT verglich, PERFECT hat verglichen) ◊ *People always compare him with his brother.* Die Leute vergleichen ihn immer mit seinem Bruder.
♦ **compared with** im Vergleich zu ◊ *Oxford is small compared with London.* Im Vergleich zu London ist Oxford klein.
**comparison** NOUN
der <u>Vergleich</u> (PL die Vergleiche)
**compartment** NOUN
das <u>Abteil</u> (PL die Abteile)
**compass** NOUN
der <u>Kompass</u> (GEN des Kompasses, PL die Kompasse)
**compensation** NOUN
der <u>Schadenersatz</u> ◊ *They got two thousand pounds compensation.* Sie bekamen zweitausend Pfund Schadenersatz.
**compere** NOUN
der <u>Conférencier</u> (PL die Conférenciers)
to **compete** VERB
<u>teilnehmen</u> (PRESENT nimmt teil, IMPERFECT nahm teil, PERFECT hat teilgenommen) ◊ *I'm competing in the marathon.* Ich nehme am Marathon teil.
♦ **to compete for something** um etwas kämpfen ◊ *They are competing for a place in the UEFA cup.* Sie kämpfen um einen Platz im UEFA-Pokal.
♦ **There are fifty students competing for six places.** Fünfzig Studenten bewerben sich auf sechs Studienplätze.
**competent** ADJECTIVE
<u>kompetent</u>
**competition** NOUN
(*organized event*)
der <u>Wettbewerb</u> (PL die Wettbewerbe)
◊ *a singing competition* ein Gesangswettbewerb

**competitive** ADJECTIVE
♦ **I'm a very competitive person.** Ich bin ein sehr ehrgeiziger Mensch.
**competitor** NOUN
(*participant*)
der <u>Teilnehmer</u> (PL die Teilnehmer)
die <u>Teilnehmerin</u>
to **complain** VERB
<u>sich beschweren</u> (PERFECT hat sich beschwert) ◊ *I'm going to complain to the manager.* Ich werde mich beim Geschäftsführer beschweren. ◊ *We complained about the noise.* Wir haben uns über den Lärm beschwert.
**complaint** NOUN
die <u>Beschwerde</u> ◊ *There were lots of complaints about the food.* Es gab viele Beschwerden über das Essen.
**complete** ADJECTIVE
<u>vollständig</u>
**completely** ADVERB
<u>völlig</u>
**complexion** NOUN
der <u>Teint</u> (PL die Teints)
**complicated** ADJECTIVE
<u>kompliziert</u>
**compliment** NOUN

> see also **compliment** VERB

das <u>Kompliment</u> (PL die Komplimente)
to **compliment** VERB

> see also **compliment** NOUN

♦ **They complimented me on my German.** Sie haben mir Komplimente zu meinem Deutsch gemacht.
**complimentary** ADJECTIVE
♦ **complimentary ticket** der Freifahrschein
to **compose** VERB
<u>komponieren</u> (*music*) (PERFECT hat komponiert)
♦ **to be composed of something** aus etwas bestehen ◊ *The team is composed of two boys and three girls.* Die Mannschaft besteht aus zwei Jungen und drei Mädchen.
**composer** NOUN
der <u>Komponist</u> (GEN des Komponisten, PL die Komponisten)
die <u>Komponistin</u>
**comprehension** NOUN
das <u>Verständnis</u> (*school exercise*)
**comprehensive** ADJECTIVE
<u>umfassend</u> ◊ *a comprehensive guide to Greece* ein umfassender Reiseführer für Griechenland
**comprehensive school** NOUN
die <u>Gesamtschule</u>

> ⓘ *Gesamtschulen* are the exception rather than the rule in Germany.

**compromise** NOUN

> see also **compromise** VERB

C

☞

der Kompromiss (GEN des Kompromisses, PL die Kompromisse) ◊ *We reached a compromise.* Wir haben einen Kompromiss gefunden.

to **compromise** VERB

see also **compromise** NOUN

einen Kompromiss schließen (IMPERFECT schloss, PERFECT hat geschlossen)

**compulsory** ADJECTIVE
obligatorisch

**computer** NOUN
der Computer (PL die Computer)

**computer game** NOUN
das Computerspiel (PL die Computerspiele)

**computer programmer** NOUN
der Programmierer (PL die Programmierer)
die Programmiererin
◊ *She's a computer programmer.* Sie ist Programmiererin.

**computer science** NOUN
die Informatik

**computing** NOUN
die Informatik

to **concentrate** VERB
sich konzentrieren (PERFECT hat sich konzentriert) ◊ *I couldn't concentrate.* Ich konnte mich nicht konzentrieren.

**concentration** NOUN
die Konzentration

**concern** NOUN

see also **concern** VERB

die Sorge ◊ *to express concern about something* Sorge über etwas ausdrücken

to **concern** VERB

see also **concern** NOUN

betreffen (PRESENT betrifft, IMPERFECT betraf, PERFECT hat betroffen) ◊ *It concerns all of us.* Es betrifft uns alle.

**concerned** ADJECTIVE
♦ **to be concerned** sich Sorgen machen ◊ *I am concerned about him.* Ich mache mir Sorgen um ihn.
♦ **as far as I'm concerned** was mich betrifft

**concerning** NOUN
bezüglich ◊ *For further information concerning the job, contact Mr Ross.* Für weitere Informationen bezüglich der Stelle wenden Sie sich an Herrn Ross.

**concert** NOUN
das Konzert (PL die Konzerte)

**concrete** NOUN
der Beton (PL die Betons)

to **condemn** VERB
verurteilen (PERFECT hat verurteilt)

**condition** NOUN
[1] die Bedingung ◊ *I'll do it, on one condition ...* Ich mache es unter einer Bedingung ...
[2] der Zustand (PL die Zustände) ◊ *in good condition* in gutem Zustand

**conditional** NOUN
der Konditional

**conditioner** NOUN
die Spülung (*for hair*)

**condom** NOUN
das Kondom (PL die Kondome)

to **conduct** VERB
dirigieren (*orchestra*) (PERFECT hat dirigiert)

**conductor** NOUN
der Dirigent (GEN des Dirigenten, PL die Dirigenten)
die Dirigentin

**cone** NOUN
[1] die Eistüte ◊ *an ice-cream cone* eine Eistüte
[2] (*geometric shape*)
der Kegel (PL die Kegel)
♦ **a traffic cone** ein Pylon MASC

**conference** NOUN
die Konferenz

to **confess** VERB
gestehen (IMPERFECT gestand, PERFECT hat gestanden) ◊ *He finally confessed.* Er hat schließlich gestanden. ◊ *He confessed to the murder.* Er hat den Mord gestanden.

**confession** NOUN
[1] das Geständnis (GEN des Geständnisses, PL die Geständnisse) ◊ *Her confession was made under duress.* Ihr Geständnis war erzwungen.
[2] (*in church*)
die Beichte ◊ *My sister doesn't like going to confession.* Meine Schwester geht ungern zur Beichte.

**confetti** NOUN
das Konfetti

**confidence** NOUN
[1] das Vertrauen ◊ *I've got confidence in you.* Ich habe Vertrauen in dich.
[2] das Selbstvertrauen ◊ *She lacks confidence.* Sie hat zu wenig Selbstvertrauen.

**confident** ADJECTIVE
[1] zuversichtlich (*sure of something*) ◊ *I'm confident everything will be okay.* Ich bin zuversichtlich, dass alles gut gehen wird.
[2] selbstbewusst (*self-assured*) ◊ *She's seems a confident person.* Sie scheint eine selbstbewusste Frau zu sein.

**confidential** ADJECTIVE
vertraulich

to **confirm** VERB
bestätigen (*booking*) (PERFECT hat bestätigt)

**confirmation** NOUN
die Bestätigung

**conflict** NOUN
der Konflikt (PL die Konflikte)

to **confuse** VERB
durcheinander bringen (IMPERFECT brachte durcheinander, PERFECT hat durcheinander gebracht) ◊ *Don't confuse me!* Bring mich nicht durcheinander!

**confused** ADJECTIVE

durcheinander
**confusing** ADJECTIVE
verwirrend
**confusion** NOUN
das Durcheinander
to **congratulate** VERB
beglückwünschen (PERFECT hat
beglückwünscht) ◊ *My friends
congratulated me on passing the test.*
Meine Freunde haben mich zur
bestandenen Prüfung beglückwünscht.
**congratulations** PL NOUN
der Glückwunsch (PL die Glückwünsche)
◊ *Congratulations on your new job!*
Herzlichen Glückwunsch zum neuen Job!
**conjunction** NOUN
die Konjunktion
**conjurer** NOUN
der Zauberkünstler (PL die
Zauberkünstler)
die Zauberkünstlerin
**connection** NOUN
[1] der Zusammenhang (PL die
Zusammenhänge) ◊ *There's no
connection between the two events.* Es
besteht kein Zusammenhang zwischen
den beiden Ereignissen.
[2] (*electrical*)
der Kontakt (PL die Kontakte) ◊ *There's a
loose connection.* Da ist ein
Wackelkontakt.
[3] (*of trains, planes*)
der Anschluss (GEN des Anschlusses, PL
die Anschlüsse) ◊ *We missed our
connection.* Wir haben unseren
Anschluss verpasst.
to **conquer** VERB
erobern (PERFECT hat erobert)
**conscience** NOUN
das Gewissen ◊ *I have a guilty
conscience.* Ich habe ein schlechtes
Gewissen.
**conscious** ADJECTIVE
bewusst ◊ *politically conscious* politisch
bewusst ◊ *a conscious effort* eine
bewusste Anstrengung
♦ **to be conscious of something (1)** (*know*)
sich einer Sache bewusst sein ◊ *I was
conscious of his disapproval.* Ich war mir
seiner Missbilligung bewusst.
♦ **to be conscious of something (2)** (*notice*)
etwas bemerken ◊ *She was conscious of
Max looking at her.* Sie hatte bemerkt,
dass Max sie ansah.
**consciousness** NOUN
das Bewusstsein
♦ **to lose consciousness** bewusstlos
werden ◊ *I lost consciousness.* Ich wurde
bewusstlos.
**consequence** NOUN
die Folge
**consequently** ADVERB
folglich

**conservation** NOUN
der Schutz ◊ *nature conservation* der
Naturschutz
**conservative** ADJECTIVE
see also **conservative** NOUN
konservativ
♦ **the Conservative Party** die Konservative
Partei
**Conservative** NOUN
see also **conservative** ADJECTIVE
der Konservative (GEN des
Konservativen, PL die Konservativen)
die Konservative
◊ *a Conservative* (*man*) ein Konservativer
♦ **to vote Conservative** die Konservativen
wählen
♦ **the Conservatives** die Konservativen
**conservatory** NOUN
der Wintergarten (PL die Wintergärten)
to **consider** VERB
in Erwägung ziehen (IMPERFECT zog in
Erwägung, PERFECT hat in Erwägung
gezogen) ◊ *We considered cancelling our
holiday.* Wir zogen in Erwägung, den
Urlaub abzusagen.
♦ **I'm considering the idea.** Ich denke
darüber nach.
♦ **He considered it a waste of time.** Er hielt
es für Zeitverschwendung.
**considerate** ADJECTIVE
aufmerksam ◊ *That was very considerate
of you.* Das war sehr aufmerksam von dir.
♦ **not very considerate** nicht sehr
rücksichtsvoll
**considering** PREPOSITION
[1] dafür, dass ◊ *Considering we were
there for a month ...* Dafür, dass wir
einen Monat da waren ...
[2] unter den Umständen ◊ *I got a good
mark, considering.* Unter den Umständen
bekam ich eine gute Note.
to **consist** VERB
♦ **to consist of** bestehen aus ◊ *The band
consists of three guitarists and a
drummer.* Die Band besteht aus drei
Gitarristen und einem Schlagzeuger.
**consistent** ADJECTIVE
beständig ◊ *He's the team's most
consistent player.* Er ist der beständigste
Spieler der Mannschaft.
**consonant** NOUN
der Konsonant (GEN des Konsonanten, PL
die Konsonanten)
**constant** ADJECTIVE
beständig
**constantly** ADVERB
dauernd
**constipated** ADJECTIVE
verstopft
to **construct** VERB
bauen
**construction** NOUN
der Bau

to **consult** VERB
⨩1⨩ (*solicitor, doctor*)
um Rat fragen
⨩2⨩ (*book*)
nachsehen in +DAT
(PRESENT sieht nach, IMPERFECT sah nach,
PERFECT hat nachgesehen) ◊ *You should
consult the dictionary.* Du solltest im
Wörterbuch nachsehen.

**consumer** NOUN
der Verbraucher (PL die Verbraucher)
die Verbraucherin

**contact** NOUN
│ *see also* **contact** VERB │
der Kontakt (PL die Kontakte) ◊ *I'm in
contact with her.* Ich bin in Kontakt mit
ihr.

to **contact** VERB
│ *see also* **contact** NOUN │
sich in Verbindung setzen mit ◊ *You
should contact us immediately.* Sie
sollten sich sofort mit uns in Verbindung
setzen.
✦ **Where can we contact you?** Wo können
wir Sie erreichen?

**contact lenses** PL NOUN
die Kontaktlinsen FEM PL

to **contain** VERB
enthalten (PRESENT enthält, IMPERFECT
enthielt, PERFECT hat enthalten)

**container** NOUN
der Behälter (PL die Behälter)

**contempt** NOUN
die Verachtung

**contents** PL NOUN
der Inhalt
✦ **table of contents** das Inhaltsverzeichnis

**contest** NOUN
der Wettbewerb (PL die Wettbewerbe)

**contestant** NOUN
der Teilnehmer (PL die Teilnehmer)
die Teilnehmerin

**context** NOUN
der Zusammenhang (PL die
Zusammenhänge)

**continent** NOUN
der Kontinent (PL die Kontinente) ◊ *How
many continents are there?* Wie viele
Kontinente gibt es?
✦ **the Continent** Kontinentaleuropa NEUT
◊ *on the Continent* in Kontinentaleuropa
✦ **I've never been to the Continent.** Ich war
noch nie auf dem Kontinent.

**continental breakfast** NOUN
das kleine Frühstück

**continental quilt** NOUN
die Steppdecke

to **continue** VERB
weitermachen (PERFECT hat
weitergemacht) ◊ *We will continue after
the break.* Wir machen nach der Pause
weiter.
✦ **Please continue!** Bitte fahren Sie fort!

✦ **She continued talking to her friend.** Sie
redete weiter mit ihrer Freundin.

**continuous** ADJECTIVE
laufend
✦ **continuous assessment** laufende
Leistungskontrolle

**contraceptive** NOUN
das Verhütungsmittel (PL die
Verhütungsmittel)

**contract** NOUN
der Vertrag (PL die Verträge)

to **contradict** VERB
widersprechen (PRESENT widerspricht,
IMPERFECT widersprach, PERFECT hat
widersprochen) ◊ *Don't contradict me!*
Widersprich mir nicht!

**contrary** NOUN
das Gegenteil
✦ **on the contrary** im Gegenteil

**contrast** NOUN
der Kontrast (PL die Kontraste)

to **contribute** VERB
⨩1⨩ beitragen (PRESENT trägt bei, IMPERFECT
trug bei, PERFECT hat beigetragen) ◊ *The
treaty will contribute to world peace.* Der
Vertrag wird zum Weltfrieden beitragen.
⨩2⨩ (*donate*)
spenden ◊ *She contributed ten pounds.*
Sie hat zehn Pfund gespendet.

**contribution** NOUN
der Beitrag (PL die Beiträge)

**control** NOUN
│ *see also* **control** VERB │
die Kontrolle
✦ **to lose control** (*of vehicle*) die Kontrolle
verlieren ◊ *He lost control of the car.* Er
hat die Kontrolle über das Auto verloren.
✦ **the controls** (*of machine*) die
Bedienelemente NEUT PL
✦ **to be in control** das Sagen haben
✦ **to keep control** (*of people*) Disziplin
halten ◊ *He can't keep control of the
class.* Er kann in der Klasse keine
Disziplin halten.
✦ **out of control** (*child, class*) außer Rand
und Band

to **control** VERB
│ *see also* **control** NOUN │
⨩1⨩ (*country, organization*)
unter Kontrolle haben (PRESENT hat unter
Kontrolle, IMPERFECT hatte unter Kontrolle,
PERFECT hat unter Kontrolle gehabt)
⨩2⨩ Disziplin halten in +DAT
(PRESENT hält Disziplin in, IMPERFECT hielt
Disziplin in, PERFECT hat Disziplin gehalten
in) ◊ *He can't control the class.* Er kann in
der Klasse keine Disziplin halten.
⨩3⨩ unter Kontrolle halten ◊ *I couldn't
control the horse.* Ich konnte das Pferd
nicht mehr unter Kontrolle halten.
⨩4⨩ (*regulate*)

regeln ◊ *You can control the volume using this knob.* Sie können mit diesem Knopf die Lautstärke regeln.
♦ **to control oneself** sich beherrschen
**controversial** ADJECTIVE
umstritten ◊ *a controversial book* ein umstrittenes Buch
**convenient** ADJECTIVE
günstig (*place*) ◊ *The hotel's convenient for the airport.* Das Hotel ist in günstiger Lage zum Flughafen. ◊ *It's not convenient for me right now.* Es ist gerade ungünstig.
♦ **Would Monday be convenient for you?** Würde dir Montag passen?
**conventional** ADJECTIVE
konventionell
**convent school** NOUN
die Klosterschule
**conversation** NOUN
die Unterhaltung
♦ **a German conversation class** deutsche Konversation
to **convert** VERB
umbauen (PERFECT hat umgebaut) ◊ *We've converted the loft into a spare room.* Wir haben den Speicher zu einem Gästezimmer umgebaut.
**convict** NOUN
| *see also* **convict** VERB |
der Häftling ◊ *an escaped convict* ein entflohener Häftling
to **convict** VERB
| *see also* **convict** NOUN |
überführen (PERFECT hat überführt) ◊ *He was convicted of the murder.* Er wurde des Mordes überführt.
**conviction** NOUN
die Überzeugung ◊ *She spoke with great conviction.* Sie sprach mit großer Überzeugung.
♦ **He has three previous convictions for robbery.** Er ist bereits dreimal wegen Raubes vorbestraft.
to **convince** VERB
überzeugen (PERFECT hat überzeugt) ◊ *I'm not convinced.* Ich bin nicht überzeugt.
to **cook** VERB
| *see also* **cook** NOUN |
kochen ◊ *I can't cook.* Ich kann nicht kochen. ◊ *She's cooking lunch.* Sie kocht das Mittagessen.
♦ **to be cooked** fertig sein ◊ *When the potatoes are cooked ...* Wenn die Kartoffeln fertig sind ...
**cook** NOUN
| *see also* **cook** VERB |
der Koch (PL die Köche)
die Köchin
◊ *Werner's an excellent cook.* Werner ist ein ausgezeichneter Koch.
**cookbook** NOUN

das Kochbuch (PL die Kochbücher)
**cooker** NOUN
der Herd (PL die Herde) ◊ *a gas cooker* ein Gasherd
**cookery** NOUN
das Kochen
♦ **a cookery class** ein Kochkurs MASC
**cookie** NOUN US
der Keks (GEN des Kekses, PL die Kekse)
**cooking** NOUN
das Kochen
♦ **I like cooking.** Ich koche gern.
**cool** ADJECTIVE
| *see also* **cool** VERB |
kühl ◊ *a cooler place* ein kühlerer Ort
♦ **to stay cool** (*keep calm*) ruhig bleiben ◊ *He stayed cool.* Er blieb ruhig.
to **cool** VERB
| *see also* **cool** ADJECTIVE |
kühlen
♦ **Just cool it!** Immer mit der Ruhe! (*informal*)
**cooperation** NOUN
die Zusammenarbeit
**cop** NOUN
der Polizist (GEN des Polizisten, PL die Polizisten)
die Polizistin
to **cope** VERB
es schaffen ◊ *It was hard, but we coped.* Es war schwer, aber wir haben es geschafft.
♦ **to cope with** bewältigen ◊ *She's got a lot of problems to cope with.* Sie hat eine Menge Probleme zu bewältigen.
**copper** NOUN
[1] das Kupfer ◊ *a copper bracelet* ein Kupferarmband
[2] (*police officer*)
der Polizist (GEN des Polizisten, PL die Polizisten)
die Polizistin
**copy** NOUN
| *see also* **copy** VERB |
[1] (*of letter, document*)
die Kopie
[2] (*of book*)
das Exemplar (PL die Exemplare)
to **copy** VERB
| *see also* **copy** NOUN |
[1] (*write down*)
abschreiben (IMPERFECT schrieb ab, PERFECT hat abgeschrieben) ◊ *She copied the sentence into her exercise book.* Sie schrieb den Satz in ihr Heft ab. ◊ *The teacher accused him of copying.* Der Lehrer warf ihm vor, abgeschrieben zu haben.
[2] (*person*)
nachmachen (PERFECT hat nachgemacht) ◊ *She always copies her sister.* Sie macht ihrer Schwester alles nach.

**C**

☞

**3** (*computer*)
kopieren (PERFECT hat kopiert) ◊ *to copy and paste* kopieren und einfügen

**core** NOUN
der Stein (*of fruit*)

**cork** NOUN
**1** (*of bottle*)
der Korken (PL die Korken)
**2** (*material*)
der Kork ◊ *a cork table mat* ein Korkuntersetzer MASC

**corkscrew** NOUN
der Korkenzieher (PL die Korkenzieher)

**corn** NOUN
**1** (*wheat*)
das Getreide (PL die Getreide)
**2** (*sweetcorn*)
der Mais
◆ **corn on the cob** der Maiskolben

**corner** NOUN
**1** die Ecke ◊ *in a corner of the room* in einer Ecke des Zimmers ◊ *the shop on the corner* das Geschäft an der Ecke ◊ *He lives just round the corner.* Er wohnt gleich um die Ecke.
**2** (*in football*)
der Eckball (PL die Eckbälle)

**cornet** NOUN
**1** das Kornett (PL die Kornette) ◊ *He plays the cornet.* Er spielt Kornett.
**2** (*ice cream*)
die Eistüte

**cornflakes** PL NOUN
die Cornflakes PL

**cornstarch** NOUN [US]
das Maismehl

**Cornwall** NOUN
Cornwall NEUT
◆ **in Cornwall** in Cornwall

**corporal** NOUN
der Stabsunteroffizier (PL die Stabsunteroffiziere)

**corporal punishment** NOUN
die Prügelstrafe

**corpse** NOUN
die Leiche

**correct** ADJECTIVE
see also **correct** VERB
richtig ◊ *That's correct.* Das ist richtig.
◊ *the correct answer* die richtige Antwort

to **correct** VERB
see also **correct** ADJECTIVE
korrigieren (PERFECT hat korrigiert)

**correction** NOUN
die Verbesserung

**correctly** ADVERB
richtig

**correspondent** NOUN
der Korrespondent (GEN des Korrespondenten, PL die Korrespondenten)
die Korrespondentin

**corridor** NOUN
der Korridor (PL die Korridore)

**corruption** NOUN
die Korruption

**Corsica** NOUN
Korsika NEUT
◆ **from Corsica** aus Korsika
◆ **to Corsica** nach Korsika

**cosmetics** PL NOUN
die Kosmetika NEUT PL

**cosmetic surgery** NOUN
die Schönheitschirurgie

to **cost** VERB
see also **cost** NOUN
kosten ◊ *The meal cost fifty marks.* Das Essen hat fünfzig Mark gekostet. ◊ *How much does it cost?* Wie viel kostet das? ◊ *It costs too much.* Das kostet zu viel.

**cost** NOUN
see also **cost** VERB
die Kosten PL ◊ *the cost of living* die Lebenshaltungskosten
◆ **at all costs** um jeden Preis

**costume** NOUN
das Kostüm (PL die Kostüme)

**cosy** ADJECTIVE
gemütlich

**cot** NOUN
**1** (*for children*)
das Kinderbett (PL die Kinderbetten)
**2** (*camp bed*)
die Campingliege

**cottage** NOUN
das kleine Haus (GEN des kleinen Hauses, PL die kleinen Häuser)
◆ **a thatched cottage** ein Haus mit Strohdach

**cottage cheese** NOUN
der Hüttenkäse

**cotton** NOUN
die Baumwolle ◊ *a cotton shirt* ein Baumwollhemd NEUT
◆ **cotton candy** die Zuckerwatte
◆ **cotton wool** die Watte

**couch** NOUN
die Couch (PL die Couches)

**couchette** NOUN
der Platz im Liegewagen (PL die Plätze im Liegewagen)

to **cough** VERB
see also **cough** NOUN
husten

**cough** NOUN
see also **cough** VERB
der Husten ◊ *a bad cough* ein schlimmer Husten ◊ *I've got a cough.* Ich habe Husten.

**could** VERB *see* **can**

**council** NOUN
der Gemeinderat (PL die Gemeinderäte)
◊ *He's on the council.* Er ist im Gemeinderat.

◆ **a council estate** eine Siedlung des sozialen Wohnungsbaus
◆ **a council house** eine Sozialwohnung

> ⓘ *In Germany the council provides flats rather than houses.*

**councillor** NOUN
der Gemeinderat (PL die Gemeinderäte)
die Gemeinderätin
◇ *She's a local councillor.* Sie ist Gemeinderätin.

to **count** VERB
zählen
◆ **to count on** zählen auf +ACC ◇ *You can count on me.* Du kannst auf mich zählen.

**counter** NOUN
[1] (*in shop*)
der Ladentisch (PL die Ladentische)
[2] (*in post office, bank*)
der Schalter (PL die Schalter)
[3] (*in game*)
die Spielmarke

**country** NOUN
das Land (PL die Länder) ◇ *the border between the two countries* die Grenze zwischen den beiden Ländern
◆ **in the country** auf dem Land ◇ *I live in the country.* Ich wohne auf dem Land.
◆ **country dancing** der Volkstanz

**countryside** NOUN
die Landschaft

**county** NOUN
die Grafschaft

> ⓘ *The nearest German equivalent of a county would be a **Bundesland**.*

◆ **the county council** der Grafschaftsrat

> ⓘ *The nearest German equivalent of a county council would be the **Landtag**.*

**couple** NOUN
das Paar (PL die Paare) ◇ *the couple who live next door* das Paar von nebenan
◆ **a couple** ein paar

> *Note that in this sense **paar** is spelt with a small "p".*

◇ *a couple of hours* ein paar Stunden
◇ *Could you wait a couple of minutes?* Könntest du ein paar Minuten warten?

**courage** NOUN
der Mut

**courgette** NOUN
die Zucchini (PL die Zucchini)

**courier** NOUN
[1] (*for tourists*)
der Reiseleiter (PL die Reiseleiter)
die Reiseleiterin
[2] (*delivery service*)

der Kurier (PL die Kuriere) ◇ *They sent it by courier.* Sie haben es mit Kurier geschickt.

**course** NOUN
[1] der Kurs (PL die Kurse) ◇ *a German course* ein Deutschkurs ◇ *to go on a course* einen Kurs machen
[2] der Gang (PL die Gänge) ◇ *the first course* der erste Gang
◆ **the main course** das Hauptgericht
[3] der Platz (PL die Plätze) ◇ *a golf course* ein Golfplatz
◆ **of course** natürlich ◇ *Do you love me? – Of course I do!* Liebst du mich? – Aber natürlich!

**court** NOUN
[1] (*of law*)
das Gericht (PL die Gerichte) ◇ *He was in court last week.* Er war letzte Woche vor Gericht.
[2] (*tennis*)
der Platz (PL die Plätze) ◇ *There are tennis and squash courts.* Es gibt Tennis- und Squashplätze.

**courtyard** NOUN
der Hof (PL die Höfe)

**cousin** NOUN
[1] (*man*)
der Vetter (PL die Vettern)
[2] (*woman*)
die Kusine

**cover** NOUN

> see also **cover** VERB

[1] (*of book*)
der Umschlag (PL die Umschläge)
[2] (*of duvet*)
der Bezug (PL die Bezüge)

to **cover** VERB

> see also **cover** NOUN

[1] bedecken (PERFECT hat bedeckt) ◇ *He covers his computer with a plastic hood.* Er bedeckt seinen Computer mit einer Plastikhülle.
◆ **My face was covered with mosquito bites.** Mein Gesicht war voller Mückenstiche.
[2] decken ◇ *Our insurance didn't cover it.* Unsere Versicherung hat das nicht gedeckt.
◆ **to cover up a scandal** einen Skandal vertuschen

**cow** NOUN
die Kuh (PL die Kühe)

**coward** NOUN
der Feigling (PL die Feiglinge)
> *der Feigling is also used for women.*
◇ *She's a coward.* Sie ist ein Feigling.

**cowardly** ADJECTIVE
feige

**cowboy** NOUN
der Cowboy (PL die Cowboys)

**crab** NOUN
die Krabbe

C

**crack** NOUN

> see also **crack** VERB

1 (*in wall*)

der Riss (GEN des Risses, PL die Risse)

2 (*in cup, window*)

der Sprung (PL die Sprünge)

3 (*drug*)

das Crack

♦ **I'll have a crack at it.** Ich werd's mal versuchen.

to **crack** VERB

> see also **crack** NOUN

1 (*nut*)

knacken

2 (*egg*)

aufschlagen (PRESENT schlägt auf, IMPERFECT schlug auf, PERFECT hat aufgeschlagen)

♦ **to crack a joke** einen Witz reißen

♦ **to crack down on** hart durchgreifen
◊ *The police are cracking down on motorists who drive too fast.* Die Polizei greift hart gegen Fahrer durch, die zu schnell fahren.

**cracked** ADJECTIVE

kaputt (*cup, window*)

**cracker** NOUN

1 (*biscuit*)

der Cracker (PL die Cracker)

2 (*Christmas cracker*)

das Knallbonbon (PL die Knallbonbons)

**cradle** NOUN

die Wiege

**craft** NOUN

das Werken ◊ *We do craft at school.* Wir haben Werken in der Schule.

♦ **a craft centre** ein Kunstgewerbezentrum NEUT

**craftsman** NOUN

der Kunsthandwerker (PL die Kunsthandwerker)

to **cram** VERB

1 stopfen ◊ *We crammed our stuff into the boot.* Wir haben unsere Sachen in den Kofferraum gestopft.

2 pauken (*for exams*)

**crane** NOUN

der Kran (*machine*)

to **crash** VERB

> see also **crash** NOUN

kaputtfahren (PRESENT fährt kaputt, IMPERFECT fuhr kaputt, PERFECT hat kaputtgefahren) ◊ *He's crashed his car.* Er hat sein Auto kaputtgefahren.

♦ **The plane crashed.** Das Flugzeug stürzte ab.

♦ **to crash into something** auf etwas fahren ◊ *My brother crashed into the back of a lorry.* Mein Bruder ist hinten auf einen Lastwagen gefahren.

**crash** NOUN

> see also **crash** VERB

1 (*of car*)

der Unfall (PL die Unfälle)

2 (*of plane*)

das Unglück (PL die Unglücke)

♦ **a crash helmet** ein Sturzhelm MASC

♦ **a crash course** ein Crashkurs MASC

to **crawl** VERB

> see also **crawl** NOUN

krabbeln (*baby*) (PERFECT ist gekrabbelt)

**crawl** NOUN

> see also **crawl** VERB

das Kraulen

♦ **to do the crawl** kraulen

**crazy** ADJECTIVE

verrückt

**cream** ADJECTIVE

> see also **cream** NOUN

cremefarben (*colour*)

**cream** NOUN

> see also **cream** ADJECTIVE

die Sahne ◊ *strawberries and cream* Erdbeeren mit Sahne ◊ *a cream cake* eine Sahnetorte

♦ **cream cheese** der Frischkäse

♦ **sun cream** die Sonnencreme

**crease** NOUN

die Falte

**creased** ADJECTIVE

zerknittert

to **create** VERB

schaffen (IMPERFECT schuf, PERFECT hat geschaffen)

**creation** NOUN

die Schöpfung

**creative** ADJECTIVE

kreativ

**creature** NOUN

das Lebewesen (PL die Lebewesen)

**crèche** NOUN

die Kinderkrippe

**credit** NOUN

der Kredit (PL die Kredite) ◊ *on credit* auf Kredit

**credit card** NOUN

die Kreditkarte

**creep** NOUN

> see also **creep** VERB

♦ **It gives me the creeps.** Es ist mir nicht geheuer.

to **creep** VERB

> see also **creep** NOUN

kriechen (IMPERFECT kroch, PERFECT ist gekrochen)

**cress** NOUN

die Kresse

**crew** NOUN

die Mannschaft

**crew cut** NOUN

der Bürstenhaarschnitt (PL die Bürstenhaarschnitte)

**cricket** NOUN

1 das Cricket

**❶** *Cricket is practically never played in Germany.*

◊ *I play cricket.* Ich spiele Cricket.
♦ **a cricket bat** ein Cricketschläger MASC
[2] die Grille (*insect*)
**crime** NOUN
[1] das Verbrechen (PL die Verbrechen)
◊ *Murder is a crime.* Mord ist ein Verbrechen.
[2] (*lawlessness*)
die Kriminalität ◊ *Crime is rising.* Die Kriminalität nimmt zu.
**criminal** NOUN
| see also **criminal** ADJECTIVE |
der Verbrecher (PL die Verbrecher)
die Verbrecherin
**criminal** ADJECTIVE
| see also **criminal** NOUN |
kriminell ◊ *It's criminal!* Das ist kriminell!
♦ **It's a criminal offence.** Das ist eine strafbare Handlung.
♦ **to have a criminal record** vorbestraft sein
**crippled** ADJECTIVE
gelähmt ◊ *He was crippled in an accident.* Er ist seit einem Unfall gelähmt.
**crisis** NOUN
die Krise
**crisp** ADJECTIVE
knusprig (*food*)
**crisps** PL NOUN
die Chips MASC PL ◊ *a bag of crisps* eine Tüte Chips
**criterion** NOUN
das Kriterium (PL die Kriterien)
**critic** NOUN
der Kritiker (PL die Kritiker)
die Kritikerin
**critical** ADJECTIVE
kritisch
**criticism** NOUN
die Kritik
to **criticize** VERB
kritisieren (PERFECT hat kritisiert)
**Croatia** NOUN
Kroatien NEUT
♦ **from Croatia** aus Kroatien
♦ **to Croatia** nach Kroatien
to **crochet** VERB
häkeln
**crocodile** NOUN
das Krokodil (PL die Krokodile)
**crook** NOUN
der Verbrecher (*criminal*) (PL die Verbrecher)
**crop** NOUN
die Ernte ◊ *a good crop of apples* eine gute Apfelernte

**cross** NOUN
| see also **cross** ADJECTIVE, VERB |
das Kreuz (PL die Kreuze)
**cross** ADJECTIVE
| see also **cross** NOUN, VERB |
böse ◊ *to be cross about something* wegen etwas böse sein
to **cross** VERB
| see also **cross** ADJECTIVE, NOUN |
überqueren (*street, bridge*) (PERFECT hat überquert)
♦ **to cross out** durchstreichen
♦ **to cross over** hinübergehen
**cross-country** NOUN
das Querfeldeinrennen (*race*) (PL die Querfeldeinrennen)
♦ **cross-country skiing** der Langlauf
**crossing** NOUN
[1] (*by boat*)
die Überfahrt ◊ *the crossing from Dover to Calais* die Überfahrt von Dover nach Calais
[2] (*for pedestrians*)
der Fußgängerüberweg (PL die Fußgängerüberwege)
**crossroads** SING NOUN
die Kreuzung
**crossword** NOUN
das Kreuzworträtsel (PL die Kreuzworträtsel) ◊ *I like doing crosswords.* Ich mache gern Kreuzworträtsel.
to **crouch down** VERB
sich niederkauern (PERFECT hat sich niedergekauert)
**crow** NOUN
die Krähe
**crowd** NOUN
| see also **crowd** VERB |
die Menge
♦ **the crowd** (*at sports match*) die Zuschauer MASC PL
to **crowd** VERB
| see also **crowd** NOUN |
sich drängen ◊ *The children crowded round the model.* Die Kinder drängten sich um das Modell.
**crowded** ADJECTIVE
voll
**crown** NOUN
die Krone
**crucifix** NOUN
das Kruzifix (PL die Kruzifixe)
**crude** ADJECTIVE
ordinär (*vulgar*)
**cruel** ADJECTIVE
grausam
**cruise** NOUN
die Kreuzfahrt ◊ *to go on a Caribbean cruise* eine Karibikkreuzfahrt machen
**crumb** NOUN
der Krümel (PL die Krümel)

C

to **crush** VERB

> see also **crush** NOUN

**1** zerquetschen (PERFECT hat zerquetscht) ◊ *The tomatoes got crushed.* Die Tomaten wurden zerquetscht.

**2** (*finger*)
quetschen ◊ *I crushed my finger in the car door.* Ich habe mir den Finger in der Autotür gequetscht.

**crush** NOUN

> see also **crush** VERB

♦**to have a crush on somebody** für jemanden schwärmen

**crutch** NOUN
die Krücke

**cry** NOUN

> see also **cry** VERB

der Schrei ◊ *With a cry, she rushed forward.* Mit einem Schrei rannte sie vorwärts.

♦**to have a good cry** sich ausweinen

to **cry** VERB

> see also **cry** NOUN

weinen ◊ *The baby cried all night.* Das Baby hat die ganze Nacht geweint.

**crystal** NOUN
der Kristall (PL die Kristalle)

**CTC** NOUN (= *city technology college*)
die technische Fachschule

**cub** NOUN

**1** (*animal*)
das Junge (GEN des Jungen, PL die Jungen) ◊ *the lioness and her cub* die Löwin und ihr Junges

**2** (*scout*)
der Wölfling (PL die Wölflinge)

**cube** NOUN
der Würfel (PL die Würfel)

**cubic** ADJECTIVE

♦**a cubic metre** ein Kubikmeter MASC

**cucumber** NOUN
die Gurke

**cuddle** NOUN

> see also **cuddle** VERB

♦**Come and give me a cuddle.** Komm und nimm mich in den Arm.

to **cuddle** VERB

> see also **cuddle** NOUN

♦**to cuddle somebody** jemanden in den Arm nehmen

**cue** NOUN
das Queue (*for snooker, pool*) (PL die Queues)
*Queue is pronounced as if spelt "Kö".*

**culottes** PL NOUN
der Hosenrock (PL die Hosenröcke) ◊ *a pair of culottes* ein Hosenrock

**culture** NOUN
die Kultur

**cunning** ADJECTIVE
schlau

**cup** NOUN

**1** die Tasse ◊ *a china cup* eine Porzellantasse ◊ *a cup of coffee* eine Tasse Kaffee

**2** (*trophy*)
der Pokal (PL die Pokale)

**cupboard** NOUN
der Schrank (PL die Schränke)

to **cure** VERB

> see also **cure** NOUN

heilen

**cure** NOUN

> see also **cure** VERB

das Mittel (PL die Mittel) ◊ *There is no simple cure for the common cold.* Es gibt kein einfaches Mittel gegen Schnupfen.

**curious** ADJECTIVE
neugierig

**curl** NOUN

> see also **curl** VERB

die Locke

to **curl** VERB

> see also **curl** NOUN

in Locken legen (*hair*)

**curly** ADJECTIVE
lockig ◊ *When I was younger my hair was curlier.* Als ich jünger war, waren meine Haare lockiger.

**currant** NOUN
die Korinthe (*dried fruit*)

**currency** NOUN
die Währung ◊ *foreign currency* ausländische Währung

**current** NOUN

> see also **current** ADJECTIVE

die Strömung ◊ *The current is very strong.* Die Strömung ist sehr stark.

**current** ADJECTIVE

> see also **current** NOUN

aktuell ◊ *the current situation* die aktuelle Lage

**current account** NOUN
das Girokonto (PL die Girokonten)

**current affairs** PL NOUN
die Tagespolitik SING

**curriculum** NOUN
der Lehrplan (PL die Lehrpläne)

**curriculum vitae** NOUN
der Lebenslauf (PL die Lebensläufe)

**curry** NOUN
das Curry (PL die Currys)

**curse** NOUN
der Fluch (*spell*) (PL die Flüche)

**curtain** NOUN
der Vorhang (PL die Vorhänge)

**cushion** NOUN
das Kissen (PL die Kissen)

**custard** NOUN
die Vanillesoße (*for pouring*)

**custody** NOUN
das Sorgerecht (*of child*) ◊ *He got custody of his son.* Er bekam das Sorgerecht für seinen Sohn.

♦ **to be remanded in custody** inhaftiert werden

**custom** NOUN
der Brauch (PL die Bräuche) ◊ *It's an old custom.* Es ist ein alter Brauch.

**customer** NOUN
der Kunde (GEN des Kunden, PL die Kunden)
die Kundin

**customs** PL NOUN
der Zoll (PL die Zölle)

**customs officer** NOUN
der Zollbeamte (GEN des Zollbeamten, PL die Zollbeamten)
die Zollbeamtin
◊ *a customs officer* (*man*) ein Zollbeamter

**cut** NOUN
☐ see also **cut** VERB
[1] die Schnittwunde ◊ *He's got a cut on his forehead.* Er hat eine Schnittwunde an der Stirn.
[2] die Senkung (*in price*)
[3] die Kürzung (*in spending*)
♦ **a cut and blow-dry** Schneiden und Föhnen

to **cut** VERB
☐ see also **cut** NOUN
[1] schneiden (IMPERFECT schnitt, PERFECT hat geschnitten) ◊ *I'll cut some bread.* Ich schneide Brot.
♦ **I cut my foot on a piece of glass.** Ich habe mir den Fuß an einer Glasscherbe verletzt.
♦ **to cut oneself** sich schneiden ◊ *Watch you don't cut yourself!* Pass auf, dass du dich nicht schneidest!
[2] (*price*)
senken
[3] (*spending*)
kürzen
♦ **to cut down (1)** (*tree*) fällen
♦ **to cut down (2)** einschränken ◊ *I'm trying to cut down on coffee and cigarettes.* Ich versuche, meinen Kaffee- und Zigarettenkonsum einzuschränken.
♦ **The electricity was cut off.** Der Strom wurde abgestellt.
♦ **to cut up** (*vegetables, meat*) klein schneiden

**cutback** NOUN
die Kürzung ◊ *Over the past year there*

*have been severe cutbacks in public services.* In den letzten Jahren gab es starke Kürzungen bei den öffentlichen Ausgaben.

**cute** ADJECTIVE
niedlich

**cutlery** NOUN
das Besteck (PL die Bestecke)

**CV** NOUN
der Lebenslauf (PL die Lebensläufe)

**cybercafé** NOUN
das Internet-Café (PL die Internet-Cafés)

to **cycle** VERB
☐ see also **cycle** NOUN
Rad fahren (PRESENT fährt Rad, IMPERFECT fuhr Rad, PERFECT ist Rad gefahren) ◊ *I like cycling.* Ich fahre gern Rad.
♦ **I cycle to school.** Ich fahre mit dem Rad zur Schule.

**cycle** NOUN
☐ see also **cycle** VERB
das Fahrrad (PL die Fahrräder) ◊ *a cycle ride* eine Fahrradfahrt

**cycling** NOUN
das Radfahren ◊ *My hobby is cycling.* Radfahren ist mein Hobby.

**cyclist** NOUN
der Radfahrer (PL die Radfahrer)
die Radfahrerin

**cylinder** NOUN
der Zylinder (PL die Zylinder)

**Cyprus** NOUN
Zypern NEUT
♦ **from Cyprus** aus Zypern
♦ **in Cyprus** auf Zypern
♦ **to Cyprus** nach Zypern

**Czech** ADJECTIVE
☐ see also **Czech** NOUN
tschechisch
♦ **the Czech Republic** die Tschechische Republik

**Czech** NOUN
☐ see also **Czech** ADJECTIVE
[1] (*person*)
der Tscheche (GEN des Tschechen, PL die Tschechen)
die Tschechin
[2] (*language*)
das Tschechisch (GEN des Tschechischen)

# D

**dad** NOUN
der Papa (PL die Papas) ◇ *his dad* sein
Papa ◇ *I'll ask Dad.* Ich werde Papa
fragen.

**daddy** NOUN
der Papa (PL die Papas) ◇ *my daddy* mein
Papa

**daffodil** NOUN
die Osterglocke

**daft** ADJECTIVE
verrückt

**daily** ADJECTIVE, ADVERB
täglich ◇ *It's part of my daily routine.* Es
gehört zu meiner täglichen Routine.
◇ *The pool is open daily from nine a.m.
to six p.m.* Das Schwimmbad ist täglich
von neun bis achtzehn Uhr geöffnet.

**dairy** NOUN
die Molkerei (*company*)

**dairy products** PL NOUN
die Milchprodukte NEUT PL

**daisy** NOUN
das Gänseblümchen (PL die
Gänseblümchen)

**dam** NOUN
der Damm (PL die Dämme)

**damage** NOUN
> see also **damage** VERB

der Schaden (PL die Schäden) ◇ *The
storm did a lot of damage.* Der Sturm hat
viel Schaden angerichtet.

to **damage** VERB
> see also **damage** NOUN

beschädigen (PERFECT hat beschädigt)

**damn** NOUN
> see also **damn** ADJECTIVE

♦ **I don't give a damn!** Das ist mir
scheißegal! (*informal*)
♦ **Damn!** Verdammt! (*informal*)

**damn** ADJECTIVE, ADVERB
> see also **damn** NOUN

♦ **It's a damn nuisance!** Es ist verdammt
ärgerlich! (*informal*)

**damp** ADJECTIVE
feucht

**dance** NOUN
> see also **dance** VERB

der Tanz (PL die Tänze) ◇ *The last dance
was a waltz.* Der letzte Tanz war ein
Walzer. ◇ *Are you going to the dance
tonight?* Gehst du heute Abend zum
Tanz?

to **dance** VERB
> see also **dance** NOUN

tanzen

**dancer** NOUN
der Tänzer (PL die Tänzer)
die Tänzerin

**dancing** NOUN
das Tanzen
♦ **to go dancing** tanzen gehen ◇ *Let's go
dancing!* Lass uns tanzen gehen!

**dandruff** NOUN
die Schuppen FEM PL

**Dane** NOUN
der Däne (GEN des Dänen, PL die Dänen)
die Dänin

**danger** NOUN
die Gefahr
♦ **in danger** in Gefahr ◇ *His life is in
danger.* Sein Leben ist in Gefahr.
♦ **I'm in danger of failing maths.** Es könnte
durchaus sein, dass ich in Mathe
durchfalle.

**dangerous** ADJECTIVE
gefährlich

**Danish** ADJECTIVE
> see also **Danish** NOUN

dänisch

**Danish** NOUN
> see also **Danish** ADJECTIVE

das Dänisch (*language*) (GEN des
Dänischen)

**Danube** NOUN
die Donau

to **dare** VERB
sich trauen
♦ **to dare to do something** sich trauen,
etwas zu tun ◇ *I didn't dare to tell my
parents.* Ich habe mich nicht getraut, es
meinen Eltern zu sagen.
♦ **I dare say it'll be okay.** Ich denke, dass
das in Ordnung ist.

**daring** ADJECTIVE
mutig

**dark** ADJECTIVE
> see also **dark** NOUN

dunkel ◇ *It's dark.* Es ist dunkel. ◇ *It's
getting dark.* Es wird dunkel. ◇ *She's got
dark hair.* Sie hat dunkle Haare. ◇ *a dark
green sweater* ein dunkelgrüner Pullover

**dark** NOUN
> see also **dark** ADJECTIVE

die Dunkelheit ◇ *after dark* nach
Einbruch der Dunkelheit
♦ **in the dark** im Dunkeln
♦ **I'm afraid of the dark.** Ich habe Angst im
Dunkeln.

**darkness** NOUN
die Dunkelheit
♦ **The room was in darkness.** Das Zimmer
war dunkel.

**darling** NOUN
der Liebling (PL die Lieblinge)
*der Liebling is also used for women.*
◇ *Thank you, darling!* Danke, Liebling!

**dart** NOUN
der Pfeil (PL die Pfeile)
♦ **to play darts** Darts spielen

**dash** NOUN
> see also **dash** VERB

der Bindestrich (*punctuation mark*)

to **dash** VERB
> see also **dash** NOUN

[1] rennen (IMPERFECT rannte, PERFECT ist gerannt) ◊ *Everyone dashed to the window.* Alle rannten zum Fenster.
[2] sich beeilen (PERFECT hat sich beeilt) ◊ *I've got to dash!* Ich muss mich beeilen!

**dashboard** NOUN
das Armaturenbrett (PL die Armaturenbretter)

**data** PL NOUN
die Daten PL

**database** NOUN
die Datenbank (*on computer*) (PL die Datenbanken)

**date** NOUN
[1] das Datum (PL die Daten) ◊ *my date of birth* mein Geburtsdatum
♦ **What's the date today?** der Wievielte ist heute?
♦ **to have a date with somebody** mit jemandem eine Verabredung haben ◊ *She's got a date with Ian tonight.* Sie hat heute Abend eine Verabredung mit Ian.
♦ **out of date (1)** (*passport*) abgelaufen
♦ **out of date (2)** (*technology*) veraltet
♦ **out of date (3)** (*clothes*) altmodisch
[2] (*fruit*)
die Dattel

**daughter** NOUN
die Tochter (PL die Töchter)

**daughter-in-law** NOUN
die Schwiegertochter (PL die Schwiegertöchter)

**dawn** NOUN
das Morgengrauen ◊ *at dawn* im Morgengrauen

**day** NOUN
der Tag (PL die Tage) ◊ *We stayed in Vienna for three days.* Wir sind drei Tage in Wien geblieben. ◊ *I stayed at home all day.* Ich war den ganzen Tag zu Hause.
♦ **every day** jeden Tag
♦ **during the day** tagsüber
♦ **the day before** der Tag davor ◊ *the day before my birthday* der Tag vor meinem Geburtstag
♦ **the day after** der Tag danach ◊ *the day after my birthday* der Tag nach meinem Geburtstag
♦ **the day before yesterday** vorgestern ◊ *He arrived the day before yesterday.* Er ist vorgestern angekommen.

♦ **the day after tomorrow** übermorgen ◊ *We're leaving the day after tomorrow.* Wir fahren übermorgen ab.

**dead** ADJECTIVE, ADVERB
[1] tot ◊ *He was already dead when the doctor came.* Er war schon tot, als der Arzt kam.
♦ **He was shot dead.** Er wurde erschossen.
[2] völlig (*totally*) ◊ *You're dead right!* Du hast völlig recht!
♦ **dead on time** ganz pünktlich ◊ *The train arrived dead on time.* Der Zug kam ganz pünktlich an.

**dead end** NOUN
die Sackgasse

**deadline** NOUN
der Termin (PL die Termine) ◊ *We'll never meet the deadline.* Den Termin schaffen wir nie.

**deaf** ADJECTIVE
taub

**deafening** ADJECTIVE
ohrenbetäubend

**deal** NOUN
> see also **deal** VERB

das Geschäft (PL die Geschäfte)
♦ **It's a deal!** Abgemacht!
♦ **a great deal** viel ◊ *a great deal of money* viel Geld

to **deal** VERB
> see also **deal** NOUN

geben (*cards*) (PRESENT gibt, IMPERFECT gab, PERFECT hat gegeben) ◊ *It's your turn to deal.* Du gibst!
♦ **to deal with something** sich um etwas kümmern ◊ *He promised to deal with it immediately.* Er versprach, sich sofort darum zu kümmern.

**dealer** NOUN
der Händler (PL die Händler)
die Händlerin
◊ *a drug dealer* ein Drogenhändler ◊ *an antique dealer* ein Antiquitätenhändler

**dear** ADJECTIVE
[1] lieb
♦ **Dear Mrs Sinclair (1)** Liebe Frau Sinclair
♦ **Dear Mrs Sinclair (2)** (*more formal*) Sehr geehrte Frau Sinclair
♦ **Dear Sir/Madam** (*in a circular*) Sehr geehrte Damen und Herren
[2] teuer (*expensive*)

**death** NOUN
der Tod (PL die Tode) ◊ *after her death* nach ihrem Tod ◊ *I was bored to death.* Ich habe mich zu Tode gelangweilt.

**debate** NOUN
> see also **debate** VERB

die Debatte

to **debate** VERB
> see also **debate** NOUN

debattieren (PERFECT hat debattiert) ◊ *We debated the issue of capital punishment.*

**D**

Wir haben die Frage der Todesstrafe debattiert.

**debt** NOUN
die Schulden FEM PL ◊ *He's got a lot of debts.* Er hat viel Schulden.
♦ **to be in debt** verschuldet sein

**decade** NOUN
das Jahrzehnt (PL die Jahrzehnte)

**decaffeinated** ADJECTIVE
entkoffeiniert

**decay** NOUN
♦ **tooth decay** die Karies

to **deceive** VERB
täuschen

**December** NOUN
der Dezember ◊ *in December* im Dezember

**decent** ADJECTIVE
ordentlich ◊ *a decent education* eine ordentliche Ausbildung

to **decide** VERB
1 beschließen (IMPERFECT beschloss, PERFECT hat beschlossen) ◊ *I decided to write to her.* Ich habe beschlossen, ihr zu schreiben. ◊ *I decided not to go.* Ich habe beschlossen, nicht hinzugehen.
2 sich entscheiden (IMPERFECT entschied sich, PERFECT hat sich entschieden) ◊ *I can't decide.* Ich kann mich nicht entscheiden. ◊ *Haven't you decided yet?* Hast du dich noch nicht entschieden?
♦ **to decide on something** über etwas entscheiden ◊ *We haven't decided on the name yet.* Wir haben noch nicht über den Namen entschieden.

**decimal** ADJECTIVE
dezimal ◊ *the decimal system* das Dezimalsystem

**decision** NOUN
die Entscheidung ◊ *to make a decision* eine Entscheidung treffen

**decisive** ADJECTIVE
entschlossen (*person*)

**deck** NOUN
1 (*of ship*)
das Deck (PL die Decks) ◊ *on deck* an Deck
2 (*of cards*)
das Spiel (PL die Spiele)

**deckchair** NOUN
der Liegestuhl (PL die Liegestühle)

to **declare** VERB
erklären (PERFECT hat erklärt)

to **decline** VERB
1 ablehnen (PERFECT hat abgelehnt) ◊ *He declined to comment.* Er lehnte einen Kommentar ab.
2 zurückgehen (IMPERFECT ging zurück, PERFECT ist zurückgegangen) ◊ *The birth rate has declined by five per cent.* Die Geburtenrate ist um fünf Prozent zurückgegangen.

to **decorate** VERB
1 dekorieren (PERFECT hat dekoriert) ◊ *I decorated the cake with glacé cherries.* Ich habe den Kuchen mit glasierten Kirschen dekoriert.
2 (*paint*)
streichen (IMPERFECT strich, PERFECT hat gestrichen)
3 (*wallpaper*)
tapezieren (PERFECT hat tapeziert)

**decorations** PLURAL NOUN
der Schmuck ◊ *Christmas decorations* der Weihnachtsschmuck

**decrease** NOUN
see also **decrease** VERB
die Abnahme ◊ *a decrease in the number of unemployed people* eine Abnahme der Arbeitslosenzahl

to **decrease** VERB
see also **decrease** NOUN
abnehmen (PRESENT nimmt ab, IMPERFECT nahm ab, PERFECT hat abgenommen)

**dedicated** ADJECTIVE
engagiert ◊ *a very dedicated teacher* ein sehr engagierter Lehrer

to **deduct** VERB
abziehen (IMPERFECT zog ab, PERFECT hat abgezogen)

**deep** ADJECTIVE
tief (*water, hole, cut*) ◊ *How deep is the lake?* Wie tief ist der See? ◊ *a hole four metres deep* ein vier Meter tiefes Loch ◊ *He's got a deep voice.* Er hat eine tiefe Stimme.
♦ **to take a deep breath** tief einatmen
♦ **The snow was really deep.** Es lag sehr viel Schnee.

**deeply** ADVERB
zutiefst (*depressed*)

**deer** NOUN
das Reh (PL die Rehe)

**defeat** NOUN
see also **defeat** VERB
die Niederlage

to **defeat** VERB
see also **defeat** NOUN
besiegen (PERFECT hat besiegt)

**defect** NOUN
der Defekt (PL die Defekte)

**defence** NOUN
die Verteidigung

to **defend** VERB
verteidigen (PERFECT hat verteidigt)

**defender** NOUN
der Verteidiger (PL die Verteidiger)
die Verteidigerin

**defense** NOUN US
die Verteidigung

to **define** VERB
definieren (PERFECT hat definiert)

**definite** ADJECTIVE
1 genau ◊ *I haven't got any definite plans.* Ich habe noch keine genauen Pläne.

[2] eindeutig ◇ *It's a definite improvement.* Es ist eine eindeutige Verbesserung.
[3] sicher ◇ *Perhaps we'll go to Spain, but it's not definite.* Vielleicht fahren wir nach Spanien, aber es ist noch nicht sicher.
♦ **He was definite about it.** Er war sich sehr sicher.

**definitely** ADVERB
eindeutig ◇ *He's definitely the best player.* Er ist eindeutig der beste Spieler.
♦ **He's the best player. – Definitely!** Er ist der beste Spieler. – Absolut!
♦ **I definitely think he'll come.** Ich bin sicher, dass er kommt.

**definition** NOUN
die Definition

**degree** NOUN
[1] der Grad (PL die Grade) ◇ *a temperature of thirty degrees* eine Temperatur von dreißig Grad
[2] der Universitätsabschluss (GEN des Universitätsabschlusses, PL die Universitätsabschlüsse) ◇ *a degree in English* ein Universitätsabschluss in Englisch

to **delay** VERB
see also **delay** NOUN
verschieben (IMPERFECT verschob, PERFECT hat verschoben) ◇ *We decided to delay our departure.* Wir haben beschlossen, unsere Abreise zu verschieben.
♦ **to be delayed** Verspätung haben ◇ *Our flight was delayed.* Unser Flug hatte Verspätung.

**delay** NOUN
see also **delay** VERB
die Verzögerung
♦ **without delay** unverzüglich

to **delete** VERB
löschen (*on computer, tape*)

**deliberate** ADJECTIVE
absichtlich

**deliberately** ADVERB
absichtlich ◇ *She did it deliberately.* Sie hat es absichtlich getan.

**delicate** ADJECTIVE
[1] zierlich ◇ *She has very delicate hands.* Sie hat sehr zierliche Hände.
[2] zerbrechlich (*object*) ◇ *That vase is very delicate.* Die Vase ist sehr zerbrechlich.
[3] anfällig (*often ill*) ◇ *She's a very delicate child.* Sie ist ein sehr anfälliges Kind.
[4] heikel (*situation*) ◇ *The situation is rather delicate.* Die Lage ist ziemlich heikel.

**delicatessen** SING NOUN
das Feinkostgeschäft (PL die Feinkostgeschäfte)

**delicious** ADJECTIVE
köstlich

**delight** NOUN
die Freude

**delighted** ADJECTIVE
hocherfreut ◇ *He'll be delighted to see you.* Er wird hocherfreut sein, dich zu sehen.

**delightful** ADJECTIVE
wunderbar (*meal, evening*)

to **deliver** VERB
[1] austragen (PRESENT trägt aus, IMPERFECT trug aus, PERFECT hat ausgetreten) ◇ *I deliver newspapers.* Ich trage Zeitungen aus.
[2] (*mail*)
ausliefern (PERFECT hat ausgeliefert)

**delivery** NOUN
die Lieferung

to **demand** VERB
see also **demand** NOUN
fordern

**demand** NOUN
see also **demand** VERB
die Nachfrage (*for product*)

**demanding** ADJECTIVE
anspruchsvoll ◇ *It's a very demanding job.* Es ist eine sehr anspruchsvolle Arbeit.

**demo** NOUN
die Demo (*protest*) (PL die Demos)

**democracy** NOUN
die Demokratie

**democratic** ADJECTIVE
demokratisch

to **demolish** VERB
abreißen (*building*) (IMPERFECT riss ab, PERFECT hat abgerissen)

to **demonstrate** VERB
[1] (*show*)
vorführen (PERFECT hat vorgeführt) ◇ *She demonstrated the technique.* Sie hat die Methode vorgeführt.
[2] (*protest*)
demonstrieren (PERFECT hat demonstriert) ◇ *to demonstrate against something* gegen etwas demonstrieren

**demonstration** NOUN
[1] die Vorführung (*of method, technique*)
[2] die Demonstration (*protest*)

**demonstrator** NOUN
(*protester*)
der Demonstrant (GEN des Demonstranten, PL die Demonstranten)
die Demonstrantin

**denim** NOUN
der Jeansstoff
♦ **a denim jacket** eine Jeansjacke

**denims** PL NOUN
die Jeans FEM PL (*jeans*) ◇ *a pair of denims* eine Jeans

D

**Denmark** NOUN
Dänemark NEUT
◆**from Denmark** aus Dänemark
◆**to Denmark** nach Dänemark

**dense** ADJECTIVE
⓵ dicht (*crowd, fog*)
⓶ dick (*smoke*)
◆**He's so dense!** Er ist furchtbar blöd!
(*informal*)

**dent** NOUN
see also **dent** VERB
die Delle

to **dent** VERB
see also **dent** NOUN
eindellen (PERFECT hat eingedellt)

**dental** ADJECTIVE
◆**dental treatment** die Zahnbehandlung
◆**dental floss** die Zahnseide
◆**dental surgeon** der Zahnarzt

**dentist** NOUN
der Zahnarzt (PL die Zahnärzte)
die Zahnärztin
◊ *Catherine is a dentist.* Catherine ist
Zahnärztin.

to **deny** VERB
leugnen ◊ *She denied everything.* Sie
hat alles geleugnet.

**deodorant** NOUN
das Deo (PL die Deos)

to **depart** VERB
⓵ (*person*)
abreisen (PERFECT ist abgereist)
⓶ (*train*)
abfahren (PRESENT fährt ab, IMPERFECT fuhr
ab, PERFECT ist abgefahren)

**department** NOUN
⓵ (*in shop*)
die Abteilung ◊ *the shoe department* die
Schuhabteilung
⓶ (*university, school*)
der Fachbereich (PL die Fachbereiche)
◊ *the English department* der
Fachbereich Englisch

**department store** NOUN
das Kaufhaus (GEN des Kaufhauses, PL die
Kaufhäuser)

**departure** NOUN
die Abfahrt

**departure lounge** NOUN
die Abflughalle

to **depend** VERB
◆**to depend on** abhängen von ◊ *The price
depends on the quality.* Der Preis hängt
von der Qualität ab.
◆**depending on the weather** je nach
Wetterlage
◆**It depends.** Das kommt drauf an.

to **deport** VERB
abschieben (IMPERFECT schob ab, PERFECT hat
abgeschoben)

**deposit** NOUN
⓵ (*part payment*)

die Anzahlung ◊ *You have to pay a
deposit when you book.* Sie müssen eine
Anzahlung leisten, wenn Sie buchen.
⓶ (*when hiring something*)
die Kaution ◊ *You get the deposit back
when you return the bike.* Sie bekommen
die Kaution zurück, wenn Sie das Fahrrad
zurückbringen.
⓷ (*on bottle*)
das Pfand (PL die Pfänder)

**depressed** ADJECTIVE
deprimiert ◊ *I'm feeling depressed.* Ich
bin deprimiert.

**depressing** ADJECTIVE
deprimierend

**depth** NOUN
die Tiefe

**deputy head** NOUN
der Konrektor (PL die Konrektoren)
die Konrektorin

to **descend** VERB
hinuntersteigen (IMPERFECT stieg hinunter,
PERFECT ist hinuntergestiegen)

to **describe** VERB
beschreiben (IMPERFECT beschrieb, PERFECT
hat beschrieben)

**description** NOUN
die Beschreibung

**desert** NOUN
die Wüste

**desert island** NOUN
die einsame Insel

to **deserve** VERB
verdienen (PERFECT hat verdient) ◊ *He
deserves a holiday.* Er hat einen Urlaub
verdient.
◆**She deserves to be punished.** Sie gehört
bestraft.

**design** NOUN
see also **design** VERB
⓵ das Design (PL die Designs) ◊ *fashion
design* das Modedesign
◆**It's a completely new design.** Es ist eine
völlig neue Konstruktion.
⓶ (*pattern*)
das Muster (PL die Muster) ◊ *a geometric
design* ein geometrisches Muster

to **design** VERB
see also **design** NOUN
entwerfen (*clothes, furniture*) (PRESENT
entwirft, IMPERFECT entwarf, PERFECT hat
entworfen)

**designer** NOUN
(*of clothes*)
der Modeschöpfer (PL die
Modeschöpfer)
die Modeschöpferin
◆**designer clothes** die Designerkleidung
SING

**desire** NOUN
see also **desire** VERB
das Verlangen (PL die Verlangen)

to **desire** VERB

> see also **desire** NOUN

wünschen ◊ *if desired* falls gewünscht

**desk** NOUN

1 (*in office*)
der Schreibtisch (PL die Schreibtische)
2 (*in school*)
die Bank (PL die Bänke)
3 (*in hotel*)
die Rezeption
4 (*at airport*)
der Schalter (PL die Schalter)

**despair** NOUN

die Verzweiflung

◆ **I was in despair.** Ich war verzweifelt.

**desperate** ADJECTIVE

verzweifelt ◊ *a desperate situation* eine
verzweifelte Lage

◆ **to get desperate** fast verzweifeln ◊ *I was
getting desperate.* Ich bin fast
verzweifelt.

◆ **I'm desperate for a drink.** Ich brauche
dringend etwas zu trinken.

**desperately** ADVERB

1 äußerst ◊ *We're desperately worried.*
Wir sind äußerst besorgt.
2 verzweifelt ◊ *He was desperately
trying to persuade her.* Er versuchte
verzweifelt, sie zu überzeugen.

to **despise** VERB

verachten (PERFECT hat verachtet)

**despite** PREPOSITION

trotz ◊ *despite the bad weather* trotz des
schlechten Wetters

**dessert** NOUN

der Nachtisch ◊ *for dessert* zum
Nachtisch

**destination** NOUN

das Ziel (PL die Ziele)

to **destroy** VERB

zerstören (PERFECT hat zerstört)

**destruction** NOUN

die Zerstörung

**detached house** NOUN

das Einzelhaus (GEN des Einzelhauses, PL
die Einzelhäuser)

**detail** NOUN

das Detail (PL die Details)

◆ **in detail** ganz genau

**detailed** ADJECTIVE

ausführlich

**detective** NOUN

der Detektiv (PL die Detektive)
die Detektivin

◆ **a private detective** ein Privatdetektiv

◆ **a detective story** eine Detektivgeschichte

**detention** NOUN

◆ **to get a detention** nachsitzen müssen
◊ *He got a detention for smoking.* Er
musste nachsitzen, weil er geraucht
hatte.

**detergent** NOUN

das Waschmittel (PL die Waschmittel)

**determined** ADJECTIVE

entschlossen

◆ **to be determined to do something**
entschlossen sein, etwas zu tun ◊ *She's
determined to marry him.* Sie ist
entschlossen, ihn zu heiraten.

**detour** NOUN

der Umweg (PL die Umwege)

**devaluation** NOUN

die Abwertung

**devastated** ADJECTIVE

am Boden zerstört ◊ *I was devastated.*
Ich war am Boden zerstört.

**devastating** ADJECTIVE

1 erschütternd (*upsetting*)
2 verheerend (*flood, storm*)

to **develop** VERB

1 entwickeln (PERFECT hat entwickelt) ◊ *to
get a film developed* einen Film
entwickeln lassen
2 sich entwickeln (PERFECT hat sich
entwickelt) ◊ *Girls develop faster than
boys.* Mädchen entwickeln sich schneller
als Jungen. ◊ *The argument developed
into a fight.* Der Streit entwickelte sich zu
einer Schlägerei.

◆ **developing country** das
Entwicklungsland

**development** NOUN

die Entwicklung ◊ *the latest
developments* die neuesten
Entwicklungen

**device** NOUN

das Gerät

**devil** NOUN

der Teufel (PL die Teufel) ◊ *Poor devil!*
Armer Teufel!

to **devise** VERB

sich ausdenken (IMPERFECT dachte sich aus,
PERFECT hat sich ausgedacht) ◊ *We have
devised a way to help him.* Wir haben uns
etwas ausgedacht, um ihm zu helfen.

**devoted** ADJECTIVE

◆ **He's completely devoted to her.** Er liebt
sie über alles.

**diabetes** NOUN

der Zucker ◊ *She's got diabetes.* Sie hat
Zucker.

**diabetic** NOUN

der Zuckerkranke (GEN des
Zuckerkranken, PL die Zuckerkranken)
die Zuckerkranke (GEN der
Zuckerkranken)

◆ **I'm a diabetic.** Ich habe Zucker.

**diagonal** ADJECTIVE

diagonal

**diagram** NOUN

das Diagramm (PL die Diagramme)

to **dial** VERB

wählen (*number*)

◆ **He dialled the wrong number.** Er hat sich
verwählt.

**dialling tone** NOUN

☞

das Amtszeichen (PL die Amtszeichen)
**dialogue** NOUN
der Dialog (PL die Dialoge)
**diamond** NOUN
der Diamant (GEN des Diamanten, PL die
Diamanten) ◊ *a diamond ring* ein
Diamantring MASC
◆**diamonds** (*in cards*) das Karo ◊ *the ace of
diamonds* das Karoass
**diaper** NOUN US
die Windel
**diarrhoea** NOUN
der Durchfall (PL die Durchfälle) ◊ *I've
got diarrhoea.* Ich habe Durchfall.
**diary** NOUN
[1] der Kalender (PL die Kalender) ◊ *I've
got her phone number in my diary.* Ich
habe ihre Telefonnummer in meinem
Kalender.
[2] das Tagebuch (PL die Tagebücher) ◊ *I
keep a diary.* Ich führe ein Tagebuch.
**dice** NOUN
der Würfel (PL die Würfel)
**dictation** NOUN
das Diktat (PL die Diktate)
**dictator** NOUN
der Diktator (PL die Diktatoren)
**dictionary** NOUN
das Wörterbuch (PL die Wörterbücher)
**did** VERB *see* **do**
to **die** VERB
sterben (PRESENT stirbt, IMPERFECT starb,
PERFECT ist gestorben) ◊ *She's dying.* Sie
stirbt. ◊ *He died last year.* Er ist letztes
Jahr gestorben.
◆**to be dying to do something** es kaum
erwarten können, etwas zu tun ◊ *I'm
dying to see you.* Ich kann es kaum
erwarten, dich zu sehen.
to **die down** VERB
nachlassen (PRESENT lässt nach, IMPERFECT
ließ nach, PERFECT hat nachgelassen) ◊ *The
wind is dying down.* Der Wind lässt nach.
**diesel** NOUN
[1] (*fuel*)
der Diesel ◊ *Thirty litres of diesel,
please.* Dreißig Liter Diesel, bitte.
[2] (*car*)
der Diesel (PL die Diesel) ◊ *Our car's a
diesel.* Unser Auto ist ein Diesel.
**diet** NOUN
*see also* **diet** VERB
[1] die Nahrung ◊ *a healthy diet* gesunde
Nahrung
[2] die Diät (*for slimming*)
◆**I'm on a diet.** Ich mache eine Diät.
to **diet** VERB
*see also* **diet** NOUN
eine Diät machen ◊ *I've been dieting for
two months.* Ich mache seit zwei
Monaten eine Diät.
**difference** NOUN

der Unterschied (PL die Unterschiede)
◊ *There's not much difference in age
between us.* Es besteht kein großer
Altersunterschied zwischen uns.
◆**It makes no difference.** Das ist egal.
**different** ADJECTIVE
verschieden ◊ *We are very different.* Wir
sind sehr verschieden.
◆**Berlin is different from London.** Berlin ist
anders als London.
**difficult** ADJECTIVE
schwierig ◊ *It's difficult to choose.* Es ist
schwierig, sich zu entscheiden.
**difficulty** NOUN
die Schwierigkeit ◊ *to have difficulty
doing something* Schwierigkeiten haben,
etwas zu tun
◆**without difficulty** problemlos
to **dig** VERB
[1] (*hole*)
graben (PRESENT gräbt, IMPERFECT grub,
PERFECT hat gegraben)
[2] (*garden*)
umgraben (PERFECT hat umgegraben)
◆**to dig something up** etwas ausgraben
**digestion** NOUN
die Verdauung
**digger** NOUN
der Bagger (PL die Bagger)
**digital** ADJECTIVE
digital ◊ *the digital revolution* die
digitale Revolution
◆**a digital camera** eine Digitalkamera
◆**a digital watch** eine Digitaluhr
◆**digital TV** das Digitalfernsehen
**dim** ADJECTIVE
[1] schwach (*light*)
[2] beschränkt (*stupid*)
**dimension** NOUN
das Maß (*measurement*) (GEN des Maßes,
PL die Maße)
to **diminish** VERB
abnehmen (PRESENT nimmt ab, IMPERFECT
nahm ab, PERFECT hat abgenommen)
**din** NOUN
der Krach (PL die Kräche)
**diner** NOUN US
die Gaststätte
**dinghy** NOUN
◆**a rubber dinghy** ein Gummiboot NEUT
◆**a sailing dinghy** ein Segelboot NEUT
**dining car** NOUN
der Speisewagen (PL die Speisewagen)
**dining room** NOUN
das Esszimmer (PL die Esszimmer)
**dinner** NOUN
[1] (*at midday*)
das Mittagessen (PL die Mittagessen)
[2] (*in the evening*)
das Abendessen (PL die Abendessen)
**dinner jacket** NOUN
die Smokingjacke
**dinner party** NOUN

die Abendgesellschaft
♦ **We're having a dinner party on Saturday.** Wir haben am Samstag Leute zum Essen eingeladen.

**dinner time** NOUN
die Essenszeit

**dinosaur** NOUN
der Dinosaurier (PL die Dinosaurier)

**dip** NOUN

| see also **dip** VERB |

der Dip (PL die Dips) ◇ *a spicy dip* ein pikanter Dip
♦ **to go for a dip** kurz mal ins Wasser gehen

to **dip** VERB

| see also **dip** NOUN |

[1] tauchen ◇ *She dipped her hand in the water.* Sie tauchte ihre Hand ins Wasser.
[2] tunken ◇ *He dipped a biscuit into his tea.* Er tunkte einen Keks in seinen Tee.

**diploma** NOUN
das Diplom (PL die Diplome)
♦ **She has a diploma in social work.** Sie hat Sozialarbeiterin gelernt.

**diplomat** NOUN
der Diplomat (GEN des Diplomaten, PL die Diplomaten)
die Diplomatin

**diplomatic** ADJECTIVE
diplomatisch

**direct** ADJECTIVE, ADVERB

| see also **direct** VERB |

direkt ◇ *the most direct route* der direkteste Weg ◇ *You can't fly to Stuttgart direct from Glasgow.* Sie können von Glasgow nicht direkt nach Stuttgart fliegen.

to **direct** VERB

| see also **direct** ADJECTIVE |

Regie führen bei (*film, play*) ◇ *Who directed the film?* Wer hat bei dem Film Regie geführt?

**direction** NOUN
die Richtung ◇ *We're going in the wrong direction.* Wir fahren in die falsche Richtung.
♦ **to ask somebody for directions** jemanden nach dem Weg fragen

**director** NOUN
[1] (*of company*)
der Direktor (PL die Direktoren)
die Direktorin
[2] (*of play, film*)
der Regisseur (PL die Regisseure)
die Regisseurin
[3] (*of programme*)
der Leiter (PL die Leiter)
die Leiterin

**directory** NOUN
[1] das Verzeichnis (GEN des Verzeichnisses, PL die Verzeichnisse) ◇ *file directory* das Dateiverzeichnis

[2] (*telephone book*)
das Telefonbuch (PL die Telefonbücher)

**dirt** NOUN
der Schmutz

**dirty** ADJECTIVE
schmutzig ◇ *to get dirty* sich schmutzig machen ◇ *to get something dirty* etwas schmutzig machen ◇ *a dirty joke* ein schmutziger Witz

**disabled** ADJECTIVE
behindert
♦ **the disabled** die Behinderten MASC PL

**disadvantage** NOUN
der Nachteil (PL die Nachteile)

to **disagree** VERB
♦ **We always disagree.** Wir sind nie einer Meinung.
♦ **I disagree!** Ich bin anderer Meinung.
♦ **He disagreed with me.** Er war anderer Meinung als ich.

**disagreement** NOUN
die Meinungsverschiedenheit

to **disappear** VERB
verschwinden (IMPERFECT verschwand, PERFECT ist verschwunden)

**disappearance** NOUN
das Verschwinden

**disappointed** ADJECTIVE
enttäuscht

**disappointing** ADJECTIVE
enttäuschend

**disappointment** NOUN
die Enttäuschung

**disaster** NOUN
die Katastrophe

**disastrous** ADJECTIVE
katastrophal

**disc** NOUN
die Platte

**discipline** NOUN
die Disziplin

**disc jockey** NOUN
der Diskjockey (PL die Diskjockeys)

**disco** NOUN
die Disko (PL die Diskos) ◇ *There's a disco at the school tonight.* Heute Abend gibt es in der Schule eine Disko.

to **disconnect** VERB
[1] (*electrical equipment*)
ausstecken (PERFECT hat ausgesteckt)
[2] (*telephone, water supply*)
abstellen (PERFECT hat abgestellt)

**discount** NOUN
der Rabatt (PL die Rabatte) ◇ *a discount of twenty per cent* zwanzig Prozent Rabatt
♦ **a discount for students** eine Studentenermäßigung

to **discourage** VERB
entmutigen (PERFECT hat entmutigt)
♦ **to get discouraged** sich entmutigen lassen ◇ *Don't get discouraged!* Lass dich nicht entmutigen!

**D**

to **discover** VERB
    entdecken (PERFECT hat entdeckt)
**discovery** NOUN
    die Entdeckung
**discrimination** NOUN
    die Diskriminierung ◊ *racial*
    *discrimination* die
    Rassendiskriminierung
to **discuss** VERB
    [1] besprechen (PRESENT bespricht, IMPERFECT
    besprach, PERFECT hat besprochen) ◊ *I'll*
    *discuss it with my parents.* Ich werde es
    mit meinen Eltern besprechen.
    [2] (*topic*)
    diskutieren über +ACC (PERFECT hat
    diskutiert) ◊ *We discussed the problem*
    *of pollution.* Wir haben über das Problem
    der Umweltverschmutzung diskutiert.
**discussion** NOUN
    die Diskussion
**disease** NOUN
    die Krankheit
**disgraceful** ADJECTIVE
    schändlich
to **disguise** VERB
    verkleiden (PERFECT hat verkleidet) ◊ *He*
    *was disguised as a policeman.* Er war als
    Polizist verkleidet.
**disgusted** ADJECTIVE
    angewidert ◊ *I was absolutely*
    *disgusted.* Ich war total angewidert.
**disgusting** ADJECTIVE
    [1] widerlich (*food, smell*) ◊ *It looks*
    *disgusting.* Es sieht widerlich aus.
    [2] abscheulich (*disgraceful*) ◊ *That's*
    *disgusting!* Das ist abscheulich!
**dish** NOUN
    [1] die Schüssel ◊ *a china dish* eine
    Porzellanschüssel
    ◆ **the dishes** das Geschirr SING
    ◆ **to do the dishes** abwaschen ◊ *He never*
    *does the dishes.* Er wäscht nie ab.
    [2] (*food*)
    das Gericht (PL die Gerichte) ◊ *a*
    *vegetarian dish* ein vegetarisches
    Gericht
**dishonest** ADJECTIVE
    unehrlich
**dish soap** NOUN [US]
    das Spülmittel (PL die Spülmittel)
**dish towel** NOUN [US]
    das Geschirrtuch (PL die Geschirrtücher)
**dishwasher** NOUN
    die Geschirrspülmaschine
**disinfectant** NOUN
    das Desinfektionsmittel (PL die
    Desinfektionsmittel)
**disk** NOUN
    die Platte
    ◆ **the hard disk** die Festplatte
    ◆ **a floppy disk** eine Diskette
**diskette** NOUN
    die Diskette

to **dislike** VERB
    see also **dislike** NOUN
    nicht mögen (PRESENT mag nicht, IMPERFECT
    mochte nicht, PERFECT hat nicht gemocht)
    ◊ *I've always disliked cabbage.* Kohl
    habe ich noch nie gemocht.
**dislike** NOUN
    see also **dislike** VERB
    ◆ **my likes and dislikes** was ich mag und
    nicht mag
**dismal** ADJECTIVE
    kläglich ◊ *a dismal failure* ein kläglicher
    Fehlschlag
to **dismiss** VERB
    entlassen (*employee*) (PRESENT entlässt,
    IMPERFECT entließ, PERFECT hat
    entlassen)
**disobedient** ADJECTIVE
    ungehorsam
**display** NOUN
    see also **display** VERB
    die Auslage (*of goods*)
    ◆ **to be on display** ausgestellt sein ◊ *Her*
    *best paintings were on display.* Ihre
    besten Bilder waren ausgestellt.
    ◆ **a firework display** ein Feuerwerk NEUT
to **display** VERB
    see also **display** NOUN
    [1] zeigen ◊ *She proudly displayed her*
    *medal.* Sie zeigte stolz ihre Medaille.
    [2] (*in shop window*)
    ausstellen (PERFECT hat ausgestellt) ◊ *The*
    *fruit displayed in the shop window ...* Das
    Obst, das im Schaufenster ausgestellt
    war ...
**disposable** ADJECTIVE
    zum Wegwerfen
    ◆ **disposable nappies** die Wegwerfwindeln
    FEM PL
to **disqualify** VERB
    disqualifizieren (PERFECT hat
    disqualifiziert)
    ◆ **to be disqualified** disqualifiziert werden
    ◊ *He was disqualified.* Er wurde
    disqualifiziert.
to **disrupt** VERB
    [1] stören ◊ *Protesters disrupted the*
    *meeting.* Protestierende haben die
    Versammlung gestört.
    [2] (*service*)
    unterbrechen (PRESENT unterbricht,
    IMPERFECT unterbrach, PERFECT hat
    unterbrochen) ◊ *Train services are being*
    *disrupted by the strike.* Der Zugverkehr
    wird vom Streik unterbrochen.
**dissatisfied** ADJECTIVE
    unzufrieden ◊ *We were dissatisfied with*
    *the service.* Wir waren mit dem Service
    unzufrieden.
to **dissolve** VERB
    [1] auflösen (PERFECT hat aufgelöst) ◊ *We*
    *dissolved the crystals in an acid solution.*

Wir lösten die Kristalle in einer Säurelösung auf.
[2] sich auflösen ◊ *Sugar dissolves quickly in hot tea.* Zucker löst sich in heißem Tee schnell auf.

**distance** NOUN
die Entfernung ◊ *a distance of forty kilometres* eine Entfernung von vierzig Kilometern
♦ **It's within walking distance.** Man kann zu Fuß hingehen.
♦ **in the distance** in der Ferne

**distant** ADJECTIVE
weit ◊ *in the distant future* in weiter Zukunft

**distillery** NOUN
die Brennerei ◊ *a whisky distillery* eine Whiskybrennerei

**distinction** NOUN
[1] die Unterscheidung ◊ *to make a distinction between ...* unterscheiden zwischen ...
[2] die Auszeichnung ◊ *I got a distinction in my piano exam.* Ich habe meine Klavierprüfung mit Auszeichnung bestanden.

**distinctive** ADJECTIVE
auffällig

to **distract** VERB
ablenken (PERFECT hat abgelenkt)

to **distribute** VERB
verteilen (PERFECT hat verteilt)

**district** NOUN
[1] (*of town*)
das Viertel (PL die Viertel)
[2] (*of country*)
die Gegend

to **disturb** VERB
stören
♦ **I'm sorry to disturb you.** Verzeihen Sie die Störung.

**ditch** NOUN
see also **ditch** VERB
der Graben (PL die Gräben)

to **ditch** VERB
see also **ditch** NOUN
Schluss machen mit (*informal*) ◊ *She's just ditched her boyfriend.* Sie hat gerade mit ihrem Freund Schluss gemacht.

**dive** NOUN
see also **dive** VERB
der Kopfsprung (PL die Kopfsprünge)

to **dive** VERB
see also **dive** NOUN
[1] tauchen (*under water*) ◊ *They are diving for pearls.* Sie tauchen nach Perlen.
[2] einen Kopfsprung machen (*into water*) ◊ *She dived into the water.* Sie machte einen Kopfsprung ins Wasser.

**diver** NOUN
(*with breathing apparatus*)
der Taucher (PL die Taucher)

die Taucherin

**diversion** NOUN
die Umleitung (*for traffic*)

to **divide** VERB
[1] teilen ◊ *Divide the pastry in half.* Teilen Sie den Teig in zwei Teile.
◊ *Twelve divided by three is four.* Zwölf geteilt durch drei macht vier.
[2] sich aufteilen (PERFECT hat sich aufgeteilt) ◊ *We divided into two groups.* Wir haben uns in zwei Gruppen aufgeteilt.

**diving** NOUN
[1] das Tauchen (*under water*)
[2] das Springen (*into water*)
♦ **diving board** das Sprungbrett

**division** NOUN
[1] das Teilen ◊ *I'm not very good at division.* Im Teilen bin ich nicht sehr gut.
♦ **the division of labour** die Arbeitsteilung
[2] (*in football*)
die Liga (PL die Ligen)

**divorce** NOUN
die Scheidung

**divorced** ADJECTIVE
geschieden ◊ *My parents are divorced.* Meine Eltern sind geschieden.

**DIY** NOUN (= *do-it-yourself*)
das Heimwerken
♦ **to do DIY** Heimwerker sein
♦ **a DIY shop** ein Geschäft für Heimwerker
♦ **DIY superstore** der Baumarkt

**dizzy** ADJECTIVE
♦ **I feel dizzy.** Mir ist schwindlig.

**DJ** NOUN (= *disc jockey*)
der Diskjockey (PL die Diskjockeys)

to **do** VERB
[1] machen ◊ *What are you doing this evening?* Was macht ihr heute Abend? ◊ *I haven't done my homework.* Ich habe meine Hausaufgaben noch nicht gemacht. ◊ *She did it by herself.* Sie hat es allein gemacht.
[2] tun (IMPERFECT tat, PERFECT hat getan)
◊ *What shall I do?* Was soll ich tun? ◊ *I'll do my best.* Ich werde mein Bestes tun.
◊ *I'll tell you what to do.* Ich sage dir, was du tun sollst.

*In combination with certain nouns and verbs* **do** *is not translated.*
◊ *I do a lot of cycling.* Ich fahre viel Rad.
◊ *She was doing her knitting.* Sie strickte.
◊ *to do the ironing* bügeln
♦ **to do well** erfolgreich sein ◊ *The firm is doing well.* Die Firma ist sehr erfolgreich.
♦ **She's doing well at school.** Sie ist gut in der Schule.
[3] (*be enough*)
reichen ◊ *It's not very good, but it'll do.* Es ist nicht besonders gut, aber es wird reichen. ◊ *That'll do, thanks.* Danke, das reicht.

*In English **do** is used to make questions. In German, questions are expressed by reversing the order of verb and subject.*
◊ *Do you like German food?* Magst du deutsches Essen? ◊ *Where does he live?* Wo wohnt er? ◊ *Do you speak English?* Sprechen Sie Englisch? ◊ *What do you do in your free time?* Was machen Sie in Ihrer Freizeit? ◊ *Where did you go for your holidays?* Wohin seid ihr in den Ferien gefahren?

*Use **nicht** in negative sentences for **don't**.*
◊ *I don't understand.* Ich verstehe nicht. ◊ *Why didn't you come?* Warum bist du nicht gekommen?

***do** is not translated when it is used in place of another verb.*
◊ *I hate maths. – So do I.* Ich hasse Mathe. – Ich auch. ◊ *I didn't like the film. – Neither did I.* Ich mochte den Film nicht. – Ich auch nicht. ◊ *Do you like horses? – No, I don't.* Magst du Pferde? – Nein.

*Questions like "doesn't it?" don't exist in German.*
◊ *The bus stops at the youth hostel, doesn't it?* Der Bus hält an der Jugendherberge, nicht wahr? ◊ *You go swimming on Fridays, don't you?* Du gehst freitags schwimmen, nicht wahr?
♦ **How do you do?** Guten Tag!
♦ **to do up (1)** (*shoes, shirt, cardigan*) zumachen ◊ *Do up your shoes!* Mach deine Schuhe zu!
♦ **to do up (2)** (*renovate*) renovieren ◊ *They're doing up an old cottage.* Sie renovieren ein altes Haus.
♦ **I could do with a holiday.** Ich könnte einen Urlaub gebrauchen.
♦ **to do without** ohne etwas auskommen ◊ *I couldn't do without my computer.* Ich käme nicht ohne meinen Computer aus.

**dock** NOUN
das <u>Dock</u> (*for ships*) (PL die Docks)
**doctor** NOUN
der <u>Arzt</u> (PL die Ärzte)
die <u>Ärztin</u>
◊ *She's a doctor.* Sie ist Ärztin. ◊ *She'd like to be a doctor.* Sie möchte gerne Ärztin werden.
**document** NOUN
das <u>Dokument</u> (PL die Dokumente)
**documentary** NOUN
der <u>Dokumentarfilm</u> (PL die Dokumentarfilme)
to **dodge** VERB
<u>ausweichen</u> (*attacker*) (IMPERFECT wich aus, PERFECT ist ausgewichen) ◊ *to dodge something* einer Sache ausweichen
**Dodgems** ® PL NOUN

der <u>Autoskooter</u> SING (PL die Autoskooter)
◊ *to go on the Dodgems* Autoskooter fahren
**does** VERB *see* **do**
**doesn't** = **does not**
**dog** NOUN
der <u>Hund</u> (PL die Hunde) ◊ *Have you got a dog?* Hast du einen Hund?
**do-it-yourself** NOUN
das <u>Heimwerken</u>
**dole** NOUN
die <u>Arbeitslosenunterstützung</u>
♦ **to be on the dole** stempeln gehen ◊ *A lot of people are on the dole.* Viele Menschen gehen stempeln.
♦ **to go on the dole** sich arbeitslos melden
**doll** NOUN
die <u>Puppe</u>
**dollar** NOUN
der <u>Dollar</u> (PL die Dollars *or* Dollar)
*When talking about amounts of money use the plural form **Dollar**.*
◊ *That costs fifty dollars.* Das kostet fünfzig Dollar.
**dolphin** NOUN
der <u>Delphin</u> (PL die Delphine)
**domestic** ADJECTIVE
♦ **a domestic flight** ein Inlandsflug MASC
**dominoes** SING NOUN
♦ **to have a game of dominoes** Domino spielen
to **donate** VERB
<u>spenden</u>
**done** VERB *see* **do**
**donkey** NOUN
der <u>Esel</u> (PL die Esel)
**donor** NOUN
der <u>Spender</u> (PL die Spender)
die <u>Spenderin</u>
**don't** = **do not**
**door** NOUN
die <u>Tür</u>
**doorbell** NOUN
die <u>Klingel</u>
♦ **to ring the doorbell** klingeln
♦ **Suddenly the doorbell rang.** Es klingelte plötzlich.
**doorman** NOUN
der <u>Portier</u> (PL die Portiers)
**doorstep** NOUN
die <u>Eingangsstufe</u>
**dormitory** NOUN
der <u>Schlafsaal</u> (PL die Schlafsäle)
**dose** NOUN
die <u>Dosis</u> (PL die Dosen)
**dosh** NOUN
die <u>Kohle</u> (*informal: money*)
**dot** NOUN
(*on letter "i", in E-mail address*)
der <u>Punkt</u> (PL die Punkte)

♦**on the dot** genau ◊ *He arrived at nine o'clock on the dot.* Er kam genau um neun Uhr.

to **double** VERB
| see also **double** ADJECTIVE |
<u>sich verdoppeln</u> (PERFECT hat sich verdoppelt) ◊ *The number of attacks has doubled.* Die Zahl der Überfälle hat sich verdoppelt.

**double** ADJECTIVE, ADVERB
| see also **double** VERB |
<u>doppelt</u> ◊ *a double helping* eine doppelte Portion
♦**to cost double** doppelt so viel kosten ◊ *First-class tickets cost double.* Fahrscheine erster Klasse kosten doppelt so viel.
♦**a double bed** ein Doppelbett NEUT
♦**a double room** ein Doppelzimmer NEUT
♦**a double-decker bus** ein Doppeldeckerbus MASC

**double bass** NOUN
der <u>Kontrabass</u> (GEN des Kontrabasses, PL die Kontrabässe) ◊ *I play the double bass.* Ich spiele Kontrabass.

to **double-click** VERB
<u>doppelklicken</u> (*computer*) (PERFECT hat doppelgeklickt)

**double glazing** NOUN
das <u>Doppelfenster</u> (PL die Doppelfenster)

**doubles** PL NOUN
das <u>Doppel</u> (*in tennis*) (PL die Doppel) ◊ *to play mixed doubles* gemischtes Doppel spielen

**doubt** NOUN
| see also **doubt** VERB |
der <u>Zweifel</u> (PL die Zweifel) ◊ *I have my doubts.* Ich habe meine Zweifel.

to **doubt** VERB
| see also **doubt** NOUN |
<u>bezweifeln</u> (PERFECT hat bezweifelt) ◊ *I doubt it.* Das bezweifle ich.
♦**to doubt that** bezweifeln, dass ◊ *I doubt he'll agree.* Ich bezweifle, dass er zustimmt.

**doubtful** ADJECTIVE
♦**to be doubtful about doing something** nicht wissen, ob man etwas tun soll ◊ *I'm doubtful about going by myself.* Ich weiß nicht, ob ich allein gehen soll.
♦**It's doubtful.** Es ist fraglich.
♦**You sound doubtful.** Du scheinst nicht sicher zu sein.

**dough** NOUN
der <u>Teig</u> (PL die Teige)

**doughnut** NOUN
der <u>Berliner</u> (PL die Berliner) ◊ *a jam doughnut* ein gefüllter Berliner

**Dover** NOUN
<u>Dover</u> NEUT ◊ *We went from Dover to Boulogne.* Wir sind von Dover nach Boulogne gefahren.

**down** ADVERB, ADJECTIVE, PREPOSITION

[1] <u>unten</u> (*below*) ◊ *His office is down on the first floor.* Sein Büro ist unten im ersten Stock. ◊ *It's down there.* Es ist da unten.
[2] <u>auf den Boden</u> (*to the ground*) ◊ *He threw down his racket.* Er warf seinen Schläger auf den Boden.
♦**They live just down the road.** Sie wohnen etwas weiter unten.
♦**to come down** herunterkommen ◊ *Come down here!* Komm herunter!
♦**to go down** hinuntergehen ◊ *They went down into the cellar.* Sie gingen in den Keller hinunter.
♦**to sit down** sich hinsetzen ◊ *Sit down!* Setz dich hin!
♦**to feel down** niedergeschlagen sein ◊ *I'm feeling a bit down.* Ich bin etwas niedergeschlagen.
♦**The computer's down.** Der Computer ist abgestürzt.

to **download** VERB
<u>runterladen</u> (*computer*) (PRESENT lädt runter, IMPERFECT lud runter, PERFECT hat runtergeladen) ◊ *to download a file* eine Datei runterladen

**downpour** NOUN
der <u>Regenguss</u> (GEN des Regengusses, PL die Regengüsse) ◊ *a sudden downpour* ein plötzlicher Regenguss

**downstairs** ADVERB, ADJECTIVE
[1] <u>unten</u> ◊ *The bathroom's downstairs.* Das Badezimmer ist unten.
♦**the people downstairs** die Leute von unten
♦**to go downstairs** nach unten gehen
[2] <u>untere</u> ◊ *the downstairs bathroom* das untere Badezimmer

**downtown** ADVERB US
im Stadtzentrum

to **doze** VERB
<u>dösen</u>
♦**to doze off** einnicken

**dozen** NOUN
das <u>Dutzend</u> (PL die Dutzende or Dutzend)
*When talking about more than one dozen use the plural form **Dutzend**.*
◊ *two dozen* zwei Dutzend ◊ *a dozen eggs* ein Dutzend Eier
♦**I've told you that dozens of times.** Ich habe dir das schon x-mal gesagt.

**drab** ADJECTIVE
<u>trist</u> (*clothes*)

**draft** NOUN US
der <u>Luftzug</u> (PL die Luftzüge)
♦**There's a draft!** Es zieht!

to **drag** VERB
| see also **drag** NOUN |
<u>schleppen</u> (*thing, person*)

**drag** NOUN
| see also **drag** VERB |

**D**

☞

◆ **It's a real drag!** Das ist echt öde!
(*informal*)

◆ **in drag** in Frauenkleidern ◇ *He was in drag.* Er hatte Frauenkleider an.

**dragon** NOUN
der Drache (GEN des Drachen, PL die Drachen)

**drain** NOUN
see also **drain** VERB
der Abfluss (GEN des Abflusses, PL die Abflüsse) ◇ *The drains are blocked.* Der Abfluss ist verstopft.

to **drain** VERB
see also **drain** NOUN
abtropfen lassen (*vegetables, pasta*) (PRESENT lässt abtropfen, IMPERFECT ließ abtropfen, PERFECT hat abtropfen lassen)

**draining board** NOUN
das Ablaufbrett (PL die Ablaufbretter)

**drainpipe** NOUN
das Regenrohr (PL die Regenrohre)

**drama** NOUN
das Drama (PL die Dramen) ◇ *Drama is my favourite subject.* Drama ist mein Lieblingsfach.

◆ **drama school** die Schauspielschule ◇ *I'd like to go to drama school.* Ich würde gerne auf die Schauspielschule gehen.

**dramatic** ADJECTIVE
dramatisch ◇ *It was really dramatic!* Es war wirklich dramatisch! ◇ *a dramatic improvement* eine dramatische Besserung

**drank** VERB see **drink**

**drapes** PL NOUN US
die Vorhänge MASC PL

**drastic** ADJECTIVE
drastisch (*change*) ◇ *to take drastic action* drastische Maßnahmen ergreifen

**draught** NOUN
der Luftzug
◆ **There's a draught!** Es zieht!

**draughts** SING NOUN
Dame FEM ◇ *to play draughts* Dame spielen

**draw** NOUN
see also **draw** VERB
[1] (*sport*)
das Unentschieden (PL die Unentschieden) ◇ *The game ended in a draw.* Das Spiel endete mit einem Unentschieden.
[2] (*in lottery*)
die Ziehung ◇ *The draw takes place on Saturday.* Die Ziehung findet am Samstag statt.

to **draw** VERB
see also **draw** NOUN
[1] malen ◇ *He's good at drawing.* Er kann gut malen. ◇ *to draw a picture* ein Bild malen
◆ **to draw a line** einen Strich machen

[2] unentschieden spielen (*sport*) ◇ *We drew two all.* Wir haben zwei zu zwei gespielt.
◆ **to draw the curtains** die Vorhänge zuziehen
◆ **to draw lots** losen

to **draw on** VERB
zurückgreifen auf (IMPERFECT griff zurück, PERFECT hat zurückgegriffen) ◇ *He drew on his own experience to write the book.* Er griff beim Schreiben des Buches auf seine eigenen Erfahrungen zurück.

to **draw up** VERB
halten (PRESENT hält, IMPERFECT hielt, PERFECT hat gehalten) ◇ *The car drew up in front of the house.* Das Auto hielt vor dem Haus.

**drawback** NOUN
der Nachteil (PL die Nachteile)

**drawer** NOUN
die Schublade

**drawing** NOUN
die Zeichnung

**drawing pin** NOUN
die Reißzwecke

**drawn** VERB see **draw**

**dreadful** ADJECTIVE
[1] furchtbar ◇ *a dreadful mistake* ein furchtbarer Fehler ◇ *You look dreadful.* (*ill*) Du siehst furchtbar aus. ◇ *I feel dreadful.* Ich fühle mich furchtbar.
[2] schrecklich ◇ *The weather was dreadful.* Das Wetter war schrecklich.

to **dream** VERB
see also **dream** NOUN
träumen ◇ *I dreamt I was in Belgium.* Ich habe geträumt, ich sei in Belgien.
*Note the use of the subjunctive.*

**dream** NOUN
see also **dream** VERB
der Traum (PL die Träume) ◇ *It was just a dream.* Es war nur ein Traum. ◇ *a bad dream* ein böser Traum

to **drench** VERB
◆ **to get drenched** klatschnass werden ◇ *We got drenched.* Wir wurden klatschnass.

**dress** NOUN
see also **dress** VERB
das Kleid (PL die Kleider)

to **dress** VERB
see also **dress** NOUN
sich anziehen (IMPERFECT zog sich an, PERFECT hat sich angezogen) ◇ *I got up, dressed, and went downstairs.* Ich stand auf, zog mich an und ging hinunter.
◆ **to dress somebody** jemanden anziehen ◇ *She dressed the children.* Sie zog die Kinder an.
◆ **to get dressed** sich anziehen ◇ *I got dressed quickly.* Ich habe mich schnell angezogen.

◆ **to dress up** sich verkleiden ◊ *I dressed up as a ghost.* Ich habe mich als Gespenst verkleidet.

**dressed** ADJECTIVE
angezogen ◊ *I'm not dressed yet.* Ich bin noch nicht angezogen. ◊ *How was she dressed?* Wie war sie angezogen?
◆ **She was dressed in a green sweater and jeans.** Sie hatte einen grünen Pullover und Jeans an.

**dresser** NOUN
die Kommode (*furniture*)

**dressing** NOUN
das Dressing (*for salad*) (PL die Dressings)

**dressing gown** NOUN
der Morgenmantel (PL die Morgenmäntel)

**dressing table** NOUN
der Frisiertisch (PL die Frisiertische)

**drew** VERB *see* **draw**

**drier** NOUN
[1] (*for washing*)
der Wäschetrockner (PL die Wäschetrockner)
[2] (*for hair*)
der Haartrockner (PL die Haartrockner)

**drift** NOUN
   see also **drift** VERB
◆ **a snow drift** eine Schneeverwehung

to **drift** VERB
   see also **drift** NOUN
treiben (*boat, snow*) (IMPERFECT trieb, PERFECT ist getrieben)

**drill** NOUN
   see also **drill** VERB
der Bohrer (PL die Bohrer)

to **drill** VERB
   see also **drill** NOUN
bohren

to **drink** VERB
   see also **drink** NOUN
trinken (IMPERFECT trank, PERFECT hat getrunken) ◊ *What would you like to drink?* Was möchtest du trinken? ◊ *She drank three cups of tea.* Sie trank drei Tassen Tee. ◊ *He'd been drinking.* Er hatte getrunken. ◊ *I don't drink.* Ich trinke nicht.

**drink** NOUN
   see also **drink** VERB
[1] das Getränk (PL die Getränke) ◊ *a cold drink* ein kaltes Getränk ◊ *a hot drink* ein heißes Getränk
[2] (*alcoholic*)
der Drink (PL die Drinks)
◆ **They've gone out for a drink.** Sie sind etwas trinken gegangen.
◆ **to have a drink** etwas trinken

**drinking water** NOUN
das Trinkwasser

**drive** NOUN
   see also **drive** VERB
[1] die Fahrt ◊ *We've got a long drive tomorrow.* Wir haben morgen eine lange Fahrt.
◆ **to go for a drive** fahren ◊ *We went for a drive in the country.* Wir sind aufs Land gefahren.
[2] die Auffahrt (*of house*) ◊ *He parked his car in the drive.* Er parkte sein Auto in der Auffahrt.

to **drive** VERB
   see also **drive** NOUN
[1] fahren (PRESENT fährt, IMPERFECT fuhr, PERFECT ist/hat gefahren) ◊ *My mother drives me to school.* Meine Mutter fährt mich in die Schule. ◊ *I drove down to London.* Ich bin nach London gefahren.
*When* **fahren** *is used with an object it takes* **haben** *not* **sein.**
◊ *He drove me home.* Er hat mich nach Hause gefahren.
[2] (*operate a car*)
Auto fahren (PRESENT fährt Auto, IMPERFECT fuhr Auto, PERFECT ist Auto gefahren) ◊ *Can you drive?* Kannst du Auto fahren?
◆ **She's learning to drive.** Sie macht den Führerschein.
[3] (*go by car*)
mit dem Auto fahren ◊ *Did you go by train? – No, we drove.* Seid ihr mit dem Zug gefahren? – Nein, wir sind mit dem Auto gefahren.
◆ **to drive somebody mad** jemanden wahnsinnig machen ◊ *He drives her mad.* Er macht sie wahnsinnig.

**driver** NOUN
der Fahrer (PL die Fahrer)
die Fahrerin
◊ *She's an excellent driver.* Sie ist eine ausgezeichnete Fahrerin. ◊ *He's a bus driver.* Er ist Busfahrer.

**driver's license** NOUN US
der Führerschein (PL die Führerscheine)

**driving instructor** NOUN
der Fahrlehrer (PL die Fahrlehrer)
die Fahrlehrerin
◊ *He's a driving instructor.* Er ist Fahrlehrer.

**driving lesson** NOUN
die Fahrstunde

**driving licence** NOUN
der Führerschein (PL die Führerscheine)

**driving test** NOUN
die Fahrprüfung
◆ **to take one's driving test** die Fahrprüfung machen ◊ *He's taking his driving test tomorrow.* Er macht morgen die Fahrprüfung.
◆ **She's just passed her driving test.** Sie hat gerade ihren Führerschein gemacht.

**drizzle** NOUN
   see also **drizzle** VERB
der Nieselregen

to **drizzle** VERB
> see also **drizzle** NOUN

nieseln
**drop** NOUN
> see also **drop** VERB

der Tropfen (PL die Tropfen) ◊ *a drop of water* ein Wassertropfen
to **drop** VERB
> see also **drop** NOUN

1 fallen lassen (PRESENT lässt fallen, IMPERFECT ließ fallen, PERFECT hat fallen lassen) ◊ *I dropped the glass and it broke.* Ich habe das Glas fallen lassen, und es ist kaputtgegangen.

2 (*abandon*)
aufgeben (PRESENT gibt auf, IMPERFECT gab auf, PERFECT hat aufgegeben) ◊ *I'm going to drop chemistry.* Ich gebe Chemie auf.

3 absetzen (PERFECT hat abgesetzt) ◊ *Could you drop me at the station?* Könntest du mich am Bahnhof absetzen?

**drought** NOUN
die Dürre
**drove** VERB see **drive**
to **drown** VERB
ertrinken (IMPERFECT ertrank, PERFECT ist ertrunken) ◊ *A young boy drowned here yesterday.* Hier ist gestern ein kleiner Junge ertrunken.

**drug** NOUN
1 (*medicine*)
das Medikament (PL die Medikamente) ◊ *They need food and drugs.* Sie brauchen Nahrung und Medikamente.

2 (*illegal*)
die Droge ◊ *hard drugs* harte Drogen ◊ *soft drugs* weiche Drogen ◊ *to take drugs* Drogen nehmen

◆ **a drug addict** (*man*) ein Drogensüchtiger
◆ **She's a drug addict.** Sie ist drogensüchtig.
◆ **a drug pusher** ein Dealer MASC
◆ **a drug smuggler** ein Drogenschmuggler MASC
◆ **the drugs squad** das Rauschgiftdezernat

**drugstore** NOUN US
der Drugstore (PL die Drugstores)
**drum** NOUN
die Trommel ◊ *an African drum* eine afrikanische Trommel

◆ **a drum kit** ein Schlagzeug NEUT
◆ **drums** das Schlagzeug SING ◊ *I play drums.* Ich spiele Schlagzeug.

**drummer** NOUN
(*in rock group*)
der Schlagzeuger (PL die Schlagzeuger)
die Schlagzeugerin
**drunk** VERB see **drink**
**drunk** ADJECTIVE
> see also **drunk** NOUN

betrunken ◊ *He was drunk.* Er war betrunken.

**drunk** NOUN
> see also **drunk** ADJECTIVE

der Betrunkene (GEN des Betrunkenen, PL die Betrunkenen)
die Betrunkene (GEN der Betrunkenen)
◊ *a drunk* (*man*) ein Betrunkener ◊ *The streets were full of drunks.* Die Straßen waren voll von Betrunkenen.

**dry** ADJECTIVE
> see also **dry** VERB

trocken ◊ *The paint isn't dry yet.* Die Farbe ist noch nicht trocken.
◆ **a long dry period** eine lange Trockenzeit
to **dry** VERB
> see also **dry** ADJECTIVE

1 trocknen ◊ *The washing will dry quickly in the sun.* Die Wäsche wird in der Sonne schnell trocknen. ◊ *some dried flowers* getrocknete Blumen

◆ **to dry one's hair** sich die Haare föhnen ◊ *I haven't dried my hair yet.* Ich habe mir noch nicht die Haare geföhnt.

2 (*clothes*)
trocknen lassen (PRESENT lässt trocknen, IMPERFECT ließ trocknen, PERFECT hat trocknen lassen) ◊ *There's nowhere to dry clothes here.* Hier kann man nirgends Kleider trocknen lassen.

◆ **to dry the dishes** das Geschirr abtrocknen
**dry-cleaner's** NOUN
die Reinigung
**dryer** NOUN
der Wäschetrockner (*for clothes*) (PL die Wäschetrockner)

◆ **a tumble dryer** ein Wäschetrockner
◆ **a hair dryer** ein Föhn MASC
**DTP** ABBREVIATION (= *Desktop Publishing*)
DTP
**dubbed** ADJECTIVE
synchronisiert ◊ *The film was dubbed into German.* Der Film war deutsch synchronisiert.

**dubious** ADJECTIVE
◆ **My parents were a bit dubious about it.** Meine Eltern hatten ihre Zweifel.
**duck** NOUN
die Ente
**due** ADJECTIVE, ADVERB
◆ **to be due to do something** etwas tun sollen ◊ *He's due to arrive tomorrow.* Er soll morgen ankommen.
◆ **The plane's due in half an hour.** Das Flugzeug sollte in einer halben Stunde ankommen.
◆ **When's the baby due?** Wann kommt das Baby?
◆ **due to** wegen ◊ *The trip was cancelled due to bad weather.* Der Ausflug wurde wegen des schlechten Wetters abgesagt.

**dug** VERB see **dig**
**dull** ADJECTIVE

1 langweilig ◊ *He's nice, but a bit dull.*
Er ist nett, aber ein bisschen langweilig.
2 trüb (*weather, day*)
**dumb** ADJECTIVE
1 taub
♦ **She's deaf and dumb.** Sie ist
taubstumm.
2 blöd (*stupid*) ◊ *That was a really dumb
thing I did!* Da habe ich etwas echt
Blödes gemacht!
**dummy** NOUN
der Schnuller (*for baby*) (PL die
Schnuller)
**dump** NOUN
  see also **dump** VERB
♦ **It's a real dump!** Das ist ein Dreckloch!
(*informal*)
♦ **a rubbish dump** eine Müllkippe
to **dump** VERB
  see also **dump** NOUN
1 (*waste*)
abladen (PRESENT lädt ab, IMPERFECT lud ab,
PERFECT hat abgeladen)
♦ **"no dumping"** "Schutt abladen verboten"
2 (*informal: get rid of*)
Schluss machen mit ◊ *He's just dumped
his girlfriend.* Er hat gerade mit seiner
Freundin Schluss gemacht.
**dungarees** PL NOUN
die Latzhose ◊ *a pair of dungarees* eine
Latzhose
**dungeon** NOUN
das Verlies (PL die Verliese)
**duration** NOUN
die Dauer
**during** PREPOSITION
während ◊ *during the holidays* während
der Ferien
♦ **during the day** tagsüber
**dusk** NOUN
die Dämmerung ◊ *at dusk* bei
Dämmerung
**dust** NOUN
  see also **dust** VERB
der Staub
to **dust** VERB
  see also **dust** NOUN
abstauben (PERFECT hat abgestaubt) ◊ *I
dusted the shelves.* Ich habe das Regal
abgestaubt.
♦ **I hate dusting!** Ich hasse Staubwischen!

**dustbin** NOUN
der Mülleimer (PL die Mülleimer)
**dustman** NOUN
der Müllmann (PL die Müllmänner)
♦ **He's a dustman.** Er arbeitet bei der
Müllabfuhr.
**dusty** ADJECTIVE
staubig
**Dutch** ADJECTIVE
  see also **Dutch** NOUN
holländisch ◊ *She's Dutch.* Sie ist
Holländerin.
**Dutch** NOUN
  see also **Dutch** ADJECTIVE
das Holländisch (*language*) (GEN des
Holländischen)
♦ **the Dutch** die Holländer MASC PL
**Dutchman** NOUN
der Holländer (PL die Holländer)
**Dutchwoman** NOUN
die Holländerin
**duty** NOUN
die Pflicht ◊ *It was his duty to tell the
police.* Es war seine Pflicht, die Polizei zu
informieren.
♦ **to be on duty** Dienst haben
**duty-free** ADJECTIVE
zollfrei
♦ **the duty-free shop** der Duty-free-Laden
**duvet** NOUN
das Deckbett (PL die Deckbetten)
**DVD** NOUN (= *digital video disc*)
die DVD (PL die DVDs)
**dwarf** NOUN
der Zwerg (PL die Zwerge)
die Zwergin
**dye** NOUN
  see also **dye** VERB
der Farbstoff
♦ **hair dye** das Haarfärbemittel
to **dye** VERB
  see also **dye** NOUN
färben ◊ *to dye sth red* etw rot färben
◊ *She has dyed her hair blonde.* Sie hat
blond gefärbte Haare.
**dynamic** ADJECTIVE
dynamisch
**dyslexia** NOUN
die Legasthenie
♦ **She has dyslexia.** Sie ist Legasthenikerin.

D

# E

**each** ADJECTIVE, PRONOUN
jeder ◇ *Each pupil has his own desk.*
Jeder Schüler hat seinen eigenen
Schreibtisch. ◇ *They have ten points
each.* Jeder hat zehn Punkte. ◇ *He gave
each of us ten pounds.* Er gab jedem von
uns zehn Pfund. ◇ *each day* jeder Tag
jede ◇ *Each dancer wore a different
costume.* Jede Tänzerin trug ein anderes
Kostüm. ◇ *He gave each of the dancers a
red rose.* Er gab jeder Tänzerin eine rote
Rose.
jedes ◇ *Each house in our street has its
own garden.* Jedes Haus in unserer
Straße hat einen eigenen Garten. ◇ *The
girls each have their own bedroom.*
Jedes der Mädchen hat sein eigenes
Zimmer.
◆ **each other** einander ◇ *They hate each
other.* Sie hassen einander. ◇ *We wrote
to each other.* Wir haben einander
geschrieben.
◆ **They don't know each other.** Sie kennen
sich nicht.
**eager** ADJECTIVE
◆ **He was eager to tell us about his
experiences.** Er wollte uns unbedingt von
seinen Erfahrungen erzählen.
**eagle** NOUN
der Adler (PL die Adler)
**ear** NOUN
das Ohr (PL die Ohren)
**earache** NOUN
die Ohrenschmerzen MASC PL ◇ *to have
earache* Ohrenschmerzen haben
**earlier** ADVERB
⒈ vorher ◇ *I saw him earlier.* Ich habe
ihn vorher gesehen.
⒉ früher (*in the morning*) ◇ *I ought to get
up earlier.* Ich sollte früher aufstehen.
**early** ADVERB, ADJECTIVE
früh ◇ *I have to get up early.* Ich muss
früh aufstehen. ◇ *I came early to get a
good seat.* Ich bin früh gekommen, um
einen guten Platz zu bekommen.
◆ **to have an early night** früh ins Bett
gehen
to **earn** VERB
verdienen (PERFECT hat verdient) ◇ *She
earns five pounds an hour.* Sie verdient
fünf Pfund in der Stunde.
**earnings** PL NOUN
der Verdienst (PL die Verdienste)
**earring** NOUN
der Ohrring (PL die Ohrringe)
**earth** NOUN
die Erde
**earthquake** NOUN
das Erdbeben (PL die Erdbeben)

**easily** ADVERB
leicht
**east** ADJECTIVE, ADVERB
see also **east** NOUN
◆ **the east coast** die Ostküste
◆ **an east wind** ein Ostwind MASC
nach Osten ◇ *We were travelling east.*
Wir sind nach Osten gefahren.
◆ **east of** östlich von ◇ *It's east of London.*
Es liegt östlich von London.
**east** NOUN
see also **east** ADJECTIVE
der Osten ◇ *in the east* im Osten
**Easter** NOUN
Ostern NEUT ◇ *at Easter* an Ostern ◇ *We
went to my grandparents' for Easter.* Wir
sind über Ostern zu meinen Großeltern
gefahren.
**Easter egg** NOUN
das Osterei (PL die Ostereier)
**eastern** ADJECTIVE
östlich ◇ *the eastern part of the island*
der östliche Teil der Insel
◆ **Eastern Europe** Osteuropa NEUT
**easy** ADJECTIVE
einfach
**easy chair** NOUN
der Sessel (PL die Sessel)
**easy-going** ADJECTIVE
locker ◇ *She's very easy-going.* Sie ist
echt locker.
to **eat** VERB
essen (PRESENT isst, IMPERFECT aß, PERFECT hat
gegessen) ◇ *Would you like something
to eat?* Möchtest du etwas essen?
**EC** NOUN (= *European Community*)
die EG (= Europäische Gemeinschaft)
**eccentric** ADJECTIVE
exzentrisch
**echo** NOUN
das Echo (PL die Echos)
**ecology** NOUN
die Ökologie
**e-commerce** NOUN
der E-Commerce (GEN des E-Commerce)
**economic** ADJECTIVE
rentabel (*profitable*)
**economical** ADJECTIVE
sparsam
**economics** SING NOUN
die Volkswirtschaft ◇ *He's studying
economics.* Er studiert Volkswirtschaft.
to **economize** VERB
sparen ◇ *to economize on something* mit
etwas sparen
**economy** NOUN
die Wirtschaft ◇ *the German economy*
die deutsche Wirtschaft

**ecstasy** NOUN
das Ecstasy (*drug*) (GEN des Ecstasy)
♦ **to be in ecstasy** entzückt sein

**ecu** NOUN (= *European Currency Unit*)
der Ecu (GEN des Ecu, PL die Ecu)

**eczema** NOUN
der Hautausschlag (PL die Hautausschläge)

**edge** NOUN
[1] der Rand (PL die Ränder) ◊ *They live on the edge of the moors.* Sie leben am Rand des Moors. ◊ *The country was on the edge of war.* Das Land stand am Rand eines Krieges.
[2] (*of table*)
die Kante
[3] (*of lake*)
das Ufer (PL die Ufer)

**edgy** ADJECTIVE
nervös

**Edinburgh** NOUN
Edinburgh NEUT

**editor** NOUN
(*of newspaper*)
der Redakteur (PL die Redakteure)
die Redakteurin

**educated** ADJECTIVE
gebildet

**education** NOUN
[1] das Bildungswesen ◊ *There should be more investment in education.* Es sollte mehr Geld ins Bildungswesen investiert werden.
[2] das Lehramt (*teaching*) ◊ *She works in education.* Sie ist im Lehramt tätig.

**educational** ADJECTIVE
lehrreich (*experience*) ◊ *It was very educational.* Das was sehr lehrreich.

**effect** NOUN
der Effekt (PL die Effekte) ◊ *special effects* Spezialeffekte

**effective** ADJECTIVE
effektiv

**efficient** ADJECTIVE
effizient

**effort** NOUN
die Bemühung
♦ **to make an effort to do something** sich bemühen, etwas zu tun

**e.g.** ABBREVIATION
z. B. (= zum Beispiel)

**egg** NOUN
das Ei (PL die Eier) ◊ *a hard-boiled egg* ein hart gekochtes Ei ◊ *a soft-boiled egg* ein weich gekochtes Ei
♦ **a fried egg** ein Spiegelei
♦ **scrambled eggs** die Rühreier NEUT PL

**egg cup** NOUN
der Eierbecher (PL die Eierbecher)

**eggplant** NOUN US
die Aubergine

**Egypt** NOUN
Ägypten NEUT ◊ *to Egypt* nach Ägypten ˊ

**eight** NUMBER
acht ◊ *She's eight.* Sie ist acht.

**eighteen** NUMBER
achtzehn ◊ *She's eighteen.* Sie ist achtzehn.

**eighteenth** ADJECTIVE
achtzehnte
♦ **the eighteenth of August** der achtzehnte August

**eighth** ADJECTIVE
achte ◊ *the eighth floor* der achte Stock
♦ **the eighth of August** der achte August

**eighty** NUMBER
achtzig ◊ *She's eighty.* Sie ist achtzig.

**Eire** NOUN
Irland NEUT
♦ **from Eire** aus Irland
♦ **in Eire** in Irland
♦ **to Eire** nach Irland

**either** ADVERB, CONJUNCTION, PRONOUN
[1] auch kein ◊ *I don't like milk, and I don't like eggs either.* Ich mag keine Milch und ich mag auch keine Eier.
[2] auch nicht ◊ *I've never been to Spain. – I haven't either.* Ich war noch nie in Spanien. – Ich auch nicht.
♦ **either ... or ...** entweder ... oder ... ◊ *You can have either ice cream or yoghurt.* Du kannst entweder Eis oder Joghurt haben.
♦ **either of them** einer von beiden ◊ *Take either of them.* Nimm einen von beiden.
♦ **I don't like either of them.** Ich mag keinen von beiden.

**elastic** NOUN
das Gummiband (PL die Gummibänder)

**elastic band** NOUN
das Gummiband (PL die Gummibänder)

**elbow** NOUN
der Ellbogen (PL die Ellbogen)

**elder** ADJECTIVE
älter ◊ *my elder sister* meine ältere Schwester

**elderly** ADJECTIVE
älter ◊ *an elderly gentleman* ein älterer Herr
♦ **the elderly** ältere Leute PL

**eldest** ADJECTIVE
älteste ◊ *my eldest brother* mein ältester Bruder ◊ *my eldest sister* meine älteste Schwester ◊ *He's the eldest.* Er ist der Älteste.

to **elect** VERB
wählen

**election** NOUN
die Wahl

**electric** ADJECTIVE
elektrisch ◊ *an electric fire* ein elektrischer Ofen ◊ *an electric guitar* eine elektrische Gitarre
♦ **an electric blanket** eine Heizdecke

**electrical** ADJECTIVE
elektrisch

E

♦ **an electrical engineer** ein
Elektrotechniker

**electrician** NOUN
der Elektriker (PL die Elektriker)
die Elektrikerin
◊ *He's an electrician.* Er ist Elektriker.

**electricity** NOUN
der Strom ◊ *They cut off our electricity.*
Sie haben den Strom abgestellt.

**electronic** ADJECTIVE
elektronisch

**electronics** SING NOUN
die Elektronik ◊ *My hobby is electronics.*
Elektronik ist mein Hobby.

**elegant** ADJECTIVE
elegant

**elementary school** NOUN US
die Grundschule

**elephant** NOUN
der Elefant (GEN des Elefanten, PL die
Elefanten)

**elevator** NOUN US
der Aufzug (PL die Aufzüge)

**eleven** NUMBER
elf ◊ *She's eleven.* Sie ist elf.

**eleventh** ADJECTIVE
elfte ◊ *the eleventh floor* der elfte Stock
♦ **the eleventh of August** der elfte August

**else** ADVERB
1 anders ◊ *somebody else* jemand
anders ◊ *nobody else* niemand anders
◊ *somewhere else* irgendwo anders
◊ *anywhere else* irgendwo anders
2 anderes ◊ *nothing else* nichts anderes
◊ *something else* etwas anderes
◊ *anything else* etwas anderes
♦ **Would you like anything else?** Möchtest
du noch etwas?
♦ **I don't want anything else.** Ich will nichts
anderes.
♦ **Give me the money, or else!** Gib mir das
Geld, sonst gibt's was!

**email** NOUN
　see also **email** VERB
die E-Mail (PL die E-Mails) ◊ *My email
address is ...* Meine E-Mail-Adresse ist ...

to **email** VERB
　see also **email** NOUN
mailen (PERFECT hat gemailt) ◊ *Did you
email it?* Hast du es gemailt?
♦ **to email somebody** jemandem eine
E-Mail senden

**embankment** NOUN
die Böschung

**embarrassed** ADJECTIVE
verlegen ◊ *He seemed to be pretty
embarrassed.* Er schien sehr verlegen.
♦ **I was really embarrassed.** Es war mir
wirklich peinlich.

**embarrassing** ADJECTIVE
peinlich ◊ *It was so embarrassing.* Es
war so peinlich.

**embassy** NOUN
die Botschaft

to **embroider** VERB
besticken (PERFECT hat bestickt)

**embroidery** NOUN
die Stickerei
♦ **I do embroidery.** Ich sticke.

**emergency** NOUN
der Notfall (PL die Notfälle) ◊ *This is an
emergency!* Dies ist ein Notfall! ◊ *in an
emergency* in einem Notfall
♦ **an emergency exit** ein Notausgang MASC
♦ **an emergency landing** eine Notlandung
♦ **the emergency services** die
Rettungsdienste MASC PL

to **emigrate** VERB
auswandern (PERFECT ist ausgewandert)

**emotion** NOUN
das Gefühl (PL die Gefühle)

**emotional** ADJECTIVE
emotional (*person*)

**emperor** NOUN
der Kaiser (PL die Kaiser)

to **emphasize** VERB
betonen (PERFECT hat betont)

**empire** NOUN
das Reich (PL die Reiche)

to **employ** VERB
beschäftigen (PERFECT hat beschäftigt)
◊ *The factory employs six hundred
people.* Die Fabrik beschäftigt
sechshundert Leute.

**employee** NOUN
der Angestellte (GEN des Angestellten, PL
die Angestellten)
die Angestellte (GEN der Angestellten)
◊ *He's an employee.* Er ist Angestellter.

**employer** NOUN
der Arbeitgeber (PL die Arbeitgeber)
die Arbeitgeberin

**employment** NOUN
die Beschäftigung

**empty** ADJECTIVE
　see also **empty** VERB
leer

to **empty** VERB
　see also **empty** ADJECTIVE
leeren
♦ **to empty something out** etwas
ausleeren

to **encourage** VERB
ermutigen (PERFECT hat ermutigt)
♦ **to encourage somebody to do
something** jemanden ermutigen, etwas
zu tun

**encouragement** NOUN
die Ermutigung

**encyclopedia** NOUN
das Lexikon (PL die Lexika)

**end** NOUN
　see also **end** VERB

das Ende (PL die Enden) ◊ *the end of the holidays* das Ende der Ferien ◊ *at the end of the street* am Ende der Straße ◊ *at the other end of the table* am anderen Ende des Tisches
♦ **the end of the film** der Schluss des Films
♦ **in the end** schließlich ◊ *In the end I decided to stay at home.* Schließlich habe ich beschlossen, zu Hause zu bleiben. ◊ *It turned out all right in the end.* Schließlich ging alles gut.
♦ **for hours on end** stundenlang
to **end** VERB

see also **end** NOUN

zu Ende sein (PRESENT ist zu Ende, IMPERFECT war zu Ende, PERFECT ist zu Ende gewesen) ◊ *What time does the film end?* Wann ist der Film zu Ende?
♦ **to end up doing something** schließlich etwas tun ◊ *I ended up walking home.* Ich bin schließlich zu Fuß nach Hause gegangen.
**ending** NOUN
der Schluss (GEN des Schlusses, PL die Schlüsse) ◊ *It was an exciting film, especially the ending.* Es war ein spannender Film, besonders am Schluss.
**endless** ADJECTIVE
endlos ◊ *The journey seemed endless.* Die Reise erschien endlos.
**enemy** NOUN
der Feind (PL die Feinde)
die Feindin
**energetic** ADJECTIVE
voller Energie (*person*)
**energy** NOUN
die Energie
**engaged** ADJECTIVE
[1] besetzt (*busy, in use*) ◊ *I phoned, but it was engaged.* Ich habe angerufen, aber es war besetzt.
[2] verlobt (*to be married*) ◊ *She's engaged to Brian.* Sie ist mit Brian verlobt.
♦ **to get engaged** sich verloben
**engagement** NOUN
die Verlobung ◊ *an engagement ring* ein Verlobungsring MASC
**engine** NOUN
der Motor (PL die Motoren)
**engineer** NOUN
[1] der Ingenieur (PL die Ingenieure)
die Ingenieurin
◊ *He's an engineer.* Er ist Ingenieur.
[2] (*train driver*)
der Lokomotivführer (PL die Lokomotivführer)
**engineering** NOUN
die Technik ◊ *genetic engineering* die Gentechnik
♦ **mechanical engineering** der Maschinenbau
**England** NOUN

England NEUT
♦ **from England** aus England
♦ **in England** in England
♦ **to England** nach England

> ℹ️ Germans frequently use **England** to mean Great Britain or the United Kingdom.

**English** ADJECTIVE

see also **English** NOUN

englisch
♦ **He's English.** Er ist Engländer.
♦ **She's English.** Sie ist Engländerin.
♦ **English people** die Engländer MASC PL
**English** NOUN

see also **English** ADJECTIVE

das Englisch (*language*) (GEN des Englischen) ◊ *Do you speak English?* Sprechen Sie Englisch?
♦ **the English** (*people*) die Engländer MASC PL
**Englishman** NOUN
der Engländer (PL die Engländer)
**Englishwoman** NOUN
die Engländerin
to **enjoy** VERB
genießen (IMPERFECT genoss, PERFECT hat genossen) ◊ *I really enjoyed my holidays.* Ich habe meine Ferien wirklich genossen.
♦ **Did you enjoy the film?** Hat dir der Film gefallen?
♦ **Did you enjoy your meal?** Hat es Ihnen geschmeckt?
♦ **to enjoy oneself** sich amüsieren ◊ *I really enjoyed myself.* Ich habe mich richtig amüsiert. ◊ *Did you enjoy yourselves at the party?* Habt ihr euch auf der Party amüsiert?
**enjoyable** ADJECTIVE
nett
**enlargement** NOUN
die Vergrößerung (*of photo*)
**enormous** ADJECTIVE
riesig
**enough** PRONOUN, ADJECTIVE
genug ◊ *enough time* genug Zeit ◊ *I didn't have enough money.* Ich hatte nicht genug Geld. ◊ *big enough* groß genug ◊ *warm enough* warm genug
♦ **Have you got enough?** Reicht dir das?
♦ **I've had enough!** Mir reicht's!
♦ **That's enough.** Das reicht.
to **enquire** VERB
sich erkundigen (PERFECT hat sich erkundigt)
♦ **to enquire about something** sich nach etwas erkundigen ◊ *I'm going to enquire about train times.* Ich werde mich nach den Abfahrtszeiten der Züge erkundigen.
**enquiry** NOUN

E

☞

die <u>Untersuchung</u> (*official investigation*)
- **to make an enquiry** sich erkundigen
  ◊ *I'd like to make an enquiry about hotels.* Ich möchte mich über Hotels erkundigen.

to **enter** VERB
<u>betreten</u> (*room*) (PRESENT betritt, IMPERFECT betrat, PERFECT hat betreten)
- **to enter a competition** an einem Wettbewerb teilnehmen

to **entertain** VERB
<u>unterhalten</u> (*guests*) (PRESENT unterhält, IMPERFECT unterhielt, PERFECT hat unterhalten)

**entertainer** NOUN
der <u>Entertainer</u> (PL die Entertainer)
die <u>Entertainerin</u>

**entertaining** ADJECTIVE
<u>unterhaltsam</u>

**enthusiasm** NOUN
die <u>Begeisterung</u>

**enthusiast** NOUN
- **a railway enthusiast** ein Eisenbahnfan MASC
- **She's a DIY enthusiast.** Sie ist begeisterte Heimwerkerin.

**enthusiastic** ADJECTIVE
<u>begeistert</u>

**entire** ADJECTIVE
<u>ganz</u> ◊ *the entire world* die ganze Welt

**entirely** ADVERB
<u>ganz</u>

**entrance** NOUN
der <u>Eingang</u> (PL die Eingänge)
- **an entrance exam** eine Aufnahmeprüfung
- **entrance fee** der Eintritt

**entry** NOUN
der <u>Eingang</u> (*way in*) (PL die Eingänge)
- **"no entry" (1)** (*on door*) "kein Zutritt"
- **"no entry" (2)** (*on road sign*) "Einfahrt verboten"
- **an entry form** ein Teilnahmeformular NEUT

**entry phone** NOUN
die <u>Gegensprechanlage</u>

**envelope** NOUN
der <u>Umschlag</u> (PL die Umschläge)

**envious** ADJECTIVE
<u>neidisch</u>

**environment** NOUN
die <u>Umwelt</u>

**environmental** ADJECTIVE
- **environmental pollution** die Umweltverschmutzung
- **environmental protection** der Umweltschutz

**environment-friendly** ADJECTIVE
<u>umweltfreundlich</u>

**envy** NOUN
| see also **envy** VERB |
der <u>Neid</u>

to **envy** VERB
| see also **envy** NOUN |
<u>beneiden</u> (PERFECT hat beneidet) ◊ *I don't envy you!* Ich beneide dich nicht!

**epileptic** NOUN
der <u>Epileptiker</u> (PL die Epileptiker)
die <u>Epileptikerin</u>

**episode** NOUN
die <u>Folge</u> (*of TV programme, story*)

**equal** ADJECTIVE
| see also **equal** VERB |
<u>gleich</u>

to **equal** VERB
| see also **equal** ADJECTIVE |
- **Ten times two equals twenty.** Zehn mal zwei ist gleich zwanzig.

**equality** NOUN
die <u>Gleichheit</u>

to **equalize** VERB
<u>ausgleichen</u> (*in sport*) (IMPERFECT glich aus, PERFECT hat ausgeglichen)

**equator** NOUN
der <u>Äquator</u>

**equipment** NOUN
die <u>Ausrüstung</u> ◊ *fishing equipment* die Anglerausrüstung ◊ *skiing equipment* die Skiausrüstung

**equipped** ADJECTIVE
- **equipped with** ausgerüstet mit
- **to be well equipped** gut ausgestattet sein

**equivalent** NOUN
das <u>Äquivalent</u> (PL die Äquivalente)
- **to be equivalent to something** einer Sache entsprechen ◊ *Twenty-five per cent is equivalent to a quarter.* Fünfundzwanzig Prozent entspricht einem Viertel.

**error** NOUN
der <u>Fehler</u> (PL die Fehler)

**escalator** NOUN
die <u>Rolltreppe</u>

**escape** NOUN
| see also **escape** VERB |
der <u>Ausbruch</u> (*from prison*) (PL die Ausbrüche)

to **escape** VERB
| see also **escape** NOUN |
<u>ausbrechen</u> (PRESENT bricht aus, IMPERFECT brach aus, PERFECT ist ausgebrochen) ◊ *A lion has escaped.* Ein Löwe ist ausgebrochen. ◊ *to escape from prison* aus dem Gefängnis ausbrechen

**escort** NOUN
die <u>Eskorte</u> ◊ *a police escort* eine Polizeieskorte

**Eskimo** NOUN
der <u>Eskimo</u> (PL die Eskimos)
die <u>Eskimofrau</u>

**especially** ADVERB

besonders ◊ *It's very hot there,
especially in the summer.* Dort ist es sehr
heiß, besonders im Sommer.

**essay** NOUN
der Aufsatz (PL die Aufsätze) ◊ *a history
essay* ein Aufsatz in Geschichte

**essential** ADJECTIVE
wichtig ◊ *It's essential to bring warm
clothes.* Es ist ganz wichtig, warme
Kleidung mitzubringen.

**estate** NOUN
die Siedlung (*housing estate*) ◊ *I live on
an estate.* Ich wohne in einer
Siedlung.

**estate agent** NOUN
der Immobilienmakler (PL die
Immobilienmakler)
die Immobilienmaklerin

**estate car** NOUN
der Kombiwagen (PL die Kombiwagen)

to **estimate** VERB
schätzen ◊ *They estimated it would take
three weeks.* Sie schätzten, dass es drei
Wochen dauern würde.

**etc** ABBREVIATION (= *et cetera*)
usw. (= und so weiter)

**Ethiopia** NOUN
Äthiopien NEUT ◊ *in Ethiopia* in Äthiopien

**ethnic** ADJECTIVE
[1] ethnisch (*racial*) ◊ *an ethnic minority*
eine ethnische Minderheit
[2] folkloristisch (*clothes, music*)

**EU** NOUN (= *European Union*)
die EU (= Europäische Union)

**euro** NOUN
der Euro (PL die Euros)

**Eurocheque** NOUN
der Euroscheck (PL die Euroschecks)

**Europe** NOUN
Europa NEUT
♦ **from Europe** aus Europa
♦ **in Europe** in Europa
♦ **to Europe** nach Europa

**European** ADJECTIVE
see also **European** NOUN
europäisch
♦ **He's European.** Er ist Europäer.

**European** NOUN
see also **European** ADJECTIVE
(*person*)
der Europäer (PL die Europäer)
die Europäerin

to **evacuate** VERB
evakuieren (PERFECT hat evakuiert)

**eve** NOUN
♦ **Christmas Eve** der Heilige Abend
♦ **New Year's Eve** Silvester NEUT

**even** ADVERB
see also **even** ADJECTIVE
sogar ◊ *I like all animals, even snakes.*
Ich mag alle Tiere, sogar Schlangen.

♦ **even if** selbst wenn ◊ *I'd never do that,
even if you asked me.* Ich würde das nie
tun, selbst wenn du mich darum bitten
würdest.
♦ **not even** nicht einmal ◊ *He never stops
working, not even at the weekend.* Er
hört nie auf zu arbeiten, nicht einmal am
Wochenende.
♦ **even though** obwohl ◊ *He's never got
any money, even though his parents are
quite rich.* Er hat nie Geld, obwohl seine
Eltern ziemlich reich sind.
♦ **I liked Hamburg even more than Munich.**
Hamburg hat mir noch besser gefallen
als München.

**even** ADJECTIVE
see also **even** ADVERB
gleichmäßig ◊ *an even layer of snow*
eine gleichmäßige Schneeschicht
♦ **an even number** eine gerade Zahl
♦ **to get even with somebody** es
jemandem heimzahlen ◊ *He wanted to
get even with her.* Er wollte es ihr
heimzahlen.

**evening** NOUN
der Abend (PL die Abende) ◊ *in the
evening* am Abend ◊ *all evening* den
ganzen Abend ◊ *yesterday evening*
gestern Abend ◊ *tomorrow evening*
morgen Abend
♦ **Good evening!** Guten Abend!

**evening class** NOUN
der Abendkurs (PL die Abendkurse)

**event** NOUN
das Ereignis (GEN des Ereignisses, PL die
Ereignisse)
♦ **a sporting event** eine Sportveranstaltung

**eventful** ADJECTIVE
ereignisreich

**eventual** ADJECTIVE
schließlich
♦ **the eventual outcome** das Endergebnis
*Be careful not to translate **eventual** by
**eventuell**.*

**eventually** ADVERB
schließlich

**ever** ADVERB
[1] schon einmal ◊ *Have you ever been
to America?* Warst du schon einmal in
Amerika? ◊ *Have you ever seen her?*
Hast du sie schon einmal gesehen?
[2] je ◊ *the best I've ever seen* das Beste,
was ich je gesehen habe
♦ **for the first time ever** das allererste
Mal
♦ **ever since** seit ◊ *ever since I met him* seit
ich ihn kenne
♦ **ever since then** seither

**every** ADJECTIVE
jeder ◊ *every pupil* jeder Schüler ◊ *every
day* jeden Tag
jede ◊ *every mother* jede Mutter ◊ *every
week* jede Woche

E

☞

jedes ◇ *every child* jedes Kind ◇ *every year* jedes Jahr

◆ **every time** jedes Mal ◇ *Every time I see him, he's depressed.* Jedes Mal, wenn ich ihn sehe, ist er deprimiert.

◆ **every now and then** ab und zu

**everybody** PRONOUN
1 alle ◇ *Everybody had a good time.* Alle hatten ihren Spaß.
2 jeder ◇ *Everybody makes mistakes.* Jeder macht mal Fehler.

**everyone** PRONOUN
1 alle ◇ *Everyone opened their presents.* Alle machten ihre Geschenke auf.
2 jeder ◇ *Everyone should have a hobby.* Jeder sollte ein Hobby haben.

**everything** PRONOUN
alles ◇ *You've thought of everything!* Du hast an alles gedacht! ◇ *Money isn't everything.* Geld ist nicht alles.

**everywhere** ADVERB
überall ◇ *I looked everywhere, but I couldn't find it.* Ich habe überall nachgesehen, habe es aber nirgends gefunden. ◇ *There were policemen everywhere.* Überall waren Polizisten.

**evil** ADJECTIVE
böse

**ex-** PREFIX
Ex- ◇ *his ex-wife* seine Ex-Frau

**exact** ADJECTIVE
genau

**exactly** ADVERB
genau ◇ *exactly the same* genau das gleiche ◇ *It's exactly ten o'clock.* Es ist genau zehn Uhr.

to **exaggerate** VERB
übertreiben (IMPERFECT übertrieb, PERFECT hat übertrieben)

**exaggeration** NOUN
die Übertreibung

**exam** NOUN
die Prüfung ◇ *a German exam* eine Deutschprüfung ◇ *the exam results* die Prüfungsergebnisse

**examination** NOUN
die Prüfung

◆ **a medical examination** eine ärztliche Untersuchung

to **examine** VERB
untersuchen (PERFECT hat untersucht) ◇ *The doctor examined him.* Der Arzt untersuchte ihn.

◆ **He examined her passport.** Er prüfte ihren Pass.

**examiner** NOUN
der Prüfer (PL die Prüfer)
die Prüferin

**example** NOUN
das Beispiel (PL die Beispiele)

◆ **for example** zum Beispiel

**excellent** ADJECTIVE

ausgezeichnet ◇ *Her results were excellent.* Ihre Noten waren ausgezeichnet.

**except** PREPOSITION
außer ◇ *everyone except me* alle außer mir

◆ **except for** abgesehen von ◇ *It was super except for the weather.* Abgesehen vom Wetter war es super.

◆ **except that** außer, dass ◇ *The weather was great, except that it was a bit cold.* Das Wetter war toll, außer dass es etwas kalt war.

**exception** NOUN
die Ausnahme ◇ *to make an exception* eine Ausnahme machen

**exceptional** ADJECTIVE
außergewöhnlich

**excess baggage** NOUN
das Übergewicht (PL die Übergewichte)

to **exchange** VERB
tauschen ◇ *I exchanged the book for a video.* Ich habe das Buch gegen ein Video getauscht.

**exchange rate** NOUN
der Wechselkurs (PL die Wechselkurse)

**excited** ADJECTIVE
aufgeregt

**exciting** ADJECTIVE
aufregend

**exclamation mark** NOUN
das Ausrufezeichen (PL die Ausrufezeichen)

**excuse** NOUN
| see also **excuse** VERB |
die Entschuldigung

to **excuse** VERB
| see also **excuse** NOUN |

◆ **Excuse me!** Entschuldigung!

**ex-directory** ADJECTIVE

◆ **She's ex-directory.** Ihre Nummer steht nicht im Telefonbuch.

to **execute** VERB
1 (*kill*)
hinrichten (PERFECT hat hingerichtet)
2 (*plan*)
ausführen (PERFECT hat ausgeführt)

**execution** NOUN
die Hinrichtung (*punishment*) ◇ *His execution took place yesterday.* Seine Hinrichtung fand gestern statt.

**executive** NOUN
(*in business*)
der leitende Angestellte (GEN des leitenden Angestellten, PL die leitenden Angestellten)
die leitende Angestellte (GEN der leitenden Angestellten) ◇ *He's an executive.* Er ist leitender Angestellter.

**exercise** NOUN
1 die Übung ◇ *an exercise book* ein Übungsheft

[2] die <u>Bewegung</u> ◊ *You need more exercise.* Sie brauchen mehr Bewegung.
♦**an exercise bike** ein Heimtrainer MASC
♦**She does her exercises every morning.** Sie macht jeden Morgen ihre Gymnastik.

**exhaust** NOUN
der <u>Auspuff</u>
♦**exhaust fumes** die Abgase PL

**exhausted** ADJECTIVE
erschöpft

**exhaust pipe** NOUN
das <u>Auspuffrohr</u> (PL die Auspuffrohre)

**exhibition** NOUN
die <u>Ausstellung</u>

to **exist** VERB
existieren (PERFECT hat existiert)
♦**It doesn't exist.** Das gibt es nicht.

**exit** NOUN
der <u>Ausgang</u> (*way out*) (PL die Ausgänge)

**exotic** ADJECTIVE
exotisch

to **expect** VERB
[1] erwarten (PERFECT hat erwartet) ◊ *I'm expecting him for dinner.* Ich erwarte ihn zum Abendessen. ◊ *She's expecting a baby.* Sie erwartet ein Kind. ◊ *I didn't expect that from him.* Das habe ich von ihm nicht erwartet.
[2] annehmen (PRESENT nimmt an, IMPERFECT nahm an, PERFECT hat angenommen) ◊ *I expect he'll be late.* Ich nehme an, dass er sich verspäten wird. ◊ *I expect so.* Das nehme ich mal an.

**expedition** NOUN
die <u>Expedition</u>

to **expel** VERB
♦**to get expelled** (*from school*) von der Schule verwiesen werden

**expenses** PL NOUN
die <u>Kosten</u> PL

**expensive** ADJECTIVE
teuer

**experience** NOUN
see also **experience** VERB
die <u>Erfahrung</u>

to **experience** VERB
see also **experience** NOUN
[1] haben (PRESENT hat, IMPERFECT hatte, PERFECT hat gehabt) ◊ *They're experiencing some problems.* Sie haben einige Probleme.
[2] (*feel*)
empfinden (IMPERFECT empfand, PERFECT hat empfunden) ◊ *He experienced fear and excitement.* Er empfand Angst und Aufregung.

**experienced** ADJECTIVE
erfahren

**experiment** NOUN
das <u>Experiment</u> (PL die Experimente)

**expert** NOUN

der <u>Fachmann</u> (PL die Fachleute)
die <u>Fachfrau</u>
◊ *He's a computer expert.* Er ist ein Computerfachmann.
♦**He's an expert cook.** Er kocht ausgezeichnet.

to **expire** VERB
ablaufen (*passport*) (PRESENT läuft ab, IMPERFECT lief ab, PERFECT ist abgelaufen)

to **explain** VERB
erklären (PERFECT hat erklärt)

**explanation** NOUN
die <u>Erklärung</u>

to **explode** VERB
explodieren (PERFECT ist explodiert)

to **exploit** VERB
ausbeuten (PERFECT hat ausgebeutet)

**exploitation** NOUN
die <u>Ausbeutung</u>

to **explore** VERB
erkunden (*place*) (PERFECT hat erkundet)

**explorer** NOUN
der <u>Forscher</u> (PL die Forscher)
die <u>Forscherin</u>

**explosion** NOUN
die <u>Explosion</u>

**explosive** ADJECTIVE
see also **explosive** NOUN
explosiv

**explosive** NOUN
see also **explosive** ADJECTIVE
der <u>Sprengstoff</u> (PL die Sprengstoffe)

to **export** VERB
exportieren (PERFECT hat exportiert)

to **express** VERB
ausdrücken (PERFECT hat ausgedrückt)
♦**to express oneself** sich ausdrücken ◊ *It's not easy to express oneself in a foreign language.* Es ist nicht einfach, sich in einer fremden Sprache auszudrücken.

**expression** NOUN
der <u>Ausdruck</u> (PL die Ausdrücke)
♦**It's an English expression.** Das ist eine englische Redewendung.

**expressway** NOUN US
die <u>Schnellstraße</u>

**extension** NOUN
[1] (*of building*)
der <u>Anbau</u> (PL die Anbauten)
[2] (*telephone*)
der <u>Apparat</u> (PL die Apparate)
♦**Extension 3137, please.** Apparat 3137, bitte.

**extensive** ADJECTIVE
[1] ausgedehnt ◊ *The hotel is situated in extensive grounds.* Das Hotel liegt auf einem ausgedehnten Gelände.
[2] umfangreich ◊ *My brother has an extensive knowledge of this subject.* Mein Bruder verfügt auf diesem Gebiet über ein umfangreiches Wissen.
♦**extensive damage** schwere Schäden PL

E

**extensively** ADVERB
viel ◊ *He has travelled extensively.* Er ist
viel gereist.

**extent** NOUN
♦ **to some extent** in gewisser Weise

**exterior** ADJECTIVE
äußere ◊ *the exterior walls* die äußeren
Wände

**extinct** ADJECTIVE
♦ **to become extinct** aussterben
♦ **to be extinct** ausgestorben sein ◊ *The
species is almost extinct.* Diese Art ist
fast ausgestorben.

**extinguisher** NOUN
der Feuerlöscher (*fire extinguisher*) (PL die
Feuerlöscher)

**extortionate** ADJECTIVE
überzogen

**extra** ADJECTIVE, ADVERB
zusätzlich ◊ *an extra blanket* eine
zusätzliche Decke
♦ **to pay extra** extra bezahlen
♦ **Breakfast is extra.** Frühstück wird extra
berechnet.
♦ **It costs extra.** Das kostet extra.

**extraordinary** ADJECTIVE
außergewöhnlich

**extravagant** ADJECTIVE
verschwenderisch (*person*)

**extreme** ADJECTIVE
extrem

**extremely** ADVERB
äußerst

**extremist** NOUN
der Extremist (GEN des Extremisten, PL die
Extremisten)
die Extremistin

**eye** NOUN
das Auge (PL die Augen) ◊ *I've got green
eyes.* Ich habe grüne Augen.
♦ **to keep an eye on something** auf etwas
aufpassen

**eyebrow** NOUN
die Augenbraue

**eyelash** NOUN
die Wimper

**eyelid** NOUN
das Augenlid (PL die Augenlider)

**eyeliner** NOUN
der Eyeliner (PL die Eyeliner)

**eye shadow** NOUN
der Lidschatten (PL die Lidschatten)

**eyesight** NOUN
das Sehvermögen ◊ *Her eyesight is
deteriorating.* Ihr Sehvermögen lässt
nach.
♦ **to have good eyesight** gute Augen
haben

# F

**fabric** NOUN
der Stoff (PL die Stoffe)

**fabulous** ADJECTIVE
traumhaft ◊ *The show was fabulous.* Die Show war traumhaft.

**face** NOUN

> see also **face** VERB

[1] (*of person*)
das Gesicht (PL die Gesichter)
[2] (*of clock*)
das Zifferblatt (PL die Zifferblätter)
[3] (*of cliff*)
die Wand (PL die Wände)

- **on the face of it** auf den ersten Blick
- **in the face of these difficulties** angesichts dieser Schwierigkeiten
- **face to face** Auge in Auge
- **a face cloth** ein Waschlappen MASC

to **face** VERB

> see also **face** NOUN

konfrontiert sein mit (*place, problem*) (PRESENT ist konfrontiert mit, IMPERFECT war konfrontiert mit, PERFECT ist konfrontiert gewesen mit)

- **to face up to something** sich einer Sache stellen ◊ *You must face up to your responsibilities.* Sie müssen sich Ihrer Verantwortung stellen.

**facilities** PL NOUN
die Einrichtungen FEM PL

- **This school has excellent facilities.** Diese Schule ist ausgezeichnet ausgestattet.
- **toilet facilities** Toiletten FEM PL
- **cooking facilities** die Kochgelegenheit SING

**fact** NOUN
die Tatsache

- **in fact** tatsächlich

**factory** NOUN
die Fabrik

to **fade** VERB

[1] (*colour*)
verblassen (PERFECT ist verblasst) ◊ *The colour has faded in the sun.* Die Farbe ist in der Sonne verblasst.

- **My jeans have faded.** Meine Jeans sind verbleicht.

[2] schwächer werden (PRESENT wird schwächer, IMPERFECT wurde schwächer, PERFECT ist schwächer geworden) ◊ *The light was fading fast.* Das Licht wurde schnell schwächer.

[3] abnehmen (PRESENT nimmt ab, IMPERFECT nahm ab, PERFECT hat abgenommen) ◊ *The noise gradually faded.* Der Lärm nahm allmählich ab.

**fag** NOUN
die Kippe (*informal: cigarette*)

to **fail** VERB

> see also **fail** NOUN

[1] durchfallen in +DAT (PRESENT fällt durch, IMPERFECT fiel durch, PERFECT ist durchgefallen) ◊ *I failed the history exam.* Ich bin in der Geschichtsprüfung durchgefallen.

[2] durchfallen ◊ *In our class, no one failed.* In unserer Klasse ist niemand durchgefallen.

[3] versagen (PERFECT hat versagt) ◊ *My brakes failed.* Meine Bremsen haben versagt.

- **to fail to do something** etwas nicht tun ◊ *She failed to return her library books.* Sie hat die Bücher aus der Bücherei nicht zurückgebracht.

**fail** NOUN

> see also **fail** VERB

- **without fail** ganz bestimmt

**failure** NOUN

[1] das Versagen ◊ *a mechanical failure* ein mechanisches Versagen

- **feelings of failure** das Gefühl zu versagen

[2] der Versager (PL die Versager)
die Versagerin
◊ *He's a failure.* Er ist ein Versager.

**faint** ADJECTIVE

> see also **faint** VERB

schwach ◊ *His voice was very faint.* Seine Stimme war sehr schwach.

- **I feel faint.** Mir ist schwindlig.

to **faint** VERB

> see also **faint** ADJECTIVE

ohnmächtig werden (PRESENT wird ohnmächtig, IMPERFECT wurde ohnmächtig, PERFECT ist ohnmächtig geworden) ◊ *All of a sudden she fainted.* Plötzlich wurde sie ohnmächtig.

**fair** ADJECTIVE

> see also **fair** NOUN

[1] fair ◊ *That's not fair.* Das ist nicht fair.
[2] blond (*hair*) ◊ *He's got fair hair.* Er hat blonde Haare.
[3] hell (*skin*) ◊ *people with fair skin* Menschen mit heller Haut
[4] schön (*weather*) ◊ *The weather was fair.* Das Wetter war schön.
[5] gut (*good enough*) ◊ *I have a fair chance of winning.* Ich habe gute Gewinnchancen.
[6] ordentlich (*sizeable*) ◊ *That's a fair distance.* Das ist eine ordentliche Entfernung.

**fair** NOUN

> see also **fair** ADJECTIVE

☞

das <u>Volksfest</u> (PL die Volksfeste) ◊ *They went to the fair.* Sie sind aufs Volksfest gegangen.
◆ **a trade fair** eine Handelsmesse
**fairground** NOUN
　der <u>Rummelplatz</u> (PL die Rummelplätze)
**fair-haired** ADJECTIVE
　<u>blond</u>
**fairly** ADVERB
　[1] <u>gerecht</u> ◊ *The cake was divided fairly.* Der Kuchen wurde gerecht verteilt.
　[2] <u>ziemlich</u> (*quite*) ◊ *That's fairly good.* Das ist ziemlich gut.
**fairness** NOUN
　die <u>Fairness</u>
**fairy** NOUN
　die <u>Fee</u>
**fairy tale** NOUN
　das <u>Märchen</u> (PL die Märchen)
**faith** NOUN
　[1] der <u>Glaube</u> (GEN des Glaubens) ◊ *the Catholic faith* der katholische Glaube
　[2] das <u>Vertrauen</u> ◊ *People have lost faith in the government.* Die Menschen haben das Vertrauen in die Regierung verloren.
**faithful** ADJECTIVE
　<u>treu</u>
**faithfully** ADVERB
◆ **Yours faithfully ...** (*in letter*) Hochachtungsvoll ...
**fake** NOUN
　see also **fake** ADJECTIVE
　die <u>Fälschung</u> ◊ *The painting was a fake.* Das Gemälde war eine Fälschung.
**fake** ADJECTIVE
　see also **fake** NOUN
　<u>gefälscht</u> ◊ *a fake certificate* eine gefälschte Urkunde
◆ **She wore fake fur.** Sie trug eine Pelzimitation.
**fall** NOUN
　see also **fall** VERB
　[1] der <u>Sturz</u> (GEN des Sturzes, PL die Stürze)
◆ **She had a nasty fall.** Sie ist übel gestürzt.
◆ **a fall of snow** ein Schneefall MASC
◆ **the Niagara Falls** die Niagarafälle
　[2] [US] (*autumn*)
　der <u>Herbst</u> (PL die Herbste)
　◊ *in fall* im Herbst
to **fall** VERB
　see also **fall** NOUN
　[1] <u>hinfallen</u> (PRESENT fällt hin, IMPERFECT fiel hin, PERFECT ist hingefallen) ◊ *He tripped and fell.* Er ist gestolpert und hingefallen.
　[2] <u>fallen</u> ◊ *Prices are falling.* Die Preise fallen.
◆ **to fall apart** auseinander fallen ◊ *The book fell apart when he opened it.* Das Buch fiel auseinander, als er es öffnete.

◆ **to fall down (1)** (*person*) hinfallen ◊ *She's fallen down.* Sie ist hingefallen.
◆ **to fall down (2)** (*building*) einfallen ◊ *The wall fell down.* Die Mauer ist eingefallen.
◆ **to fall for (1)** hereinfallen auf +ACC ◊ *They fell for it.* Sie sind darauf hereingefallen.
◆ **to fall for (2)** sich verlieben in +ACC ◊ *She's falling for him.* Sie ist dabei, sich in ihn zu verlieben.
◆ **to fall off** herunterfallen von ◊ *The book fell off the shelf.* Das Buch ist vom Regal heruntergefallen.
◆ **to fall out** sich zerstreiten ◊ *Sarah's fallen out with her boyfriend.* Sarah hat sich mit ihrem Freund zerstritten.
◆ **to fall through** ins Wasser fallen ◊ *Our plans have fallen through.* Unsere Pläne sind ins Wasser gefallen.
**false** ADJECTIVE
　<u>falsch</u>
◆ **a false alarm** falscher Alarm
◆ **false teeth** das Gebiss
**fame** NOUN
　der <u>Ruhm</u>
**familiar** ADJECTIVE
　<u>vertraut</u> ◊ *a familiar face* ein vertrautes Gesicht
◆ **to be familiar with something** mit etwas vertraut sein ◊ *I'm familiar with his work.* Ich bin mit seiner Arbeit vertraut.
**family** NOUN
　die <u>Familie</u>
◆ **the Airlie family** die Familie Airlie
**famine** NOUN
　die <u>Hungersnot</u> (PL die Hungersnöte)
**famous** ADJECTIVE
　<u>berühmt</u>
**fan** NOUN
　[1] (*hand-held*)
　der <u>Fächer</u> (PL die Fächer)
　[2] (*electric*)
　der <u>Ventilator</u> (PL die Ventilatoren)
　[3] (*of person, band, sport*)
　der <u>Fan</u> (PL die Fans)
　*der Fan is also used for women.*
　◊ *I'm a fan of Oasis.* Ich bin ein Fan von Oasis. ◊ *football fans* Fußballfans
**fanatic** NOUN
　der <u>Fanatiker</u> (PL die Fanatiker)
　die <u>Fanatikerin</u>
to **fancy** VERB
◆ **to fancy something** Lust auf etwas haben ◊ *I fancy an ice cream.* Ich habe Lust auf ein Eis.
◆ **to fancy doing something** Lust haben, etwas zu tun
◆ **He fancies her.** Er steht auf sie.
**fancy dress** NOUN
　das <u>Kostüm</u> (PL die Kostüme)
◆ **He was wearing fancy dress.** Er war kostümiert.
◆ **a fancy-dress ball** ein Kostümball MASC
**fantastic** ADJECTIVE

fantastisch

**far** ADJECTIVE, ADVERB
weit ◊ *Is it far?* Ist es weit? ◊ *How far is it?* Wie weit ist es? ◊ *How far is it to Geneva?* Wie weit ist es nach Genf?
♦ **far from (1)** weit entfernt von ◊ *It's not far from London.* Es ist nicht weit von London entfernt.
♦ **far from (2)** überhaupt nicht ◊ *It's far from easy.* Es ist überhaupt nicht einfach.
♦ **How far have you got?** (*with a task*) Wie weit bist du gekommen?
♦ **at the far end** am anderen Ende ◊ *at the far end of the room* am anderen Ende des Zimmers
♦ **far better** viel besser
♦ **as far as I know** soviel ich weiß

**fare** NOUN
der Fahrpreis (PL die Fahrpreise)
♦ **half fare** halber Preis
♦ **full fare** voller Preis

**Far East** NOUN
der Ferne Osten ◊ *in the Far East* im Fernen Osten

**farm** NOUN
der Bauernhof (PL die Bauernhöfe)

**farmer** NOUN
der Bauer (GEN des Bauern, PL die Bauern)
die Bäuerin
◊ *He's a farmer.* Er ist Bauer.

**farmhouse** NOUN
das Bauernhaus (GEN des Bauernhauses, PL die Bauernhäuser)

**farming** NOUN
die Landwirtschaft
♦ **dairy farming** die Milchwirtschaft

**fascinating** ADJECTIVE
faszinierend

**fashion** NOUN
die Mode
♦ **in fashion** in Mode

**fashionable** ADJECTIVE
modisch ◊ *Jane wears very fashionable clothes.* Jane trägt sehr modische Kleidung.
♦ **a fashionable restaurant** ein Restaurant, das in Mode ist

**fast** ADJECTIVE, ADVERB
schnell ◊ *He can run fast.* Er kann schnell laufen. ◊ *a fast car* ein schnelles Auto
♦ **That clock's fast.** Die Uhr geht vor.
♦ **He's fast asleep.** Er schläft fest.
*Be careful not to translate **fast** by the German word **fast**.*

**fat** ADJECTIVE
see also **fat** NOUN
dick (*person*)

**fat** NOUN
see also **fat** ADJECTIVE
das Fett (PL die Fette)
♦ **It's very high in fat.** Es ist sehr fett.

**fatal** ADJECTIVE

[1] tödlich (*causing death*) ◊ *a fatal accident* ein tödlicher Unfall
[2] fatal (*disastrous*) ◊ *He made a fatal mistake.* Er machte einen fatalen Fehler.

**father** NOUN
der Vater (PL die Väter) ◊ *my father* mein Vater
♦ **Father Christmas** der Weihnachtsmann

**father-in-law** NOUN
der Schwiegervater (PL die Schwiegerväter)

**faucet** NOUN US
der Wasserhahn (PL die Wasserhähne)

**fault** NOUN
[1] (*mistake*)
die Schuld ◊ *It's my fault.* Es ist meine Schuld.
[2] (*defect*)
der Fehler (PL die Fehler) ◊ *a mechanical fault* ein mechanischer Fehler

**faulty** ADJECTIVE
defekt ◊ *This machine is faulty.* Die Maschine ist defekt.

**favour** NOUN (US **favor**)
der Gefallen (PL die Gefallen)
♦ **to do somebody a favour** jemandem einen Gefallen tun ◊ *Could you do me a favour?* Könntest du mir einen Gefallen tun?
♦ **to be in favour of something** für etwas sein ◊ *I'm in favour of nuclear disarmament.* Ich bin für nukleare Abrüstung.

**favourite** ADJECTIVE (US **favorite**)
see also **favourite** NOUN
♦ **Blue's my favourite colour.** Blau ist meine Lieblingsfarbe.

**favourite** NOUN (US **favorite**)
see also **favourite** ADJECTIVE
[1] der Liebling (PL die Lieblinge)
*der Liebling is also used for women.*
◊ *She's his favourite.* Sie ist sein Liebling.
[2] der Favorit (PL die Favoriten)
die Favoritin
◊ *Liverpool are favourites to win the Cup.* Der FC Liverpool ist Favorit für den Pokal.

**fax** NOUN
see also **fax** VERB
das Fax (GEN des Fax, PL die Faxe)

to **fax** VERB
see also **fax** NOUN
faxen

**fear** NOUN
see also **fear** VERB
die Furcht

to **fear** VERB
see also **fear** NOUN
befürchten (PERFECT hat befürchtet) ◊ *You have nothing to fear.* Sie haben nichts zu befürchten.

**feather** NOUN

☞

**F**

die Feder
**feature** NOUN
die Eigenschaft (*of person, object*) ◊ *an important feature* eine wichtige Eigenschaft
**February** NOUN
der Februar ◊ *in February* im Februar
**fed** VERB *see* **feed**
**fed up** ADJECTIVE
◆**to be fed up with something** etwas satt haben ◊ *I'm fed up with him.* Ich habe ihn satt.
to **feed** VERB
füttern ◊ *Have you fed the cat?* Hast du die Katze gefüttert?
◆**He worked hard to feed his family.** Er arbeitete hart, um seine Familie zu ernähren.
to **feel** VERB
[1] sich fühlen ◊ *I don't feel well.* Ich fühle mich nicht wohl. ◊ *I feel a bit lonely.* Ich fühle mich etwas einsam.
[2] spüren ◊ *I didn't feel much pain.* Ich habe keine großen Schmerzen gespürt.
[3] befühlen (PERFECT hat befühlt) ◊ *The doctor felt his forehead.* Der Arzt hat ihm die Stirn befühlt.
◆**I was feeling hungry.** Ich hatte Hunger.
◆**I was feeling cold, so I went inside.** Mir war kalt, also bin ich ins Haus gegangen.
◆**I feel like ...** (*want*) Ich habe Lust auf ... ◊ *Do you feel like an ice cream?* Hast du Lust auf ein Eis?
**feeling** NOUN
das Gefühl (PL die Gefühle) ◊ *a feeling of satisfaction* ein Gefühl der Befriedigung
◆**an itchy feeling** ein Jucken NEUT
**feet** PL NOUN *see* **foot**
**fell** VERB *see* **fall**
**felt** VERB *see* **feel**
**felt-tip pen** NOUN
der Filzschreiber (PL die Filzschreiber)
**female** ADJECTIVE
| *see also* **female** NOUN |
weiblich ◊ *a female animal* ein weibliches Tier ◊ *the female sex* das weibliche Geschlecht
*In many cases, the ending indicates clearly whether the noun refers to a man or a woman and there is therefore no need for the word* **female**.
◊ *male and female students* Studenten und Studentinnen
**female** NOUN
| *see also* **female** ADJECTIVE |
das Weibchen (*animal*) (PL die Weibchen)
**feminine** ADJECTIVE
feminin
**feminist** NOUN
der Feminist (GEN des Feministen, PL die Feministen)
die Feministin

**fence** NOUN
der Zaun (PL die Zäune)
**fern** NOUN
der Farn (PL die Farne)
**ferocious** ADJECTIVE
wild
**ferry** NOUN
die Fähre
**fertile** ADJECTIVE
fruchtbar
**fertilizer** NOUN
das Düngemittel (PL die Düngemittel)
**festival** NOUN
das Festival (PL die Festivals) ◊ *a jazz festival* ein Jazzfestival
to **fetch** VERB
[1] holen ◊ *Fetch the bucket.* Hol den Eimer.
[2] (*sell for*)
einbringen (IMPERFECT brachte ein, PERFECT hat eingebracht) ◊ *His painting fetched five thousand pounds.* Sein Bild hat fünftausend Pfund eingebracht.
**fever** NOUN
das Fieber (*temperature*)
**few** ADJECTIVE, PRONOUN
wenige (*not many*) ◊ *few books* wenige Bücher
◆**a few** ein paar ◊ *a few hours* ein paar Stunden ◊ *How many apples do you want? – A few.* Wie viele Äpfel willst du? – Ein paar.
◆**quite a few people** einige Leute
**fewer** ADJECTIVE
weniger ◊ *There are fewer people than there were yesterday.* Es sind weniger Leute da als gestern. ◊ *There are fewer pupils in this class.* In dieser Klasse sind weniger Schüler.
**fiancé** NOUN
der Verlobte (GEN des Verlobten, PL die Verlobten) ◊ *He's my fiancé.* Er ist mein Verlobter.
**fiancée** NOUN
die Verlobte (GEN der Verlobten, PL die Verlobten) ◊ *She's my fiancée.* Sie ist meine Verlobte.
**fiction** NOUN
die Romane MASC PL (*novels*)
**field** NOUN
[1] (*in countryside*)
das Feld (PL die Felder) ◊ *a field of wheat* ein Weizenfeld
[2] (*for sport*)
der Platz (GEN des Platzes, PL die Plätze) ◊ *a football field* ein Fußballplatz
[3] (*subject*)
das Gebiet (PL die Gebiete) ◊ *He's an expert in his field.* Er ist Fachmann auf seinem Gebiet.
**fierce** ADJECTIVE
[1] gefährlich ◊ *The dog looked very fierce.* Der Hund sah sehr gefährlich aus.

2 heftig ◊ *a fierce attack* ein heftiger Angriff
♦**The wind was very fierce.** Es wehte ein sehr scharfer Wind.

**fifteen** NUMBER
fünfzehn ◊ *I'm fifteen.* Ich bin fünfzehn.

**fifteenth** ADJECTIVE
fünfzehnte
♦**the fifteenth of August** der fünfzehnte August

**fifth** ADJECTIVE
fünfte ◊ *the fifth floor* der fünfte Stock
♦**the fifth of August** der fünfte August

**fifty** NUMBER
fünfzig ◊ *He's fifty.* Er ist fünfzig.

**fifty-fifty** ADJECTIVE, ADVERB
halbe-halbe ◊ *They split the prize money fifty-fifty.* Sie teilten das Preisgeld halbe-halbe.
♦**a fifty-fifty chance** eine fifty-fifty Chance

**fight** NOUN
see also **fight** VERB
1 die Schlägerei ◊ *There was a fight in the pub.* In der Kneipe gab es eine Schlägerei.
2 der Kampf (PL die Kämpfe) ◊ *the fight against cancer* der Kampf gegen Krebs

to **fight** VERB
see also **fight** NOUN
1 (*physically*)
sich prügeln ◊ *They were fighting.* Sie haben sich geprügelt.
2 (*quarrel*)
streiten (IMPERFECT stritt, PERFECT hat gestritten) ◊ *He's always fighting with his wife.* Er streitet dauernd mit seiner Frau.
3 (*combat*)
bekämpfen (PERFECT hat bekämpft) ◊ *The doctors tried to fight the disease.* Die Ärzte versuchten, die Krankheit zu bekämpfen.

to **fight back** VERB
sich wehren

**fighting** NOUN
die Schlägerei ◊ *Fighting broke out outside the pub.* Vor der Kneipe kam es zu einer Schlägerei.

**figure** NOUN
1 die Zahl (*number*) ◊ *Can you give me the exact figures?* Können Sie mir genaue Zahlen nennen?
2 die Gestalt (*outline of person*) ◊ *Mary saw the figure of a man on the bridge.* Mary sah die Gestalt eines Mannes auf der Brücke.
3 die Figur (*shape*) ◊ *She's got a good figure.* Sie hat eine gute Figur. ◊ *I have to watch my figure.* Ich muss auf meine Figur achten.
4 die Persönlichkeit (*personality*) ◊ *She's an important political figure.* Sie ist eine wichtige politische Persönlichkeit.

to **figure out** VERB
1 ausrechnen (PERFECT hat ausgerechnet) ◊ *I'll try to figure out how much it'll cost.* Ich versuche auszurechnen, wie viel das kostet.
2 herausfinden (IMPERFECT fand heraus, PERFECT hat herausgefunden) ◊ *I couldn't figure out what it meant.* Ich konnte nicht herausfinden, was das bedeutet.
3 schlau werden aus (PRESENT wird schlau, IMPERFECT wurde schlau, PERFECT ist schlau geworden) ◊ *I can't figure him out at all.* Ich werde aus ihm überhaupt nicht schlau.

**file** NOUN
see also **file** VERB
1 (*document*)
die Akte ◊ *Have we got a file on the suspect?* Haben wir über den Verdächtigen eine Akte?
2 (*folder*)
die Aktenmappe ◊ *She keeps all her letters in a cardboard file.* Sie bewahrt all ihre Briefe in einer Aktenmappe auf.
3 (*ring binder*)
der Aktenordner (PL die Aktenordner)
4 (*on computer*)
die Datei
5 (*for nails, metal*)
die Feile

to **file** VERB
see also **file** NOUN
1 (*papers*)
abheften (PERFECT hat abgeheftet)
2 (*nails, metal*)
feilen ◊ *I'll have to file my nails.* Ich muss mir die Nägel feilen.

to **fill** VERB
füllen ◊ *She filled the glass with water.* Sie füllte das Glas mit Wasser.
♦**to fill in (1)** ausfüllen ◊ *Can you fill this form in, please?* Können Sie bitte dieses Formular ausfüllen?
♦**to fill in (2)** auffüllen ◊ *He filled the hole in with soil.* Er füllte das Loch mit Erde auf.
♦**to fill up** voll machen ◊ *He filled the cup up to the brim.* Er machte die Tasse bis zum Rand voll.
♦**Fill it up, please.** (*at petrol station*) Voll tanken, bitte.

**film** NOUN
der Film (PL die Filme)

**film star** NOUN
der Filmstar (PL die Filmstars)
*der Filmstar is also used for women.*
◊ *She's a film star.* Sie ist ein Filmstar.

**filthy** ADJECTIVE
schmutzig

**final** ADJECTIVE
see also **final** NOUN
1 letzte (*last*) ◊ *our final match of the season* unser letztes Spiel der Saison

F

☞

[2] endgültig (*definite*) ◊ *a final decision*
eine endgültige Entscheidung
◆ **I'm not going and that's final.** Ich gehe
nicht, und damit basta.
**final** NOUN
see also **final** ADJECTIVE
das Finale (PL die Finale) ◊ *Boris Becker
is in the final.* Boris Becker ist im Finale.
**finally** ADVERB
[1] schließlich (*lastly*) ◊ *Finally, I would
like to say ...* Und schließlich möchte ich
sagen ...
[2] letztendlich (*eventually*) ◊ *They finally
decided to leave on Saturday instead of
Friday.* Sie haben letztendlich
beschlossen, am Samstag statt am
Freitag zu fahren.
**financial** ADJECTIVE
finanziell
to **find** VERB
finden (IMPERFECT fand, PERFECT hat
gefunden) ◊ *I can't find the exit.* Ich kann
den Ausgang nicht finden. ◊ *Did you find
your pen?* Hast du deinen Schreiber
gefunden?
◆ **to find something out** etwas
herausfinden ◊ *I'm determined to find
out the truth.* Ich bin entschlossen, die
Wahrheit herauszufinden.
◆ **to find out about (1)** (*make enquiries*) sich
erkundigen nach ◊ *Try to find out about
the cost of a hotel.* Versuche, dich nach
dem Preis für ein Hotel zu erkundigen.
◆ **to find out about (2)** (*by chance*) erfahren
◊ *I found out about their affair.* Ich habe
von ihrem Verhältnis erfahren.
**fine** ADJECTIVE, ADVERB
see also **fine** NOUN
[1] ausgezeichnet (*very good*) ◊ *He's a
fine musician.* Er ist ein ausgezeichneter
Musiker.
◆ **How are you? – I'm fine.** Wie geht's? –
Gut!
◆ **I feel fine.** Mir geht's gut.
◆ **The weather is fine today.** Das Wetter ist
heute schön.
[2] fein (*not coarse*) ◊ *She's got very fine
hair.* Sie hat sehr feine Haare.
**fine** NOUN
see also **fine** ADJECTIVE
[1] die Geldbuße ◊ *She got a fifty-pound
fine.* Sie hat eine Geldbuße von fünfzig
Pfund bekommen.
[2] (*for traffic offence*)
der Strafzettel (PL die Strafzettel) ◊ *I got a
fine for driving through a red light.* Ich
habe einen Strafzettel bekommen, weil
ich bei Rot über die Ampel gefahren bin.
**finger** NOUN
der Finger (PL die Finger)
◆ **my little finger** mein kleiner Finger
**fingernail** NOUN
der Fingernagel (PL die Fingernägel)

**finish** NOUN
see also **finish** VERB
das Finish (*of race*) (PL die Finishs) ◊ *We
saw the finish of the London Marathon.*
Wir sahen das Finish des Londoner
Marathonlaufs.
to **finish** VERB
see also **finish** NOUN
[1] fertig sein (PRESENT ist fertig, IMPERFECT
war fertig, PERFECT ist fertig gewesen)
◊ *I've finished!* Ich bin fertig!
[2] zu Ende sein (PRESENT ist zu Ende,
IMPERFECT war zu Ende, PERFECT ist zu Ende
gewesen) ◊ *The film has finished.* Der
Film ist zu Ende.
◆ **I've finished the book.** Ich habe das Buch
zu Ende gelesen.
◆ **to finish doing something** etwas zu Ende
machen ◊ *Let me finish writing this
letter.* Lass mich den Brief zu Ende
schreiben.
**Finland** NOUN
Finnland NEUT
◆ **from Finland** aus Finnland
◆ **to Finland** nach Finnland
**Finn** NOUN
der Finne (GEN des Finnen, PL die
Finnen)
die Finnin
**Finnish** ADJECTIVE
see also **Finnish** NOUN
finnisch
◆ **She's Finnish.** Sie ist Finnin.
**Finnish** NOUN
see also **Finnish** ADJECTIVE
(*language*)
das Finnisch (GEN des Finnischen)
**fir** NOUN
die Tanne
◆ **fir cone** der Tannenzapfen
◆ **fir tree** der Tannenbaum
**fire** NOUN
see also **fire** VERB
[1] das Feuer (PL die Feuer) ◊ *He made a
fire to warm himself up.* Er machte ein
Feuer, um sich aufzuwärmen.
◆ **to be on fire** brennen
[2] (*accidental*)
der Brand (PL die Brände)
◆ **The house was destroyed by fire.** Das
Haus ist abgebrannt.
[3] (*heater*)
die Heizung ◊ *Turn the fire on.* Mach die
Heizung an.
◆ **the fire brigade** die Feuerwehr
◆ **a fire alarm** ein Feueralarm MASC
◆ **a fire engine** ein Feuerwehrauto NEUT
◆ **a fire escape** (*stairs*) eine Feuertreppe
◆ **a fire extinguisher** ein Feuerlöscher
MASC
◆ **a fire station** eine Feuerwehrstation
to **fire** VERB
see also **fire** NOUN

schießen (*shoot*) (IMPERFECT schoss, PERFECT hat geschossen) ◊ *She fired twice.* Sie hat zweimal geschossen.

♦ **to fire at somebody** auf jemanden schießen ◊ *The terrorist fired at the crowd.* Der Terrorist hat in die Menge geschossen.

♦ **to fire a gun** einen Schuss abgeben

♦ **to fire somebody** jemanden feuern ◊ *He was fired from his job.* Er wurde aus seinem Job gefeuert.

**fireman** NOUN
der Feuerwehrmann (PL die Feuerwehrleute) ◊ *He's a fireman.* Er ist Feuerwehrmann.

**fireplace** NOUN
der offene Kamin (PL die offenen Kamine)

**fireworks** PL NOUN
das Feuerwerk (PL die Feuerwerke) ◊ *Are you going to see the fireworks?* Seht ihr euch das Feuerwerk an?

**firm** ADJECTIVE
see also **firm** NOUN
streng ◊ *to be firm with somebody* streng mit jemandem sein

**firm** NOUN
see also **firm** ADJECTIVE
die Firma (PL die Firmen) ◊ *He works for a large firm in London.* Er arbeitet für eine große Firma in London.

**first** ADJECTIVE, ADVERB
see also **first** NOUN
[1] erste ◊ *my first boyfriend* mein erster Freund ◊ *the first time* das erste Mal

♦ **Rachel came first.** (*in exam, race*) Rachel war Erste.

♦ **John came first.** (*in exam, race*) John war Erster. ◊ *the first of August* der erste August

[2] zuerst ◊ *I want to get a job, but first I have to pass my exams.* Ich will mir einen Job suchen, aber zuerst muss ich meine Prüfung bestehen.

♦ **first of all** zuallererst

**first** NOUN
see also **first** ADJECTIVE
der Erste (GEN des Ersten, PL die Ersten)
die Erste (GEN der Ersten) ◊ *She was the first to arrive.* Sie ist als Erste angekommen.

♦ **at first** zuerst

**first aid** NOUN
die erste Hilfe

♦ **a first aid kit** ein Verbandszeug NEUT

**first-class** ADJECTIVE
[1] erster Klasse ◊ *She has booked a first-class ticket.* Sie hat ein Ticket erster Klasse gebucht.

[2] erstklassig ◊ *a first-class meal* ein erstklassiges Essen

🛈 *In Germany there is no first-class or second-class post. However, letters cost more to send than postcards, so you have to remember to say what you are sending when buying stamps. There is also an express service.*

**firstly** ADVERB
[1] zuerst ◊ *Firstly, let's see what the book is about.* Wir wollen erst mal sehen, wovon das Buch handelt.

[2] erstens ◊ *firstly ... secondly ...* erstens ... zweitens ...

**fish** NOUN
see also **fish** VERB
der Fisch (PL die Fische) ◊ *I caught three fish.* Ich habe drei Fische gefangen.

to **fish** VERB
see also **fish** NOUN
fischen

♦ **to go fishing** fischen gehen ◊ *We went fishing in the River Dee.* Wir haben im River Dee gefischt.

**fisherman** NOUN
der Fischer (PL die Fischer) ◊ *He's a fisherman.* Er ist Fischer.

**fish finger** NOUN
das Fischstäbchen (PL die Fischstäbchen)

**fishing** NOUN
das Angeln ◊ *My hobby is fishing.* Angeln ist mein Hobby.

**fishing boat** NOUN
das Fischerboot (PL die Fischerboote)

**fishing rod** NOUN
die Angel

**fishing tackle** NOUN
das Angelzeug

**fishmonger's** NOUN
der Fischladen (PL die Fischläden)

**fish sticks** PL NOUN US
die Fischstäbchen

**fist** NOUN
die Faust (PL die Fäuste)

to **fit** VERB
see also **fit** ADJECTIVE, NOUN
[1] (*be the right size*)
passen (PERFECT hat gepasst) ◊ *Does it fit?* Passt es?

[2] (*fix up*)
einbauen (PERFECT hat eingebaut) ◊ *He fitted an alarm in his car.* Er hat eine Alarmanlage in sein Auto eingebaut.

[3] (*attach*)
anbringen (IMPERFECT brachte an, PERFECT hat angebracht) ◊ *She fitted a plug to the hair dryer.* Sie brachte am Föhn einen Stecker an.

♦ **to fit in (1)** (*match up*) passen zu ◊ *That story doesn't fit in with what he told us.* Diese Geschichte passt nicht zu dem, was er uns gesagt hat.

F

☞

◆**to fit in (2)** (*person*) sich einpassen ◊ *She fitted in well at her new school.* Sie hat sich in ihrer neuen Schule gut eingepasst.

**fit** ADJECTIVE
> see also **fit** VERB, NOUN

**fit** (*healthy*) ◊ *He felt relaxed and fit after his holiday.* Nach seinem Urlaub fühlte er sich entspannt und fit.

**fit** NOUN
> see also **fit** ADJECTIVE, VERB

◆**to have a fit (1)** (*epileptic*) einen Anfall haben

◆**to have a fit (2)** (*be angry*) Zustände bekommen ◊ *My Mum will have a fit when she sees the carpet!* Meine Mutter bekommt Zustände, wenn sie den Teppich sieht!

**fitted carpet** NOUN
der Teppichboden (PL die Teppichböden)

**fitted kitchen** NOUN
die Einbauküche

**fitting room** NOUN
die Umkleidekabine

**five** NUMBER
fünf ◊ *He's five.* Er ist fünf.

to **fix** VERB
[1] (*mend*)
reparieren (PERFECT hat repariert) ◊ *Can you fix my bike?* Kannst du mein Fahrrad reparieren?
[2] (*decide*)
festlegen (PERFECT hat festgelegt) ◊ *Let's fix a date for the party.* Lass uns einen Tag für die Party festlegen. ◊ *They fixed a price for the car.* Sie haben einen Preis für das Auto festgelegt.
[3] machen ◊ *Janice fixed some food for us.* Janice hat uns etwas zum Essen gemacht.

**fixed** ADJECTIVE
festgesetzt ◊ *at a fixed price* zu einem festgesetzten Preis

◆**at a fixed time** zu einer bestimmten Zeit
◆**My parents have very fixed ideas.** Meine Eltern haben ziemlich festgelegte Ansichten.

**fizzy** ADJECTIVE
mit Kohlensäure ◊ *I don't like fizzy drinks.* Ich mag keine Getränke mit Kohlensäure.

**flabby** ADJECTIVE
wabbelig

**flag** NOUN
die Fahne

**flame** NOUN
die Flamme

**flamingo** NOUN
der Flamingo (PL die Flamingos)

**flan** NOUN
[1] (*sweet*)
der Kuchen (PL die Kuchen) ◊ *a raspberry flan* ein Himbeerkuchen

[2] (*savoury*)
die Quiche (PL die Quiches) ◊ *a cheese and onion flan* eine Käse-Zwiebel-Quiche

**flannel** NOUN
der Waschlappen (*for face*) (PL die Waschlappen)

to **flap** VERB
flattern mit ◊ *The bird flapped its wings.* Der Vogel flatterte mit den Flügeln.

**flash** NOUN
> see also **flash** VERB

das Blitzlicht (PL die Blitzlichter) ◊ *Has your camera got a flash?* Hat dein Fotoapparat ein Blitzlicht?

◆**a flash of lightning** ein Blitz MASC
◆**in a flash** blitzschnell

to **flash** VERB
> see also **flash** NOUN

[1] blinken ◊ *The police car's blue light was flashing.* Das Blaulicht des Polizeiautos blinkte.
[2] leuchten mit ◊ *They flashed a torch in his face.* Sie leuchteten ihm mit einer Taschenlampe ins Gesicht.

◆**She flashed her headlights.** Sie betätigte die Lichthupe.

**flask** NOUN
die Thermosflasche ®

**flat** ADJECTIVE
> see also **flat** NOUN

[1] flach ◊ *flat shoes* flache Schuhe
◆**a flat roof** ein Flachdach NEUT
[2] platt (*tyre*) ◊ *I've got a flat tyre.* Ich habe einen platten Reifen.

**flat** NOUN
> see also **flat** ADJECTIVE

die Wohnung ◊ *She lives in a flat.* Sie wohnt in einer Wohnung.

to **flatter** VERB
schmeicheln ◊ *Are you trying to flatter me?* Willst du mir schmeicheln? ◊ *I feel flattered.* Ich fühle mich geschmeichelt.

**flavour** NOUN
der Geschmack (PL die Geschmäcke) ◊ *This cheese has a very strong flavour.* Dieser Käse hat einen sehr pikanten Geschmack.

◆**Which flavour of ice cream would you like?** Was für ein Eis möchtest du?

**flavouring** NOUN
das Aroma (PL die Aromen)

**flea** NOUN
der Floh (PL die Flöhe)

**flew** VERB *see* **fly**

**flexible** ADJECTIVE
flexibel
◆**flexible working hours** gleitende Arbeitszeit

to **flick** VERB
schnipsen ◊ *She flicked the ash off her jumper.* Sie schnipste die Asche von ihrem Pullover.

◆ **to flick through a book** ein Buch durchblättern

to **flicker** VERB
flackern ◇ *The light flickered.* Das Licht flackerte.

**flight** NOUN
der Flug (PL die Flüge) ◇ *What time is the flight to Munich?* Um wie viel Uhr geht der Flug nach München?
◆ **a flight of stairs** eine Treppe

**flight attendant** NOUN
der Flugbegleiter (PL die Flugbegleiter)
die Flugbegleiterin

to **fling** VERB
schmeißen (IMPERFECT schmiss, PERFECT hat geschmissen) ◇ *He flung the dictionary onto the floor.* Er schmiss das Wörterbuch auf den Boden.

to **float** VERB
schwimmen (IMPERFECT schwamm, PERFECT ist geschwommen) ◇ *A leaf was floating on the water.* Auf dem Wasser schwamm ein Blatt.

**flock** NOUN
◆ **a flock of sheep** eine Schafherde
◆ **a flock of birds** ein Vogelschwarm NEUT

**flood** NOUN
see also **flood** VERB

1 die Überschwemmung ◇ *The rain has caused many floods.* Der Regen hat zu vielen Überschwemmungen geführt.
2 die Flut ◇ *He received a flood of letters.* Er erhielt eine Flut von Briefen.

to **flood** VERB
see also **flood** NOUN
überschwemmen (PERFECT hat überschwemmt) ◇ *The river has flooded the village.* Der Fluss hat das Dorf überschwemmt.

**flooding** NOUN
die Überschwemmung

**floor** NOUN
1 der Fußboden (PL die Fußböden)
◆ **a tiled floor** ein Fliesenboden
◆ **on the floor** auf dem Boden
2 (*storey*)
der Stock (PL die Stock)
◆ **the first floor** der erste Stock ◇ *on the first floor* im ersten Stock
◆ **the ground floor** das Erdgeschoss
Be careful not to translate **floor** by **Flur**.

**flop** NOUN
der Flop (PL die Flops) ◇ *The film was a flop.* Der Film war ein Flop.

**floppy disk** NOUN
die Diskette

**florist** NOUN
der Florist (GEN des Floristen, PL die Floristen)
die Floristin

**flour** NOUN
das Mehl (PL die Mehle)

to **flow** VERB
fließen (IMPERFECT floss, PERFECT ist geflossen) ◇ *Water was flowing from the pipe.* Aus dem Rohr floss Wasser.

**flower** NOUN
see also **flower** VERB
die Blume

to **flower** VERB
see also **flower** NOUN
blühen

**flown** VERB see **fly**

**flu** NOUN
die Grippe ◇ *She's got flu.* Sie hat Grippe.

**fluent** ADJECTIVE
◆ **He speaks fluent German.** Er spricht fließend Deutsch.

**flung** VERB see **fling**

**flush** NOUN
see also **flush** VERB
die Spülung (*of toilet*)

to **flush** VERB
see also **flush** NOUN
◆ **to flush the toilet** spülen

**flute** NOUN
die Querflöte ◇ *I play the flute.* Ich spiele Querflöte.

**fly** NOUN
see also **fly** VERB
die Fliege (*insect*)

to **fly** VERB
see also **fly** NOUN
fliegen (IMPERFECT flog, PERFECT ist geflogen) ◇ *He flew from Berlin to New York.* Er flog von Berlin nach New York.
◆ **to fly away** wegfliegen ◇ *The bird flew away.* Der Vogel flog weg.

**foal** NOUN
das Fohlen (PL die Fohlen)

**focus** NOUN
see also **focus** VERB
◆ **to be out of focus** unscharf sein ◇ *The house is out of focus in this photo.* Das Haus ist auf diesem Foto unscharf.

to **focus** VERB
see also **focus** NOUN
scharf einstellen (PERFECT hat scharf eingestellt) ◇ *Try to focus the binoculars.* Versuch, das Fernglas scharf einzustellen.
◆ **to focus on something (1)** (*with camera, telescope*) etwas auf etwas einstellen ◇ *The cameraman focused on the bird.* Der Kameramann stellte die Kamera auf den Vogel ein.
◆ **to focus on something (2)** (*concentrate*) sich auf etwas konzentrieren ◇ *Let's focus on the plot of the play.* Wir wollen uns auf die Handlung des Stücks konzentrieren.

**fog** NOUN
der Nebel (PL die Nebel)

**foggy** ADJECTIVE

**F**

neblig ◇ *a foggy day* ein nebliger Tag

**foil** NOUN
die Alufolie (*kitchen foil*) ◇ *She wrapped the meat in foil.* Sie wickelte das Fleisch in Alufolie.

**fold** NOUN
see also **fold** VERB
die Falte

to **fold** VERB
see also **fold** NOUN
falten ◇ *He folded the newspaper in half.* Er faltete die Zeitung in der Mitte zusammen.
♦ **to fold up (1)** zusammenfalten (*paper*)
♦ **to fold up (2)** zusammenklappen (*chair*)
♦ **to fold one's arms** verschränken ◇ *She folded her arms.* Sie verschränkte die Arme.

**folder** NOUN
1 die Mappe ◇ *She kept all her letters in a folder.* Sie bewahrte all ihre Briefe in einer Mappe auf.
2 (*ring binder*)
der Ordner (PL die Ordner)

**folding** ADJECTIVE
♦ **a folding chair** ein Klappstuhl MASC
♦ **a folding bed** ein Klappbett NEUT

to **follow** VERB
folgen (PERFECT ist gefolgt) ◇ *She followed him.* Sie folgte ihm.
♦ **You go first and I'll follow.** Geh du vor, ich komme nach.

**following** ADJECTIVE
folgend ◇ *the following day* am folgenden Tag

**fond** ADJECTIVE
♦ **to be fond of somebody** jemanden gern haben ◇ *I'm very fond of her.* Ich habe sie sehr gern.

**food** NOUN
die Nahrung
♦ **We need to buy some food.** Wir müssen etwas zum Essen kaufen.
♦ **cat food** das Katzenfutter
♦ **dog food** das Hundefutter

**food processor** NOUN
die Küchenmaschine

**fool** NOUN
der Idiot (GEN des Idioten, PL die Idioten)
die Idiotin

**foot** NOUN
1 (*of person*)
der Fuß (GEN des Fußes, PL die Füße) ◇ *My feet are aching.* Mir tun die Füße weh.
♦ **on foot** zu Fuß
2 (*12 inches*)
der Fuß (PL die Fuß)

> ℹ *In Germany measurements are in metres and centimetres rather than feet and inches. A foot is about 30 centimetres.*

◇ *Dave is six foot tall.* Dave ist ein Meter achtzig groß. ◇ *That mountain is five thousand feet high.* Dieser Berg ist eintausendsechshundert Meter hoch.

**football** NOUN
der Fußball (PL die Fußbälle) ◇ *I like playing football.* Ich spiele gern Fußball. ◇ *Paul threw the football over the fence.* Paul warf den Fußball über den Zaun.

**footballer** NOUN
der Fußballer (PL die Fußballer)
die Fußballerin

**football player** NOUN
der Fußballspieler (PL die Fußballspieler)
die Fußballspielerin
◇ *He's a famous football player.* Er ist ein bekannter Fußballspieler.

**footpath** NOUN
der Fußweg (PL die Fußwege) ◇ *Jane followed the footpath through the forest.* Jane ging den Fußweg durch den Wald entlang.

**footprint** NOUN
der Fußabdruck (PL die Fußabdrücke)
◇ *He saw some footprints in the sand.* Er sah Fußabdrücke im Sand.

**footstep** NOUN
der Schritt (PL die Schritte) ◇ *I can hear footsteps on the stairs.* Ich höre Schritte auf der Treppe.

**for** PREPOSITION

> *There are several ways of translating* **for**. *Scan the examples to find one that is similar to what you want to say.*

1 für ◇ *a present for me* ein Geschenk für mich ◇ *He works for the government.* Er arbeitet für die Regierung. ◇ *I'll do it for you.* Ich mache es für dich. ◇ *Are you for or against the idea?* Bist du für oder gegen die Idee? ◇ *Oxford is famous for its university.* Oxford ist für seine Universität berühmt. ◇ *I sold it for five pounds.* Ich habe es für fünf Pfund verkauft.
♦ **What for?** Wofür? ◇ *Give me some money! – What for?* Gib mir Geld! – Wofür? ◇ *What's it for?* Wofür ist das?

> *When referring to periods of time, use* **lang** *for the future and completed action in the past, and* **seit** *(with the German verb in the present tense) for something that started in the past and is still going on.*

2 lang ◇ *He worked in Germany for two years.* Er hat zwei Jahre lang in Deutschland gearbeitet. ◇ *She will be away for a month.* Sie wird einen Monat lang weg sein.
♦ **There are road works for three kilometres.** Es gibt dort über drei Kilometer Bauarbeiten.
3 seit ◇ *He's been learning German for two years.* Er lernt seit zwei Jahren

Deutsch. ◊ *She's been away for a month.*
Sie ist seit einem Monat weg.
◆ **What's the German for "lion"?** Wie sagt
man "lion" auf Deutsch?
◆ **It's time for lunch.** Es ist Zeit zum
Mittagessen.
◆ **the train for London** der Zug nach
London
◆ **for sale** zu verkaufen ◊ *The factory's for
sale.* Die Fabrik ist zu verkaufen.
to **forbid** VERB
   <u>verbieten</u> (IMPERFECT verbot, PERFECT hat
verboten)
◆ **to forbid somebody to do something**
jemandem verbieten, etwas zu tun ◊ *I
forbid you to go out tonight!* Ich verbiete
dir, heute Abend auszugehen!
**forbidden** ADJECTIVE
   <u>verboten</u> ◊ *Smoking is strictly forbidden.*
Rauchen ist streng verboten.
**force** NOUN
   | *see also* **force** VERB |
   die <u>Gewalt</u> ◊ *the forces of nature* die
Naturgewalten
◆ **The force of the explosion blew out all
the windows.** Die Explosion war so stark,
dass alle Fenster kaputtgingen.
◆ **in force** in Kraft ◊ *The new law has been
in force since May.* Das neue Gesetz ist
seit Mai in Kraft.
to **force** VERB
   | *see also* **force** NOUN |
   <u>zwingen</u> (IMPERFECT zwang, PERFECT hat
gezwungen) ◊ *They forced him to open
the safe.* Sie zwangen ihn, den Safe
aufzumachen.
**forecast** NOUN
◆ **the weather forecast** die
Wettervorhersage
**foreground** NOUN
   der <u>Vordergrund</u> ◊ *in the foreground* im
Vordergrund
**forehead** NOUN
   die <u>Stirn</u>
**foreign** ADJECTIVE
   <u>ausländisch</u>
**foreigner** NOUN
   der <u>Ausländer</u> (PL die Ausländer)
   die <u>Ausländerin</u>
to **foresee** VERB
   <u>vorhersehen</u> (PRESENT sieht vorher,
IMPERFECT sah vorher, PERFECT hat
vorhergesehen) ◊ *He had foreseen the
problem.* Er hatte das Problem
vorhergesehen.
**forest** NOUN
   der <u>Wald</u> (PL die Wälder)
**forever** ADVERB
   [1] <u>für immer</u> ◊ *He's gone forever.* Er ist
für immer weg.
   [2] <u>dauernd</u> (*always*) ◊ *She's forever
complaining.* Sie beklagt sich dauernd.
**forgave** VERB *see* **forgive**

to **forge** VERB
   <u>fälschen</u> ◊ *She tried to forge his
signature.* Sie versuchte, seine
Unterschrift zu fälschen.
**forged** ADJECTIVE
   <u>gefälscht</u> ◊ *forged banknotes* gefälschte
Banknoten
to **forget** VERB
   <u>vergessen</u> (PRESENT vergisst, IMPERFECT
vergaß, PERFECT hat vergessen) ◊ *I've
forgotten his name.* Ich habe seinen
Namen vergessen. ◊ *I'm sorry, I
completely forgot!* Tut mir Leid, das
habe ich total vergessen!
**forgetful** ADJECTIVE
   <u>vergesslich</u>
to **forgive** VERB
◆ **to forgive somebody** jemandem
verzeihen ◊ *I forgive you.* Ich verzeihe
dir.
◆ **to forgive somebody for doing
something** jemandem verzeihen, etwas
getan zu haben ◊ *She forgave him for
forgetting her birthday.* Sie verzieh ihm,
dass er ihren Geburtstag vergessen hat.
**forgot, forgotten** VERB *see* **forget**
**fork** NOUN
   [1] die <u>Gabel</u> (*for eating, gardening*) ◊ *He
ate his chips with a fork.* Er aß seine
Pommes frites mit einer Gabel.
   [2] die <u>Gabelung</u> (*in road*)
◆ **There was a fork in the road.** Die Straße
gabelte sich.
**form** NOUN
   [1] (*paper*)
   das <u>Formular</u> (PL die Formulare) ◊ *to fill
in a form* ein Formular ausfüllen
   [2] (*type*)
   die <u>Form</u> ◊ *I'm against hunting in any
form.* Ich bin gegen die Jagd in jeglicher
Form.
◆ **in top form** in Topform
◆ **She's in the fourth form.** Sie ist in der
zehnten Klasse.
**formal** ADJECTIVE
   [1] <u>formell</u> (*occasion*) ◊ *a formal dinner*
ein formelles Abendessen
   [2] <u>förmlich</u> (*person*)
   [3] <u>gehoben</u> (*language*) ◊ *In English,
"residence" is a formal term.* Auf
Englisch ist "residence" ein gehobener
Ausdruck.
◆ **formal clothes** die Gesellschaftskleidung
SING
◆ **He's got no formal qualifications.** Er hat
keinen offiziellen Abschluss.
**former** ADJECTIVE
   <u>früher</u> ◊ *a former pupil* ein früherer
Schüler ◊ *the former Prime Minister* der
frühere Premierminister
**formerly** ADVERB
   <u>früher</u>
**fort** NOUN

**F**

☞

das <u>Fort</u> (PL die Forts)
**forth** ADVERB
- ◆ **to go back and forth** hin- und hergehen
- ◆ **and so forth** und so weiter

**forthcoming** ADJECTIVE
<u>kommend</u> ◊ *It will be discussed at the forthcoming meeting.* Darüber wird auf der kommenden Besprechung diskutiert werden.

**fortnight** NOUN
- ◆ **a fortnight** vierzehn Tage ◊ *I'm going on holiday for a fortnight.* Ich verreise für vierzehn Tage.

**fortunate** ADJECTIVE
- ◆ **to be fortunate** Glück haben ◊ *He was extremely fortunate to survive.* Es war Glück, dass er überlebt hat.
- ◆ **It's fortunate that I remembered the map.** Zum Glück habe ich an die Landkarte gedacht.

**fortunately** ADVERB
<u>zum Glück</u> ◊ *Fortunately, it didn't rain.* Zum Glück hat es nicht geregnet.

**fortune** NOUN
das <u>Vermögen</u> (PL die Vermögen) ◊ *Kate earns a fortune!* Kate verdient ein Vermögen!
- ◆ **to tell somebody's fortune** jemandem wahrsagen

**forty** NUMBER
<u>vierzig</u> ◊ *He's forty.* Er ist vierzig.

**forward** ADVERB
> see also **forward** VERB
- ◆ **to move forward** sich vorwärts bewegen

to **forward** VERB
> see also **forward** ADVERB
<u>nachsenden</u> (IMPERFECT sandte nach, PERFECT hat nachgesandt) ◊ *He forwarded all her letters.* Er sandte alle ihre Briefe nach.

to **foster** VERB
<u>in Pflege nehmen</u> (PRESENT nimmt, IMPERFECT nahm, PERFECT hat genommen) ◊ *She has fostered more than fifteen children.* Sie hat mehr als fünfzehn Kinder in Pflege genommen.

**foster child** NOUN
das <u>Pflegekind</u> (PL die Pflegekinder) ◊ *She's their foster child.* Sie ist ihr Pflegekind.

**fought** VERB *see* **fight**

**foul** ADJECTIVE
> see also **foul** NOUN
<u>furchtbar</u> ◊ *The weather was foul.* Das Wetter war furchtbar. ◊ *What a foul smell!* Was für ein furchtbarer Gestank!

**foul** NOUN
> see also **foul** ADJECTIVE
das <u>Foul</u> (PL die Fouls) ◊ *Ferguson committed a foul.* Ferguson hat ein Foul begangen.

**found** VERB *see* **find**

to **found** VERB

<u>gründen</u> ◊ *Baden-Powell founded the Scout Movement.* Baden-Powell hat die Pfadfinderbewegung gegründet.

**foundations** PL NOUN
das <u>Fundament</u> (PL die Fundamente)

**fountain** NOUN
der <u>Brunnen</u> (PL die Brunnen)

**fountain pen** NOUN
der <u>Füllfederhalter</u> (PL die Füllfederhalter)

**four** NUMBER
<u>vier</u> ◊ *She's four.* Sie ist vier.

**fourteen** NUMBER
<u>vierzehn</u> ◊ *I'm fourteen.* Ich bin vierzehn.

**fourteenth** ADJECTIVE
<u>vierzehnte</u>
- ◆ **the fourteenth of August** der vierzehnte August

**fourth** ADJECTIVE
<u>vierte</u> ◊ *the fourth floor* der vierte Stock
- ◆ **the fourth of August** der vierte August

**fox** NOUN
der <u>Fuchs</u> (GEN des Fuchses, PL die Füchse)

**fragile** ADJECTIVE
<u>zerbrechlich</u>

**frame** NOUN
(*for picture*)
der <u>Rahmen</u> (PL die Rahmen)

**France** NOUN
<u>Frankreich</u> NEUT
- ◆ **from France** aus Frankreich
- ◆ **in France** in Frankreich
- ◆ **to France** nach Frankreich

**frantic** ADJECTIVE
- ◆ **I was going frantic.** Ich bin fast durchgedreht.
- ◆ **I was frantic with worry.** Ich habe mir furchtbare Sorgen gemacht.

**fraud** NOUN
1 (*crime*)
der <u>Betrug</u> ◊ *He was jailed for fraud.* Er kam wegen Betrugs ins Gefängnis.
2 (*person*)
der <u>Betrüger</u> (PL die Betrüger)
die <u>Betrügerin</u>
◊ *He's not a real doctor, he's a fraud.* Er ist kein echter Arzt, er ist ein Betrüger.

**freckles** PL NOUN
die <u>Sommersprossen</u> PL

**free** ADJECTIVE
> see also **free** VERB
1 <u>kostenlos</u> (*free of charge*) ◊ *a free brochure* eine kostenlose Broschüre
2 <u>frei</u> (*not busy, not taken*) ◊ *Is this seat free?* Ist dieser Platz frei?
- ◆ **"admission free"** "Eintritt frei"
- ◆ **Are you free after school?** Hast du nach der Schule Zeit?

to **free** VERB
> see also **free** ADJECTIVE
<u>befreien</u> (PERFECT hat befreit)

**freedom** NOUN

die Freiheit
**freeway** NOUN US
die Autobahn
to **freeze** VERB
1 gefrieren (IMPERFECT gefror, PERFECT ist
gefroren) ◊ *The water had frozen.* Das
Wasser war gefroren.
2 (*food*)
einfrieren ◊ *She froze the rest of the*
*raspberries.* Sie hat die restlichen
Himbeeren eingefroren.
**freezer** NOUN
der Gefrierschrank (PL die
Gefrierschränke)
**freezing** ADJECTIVE
♦ **It's freezing!** Es ist eiskalt! (*informal*)
♦ **I'm freezing!** Mir ist eiskalt! (*informal*)
♦ **three degrees below freezing** drei Grad
minus
**freight** NOUN
der Fracht (*goods*)
♦ **a freight train** ein Güterzug MASC
**French** ADJECTIVE
see also **French** NOUN
französisch ◊ *He's French.* Er ist
Franzose. ◊ *She's French.* Sie ist
Französin.
**French** NOUN
see also **French** ADJECTIVE
das Französisch (*language*) (GEN des
Französischen) ◊ *Do you speak French?*
Sprechen Sie Französisch?
♦ **the French** (*people*) die Franzosen MASC
PL
**French beans** PL NOUN
die grünen Bohnen FEM PL ◊ *She's very*
*fond of French beans.* Sie mag grüne
Bohnen besonders gern.
**French fries** PL NOUN
die Pommes frites PL
**French horn** NOUN
das Waldhorn (PL die Waldhörner) ◊ *I*
*play the French horn.* Ich spiele
Waldhorn.
**French kiss** NOUN
der Zungenkuss (GEN des Zungenkusses,
PL die Zungenküsse)
**French loaf** NOUN
das Stangenbrot (PL die Stangenbrote)
**Frenchman** NOUN
der Franzose (GEN des Franzosen, PL die
Franzosen)
**French windows** PL NOUN
die Verandatür
**Frenchwoman** NOUN
die Französin
**frequent** ADJECTIVE
häufig ◊ *frequent showers* häufige
Niederschläge
♦ **There are frequent buses to the town**
**centre.** Es gehen häufig Busse ins
Stadtzentrum.

**fresh** ADJECTIVE
frisch ◊ *I need some fresh air.* Ich
brauche frische Luft.
to **freshen up** VERB
sich frisch machen ◊ *I'd like to go and*
*freshen up.* Ich würde mich gerne frisch
machen.
to **fret** VERB
sich verrückt machen ◊ *Don't fret about*
*your exams.* Mach dich wegen der
Prüfung nicht verrückt.
**Friday** NOUN
der Freitag (PL die Freitage) ◊ *on Friday*
am Freitag ◊ *every Friday* jeden Freitag
◊ *last Friday* letzten Freitag ◊ *next Friday*
nächsten Freitag
♦ **on Fridays** freitags
**fridge** NOUN
der Kühlschrank (PL die Kühlschränke)
**fried** ADJECTIVE
gebraten ◊ *fried onions* gebratene
Zwiebeln
♦ **a fried egg** ein Spiegelei NEUT
**friend** NOUN
der Freund (PL die Freunde)
die Freundin
**friendly** ADJECTIVE
freundlich ◊ *She's really friendly.* Sie ist
wirklich freundlich. ◊ *Liverpool is a very*
*friendly city.* Liverpool ist eine sehr
freundliche Stadt.
**friendship** NOUN
die Freundschaft
**fright** NOUN
der Schrecken (PL die Schrecken) ◊ *I got*
*a terrible fright!* Ich habe einen
furchtbaren Schrecken bekommen!
to **frighten** VERB
Angst machen ◊ *Horror films frighten*
*him.* Horrorfilme machen ihm Angst.
**frightened** ADJECTIVE
♦ **to be frightened** Angst haben ◊ *I'm*
*frightened!* Ich habe Angst!
♦ **to be frightened of something** vor
etwas Angst haben ◊ *Anna's frightened*
*of spiders.* Anna hat Angst vor
Spinnen.
**frightening** ADJECTIVE
beängstigend
**fringe** NOUN
der Pony (*of hair*) (PL die Ponys) ◊ *She's*
*got a fringe.* Sie hat einen Pony.
**Frisbee** ® NOUN
das Frisbee ®
(PL die Frisbees) ◊ *to play Frisbee* Frisbee
spielen
**fro** ADVERB
♦ **to and fro** hin und her
**frog** NOUN
der Frosch (PL die Frösche)
**from** PREPOSITION

☞

⊓ aus (*from country, town*) ◊ *I'm from Yorkshire.* Ich bin aus Yorkshire. ◊ *I come from Perth.* Ich bin aus Perth.

◆ **Where do you come from?** Woher sind Sie?

⊔ von (*from person*) ◊ *a letter from my sister* ein Brief von meiner Schwester

◆ **The hotel is one kilometre from the beach.** Das Hotel ist einen Kilometer vom Strand entfernt.

⊡ ab (*number*) ◊ *from ten pounds* ab zehn Pfund ◊ *from the age of fourteen* ab vierzehn

◆ **from ... to ... (1)** (*distance*) von ... nach ... ◊ *He flew from London to Paris.* Er flog von London nach Paris.

◆ **from ... to ... (2)** (*time*) von ... bis ... ◊ *from one o'clock to two* von eins bis zwei

◆ **The price was reduced from ten pounds to five.** Der Preis war von zehn auf fünf Pfund herabgesetzt.

◆ **from ... onwards** ab ... ◊ *We'll be at home from seven o'clock onwards.* Wir werden ab sieben Uhr zu Hause sein.

**front** NOUN

| see also **front** ADJECTIVE |

die Vorderseite ◊ *the front of the house* die Vorderseite des Hauses

◆ **in front** davor ◊ *a house with a car in front* ein Haus mit einem Auto davor

◆ **in front of** vor

Use the accusative to express movement or a change of place. Use the dative when there is no change of place.

◊ *He stood in front of the house.* Er stand vor dem Haus. ◊ *He ran in front of a bus.* Er lief vor einen Bus. ◊ *the car in front of us* das Auto vor uns

◆ **in the front** (*of car*) vorn ◊ *I was sitting in the front.* Ich saß vorn.

◆ **at the front of the train** vorn im Zug

**front** ADJECTIVE

| see also **front** NOUN |

vordere ◊ *the front row* die vordere Reihe ◊ *the front seats of the car* die vorderen Sitze des Autos

◆ **the front door** die Haustür

**frontier** NOUN
die Grenze

**frost** NOUN
der Frost (PL die Fröste)

**frosting** NOUN US
der Zuckerguss (GEN des Zuckergusses)

**frosty** ADJECTIVE
frostig ◊ *It's frosty today.* Heute ist es frostig.

to **frown** VERB
die Stirn runzeln ◊ *He frowned.* Er runzelte die Stirn.

**froze, frozen** VERB *see* **freeze**

**frozen** ADJECTIVE

| see also **freeze** |

tiefgefroren (*food*) ◊ *frozen chips* tiefgefrorene Pommes frites

**fruit** NOUN

⊓ die Frucht (PL die Früchte) ◊ *an exotic fruit* eine exotische Frucht

⊔ das Obst ◊ *Fruit is very healthy.* Obst ist sehr gesund.

◆ **fruit juice** der Fruchtsaft

◆ **a fruit salad** ein Obstsalat MASC

**fruit machine** NOUN
der Spielautomat (GEN des Spielautomaten, PL die Spielautomaten)

**frustrated** ADJECTIVE
frustriert

to **fry** VERB
braten (PRESENT brät, IMPERFECT briet, PERFECT hat gebraten) ◊ *Fry the onions for five minutes.* Braten Sie die Zwiebeln fünf Minuten lang.

**frying pan** NOUN
die Bratpfanne

**fuel** NOUN
das Benzin (*for car, aeroplane*) (PL die Benzine) ◊ *to run out of fuel* kein Benzin mehr haben

to **fulfil** VERB
erfüllen (PERFECT hat erfüllt) ◊ *Robert fulfilled his dream of becoming a pilot.* Robert hat sich seinen Traum erfüllt und ist Pilot geworden.

**full** ADJECTIVE, ADVERB

⊓ voll ◊ *The tank's full.* Der Tank ist voll.

⊔ ausführlich ◊ *He asked for full information on the job.* Er bat um ausführliche Informationen über die Stelle.

◆ **your full name** Name und Vornamen

◆ **My full name is Ian John Marr.** Ich heiße Ian John Marr.

◆ **I'm full.** (*after meal*) Ich bin satt.

◆ **at full speed** mit Höchstgeschwindigkeit ◊ *He drove at full speed.* Er fuhr Höchstgeschwindigkeit.

◆ **There was a full moon.** Es war Vollmond.

**full stop** NOUN
der Punkt (PL die Punkte)

**full-time** ADJECTIVE, ADVERB
ganztags ◊ *She works full-time.* Sie arbeitet ganztags.

◆ **She's got a full-time job.** Sie hat einen Ganztagsjob.

**fully** ADVERB
ganz ◊ *He hasn't fully recovered from his illness.* Er hat sich noch nicht ganz von seiner Krankheit erholt.

**fumes** PL NOUN
die Abgase NEUT PL ◊ *The factory gave out dangerous fumes.* Die Fabrik stieß gefährliche Abgase aus.

◆ **exhaust fumes** Autoabgase

**fun** ADJECTIVE

| see also **fun** NOUN |

lustig ◊ *She's a fun person.* Sie ist ein lustiger Mensch.

**fun** NOUN
⎣ *see also* **fun** ADJECTIVE ⎦

♦**to have fun** Spaß haben ◊ *We had great fun playing in the snow.* Wir hatten beim Spielen im Schnee unseren Spaß.

♦**for fun** zum Spaß ◊ *He entered the competition just for fun.* Er hat am Wettbewerb nur zum Spaß mitgemacht.

♦**to make fun of somebody** sich über jemanden lustig machen ◊ *They made fun of him.* Sie machten sich über ihn lustig.

♦**It's fun!** Das macht Spaß!

♦**Have fun!** Viel Spaß!

**funds** PL NOUN

♦**to raise funds** Spenden sammeln

**funeral** NOUN
die Beerdigung

**funfair** NOUN
das Volksfest (PL die Volksfeste)

**funny** ADJECTIVE
[1] lustig (*amusing*) ◊ *It was really funny.* Es war wirklich lustig.
[2] komisch (*strange*) ◊ *There's something funny about him.* Er hat etwas Komisches an sich.

**fur** NOUN
[1] der Pelz (GEN des Pelzes, PL die Pelze) ◊ *a fur coat* ein Pelzmantel MASC
[2] das Fell (PL die Felle) ◊ *the dog's fur* das Fell des Hundes

**furious** ADJECTIVE
wütend ◊ *Dad was furious with me.* Papa war wütend auf mich.

**furniture** NOUN
die Möbel NEUT PL ◊ *a piece of furniture* ein Möbelstück NEUT

**further** ADVERB, ADJECTIVE
weiter entfernt ◊ *London is further from Manchester than Leeds is.* London ist weiter von Manchester entfernt als Leeds.

♦**How much further is it?** Wie weit ist es noch?

**further education** NOUN
die Weiterbildung

**fuse** NOUN
die Sicherung ◊ *The fuse has blown.* Die Sicherung ist durchgebrannt.

**fuss** NOUN
die Aufregung ◊ *What's all the fuss about?* Was soll die ganze Aufregung?

♦**to make a fuss** Theater machen ◊ *He's always making a fuss about nothing.* Er macht immer Theater wegen nichts.

**fussy** ADJECTIVE
pingelig ◊ *She is very fussy about her food.* Sie ist mit dem Essen sehr pingelig.

**future** NOUN
[1] die Zukunft

♦**in future** in Zukunft ◊ *Be more careful in future.* Sei in Zukunft vorsichtiger.

♦**What are your plans for the future?** Was für Zukunftspläne haben Sie?
[2] das Futur (*in grammar*) ◊ *Put this sentence into the future.* Setzt diesen Satz ins Futur.

**F**

# G

---

to **gain** VERB
  ♦ **to gain weight** zunehmen
  ♦ **to gain speed** schneller werden
**gallery** NOUN
  die Galerie ◊ *an art gallery* eine
  Kunstgalerie
to **gamble** VERB
  spielen
**gambler** NOUN
  der Spieler (PL die Spieler)
  die Spielerin
**gambling** NOUN
  das Glücksspiel (PL die Glücksspiele)
  ♦ **He likes gambling.** Er spielt gern.
**game** NOUN
  das Spiel (PL die Spiele) ◊ *The children
  were playing a game.* Die Kinder spielten
  ein Spiel. ◊ *a game of football* ein
  Fußballspiel ◊ *a game of cards* ein
  Kartenspiel
**gang** NOUN
  die Gang (PL die Gangs)
**gangster** NOUN
  der Gangster (PL die Gangster)
**gap** NOUN
  [1] die Lücke ◊ *There's a gap in the
  hedge.* In der Hecke ist eine Lücke.
  [2] die Pause ◊ *a gap of four years* eine
  Pause von vier Jahren
**garage** NOUN
  [1] (*for parking cars*)
  die Garage
  [2] (*for repairs*)
  die Werkstatt (PL die Werkstätten)
**garbage** NOUN
  der Müll ◊ *the garbage can* die
  Mülltonne
  ♦ **That's garbage!** Das ist Blödsinn!
**garden** NOUN
  der Garten (PL die Gärten)
**gardener** NOUN
  der Gärtner (PL die Gärtner)
  die Gärtnerin
  ◊ *He's a gardener.* Er ist Gärtner.
**gardening** NOUN
  die Gartenarbeit ◊ *Margaret loves
  gardening.* Margaret liebt
  Gartenarbeit.
**gardens** PL NOUN
  der Park SING (PL die Parks)
**garlic** NOUN
  der Knoblauch
**garment** NOUN
  das Kleidungsstück (PL die
  Kleidungsstücke)
**gas** NOUN
  [1] das Gas (PL die Gase)
  ♦ **a gas cooker** ein Gasherd MASC

♦ **a gas cylinder** eine Gasflasche
♦ **a gas fire** ein Gasofen MASC
♦ **a gas leak** eine undichte Stelle in der
  Gasleitung
  [2] das Benzin [US]
♦ **a gas station** eine Tankstelle
**gasoline** NOUN [US]
  das Benzin
**gate** NOUN
  [1] (*of garden*)
  das Tor (PL die Tore)
  [2] (*of field*)
  das Gatter (PL die Gatter)
  [3] (*at airport*)
  der Flugsteig (PL die Flugsteige)
**gateau** NOUN
  die Torte
to **gather** VERB
  sich versammeln (*assemble*) (PERFECT
  haben sich versammelt) ◊ *People
  gathered in front of Buckingham Palace.*
  Menschen versammelten sich vor dem
  Buckingham-Palast.
  ♦ **to gather speed** schneller werden ◊ *The
  train gathered speed.* Der Zug wurde
  schneller.
**gave** VERB *see* **give**
**gay** ADJECTIVE
  schwul (*homosexual*)
to **gaze** VERB
  ♦ **to gaze at something** etwas anstarren
  ◊ *He gazed at her.* Er starrte sie an.
**GCSE** NOUN (= *General Certificate of
  Secondary Education*)
  die mittlere Reife
**gear** NOUN
  [1] (*in car*)
  der Gang (PL die Gänge) ◊ *in first gear* im
  ersten Gang
  ♦ **to change gear** schalten
  [2] die Ausrüstung ◊ *camping gear* die
  Campingausrüstung
  ♦ **your sports gear** (*clothes*) dein Sportzeug
  NEUT
**gear lever** NOUN
  der Schalthebel (PL die Schalthebel)
**gearshift** NOUN [US]
  der Schaltknüppel (PL die Schaltknüppel)
**geese** PL NOUN *see* **goose**
**gel** NOUN
  das Gel (PL die Gele)
  *Note that in German the "g" in* **Gel** *is
  pronounced like the "g" in girl.*
  ◊ *hair gel* das Haargel
**gem** NOUN
  der Edelstein (PL die Edelsteine)
**Gemini** SING NOUN

die Zwillinge MASC PL ◊ *I'm Gemini.* Ich bin Zwilling.

**gender** NOUN
das Geschlecht (PL die Geschlechter)

**general** NOUN
see also **general** ADJECTIVE
der General (PL die Generäle)

**general** ADJECTIVE
see also **general** NOUN
allgemein
♦ **in general** im Allgemeinen

**general election** NOUN
die allgemeinen Wahlen FEM PL

**general knowledge** NOUN
die Allgemeinbildung

**generally** ADVERB
normalerweise ◊ *I generally go shopping on Saturday.* Ich gehe normalerweise samstags einkaufen.

**generation** NOUN
die Generation ◊ *the younger generation* die jüngere Generation

**generator** NOUN
der Generator (PL die Generatoren)

**generous** ADJECTIVE
großzügig ◊ *That's very generous of you.* Das ist sehr großzügig von Ihnen.

**genetic** ADJECTIVE
genetisch

**genetically** ADVERB
genetisch
♦ **genetically modified** genmanipuliert

**Geneva** NOUN
Genf NEUT ◊ *to Geneva* nach Genf
♦ **Lake Geneva** der Genfer See

**genius** NOUN
das Genie (PL die Genies) ◊ *She's a genius!* Sie ist ein Genie!

**gentle** ADJECTIVE
sanft

**gentleman** NOUN
der Gentleman (PL die Gentlemen)
♦ **Good morning, gentlemen.** Guten Morgen, meine Herren.

**gently** ADVERB
sanft

**gents** SING NOUN
die Herrentoilette ◊ *Can you tell me where the gents is, please?* Können Sie mir bitte sagen, wo die Herrentoilette ist?
♦ **"gents"** (*on sign*) "Herren"

**genuine** ADJECTIVE
1 echt (*real*) ◊ *These are genuine diamonds.* Das sind echte Diamanten.
2 geradlinig (*sincere*) ◊ *She's a very genuine person.* Sie ist ein sehr geradliniger Mensch.

**geography** NOUN
die Geografie

**germ** NOUN
die Bazille

**German** ADJECTIVE
see also **German** NOUN
deutsch ◊ *He is German.* Er ist Deutscher. ◊ *She is German.* Sie ist Deutsche.
♦ **German shepherd** der Schäferhund

**German** NOUN
see also **German** ADJECTIVE
1 (*person*)
der Deutsche (GEN des Deutschen, PL die Deutschen)
die Deutsche (GEN der Deutschen) ◊ *a German* (*man*) ein Deutscher
♦ **the Germans** die Deutschen
2 (*language*)
das Deutsch (GEN des Deutschen) ◊ *Do you speak German?* Sprechen sie Deutsch?

**German measles** NOUN
die Röteln PL ◊ *to have German measles* die Röteln haben

**Germany** NOUN
Deutschland NEUT
♦ **from Germany** aus Deutschland
♦ **in Germany** in Deutschland
♦ **to Germany** nach Deutschland

**gesture** NOUN
die Geste

to **get** VERB
1 (*receive*)
bekommen (IMPERFECT bekam, PERFECT hat bekommen) ◊ *I got lots of presents.* Ich habe viele Geschenke bekommen. ◊ *He got first prize.* Er hat den ersten Preis bekommen. ◊ *Jackie got good exam results.* Jackie hat gute Noten bekommen.
♦ **have got** haben ◊ *How many have you got?* Wie viele hast du?
2 (*fetch*)
holen ◊ *Quick, get help!* Schnell, hol Hilfe!
3 (*catch*)
fassen ◊ *They've got the thief.* Sie haben den Dieb gefasst.
4 (*train, bus*)
nehmen (PRESENT nimmt, IMPERFECT nahm, PERFECT hat genommen) ◊ *I'm getting the bus into town.* Ich nehme den Bus in die Stadt.
5 (*understand*)
verstehen (IMPERFECT verstand, PERFECT hat verstanden) ◊ *I don't get the joke.* Ich verstehe den Witz nicht.
6 (*go*)
kommen (IMPERFECT kam, PERFECT ist gekommen) ◊ *How do you get to the castle?* Wie kommt man zur Burg?
7 (*become*)
werden (PRESENT wird, IMPERFECT wurde, PERFECT ist geworden) ◊ *to get old* alt werden
♦ **to get something done** etwas machen lassen ◊ *to get something repaired* etwas

**G**

reparieren lassen ◊ *to get one's hair cut* sich die Haare schneiden lassen

♦ **to get something for somebody** etwas für jemanden holen ◊ *The librarian got the book for me.* Die Bibliothekarin holte mir das Buch.

♦ **to have got to do something** etwas tun müssen ◊ *I've got to tell him.* Ich muss es ihm sagen.

♦ **to get away** entkommen ◊ *One of the burglars got away.* Einer der Einbrecher ist entkommen.

♦ **You'll never get away with it.** Das wird man dir niemals durchgehen lassen.

♦ **to get back (1)** zurückkommen ◊ *What time did you get back?* Wann seid ihr zurückgekommen?

♦ **to get back (2)** zurückbekommen ◊ *He got his money back.* Er hat sein Geld zurückbekommen.

♦ **to get down** herunterkommen ◊ *Get down from there!* Komm da runter!

♦ **to get in** heimkommen ◊ *What tim... ...you get in last night?* Wann bist ... Nacht nach Hause gekomme...

♦ **to get into** einsteigen in +ACC ... *into the car.* Sharon stieg ins A...

♦ **to get off (1)** (*vehicle*) aussteigen ... ◊ *Isobel got off the train.* Isobel sti... aus dem Zug aus.

♦ **to get off (2)** (*bike*) absteigen von ◊ *He got off his bike.* Er stieg vom Fahrrad ab.

♦ **to get on (1)** (*vehicle*) einsteigen in +ACC ◊ *Phyllis got on the bus.* Phyllis stieg in den Bus ein.

♦ **to get on (2)** (*bike*) steigen auf +ACC ◊ *Carol got on her bike.* Carol stieg auf ihr Fahrrad.

♦ **to get on with somebody** sich mit jemandem verstehen ◊ *He doesn't get on with his parents.* Er versteht sich nicht mit seinen Eltern. ◊ *We got on really well.* Wir haben uns wirklich gut verstanden.

♦ **to get out** aussteigen aus ◊ *Jason got out of the car.* Jason stieg aus dem Auto aus.

♦ **Get out!** Raus!

♦ **to get something out** etwas hervorholen ◊ *She got the map out.* Sie holte die Karte hervor.

♦ **to get over something (1)** sich von etwas erholen ◊ *It took her a long time to get over the illness.* Sie brauchte lange Zeit, um sich von der Krankheit zu erholen.

♦ **to get over something (2)** etwas überwinden ◊ *He managed to get over the problem.* Er konnte das Problem überwinden.

♦ **to get round to something** zu etwas kommen ◊ *I'll get round to it eventually.* Ich werde schon noch dazu kommen.

♦ **to get together** sich treffen ◊ *Could we get together this evening?* Könnten wir uns heute abend treffen?

♦ **to get up** aufstehen ◊ *What time do you get up?* Wann stehst du auf?

**ghetto blaster** NOUN
das <u>tragbare Kofferradio</u> (PL die tragbaren Kofferradios)

**ghost** NOUN
das <u>Gespenst</u> (PL die Gespenster)

**giant** ADJECTIVE
| *see also* **giant** NOUN |

<u>riesig</u> ◊ *They ate a giant meal.* Sie haben ein riesiges Essen vertilgt.

**giant** NOUN
| *see also* **giant** ADJECTIVE |

der <u>Riese</u> (GEN des Riesen, PL die Riesen)
die <u>Riesin</u>

**gift** N...
...ie Geschenke)

...ung
... **a gift for something** für etwas ...abt sein ◊ *Dave has a gift for painting.* Dave ist künstlerisch begabt.
*Be careful not to translate* **gift** *by the German word* **Gift**.

**gifted** ADJECTIVE
<u>begabt</u> ◊ *Janice is a gifted pianist.* Janice ist eine begabte Pianistin.

**gift shop** NOUN
der <u>Geschenkladen</u> (PL die Geschenkläden)

**gigantic** ADJECTIVE
<u>riesengroß</u>

to **giggle** VERB
<u>kichern</u>

**gin** NOUN
der <u>Gin</u> (PL die Gins *or* Gin)
*When ordering more than one gin use the plural form* **Gin**.
◊ *Three gins, please.* Drei Gin bitte.

♦ **a gin and tonic** ein Gin Tonic

**ginger** NOUN
| *see also* **ginger** ADJECTIVE |

der <u>Ingwer</u> ◊ *Add a teaspoon of ginger.* Fügen Sie einen Teelöffel Ingwer zu.

**ginger** ADJECTIVE
| *see also* **ginger** NOUN |

<u>rot</u> ◊ *David has ginger hair.* David hat rote Haare.

**gipsy** NOUN
der <u>Zigeuner</u> (PL die Zigeuner)
die <u>Zigeunerin</u>

**giraffe** NOUN
die <u>Giraffe</u>

**girl** NOUN
das <u>Mädchen</u> (PL die Mädchen)
◊ *They've got a girl and two boys.* Sie haben ein Mädchen und zwei Jungen.

◇ *a five-year-old girl* ein fünfjähriges Mädchen
♦ **an English girl** eine junge Engländerin

**girlfriend** NOUN
die <u>Freundin</u> ◇ *Damon's girlfriend is called Justine.* Damons Freundin heißt Justine. ◇ *She often went out with her girlfriends.* Sie ging oft mit ihren Freundinnen aus.

to **give** VERB
<u>geben</u> (PRESENT gibt, IMPERFECT gab, PERFECT hat gegeben)
♦ **to give something to somebody** jemandem etwas geben ◇ *He gave me ten pounds.* Er gab mir zehn Pfund.
♦ **to give something back to somebody** jemandem etwas zurückgeben ◇ *I gave the book back to him.* Ich habe ihm das Buch zurückgegeben.
♦ **to give in** nachgeben ◇ *His mum gave in and let him watch TV.* Seine Mama hat nachgegeben und ihn fernsehen lassen.
♦ **to give out** austeilen ◇ *The teacher gave out the books.* Der Lehrer hat die Bücher ausgeteilt.
♦ **to give up** aufgeben ◇ *I couldn't do it, so I gave up.* Ich habe es nicht gekonnt, also habe ich aufgegeben.
♦ **to give up doing something** etwas aufgeben ◇ *He gave up smoking.* Er hat das Rauchen aufgegeben.
♦ **to give oneself up** sich ergeben ◇ *The thief gave himself up.* Der Dieb hat sich ergeben.
♦ **to give way** (*in traffic*) die Vorfahrt achten

**glad** ADJECTIVE
<u>froh</u> ◇ *She's glad she's done it.* Sie ist froh, dass sie es getan hat.

**glamorous** ADJECTIVE
<u>glamourös</u> (*person*)

to **glance** VERB
| *see also* **glance** NOUN |
♦ **to glance at something** einen Blick auf etwas werfen ◇ *Peter glanced at his watch.* Peter warf einen Blick auf seine Uhr.

**glance** NOUN
| *see also* **glance** VERB |
der <u>Blick</u> (PL die Blicke) ◇ *at first glance* auf den ersten Blick

to **glare** VERB
♦ **to glare at somebody** jemanden wütend ansehen ◇ *He glared at me.* Er sah mich wütend an.

**glaring** ADJECTIVE
♦ **a glaring mistake** ein eklatanter Fehler

**glass** NOUN
das <u>Glas</u> (GEN des Glases, PL die Gläser) ◇ *a glass of milk* ein Glas Milch

**glasses** PL NOUN
die <u>Brille</u> ◇ *Veronika wears glasses.* Veronika trägt eine Brille.

to **gleam** VERB

funkeln ◇ *Her eyes gleamed with excitement.* Ihre Augen funkelten vor Aufregung.

**glider** NOUN
das <u>Segelflugzeug</u> (PL die Segelflugzeuge)

**gliding** NOUN
das <u>Segelfliegen</u> ◇ *My hobby is gliding.* Segelfliegen ist mein Hobby.

**glimpse** NOUN
♦ **to catch a glimpse of somebody** jemanden kurz zu sehen bekommen

to **glitter** VERB
glitzern

**global** ADJECTIVE
<u>weltweit</u>
♦ **on a global scale** weltweit

**global warming** NOUN
die <u>Erwärmung der Erdatmosphäre</u>

**globe** NOUN
der <u>Globus</u> (GEN des Globus, PL die Globen)

**gloomy** ADJECTIVE
1 <u>düster</u> ◇ *He lives in a small gloomy flat.* Er wohnt in einer kleinen, düsteren Wohnung.
2 <u>niedergeschlagen</u> ◇ *She's been feeling very gloomy recently.* Sie fühlt sich in letzter Zeit sehr niedergeschlagen.

**glorious** ADJECTIVE
<u>herrlich</u>

**glove** NOUN
der <u>Handschuh</u> (PL die Handschuhe)

**glove compartment** NOUN
das <u>Handschuhfach</u> (PL die Handschuhfächer)

to **glow** VERB
leuchten ◇ *He bought a watch which glows in the dark.* Er kaufte eine Uhr, die im Dunkeln leuchtet.

**glue** NOUN
| *see also* **glue** VERB |
der <u>Klebstoff</u> (PL die Klebstoffe)

to **glue** VERB
| *see also* **glue** NOUN |
kleben ◇ *to glue something together* etwas zusammenkleben

**GM** ABBREVIATION (= *genetically modified*)
<u>genmanipuliert</u> ◇ *GM food* genmanipulierte Lebensmittel PL

**GMO** NOUN (= *genetically modified organism*)
der <u>genmanipulierte Organismus</u> (GEN des genmanipulierten Organismus, PL die genmanipulierten Organismen)

**go** NOUN
| *see also* **go** VERB |
♦ **to have a go at doing something** etwas versuchen ◇ *He had a go at making a cake.* Er hat versucht, einen Kuchen zu backen.
♦ **Whose go is it?** Wer ist dran?

G

to **go** VERB

see also **go** NOUN

**1** gehen (IMPERFECT ging, PERFECT ist gegangen) ◊ *I'm going to the cinema tonight.* Ich gehe heute Abend ins Kino. ◊ *I'm going now.* Ich gehe jetzt.

**2** (*leave*)
weggehen ◊ *Where's Thomas? – He's gone.* Wo ist Thomas? – Er ist weggegangen.

**3** (*vehicle*)
fahren (PRESENT fährt, IMPERFECT fuhr, PERFECT ist gefahren) ◊ *My car won't go.* Mein Auto fährt nicht.

◆ **to go home** nach Hause gehen ◊ *I go home at about four o'clock.* Ich gehe um etwa vier Uhr nach Hause.

◆ **to go for a walk** einen Spaziergang machen ◊ *Shall we go for a walk?* Sollen wir einen Spaziergang machen?

◆ **How did it go?** Wie ist es gelaufen?

◆ **I'm going to do it tomorrow.** Ich werde es morgen tun.

◆ **It's going to be difficult.** Es wird schwierig werden.

to **go after** VERB
nachgehen (*follow*)
+DAT (IMPERFECT ging nach, PERFECT ist nachgegangen) ◊ *I went after him.* Ich ging ihm nach.

◆ **Quick, go after them!** Schnell, ihnen nach!

to **go ahead** VERB
vorangehen (IMPERFECT ging voran, PERFECT ist vorangegangen)

◆ **to go ahead with something** etwas durchführen

to **go around** VERB
herumgehen (IMPERFECT ging herum, PERFECT ist herumgegangen) ◊ *There's a rumour going around that they're getting married.* Es geht das Gerücht um, sie würden heiraten.

to **go away** VERB
weggehen (IMPERFECT ging weg, PERFECT ist weggegangen) ◊ *Go away!* Geh weg!

to **go back** VERB
zurückgehen (IMPERFECT ging zurück, PERFECT ist zurückgegangen) ◊ *We went back to the same place.* Wir sind an denselben Ort zurückgegangen.

◆ **Is he still here? – No, he's gone back home.** Ist er noch hier? – Nein, er ist nach Hause gegangen.

to **go by** VERB
vorbeigehen (IMPERFECT ging vorbei, PERFECT ist vorbeigegangen) ◊ *Two policemen went by.* Zwei Polizisten gingen vorbei.

to **go down** VERB
**1** (*person*)
hinuntergehen (IMPERFECT ging hinunter, PERFECT ist hinuntergegangen) ◊ *to go down the stairs* die Treppe hinuntergehen

**2** (*decrease*)
sinken (IMPERFECT sank, PERFECT ist gesunken) ◊ *The price of computers has gone down.* Die Preise für Computer sind gesunken.

**3** (*deflate*)
Luft verlieren (IMPERFECT verlor Luft, PERFECT hat Luft verloren) ◊ *My airbed kept going down.* Meine Luftmatratze verlor dauernd Luft.

◆ **My brother's gone down with flu.** Mein Bruder hat die Grippe bekommen.

to **go for** VERB
angreifen (*attack*) (IMPERFECT griff an, PERFECT hat angegriffen) ◊ *Suddenly the dog went for me.* Der Hund griff mich plötzlich an.

◆ **Go for it!** (*go on!*) Na los!

to **go in** VERB
hineingehen (IMPERFECT ging hinein, PERFECT ist hineingegangen) ◊ *He knocked on the door and went in.* Er klopfte und ging hinein.

to **go off** VERB
**1** losgehen (IMPERFECT ging los, PERFECT ist losgegangen) ◊ *The bomb went off.* Die Bombe ging los. ◊ *The fire alarm went off.* Der Feueralarm ging los.

**2** klingeln ◊ *My alarm clock goes off at seven every morning.* Mein Wecker klingelt jeden Morgen um sieben Uhr.

**3** schlecht werden (PRESENT wird schlecht, IMPERFECT wurde schlecht, PERFECT ist schlecht geworden)

◆ **The milk's gone off.** Die Milch ist sauer geworden.

**4** (*go away*)
weggehen ◊ *He went off in a huff.* Er ist beleidigt weggegangen.

to **go on** VERB
**1** (*happen*)
los sein (PRESENT ist los, IMPERFECT war los, PERFECT ist los gewesen) ◊ *What's going on?* Was ist los?

**2** (*carry on*)
dauern ◊ *The concert went on until eleven o'clock at night.* Das Konzert hat bis nach elf Uhr nachts gedauert.

◆ **to go on doing something** etwas weiter tun ◊ *He went on reading.* Er las weiter.

◆ **to go on at somebody** an jemandem herumkritisieren ◊ *My parents always go on at me.* Meine Eltern kritisieren dauernd an mir herum.

◆ **Go on!** Na los! ◊ *Go on, tell me what the problem is!* Na los, sag mir, wo das Problem ist!

to **go out** VERB
ausgehen (IMPERFECT ging aus, PERFECT ist ausgegangen) ◊ *Are you going out*

tonight? Gehst du heute Abend aus?
◊ *Suddenly the lights went out.* Plötzlich ging das Licht aus.
- ◆ **to go out with somebody** mit jemandem ausgehen ◊ *Are you going out with him?* Gehst du mit ihm aus?

to **go past** VERB
- ◆ **to go past something** an etwas vorbeigehen ◊ *He went past the shop.* Er ging an dem Geschäft vorbei.

to **go round** VERB
- ◆ **to go round a corner** um die Ecke biegen
- ◆ **to go round to somebody's house** jemanden besuchen
- ◆ **to go round a museum** sich ein Museum ansehen
- ◆ **to go round the shops** einen Einkaufsbummel machen

to **go through** VERB
  fahren durch (*by car*) (PRESENT fährt, IMPERFECT fuhr, PERFECT ist gefahren)
- ◆ **We went through London to get to Birmingham.** Wir sind über London nach Birmingham gefahren.

to **go up** VERB
  1 (*person*)
  hinaufgehen (IMPERFECT ging hinauf, PERFECT ist hinaufgegangen) ◊ *to go up the stairs* die Treppe hinaufgehen
  2 (*increase*)
  steigen (IMPERFECT stieg, PERFECT ist gestiegen) ◊ *The price has gone up.* Der Preis ist gestiegen.
- ◆ **to go up in flames** in Flammen aufgehen ◊ *The whole factory went up in flames.* Die ganze Fabrik ist in Flammen aufgegangen.

to **go** VERB
  passen zu ◊ *Does this blouse go with that skirt?* Passt diese Bluse zu dem Rock?

**goal** NOUN
  1 (*sport*)
  das Tor (PL die Tore) ◊ *to score a goal* ein Tor schießen
  2 (*aim*)
  das Ziel (PL die Ziele) ◊ *His goal is to become the world champion.* Sein Ziel ist es, Weltmeister zu werden.

**goalkeeper** NOUN
  der Torwart (PL die Torwarte)

**goat** NOUN
  die Ziege
- ◆ **goat's cheese** der Ziegenkäse

**god** NOUN
  der Gott (PL die Götter) ◊ *I believe in God.* Ich glaube an Gott.

**goddaughter** NOUN
  die Patentochter (PL die Patentöchter)

**godfather** NOUN
  der Patenonkel (PL die Patenonkel) ◊ *my godfather* mein Patenonkel

**godmother** NOUN

die Patentante ◊ *my godmother* meine Patentante

**godson** NOUN
  der Patensohn (PL die Patensöhne)

**goes** VERB *see* **go**

**goggles** PL NOUN
  die Schutzbrille

**gold** NOUN
  das Gold ◊ *They found some gold.* Sie haben Gold gefunden. ◊ *a gold necklace* eine goldene Halskette

**goldfish** NOUN
  der Goldfisch (PL die Goldfische) ◊ *I've got five goldfish.* Ich habe fünf Goldfische.

**gold-plated** ADJECTIVE
  vergoldet

**golf** NOUN
  das Golf ◊ *My dad plays golf.* Mein Papa spielt Golf.
- ◆ **a golf club (1)** (*stick*) ein Golfschläger MASC
- ◆ **a golf club (2)** (*place*) ein Golfklub MASC

**golf course** NOUN
  der Golfplatz (GEN des Golfplatzes, PL die Golfplätze)

**gone** VERB *see* **go**

**good** ADJECTIVE
  1 gut ◊ *It's a very good film.* Das ist ein sehr guter Film.
- ◆ **Vegetables are good for you.** Gemüse ist gesund.
- ◆ **to be good at something** gut in etwas sein ◊ *Maree's very good at maths.* Maree ist sehr gut in Mathe.
  2 freundlich (*kind*) ◊ *They were very good to me.* Sie waren sehr freundlich zu mir. ◊ *That's very good of you.* Das ist sehr freundlich von Ihnen.
  3 artig (*not naughty*) ◊ *Be good!* Sei artig!
- ◆ **for good** für immer ◊ *One day he left for good.* Eines Tages ist er für immer weggegangen.
- ◆ **Good morning!** Guten Morgen!
- ◆ **Good afternoon!** Guten Tag!
- ◆ **Good evening!** Guten Abend!
- ◆ **Good night!** Gute Nacht!
- ◆ **It's no good complaining.** Es hat keinen Wert, sich zu beklagen.

**goodbye** EXCLAMATION
  auf Wiedersehen

**Good Friday** NOUN
  der Karfreitag (PL die Karfreitage)

**good-looking** ADJECTIVE
  gut aussehend
- ◆ **Andrew's very good-looking.** Andrew sieht sehr gut aus.

**good-natured** ADJECTIVE
  gutmütig

**goods** PL NOUN
  die Ware (*in shop*)
- ◆ **a goods train** ein Güterzug MASC

**goose** NOUN

**G**

☞

die <u>Gans</u> (PL die Gänse)
**gooseberry** NOUN
die <u>Stachelbeere</u>
**gorgeous** ADJECTIVE
  [1] <u>hinreißend</u> ◊ *She's gorgeous!* Sie
  sieht hinreißend aus!
  [2] <u>herrlich</u> ◊ *The weather was gorgeous.*
  Das Wetter war herrlich.
**gorilla** NOUN
der <u>Gorilla</u> (PL die Gorillas)
**gospel** NOUN
das <u>Evangelium</u> (PL die Evangelien)
**gossip** NOUN
  see also **gossip** VERB
  [1] (*rumours*)
  der <u>Tratsch</u> ◊ *Tell me the gossip!* Erzähl
  mir den neuesten Tratsch!
  [2] (*woman*)
  die <u>Klatschtante</u> ◊ *She's such a gossip!*
  Sie ist eine furchtbare Klatschtante!
  [3] (*man*)
  das <u>Klatschweib</u> (PL die Klatschweiber)
  ◊ *What a gossip!* So ein Klatschweib!
to **gossip** VERB
  see also **gossip** NOUN
  [1] <u>schwatzen</u> (*chat*) ◊ *They were always*
  *gossiping.* Sie haben dauernd
  geschwatzt.
  [2] <u>tratschen</u> (*about somebody*) ◊ *They*
  *gossiped about her.* Sie haben über sie
  getratscht.
**got** VERB *see* **get**
**gotten** VERB *see* **get**
**government** NOUN
die <u>Regierung</u>
**GP** NOUN (= *General Practitioner*)
der <u>praktische Arzt</u> (PL die praktischen
Ärzte)
die <u>praktische Ärztin</u>
to **grab** VERB
<u>packen</u> ◊ *She grabbed her umbrella and*
*ran out of the door.* Sie packte ihren
Schirm und lief zur Tür hinaus.
**graceful** ADJECTIVE
<u>anmutig</u>
**grade** NOUN
  [1] die <u>Note</u> (*mark*) ◊ *He got good grades*
  *in his exams.* Er hat in der Prüfung gute
  Noten bekommen.
  [2] die <u>Klasse</u> (*class*) ◊ *Which grade are*
  *you in?* In welcher Klasse bist du?
**grade school** NOUN US
die <u>Grundschule</u>
**gradual** ADJECTIVE
<u>allmählich</u>
**gradually** ADVERB
<u>allmählich</u> ◊ *We got used to it.* Wir
haben uns daran gewöhnt.
**graduate** NOUN
  see also **graduate** VERB

der <u>Hochschulabsolvent</u> (GEN des
Hochschulabsolventen, PL die
Hochschulabsolventen)
die <u>Hochschulabsolventin</u>
to **graduate** VERB
  see also **graduate** NOUN
  das <u>Examen machen</u>
**graffiti** PL NOUN
die <u>Graffiti</u> PL
**grain** NOUN
das <u>Korn</u> (PL die Körner)
**gram** NOUN
das <u>Gramm</u> (PL die Gramme *or* Gramm)
*When specifying a quantity of*
*something use the plural form* **Gramm.**
  ◊ *five hundred grams of cheese*
  fünfhundert Gramm Käse
**grammar** NOUN
die <u>Grammatik</u>
**grammar school** NOUN
das <u>Gymnasium</u> (PL die Gymnasien)

> **ⓘ Gymnasium** *education begins after*
> *year 4 of the* **Grundschule** *and lasts*
> *until year 13 (however, pupils can leave*
> *after year 10). It mainly prepares*
> *children for university education.*

**grammatical** ADJECTIVE
<u>grammatisch</u>
**gramme** NOUN
das <u>Gramm</u> (PL die Gramme *or* Gramm)
*When specifying a quantity of*
*something use the plural form* **Gramm.**
  ◊ *five hundred grammes of cheese*
  fünfhundert Gramm Käse
**grand** ADJECTIVE
<u>prachtvoll</u> ◊ *Samantha lives in a very*
*grand house.* Samantha wohnt in einem
prachtvollen Haus.
**grandchild** NOUN
der <u>Enkel</u> (PL die Enkel)
**granddad** NOUN
der <u>Opa</u> (PL die Opas) ◊ *my granddad*
mein Opa
**granddaughter** NOUN
die <u>Enkelin</u>
**grandfather** NOUN
der <u>Großvater</u> (PL die Großväter) ◊ *my*
*grandfather* mein Großvater
**grandma** NOUN
die <u>Oma</u> (PL die Omas) ◊ *my grandma*
meine Oma
**grandmother** NOUN
die <u>Großmutter</u> (PL die Großmütter)
  ◊ *my grandmother* meine Großmutter
**grandpa** NOUN
der <u>Opa</u> (PL die Opas) ◊ *my grandpa*
mein Opa
**grandparents** PL NOUN
die <u>Großeltern</u> PL ◊ *my grandparents*
meine Großeltern

**grandson** NOUN
der Enkel (PL die Enkel)
**granny** NOUN
die Oma (PL die Omas) ◊ *my granny*
meine Oma
**grant** NOUN
[1] (*for study*)
das Stipendium (PL die Stipendien)
[2] (*for industry, organization*)
die Unterstützung
**grape** NOUN
die Traube
**grapefruit** NOUN
die Grapefruit (PL die Grapefruits)
**graph** NOUN
die grafische Darstellung
**graphics** PL NOUN
die Grafik SING
to **grasp** VERB
[1] (*with hand*)
packen
[2] verstehen (IMPERFECT verstand, PERFECT
hat verstanden) ◊ *I couldn't grasp the
difference.* Ich habe den Unterschied
nicht verstanden.
**grass** NOUN
das Gras (GEN des Grases) ◊ *The grass is
long.* Das Gras ist hoch.
♦ **to cut the grass** den Rasen mähen
**grasshopper** NOUN
die Heuschrecke
to **grate** VERB
reiben (IMPERFECT rieb, PERFECT hat gerieben)
◊ *to grate some cheese* Käse reiben
**grateful** ADJECTIVE
dankbar
**grave** NOUN
das Grab (PL die Gräber)
**gravel** NOUN
der Kies
**graveyard** NOUN
der Friedhof (PL die Friedhöfe)
**gravy** NOUN
die Bratensoße
**grease** NOUN
das Fett (PL die Fette)
**greasy** ADJECTIVE
fettig ◊ *He has greasy hair.* Er hat fettige
Haare.
♦ **The food was very greasy.** Das Essen
war sehr fett.
**great** ADJECTIVE
[1] toll ◊ *That's great!* Das ist toll!
[2] groß (*big*) ◊ *a great mansion* eine
große Villa
**Great Britain** NOUN
Großbritannien NEUT
♦ **from Great Britain** aus Großbritannien
♦ **in Great Britain** in Großbritannien
♦ **to Great Britain** nach Großbritannien
**great-grandfather** NOUN
der Urgroßvater (PL die Urgroßväter)

**great-grandmother** NOUN
die Urgroßmutter (PL die Urgroßmütter)
**Greece** NOUN
Griechenland NEUT
♦ **from Greece** aus Griechenland
♦ **to Greece** nach Griechenland
**greedy** ADJECTIVE
gierig ◊ *I want some more cake. – Don't
be so greedy!* Ich möchte noch etwas
Kuchen. – Sei nicht so gierig!
**Greek** ADJECTIVE
| see also **Greek** NOUN |
griechisch ◊ *I love Greek food.* Ich mag
griechisches Essen sehr gern. ◊ *Dionysis
is Greek.* Dionysis ist Grieche. ◊ *She's
Greek.* Sie ist Griechin.
**Greek** NOUN
| see also **Greek** ADJECTIVE |
[1] (*person*)
der Grieche (GEN des Griechen, PL die
Griechen)
die Griechin
[2] (*language*)
das Griechisch (GEN des Griechischen)
**green** ADJECTIVE
| see also **green** NOUN |
grün ◊ *a green car* ein grünes Auto ◊ *a
green salad* ein grüner Salat
♦ **the Green Party** die Grünen MASC PL
**green** NOUN
| see also **green** ADJECTIVE |
das Grün ◊ *a dark green* ein dunkles
Grün
♦ **greens** (*vegetables*) das Grüngemüse SING
♦ **the Greens** (*party*) die Grünen
**greengrocer's** NOUN
der Gemüsehändler (PL die
Gemüsehändler)
**greenhouse** NOUN
das Treibhaus (GEN des Treibhauses, PL
die Treibhäuser)
♦ **the greenhouse effect** der
Treibhauseffekt
**Greenland** NOUN
Grönland NEUT
to **greet** VERB
begrüßen (PERFECT hat begrüßt) ◊ *He
greeted me with a kiss.* Er begrüßte mich
mit einem Kuss.
**greeting** NOUN
♦ **Greetings from Bangor!** Grüße aus
Bangor!
**greetings card** NOUN
die Grußkarte
**grew** VERB *see* **grow**
**grey** ADJECTIVE
grau ◊ *She's got grey hair.* Sie hat graue
Haare. ◊ *He's going grey.* Er wird grau.
**grey-haired** ADJECTIVE
grauhaarig
**grid** NOUN
[1] (*on map*)

**G**

☞

das Gitter (PL die Gitter)
[2] (of electricity)
das Netz (GEN des Netzes, PL die Netze)

**grief** NOUN
der Kummer

**grill** NOUN
see also **grill** VERB
der Grill (of cooker) (PL die Grills)
♦ **a mixed grill** ein Grillteller MASC

to **grill** VERB
see also **grill** NOUN
grillen

**grim** ADJECTIVE
schlimm ◇ Things look grim. Es sieht schlimm aus.

to **grin** VERB
see also **grin** NOUN
grinsen ◇ Dave grinned at me. Dave grinste mich an.

**grin** NOUN
see also **grin** VERB
das Grinsen

to **grind** VERB
[1] (coffee, pepper)
mahlen (PERFECT hat gemahlen)
[2] (meat)
hacken

to **grip** VERB
packen ◇ I gripped his shirt and pulled him to the ground. Ich packte ihn am Hemd und zog ihn zu Boden.

**gripping** ADJECTIVE
spannend (exciting)

**grit** NOUN
der Splitt (PL die Splitte)

to **groan** VERB
see also **groan** NOUN
stöhnen ◇ He groaned with pain. Er stöhnte vor Schmerzen.

**groan** NOUN
see also **groan** VERB
das Stöhnen (of pain)

**grocer** NOUN
der Lebensmittelhändler (PL die Lebensmittelhändler)
die Lebensmittelhändlerin
◇ He's a grocer. Er ist Lebensmittelhändler.

**groceries** PL NOUN
die Einkäufe MASC PL

**grocer's (shop)** NOUN
das Lebensmittelgeschäft (PL die Lebensmittelgeschäfte)

**grocery store** NOUN US
das Lebensmittelgeschäft (PL die Lebensmittelgeschäfte)

**groom** NOUN
der Bräutigam (bridegroom) (PL die Bräutigame) ◇ the groom and his best man der Bräutigam und sein Trauzeuge

to **grope** VERB

♦ **to grope for something** nach etwas tasten ◇ He groped for the light switch. Er tastete nach dem Lichtschalter.

**gross** ADJECTIVE
abscheulich (revolting) ◇ It was really gross! Es war wirklich abscheulich!

**grossly** ADVERB
total ◇ We're grossly underpaid. Wir sind total unterbezahlt.

**ground** NOUN
see also **ground** VERB
[1] (earth)
der Boden (PL die Böden) ◇ The ground's wet. Der Boden ist nass.
[2] (for sport)
der Platz (GEN des Platzes, PL die Plätze)
◇ a football ground ein Fußballplatz
[3] (reason)
der Grund (PL die Gründe) ◇ We've got grounds for complaint. Wir haben Grund zur Klage.
♦ **on the ground** auf dem Boden ◇ We sat on the ground. Wir saßen auf dem Boden.

**ground** VERB see **grind**
see also **ground** NOUN
♦ **ground coffee** gemahlener Kaffee

**group** NOUN
die Gruppe

to **grow** VERB
[1] (plant, person, animal)
wachsen (PRESENT wächst, IMPERFECT wuchs, PERFECT ist gewachsen) ◇ Grass grows quickly. Gras wächst schnell. ◇ Haven't you grown! Bist du aber gewachsen!
♦ **to grow a beard** sich einen Bart wachsen lassen ◇ You should grow a beard. Du solltest dir einen Bart wachsen lassen.
♦ **He's grown out of his jacket.** Er ist aus der Jacke herausgewachsen.
[2] (increase)
zunehmen (PRESENT nimmt zu, IMPERFECT nahm zu, PERFECT hat zugenommen) ◇ The number of unemployed people has grown. Die Zahl der Arbeitslosen hat zugenommen.
[3] (cultivate)
anbauen (PERFECT hat angebaut) ◇ My Dad grows potatoes. Mein Papa baut Kartoffeln an.
♦ **to grow up** erwachsen werden ◇ Oh, grow up! Werd endlich erwachsen!

to **growl** VERB
knurren

**grown** VERB see **grow**

**growth** NOUN
das Wachstum ◇ economic growth das Wirtschaftswachstum

**grub** NOUN
die Fressalien FEM PL (informal)

**grudge** NOUN
♦ **to bear a grudge against somebody** einen Groll gegen jemanden haben

◊ *He's always borne a grudge against me.* Er hat schon immer einen Groll gegen mich gehabt.

**gruesome** ADJECTIVE
furchtbar

**guarantee** NOUN
> see also **guarantee** VERB

die Garantie ◊ *a five-year guarantee* eine Garantie von fünf Jahren

to **guarantee** VERB
> see also **guarantee** NOUN

garantieren (PERFECT hat garantiert) ◊ *I can't guarantee he'll come.* Ich kann nicht garantieren, dass er kommt.

to **guard** VERB
> see also **guard** NOUN

bewachen (PERFECT hat bewacht) ◊ *They guarded the palace.* Sie bewachten den Palast.

◆ **to guard against something** gegen etwas Vorsichtsmaßnahmen ergreifen

**guard** NOUN
> see also **guard** VERB

(*of train*)
der Zugbegleiter (PL die Zugbegleiter)
die Zugbegleiterin

◆ **a security guard** ein Wachtmann MASC
◆ **a guard dog** ein Wachhund MASC

to **guess** VERB
> see also **guess** NOUN

raten (PRESENT rät, IMPERFECT riet, PERFECT hat geraten) ◊ *Can you guess what it is?* Rate mal, was das ist. ◊ *to guess wrong* falsch raten

**guess** NOUN
> see also **guess** VERB

die Vermutung ◊ *It's just a guess.* Es ist nur eine Vermutung.

◆ **Have a guess!** Rate mal!

**guest** NOUN
der Gast (PL die Gäste)
*der Gast is also used for women.*
◊ *She is our guest.* Sie ist unser Gast.
◊ *We have guests staying with us.* Wir haben Gäste.

**guesthouse** NOUN
die Pension ◊ *We stayed overnight in a guesthouse.* Wir haben in einer Pension übernachtet.

**guide** NOUN
[1] (*book*)
der Führer (PL die Führer) ◊ *We bought a guide to Cologne.* Wir haben einen Führer von Köln gekauft.
[2] (*person*)
der Führer (PL die Führer)

die Führerin
◊ *The guide showed us round the castle.* Unser Führer hat uns die Burg gezeigt.
[3] (*Girl Guide*)
die Pfadfinderin
◆ **the Guides** die Pfadfinderinnen

**guidebook** NOUN
der Führer (PL die Führer)

**guide dog** NOUN
der Blindenhund (PL die Blindenhunde)

**guilty** ADJECTIVE
schuldig ◊ *to feel guilty* sich schuldig fühlen ◊ *She was found guilty.* Sie wurde schuldig gesprochen.

**guinea pig** NOUN
das Meerschweinchen (PL die Meerschweinchen)

**guitar** NOUN
die Gitarre ◊ *I play the guitar.* Ich spiele Gitarre.

**gum** NOUN
der Kaugummi (*chewing gum*) (PL die Kaugummis)
◆ **gums** (*in mouth*) das Zahnfleisch SING

**gun** NOUN
[1] (*small*)
die Pistole
[2] (*rifle*)
das Gewehr (PL die Gewehre)

**gunpoint** NOUN
◆ **at gunpoint** mit Waffengewalt

**gust** NOUN
◆ **a gust of wind** ein Windstoß MASC

**guts** PL NOUN
der Mumm (*informal: courage*) ◊ *He's certainly got guts.* Er hat wirklich Mumm.
◆ **I hate his guts.** Ich kann ihn nicht ausstehen.

**guy** NOUN
der Typ (PL die Typen) ◊ *Who's that guy?* Wer ist der Typ?
◆ **He's a nice guy.** Er ist ein netter Kerl.

**gym** NOUN
die Turnhalle
◆ **gym classes** die Turnstunden

**gymnast** NOUN
der Turner (PL die Turner)
die Turnerin
◊ *She's a gymnast.* Sie ist Turnerin.

**gymnastics** NOUN
das Turnen
◆ **to do gymnastics** turnen

**gypsy** NOUN
der Zigeuner (PL die Zigeuner)
die Zigeunerin

**G**

# H

**habit** NOUN
die Angewohnheit ◊ *a bad habit* eine
schlechte Angewohnheit
**hacker** NOUN
der Hacker (PL die Hacker)
die Hackerin
**had** VERB *see* **have**
**haddock** NOUN
der Schellfisch
**hadn't** = **had not**
**hail** NOUN
see also **hail** VERB
der Hagel
to **hail** VERB
see also **hail** NOUN
hageln ◊ *It's hailing.* Es hagelt.
**hair** NOUN
die Haare NEUT PL ◊ *She's got long hair.*
Sie hat lange Haare. ◊ *He's got black
hair.* Er hat schwarze Haare. ◊ *He's losing
his hair.* Ihm gehen die Haare aus.
♦ **to brush one's hair** sich die Haare
bürsten ◊ *I brush my hair every morning.*
Ich bürste mir jeden Morgen die Haare.
♦ **to wash one's hair** sich die Haare
waschen ◊ *I need to wash my hair.* Ich
muss mir die Haare waschen.
♦ **to have one's hair cut** sich die Haare
schneiden lassen ◊ *I've just had my hair
cut.* Ich habe mir gerade die Haare
schneiden lassen.
♦ **a hair** ein Haar NEUT
**hairbrush** NOUN
die Haarbürste
**hair clip** NOUN
die Haarspange
**haircut** NOUN
der Haarschnitt (PL die Haarschnitte)
♦ **to have a haircut** sich die Haare
schneiden lassen ◊ *I've just had a
haircut.* Ich habe mir gerade die Haare
schneiden lassen.
**hairdresser** NOUN
der Friseur (PL die Friseure)
die Friseuse
◊ *He's a hairdresser.* Er ist Friseur.
**hairdresser's** NOUN
der Friseur (PL die Friseure) ◊ *at the
hairdresser's* beim Friseur
**hair dryer** NOUN
der Haartrockner (PL die Haartrockner)
**hair gel** NOUN
das Haargel (PL die Haargele)
*In German the "g" in* **Haargel** *is
pronounced like the "g" in girl.*
**hairgrip** NOUN
die Haarklemme
**hair spray** NOUN

der Haarspray (PL die Haarsprays)
**hairstyle** NOUN
die Frisur
**hairy** ADJECTIVE
haarig ◊ *He's got hairy legs.* Er hat die
haarige Beine.
**half** NOUN
see also **half** ADJECTIVE
[1] die Hälfte ◊ *half of the cake* die Hälfte
des Kuchens
[2] die Kinderfahrkarte (*ticket*) ◊ *A half to
York, please.* Ein Kinderfahrkarte nach
York bitte.
♦ **two and a half** zweieinhalb
♦ **half an hour** eine halbe Stunde
♦ **half past ten** halb elf
♦ **half a kilo** ein halbes Kilo
♦ **to cut something in half** etwas in zwei
Teile schneiden
**half** ADJECTIVE, ADVERB
see also **half** NOUN
[1] halb ◊ *a half chicken* ein halbes
Hähnchen
[2] fast ◊ *He was half asleep.* Er schlief
fast.
**half-hour** NOUN
die halbe Stunde
**half-price** ADJECTIVE, ADVERB
♦ **at half-price** zum halben Preis
**half-term** NOUN
die kleinen Ferien PL
**half-time** NOUN
die Halbzeit
**halfway** ADVERB
[1] auf halber Strecke ◊ *halfway between
Oxford and London* auf halber Strecke
zwischen Oxford und London
[2] in der Mitte ◊ *halfway through the
chapter* in der Mitte des Kapitels
**hall** NOUN
[1] (*in house*)
der Flur (PL die Flure)
[2] der Saal (PL die Säle) ◊ *the village hall*
der Gemeindesaal
♦ **hall of residence** das Wohnheim
**Hallowe'en** NOUN
der Abend vor Allerheiligen
**hallway** NOUN
der Flur (PL die Flure)
**halt** NOUN
♦ **to come to a halt** zum Stehen kommen
**ham** NOUN
der Schinken (PL die Schinken) ◊ *a ham
sandwich* ein Schinkensandwich NEUT
**hamburger** NOUN
der Hamburger (PL die Hamburger)
**hammer** NOUN
der Hammer (PL die Hämmer)

**hamster** NOUN
der Hamster (PL die Hamster)
**hand** NOUN
see also **hand** VERB
1 (of person)
die Hand (PL die Hände)
◆to give somebody a hand jemandem
helfen ◊ Can you give me a hand?
Kannst du mir mal helfen?
◆on the one hand ..., on the other hand ...
einerseits ..., anderseits ...
2 (of clock)
der Zeiger (PL die Zeiger)
to **hand** VERB
see also **hand** NOUN
reichen ◊ He handed me the book. Er
reichte mir das Buch.
◆to hand something in etwas abgeben
◊ Martin handed his exam paper in.
Martin gab seine Prüfungsarbeit ab.
◆to hand something out etwas austeilen
◊ The teacher handed out the books. Der
Lehrer teilte die Bücher aus.
◆to hand something over etwas
übergeben ◊ She handed the keys over
to me. Sie übergab mir die Schlüssel.
**handbag** NOUN
die Handtasche
**handball** NOUN
1 der Handball (sport)
2 das Handspiel (foul)
**handbook** NOUN
das Handbuch (PL die Handbücher)
**handcuffs** PL NOUN
die Handschellen FEM PL
**handkerchief** NOUN
das Taschentuch (PL die Taschentücher)
**handle** NOUN
see also **handle** VERB
1 (of door)
die Klinke
2 (of cup)
der Henkel (PL die Henkel)
3 (of knife)
der Griff (PL die Griffe)
4 (of saucepan)
der Stiel (PL die Stiele)
to **handle** VERB
see also **handle** NOUN
◆He handled it well. Er hat das gut
gemacht.
◆Kath handled the travel arrangements.
Kath hat sich um die
Reisevorbereitungen gekümmert.
◆She's good at handling children. Sie
kann gut mit Kindern umgehen.
**handlebars** PL NOUN
die Lenkstange SING
**handmade** ADJECTIVE
handgemacht
**handsome** ADJECTIVE
gut aussehend ◊ a handsome man ein
gut aussehender Mann

◆He's very handsome. Er sieht sehr gut
aus.
**handwriting** NOUN
die Handschrift
**handy** ADJECTIVE
1 praktisch ◊ This knife's very handy.
Dieses Messer ist sehr praktisch.
2 zur Hand ◊ Have you got a pen
handy? Hast du einen Schreiber zur
Hand?
to **hang** VERB
1 aufhängen (PERFECT hat aufgehängt)
◊ Mike hung the painting on the wall.
Mike hängte das Bild an der Wand
auf.
2 hängen ◊ They hanged the criminal.
Sie hängten den Verbrecher.
◆to hang around rumhängen ◊ On
Saturdays we hang around in the park.
Samstags hängen wir im Park rum.
◆to hang on warten ◊ Hang on a minute,
please. Bitte warte einen Moment.
◆to hang up (1) (clothes) aufhängen
◊ Hang your jacket up on the hook. Häng
deine Jacke am Haken auf.
◆to hang up (2) (phone) auflegen ◊ I tried
to phone him but he hung up on me. Ich
habe versucht, mit ihm zu telefonieren,
aber er hat einfach aufgelegt.
**hanger** NOUN
der Bügel (for clothes) (PL die Bügel)
**hang-gliding** NOUN
das Drachenfliegen
◆to go hang-gliding Drachen fliegen
gehen
**hangover** NOUN
der Kater (PL die Kater) ◊ to have a
hangover einen Kater haben
to **happen** VERB
passieren (PERFECT ist passiert) ◊ What's
happened? Was ist passiert?
◆as it happens zufälligerweise ◊ As it
happens I saw him yesterday.
Zufälligerweise habe ich ihn gestern
gesehen.
**happily** ADVERB
1 fröhlich ◊ "Don't worry!" he said
happily. "Mach dir keine Sorgen!" sagte
er fröhlich.
2 zum Glück (fortunately) ◊ Happily,
everything went well. Zum Glück ging
alles gut.
**happiness** NOUN
das Glück
**happy** ADJECTIVE
glücklich ◊ Janet looks happy. Janet
sieht glücklich aus.
◆I'm very happy with your work. Ich bin
sehr zufrieden mit Ihrer Arbeit.
◆Happy birthday! Herzlichen
Glückwunsch zum Geburtstag!
**harbour** NOUN
der Hafen (PL die Häfen)

H

**hard** ADJECTIVE, ADVERB

[1] hart ◊ *This cheese is very hard.* Dieser Käse ist sehr hart. ◊ *He's worked very hard.* Er hat sehr hart gearbeitet.

[2] schwierig ◊ *This question's too hard for me.* Diese Frage ist für mich zu schwierig.

**hard disk** NOUN
die Festplatte (*of computer*)

**hardly** ADVERB
kaum ◊ *I've hardly got any money.* Ich habe kaum Geld. ◊ *I hardly know you.* Ich kenne Sie kaum.
◆ **hardly ever** fast nie

**hard up** ADJECTIVE
pleite

**hardware** NOUN
die Hardware

**hare** NOUN
der Feldhase (GEN des Feldhasen, PL die Feldhasen)

to **harm** VERB
◆ **to harm somebody** jemandem wehtun ◊ *I didn't mean to harm you.* Ich wollte Ihnen nicht wehtun.
◆ **to harm something** einer Sache schaden ◊ *Chemicals harm the environment.* Chemikalien schaden der Umwelt.

**harmful** ADJECTIVE
schädlich ◊ *harmful chemicals* schädliche Chemikalien

**harmless** ADJECTIVE
harmlos ◊ *Most spiders are harmless.* Die meisten Spinnen sind harmlos.

**harsh** ADJECTIVE
[1] hart ◊ *He deserves a harsh punishment for what he did.* Er verdient es, hart bestraft zu werden für das, was er getan hat.
[2] rau ◊ *She's got a very harsh voice.* Sie hat eine sehr raue Stimme.

**harvest** NOUN
die Ernte

**has** VERB *see* **have**

**hasn't** = **has not**

**hat** NOUN
der Hut (PL die Hüte)

to **hate** VERB
hassen ◊ *I hate maths.* Ich hasse Mathe.

**hatred** NOUN
der Hass (GEN des Hasses)

**haunted** ADJECTIVE
verwunschen ◊ *a haunted house* ein verwunschenes Haus

to **have** VERB
[1] haben (PRESENT hat, IMPERFECT hatte, PERFECT hat gehabt) ◊ *Have you got a sister?* Hast du eine Schwester? ◊ *He's got blue eyes.* Er hat blaue Augen. ◊ *I've got a cold.* Ich habe eine Erkältung.
*The perfect tense of most verbs is formed with* **haben**.

◊ *They have eaten.* Sie haben gegessen.
◊ *Have you done your homework?* Hast du deine Hausaufgaben gemacht?
*Questions like "hasn't he?" don't exist in German.*
◊ *He's done it, hasn't he?* Er hat es getan, nicht wahr?
**have** *is not translated when it is used in place of another verb.*
◊ *Have you got any money? – No, I haven't.* Hast du Geld? – Nein. ◊ *Does she have any pets? – Yes, she has.* Hat sie Haustiere? – Ja. ◊ *He hasn't done his homework. – Yes, he has.* Er hat seine Hausaufgaben nicht gemacht. – Doch.
[2] sein (PRESENT ist, IMPERFECT war, PERFECT ist gewesen)
*The perfect tense of some verbs is formed with* **sein**.
◊ *They have arrived.* Sie sind angekommen. ◊ *Has he gone?* Ist er gegangen?
**have** *plus noun is sometimes translated by a German verb.*
◊ *He had his breakfast.* Er hat gefrühstückt. ◊ *to have a shower* duschen ◊ *to have a bath* baden
◆ **to have got to do something** etwas tun müssen ◊ *She's got to do it.* Sie muss es tun.
◆ **to have a party** eine Party machen
◆ **I had my hair cut yesterday.** Ich habe mir gestern die Haare schneiden lassen.

**haven't** = **have not**

**hay** NOUN
das Heu

**hay fever** NOUN
der Heuschnupfen ◊ *Do you get hay fever?* Hast du manchmal Heuschnupfen?

**hazelnut** NOUN
die Haselnuss (PL die Haselnüsse)

**he** PRONOUN
er ◊ *He loves dogs.* Er liebt Hunde.

**head** NOUN
see also **head** VERB
[1] (*of person*)
der Kopf (PL die Köpfe) ◊ *The wine went to my head.* Der Wein ist mir in den Kopf gestiegen.
[2] (*of private or primary school*)
der Rektor (PL die Rektoren)
die Rektorin
[3] (*of state secondary school*)
der Direktor (PL die Direktoren)
die Direktorin
[4] (*leader*)
das Oberhaupt (PL die Oberhäupter) ◊ *a head of state* ein Staatsoberhaupt
◆ **to have a head for figures** gut mit Zahlen umgehen können
◆ **Heads or tails? – Heads.** Kopf oder Wappen? – Kopf.

to **head** VERB

see also **head** NOUN

◆ **to head for something** auf etwas
zugehen ◊ *He headed straight for the
bar.* Er ging direkt auf die Theke zu.

**headache** NOUN
die Kopfschmerzen MASC PL ◊ *I've got a
headache.* Ich habe Kopfschmerzen.

**headlight** NOUN
der Scheinwerfer (PL die Scheinwerfer)

**headline** NOUN
die Schlagzeile

**headmaster** NOUN
[1] (*of private or primary school*)
der Rektor (PL die Rektoren)
[2] (*of state secondary school*)
der Direktor (PL die Direktoren)

**headmistress** NOUN
[1] (*of private or primary school*)
die Rektorin
[2] (*of state secondary school*)
die Direktorin

**headphones** PL NOUN
der Kopfhörer (PL die Kopfhörer) ◊ *a set
of headphones* ein Kopfhörer

**headquarters** PL NOUN
das Hauptquartier ◊ *The bank's
headquarters are in London.* Das
Hauptquartier der Bank ist in London.

**headteacher** NOUN
[1] (*of private or primary school*)
der Rektor (PL die Rektoren)
die Rektorin
[2] (*of state secondary school*)
der Direktor (PL die Direktoren)
die Direktorin

to **heal** VERB
heilen

**health** NOUN
die Gesundheit

**healthy** ADJECTIVE
gesund ◊ *Lesley's a healthy person.*
Lesley ist gesund. ◊ *a healthy diet* eine
gesunde Ernährung

**heap** NOUN
der Haufen (PL die Haufen) ◊ *a rubbish
heap* ein Müllhaufen

to **hear** VERB
hören ◊ *He heard the dog bark.* Er hörte
den Hund bellen. ◊ *She can't hear very
well.* Sie hört nicht gut. ◊ *I heard that she
was ill.* Ich habe gehört, dass sie krank
war. ◊ *Did you hear the good news?* Hast
du die gute Nachricht gehört?

◆ **to hear about something** von etwas
hören

◆ **to hear from somebody** von jemandem
hören ◊ *I haven't heard from him
recently.* Ich habe in letzter Zeit nichts
von ihm gehört.

**heart** NOUN
das Herz (GEN des Herzens, PL die Herzen)

◆ **to learn something by heart** etwas
auswendig lernen

◆ **the ace of hearts** das Herzass

**heart attack** NOUN
der Herzinfarkt (PL die Herzinfarkte)

**heartbroken** ADJECTIVE
zutiefst betrübt

**heat** NOUN
see also **heat** VERB
die Hitze

to **heat** VERB
see also **heat** NOUN
erhitzen (PERFECT hat erhitzt) ◊ *Heat gently
for five minutes.* Erhitzen Sie es bei
schwacher Hitze fünf Minuten lang.

◆ **to heat up (1)** (*cooked food*) aufwärmen
◊ *He heated the soup up.* Er hat die
Suppe aufgewärmt.

◆ **to heat up (2)** (*water, oven*) heiß werden
◊ *The water is heating up.* Das Wasser
wird heiß.

**heater** NOUN
der Heizofen (PL die Heizöfen) ◊ *an
electric heater* ein elektrischer Heizofen

**heather** NOUN
das Heidekraut (PL die Heidekräuter)

**heating** NOUN
die Heizung

**heaven** NOUN
der Himmel (PL die Himmel)

**heavily** ADVERB
schwer ◊ *The car was heavily loaded.*
Das Auto war schwer beladen.

◆ **He drinks heavily.** Er trinkt viel.

◆ **It was raining heavily.** Es regnete stark.

**heavy** ADJECTIVE
[1] schwer ◊ *This bag's very heavy.* Diese
Tasche ist sehr schwer.

◆ **heavy rain** starker Regen
[2] anstrengend (*busy*) ◊ *I've got a very
heavy week ahead.* Ich habe eine
anstrengende Woche vor mir.

◆ **to be a heavy drinker** viel trinken

**he'd** = **he would**, = **he had**

**hedge** NOUN
die Hecke

**hedgehog** NOUN
der Igel (PL die Igel)

**heel** NOUN
der Absatz (GEN des Absatzes, PL die
Absätze)

**height** NOUN
[1] die Größe (*of person*)
[2] die Höhe (*of object, mountain*)

**heir** NOUN
der Erbe (GEN des Erben, PL die Erben)

**heiress** NOUN
die Erbin

**held** VERB *see* **hold**

**helicopter** NOUN
der Hubschrauber (PL die Hubschrauber)

**hell** NOUN

**H**

die <u>Hölle</u>
◆ **Hell!** Mist! (*informal*)
**he'll** = **he will**, = **he shall**
**hello** EXCLAMATION
<u>hallo</u>
**helmet** NOUN
der <u>Helm</u> (PL die Helme)
to **help** VERB

| see also **help** NOUN |

<u>helfen</u> (PRESENT hilft, IMPERFECT half, PERFECT
hat geholfen)
◆ **to help somebody** jemandem helfen
◇ *Can you help me?* Kannst du mir
helfen?
◆ **Help!** Hilfe!
◆ **Help yourself!** Bedienen Sie sich!
◆ **He can't help it.** Er kann nichts dafür.
**help** NOUN

| see also **help** VERB |

die <u>Hilfe</u> ◇ *Do you need any help?*
Brauchst du Hilfe?
**helpful** ADJECTIVE
<u>hilfreich</u> ◇ *a helpful suggestion* ein
hilfreicher Vorschlag
◆ **He was very helpful.** Er war eine große
Hilfe.
**help menu** NOUN
das <u>Hilfemenü</u> (PL die Hilfemenüs)
**hen** NOUN
die <u>Henne</u>
**her** ADJECTIVE

| see also **her** PRONOUN |

<u>ihr</u> ◇ *her father* ihr Vater ◇ *her mother*
ihre Mutter ◇ *her child* ihr Kind ◇ *her
parents* ihre Eltern

*Do not use ihr with parts of the body.*

◇ *She's going to wash her hair.* Sie
wäscht sich die Haare. ◇ *She's cleaning
her teeth.* Sie putzt sich die Zähne.
◇ *She's hurt her foot.* Sie hat sich am
Fuß verletzt.
**her** PRONOUN

| see also **her** ADJECTIVE |

1 <u>sie</u> ◇ *I can see her.* Ich kann sie sehen.
◇ *Look at her!* Sieh sie an! ◇ *Who is it? –
It's her again.* Wer ist da? – Sie ist es
schon wieder. ◇ *I'm older than her.* Ich
bin älter als sie.

*Use sie after prepositions which take the
accusative.*

◇ *I was thinking of her.* Ich habe an sie
gedacht.
2 <u>ihr</u>

*Use ihr after prepositions which take the
dative.*

◇ *I'm going with her.* Ich gehe mit ihr mit.
◇ *He sat next to her.* Er saß neben ihr.

*Use ihr when her means to her.*

◇ *I gave her a book.* Ich gab ihr ein Buch.
◇ *I told her the truth.* Ich habe ihr die
Wahrheit gesagt.
**herb** NOUN

das <u>Kraut</u> (PL die Kräuter)
**here** ADVERB
<u>hier</u> ◇ *I live here.* Ich wohne hier.
◇ *Here's Helen.* Hier ist Helen. ◇ *Here are
the books.* Hier sind die Bücher. ◇ *Here
he is!* Da ist er ja!
**hero** NOUN
der <u>Held</u> (GEN des Helden, PL die Helden)
◇ *He's a real hero!* Er ist ein echter Held!
**heroin** NOUN
das <u>Heroin</u> ◇ *Heroin is a hard drug.*
Heroin ist eine harte Droge.
◆ **a heroin addict** (*man*) ein
Heroinsüchtiger
◆ **She's a heroin addict.** Sie ist
heroinsüchtig.
**heroine** NOUN
die <u>Heldin</u> ◇ *the heroine of the novel* die
Heldin des Romans
**hers** PRONOUN
1 <u>ihrer</u> ◇ *Is this her coat? – No, hers is
black.* Ist das ihr Mantel? – Nein, ihrer ist
schwarz.
<u>ihre</u> ◇ *Is this her cup? – No, hers is red.*
Ist das ihre Tasse? – Nein, ihre ist rot.
<u>ihres</u> ◇ *Is this her car? – No, hers is white.*
Ist das ihr Auto? – Nein, ihres ist weiß.
2 <u>ihre</u> ◇ *my parents and hers* meine
Eltern und ihre ◇ *I have my reasons and
she has hers.* Ich habe meine Gründe
und sie hat ihre.
◆ **Is this hers?** Gehört das ihr? ◇ *This book
is hers.* Dieses Buch gehört ihr. ◇ *Whose
is this? – It's hers.* Wem gehört das? – Es
gehört ihr.
**herself** PRONOUN
1 <u>sich</u> ◇ *She's hurt herself.* Sie hat sich
verletzt. ◇ *She talked mainly about
herself.* Sie redete hauptsächlich über
sich selbst.
2 <u>selbst</u> ◇ *She did it herself.* Sie hat es
selbst gemacht.
◆ **by herself** allein ◇ *She doesn't like
travelling by herself.* Sie verreist nicht
gern allein.
**he's** = **he is**, = **he has**
to **hesitate** VERB
<u>zögern</u>
**heterosexual** ADJECTIVE
<u>heterosexuell</u>
**hi** EXCLAMATION
<u>hallo</u>
**hiccups** PL NOUN
der <u>Schluckauf</u> SING ◇ *He had the hiccups.*
Er hatte einen Schluckauf.
to **hide** VERB
<u>sich verstecken</u> (PERFECT hat sich
versteckt) ◇ *He hid behind a bush.* Er
versteckte sich hinter einem Busch.
◆ **to hide something** etwas verstecken
◇ *Paula hid the present.* Paula hat das
Geschenk versteckt.
**hide-and-seek** NOUN

◆**to play hide-and-seek** Versteck en spielen
**hideous** ADJECTIVE
  scheußlich
**hi-fi** NOUN
  die Hi-Fi-Anlage
**high** ADJECTIVE, ADVERB
  hoch ◊ *It's too high.* Es ist zu hoch.
  ◊ *How high is the wall?* Wie hoch ist die
  Mauer? ◊ *The wall's two metres high.*
  Die Mauer ist zwei Meter hoch.
  *Before a noun or after an article, use*
  *hohe.*
  ◊ *She's got a very high voice.* Sie hat
  eine sehr hohe Stimme. ◊ *a high price*
  ein hoher Preis ◊ *a high temperature*
  eine hohe Temperatur ◊ *at high speed*
  mit hoher Geschwindigkeit
◆**It's very high in fat.** Es ist sehr fetthaltig.
◆**to be high** (*on drugs*) high sein (*informal*)
◆**to get high** (*on drugs*) high werden
  (*informal*) ◊ *to get high on crack* von
  Crack high werden
**higher education** NOUN
  die Hochschulbildung
**high-heeled** ADJECTIVE
◆**high-heeled shoes** hochhackige Schuhe
**high jump** NOUN
  der Hochsprung (*sport*) (PL die
  Hochsprünge)
**highlight** NOUN
  see also **highlight** VERB
  der Höhepunkt (PL die Höhepunkte) ◊ *the*
  *highlight of the evening* der Höhepunkt
  des Abends
to **highlight** VERB
  see also **highlight** NOUN
  markieren (PERFECT hat markiert) ◊ *She*
  *highlighted the word in yellow.* Sie
  markierte das Wort in Gelb.
**highlighter** NOUN
  der Textmarker (PL die Textmarker)
**high-rise** NOUN
  das Hochhaus (GEN des Hochhauses, PL
  die Hochhäuser) ◊ *I live in a high-rise.* Ich
  wohne in einem Hochhaus.
**high school** NOUN
  das Gymnasium (PL die Gymnasien)
to **hijack** VERB
  entführen (PERFECT hat entführt)
**hijacker** NOUN
  der Entführer (PL die Entführer)
  die Entführerin
**hike** NOUN
  die Wanderung
**hiking** NOUN
◆**to go hiking** wandern gehen
**hilarious** ADJECTIVE
  urkomisch ◊ *It was hilarious!* Es war
  urkomisch!
**hill** NOUN
  der Hügel (PL die Hügel) ◊ *She walked up*
  *the hill.* Sie ging den Hügel hinauf.

**hill-walking** NOUN
  das Bergwandern
◆**to go hill-walking** Bergwanderungen
  machen
**him** PRONOUN
  [1] ihn ◊ *I can see him.* Ich kann ihn
  sehen. ◊ *Look at him!* Sieh ihn an!
  *Use **ihn** after prepositions which take the*
  *accusative.*
  ◊ *I did it for him.* Ich habe es für ihn getan.
  [2] ihm
  *Use **ihm** after prepositions which take*
  *the dative.*
  ◊ *I travelled with him.* Ich bin mit ihm
  gereist. ◊ *I haven't heard from him.* Ich
  habe nichts von ihm gehört.
  *Use **ihm** when **him** means to him.*
  ◊ *I gave him a book.* Ich gab ihm ein
  Buch. ◊ *I told him the truth.* Ich habe ihm
  die Wahrheit gesagt.
  [3] er ◊ *It's him again.* Er ist es schon
  wieder. ◊ *I'm older than him.* Ich bin älter
  als er.
**himself** PRONOUN
  [1] sich ◊ *He's hurt himself.* Er hat sich
  verletzt. ◊ *He talked mainly about*
  *himself.* Er redete hauptsächlich über
  sich selbst.
  [2] selbst ◊ *He did it himself.* Er hat es
  selbst gemacht.
◆**by himself** allein ◊ *He was travelling by*
  *himself.* Er reiste allein.
**Hindu** ADJECTIVE
  hinduistisch
◆**a Hindu temple** ein Hindutempel MASC
**hint** NOUN
  see also **hint** VERB
  die Andeutung ◊ *to drop a hint* eine
  Andeutung machen
◆**I can take a hint.** Ich verstehe schon.
to **hint** VERB
  see also **hint** NOUN
  andeuten (PERFECT hat angedeutet) ◊ *He*
  *hinted that I had a good chance of*
  *getting the job.* Er deutete an, dass ich
  gute Chancen habe, die Stelle zu
  bekommen.
**hip** NOUN
  die Hüfte
**hippie** NOUN
  der Hippie (PL die Hippies)
  *der Hippie is also used for women.*
  ◊ *She was a hippie.* Sie war ein Hippie.
**hippo** NOUN
  das Nilpferd (PL die Nilpferde)
to **hire** VERB
  see also **hire** NOUN
  [1] mieten ◊ *to hire a car* ein Auto mieten
  [2] (*person*)
  anstellen (PERFECT hat angestellt) ◊ *They*
  *hired a cleaner.* Sie haben eine Putzfrau
  angestellt.
**hire** NOUN

**H**

☞

see also **hire** VERB

der Verleih (PL die Verleihe)
- **car hire** der Autoverleih
- **for hire** zu vermieten

**hire car** NOUN
der Mietwagen (PL die Mietwagen)

**his** ADJECTIVE

see also **his** PRONOUN

sein ◊ *his father* sein Vater ◊ *his mother* seine Mutter ◊ *his child* sein Kind ◊ *his parents* seine Eltern
*Do not use sein with parts of the body.*
◊ *He's going to wash his hair.* Er wäscht sich die Haare. ◊ *He's cleaning his teeth.* Er putzt sich die Zähne. ◊ *He's hurt his foot.* Er hat sich am Fuß verletzt.

**his** PRONOUN

see also **his** ADJECTIVE

[1] seiner ◊ *Is this his coat? – No, his is black.* Ist das sein Mantel? – Nein, seiner ist schwarz.
seine ◊ *Is this his cup? – No, his is red.* Ist das seine Tasse? – Nein, seine ist rot.
seines ◊ *Is this his car? – No, his is white.* Ist das sein Auto? – Nein, seines ist weiß.
[2] seine ◊ *my parents and his* meine Eltern und seine ◊ *I have my reasons and he has his.* Ich habe meine Gründe und er hat seine.
- **Is this his?** Gehört das ihm? ◊ *This book is his.* Dieses Buch gehört ihm. ◊ *Whose is this? – It's his.* Wem gehört das? – Das gehört ihm.

**history** NOUN
die Geschichte

to **hit** VERB

see also **hit** NOUN

[1] schlagen (PRESENT schlägt, IMPERFECT schlug, PERFECT hat geschlagen) ◊ *Andrew hit him.* Andrew hat ihn geschlagen.
[2] anfahren (PRESENT fährt an, IMPERFECT fuhr an, PERFECT hat angefahren) ◊ *He was hit by a car.* Er wurde von einem Auto angefahren.
[3] treffen (PRESENT trifft, IMPERFECT traf, PERFECT hat getroffen) ◊ *The arrow hit the target.* Der Pfeil traf sein Ziel.
- **to hit it off with somebody** sich gut mit jemandem verstehen ◊ *She hit it off with his parents.* Sie hat sich mit seinen Eltern gut verstanden.

**hit** NOUN

see also **hit** VERB

[1] (*song*)
der Hit (PL die Hits) ◊ *Blur's latest hit* Blurs neuester Hit
[2] (*success*)
der Erfolg (PL die Erfolge) ◊ *The film was a massive hit.* Der Film war ein enormer Erfolg.

**hitch** NOUN

das Problem (PL die Probleme) ◊ *There's been a slight hitch.* Es gab ein kleineres Problem.

to **hitchhike** VERB
per Anhalter fahren (PRESENT fährt, IMPERFECT fuhr, PERFECT ist gefahren)

**hitchhiker** NOUN
der Anhalter (PL die Anhalter)
die Anhalterin

**hitchhiking** NOUN
das Trampen ◊ *Hitchhiking can be dangerous.* Trampen kann gefährlich sein.

**hit man** NOUN
der Killer (PL die Killer)

**HIV-negative** ADJECTIVE
HIV-negativ

**HIV-positive** ADJECTIVE
HIV-positiv

**hobby** NOUN
das Hobby (PL die Hobbys) ◊ *What are your hobbies?* Welche Hobbys haben Sie?

**hockey** NOUN
das Hockey ◊ *I play hockey.* Ich spiele Hockey.

to **hold** VERB
[1] (*hold on to*)
halten (PRESENT hält, IMPERFECT hielt, PERFECT hat gehalten) ◊ *Hold this end of the rope, please.* Halt bitte dieses Ende des Seils.
- **She held a bottle in her hand.** Sie hatte eine Flasche in der Hand.
[2] (*contain*)
fassen ◊ *This bottle holds two litres.* Diese Flasche fasst zwei Liter.
- **to hold a meeting** eine Versammlung abhalten
- **Hold the line!** (*on telephone*) Bleiben Sie am Apparat!
- **Hold it!** (*wait*) Sekunde!
- **to get hold of something** (*obtain*) etwas bekommen ◊ *I couldn't get hold of it.* Ich habe es nicht bekommen.

to **hold on** VERB
[1] (*keep hold*)
sich festhalten (PRESENT hält sich fest, IMPERFECT hielt sich fest, PERFECT hat sich festgehalten) ◊ *The cliff was slippery, but he managed to hold on.* Die Klippe war sehr rutschig, aber er konnte sich festhalten.
- **to hold on to something (1)** sich an etwas klammern ◊ *He held on to the railing.* Er klammerte sich an das Geländer.
- **to hold on to something (2)** etwas behalten ◊ *He held on to the book, just in case.* Er hat das Buch vorsichtshalber behalten.
[2] (*wait*)
warten ◊ *Hold on, I'm coming!* Warte, ich komme!

◆**Hold on!** (*on telephone*) Bleiben Sie am Apparat!

to **hold up** VERB

◆**to hold up one's hand** die Hand heben ◊ *Peter held up his hand.* Peter hob die Hand.

◆**to hold somebody up** (*delay*) jemanden aufhalten ◊ *I was held up at the office.* Ich wurde im Büro aufgehalten.

◆**to hold up a bank** (*rob*) eine Bank überfallen

**hold-up** NOUN

1 (*at bank*)
der <u>Überfall</u> (PL die Überfälle)
2 (*delay*)
die <u>Verzögerung</u>
3 (*traffic jam*)
der <u>Stau</u> (PL die Staus)

**hole** NOUN
das <u>Loch</u> (PL die Löcher)

**holiday** NOUN

1 (*from school*)
die <u>Ferien</u> PL ◊ *Did you have a good holiday?* Hattet ihr schöne Ferien?

◆**on holiday** in den Ferien ◊ *to go on holiday* in die Ferien fahren ◊ *We are on holiday.* Wir haben Ferien.

◆**the school holidays** die Schulferien
2 (*from work*)
der <u>Urlaub</u> (PL die Urlaube) ◊ *Did you have a good holiday?* Hattet ihr einen schönen Urlaub?

◆**on holiday** im Urlaub ◊ *to go on holiday* in Urlaub fahren ◊ *We are on holiday.* Wir sind im Urlaub.
3 (*public holiday*)
der <u>Feiertag</u> (PL die Feiertage) ◊ *Next Wednesday is a holiday.* Nächsten Mittwoch ist ein Feiertag.
4 (*day off*)
der <u>freie Tag</u> (PL die freien Tage)

◆**He took a day's holiday.** Er nahm einen Tag frei.

◆**a holiday camp** ein Ferienlager NEUT

**Holland** NOUN
<u>Holland</u> NEUT

◆**from Holland** aus Holland
◆**in Holland** in Holland
◆**to Holland** nach Holland

**hollow** ADJECTIVE
<u>hohl</u>

**holly** NOUN
die <u>Stechpalme</u>

**holy** ADJECTIVE
<u>heilig</u>

**home** NOUN

see also **home** ADVERB

das <u>Zuhause</u> (GEN des Zuhause)

◆**at home** zu Hause
◆**Make yourself at home.** Machen Sie es sich bequem.

**home** ADVERB

see also **home** NOUN

1 <u>zu Hause</u> ◊ *to be at home* zu Hause sein
2 <u>nach Hause</u> ◊ *to go home* nach Hause gehen

◆**to get home** nach Hause kommen ◊ *What time did he get home?* Wann ist er nach Hause gekommen?

**home address** NOUN
die <u>Adresse</u> ◊ *What's your home address?* Wie ist Ihre Adresse?

**homeland** NOUN
das <u>Heimatland</u> (PL die Heimatländer)

**homeless** ADJECTIVE
<u>obdachlos</u>

◆**the homeless** die Obdachlosen MASC PL

**home match** NOUN
das <u>Heimspiel</u> (PL die Heimspiele)

**homeopathy** NOUN
die <u>Homöopathie</u>

**home page** NOUN
die <u>Homepage</u> (*Internet*) (PL die Homepages)

**homesick** ADJECTIVE

◆**to be homesick** Heimweh haben

**homework** NOUN
die <u>Hausaufgaben</u> FEM PL ◊ *Have you done your homework?* Hast du deine Hausaufgaben gemacht? ◊ *my geography homework* meine Erdkundeaufgaben

**homosexual** ADJECTIVE

see also **homosexual** NOUN

<u>homosexuell</u>

**homosexual** NOUN

see also **homosexual** ADJECTIVE

der <u>Homosexuelle</u> (GEN des Homosexuellen, PL die Homosexuellen) ◊ *a homosexual (man)* ein Homosexueller

**honest** ADJECTIVE
<u>ehrlich</u> ◊ *She's an honest person.* Sie ist ein ehrlicher Mensch. ◊ *He was very honest with her.* Er war sehr ehrlich zu ihr.

**honestly** ADVERB
<u>ehrlich</u> ◊ *I honestly don't know.* Ich weiß es ehrlich nicht.

**honesty** NOUN
die <u>Ehrlichkeit</u>

**honey** NOUN
der <u>Honig</u>

**honeymoon** NOUN
die <u>Flitterwochen</u> FEM PL

**honour** NOUN
die <u>Ehre</u>

**hood** NOUN
1 die <u>Kapuze</u> ◊ *a coat with a hood* ein Mantel mit Kapuze
2 die <u>Motorhaube</u> (*of car*)

**hook** NOUN
der <u>Haken</u> (PL die Haken) ◊ *He hung the painting on the hook.* Er hängte das Bild an den Haken.

H

◆ **to take the phone off the hook** das Telefon aushängen

◆ **a fish-hook** ein Angelhaken

**hooligan** NOUN
der <u>Rowdy</u> (PL die Rowdys)

**hooray** EXCLAMATION
<u>hurra</u>

**Hoover** ® NOUN
der <u>Staubsauger</u> (PL die Staubsauger)

to **hoover** VERB
<u>staubsaugen</u> ◊ *She hoovered the lounge.* Sie hat im Wohnzimmer gestaubsaugt.

to **hop** VERB
<u>hüpfen</u> (PERFECT ist gehüpft)

to **hope** VERB

| see also **hope** NOUN |

<u>hoffen</u> ◊ *I hope he comes.* Ich hoffe, er kommt. ◊ *I'm hoping for good results.* Ich hoffe, dass ich gute Noten bekomme.

◆ **I hope so.** Hoffentlich.

◆ **I hope not.** Hoffentlich nicht.

**hope** NOUN

| see also **hope** VERB |

die <u>Hoffnung</u>

◆ **to give up hope** die Hoffnung aufgeben ◊ *Don't give up hope!* Gib die Hoffnung nicht auf!

**hopeful** ADJECTIVE
1 <u>zuversichtlich</u> ◊ *I'm hopeful.* Ich bin zuversichtlich.

◆ **He's hopeful of winning.** Er rechnet sich Gewinnchancen aus.

2 <u>aussichtsreich</u> (*situation*)

◆ **The prospects look hopeful.** Die Aussichten sind gut.

**hopefully** ADVERB
<u>hoffentlich</u> ◊ *Hopefully he'll make it in time.* Hoffentlich schafft er es noch.

**hopeless** ADJECTIVE
<u>hoffnungslos</u> ◊ *I'm hopeless at maths.* In Mathe bin ich ein hoffnungsloser Fall.

**horizon** NOUN
der <u>Horizont</u> (PL die Horizonte)

**horizontal** ADJECTIVE
<u>horizontal</u>

**horn** NOUN
1 (*of car*)
die <u>Hupe</u>

◆ **He sounded his horn.** Er hat gehupt.

2 das <u>Horn</u> (PL die Hörner) ◊ *I play the horn.* Ich spiele Horn.

**horoscope** NOUN
das <u>Horoskop</u> (PL die Horoskope)

**horrible** ADJECTIVE
<u>furchtbar</u> ◊ *What a horrible dress!* Was für ein furchtbares Kleid!

to **horrify** VERB
<u>entsetzen</u> ◊ *I was horrified by the news.* Ich war über die Neuigkeiten entsetzt.

**horrifying** ADJECTIVE

<u>schrecklich</u> ◊ *a horrifying accident* ein schrecklicher Unfall

**horror** NOUN
der <u>Horror</u>

**horror film** NOUN
der <u>Horrorfilm</u> (PL die Horrorfilme)

**horse** NOUN
das <u>Pferd</u> (PL die Pferde)

**horse-racing** NOUN
das <u>Pferderennen</u> (PL die Pferderennen)

**horseshoe** NOUN
das <u>Hufeisen</u> (PL die Hufeisen)

**hose** NOUN
der <u>Schlauch</u> (PL die Schläuche) ◊ *a garden hose* ein Gartenschlauch

*Be careful not to translate **hose** by the German word **Hose**.*

**hosepipe** NOUN
der <u>Schlauch</u> (PL die Schläuche)

**hospital** NOUN
das <u>Krankenhaus</u> (GEN des Krankenhauses, PL die Krankenhäuser) ◊ *Take me to the hospital!* Bringen Sie mich ins Krankenhaus! ◊ *in hospital* im Krankenhaus

**hospitality** NOUN
die <u>Gastfreundschaft</u>

**host** NOUN
1 der <u>Gastgeber</u> (PL die Gastgeber)
die <u>Gastgeberin</u>
2 (*television*)
der <u>Moderator</u> (PL die Moderatoren)
die <u>Moderatorin</u>

**hostage** NOUN
die <u>Geisel</u> ◊ *to take somebody hostage* jemanden als Geisel nehmen

**hostel** NOUN
die <u>Herberge</u>

**hostile** ADJECTIVE
<u>feindlich</u>

**hot** ADJECTIVE
1 <u>heiß</u> (*warm*) ◊ *a hot bath* ein heißes Bad ◊ *a hot country* ein heißes Land ◊ *It's hot.* Es ist heiß. ◊ *It's very hot today.* Heute ist es sehr heiß.

*When you talk about a person being **hot**, you use the impersonal construction.*
◊ *I'm hot.* Mir ist heiß. ◊ *I'm too hot.* Mir ist es zu heiß.

2 <u>scharf</u> (*spicy*) ◊ *a very hot curry* ein sehr scharfes Curry

**hot dog** NOUN
der <u>Hotdog</u> (PL die Hotdogs)

**hotel** NOUN
das <u>Hotel</u> (PL die Hotels) ◊ *We stayed in a hotel.* Wir haben in einem Hotel übernachtet.

**hour** NOUN
die <u>Stunde</u> ◊ *She always takes hours to get ready.* Sie braucht immer Stunden, bis sie fertig ist.

◆ **a quarter of an hour** eine Viertelstunde

◆ **half an hour** eine halbe Stunde

♦ **two and a half hours** zweieinhalb Stunden

**hourly** ADJECTIVE, ADVERB
stündlich ◊ *There are hourly buses.* Der Bus verkehrt stündlich.
♦ **to be paid hourly** stundenweise bezahlt werden

**house** NOUN
das Haus (GEN des Hauses, PL die Häuser)
♦ **at his house** bei ihm zu Hause
♦ **We stayed at their house.** Wir haben bei ihnen übernachtet.

**housewife** NOUN
die Hausfrau ◊ *She's a housewife.* Sie ist Hausfrau.

**housework** NOUN
die Hausarbeit ◊ *to do the housework* die Hausarbeit machen

**hovercraft** NOUN
das Luftkissenfahrzeug (PL die Luftkissenfahrzeuge)

**how** ADVERB
wie ◊ *How old are you?* Wie alt bist du?
◊ *How far is it to Edinburgh?* Wie weit ist es nach Edinburgh? ◊ *How long have you been here?* Wie lange sind Sie schon hier? ◊ *How are you?* Wie geht's?
♦ **How much?** Wie viel? ◊ *How much sugar do you want?* Wie viel Zucker willst du?
♦ **How many?** Wie viele? ◊ *How many pupils are there in the class?* Wie viele Schüler sind in der Klasse?

**however** CONJUNCTION
aber ◊ *This, however, isn't true.* Das ist aber nicht wahr.

to **howl** VERB
heulen

**HTML** ABBREVIATION (= *hypertext markup language*)
HTML

to **hug** VERB
see also **hug** NOUN
umarmen (PERFECT hat umarmt) ◊ *He hugged her.* Er umarmte sie.

**hug** NOUN
see also **hug** VERB
♦ **to give somebody a hug** jemanden umarmen ◊ *She gave them a hug.* Sie umarmte sie.

**huge** ADJECTIVE
riesig

to **hum** VERB
summen ◊ *She hummed to herself.* Sie summte vor sich hin.

**human** ADJECTIVE
menschlich ◊ *the human body* der menschliche Körper

**human being** NOUN
der Mensch (GEN des Menschen, PL die Menschen)

**humble** ADJECTIVE
bescheiden

**humour** NOUN
der Humor
♦ **to have a sense of humour** Humor haben

**hundred** NUMBER
♦ **a hundred** einhundert ◊ *a hundred marks* einhundert Mark
♦ **five hundred** fünfhundert
♦ **five hundred and one** fünfhundertundeins
♦ **hundreds of people** Hunderte von Menschen

**hung** VERB see **hang**

**Hungarian** ADJECTIVE
ungarisch

**Hungary** NOUN
Ungarn NEUT
♦ **from Hungary** aus Ungarn
♦ **to Hungary** nach Ungarn

**hunger** NOUN
der Hunger

**hungry** ADJECTIVE
♦ **to be hungry** Hunger haben

to **hunt** VERB
jagen ◊ *People used to hunt wild boar.* Menschen haben früher Wildschweine gejagt.
♦ **to go hunting** auf die Jagd gehen
♦ **The police are hunting the killer.** Die Polizei sucht den Mörder.
♦ **to hunt for something** (*search*) nach etwas suchen ◊ *I hunted everywhere for that book.* Ich habe überall nach diesem Buch gesucht.

**hunting** NOUN
das Jagen ◊ *I'm against hunting.* Ich bin gegen Jagen.
♦ **fox-hunting** die Fuchsjagd

**hurdle** NOUN
die Hürde ◊ *the 100 metres hurdles* die 100 Meter Hürden

**hurricane** NOUN
der Orkan (PL die Orkane)

to **hurry** VERB
see also **hurry** NOUN
eilen (PERFECT ist geeilt) ◊ *Sharon hurried back home.* Sharon eilte nach Hause.
♦ **Hurry up!** Beeil dich!

**hurry** NOUN
see also **hurry** VERB
♦ **to be in a hurry** in Eile sein
♦ **to do something in a hurry** etwas auf die Schnelle machen
♦ **There's no hurry.** Das eilt nicht.

to **hurt** VERB
see also **hurt** ADJECTIVE
wehtun (IMPERFECT tat weh, PERFECT hat wehgetan) ◊ *That hurts.* Das tut weh.
◊ *My leg hurts.* Mein Bein tut weh. ◊ *It hurts to have a tooth out.* Es tut weh, wenn einem ein Zahn gezogen wird.
♦ **to hurt somebody (1)** jemandem wehtun ◊ *You're hurting me!* Du tust mir weh!

**H**

☞

♦ **to hurt somebody (2)** (*offend*) jemanden verletzen ◊ *His remarks hurt me.* Seine Bemerkungen haben mich verletzt.

♦ **to hurt oneself** sich wehtun ◊ *I fell over and hurt myself.* Ich bin hingefallen und habe mir wehgetan.

**hurt** ADJECTIVE

see also **hurt** VERB

verletzt ◊ *Is he badly hurt?* Ist er schlimm verletzt? ◊ *He was hurt in the leg.* Er hatte ein verletztes Bein. ◊ *Luckily, nobody got hurt.* Zum Glück wurde niemand verletzt. ◊ *I was hurt by what he said.* Was er sagte hat mich verletzt.

**husband** NOUN
  der Ehemann (PL die Ehemänner)
**hut** NOUN
  die Hütte

**hymn** NOUN
  das Kirchenlied (PL die Kirchenlieder)
**hypermarket** NOUN
  der Verbrauchermarkt (PL die Verbrauchermärkte)
**hyphen** NOUN
  der Bindestrich (PL die Bindestriche)

**I** PRONOUN
ich ◊ *I speak German.* Ich spreche
Deutsch. ◊ *Ann and I* Ann und ich
**ice** NOUN
[1] das Eis
♦ **There was ice on the lake.** Der See war
gefroren.
[2] das Glatteis (*on road*)
**iceberg** NOUN
der Eisberg (PL die Eisberge)
**icebox** NOUN US
der Kühlschrank (PL die
Kühlschränke)
**ice cream** NOUN
das Eis (PL die Eis) ◊ *vanilla ice cream*
das Vanilleeis
**ice cube** NOUN
der Eiswürfel (PL die Eiswürfel)
**ice hockey** NOUN
das Eishockey ◊ *I like ice hockey.* Ich
mag Eishockey.
**Iceland** NOUN
Island NEUT
♦ **from Iceland** aus Island
♦ **to Iceland** nach Island
**ice lolly** NOUN
das Eis am Stiel
**ice rink** NOUN
die Eisbahn
**ice-skating** NOUN
das Schlittschuhlaufen
♦ **I like ice-skating.** Ich laufe gern
Schlittschuh.
♦ **to go ice-skating** Schlittschuh laufen
gehen
**icing** NOUN
der Zuckerguss (*on cake*) (GEN des
Zuckergusses)
♦ **icing sugar** der Puderzucker
**icon** NOUN
das Icon (*computer*) (PL die Icons) ◊ *to
click on an icon* ein Icon anklicken
**icy** ADJECTIVE
eiskalt ◊ *There was an icy wind.* Es
wehte ein eiskalter Wind.
♦ **The roads are icy.** Die Straßen sind
vereist.
**I'd** = I had, = I would
**idea** NOUN
die Idee ◊ *Good idea!* Gute Idee!
**ideal** ADJECTIVE
ideal
**identical** ADJECTIVE
identisch ◊ *identical to* identisch mit
**identification** NOUN
die Identifikation
♦ **Have you got any identification?** Können
Sie sich ausweisen?

to **identify** VERB
identifizieren (PERFECT hat identifiziert)
**identity card** NOUN
der Personalausweis (PL die
Personalausweise)
**idiom** NOUN
die Redewendung
**idiot** NOUN
der Idiot (GEN des Idioten, PL die Idioten)
die Idiotin
**idiotic** ADJECTIVE
idiotisch
**idle** ADJECTIVE
faul (*lazy*) ◊ *to be idle* faul sein
♦ **It's just idle gossip.** Das ist nur sinnloses
Geschwätz.
♦ **I asked out of idle curiosity.** Ich habe aus
reiner Neugier gefragt.
**i.e.** ABBREVIATION
d. h. (= das heißt)
**if** CONJUNCTION
[1] wenn ◊ *You can have it if you like.*
Wenn du willst, kannst du es haben.
[2] ob (*whether*) ◊ *Do you know if he's
there?* Weißt du, ob er da ist?
♦ **if only** wenn doch nur ◊ *If only I had
more money!* Wenn ich doch nur mehr
Geld hätte!
♦ **if not** falls nicht ◊ *Are you coming? If
not, I'll go with Mark.* Kommst du? Falls
nicht, gehe ich mit Mark.
**ignorant** ADJECTIVE
unwissend
to **ignore** VERB
[1] nicht beachten (PERFECT hat nicht
beachtet) ◊ *She ignored my advice.* Sie
hat meinen Rat nicht beachtet.
[2] ignorieren (PERFECT hat ignoriert) ◊ *She
saw me, but she ignored me.* Sie sah
mich, hat mich aber ignoriert.
♦ **Just ignore him!** Beachte ihn einfach
nicht!
**ill** ADJECTIVE
krank (*sick*)
♦ **to be taken ill** krank werden ◊ *She was
taken ill while on holiday.* Sie wurde im
Urlaub krank.
**I'll** = I will
**illegal** ADJECTIVE
illegal
**illegible** ADJECTIVE
unleserlich
**illness** NOUN
die Krankheit
to **ill-treat** VERB
misshandeln (PERFECT hat misshandelt)
**illusion** NOUN
die Illusion

**illustration** NOUN
die Illustration

**I'm** = **I am**

**image** NOUN
das Image (*public image*) (GEN des Image,
PL die Images) ◊ *The company has
changed its image.* Die Firma hat sich ein
anderes Image zugelegt.

**imagination** NOUN
die Fantasie ◊ *You need a lot of
imagination to be a writer.* Als
Schriftsteller braucht man viel Fantasie.
♦ **It's just your imagination!** Das bildest du
dir nur ein!

to **imagine** VERB
sich vorstellen (PERFECT hat sich
vorgestellt) ◊ *You can imagine how I felt!*
Du kannst dir vorstellen, wie mir zumute
war!
♦ **Is he angry? – I imagine so.** Ist er böse? –
Ich denke schon.

to **imitate** VERB
nachmachen (PERFECT hat nachgemacht)

**imitation** NOUN
die Imitation

**immediate** ADJECTIVE
sofortig ◊ *We need an immediate
answer.* Wir brauchen eine sofortige
Antwort.
♦ **in the immediate future** in unmittelbarer
Zukunft

**immediately** ADVERB
sofort ◊ *I'll do it immediately.* Ich mache
es sofort.

**immigrant** NOUN
der Einwanderer (PL die Einwanderer)
die Einwanderin

**immigration** NOUN
die Einwanderung

**immoral** ADJECTIVE
unmoralisch

**immune** ADJECTIVE
♦ **to be immune to something** gegen
etwas immun sein ◊ *She is immune to
measles.* Sie ist gegen Masern
immun.

**impartial** ADJECTIVE
unparteiisch

**impatience** NOUN
die Ungeduld

**impatient** ADJECTIVE
ungeduldig ◊ *People are getting
impatient.* Die Leute werden ungeduldig.

**impersonal** ADJECTIVE
unpersönlich

to **implement** VERB
ausführen (PERFECT hat ausgeführt) ◊ *It'll
take a few months to implement the
plan.* Es wird ein paar Monate dauern,
bis der Plan ausgeführt ist.

to **imply** VERB

[1] andeuten (PERFECT hat angedeutet)
◊ *Are you implying I did it on purpose?*
Wollen Sie damit andeuten, ich hätte das
absichtlich getan?
[2] bedeuten (PERFECT hat bedeutet) ◊ *It
implies a lot of work.* Das bedeutet viel
Arbeit.

to **import** VERB
importieren (PERFECT hat importiert)

**importance** NOUN
die Wichtigkeit ◊ *the importance of a
good knowledge of German* die
Wichtigkeit guter Deutschkenntnisse

**important** ADJECTIVE
wichtig

to **impose** VERB
auferlegen (PERFECT hat auferlegt) ◊ *to
impose a penalty* eine Strafe auferlegen

**impossible** ADJECTIVE
unmöglich

to **impress** VERB
beeindrucken (PERFECT hat beeindruckt)
◊ *She's trying to impress you.* Sie will
dich beeindrucken.

**impressed** ADJECTIVE
beeindruckt ◊ *I'm very impressed!* Ich
bin sehr beeindruckt!

**impression** NOUN
der Eindruck (PL die Eindrücke) ◊ *I was
under the impression that ...* Ich hatte
den Eindruck, dass ...

**impressive** ADJECTIVE
beeindruckend

to **improve** VERB
[1] (*make better*)
verbessern (PERFECT hat verbessert) ◊ *The
hotel has improved its service.* Das Hotel
hat den Service verbessert.
[2] (*get better*)
besser werden (PRESENT wird besser,
IMPERFECT wurde besser, PERFECT ist besser
geworden) ◊ *The weather is improving.*
Das Wetter wird besser. ◊ *My German
has improved.* Mein Deutsch ist besser
geworden.

**improvement** NOUN
[1] (*of condition*)
die Verbesserung ◊ *It's a great
improvement.* Das ist eine gewaltige
Verbesserung.
[2] (*of learner*)
der Fortschritt (PL die Fortschritte)
◊ *There's been an improvement in his
German.* Er hat in Deutsch Fortschritte
gemacht.

**in** PREPOSITION, ADVERB
*Use the accusative to express movement
or a change of place. Use the dative
when there is no change of place.*
[1] in ◊ *It's in my bag.* Es ist in meiner
Tasche. ◊ *Put it in my bag.* Tu es in
meine Tasche. ◊ *I read it in this book.* Ich
habe es in diesem Buch gelesen. ◊ *Write*

it in your address book. Schreib es in dein Adressbuch. ◊ *in hospital* im Krankenhaus ◊ *in school* in der Schule ◊ *in London* in London ◊ *in Germany* in Deutschland ◊ *in Switzerland* in der Schweiz ◊ *in May* im Mai ◊ *in spring* im Frühling ◊ *in the rain* im Regen ◊ *I'll see you in three weeks.* Ich sehe dich in drei Wochen.

*Sometimes in is not translated.*

◊ *It happened in 1996.* Es geschah 1996. ◊ *in the morning* morgens ◊ *in the afternoon* nachmittags ◊ *at six in the evening* um sechs Uhr abends

[2] mit ◊ *the boy in the blue shirt* der Junge mit dem blauen Hemd ◊ *It was written in pencil.* Es war mit Bleistift geschrieben. ◊ *in a loud voice* mit lauter Stimme ◊ *She paid in dollars.* Sie hat mit Dollar bezahlt.

[3] auf ◊ *in German* auf Deutsch ◊ *in English* auf Englisch

*in is sometimes translated using the genitive.*

◊ *the best pupil in the class* der beste Schüler der Klasse ◊ *the tallest person in the family* der Größte der Familie

♦ **in the beginning** am Anfang
♦ **in the country** auf dem Land
♦ **in time** rechtzeitig ◊ *We arrived in time for dinner.* Wir kamen rechtzeitig zum Abendessen.
♦ **in here** hier drin ◊ *It's hot in here.* Hier drin ist es heiß.
♦ **one person in ten** einer von zehn
♦ **to be in** (*at home, work*) da sein ◊ *He wasn't in.* Er war nicht da.
♦ **to ask somebody in** jemanden hereinbitten

**inaccurate** ADJECTIVE
[1] ungenau (*not precise*) ◊ *an inaccurate translation* eine ungenaue Übersetzung
[2] unrichtig (*not correct*) ◊ *What he said was inaccurate.* Was er sagte war unrichtig.

**inadequate** ADJECTIVE
unzulänglich

**incentive** NOUN
die Motivation ◊ *There is no incentive to work.* Es gibt keine Motivation zu arbeiten.

**inch** NOUN
der Zoll (PL die Zoll)

> 🛈 *In Germany measurements are given in metres and centimetres rather than feet and inches. An inch is about 2.5 centimetres.*

♦ **six inches** fünfzehn Zentimeter
**incident** NOUN
der Vorfall (PL die Vorfälle)
**inclined** ADJECTIVE

♦ **to be inclined to do something** dazu tendieren, etwas zu tun ◊ *He's inclined to arrive late.* Er tendiert dazu, zu spät zu kommen.

to **include** VERB
einschließen (IMPERFECT schloss ein, PERFECT hat eingeschlossen) ◊ *Service is not included.* Bedienung ist nicht eingeschlossen.

**including** PREPOSITION
inklusive ◊ *That will be two hundred marks, including VAT.* Das macht zweihundert Mark, inklusive Mehrwertsteuer.

**inclusive** ADJECTIVE
♦ **The inclusive price is two hundred marks.** Das kostet alles in allem zweihundert Mark.
♦ **inclusive of VAT** inklusive Mehrwertsteuer

**income** NOUN
das Einkommen (PL die Einkommen)
**income tax** NOUN
die Einkommensteuer
**incompetent** ADJECTIVE
inkompetent
**incomplete** ADJECTIVE
unvollständig
**inconsistent** ADJECTIVE
[1] widersprüchlich
♦ **to be inconsistent with ...** im Widerspruch stehen zu ...
[2] unbeständig ◊ *Your work this year has been very inconsistent.* Die Qualität deiner Arbeit war dieses Jahr sehr unbeständig.

**inconvenience** NOUN
♦ **I don't want to cause any inconvenience.** Ich möchte keine Umstände machen.

**inconvenient** ADJECTIVE
♦ **That's very inconvenient for me.** Das passt mir gar nicht.

**incorrect** ADJECTIVE
unrichtig

**increase** NOUN
see also **increase** VERB
die Zunahme ◊ *an increase in road accidents* eine Zunahme an Verkehrsunfällen

to **increase** VERB
see also **increase** NOUN
[1] (*traffic, number*)
zunehmen (PRESENT nimmt zu, IMPERFECT nahm zu, PERFECT hat zugenommen) ◊ *Traffic on motorways has increased.* Der Verkehr auf den Autobahnen hat zugenommen.
[2] (*price, demand*)
steigen (IMPERFECT stieg, PERFECT ist gestiegen) ◊ *with increasing demand* bei steigender Nachfrage
[3] (*pain, wind*)

stärker werden (PRESENT wird stärker, IMPERFECT wurde stärker, PERFECT ist stärker geworden) ◊ *The wind has increased.* Der Wind ist stärker geworden.

◆ **to increase in size** größer werden

◆ **to increase something** etwas erhöhen ◊ *They have increased the price.* Sie haben den Preis erhöht.

◆ **increased cost of living** höhere Lebenshaltungskosten

**incredible** ADJECTIVE
unglaublich

**indecisive** ADJECTIVE
unentschlossen (*person*)

**indeed** ADVERB
wirklich ◊ *It's very hard indeed.* Es ist wirklich schwer.

◆ **Know what I mean? – Indeed I do.** Weißt du, was ich meine? – Ja, ganz genau.

◆ **Thank you very much indeed!** Ganz herzlichen Dank!

**independence** NOUN
die Unabhängigkeit

**independent** ADJECTIVE
unabhängig

◆ **an independent school** eine Privatschule

**index** NOUN
das Verzeichnis (*in book*) (GEN des Verzeichnisses, PL die Verzeichnisse)

**India** NOUN
Indien NEUT

◆ **from India** aus Indien

◆ **to India** nach Indien

**Indian** ADJECTIVE
| see also **Indian** NOUN |
[1] indisch
[2] indianisch (*American Indian*)

**Indian** NOUN
| see also **Indian** ADJECTIVE |
(*person*)
der Inder (PL die Inder)
die Inderin

◆ **an American Indian** ein Indianer MASC

to **indicate** VERB
[1] zeigen ◊ *His reaction indicates how he feels about it.* Seine Reaktion zeigt, was er davon hält.

[2] (*make known*)
andeuten (PERFECT hat angedeutet) ◊ *He indicated that he may resign.* Er hat angedeutet, dass er vielleicht zurücktritt.

[3] (*technical device*)
anzeigen (PERFECT hat angezeigt) ◊ *The gauge indicated a very high temperature.* Das Messgerät zeigte eine sehr hohe Temperatur an.

◆ **to indicate left** links blinken

**indicator** NOUN
der Blinker (*in car*) (PL die Blinker)

**indigestion** NOUN
die Magenverstimmung

◆ **I've got indigestion.** Ich habe eine Magenverstimmung.

**individual** NOUN
| see also **individual** ADJECTIVE |
das Individuum (PL die Individuen)

**individual** ADJECTIVE
| see also **individual** NOUN |
individuell

**indoor** ADJECTIVE

◆ **an indoor swimming pool** ein Hallenbad

**indoors** ADVERB
im Haus ◊ *They're indoors.* Sie sind im Haus.

◆ **to go indoors** hineingehen ◊ *We'd better go indoors.* Wir gehen besser hinein.

**industrial** ADJECTIVE
industriell

**industrial estate** NOUN
das Industriegebiet (PL die Industriegebiete)

**industry** NOUN
die Industrie ◊ *the tourist industry* die Tourismusindustrie ◊ *the oil industry* die Erdölindustrie

◆ **I'd like to work in industry.** Ich würde gern in der freien Wirtschaft arbeiten.

**inefficient** ADJECTIVE
ineffizient

**inevitable** ADJECTIVE
unvermeidlich

**inexpensive** ADJECTIVE
preiswert ◊ *an inexpensive hotel* ein preiswertes Hotel

◆ **inexpensive holidays** günstige Ferien

**inexperienced** ADJECTIVE
unerfahren

**infant school** NOUN
die Grundschule

> **ⓘ** The **Grundschule** is a primary school which children attend from the age of 6 to 10. Many children attend **Kindergarten** before going to the **Grundschule**.

**infection** NOUN
die Entzündung ◊ *an ear infection* eine Ohrenentzündung ◊ *a throat infection* eine Halsentzündung

**infectious** ADJECTIVE
ansteckend ◊ *It's not infectious.* Es ist nicht ansteckend.

**infinitive** NOUN
der Infinitiv (PL die Infinitive)

**infirmary** NOUN
das Krankenhaus (GEN des Krankenhauses, PL die Krankenhäuser)

**inflatable** ADJECTIVE

◆ **an inflatable mattress** eine Luftmatratze

◆ **an inflatable dinghy** ein Gummiboot NEUT

**inflation** NOUN
die Inflation

**influence** NOUN

| *see also* **influence** VERB |
| --- |

der Einfluss (GEN des Einflusses, PL die Einflüsse) ◊ *He's a bad influence on her.* Er hat einen schlechten Einfluss auf sie.

to **influence** VERB

| *see also* **influence** NOUN |
| --- |

beeinflussen (PERFECT hat beeinflusst)

**influenza** NOUN
die Grippe

to **inform** VERB
informieren (PERFECT hat informiert)
♦ **to inform somebody of something** jemanden über etwas informieren ◊ *Nobody informed me of the new plan.* Niemand hat mich über den neuen Plan informiert.

**informal** ADJECTIVE
[1] locker (*person*)
[2] zwanglos (*party*) ◊ *"informal dress"* "zwanglose Kleidung"
[3] umgangssprachlich (*colloquial*)
♦ **informal language** die Umgangssprache
♦ **an informal visit** ein inoffizieller Besuch

**information** NOUN
die Information ◊ *important information* wichtige Informationen
♦ **a piece of information** eine Information
♦ **Could you give me some information about trains to Berlin?** Können Sie mir Auskunft über Zugverbindungen nach Berlin geben?

**information office** NOUN
die Auskunft (PL die Auskünfte)

**information technology** NOUN
die Informationstechnik

**infuriating** ADJECTIVE
äußerst ärgerlich

**ingenious** ADJECTIVE
genial

**ingredient** NOUN
die Zutat

**inhabitant** NOUN
(*of country, town*)
der Einwohner (PL die Einwohner)
die Einwohnerin

to **inherit** VERB
erben ◊ *She inherited her father's house.* Sie erbte das Haus ihres Vaters.

**initials** PL NOUN
die Initialen FEM PL ◊ *Her initials are CDT.* Ihre Initialen sind CDT.

**initiative** NOUN
die Initiative

to **inject** VERB
spritzen (*drug*) ◊ *He injected himself with heroin.* Er hat sich Heroin gespritzt.

**injection** NOUN
die Spritze

to **injure** VERB
verletzen (PERFECT hat verletzt)

**injured** ADJECTIVE
verletzt

**injury** NOUN
die Verletzung

**injury time** NOUN
♦ **to play injury time** nachspielen

**injustice** NOUN
die Ungerechtigkeit

**ink** NOUN
die Tinte

**in-laws** PL NOUN
die Schwiegereltern PL

**inn** NOUN
das Gasthaus (GEN des Gasthauses, PL die Gasthäuser)

**inner** ADJECTIVE
♦ **the inner city** die Innenstadt

**inner tube** NOUN
der Schlauch (PL die Schläuche)

**innocent** ADJECTIVE
unschuldig

**inquest** NOUN
die gerichtliche Untersuchung

to **inquire** VERB
♦ **to inquire about something** sich nach etwas erkundigen

**inquiries office** NOUN
die Auskunft (PL die Auskünfte)

**inquiry** NOUN
die Untersuchung (*official investigation*)

**inquisitive** ADJECTIVE
neugierig

**insane** ADJECTIVE
wahnsinnig

**inscription** NOUN
die Inschrift

**insect** NOUN
das Insekt (PL die Insekten)

**insect repellent** NOUN
das Insektenschutzmittel (PL die Insektenschutzmittel)

**insensitive** ADJECTIVE
gefühllos

to **insert** VERB
einwerfen (PRESENT wirft ein, IMPERFECT warf ein, PERFECT hat eingeworfen) ◊ *I inserted a coin.* Ich warf eine Münze ein.

**inside** NOUN

| *see also* **inside** ADVERB |
| --- |

das Innere (GEN des Inneren)

**inside** ADVERB, PREPOSITION

| *see also* **inside** NOUN |
| --- |

innen ◊ *inside and outside* innen und außen
♦ **They're inside.** Sie sind drinnen.
♦ **to go inside** hineingehen
♦ **Come inside!** Kommt herein!
*Use the accusative to express movement or a change of place. Use the dative when there is no change of place.*
♦ **inside the house (1)** im Haus ◊ *She was inside the house.* Sie war im Haus.
♦ **inside the house (2)** ins Haus ◊ *She went inside the house.* Sie ging ins Haus.

**insincere** ADJECTIVE
unaufrichtig

to **insist** VERB
darauf bestehen (IMPERFECT bestand darauf, PERFECT hat darauf bestanden) ◊ *I didn't want to, but he insisted.* Ich wollte nicht, aber er hat darauf bestanden.
♦ **to insist on doing something** darauf bestehen, etwas zu tun ◊ *She insisted on paying.* Sie hat darauf bestanden zu bezahlen.
♦ **He insisted he was innocent.** Er beteuerte seine Unschuld.

to **inspect** VERB
kontrollieren (PERFECT hat kontrolliert)

**inspector** NOUN
(*police*)
der Kommissar (PL die Kommissare)
die Kommissarin
◊ *Inspector Jill Brown* Kommissarin Jill Brown

to **install** VERB
installieren (PERFECT hat installiert)

**instalment** NOUN (US **installment**)
① die Rate ◊ *to pay in instalments* in Raten zahlen
② die Folge (*of TV, radio serial*)
③ der Teil (*of publication*)

**instance** NOUN
♦ **for instance** zum Beispiel

**instant** ADJECTIVE
sofortig ◊ *It was an instant success.* Es war ein sofortiger Erfolg.
♦ **instant coffee** der Pulverkaffee

**instantly** ADVERB
sofort

**instead** ADVERB
♦ **instead of (1)** (*followed by noun*) anstelle von ◊ *Use honey instead of sugar.* Nehmen Sie Honig anstelle von Zucker.
♦ **instead of (2)** (*followed by verb*) statt ◊ *We played tennis instead of going swimming.* Wir spielten Tennis statt schwimmen zu gehen.
♦ **The pool was closed, so we played tennis instead.** Das Schwimmbad war zu, also spielten wir stattdessen Tennis.

**instinct** NOUN
der Instinkt (PL die Instinkte)

**institute** NOUN
das Institut

**institution** NOUN
die Institution

to **instruct** VERB
anweisen (IMPERFECT wies an, PERFECT hat angewiesen)
♦ **to instruct somebody to do something** jemanden anweisen, etwas zu tun ◊ *She instructed us to wait outside.* Sie wies uns an, draußen zu warten.

**instructions** PL NOUN

① die Anweisungen FEM PL ◊ *Follow the instructions carefully.* Befolgen Sie die Anweisungen genau.
② die Gebrauchsanweisung (*manual*)
◊ *Where are the instructions?* Wo ist die Gebrauchsanweisung?

**instructor** NOUN
der Lehrer (PL die Lehrer)
die Lehrerin
◊ *a skiing instructor* ein Skilehrer ◊ *a driving instructor* ein Fahrlehrer

**instrument** NOUN
das Instrument (PL die Instrumente) ◊ *Do you play an instrument?* Spielst du ein Instrument?

**insufficient** ADJECTIVE
unzureichend

**insulin** NOUN
das Insulin

**insult** NOUN
see also **insult** VERB
die Beleidigung

to **insult** VERB
see also **insult** NOUN
beleidigen (PERFECT hat beleidigt)

**insurance** NOUN
die Versicherung ◊ *his car insurance* seine Kraftfahrzeugversicherung
♦ **an insurance policy** eine Versicherungspolice

**intelligent** ADJECTIVE
intelligent

to **intend** VERB
♦ **to intend to do something** beabsichtigen, etwas zu tun ◊ *I intend to do German at university.* Ich beabsichtige, Deutsch zu studieren.

**intense** ADJECTIVE
stark

**intensive** ADJECTIVE
intensiv

**intention** NOUN
die Absicht

**intercom** NOUN
die Sprechanlage

**interest** NOUN
see also **interest** VERB
das Interesse (PL die Interessen) ◊ *to show an interest in something* Interesse an etwas zeigen ◊ *What interests do you have?* Welche Interessen hast du?
♦ **My main interest is music.** Ich interessiere mich hauptsächlich für Musik.

to **interest** VERB
see also **interest** NOUN
interessieren (PERFECT hat interessiert) ◊ *It doesn't interest me.* Das interessiert mich nicht.
♦ **to be interested in something** sich für etwas interessieren ◊ *I'm not interested*

*in politics.* Ich interessiere mich nicht für Politik.

**interesting** ADJECTIVE
interessant

**interior** NOUN
das Innere (GEN des Inneren)

**interior designer** NOUN
der Innenarchitekt (GEN des Innenarchitekten, PL die Innenarchitekten)
die Innenarchitektin

**intermediate** ADJECTIVE
♦ **an intermediate course** ein Kurs für fortgeschrittene Anfänger

**internal** ADJECTIVE
innere ◊ *the internal organs* die inneren Organe

**international** ADJECTIVE
international

**Internet** NOUN
das Internet ◊ *on the Internet* im Internet

**Internet café** NOUN
das Internet-Café (PL die Internet-Cafés)

**Internet user** NOUN
der Internetbenutzer (PL die Internetbenutzer)
die Internetbenutzerin

to **interpret** VERB
übersetzen (PERFECT hat übersetzt) ◊ *Steve couldn't speak German, so his friend interpreted.* Steve konnte kein Deutsch, also übersetzte sein Freund.

**interpreter** NOUN
der Dolmetscher (PL die Dolmetscher)
die Dolmetscherin

to **interrupt** VERB
unterbrechen (PRESENT unterbricht, IMPERFECT unterbrach, PERFECT hat unterbrochen)

**interruption** NOUN
die Unterbrechung

**interval** NOUN
die Pause (*in play, concert*)

**interview** NOUN
| see also **interview** VERB |
1 das Interview (*on TV, radio*) (PL die Interviews)
2 (*for job*)
das Vorstellungsgespräch (PL die Vorstellungsgespräche)

to **interview** VERB
| see also **interview** NOUN |
interviewen (*on TV, radio*) (PERFECT hat interviewt) ◊ *I was interviewed on the radio.* Ich wurde im Radio interviewt.

**interviewer** NOUN
(*on TV, radio*)
der Moderator (PL die Moderatoren)
die Moderatorin

**intimate** ADJECTIVE
eng ◊ *an intimate friendship* eine enge Freundschaft

♦ **my intimate feelings** meine innersten Gefühle

**into** PREPOSITION
in
*In this sense **in** is followed by the accusative.*
◊ *He got into the car.* Er stieg ins Auto.
◊ *I'm going into town.* Ich gehe in die Stadt. ◊ *Translate it into German.* Übersetze das ins Deutsche. ◊ *Divide into two groups.* Teilt euch in zwei Gruppen.

**intranet** NOUN
das Intranet (PL die Intranets)

to **introduce** VERB
vorstellen (PERFECT hat vorgestellt) ◊ *He introduced me to his parents.* Er stellte mich seinen Eltern vor.

**introduction** NOUN
die Einleitung (*in book*)

**intruder** NOUN
der Eindringling (PL die Eindringlinge)
*der Eindringling is also used for women.*

**intuition** NOUN
die Intuition

to **invade** VERB
eindringen in +ACC (IMPERFECT drang ein, PERFECT ist eingedrungen) ◊ *to invade a country* in ein Land eindringen

**invalid** NOUN
der Kranke (GEN des Kranken, PL die Kranken)
die Kranke (GEN der Kranken) ◊ *an invalid (man)* ein Kranker

to **invent** VERB
erfinden (IMPERFECT erfand, PERFECT hat erfunden)

**invention** NOUN
die Erfindung

**inventor** NOUN
der Erfinder (PL die Erfinder)
die Erfinderin

to **invest** VERB
investieren (PERFECT hat investiert)

**investigation** NOUN
die Untersuchung (*police*)

**investment** NOUN
die Investition

**invigilator** NOUN
die Aufsicht
*die Aufsicht is also used for men.*
◊ *You have to ask the invigilator.* Du musst die Aufsicht fragen.

**invisible** ADJECTIVE
unsichtbar

**invitation** NOUN
die Einladung

to **invite** VERB
einladen (PRESENT lädt ein, IMPERFECT lud ein, PERFECT hat eingeladen) ◊ *He's not invited.* Er ist nicht eingeladen. ◊ *to invite somebody to a party* jemanden zu einer Party einladen

to **involve** VERB

mit sich bringen (IMPERFECT brachte mit sich, PERFECT hat mit sich gebracht) ◊ *This will involve a lot of work.* Das wird viel Arbeit mit sich bringen.

♦ **His job involves a lot of travelling.** Er muss in seinem Job viel reisen.

♦ **to be involved in something** (*crime, drugs*) in etwas verwickelt sein ◊ *He was involved in the murder.* Er war in den Mord verwickelt.

♦ **to be involved with somebody** (*in relationship*) mit jemandem eine Beziehung haben

♦ **I don't want to get involved.** Ich will damit nichts zu tun haben.

**IQ** NOUN (= *intelligence quotient*)

der IQ (GEN des IQ, PL die IQ) (= Intelligenzquotient)

**Iran** NOUN

der Iran

> *Note that the definite article is used in German for countries which are masculine.*

♦ **from Iran** aus dem Iran
♦ **in Iran** im Iran
♦ **to Iran** in den Iran

**Iraq** NOUN

der Irak

> *Note that the definite article is used in German for countries which are masculine.*

♦ **from Iraq** aus dem Irak
♦ **in Iraq** im Irak
♦ **to Iraq** in den Irak

**Iraqi** NOUN

see also **Iraqi** ADJECTIVE

der Iraker (PL die Iraker)
die Irakerin

**Iraqi** ADJECTIVE

see also **Iraqi** NOUN

irakisch

**Ireland** NOUN

Irland NEUT

♦ **from Ireland** aus Irland
♦ **in Ireland** in Irland
♦ **to Ireland** nach Irland

**Irish** ADJECTIVE

see also **Irish** NOUN

irisch ◊ *Irish music* irische Musik
♦ **He's Irish.** Er ist Ire.
♦ **She's Irish.** Sie ist Irin.

**Irish** NOUN

see also **Irish** ADJECTIVE

das Irisch (*language*) (GEN des Irischen)
♦ **the Irish** (*people*) die Iren MASC PL

**Irishman** NOUN

der Ire (GEN des Iren, PL die Iren)

**Irishwoman** NOUN

die Irin

**iron** NOUN

see also **iron** VERB

**1** (*metal*)

das Eisen

**2** (*for clothes*)

das Bügeleisen (PL die Bügeleisen)

to **iron** VERB

see also **iron** NOUN

bügeln

**ironic** ADJECTIVE

ironisch

**ironing** NOUN

das Bügeln
♦ **to do the ironing** bügeln

**ironing board** NOUN

das Bügelbrett (PL die Bügelbretter)

**ironmonger's (shop)** NOUN

die Eisenwarenhandlung

**irrelevant** ADJECTIVE

irrelevant ◊ *That's irrelevant.* Das ist irrelevant.

**irresponsible** ADJECTIVE

verantwortungslos (*person*)
♦ **That was irresponsible of him.** Das war unverantwortlich von ihm.

**irritating** ADJECTIVE

nervend

**is** VERB *see* **be**

**Islam** NOUN

> *Note that the definite article is used in German.*

der Islam

**Islamic** ADJECTIVE

islamisch ◊ *Islamic fundamentalists* islamische Fundamentalisten
♦ **Islamic law** das Recht des Islams

**island** NOUN

die Insel

**isle** NOUN

♦ **the Isle of Man** die Insel Man
♦ **the Isle of Wight** die Insel Wight

**isolated** ADJECTIVE

abgelegen (*place*)
♦ **She feels very isolated.** Sie fühlt sich sehr isoliert.
♦ **an isolated case** ein Einzelfall MASC

**ISP** ABBREVIATION (= *Internet Service Provider*)

der Internet-Anbieter (PL die Internet-Anbieter)

**Israel** NOUN

Israel NEUT

♦ **from Israel** aus Israel
♦ **to Israel** nach Israel

**Israeli** NOUN

see also **Israeli** ADJECTIVE

der Israeli (GEN des Israeli, PL die Israeli)
die Israeli (GEN der Israeli)

**Israeli** ADJECTIVE

see also **Israeli** NOUN

israelisch
♦ **He's Israeli.** Er ist Israeli.

**issue** NOUN

see also **issue** VERB

boxed{1} die <u>Frage</u> (*matter*) ◊ *a controversial issue* eine umstrittene Frage
boxed{2} die <u>Ausgabe</u> (*of magazine*)

to **issue** VERB

| *see also* **issue** NOUN |

**ausgeben** (*equipment, supplies*) (PRESENT gibt aus, IMPERFECT gab aus, PERFECT hat ausgegeben)

**it** PRONOUN

*Remember to check if* **it** *stands for a masculine, feminine or neuter noun, and use the appropriate gender and case.*

boxed{1} **er** ◊ *Where's my hat? – It's on the table.* Wo ist mein Hut? – Er ist auf dem Tisch.
**sie**
◊ *What happened to your watch? – It broke.* Was ist mit deiner Uhr passiert? – Sie ist kaputtgegangen.
**es**
◊ *Have you seen her new dress, it's very pretty.* Hast du ihr neues Kleid gesehen, es ist sehr hübsch.
boxed{2} **ihn** ◊ *Where's my hat? – I haven't seen it.* Wo ist mein Hut? – Ich habe ihn nicht gesehen.
**sie**
◊ *Where's your jacket? – I've lost it.* Wo ist deine Jacke? – Ich habe sie verloren.
**es**
◊ *You can have my ruler, I don't need it anymore.* Du kannst mein Lineal haben, ich brauche es nicht mehr.
♦ **It's raining.** Es regnet.
♦ **It's six o'clock.** Es ist sechs Uhr.
♦ **It's Friday tomorrow.** Morgen ist Freitag.
♦ **Who is it? – It's me.** Wer ist's? – Ich bin's.
♦ **It's expensive.** Das ist teuer.

**Italian** ADJECTIVE

| *see also* **Italian** NOUN |

**italienisch**
♦ **She's Italian.** Sie ist Italienerin.

**Italian** NOUN

| *see also* **Italian** ADJECTIVE |

boxed{1} (*person*)
der <u>Italiener</u> (PL die Italiener)
die <u>Italienerin</u>
boxed{2} (*language*)
das <u>Italienisch</u> (GEN des Italienischen)

**italics** PL NOUN

die <u>Kursivschrift</u>
♦ **in italics** kursiv

**Italy** NOUN

<u>Italien</u> NEUT
♦ **from Italy** aus Italien
♦ **in Italy** in Italien
♦ **to Italy** nach Italien

to **itch** VERB

**jucken** ◊ *It itches.* Es juckt. ◊ *My head's itching.* Mein Kopf juckt.

**itchy** ADJECTIVE
♦ **My arm is itchy.** Mein Arm juckt.

**it'd** = **it had**, = **it would**

**item** NOUN

der <u>Artikel</u> (*object*) (PL die Artikel)

**itinerary** NOUN

die <u>Reiseroute</u>

**it'll** = **it will**

**its** ADJECTIVE

*Remember to check if* **its** *refers back to a masculine, feminine or neuter noun, and use the appropriate gender and case.*

**sein** ◊ *The dog is in its kennel.* Der Hund ist in seiner Hütte.
**ihr** ◊ *The cup is in its usual place.* Die Tasse ist an ihrem üblichen Platz.
**sein** ◊ *The baby is in its cot.* Das Baby ist in seinem Bett.

**it's** = **it is**, = **it has**

**itself** PRONOUN

boxed{1} **sich** ◊ *The dog scratched itself.* Der Hund kratzte sich.
boxed{2} **selbst** ◊ *The heating switches itself off.* Die Heizung schaltet von selbst aus.

**I've** = **I have**

# J

jab NOUN
die <u>Spritze</u> (*injection*)

jack NOUN
[1] (*for car*)
der <u>Wagenheber</u> (PL die Wagenheber)
[2] (*playing card*)
der <u>Bube</u> (GEN des Buben, PL die Buben)

jacket NOUN
die <u>Jacke</u>
♦ **jacket potatoes** gebackene Kartoffeln

jackpot NOUN
der <u>Jackpot</u> (PL die Jackpots) ◊ *to win the jackpot* den Jackpot gewinnen

jail NOUN
| see also **jail** VERB |
das <u>Gefängnis</u> (GEN des Gefängnisses, PL die Gefängnisse)
♦ **She was sent to jail.** Sie musste ins Gefängnis.

to jail VERB
| see also **jail** NOUN |
<u>einsperren</u> (PERFECT hat eingesperrt)
♦ **He was jailed for ten years.** Er hat zehn Jahre Gefängnis bekommen.

jam NOUN
die <u>Marmelade</u> ◊ *strawberry jam* Erdbeermarmelade
♦ **a traffic jam** ein Verkehrsstau MASC

jam jar NOUN
das <u>Marmeladenglas</u> (GEN des Marmeladenglases, PL die Marmeladengläser)

jammed ADJECTIVE
♦ **The window's jammed.** Das Fenster klemmt.

jam-packed ADJECTIVE
<u>brechend voll</u> ◊ *The room was jam-packed.* Der Raum war brechend voll.

janitor NOUN
der <u>Hausmeister</u> (PL die Hausmeister)
die <u>Hausmeisterin</u>
◊ *He's a janitor.* Er ist Hausmeister.

January NOUN
der <u>Januar</u> ◊ *in January* im Januar

Japan NOUN
<u>Japan</u> NEUT
♦ **from Japan** aus Japan
♦ **to Japan** nach Japan

Japanese ADJECTIVE
| see also **Japanese** NOUN |
<u>japanisch</u>

Japanese NOUN
| see also **Japanese** ADJECTIVE |
[1] (*person*)
der <u>Japaner</u> (PL die Japaner)
die <u>Japanerin</u>
♦ **the Japanese** die Japaner MASC PL
[2] (*language*)

das <u>Japanisch</u> (GEN des Japanischen)

jar NOUN
das <u>Glas</u> (GEN des Glases, PL die Gläser)
◊ *an empty jar* ein leeres Glas ◊ *a jar of honey* ein Glas Honig

jaundice NOUN
die <u>Gelbsucht</u> ◊ *She's suffering from jaundice.* Sie hat Gelbsucht.

javelin NOUN
der <u>Speer</u> (PL die Speere)

jaw NOUN
der <u>Kiefer</u> (PL die Kiefer)

jazz NOUN
der <u>Jazz</u> (GEN des Jazz)

jealous ADJECTIVE
<u>eifersüchtig</u>

jeans PL NOUN
die <u>Jeans</u> FEM PL ◊ *a pair of jeans* eine Jeans

Jehovah's Witness NOUN
der <u>Zeuge Jehovas</u> (GEN des Zeugen Jehovas, PL die Zeugen Jehovas)
die <u>Zeugin Jehovas</u>
◊ *She's a Jehovah's Witness.* Sie ist Zeugin Jehovas.

Jello ® NOUN US
der <u>Wackelpudding</u>

jelly NOUN
[1] der <u>Wackelpudding</u> (*dessert*)
[2] die <u>Marmelade</u> (*jam*)

jellyfish NOUN
die <u>Qualle</u>

jersey NOUN
der <u>Pullover</u> (PL die Pullover)

Jesus NOUN
<u>Jesus</u> MASC (GEN des Jesus)

jet NOUN
das <u>Düsenflugzeug</u> (*plane*) (PL die Düsenflugzeuge)

jetlag NOUN
♦ **to be suffering from jetlag** unter der Zeitverschiebung leiden

jetty NOUN
die <u>Mole</u>

Jew NOUN
der <u>Jude</u> (GEN des Juden, PL die Juden)
die <u>Jüdin</u>

jewel NOUN
der <u>Edelstein</u> (*stone*) (PL die Edelsteine)

jeweller NOUN
der <u>Juwelier</u> (PL die Juweliere)
die <u>Juwelierin</u>
◊ *He's a jeweller.* Er ist Juwelier.

jeweller's shop NOUN

das Juweliergeschäft (PL die
Juweliergeschäfte)
**jewellery** NOUN
der Schmuck
**Jewish** ADJECTIVE
jüdisch
**jigsaw** NOUN
das Puzzle (PL die Puzzles)
**job** NOUN
[1] der Job (PL die Jobs) ◊ *He's lost his
job.* Er hat seinen Job verloren. ◊ *I've got
a Saturday job.* Ich habe einen
Samstagsjob.
[2] (*chore, task*)
die Arbeit ◊ *That was a difficult job.* Das
war eine schwierige Arbeit.
**job centre** NOUN
das Arbeitsamt (PL die Arbeitsämter)
**jobless** ADJECTIVE
arbeitslos
**jockey** NOUN
der Jockey (PL die Jockeys)
to **jog** VERB
joggen
**jogging** NOUN
das Jogging ◊ *I like jogging.* Ich mag
Jogging.
◆ **to go jogging** joggen
**john** NOUN US
das Klo (*informal*) (PL die Klos)
to **join** VERB
[1] (*become member of*)
beitreten (PRESENT tritt bei, IMPERFECT trat
bei, PERFECT ist beigetreten) ◊ *I'm going to
join the tennis club.* Ich trete dem
Tennisklub bei.
[2] (*accompany*)
sich anschließen (IMPERFECT schloss sich
an, PERFECT hat sich angeschlossen) ◊ *Do
you mind if I join you?* Macht es dir
etwas aus, wenn ich mich dir
anschließe?
to **join in** VERB
[1] mitmachen (PERFECT hat mitgemacht)
◊ *He doesn't join in with what we do.* Er
macht nicht mit bei den Dingen, die wir
tun.
[2] einstimmen (PERFECT hat eingestimmt)
◊ *She started singing, and the audience
joined in.* Sie begann zu singen, und das
Publikum stimmte mit ein.
**joiner** NOUN
der Schreiner (PL die Schreiner)
die Schreinerin
◊ *She's a joiner.* Sie ist Schreinerin.
**joint** NOUN
[1] (*in body*)
das Gelenk (PL die Gelenke)
[2] (*of meat*)
der Braten (PL die Braten)
[3] (*drugs*)
der Joint (PL die Joints)
**joke** NOUN

see also **joke** VERB

der Witz (GEN des Witzes, PL die Witze)
◊ *to tell a joke* einen Witz erzählen
to **joke** VERB

see also **joke** NOUN

Spaß machen ◊ *I'm only joking.* Ich
mache nur Spaß.
**jolly** ADJECTIVE
fröhlich
**Jordan** NOUN
Jordanien NEUT (*country*)
◆ **from Jordan** aus Jordanien
◆ **to Jordan** nach Jordanien
to **jot down** VERB
notieren (PERFECT hat notiert)
**jotter** NOUN
der Notizblock (*pad*) (PL die
Notizblöcke)
**journalism** NOUN
der Journalismus (GEN des
Journalismus)
**journalist** NOUN
der Journalist (GEN des Journalisten, PL
die Journalisten)
die Journalistin
◊ *She's a journalist.* Sie ist Journalistin.
**journey** NOUN
[1] die Reise ◊ *I don't like long journeys.*
Ich mag lange Reisen nicht.
◆ **to go on a journey** eine Reise machen
[2] die Fahrt (*to school, work*) ◊ *The
journey to school takes about half an
hour.* Die Fahrt zur Schule dauert etwa
eine halbe Stunde.
◆ **a bus journey** eine Busfahrt
**joy** NOUN
die Freude
**joystick** NOUN
der Joystick (*for computer game*) (PL die
Joysticks)
**judge** NOUN

see also **judge** VERB

der Richter (PL die Richter)
die Richterin
◊ *She's a judge.* Sie ist Richterin.
to **judge** VERB

see also **judge** NOUN

beurteilen (*assess*) (PERFECT hat beurteilt)
◊ *You can judge for yourself which is
better.* Du kannst das selbst beurteilen,
welches besser ist.
**judo** NOUN
das Judo (GEN des Judo) ◊ *My hobby is
judo.* Judo ist mein Hobby.
**jug** NOUN
der Krug (PL die Krüge)
**juggler** NOUN
der Jongleur
die Jongleurin
**juice** NOUN
der Saft (PL die Säfte) ◊ *orange juice* der
Orangensaft

J

**July** NOUN
der Juli ◊ *in July* im Juli
**jumble sale** NOUN
der Flohmarkt (PL die Flohmärkte)
to **jump** VERB
springen (IMPERFECT sprang, PERFECT ist
gesprungen) ◊ *to jump out of the
window* aus dem Fenster springen ◊ *to
jump off the roof* vom Dach
springen
♦ **to jump over something** über etwas
springen ◊ *He jumped over the fence.* Er
sprang über den Zaun.
**jumper** NOUN
[1] der Pullover (PL die Pullover)
[2] (*dress*)
das Trägerkleid (PL die
Trägerkleider)
**junction** NOUN
[1] (*of roads*)
die Kreuzung
[2] (*motorway exit*)
die Ausfahrt
**June** NOUN
der Juni ◊ *in June* im Juni
**jungle** NOUN
der Dschungel (PL die Dschungel)
**junior** NOUN
♦ **the juniors** die Grundschüler MASC PL
**junior school** NOUN
die Grundschule

---

*i* The **Grundschule** *is a primary
school which children attend from the
age of 6 to 10.*

---

**junk** NOUN
der Krempel (*old things*) ◊ *The attic's full
of junk.* Der Speicher ist voller Krempel.
♦ **to eat junk food** Junkfood essen
♦ **a junk shop** ein Trödelladen MASC
**jury** NOUN
die Geschworenen MASC PL (*in court*)
**just** ADVERB
[1] gerade (*barely*) ◊ *We had just enough
money.* Wir hatten gerade genug Geld.
◊ *just in time* gerade noch rechtzeitig
[2] kurz (*shortly*) ◊ *just after Christmas*
kurz nach Weihnachten
[3] genau (*exactly*) ◊ *just here* genau hier
[4] eben (*this minute*) ◊ *I did it just now.*
Ich habe es eben gemacht. ◊ *He's just
arrived.* Er ist eben angekommen.
♦ **I'm rather busy just now.** Ich bin gerade
ziemlich beschäftigt.
♦ **I'm just coming!** Ich komme schon!
[5] nur (*only*) ◊ *It's just a suggestion.* Es
ist nur ein Vorschlag.
**justice** NOUN
die Gerechtigkeit
to **justify** VERB
rechtfertigen

# K

**kangaroo** NOUN
das Känguru (PL die Kängurus)
**karate** NOUN
das Karate (GEN des Karate) ◊ *I like
karate.* Ich mag Karate.
**kebab** NOUN
der Kebab (PL die Kebabs)
**keen** ADJECTIVE
⬜1⬜ begeistert (*enthusiastic*) ◊ *He doesn't
seem very keen.* Er scheint nicht gerade
begeistert.
⬜2⬜ eifrig (*hardworking*) ◊ *She's a keen
student.* Sie ist eine eifrige Studentin.
◆ **to be keen on something** etwas mögen
◊ *I'm keen on maths.* Ich mag Mathe.
◊ *I'm not very keen on maths.* Ich mag
Mathe nicht besonders.
◆ **to be keen on somebody** (*fancy them*) auf
jemanden stehen ◊ *He's keen on her.* Er
steht auf sie.
◆ **to be keen on doing something** Lust
haben, etwas zu tun ◊ *I'm not very keen
on going.* Ich habe keine große Lust zu
gehen.
to **keep** VERB
⬜1⬜ (*retain*)
behalten (PRESENT behält, IMPERFECT behielt,
PERFECT hat behalten) ◊ *You can keep it.*
Das kannst du behalten.
⬜2⬜ (*remain*)
sein (PRESENT ist, IMPERFECT war, PERFECT ist
gewesen) ◊ *Keep quiet!* Sei still!
◆ **Keep still!** Halt still!
◆ **I keep forgetting my keys.** Ich vergesse
dauernd meine Schlüssel.
◆ **to keep on doing something (1)**
(*continue*) etwas weiter tun ◊ *He kept on
reading.* Er las weiter.
◆ **to keep on doing something (2)**
(*repeatedly*) etwas dauernd tun ◊ *The car
keeps on breaking down.* Das Auto ist
dauernd kaputt.
◆ **"keep out"** "Kein Zutritt"
◆ **to keep up** mithalten ◊ *Matthew walks so
fast I can't keep up.* Matthew geht so
schnell, da kann ich nicht mithalten.
**keep-fit** NOUN
die Gymnastik ◊ *I like keep-fit.* Ich
mache gern Gymnastik.
◆ **I go to keep-fit classes.** Ich gehe zur
Gymnastik.
**kennel** NOUN
die Hundehütte
**kept** VERB *see* **keep**
**kerosene** NOUN US
das Petroleum
**kettle** NOUN
der
Wasserkessel (PL die Wasserkessel)

**key** NOUN
der Schlüssel (PL die Schlüssel)
**keyboard** NOUN
⬜1⬜ (*of piano, computer*)
die Tastatur
⬜2⬜ (*of electric organ*)
das Keyboard (PL die Keyboards)
◊ *... with Mike Moran on keyboards*
... mit Mike Moran am Keyboard
**keyring** NOUN
der Schlüsselring (PL die Schlüsselringe)
**kick** NOUN
> *see also* **kick** VERB
der Tritt (PL die Tritte)
to **kick** VERB
> *see also* **kick** NOUN
treten (PRESENT tritt, IMPERFECT trat, PERFECT hat
getreten) ◊ *He kicked me.* Er hat mich
getreten. ◊ *He kicked the ball hard.* Er trat
kräftig gegen den Ball.
◆ **to kick off** (*in football*) anfangen
**kick-off** NOUN
der Anstoß (GEN des Anstoßes, PL die
Anstöße) ◊ *Kick-off is at ten o'clock.* Um
zehn Uhr ist Anstoß.
**kid** NOUN
> *see also* **kid** VERB
das Kind (*child*) (PL die Kinder)
to **kid** VERB
> *see also* **kid** NOUN
Spaß machen ◊ *I'm just kidding.* Ich
mache nur Spaß.
to **kidnap** VERB
entführen (PERFECT hat entführt)
**kidney** NOUN
die Niere ◊ *He's got kidney trouble.* Er
hat Nierenprobleme. ◊ *I don't like
kidneys.* Ich mag Nieren nicht.
to **kill** VERB
töten
◆ **to be killed** umkommen ◊ *He was killed
in a car accident.* Er kam bei einem Unfall
um. ◊ *Luckily, nobody was killed.* Zum
Glück ist niemand dabei umgekommen.
◆ **to kill oneself** sich umbringen ◊ *He killed
himself.* Er hat sich umgebracht.
**killer** NOUN
⬜1⬜ (*murderer*)
der Mörder (PL die Mörder)
die Mörderin
◊ *The police are searching for the killer.*
Die Polizei sucht nach dem Mörder.
⬜2⬜ (*hitman*)
der Killer (PL die Killer) ◊ *a hired killer* ein
Auftragskiller
◆ **Meningitis can be a killer.**
Hirnhautentzündung kann tödlich sein.
**kilo** NOUN

☞

das Kilo (PL die Kilos or Kilo)
*When specifying a quantity of something use the plural form Kilo.*
◊ *ten marks a kilo* zehn Mark das Kilo
◊ *three kilos of tomatoes* drei Kilo Tomaten

**kilometre** NOUN
der Kilometer (PL die Kilometer) ◊ *a hundred kilometres* hundert Kilometer

**kilt** NOUN
der Kilt (PL die Kilts)

**kind** ADJECTIVE
| see also **kind** NOUN |

nett
♦ **to be kind to somebody** zu jemandem nett sein
♦ **Thank you for being so kind.** Vielen Dank, dass Sie so nett waren.

**kind** NOUN
| see also **kind** ADJECTIVE |

die Art ◊ *It's a kind of sausage.* Es ist eine Art Wurst.
♦ **a new kind of dictionary** ein neuartiges Wörterbuch

**kindergarten** NOUN
der Kindergarten (PL die Kindergärten)

*ℹ Many German children go to **Kindergarten** from the age of 3 to 6.*

**kindly** ADVERB
freundlicherweise

**kindness** NOUN
die Freundlichkeit

**king** NOUN
der König (PL die Könige)

**kingdom** NOUN
das Königreich (PL die Königreiche)

**kiosk** NOUN
1 (*phone box*)
die Telefonzelle
2 der Kiosk (PL die Kioske) ◊ *a newspaper kiosk* ein Zeitungskiosk

**kipper** NOUN
der Räucherhering (PL die Räucherheringe)

**kiss** NOUN
| see also **kiss** VERB |

der Kuss (GEN des Kusses, PL die Küsse)
◊ *a passionate kiss* ein leidenschaftlicher Kuss

to **kiss** VERB
| see also **kiss** NOUN |

1 küssen ◊ *He kissed her passionately.* Er küsste sie leidenschaftlich.
2 sich küssen ◊ *They kissed.* Sie küssten sich.

**kit** NOUN
1 (*clothes for sport*)
das Zeug ◊ *I've forgotten my gym kit.* Ich habe mein Sportzeug vergessen.

2 der Kasten (PL die Kästen) ◊ *a tool kit* ein Werkzeugkasten ◊ *a first-aid kit* ein Erste-Hilfe-Kasten
♦ **puncture repair kit** das Flickzeug
♦ **sewing kit** das Nähzeug

**kitchen** NOUN
die Küche ◊ *a fitted kitchen* eine Einbauküche
♦ **the kitchen units** die Küchenschränke
♦ **a kitchen knife** ein Küchenmesser NEUT

**kite** NOUN
der Drachen (PL die Drachen)

**kitten** NOUN
das Kätzchen (PL die Kätzchen)

**knee** NOUN
das Knie (PL die Knie) ◊ *He was on his knees.* Er lag auf den Knien.

to **kneel (down)** VERB
sich hinknien (PERFECT hat sich hingekniet)

**knew** VERB *see* **know**

**knickers** PL NOUN
die Unterhose ◊ *a pair of knickers* eine Unterhose

**knife** NOUN
das Messer (PL die Messer)
♦ **a sheath knife** ein Fahrtenmesser
♦ **a penknife** ein Taschenmesser

to **knit** VERB
stricken

**knitting** NOUN
das Stricken
♦ **I like knitting.** Ich stricke gern.

**knives** PL NOUN *see* **knife**

**knob** NOUN
1 (*on door*)
der Griff
2 (*on radio, TV*)
der Knopf (PL die Knöpfe)

to **knock** VERB
| see also **knock** NOUN |

klopfen ◊ *to knock on the door* an die Tür klopfen
♦ **Someone's knocking at the door.** Es klopft.
♦ **She was knocked down by a car.** Ein Auto hat sie umgefahren.
♦ **to knock somebody out (1)** (*stun*) jemanden bewusstlos schlagen ◊ *They knocked out the watchman.* Sie haben den Wächter bewusstlos geschlagen.
♦ **to knock somebody out (2)** (*defeat*) jemanden schlagen ◊ *Liverpool knocked Aston Villa out of the cup.* Der FC Liverpool hat Aston Villa im Pokalspiel geschlagen.
♦ **They were knocked out early in the tournament.** Sie schieden beim Turnier früh aus.
♦ **to knock something over** etwas umstoßen ◊ *I accidentally knocked the milk over.* Ich habe aus Versehen die Milch umgestoßen.

**knock** NOUN

see also **knock** VERB

♦**There was a knock on the door.** Es hat geklopft.

**knot** NOUN
der Knoten (PL die Knoten)

to **know** VERB

*Use **wissen** for knowing facts, **kennen** for knowing people and places.*

[1] wissen (PRESENT weiß, IMPERFECT wusste, PERFECT hat gewusst) ◊ *It's a long way. – Yes, I know.* Es ist weit. – Ja, ich weiß. ◊ *I don't know.* Ich weiß nicht. ◊ *I don't know what to do.* Ich weiß nicht, was ich tun soll. ◊ *I don't know how to do it.* Ich weiß nicht, wie ich es machen soll.

[2] kennen (IMPERFECT kannte, PERFECT hat gekannt) ◊ *I know her.* Ich kenne sie. ◊ *I know Berlin well.* Ich kenne Berlin gut.

♦**I don't know any French.** Ich kann kein Französisch.

♦**to know that ...** wissen, dass ... ◊ *I know that you like chocolate.* Ich weiß, dass du Schokolade magst. ◊ *I didn't know that your dad was a policeman.* Ich wusste nicht, dass dein Vater Polizist ist.

♦**to know about something (1)** (*be aware of*) von etwas wissen ◊ *Do you know about the meeting this afternoon?* Weißt du von dem Treffen heute Nachmittag?

♦**to know about something (2)** (*be knowledgeable about*) sich mit etwas auskennen ◊ *He knows a lot about cars.* Er kennt sich mit Autos aus. ◊ *I don't know much about computers.* Mit Computern kenne ich mich nicht besonders aus.

♦**to get to know somebody** jemanden kennen lernen

♦**How should I know?** (*I don't know!*) Wie soll ich das wissen?

♦**You never know!** Man kann nie wissen!

**know-all** NOUN
der Besserwisser (PL die Besserwisser)
die Besserwisserin
◊ *He's such a know-all!* So ein Besserwisser!

**know-how** NOUN
das Know-how (GEN des Know-how)

**knowledge** NOUN
[1] das Wissen (*general knowledge*) ◊ *Our knowledge of the universe is limited.* Unser Wissen über das Universum ist begrenzt.
[2] die Kenntnisse FEM PL (*things learnt*) ◊ *my knowledge of German* meine Deutschkenntnisse

**knowledgeable** ADJECTIVE
♦**to be knowledgeable about something** viel über etwas wissen ◊ *She is very knowledgeable about physics.* Sie weiß viel über Physik.
♦**She's very knowledgeable about computers.** Sie kennt sich mit Computern gut aus.

**known** VERB *see* **know**

**Koran** NOUN
der Koran

**Korea** NOUN
Korea NEUT
♦**from Korea** aus Korea
♦**to Korea** nach Korea

**kosher** ADJECTIVE
koscher

**K**

# L

**lab** NOUN (= *laboratory*)
das Labor (PL die Labors)
♦ **a lab technician** ein Laborant MASC

**label** NOUN
1 (*sticker*)
der Aufkleber (PL die Aufkleber)
2 (*on clothes*)
das Etikett (PL die Etiketts)
3 (*for luggage*)
der Anhänger (PL die
Anhänger)

**laboratory** NOUN
das Labor (PL die Labors)

**labor union** NOUN US
die Gewerkschaft

**Labour** NOUN
die Labour-Party ◊ *My parents vote
Labour. Meine Eltern wählen die
Labour-Party.*
♦ **the Labour Party** die Labour-Party

**labourer** NOUN
der Arbeiter (PL die Arbeiter)
die Arbeiterin
♦ **a farm labourer** ein Landarbeiter

**lace** NOUN
1 (*of shoe*)
der Schnürsenkel (PL die
Schnürsenkel)
2 die Spitze ◊ *a lace collar* ein
Spitzenkragen

**lack** NOUN
der Mangel (PL die Mängel) ◊ *He got the
job, despite his lack of experience.* Er
bekam die Stelle trotz seines Mangels an
Erfahrung.

**lacquer** NOUN
der Lack (PL die Lacke)

**lad** NOUN
der Junge (GEN des Jungen, PL die
Jungen)

**ladder** NOUN
1 die Leiter
2 die Laufmasche (*in tights*)

**lady** NOUN
die Dame ◊ *a young lady* eine junge
Dame
♦ **Ladies and gentlemen** ... Meine Damen
und Herren ...
♦ **the ladies'** die Damentoilette

**ladybird** NOUN
der Marienkäfer (PL die
Marienkäfer)

to **lag behind** VERB
hinterherhinken (PERFECT ist
hinterhergehinkt)

**lager** NOUN
das helle Bier (PL die hellen Biere)

> ***ⓘ*** *German beers are completely
> different from British ones. There is no
> real equivalent to **lager**.*

**laid** VERB *see* lay

**laid-back** ADJECTIVE
locker

**lain** VERB *see* lie

**lake** NOUN
der See (PL die Seen)
♦ **Lake Geneva** der Genfer See
♦ **Lake Constance** der Bodensee

**lamb** NOUN
das Lamm (PL die Lämmer)
♦ **a lamb chop** ein Lammkotelett NEUT

**lame** ADJECTIVE
lahm
♦ **My pony is lame.** Mein Pony lahmt.

**lamp** NOUN
die Lampe

**lamppost** NOUN
der Laternenpfahl (PL die
Laternenpfähle)

**lampshade** NOUN
der Lampenschirm

**land** NOUN
| *see also* **land** VERB |
das Land (PL die Länder) ◊ *a piece of land*
ein Stück Land

to **land** VERB
| *see also* **land** NOUN |
(*plane, passenger*)
landen (PERFECT ist gelandet)

**landing** NOUN
1 (*of plane*)
die Landung
2 (*of staircase*)
der Treppenabsatz (GEN des
Treppenabsatzes, PL die Treppenabsätze)

**landlady** NOUN
die Vermieterin

**landlord** NOUN
der Vermieter (PL die Vermieter)

**landmark** NOUN
das Wahrzeichen (PL die Wahrzeichen)
◊ *Big Ben is one of London's landmarks.*
Big Ben ist eines der Wahrzeichen
Londons.

**landowner** NOUN
der Grundbesitzer (PL die Grundbesitzer)
die Grundbesitzerin

**landscape** NOUN
die Landschaft

**lane** NOUN
1 (*in country*)
das Sträßchen (PL die Sträßchen)
2 (*on motorway*)

die <u>Spur</u>
**language** NOUN
  die <u>Sprache</u> ◊ *Greek is a difficult
  language.* Griechisch ist eine schwierige
  Sprache.
♦ **to use bad language** Kraftausdrücke
  benutzen
**language laboratory** NOUN
  das <u>Sprachlabor</u> (PL die Sprachlabors)
**lap** NOUN
  die <u>Runde</u> (*sport*) ◊ *I ran ten laps.* Ich bin
  zehn Runden gelaufen.
♦ **on my lap** auf meinem Schoß
**laptop** NOUN
  der <u>Laptop</u> (*computer*) (PL die Laptops)
**larder** NOUN
  die <u>Speisekammer</u>
**large** ADJECTIVE
  <u>groß</u> ◊ *a large house* ein großes Haus
  ◊ *a large dog* ein großer Hund
**largely** ADVERB
  <u>größtenteils</u>
**laser** NOUN
  der <u>Laser</u> (PL die Laser)
**lass** NOUN
  das <u>Mädchen</u> (PL die Mädchen)
**last** ADJECTIVE, ADVERB
  | *see also* **last** VERB |
  [1] <u>letzte</u> ◊ *one last time* ein letztes Mal
  ◊ *the last question* die letzte Frage ◊ *last
  Friday* letzten Freitag ◊ *last week* letzte
  Woche
  [2] <u>als Letzte</u> ◊ *He arrived last.* Er kam als
  Letzter an.
  [3] <u>zuletzt</u> ◊ *I've lost my bag. – When did
  you see it last?* Ich habe meine Tasche
  verloren. – Wann hast du sie zuletzt
  gesehen?
♦ **When I last saw him, he was wearing a
  blue shirt.** Als ich ihn das letzte Mal sah,
  trug er ein blaues Hemd.
♦ **the last time** das letzte Mal ◊ *the last
  time I saw her* als ich sie das letzte Mal
  sah ◊ *That's the last time I take your
  advice!* Das ist das letzte Mal, dass ich
  auf deinen Rat höre!
♦ **last night (1)** (*evening*) gestern Abend ◊ *I
  got home at midnight last night.* Ich bin
  gestern Abend um Mitternacht nach
  Hause gekommen.
♦ **last night (2)** (*sleeping hours*) heute Nacht
  ◊ *I couldn't sleep last night.* Ich konnte
  heute Nacht nicht schlafen.
♦ **at last** endlich
to **last** VERB
  | *see also* **last** ADJECTIVE |
  <u>dauern</u> ◊ *The concert lasts two hours.*
  Das Konzert dauert zwei Stunden.
**lastly** ADVERB
  <u>schließlich</u> ◊ *Lastly I'd like to mention
  that ...* Und schließlich möchte ich
  erwähnen, dass ...
**late** ADJECTIVE, ADVERB

[1] zu spät ◊ *Hurry up or you'll be late!*
  Beeil dich, du kommst sonst zu spät!
  ◊ *I'm often late for school.* Ich komme oft
  zu spät zur Schule.
♦ **to arrive late** zu spät kommen ◊ *She
  arrived late.* Sie kam zu spät.
  [2] spät ◊ *I went to bed late.* Ich bin spät
  ins Bett gegangen. ◊ *in the late afternoon*
  am späten Nachmittag
♦ **in late May** Ende Mai
**lately** ADVERB
  <u>in letzter Zeit</u> ◊ *I haven't seen him lately.*
  Ich habe ihn in letzter Zeit nicht gesehen.
**later** ADVERB
  <u>später</u> ◊ *I'll do it later.* Ich mache es
  später.
♦ **See you later!** Bis später!
**latest** ADJECTIVE
  <u>neueste</u> ◊ *the latest news* die neuesten
  Nachrichten ◊ *their latest album* ihr
  neuestes Album
♦ **at the latest** spätestens ◊ *by ten o'clock
  at the latest* bis spätestens zehn Uhr
**Latin** NOUN
  das <u>Latein</u> ◊ *I do Latin.* Ich lerne Latein.
**Latin America** NOUN
  <u>Lateinamerika</u> NEUT
♦ **from Latin America** aus Lateinamerika
♦ **to Latin America** nach Lateinamerika
**Latin American** ADJECTIVE
  <u>lateinamerikanisch</u>
**laugh** NOUN
  | *see also* **laugh** VERB |
  das <u>Lachen</u>
♦ **It was a good laugh.** (*it was fun*) Es war
  lustig.
to **laugh** VERB
  | *see also* **laugh** NOUN |
  <u>lachen</u>
♦ **to laugh at something** über etwas lachen
  ◊ *She didn't laugh at my joke.* Sie hat
  über meinen Witz nicht gelacht.
♦ **to laugh at somebody** jemanden
  auslachen ◊ *They laughed at her.* Sie
  lachten sie aus.
to **launch** VERB
  [1] <u>auf den Markt bringen</u> (*product*)
  (IMPERFECT brachte, PERFECT hat gebracht)
  [2] <u>abschießen</u> (*rocket*) (IMPERFECT schoss
  ab, PERFECT hat abgeschossen)
**Launderette** ® NOUN
  der <u>Waschsalon</u> (PL die Waschsalons)
**Laundromat** ® NOUN US
  der <u>Waschsalon</u> (PL die Waschsalons)
**laundry** NOUN
  die <u>Wäsche</u> (*clothes*)
**lavatory** NOUN
  die <u>Toilette</u>
**lavender** NOUN
  der <u>Lavendel</u>
**law** NOUN

**L**

① das Gesetz (GEN des Gesetzes, PL die Gesetze) ◊ *It's against the law.* Das ist gegen das Gesetz.
② (*subject*)
Jura ◊ *My sister's studying law.* Meine Schwester studiert Jura.

**lawn** NOUN
der Rasen (PL die Rasen)

**lawnmower** NOUN
der Rasenmäher (PL die Rasenmäher)

**law school** NOUN [US]
die juristische Fakultät

**lawyer** NOUN
der Rechtsanwalt (PL die Rechtsanwälte)
die Rechtsanwältin
◊ *My mother's a lawyer.* Meine Mutter ist Rechtsanwältin.

to **lay** VERB
*lay is also a form of **lie (2)** VERB.*
legen ◊ *She laid the baby in her cot.* Sie legte das Baby ins Bettchen.
◆ **to lay the table** den Tisch decken
◆ **to lay something on (1)** (*provide*) etwas bereitstellen ◊ *They laid on extra buses.* Sie stellten zusätzliche Busse bereit.
◆ **to lay something on (2)** (*prepare*) etwas vorbereiten ◊ *They had laid on a meal.* Sie hatten ein Essen vorbereitet.
◆ **to lay off** entlassen ◊ *My father's been laid off.* Mein Vater ist entlassen worden.

**lay-by** NOUN
der Rastplatz (GEN des Rastplatzes, PL die Rastplätze)

**layer** NOUN
die Schicht

**layout** NOUN
das Design (*of house, garden*) (PL die Designs)

**lazy** ADJECTIVE
faul

**lb.** ABBREVIATION (= *pound*)
Pfund

to **lead** VERB
*see also **lead (1)** NOUN AND **lead (2)** NOUN*
führen ◊ *the street that leads to the station* die Straße, die zum Bahnhof führt
◆ **to lead the way** vorangehen ◊ *She led the way.* Sie ist vorangegangen.
◆ **to lead somebody away** jemanden abführen ◊ *The police led the man away.* Die Polizei führte den Mann ab.

**lead (1)** NOUN
*see also **lead** VERB AND **lead (2)** NOUN*
① (*cable*)
das Kabel (PL die Kabel)
② (*for dog*)
die Hundeleine
◆ **to be in the lead** in Führung sein ◊ *Our team is in the lead.* Unsere Mannschaft ist in Führung.

**lead (2)** NOUN
*see also **lead** VERB AND **lead (1)** NOUN*
das Blei (*metal*)

**leaded petrol** NOUN
das verbleite Benzin

**leader** NOUN
① (*of expedition, gang*)
der Führer (PL die Führer)
die Führerin
② (*of political party*)
der Anführer (PL die Anführer)
die Anführerin

**lead-free** ADJECTIVE
◆ **lead-free petrol** das bleifreie Benzin

**lead singer** NOUN
der Leadsinger (PL die Leadsinger)
die Leadsingerin

**leaf** NOUN
das Blatt (PL die Blätter)

**leaflet** NOUN
der Prospekt (*advertising*) (PL die Prospekte) ◊ *They sent me a leaflet describing their products.* Sie haben mir einen Prospekt über ihre Produkte geschickt.

**league** NOUN
die Liga (GEN der Liga, PL die Ligen) ◊ *the Premier League* die erste Liga

> ⓘ The **Premier League** is similar to the German **Bundesliga**.

◆ **They are at the top of the league.** Sie sind Tabellenführer.

**leak** NOUN
*see also **leak** VERB*
die undichte Stelle ◊ *a gas leak* eine undichte Stelle in der Gasleitung

to **leak** VERB
*see also **leak** NOUN*
① (*pipe*)
undicht sein (PRESENT ist undicht, IMPERFECT war undicht, PERFECT ist undicht gewesen)
② (*water*)
auslaufen (PRESENT läuft aus, IMPERFECT lief aus, PERFECT ist ausgelaufen)
③ (*gas*)
austreten (PRESENT tritt aus, IMPERFECT trat aus, PERFECT ist ausgetreten)

to **lean** VERB
sich lehnen ◊ *Don't lean over too far.* Lehn dich nicht zu weit vor. ◊ *She leant out of the window.* Sie lehnte sich zum Fenster hinaus.
◆ **to lean forward** sich nach vorn beugen
◆ **to lean on something** sich auf etwas stützen ◊ *He leant on the wall.* Er stützte sich auf die Mauer.
◆ **to be leaning against something** gegen etwas gelehnt sein ◊ *The ladder was leaning against the wall.* Die Leiter war gegen die Wand gelehnt.
◆ **to lean something against a wall** etwas an einer Mauer anlehnen ◊ *He leant his bike against the wall.* Er lehnte sein Fahrrad an der Mauer an.

to **leap** VERB
　　springen (IMPERFECT sprang, PERFECT ist gesprungen) ◊ *He leapt out of his chair when his team scored.* Er sprang vom Stuhl auf, als seine Mannschaft ein Tor schoss.

**leap year** NOUN
　　das Schaltjahr (PL die Schaltjahre)

to **learn** VERB
　　lernen ◊ *I'm learning to ski.* Ich lerne Ski fahren.

**learner** NOUN
　　◆**She's a quick learner.** Sie lernt schnell.
　　◆**German learners** (*people learning German*) Deutschschüler MASC PL

**learner driver** NOUN
　　der Fahrschüler (PL die Fahrschüler)
　　die Fahrschülerin

**learnt** VERB *see* **learn**

**least** ADVERB, ADJECTIVE, PRONOUN
　　◆**the least (1)** (*followed by noun*) wenigste ◊ *It takes the least time to do.* Das braucht die wenigste Zeit. ◊ *She has the least money.* Sie hat das wenigste Geld.
　　◆**the least (2)** (*followed by adjective*) am wenigsten ... ◊ *the least intelligent pupil* der am wenigsten intelligente Schüler ◊ *the least attractive woman* die am wenigsten attraktive Frau ◊ *the least interesting book* das am wenigsten interessante Buch
　　◆**the least (3)** (*after a verb*) am wenigsten ◊ *Maths is the subject I like the least.* Mathe ist das Fach, das ich am wenigsten mag.
　　◆**It's the least I can do.** Das ist das wenigste, was ich tun kann.
　　◆**at least (1)** mindestens ◊ *It'll cost at least two hundred pounds.* Das kostet mindestens zweihundert Pfund.
　　◆**at least (2)** wenigstens ◊ *... but at least nobody was hurt.* ... aber wenigstens wurde niemand verletzt.
　　◆**It's totally unfair – at least, that's my opinion.** Das ist total ungerecht – zumindest meiner Meinung nach.

**leather** NOUN
　　das Leder (PL die Leder) ◊ *a black leather jacket* eine schwarze Lederjacke

to **leave** VERB
　　| see also **leave** NOUN |
　　⑴ (*deliberately*)
　　lassen (PRESENT lässt, IMPERFECT ließ, PERFECT hat gelassen) ◊ *He always leaves his camera in the car.* Er lässt immer seinen Fotoapparat im Auto.
　　⑵ (*by mistake*)
　　vergessen (PRESENT vergisst, IMPERFECT vergaß, PERFECT hat vergessen) ◊ *I've left my book at home.* Ich habe mein Buch zu Hause vergessen.

　　◆**Make sure you don't leave anything behind.** Passen Sie auf, dass Sie nichts liegen lassen.
　　③ (*bus, train*)
　　abfahren (PRESENT fährt ab, IMPERFECT fuhr ab, PERFECT ist abgefahren) ◊ *The bus leaves at eight.* Der Bus fährt um acht ab.
　　④ (*plane*)
　　abfliegen (IMPERFECT flog ab, PERFECT ist abgeflogen) ◊ *The plane leaves at six.* Das Flugzeug fliegt um sechs ab.
　　⑤ (*person*)
　　weggehen (IMPERFECT ging weg, PERFECT ist weggegangen) ◊ *She's just left.* Sie ist eben weggegangen.
　　◆**My sister left home last year.** Meine Schwester ist letztes Jahr von zu Hause weggezogen.
　　⑥ (*abandon*)
　　verlassen (PRESENT verlässt, IMPERFECT verließ, PERFECT hat verlassen) ◊ *She left her husband.* Sie hat ihren Mann verlassen.
　　◆**to leave somebody alone** jemanden in Ruhe lassen ◊ *Leave me alone!* Lass mich in Ruhe!
　　◆**to leave out** auslassen ◊ *You've left out a comma.* Du hast ein Komma ausgelassen.
　　◆**I felt really left out.** Ich fühlte mich richtig ausgeschlossen.

**leave** NOUN
　　| see also **leave** VERB |
　　der Urlaub (*from job, army*) (PL die Urlaube) ◊ *My brother is on leave for a week.* Mein Bruder hat eine Woche Urlaub.

**leaves** PL NOUN *see* **leaf**

**Lebanon** NOUN
　　der Libanon
　　*Note that the definite article is used in German for countries which are masculine.*
　　◆**from Lebanon** aus dem Libanon
　　◆**in Lebanon** im Libanon
　　◆**to Lebanon** in den Libanon

**lecture** NOUN
　　| see also **lecture** VERB |
　　① (*public*)
　　der Vortrag (PL die Vorträge)
　　② (*at university*)
　　die Vorlesung
　　*Be careful not to translate **lecture** by **Lektüre**.*

to **lecture** VERB
　　| see also **lecture** NOUN |
　　① unterrichten (PERFECT hat unterrichtet) ◊ *She lectures at the technical college.* Sie unterrichtet an der Fachschule.
　　② (*tell off*)
　　belehren (PERFECT hat belehrt) ◊ *He's always lecturing us.* Er belehrt uns andauernd.

**L**

**lecturer** NOUN
der <u>Dozent</u> (GEN des Dozenten, PL die Dozenten)
die <u>Dozentin</u>
◊ *She's a lecturer.* Sie ist Dozentin.

**led** VERB *see* **lead**

**leek** NOUN
der <u>Lauch</u> (PL die Lauche)

**left** VERB *see* **leave**

**left** ADJECTIVE, ADVERB
see also **left** NOUN
[1] <u>linke</u> ◊ *the left foot* der linke Fuß ◊ *my left arm* mein linker Arm ◊ *your left hand* deine linke Hand ◊ *her left eye* ihr linkes Auge
[2] <u>links</u> ◊ *Turn left at the traffic lights.* Biegen Sie an der Ampel links ab.
♦ **Look left!** Sehen Sie nach links!
♦ **I haven't got any money left.** Ich habe kein Geld mehr.

**left** NOUN
see also **left** ADJECTIVE
die <u>linke Seite</u>
♦ **on the left** links ◊ *Remember to drive on the left.* Vergiss nicht, links zu fahren.

**left-hand** ADJECTIVE
♦ **the left-hand side** die linke Seite
♦ **It's on the left-hand side.** Es liegt links.

**left-handed** ADJECTIVE
<u>linkshändig</u>

**left-luggage office** NOUN
die <u>Gepäckaufbewahrung</u>

**leg** NOUN
das <u>Bein</u> (PL die Beine) ◊ *I've broken my leg.* Ich habe mir das Bein gebrochen.
♦ **a chicken leg** eine Hähnchenkeule
♦ **a leg of lamb** eine Lammkeule

**legal** ADJECTIVE
<u>legal</u>

**leggings** PL NOUN
die <u>Leggings</u> PL

**leisure** NOUN
die <u>Freizeit</u> ◊ *What do you do in your leisure time?* Was machen Sie in Ihrer Freizeit?

**leisure centre** NOUN
das <u>Freizeitzentrum</u> (PL die Freizeitzentren)

**lemon** NOUN
die <u>Zitrone</u>

**lemonade** NOUN
die <u>Limonade</u>

to **lend** VERB
<u>leihen</u> (IMPERFECT lieh, PERFECT hat geliehen) ◊ *I can lend you some money.* Ich kann dir Geld leihen.

**length** NOUN
die <u>Länge</u>
♦ **It's about a metre in length.** Es ist etwa einen Meter lang.

**lens** NOUN
[1] (*contact lens*)

die <u>Kontaktlinse</u>
[2] (*of spectacles*)
das <u>Glas</u> (GEN des Glases, PL die Gläser)
[3] (*of camera*)
das <u>Objektiv</u> (PL die Objektive)

**Lent** NOUN
die <u>Fastenzeit</u> ◊ *during Lent* während der Fastenzeit

**lent** VERB *see* **lend**

**lentil** NOUN
die <u>Linse</u>

**Leo** NOUN
der <u>Löwe</u> (GEN des Löwen) ◊ *I'm Leo.* Ich bin Löwe.

**leotard** NOUN
der <u>Gymnastikanzug</u> (PL die Gymnastikanzüge)

**lesbian** NOUN
die <u>Lesbierin</u>
♦ **She's a lesbian.** Sie ist lesbisch.

**less** PRONOUN, ADVERB, ADJECTIVE
<u>weniger</u> ◊ *A bit less, please.* Etwas weniger, bitte. ◊ *I've got less time for hobbies now.* Ich habe jetzt weniger Zeit für Hobbys.
♦ **He's less intelligent than his brother.** Er ist nicht so intelligent wie sein Bruder.
♦ **less than** weniger als ◊ *It costs less than a hundred marks.* Es kostet weniger als hundert Mark. ◊ *less than half* weniger als die Hälfte ◊ *He spent less than me.* Er hat weniger als ich ausgegeben. ◊ *I've got less than you.* Ich habe weniger als du.

**lesson** NOUN
[1] die <u>Lektion</u> ◊ *"Lesson Sixteen"* (*in textbook*) "Lektion sechzehn"
[2] die <u>Stunde</u> (*class*) ◊ *The lessons last forty minutes each.* Eine Stunde dauert je vierzig Minuten.

to **let** VERB
[1] (*allow*)
<u>lassen</u> (PRESENT lässt, IMPERFECT ließ, PERFECT hat gelassen)
♦ **to let somebody do something** jemanden etwas tun lassen ◊ *Let me have a look.* Lass mich mal sehen. ◊ *My mother won't let me go out tonight.* Meine Mutter lässt mich heute Abend nicht ausgehen.
♦ **to let somebody down** jemanden enttäuschen ◊ *I won't let you down.* Ich werde dich nicht enttäuschen.
♦ **to let somebody know** jemandem Bescheid sagen ◊ *I'll let you know as soon as possible.* Ich sage Ihnen sobald wie möglich Bescheid.
♦ **to let go** (*release*) loslassen ◊ *Let me go!* Lass mich los!
♦ **to let in** hineinlassen ◊ *They wouldn't let me in because I was under eighteen.* Sie wollten mich nicht hineinlassen, weil ich noch nicht achtzehn bin.

◆**Let's go to the cinema!** Lass uns ins Kino gehen!
◆**Let's go!** Gehen wir!
2 (*hire out*)
vermieten (PERFECT hat vermietet)
◆**"to let"** "zu vermieten"
**letter** NOUN
1 der Brief (PL die Briefe) ◇ *She wrote me a long letter.* Sie hat mir einen langen Brief geschrieben.
2 (*of alphabet*)
der Buchstabe (GEN des Buchstaben, PL die Buchstaben) ◇ *A is the first letter of the alphabet.* A ist der erste Buchstabe des Alphabets.
**letterbox** NOUN
der Briefkasten (PL die Briefkästen)
**lettuce** NOUN
der Kopfsalat (PL die Kopfsalate)
**leukaemia** NOUN
die Leukämie ◇ *He suffers from leukaemia.* Er leidet an Leukämie.
**level** ADJECTIVE
see also **level** NOUN
eben ◇ *A snooker table must be perfectly level.* Ein Snookertisch muss ganz eben sein.
**level** NOUN
see also **level** ADJECTIVE
1 (*of river, lake*)
der Wasserstand (PL die Wasserstände) ◇ *The level of the river is rising.* Der Wasserstand des Flusses steigt.
2 (*height*)
die Höhe ◇ *at eye level* in Augenhöhe
◆**A levels** das Abitur

🛈 Germans take their **Abitur** at the age of 19. The students sit examinations in a variety of subjects to attain an overall grade. If you pass, you have the right to a place at university.

**level crossing** NOUN
der Bahnübergang (PL die Bahnübergänge)
**lever** NOUN
der Hebel (PL die Hebel)
**liable** ADJECTIVE
◆**He's liable to lose his temper.** Er wird leicht wütend.
**liar** NOUN
der Lügner (PL die Lügner)
die Lügnerin
**liberal** ADJECTIVE
liberal (*opinions*)
◆**the Liberal Democrats** die Liberaldemokraten
**liberation** NOUN
die Befreiung
**Libra** NOUN
die Waage ◇ *I'm Libra.* Ich bin Waage.
**librarian** NOUN

der Bibliothekar (PL die Bibliothekare)
die Bibliothekarin
◇ *She's a librarian.* Sie ist Bibliothekarin.
**library** NOUN
1 die Bücherei (*public lending library*)
2 die Bibliothek (*of school, university*)
**Libya** NOUN
Libyen NEUT
◆**from Libya** aus Libyen
◆**to Libya** nach Libyen
**licence** NOUN
der Schein (PL die Scheine)
◆**a driving licence** ein Führerschein
to **lick** VERB
lecken
**lid** NOUN
der Deckel (PL die Deckel)
**lie** NOUN
see also **lie (1)** VERB AND **lie (2)** VERB
die Lüge ◇ *That's a lie!* Das ist eine Lüge!
◆**to tell a lie** lügen
to **lie (1)** VERB
see also **lie** NOUN AND **lie (2)** VERB
lügen (*not tell the truth*) (IMPERFECT log, PERFECT hat gelogen) ◇ *I know she's lying.* Ich weiß, dass sie lügt.
to **lie (2)** VERB
see also **lie** NOUN AND **lie (1)** VERB
liegen (IMPERFECT lag, PERFECT hat gelegen) ◇ *He was lying on the sofa.* Er lag auf dem Sofa. ◇ *When I'm on holiday I lie on the beach all day.* In den Ferien liege ich den ganzen Tag am Strand.
◆**to lie down** sich hinlegen
◆**to be lying down** liegen
**lie-in** NOUN
◆**to have a lie-in** ausschlafen ◇ *She has a lie-in on Sundays.* Sonntags schläft sie aus.
**lieutenant** NOUN
der Leutnant (PL die Leutnants)
**life** NOUN
das Leben (PL die Leben)
**lifebelt** NOUN
der Rettungsring (PL die Rettungsringe)
**lifeboat** NOUN
das Rettungsboot (PL die Rettungsboote)
**lifeguard** NOUN
1 (*at beach*)
der Rettungsschwimmer (PL die Rettungsschwimmer)
die Rettungsschwimmerin
2 (*at swimming pool*)
der Bademeister (PL die Bademeister)
die Bademeisterin
**life jacket** NOUN
die Schwimmweste
**life-saving** NOUN
das Rettungsschwimmen ◇ *I've done a course in life-saving.* Ich habe einen Kurs im Rettungsschwimmen gemacht.

**L**

**lifestyle** NOUN
der Lebensstil (PL die Lebensstile)

to **lift** VERB
see also **lift** NOUN

hochheben (IMPERFECT hob hoch, PERFECT hat hochgehoben) ◊ *It's too heavy, I can't lift it.* Es ist zu schwer, ich kann es nicht hochheben.

**lift** NOUN
see also **lift** VERB

der Aufzug (PL die Aufzüge) ◊ *The lift isn't working.* Der Aufzug geht nicht.
◆**He gave me a lift to the cinema.** Er hat mich zum Kino gefahren.
◆**Would you like a lift?** Wollen Sie mitfahren?

**light** ADJECTIVE
see also **light** NOUN, VERB

[1] leicht (*not heavy*) ◊ *a light jacket* eine leichte Jacke ◊ *a light meal* ein leichtes Essen
[2] hell (*colour*) ◊ *a light blue sweater* ein hellblauer Pullover

**light** NOUN
see also **light** ADJECTIVE, VERB

[1] das Licht (PL die Lichter) ◊ *to switch on the light* das Licht anmachen ◊ *to switch off the light* das Licht ausmachen
[2] die Lampe ◊ *There's a light by my bed.* Ich habe am Bett eine Lampe.
◆**the traffic lights** die Ampel SING
◆**Have you got a light?** (*for cigarette*) Haben Sie Feuer?

to **light** VERB
see also **light** ADJECTIVE, NOUN

anzünden (*candle, cigarette, fire*) (PERFECT hat angezündet)

**light bulb** NOUN
die Glühbirne

**lighter** NOUN
das Feuerzeug (*for cigarettes*) (PL die Feuerzeuge)

**lighthouse** NOUN
der Leuchtturm (PL die Leuchttürme)

**lightning** NOUN
der Blitz (GEN des Blitzes, PL die Blitze)
◆**a flash of lightning** ein Blitz
◆**There was a flash of lightning.** Es hat geblitzt.

to **like** VERB
see also **like** PREPOSITION

mögen (PRESENT mag, IMPERFECT mochte, PERFECT hat gemocht) ◊ *I don't like mustard.* Ich mag Senf nicht. ◊ *I like Paul, but I don't want to go out with him.* Ich mag Paul, aber ich will nicht mit ihm ausgehen.
◆**I like riding.** Ich reite gern.
◆**Would you like ...?** Möchtest du ...?
◊ *Would you like some coffee?* Möchtest du Kaffee? ◊ *Would you like to go for a walk?* Möchtest du einen Spaziergang machen?
◆**I'd like ...** Ich hätte gern ... ◊ *I'd like an orange juice, please.* Ich hätte gern einen Orangensaft, bitte.
◆**I'd like to ...** Ich würde gern ... ◊ *I'd like to go to Russia one day.* Eines Tages würde ich gern nach Russland fahren. ◊ *I'd like to wash my hands.* Ich würde mir gern die Hände waschen.
◆**... if you like ...** wenn du möchtest

**like** PREPOSITION
see also **like** VERB

[1] so (*this way*) ◊ *It's fine like that.* So ist es gut. ◊ *Do it like this.* Mach das so.
[2] wie (*similar to*) ◊ *a city like Munich* eine Stadt wie München ◊ *It's a bit like salmon.* Es ist ein bisschen wie Lachs.
◆**What's the weather like?** Wie ist das Wetter?
◆**to look like somebody** jemandem ähnlich sehen ◊ *You look like my brother.* Du siehst meinem Bruder ähnlich.

**likely** ADJECTIVE
wahrscheinlich ◊ *That's not very likely.* Das ist nicht sehr wahrscheinlich.
◆**She's likely to come.** Sie kommt wahrscheinlich.
◆**She's not likely to come.** Sie kommt wahrscheinlich nicht.

**Lilo** ® NOUN
die Luftmatratze

**lime** NOUN
die Limone (*fruit*)

**limit** NOUN
die Grenze
◆**the speed limit** die Geschwindigkeitsbegrenzung

**limousine** NOUN
die Limousine

to **limp** VERB
hinken

**line** NOUN
[1] die Linie ◊ *a straight line* eine gerade Linie
[2] (*to divide, cancel*)
der Strich (PL die Striche) ◊ *Draw a line under each answer.* Machen Sie unter jede Antwort einen Strich.
[3] (*railway track*)
das Gleis (GEN des Gleises, PL die Gleise)
[4] die Schlange ◊ *to stand in line* Schlange stehen
◆**Hold the line, please.** (*on telephone*) Bleiben Sie bitte am Apparat.
◆**It's a very bad line.** (*on telephone*) Die Verbindung ist sehr schlecht.

**linen** NOUN
das Leinen ◊ *a linen jacket* eine Leinenjacke

**liner** NOUN

der Überseedampfer (*ship*) (PL die Überseedampfer)

**linguist** NOUN
♦ **to be a good linguist** sprachbegabt sein ◊ *She's a good linguist.* Sie ist sehr sprachbegabt.

**lining** NOUN
das Futter (*of clothes*) (PL die Futter)

**link** NOUN
see also **link** VERB

1 der Zusammenhang (PL die Zusammenhänge) ◊ *the link between smoking and cancer* der Zusammenhang zwischen Rauchen und Krebs
2 (*computer*)
der Link (PL die Links)

to **link** VERB
see also **link** NOUN

verbinden (IMPERFECT verband, PERFECT hat verbunden)

**lino** NOUN
das Linoleum

**lion** NOUN
der Löwe (GEN des Löwen, PL die Löwen)

**lioness** NOUN
die Löwin

**lip** NOUN
die Lippe

to **lip-read** VERB
von den Lippen ablesen (PRESENT liest von den Lippen ab, IMPERFECT las von den Lippen ab, PERFECT hat von den Lippen abgelesen)
♦ **I'm learning how to lip-read.** Ich lerne gerade Lippenlesen.

**lip salve** NOUN
der Lippenpflegestift (PL die Lippenpflegestifte)

**lipstick** NOUN
der Lippenstift (PL die Lippenstifte)

**liqueur** NOUN
der Likör (PL die Liköre)

**liquid** NOUN
die Flüssigkeit

**liquidizer** NOUN
der Mixer (PL die Mixer)

**list** NOUN
see also **list** VERB

die Liste

to **list** VERB
see also **list** NOUN

aufzählen (PERFECT hat aufgezählt) ◊ *List your hobbies.* Zählen Sie Ihre Hobbys auf.

to **listen** VERB
zuhören (PERFECT hat zugehört) ◊ *Listen to me!* Hör mir zu!
♦ **Listen to this!** Hör dir das an!

**listener** NOUN
der Zuhörer (PL die Zuhörer)
die Zuhörerin

**lit** VERB *see* **light**

**liter** NOUN [US]
der Liter (PL die Liter)

**literally** ADVERB
buchstäblich (*completely*) ◊ *It was literally impossible to find a seat.* Es war buchstäblich unmöglich, einen Platz zu finden.
♦ **to translate literally** wörtlich übersetzen

**literature** NOUN
die Literatur ◊ *I'm studying English Literature.* Ich studiere englische Literatur.

**litre** NOUN
der Liter (PL die Liter) ◊ *three litres* drei Liter

**litter** NOUN
der Abfall (PL die Abfälle)

**litter bin** NOUN
der Abfallkorb (PL die Abfallkörbe)

**little** ADJECTIVE
klein ◊ *a little girl* ein kleines Mädchen
♦ **a little** ein bisschen ◊ *How much would you like? – Just a little.* Wie viel möchtest du? – Nur ein bisschen.
♦ **very little** sehr wenig ◊ *We've got very little time.* Wir haben sehr wenig Zeit.
♦ **little by little** nach und nach

**live** ADJECTIVE
see also **live** VERB

1 lebendig (*animal*)
2 live (*broadcast*)
♦ **There's live music on Fridays.** Freitags gibt es Live-Musik.

to **live** VERB
see also **live** ADJECTIVE

1 leben ◊ *I live with my grandmother.* Ich lebe bei meiner Großmutter. ◊ *They're not married, they're living together.* Sie sind nicht verheiratet, sie leben zusammen.
♦ **to live on something** von etwas leben ◊ *He had to live on bread and water.* Er musste von Brot und Wasser leben. ◊ *He lives on benefit.* Er lebt von der Unterstützung.
2 wohnen (*in house, town*) ◊ *Where do you live?* Wo wohnst du? ◊ *I live in Edinburgh.* Ich wohne in Edinburgh.

**lively** ADJECTIVE
lebhaft ◊ *She's got a lively personality.* Sie ist ein lebhafter Typ.

**liver** NOUN
die Leber
♦ **liver sausage** die Leberwurst

**lives** PL NOUN *see* **life**

**living** NOUN
♦ **to make a living** sich seinen Lebensunterhalt verdienen ◊ *How do you make your living?* Wie verdienst du dir deinen Lebensunterhalt?
♦ **What does she do for a living?** Was macht sie beruflich?

**living room** NOUN

**L**

☞

das Wohnzimmer (PL die Wohnzimmer)
**lizard** NOUN
die Echse
**load** NOUN
> see also **load** VERB

♦ **loads of** eine Menge ◇ *loads of people* eine Menge Leute ◇ *loads of money* eine Menge Geld

♦ **You're talking a load of rubbish!** Du redest vielleicht einen Unsinn!

to **load** VERB
> see also **load** NOUN

beladen (PRESENT belädt, IMPERFECT belud, PERFECT hat beladen) ◇ *He's loading the van right now.* Er belädt gerade den Lieferwagen.

**loaf** NOUN
der Laib (PL die Laibe)

♦ **a loaf of bread** ein Brot NEUT

**loan** NOUN
> see also **loan** VERB

das Darlehen (*money*) (PL die Darlehen)

to **loan** VERB
> see also **loan** NOUN

ausleihen (IMPERFECT lieh aus, PERFECT hat ausgeliehen)

to **loathe** VERB
verabscheuen (PERFECT hat verabscheut) ◇ *I loathe her.* Ich verabscheue sie.

**loaves** PL NOUN *see* **loaf**

**lobster** NOUN
der Hummer (PL die Hummer)

**local** ADJECTIVE
örtlich ◇ *the local police* die örtliche Polizei

♦ **the local paper** das Lokalblatt

♦ **a local call** ein Ortsgespräch NEUT

**loch** NOUN
der See (PL die Seen)

**lock** NOUN
> see also **lock** VERB

das Schloss (GEN des Schlosses, PL die Schlösser) ◇ *The lock is broken.* Das Schloss ist kaputt.

to **lock** VERB
> see also **lock** NOUN

abschließen (IMPERFECT schloss ab, PERFECT hat abgeschlossen) ◇ *Make sure you lock your door.* Schließen Sie die Tür ab.

♦ **to lock somebody out** jemanden aussperren ◇ *The door slammed and I was locked out.* Die Tür schlug zu und ich war ausgesperrt.

**locker** NOUN
das Schließfach (PL die Schließfächer)

♦ **the locker room** der Umkleideraum

♦ **the left-luggage lockers** die Gepäckschließfächer

**locket** NOUN
das Medaillon (PL die Medaillons)

**lodger** NOUN
der Untermieter (PL die Untermieter)

die Untermieterin
**loft** NOUN
der Speicher (PL die Speicher)
**log** NOUN
das Scheit (*of wood*) (PL die Scheite)
**logical** ADJECTIVE
logisch
to **log in** VERB
einloggen (*computer*) (PERFECT hat eingeloggt)
to **log off** VERB
ausloggen (*computer*) (PERFECT hat ausgeloggt)
to **log on** VERB
einloggen (*computer*) (PERFECT hat eingeloggt)
to **log out** VERB
ausloggen (*computer*) (PERFECT hat ausgeloggt)
**lollipop** NOUN
der Lutscher (PL die Lutscher)
**lolly** NOUN
das Eis am Stiel (*ice lolly*)
**London** NOUN
London NEUT

♦ **from London** aus London

♦ **to London** nach London

**Londoner** NOUN
der Londoner (PL die Londoner)
die Londonerin
**loneliness** NOUN
die Einsamkeit
**lonely** ADJECTIVE
einsam

♦ **to feel lonely** sich einsam fühlen ◇ *She feels a bit lonely.* Sie fühlt sich ein bisschen einsam.

**long** ADJECTIVE, ADVERB
> see also **long** VERB

lang ◇ *She's got long hair.* Sie hat lange Haare. ◇ *The room is six metres long.* Das Zimmer ist sechs Meter lang.

♦ **how long?** (*time*) wie lange? ◇ *How long did you stay there?* Wie lange bist du dort geblieben? ◇ *How long is the flight?* Wie lange dauert der Flug?

*When you want to say how long you have been doing something, use the present tense in German.*

◇ *How long have you been here?* Wie lange bist du schon da? ◇ *I've been waiting a long time.* Ich warte schon lange.

♦ **It takes a long time.** Das dauert lange.

♦ **as long as** solange ◇ *I'll come as long as it's not too expensive.* Ich komme mit, solange es nicht zu teuer ist.

to **long** VERB
> see also **long** ADJECTIVE

♦ **to long to do something** es kaum erwarten können, etwas zu tun ◇ *I'm* *longing to see my boyfriend again.* Ich kann es kaum erwarten, bis ich meinen Freund wiedersehe.

**long-distance** ADJECTIVE
◆ **a long-distance call** ein Ferngespräch NEUT

**longer** ADVERB
see also **long** ADJECTIVE
◆ **They're no longer going out together.** Sie gehen nicht mehr miteinander.
◆ **I can't stand it any longer.** Ich halte das nicht länger aus.

**long jump** NOUN
der Weitsprung (PL die Weitsprünge)

**loo** NOUN
das Klo (*informal*) (PL die Klos) ◊ *Where's the loo?* Wo ist das Klo?
◆ **I need the loo.** (*informal*)
Ich muss mal.

**look** NOUN
see also **look** VERB
◆ **to have a look** ansehen ◊ *Have a look at this!* Sieh dir das mal an!
◆ **I don't like the look of it.** Das gefällt mir nicht.

to **look** VERB
see also **look** NOUN
1 sehen (PRESENT sieht, IMPERFECT sah, PERFECT hat gesehen)
◆ **Look!** Sieh mal!
◆ **to look at something** etwas ansehen ◊ *Look at the picture.* Sieh dir das Bild an.
2 (*seem*)
aussehen (PERFECT hat ausgesehen) ◊ *She looks surprised.* Sie sieht überrascht aus. ◊ *That cake looks nice.* Der Kuchen sieht gut aus. ◊ *It looks fine.* Es sieht gut aus.
◆ **to look like somebody** jemandem ähnlich sehen ◊ *He looks like his brother.* Er sieht seinem Bruder ähnlich.
◆ **What does she look like?** Wie sieht sie aus?
◆ **Look out!** Pass auf!
◆ **to look after** sich kümmern um ◊ *I look after my little sister.* Ich kümmere mich um meine kleine Schwester.
◆ **to look for** suchen ◊ *I'm looking for my passport.* Ich suche meinen Pass.
◆ **to look forward to something** sich auf etwas freuen ◊ *I'm looking forward to the holidays.* Ich freue mich auf die Ferien.
◆ **Looking forward to hearing from you ...** In der Hoffnung, bald etwas von dir zu hören, ...
◆ **to look round** sich umsehen ◊ *I shouted and he looked round.* Ich habe gerufen, und er sah sich um. ◊ *I'm just looking round.* Ich sehe mich nur um. ◊ *I like looking round the shops.* Ich sehe mich gern in den Geschäften um.
◆ **to look round a museum** ein Museum ansehen

◆ **to look up** (*word, name*) nachschlagen ◊ *If you don't know a word, look it up in the dictionary.* Wenn du ein Wort nicht weißt, schlage es im Wörterbuch nach.

**loose** ADJECTIVE
weit (*clothes*)
◆ **loose change** das Kleingeld

**lord** NOUN
der Lord (*feudal*) (PL die Lords)
◆ **the House of Lords** das Oberhaus
◆ **the Lord** (*god*) Gott
◆ **Good Lord!** Großer Gott!

**lorry** NOUN
der Lastwagen (PL die Lastwagen)

**lorry driver** NOUN
der Lastwagenfahrer (PL die Lastwagenfahrer)
die Lastwagenfahrerin
◊ *He's a lorry driver.* Er ist Lastwagenfahrer.

to **lose** VERB
verlieren (IMPERFECT verlor, PERFECT hat verloren) ◊ *I've lost my purse.* Ich habe meinen Geldbeutel verloren.
◆ **to get lost** sich verlaufen ◊ *I was afraid of getting lost.* Ich hatte Angst, mich zu verlaufen.

**loss** NOUN
der Verlust (PL die Verluste)

**lost** VERB see **lose**

**lost** ADJECTIVE
verloren

**lost-and-found** NOUN US
das Fundbüro (PL die Fundbüros)

**lost property office** NOUN
das Fundbüro (PL die Fundbüros)

**lot** NOUN
◆ **a lot** viel
◆ **a lot of** (1) viel ◊ *He earns a lot of money.* Er verdient viel Geld.
◆ **a lot of** (2) viele ◊ *We saw a lot of interesting things.* Wir haben viele interessante Dinge gesehen.
◆ **lots of** eine Menge ◊ *She's got lots of money.* Sie hat eine Menge Geld. ◊ *He's got lots of friends.* Er hat eine Menge Freunde.
◆ **What did you do at the weekend? – Not a lot.** Was hast du am Wochenende gemacht? – Nicht viel.
◆ **Do you like football? – Not a lot.** Magst du Fußball? – Nicht besonders.
◆ **That's the lot.** Das ist alles.

**lottery** NOUN
das Lotto
◆ **to win the lottery** im Lotto gewinnen

**loud** ADJECTIVE
laut ◊ *The television is too loud.* Der Fernseher ist zu laut.

**loudly** ADVERB
laut

**loudspeaker** NOUN
der Lautsprecher (PL die Lautsprecher)

L

**lounge** NOUN
das Wohnzimmer (PL die Wohnzimmer)

**lousy** ADJECTIVE
lausig schlecht (*informal*) ◊ *The food in the canteen is lousy.* Das Essen in der Kantine ist lausig schlecht.
♦ **I feel lousy.** Mir geht's lausig schlecht.

**love** NOUN
> see also **love** VERB

die Liebe
♦ **to be in love** verliebt sein ◊ *She's in love with Paul.* Sie ist in Paul verliebt.
♦ **to make love** sich lieben
♦ **Give Heike my love.** Grüß Heike von mir.
♦ **Love, Rosemary.** Alles Liebe, Rosemary.

to **love** VERB
> see also **love** NOUN

1 (*person, thing*)
lieben ◊ *I love you.* Ich liebe dich. ◊ *I love chocolate.* Ich liebe Schokolade.
2 (*like a lot*)
mögen (PRESENT mag, IMPERFECT mochte, PERFECT hat gemocht) ◊ *Everybody loves her.* Alle mögen sie.
♦ **I'd love to come.** Ich würde liebend gern kommen.
♦ **I love skiing.** Ich fahre unheimlich gern Ski.

**lovely** ADJECTIVE
1 wunderbar ◊ *What a lovely surprise!* Was für eine wunderbare Überraschung!
2 schön (*pretty*) ◊ *They've got a lovely house.* Sie haben ein schönes Haus.
♦ **It's a lovely day.** Es ist ein herrlicher Tag.
♦ **She's a lovely person.** Sie ist ein sehr netter Mensch.
♦ **Is your meal OK? – Yes, it's lovely.** Schmeckt dein Essen? – Ja, prima.
♦ **Have a lovely time!** Viel Spaß!

**lover** NOUN
der Liebhaber (PL die Liebhaber)
die Liebhaberin

**low** ADJECTIVE, ADVERB
niedrig ◊ *low prices* niedrige Preise
♦ **That plane is flying very low.** Das Flugzeug fliegt sehr tief.
♦ **the low season** die Nebensaison ◊ *in the low season* in der Nebensaison

**lower sixth** NOUN
die zwölfte Klasse ◊ *He's in the lower sixth.* Er ist in der zwölften Klasse.

**low-fat** ADJECTIVE
mager
♦ **a low-fat yoghurt** ein Magerjoghurt MASC

**loyalty** NOUN
die Treue

**loyalty card** NOUN
die Kundenkarte

**L-plates** PL NOUN
das L-Schild (PL die L-Schilder)

**luck** NOUN
das Glück ◊ *She hasn't had much luck.* Sie hat nicht viel Glück gehabt.

♦ **Good luck!** Viel Glück!
♦ **Bad luck!** So ein Pech!

**luckily** ADVERB
zum Glück

**lucky** ADJECTIVE
♦ **to be lucky (1)** (*be fortunate*) Glück haben ◊ *He's lucky, he's got a job.* Er hat Glück, er hat Arbeit.
♦ **He wasn't hurt. – That was lucky!** Er wurde nicht verletzt. – Das war Glück!
♦ **to be lucky (2)** (*bring luck*) Glück bringen ◊ *Black cats are lucky in Britain.* In Großbritannien bringen schwarze Katzen Glück.
♦ **a lucky horseshoe** ein Glückshufeisen NEUT

**luggage** NOUN
das Gepäck

**lukewarm** ADJECTIVE
lauwarm

**lump** NOUN
1 das Stück (PL die Stücke) ◊ *a lump of coal* ein Stück Kohle
2 (*swelling*)
die Beule ◊ *He's got a lump on his forehead.* Er hat eine Beule an der Stirn.

**lunatic** NOUN
der Verrückte (GEN des Verrückten, PL die Verrückten)
die Verrückte (GEN der Verrückten) ◊ *a lunatic* (*man*) ein Verrückter
♦ **He's an absolute lunatic.** Er ist total verrückt.

**lunch** NOUN
das Mittagessen (PL die Mittagessen)
♦ **to have lunch** zu Mittag essen ◊ *We have lunch at twelve o'clock.* Wir essen um zwölf Uhr zu Mittag.

**luncheon voucher** NOUN
die Essensmarke

**lung** NOUN
die Lunge ◊ *lung cancer* der Lungenkrebs

**luscious** ADJECTIVE
köstlich

**lush** ADJECTIVE
üppig

**lust** NOUN
das Verlangen

**Luxembourg** NOUN
Luxemburg NEUT (*country, city*)
♦ **from Luxembourg** aus Luxemburg
♦ **to Luxembourg** nach Luxemburg

**luxurious** ADJECTIVE
luxuriös

**luxury** NOUN
der Luxus (GEN des Luxus) ◊ *It was luxury!* Das war wirklich ein Luxus!
♦ **a luxury hotel** ein Luxushotel NEUT

**lying** VERB *see* lie

**lyrics** PL NOUN
der Text SING (*of song*) (PL die Texte)

# M

mac NOUN
der Regenmantel (PL die Regenmäntel)
macaroni SING NOUN
die Makkaroni PL
machine NOUN
die Maschine
machine gun NOUN
das Maschinengewehr
machinery NOUN
die Maschinen FEM PL
mackerel NOUN
die Makrele
mad ADJECTIVE
[1] verrückt (insane) ◊ You're mad! Du
bist verrückt!
♦ to be mad about verrückt sein nach
◊ Ann is mad about John. Ann ist
verrückt nach John. ◊ He's mad about
football. Er ist verrückt nach Fußball.
[2] wütend (angry) ◊ She'll be mad when
she finds out. Wenn sie das erfährt, wird
sie wütend sein.
♦ to be mad at somebody wütend auf
jemanden sein ◊ She was mad at me. Sie
war wütend auf mich.
madam NOUN
*In German no form of address is
normally used apart from Sie.*
◊ Would you like to order, Madam?
Möchten Sie bestellen?
made VERB see make
madly ADVERB
♦ They're madly in love. Sie sind
wahnsinnig verliebt.
madman NOUN
der Verrückte (GEN des Verrückten, PL die
Verrückten) ◊ a madman ein Verrückter
madness NOUN
der Wahnsinn ◊ It's absolute madness.
Das ist totaler Wahnsinn.
magazine NOUN
die Zeitschrift
maggot NOUN
die Made
magic ADJECTIVE
see also **magic** NOUN
[1] magisch (magical) ◊ magic powers
magische Kräfte
♦ a magic trick ein Zaubertrick MASC
♦ a magic wand ein Zauberstab MASC
[2] echt toll (brilliant) ◊ It was magic! Es
war echt toll!
magic NOUN
see also **magic** ADJECTIVE
das Zaubern ◊ My hobby is magic.
Zaubern ist mein Hobby.
magician NOUN
(conjurer)

der Zauberkünstler (PL die
Zauberkünstler)
die Zauberkünstlerin
magnet NOUN
der Magnet
magnificent ADJECTIVE
[1] wundervoll (beautiful) ◊ a magnificent
view eine wundervolle Aussicht
[2] ausgezeichnet (outstanding) ◊ It was a
magnificent film. Es war ein
ausgezeichneter Film.
magnifying glass NOUN
die Lupe
maid NOUN
die Hausangestellte (servant) (GEN der
Hausangestellten)
♦ an old maid (spinster) eine alte Jungfer
maiden name NOUN
der Mädchenname (GEN des
Mädchennamens, PL die
Mädchennamen)
mail NOUN
die Post ◊ Here's your mail. Hier ist
deine Post.
♦ by mail per Post
♦ e-mail (electronic mail) die E-Mail
mailbox NOUN US
der Briefkasten (PL die Briefkästen)
mailing list NOUN
die Mailingliste
mailman NOUN US
der Briefträger (PL die Briefträger)
main ADJECTIVE
♦ the main problem das Hauptproblem
♦ the main thing die Hauptsache
mainly ADVERB
hauptsächlich
main road NOUN
die Hauptstraße ◊ I don't like cycling on
main roads. Ich fahre nicht gern auf
Hauptstraßen Rad.
to maintain VERB
instand halten (machine, building) (PRESENT
hält instand, IMPERFECT hielt instand, PERFECT
hat instand gehalten)
maintenance NOUN
die Instandhaltung (of machine,
building)
maize NOUN
der Mais
majesty NOUN
die Majestät
♦ Your Majesty Eure Majestät
major ADJECTIVE
groß ◊ a major problem ein großes
Problem
♦ in C major in C-Dur
Majorca NOUN

☞

Mallorca NEUT ◊ *to Majorca* nach Mallorca

**majority** NOUN
die Mehrheit

**make** NOUN
see also **make** VERB
die Marke ◊ *What make is that car?*
Welche Marke ist das Auto?

to **make** VERB
see also **make** NOUN
[1] machen ◊ *He made it himself.* Er hat
es selbst gemacht. ◊ *I make my bed*
*every morning.* Ich mache jeden Morgen
mein Bett. ◊ *Two and two make four.*
Zwei und zwei macht vier.
♦ **to make lunch** das Mittagessen machen
◊ *She's making lunch.* Sie macht das
Mittagessen.
♦ **I'm going to make a cake.** Ich werde
einen Kuchen backen.
[2] (*manufacture*)
herstellen (PERFECT hat hergestellt) ◊ *made*
*in Germany* in Deutschland hergestellt
[3] (*earn*)
verdienen (PERFECT hat verdient) ◊ *He*
*makes a lot of money.* Er verdient viel
Geld.
♦ **to make somebody do something**
jemanden zwingen, etwas zu tun ◊ *My*
*mother makes me do my homework.*
Meine Mutter zwingt mich, meine
Hausaufgaben zu machen.
♦ **to make a phone call** telefonieren ◊ *I'd*
*like to make a phone call.* Ich würde gern
telefonieren.
♦ **to make fun of somebody** sich über
jemanden lustig machen ◊ *They made*
*fun of him.* Sie haben sich über ihn lustig
gemacht.
♦ **What time do you make it?** Wie viel Uhr
hast du?

to **make out** VERB
[1] entziffern (PERFECT hat entziffert) ◊ *I*
*can't make out the address on the label.*
Ich kann die Anschrift auf dem Anhänger
nicht entziffern.
[2] verstehen (IMPERFECT verstand, PERFECT
hat verstanden) ◊ *I can't make her out at*
*all.* Ich kann sie überhaupt nicht
verstehen.
[3] behaupten (PERFECT hat behauptet)
◊ *They're making out it was my fault.* Sie
behaupten, es wäre meine Schuld
gewesen.
♦ **to make a cheque out to somebody**
jemandem einen Scheck ausstellen

to **make up** VERB
[1] (*invent*)
erfinden (IMPERFECT erfand, PERFECT hat
erfunden) ◊ *He made up the whole story.*
Er hat die ganze Geschichte erfunden.
[2] (*after argument*)
sich versöhnen (PERFECT haben sich
versöhnt) ◊ *They had a quarrel, but soon*

made up. Sie haben sich gestritten, sich
aber bald wieder versöhnt.
♦ **to make oneself up** sich schminken
◊ *She spends hours making herself up.*
Sie schminkt sich immer stundenlang.

**maker** NOUN
der Hersteller (PL die Hersteller)
◊ *Germany's biggest car maker*
Deutschlands größter Autohersteller

**make-up** NOUN
das Make-up (PL die Make-ups)

**Malaysia** NOUN
Malaysia NEUT ◊ *to Malaysia* nach
Malaysia

**male** ADJECTIVE
männlich ◊ *a male kitten* ein männliches
Katzenjunges ◊ *Sex: male.* Geschlecht:
männlich

*In many cases, the ending in German*
*indicates clearly whether the noun refers*
*to a man or a woman and there is*
*therefore no need for the word **male**.*
◊ *male and female students* Studenten
und Studentinnen
♦ **a male chauvinist** ein Macho MASC
♦ **a male nurse** ein Krankenpfleger MASC

**mall** NOUN
das Einkaufszentrum (PL die
Einkaufszentren)

**Malta** NOUN
Malta NEUT
♦ **from Malta** aus Malta
♦ **to Malta** nach Malta

**mammoth** ADJECTIVE
monumental ◊ *a mammoth task* eine
monumentale Aufgabe

**man** NOUN
der Mann (PL die Männer) ◊ *an old man*
ein alter Mann

to **manage** VERB
[1] (*be in charge of*)
leiten ◊ *She manages a big store.* Sie
leitet ein großes Geschäft.
[2] (*band, football team*)
managen ◊ *He manages our band.* Er
managt unsere Band.
[3] (*get by*)
klar kommen (IMPERFECT kam klar, PERFECT
ist klar gekommen) ◊ *We haven't got*
*much money, but we manage.* Wir haben
nicht viel Geld, aber wir kommen klar.
◊ *It's okay, I can manage.* Das ist okay,
ich komme klar.
[4] schaffen ◊ *Can you manage okay?*
Schaffst du es? ◊ *I can't manage all that.*
(*food*) Das schaffe ich nicht alles.
♦ **to manage to do something** es schaffen,
etwas zu tun
♦ **Luckily I managed to pass the exam.**
Zum Glück habe ich die Prüfung
geschafft.

**manageable** ADJECTIVE
machbar (*task*)

**management** NOUN
die <u>Leitung</u> (*organization*) ◇ *He's responsible for the management of the company.* Er ist für die Leitung des Unternehmens verantwortlich. ◇ *"under new management"* "unter neuer Leitung"

**manager** NOUN
1 (*of company, shop, restaurant*)
der <u>Geschäftsführer</u> (PL die Geschäftsführer)
die <u>Geschäftsführerin</u>
2 (*of performer, football team*)
der <u>Manager</u> (PL die Manager)
die <u>Managerin</u>

**manageress** NOUN
die <u>Geschäftsführerin</u>

**mandarin** NOUN
die <u>Mandarine</u> (*fruit*)

**mango** NOUN
die <u>Mango</u> (PL die Mangos)

**mania** NOUN
die <u>Manie</u>

**maniac** NOUN
der <u>Verrückte</u> (GEN des Verrückten, PL die Verrückten)
die <u>Verrückte</u> (GEN der Verrückten) ◇ *He drives like a maniac.* Er fährt wie ein Verrückter.

to **manipulate** VERB
<u>manipulieren</u> (PERFECT hat manipuliert)

**mankind** NOUN
die <u>Menschheit</u> ◇ *Is there any hope for mankind?* Gibt es noch Hoffnung für die Menschheit?

**man-made** ADJECTIVE
<u>synthetisch</u> (*fibre*)

**manner** NOUN
die <u>Art und Weise</u> ◇ *in this manner* auf diese Art und Weise
♦ **She behaves in an odd manner.** Sie benimmt sich eigenartig.
♦ **He has a confident manner.** Er wirkt selbstsicher.

**manners** PL NOUN
das <u>Benehmen</u> SING ◇ *good manners* gutes Benehmen
♦ **Her manners are appalling.** Sie benimmt sich schrecklich.
♦ **It's bad manners to speak with your mouth full.** Es gehört sich nicht, mit vollem Mund zu sprechen.

**manpower** NOUN
die <u>Arbeitskräfte</u> FEM PL

**mansion** NOUN
die <u>Villa</u> (PL die Villen)

**mantelpiece** NOUN
der <u>Kaminsims</u> (GEN des Kaminsimses, PL die Kaminsimse)

**manual** NOUN
das <u>Handbuch</u> (PL die Handbücher)

to **manufacture** VERB
<u>herstellen</u> (PERFECT hat hergestellt)

**manufacturer** NOUN
der <u>Hersteller</u> (PL die Hersteller)

**manure** NOUN
der <u>Mist</u>

**manuscript** NOUN
das <u>Manuskript</u> (PL die Manuskripte)

**many** ADJECTIVE, PRONOUN
<u>viele</u> ◇ *The film has many special effects.* In dem Film gibt es viele Spezialeffekte. ◇ *He hasn't got many friends.* Er hat nicht viele Freunde. ◇ *Were there many people at the concert?* Waren viele Leute in dem Konzert?
♦ **very many** sehr viele ◇ *I haven't got very many CDs.* Ich habe nicht sehr viele CDs.
♦ **Not many.** Nicht viele.
♦ **How many?** Wie viele? ◇ *How many do you want?* Wie viele möchten Sie?
♦ **How many marks do you get for one pound?** Wie viel Mark bekommt man für ein Pfund?
♦ **too many** zu viele ◇ *That's too many.* Das sind zu viele. ◇ *She makes too many mistakes.* Sie macht zu viele Fehler.
♦ **so many** so viele ◇ *I didn't know that so many would come.* Ich wusste nicht, dass so viele kommen würden. ◇ *I've never seen so many policemen.* Ich habe noch nie so viele Polizisten gesehen.

**map** NOUN
1 (*of country, area*)
die <u>Landkarte</u>
2 (*of town*)
der <u>Stadtplan</u> (PL die Stadtpläne)
*Be careful not to translate* **map** *by* **Mappe**.

**marathon** NOUN
der <u>Marathonlauf</u> (PL die Marathonläufe) ◇ *the London marathon* der Londoner Marathonlauf

**marble** NOUN
der <u>Marmor</u> ◇ *a marble statue* eine Marmorstatue
♦ **to play marbles** Murmeln spielen

**March** NOUN
der <u>März</u> ◇ *in March* im März

**march** NOUN
see also **march** VERB
der <u>Protestmarsch</u> (*demonstration*) (GEN des Protestmarsches, PL die Protestmärsche)

to **march** VERB
see also **march** NOUN
1 (*soldiers*)
<u>marschieren</u> (PERFECT ist marschiert)
2 (*protesters*)
<u>aufmarschieren</u> (PERFECT ist aufmarschiert)

**mare** NOUN
die <u>Stute</u>

**margarine** NOUN
die <u>Margarine</u>

**margin** NOUN

**M**

☞

der <u>Rand</u> (PL die Ränder) ◊ *I wrote notes in the margin.* Ich schrieb Notizen an den Rand.

**marijuana** NOUN
das <u>Marihuana</u>

**marital status** NOUN
der <u>Familienstand</u>

**mark** NOUN
see also **mark** VERB
**1** (*in school*)
die <u>Note</u> ◊ *I get good marks for German.* Ich habe in Deutsch gute Noten.
**2** (*stain*)
der <u>Fleck</u> (PL die Flecken) ◊ *You've got a mark on your shirt.* Du hast einen Fleck auf dem Hemd.
**3** (*German currency*)
die <u>Mark</u> (PL die Mark) ◊ *It costs thirty marks.* Es kostet dreißig Mark.

to **mark** VERB
see also **mark** NOUN
<u>korrigieren</u> (PERFECT hat korrigiert) ◊ *The teacher hasn't marked my homework yet.* Der Lehrer hat meine Hausarbeit noch nicht korrigiert.

**market** NOUN
der <u>Markt</u> (PL die Märkte)

**marketing** NOUN
das <u>Marketing</u> (GEN des Marketing)

**marketplace** NOUN
der <u>Marktplatz</u> (GEN des Marktplatzes, PL die Marktplätze)

**marmalade** NOUN
die <u>Orangenmarmelade</u>

**maroon** ADJECTIVE
<u>burgunderrot</u> (*colour*)

**marriage** NOUN
die <u>Ehe</u>

**married** ADJECTIVE
<u>verheiratet</u> ◊ *They are not married.* Sie sind nicht verheiratet. ◊ *They have been married for fifteen years.* Sie sind seit fünfzehn Jahren verheiratet.
♦ **a married couple** ein Ehepaar NEUT

**marrow** NOUN
der <u>Kürbis</u> (*vegetable*) (GEN des Kürbisses, PL die Kürbisse)

to **marry** VERB
<u>heiraten</u> ◊ *He wants to marry her.* Er will sie heiraten.
♦ **to get married** heiraten ◊ *My sister's getting married in June.* Meine Schwester heiratet im Juni.

**marvellous** ADJECTIVE
<u>wunderbar</u> ◊ *She's a marvellous cook.* Sie ist eine wunderbare Köchin. ◊ *The weather was marvellous.* Das Wetter war wunderbar.

**marzipan** NOUN
der <u>Marzipan</u> (PL die Marzipane)

**mascara** NOUN
die <u>Wimperntusche</u>

**masculine** ADJECTIVE

<u>männlich</u>

**mashed potatoes** PL NOUN
der <u>Kartoffelbrei</u> ◊ *sausages and mashed potatoes* Würstchen mit Kartoffelbrei

**mask** NOUN
die <u>Maske</u>

**masked** ADJECTIVE
<u>maskiert</u> ◊ *a masked man* ein maskierter Mann

**mass** NOUN
**1** der <u>Haufen</u> (PL die Haufen) ◊ *a mass of books and papers* ein Haufen Bücher und Papiere
**2** (*in church*)
die <u>Messe</u> ◊ *We go to mass on Sunday.* Wir gehen am Sonntag zur Messe.
♦ **the mass media** die Massenmedien

**massage** NOUN
die <u>Massage</u>

**massive** ADJECTIVE
<u>enorm</u>

to **master** VERB
<u>beherrschen</u> (PERFECT hat beherrscht) ◊ *to master a language* eine Sprache beherrschen

**masterpiece** NOUN
das <u>Meisterstück</u> (PL die Meisterstücke)

**mat** NOUN
der <u>Vorleger</u> (*doormat*) (PL die Vorleger)
♦ **a table mat** ein Untersetzer MASC
♦ **a place mat** ein Set NEUT

**match** NOUN
see also **match** VERB
**1** das <u>Streichholz</u> (GEN des Streichholzes, PL die Streichhölzer) ◊ *a box of matches* eine Schachtel Streichhölzer
**2** (*sport*)
das <u>Spiel</u> (PL die Spiele) ◊ *a football match* ein Fußballspiel

to **match** VERB
see also **match** NOUN
<u>passen zu</u> ◊ *The jacket matches the trousers.* Die Jacke passt zu der Hose. ◊ *These colours don't match.* Diese Farben passen nicht zueinander.

**matching** ADJECTIVE
<u>farblich aufeinander abgestimmt</u> ◊ *My bedroom has matching wallpaper and curtains.* Mein Schlafzimmer hat farblich aufeinander abgestimmte Tapeten und Vorhänge.

**mate** NOUN
der <u>Kumpel</u> (*informal*) (PL die Kumpel)
*der Kumpel is also used for women.*
◊ *On Friday night I go out with my mates.* Freitag Abend gehe ich mit meinen Kumpels aus.

**material** NOUN

[1] (*cloth*)
der Stoff (PL die Stoffe)
[2] (*information, data*)
das Material (PL die Materialien) ◊ *I'm
collecting material for my project.* Ich
sammle Material für mein Referat.
♦ **raw materials** die Rohstoffe
**mathematics** SING NOUN
der Mathematik
**maths** SING NOUN
die Mathe
**matron** NOUN
die Oberschwester (*in hospital*)
**matter** NOUN
│ *see also* **matter** VERB │
die Angelegenheit ◊ *It's a serious
matter.* Das ist eine ernste
Angelegenheit.
♦ **It's a matter of life and death.** Es geht
um Leben und Tod.
♦ **What's the matter?** Was ist los?
♦ **as a matter of fact** tatsächlich
to **matter** VERB
│ *see also* **matter** NOUN │
♦ **it doesn't matter (1)** (*I don't mind*) das
macht nichts ◊ *I can't give you the
money today. – It doesn't matter.* Ich
kann dir das Geld heute nicht geben. –
Das macht nichts.
♦ **it doesn't matter (2)** (*makes no difference*)
das ist egal ◊ *Shall I phone today or
tomorrow? – Whenever, it doesn't
matter.* Soll ich heute oder morgen
anrufen? – Wann du willst, das ist egal.
♦ **It matters a lot to me.** Das ist mir sehr
wichtig.
**mattress** NOUN
die Matratze
**mature** ADJECTIVE
reif ◊ *She's very mature for her age.* Sie
ist sehr reif für ihr Alter.
**maximum** NOUN
│ *see also* **maximum** ADJECTIVE │
das Maximum (PL die Maxima)
**maximum** ADJECTIVE
│ *see also* **maximum** NOUN │
♦ **The maximum speed is a hundred
kilometres per hour.** Die
Höchstgeschwindigkeit beträgt hundert
Stundenkilometer.
♦ **the maximum amount** der Höchstbetrag
**May** NOUN
der Mai ◊ *in May* im Mai
♦ **May Day** der Erste Mai
**may** VERB
♦ **He may come.** Er kommt vielleicht. ◊ *It
may rain.* Es regnet vielleicht.
♦ **Are you going to the party? – I don't
know, I may.** Gehst du zur Party? – Ich
weiß nicht, vielleicht.
♦ **May I smoke?** Darf ich rauchen?
**maybe** ADVERB

vielleicht ◊ *maybe not* vielleicht nicht ◊ *a
bit boring, maybe* vielleicht etwas
langweilig ◊ *Maybe she's at home.*
Vielleicht ist sie zu Hause. ◊ *Maybe he'll
change his mind.* Vielleicht überlegt er es
sich anders.
**mayonnaise** NOUN
die Mayonnaise
**mayor** NOUN
der Bürgermeister (PL die Bürgermeister)
die Bürgermeisterin
**maze** NOUN
der Irrgarten (PL die Irrgärten)
**me** PRONOUN
[1] mich ◊ *Can you hear me?* Kannst du
mich hören? ◊ *Look at me!* Sieh mich an!
*Use* **mich** *after prepositions which take
the accusative.*
◊ *Is this present for me?* Ist das
Geschenk für mich? ◊ *Wait for me!* Warte
auf mich!
[2] mir
*Use* **mir** *after prepositions which take
the dative.*
◊ *Will you come with me?* Kommst du
mit mir mit? ◊ *He sat next to me.* Er saß
neben mir.
*Use* **mir** *when* **me** *means* **to me.**
◊ *Give me the book, please!* Gib mir bitte
das Buch! ◊ *She told me the truth.* Sie
hat mir die Wahrheit erzählt.
[3] ich ◊ *It's me!* Ich bin's! ◊ *Me too!* Ich
auch! ◊ *She's older than me.* Sie ist älter
als ich.
**meal** NOUN
das Essen (PL die Essen)
**mealtime** NOUN
♦ **at mealtimes** zur Essenszeit
to **mean** VERB
│ *see also* **mean** ADJECTIVE AND **means** NOUN │
[1] (*signify*)
bedeuten (PERFECT hat bedeutet) ◊ *What
does "besetzt" mean?* Was bedeutet
"besetzt"? ◊ *I don't know what it means.*
Ich weiß nicht, was es bedeutet.
[2] (*mean to say*)
meinen ◊ *What do you mean?* Was
meinst du damit? ◊ *That's not what I
meant.* Das habe ich nicht gemeint.
◊ *Which one do you mean?* Welchen
meinst du? ◊ *Do you really mean it?*
Meinst du das wirklich?
♦ **to mean to do something** etwas tun
wollen ◊ *I didn't mean to offend you.* Ich
wollte dich nicht kränken.
**mean** ADJECTIVE
│ *see also* **mean** VERB AND **means** NOUN │
[1] geizig (*with money*) ◊ *He's too mean to
buy Christmas presents.* Er ist zu geizig,
um Weihnachtsgeschenke zu kaufen.
[2] gemein (*unkind*) ◊ *You're being mean
to me.* Du bist gemein zu mir. ◊ *That's a*

**M**

☞

*really mean thing to say!* Das ist gemein,
so etwas zu sagen!
**meaning** NOUN
  die Bedeutung
  *Be careful not to translate **meaning** by
  **Meinung**.*
**means** NOUN
  see also **mean** VERB AND ADJECTIVE
  [1] die Möglichkeit ◊ *a means of storing
  power* eine Möglichkeit, Energie zu
  speichern ◊ *We have the means to do
  that.* Wir haben die Möglichkeit, das zu
  tun.
  [2] das Mittel (PL die Mittel) ◊ *We have
  the means to renovate the house.* Wir
  haben die Mittel, um das Haus zu
  renovieren. ◊ *a means of transport* ein
  Transportmittel NEUT
  ◆**He'll do it by any possible means.** Er
  wird es tun, egal wie.
  ◆**by means of** mit ◊ *He got in by means of
  a stolen key.* Er kam mit einem
  gestohlenen Schlüssel hinein.
  ◆**by all means** selbstverständlich ◊ *Can I
  come? – By all means!* Kann ich
  kommen? – Selbstverständlich!
  ◆**by no means** keineswegs ◊ *That was by
  no means the end of the matter.* Damit
  war die Sache keineswegs erledigt.
**meant** VERB *see* **mean**
**meanwhile** ADVERB
  inzwischen
**measles** SING NOUN
  die Masern PL ◊ *She's got measles.* Sie
  hat Masern.
to **measure** VERB
  [1] ausmessen (PRESENT misst aus, IMPERFECT
  maß aus, PERFECT hat ausgemessen) ◊ *I
  measured the page.* Ich habe die Seite
  ausgemessen.
  [2] messen ◊ *The room measures three
  metres by four.* Das Zimmer misst drei
  auf vier Meter.
**measurement** NOUN
  das Maß (*of object*) (PL die Maße) ◊ *What
  are the measurements of the room?* Wie
  sind die Maße des Zimmers? ◊ *What are
  your measurements?* Was sind Ihre
  Maße?
  ◆**my waist measurement** meine
  Taillenweite
  ◆**What's your neck measurement?** Welche
  Kragenweite haben Sie?
**meat** NOUN
  das Fleisch ◊ *I don't eat meat.* Ich esse
  kein Fleisch.
**Mecca** NOUN
  Mekka NEUT
**mechanic** NOUN
  der Mechaniker (PL die Mechaniker)
  die Mechanikerin
  ◊ *He's a mechanic.* Er ist Mechaniker.
**mechanical** ADJECTIVE

mechanisch
**medal** NOUN
  die Medaille
  ◆**the gold medal** die Goldmedaille
**media** PL NOUN
  die Medien NEUT PL
**median strip** NOUN [US]
  der Mittelstreifen (PL die Mittelstreifen)
**medical** ADJECTIVE
  see also **medical** NOUN
  medizinisch ◊ *medical treatment* die
  medizinische Behandlung
  ◆**medical insurance** die
  Krankenversicherung
  ◆**to have medical problems**
  gesundheitliche Probleme haben
  ◆**She's a medical student.** Sie ist
  Medizinstudentin.
**medical** NOUN
  see also **medical** ADJECTIVE
  ◆**to have a medical** sich ärztlich
  untersuchen lassen
**medicine** NOUN
  die Medizin ◊ *I want to study medicine.*
  Ich möchte Medizin studieren.
  ◊ *alternative medicine* die alternative
  Medizin ◊ *I need some medicine.* Ich
  brauche Medizin.
**Mediterranean** ADJECTIVE
  südländisch (*person, character, scenery*)
  ◆**the Mediterranean** das Mittelmeer
**medium** ADJECTIVE
  mittlere ◊ *a man of medium height* ein
  Mann von mittlerer Größe
**medium-sized** ADJECTIVE
  mittelgroß ◊ *a medium-sized town* eine
  mittelgroße Stadt
to **meet** VERB
  [1] (*by chance*)
  treffen (PRESENT trifft, IMPERFECT traf, PERFECT
  hat getroffen) ◊ *I met Paul when I was
  walking the dog.* Ich habe Paul getroffen,
  als ich mit dem Hund spazieren war.
  [2] (*by arrangement*)
  sich treffen ◊ *Let's meet in front of the
  tourist office.* Treffen wir uns doch vor
  dem Verkehrsbüro. ◊ *I'm going to meet
  my friends.* Ich treffe mich mit meinen
  Freunden.
  [3] (*get to know*)
  kennen lernen (PERFECT hat kennen
  gelernt) ◊ *I like meeting new people.* Ich
  lerne gerne neue Leute kennen.
  ◆**Have you met him before?** Kennen Sie
  ihn?
  [4] (*pick up*)
  abholen (PERFECT hat abgeholt) ◊ *I'll meet
  you at the station.* Ich hole dich am
  Bahnhof ab.
**meeting** NOUN
  [1] (*for work*)
  die Besprechung ◊ *a business meeting*
  eine geschäftliche Besprechung

[2] (*socially*)
das Treffen (PL die Treffen) ◊ *their first meeting* ihr erstes Treffen

**mega** ADJECTIVE
♦**He's mega rich.** Er ist superreich. (*informal*)

**melody** NOUN
die Melodie

**melon** NOUN
die Melone

to **melt** VERB
schmelzen (PRESENT schmilzt, IMPERFECT schmolz, PERFECT ist geschmolzen) ◊ *The snow is melting.* Der Schnee schmilzt.

**member** NOUN
das Mitglied (PL die Mitglieder)
♦**a Member of Parliament (1)** (*man*) ein Abgeordneter
♦**a Member of Parliament (2)** (*woman*) eine Abgeordnete

**membership** NOUN
die Mitgliedschaft (*of party, union*) ◊ *I'm going to apply for membership.* Ich werde mich um Mitgliedschaft bewerben.

**membership card** NOUN
der Mitgliedsausweis (PL die Mitgliedsausweise)

**memento** NOUN
das Andenken (PL die Andenken)

**memorial** NOUN
das Denkmal (PL die Denkmäler) ◊ *a war memorial* ein Kriegerdenkmal

to **memorize** VERB
auswendig lernen

**memory** NOUN
[1] das Gedächtnis (GEN des Gedächtnisses) ◊ *I haven't got a good memory.* Ich habe kein gutes Gedächtnis.
[2] (*recollection*)
die Erinnerung ◊ *to bring back memories* Erinnerungen wachrufen
[3] (*computer*)
der Speicher (GEN die Speicher)

**men** PL NOUN *see* **man**

to **mend** VERB
flicken

**meningitis** NOUN
die Hirnhautentzündung

**mental** ADJECTIVE
[1] geistig
♦**a mental illness** eine Geisteskrankheit
[2] wahnsinnig (*mad*) ◊ *You're mental!* Du bist wahnsinnig!
♦**a mental hospital** eine psychiatrische Klinik

to **mention** VERB
erwähnen (PERFECT hat erwähnt)
♦**Thank you! – Don't mention it!** Danke! – Bitte!

**menu** NOUN

[1] die Speisekarte ◊ *Could I have the menu please?* Könnte ich bitte die Speisekarte haben?
[2] (*on computer*)
das Menü (PL die Menüs)

**merchant** NOUN
der Händler (PL die Händler)
die Händlerin
◊ *a wine merchant* ein Weinhändler

**mercy** NOUN
die Gnade

**mere** ADJECTIVE
bloß ◊ *It's a mere formality.* Das ist eine bloße Formalität.
♦**a mere five percent** ganze fünf Prozent

**meringue** NOUN
die Meringe

**merry** ADJECTIVE
♦**Merry Christmas!** Fröhliche Weihnachten!

**merry-go-round** NOUN
das Karussell (PL die Karussells)

**mess** NOUN
die Unordnung ◊ *His bedroom's always in a mess.* In seinem Schlafzimmer herrscht ständig Unordnung.

to **mess about** VERB
♦**to mess about with something** (*interfere with*) an etwas herumfummeln ◊ *Stop messing about with my computer!* Hör auf, an meinem Computer herumzufummeln!
♦**Don't mess about with my things!** Lass meine Sachen in Ruhe!

to **mess up** VERB
♦**to mess something up** etwas durcheinander bringen ◊ *My little brother has messed up my cassettes.* Mein kleiner Bruder hat meine Kassetten durcheinander gebracht.

**message** NOUN
die Nachricht

**messenger** NOUN
der Bote (GEN des Boten, PL die Boten)
die Botin

**messy** ADJECTIVE
[1] schmutzig (*dirty*) ◊ *a messy job* eine schmutzige Arbeit
[2] unordentlich (*untidy*) ◊ *Your room's really messy.* Dein Zimmer ist wirklich unordentlich. ◊ *She's so messy!* Sie ist so unordentlich!
♦**My writing is terribly messy.** Ich habe eine schreckliche Schrift.

**met** VERB *see* **meet**

**metal** NOUN
das Metall (PL die Metalle)

**meter** NOUN
[1] (*for gas, electricity, taxi*)
der Zähler (PL die Zähler)
[2] (*parking meter*)
die Parkuhr

**method** NOUN

**M**

☞

die <u>Methode</u>

**Methodist** NOUN
der <u>Methodist</u> (GEN des Methodisten, PL die Methodisten)
die <u>Methodistin</u>
◊ *She's a Methodist.* Sie ist Methodistin.

**metre** NOUN
der <u>Meter</u> (PL die Meter)
**metric** ADJECTIVE
<u>metrisch</u>

**Mexico** NOUN
<u>Mexiko</u> NEUT
♦**from Mexico** aus Mexiko
♦**to Mexico** nach Mexiko

to **miaow** VERB
<u>miauen</u> (PERFECT hat miaut)
**mice** PL NOUN *see* **mouse**

**microchip** NOUN
der <u>Mikrochip</u> (PL die Mikrochips)
**microphone** NOUN
das <u>Mikrofon</u> (PL die Mikrofone)
**microscope** NOUN
das <u>Mikroskop</u> (PL die Mikroskope)
**microwave** NOUN
die <u>Mikrowelle</u>

**microwave oven** NOUN
der <u>Mikrowellenherd</u> (PL die Mikrowellenherde)
**mid** ADJECTIVE
♦**in mid May** Mitte Mai

**midday** NOUN
der <u>Mittag</u> (PL die Mittage)
♦**at midday** um zwölf Uhr mittags

**middle** NOUN
die <u>Mitte</u>
♦**in the middle of the road** mitten auf der Straße
♦**in the middle of the night** mitten in der Nacht
♦**the middle seat** der mittlere Sitz

**middle-aged** ADJECTIVE
<u>mittleren Alters</u> ◊ *a middle-aged man* ein Mann mittleren Alters ◊ *She's middle-aged.* Sie ist mittleren Alters.

**Middle Ages** PL NOUN
♦**the Middle Ages** das Mittelalter

**middle-class** ADJECTIVE
♦**a middle-class family** eine Familie der Mittelschicht

**Middle East** NOUN
der <u>Nahe Osten</u> ◊ *in the Middle East* im Nahen Osten

**middle name** NOUN
der <u>zweite Vorname</u> (GEN des zweiten Vornamens, PL die zweiten Vornamen)
**midge** NOUN
die <u>Mücke</u>

**midnight** NOUN
die <u>Mitternacht</u>
♦**at midnight** um Mitternacht

**midwife** NOUN

die <u>Hebamme</u> ◊ *She's a midwife.* Sie ist Hebamme.

**might** VERB
*Use* **vielleicht** *to express possibility.*
◊ *He might come later.* Er kommt vielleicht später. ◊ *We might go to Spain next year.* Wir fahren nächstes Jahr vielleicht nach Spanien. ◊ *She might not have understood.* Sie hat es vielleicht nicht verstanden.

**migraine** NOUN
die <u>Migräne</u> ◊ *I've got a migraine.* Ich habe Migräne.

**mike** NOUN
das <u>Mikro</u> (PL die Mikros)
**mild** ADJECTIVE
<u>mild</u> ◊ *The winters are quite mild.* Die Winter sind ziemlich mild.

**mile** NOUN
die <u>Meile</u>

> ℹ *In Germany distances and speeds are expressed in kilometres. A mile is about 1.6 kilometres.*

◊ *It's five miles from here.* Es ist acht Kilometer von hier. ◊ *at fifty miles per hour* mit achtzig Kilometern pro Stunde
♦**We walked miles!** Wir sind meilenweit gegangen!

**military** ADJECTIVE
<u>militärisch</u>
**milk** NOUN
[see also **milk** VERB]
die <u>Milch</u> ◊ *tea with milk* der Tee mit Milch

to **milk** VERB
[see also **milk** NOUN]
<u>melken</u> (PERFECT hat gemolken)
**milk chocolate** NOUN
die <u>Milchschokolade</u>

**milkman** NOUN
der <u>Milchmann</u> (PL die Milchmänner)
◊ *He's a milkman.* Er ist Milchmann.

**milk shake** NOUN
der <u>Milchshake</u> (PL die Milchshakes)
**mill** NOUN
die <u>Mühle</u> (for grain)
**millennium** NOUN
das <u>Jahrtausend</u>
**millimetre** NOUN
der <u>Millimeter</u> (PL die Millimeter)
**million** NOUN
die <u>Million</u>
**millionaire** NOUN
der <u>Millionär</u> (PL die Millionäre)
die <u>Millionärin</u>

to **mimic** VERB
<u>nachmachen</u> (PERFECT hat nachgemacht)
**mince** NOUN
das <u>Hackfleisch</u>
to **mind** VERB

see also **mind** NOUN

aufpassen auf +ACC (PERFECT hat
aufgepasst) ◊ *Could you mind the baby
this afternoon?* Kannst du heute
Nachmittag auf das Baby aufpassen?
◊ *Could you mind my bags for a few
minutes?* Können Sie für ein paar
Minuten auf mein Gepäck aufpassen?

◆ **Do you mind if I open the window?**
Macht es Ihnen etwas aus, wenn ich das
Fenster aufmache?

◆ **I don't mind.** Es macht mir nichts aus. ◊ *I
don't mind the noise.* Der Lärm macht
mir nichts aus.

◆ **Never mind!** Macht nichts!

◆ **Mind that bike!** Pass auf das Fahrrad
auf!

◆ **Mind the step!** Vorsicht Stufe!

**mind** NOUN

see also **mind** VERB

◆ **to make up one's mind** sich entscheiden
◊ *I haven't made up my mind yet.* Ich
habe mich noch nicht entschieden.

◆ **to change one's mind** es sich anders
überlegen ◊ *I've changed my mind.* Ich
habe es mir anders überlegt.

◆ **Are you out of your mind?** Bist du
wahnsinnig?

**mine** PRONOUN

see also **mine** NOUN

1 meiner ◊ *Is this your coat? – No,
mine's black.* Ist das dein Mantel? – Nein,
meiner ist schwarz.

meine ◊ *Is this your cup? – No, mine's
red.* Ist das deine Tasse? – Nein, meine
ist rot.

meines ◊ *Is this your car? – No, mine's
green.* Ist das dein Auto? – Nein, meines
ist grün.

2 meine ◊ *her parents and mine* ihre
Eltern und meine ◊ *Your hands are dirty,
mine are clean.* Deine Hände sind
schmutzig, meine sind sauber.

◆ **It's mine.** Das gehört mir. ◊ *This book is
mine.* Dieses Buch gehört mir. ◊ *Whose
is this? – It's mine.* Wem gehört das? – Es
gehört mir.

**mine** NOUN

see also **mine** PRONOUN

die Mine ◊ *a land mine* eine Landmine

◆ **a coal mine** ein Kohlebergwerk NEUT

**miner** NOUN
der Bergarbeiter (PL die Bergarbeiter)

**mineral water** NOUN
das Mineralwasser (PL die
Mineralwasser)

**miniature** NOUN
die Miniatur

**minibus** NOUN
der Minibus (GEN des Minibusses, PL die
Minibusse)

**minicab** NOUN
das Kleintaxi (PL die Kleintaxis)

**Minidisc** ® NOUN
die Minidisc ® (PL die Minidiscs)

**minimum** NOUN

see also **minimum** ADJECTIVE

das Mininum (PL die Minima)

**minimum** ADJECTIVE

see also **minimum** NOUN

◆ **minimum age** das Mindestalter

◆ **minimum amount** der Mindestbetrag

◆ **minimum wage** der Mindestlohn

**miniskirt** NOUN
der Minirock (PL die Miniröcke)

**minister** NOUN
1 (*in government*)
der Minister (PL die Minister)
die Ministerin

2 (*of church*)
der Pfarrer (PL die Pfarrer)
die Pfarrerin

**ministry** NOUN
das Ministerium (*in politics*) (PL die
Ministerien)

**mink** NOUN
der Nerz ◊ *a mink coat* ein Nerzmantel
MASC

**minor** ADJECTIVE
kleiner ◊ *a minor problem* ein kleineres
Problem ◊ *a minor operation* eine
kleinere Operation

◆ **in D minor** in d-Moll

**minority** NOUN
die Minderheit

**mint** NOUN
1 (*plant*)
die Pfefferminze ◊ *mint sauce* die
Pfefferminzsoße

2 (*sweet*)
das Pfefferminzbonbon (PL die
Pfefferminzbonbons)

**minus** PREPOSITION
minus ◊ *Sixteen minus three is thirteen.*
Sechzehn minus drei ist dreizehn. ◊ *It's
minus two degrees outside.* Draußen
hat es zwei Grad minus. ◊ *I got a B
minus.* Ich habe eine Zwei minus
bekommen.

ⓘ *In Germany, grades are given from
1 to 6, with 1 being the best.*

**minute** NOUN

see also **minute** ADJECTIVE

die Minute

◆ **Wait a minute!** Einen Augenblick!

**minute** ADJECTIVE

see also **minute** NOUN

winzig ◊ *Her flat is minute.* Ihre
Wohnung ist winzig.

**miracle** NOUN
das Wunder (PL die Wunder)

**mirror** NOUN
der Spiegel (PL die Spiegel)

to **misbehave** VERB

M

sich schlecht benehmen (PRESENT benimmt sich schlecht, IMPERFECT benahm sich schlecht, PERFECT hat sich schlecht benommen)

**miscellaneous** ADJECTIVE
verschieden ◊ *miscellaneous items* verschiedene Artikel

**mischief** NOUN
die Dummheiten FEM PL ◊ *My little sister's always up to mischief.* Meine kleine Schwester macht dauernd Dummheiten.

**mischievous** ADJECTIVE
verschmitzt

**miser** NOUN
der Geizhals (GEN des Geizhalses, PL die Geizhälse)

**miserable** ADJECTIVE
[1] unglücklich (*person*) ◊ *You're looking miserable.* Du siehst richtig unglücklich aus.
[2] schrecklich (*weather*) ◊ *The weather was miserable.* Das Wetter war schrecklich.
◆ **to feel miserable** sich miserabel fühlen ◊ *I'm feeling miserable.* Ich fühle mich miserabel.

**misery** NOUN
[1] das Elend ◊ *All that money brought nothing but misery.* All das Geld hat nichts als Elend gebracht.
[2] der Miesepeter (*informal*) (PL die Miesepeter) ◊ *She's a real misery.* Sie ist ein richtiger Miesepeter.

**misfortune** NOUN
das Unglück (PL die Unglücke)

**mishap** NOUN
das Missgeschick (PL die Missgeschicke)

to **misjudge** VERB
falsch einschätzen (*person*) (PERFECT hat falsch eingeschätzt) ◊ *I've misjudged her.* Ich habe sie falsch eingeschätzt.
◆ **He misjudged the bend.** Er hat sich in der Kurve verschätzt.

to **mislay** VERB
verlegen (PERFECT hat verlegt) ◊ *I've mislaid my passport.* Ich habe meinen Pass verlegt.

to **mislead** VERB
irreführen (PERFECT hat irregeführt)

**misleading** ADJECTIVE
irreführend

**misprint** NOUN
der Druckfehler (PL die Druckfehler)

**Miss** NOUN
das Fräulein

> ℹ *Nowadays it is regarded as old-fashioned to call somebody **Fräulein** and **Frau** is used instead.*

◊ *Miss Jones* Frau Jones

to **miss** VERB

verpassen (PERFECT hat verpasst) ◊ *Hurry or you'll miss the bus.* Beeil dich, sonst verpasst du den Bus! ◊ *to miss an opportunity* eine Gelegenheit verpassen
◆ **I miss you.** Du fehlst mir. ◊ *I'm missing my family.* Meine Familie fehlt mir.
◆ **He missed the target.** Er hat nicht getroffen.

**missing** ADJECTIVE
fehlend ◊ *the missing part* das fehlende Teil
◆ **to be missing** fehlen ◊ *My rucksack is missing.* Mein Rucksack fehlt. ◊ *Two members of the group are missing.* Zwei Mitglieder der Gruppe fehlen.

**missionary** NOUN
der Missionar (PL die Missionare)
die Missionarin

**mist** NOUN
der Nebel (PL die Nebel)
> *Be careful not to translate **mist** by the German word **Mist**.*

**mistake** NOUN
> see also **mistake** VERB

der Fehler (PL die Fehler) ◊ *It was a mistake to buy those yellow shoes.* Es war ein Fehler, diese gelben Schuhe zu kaufen. ◊ *a spelling mistake* ein Rechtschreibfehler
◆ **to make a mistake (1)** (*in writing, speaking*) einen Fehler machen
◆ **to make a mistake (2)** (*get mixed up*) sich vertun ◊ *I'm sorry, I made a mistake.* Tut mir Leid, ich habe mich vertan.
◆ **by mistake** aus Versehen ◊ *I took his bag by mistake.* Ich habe aus Versehen seine Tasche genommen.

to **mistake** VERB
> see also **mistake** NOUN

◆ **He mistook me for my sister.** Er hat mich mit meiner Schwester verwechselt.

**mistaken** ADJECTIVE
◆ **to be mistaken** sich irren ◊ *If you think I'm going to get up at six o'clock, you're mistaken.* Wenn du meinst, ich würde um sechs Uhr aufstehen, dann irrst du dich.

**mistakenly** ADVERB
irrtümlicherweise

**mistletoe** NOUN
die Mistel

**mistook** VERB see **mistake**

**mistress** NOUN
[1] (*teacher*)
die Lehrerin ◊ *our German mistress* unsere Deutschlehrerin
[2] (*lover*)
die Geliebte (GEN der Geliebten) ◊ *He's got a mistress.* Er hat eine Geliebte.

to **mistrust** VERB
misstrauen (PERFECT hat misstraut) ◊ *I mistrust her.* Ich misstraue ihr.

**misty** ADJECTIVE

neblig ◊ *a misty morning* ein nebliger Morgen

to **misunderstand** VERB
missverstehen (IMPERFECT missverstand, PERFECT hat missverstanden) ◊ *Sorry, I misunderstood you.* Entschuldigung, ich habe Sie missverstanden.

**misunderstanding** NOUN
das Missverständnis (GEN des Missverständnisses, PL die Missverständnisse)

**misunderstood** VERB *see* **misunderstand**

**mix** NOUN
see also **mix** VERB
die Mischung ◊ *It's a mix of science fiction and comedy.* Es ist eine Mischung aus Sciencefiction und Komödie.
♦ **a cake mix** eine Backmischung

to **mix** VERB
see also **mix** NOUN
[1] vermischen (PERFECT hat vermischt) ◊ *Mix the flour with the sugar.* Vermischen Sie das Mehl mit dem Zucker.
[2] verbinden (IMPERFECT verband, PERFECT hat verbunden) ◊ *He's mixing business with pleasure.* Er verbindet das Geschäftliche mit dem Vergnügen.
♦ **to mix with somebody** (*associate*) mit jemandem verkehren
♦ **He doesn't mix much.** Er geht nicht viel unter Menschen.
♦ **to mix up** verwechseln ◊ *He always mixes me up with my sister.* Er verwechselt mich immer mit meiner Schwester. ◊ *The travel agent mixed up the bookings.* Das Reisebüro hat die Buchungen verwechselt.
♦ **I'm getting mixed up.** Ich werde ganz konfus.

**mixed** ADJECTIVE
gemischt ◊ *a mixed salad* ein gemischter Salat ◊ *a mixed school* eine gemischte Schule
♦ **a mixed grill** ein Grillteller MASC

**mixer** NOUN
der Mixer (*for food*) (PL die Mixer)

**mixture** NOUN
die Mischung ◊ *a mixture of spices* eine Gewürzmischung
♦ **cough mixture** der Hustensaft

**mix-up** NOUN
die Verwechslung

to **moan** VERB
sich beklagen (PERFECT hat sich beklagt) ◊ *She's always moaning.* Sie beklagt sich dauernd.

**mobile** NOUN
(*phone*)
das Handy (PL die Handys)

**mobile home** NOUN
das Wohnmobil (PL die Wohnmobile)

to **mock** VERB

see also **mock** ADJECTIVE
sich lustig machen über +ACC ◊ *Stop mocking him!* Mach dich nicht über ihn lustig!

**mock** ADJECTIVE
see also **mock** VERB
♦ **a mock exam** eine Übungsprüfung

**mod cons** PL NOUN
♦ **with all mod cons** mit allem Komfort

**model** NOUN
see also **model** ADJECTIVE, VERB
[1] das Modell (PL die Modelle) ◊ *His car is the latest model.* Sein Auto ist das neueste Modell. ◊ *a model of the castle* ein Modell der Burg
[2] (*fashion*)
das Mannequin (PL die Mannequins) ◊ *She's a famous model.* Sie ist ein berühmtes Mannequin.

**model** ADJECTIVE
see also **model** NOUN, VERB
♦ **a model plane** ein Modellflugzeug NEUT
♦ **a model railway** eine Modelleisenbahn
♦ **He's a model pupil.** Er ist ein vorbildlicher Schüler.

to **model** VERB
see also **model** NOUN, ADJECTIVE
als Model arbeiten ◊ *She was modelling in New York.* Sie arbeitete in New York als Model.
♦ **She was modelling a Paul Costello outfit.** Sie führte ein Outfit von Paul Costello vor.

**modem** NOUN
das Modem (PL die Modems)

**moderate** ADJECTIVE
gemäßigt ◊ *His views are quite moderate.* Er hat sehr gemäßigte Ansichten.
♦ **a moderate amount of alcohol** wenig Alkohol
♦ **a moderate price** ein annehmbarer Preis

**modern** ADJECTIVE
modern

to **modernize** VERB
modernisieren (PERFECT hat modernisiert)

**modest** ADJECTIVE
bescheiden

to **modify** VERB
ändern

**moist** ADJECTIVE
feucht ◊ *This cake is very moist.* Dieser Kuchen ist sehr feucht. ◊ *Sow the seeds in moist compost.* Säen Sie den Samen in feuchten Kompost.

**moisture** NOUN
die Feuchtigkeit

**moisturizer** NOUN
[1] (*cream*)
die Feuchtigkeitscreme (PL die Feuchtigkeitscremes)
[2] (*lotion*)

**M**

die <u>Feuchtigkeitslotion</u>
**moldy** ADJECTIVE US
<u>schimmlig</u>
**mole** NOUN
[1] (*animal*)
der <u>Maulwurf</u> (PL die Maulwürfe)
[2] (*on skin*)
der <u>Leberfleck</u> (PL die Leberflecke)
**moment** NOUN
der <u>Augenblick</u> (PL die Augenblicke)
◊ *Could you wait a moment?* Können Sie
einen Augenblick warten? ◊ *in a moment*
in einem Augenblick ◊ *Just a moment!*
Einen Augenblick!
♦ **at the moment** momentan
♦ **any moment now** jeden Moment
◊ *They'll be arriving any moment now.*
Sie können jeden Moment kommen.
**momentous** ADJECTIVE
<u>bedeutsam</u>
**monarch** NOUN
der <u>Monarch</u> (GEN des Monarchen, PL die
Monarchen)
die <u>Monarchin</u>
**monarchy** NOUN
die <u>Monarchie</u>
**monastery** NOUN
das <u>Kloster</u> (PL die Klöster)
**Monday** NOUN
der <u>Montag</u> (PL die Montage) ◊ *on
Monday* am Montag ◊ *every Monday*
jeden Montag ◊ *last Monday* letzten
Montag ◊ *next Monday* nächsten Montag
♦ **on Mondays** montags
**money** NOUN
das <u>Geld</u> (PL die Gelder) ◊ *I need to
change some money.* Ich muss Geld
wechseln.
♦ **to make money** Geld verdienen
**mongrel** NOUN
die <u>Promenadenmischung</u> ◊ *My dog's a
mongrel.* Mein Hund ist eine
Promenadenmischung.
**monitor** NOUN
der <u>Monitor</u> (*of computer*) (PL die
Monitore)
**monk** NOUN
der <u>Mönch</u> (PL die Mönche)
**monkey** NOUN
der <u>Affe</u> (GEN des Affen, PL die Affen)
**monopoly** NOUN
das <u>Monopol</u>
♦ **to play Monopoly** ® Monopoly spielen
**monotonous** ADJECTIVE
<u>monoton</u>
**monster** NOUN
das <u>Monster</u> (PL die Monster)
**month** NOUN
der <u>Monat</u> (PL die Monate) ◊ *this month*
diesen Monat ◊ *next month* nächsten
Monat ◊ *last month* letzten Monat
◊ *every month* jeden Monat ◊ *at the end
of the month* Ende des Monats

**monthly** ADJECTIVE
<u>monatlich</u>
**monument** NOUN
das <u>Denkmal</u> (PL die Denkmäler)
**mood** NOUN
die <u>Laune</u>
♦ **to be in a bad mood** schlechte Laune
haben
♦ **to be in a good mood** gute Laune haben
**moody** ADJECTIVE
[1] <u>launisch</u> (*temperamental*)
[2] <u>schlecht gelaunt</u> (*in a bad mood*)
**moon** NOUN
der <u>Mond</u> (PL die Monde)
♦ **There's a full moon tonight.** Heute ist
Vollmond.
♦ **to be over the moon** (*happy*)
überglücklich sein
**moor** NOUN
see also **moor** VERB
das <u>Moor</u> (PL die Moore)
to **moor** VERB
see also **moor** NOUN
<u>festmachen</u> (*boat*) (PERFECT hat
festgemacht)
**mop** NOUN
der <u>Mopp</u> (PL die Mopps)
(*for floor*)
**moped** NOUN
das <u>Moped</u> (PL die Mopeds)
**moral** ADJECTIVE
see also **moral** NOUN
<u>moralisch</u>
**moral** NOUN
see also **moral** ADJECTIVE
die <u>Moral</u> ◊ *the moral of the story* die
Moral der Geschichte
♦ **morals** die Moral SING
**morale** NOUN
die <u>Stimmung</u> ◊ *Their morale is very
low.* Ihre Stimmung ist sehr schlecht.
**more** ADJECTIVE, PRONOUN, ADVERB
<u>mehr</u> ◊ *a bit more* etwas mehr ◊ *There
are more girls in the class.* In der Klasse
sind mehr Mädchen.
♦ **more than** mehr als ◊ *She practises
more than I do.* Sie übt mehr als ich. ◊ *I
spent more than two hundred marks.* Ich
habe mehr als zweihundert Mark
ausgegeben. ◊ *More girls than boys do
German.* Mehr Mädchen als Jungen
lernen Deutsch.

*In comparisons you usually add* **-er** *to
the adjective.*

◊ *Could you speak more slowly?*
Könnten Sie langsamer sprechen? ◊ *He's
more intelligent than me.* Er ist
intelligenter als ich. ◊ *Beer is more
expensive in Britain.* Bier ist in
Großbritannien teurer.

*When referring to an additional amount,
over and above what there already is,
you usually use* **noch**.

◊ *Is there any more?* Gibt es noch mehr? ◊ *Would you like some more?* Möchten Sie noch etwas? ◊ *It'll take a few more days.* Es braucht noch ein paar Tage. ◊ *Could I have some more chips?* Kann ich noch Pommes frites haben? ◊ *Do you want some more tea?* Möchten sie noch Tee?

♦ **There isn't any more.** Es ist nichts mehr da.

♦ **more or less** mehr oder weniger

♦ **more than ever** mehr denn je

**moreover** ADVERB
  außerdem

**morning** NOUN
  der Morgen (PL die Morgen) ◊ *every morning* jeden Morgen

♦ **this morning** heute Morgen

♦ **tomorrow morning** morgen früh ◊ *I have to get up at six tomorrow morning.* Ich muss morgen früh um sechs aufstehen.

♦ **in the morning** morgens ◊ *at seven o'clock in the morning* um sieben Uhr morgens

♦ **a morning paper** eine Morgenzeitung

**Morocco** NOUN
  Marokko NEUT

♦ **from Morocco** auf Marokko

♦ **to Morocco** nach Marokko

**mortgage** NOUN
  die Hypothek (PL die Hypotheken)

**Moscow** NOUN
  Moskau NEUT

♦ **to Moscow** nach Moskau

**Moslem** NOUN
  der Moslem (PL die Moslems)
  die Moslime
  ◊ *He's a Moslem.* Er ist Moslem.

**mosque** NOUN
  die Moschee

**mosquito** NOUN
  die Stechmücke

♦ **a mosquito bite** ein Mückenstich MASC

**most** ADVERB, ADJECTIVE, PRONOUN
  1 die meisten ◊ *most of my friends* die meisten meiner Freunde ◊ *most of them* die meisten von ihnen ◊ *most people* die meisten Menschen ◊ *Most cats are affectionate.* Die meisten Katzen sind anhänglich.
  2 am meisten ◊ *what I hate most* was ich am meisten hasse

♦ **most of the time** meist

♦ **most of the evening** fast den ganzen Abend

♦ **most of the money** fast das ganze Geld

♦ **the most** am meisten ◊ *He's the one who talks the most.* Er ist derjenige, der am meisten redet.

♦ **to make the most of something** das Beste aus etwas machen

♦ **at the most** höchstens ◊ *Two hours at the most.* Höchstens zwei Stunden.

*For the superlative you usually add* **-ste** *to the adjective.*

◊ *the most expensive seat* der teuerste Platz ◊ *the most boring work* die langweiligste Arbeit ◊ *the most expensive restaurant* das teuerste Restaurant

**mostly** ADVERB

♦ **The teachers are mostly quite nice.** Die meisten unserer Lehrer sind ganz nett.

**MOT** NOUN
  der TÜV (= Technischer Überwachungsverein) ◊ *My car failed its MOT.* Mein Auto ist nicht durch den TÜV gekommen.

**motel** NOUN
  das Motel (PL die Motels)

**moth** NOUN
  die Motte

**mother** NOUN
  die Mutter (PL die Mütter) ◊ *my mother* meine Mutter

♦ **mother tongue** die Muttersprache

**mother-in-law** NOUN
  die Schwiegermutter (PL die Schwiegermütter)

**Mother's Day** NOUN
  der Muttertag (PL die Muttertage)

> ❶ In Germany **Muttertag** is on the second Sunday in May.

**M**

**motionless** ADJECTIVE
  bewegungslos

**motivated** ADJECTIVE
  motiviert ◊ *He is highly motivated.* Er ist höchst motiviert.

**motivation** NOUN
  die Motivation

**motive** NOUN
  das Motiv (PL die Motive) ◊ *the motive for the killing* das Motiv für den Mord

**motor** NOUN
  der Motor (PL die Motoren) ◊ *The boat has a motor.* Das Boot hat einen Motor.

**motorbike** NOUN
  das Motorrad (PL die Motorräder)

**motorboat** NOUN
  das Motorboot (PL die Motorboote)

**motorcycle** NOUN
  das Motorrad (PL die Motorräder)

**motorcyclist** NOUN
  der Motorradfahrer (PL die Motorradfahrer)
  die Motorradfahrerin

**motorist** NOUN
  der Autofahrer (PL die Autofahrer)
  die Autofahrerin

**motor mechanic** NOUN
  der Automechaniker (PL die Automechaniker)
  die Automechanikerin

**motor racing** NOUN

das Autorennen (PL die Autorennen)
**motorway** NOUN
die Autobahn ◊ *on the motorway* auf
der Autobahn
**mouldy** ADJECTIVE
schimmlig
**mountain** NOUN
der Berg (PL die Berge)
♦ **a mountain bike** ein Mountainbike
NEUT
**mountaineer** NOUN
der Bergsteiger (PL die Bergsteiger)
die Bergsteigerin
**mountaineering** NOUN
das Bergsteigen
♦ **I go mountaineering.** Ich gehe
bergsteigen.
**mountainous** ADJECTIVE
bergig
**mouse** NOUN
die Maus (*also for computer*) (PL die
Mäuse) ◊ *white mice* weiße Mäuse
**mouse mat** NOUN
das Mousepad (*computer*) (PL die
Mousepads)
**mousse** NOUN
[1] (*food*)
die Creme (PL die Cremes) ◊ *chocolate
mousse* die Schokoladencreme
[2] (*for hair*)
der Schaumfestiger (PL die
Schaumfestiger)
**moustache** NOUN
der Schnurrbart (PL die Schnurrbärte)
◊ *He's got a moustache.* Er hat einen
Schnurrbart.
**mouth** NOUN
der Mund (PL die Münder)
**mouthful** NOUN
der Bissen (PL die Bissen)
**mouth organ** NOUN
die Mundharmonika (PL die
Mundharmonikas) ◊ *I play the mouth
organ.* Ich spiele Mundharmonika.
**mouthwash** NOUN
das Mundwasser (PL die Mundwasser)
**move** NOUN
see also **move** VERB
[1] der Zug (PL die Züge) ◊ *That was a
good move.* Das war ein guter Zug.
♦ **It's your move.** Du bist dran.
[2] der Umzug (PL die Umzüge) ◊ *our
move from Oxford to Luton* unser
Umzug von Oxford nach Luton
♦ **to get a move on** schneller machen
♦ **Get a move on!** Nun mach schon!
to **move** VERB
see also **move** NOUN
[1] bewegen (PERFECT hat bewegt) ◊ *I can't
move my arm.* Ich kann den Arm nicht
bewegen. ◊ *I was very moved by the
film.* Der Film hat mich sehr bewegt.

♦ **Could you move your stuff?** Könntest du
dein Zeug wegtun?
♦ **Could you move your car?** Könnten Sie
Ihr Auto wegfahren?
[2] sich bewegen ◊ *Try not to move.*
Versuche, dich nicht zu bewegen.
♦ **Don't move!** Keine Bewegung!
[3] (*vehicle*)
fahren (PRESENT fährt, IMPERFECT fuhr, PERFECT
ist gefahren) ◊ *The car was moving very
slowly.* Das Auto fuhr sehr langsam.
♦ **to move house** umziehen ◊ *We're
moving in July.* Wir ziehen im Juli um.
♦ **to move forward** sich vorwärts bewegen
♦ **to move in** einziehen ◊ *They're moving
in tomorrow.* Sie ziehen morgen ein.
♦ **to move over** rücken ◊ *Could you move
over a bit?* Könnten Sie ein Stückchen
rücken?
**movement** NOUN
die Bewegung
**movie** NOUN
der Film (PL die Filme)
♦ **the movies** das Kino SING ◊ *Let's go to the
movies!* Lass uns ins Kino gehen!
**moving** ADJECTIVE
[1] fahrend (*not stationary*) ◊ *a moving bus*
ein fahrender Bus
[2] ergreifend (*touching*) ◊ *a moving story*
eine ergreifende Geschichte
to **mow** VERB
mähen ◊ *to mow the lawn* den Rasen
mähen
**mower** NOUN
der Rasenmäher (PL die Rasenmäher)
**mown** VERB *see* **mow**
**MP** NOUN (= *Member of Parliament*)
der Abgeordnete (GEN des
Abgeordneten, PL die Abgeordneten)
die Abgeordnete (GEN der Abgeordneten)
◊ *an MP* (*man*) ein Abgeordneter ◊ *She's
an MP.* Sie ist Abgeordnete.
**mph** ABBREVIATION (= *miles per hour*)
Meilen pro Stunde
**Mr** NOUN (= *Mister*)
Herr
**Mrs** NOUN
Frau
**MS** NOUN (= *multiple sclerosis*)
MS ◊ *She's got MS.* Sie hat MS.
**Ms** NOUN
Frau

🛈 *Generally* **Frau** *is used to address all
women whether married or not.*

**much** ADJECTIVE, ADVERB, PRONOUN
[1] viel ◊ *I haven't got much money.* Ich
habe nicht viel Geld. ◊ *I haven't got very
much money.* Ich habe nicht sehr viel
Geld. ◊ *This is much better.* Das ist viel
besser. ◊ *I feel much better now.* Ich
fühle mich jetzt viel besser.

**2** sehr
*Use **sehr** with most verbs.*
◇ I didn't like it much. Es hat mir nicht sehr gefallen. ◇ I enjoyed the film very much. Der Film hat mir sehr gefallen.
**3** viel
*Use **viel** with verbs implying physical activity.*
◇ She doesn't travel much. Sie reist nicht viel. ◇ We didn't laugh much. Wir haben nicht viel gelacht.
♦ **Do you go out much?** Gehst du oft aus?
♦ **Thank you very much.** Vielen Dank!
♦ **Not much.** Nicht viel. ◇ What's on TV? – Not much. Was kommt im Fernsehen? – Nicht viel. ◇ What do you think of it? – Not much. Was hältst du davon? – Nicht viel.
♦ **How much?** Wie viel? ◇ How much do you want? Wie viel möchtest du? ◇ How much time have you got? Wie viel Zeit hast du? ◇ How much is it? (cost) Wie viel kostet das?
♦ **too much** zu viel ◇ That's too much! Das ist zu viel! ◇ It costs too much. Das kostet zu viel. ◇ They gave us too much homework. Sie haben uns zu viele Hausaufgaben aufgegeben.
♦ **so much** so viel ◇ I didn't think it would cost so much. Ich hatte nicht gedacht, dass es so viel kosten würde. ◇ I've never seen so much traffic. Ich habe noch nie so viel Verkehr erlebt.

**mud** NOUN
der Schlamm
**muddle** NOUN
das Durcheinander
♦ **to be in a muddle** durcheinander sein ◇ The photos are in a muddle. Die Fotos sind durcheinander.
to **muddle up** VERB
verwechseln (people) (PERFECT hat verwechselt) ◇ He muddles me up with my sister. Er verwechselt mich mit meiner Schwester.
♦ **to get muddled up** durcheinander kommen ◇ I'm getting muddled up. Ich komme durcheinander.
**muddy** ADJECTIVE
schlammig
**muesli** NOUN
das Müsli (PL die Müsli)
**muffler** NOUN US
der Schalldämpfer (PL die Schalldämpfer)
**mug** NOUN
see also **mug** VERB
der Becher (PL die Becher) ◇ Do you want a cup or a mug? Möchtest du eine Tasse oder einen Becher?
♦ **a beer mug** ein Bierkrug MASC
to **mug** VERB
see also **mug** NOUN

überfallen (PRESENT überfällt, IMPERFECT überfiel, PERFECT hat überfallen) ◇ He was mugged in the city centre. Er wurde in der Innenstadt überfallen.
**mugger** NOUN
der Straßenräuber (PL die Straßenräuber)
die Straßenräuberin
**mugging** NOUN
der Überfall (PL die Überfälle) ◇ Mugging has increased in recent years. Die Zahl der Überfälle hat in den letzten Jahren zugenommen.
**muggy** ADJECTIVE
schwül ◇ It's muggy today. Es ist schwül heute.
**multiple choice test** NOUN
der Multiple-Choice-Test (PL die Multiple-Choice-Tests)
**multiple sclerosis** NOUN
die multiple Sklerose ◇ She's got multiple sclerosis. Sie hat multiple Sklerose.
**multiplication** NOUN
die Multiplikation
to **multiply** VERB
multiplizieren (PERFECT hat multipliziert) ◇ to multiply six by three sechs mit drei multiplizieren
**multi-storey car park** NOUN
das Parkhaus (GEN des Parkhauses, PL die Parkhäuser)
**mum** NOUN
die Mama (PL die Mamas) ◇ my mum meine Mama ◇ I'll ask Mum. Ich frage Mama.
**mummy** NOUN
**1** (mum)
die Mutti (PL die Muttis) ◇ Mummy says I can go. Mutti sagt, ich kann gehen.
**2** (Egyptian)
die Mumie
**mumps** SING NOUN
der Mumps ◇ My brother's got mumps. Mein Bruder hat Mumps.
**Munich** NOUN
München NEUT
♦ **to Munich** nach München
**murder** NOUN
see also **murder** VERB
der Mord (PL die Morde)
*Be careful not to translate **murder** by **Mörder**.*
to **murder** VERB
see also **murder** NOUN
ermorden (PERFECT hat ermordet) ◇ He was murdered. Er wurde ermordet.
**murderer** NOUN
der Mörder (PL die Mörder)
die Mörderin
**muscle** NOUN
der Muskel (PL die Muskeln)

M

**muscular** ADJECTIVE
  muskulös
**museum** NOUN
  das Museum (PL die Museen)
**mushroom** NOUN
  **1** der Pilz (PL die Pilze)
  **2** (*button mushroom*)
  der Champignon (PL die Champignons)
  ◊ *mushroom omelette* das
  Champignonomelett
**music** NOUN
  die Musik
**musical** ADJECTIVE
  see also **musical** NOUN
  musikalisch ◊ *I'm not musical.* Ich bin
  nicht musikalisch.
♦ **a musical instrument** ein
  Musikinstrument NEUT
**musical** NOUN
  see also **musical** ADJECTIVE
  das Musical (PL die Musicals)
**music centre** NOUN
  die Stereoanlage
**musician** NOUN
  der Musiker (PL die Musiker)
  die Musikerin
**Muslim** NOUN
  der Moslem (PL die Moslems)
  die Moslime
  ◊ *He's a Muslim.* Er ist Moslem.
**mussel** NOUN
  die Miesmuschel
**must** VERB
  **1** müssen (PRESENT muss, IMPERFECT
  musste, PERFECT hat gemusst) ◊ *I must buy
  some presents.* Ich muss Geschenke
  kaufen. ◊ *I really must go now.* Ich muss
  jetzt wirklich gehen. ◊ *You must be tired.*
  Du musst müde sein. ◊ *They must have
  plenty of money.* Sie müssen viel Geld
  haben. ◊ *You must come and see us.* Sie
  müssen uns besuchen.
  **2** dürfen (PRESENT darf, IMPERFECT durfte,
  PERFECT hat gedurft)
  *Use **dürfen** in negative sentences.*
  ◊ *You mustn't say things like that.* So
  was darfst du nicht sagen.
♦ **You mustn't forget to send her a card.**
  Vergiss nicht, ihr eine Karte zu schicken.
**mustard** NOUN

der Senf (PL die Senfe)
to **mutter** VERB
  murmeln
**mutton** NOUN
  das Hammelfleisch
**mutual** ADJECTIVE
  gegenseitig ◊ *The feeling was mutual.*
  Das Gefühl war gegenseitig.
♦ **a mutual friend** ein gemeinsamer Freund
**my** ADJECTIVE
  mein ◊ *my father* mein Vater ◊ *my aunt*
  meine Tante ◊ *my car* mein Auto ◊ *my
  parents* meine Eltern
♦ **my friend (1)** (*male*) mein Freund
♦ **my friend (2)** (*female*) meine Freundin
  *Do not use **mein** with parts of the body.*
  ◊ *I want to wash my hair.* Ich will mir die
  Haare waschen. ◊ *I'm going to clean my
  teeth.* Ich putze mir die Zähne. ◊ *I've hurt
  my foot.* Ich habe mich am Fuß verletzt.
**myself** PRONOUN
  **1** mich ◊ *I've hurt myself.* Ich habe mich
  verletzt. ◊ *When I look at myself in the
  mirror ...* Wenn ich mich im Spiegel
  ansehe ... ◊ *I don't like talking about
  myself.* Ich rede nicht gern über mich
  selbst.
  **2** mir ◊ *I said to myself ...* Ich sagte mir
  ... ◊ *I am not very pleased with myself.*
  Ich bin mit mir selbst nicht sehr
  zufrieden.
  **3** selbst ◊ *I made it myself.* Ich habe es
  selbst gemacht.
♦ **by myself** allein ◊ *I don't like travelling
  by myself.* Ich verreise nicht gern allein.
**mysterious** ADJECTIVE
  rätselhaft
**mystery** NOUN
  das Rätsel (PL die Rätsel)
♦ **a murder mystery** (*novel*) ein Krimi MASC
**myth** NOUN
  **1** (*legend*)
  der Mythos (GEN des Mythos, PL die
  Mythen) ◊ *a Greek myth* ein griechischer
  Mythos
  **2** (*untrue idea*)
  das Märchen (PL die Märchen) ◊ *That's a
  myth.* Das ist ein Märchen.
**mythology** NOUN
  die Mythologie

# N

**to nag** VERB
herumnörgeln an (scold) (PERFECT hat
herumgenörgelt) ◇ She's always nagging
me. Sie nörgelt dauernd an mir herum.

**nail** NOUN
der Nagel (PL die Nägel) ◇ Don't bite your
nails! Kau nicht an den Nägeln!

**nailbrush** NOUN
die Nagelbürste

**nailfile** NOUN
die Nagelfeile

**nail scissors** PL NOUN
die Nagelschere ◇ a pair of nail scissors
eine Nagelschere

**nail varnish** NOUN
der Nagellack (PL die Nagellacke)
♦ **nail varnish remover** der
Nagellackentferner

**naked** ADJECTIVE
nackt

**name** NOUN
der Name (GEN des Namens, PL die
Namen)
♦ **What's your name?** Wie heißt du?

**nanny** NOUN
das Kindermädchen (PL die
Kindermädchen) ◇ She's a nanny. Sie ist
Kindermädchen.

**nap** NOUN
das Nickerchen (PL die Nickerchen)
♦ **to have a nap** ein Nickerchen machen

**napkin** NOUN
die Serviette

**nappy** NOUN
die Windel

**narrow** ADJECTIVE
eng

**narrow-minded** ADJECTIVE
engstirnig

**nasty** ADJECTIVE
[1] übel (bad) ◇ a nasty cold eine üble
Erkältung ◇ a nasty smell ein übler
Geruch
[2] böse (unfriendly) ◇ He gave me a nasty
look. Er warf mir einen bösen Blick zu.

**nation** NOUN
die Nation

**national** ADJECTIVE
national
♦ **a national newspaper** eine überregionale
Zeitung
♦ **the national elections** die
Parlamentswahlen

> **ⓘ** In Germany the national elections
> are called **Bundestagswahlen**.

**national anthem** NOUN

die Nationalhymne

**National Health Service** NOUN
der staatliche Gesundheitsdienst

> **ⓘ** In Germany there are a large
> number of health schemes, not just a
> single service.

**nationalism** NOUN
der Nationalismus (GEN des
Nationalismus) ◇ Scottish Nationalism
der schottische Nationalismus

**nationalist** NOUN
der Nationalist (GEN des Nationalisten, PL
die Nationalisten)

**nationality** NOUN
die Staatsangehörigkeit

**National Lottery** NOUN
das Lotto

**national park** NOUN
der Nationalpark (PL die Nationalparks)

**native** ADJECTIVE
♦ **my native country** mein Heimatland
NEUT
♦ **native language** die Muttersprache
◇ English is not their native language.
Englisch ist nicht ihre Muttersprache.
♦ **a Native American** ein Indianer MASC

**natural** ADJECTIVE
natürlich

**naturalist** NOUN
der Naturforscher (PL die Naturforscher)
die Naturforscherin

**naturally** ADVERB
natürlich ◇ Naturally, we were very
disappointed. Natürlich waren wir sehr
enttäuscht.

**nature** NOUN
die Natur

**naughty** ADJECTIVE
böse ◇ Naughty girl! Böses Mädchen!
♦ **Don't be so naughty!** Sei nicht so
ungezogen!

**navy** NOUN
die Marine ◇ He's in the navy. Er ist bei
der Marine.

**navy-blue** ADJECTIVE
marineblau ◇ a navy-blue shirt ein
marineblaues Hemd

**Nazi** NOUN
der Nazi (PL die Nazis) ◇ the Nazis die
Nazis
**der Nazi** is also used for women.
◇ She was a Nazi. Sie war ein Nazi.

**near** ADJECTIVE
see also **near** PREPOSITION

☞

nah ◊ *It's fairly near.* Es ist ziemlich nah.
◊ *It's near enough to walk.* Es ist nah
genug, um zu Fuß zu gehen.
♦**nearest** nächste ◊ *Where's the nearest
service station?* Wo ist die nächste
Tankstelle? ◊ *The nearest shops were
three kilometres away.* Die nächsten
Geschäfte waren drei Kilometer weg.

**near** PREPOSITION, ADVERB
see also **near** ADJECTIVE
in der Nähe von ◊ *I live near Liverpool.*
Ich wohne in der Nähe von Liverpool.
◊ *near my house* in der Nähe meines
Hauses
♦**near here** hier in der Nähe ◊ *Is there a
bank near here?* Ist hier in der Nähe eine
Bank?
♦**near to** in der Nähe +GEN ◊ *It's very near to
the school.* Es ist ganz in der Nähe der
Schule.

**nearby** ADVERB, ADJECTIVE
1 in der Nähe ◊ *There's a supermarket
nearby.* Es gibt einen Supermarkt in der
Nähe.
2 nahe gelegen (*close*) ◊ *a nearby
garage* eine nahe gelegene Tankstelle

**nearly** ADVERB
fast ◊ *Dinner's nearly ready.* Das Essen
ist fast fertig. ◊ *I'm nearly fifteen.* Ich bin
fast fünfzehn. ◊ *I nearly missed the train.*
Ich habe fast meinen Zug verpasst.

**neat** ADJECTIVE
ordentlich ◊ *She has very neat writing.*
Sie hat eine sehr ordentliche Schrift.
♦**a neat whisky** ein Whisky pur

**neatly** ADVERB
ordentlich ◊ *neatly folded* ordentlich
gefaltet ◊ *neatly dressed* ordentlich
gekleidet

**necessarily** ADVERB
♦**not necessarily** nicht unbedingt

**necessary** ADJECTIVE
nötig

**necessity** NOUN
die Notwendigkeit ◊ *A car is a necessity,
not a luxury.* Ein Auto ist eine
Notwendigkeit und kein Luxus.

**neck** NOUN
1 (*of body*)
der Hals (GEN des Halses, PL die Hälse)
2 (*of garment*)
der Ausschnitt (PL die Ausschnitte) ◊ *a
V-neck sweater* ein Pullover mit
V-Ausschnitt

**necklace** NOUN
die Halskette

to **need** VERB
see also **need** NOUN
brauchen ◊ *I need a bigger size.* Ich
brauche eine größere Größe.
♦**to need to do something** etwas tun
müssen ◊ *I need to change some money.*
Ich muss Geld wechseln.

**need** NOUN
see also **need** VERB
♦**There's no need to book.** Man braucht
nicht zu buchen.

**needle** NOUN
die Nadel

**needlework** NOUN
die Handarbeit ◊ *We have needlework
lessons at school.* Wir haben
Handarbeitsunterricht an der Schule.

**negative** NOUN
see also **negative** ADJECTIVE
das Negativ (*photo*) (PL die Negative)

**negative** ADJECTIVE
see also **negative** NOUN
negativ ◊ *He's got a very negative
attitude.* Er hat eine sehr negative
Einstellung.

**neglected** ADJECTIVE
ungepflegt (*untidy*) ◊ *The garden is
neglected.* Der Garten ist ungepflegt.

**negligee** NOUN
das Negligé (PL die Negligés)

to **negotiate** VERB
verhandeln

**negotiations** PL NOUN
die Verhandlungen PL

**neighbour** NOUN
der Nachbar (GEN des Nachbarn, PL die
Nachbarn)
die Nachbarin
◊ *the neighbours' garden* der Garten der
Nachbarn

**neighbourhood** NOUN
die Nachbarschaft

**neither** PRONOUN, CONJUNCTION, ADVERB
weder noch ◊ *Carrots or peas? –
Neither, thanks.* Karotten oder Erbsen? –
Weder noch, danke.
♦**Neither of them is coming.** Keiner von
beiden kommt.
♦**neither ... nor ...** weder ... noch ...
◊ *Neither Sarah nor Tamsin is coming to
the party.* Weder Sarah noch Tamsin
kommen zur Party.
♦**Neither do I.** Ich auch nicht. ◊ *I don't like
him. – Neither do I!* Ich mag ihn nicht. –
Ich auch nicht!
♦**Neither have I.** Ich auch nicht. ◊ *I've
never been to Spain. – Neither have I.*
Ich war noch nie in Spanien. – Ich auch
nicht.

**neon** NOUN
das Neon ◊ *a neon light* eine
Neonlampe

**nephew** NOUN
der Neffe (GEN des Neffen, PL die Neffen)
◊ *my nephew* mein Neffe

**nerve** NOUN
der Nerv (PL die Nerven) ◊ *She
sometimes gets on my nerves.* Sie geht
mir manchmal auf die Nerven.

**♦ He's got a nerve!** Der hat vielleicht Nerven!

**nerve-racking** ADJECTIVE
nervenaufreibend

**nervous** ADJECTIVE
nervös (*tense*) ◊ *I bite my nails when I'm nervous.* Wenn ich nervös bin, kaue ich an den Nägeln.

**♦ to be nervous about something** vor etwas Angst haben ◊ *I'm a bit nervous about flying to Paris by myself.* Ich habe etwas Angst, allein nach Paris zu fliegen.

**nest** NOUN
das Nest (PL die Nester)

**net** NOUN
das Netz (GEN des Netzes, PL die Netze) ◊ *a fishing net* ein Fischnetz

**Net** NOUN
**♦ the Net** das Internet

**netball** NOUN
der Netzball

**Netherlands** PL NOUN
die Niederlande PL

*Note that the definite article is used in German for countries which are plural.*

**♦ from the Netherlands** aus den Niederlanden
**♦ in the Netherlands** in den Niederlanden
**♦ to the Netherlands** in die Niederlande

**network** NOUN
[1] das Netz (GEN des Netzes, PL die Netze)
[2] (*for computers*) das Netzwerk (PL die Netzwerke)

**neurotic** ADJECTIVE
neurotisch

**never** ADVERB
nie ◊ *Have you ever been to Germany? – No, never.* Waren Sie schon mal in Deutschland? – Nein, nie. ◊ *I never write letters.* Ich schreibe nie Briefe. ◊ *Never again!* Nie wieder!
**♦ Never mind.** Macht nichts!

**new** ADJECTIVE
neu ◊ *her new boyfriend* ihr neuer Freund ◊ *I need a new dress.* Ich brauche ein neues Kleid.

**newborn** ADJECTIVE
**♦ a newborn baby** ein neugeborenes Kind

**newcomer** NOUN
der Neuling (PL die Neulinge)
*der Neuling is also used for women.*

**news** SING NOUN
*Nachricht is a piece of news;*
*Nachrichten is the news, for example on TV.*

[1] die Nachrichten FEM PL ◊ *good news* gute Nachrichten ◊ *I've had some bad news.* Ich habe schlechte Nachrichten bekommen. ◊ *I watch the news every evening.* Ich sehe mir jeden Abend die Nachrichten an. ◊ *I listen to the news every morning.* Ich höre jeden Morgen die Nachrichten.

[2] die Nachricht ◊ *That's wonderful news!* Das ist eine wunderbare Nachricht!

**newsagent** NOUN
der Zeitungshändler (PL die Zeitungshändler)
die Zeitungshändlerin

**news dealer** NOUN US
der Zeitungshändler (PL die Zeitungshändler)
die Zeitungshändlerin

**newspaper** NOUN
die Zeitung ◊ *I deliver newspapers.* Ich trage Zeitungen aus.

**newsreader** NOUN
der Nachrichtensprecher (PL die Nachrichtensprecher)
die Nachrichtensprecherin

**New Year** NOUN
das Neujahr ◊ *to celebrate New Year* Neujahr feiern
**♦ Happy New Year!** Ein gutes neues Jahr!
**♦ New Year's Day** der Neujahrstag
**♦ New Year's Eve** das Silvester ◊ *a New Year's Eve party* eine Silvesterparty

**New Zealand** NOUN
Neuseeland NEUT
**♦ from New Zealand** aus Neuseeland
**♦ in New Zealand** in Neuseeland
**♦ to New Zealand** nach Neuseeland

**New Zealander** NOUN
der Neuseeländer (PL die Neuseeländer)
die Neuseeländerin

**next** ADJECTIVE, ADVERB, PREPOSITION
[1] nächste ◊ *next Saturday* nächsten Samstag ◊ *next week* nächste Woche ◊ *next year* nächstes Jahr ◊ *the next train* der nächste Zug
**♦ Next please!** Der Nächste, bitte!
[2] danach (*afterwards*) ◊ *What happened next?* Was ist danach passiert?
**♦ What shall I do next?** Was soll ich als nächstes machen?
**♦ next to** neben

*Use the accusative to express movement or a change of place. Use the dative when there is no change of place.*

◊ *I sat down next to my sister.* Ich setzte mich neben meine Schwester. ◊ *The post office is next to the bank.* Die Post ist neben der Bank.
**♦ the next day** am nächsten Tag ◊ *The next day we visited Heidelberg.* Am nächsten Tag haben wir Heidelberg besucht.
**♦ the next time** das nächste Mal ◊ *the next time you see her* wenn du sie das nächste Mal siehst
**♦ next door** nebenan ◊ *They live next door.* Sie wohnen nebenan. ◊ *the people next door* die Leute von nebenan
**♦ the next room** das Nebenzimmer

**N**

**NHS** NOUN (= *National Health Service*)
der <u>staatliche Gesundheitsdienst</u>

> ❶ *In Germany there are a large number of health schemes, not just a single service.*

**nice** ADJECTIVE
[1] <u>nett</u> (*kind*) ◊ *Your parents are nice.* Deine Eltern sind nett. ◊ *It was nice of you to remember my birthday.* Es war nett, dass du an meinen Geburtstag gedacht hast. ◊ *to be nice to somebody* nett zu jemandem sein
[2] <u>hübsch</u> (*pretty*) ◊ *That's a nice dress!* Das ist ein hübsches Kleid! ◊ *Ulm is a nice town.* Ulm ist eine hübsche Stadt.
[3] <u>schön</u> ◊ *nice weather* schönes Wetter ◊ *It's a nice day.* Es ist ein schöner Tag.
[4] <u>lecker</u> (*food*) ◊ *This pizza's very nice.* Diese Pizza ist sehr lecker.
◆ **Have a nice time!** Viel Spaß!

**nickname** NOUN
der <u>Spitzname</u> (GEN des Spitznamens, PL die Spitznamen)

**niece** NOUN
die <u>Nichte</u> ◊ *my niece* meine Nichte

**Nigeria** NOUN
<u>Nigeria</u> NEUT ◊ *in Nigeria* in Nigeria

**night** NOUN
[1] die <u>Nacht</u> (PL die Nächte) ◊ *I want a single room for two nights.* Ich möchte ein Einzelzimmer für zwei Nächte.
◆ **at night** nachts
◆ **Good night!** Gute Nacht!
◆ **a night club** ein Nachtklub MASC
[2] (*evening*)
der <u>Abend</u> (PL die Abende) ◊ *last night* gestern Abend

**nightdress** NOUN
das <u>Nachthemd</u> (PL die Nachthemden)

**nightie** NOUN
das <u>Nachthemd</u> (PL die Nachthemden)

**nightlife** NOUN
das <u>Nachtleben</u> ◊ *There's plenty of nightlife.* Dort gibt es ein reges Nachtleben.

**nightmare** NOUN
der <u>Alptraum</u> (PL die Alpträume) ◊ *I had a nightmare.* Ich hatte einen Alptraum. ◊ *It was a real nightmare!* Es war ein Alptraum!

**nightshirt** NOUN
das <u>Nachthemd</u> (PL die Nachthemden)

**nil** NOUN
<u>null</u> ◊ *We won one nil.* Wir haben eins zu null gewonnen.

**nine** NUMBER
<u>neun</u> ◊ *She's nine.* Sie ist neun.

**nineteen** NUMBER
<u>neunzehn</u> ◊ *She's nineteen.* Sie ist neunzehn.

**nineteenth** ADJECTIVE

<u>neunzehnte</u>
◆ **the nineteenth of August** der neunzehnte August

**ninety** NUMBER
<u>neunzig</u> ◊ *She's ninety.* Sie ist neunzig.

**ninth** ADJECTIVE
<u>neunte</u> ◊ *the ninth floor* der neunte Stock
◆ **the ninth of August** der neunte August

**no** ADVERB, ADJECTIVE
[1] <u>nein</u> ◊ *Are you coming? – No.* Kommst du? – Nein. ◊ *Would you like some more? – No thank you.* Möchten Sie noch etwas? – Nein danke.
[2] <u>kein</u> (*not any*) ◊ *There's no hot water.* Es gibt kein heißes Wasser. ◊ *There are no trains on Sundays.* Sonntags verkehren keine Züge. ◊ *No problem.* Kein Problem. ◊ *I've got no idea.* Ich habe keine Ahnung.
◆ **No way!** Auf keinen Fall!
◆ **"no smoking"** "Rauchen verboten"

**nobody** PRONOUN
<u>niemand</u> ◊ *Who's going with you? – Nobody.* Wer geht mit dir mit? – Niemand. ◊ *There was nobody in the office.* Es war niemand im Büro.

to **nod** VERB
<u>nicken</u>

**noise** NOUN
der <u>Lärm</u> ◊ *Please make less noise.* Macht bitte weniger Lärm.

**noisy** ADJECTIVE
<u>laut</u> ◊ *It's too noisy here.* Hier ist es zu laut.

to **nominate** VERB
<u>nominieren</u> (PERFECT hat nominiert) ◊ *She was nominated for the post.* Sie wurde für den Posten nominiert. ◊ *He was nominated for an Oscar.* Er war für einen Oskar nominiert.

**none** PRONOUN
<u>keiner</u> ◊ *None of my friends wanted to come.* Keiner meiner Freunde wollte kommen. ◊ *How many brothers have you got? – None.* Wie viele Brüder hast du? – Keinen.
<u>keine</u> ◊ *Where is the milk? – There's none left.* Wo ist die Milch? – Es ist keine mehr da.
<u>keines</u> ◊ *Which of the books have you read? – None.* Welches der Bücher hast du gelesen? – Keines.
◆ **There are none left.** Es sind keine mehr da.

**nonsense** NOUN
der <u>Unsinn</u> ◊ *She talks a lot of nonsense.* Sie redet viel Unsinn. ◊ *Nonsense!* Unsinn!

**nonsmoker** NOUN
der <u>Nichtraucher</u> (PL die Nichtraucher) die <u>Nichtraucherin</u>

◊ *She's a nonsmoker.* Sie ist
Nichtraucherin.

**nonsmoking** ADJECTIVE
♦ **a nonsmoking carriage** ein
Nichtraucherabteil NEUT

**nonstop** ADJECTIVE, ADVERB
[1] nonstop ◊ *We flew nonstop.* Wir sind
nonstop geflogen.
♦ **a nonstop flight** ein Nonstopflug MASC
[2] ununterbrochen ◊ *Liz talks nonstop.*
Liz redet ununterbrochen.

**noodles** PL NOUN
die Nudeln FEM PL

**noon** NOUN
der Mittag (PL die Mittage)
♦ **at noon** um zwölf Uhr mittags

**no one** PRONOUN
niemand ◊ *Who's going with you? – No
one.* Wer geht mit dir mit? – Niemand.
◊ *There was no one in the office.* Es war
niemand im Büro.

**nor** CONJUNCTION
♦ **neither ... nor** weder ... noch ◊ *neither
the cinema nor the swimming pool*
weder das Kino noch das Schwimmbad
♦ **Nor do I.** Ich auch nicht. ◊ *I didn't like the
film. – Nor did I.* Der Film hat mir nicht
gefallen. – Mir auch nicht.
♦ **Nor have I.** Ich auch nicht. ◊ *I haven't
seen him. – Nor have I.* Ich habe ihn nicht
gesehen. – Ich auch nicht.

**normal** ADJECTIVE
normal ◊ *at the normal time* zur
normalen Zeit ◊ *a normal car* ein
normales Auto

**normally** ADVERB
[1] normalerweise (*usually*) ◊ *I normally
arrive at nine o'clock.* Normalerweise
komme ich um neun Uhr.
[2] normal (*as normal*) ◊ *In spite of the
strike, the airports are working normally.*
Trotz des Streiks arbeiten die Flughäfen
normal.

**Normandy** NOUN
die Normandie
♦ **in Normandy** in der Normandie

**north** ADJECTIVE, ADVERB
see also **north** NOUN
♦ **the north coast** die Nordküste
♦ **a north wind** ein Nordwind MASC
nach Norden ◊ *We were travelling
north.* Wir sind nach Norden gefahren.
♦ **north of** nördlich von ◊ *It's north of
London.* Es liegt nördlich von London.

**north** NOUN
see also **north** ADJECTIVE
der Norden ◊ *in the north* im Norden

**North America** NOUN
Nordamerika NEUT
♦ **from North America** aus Nordamerika
♦ **to North America** nach Nordamerika

**northbound** ADJECTIVE

in Richtung Norden ◊ *Northbound
traffic is moving very slowly.* Der Verkehr
in Richtung Norden kommt nur sehr
langsam voran.

**northeast** NOUN
der Nordosten ◊ *in the northeast* im
Nordosten

**northern** ADJECTIVE
nördlich ◊ *the northern part of the island*
der nördliche Teil der Insel
♦ **Northern Europe** Nordeuropa NEUT

**Northern Ireland** NOUN
Nordirland NEUT
♦ **from Northern Ireland** aus Nordirland
♦ **in Northern Ireland** in Nordirland
♦ **to Northern Ireland** nach Nordirland

**North Pole** NOUN
der Nordpol

**North Sea** NOUN
die Nordsee

**northwest** NOUN
der Nordwesten ◊ *in the northwest* im
Nordwesten

**Norway** NOUN
Norwegen NEUT
♦ **from Norway** aus Norwegen
♦ **to Norway** nach Norwegen

**Norwegian** ADJECTIVE
see also **Norwegian** NOUN
norwegisch
♦ **He's Norwegian.** Er ist Norweger.

**Norwegian** NOUN
see also **Norwegian** ADJECTIVE
[1] (*person*)
der Norweger (PL die Norweger)
die Norwegerin
[2] (*language*)
das Norwegisch (GEN des Norwegischen)

**nose** NOUN
die Nase

**nosebleed** NOUN
das Nasenbluten ◊ *I often get
nosebleeds.* Ich habe oft Nasenbluten.

**nosey** ADJECTIVE
neugierig ◊ *She's very nosey.* Sie ist
sehr neugierig.

**not** ADVERB
[1] nicht ◊ *Are you coming or not?*
Kommst du oder nicht? ◊ *I'm not sure.*
Ich bin nicht sicher. ◊ *It's not raining.* Es
regnet nicht.
♦ **not really** eigentlich nicht
♦ **not at all** überhaupt nicht
♦ **not yet** noch nicht ◊ *Have you finished?
– Not yet.* Bist du fertig? – Noch nicht.
◊ *They haven't arrived yet.* Sie sind noch
nicht angekommen.
[2] nein ◊ *Can you lend me ten pounds? –
I'm afraid not.* Können Sie mir zehn
Pfund leihen? – Leider nein.

**note** NOUN
[1] die Notiz

**N**

☞

◆ **to take notes** sich Notizen machen ◊ *You should take notes.* Du solltest dir Notizen machen.

[2] (*letter*)
der Brief (PL die Briefe)

◆ **I'll write her a note.** Ich werde ihr schreiben.

[3] (*banknote*)
der Schein (PL die Scheine) ◊ *a five-pound note* ein Fünfpfundschein

to **note down** VERB
aufschreiben (IMPERFECT schrieb auf, PERFECT hat aufgeschrieben)

**notebook** NOUN
[1] das Notizbuch (PL die Notizbücher)
[2] (*computer*)
der Notebookcomputer (PL die Notebookcomputer)

**notepad** NOUN
der Notizblock (PL die Notizblöcke)

**notepaper** NOUN
das Briefpapier

**nothing** NOUN
nichts ◊ *What's wrong? – Nothing.* Was ist los? – Nichts. ◊ *nothing special* nichts Besonderes ◊ *He does nothing.* Er tut nichts. ◊ *He ate nothing for breakfast.* Er hat nichts zum Frühstück gegessen.

**notice** NOUN
see also **notice** VERB
die Notiz (*sign*) ◊ *to put up a notice* eine Notiz aushängen ◊ *Don't take any notice of him!* Nimm keine Notiz von ihm!

◆ **a warning notice** ein Warnschild NEUT

to **notice** VERB
see also **notice** NOUN
bemerken (PERFECT hat bemerkt)

**notice board** NOUN
das Anschlagbrett (PL die Anschlagbretter)

**nought** NOUN
die Null

**noun** NOUN
das Substantiv (PL die Substantive)

**novel** NOUN
der Roman (PL die Romane)

**novelist** NOUN
der Romanautor (PL die Romanautoren)
die Romanautorin

**November** NOUN
der November ◊ *in November* im November

**now** ADVERB, CONJUNCTION
jetzt ◊ *What are you doing now?* Was tust du jetzt?

◆ **just now** gerade ◊ *I'm rather busy just now.* Ich bin gerade ziemlich beschäftigt. ◊ *I did it just now.* Ich habe es gerade getan.

◆ **by now** inzwischen ◊ *He should be there by now.* Er müsste inzwischen dort sein. ◊ *It should be ready by now.* Es müsste inzwischen fertig sein.

◆ **now and then** ab und zu

**nowhere** ADVERB
nirgends ◊ *nowhere else* sonst nirgends

**nuclear** ADJECTIVE
nuklear

◆ **nuclear power** die Kernkraft ◊ *a nuclear power station* ein Kernkraftwerk NEUT

**nude** ADJECTIVE
see also **nude** NOUN
nackt ◊ *to sunbathe nude* nackt sonnenbaden

**nude** NOUN
see also **nude** ADJECTIVE

◆ **in the nude** nackt

**nudist** NOUN
der Nudist (GEN des Nudisten, PL die Nudisten)
die Nudistin

**nuisance** NOUN
◆ **It's a nuisance.** Es ist sehr lästig.
◆ **Sorry to be a nuisance.** Tut mir Leid, dass ich schon wieder ankomme.

**numb** ADJECTIVE
taub ◊ *numb with cold* taub vor Kälte

**number** NOUN
[1] die Anzahl (*total amount*) ◊ *a large number of people* eine große Anzahl von Menschen
[2] die Nummer (*of house, telephone, bank account*) ◊ *They live at number five.* Sie wohnen in der Nummer fünf. ◊ *What's your phone number?* Wie ist Ihre Telefonnummer?

◆ **You've got the wrong number.** Sie sind falsch verbunden.

[3] die Zahl (*figure, digit*) ◊ *I can't read the second number.* Ich kann die zweite Zahl nicht lesen.

**number plate** NOUN
das Nummernschild (PL die Nummernschilder)

---

*ℹ The first letters of a German number plate allow you to tell where the car's owner lives. Thus L stands for Leipzig, LB for Ludwigsburg, LU for Ludwigshafen, etc.*

---

**nun** NOUN
die Nonne ◊ *She's a nun.* Sie ist Nonne.

**nurse** NOUN
die Krankenschwester ◊ *She's a nurse.* Sie ist Krankenschwester.
der Krankenpfleger
◊ *He's a nurse.* Er ist Krankenpfleger.

**nursery** NOUN
[1] (*for children*)
die Kindergarten (PL die Kindergärten)
[2] (*for plants*)
die Baumschule

**nursery school** NOUN
der Kindergarten (PL die Kindergärten)

> ⓘ *German children go to **Kindergarten** from the age of 3 to 6.*

**nursery slope** NOUN
  der Idiotenhügel (PL die Idiotenhügel)
**nut** NOUN
  1 die Nuss (PL die Nüsse)
  2 (*made of metal*)
  die Mutter
**nutmeg** NOUN

  der Muskat
**nutritious** ADJECTIVE
  nahrhaft
**nuts** ADJECTIVE
  ♦He's nuts. Er spinnt. (*informal*)
**nutter** NOUN
  ♦He's a nutter. Er ist völlig durchgeknallt.
  (*informal*)
**nylon** NOUN
  das Nylon

N

# O

**oak** NOUN
die Eiche ◊ *an oak table* ein Eichentisch
MASC

**oar** NOUN
das Ruder (PL die Ruder)

**oats** PL NOUN
der Hafer

**obedient** ADJECTIVE
gehorsam

to **obey** VERB
gehorchen (PERFECT hat gehorcht) ◊ *She didn't obey her mother.* Sie hat ihrer Mutter nicht gehorcht.
♦ **to obey the rules** die Regeln befolgen

**object** NOUN
der Gegenstand (PL die Gegenstände)
◊ *a familiar object* ein vertrauter Gegenstand

**objection** NOUN
der Einspruch (PL die Einsprüche)

**objective** NOUN
das Ziel (PL die Ziele)

**oblong** ADJECTIVE
länglich

**oboe** NOUN
die Oboe ◊ *I play the oboe.* Ich spiele Oboe.

**obscene** ADJECTIVE
obszön

**observant** ADJECTIVE
aufmerksam

to **observe** VERB
beobachten (PERFECT hat beobachtet)

**obsessed** ADJECTIVE
besessen ◊ *He's completely obsessed with trains.* Er ist von Zügen ganz besessen.

**obsession** NOUN
die Leidenschaft ◊ *Football's an obsession of mine.* Fußball ist meine Leidenschaft.

**obsolete** ADJECTIVE
veraltet

**obstacle** NOUN
das Hindernis (GEN des Hindernisses, PL die Hindernisse)

**obstinate** ADJECTIVE
stur

to **obstruct** VERB
behindern (PERFECT hat behindert) ◊ *A lorry was obstructing the traffic.* Ein Lastwagen hat den Verkehr behindert.

to **obtain** VERB
erhalten (IMPERFECT erhielt, PERFECT hat erhalten)

**obvious** ADJECTIVE
offensichtlich

**obviously** ADVERB
[1] natürlich (*of course*) ◊ *Do you want to pass the exam? – Obviously!* Willst du die Prüfung bestehen? – Natürlich!
◊ *Obviously not!* Natürlich nicht!
[2] offensichtlich (*visibly*) ◊ *She was obviously exhausted.* Sie war offensichtlich erschöpft.

**occasion** NOUN
die Gelegenheit ◊ *a special occasion* eine besondere Gelegenheit
♦ **on several occasions** mehrmals

**occasionally** ADVERB
ab und zu

**occupation** NOUN
die Beschäftigung

to **occupy** VERB
besetzen (PERFECT hat besetzt) ◊ *That seat is occupied.* Der Platz ist besetzt.

to **occur** VERB
passieren (*happen*) (PERFECT ist passiert)
◊ *The accident occurred yesterday.* Der Unfall ist gestern passiert.
♦ **It suddenly occurred to me that ...** Plötzlich ist mir eingefallen, dass ...

**ocean** NOUN
der Ozean (PL die Ozeane)

**o'clock** ADVERB
♦ **at four o'clock** um vier Uhr
♦ **It's five o'clock.** Es ist fünf Uhr.

**October** NOUN
der Oktober ◊ *in October* im Oktober

**octopus** NOUN
der Tintenfisch (PL die Tintenfische)

**odd** ADJECTIVE
[1] eigenartig ◊ *That's odd!* Das ist eigenartig!
[2] ungerade ◊ *an odd number* eine ungerade Zahl

**of** PREPOSITION
von ◊ *some photos of my holiday* Fotos von meinen Ferien ◊ *three of us* drei von uns ◊ *a friend of mine* ein Freund von mir ◊ *That's very kind of you.* Das ist sehr nett von Ihnen. ◊ *Can I have half of that?* Kann ich die Hälfte davon haben?
*of is not translated when specifying a quantity of something.*
◊ *a kilo of oranges* ein Kilo Orangen
*of is often expressed by using the genitive.*
◊ *the end of the film* das Ende des Films
◊ *the top of the stairs* das obere Ende der Treppe ◊ *the front of the house* die Vorderseite des Hauses
♦ **a boy of ten** ein zehnjähriger Junge
♦ **the fourteenth of September** der vierzehnte September

♦ **It's made of wood.** Es ist aus Holz.
**off** ADVERB, PREPOSITION, ADJECTIVE

*For other expressions with **off**, see the verbs **get, take, turn** etc.*

1 aus *(heater, light, TV)* ◊ *All the lights are off.* Alle Lichter sind aus.

2 zu *(tap, gas)* ◊ *Are you sure the tap is off?* Bist du sicher, dass der Hahn zu ist?

3 abgesagt *(cancelled)* ◊ *The match is off.* Das Spiel wurde abgesagt.

♦ **to be off sick** krank sein
♦ **a day off** ein freier Tag
♦ **to take a day off work** sich einen Tag freinehmen ◊ *I'm taking a day off work tomorrow.* Ich werde mir morgen einen Tag freinehmen.
♦ **She's off school today.** Sie ist heute nicht in der Schule.
♦ **I must be off now.** Ich muss jetzt gehen.
♦ **I'm off.** Ich gehe jetzt.
**offence** NOUN
das Vergehen *(crime)* (PL die Vergehen)
**offensive** ADJECTIVE
anstößig
**offer** NOUN

see also **offer** VERB

das Angebot (PL die Angebote) ◊ *a good offer* ein günstiges Angebot
♦ **"on special offer"** "im Sonderangebot"
to **offer** VERB

see also **offer** NOUN

anbieten (IMPERFECT bot an, PERFECT hat angeboten) ◊ *He offered to help me.* Er bot mir seine Hilfe an. ◊ *I offered to go with them.* Ich habe ihnen angeboten mitzugehen.
**office** NOUN
das Büro (PL die Büros) ◊ *She works in an office.* Sie arbeitet in einem Büro.
♦ **doctor's office** die Arztpraxis
**officer** NOUN
der Offizier *(in army)* (PL die Offiziere)
♦ **a police officer** *(man)* ein Polizeibeamter
**official** ADJECTIVE
offiziell
**off-licence** NOUN
die Wein- und Spirituosenhandlung
**off-peak** ADJECTIVE
außerhalb der Stoßzeiten ◊ *It's cheaper to travel off-peak.* Es ist billiger, außerhalb der Stoßzeiten zu fahren.
♦ **off-peak calls** Gespräche zum Billigtarif
**offside** ADJECTIVE
im Abseits *(in football)*
**often** ADVERB
oft ◊ *It often rains.* Es regnet oft. ◊ *How often do you go to church?* Wie oft gehst du in die Kirche? ◊ *I'd like to go skiing more often.* Ich würde gern öfter Ski fahren.
**oil** NOUN

see also **oil** VERB

1 *(for lubrication, cooking)*
das Öl (PL die Öle)
♦ **an oil painting** ein Ölgemälde NEUT
2 *(petroleum)*
das Erdöl ◊ *North Sea oil* Erdöl aus der Nordsee
to **oil** VERB

see also **oil** NOUN

ölen
**oil rig** NOUN
die Bohrinsel ◊ *He works on an oil rig.* Er arbeitet auf einer Bohrinsel.
**oil slick** NOUN
der Ölteppich (PL die Ölteppiche)
**oil well** NOUN
die Ölquelle
**ointment** NOUN
die Salbe
**okay** EXCLAMATION, ADJECTIVE
okay ◊ *Could you call back later? – Okay!* Kannst du später anrufen? – Okay! ◊ *I'll meet you at six o'clock, okay?* Ich treffe dich um sechs Uhr, okay? ◊ *Is that okay?* Ist das okay? ◊ *How was your holiday? – It was okay.* Wie waren die Ferien? – Okay.
♦ **I'll do it tomorrow, if that's okay with you.** Ich mache das morgen, wenn du einverstanden bist.
♦ **Are you okay?** Bist du in Ordnung?
**old** ADJECTIVE
alt ◊ *an old dog* ein alter Hund ◊ *old people* alte Menschen ◊ *my old English teacher* mein alter Englischlehrer ◊ *How old are you?* Wie alt bist du? ◊ *He's ten years old.* Er ist zehn Jahre alt. ◊ *my older brother* mein älterer Bruder ◊ *my older sister* meine ältere Schwester ◊ *She's two years older than me.* Sie ist zwei Jahre älter als ich. ◊ *He's the oldest in the family.* Er ist der Älteste der Familie.
**old age pensioner** NOUN
der Rentner (PL die Rentner)
die Rentnerin
◊ *She's an old age pensioner.* Sie ist Rentnerin.
**old-fashioned** ADJECTIVE
altmodisch ◊ *She wears old-fashioned clothes.* Sie trägt altmodische Kleidung. ◊ *My parents are rather old-fashioned.* Meine Eltern sind ziemlich altmodisch.
**olive** NOUN
die Olive
**olive oil** NOUN
das Olivenöl (PL die Olivenöle)
**Olympic** ADJECTIVE
olympisch
♦ **the Olympics** die Olympischen Spiele
**omelette** NOUN
das Omelett (PL die Omeletts)
**on** PREPOSITION, ADVERB

**O**

☞

*see also* **on** ADJECTIVE

*There are several ways of translating* **on***. Scan the examples to find one that is similar to what you want to say. For other expressions with* **on** *see the verbs* **go, put, turn** *etc.*

**1** auf

*Use the accusative to express movement or a change of place. Use the dative when there is no change of place.*

◊ *It's on the table.* Es ist auf dem Tisch. ◊ *Please, put it on the table.* Stell es bitte auf den Tisch. ◊ *on an island* auf einer Insel ◊ *on the left* auf der linken Seite

**2** an ◊ *on Friday* am Freitag ◊ *on Christmas Day* am ersten Weihnachtsfeiertag ◊ *on the twentieth of June* am zwanzigsten Juni ◊ *on my birthday* an meinem Geburtstag

♦ **on Fridays** freitags

*Use the accusative to express movement or a change of place. Use the dative when there is no change of place.*

◊ *There was not a single picture on the wall.* An der Wand hing kein einziges Bild. ◊ *She hung a picture up on the wall.* Sie hängte ein Bild an die Wand.

**3** in ◊ *on the second floor* im zweiten Stock ◊ *on TV* im Fernsehen ◊ *What's on TV?* Was kommt im Fernsehen? ◊ *I heard it on the radio.* Ich habe es im Radio gehört.

♦ **on the bus (1)** (*by bus*) mit dem Bus ◊ *I go into town on the bus.* Ich fahre mit dem Bus in die Stadt.

♦ **on the bus (2)** (*inside*) im Bus ◊ *There were no empty seats on the bus.* Es gab keinen freien Platz im Bus.

♦ **I go to school on my bike.** Ich fahre mit dem Fahrrad zur Schule.

♦ **on holiday** in den Ferien ◊ *They're on holiday.* Sie sind in den Ferien.

♦ **They are on strike.** Sie streiken.

**on** ADJECTIVE

*see also* **on** PREPOSITION

**1** an (*heater, light, TV*) ◊ *I think I left the light on.* Ich glaube, ich habe das Licht angelassen. ◊ *Is the dishwasher on?* Ist die Spülmaschine an?

**2** auf (*tap, gas*) ◊ *Leave the tap on.* Lass den Hahn auf.

♦ **What's on at the cinema?** Was gibt's im Kino?

**once** ADVERB

einmal ◊ *once a week* einmal pro Woche ◊ *once more* noch einmal ◊ *I've been to Germany once before.* Ich war schon einmal in Deutschland.

♦ **Once upon a time ...** Es war einmal ...

♦ **at once** sofort

♦ **once in a while** ab und zu

**one** NUMBER, PRONOUN

*Use* **ein** *for masculine and neuter nouns,* **eine** *for feminine nouns.*

**1** ein ◊ *one man* ein Mann ◊ *one child* ein Kind ◊ *We stayed there for one day.* Wir sind einen Tag dort geblieben.

**2** eine ◊ *one minute* eine Minute ◊ *Do you need a stamp? – No thanks, I've got one.* Brauchst du eine Briefmarke? – Nein danke, ich habe eine. ◊ *I've got one brother and one sister.* Ich habe einen Bruder und eine Schwester.

**3** eins

*Use* **eins** *when counting.*

◊ *one, two, three* eins, zwei, drei

**4** man (*impersonal*) ◊ *One never knows.* Man kann nie wissen.

♦ **this one (1)** (*masculine*) dieser ◊ *Which foot hurts? – This one.* Welcher Fuß tut weh? – Dieser.

♦ **this one (2)** (*feminine*) diese ◊ *Which is your cup? – This one.* Welche ist deine Tasse? – Diese.

♦ **this one (3)** (*neuter*) dieses ◊ *Which is the best photo? – This one.* Welches ist das beste Foto? – Dieses.

♦ **that one (1)** (*masculine*) der da ◊ *Which pen did you use? – That one.* Welchen Schreiber hast du benützt? – Den da.

♦ **that one (2)** (*feminine*) die da ◊ *Which bag is yours? – That one.* Welche ist deine Tasche? – Die da.

♦ **that one (3)** (*neuter*) das da ◊ *Which is your car? – That one.* Welches ist Ihr Auto? – Das da.

**oneself** PRONOUN

**1** sich ◊ *to hurt oneself* sich wehtun

**2** selbst ◊ *It's quicker to do it oneself.* Es geht schneller, wenn man es selbst macht.

**one-way** ADJECTIVE

♦ **a one-way street** eine Einbahnstraße

**onion** NOUN

die Zwiebel ◊ *onion soup* die Zwiebelsuppe

**on-line** ADJECTIVE

online

**only** ADVERB, ADJECTIVE, CONJUNCTION

**1** einzig ◊ *Monday is the only day I'm free.* Montag ist mein einziger freier Tag. ◊ *German is the only subject I like.* Deutsch ist das einzige Fach, das ich mag.

**2** nur ◊ *How much was it? – Only ten marks.* Wie viel hat es gekostet? – Nur zehn Mark. ◊ *We only want to stay for one night.* Wir wollen nur eine Nacht bleiben. ◊ *I'd like the same sweater, only in black.* Ich möchte den gleichen Pullover, nur in Schwarz.

♦ **an only child** ein Einzelkind NEUT

**onwards** ADVERB

ab ◊ *from July onwards* ab Juli

**open** ADJECTIVE

see also **open** VERB

offen ◊ *The window was open.* Das Fenster war offen.
- ◆**The baker's is open on Sunday morning.** Die Bäckerei hat am Sonntagmorgen auf.
- ◆**in the open air** im Freien

to **open** VERB

see also **open** ADJECTIVE

[1] aufmachen (PERFECT hat aufgemacht) ◊ *Can I open the window?* Kann ich das Fenster aufmachen? ◊ *What time do the shops open?* Um wie viel Uhr machen die Geschäfte auf?
[2] aufgehen (IMPERFECT ging auf, PERFECT ist aufgegangen) ◊ *The door opens automatically.* Die Tür geht automatisch auf. ◊ *The door opened and in came the teacher.* Die Tür ging auf, und der Lehrer kam herein.

**opening hours** PL NOUN
die Öffnungszeiten FEM PL

**opera** NOUN
die Oper

to **operate** VERB
bedienen (*machine*) (PERFECT hat bedient)
- ◆**to operate on someone** jemanden operieren

**operation** NOUN
die Operation ◊ *a major operation* eine größere Operation
- ◆**to have an operation** operiert werden ◊ *I have never had an operation.* Ich bin noch nie operiert worden.

**operator** NOUN
(*on telephone*)
der Telefonist (GEN des Telefonisten, PL die Telefonisten)
die Telefonistin

**opinion** NOUN
die Meinung ◊ *He asked me my opinion.* Er fragte mich nach meiner Meinung. ◊ *What's your opinion?* Was ist deine Meinung?
- ◆**in my opinion** meiner Meinung nach

**opinion poll** NOUN
die Meinungsumfrage

**opponent** NOUN
der Gegner (PL die Gegner)
die Gegnerin

**opportunity** NOUN
die Gelegenheit
- ◆**to have the opportunity to do something** die Gelegenheit haben, etwas zu tun ◊ *I've never had the opportunity to go to Germany.* Ich hatte noch nie die Gelegenheit, nach Deutschland zu fahren.

**opposed** ADJECTIVE
- ◆**to be opposed to something** gegen etwas sein ◊ *I've always been opposed to violence.* Ich bin immer gegen Gewalt gewesen.

**opposing** ADJECTIVE
gegnerisch (*team*)

**opposite** ADJECTIVE, ADVERB, PREPOSITION
[1] entgegengesetzt ◊ *It's in the opposite direction.* Es ist in der entgegengesetzten Richtung.
[2] gegenüber ◊ *They live opposite.* Sie wohnen gegenüber. ◊ *the girl who was sitting opposite me* das Mädchen, das mir gegenüber saß
- ◆**the opposite sex** das andere Geschlecht

**opposition** NOUN
die Opposition

**optician** NOUN
der Optiker (PL die Optiker)
die Optikerin
◊ *She's an optician.* Sie ist Optikerin.

**optimist** NOUN
der Optimist (GEN des Optimisten, PL die Optimisten)
die Optimistin
◊ *She's an optimist.* Sie ist Optimistin.

**optimistic** ADJECTIVE
optimistisch

**option** NOUN
[1] (*choice*)
die Wahl ◊ *I've got no option.* Ich habe keine andere Wahl.
[2] (*optional subject*)
das Wahlfach (PL die Wahlfächer) ◊ *I'm doing geology as my option.* Ich habe Geologie als Wahlfach.

**optional** ADJECTIVE
fakultativ

**or** CONJUNCTION
[1] oder ◊ *Would you like tea or coffee?* Möchten Sie Tee oder Kaffee?
Use **weder ... noch** in negative sentences.
◊ *I don't eat meat or fish.* Ich esse weder Fleisch noch Fisch.
[2] sonst (*otherwise*) ◊ *Hurry up or you'll miss the bus.* Beeil dich, sonst verpasst du den Bus.
- ◆**Give me the money, or else!** Gib mir das Geld, sonst gibt's was!

**oral** ADJECTIVE

see also **oral** NOUN

mündlich ◊ *an oral exam* eine mündliche Prüfung

**oral** NOUN

see also **oral** ADJECTIVE

die mündliche Prüfung ◊ *I've got my German oral soon.* Ich habe bald meine mündliche Prüfung in Deutsch.

**orange** NOUN

see also **orange** ADJECTIVE

die Orange
- ◆**an orange juice** ein Orangensaft MASC

**orange** ADJECTIVE

see also **orange** NOUN

orangerot (*colour*)

O

**orchard** NOUN
der Obstgarten (PL die Obstgärten)

**orchestra** NOUN
[1] das Orchester (PL die Orchester) ◊ *I play in the school orchestra.* Ich spiele im Schulorchester.
[2] (*stalls*)
das Parkett ◊ *We sat in the orchestra.* Wir saßen im Parkett.

**order** NOUN

| see also **order** VERB |

[1] (*sequence*)
die Reihenfolge ◊ *in alphabetical order* in alphabetischer Reihenfolge
[2] (*at restaurant, in shop*)
die Bestellung ◊ *The waiter took our order.* Der Ober nahm unsere Bestellung auf.
[3] (*instruction*)
der Befehl (PL die Befehle) ◊ *That's an order.* Das ist ein Befehl.
♦ **in order to** um zu ◊ *He does it in order to earn money.* Er tut es, um Geld zu verdienen.
♦ **"out of order"** "außer Betrieb"

to **order** VERB

| see also **order** NOUN |

bestellen (PERFECT hat bestellt) ◊ *We ordered steak and chips.* Wir haben Steak mit Pommes frites bestellt. ◊ *Are you ready to order?* Möchten Sie bestellen?

to **order about** VERB
herumkommandieren (PERFECT hat herumkommandiert) ◊ *She was fed up with being ordered about.* Sie hatte es satt, herumkommandiert zu werden.

**ordinary** ADJECTIVE
[1] gewöhnlich ◊ *an ordinary day* ein gewöhnlicher Tag
[2] normal (*people*) ◊ *an ordinary family* eine normale Familie ◊ *He's just an ordinary guy.* Er ist ein ganz normaler Mensch.

**organ** NOUN
die Orgel (*instrument*) ◊ *I play the organ.* Ich spiele Orgel.

**organic** ADJECTIVE
biodynamisch (*fruit*)
♦ **organic vegetables** das Biogemüse SING

**organization** NOUN
die Organisation

to **organize** VERB
organisieren (PERFECT hat organisiert)

**origin** NOUN
der Ursprung (PL die Ursprünge)

**original** ADJECTIVE
originell ◊ *It's a very original idea.* Das ist eine sehr originelle Idee.
♦ **Our original plan was to go camping.** Ursprünglich wollten wir zelten.

**originally** ADVERB
ursprünglich

**Orkney** NOUN
die Orkneyinseln FEM PL
♦ **in Orkney** auf den Orkneyinseln

**ornament** NOUN
die Verzierung

**orphan** NOUN
das Waisenkind (PL die Waisenkinder) ◊ *She's an orphan.* Sie ist ein Waisenkind.

**ostrich** NOUN
der Strauß (GEN des Straußes, PL die Strauße)

**other** ADJECTIVE, PRONOUN
andere ◊ *Have you got these jeans in other colours?* Haben Sie diese Jeans in anderen Farben? ◊ *on the other side of the street* auf der anderen Straßenseite
♦ **the other day** neulich
♦ **the other one (1)** (*masculine*) der andere ◊ *This hat? – No, the other one.* Dieser Hut? – Nein, der andere.
♦ **the other one (2)** (*feminine*) die andere ◊ *This cup? – No, the other one.* Diese Tasse? – Nein, die andere.
♦ **the other one (3)** (*neuter*) das andere ◊ *This photo? – No, the other one.* Dieses Foto? – Nein, das andere.
♦ **the others** die anderen ◊ *The others are going but I'm not.* Die anderen gehen, ich nicht.

**otherwise** ADVERB, CONJUNCTION
sonst ◊ *Note down the number, otherwise you'll forget it.* Schreib dir die Nummer auf, sonst vergisst du sie. ◊ *Put some sunscreen on, you'll get burned otherwise.* Creme dich ein, sonst bekommst du einen Sonnenbrand. ◊ *I'm tired, but otherwise I'm fine.* Ich bin müde, aber sonst geht's mir gut.

**ought** VERB
*If you want to say that you feel obliged to do something, use the conditional tense of **sollen**.*
◊ *I ought to phone my parents.* Ich sollte meine Eltern anrufen. ◊ *You ought not to do that.* Du solltest das nicht tun.
*If you want to say that something is likely, use the conditional tense of **müssen**.*
◊ *He ought to win.* Er müsste gewinnen.

**ounce** NOUN
die Unze

**our** ADJECTIVE
unser ◊ *Our boss is quite nice.* Unser Chef ist ganz nett. ◊ *Our company is going to expand.* Unsere Firma wird expandieren. ◊ *Our house is quite big.* Unser Haus ist ziemlich groß. ◊ *Our neighbours are very nice.* Unsere Nachbarn sind sehr nett.
*Do not use **unser** with parts of the body.*
◊ *We had to shut our eyes.* Wir mussten die Augen zumachen.

**ours** PRONOUN
  1 unserer ◇ *Your garden is very big,
ours is much smaller.* Euer Garten ist
sehr groß, unserer ist viel kleiner.
  unsere ◇ *Your school is very different
from ours.* Eure Schule ist ganz anderes
als unsere.
  unseres ◇ *Your house is bigger than
ours.* Euer Haus ist größer als unseres.
  2 unsere ◇ *Our teachers are strict. –
Ours are too.* Unsere Lehrer sind streng.
– Unsere auch.
◆ **Is this ours?** Gehört das uns? ◇ *This car
is ours.* Das Auto gehört uns. ◇ *Whose is
this? – It's ours.* Wem gehört das? – Uns.

**ourselves** PRONOUN
  1 uns ◇ *We really enjoyed ourselves.*
Wir haben uns wirklich amüsiert.
  2 selbst ◇ *We built our garage
ourselves.* Wir haben die Garage selbst
gebaut.

**out** ADVERB
*There are several ways of translating
**out**. Scan the examples to find one that
is similar to what you want to say. For
other expressions with **out**, see the
verbs **go**, **put**, **turn** etc.*
  1 draußen (*outside*) ◇ *It's cold out.* Es ist
kalt draußen.
  2 aus (*light, fire*) ◇ *All the lights are out.*
Alle Lichter sind aus.
◆ **She's out.** Sie ist weg. ◇ *She's out for the
afternoon.* Sie ist den ganzen Nachmittag
weg.
◆ **She's out shopping.** Sie ist zum
Einkaufen.
◆ **out there** da draußen ◇ *It's cold out
there.* Es ist kalt da draußen.
◆ **to go out** ausgehen ◇ *I'm going out
tonight.* Ich gehe heute Abend aus.
◆ **to go out with somebody** mit jemandem
gehen ◇ *I've been going out with him for
two months.* Ich gehe seit zwei Monaten
mit ihm.
◆ **out of (1)** aus ◇ *to drink out of a glass*
aus einem Glas trinken
◆ **out of (2)** von ◇ *in nine cases out of ten*
in neun von zehn Fällen
◆ **out of (3)** außerhalb ◇ *He lives out of
town.* Er wohnt außerhalb der Stadt.
◇ *three kilometres out of town* drei
Kilometer außerhalb der Stadt
◆ **out of curiosity** aus Neugier
◆ **out of work** arbeitslos
◆ **That is out of the question.** Das kommt
nicht in Frage.
◆ **You're out!** (*in game*) Du bist draußen!
◆ **"way out"** "Ausgang"

**outbreak** NOUN
  der Ausbruch (PL die Ausbrüche) ◇ *a
salmonella outbreak* ein Ausbruch von
Salmonellenvergiftung ◇ *the outbreak of
war* der Kriegsausbruch

**outcome** NOUN
  das Ergebnis (PL die Ergebnisse)

**outdoor** ADJECTIVE
  im Freien ◇ *outdoor activities* Aktivitäten
im Freien
◆ **an outdoor swimming pool** ein Freibad
NEUT

**outdoors** ADVERB
  im Freien

**outfit** NOUN
  das Outfit (PL die Outfits) ◇ *a cowboy
outfit* ein Cowboyoutfit

**outgoing** ADJECTIVE
  aufgeschlossen ◇ *She's very outgoing.*
Sie ist sehr aufgeschlossen.

**outing** NOUN
  der Ausflug (PL die Ausflüge) ◇ *to go on
an outing* einen Ausflug machen

**outline** NOUN
  1 (*summary*)
  der Grundriss (GEN des Grundrisses, PL
die Grundrisse)
◆ **This is an outline of the plan.** Das ist der
Grundriss des Plans.
  2 (*shape*)
  der Umriss (GEN des Umrisses, PL die
Umrisse) ◇ *We could see the outline of
the mountain in the mist.* Wir konnten im
Nebel den Umriss des Berges erkennen.

**outlook** NOUN
  1 die Einstellung (*attitude*) ◇ *my outlook
on life* meine Einstellung zum Leben
  2 die Aussichten PL (*prospects*)

**outrageous** ADJECTIVE
  1 unerhört (*behaviour*)
  2 unverschämt (*price*)

**outset** NOUN
  der Anfang (PL die Anfänge) ◇ *at the
outset* am Anfang

**outside** NOUN
  see also **outside** ADJECTIVE
  die Außenseite

**outside** ADJECTIVE, ADVERB, PREPOSITION
  see also **outside** NOUN
  1 äußere ◇ *the outside walls* die
äußeren Mauern
  2 draußen ◇ *It's very cold outside.*
Draußen ist es sehr kalt.
  3 außerhalb ◇ *outside the school*
außerhalb der Schule ◇ *outside school
hours* außerhalb der Schulzeit

**outsize** ADJECTIVE
  übergroß

**outskirts** PL NOUN
  der Stadtrand SING ◇ *on the outskirts of
the town* am Stadtrand

**outstanding** ADJECTIVE
  bemerkenswert

**oval** ADJECTIVE
  oval

**oven** NOUN
  der Backofen (PL die Backöfen)

**O**

**over** PREPOSITION, ADVERB, ADJECTIVE

1 über

*Use the accusative to express movement or a change of place. Use the dative when there is no change of place.*

◇ *The ball went over the wall.* Der Ball flog über die Mauer. ◇ *There's a mirror over the washbasin.* Über dem Becken ist ein Spiegel.

2 über +ACC (*more than*) ◇ *It's over ten kilos.* Es ist über zehn Kilo schwer. ◇ *The temperature was over thirty degrees.* Die Temperatur lag über dreißig Grad.

3 vorbei (*finished*) ◇ *I'll be happy when the exams are over.* Ich bin froh, wenn die Prüfungen vorbei sind.

♦ **over the holidays** die Ferien über
♦ **over Christmas** über Weihnachten
♦ **over here** hier
♦ **over there** dort
♦ **all over Scotland** in ganz Schottland

**overall** ADVERB
insgesamt (*generally*) ◇ *My results were quite good overall.* Insgesamt hatte ich ganz gute Noten.

**overalls** PL NOUN
der Overall SING (PL die Overalls)

**overcast** ADJECTIVE
bedeckt ◇ *The sky was overcast.* Der Himmel war bedeckt.

to **overcharge** VERB
zu viel berechnen (PERFECT hat zu viel berechnet) ◇ *He overcharged me.* Er hat mir zu viel berechnet. ◇ *They overcharged us for the meal.* Sie haben uns für das Essen zu viel berechnet.

**overcoat** NOUN
der Mantel (PL die Mäntel)

**overdone** ADJECTIVE
verkocht (*food*)

**overdose** NOUN
die Überdosis (*of drugs*) (PL die Überdosen) ◇ *to take an overdose* eine Überdosis nehmen

**overdraft** NOUN
der Überziehungskredit

to **overestimate** VERB
überschätzen (PERFECT hat überschätzt)

**overhead projector** NOUN
der Tageslichtprojektor (PL die Tageslichtprojektoren)

to **overlook** VERB

1 (*have view of*)
einen Blick haben auf +ACC (PRESENT hat einen Blick auf, IMPERFECT hatte einen Blick auf, PERFECT hat einen Blick auf gehabt) ◇ *The hotel overlooked the beach.* Vom Hotel hat man einen Blick auf den Strand.

2 (*forget about*)
übersehen (PRESENT übersieht, IMPERFECT übersah, PERFECT hat übersehen) ◇ *He had overlooked one important problem.* Er hatte ein wichtiges Problem übersehen.

**overseas** ADVERB

1 im Ausland ◇ *I'd like to work overseas.* Ich würde gern im Ausland arbeiten.

2 ins Ausland ◇ *His company has sent him overseas.* Seine Firma hat ihn ins Ausland geschickt.

**oversight** NOUN
das Versehen (PL die Versehen)

to **oversleep** VERB
verschlafen (PRESENT verschläft, IMPERFECT verschlief, PERFECT hat verschlafen) ◇ *I overslept this morning.* Ich habe heute morgen verschlafen.

to **overtake** VERB
überholen (PERFECT hat überholt) ◇ *He overtook me.* Er hat mich überholt.

**overtime** NOUN
die Überstunden FEM PL ◇ *to work overtime* Überstunden machen

**overtook** VERB *see* **overtake**

**overweight** ADJECTIVE
♦ **to be overweight** Übergewicht haben

to **owe** VERB
schulden
♦ **to owe somebody something** jemandem etwas schulden ◇ *You owe me five pounds.* Du schuldest mir fünf Pfund.

**owing to** PREPOSITION
wegen ◇ *owing to bad weather* wegen des schlechten Wetters

**owl** NOUN
die Eule

**own** ADJECTIVE

see also **own** VERB

eigen ◇ *I've got my own bathroom.* Ich habe mein eigenes Badezimmer.
♦ **I'd like a room of my own.** Ich hätte gern ein eigenes Zimmer.
♦ **on one's own** allein ◇ *on her own* allein ◇ *on our own* allein

to **own** VERB

see also **own** ADJECTIVE

besitzen (IMPERFECT besaß, PERFECT hat besessen) ◇ *My father owns a small business.* Mein Vater besitzt ein kleines Geschäft.

to **own up** VERB
zugeben (PRESENT gibt zu, IMPERFECT gab zu, PERFECT hat zugegeben) ◇ *to own up to something* etwas zugeben

**owner** NOUN
der Besitzer (PL die Besitzer)
die Besitzerin

**oxygen** NOUN
der Sauerstoff

**oyster** NOUN
die Auster

**ozone layer** NOUN
die Ozonschicht

# P

**PA** NOUN (= *personal assistant*)
der Chefsekretär (PL die Chefsekretäre)
die Chefsekretärin
◊ *She's a PA.* Sie ist Chefsekretärin.
♦ **the PA system** (*public address*) die
Lautsprecheranlage

**pace** NOUN
das Tempo (*speed*) ◊ *Technology is
developing at a rapid pace.* Die
Technologie entwickelt sich in schnellem
Tempo.
♦ **He was walking at a brisk pace.** Er ging
mit schnellen Schritten.

**Pacific** NOUN
der Pazifik

**pacifier** NOUN US
der Schnuller (PL die Schnuller)

to **pack** VERB
see also **pack** NOUN
packen ◊ *I'll help you pack.* Ich helfe
dir packen. ◊ *I've already packed my
case.* Ich habe meinen Koffer schon
gepackt.
♦ **Pack it in!** (*stop it*) Lass es!

**pack** NOUN
see also **pack** VERB
1 (*packet*)
die Packung ◊ *a pack of cigarettes* eine
Packung Zigaretten
2 (*of yoghurts, cans*)
der Pack (PL die Packs) ◊ *a six-pack* ein
Sechserpack
♦ **a pack of cards** ein Spiel Karten NEUT

**package** NOUN
das Paket (PL die Pakete)
♦ **a package holiday** eine Pauschalreise

**packed** ADJECTIVE
gerammelt voll ◊ *The cinema was
packed.* Das Kino war gerammelt voll.

**packed lunch** NOUN
das Lunchpaket (PL die Lunchpakete)
♦ **I take a packed lunch to school.** Ich
nehme für mittags etwas zum Essen in
die Schule mit.

**packet** NOUN
die Packung ◊ *a packet of cigarettes* eine
Packung Zigaretten

**pad** NOUN
der Notizblock (*notepad*) (PL die
Notizblöcke)

to **paddle** VERB
see also **paddle** NOUN
1 paddeln (*canoe*)
2 planschen (*in water*)

**paddle** NOUN
see also **paddle** VERB
das Paddel (*for canoe*) (PL die Paddel)
♦ **to go for a paddle** planschen gehen

**padlock** NOUN
das Vorhängeschloss (GEN des
Vorhängeschlosses, PL die
Vorhängeschlösser)

**page** NOUN
see also **page** VERB
die Seite (*of book*)

to **page** VERB
see also **page** NOUN
♦ **to page somebody** jemanden per Pager
benachrichtigen

**pager** NOUN
der Pager (PL die Pager)

**paid** VERB see pay

**paid** ADJECTIVE
bezahlt ◊ *three weeks' paid holiday* drei
Wochen bezahlter Urlaub

**pail** NOUN
der Eimer (PL die Eimer)

**pain** NOUN
der Schmerz (GEN des Schmerzes, PL die
Schmerzen) ◊ *a terrible pain* ein
furchtbarer Schmerz
♦ **I've got pains in my stomach.** Ich habe
Bauchschmerzen.
♦ **to be in pain** Schmerzen haben ◊ *She's
in a lot of pain.* Sie hat starke Schmerzen.
♦ **He's a real pain.** Er geht einem echt auf
die Nerven. (*informal*)

**painful** ADJECTIVE
schmerzhaft
♦ **to suffer from painful periods** starke
Periodenschmerzen haben
♦ **to be painful** wehtun ◊ *Is it painful?* Tut
es weh?

**painkiller** NOUN
das Schmerzmittel (PL die
Schmerzmittel)

**paint** NOUN
see also **paint** VERB
die Farbe

to **paint** VERB
see also **paint** NOUN
1 streichen (IMPERFECT strich, PERFECT hat
gestrichen) ◊ *to paint something green*
etwas grün streichen
2 (*pictures*)
malen ◊ *She painted a picture of the
house.* Sie hat von dem Haus ein Bild
gemalt.

**paintbrush** NOUN
der Pinsel (PL die Pinsel)

**painter** NOUN
der Maler (PL die Maler)
die Malerin
♦ **a painter and decorator** ein Anstreicher

**painting** NOUN

☞

1 das <u>Malen</u> ◊ *My hobby is painting.*
Malen ist mein Hobby.

2 (*picture*)
das <u>Bild</u> (PL die Bilder) ◊ *a painting by
Picasso* ein Bild von Picasso

**pair** NOUN
das <u>Paar</u> (PL die Paare) ◊ *a pair of shoes*
ein Paar Schuhe
♦ **a pair of scissors** eine Schere
♦ **a pair of trousers** eine Hose
♦ **a pair of jeans** eine Jeans
♦ **in pairs** paarweise ◊ *We work in pairs.*
Wir arbeiten paarweise.

**pajamas** PL NOUN US
der <u>Schlafanzug</u> (PL die Schlafanzüge)
◊ *my pajamas* mein Schlafanzug
♦ **a pair of pajamas** ein Schlafanzug

**Pakistan** NOUN
<u>Pakistan</u> NEUT
♦ **from Pakistan** aus Pakistan
♦ **to Pakistan** nach Pakistan

**Pakistani** NOUN
see also **Pakistani** ADJECTIVE
der <u>Pakistani</u> (PL die Pakistani)
die <u>Pakistani</u>

**Pakistani** ADJECTIVE
see also **Pakistani** NOUN
pakistanisch
♦ **He's Pakistani.** Er ist Pakistani.

**pal** NOUN
der <u>Kumpel</u> (*informal*) (PL die
Kumpel)
*der Kumpel is also used for women.*

**palace** NOUN
der <u>Palast</u> (PL die Paläste)

**pale** ADJECTIVE
<u>blass</u> ◊ *You're very pale.* Du bist sehr
blass.
♦ **a pale blue shirt** ein hellblaues Hemd

**Palestine** NOUN
<u>Palästina</u> NEUT
♦ **from Palestine** aus Palästina
♦ **to Palestine** nach Palästina

**Palestinian** ADJECTIVE
see also **Palestinian** NOUN
palästinensisch
♦ **He's Palestinian.** Er ist Palästinenser.

**Palestinian** NOUN
see also **Palestinian** ADJECTIVE
der <u>Palästinenser</u> (PL die Palästinenser)
die <u>Palästinenserin</u>

**palm** NOUN
der <u>Handteller</u> (*of hand*) (PL die
Handteller)
♦ **a palm tree** eine Palme

**pamphlet** NOUN
die <u>Broschüre</u>

**pan** NOUN
1 (*saucepan*)
der <u>Topf</u> (PL die Töpfe)
2 (*frying pan*)
die <u>Pfanne</u>

**pancake** NOUN
der <u>Pfannkuchen</u> (PL die Pfannkuchen)

**panic** NOUN
see also **panic** VERB
die <u>Panik</u>

to **panic** VERB
see also **panic** NOUN
in <u>Panik geraten</u> (PRESENT gerät in Panik,
IMPERFECT geriet in Panik, PERFECT ist in Panik
geraten) ◊ *She panicked.* Sie geriet in
Panik.
♦ **Don't panic!** Nur keine Panik!

**panther** NOUN
der <u>Panther</u> (PL die Panther)

**panties** PL NOUN
der <u>Slip</u> (PL die Slips) ◊ *a pair of panties*
ein Slip

**pantomime** NOUN
das <u>Weihnachtsmärchen</u> (PL die
Weihnachtsmärchen)

**pants** PL NOUN
1 die <u>Unterhose</u> (*underwear*) ◊ *a pair of
pants* eine Unterhose
2 die <u>Hose</u> (*trousers*) ◊ *a pair of pants*
eine Hose

**pantyhose** PL NOUN US
die <u>Strumpfhose</u>

**paper** NOUN
1 das <u>Papier</u> (PL die Papiere) ◊ *a piece of
paper* ein Stück Papier ◊ *a paper towel*
ein Papierhandtuch
2 (*newspaper*)
die <u>Zeitung</u> ◊ *I saw an advert in the
paper.* Ich habe eine Anzeige in der
Zeitung gesehen.
♦ **an exam paper** eine Klausur

**paperback** NOUN
das <u>Taschenbuch</u> (PL die
Taschenbücher)

**paper boy** NOUN
der <u>Zeitungsjunge</u> (GEN des
Zeitungsjungen, PL die Zeitungsjungen)

**paper clip** NOUN
die <u>Büroklammer</u>

**paper girl** NOUN
das <u>Zeitungsmädchen</u> (PL die
Zeitungsmädchen)

**paper round** NOUN
♦ **to do a paper round** Zeitungen austragen

**paperweight** NOUN
der <u>Briefbeschwerer</u> (PL die
Briefbeschwerer)

**paperwork** NOUN
die <u>Schreibarbeit</u> ◊ *I've got a lot of
paperwork to do.* Ich habe eine Menge
Schreibarbeit zu erledigen.

**parachute** NOUN
der <u>Fallschirm</u> (PL die Fallschirme)

**parade** NOUN
die <u>Parade</u>

**paradise** NOUN
das <u>Paradies</u> (GEN des Paradieses, PL die
Paradiese)

**paraffin** NOUN
das Petroleum ◊ *a paraffin lamp* eine
Petroleumlampe

**paragraph** NOUN
der Paragraf (GEN des Paragrafen, PL die
Paragrafen)

**parallel** ADJECTIVE
parallel

**paralyzed** ADJECTIVE
gelähmt

**paramedic** NOUN
der Sanitäter (PL die Sanitäter)
die Sanitäterin

**parcel** NOUN
das Paket (PL die Pakete)

**pardon** NOUN
♦**Pardon?** Wie bitte?

**parent** NOUN
[1] der Vater (*father*)
[2] die Mutter (*mother*)
♦**my parents** meine Eltern

**Paris** NOUN
Paris NEUT

**park** NOUN
| *see also* **park** VERB |
der Park (PL die Parks) ◊ *a national park*
ein Nationalpark ◊ *a theme park* ein
Themenpark
♦**a car park** ein Parkplatz MASC

to **park** VERB
| *see also* **park** NOUN |
parken ◊ *Where can I park my car?* Wo
kann ich mein Auto parken?
♦**We couldn't find anywhere to park.** Wir
haben nirgends einen Parkplatz
gefunden.

**parking** NOUN
das Parken ◊ *"no parking"* "Parken
verboten"

**parking lot** NOUN [US]
der Parkplatz (GEN des Parkplatzes, PL die
Parkplätze)

**parking meter** NOUN
die Parkuhr

**parking ticket** NOUN
der Strafzettel (PL die Strafzettel)

**parliament** NOUN
das Parlament (PL die Parlamente)

**parole** NOUN
♦**on parole** auf Bewährung

**parrot** NOUN
der Papagei (PL die Papageien)

**parsley** NOUN
die Petersilie

**part** NOUN
[1] (*section*)
der Teil (PL die Teile) ◊ *The first part of
the film was boring.* Der erste Teil des
Films war langweilig.
[2] (*component*)
das Teil (PL die Teile) ◊ *spare parts*
Ersatzteile

[3] (*in play, film*)
die Rolle
♦**to take part in something** an etwas
teilnehmen ◊ *A lot of people took part in
the demonstration.* An der
Demonstration haben viele Menschen
teilgenommen.

**particular** ADJECTIVE
bestimmt ◊ *I am looking for a particular
book.* Ich suche ein bestimmtes Buch.
♦**Are you looking for anything particular?**
Suchen Sie nach etwas Bestimmtem?
♦**nothing in particular** nichts Bestimmtes

**particularly** ADVERB
besonders

**parting** NOUN
der Scheitel (*in hair*) (PL die Scheitel)

**partly** ADVERB
zum Teil

**partner** NOUN
der Partner (PL die Partner)
die Partnerin

**part-time** ADJECTIVE, ADVERB
Teilzeit ◊ *a part-time job* eine
Teilzeitarbeit ◊ *She works part-time.* Sie
arbeitet Teilzeit.

**party** NOUN
[1] die Party (PL die Partys) ◊ *a birthday
party* eine Geburtstagsparty ◊ *a
Christmas party* eine Weihnachtsparty
◊ *a New Year party* eine Silvesterparty
[2] (*political*)
die Partei ◊ *the Conservative Party* die
Konservative Partei
[3] (*group*)
die Gruppe ◊ *a party of tourists* eine
Gruppe Touristen

**pass** NOUN
| *see also* **pass** VERB |
der Pass (GEN des Passes, PL die Pässe)
◊ *The pass was blocked with snow.* Der
Pass war zugeschneit. ◊ *That was a good
pass by Ferguson.* Das war ein guter
Pass von Ferguson.
♦**to get a pass** (*in exam*) bestehen ◊ *She
got a pass in her piano exam.* Sie hat
ihre Klavierprüfung bestanden. ◊ *I got six
passes.* Ich habe in sechs Fächern
bestanden.
♦**a bus pass (1)** (*monthly*) eine Monatskarte
für den Bus
♦**a bus pass (2)** (*for old-age pensioners*) eine
Seniorenkarte für den Bus

P

> ❶ *Almost all German cities operate an
> integrated public transport system; you
> can buy a weekly (**Wochenkarte**),
> monthly (**Monatskarte**) or yearly
> (**Jahreskarte**) pass which are valid for
> that period on all buses, trams and
> light railway vehicles in a particular
> zone.*

to **pass** VERB

see also **pass** NOUN

**1** (*give*)
**geben** (PRESENT **gibt**, IMPERFECT **gab**, PERFECT hat gegeben) ◊ *Could you pass me the salt, please?* Könntest du mir bitte das Salz geben?

**2** (*go by*)
**vergehen** (IMPERFECT **verging**, PERFECT ist vergangen) ◊ *The time has passed quickly.* Die Zeit ist schnell vergangen.

**3** (*on foot*)
**vorbeigehen an** +DAT (IMPERFECT **ging vorbei**, PERFECT **ist vorbeigegangen**) ◊ *I pass his house on my way to school.* Auf dem Weg zur Schule gehe ich an seinem Haus vorbei.

**4** (*in vehicle*)
**vorbeifahren an** +DAT (PRESENT **fährt vorbei**, IMPERFECT **fuhr vorbei**, PERFECT ist vorbeigefahren) ◊ *We passed the post office.* Wir sind an der Post vorbeigefahren.

**5** (*exam*)
**bestehen** (IMPERFECT **bestand**, PERFECT hat bestanden) ◊ *Did you pass?* Hast du bestanden?

♦ **to pass an exam** eine Prüfung bestehen ◊ *I hope I'll pass the exam.* Ich hoffe, dass ich die Prüfung bestehe.

to **pass out** VERB
**ohnmächtig werden** (*faint*) (PRESENT **wird ohnmächtig**, IMPERFECT **wurde ohnmächtig**, PERFECT ist ohnmächtig geworden)

**passage** NOUN
**1** (*piece of writing*)
der **Abschnitt** (PL die Abschnitte) ◊ *Read the passage carefully.* Lest den Abschnitt sorgfältig durch.
**2** (*corridor*)
der **Gang** (PL die Gänge)

**passenger** NOUN
der **Passagier** (PL die Passagiere)
die **Passagierin**

**passion** NOUN
die **Leidenschaft**

**passive** ADJECTIVE
**passiv**
♦ **passive smoking** das Passivrauchen

**Passover** NOUN
das **Passahfest**

**passport** NOUN
der **Pass** (GEN des Passes, PL die Pässe)
◊ *passport control* die Passkontrolle

**password** NOUN
das **Passwort** (PL die Passwörter)

**past** ADVERB, PREPOSITION

see also **past** NOUN

**nach** (*beyond*) ◊ *It's on the right, just past the station.* Es ist auf der rechten Seite, gleich nach dem Bahnhof. ◊ *It's quarter past nine.* Es ist Viertel nach neun.

♦ **It's past midnight.** Es ist schon nach Mitternacht.
♦ **It's half past ten.** Es ist halb elf.
♦ **to go past (1)** (*vehicle*) vorbeifahren ◊ *The bus went past without stopping.* Der Bus ist vorbeigefahren, ohne anzuhalten. ◊ *The bus goes past our house.* Der Bus fährt an unserem Haus vorbei.
♦ **to go past (2)** (*on foot*) vorbeigehen ◊ *He went past without saying hello.* Er ging vorbei, ohne hallo zu sagen. ◊ *I went past your house yesterday.* Ich bin gestern an eurem Haus vorbeigegangen.

**past** NOUN

see also **past** ADVERB

die **Vergangenheit** ◊ *She lives in the past.* Sie lebt in der Vergangenheit.
♦ **in the past** (*previously*) früher ◊ *That was common in the past.* Das war früher üblich.

**pasta** NOUN
die **Teigwaren** FEM PL ◊ *Pasta is easy to cook.* Teigwaren sind leicht zu kochen.

**paste** NOUN
der **Leim** (*glue*) (PL die Leime)

**pasteurized** ADJECTIVE
**pasteurisiert**

**pastime** NOUN
der **Zeitvertreib** (PL die Zeitvertreibe)
◊ *Crossword puzzles are a popular pastime.* Kreuzworträtsel sind ein beliebter Zeitvertreib.
♦ **Her favourite pastime is knitting.** Stricken ist ihre Lieblingsbeschäftigung.

**pastry** NOUN
der **Teig**
♦ **pastries** (*cakes*) das Gebäck SING

to **pat** VERB
**streicheln** (*dog, cat*) (PERFECT hat gestreichelt)

**patch** NOUN
**1** das **Stück** (PL die Stücke) ◊ *a patch of material* ein Stück Stoff
**2** (*for flat tyre*)
der **Flicken** (PL die Flicken)
♦ **He's got a bald patch.** Er hat eine kahle Stelle.

**patched** ADJECTIVE
**geflickt** ◊ *a pair of patched jeans* eine geflickte Jeans

**pâté** NOUN
die **Fleischpastete**
♦ **liver pâté** die Leberwurst

**path** NOUN
der **Weg** (PL die Wege)

**pathetic** ADJECTIVE
**schrecklich schlecht** ◊ *Our team was pathetic.* Unsere Mannschaft war schrecklich schlecht.

**patience** NOUN

**[1]** die Geduld ◊ *He hasn't got much patience.* Er hat nicht viel Geduld.
**[2]** die Patience (*card game*) ◊ *to play patience* Patience spielen

**patient** NOUN

see also **patient** ADJECTIVE

der Patient (GEN des Patienten, PL die Patienten)
die Patientin

**patient** ADJECTIVE

see also **patient** NOUN

geduldig

**patio** NOUN
die Terrasse

**patriotic** ADJECTIVE
patriotisch

**patrol** NOUN
**[1]** die Patrouille (*military*)
**[2]** die Streife (*of police*)

**patrol car** NOUN
der Streifenwagen (PL die Streifenwagen)

**pattern** NOUN
das Muster (PL die Muster) ◊ *a geometric pattern* ein geometrisches Muster ◊ *a sewing pattern* ein Nähmuster

**pause** NOUN
die Pause

**pavement** NOUN
der Bürgersteig (PL die Bürgersteige)

**pavilion** NOUN
der Pavillon (PL die Pavillons)

**paw** NOUN
die Pfote

**pay** NOUN

see also **pay** VERB

die Bezahlung

to **pay** VERB

see also **pay** NOUN

bezahlen (PERFECT hat bezahlt) ◊ *They pay me more on Sundays.* Sie bezahlen mir sonntags mehr. ◊ *to pay by cheque* mit Scheck bezahlen ◊ *to pay by credit card* mit Kreditkarte bezahlen
♦ **to pay for something** für etwas bezahlen ◊ *I paid fifty marks for it.* Ich habe fünfzig Mark dafür bezahlt. ◊ *I paid for my ticket.* Ich habe meine Fahrkarte bezahlt.
♦ **to pay extra for something** für etwas extra bezahlen ◊ *You have to pay extra for parking.* Fürs Parken müssen Sie extra bezahlen.
♦ **to pay attention** aufpassen ◊ *You should pay more attention.* Du solltest besser aufpassen.
♦ **Don't pay any attention to him.** Beachte ihn einfach nicht.
♦ **to pay somebody a visit** jemanden besuchen ◊ *Paul paid us a visit last night.* Paul hat uns gestern Abend besucht.
♦ **to pay somebody back** (*money*) es jemandem zurückzahlen ◊ *I'll pay you*

**patient → pedestrian crossing**

*back tomorrow.* Ich zahle es dir morgen zurück.

**payment** NOUN
die Bezahlung

**payphone** NOUN
der Münzfernsprecher (PL die Münzfernsprecher)

**PC** NOUN (= *personal computer*)
der PC (PL die PCs) ◊ *She typed the report on her PC.* Sie hat den Bericht am PC erfasst.

**PE** NOUN (= *physical education*)
der Sportunterricht

**pea** NOUN
die Erbse

**peace** NOUN
**[1]** der Frieden (*after war*)
**[2]** die Stille (*quietness*)

**peaceful** ADJECTIVE
**[1]** ruhig (*calm*) ◊ *a peaceful afternoon* ein ruhiger Nachmittag
**[2]** friedlich (*not violent*) ◊ *a peaceful protest* ein friedlicher Protest

**peach** NOUN
der Pfirsich (PL die Pfirsiche)

**peacock** NOUN
der Pfau (PL die Pfauen)

**peak** NOUN
der Gipfel (*of mountain*) (PL die Gipfel)
♦ **the peak rate** der Spitzentarif ◊ *You pay the peak rate for calls at this time of day.* Um diese Tageszeit zahlt man fürs Telefonieren den Spitzentarif.
♦ **in peak season** in der Hochsaison

**peanut** NOUN
die Erdnuss (PL die Erdnüsse) ◊ *a packet of peanuts* eine Packung Erdnüsse

**peanut butter** NOUN
die Erdnussbutter ◊ *a peanut butter sandwich* ein Brot mit Erdnussbutter

**pear** NOUN
die Birne

**pearl** NOUN
die Perle

**pebble** NOUN
der Kieselstein (PL die Kieselsteine)
♦ **a pebble beach** ein Kieselstrand MASC

**peckish** ADJECTIVE
♦ **to feel a bit peckish** ein bisschen Hunger haben

**peculiar** ADJECTIVE
eigenartig ◊ *He's a peculiar person.* Er ist ein eigenartiger Mensch. ◊ *It tastes peculiar.* Es schmeckt eigenartig.

**pedal** NOUN
das Pedal (PL die Pedale)

**pedestrian** NOUN
der Fußgänger (PL die Fußgänger)
die Fußgängerin

**pedestrian crossing** NOUN
der Fußgängerüberweg (PL die Fußgängerüberwege)

**P**

**pedestrianized** ADJECTIVE
◆**a pedestrianized street** eine Fußgängerzone
**pedigree** ADJECTIVE
reinrassig (*animal*) ◊ *a pedigree labrador* ein reinrassiger Labrador
**pee** NOUN
◆**to have a pee** pinkeln (*informal*)
**peek** NOUN
◆**to have a peek at something** einen kurzen Blick auf etwas werfen ◊ *I had a peek at your new dress.* Ich habe einen kurzen Blick auf dein neues Kleid geworfen.
**peel** NOUN
[see also **peel** VERB]
die Schale (*of orange*)
to **peel** VERB
[see also **peel** NOUN]
[1] schälen ◊ *Shall I peel the potatoes?* Soll ich die Kartoffeln schälen?
[2] sich schälen ◊ *My nose is peeling.* Meine Nase schält sich.
**peg** NOUN
[1] (*for coats*)
der Haken (PL die Haken)
[2] (*clothes peg*)
die Wäscheklammer
[3] (*tent peg*)
der Hering (PL die Heringe)
**Pekinese** NOUN
der Pekinese (GEN des Pekinesen, PL die Pekinesen)
**pelican crossing** NOUN
die Fußgängerampel
**pellet** NOUN
die Schrotkugel (*for gun*)
**pelvis** NOUN
das Becken (PL die Becken)
**pen** NOUN
der Schreiber (PL die Schreiber)
to **penalize** VERB
bestrafen (PERFECT hat bestraft)
**penalty** NOUN
[1] (*punishment*)
die Strafe ◊ *the death penalty* die Todesstrafe
[2] (*in football*)
der Elfmeter (PL die Elfmeter)
[3] (*in rugby*)
der Strafstoß (GEN des Strafstoßes, PL die Strafstöße)
◆**a penalty shoot-out** ein Elfmeterschießen NEUT
**pence** PL NOUN
die Pence MASC PL
**pencil** NOUN
der Bleistift (PL die Bleistifte)
◆**in pencil** mit Bleistift
**pencil case** NOUN
das Federmäppchen (PL die Federmäppchen)
**pencil sharpener** NOUN

der Bleistiftspitzer (PL die Bleistiftspitzer)
**pendant** NOUN
der Anhänger (PL die Anhänger)
**pen friend** NOUN
der Brieffreund (PL die Brieffreunde)
die Brieffreundin
**penguin** NOUN
der Pinguin (PL die Pinguine)
**penicillin** NOUN
das Penizillin
**penis** NOUN
der Penis (GEN des Penis, PL die Penisse)
**penitentiary** NOUN [US]
das Gefängnis (GEN des Gefängnisses, PL die Gefängnisse)
**penknife** NOUN
das Taschenmesser (PL die Taschenmesser)
**penny** NOUN
der Penny (PL die Pennys *or* Pence)
**pension** NOUN
die Rente
**pensioner** NOUN
der Rentner (PL die Rentner)
die Rentnerin
**pentathlon** NOUN
der Fünfkampf (PL die Fünfkämpfe)
**people** PL NOUN
[1] die Leute PL ◊ *The people were nice.* Die Leute waren nett. ◊ *a lot of people* viele Leute
[2] die Menschen MASC PL (*individuals*) ◊ *six people* sechs Menschen ◊ *several people* mehrere Menschen
◆**German people** die Deutschen
◆**black people** die Schwarzen
◆**People say that ...** Man sagt, dass ...
**pepper** NOUN
[1] der Pfeffer (*spice*) ◊ *Pass the pepper, please.* Gib mir mal bitte den Pfeffer.
[2] die Paprikaschote (*vegetable*) ◊ *a green pepper* eine grüne Paprikaschote
**peppermill** NOUN
die Pfeffermühle
**peppermint** NOUN
das Pfefferminzbonbon (*sweet*) (PL die Pfefferminzbonbons)
◆**peppermint chewing gum** der Kaugummi mit Pfefferminzgeschmack
**per** PREPOSITION
pro ◊ *per day* pro Tag ◊ *per week* pro Woche
◆**thirty miles per hour** dreißig Meilen in der Stunde
**per cent** ADVERB
das Prozent ◊ *fifty per cent* fünfzig Prozent
**percentage** NOUN
der Prozentsatz (GEN des Prozentsatzes, PL die Prozentsätze)
**percolator** NOUN
die Kaffeemaschine

**percussion** NOUN
das <u>Schlagzeug</u> (PL die Schlagzeuge)
◊ *I play percussion.* Ich spiele
Schlagzeug.

**perfect** I ADJECTIVE
<u>perfekt</u> ◊ *Manfred speaks perfect
English.* Manfred spricht perfekt
Englisch.

**perfectly** ADVERB
[1] <u>ganz</u> ◊ *You know perfectly well what
happened.* Du weißt ganz genau, was
passiert ist.
[2] <u>perfekt</u> (*very well*) ◊ *The system
worked perfectly.* Das System hat perfekt
funktioniert.

to **perform** VERB
<u>spielen</u> (*act, play*)

**performance** NOUN
[1] die <u>Vorstellung</u> (*show*) ◊ *The
performance lasts two hours.* Die
Vorstellung dauert zwei Stunden.
[2] die <u>Darstellung</u> (*acting*) ◊ *his
performance as Hamlet* seine Darstellung
des Hamlet
[3] die <u>Leistung</u> (*results*) ◊ *the team's
poor performance* die schwache Leistung
der Mannschaft

**perfume** NOUN
das <u>Parfüm</u> (PL die Parfüme)

**perhaps** ADVERB
<u>vielleicht</u> ◊ *a bit boring, perhaps* etwas
langweilig vielleicht ◊ *Perhaps he's ill.*
Vielleicht ist er krank. ◊ *perhaps not*
vielleicht nicht

**period** NOUN
[1] die <u>Zeit</u> ◊ *for a limited period* für eine
begrenzte Zeit
[2] die <u>Epoche</u> (*in history*) ◊ *the Victorian
period* die viktorianische Epoche
[3] die <u>Periode</u> (*menstruation*) ◊ *I'm
having my period.* Ich habe meine
Periode.
[4] die <u>Stunde</u> (*lesson time*) ◊ *Each period
lasts forty minutes.* Jede Stunde dauert
vierzig Minuten.

**perm** NOUN
die <u>Dauerwelle</u> ◊ *She's got a perm.* Sie
hat eine Dauerwelle.
♦ **to have a perm** sich eine Dauerwelle
machen lassen ◊ *I'm going to have a
perm.* Ich lasse mir eine Dauerwelle
machen.

**permanent** ADJECTIVE
[1] <u>dauerhaft</u> (*damage, solution,
relationship*) ◊ *We need a permanent
solution.* Wir brauchen eine dauerhafte
Lösung.
[2] <u>dauernd</u> (*difficulties, tension*) ◊ *a
permanent headache* dauernde
Kopfschmerzen
[3] <u>fest</u> (*job, address*) ◊ *I'm hoping to get a
permanent job.* Ich hoffe, ich finde eine
feste Arbeit.

**permission** NOUN
die <u>Erlaubnis</u> (PL die Erlaubnisse) ◊ *to
ask somebody's permission* jemanden
um Erlaubnis bitten
♦ **Could I have permission to leave early?**
Darf ich früher gehen?

**permit** NOUN
der <u>Schein</u> (PL die Scheine) ◊ *a fishing
permit* ein Angelschein

to **persecute** VERB
<u>verfolgen</u> (PERFECT hat verfolgt)

**Persian** ADJECTIVE
♦ **a Persian cat** eine Perserkatze

**persistent** ADJECTIVE
<u>hartnäckig</u> (*person*)

**person** NOUN
[1] der <u>Mensch</u> (GEN des Menschen, PL die
Menschen) ◊ *She's a very nice person.*
Sie ist ein netter Mensch.
[2] (*in grammar*)
die <u>Person</u> ◊ *first person singular* erste
Person Singular
♦ **in person** persönlich

**personal** ADJECTIVE
<u>persönlich</u>

**personality** NOUN
die <u>Persönlichkeit</u>

**personally** ADVERB
<u>persönlich</u> ◊ *I don't know him
personally.* Ich kenne ihn nicht
persönlich. ◊ *Personally I don't agree.* Ich
persönlich bin nicht einverstanden.

**personal stereo** NOUN
der <u>Walkman</u> ® (PL die Walkmans)

**personnel** NOUN
das <u>Personal</u>

**perspiration** NOUN
der <u>Schweiß</u>

to **persuade** VERB
<u>überreden</u> (PERFECT hat überredet)
♦ **to persuade somebody to do something**
jemanden überreden, etwas zu tun ◊ *She
persuaded me to go with her.* Sie hat
mich überredet mitzukommen.

**Peru** NOUN
<u>Peru</u> NEUT

**Peruvian** ADJECTIVE
<u>peruanisch</u>

**pessimist** NOUN
der <u>Pessimist</u> (GEN des Pessimisten, PL die
Pessimisten)
die <u>Pessimistin</u>
◊ *I'm a pessimist.* Ich bin Pessimist.

**pessimistic** ADJECTIVE
<u>pessimistisch</u>

**pest** NOUN
die <u>Nervensäge</u> (*person*) ◊ *He's a real
pest!* Er ist eine echte Nervensäge!

to **pester** VERB
<u>belästigen</u> (PERFECT hat belästigt) ◊ *I wish
she would stop pestering me.* Ich

**P**

☞

wünschte, sie würde aufhören, mich zu belästigen.

♦ **The children pestered her to take them to the zoo.** Die Kinder ließen ihr keine Ruhe, mit ihnen in den Zoo zu gehen.

**pesticide** NOUN
das Pestizid

**pet** NOUN
das Haustier (PL die Haustiere) ◊ *Have you got a pet?* Hast du ein Haustier?

♦ **She's the teacher's pet.** Sie ist das Schätzchen der Lehrerin.

**petition** NOUN
die Petition ◊ *a petition for the abolition of school uniform* eine Petition für die Abschaffung der Schuluniform

**petrified** ADJECTIVE
♦ **to be petrified of something** panische Angst vor etwas haben ◊ *She's petrified of spiders.* Sie hat panische Angst vor Spinnen.

**petrol** NOUN
das Benzin (PL die Benzine)
♦ **unleaded petrol** bleifreies Benzin
♦ **leaded petrol** verbleites Benzin
♦ **Four-star petrol, please.** Super, bitte.

**petrol station** NOUN
die Tankstelle

**petrol tank** NOUN
der Benzintank (PL die Benzintanks)

**phantom** NOUN
der Geist (PL die Geister)

**pharmacy** NOUN
die Apotheke

**pheasant** NOUN
der Fasan (PL die Fasane)

**philosophy** NOUN
die Philosophie

**phobia** NOUN
die Phobie

**phone** NOUN
see also **phone** VERB
das Telefon (PL die Telefone) ◊ *Where's the phone?* Wo ist das Telefon? ◊ *Is there a phone here?* Gibt es hier ein Telefon?

♦ **by phone** telefonisch
♦ **to be on the phone (1)** (*speaking*) telefonieren ◊ *She's on the phone at the moment.* Sie telefoniert gerade.
♦ **to be on the phone (2)** (*connected*) Telefonanschluss haben ◊ *They're not on the phone.* Sie haben keinen Telefonanschluss.
♦ **Can I use the phone, please?** Kann ich mal bitte telefonieren?

to **phone** VERB
see also **phone** NOUN
anrufen (IMPERFECT rief an, PERFECT hat angerufen) ◊ *I tried to phone you yesterday.* Ich habe gestern versucht, dich anzurufen.

**phone bill** NOUN
die Telefonrechnung

**phone book** NOUN
das Telefonbuch (PL die Telefonbücher)

**phone box** NOUN
die Telefonzelle

**phone call** NOUN
der Anruf (PL die Anrufe) ◊ *There's a phone call for you.* Da ist ein Anruf für Sie.

♦ **to make a phone call** telefonieren ◊ *Can I make a phone call?* Kann ich telefonieren?

**phonecard** NOUN
die Telefonkarte

**phone number** NOUN
die Telefonnummer

**photo** NOUN
das Foto (PL die Fotos) ◊ *to take a photo* ein Foto machen ◊ *to take a photo of somebody* ein Foto von jemandem machen

**photocopier** NOUN
der Fotokopierer (PL die Fotokopierer)

**photocopy** NOUN
see also **photocopy** VERB
die Fotokopie

to **photocopy** VERB
see also **photocopy** NOUN
fotokopieren (PERFECT hat fotokopiert)

**photograph** NOUN
see also **photograph** VERB
das Foto (PL die Fotos) ◊ *to take a photograph* ein Foto machen ◊ *to take a photograph of somebody* ein Foto von jemandem machen

Be careful not to translate **photograph** by **Fotograf**.

to **photograph** VERB
see also **photograph** NOUN
fotografieren (PERFECT hat fotografiert)

**photographer** NOUN
der Fotograf (GEN des Fotografen, PL die Fotografen)
die Fotografin
◊ *She's a photographer.* Sie ist Fotografin.

**photography** NOUN
die Fotografie ◊ *My hobby is photography.* Mein Hobby ist die Fotografie.

**phrase** NOUN
die Wendung

**phrase book** NOUN
der Sprachführer (PL die Sprachführer)

**physical** ADJECTIVE
see also **physical** NOUN
körperlich (*of the body*) ◊ *physical exercise* körperliche Bewegung
♦ **physical education** der Sportunterricht
♦ **physical therapist** (*man*) der Krankengymnast

**physical** NOUN US
see also **physical** ADJECTIVE

die ärztliche Untersuchung
**physicist** NOUN
der Physiker (PL die Physiker)
die Physikerin
◊ *He's a physicist.* Er ist Physiker.
**physics** NOUN
die Physik ◊ *She teaches physics.* Sie
unterrichtet Physik.
**physiotherapist** NOUN
der Krankengymnast (GEN des
Krankengymnasten, PL die
Krankengymnasten)
die Krankengymnastin
**physiotherapy** NOUN
die Krankengymnastik
**pianist** NOUN
der Pianist (GEN des Pianisten, PL die
Pianisten)
die Pianistin
**piano** NOUN
das Klavier (PL die Klaviere) ◊ *I play the
piano.* Ich spiele Klavier. ◊ *I have piano
lessons.* Ich nehme Klavierstunden.
**pick** NOUN
⬚ *see also* **pick** VERB
♦**Take your pick!** Du hast die Wahl!
to **pick** VERB
⬚ *see also* **pick** NOUN
[1] (*choose*)
auswählen (PERFECT hat ausgewählt) ◊ *I
picked the biggest piece.* Ich habe das
größte Stück ausgewählt. ◊ *I've been
picked for the team.* Ich bin für die
Mannschaft ausgewählt worden.
[2] (*fruit, flowers*)
pflücken
♦**to pick on somebody** auf jemandem
herumhacken ◊ *She's always picking on
me.* Sie hackt dauernd auf mir herum.
♦**to pick out** auswählen ◊ *I like them all –
it's difficult to pick one out.* Sie gefallen
mir alle – es ist schwierig, eins
auszuwählen.
♦**to pick up (1)** (*collect*) abholen ◊ *We'll
come to the airport to pick you up.* Wir
holen dich am Flughafen ab.
♦**to pick up (2)** (*from floor*) aufheben
◊ *Could you help me pick up the toys?*
Kannst du mir helfen, die Spielsachen
aufzuheben?
♦**to pick up (3)** (*learn*) aufschnappen
(*informal*) ◊ *I picked up some Spanish
during my holiday.* Ich habe während der
Ferien etwas Spanisch aufgeschnappt.
**pickpocket** NOUN
der Taschendieb (PL die Taschendiebe)
die Taschendiebin
**picnic** NOUN
das Picknick (PL die Picknicke)
♦**to have a picnic** picknicken ◊ *We had a
picnic on the beach.* Wir haben am
Strand gepicknickt.
**picture** NOUN

[1] das Bild (PL die Bilder) ◊ *Children's
books have lots of pictures.*
Kinderbücher sind voller Bilder.
♦**to draw a picture of something** etwas
zeichnen
[2] das Foto (PL die Fotos) ◊ *My picture
was in the paper.* Mein Foto war in der
Zeitung.
[3] (*painting*)
das Gemälde (PL die Gemälde) ◊ *a
famous picture* ein berühmtes Gemälde
♦**to paint a picture of something** etwas
malen
♦**the pictures** (*cinema*) das Kino ◊ *Shall we
go to the pictures?* Sollen wir ins Kino
gehen?
**picturesque** ADJECTIVE
malerisch
**pie** NOUN
[1] (*savoury*)
die Pastete
[2] (*sweet*)
der Obstkuchen (PL die Obstkuchen)
♦**an apple pie** ein gedeckter Apfelkuchen
**piece** NOUN
das Stück (PL die Stücke) ◊ *A small piece,
please.* Ein kleines Stück, bitte.
♦**a piece of furniture** ein Möbelstück
♦**a piece of advice** ein Ratschlag MASC
**pier** NOUN
der Pier (PL die Piere)
**pierced** ADJECTIVE
[1] durchstochen ◊ *I've got pierced ears.*
Ich habe durchstochene Ohrläppchen.
[2] gepierct ◊ *She's got a pierced nose.*
Sie hat eine gepiercte Nase.
**piercing** ADJECTIVE
durchdringend (*cry*)
**pig** NOUN
das Schwein (PL die Schweine)
**pigeon** NOUN
die Taube
**piggyback** NOUN
♦**to give somebody a piggyback**
jemanden huckepack nehmen
**piggy bank** NOUN
das Sparschwein (PL die Sparschweine)
**pigtail** NOUN
der Zopf (PL die Zöpfe)
**pile** NOUN
[1] (*tidy*)
der Stapel (PL die Stapel)
[2] (*untidy*)
der Haufen (PL die Haufen)
**piles** PL NOUN
die Hämorrhoiden PL
**pile-up** NOUN
der Auffahrunfall (PL die Auffahrunfälle)
**pill** NOUN
die Pille
♦**to be on the pill** die Pille nehmen
**pillar** NOUN
die Säule

**P**

**pillar box** NOUN
der Briefkasten (PL die Briefkästen)
**pillow** NOUN
das Kopfkissen (PL die Kopfkissen)
**pilot** NOUN
der Pilot (GEN des Piloten, PL die Piloten)
die Pilotin
◊ *He's a pilot.* Er ist Pilot.
**pimple** NOUN
der Pickel (PL die Pickel)
**pin** NOUN
die Stecknadel
♦ **I've got pins and needles in my foot.**
Mein Fuß ist eingeschlafen.
**PIN** NOUN (= *personal identification
number*)
die PIN-Nummer
**pinafore** NOUN
die Schürze
**pinball** NOUN
der Flipper (PL die Flipper)
♦ **to play pinball** flippern
♦ **a pinball machine** ein Flipper
to **pinch** VERB
[1] kneifen (IMPERFECT kniff, PERFECT hat
gekniffen) ◊ *He pinched me!* Er hat mich
gekniffen!
[2] klauen (*informal: steal*) ◊ *Who's
pinched my pen?* Wer hat meinen
Schreiber geklaut?
**pine** NOUN
die Kiefer ◊ *a pine table* ein Kieferntisch
MASC
**pineapple** NOUN
die Ananas (PL die Ananas)
**pink** ADJECTIVE
rosa
*rosa is invariable.*
◊ *a pink shirt* ein rosa Hemd
**pint** NOUN
das Pint (PL die Pints)

> ⓘ *In Germany measurements are in
> litres and centilitres. A pint is about 0.6
> litres. German people don't drink pints
> of beer, they are more likely to order
> **ein großes Bier**.*

♦ **to have a pint** ein Bier trinken ◊ *He's
gone out for a pint.* Er ist ein Bier trinken
gegangen.
**pipe** NOUN
[1] (*for water, gas*)
das Rohr (PL die Rohre) ◊ *The pipes
froze.* Die Rohre sind eingefroren.
[2] (*for smoking*)
die Pfeife ◊ *He smokes a pipe.* Er raucht
Pfeife.
♦ **the pipes** (*bagpipes*) der Dudelsack SING
◊ *He plays the pipes.* Er spielt Dudelsack.
**pirate** NOUN
der Pirat (GEN des Piraten, PL die Piraten)
**pirated** ADJECTIVE

♦ **a pirated video** ein Raubvideo NEUT
**Pisces** SING NOUN
die Fische MASC PL ◊ *I'm Pisces.* Ich bin
Fisch.
**pissed** ADJECTIVE
besoffen (*informal*)
**pissed off** ADJECTIVE
♦ **I'm pissed off with him.** Ich hab die
Schnauze voll von ihm. (*rude*)
**pistol** NOUN
die Pistole
**pitch** NOUN
│ *see also* **pitch** VERB │
der Platz (GEN des Platzes, PL die Plätze)
◊ *a football pitch* ein Fußballplatz
to **pitch** VERB
│ *see also* **pitch** NOUN │
aufschlagen (*tent*) (PRESENT schlägt auf,
IMPERFECT schlug auf, PERFECT hat
aufgeschlagen) ◊ *We pitched our tent
near the beach.* Wir haben unser Zelt in
der Nähe des Strandes aufgeschlagen.
**pity** NOUN
│ *see also* **pity** VERB │
das Mitleid
♦ **What a pity!** Wie schade!
to **pity** VERB
│ *see also* **pity** NOUN │
bemitleiden (PERFECT hat bemitleidet)
**pizza** NOUN
die Pizza (PL die Pizzas)
**place** NOUN
│ *see also* **place** VERB │
[1] (*location*)
der Ort (PL die Orte) ◊ *It's a quiet place.*
Es ist ein ruhiger Ort. ◊ *There are a lot of
interesting places to visit.* Es gibt viele
interessante Orte zu besuchen.
[2] (*space*)
der Platz (GEN des Platzes, PL die Plätze)
◊ *a parking place* ein Parkplatz ◊ *a
university place* ein Studienplatz
♦ **to change places** die Plätze tauschen
◊ *Tamsin, change places with Christine!*
Tamsin, tausch die Plätze mit Christine!
♦ **to take place** stattfinden
♦ **at your place** bei dir ◊ *Shall we meet at
your place?* Sollen wir uns bei dir
treffen?
♦ **to my place** zu mir ◊ *Do you want to
come round to my place?* Willst du noch
zu mir mitkommen?
to **place** VERB
│ *see also* **place** NOUN │
legen ◊ *He placed his hand on hers.* Er
legte seine Hand auf ihre.
♦ **He was placed third.** Er wurde Dritter.
**plaid** ADJECTIVE
kariert ◊ *a plaid shirt* ein kariertes Hemd
**plain** NOUN
│ *see also* **plain** ADJECTIVE │
die Ebene

**plain** ADJECTIVE, ADVERB

see also **plain** NOUN

[1] einfarbig (*self-coloured*) ◊ *a plain carpet* ein einfarbiger Teppich
[2] einfach (*not fancy*) ◊ *a plain white blouse* eine einfache weiße Bluse

**plain chocolate** NOUN
die bittere Schokolade

**plait** NOUN
der Zopf (PL die Zöpfe) ◊ *She wears her hair in a plait.* Sie trägt einen Zopf.

**plan** NOUN

see also **plan** VERB

der Plan (PL die Pläne) ◊ *What are your plans for the holidays?* Welche Ferienpläne habt ihr? ◊ *to make plans* Pläne machen ◊ *a plan of the campsite* ein Plan des Zeltplatzes
♦ **Everything went according to plan.** Alles lief nach Plan.
♦ **my essay plan** das Konzept für meinen Aufsatz

to **plan** VERB

see also **plan** NOUN

planen ◊ *We're planning a trip to Germany.* Wir planen eine Reise nach Deutschland. ◊ *Plan your revision carefully.* Plant eure Stoffwiederholung sorgfältig.
♦ **to plan to do something** vorhaben, etwas zu tun ◊ *I'm planning to get a job in the holidays.* Ich habe vor, mir einen Ferienjob zu suchen.

**plane** NOUN
das Flugzeug (PL die Flugzeuge) ◊ *by plane* mit dem Flugzeug

**planet** NOUN
der Planet (GEN des Planeten, PL die Planeten)

**planning** NOUN
die Planung ◊ *family planning* die Familienplanung
♦ **The trip needs careful planning.** Die Reise muss sorgfältig geplant werden.

**plant** NOUN

see also **plant** VERB

[1] die Pflanze ◊ *to water the plants* die Pflanzen gießen
[2] die Fabrik (*factory*)

to **plant** VERB

see also **plant** NOUN

pflanzen

**plant pot** NOUN
der Blumentopf (PL die Blumentöpfe)

**plaque** NOUN
[1] die Gedenktafel (*to famous person, event*)
[2] der Zahnbelag (*on teeth*)

**plaster** NOUN
[1] (*sticking plaster*)

das Pflaster (PL die Pflaster) ◊ *Have you got a plaster, by any chance?* Hast du zufälligerweise ein Pflaster?
[2] (*for fracture*)
der Gips (GEN des Gipses, PL die Gipse) ◊ *Her leg's in plaster.* Sie hat das Bein in Gips.

**plastic** NOUN

see also **plastic** ADJECTIVE

das Plastik ◊ *It's made of plastic.* Es ist aus Plastik.

**plastic** ADJECTIVE

see also **plastic** NOUN

aus Plastik ◊ *a plastic mac* ein Regenmantel aus Plastik
♦ **a plastic bag** eine Plastiktüte

**plate** NOUN
der Teller (*for food*) (PL die Teller)

**platform** NOUN
[1] (*at station*)
der Bahnsteig (PL die Bahnsteige) ◊ *on platform seven* auf Bahnsteig sieben
[2] (*for performers*)
das Podium (PL die Podien)

**play** NOUN

see also **play** VERB

das Stück (PL die Stücke) ◊ *a play by Shakespeare* ein Stück von Shakespeare ◊ *to put on a play* ein Stück aufführen

to **play** VERB

see also **play** NOUN

[1] spielen ◊ *He's playing with his friends.* Er spielt mit seinen Freunden. ◊ *What sort of music do they play?* Welche Art von Musik spielen sie? ◊ *I play hockey.* Ich spiele Hockey. ◊ *I play the guitar.* Ich spiele Gitarre. ◊ *She's always playing that record.* Sie spielt dauernd diese Platte.
[2] spielen gegen (*against person, team*) ◊ *Germany will play Scotland next month.* Deutschland spielt nächsten Monat gegen Schottland.

to **play down** VERB
herunterspielen (PERFECT hat heruntergespielt) ◊ *He tried to play down his illness.* Er versuchte, die Schwere seiner Krankheit herunterzuspielen.

**player** NOUN
der Spieler (PL die Spieler)
die Spielerin
◊ *a football player* ein Fußballspieler

**playful** ADJECTIVE
verspielt

**playground** NOUN
[1] (*at school*)
der Schulhof (PL die Schulhöfe)
[2] (*in park*)
der Spielplatz (GEN des Spielplatzes, PL die Spielplätze)

**playgroup** NOUN
die Spielgruppe

P

**playing card** NOUN
die Spielkarte

**playing field** NOUN
der Sportplatz (GEN des Sportplatzes, PL
die Sportplätze)

**playtime** NOUN
die Pause

to **play up** VERB
♦ **The engine's playing up again.** Der
Motor macht schon wieder
Schwierigkeiten.

**playwright** NOUN
der Dramatiker (PL die Dramatiker)
die Dramatikerin

**pleasant** ADJECTIVE
angenehm

**please** EXCLAMATION
bitte ◊ *Two coffees, please.* Zwei Kaffee
bitte.

**pleased** ADJECTIVE
1 erfreut (*happy*) ◊ *My mother's not
going to be very pleased.* Meine Mutter
wird nicht sehr erfreut sein.
2 zufrieden (*satisfied*) ◊ *It's beautiful,
she'll be pleased with it.* Es ist
wunderschön, sie wird damit sehr
zufrieden sein.
♦ **to be pleased about something** sich über
etwas freuen ◊ *Are you pleased about
the exam results?* Freust du dich über die
Prüfungsergebnisse?
♦ **Pleased to meet you!** Angenehm!

**pleasure** NOUN
das Vergnügen (PL die Vergnügen) ◊ *I
read for pleasure.* Ich lese zum
Vergnügen.

**plenty** NOUN
mehr als genug ◊ *I've got plenty.* Ich
habe mehr als genug. ◊ *That's plenty,
thanks.* Danke, das ist mehr als genug.
♦ **I've got plenty to do.** Ich habe viel zu tun.
♦ **plenty of (1)** viele ◊ *There were plenty of
opportunities.* Es gab viele
Möglichkeiten.
♦ **plenty of (2)** (*more than enough*)
genügend ◊ *I've got plenty of money.* Ich
habe genügend Geld. ◊ *We've got plenty
of time.* Wir haben genügend Zeit.

**pliers** PL NOUN
die Zange SING
♦ **a pair of pliers** eine Zange

**plot** NOUN
see also **plot** VERB
1 die Handlung (*of story, play*)
2 die Verschwörung (*against somebody*)
◊ *a plot against the president* eine
Verschwörung gegen den Präsidenten
♦ **a plot of land** ein Stück Land NEUT
♦ **a vegetable plot** ein Gemüsebeet NEUT

to **plot** VERB
see also **plot** NOUN
planen ◊ *They were plotting to kill him.*
Sie planten, ihn zu töten.

**plough** NOUN
see also **plough** VERB
der Pflug (PL die Pflüge)

to **plough** VERB
see also **plough** NOUN
pflügen

**plug** NOUN
1 (*electrical*)
der Stecker (PL die Stecker) ◊ *The plug is
faulty.* Der Stecker ist kaputt.
2 (*for sink*)
der Stöpsel (PL die Stöpsel)

to **plug in** VERB
einstecken (PERFECT hat eingesteckt) ◊ *Is it
plugged in?* Ist es eingesteckt?

**plum** NOUN
die Pflaume ◊ *plum jam* die
Pflaumenmarmelade

**plumber** NOUN
der Klempner (PL die Klempner)
die Klempnerin
◊ *He's a plumber.* Er ist Klempner.

**plump** ADJECTIVE
rundlich

to **plunge** VERB
tauchen

**plural** NOUN
der Plural (PL die Plurale)

**plus** PREPOSITION, ADJECTIVE
plus ◊ *Four plus three equals seven.* Vier
plus drei macht sieben. ◊ *I got a B plus.*
Ich habe eine Zwei plus bekommen.

ⓘ *In Germany, grades are given from
1 to 6, with 1 being the best.*

♦ **three children plus a dog** drei Kinder und
ein Hund

**p.m.** ABBREVIATION
♦ **at eight p.m.** um acht Uhr abends

ⓘ *In Germany times are often given
using the 24-hour clock.*

◊ *at two p.m.* um vierzehn Uhr

**pneumonia** NOUN
die Lungenentzündung

**poached** ADJECTIVE
♦ **a poached egg** ein verlorenes Ei NEUT

**pocket** NOUN
die Tasche
♦ **pocket money** das Taschengeld ◊ *eight
pounds a week pocket money* acht Pfund
Taschengeld pro Woche

**pocket calculator** NOUN
der Taschenrechner (PL die
Taschenrechner)

**poem** NOUN
das Gedicht (PL die Gedichte)

**poet** NOUN
der Dichter (PL die Dichter)
die Dichterin

**poetry** NOUN
die Gedichte NEUT PL ◊ *to write poetry*
Gedichte schreiben

**point** NOUN
see also **point** VERB
1 (*spot, score*)
der Punkt (PL die Punkte) ◊ *a point on the
horizon* ein Punkt am Horizont ◊ *They
scored five points.* Sie machten fünf
Punkte.
2 (*comment*)
die Bemerkung ◊ *He made some
interesting points.* Er machte ein paar
interessante Bemerkungen.
3 (*tip*)
die Spitze ◊ *a pencil with a sharp point*
ein Bleistift mit einer scharfen Spitze
4 (*in time*)
der Zeitpunkt ◊ *At that point, our team
was three one up.* Zu dem Zeitpunkt lag
unsere Mannschaft mit drei zu eins in
Führung.
♦ **a point of view** ein Gesichtspunkt MASC
♦ **to get the point** begreifen ◊ *Sorry, I don't
get the point.* Entschuldigung, ich
begreife das nicht.
♦ **That's a good point!** Da hast du Recht.
♦ **There's no point.** Das hat keinen Wert.
◊ *There's no point in waiting.* Es hat
keinen Wert zu warten.
♦ **What's the point?** Wozu? ◊ *What's the
point of leaving now?* Wozu jetzt gehen?
♦ **Punctuality isn't my strong point.**
Pünktlichkeit ist nicht meine Stärke.
♦ **two point five (2.5)** zwei Komma fünf
(2,5)

to **point** VERB
see also **point** NOUN
mit dem Finger zeigen ◊ *Don't point!*
Man zeigt nicht mit dem Finger!
♦ **to point at somebody** auf jemanden
zeigen ◊ *She pointed at Anne.* Sie zeigte
auf Anne.
♦ **to point a gun at somebody** auf
jemanden mit der Waffe zielen
♦ **to point something out (1)** (*show*) auf
etwas zeigen ◊ *The guide pointed out Big
Ben to us.* Unser Führer zeigte auf Big
Ben.
♦ **to point something out (2)** (*mention*) auf
etwas hinweisen ◊ *I should point out
that ...* Ich möchte darauf hinweisen,
dass ...

**pointless** ADJECTIVE
nutzlos ◊ *It's pointless to argue.* Es ist
nutzlos zu streiten.

**poison** NOUN
see also **poison** VERB
das Gift (PL die Gifte)

to **poison** VERB
see also **poison** NOUN
vergiften (PERFECT hat vergiftet)

**poisonous** ADJECTIVE

giftig

to **poke** VERB
♦ **He poked me in the eye.** Er stieß mir ins
Auge.

**poker** NOUN
das Poker ◊ *I play poker.* Ich spiele
Poker.

**Poland** NOUN
Polen NEUT
♦ **from Poland** aus Polen
♦ **to Poland** nach Polen

**polar bear** NOUN
der Eisbär (GEN des Eisbären, PL die
Eisbären)

**Pole** NOUN
(*Polish person*)
der Pole (GEN des Polen, PL die Polen)
die Polin

**pole** NOUN
der Mast (PL die Masten) ◊ *a telegraph
pole* ein Telegrafenmast
♦ **a tent pole** eine Zeltstange
♦ **a ski pole** ein Skistock MASC
♦ **the North Pole** der Nordpol
♦ **the South Pole** der Südpol

**pole vault** NOUN
das Stabhochspringen

**police** PL NOUN
die Polizei ◊ *We called the police.* Wir
haben die Polizei gerufen.
*Note that **police** is used with a plural
verb and **Polizei** with a singular verb.*
◊ *The police haven't arrived yet.* Die
Polizei ist noch nicht da.
♦ **a police car** ein Polizeiwagen MASC
♦ **a police station** ein Polizeirevier NEUT

**policeman** NOUN
der Polizist (GEN des Polizisten, PL die
Polizisten) ◊ *He's a policeman.* Er ist
Polizist.

**policewoman** NOUN
die Polizistin ◊ *She's a policewoman.*
Sie ist Polizistin.

**polio** NOUN
die Kinderlähmung

**Polish** ADJECTIVE
see also **Polish** NOUN
polnisch
♦ **He's Polish.** Er ist Pole.
♦ **She's Polish.** Sie ist Polin.

**Polish** NOUN
see also **Polish** ADJECTIVE
das Polnisch (*language*) (GEN des
Polnischen)

**polish** NOUN
see also **polish** VERB
1 (*for shoes*)
die Schuhcreme (PL die Schuhcremes)
2 (*for furniture*)
die Politur

to **polish** VERB
see also **polish** NOUN

P

1 (*shoes*)
eincremen (PERFECT hat eingecremt)
2 (*glass, furniture*)
polieren (PERFECT hat poliert)
**polite** ADJECTIVE
höflich
**politely** ADVERB
höflich
**politeness** NOUN
die Höflichkeit
**political** ADJECTIVE
politisch
**politician** NOUN
der Politiker (PL die Politiker)
die Politikerin
**politics** PL NOUN
die Politik ◊ *I'm not interested in politics.*
Ich interessiere mich nicht für Politik.
**poll** NOUN
die Umfrage ◊ *A recent poll revealed
that ...* Eine Umfrage ergab vor kurzem,
dass ...
**pollen** NOUN
der Pollen (PL die Pollen)
to **pollute** VERB
verschmutzen (PERFECT hat verschmutzt)
**polluted** ADJECTIVE
verschmutzt
**pollution** NOUN
die Umweltverschmutzung
♦ **air pollution** die Luftverschmutzung
**polo-necked sweater** NOUN
der Rollkragenpullover (PL die
Rollkragenpullover)
**polo shirt** NOUN
das Polohemd (PL die Polohemden)
**polythene bag** NOUN
die Plastiktüte
**pond** NOUN
der Teich (PL die Teiche) ◊ *We've got a
pond in our garden.* Wir haben einen
Teich im Garten.
**pony** NOUN
das Pony (PL die Ponys)
**ponytail** NOUN
der Pferdeschwanz (GEN des
Pferdeschwanzes, PL die Pferdeschwänze)
◊ *He's got a ponytail.* Er hat einen
Pferdeschwanz.
**pony trekking** NOUN
♦ **to go pony trekking** Pony reiten gehen
**poodle** NOUN
der Pudel (PL die Pudel)
**pool** NOUN
1 (*puddle*)
die Pfütze
2 (*pond*)
der Teich (PL die Teiche)
3 (*for swimming*)
das Schwimmbecken (PL die
Schwimmbecken)
4 (*game*)

das Poolbillard ◊ *Shall we have a game
of pool?* Sollen wir eine Partie Poolbillard
spielen?
♦ **the pools** (*football*) das Toto ◊ *to do the
pools* Toto spielen
**poor** ADJECTIVE
1 arm ◊ *a poor family* eine arme Familie
◊ *They are poorer than we are.* Sie sind
ärmer als wir. ◊ *Poor David, he's very
unlucky!* Der arme David, er hat wirklich
kein Glück!
♦ **the poor** die Armen MASC PL
2 schlecht (*bad*) ◊ *a poor mark* eine
schlechte Note
**poorly** ADJECTIVE
♦ **She's poorly.** Es geht ihr schlecht.
**pop** ADJECTIVE
♦ **pop music** die Popmusik
♦ **a pop star** ein Popstar MASC
♦ **a pop group** eine Popgruppe
♦ **a pop song** ein Popsong MASC
to **pop in** VERB
vorbeikommen (IMPERFECT kam vorbei,
PERFECT ist vorbeigekommen)
to **pop out** VERB
kurz weggehen (IMPERFECT ging weg,
PERFECT ist weggegangen) ◊ *I'm just
popping out for an hour.* Ich gehe nur
mal kurz für eine Stunde weg.
to **pop round** VERB
♦ **I'm just popping round to John's.** Ich
gehe nur mal kurz zu John.
**popcorn** NOUN
das Popcorn
**pope** NOUN
der Papst (PL die Päpste)
**poppy** NOUN
der Mohn
**Popsicle** ® NOUN US
das Eis am Stiel (GEN des Eises am Stiel,
PL die Eis am Stiel)
**popular** ADJECTIVE
beliebt ◊ *She's a very popular girl.* Sie
ist sehr beliebt.
**population** NOUN
die Bevölkerung
**porch** NOUN
die Veranda (PL die Veranden)
**pork** NOUN
das Schweinefleisch ◊ *I don't eat pork.*
Ich esse kein Schweinefleisch.
♦ **a pork chop** ein Schweinekotelett NEUT
**porn** NOUN
see also **porn** ADJECTIVE
die Pornografie
**porn** ADJECTIVE
see also **porn** NOUN
♦ **a porn film** ein Pornofilm MASC
♦ **a porn mag** ein Pornoheft NEUT
**pornographic** ADJECTIVE
pornografisch ◊ *a pornographic
magazine* eine pornografische Zeitschrift

**pornography** NOUN
die Pornografie

**porridge** NOUN
der Haferbrei

**port** NOUN
[1] (*harbour*)
der Hafen (PL die Häfen)
[2] (*wine*)
der Portwein ◊ *a glass of port* ein Glas
Portwein

**portable** ADJECTIVE
tragbar ◊ *a portable TV* ein tragbarer
Fernseher

**porter** NOUN
[1] (*in hotel*)
der Portier (PL die Portiers)
[2] (*at station*)
der Gepäckträger (PL die Gepäckträger)

**portion** NOUN
die Portion ◊ *a large portion of chips*
eine große Portion Pommes frites

**portrait** NOUN
das Porträt (PL die Porträts)

**Portugal** NOUN
Portugal NEUT
♦**from Portugal** aus Portugal
♦**to Portugal** nach Portugal

**Portuguese** ADJECTIVE
| see also **Portuguese** NOUN |
portugiesisch
♦**She's Portuguese.** Sie ist Portugiesin.

**Portuguese** NOUN
| see also **Portuguese** ADJECTIVE |
[1] (*person*)
der Portugiese (GEN des Portugiesen, PL
die Portugiesen)
die Portugiesin
[2] (*language*)
das Portugiesisch (GEN des
Portugiesischen)

**posh** ADJECTIVE
vornehm ◊ *a posh hotel* ein vornehmes
Hotel

**position** NOUN
die Stellung ◊ *an uncomfortable
position* eine unbequeme Stellung

**positive** ADJECTIVE
[1] positiv (*good*) ◊ *a positive attitude*
eine positive Einstellung
[2] ganz sicher (*sure*) ◊ *I'm positive.* Ich
bin ganz sicher.

to **possess** VERB
besitzen (IMPERFECT besaß, PERFECT hat
besessen)

**possession** NOUN
♦**Have you got all your possessions?** Hast
du all deine Sachen?

**possibility** NOUN
die Möglichkeit ◊ *It's a possibility.* Das
ist eine Möglichkeit.

**possible** ADJECTIVE
möglich ◊ *as soon as possible* sobald
wie möglich

**possibly** ADVERB
vielleicht (*perhaps*) ◊ *Are you coming to
the party? – Possibly.* Kommst du zur
Party? – Vielleicht.
♦**... if you possibly can.** ... wenn du irgend
kannst.
♦**I can't possibly come.** Ich kann
unmöglich kommen.

**post** NOUN
| see also **post** VERB |
[1] (*letters*)
die Post ◊ *Is there any post for me?* Ist
Post für mich da?
[2] (*pole*)
der Pfosten (PL die Pfosten) ◊ *The ball hit
the post.* Der Ball traf den Pfosten.

to **post** VERB
| see also **post** NOUN |
aufgeben (PRESENT gibt auf, IMPERFECT gab
auf, PERFECT hat aufgegeben) ◊ *I've got
some cards to post.* Ich muss ein paar
Karten aufgeben.

**postage** NOUN
das Porto (PL die Portos)

**postbox** NOUN
der Briefkasten (PL die Briefkästen)

**postcard** NOUN
die Postkarte

**postcode** NOUN
die Postleitzahl

> *ⓘ German postcodes consist of a
> 5-figure number which precedes the
> name of the city.*

**poster** NOUN
[1] das Poster (PL die Poster) ◊ *I've got
posters on my bedroom walls.* Ich habe
in meinem Zimmer Poster an den
Wänden.
[2] (*advertising*)
das Plakat (PL die Plakate) ◊ *There are
posters all over town.* In der ganzen
Stadt hängen Plakate.

**postman** NOUN
der Briefträger (PL die Briefträger) ◊ *He's
a postman.* Er ist Briefträger.

**postmark** NOUN
der Stempel (PL die Stempel)

**post office** NOUN
das Postamt (PL die Postämter)
◊ *Where's the post office, please?* Wo ist
das Postamt, bitte?
♦**She works for the post office.** Sie
arbeitet bei der Post.

to **postpone** VERB
verschieben (IMPERFECT verschob, PERFECT
hat verschoben) ◊ *The match has been
postponed.* Das Spiel wurde verschoben.

**postwoman** NOUN

**P**

☞

die Briefträgerin ◊ *She's a postwoman.*
Sie ist Briefträgerin.

**pot** NOUN
1 der Topf (PL die Töpfe) ◊ *a pot of jam*
ein Marmeladentopf
2 (*for hot drinks*)
die Kanne
3 (*marijuana*)
das Gras ◊ *to smoke pot* Gras rauchen
♦ **the pots and pans** Töpfe und Pfannen

**potato** NOUN
die Kartoffel ◊ *a baked potato* eine
gebackene Kartoffel ◊ *potato salad* der
Kartoffelsalat
♦ **mashed potatoes** der Kartoffelbrei
♦ **potato chips** die Kartoffelchips MASC PL

**potential** NOUN
see also **potential** ADJECTIVE
♦ **He has great potential.** Er ist sehr viel
versprechend.

**potential** ADJECTIVE
see also **potential** NOUN
möglich ◊ *a potential problem* ein
mögliches Problem

**pothole** NOUN
das Schlagloch (*in road*) (PL die
Schlaglöcher)

**pot plant** NOUN
die Topfpflanze

**pottery** NOUN
die Keramik

**pound** NOUN
see also **pound** VERB
das Pfund (*weight, money*) (PL die Pfunde
or Pfund)

*When talking about an amount of money
or specifying a quantity of something
use the plural form **Pfund**.*

◊ *two pounds of carrots* zwei Pfund
Karotten ◊ *How many marks do you get
for a pound?* Wie viel Mark bekommt
man für ein Pfund? ◊ *a pound coin* eine
Pfundmünze

to **pound** VERB
see also **pound** NOUN
pochen ◊ *My heart was pounding.* Mein
Herz hat gepocht.

to **pour** VERB
gießen (*liquid*) (IMPERFECT goss, PERFECT hat
gegossen) ◊ *She poured some water into
the pan.* Sie goss etwas Wasser in den
Topf.
♦ **She poured him a drink.** Sie goss ihm
einen Drink ein.
♦ **Shall I pour you a cup of tea?** Soll ich
Ihnen eine Tasse Tee einschenken?
♦ **It's pouring.** Es gießt.
♦ **in the pouring rain** im strömenden
Regen

**poverty** NOUN
die Armut

**powder** NOUN
1 das Pulver
2 (*face powder*)
der Puder (PL die Puder)

**power** NOUN
1 (*electricity*)
der Strom ◊ *The power's off. Es gibt
keinen Strom.*
♦ **a power cut** ein Stromausfall MASC
♦ **a power point** eine Steckdose
♦ **a power station** ein Kraftwerk NEUT
2 (*energy*)
die Energie ◊ *nuclear power* die
Kernenergie ◊ *solar power* die
Sonnenenergie
3 (*authority*)
die Macht (PL die Mächte) ◊ *to be in
power* an der Macht sein

**powerful** ADJECTIVE
1 mächtig ◊ *a powerful man* ein
mächtiger Mann
2 kräftig (*physically*)
3 leistungsstark (*machine*)

**practical** ADJECTIVE
praktisch ◊ *a practical suggestion* ein
praktischer Vorschlag ◊ *She's very
practical.* Sie ist sehr praktisch.

**practically** ADVERB
praktisch ◊ *It's practically impossible.* Es
ist praktisch unmöglich.

**practice** NOUN
1 das Training (*for sport*) ◊ *football
practice* das Fußballtraining
2 die Übung ◊ *You need more practice.*
Du brauchst mehr Übung.
♦ **I've got to do my piano practice.** Ich
muss Klavier üben.
♦ **It's normal practice in our school.** Das ist
in unserer Schule so üblich.
♦ **in practice** in der Praxis
♦ **a medical practice** eine Arztpraxis

to **practise** VERB
1 (*music, hobby, language*)
üben ◊ *I ought to practise more.* Ich
sollte mehr üben. ◊ *I practise the flute
every evening.* Ich übe jeden Abend
Flöte. ◊ *I practised my German when we
were on holiday.* Ich habe in den Ferien
mein Deutsch geübt.
2 (*sport*)
trainieren (PERFECT hat trainiert) ◊ *The
team practises on Thursdays.* Die
Mannschaft trainiert donnerstags. ◊ *I
don't practise enough.* Ich trainiere nicht
genug.

**practising** ADJECTIVE
praktizierend ◊ *She's a practising
Catholic.* Sie ist praktizierende Katholikin.

to **praise** VERB
loben ◊ *The teacher praised her work.*
Der Lehrer lobte ihre Arbeit.

**pram** NOUN
der Kinderwagen (PL die Kinderwagen)

**prawn** NOUN

die <u>Garnele</u>
**prawn cocktail** NOUN
  der <u>Krabbencocktail</u> (PL die
  Krabbencocktails)
to **pray** VERB
  <u>beten</u> ◊ *to pray for something* für etwas
  beten
**prayer** NOUN
  das <u>Gebet</u> (PL die Gebete)
**precaution** NOUN
  die <u>Vorsichtsmaßnahme</u> ◊ *to take
  precautions* Vorsichtsmaßnahmen
  treffen
**preceding** ADJECTIVE
  <u>vorherig</u>
**precinct** NOUN
◆ **a shopping precinct** ein Einkaufsviertel
  NEUT
◆ **a pedestrian precinct** eine
  Fußgängerzone
**precious** ADJECTIVE
  <u>kostbar</u>
**precise** ADJECTIVE
  <u>genau</u> ◊ *at that precise moment* genau
  in diesem Augenblick
**precisely** ADVERB
  <u>genau</u> ◊ *Precisely!* Genau!
◆ **at ten o'clock precisely** um Punkt zehn
  Uhr
to **predict** VERB
  <u>vorhersagen</u> (PERFECT hat vorhergesagt)
**predictable** ADJECTIVE
  <u>vorhersehbar</u>
**prefect** NOUN

> **ⓘ** *German schools do not have
> prefects.*

◆ **My sister's a prefect.** Meine Schwester
  ist im letzten Schuljahr und führt die
  Aufsicht bei den Jüngeren.
to **prefer** VERB
  <u>lieber mögen</u> (PRESENT mag lieber, IMPERFECT
  mochte lieber, PERFECT hat lieber gemocht)
  ◊ *Which would you prefer?* Was magst
  du lieber? ◊ *I prefer German to
  chemistry.* Ich mag Deutsch lieber als
  Chemie.
◆ **I preferred the first version.** Die erste
  Version hat mir besser gefallen.
**preference** NOUN
  die <u>Vorliebe</u> ◊ *his preference for
  detective stories* seine Vorliebe für
  Kriminalromane
**pregnant** ADJECTIVE
  <u>schwanger</u> ◊ *She's six months
  pregnant.* Sie ist im siebten Monat
  schwanger.
**prehistoric** ADJECTIVE
  <u>prähistorisch</u>
**prejudice** NOUN

**1** das <u>Vorurteil</u> (PL die Vorurteile)
  ◊ *That's just a prejudice.* Das ist ein
  Vorurteil.
**2** die <u>Vorurteile</u> NEUT PL ◊ *There's a lot of
  racial prejudice.* Es gibt viele
  Rassenvorurteile.
**prejudiced** ADJECTIVE
  <u>voreingenommen</u>
◆ **to be prejudiced against somebody**
  gegen jemanden voreingenommen sein
**premature** ADJECTIVE
  <u>verfrüht</u>
◆ **a premature baby** eine Frühgeburt
**Premier League** NOUN
  die <u>erste Liga</u> ◊ *in the Premier League* in
  der ersten Liga

> **ⓘ** *The **Premier League** is similar to the
> German **Bundesliga**.*

**premises** PL NOUN
  die <u>Geschäftsräume</u> MASC PL ◊ *They're
  moving to new premises.* Sie ziehen in
  neue Geschäftsräume um.
**premonition** NOUN
  die <u>Vorahnung</u>
**preoccupied** ADJECTIVE
◆ **He's very preoccupied with his exams at
  the moment.** Er denkt im Moment nur an
  seine Prüfungen.
**prep** NOUN
  die <u>Hausaufgaben</u> FEM PL (*homework*)
  ◊ *history prep* die Hausaufgaben in
  Geschichte
**preparation** NOUN
  die <u>Vorbereitung</u>
to **prepare** VERB
  <u>vorbereiten</u> (PERFECT hat vorbereitet)
  ◊ *She has to prepare lessons in the
  evening.* Sie muss abends Stunden
  vorbereiten.
◆ **to prepare for something**
  Vorbereitungen für etwas treffen ◊ *We're
  preparing for our skiing holiday.* Wir
  treffen Vorbereitungen für unseren
  Skiurlaub.
**prepared** ADJECTIVE
◆ **to be prepared to do something** bereit
  sein, etwas zu tun ◊ *I'm prepared to help
  you.* Ich bin bereit, dir zu helfen.
**prep school** NOUN
  die <u>private Grundschule</u>
**Presbyterian** NOUN

  see also **Presbyterian** ADJECTIVE

  der <u>Presbyterianer</u> (PL die
  Presbyterianer)
  die <u>Presbyterianerin</u>
  ◊ *She is a Presbyterian.* Sie ist
  Presbyterianerin.
**Presbyterian** ADJECTIVE

  see also **Presbyterian** NOUN

  <u>presbyterianisch</u>

**P**

to **prescribe** VERB
  verschreiben (*medicine*) (IMPERFECT
  verschrieb, PERFECT hat verschrieben)
  ◊ *He prescribed me a course of
  antibiotics.* Er hat mir eine Antibiotikakur
  verschrieben.

**prescription** NOUN
  das Rezept (PL die Rezepte) ◊ *You can't
  get it without a prescription.* Das
  bekommt man nicht ohne Rezept.

**presence** NOUN
  die Anwesenheit
  ◆ **presence of mind** die Geistesgegenwart

**present** ADJECTIVE
  | see also **present** NOUN, VERB |
  [1] anwesend (*in attendance*) ◊ *He wasn't
  present at the meeting.* Er war bei der
  Besprechung nicht anwesend.
  [2] gegenwärtig (*current*) ◊ *the present
  situation* die gegenwärtige Situation
  ◆ **the present tense** die Gegenwart

**present** NOUN
  | see also **present** ADJECTIVE, VERB |
  [1] (*gift*)
  das Geschenk (PL die Geschenke) ◊ *I'm
  going to buy presents.* Ich kaufe
  Geschenke.
  ◆ **to give somebody a present** jemandem
  etwas schenken
  [2] (*time*)
  die Gegenwart ◊ *She was living in the
  past not the present.* Sie lebte in der
  Vergangenheit, nicht in der Gegenwart.
  ◆ **up to the present** bis heute
  ◆ **for the present** momentan
  ◆ **at present** im Augenblick
  ◆ **the present tense** das Präsens

to **present** VERB
  | see also **present** ADJECTIVE, NOUN |
  ◆ **to present somebody with something**
  (*prize, medal*) jemandem etwas verleihen

**presenter** NOUN
  (*on TV*)
  der Moderator (PL die Moderatoren)
  die Moderatorin

**presently** ADVERB
  [1] sofort (*soon*) ◊ *You'll feel better
  presently.* Sie werden sich sofort besser
  fühlen.
  [2] im Moment (*at present*) ◊ *They're
  presently on tour.* Sie sind im Moment
  auf Tournee.

**president** NOUN
  der Präsident (GEN des Präsidenten, PL die
  Präsidenten)
  die Präsidentin

**press** NOUN
  | see also **press** VERB |
  die Presse
  ◆ **a press conference** eine Pressekonferenz

to **press** VERB
  | see also **press** NOUN |

[1] drücken ◊ *Don't press too hard!* Nicht
zu fest drücken!
[2] treten auf +ACC (PRESENT tritt auf, IMPERFECT
trat, PERFECT hat getreten) ◊ *He pressed the
accelerator.* Er trat aufs Gaspedal.

**pressed** ADJECTIVE
  ◆ **We are pressed for time.** Wir haben
  wenig Zeit.

**press-up** NOUN
  der Liegestütz (GEN des Liegestützes, PL
  die Liegestütze) ◊ *I do twenty press-ups
  every morning.* Ich mache jeden Morgen
  zwanzig Liegestütze.

**pressure** NOUN
  | see also **pressure** VERB |
  der Druck ◊ *He's under a lot of pressure
  at work.* Er steht unter viel Druck bei
  seiner Arbeit.
  ◆ **a pressure group (1)** (*small-scale, local*)
  eine Bürgerinitiative
  ◆ **a pressure group (2)** (*large-scale, more
  political*) eine Pressuregroup

to **pressure** VERB
  | see also **pressure** NOUN |
  Druck ausüben auf +ACC (PERFECT hat Druck
  ausgeübt) ◊ *My parents are pressuring
  me.* Meine Eltern üben Druck auf mich
  aus.

**prestige** NOUN
  das Ansehen

**prestigious** ADJECTIVE
  angesehen

**presumably** ADVERB
  vermutlich

to **presume** VERB
  annehmen (PRESENT nimmt an, IMPERFECT
  nahm an, PERFECT hat angenommen) ◊ *I
  presume so.* Das nehme ich an.

to **pretend** VERB
  ◆ **to pretend to do something** so tun, als
  ob man etwas täte
  *Note that **als ob** is followed by the
  subjunctive.*
  ◊ *He pretended to be asleep.* Er tat so,
  als ob er schliefe.

**pretty** ADJECTIVE, ADVERB
  [1] hübsch ◊ *She's very pretty.* Sie ist
  sehr hübsch.
  [2] ziemlich (*rather*) ◊ *That film was pretty
  bad.* Der Film war ziemlich schlecht.
  ◆ **It's pretty much the same.** Das ist mehr
  oder weniger dasselbe.

to **prevent** VERB
  verhindern (PERFECT hat verhindert)
  ◆ **to prevent somebody from doing
  something** jemanden davon abhalten,
  etwas zu tun ◊ *They tried to prevent us
  from smoking.* Sie haben versucht, uns
  vom Rauchen abzuhalten.

**previous** ADJECTIVE
  vorherig

**previously** ADVERB

früher

**prey** NOUN
die <u>Beute</u>
♦ **a bird of prey** ein Raubvogel MASC

**price** NOUN
der <u>Preis</u> (GEN des Preises, PL die Preise)

**price list** NOUN
die <u>Preisliste</u>

to **prick** VERB
<u>stechen</u> (PRESENT sticht, IMPERFECT stach,
PERFECT hat gestochen) ◊ *I've pricked my
finger.* Ich habe mir in den Finger
gestochen.     '

**pride** NOUN
der <u>Stolz</u> (GEN des Stolzes)

**priest** NOUN
der <u>Priester</u> (PL die Priester) ◊ *He's a
priest.* Er ist Priester.

**primarily** ADVERB
<u>vor allem</u>

**primary** ADJECTIVE
<u>hauptsächlich</u>

**primary school** NOUN
die <u>Grundschule</u>

> ⓘ *Children in Germany begin*
> ***Grundschule*** *at the age of 6. The*
> ***Grundschule*** *provides primary*
> *education in school years 1 to 4.*

◊ *She's still at primary school.* Sie ist
noch in der Grundschule.

**prime minister** NOUN
der <u>Premierminister</u> (PL die
Premierminister)
die <u>Premierministerin</u>

**primitive** ADJECTIVE
<u>primitiv</u>

**prince** NOUN
der <u>Prinz</u> (GEN des Prinzen, PL die Prinzen)
◊ *the Prince of Wales* der Prinz von
Wales

**princess** NOUN
die <u>Prinzessin</u> ◊ *Princess Anne*
Prinzessin Anne

**principal** ADJECTIVE
| see also **principal** NOUN |
♦ **the principal reason** der Hauptgrund
♦ **my principal concern** mein
Hauptanliegen NEUT

**principal** NOUN
| see also **principal** ADJECTIVE |
(*of college*)
der <u>Direktor</u> (PL die Direktoren)
die <u>Direktorin</u>

**principle** NOUN
das <u>Prinzip</u> (PL die Prinzipien)
♦ **on principle** aus Prinzip

**print** NOUN
[1] (*photo*)
der <u>Abzug</u> (PL die Abzüge) ◊ *colour prints*
Farbabzüge

[2] (*letters*)
die <u>Schrift</u>
♦ **in small print** klein gedruckt

[3] (*fingerprint*)
der <u>Fingerabdruck</u> (PL die
Fingerabdrücke)

[4] (*picture*)
der <u>Kunstdruck</u> (PL die Kunstdrucke) ◊ *a
framed print* ein gerahmter Kunstdruck

**printer** NOUN
der <u>Drucker</u> (*machine*) (PL die Drucker)

**printout** NOUN
der <u>Ausdruck</u> (PL die Ausdrucke)

**priority** NOUN
die <u>Priorität</u>

**prison** NOUN
das <u>Gefängnis</u> (GEN des Gefängnisses, PL
die Gefängnisse)
♦ **in prison** im Gefängnis

**prisoner** NOUN
der <u>Gefangene</u> (GEN des Gefangenen, PL
die Gefangenen)
die <u>Gefangene</u> (GEN der Gefangenen) ◊ *a
prisoner* (*man*) ein Gefangener

**prison officer** NOUN
der <u>Gefängniswärter</u> (PL die
Gefängniswärter)
die <u>Gefängniswärterin</u>

**privacy** NOUN
das <u>Privatleben</u> ◊ *an invasion of my
privacy* ein Eingriff in mein Privatleben

**private** ADJECTIVE
<u>privat</u>
♦ **a private school** eine Privatschule
♦ **private property** das Privateigentum
♦ **"private"** (*on envelope*) "persönlich"
♦ **a private bathroom** ein eigenes
Badezimmer
♦ **I have private lessons.** Ich bekomme
Nachhilfestunden.

to **privatize** VERB
<u>privatisieren</u> (PERFECT hat privatisiert)

**privilege** NOUN
das <u>Privileg</u> (PL die Privilegien)

**prize** NOUN
der <u>Preis</u> (GEN des Preises, PL die Preise)
◊ *to win a prize* einen Preis gewinnen

**prize-giving** NOUN
die <u>Preisverleihung</u>

**prizewinner** NOUN
der <u>Preisträger</u> (PL die Preisträger)
die <u>Preisträgerin</u>

**pro** NOUN
der <u>Profi</u> (PL die Profis)
> ***der Profi*** *is also used for women.*
◊ *This was her first year as a pro.* Dies
war ihr erstes Jahr als Profi.
♦ **the pros and cons** das Für und Wider
◊ *We weighed up the pros and cons.* Wir
haben das Für und Wider abgewogen.

**probability** NOUN
die <u>Wahrscheinlichkeit</u>

**probable** ADJECTIVE

**P**

wahrscheinlich

**probably** ADVERB
wahrscheinlich ◊ *probably not*
wahrscheinlich nicht

**problem** NOUN
das Problem (PL die Probleme) ◊ *No problem!* Kein Problem!

**proceeds** PL NOUN
der Erlös SING (GEN des Erlöses, PL die Erlöse)

**process** NOUN
der Prozess (GEN des Prozesses, PL die Prozesse) ◊ *the peace process* der Friedensprozess
♦ **to be in the process of doing something** gerade dabei sein, etwas zu tun ◊ *We're in the process of painting the kitchen.* Wir sind gerade dabei, die Küche zu streichen.

**procession** NOUN
die Prozession (*religious*)

to **produce** VERB
⑴ (*manufacture*)
herstellen (PERFECT hat hergestellt)
⑵ (*play, show*)
inszenieren (PERFECT hat inszeniert)
⑶ (*film*)
produzieren (PERFECT hat produziert)

**producer** NOUN
⑴ (*of play, show*)
der Regisseur (PL die Regisseure)
die Regisseurin
⑵ (*of film*)
der Produzent (GEN des Produzenten, PL die Produzenten)
die Produzentin

**product** NOUN
das Produkt (PL die Produkte)

**production** NOUN
⑴ die Produktion ◊ *They're increasing production of luxury models.* Sie erhöhen die Produktion der Luxusmodelle.
⑵ die Inszenierung (*play, show*) ◊ *a production of "Hamlet"* eine Hamletinszenierung

**profession** NOUN
der Beruf (PL die Berufe)

**professional** NOUN
see also **professional** ADJECTIVE
der Profi (PL die Profis)
*der Profi is also used for women.*
◊ *She now plays as a professional.* Sie spielt jetzt als Profi.

**professional** ADJECTIVE
see also **professional** NOUN
professionell (*player*) ◊ *a very professional piece of work* eine sehr professionelle Arbeit
♦ **a professional musician** ein Berufsmusiker MASC

**professionally** ADVERB

♦**She sings professionally.** Sie ist Sängerin von Beruf.

**professor** NOUN
der Professor (PL die Professoren)
die Professorin
♦**He's the German professor.** Er hat den Lehrstuhl für Deutsch inne.

**profit** NOUN
der Gewinn (PL die Gewinne)

**profitable** ADJECTIVE
Gewinn bringend

**program** NOUN
see also **program** VERB
das Programm (PL die Programme) ◊ *a computer program* ein Computerprogramm

to **program** VERB
see also **program** NOUN
programmieren (PERFECT hat programmiert) ◊ *to program a computer* einen Computer programmieren

**programme** NOUN
das Programm (PL die Programme)

**programmer** NOUN
der Programmierer (PL die Programmierer)
die Programmiererin
◊ *She's a programmer.* Sie ist Programmiererin.

**programming** NOUN
das Programmieren

**progress** NOUN
der Fortschritt (PL die Fortschritte)
◊ *You're making progress!* Du machst Fortschritte!

to **prohibit** VERB
verbieten (IMPERFECT verbat, PERFECT hat verboten) ◊ *Smoking is prohibited.* Das Rauchen ist verboten.

**project** NOUN
⑴ (*plan*)
das Projekt (PL die Projekte)
⑵ (*at school*)
das Referat (PL die Referate) ◊ *I'm doing a project on education in Germany.* Ich schreibe ein Referat über das deutsche Schulwesen.

**projector** NOUN
der Projektor (PL die Projektoren)

**promenade** NOUN
die Strandpromenade

**promise** NOUN
see also **promise** VERB
das Versprechen (PL die Versprechen) ◊ *You didn't keep your promise.* Du hast dein Versprechen nicht gehalten.
♦**That's a promise!** Versprochen!

to **promise** VERB
see also **promise** NOUN
versprechen (PRESENT verspricht, IMPERFECT versprach, PERFECT hat versprochen) ◊ *She promised to write.* Sie hat versprochen

zu schreiben. ◊ *I'll write, I promise!* Ich
schreibe, das verspreche ich!

**promising** ADJECTIVE
viel versprechend

to **promote** VERB
♦ **to be promoted** befördert werden ◊ *She
was promoted after six months.* Sie
wurde nach sechs Monaten befördert.

**promotion** NOUN
⑴ die Beförderung (*in job*)
⑵ die Werbung (*advertising*)

**prompt** ADJECTIVE, ADVERB
schnell ◊ *a prompt reply* eine schnelle
Antwort
♦ **at eight o'clock prompt** genau um acht
Uhr

**promptly** ADVERB
pünktlich ◊ *We left promptly at seven.*
Wir sind pünktlich um sieben gegangen.

**pronoun** NOUN
das Pronomen (PL die Pronomen)

to **pronounce** VERB
aussprechen (PRESENT spricht aus, IMPERFECT
sprach aus, PERFECT hat ausgesprochen)
◊ *How do you pronounce that word?* Wie
spricht man das Wort aus?

**pronunciation** NOUN
die Aussprache

**proof** NOUN
der Beweis (GEN des Beweises, PL die
Beweise)

**proper** ADJECTIVE
⑴ echt (*genuine*) ◊ *proper German bread*
echtes deutsches Brot
⑵ ordentlich (*decent*) ◊ *We didn't have a
proper lunch, just sandwiches.* Wir
hatten kein ordentliches Mittagessen, nur
belegte Brote. ◊ *It's difficult to get a
proper job.* Es ist schwierig, einen
ordentlichen Job zu bekommen. ◊ *We
need proper training.* Wir brauchen eine
ordentliche Ausbildung.
⑶ richtig (*appropriate*) ◊ *You have to
have the proper equipment.* Sie
brauchen die richtige Ausrüstung.
♦ **If you had come at the proper time ...**
Wenn du zur rechten Zeit gekommen
wärst ...

**properly** ADVERB
⑴ richtig (*correctly*) ◊ *You're not doing it
properly.* Du machst das nicht richtig.
⑵ anständig (*appropriately*) ◊ *Dress
properly for your interview.* Zieh dich
zum Vorstellungsgespräch anständig an.

**property** NOUN
das Eigentum
♦ **"private property"** "Privateigentum"
♦ **stolen property** das Diebesgut

**proportional** ADJECTIVE
♦ **proportional representation** das
Verhältniswahlrecht

**proposal** NOUN

der Vorschlag (*suggestion*) (PL die
Vorschläge)

to **propose** VERB
vorschlagen (PRESENT schlägt vor, IMPERFECT
schlug vor, PERFECT hat vorgeschlagen) ◊ *I
propose a new plan.* Ich schlage einen
neuen Plan vor.
♦ **to propose to do something** vorhaben,
etwas zu tun ◊ *What do you propose to
do?* Was haben Sie zu tun vor?
♦ **to propose to somebody** (*for marriage*)
jemandem einen Heiratsantrag machen
◊ *He proposed to her at the restaurant.*
Er hat ihr im Restaurant einen
Heiratsantrag gemacht.

to **prosecute** VERB
strafrechtlich verfolgen (PERFECT hat
verfolgt) ◊ *They were prosecuted for
murder.* Sie wurden wegen Mordes
strafrechtlich verfolgt.
♦ **"Shoplifters will be prosecuted"** "Jeder
Diebstahl wird zur Anzeige gebracht"

**prospect** NOUN
die Aussicht ◊ *It'll improve my career
prospects.* Das wird meine
Berufsaussichten verbessern.
*Be careful not to translate **prospect** by
**Prospekt**.*

**prospectus** NOUN
das Lehrprogramm (*for school, university*)
(PL die Lehrprogramme)

**prostitute** NOUN
die Prostituierte (GEN der Prostituierten)
♦ **a male prostitute** ein Prostituierter

to **protect** VERB
schützen

**protection** NOUN
der Schutz (GEN des Schutzes)

**protein** NOUN
das Protein (PL die Proteine)

**protest** NOUN
see also **protest** VERB
der Protest (PL die Proteste) ◊ *He ignored
their protests.* Er hat ihre Proteste
ignoriert. ◊ *a protest march* ein
Protestmarsch MASC

to **protest** VERB
see also **protest** NOUN
protestieren (PERFECT hat protestiert)

**Protestant** NOUN
see also **Protestant** ADJECTIVE
der Protestant (GEN des Protestanten, PL
die Protestanten)
die Protestantin
◊ *She's a Protestant.* Sie ist Protestantin.

**Protestant** ADJECTIVE
see also **Protestant** NOUN
protestantisch ◊ *a Protestant church*
eine protestantische Kirche

**protester** NOUN
der Demonstrant (GEN des
Demonstranten, PL die Demonstranten)
die Demonstrantin

**P**

**proud** ADJECTIVE
stolz ◊ Her parents are proud of her. Ihre Eltern sind stolz auf sie.

to **prove** VERB
beweisen (IMPERFECT bewies, PERFECT hat bewiesen) ◊ The police couldn't prove it. Die Polizei konnte es nicht beweisen.

**proverb** NOUN
das Sprichwort (PL die Sprichwörter)

to **provide** VERB
stellen ◊ We'll provide the food if you see to the drinks. Wir stellen das Essen, wenn ihr euch um die Getränke kümmert.

♦ **to provide somebody with something** jemandem etwas zur Verfügung stellen ◊ They provided us with maps. Sie haben uns Karten zur Verfügung gestellt.

to **provide for** VERB
versorgen (PERFECT hat versorgt) ◊ He can't provide for his family any more. Er kann seine Familie nicht mehr versorgen.

**provided** CONJUNCTION
vorausgesetzt, dass ◊ He'll play in the next match provided he's fit. Er spielt im nächsten Spiel, vorausgesetzt, dass er fit ist.

**provisional** ADJECTIVE
vorläufig

**prowler** NOUN
der Herumtreiber (PL die Herumtreiber)
die Herumtreiberin

**prune** NOUN
die Backpflaume

**pseudonym** NOUN
das Pseudonym (PL die Pseudonyme)

**psychiatrist** NOUN
der Psychiater (PL die Psychiater)
die Psychiaterin
◊ She's a psychiatrist. Sie ist Psychiaterin.

**psychoanalyst** NOUN
der Psychoanalytiker (PL die Psychoanalytiker)
die Psychoanalytikerin

**psychological** ADJECTIVE
psychologisch

**psychologist** NOUN
der Psychologe (GEN des Psychologen, PL die Psychologen)
die Psychologin
◊ He's a psychologist. Er ist Psychologe.

**psychology** NOUN
die Psychologie

**PTO** ABBREVIATION (= please turn over)
b. w. (= bitte wenden)

**pub** NOUN
die Kneipe

**public** NOUN
see also **public** ADJECTIVE
die Öffentlichkeit ◊ open to the public der Öffentlichkeit zugänglich

♦ **in public** in der Öffentlichkeit

**public** ADJECTIVE
see also **public** NOUN
öffentlich ◊ public opinion die öffentliche Meinung

♦ **a public holiday** ein gesetzlicher Feiertag

♦ **the public address system** die Lautsprecheranlage

**publican** NOUN
der Gastwirt
die Gastwirtin
◊ He's a publican. Er ist Gastwirt.

**publicity** NOUN
die Publicity

**public school** NOUN
die Privatschule

**public transport** NOUN
die öffentlichen Verkehrsmittel NEUT PL

> ❶ Almost all German cities operate an integrated public transport system; you buy a single ticket which is valid on all buses, trams and light railway vehicles in a particular zone. You can buy a weekly **Wochenkarte**, monthly **Monatskarte** or yearly **Jahreskarte**.

to **publish** VERB
veröffentlichen (PERFECT hat veröffentlicht)

**publisher** NOUN
der Verlag (company) (PL die Verlage)

**pudding** NOUN
der Nachtisch ◊ What's for pudding? Was gibt's zum Nachtisch?

♦ **rice pudding** der Milchreis

♦ **black pudding** die Blutwurst

**puddle** NOUN
die Pfütze

**puff pastry** NOUN
der Blätterteig

to **pull** VERB
ziehen (IMPERFECT zog, PERFECT hat gezogen) ◊ Pull! Zieh!

♦ **He pulled the trigger.** Er drückte ab.

♦ **to pull a muscle** sich einen Muskel zerren ◊ I pulled a muscle when I was training. Ich habe mir beim Training einen Muskel gezerrt.

♦ **You're pulling my leg!** Du willst mich wohl auf den Arm nehmen! (informal)

♦ **to pull down** abreißen

♦ **to pull out (1)** (tooth, weed) herausziehen

♦ **to pull out (2)** (car) ausscheren ◊ The car pulled out to overtake. Das Auto scherte aus, um zu überholen.

♦ **to pull out (3)** (withdraw) aussteigen ◊ She pulled out of the tournament. Sie ist aus dem Turnier ausgestiegen.

♦ **to pull through** (survive) durchkommen ◊ They think he'll pull through. Sie meinen, er kommt durch.

♦ **to pull up** (car)

anhalten ◊ *A black car pulled up beside me.* Ein schwarzes Auto hielt neben mir an.

**pullover** NOUN
der Pullover (PL die Pullover)

**pulse** NOUN
der Puls (GEN des Pulses, PL die Pulse) ◊ *The nurse felt his pulse.* Die Schwester fühlte ihm den Puls.

**pulses** PL NOUN
die Hülsenfrüchte FEM PL

**pump** NOUN
*see also* **pump** VERB
1 die Pumpe ◊ *a bicycle pump* eine Fahrradpumpe
◆ **a petrol pump** eine Zapfsäule
2 (*shoe*)
der Sportschuh (PL die Sportschuhe)

to **pump** VERB
*see also* **pump** NOUN
pumpen
◆ **to pump up** (*tyre*) aufpumpen

**pumpkin** NOUN
der Kürbis (GEN des Kürbisses, PL die Kürbisse)

**punch** NOUN
*see also* **punch** VERB
1 (*blow*)
der Schlag (PL die Schläge) ◊ *Tyson went down on the third punch.* Beim dritten Schlag ging Tyson zu Boden.
2 (*drink*)
der Punsch

to **punch** VERB
*see also* **punch** NOUN
1 (*hit*)
schlagen (PRESENT schlägt, IMPERFECT schlug, PERFECT hat geschlagen) ◊ *He punched me!* Er hat mich geschlagen!
2 (*in ticket machine*)
entwerten (PERFECT hat entwertet) ◊ *Punch your ticket before you get on the train.* Entwerten Sie Ihre Fahrkarte, bevor Sie in den Zug steigen.
3 (*by ticket inspector*)
knipsen ◊ *He forgot to punch my ticket.* Er hat vergessen, meine Fahrkarte zu knipsen.

**punch-up** NOUN
die Schlägerei (*informal*)

**punctual** ADJECTIVE
pünktlich

**punctuation** NOUN
die Zeichensetzung

**puncture** NOUN
die Reifenpanne ◊ *to have a puncture* eine Reifenpanne haben

to **punish** VERB
bestrafen (PERFECT hat bestraft) ◊ *The teacher punished him for forgetting to do his homework.* Der Lehrer bestrafte ihn,

weil er vergessen hatte, seine Hausaufgaben zu machen.

**punishment** NOUN
die Strafe

**punk** NOUN
(*person*)
der Punker (PL die Punker)
die Punkerin
◆ **a punk rock band** eine Punkband

**pupil** NOUN
der Schüler (PL die Schüler)
die Schülerin

**puppet** NOUN
die Marionette

**puppy** NOUN
der junge Hund (PL die jungen Hunde)

to **purchase** VERB
erwerben (PRESENT erwirbt, IMPERFECT erwarb, PERFECT hat erworben)

**pure** ADJECTIVE
rein ◊ *pure orange juice* reiner Orangensaft
◆ **He's doing pure maths.** Er macht rein theoretische Mathematik.

**purple** ADJECTIVE
violett

**purpose** NOUN
der Zweck (PL die Zwecke) ◊ *What is the purpose of these changes?* Welchen Zweck haben diese Veränderungen?
◆ **his purpose in life** sein Lebensinhalt
◆ **on purpose** absichtlich ◊ *He did it on purpose.* Er hat es absichtlich getan.

to **purr** VERB
schnurren

**purse** NOUN
1 (*for money*)
der Geldbeutel (PL die Geldbeutel)
2 (*handbag*)
die Handtasche

to **pursue** VERB
verfolgen (PERFECT hat verfolgt)

**pursuit** NOUN
die Aktivität ◊ *outdoor pursuits* Aktivitäten im Freien

**push** NOUN
*see also* **push** VERB
◆ **to give somebody a push** jemanden stoßen ◊ *He gave me a push.* Er hat mich gestoßen.

to **push** VERB
*see also* **push** NOUN
1 drücken (*button*)
2 drängeln ◊ *Don't push!* Nicht drängeln!
◆ **to push somebody to do something** jemanden drängen, etwas zu tun ◊ *My parents are pushing me to go to university.* Meine Eltern drängen mich zu studieren.
◆ **to push drugs** mit Drogen handeln

**P**

☞

♦**to push around** herumkommandieren ◊ *He likes pushing people around.* Er kommandiert die Leute gern herum.
♦**Push off!** Hau ab! (*informal*)
♦**I pushed my way through.** Ich drängelte mich durch.

**pushchair** NOUN
der Sportwagen (PL die Sportwagen)
**pusher** NOUN
(*of drugs*)
der Drogenhändler (PL die Drogenhändler)
die Drogenhändlerin

**push-up** NOUN
der Liegestütz (GEN des Liegestützes, PL die Liegestütze) ◊ *I do twenty push-ups every morning.* Ich mache jeden Morgen zwanzig Liegestütze.

to **put** VERB
> Use **legen** when you're putting something down flat, use **stellen** when you're standing something upright.

[1] legen ◊ *Where shall I put my things?* Wohin soll ich meine Sachen legen?
◊ *She's putting the baby to bed.* Sie legt das Baby ins Bett.
[2] stellen ◊ *Put the vase on the table.* Stell die Vase auf den Tisch.
♦**Don't forget to put your name on the paper.** Vergiss nicht, deinen Namen auf das Papier zu schreiben.

to **put aside** VERB
zurücklegen (PERFECT hat zurückgelegt) ◊ *Can you put this aside for me till tomorrow?* Können Sie mir das bis morgen zurücklegen?

to **put away** VERB
wegräumen (PERFECT hat weggeräumt) ◊ *Can you put away the dishes, please?* Kannst du bitte das Geschirr wegräumen?

to **put back** VERB
[1] zurücklegen (PERFECT hat zurückgelegt) ◊ *Put it back when you've finished with it.* Leg es zurück, wenn du es nicht mehr brauchst.
[2] zurückstellen (PERFECT hat zurückgestellt) ◊ *to put the clock back* die Uhr zurückstellen ◊ *Put the milk back in the fridge.* Stell die Milch in den Kühlschrank zurück.

to **put down** VERB
[1] abstellen (PERFECT hat abgestellt) ◊ *I'll put these bags down for a minute.* Ich stelle diese Taschen für eine Minute ab.
[2] (*in writing*)
aufschreiben (IMPERFECT schrieb auf, PERFECT hat aufgeschrieben) ◊ *I've put down a few ideas.* Ich habe ein paar Ideen aufgeschrieben.
♦**to have an animal put down** ein Tier einschläfern lassen ◊ *We had to have our*

*old dog put down.* Wir mussten unseren alten Hund einschläfern lassen.

to **put forward** VERB
vorstellen (PERFECT hat vorgestellt) ◊ *to put the clock forward* die Uhr vorstellen

to **put in** VERB
einbauen (*install*) (PERFECT hat eingebaut) ◊ *We're going to get central heating put in.* Wir werden eine Zentralheizung einbauen lassen.
♦**He has put in a lot of work on this project.** Er hat viel Arbeit in dieses Projekt gesteckt.

to **put off** VERB
[1] (*switch off*)
ausmachen (PERFECT hat ausgemacht) ◊ *Shall I put the light off?* Soll ich das Licht ausmachen?
[2] (*postpone*)
verschieben (IMPERFECT verschob, PERFECT hat verschoben) ◊ *I keep putting it off.* Ich verschiebe es dauernd.
[3] (*distract*)
stören ◊ *Stop putting me off!* Hör auf, mich zu stören!
[4] (*discourage*)
entmutigen (PERFECT hat entmutigt) ◊ *He's not easily put off.* Er lässt sich nicht so schnell entmutigen.

to **put on** VERB
[1] (*clothes*)
anziehen (IMPERFECT zog an, PERFECT hat angezogen) ◊ *I'll put my coat on.* Ich ziehe mir den Mantel an.
[2] (*lipstick*)
auftragen (PRESENT trägt auf, IMPERFECT trug auf, PERFECT hat aufgetragen)
[3] (*record*)
auflegen (PERFECT hat aufgelegt)
[4] (*light, heater, TV*)
anmachen (PERFECT hat angemacht) ◊ *Shall I put the heater on?* Soll ich den Heizofen anmachen?
[5] (*play, show*)
aufführen (PERFECT hat aufgeführt) ◊ *We're putting on "Bugsy Malone".* Wir führen "Bugsy Malone" auf.
[6] aufstellen (PERFECT hat aufgestellt) ◊ *I'll put the potatoes on.* Ich stelle die Kartoffeln auf.
♦**to put on weight** zunehmen ◊ *He's put on a lot of weight.* Er hat viel zugenommen.

to **put out** VERB
[1] (*light, cigarette*)
ausmachen (PERFECT hat ausgemacht) ◊ *Put the light out.* Mach das Licht aus.
[2] (*fire*)
löschen ◊ *It took them five hours to put out the fire.* Sie haben fünf Stunden gebraucht, um das Feuer zu löschen.

to **put through** VERB

verbinden (IMPERFECT verband, PERFECT hat
verbunden) ◊ *Can you put me through to
the manager?* Können Sie mich mit dem
Geschäftsführer verbinden?
♦ **I'm putting you through.** Ich verbinde.

to **put up** VERB
1 (*pin up*)
<u>aufhängen</u> (PERFECT hat aufgehängt) ◊ *The
poster's great. I'll put it up in my room.*
Das Poster ist toll. Ich hänge es bei mir
im Zimmer auf.
2 (*tent*)
<u>aufschlagen</u> (PRESENT schlägt auf, IMPERFECT
schlug auf, PERFECT hat aufgeschlagen)
◊ *We put up our tent in a field.* Wir haben
unser Zelt auf einem Feld aufgeschlagen.
3 (*price*)
<u>erhöhen</u> (PERFECT hat erhöht) ◊ *They've
put up the price.* Sie haben den Preis
erhöht.
4 (*accommodate*)
<u>übernachten lassen</u> (PRESENT lässt
übernachten, IMPERFECT ließ übernachten,
PERFECT hat übernachten lassen) ◊ *My
friend will put me up for the night.* Mein
Freund lässt mich bei sich übernachten.

♦ **to put one's hand up** sich melden ◊ *If
you have any questions, put up your
hand.* Wenn ihr Fragen habt, dann
meldet euch.
♦ **to put up with something** sich etwas
gefallen lassen ◊ *I'm not going to put up
with it any longer.* Ich lasse mir das nicht
länger gefallen.

**puzzle** NOUN
das <u>Puzzle</u> (*jigsaw*) (PL die Puzzles)
**puzzled** ADJECTIVE
<u>verdutzt</u> ◊ *You look puzzled!* Du siehst
verdutzt aus!
**puzzling** ADJECTIVE
<u>rätselhaft</u>
**pyjamas** PL NOUN
der <u>Schlafanzug</u> (PL die Schlafanzüge)
◊ *my pyjamas* mein Schlafanzug
♦ **a pair of pyjamas** ein Schlafanzug
♦ **a pyjama top** ein Schlafanzugoberteil
NEUT
**pyramid** NOUN
die <u>Pyramide</u>
**Pyrenees** PL NOUN
♦ **the Pyrenees** die Pyrenäen PL

P

# Q

**quaint** ADJECTIVE
   malerisch (*house, village*)
**qualification** NOUN
   die Qualifikation ◊ *vocational qualifications* die beruflichen Qualifikationen
   ♦ **to leave school without any qualifications** die Schule ohne einen Abschluss verlassen
**qualified** ADJECTIVE
   ausgebildet ◊ *a qualified driving instructor* ein ausgebildeter Fahrlehrer ◊ *a qualified nurse* eine ausgebildete Krankenschwester
to **qualify** VERB
   ⬚1⬚ (*for job*)
   seinen Abschluss machen ◊ *She qualified as a teacher last year.* Sie hat letztes Jahr ihren Abschluss als Lehrerin gemacht.
   ⬚2⬚ (*in competition*)
   sich qualifizieren (PERFECT hat sich qualifiziert) ◊ *Our team didn't qualify.* Unsere Mannschaft konnte sich nicht qualifizieren.
**quality** NOUN
   ⬚1⬚ die Qualität ◊ *a good quality of life* eine gute Lebensqualität
   ♦ **good-quality ingredients** qualitativ hochwertige Zutaten
   ⬚2⬚ die Eigenschaft (*of person*) ◊ *She's got lots of good qualities.* Sie hat viele gute Eigenschaften.
**quantity** NOUN
   die Menge
**quarantine** NOUN
   die Quarantäne ◊ *in quarantine* in Quarantäne
**quarrel** NOUN
   *see also* **quarrel** VERB
   der Streit (PL die Streite)
to **quarrel** VERB
   *see also* **quarrel** NOUN
   sich streiten (IMPERFECT stritt sich, PERFECT hat sich gestritten)
**quarry** NOUN
   der Steinbruch (*for stone*) (PL die Steinbrüche)
**quarter** NOUN
   das Viertel (PL die Viertel) ◊ *three quarters* drei Viertel ◊ *a quarter of an hour* eine viertel Stunde
   ♦ **three quarters of an hour** eine Dreiviertelstunde
   ♦ **a quarter past ten** Viertel nach zehn
   ♦ **a quarter to eleven** Viertel vor elf
**quarter final** NOUN
   das Viertelfinale (PL die Viertelfinale)

**quartet** NOUN
   das Quartett (PL die Quartette) ◊ *a string quartet* ein Streichquartett
**quay** NOUN
   der Kai (PL die Kais)
**queasy** ADJECTIVE
   ♦ **I'm feeling queasy.** Mir ist schlecht.
**queen** NOUN
   ⬚1⬚ die Königin ◊ *Queen Elizabeth* Königin Elisabeth
   ⬚2⬚ die Dame (*playing card*) ◊ *the queen of hearts* die Herzdame
   ♦ **the Queen Mother** die Königinmutter
**query** NOUN
   *see also* **query** VERB
   die Frage
to **query** VERB
   *see also* **query** NOUN
   in Frage stellen ◊ *No one queried my decision.* Niemand hat meine Entscheidung in Frage gestellt.
   ♦ **They queried the bill.** Sie reklamierten die Rechnung.
**question** NOUN
   *see also* **question** VERB
   die Frage ◊ *That's a difficult question.* Das ist eine schwierige Frage.
   ♦ **Can I ask a question?** Kann ich etwas fragen?
   ♦ **It's out of the question.** Das kommt nicht in Frage.
to **question** VERB
   *see also* **question** NOUN
   befragen (PERFECT hat befragt)
   ♦ **He was questioned by the police.** Die Polizei hat ihn vernommen.
**question mark** NOUN
   das Fragezeichen (PL die Fragezeichen)
**questionnaire** NOUN
   der Fragebogen (PL die Fragebögen)
**queue** NOUN
   *see also* **queue** VERB
   die Schlange
to **queue** VERB
   *see also* **queue** NOUN
   Schlange stehen (IMPERFECT stand Schlange, PERFECT hat Schlange gestanden) ◊ *We had to queue for an hour.* Wir mussten eine Stunde lang Schlange stehen.
   ♦ **to queue for something** für etwas anstehen ◊ *We had to queue for tickets.* Wir mussten für Karten anstehen.
**quick** ADJECTIVE, ADVERB
   schnell ◊ *a quick lunch* ein schnelles Mittagessen ◊ *Quick, phone the police!* Schnell, rufen Sie die Polizei! ◊ *It's*

*quicker by train.* Mit dem Zug geht es schneller.

◆ **Be quick!** Beeil dich!

◆ **She's a quick learner.** Sie lernt schnell.

**quickly** ADVERB

schnell ◊ *It was all over very quickly.* Es war alles sehr schnell vorbei.

**quiet** ADJECTIVE

1 ruhig (*not talkative, peaceful*) ◊ *You're very quiet today.* Du bist heute sehr ruhig. ◊ *a quiet little town* eine ruhige, kleine Stadt

2 leise (*not noisy*) ◊ *The engine's very quiet.* Der Motor ist sehr leise.

◆ **Be quiet!** Sei still!

◆ **Quiet!** Ruhe!

**quietly** ADVERB

leise ◊ *He quietly opened the door.* Er öffnete leise die Tür.

**quilt** NOUN

die Steppdecke (*duvet*)

to **quit** VERB

1 aufgeben (PRESENT gibt auf, IMPERFECT gab auf, PERFECT hat aufgegeben) ◊ *I quit my job last week.* Ich habe meine Stelle letzte Woche aufgegeben.

2 aufhören ◊ *I quit smoking.* Ich habe mit dem Rauchen aufgehört.

**quite** ADVERB

1 ziemlich (*rather*) ◊ *It's quite warm today.* Heute ist es ziemlich warm. ◊ *I've been there quite a lot.* Ich war schon ziemlich oft da. ◊ *quite a lot of money* ziemlich viel Geld ◊ *There were quite a*

*few people there.* Es waren ziemlich viele Leute da. ◊ *It costs quite a lot to go abroad.* Es ist ziemlich teuer, ins Ausland zu fahren. ◊ *It's quite a long way.* Es ist ziemlich weit.

◆ **It was quite a shock.** Es war ein ziemlicher Schock.

◆ **I quite liked the film, but ...** Der Film hat mir ganz gut gefallen, aber ...

2 ganz (*entirely*) ◊ *I'm not quite sure.* Ich bin mir nicht ganz sicher. ◊ *It's not quite the same.* Das ist nicht ganz das Gleiche.

◆ **quite good** ganz gut

**quiz** NOUN

das Quiz (GEN des Quiz, PL die Quiz)

**quota** NOUN

die Quote

**quotation** NOUN

das Zitat (PL die Zitate) ◊ *a quotation from Shakespeare* ein Shakespearezitat

**quotation marks** PL NOUN

die Anführungszeichen PL

**quote** NOUN

see also **quote** VERB

das Zitat (PL die Zitate) ◊ *a Shakespeare quote* ein Shakespearezitat

◆ **quotes** (*quotation marks*) die Anführungszeichen ◊ *in quotes* in Anführungszeichen

to **quote** VERB

see also **quote** NOUN

zitieren (PERFECT hat zitiert)

Q

# R

**rabbi** NOUN
der Rabbiner (PL die Rabbiner)
**rabbit** NOUN
das Kaninchen (PL die Kaninchen) ◊ *a rabbit hutch* ein Kaninchenstall MASC
**rabies** SING NOUN
die Tollwut
♦ **a dog with rabies** ein tollwütiger Hund
**race** NOUN

> see also **race** VERB

[1] (*sport*)
das Rennen (PL die Rennen) ◊ *a cycle race* ein Radrennen
[2] (*species*)
die Rasse ◊ *the human race* die Menschheit
♦ **race relations** Rassenbeziehungen FEM PL
to **race** VERB

> see also **race** NOUN

[1] rennen (IMPERFECT rannte, PERFECT ist gerannt) ◊ *We raced to catch the bus.* Wir sind gerannt, um den Bus zu erreichen.
[2] (*have a race*)
um die Wette laufen mit (PRESENT läuft um die Wette, IMPERFECT lief um die Wette, PERFECT ist um die Wette gelaufen) ◊ *I'll race you!* Ich laufe mit dir um die Wette!
**racecourse** NOUN
die Pferderennbahn
**racehorse** NOUN
das Rennpferd (PL die Rennpferde)
**racer** NOUN
das Rennrad (*bike*) (PL die Rennräder)
**racetrack** NOUN
die Rennbahn
**racial** ADJECTIVE
♦ **racial discrimination** die Rassendiskriminierung
**racing car** NOUN
der Rennwagen (PL die Rennwagen)
**racing driver** NOUN
der Rennfahrer (PL die Rennfahrer)
die Rennfahrerin
**racism** NOUN
der Rassismus (GEN des Rassismus)
**racist** ADJECTIVE

> see also **racist** NOUN

rassistisch
♦ **He's racist.** Er ist ein Rassist.
**racist** NOUN

> see also **racist** ADJECTIVE

der Rassist (GEN des Rassisten, PL die Rassisten)
die Rassistin
**rack** NOUN
der Gepäckträger (*for luggage*) (PL die Gepäckträger)

**racket** NOUN
[1] (*for sport*)
der Schläger (PL die Schläger) ◊ *my tennis racket* mein Tennisschläger
[2] (*noise*)
der Krach ◊ *They're making a terrible racket.* Sie machen einen furchtbaren Krach.
**racquet** NOUN
der Schläger (PL die Schläger)
**radar** NOUN
das Radar
**radiation** NOUN
die Strahlung
**radiator** NOUN
der Heizkörper (PL die Heizkörper)
**radio** NOUN
das Radio (PL die Radios)
♦ **on the radio** im Radio
♦ **a radio station** ein Rundfunksender MASC
**radioactive** ADJECTIVE
radioaktiv
**radio cassette** NOUN
der Radiorekorder (PL die Radiorekorder)
**radio-controlled** ADJECTIVE
ferngesteuert (*model plane, car*)
**radish** NOUN
[1] (*small red*)
das Radieschen (PL die Radieschen)
[2] (*long white*)
der Rettich (PL die Rettiche)
**RAF** NOUN (= Royal Air Force)
die britische Luftwaffe ◊ *He's in the RAF.* Er ist bei der britischen Luftwaffe.
**raffle** NOUN
die Tombola (PL die Tombolas) ◊ *a raffle ticket* ein Tombolalos NEUT
**raft** NOUN
das Floß (GEN des Floßes, PL die Flöße)
**rag** NOUN
der Lumpen (PL die Lumpen) ◊ *dressed in rags* in Lumpen gekleidet
♦ **a piece of rag** ein Lappen MASC
**rage** NOUN
die Wut ◊ *mad with rage* wild vor Wut
♦ **to be in a rage** wütend sein ◊ *She was in a rage.* Sie war wütend.
♦ **It's all the rage.** Es ist große Mode.
**raid** NOUN

> see also **raid** VERB

[1] (*burglary*)
der Überfall (PL die Überfälle) ◊ *There was a bank raid near my house.* Es gab einen Banküberfall in der Nähe meines Hauses.
[2] die Razzia (PL die Razzien) ◊ *a police raid* eine Polizeirazzia

to **raid** VERB

> see also **raid** NOUN

eine Razzia machen in +DAT (police) ◊ The police raided a club in Soho. Die Polizei machte in einem Klub in Soho eine Razzia.

**rail** NOUN

[1] (on stairs, bridge, balcony)
das Geländer (PL die Geländer) ◊ Don't lean over the rail! Nicht über das Geländer lehnen!

[2] (on railway line)
die Schiene

♦ **by rail** mit dem Zug

**railcard** NOUN
die Bahncard ® (PL die Bahncards)

**railroad** NOUN US
die Eisenbahn

♦ **a railroad station** ein Bahnhof MASC

**railway** NOUN
die Eisenbahn ◊ the privatization of the railways die Privatisierung der Eisenbahn

♦ **a railway line** eine Eisenbahnlinie

♦ **a railway station** ein Bahnhof MASC

**rain** NOUN

> see also **rain** VERB

der Regen ◊ in the rain im Regen

to **rain** VERB

> see also **rain** NOUN

regnen ◊ It rains a lot here. Hier regnet es viel.

♦ **It's raining.** Es regnet.

**rainbow** NOUN
der Regenbogen (PL die Regenbogen)

**raincoat** NOUN
der Regenmantel (PL die Regenmäntel)

**rainfall** NOUN
der Niederschlag (PL die Niederschläge)

**rainforest** NOUN
der Regenwald (PL die Regenwälder)

**rainy** ADJECTIVE
regnerisch

to **raise** VERB

[1] (lift)
hochheben (IMPERFECT hob hoch, PERFECT hat hochgehoben) ◊ He raised his hand. Er hob die Hand hoch.

[2] (improve)
heben (IMPERFECT hob, PERFECT hat gehoben) ◊ They want to raise standards in schools. Sie wollen das Niveau in den Schulen heben.

♦ **to raise money** Spenden sammeln ◊ The school is raising money for a new gym. Die Schule sammelt Spenden für eine neue Turnhalle.

**raisin** NOUN
die Rosine

**rake** NOUN
der Rechen (PL die Rechen)

**rally** NOUN

[1] (of people)
die Kundgebung

[2] (sport)
die Rallye (PL die Rallyes) ◊ a rally driver ein Rallyefahrer MASC

[3] (in tennis)
der Ballwechsel (PL die Ballwechsel)

**ramble** NOUN
die Wanderung ◊ to go for a ramble eine Wanderung machen

**rambler** NOUN
der Wanderer (PL die Wanderer)
die Wanderin

**ramp** NOUN
die Rampe (for wheelchairs)

**ran** VERB see **run**

**ranch** NOUN
die Ranch (PL die Ranches)

**random** ADJECTIVE

♦ **a random selection** eine Zufallsauswahl

♦ **at random** aufs Geratewohl ◊ We picked the number at random. Wir haben die Nummer aufs Geratewohl ausgewählt.

**rang** VERB see **ring**

**range** NOUN

> see also **range** VERB

die Auswahl ◊ There's a wide range of colours. Es gibt eine große Auswahl an Farben.

♦ **a range of subjects** verschiedene Themen ◊ We study a range of subjects. Wir studieren verschiedene Themen.

♦ **a mountain range** eine Bergkette

to **range** VERB

> see also **range** NOUN

♦ **to range from ... to** gehen von ... bis ◊ Temperatures in summer range from twenty to thirty-five degrees. Die Temperaturen im Sommer gehen von zwanzig bis fünfunddreißig Grad.

♦ **Tickets range from two to twenty pounds.** Karten kosten von zwei bis zwanzig Pfund.

**rank** NOUN

> see also **rank** VERB

♦ **a taxi rank** ein Taxistand MASC

to **rank** VERB

> see also **rank** NOUN

rangieren (PERFECT hat rangiert) ◊ He's ranked third in the United States. Er rangiert in den Vereinigten Staaten an dritter Stelle.

**ransom** NOUN
das Lösegeld (PL die Lösegelder)

**rap** NOUN
der Rap (music)

**rape** NOUN

> see also **rape** VERB

die Vergewaltigung

to **rape** VERB

> see also **rape** NOUN

vergewaltigen (PERFECT hat vergewaltigt)

**rapids** PL NOUN
die Stromschnellen FEM PL

**R**

**rapist** NOUN
der Vergewaltiger (PL die Vergewaltiger)

**rare** ADJECTIVE
[1] selten (*unusual*) ◊ *a rare plant* eine seltene Pflanze
[2] blutig (*steak*)

**rash** NOUN
der Ausschlag (PL die Ausschläge) ◊ *I've got a rash on my chest.* Ich habe einen Ausschlag auf der Brust.

**rasher** NOUN
♦**an egg and two rashers of bacon** ein Ei und zwei Streifen Speck

**raspberry** NOUN
die Himbeere ◊ *raspberry jam* die Himbeermarmelade

**rat** NOUN
die Ratte

**rate** NOUN
see also **rate** VERB
[1] (*price*)
der Preis (GEN des Preises, PL die Preise) ◊ *There are reduced rates for students.* Studenten bekommen ermäßigte Preise.
[2] (*level*)
die Rate ◊ *the divorce rate* die Scheidungsrate
♦**a high rate of interest** ein hoher Zinssatz

to **rate** VERB
see also **rate** NOUN
einschätzen (PERFECT hat eingeschätzt) ◊ *He was rated the best.* Man schätzte ihn als den Besten ein.

**rather** ADVERB
ziemlich ◊ *I was rather disappointed.* Ich war ziemlich enttäuscht. ◊ *Twenty pounds! That's rather a lot!* Zwanzig Pfund! Das ist aber ziemlich viel!
♦**rather a lot of** ziemlich viel ◊ *I've got rather a lot of work to do.* Ich habe ziemlich viel Arbeit.
♦**rather than** statt ◊ *We decided to camp, rather than stay at a hotel.* Wir haben beschlossen zu zelten statt im Hotel zu übernachten.
♦**I'd rather ...** Ich würde lieber ... ◊ *I'd rather stay in tonight.* Ich würde heute Abend lieber zu Hause bleiben. ◊ *Would you like a sweet? – I'd rather have an apple.* Möchtest du ein Bonbon? – Ich hätte lieber einen Apfel.

**rattle** NOUN
die Rassel (*for baby*)

**rattlesnake** NOUN
die Klapperschlange

to **rave** VERB
see also **rave** NOUN
schwärmen ◊ *They raved about the film.* Sie schwärmten von dem Film.

**rave** NOUN
see also **rave** VERB

die Raveparty (*party*) (PL die Ravepartys)
♦**rave music** die Ravemusik

**raven** NOUN
der Rabe (GEN des Raben, PL die Raben)

**ravenous** ADJECTIVE
♦**to be ravenous** einen Riesenhunger haben ◊ *I'm ravenous!* Ich habe einen Riesenhunger!

**raving** ADVERB
♦**raving mad** total verrückt (*informal*)

**raw** ADJECTIVE
roh (*food*)
♦**raw materials** die Rohstoffe MASC PL

**razor** NOUN
der Rasierapparat (PL die Rasierapparate)
♦**a razor blade** eine Rasierklinge

**RE** NOUN (= *religious education*)
der Religionsunterricht

**reach** NOUN
see also **reach** VERB
♦**out of reach** außer Reichweite ◊ *The light switch was out of reach.* Der Lichtschalter war außer Reichweite.
♦**within easy reach** leicht zu erreichen ◊ *The hotel is within easy reach of the town centre.* Das Hotel ist vom Stadtzentrum leicht zu erreichen.

to **reach** VERB
see also **reach** NOUN
[1] ankommen in +DAT (IMPERFECT kam an, PERFECT ist angekommen) ◊ *We reached the hotel at ten o'clock.* Wir sind um zehn Uhr im Hotel angekommen.
♦**We hope to reach the final.** Wir wollen ins Endspiel kommen.
[2] (*decision*)
treffen (PRESENT trifft, IMPERFECT traf, PERFECT hat getroffen) ◊ *Eventually they reached a decision.* Sie haben schließlich eine Entscheidung getroffen.
♦**He reached for his gun.** Er griff nach seiner Pistole.

to **react** VERB
reagieren (PERFECT hat reagiert)

**reaction** NOUN
die Reaktion

**reactor** NOUN
der Reaktor (PL die Reaktoren) ◊ *a nuclear reactor* ein Kernreaktor

to **read** VERB
lesen (PRESENT liest, IMPERFECT las, PERFECT hat gelesen) ◊ *I don't read much.* Ich lese nicht viel. ◊ *Have you read "Animal Farm"?* Hast du "Die Farm der Tiere" gelesen? ◊ *Read the text out loud.* Lies den Text laut.

**reader** NOUN
(*person*)
der Leser (PL die Leser)
die Leserin

**readily** ADVERB

bereitwillig ◊ *She readily agreed.* Sie stimmte bereitwillig zu.

**reading** NOUN
das Lesen ◊ *Reading is one of my hobbies.* Lesen ist eines meiner Hobbies.

**ready** ADJECTIVE
fertig ◊ *She's nearly ready.* Sie ist fast fertig.
◆ **He's always ready to help.** Er ist immer bereit zu helfen.
◆ **a ready meal** ein Fertiggericht NEUT
◆ **to get ready** sich fertig machen ◊ *She's getting ready to go out.* Sie macht sich zum Ausgehen fertig.
◆ **to get something ready** etwas machen ◊ *He's getting the dinner ready.* Er macht das Abendessen.

**real** ADJECTIVE
[1] echt (*not fake*) ◊ *He wasn't a real policeman.* Er war kein echter Polizist. ◊ *It's real leather.* Es ist echtes Leder.
[2] wirklich ◊ *Her real name is Cordelia.* Ihr wirklicher Name ist Cordelia. ◊ *in real life* im wirklichen Leben
◆ **It was a real nightmare.** Es war wirklich ein Alptraum.

**realistic** ADJECTIVE
realistisch

**reality** NOUN
die Wirklichkeit

to **realize** VERB
◆ **to realize that ...** bemerken, dass ... ◊ *We realized that something was wrong.* Wir bemerkten, dass irgendetwas nicht stimmte.

**really** ADVERB
wirklich ◊ *She's really nice.* Sie ist wirklich nett. ◊ *I'm learning Italian. – Really?* Ich lerne Italienisch. – Wirklich? ◊ *Do you really think so?* Meinst du wirklich?
◆ **Do you want to go? – Not really.** Willst du gehen? – Eigentlich nicht.

**realtor** NOUN US
der Immobilienhändler (PL die Immobilienhändler)
die Immobilienhändlerin

**rear** ADJECTIVE
see also **rear** NOUN
hintere ◊ *the rear windows* die hinteren Fenster
◆ **the rear wheel** das Hinterrad

**rear** NOUN
see also **rear** ADJECTIVE
das hintere Ende (PL die hinteren Enden) ◊ *at the rear of the train* am hinteren Ende des Zuges

**reason** NOUN
der Grund (PL die Gründe) ◊ *There's no reason to think that ...* Es gibt keinen Grund zu meinen, dass ...
◆ **for security reasons** aus Sicherheitsgründen

◆ **That was the main reason I went.** Das war der Hauptgrund, warum ich gegangen bin.

**reasonable** ADJECTIVE
[1] vernünftig (*sensible*) ◊ *Be reasonable!* Sei vernünftig!
[2] ganz ordentlich (*not bad*) ◊ *He wrote a reasonable essay.* Er hat einen ganz ordentlichen Aufsatz geschrieben.

**reasonably** ADVERB
ziemlich ◊ *The team played reasonably well.* Die Mannschaft hat ziemlich gut gespielt.
◆ **reasonably priced accommodation** preiswerte Unterbringung

to **reassure** VERB
beruhigen (PERFECT hat beruhigt)

**reassuring** ADJECTIVE
beruhigend

**rebel** NOUN
see also **rebel** VERB
der Rebell (PL die Rebellen)
die Rebellin

to **rebel** VERB
see also **rebel** NOUN
rebellieren (PERFECT hat rebelliert)

**rebellious** ADJECTIVE
aufmüpfig

**receipt** NOUN
die Quittung

to **receive** VERB
erhalten (PRESENT erhält, IMPERFECT erhielt, PERFECT hat erhalten)

**receiver** NOUN
der Hörer (*of phone*) (PL die Hörer) ◊ *to pick up the receiver* den Hörer abnehmen

**recent** ADJECTIVE
neueste ◊ *the recent developments in ...* die neuesten Entwicklungen in ...
◆ **in recent years** in den letzten Jahren

**recently** ADVERB
in letzter Zeit ◊ *I've been doing a lot of training recently.* Ich habe in letzter Zeit viel trainiert.

**reception** NOUN
[1] (*in hotel*)
die Rezeption ◊ *Please leave your key at reception.* Bitte geben Sie Ihren Schlüssel an der Rezeption ab.
[2] (*party*)
der Empfang (PL die Empfänge) ◊ *The reception will be at a big hotel.* Der Empfang findet in einem großen Hotel statt.

**receptionist** NOUN
der Empfangschef (PL die Empfangschefs)
die Empfangsdame

**recession** NOUN
die Rezession

**recipe** NOUN
das Rezept (PL die Rezepte)

**R**

**to reckon** VERB
meinen ◊ *What do you reckon?* Was
meinst du?

**reclining** ADJECTIVE
♦ **a reclining seat** ein Liegesitz MASC

**recognizable** ADJECTIVE
[1] wieder zu erkennen ◊ *He was
scarcely recognizable after the accident.*
Er war nach dem Unfall kaum wieder zu
erkennen.
[2] erkennbar (*noticeable*) ◊ *There was a
recognizable improvement in his work.*
Seine Arbeit hat erkennbare Fortschritte
gemacht.

**to recognize** VERB
erkennen (IMPERFECT erkannte, PERFECT hat
erkannt) ◊ *You'll recognize me by my red
hair.* Du wirst mich an meinen roten
Haaren erkennen.

**to recommend** VERB
empfehlen (PRESENT empfiehlt, IMPERFECT
empfahl, PERFECT hat empfohlen) ◊ *What
do you recommend?* Was können Sie
empfehlen?

**to reconsider** VERB
♦ **to reconsider something** sich etwas noch
einmal überlegen ◊ *I think you should
reconsider your decision.* Ich denke, du
solltest dir die Entscheidung noch einmal
überlegen.

**record** NOUN
| see also **record** VERB |
[1] (*recording*)
die Schallplatte ◊ *my favourite record*
meine Lieblingsschallplatte
[2] (*sport*)
der Rekord (PL die Rekorde) ◊ *the world
record* der Weltrekord
♦ **in record time** in Rekordzeit ◊ *She
finished the job in record time.* Sie war in
Rekordzeit mit der Arbeit fertig.
♦ **He's got a criminal record.** Er ist
vorbestraft.
♦ **records** (*of police, hospital*) die Akten ◊ *I'll
check in the records.* Ich sehe in den
Akten nach.
♦ **There is no record of your booking.** Ihre
Buchung ist nirgends belegt.

**to record** VERB
| see also **record** NOUN |
aufnehmen (*on film, tape*) (PRESENT nimmt
auf, IMPERFECT nahm auf, PERFECT hat
aufgenommen) ◊ *They've just recorded
their new album.* Sie haben eben ihr
neues Album aufgenommen.

**recorded delivery** NOUN
♦ **to send something recorded delivery**
etwas per Einschreiben senden

**recorder** NOUN
die Blockflöte (*instrument*) ◊ *She plays
the recorder.* Sie spielt Blockflöte.
♦ **a cassette recorder** ein
Kassettenrekorder MASC

♦ **a video recorder** ein Videorekorder MASC

**recording** NOUN
die Aufnahme

**record player** NOUN
der Plattenspieler (PL die Plattenspieler)

**to recover** VERB
sich erholen (PERFECT hat sich erholt)
◊ *He's recovering from a knee injury.* Er
erholt sich von einer Knieverletzung.

**recovery** NOUN
die Erholung
♦ **Best wishes for a speedy recovery!** Gute
Besserung!

**rectangle** NOUN
das Rechteck (PL die Rechtecke)

**rectangular** ADJECTIVE
rechteckig

**to recycle** VERB
wieder verwerten (PERFECT hat wieder
verwertet)

**recycling** NOUN
das Recycling

**red** ADJECTIVE
rot ◊ *a red rose* eine rote Rose ◊ *red
meat* rotes Fleisch ◊ *Peter's got red hair.*
Peter hat rote Haare.
♦ **to go through a red light** bei Rot über die
Ampel fahren

**Red Cross** NOUN
das Rote Kreuz

**redcurrant** NOUN
die Rote Johannisbeere

**to redecorate** VERB
renovieren (PERFECT hat renoviert)

**red-haired** ADJECTIVE
rothaarig

**red-handed** ADJECTIVE
♦ **to catch somebody red-handed**
jemanden auf frischer Tat ertappen ◊ *He
was caught red-handed.* Er wurde auf
frischer Tat ertappt.

**redhead** NOUN
der Rothaarige (GEN des Rothaarigen, PL
die Rothaarigen)
die Rothaarige (GEN der Rothaarigen) ◊ *a
redhead* (*man*) ein Rothaariger

**to redo** VERB
noch einmal machen

**to reduce** VERB
ermäßigen (PERFECT hat ermäßigt) ◊ *at a
reduced price* zu ermäßigtem Preis
♦ **"reduce speed now"** "Geschwindigkeit
verringern"

**reduction** NOUN
der Nachlass (GEN des Nachlasses, PL die
Nachlässe) ◊ *a five per cent reduction* ein
Nachlass von fünf Prozent
♦ **"Huge reductions!"** "Stark reduzierte
Preise!"

**redundancy** NOUN

die <u>Entlassung</u> ◊ *There were fifty redundancies.* Es gab fünfzig Entlassungen.
◆ **his redundancy payment** seine Abfindung

**redundant** ADJECTIVE
◆ **to be made redundant** entlassen werden ◊ *He was made redundant yesterday.* Er wurde gestern entlassen.

**reed** NOUN
das <u>Schilf</u> (*plant*)

**reel** NOUN
die <u>Spule</u> (*of thread*)

to **refer** VERB
◆ **to refer to** anspielen auf +ACC ◊ *What are you referring to?* Auf was spielst du an?

**referee** NOUN
der <u>Schiedsrichter</u> (PL die Schiedsrichter)
die <u>Schiedsrichterin</u>

**reference** NOUN
das <u>Arbeitszeugnis</u> (*for job application*) (GEN des Arbeitszeugnisses, PL die Arbeitszeugnisse) ◊ *Would you please give me a reference?* Können Sie mir bitte ein Arbeitszeugnis geben?
◆ **With reference to your letter of ...** Mit Bezug auf Ihren Brief vom ...
◆ **a reference book** ein Nachschlagewerk NEUT

to **refill** VERB
<u>nachfüllen</u> (PERFECT hat nachgefüllt) ◊ *He refilled my glass.* Er füllte mein Glas nach.

**refinery** NOUN
die <u>Raffinerie</u>

to **reflect** VERB
<u>reflektieren</u> (*light, image*) (PERFECT hat reflektiert)

**reflection** NOUN
das <u>Spiegelbild</u> (*in mirror*) (PL die Spiegelbilder)

**reflex** NOUN
der <u>Reflex</u> (GEN des Reflexes, PL die Reflexe)

**reflexive** ADJECTIVE
<u>reflexiv</u> ◊ *a reflexive verb* ein reflexives Verb

**refresher course** NOUN
der <u>Wiederholungskurs</u> (GEN des Wiederholungskurses, PL die Wiederholungskurse)

**refreshing** ADJECTIVE
<u>erfrischend</u>

**refreshments** PL NOUN
die <u>Erfrischungen</u> FEM PL

**refrigerator** NOUN
der <u>Kühlschrank</u> (PL die Kühlschränke)

to **refuel** VERB
<u>auftanken</u> (PERFECT hat aufgetankt) ◊ *Our plane refuelled in Boston.* Unser Flugzeug hat in Boston aufgetankt.

**refuge** NOUN

die <u>Zuflucht</u>

**refugee** NOUN
der <u>Flüchtling</u> (PL die Flüchtlinge)
*der Flüchtling is also used for women.*

**refund** NOUN
see also **refund** VERB
die <u>Rückvergütung</u>

to **refund** VERB
see also **refund** NOUN
<u>zurückerstatten</u> (PERFECT hat zurückerstattet)

**refusal** NOUN
die <u>Weigerung</u>

to **refuse** VERB
see also **refuse** NOUN
<u>sich weigern</u>

**refuse** NOUN
see also **refuse** VERB
der <u>Müll</u>
◆ **refuse collection** die Müllabfuhr

to **regain** VERB
◆ **to regain consciousness** wieder zu Bewusstsein kommen

**regard** NOUN
see also **regard** VERB
◆ **Give my regards to Alice.** Grüße an Alice.
◆ **Martin sends his regards.** Martin lässt grüßen.
◆ **"with kind regards"** "mit freundlichen Grüßen"

to **regard** VERB
see also **regard** NOUN
◆ **to regard something as** etwas betrachten als
◆ **as regards ...** was ... betrifft ◊ *As regards offensive weapons ...* Was Angriffswaffen betrifft, ...

**regarding** PREPOSITION
<u>betreffend</u> ◊ *the laws regarding the export of animals* die Gesetze den Export von Tieren betreffend
◆ **Regarding John, ...** Was John betrifft, ...

**regardless** ADVERB
<u>trotzdem</u> ◊ *to carry on regardless* trotzdem weitermachen

**regiment** NOUN
das <u>Regiment</u> (PL die Regimenter)

**region** NOUN
die <u>Gegend</u>

**regional** ADJECTIVE
<u>regional</u>

**register** NOUN
see also **register** VERB
das <u>Klassenbuch</u> (*in school*) (PL die Klassenbücher)

to **register** VERB
see also **register** NOUN
<u>sich einschreiben</u> (*at school, college*) (IMPERFECT schrieb sich ein, PERFECT hat sich eingeschrieben)

**registered** ADJECTIVE

R

♦ **a registered letter** ein eingeschriebener Brief

**registration** NOUN

☐1 (*in school*)
der Namensaufruf (PL die Namensaufrufe)

☐2 (*of car*)
das polizeiliche Kennzeichen (PL die polizeilichen Kennzeichen)

**regret** NOUN

see also **regret** VERB

das Bedauern

♦ **I've got no regrets.** Ich bedaure nichts.

to **regret** VERB

see also **regret** NOUN

bedauern (PERFECT hat bedauert) ◊ *Give me the money or you'll regret it!* Gib mir das Geld oder du wirst es bedauern!

♦ **to regret doing something** es bedauern, etwas getan zu haben ◊ *I regretted having said that.* Ich habe bedauert, dass ich das gesagt habe.

**regular** ADJECTIVE

☐1 regelmäßig ◊ *at regular intervals* in regelmäßigen Abständen ◊ *a regular verb* ein regelmäßiges Verb

♦ **to take regular exercise** regelmäßig Sport machen

☐2 normal (*average*) ◊ *a regular portion of fries* eine normale Portion Pommes frites

**regularly** ADVERB

regelmäßig

**regulation** NOUN

die Bestimmung

**rehearsal** NOUN

die Probe

to **rehearse** VERB

proben

**rein** NOUN

der Zügel (PL die Zügel) ◊ *the reins* die Zügel

**reindeer** NOUN

das Rentier (PL die Rentiere)

to **reject** VERB

verwerfen (*idea, suggestion*) (PRESENT verwirft, IMPERFECT verwarf, PERFECT hat verworfen) ◊ *We rejected that idea straight away.* Wir haben die Idee sofort verworfen.

♦ **I applied but they rejected me.** Ich habe mich beworben, wurde aber abgelehnt.

**relapse** NOUN

der Rückfall (PL die Rückfälle) ◊ *to have a relapse* einen Rückfall haben

**related** ADJECTIVE

verwandt (*people*) ◊ *Are you related to her?* Bist du mit ihr verwandt? ◊ *We're related.* Wir sind miteinander verwandt.

♦ **The two events were not related.** Es bestand kein Zusammenhang zwischen den beiden Ereignissen.

**relation** NOUN

☐1 (*person*)
der Verwandte (GEN des Verwandten, PL die Verwandten)
die Verwandte (GEN der Verwandten)
◊ *He's a distant relation.* Er ist ein entfernter Verwandter. ◊ *I've got relations in London.* Ich habe Verwandte in London. ◊ *my close relations* meine engsten Verwandten

☐2 (*connection*)
der Bezug (PL die Bezüge) ◊ *It has no relation to reality.* Es hat keinen Bezug zur Wirklichkeit.

♦ **in relation to** verglichen mit

**relationship** NOUN

die Beziehung ◊ *We have a good relationship.* Wir haben eine gute Beziehung. ◊ *I'm not in a relationship at the moment.* Ich habe im Moment keine Beziehung.

**relative** NOUN

der Verwandte (GEN des Verwandten, PL die Verwandten)
die Verwandte (GEN der Verwandten) ◊ *a relative (man)* ein Verwandter ◊ *my close relatives* meine engsten Verwandten

♦ **all her relatives** ihre ganze Verwandtschaft

**relatively** ADVERB

relativ

to **relax** VERB

sich entspannen (PERFECT hat sich entspannt) ◊ *I relax listening to music.* Ich entspanne mich beim Musikhören.

♦ **Relax! Everything's fine.** Immer mit der Ruhe! Alles ist in Ordnung.

**relaxation** NOUN

die Entspannung ◊ *I don't have much time for relaxation.* Ich habe nicht viel Zeit für Entspannung.

**relaxed** ADJECTIVE

entspannt

**relaxing** ADJECTIVE

entspannend ◊ *I find cooking relaxing.* Ich finde Kochen entspannend.

**relay** NOUN

♦ **a relay race** ein Staffellauf MASC

to **release** VERB

see also **release** NOUN

☐1 (*prisoner*)
freilassen (PRESENT lässt frei, IMPERFECT ließ frei, PERFECT hat freigelassen)

☐2 (*report, news*)
veröffentlichen (PERFECT hat veröffentlicht)

☐3 (*record, video*)
herausbringen (IMPERFECT brachte heraus, PERFECT hat herausgebracht)

**release** NOUN

see also **release** VERB

die Freilassung (*from prison*) ◊ *the release of Nelson Mandela* die Freilassung Nelson Mandelas

◆ **the band's latest release** die neueste Platte der Band

**relegated** ADJECTIVE
abgestiegen (*sport*) ◊ *Our team was relegated.* Unsere Mannschaft ist abgestiegen.

**relevant** ADJECTIVE
entsprechend (*documents*)
◆ **That's not relevant.** Das ist nicht relevant.
◆ **to be relevant to something** einen Bezug zu etwas haben ◊ *Education should be relevant to real life.* Die Ausbildung sollte einen Bezug zum wirklichen Leben haben.

**reliable** ADJECTIVE
zuverlässig ◊ *a reliable car* ein zuverlässiges Auto ◊ *He's not very reliable.* Er ist nicht sehr zuverlässig.

**relief** NOUN
die Erleichterung ◊ *That's a relief!* Das ist eine Erleichterung!

to **relieve** VERB
lindern ◊ *This injection will relieve the pain.* Diese Spritze wird den Schmerz lindern.

**relieved** ADJECTIVE
erleichtert ◊ *I was relieved to hear ...* Ich war erleichtert zu hören ...

**religion** NOUN
die Religion ◊ *What religion are you?* Welche Religion hast du?

**religious** ADJECTIVE
religiös ◊ *I'm not religious.* Ich bin nicht religiös.
◆ **my religious beliefs** mein Glaube MASC

**reluctant** ADJECTIVE
◆ **to be reluctant to do something** etwas nur ungern tun ◊ *They were reluctant to help us.* Sie haben uns nur ungern geholfen.

**reluctantly** ADVERB
ungern ◊ *She reluctantly accepted.* Sie hat ungern angenommen.

to **rely on** VERB
sich verlassen auf +ACC (PRESENT verlässt sich, IMPERFECT verließ sich, PERFECT hat sich verlassen) ◊ *I'm relying on you.* Ich verlasse mich auf dich.

to **remain** VERB
bleiben (IMPERFECT blieb, PERFECT ist geblieben)
◆ **to remain silent** schweigen

**remaining** ADJECTIVE
restlich ◊ *the remaining ingredients* die restlichen Zutaten

**remains** PL NOUN
die Reste MASC PL ◊ *the remains of the picnic* die Reste des Picknicks
◆ **human remains** die menschlichen Überreste
◆ **Roman remains** römische Ruinen

**remake** NOUN
das Remake (*of film*) (PL die Remakes)

**remark** NOUN
die Bemerkung

**remarkable** ADJECTIVE
bemerkenswert

**remarkably** ADVERB
bemerkenswert

to **remarry** VERB
wieder heiraten ◊ *She remarried three years ago.* Sie hat vor drei Jahren wieder geheiratet.

**remedy** NOUN
das Mittel (PL die Mittel) ◊ *a good remedy for a sore throat* ein gutes Mittel gegen Halsschmerzen

to **remember** VERB
sich erinnern (PERFECT hat sich erinnert) ◊ *I can't remember his name.* Ich kann mich nicht an seinen Namen erinnern. ◊ *I don't remember.* Ich erinnere mich nicht.

*In German you often say "don't forget" rather than* **remember** *when reminding somebody about something.*

◊ *Remember your passport!* Vergiss deinen Pass nicht! ◊ *Remember to write your name on the form.* Vergiss nicht, deinen Namen auf das Formular zu schreiben.

**Remembrance Day** NOUN
der Volkstrauertag ◊ *on Remembrance Day* am Volkstrauertag

to **remind** VERB
erinnern (PERFECT hat erinnert) ◊ *It reminds me of Scotland.* Es erinnert mich an Schottland. ◊ *I'll remind you tomorrow.* Ich werde dich morgen daran erinnern. ◊ *Remind me to speak to Daniel.* Erinnere mich, dass ich mit Daniel sprechen will.

**remorse** NOUN
die Reue ◊ *He showed no remorse.* Er zeigte keine Reue.

**remote** ADJECTIVE
abgelegen ◊ *a remote village* ein abgelegenes Dorf

**remote control** NOUN
die Fernbedienung

**remotely** ADVERB
entfernt ◊ *There was nobody remotely resembling this description.* Niemand sah dieser Beschreibung auch nur entfernt ähnlich.
◆ **I suppose it is remotely possible that ...** Ich denke, es it gerade eben noch möglich, dass ...

**removable** ADJECTIVE
abnehmbar

**removal** NOUN
der Umzug (*from house*) (PL die Umzüge)
◆ **a removal van** ein Möbelwagen MASC

to **remove** VERB

**R**

☞

entfernen (PERFECT hat entfernt) ◊ *Did you remove the stain?* Hast du den Fleck entfernt?

**rendezvous** NOUN
das Treffen (PL die Treffen)

to **renew** VERB
verlängern lassen (*passport, licence*) (PRESENT lässt verlängern, IMPERFECT ließ verlängern, PERFECT hat verlängern lassen) ◊ *You'll need to renew your passport.* Du musst deinen Pass verlängern lassen.
♦**to renew a contract** einen Vertrag verlängern

**renewable** ADJECTIVE
erneuerbar (*energy, resource, passport*)

to **renovate** VERB
renovieren (PERFECT hat renoviert) ◊ *The building's been renovated.* Das Gebäude ist renoviert worden.

**renowned** ADJECTIVE
berühmt

**rent** NOUN
see also **rent** VERB
die Miete
*Be careful not to translate **rent** by **Rente**.*

to **rent** VERB
see also **rent** NOUN
mieten ◊ *We rented a car.* Wir haben ein Auto gemietet.

**rental** NOUN
die Miete ◊ *Car rental is included in the price.* Die Automiete ist im Preis inbegriffen.

**rental car** NOUN US
der Mietwagen (PL die Mietwagen)

to **reorganize** VERB
umorganisieren (PERFECT hat umorganisiert)

**rep** NOUN (= *representative*)
der Vertreter (PL die Vertreter)
die Vertreterin

**repaid** VERB *see* **repay**

to **repair** VERB
see also **repair** NOUN
reparieren (PERFECT hat repariert)
♦**to get something repaired** etwas reparieren lassen ◊ *I got the washing machine repaired.* Ich habe die Waschmaschine reparieren lassen.

**repair** NOUN
see also **repair** VERB
die Reparatur

to **repay** VERB
zurückzahlen (*money*) (PERFECT hat zurückgezahlt)

**repayment** NOUN
die Rückzahlung

to **repeat** VERB
see also **repeat** NOUN
wiederholen (PERFECT hat wiederholt)

**repeat** NOUN
see also **repeat** VERB

die Wiederholung ◊ *There are too many repeats on TV.* Es gibt zu viele Wiederholungen im Fernsehen.

**repeatedly** ADVERB
wiederholt

**repellent** NOUN
♦**insect repellent** das Insektenschutzmittel

**repetitive** ADJECTIVE
monoton (*movement, work*)

to **replace** VERB
ersetzen (PERFECT hat ersetzt)

**replay** NOUN
see also **replay** VERB
♦**There will be a replay on Friday.** Das Spiel wird am Freitag wiederholt.

to **replay** VERB
see also **replay** NOUN
wiederholen (*match*) (PERFECT hat wiederholt)

**replica** NOUN
die Kopie

**reply** NOUN
see also **reply** VERB
die Antwort

to **reply** VERB
see also **reply** NOUN
antworten

**report** NOUN
see also **report** VERB
1 (*of event*)
der Bericht (PL die Berichte) ◊ *a report in the paper* ein Zeitungsbericht
2 (*at school*)
das Zeugnis (GEN des Zeugnisses, PL die Zeugnisse) ◊ *I got a good report this year.* Ich habe in diesem Jahr ein gutes Zeugnis.
♦**report card** das Zeugnis

to **report** VERB
see also **report** NOUN
1 melden ◊ *I reported the theft to the police.* Ich habe den Diebstahl bei der Polizei gemeldet.
2 sich melden ◊ *Report to reception when you arrive.* Melden Sie sich bei Ihrer Ankunft am Empfang.

**reporter** NOUN
der Reporter (PL die Reporter)
die Reporterin
◊ *She'd like to be a reporter.* Sie möchte gern Reporterin werden.

to **represent** VERB
vertreten (*person*) (PRESENT vertritt, IMPERFECT vertrat, PERFECT hat vertreten) ◊ *my lawyer represented me in court.* Mein Anwalt hat mich vor Gericht vertreten.

**representative** ADJECTIVE
repräsentativ

**reproduction** NOUN
die Reproduktion

**reptile** NOUN
das Reptil (PL die Reptilien)

**republic** NOUN
die Republik
**repulsive** ADJECTIVE
abstoßend
**reputable** ADJECTIVE
angesehen
**reputation** NOUN
der Ruf
**request** NOUN
see also **request** VERB
die Bitte
to **request** VERB
see also **request** NOUN
bitten um (IMPERFECT bat, PERFECT hat
gebeten) ◊ He requested information. Er
bat um Informationen.
to **require** VERB
erfordern (PERFECT hat erfordert) ◊ Her job
requires a lot of patience. Ihre Arbeit
erfordert viel Geduld.
**requirement** NOUN
die Voraussetzung ◊ What are the
requirements for the job? Was sind die
Voraussetzungen für diese Arbeit?
♦ **entry requirements** (for university) die
Aufnahmebedingungen
**resat** VERB see **resit**
to **rescue** VERB
see also **rescue** NOUN
retten
**rescue** NOUN
see also **rescue** VERB
die Rettung ◊ a rescue operation eine
Rettungsaktion
♦ **a mountain rescue team** ein Team der
Bergwacht
♦ **the rescue services** der Rettungsdienst
SING
♦ **to come to somebody's rescue**
jemandem zu Hilfe kommen ◊ He came
to my rescue. Er kam mir zu Hilfe.
**research** NOUN
die Forschung (experimental) ◊ He's
doing research. Er ist in der Forschung
tätig.
♦ **Research has shown that ...**
Forschungen haben ergeben, dass ...
♦ **She's doing some research in the library.**
Sie sammelt in der Bibliothek Material.
**resemblance** NOUN
die Ähnlichkeit
to **resent** VERB
übel nehmen (PRESENT nimmt übel,
IMPERFECT nahm übel, PERFECT hat übel
genommen) ◊ I really resent your
criticism. Ich nehme Ihnen Ihre Kritik
wirklich übel.
♦ **I resent being dependent on her.** Ich
ärgere mich darüber, von ihr abhängig
zu sein.
**resentful** ADJECTIVE

verärgert ◊ He was resentful at the way
they had been treated. Er war verärgert
darüber, wie man sie behandelt hatte.
**reservation** NOUN
[1] die Reservierung (at restaurant)
♦ **I'd like to make a reservation for this
evening.** Ich möchte für heute Abend
einen Tisch reservieren.
[2] die Buchung (for journey, at hotel)
♦ **I've got a reservation for two nights.** Ich
habe für zwei Nächte gebucht.
**reserve** NOUN
see also **reserve** VERB
[1] (place)
das Schutzgebiet (PL die Schutzgebiete)
◊ a nature reserve ein Naturschutzgebiet
[2] (person)
der Reservespieler (PL die
Reservespieler)
die Reservespielerin
◊ She was reserve in the game last
Saturday. Sie war beim Spiel letzten
Samstag Reservespielerin.
to **reserve** VERB
see also **reserve** NOUN
reservieren (PERFECT hat reserviert) ◊ I'd
like to reserve a table for tomorrow
evening. Ich möchte für morgen Abend
einen Tisch reservieren.
**reserved** ADJECTIVE
reserviert ◊ a reserved seat ein
reservierter Platz ◊ He's quite reserved.
Er ist ziemlich reserviert.
**reservoir** NOUN
das Reservoir (PL die Reservoire)
**resident** NOUN
der Bewohner (PL die Bewohner)
die Bewohnerin
**residential** ADJECTIVE
♦ **a residential area** ein Wohngebiet NEUT
to **resign** VERB
[1] zurücktreten (PRESENT tritt zurück,
IMPERFECT trat zurück, PERFECT ist
zurückgetreten) ◊ The foreign minister
has resigned. Der Außenminister ist
zurückgetreten.
[2] (employee)
kündigen ◊ She resigned to take up a
post abroad. Sie kündigte, um einen
Posten im Ausland zu übernehmen.
**resistance** NOUN
der Widerstand (PL die Widerstände)
to **resit** VERB
wiederholen (PERFECT hat wiederholt)
◊ I'm resitting the exam in December.
Ich wiederhole die Prüfung im
Dezember.
**resolution** NOUN
der Beschluss (decision) (GEN des
Beschlusses, PL die Beschlüsse)
♦ **Have you made any New Year's
resolutions?** Hast du zum neuen Jahr
gute Vorsätze gefasst?

**R**

**resort** NOUN
der Badeort (*at seaside*) (PL die Badeorte) ◊ *It's a resort on the Costa del Sol.* Es ist ein Badeort an der Costa del Sol.
♦ **a ski resort** ein Skiort
♦ **as a last resort** als letzter Ausweg

**resources** PL NOUN
die Mittel NEUT PL (*financial*) ◊ *We do not have the resources to build a new swimming pool.* Wir haben nicht die Mittel, um ein neues Schwimmbad zu bauen.
♦ **natural resources** Bodenschätze MASC PL

**respect** NOUN
see also **respect** VERB
der Respekt

to **respect** VERB
see also **respect** NOUN
respektieren (PERFECT hat respektiert)

**respectable** ADJECTIVE
[1] anständig ◊ *respectable people* anständige Leute PL
[2] ordentlich (*standard, marks*)

**respectively** ADVERB
beziehungsweise ◊ *Britain and Germany were third and fourth respectively.* Großbritannien und Deutschland belegten den dritten beziehungsweise vierten Platz.

**responsibility** NOUN
die Verantwortung

**responsible** ADJECTIVE
[1] verantwortlich ◊ *to be responsible for something* für etwas verantwortlich sein
♦ **It's a responsible job.** Es ist ein verantwortungsvoller Posten.
[2] verantwortungsbewusst (*mature*) ◊ *You should be more responsible.* Du solltest verantwortungsbewusster sein.

**rest** NOUN
see also **rest** VERB
[1] (*relaxation*)
die Pause ◊ *five minutes' rest* eine fünfminütige Pause
♦ **to have a rest** sich ausruhen ◊ *We stopped to have a rest.* Wir haben Halt gemacht, um uns auszuruhen.
[2] (*remainder*)
der Rest (PL die Reste) ◊ *I'll do the rest.* Ich mache den Rest. ◊ *the rest of the money* der Rest des Geldes
♦ **the rest of them** die anderen ◊ *The rest of them went swimming.* Die anderen sind schwimmen gegangen.

to **rest** VERB
see also **rest** NOUN
[1] (*relax*)
sich ausruhen (PERFECT hat sich ausgeruht) ◊ *She's resting in her room.* Sie ruht sich in ihrem Zimmer aus.
[2] (*not overstrain*)

schonen ◊ *He has to rest his knee.* Er muss sein Knie schonen.
[3] (*lean*)
lehnen ◊ *I rested my bike against the window.* Ich habe mein Fahrrad ans Fenster gelehnt.

**restaurant** NOUN
das Restaurant (PL die Restaurants) ◊ *We don't often go to restaurants.* Wir gehen nicht oft ins Restaurant.
♦ **a restaurant car** ein Speisewagen MASC

**restful** ADJECTIVE
ruhig

**restless** ADJECTIVE
unruhig

**restoration** NOUN
die Restauration

to **restore** VERB
restaurieren (*building, picture*) (PERFECT hat restauriert)

to **restrict** VERB
beschränken (PERFECT hat beschränkt)

**rest room** NOUN US
die Toilette

**result** NOUN
das Ergebnis (GEN des Ergebnisses, PL die Ergebnisse) ◊ *my exam results* meine Prüfungsergebnisse
♦ **What was the result? – One nil.** Wie ist das Spiel ausgegangen? – Eins zu null.

**résumé** NOUN US
[1] die Zusammenfassung ◊ *a résumé of her speech* eine Zusammenfassung ihrer Rede
[2] (*CV*)
der Lebenslauf (PL die Lebensläufe)

to **retire** VERB
in Rente gehen (IMPERFECT ging in Rente, PERFECT ist in Rente gegangen) ◊ *He retired last year.* Er ist letztes Jahr in Rente gegangen.

**retired** ADJECTIVE
im Ruhestand ◊ *She's retired.* Sie ist im Ruhestand. ◊ *a retired teacher* ein Lehrer im Ruhestand

**retirement** NOUN
der Ruhestand

to **retrace** VERB
♦ **to retrace one's steps** zurückgehen ◊ *I retraced my steps.* Ich bin zurückgegangen.

**return** NOUN
see also **return** VERB
[1] die Rückkehr ◊ *after our return* nach unserer Rückkehr
♦ **the return journey** die Rückfahrt
♦ **a return match** ein Rückspiel NEUT
[2] die Rückfahrkarte (*ticket*) ◊ *A return to Freiburg, please.* Eine Rückfahrkarte nach Freiburg, bitte.
♦ **in return** dafür ◊ *... and I help her in return* ... und dafür helfe ich ihr
♦ **in return for** für

♦ **Many happy returns!** Herzlichen Glückwunsch zum Geburtstag!

to **return** VERB

| see also **return** NOUN |

**1** (*come back*)
zurückkommen (IMPERFECT kam zurück, PERFECT ist zurückgekommen) ◊ *I've just returned from holiday.* Ich bin gerade aus den Ferien zurückgekommen.

♦ **to return home** wieder nach Hause kommen

**2** (*go back*)
zurückkehren (PERFECT ist zurückgekehrt) ◊ *He returned to Germany the following year.* Er ist im Jahr danach nach Deutschland zurückgekehrt.

**3** (*give back*)
zurückgeben (PRESENT gibt zurück, IMPERFECT gab zurück, PERFECT hat zurückgegeben) ◊ *She borrows my things and doesn't return them.* Sie leiht sich meine Sachen aus und gibt sie dann nicht zurück.

**reunion** NOUN
das Treffen (PL die Treffen)

to **reuse** VERB
wieder verwenden (PERFECT hat wieder verwendet)

to **reveal** VERB
ans Licht bringen (*truth, facts*) (IMPERFECT brachte ans Licht, PERFECT hat ans Licht gebracht) ◊ *The survey reveals that too many people are overweight.* Die Untersuchung bringt ans Licht, dass zu viele Menschen Übergewicht haben.

♦ **She refused to reveal the whereabouts of her daughter.** Sie weigerte sich, den Aufenthaltsort ihrer Tochter preiszugeben.

♦ **It was revealed that ...** Es wurde bekannt gegeben, dass ...

**revenge** NOUN
die Rache ◊ *in revenge* aus Rache

♦ **to take revenge** sich rächen ◊ *They planned to take revenge on him.* Sie haben geplant, sich an ihm zu rächen.

to **reverse** VERB

| see also **reverse** ADJECTIVE |

rückwärts fahren (*car*) (PRESENT fährt rückwärts, IMPERFECT fuhr rückwärts, PERFECT ist rückwärts gefahren) ◊ *He reversed without looking.* Er fuhr rückwärts ohne zu sehen.

♦ **to reverse the charges** (*telephone*) ein R-Gespräch führen ◊ *I'd like to make a reverse charge call to Britain.* Ich möchte gern ein R-Gespräch nach Großbritannien führen.

**reverse** ADJECTIVE

| see also **reverse** VERB |

umgekehrt ◊ *in reverse order* in umgekehrter Reihenfolge

♦ **in reverse gear** im Rückwärtsgang

**review** NOUN
**1** die Überprüfung (*of policy, salary*)
**2** die Prüfung (*of subject*)

♦ **to be under review** überprüft werden

to **revise** VERB
den Stoff wiederholen

♦ **I haven't started revising yet.** Ich habe noch nicht angefangen, den Stoff zu wiederholen.

♦ **I've revised my opinion.** Ich habe meine Meinung geändert.

**revision** NOUN
die Wiederholung des Stoffes

♦ **Have you done a lot of revision?** Hast du schon viel Stoff wiederholt?

to **revive** VERB
wieder beleben (PERFECT hat wieder belebt) ◊ *The nurses tried to revive him.* Die Schwestern versuchten, ihn wieder zu beleben.

**revolting** ADJECTIVE
ekelhaft

**revolution** NOUN
die Revolution ◊ *the French Revolution* die Französische Revolution

**revolutionary** ADJECTIVE
revolutionär

**revolver** NOUN
der Revolver (PL die Revolver)

**reward** NOUN
die Belohnung

**rewarding** ADJECTIVE
dankbar ◊ *a rewarding job* eine dankbare Arbeit

to **rewind** VERB
zurückspulen (PERFECT hat zurückgespult) ◊ *to rewind a cassette* eine Kassette zurückspulen

**rheumatism** NOUN
das Rheuma

**Rhine** NOUN
der Rhein

**rhinoceros** NOUN
das Nashorn (PL die Nashörner)

**rhubarb** NOUN
der Rhabarber ◊ *a rhubarb tart* ein Rhabarberkuchen

**rhythm** NOUN
der Rhythmus (GEN des Rhythmus, PL die Rhythmen)

**rib** NOUN
die Rippe

**ribbon** NOUN
das Band (PL die Bänder)

**rice** NOUN
der Reis

♦ **rice pudding** der Milchreis

**rich** ADJECTIVE
reich

♦ **the rich** die Reichen MASC PL

to **rid** VERB

**R**

☞

◆**to get rid of** loswerden ◇ *I want to get rid of some old clothes.* Ich will ein paar alte Kleider loswerden.

**ride** NOUN

> see also **ride** VERB

◆**to go for a ride (1)** (*on horse*) reiten gehen
◆**to go for a ride (2)** (*on bike*) mit dem Fahrrad fahren
◆**We went for a bike ride.** Wir haben eine Fahrt mit dem Fahrrad gemacht.
◆**It's a short bus ride to the town centre.** Die Stadtmitte ist nur eine kurze Busfahrt entfernt.

to **ride** VERB

> see also **ride** NOUN

reiten (*on horse*) (IMPERFECT ritt, PERFECT ist geritten) ◇ *I'm learning to ride.* Ich lerne reiten.
◆**to ride a bike** Fahrrad fahren ◇ *Can you ride a bike?* Kannst du Fahrrad fahren?

**rider** NOUN

1 (*on horse*)
der Reiter (PL die Reiter)
die Reiterin
◇ *She's a good rider.* Sie ist eine gute Reiterin.
2 (*on bike*)
der Fahrradfahrer (PL die Fahrradfahrer)
die Fahrradfahrerin

**ridiculous** ADJECTIVE
lächerlich ◇ *Don't be ridiculous!* Mach dich nicht lächerlich!

**riding** NOUN
das Reiten
◆**to go riding** reiten gehen
◆**a riding school** eine Reitschule

**rifle** NOUN
das Gewehr (PL die Gewehre) ◇ *a hunting rifle* ein Jagdgewehr

**rig** NOUN
◆**an oil rig** eine Bohrinsel

**right** ADJECTIVE, ADVERB

> see also **right** NOUN

*There are several ways of translating **right**. Scan the examples to find one that is similar to what you want to say.*
1 richtig (*correct, suitable*) ◇ *the right answer* die richtige Antwort ◇ *Am I pronouncing it right?* Spreche ich das richtig aus? ◇ *It isn't the right size.* Es ist nicht die richtige Größe. ◇ *We're on the right train.* Wir sind im richtigen Zug. ◇ *It's not right to behave like that.* Es ist nicht richtig, sich so zu benehmen.
◆**Is this the right road for Hamburg?** Sind wir hier richtig nach Hamburg?
◆**I think you did the right thing.** Ich glaube, du hast das Richtige getan.
◆**to be right (1)** (*person*) Recht haben ◇ *You were right!* Du hattest Recht!
◆**to be right (2)** (*statement, opinion*) richtig sein ◇ *That's right!* Das ist richtig!

2 genau (*accurate*) ◇ *Do you have the right time?* Haben Sie die genaue Zeit?
3 rechte (*not left*) ◇ *the right foot* der rechte Fuß ◇ *my right arm* mein rechter Arm ◇ *your right hand* deine rechte Hand ◇ *her right eye* ihr rechtes Auge
4 rechts (*turn*) ◇ *Turn right at the traffic lights.* Biegen Sie an der Ampel rechts ab.
◆**Look right!** Sehen Sie nach rechts!
◆**Right! Let's get started.** Okay! Fangen wir an.
◆**right away** sofort ◇ *I'll do it right away.* Ich mache es sofort.

**right** NOUN

> see also **right** ADJECTIVE

1 das Recht (PL die Rechte) ◇ *You've got no right to do that.* Du hast kein Recht, das zu tun.
2 (*not left*)
die rechte Seite
◆**on the right** rechts ◇ *Remember to drive on the right.* Vergiss nicht, rechts zu fahren.
◆**right of way** die Vorfahrt ◇ *We had right of way.* Wir hatten Vorfahrt.

**right-hand** ADJECTIVE
◆**the right-hand side** die rechte Seite
◆**It's on the right-hand side.** Es liegt rechts.

**right-handed** ADJECTIVE
rechtshändig

**rightly** ADVERB
richtig ◇ *If I remember rightly, his name was Jeremy.* Wenn ich mich richtig erinnere, hieß er Jeremy. ◇ *She rightly decided that he was lying.* Sie kam zu dem richtigen Schluss, dass er log.

**rim** NOUN
der Rand (PL die Ränder) ◇ *glasses with wire rims* eine Brille mit Metallrand

**ring** NOUN

> see also **ring** VERB

1 der Ring (PL die Ringe) ◇ *a gold ring* ein goldener Ring ◇ *a diamond ring* ein Diamantring
◆**a wedding ring** ein Ehering
2 (*circle*)
der Kreis (GEN des Kreises, PL die Kreise) ◇ *to stand in a ring* im Kreis stehen
3 (*of bell*)
das Klingeln
◆**There's a ring at the door.** Es klingelt.
◆**to give somebody a ring** jemanden anrufen ◇ *I'll give you a ring this evening.* Ich rufe dich heute Abend an.

to **ring** VERB

> see also **ring** NOUN

1 anrufen (IMPERFECT rief an, PERFECT hat angerufen) ◇ *Your mother rang this morning.* Deine Mutter hat heute früh angerufen.

♦ **to ring somebody** jemanden anrufen
◊ *I'll ring you tomorrow morning.* Ich
rufe dich morgen früh an.
♦ **to ring somebody up** jemanden anrufen
[2] klingeln ◊ *The phone's ringing.* Das
Telefon klingelt.
♦ **to ring the bell** (*doorbell*) klingeln ◊ *I rang
the bell three times.* Ich habe dreimal
geklingelt.
♦ **to ring back** zurückrufen ◊ *I'll ring back
later.* Ich rufe später zurück.
**ring binder** NOUN
das Ringheft (PL die Ringhefte)
**ring road** NOUN
die Ringstraße
**rink** NOUN
[1] die Eisbahn (*for ice-skating*)
[2] die Rollschuhbahn (*for roller-skating*)
to **rinse** VERB
spülen
**riot** NOUN
| *see also* **riot** VERB |
die Krawalle MASC PL
to **riot** VERB
| *see also* **riot** NOUN |
randalieren (PERFECT hat randaliert)
to **rip** VERB
zerreißen (IMPERFECT zerriss, PERFECT hat
zerrissen) ◊ *I've ripped my jeans.* Ich
habe meine Jeans zerrissen. ◊ *My skirt's
ripped.* Mein Rock ist zerrissen.
to **rip off** VERB
ausnehmen (*informal*) (PRESENT nimmt aus,
IMPERFECT nahm aus, PERFECT hat
ausgenommen) ◊ *The hotel ripped us
off.* Das Hotel hat uns ausgenommen.
to **rip up** VERB
zerreißen (IMPERFECT zerriss, PERFECT hat
zerrissen) ◊ *He read the note and then
ripped it up.* Er las die Notiz und zerriss
sie dann.
**ripe** ADJECTIVE
reif
**rip-off** NOUN
♦ **It's a rip-off!** Das ist Nepp! (*informal*)
**rise** NOUN
| *see also* **rise** VERB |
[1] (*in prices, temperature*)
der Anstieg (PL die Anstiege) ◊ *a sudden
rise in temperature* ein plötzlicher
Temperaturanstieg
[2] (*pay rise*)
die Gehaltserhöhung
to **rise** VERB
| *see also* **rise** NOUN |
[1] (*increase*)
steigen (IMPERFECT stieg, PERFECT ist
gestiegen) ◊ *Prices are rising.* Die Preise
steigen.
[2] aufgehen (IMPERFECT ging auf, PERFECT ist
aufgegangen) ◊ *The sun rises early in
June.* Die Sonne geht im Juni früh auf.

**riser** NOUN
♦ **to be an early riser** ein Frühaufsteher
sein
**risk** NOUN
| *see also* **risk** VERB |
das Risiko (PL die Risiken)
♦ **to take risks** Risiken eingehen ◊ *I don't
want to take risks.* Ich möchte kein Risiko
eingehen.
♦ **It's at your own risk.** Auf eigene Gefahr.
to **risk** VERB
| *see also* **risk** NOUN |
riskieren (PERFECT hat riskiert) ◊ *You risk
getting a fine.* Du riskierst einen
Strafzettel. ◊ *I wouldn't risk it if I were
you.* Das würde ich an deiner Stelle nicht
riskieren.
**risky** ADJECTIVE
gefährlich
**rival** NOUN
| *see also* **rival** ADJECTIVE |
der Rivale (GEN des Rivalen, PL die
Rivalen)
die Rivalin
**rival** ADJECTIVE
| *see also* **rival** NOUN |
rivalisierend ◊ *a rival gang* eine
rivalisierende Bande
♦ **a rival company** ein
Konkurrenzunternehmen NEUT
**rivalry** NOUN
die Rivalität (*between towns, schools*)
**river** NOUN
der Fluss (GEN des Flusses, PL die Flüsse)
♦ **the river Rhine** der Rhein
**Riviera** NOUN
die Riviera ◊ *the Italian Riviera* die
italienische Riviera
♦ **the French Riviera** die Côte d'Azur
**road** NOUN
die Straße ◊ *There's a lot of traffic on
the roads.* Es herrscht viel Verkehr auf
den Straßen.
♦ **They live across the road.** Sie wohnen
gegenüber.
**road map** NOUN
die Straßenkarte
**road rage** NOUN
die Aggressivität im Straßenverkehr
**road sign** NOUN
das Verkehrsschild (PL die
Verkehrsschilder)
**roadworks** PL NOUN
die Bauarbeiten FEM PL
**roast** ADJECTIVE
♦ **roast chicken** das Brathähnchen
♦ **roast potatoes** die Bratkartoffeln
♦ **roast pork** der Schweinebraten
♦ **roast beef** der Rindsbraten
to **rob** VERB

**R**

☞

♦ **to rob somebody** jemanden berauben ◊ *I've been robbed.* Ich bin beraubt worden.

♦ **to rob a bank** eine Bank ausrauben

♦ **to rob somebody of something** jemandem etwas rauben ◊ *He was robbed of his wallet.* Man hat ihm seine Brieftasche geraubt.

**robber** NOUN
der Räuber (PL die Räuber)
die Räuberin

♦ **a bank robber** ein Bankräuber

**robbery** NOUN
der Raub (PL die Raube)

♦ **a bank robbery** ein Bankraub

♦ **armed robbery** der bewaffnete Raubüberfall

**robin** NOUN
das Rotkehlchen (PL die Rotkehlchen)

**robot** NOUN
der Roboter (PL die Roboter)

**rock** NOUN
see also **rock** VERB

[1] (*substance*)
der Fels (GEN des Fels) ◊ *They tunnelled through the rock.* Sie gruben einen Tunnel durch den Fels.

[2] (*boulder*)
der Felsbrocken (PL die Felsbrocken) ◊ *I sat on a rock.* Ich saß auf einem Felsbrocken.

[3] (*stone*)
der Stein (PL die Steine) ◊ *The crowd started to throw rocks.* Die Menge fing an, Steine zu werfen.

[4] (*music*)
der Rock ◊ *a rock concert* ein Rockkonzert ◊ *He's a rock star.* Er ist ein Rockstar.

[5] (*sweet*)
die Zuckerstange ◊ *a stick of rock* eine Zuckerstange

♦ **rock and roll** der Rock 'n' Roll

to **rock** VERB
see also **rock** NOUN
erschüttern (PERFECT hat erschüttert) ◊ *The explosion rocked the building.* Die Explosion erschütterte das Gebäude.

**rockery** NOUN
der Steingarten (PL die Steingärten)

**rocket** NOUN
die Rakete (*firework, spacecraft*)

**rocking chair** NOUN
der Schaukelstuhl (PL die Schaukelstühle)

**rocking horse** NOUN
das Schaukelpferd (PL die Schaukelpferde)

**rod** NOUN
die Angel (*for fishing*)

**rode** VERB see **ride**

**role** NOUN
die Rolle

**role play** NOUN
das Rollenspiel (PL die Rollenspiele) ◊ *to do a role play* ein Rollenspiel machen

**roll** NOUN
see also **roll** VERB

[1] die Rolle ◊ *a roll of tape* eine Rolle Klebstreifen ◊ *a toilet roll* eine Rolle Toilettenpapier

[2] (*bread*)
das Brötchen (PL die Brötchen)

to **roll** VERB
see also **roll** NOUN
rollen

♦ **to roll out the pastry** den Teig ausrollen

**roll call** NOUN
der Namensaufruf (PL die Namensaufrufe)

**roller** NOUN
die Walze

**Rollerblade** ® NOUN
der Rollerblade ® (PL die Rollerblades)

**roller coaster** NOUN
die Achterbahn

**roller skates** PL NOUN
die Rollschuhe MASC PL

**roller-skating** NOUN
das Rollschuhlaufen

♦ **to go roller-skating** Rollschuh laufen

**rolling pin** NOUN
das Nudelholz (PL die Nudelhölzer)

**Roman** ADJECTIVE, NOUN
römisch (*ancient*) ◊ *a Roman villa* eine römische Villa ◊ *the Roman empire* das Römische Reich

♦ **the Romans** die Römer MASC PL

**Roman Catholic** NOUN
der Katholik (GEN des Katholiken, PL die Katholiken)
die Katholikin
◊ *He's a Roman Catholic.* Er ist Katholik.

**romance** NOUN

[1] (*novels*)
der Liebesroman (PL die Liebesromane) ◊ *I read a lot of romances.* Ich lese viele Liebesromane.

[2] (*glamour*)
der romantische Zauber ◊ *the romance of Venice* der romantische Zauber von Venedig

♦ **a holiday romance** ein Ferienflirt MASC

**Romania** NOUN
Rumänien NEUT

♦ **from Romania** aus Rumänien

♦ **to Romania** nach Rumänien

**Romanian** ADJECTIVE
rumänisch

**romantic** ADJECTIVE
romantisch

**roof** NOUN
das Dach (PL die Dächer)

**roof rack** NOUN
der Dachträger (PL die Dachträger)

**room** NOUN

1 das Zimmer (PL die Zimmer) ◊ *the
biggest room in the house* das größte
Zimmer des Hauses ◊ *She's in her room.*
Sie ist in ihrem Zimmer. ◊ *the music
room* das Musikzimmer
♦ **a single room** ein Einzelzimmer
♦ **a double room** ein Doppelzimmer
2 (*space*)
der Platz (GEN des Platzes) ◊ *There's no
room for that box.* Es ist kein Platz für
diese Schachtel.
**roommate** NOUN
der Zimmergenosse (GEN des
Zimmergenossen, PL die
Zimmergenossen)
die Zimmergenossin
**root** NOUN
die Wurzel
**rope** NOUN
das Seil (PL die Seile)
**rose** VERB *see* **rise**
**rose** NOUN
die Rose (*flower*)
to **rot** VERB
verfaulen (PERFECT ist verfault)
**rotten** ADJECTIVE
faulig (*decayed*) ◊ *a rotten apple* ein
fauliger Apfel
♦ **rotten weather** das Mistwetter (*informal*)
♦ **That's a rotten thing to do.** Das ist
gemein.
♦ **to feel rotten** sich mies fühlen *informal*
**rough** ADJECTIVE
1 rau ◊ *My hands are rough.* Meine
Hände sind rau. ◊ *It's a rough area.* Das
ist eine raue Gegend.
2 hart (*game*) ◊ *Rugby's a rough sport.*
Rugby ist ein harter Sport.
3 stürmisch (*water*) ◊ *The sea was
rough.* Das Meer war stürmisch.
4 ungefähr ◊ *I've got a rough idea.* Ich
habe eine ungefähre Vorstellung.
♦ **to feel rough** sich nicht wohl fühlen ◊ *I
feel rough.* Ich fühle mich nicht wohl.
**roughly** ADVERB
ungefähr ◊ *It weighs roughly twenty
kilos.* Es wiegt ungefähr zwanzig Kilo.
**round** ADJECTIVE, ADVERB, PREPOSITION
see also **round** NOUN
1 rund ◊ *a round table* ein runder Tisch
2 um (*around*) ◊ *We were sitting round
the table.* Wir saßen um den Tisch
herum. ◊ *She wore a scarf round her
neck.* Sie trug einen Schal um den Hals.
♦ **It's just round the corner.** (*very near*) Es
ist gleich um die Ecke.
♦ **to go round to somebody's house** bei
jemandem vorbeigehen ◊ *I went round
to my friend's house.* Ich bin bei meiner
Freundin vorbeigegangen.
♦ **to have a look round** sich umsehen
◊ *We're going to have a look round.* Wir
möchten uns umsehen.

♦ **to go round a museum** sich ein Museum
ansehen ◊ *I went round the local
museum.* Ich habe mir das örtliche
Museum angesehen.
♦ **round here** hier in der Gegend ◊ *Is there
a chemist's round here?* Gibt es hier in
der Gegend eine Apotheke? ◊ *He lives
round here.* Er wohnt hier in der Gegend.
♦ **all round** ringsherum ◊ *There were
vineyards all round.* Ringsherum waren
Weinberge.
♦ **all year round** das ganze Jahr über
♦ **round about** (*roughly*) etwa ◊ *It costs
round about a hundred pounds.* Es kostet
etwa hundert Pfund. ◊ *round about eight
o'clock* etwa um acht Uhr
**round** NOUN
see also **round** ADJECTIVE
die Runde (*of tournament, boxing match*)
◊ *a round of golf* eine Runde Golf
♦ **a round of drinks** eine Runde ◊ *He
bought a round of drinks.* Er hat eine
Runde ausgegeben.
**roundabout** NOUN
1 (*at junction*)
der Kreisverkehr (PL die Kreisverkehre)
2 (*at funfair*)
das Karussell (PL die Karussells)
**rounders** SING NOUN
der Schlagball
**round trip** NOUN US
die Hin- und Rückfahrt
♦ **a round-trip ticket** eine Rückfahrkarte
**route** NOUN
die Route ◊ *We're planning our route.*
Wir planen unsere Route.
**routine** NOUN
die Routine
**row (1)** NOUN
see also **row** VERB AND **row (2)** NOUN
die Reihe ◊ *a row of houses* eine Reihe
Häuser ◊ *Our seats are in the front row.*
Unsere Plätze sind in der ersten Reihe.
♦ **five times in a row** fünfmal
hintereinander
**row (2)** NOUN
see also **row** VERB AND **row (1)** NOUN
1 (*noise*)
der Krach ◊ *What's that terrible row?*
Was ist das für ein furchtbarer Krach?
2 (*quarrel*)
der Streit (PL die Streite)
♦ **to have a row** Streit haben ◊ *They've
had a row.* Sie haben Streit gehabt.
to **row** VERB
see also **row (1)** NOUN AND **row (2)** NOUN
rudern ◊ *We took turns to row.* Wir
haben abwechselnd gerudert.
**rowboat** NOUN US
das Ruderboot (PL die Ruderboote)
**rowing** NOUN
das Rudern (*sport*) ◊ *My hobby is
rowing.* Rudern ist mein Hobby.

**R**

☞

♦ **a rowing boat** ein Ruderboot NEUT

**royal** ADJECTIVE

königlich ◊ *the royal family* die königliche Familie

to **rub** VERB

**1** (*stain*)

reiben (IMPERFECT rieb, PERFECT hat gerieben)

**2** (*part of body*)

sich reiben ◊ *Don't rub your eyes!* Reib dir nicht die Augen!

♦ **I rubbed myself dry with a towel.** Ich rieb mich mit einem Handtuch trocken.

♦ **to rub something out** etwas ausradieren

**rubber** NOUN

**1** der Gummi (PL die Gummis) ◊ *rubber soles* die Gummisohlen

**2** (*eraser*)

der Radiergummi (PL die Radiergummis) ◊ *Can I borrow your rubber?* Kann ich deinen Radiergummi ausleihen?

♦ **a rubber band** ein Gummiband NEUT

**rubbish** NOUN

see also **rubbish** ADJECTIVE

**1** der Müll (*refuse*) ◊ *When do they collect the rubbish?* Wann wird der Müll abgeholt?

**2** der Krempel (*junk*) ◊ *They sell a lot of rubbish at the market.* Sie verkaufen eine Menge Krempel auf dem Markt.

**3** der Unsinn (*nonsense*) ◊ *Don't talk rubbish!* Red keinen Unsinn!

♦ **That's a load of rubbish!** Das ist doch Unsinn! (*informal*)

♦ **This magazine is rubbish!** Die Zeitschrift ist Schrott! (*informal*)

♦ **a rubbish bin** ein Mülleimer MASC

♦ **a rubbish dump** eine Müllkippe

**rubbish** ADJECTIVE

see also **rubbish** NOUN

miserabel (*informal*) ◊ *They're a rubbish team!* Sie sind eine miserable Mannschaft!

**rucksack** NOUN

der Rucksack (PL die Rucksäcke)

**rude** ADJECTIVE

**1** unhöflich (*impolite*) ◊ *It's rude to interrupt.* Es ist unhöflich dazwischenzureden. ◊ *He was very rude to me.* Er war sehr unhöflich zu mir.

**2** unanständig (*offensive*) ◊ *a rude joke* ein unanständiger Witz

♦ **a rude word** ein Schimpfwort NEUT

**rug** NOUN

**1** der Teppich (PL die Teppiche) ◊ *a Persian rug* ein Perserteppich

**2** (*blanket*)

die Decke ◊ *a tartan rug* eine karierte Decke

**rugby** NOUN

das Rugby ◊ *I play rugby.* Ich spiele Rugby.

**ruin** NOUN

see also **ruin** VERB

die Ruine ◊ *the ruins of the castle* die Ruine der Burg

♦ **My life is in ruins.** Mein Leben ist ruiniert.

to **ruin** VERB

see also **ruin** NOUN

ruinieren (PERFECT hat ruiniert) ◊ *You'll ruin your shoes.* Du ruinierst dir deine Schuhe. ◊ *That's far too expensive. You are ruining me!* Das ist viel zu teuer. Du ruinierst mich noch!

♦ **It ruined our holiday.** Es hat uns den Urlaub verdorben.

**rule** NOUN

see also **rule** VERB

**1** die Regel ◊ *the rules of grammar* die Grammatikregeln

♦ **as a rule** in der Regel

**2** die Vorschrift (*regulation*) ◊ *It's against the rules.* Das ist gegen die Vorschriften.

to **rule** VERB

see also **rule** NOUN

regieren (PERFECT hat regiert)

to **rule out** VERB

ausschließen (*possibility*) (IMPERFECT schloss aus, PERFECT hat ausgeschlossen)

**ruler** NOUN

das Lineal (PL die Lineale) ◊ *Can I borrow your ruler?* Kann ich dein Lineal ausleihen?

**rum** NOUN

der Rum

**rumour** NOUN

das Gerücht (PL die Gerüchte) ◊ *It's just a rumour.* Es ist nur ein Gerücht.

**rump steak** NOUN

das Rumpsteak (PL die Rumpsteaks)

**run** NOUN

see also **run** VERB

der Lauf (*in cricket*) (PL die Läufe) ◊ *to score a run* einen Lauf machen

♦ **to go for a run** einen Dauerlauf machen ◊ *I go for a run every morning.* Ich mache jeden Morgen einen Dauerlauf.

♦ **I did a ten-kilometre run.** Ich bin zehn Kilometer gelaufen.

♦ **on the run** auf der Flucht ◊ *The criminals are still on the run.* Die Verbrecher sind noch auf der Flucht.

♦ **in the long run** auf Dauer

to **run** VERB

see also **run** NOUN

**1** laufen (PRESENT läuft, IMPERFECT lief, PERFECT ist gelaufen) ◊ *I ran five kilometres.* Ich bin fünf Kilometer gelaufen.

♦ **to run a marathon** an einem Marathonlauf teilnehmen

**2** (*manage*)

leiten ◊ *He runs a large company.* Er leitet ein großes Unternehmen.

**3** (*organize*)

veranstalten (PERFECT hat veranstaltet) ◊ *They run music courses in the holidays.* Sie veranstalten Musikkurse während der Ferien.

4 (*water*)

laufen ◊ *Don't leave the tap running.* Lass das Wasser nicht laufen.

◆ **to run a bath** ein Bad einlaufen lassen

5 (*by car*)

fahren (PRESENT fährt, IMPERFECT fuhr, PERFECT hat gefahren) ◊ *I can run you to the station.* Ich kann dich zum Bahnhof fahren.

◆ **to run away** weglaufen ◊ *They ran away before the police came.* Sie sind weggelaufen, bevor die Polizei kam.

◆ **Time is running out.** Die Zeit wird knapp.

◆ **We ran out of money.** Uns ist das Geld ausgegangen.

◆ **to run somebody over** jemanden überfahren

◆ **to get run over** überfahren werden ◊ *Be careful, or you'll get run over!* Pass auf, sonst wirst du überfahren!

**rung** VERB *see* **ring**

**runner** NOUN
der Läufer (PL die Läufer)
die Läuferin

**runner beans** PL NOUN
die Stangenbohnen FEM PL

**runner-up** NOUN
der Zweite (GEN des Zweiten, PL die Zweiten)
die Zweite (GEN der Zweiten)

**running** NOUN
das Laufen ◊ *Running is my favourite sport.* Laufen ist mein Lieblingssport.

**run-up** NOUN
◆ **in the run-up to Christmas** in der Zeit vor Weihnachten

**runway** NOUN
die Startbahn

**rural** ADJECTIVE
ländlich

**rush** NOUN
see also **rush** VERB
die Eile

◆ **in a rush** in Eile

to **rush** VERB
see also **rush** NOUN

1 (*run*)

rennen (IMPERFECT rannte, PERFECT ist gerannt) ◊ *Everyone rushed outside.* Alle rannten hinaus.

2 (*hurry*)

sich beeilen (PERFECT hat sich beeilt)
◊ *There's no need to rush.* Wir brauchen uns nicht zu beeilen.

**rush hour** NOUN
die Hauptverkehrszeit ◊ *in the rush hour* in der Hauptverkehrszeit

**rusk** NOUN
der Zwieback (PL die Zwiebacke)

**Russia** NOUN
Russland NEUT

◆ **from Russia** aus Russland

◆ **to Russia** nach Russland

**Russian** ADJECTIVE
see also **Russian** NOUN
russisch

◆ **He's Russian.** Er ist Russe.

◆ **She's Russian.** Sie ist Russin.

**Russian** NOUN
see also **Russian** ADJECTIVE

1 (*person*)

der Russe (GEN des Russen, PL die Russen)
die Russin

2 (*language*)

das Russisch (GEN des Russischen)

**rust** NOUN
der Rost

**rusty** ADJECTIVE
rostig ◊ *a rusty bike* ein rostiges Fahrrad
◆ **My German is very rusty.** Mein Deutsch ist ziemlich eingerostet.

**ruthless** ADJECTIVE
rücksichtslos

**rye** NOUN
der Roggen
◆ **rye bread** das Roggenbrot

R

# S

**Sabbath** NOUN
1 (*Christian*)
der Sonntag (PL die Sonntage)
2 (*Jewish*)
der Sabbat (PL die Sabbate)
**sack** NOUN

see also **sack** VERB

der Sack (PL die Säcke)
♦ **to get the sack** gefeuert werden
to **sack** VERB

see also **sack** NOUN

♦ **to sack somebody** jemanden feuern ◊ *He was sacked.* Er wurde gefeuert.
**sacred** ADJECTIVE
heilig
**sacrifice** NOUN
das Opfer (PL die Opfer)
**sad** ADJECTIVE
traurig
**saddle** NOUN
der Sattel (PL die Sättel)
**saddlebag** NOUN
die Satteltasche
**sadly** ADVERB
1 traurig ◊ *"She's gone," he said sadly.* "Sie ist weg", sagte er traurig.
2 leider (*unfortunately*) ◊ *Sadly, it was too late.* Leider war es zu spät.
**safe** NOUN

see also **safe** ADJECTIVE

der Safe (PL die Safes) ◊ *She put the money in the safe.* Sie tat das Geld in den Safe.
**safe** ADJECTIVE

see also **safe** NOUN

1 sicher ◊ *Don't worry, it's perfectly safe.* Mach dir keine Sorgen, es ist völlig sicher. ◊ *This car isn't safe.* Das Auto ist nicht sicher.
2 in Sicherheit (*out of danger*) ◊ *You're safe now.* Sie sind jetzt in Sicherheit.
♦ **to feel safe** sich sicher fühlen
♦ **safe sex** Safer Sex
**safety** NOUN
die Sicherheit
♦ **a safety belt** ein Sicherheitsgurt MASC
♦ **a safety pin** eine Sicherheitsnadel
**Sagittarius** NOUN
der Schütze (GEN des Schützen) ◊ *I'm Sagittarius.* Ich bin Schütze.
**Sahara** NOUN
♦ **the Sahara Desert** die Wüste Sahara
**said** VERB *see* **say**
**sail** NOUN

see also **sail** VERB

das Segel (PL die Segel)
to **sail** VERB

see also **sail** NOUN

1 (*travel*)
segeln (PERFECT ist gesegelt)
2 (*set off*)
abfahren (PRESENT fährt ab, IMPERFECT fuhr ab, PERFECT ist abgefahren) ◊ *The boat sails at eight o'clock.* Das Schiff fährt um acht Uhr ab.
**sailing** NOUN
das Segeln ◊ *His hobby is sailing.* Segeln ist sein Hobby.
♦ **to go sailing** segeln gehen
♦ **a sailing boat** ein Segelboot NEUT
♦ **a sailing ship** ein Segelschiff NEUT
**sailor** NOUN
der Matrose (GEN des Matrosen, PL die Matrosen)
die Matrosin
◊ *He's a sailor.* Er ist Matrose.
**saint** NOUN
der Heilige (GEN des Heiligen, PL die Heiligen)
die Heilige (GEN der Heiligen) ◊ *a saint* (*man*) ein Heiliger
**sake** NOUN
♦ **for the sake of** um ... willen ◊ *for the sake of your parents* um deiner Eltern willen
**salad** NOUN
der Salat (PL die Salate)
♦ **salad cream** die Salatmayonnaise
♦ **salad dressing** die Salatsoße
**salami** NOUN
die Salami (GEN der Salami, PL die Salamis)
**salary** NOUN
das Gehalt (PL die Gehälter)
**sale** NOUN
der Schlussverkauf (*end of season reductions*) (PL die Schlussverkäufe) ◊ *There's a sale on at Harrods.* Bei Harrods ist Schlussverkauf.
♦ **on sale** erhältlich
♦ **"for sale"** "zu verkaufen"
**sales assistant** NOUN
der Verkäufer (PL die Verkäufer)
die Verkäuferin
◊ *She's a sales assistant.* Sie ist Verkäuferin.
**salesman** NOUN
1 (*sales rep*)
der Vertreter (PL die Vertreter) ◊ *He's a salesman.* Er ist Vertreter.
♦ **a double-glazing salesman** ein Vertreter für Doppelfenster
2 (*sales assistant*)
der Verkäufer (PL die Verkäufer)
**sales rep** NOUN
der Vertreter (PL die Vertreter)

die <u>Vertreterin</u>
**saleswoman** NOUN
[1] die <u>Vertreterin</u> (*sales rep*) ◊ *She's a saleswoman.* Sie ist Vertreterin.
[2] die <u>Verkäuferin</u> (*sales assistant*)
**salmon** NOUN
der <u>Lachs</u> (GEN des Lachses, PL die Lachse)
**salon** NOUN
der <u>Salon</u> (PL die Salons) ◊ *a hair salon* ein Friseursalon ◊ *a beauty salon* ein Kosmetiksalon
**saloon car** NOUN
die <u>Limousine</u>
**salt** NOUN
das <u>Salz</u> (GEN des Salzes, PL die Salze)
**salty** ADJECTIVE
<u>salzig</u>
to **salute** VERB
<u>grüßen</u>
**Salvation Army** NOUN
die <u>Heilsarmee</u>
**same** ADJECTIVE
<u>gleiche</u> ◊ *The same coat is cheaper elsewhere.* Der gleiche Mantel ist anderswo billiger. ◊ *He asked me the same question.* Er hat mir die gleiche Frage gestellt. ◊ *I have the same car.* Ich habe das gleiche Auto. ◊ *We obviously have the same problems.* Wir haben offensichtlich die gleichen Probleme.
♦ **at the same time** zur gleichen Zeit
♦ **It's not the same.** Das ist nicht das Gleiche.
♦ **They're exactly the same.** Sie sind genau gleich.
**sample** NOUN
die <u>Probe</u> ◊ *a free sample of perfume* eine kostenlose Parfümprobe
**sand** NOUN
der <u>Sand</u>
**sandal** NOUN
die <u>Sandale</u> ◊ *a pair of sandals* ein Paar Sandalen
**sand castle** NOUN
die <u>Sandburg</u>
**sandwich** NOUN
das <u>belegte Brot</u> (PL die belegten Brote)
♦ **a cheese sandwich** ein Käsebrot
**sang** VERB see **sing**
**sanitary napkin** NOUN US
die <u>Damenbinde</u>
**sanitary towel** NOUN
die <u>Damenbinde</u>
**sank** VERB see **sink**
**Santa Claus** NOUN
der <u>Weihnachtsmann</u> (PL die Weihnachtsmänner)
**sarcastic** ADJECTIVE
<u>sarkastisch</u>
**sardine** NOUN
die <u>Sardine</u>

**sat** VERB see **sit**
**satchel** NOUN
der <u>Schulranzen</u> (PL die Schulranzen)
**satellite** NOUN
der <u>Satellit</u> (GEN des Satelliten, PL die Satelliten)
♦ **a satellite dish** eine Satellitenschüssel
♦ **satellite television** das Satellitenfernsehen
**satisfactory** ADJECTIVE
<u>befriedigend</u>
**satisfied** ADJECTIVE
<u>zufrieden</u>
**Saturday** NOUN
der <u>Samstag</u> (PL die Samstage) ◊ *on Saturday* am Samstag ◊ *every Saturday* jeden Samstag ◊ *last Saturday* letzten Samstag ◊ *next Saturday* nächsten Samstag
♦ **on Saturdays** samstags
♦ **I've got a Saturday job.** Ich habe einen Samstagsjob.
**sauce** NOUN
die <u>Soße</u>
**saucepan** NOUN
der <u>Kochtopf</u> (PL die Kochtöpfe)
**saucer** NOUN
die <u>Untertasse</u>
**Saudi Arabia** NOUN
<u>Saudi-Arabien</u> NEUT
♦ **to Saudi Arabia** nach Saudi-Arabien
**sauna** NOUN
die <u>Sauna</u> (PL die Saunas)
**sausage** NOUN
die <u>Wurst</u> (PL die Würste)
♦ **a sausage roll** eine Wurst im Blätterteig
to **save** VERB
[1] <u>sparen</u> (*money, time*) ◊ *I've saved fifty pounds already.* Ich habe schon fünfzig Pfund gespart. ◊ *I saved twenty pounds by waiting for the sales.* Ich habe zwanzig Pfund gespart, weil ich bis zum Schlussverkauf gewartet habe. ◊ *We took a taxi to save time.* Wir haben ein Taxi genommen, um Zeit zu sparen.
[2] <u>retten</u> (*rescue*) ◊ *Luckily, all the passengers were saved.* Zum Glück wurden alle Passagiere gerettet.
[3] <u>sichern</u> (*on computer*) ◊ *I saved the file onto a diskette.* Ich habe die Datei auf Diskette gesichert.
♦ **to save up** sparen ◊ *I'm saving up for a new bike.* Ich spare für ein neues Fahrrad.
**savings** PL NOUN
die <u>Ersparnisse</u> FEM PL ◊ *She spent all her savings on a computer.* Sie gab all ihre Ersparnisse für einen Computer aus.
**savoury** ADJECTIVE
<u>pikant</u> (*spicy*)
**saw** VERB see **see**
**saw** NOUN
die <u>Säge</u>

**S**

**sax** NOUN
das <u>Saxophon</u> (PL die Saxophone) ◊ *I
play the sax.* Ich spiele Saxophon.

**saxophone** NOUN
das <u>Saxophon</u> (PL die Saxophone) ◊ *I
play the saxophone.* Ich spiele
Saxophon.

to **say** VERB
<u>sagen</u> ◊ *What did he say?* Was hat er
gesagt? ◊ *Did you hear what she said?*
Hast du gehört, was sie gesagt hat?
◊ *Could you say that again?* Können Sie
das noch einmal sagen?
♦ **That goes without saying.** Das ist
selbstverständlich.

**saying** NOUN
die <u>Redensart</u> ◊ *It's just a saying.* Das ist
so eine Redensart.

**scale** NOUN
⊞ (*of map*)
der <u>Maßstab</u> (PL die Maßstäbe) ◊ *a
large-scale map* eine Karte großen
Maßstabs
⊡ (*size, extent*)
das <u>Ausmaß</u> (GEN des Ausmaßes, PL die
Ausmaße) ◊ *a disaster on a massive
scale* eine Katastrophe von riesigem
Ausmaß
⊟ (*in music*)
die <u>Tonleiter</u>

**scales** PL NOUN
die <u>Waage</u> SING (*in kitchen, shop*)
♦ **bathroom scales** die Personenwaage

**scampi** PL NOUN
die <u>Scampi</u> PL

**scandal** NOUN
⊞ (*outrage*)
der <u>Skandal</u> (PL die Skandale) ◊ *It caused
a scandal.* Es hat einen Skandal
verursacht.
⊡ (*gossip*)
der <u>Tratsch</u> ◊ *It's just scandal.* Das ist
nur Tratsch.

**Scandinavia** NOUN
<u>Skandinavien</u> NEUT
♦ **from Scandinavia** aus Skandinavien
♦ **to Scandinavia** nach Skandinavien

**Scandinavian** ADJECTIVE
<u>skandinavisch</u>
♦ **He's Scandinavian.** Er ist
Skandinavier.

**scar** NOUN
die <u>Narbe</u>

**scarce** ADJECTIVE
⊞ <u>knapp</u> ◊ *scarce resources* knappe
Geldmittel
⊡ <u>rar</u> ◊ *Jobs are scarce.* Jobs sind rar.

**scarcely** ADVERB
<u>kaum</u> ◊ *I scarcely knew him.* Ich kannte
ihn kaum.

**scare** NOUN
| see also **scare** VERB |
der <u>Schrecken</u> (PL die Schrecken)

♦ **a bomb scare** ein Bombenalarm MASC

to **scare** VERB
| see also **scare** NOUN |
♦ **to scare somebody** jemandem Angst
machen ◊ *He scares me.* Er macht mir
Angst.

**scarecrow** NOUN
die <u>Vogelscheuche</u>

**scared** ADJECTIVE
♦ **to be scared** Angst haben ◊ *I was scared
stiff.* Ich hatte furchtbar Angst.
♦ **to be scared of** Angst haben vor ◊ *Are
you scared of him?* Hast du vor ihm
Angst?

**scarf** NOUN
⊞ (*long*)
der <u>Schal</u> (PL die Schals)
⊡ (*square*)
das <u>Halstuch</u> (PL die Halstücher)

**scary** ADJECTIVE
<u>Furcht erregend</u> ◊ *It was really scary.* Es
war wirklich Furcht erregend.

**scene** NOUN
⊞ (*place*)
der <u>Ort</u> (PL die Orte) ◊ *The police were
soon on the scene.* Die Polizei war
schnell vor Ort. ◊ *the scene of the crime*
der Ort des Verbrechens
⊡ (*event, sight*)
das <u>Spektakel</u> (PL die Spektakel) ◊ *It was
an amazing scene.* Es war ein
erstaunliches Spektakel.
♦ **to make a scene** eine Szene machen

**scenery** NOUN
die <u>Landschaft</u> (*landscape*)

**scent** NOUN
der <u>Duft</u> (*perfume*) (PL die Düfte)

**schedule** NOUN
das <u>Programm</u> (PL die Programme)
◊ *a busy schedule* ein volles
Programm
♦ **on schedule** planmäßig
♦ **to be behind schedule** Verspätung haben

**scheduled flight** NOUN
der <u>Linienflug</u> (PL die Linienflüge)

**scheme** NOUN
⊞ (*idea*)
der <u>Plan</u> (PL die Pläne) ◊ *a crazy scheme
he dreamed up* ein völlig verrückter Plan,
den er sich ausgedacht hat
⊡ (*project*)
das <u>Projekt</u> (PL die Projekte) ◊ *a council
road-widening scheme* ein
Straßenverbreiterungsprojekt der
Gemeinde

**scholarship** NOUN
das <u>Stipendium</u> (PL die Stipendien)

**school** NOUN
die <u>Schule</u>
♦ **to go to school** in die Schule gehen

**schoolbook** NOUN
das <u>Schulbuch</u> (PL die Schulbücher)

**schoolboy** NOUN

der Schuljunge (GEN des Schuljungen, PL
die Schuljungen)
schoolchildren NOUN
die Schulkinder NEUT PL
schoolgirl NOUN
das Schulmädchen (PL die
Schulmädchen)
science NOUN
die Wissenschaft
science fiction NOUN
die Sciencefiction
scientific ADJECTIVE
wissenschaftlich
scientist NOUN
der Wissenschaftler (PL die
Wissenschaftler)
die Wissenschaftlerin
◊ She's a scientist. Sie ist
Wissenschaftlerin.
♦ He trained as a scientist. Er hat eine
wissenschaftliche Ausbildung.
scissors PL NOUN
die Schere ◊ a pair of scissors eine
Schere
to scoff VERB
futtern (informal: eat) ◊ My brother
scoffed all the sandwiches. Mein Bruder
hat alle Brote gefuttert.
scooter NOUN
1 der Motorroller (PL die Motorroller)
2 (child's toy)
der Roller (PL die Roller)
score NOUN
see also score VERB
der Spielstand (PL die Spielstände)
♦ What's the score? Wie steht das Spiel?
♦ The score was three nil. Es stand drei zu
null.
to score VERB
see also score NOUN
1 (goal)
schießen (IMPERFECT schoss, PERFECT hat
geschossen) ◊ to score a goal ein Tor
schießen
2 (point)
machen ◊ to score six out of ten sechs
von zehn Punkten machen
3 (keep score)
zählen ◊ Who's going to score? Wer
zählt?
Scorpio NOUN
der Skorpion ◊ I'm Scorpio. Ich bin
Skorpion.
Scot NOUN
der Schotte (GEN des Schotten, PL die
Schotten)
die Schottin
Scotch tape ® NOUN US
der Tesafilm ®
Scotland NOUN
Schottland NEUT
♦ from Scotland aus Schottland
♦ in Scotland in Schottland

♦ to Scotland nach Schottland
Scots ADJECTIVE
schottisch ◊ a Scots accent ein
schottischer Akzent
Scotsman NOUN
der Schotte (GEN des Schotten, PL die
Schotten)
Scotswoman NOUN
die Schottin
Scottish ADJECTIVE
schottisch ◊ a Scottish accent ein
schottischer Akzent
♦ He's Scottish. Er ist Schotte.
♦ She's Scottish. Sie ist Schottin.
scout NOUN
der Pfadfinder (PL die Pfadfinder) ◊ I'm in
the Scouts. Ich bin bei den Pfadfindern.
♦ girl scout die Pfadfinderin
scrambled eggs PL NOUN
die Rühreier NEUT PL
scrap NOUN
see also scrap VERB
1 das Stück (PL die Stücke) ◊ a scrap of
paper ein Stück Papier
2 (fight)
die Schlägerei
♦ scrap iron das Alteisen
to scrap VERB
see also scrap NOUN
verwerfen (plan, idea) (PRESENT verwirft,
IMPERFECT verwarf, PERFECT hat verworfen)
◊ In the end the plan was scrapped. Am
Ende wurde der Plan verworfen.
scrapbook NOUN
das Album (PL die Alben)
to scratch VERB
see also scratch NOUN
kratzen ◊ Stop scratching! Hör auf zu
kratzen!
scratch NOUN
see also scratch VERB
(on skin)
der Kratzer (PL die Kratzer)
♦ to start from scratch von vorn anfangen
scream NOUN
see also scream VERB
der Schrei (PL die Schreie)
to scream VERB
see also scream NOUN
schreien (IMPERFECT schrie, PERFECT hat
geschrien)
screen NOUN
1 (cinema)
die Leinwand (PL die Leinwände)
2 (television, computer)
der Bildschirm (PL die Bildschirme) ◊ An
error message appeared on the screen.
Auf dem Bildschirm erschien eine
Fehlermeldung.
screen saver NOUN
der Bildschirmschoner (PL die
Bildschirmschoner)

**S**

**screw** NOUN
die Schraube
**screwdriver** NOUN
der Schraubenzieher (PL die Schraubenzieher)
to **scribble** VERB
kritzeln
to **scrub** VERB
schrubben ◊ *He scrubbed the floor.* Er schrubbte den Boden.
**sculpture** NOUN
die Skulptur
**sea** NOUN
das Meer (PL die Meere)
**seafood** NOUN
die Meeresfrüchte FEM PL ◊ *I don't like seafood.* Ich mag Meeresfrüchte nicht.
**seagull** NOUN
die Möwe
**seal** NOUN
see also **seal** VERB
[1] (*animal*)
der Seehund (PL die Seehunde)
[2] (*on container*)
das Siegel (PL die Siegel)
to **seal** VERB
see also **seal** NOUN
[1] (*container*)
versiegeln (PERFECT hat versiegelt)
[2] (*letter*)
zukleben (PERFECT hat zugeklebt)
**seaman** NOUN
der Seemann (PL die Seeleute)
to **search** VERB
see also **search** NOUN
durchsuchen (PERFECT hat durchsucht)
◊ *They searched the woods for her.* Sie haben den Wald nach ihr durchsucht.
♦ **to search for something** nach etwas suchen ◊ *He was searching for gold.* Er suchte nach Gold.
**search** NOUN
see also **search** VERB
die Suche
**search engine** NOUN
die Suchmaschine (*Internet*)
**search party** NOUN
der Suchtrupp (PL die Suchtrupps)
**seashore** NOUN
der Strand (PL die Strände) ◊ *on the seashore* am Strand
**seasick** ADJECTIVE
seekrank ◊ *to be seasick* seekrank sein
**seaside** NOUN
♦ **at the seaside** am Meer
♦ **We're going to the seaside.** Wir fahren ans Meer.
**season** NOUN
die Jahreszeit ◊ *What's your favourite season?* Welche Jahreszeit hast du am liebsten?

♦ **out of season** außerhalb der Saison ◊ *It's cheaper to go there out of season.* Es ist billiger, wenn man außerhalb der Saison dorthin fährt.
♦ **during the holiday season** während der Ferienzeit
♦ **a season ticket** eine Dauerkarte
**seat** NOUN
der Platz (GEN des Platzes, PL die Plätze)
**seat belt** NOUN
der Sicherheitsgurt (PL die Sicherheitsgurte)
♦ **You should fasten your seat belt.** Du solltest dich anschnallen.
**sea water** NOUN
das Meerwasser
**seaweed** NOUN
die Alge
**second** ADJECTIVE
see also **second** NOUN
zweite ◊ *the second man from the right* der zweite Mann von rechts ◊ *her second husband* ihr zweiter Mann ◊ *on the second page* auf der zweiten Seite ◊ *my second child* mein zweites Kind
♦ **to come second** (*in race*) Zweiter werden ◊ *She came second.* Sie wurde Zweite.
♦ **the second of August** der zweite August
**second** NOUN
see also **second** ADJECTIVE
die Sekunde ◊ *It'll only take a second.* Es dauert nur eine Sekunde.
**secondary school** NOUN
[1] das Gymnasium (PL die Gymnasien)
[2] die Realschule

> ⓘ Germans always specify the type of secondary school. **Gymnasium** takes nine years and leads to **Abitur,** **Realschule** takes six years and leads to **mittlere Reife.**

**second-class** ADJECTIVE, ADVERB
[1] zweiter Klasse (*ticket, compartment*)
◊ *to travel second-class* zweiter Klasse fahren
[2] normal (*stamp, letter*)

> ⓘ In Germany there is no first-class or second-class post. However, letters cost more to send than postcards, so you have to remember to say what you are sending when buying stamps. There is also an express service.

◊ *to send something second-class* etwas mit normaler Post schicken
**second-hand** ADJECTIVE
gebraucht
♦ **a second-hand car** ein Gebrauchtwagen MASC
**secondly** ADVERB

zweitens ◊ *firstly ... secondly ...* erstens
... zweitens ...
**secret** ADJECTIVE
| see also **secret** NOUN |
geheim ◊ *a secret mission* eine geheime
Mission
**secret** NOUN
| see also **secret** ADJECTIVE |
das Geheimnis (GEN des Geheimnisses, PL
die Geheimnisse) ◊ *It's a secret.* Es ist ein
Geheimnis. ◊ *Can you keep a secret?*
Kannst du ein Geheimnis für dich
behalten?
♦ **in secret** heimlich
**secretary** NOUN
der Sekretär (PL die Sekretäre)
die Sekretärin
◊ *She's a secretary.* Sie ist Sekretärin.
**secretly** ADVERB
heimlich
**section** NOUN
[1] der Teil (PL die Teile) ◊ *I passed the
written section of the exam very easily.*
Ich habe den schriftlichen Teil der
Prüfung leicht bestanden.
[2] (*in shop*)
die Abteilung ◊ *the food section* die
Lebensmittelabteilung
**security** NOUN
die Sicherheit ◊ *They are trying to
improve airport security.* Man versucht,
die Sicherheit auf den Flughäfen zu
erhöhen.
♦ **to have no job security** keinen sicheren
Job haben
♦ **a security guard** ein Sicherheitsbeamter
**security guard** NOUN
der Wächter (PL die Wächter)
die Wächterin
♦ **She's a security guard.** Sie ist beim
Sicherheitsdienst.
**sedan** NOUN US
die Limousine
to **see** VERB
sehen (PRESENT sieht, IMPERFECT sah, PERFECT
hat gesehen) ◊ *I can't see.* Ich kann
nichts sehen. ◊ *I saw him yesterday.* Ich
habe ihn gestern gesehen. ◊ *Have you
seen him?* Hast du ihn gesehen?
♦ **See you!** Tschüs! (*informal*)
♦ **See you soon!** Bis bald!
♦ **to see to something** sich um etwas
kümmern ◊ *The window's stuck. Can you
see to it please?* Das Fenster klemmt.
Kannst du dich bitte darum kümmern?
**seed** NOUN
der Samen (PL die Samen)
♦ **sunflower seeds** die
Sonnenblumenkerne MASC PL
to **seem** VERB
scheinen (IMPERFECT schien, PERFECT hat
geschienen) ◊ *The shop seemed to be
closed.* Das Geschäft schien geschlossen

zu haben. ◊ *That seems like a good idea.*
Das scheint eine gute Idee zu sein.
♦ **She seems tired.** Sie wirkt müde.
♦ **It seems that ...** Es sieht so aus, dass ...
◊ *It seems she's getting married.* Es sieht
so aus, dass sie heiratet.
♦ **There seems to be a problem.**
Anscheinend gibt's ein Problem.
**seen** VERB *see* **see**
**seesaw** NOUN
die Wippe
**see-through** ADJECTIVE
durchsichtig
**seldom** ADVERB
selten
to **select** VERB
auswählen (PERFECT hat ausgewählt)
**selection** NOUN
die Auswahl
**self-assured** ADJECTIVE
selbstsicher ◊ *He's very self-assured.* Er
ist sehr selbstsicher.
**self-catering** ADJECTIVE
♦ **a self-catering apartment** eine Wohnung
für Selbstversorger
**self-centred** ADJECTIVE
egozentrisch
**self-confidence** NOUN
das Selbstvertrauen ◊ *He hasn't got
much self-confidence.* Er hat nicht viel
Selbstvertrauen.
**self-conscious** ADJECTIVE
gehemmt
**self-contained** ADJECTIVE
♦ **a self-contained flat** eine separate
Wohnung
**self-control** NOUN
die Selbstbeherrschung
**self-defence** NOUN
die Selbstverteidigung ◊ *self-defence
classes* der Selbstverteidigungskurs
♦ **She killed him in self-defence.** Sie hat
ihn in Notwehr getötet.
**self-discipline** NOUN
die Selbstdisziplin
**self-employed** ADJECTIVE
♦ **to be self-employed** selbstständig sein
◊ *He's self-employed.* Er ist
selbstständig.
♦ **the self-employed** die Selbstständigen
MASC PL
**selfish** ADJECTIVE
egoistisch ◊ *Don't be so selfish.* Sei
nicht so egoistisch.
**self-respect** NOUN
die Selbstachtung
**self-service** ADJECTIVE
♦ **It's self-service.** (*café, shop*) Da ist
Selbstbedienung.
♦ **a self-service restaurant** ein
Selbstbedienungsrestaurant NEUT
to **sell** VERB

**S**

☞

verkaufen (PERFECT hat verkauft) ◊ *He sold it to me.* Er hat es mir verkauft.
◆ **to sell off** verkaufen
◆ **The tickets are all sold out.** Alle Karten sind ausverkauft.
◆ **The tickets sold out in three hours.** Die Karten waren in drei Stunden ausverkauft.
**sell-by date** NOUN
das Verfallsdatum (PL die Verfallsdaten)
**selling price** NOUN
der Verkaufspreis (GEN des Verkaufspreises, PL die Verkaufspreise)
**Sellotape** ® NOUN
der Tesafilm ®
**semi** NOUN
die Doppelhaushälfte ◊ *We live in a semi.* Wir wohnen in einer Doppelhaushälfte.
**semicircle** NOUN
der Halbkreis (GEN des Halbkreises, PL die Halbkreise)
**semicolon** NOUN
der Strichpunkt (PL die Strichpunkte)
**semi-detached house** NOUN
die Doppelhaushälfte ◊ *We live in a semi-detached house.* Wir wohnen in einer Doppelhaushälfte.
**semi-final** NOUN
das Halbfinale (PL die Halbfinale)
**semi-skimmed milk** NOUN
die fettarme Milch
to **send** VERB
schicken ◊ *She sent me a birthday card.* Sie hat mir eine Geburtstagskarte geschickt.
◆ **to send back** zurückschicken
◆ **to send off (1)** (*goods, letter*) abschicken
◆ **to send off (2)** (*in sports match*) vom Platz schicken ◊ *He was sent off.* Er wurde vom Platz geschickt.
◆ **to send off for something (1)** (*free*) etwas kommen lassen ◊ *I've sent off for a brochure.* Ich habe mir eine Broschüre kommen lassen.
◆ **to send off for something (2)** (*paid for*) bestellen ◊ *She sent off for a book.* Sie hat ein Buch bestellt.
◆ **to send out** verschicken
**sender** NOUN
der Absender (PL die Absender)
die Absenderin
**senior** ADJECTIVE
leitend ◊ *senior management* die leitenden Angestellten
◆ **senior school** die weiterführende Schule
◆ **senior pupils** die Oberstufenschüler
**senior citizen** NOUN
der Senior (PL die Senioren)
die Seniorin
**sensational** ADJECTIVE
sensationell
**sense** NOUN

[1] (*faculty*)
der Sinn (PL die Sinne) ◊ *the five senses* die fünf Sinne ◊ *the sixth sense* der sechste Sinn
◆ **the sense of touch** der Tastsinn
◆ **the sense of smell** der Geschmacksinn
◆ **sense of humour** der Sinn für Humor ◊ *He's got no sense of humour.* Er hat keinen Sinn für Humor.
[2] (*wisdom*)
der Verstand
◆ **Use your common sense!** Benutze deinen gesunden Menschenverstand!
◆ **It makes sense.** Das macht Sinn.
◆ **It doesn't make sense.** Das macht keinen Sinn.
**senseless** ADJECTIVE
sinnlos
**sensible** ADJECTIVE
vernünftig ◊ *Be sensible!* Sei vernünftig! ◊ *It would be sensible to check first.* Es wäre vernünftig, zuerst nachzusehen.
*Be careful not to translate **sensible** by sensibel.*
**sensitive** ADJECTIVE
sensibel ◊ *She's very sensitive.* Sie ist sehr sensibel.
**sensuous** ADJECTIVE
sinnlich
**sent** VERB *see* **send**
**sentence** NOUN
*see also* **sentence** VERB
[1] der Satz (GEN des Satzes, PL die Sätze) ◊ *What does this sentence mean?* Was bedeutet dieser Satz?
[2] (*judgment*)
das Urteil (PL die Urteile) ◊ *The court will pass sentence tomorrow.* Das Gericht wird morgen das Urteil verkünden.
[3] (*punishment*)
die Strafe ◊ *the death sentence* die Todesstrafe
◆ **He got a life sentence.** Er hat lebenslänglich bekommen.
to **sentence** VERB
*see also* **sentence** NOUN
verurteilen (PERFECT hat verurteilt) ◊ *to sentence somebody to life imprisonment* jemanden zu einer lebenslangen Gefängnisstrafe verurteilen ◊ *to sentence somebody to death* jemanden zum Tode verurteilen
**sentimental** ADJECTIVE
sentimental
**separate** ADJECTIVE
*see also* **separate** VERB
getrennt ◊ *The children have separate rooms.* Die Kinder haben getrennte Zimmer.
◆ **I wrote it on a separate sheet.** Ich habe es auf ein extra Blatt geschrieben.
◆ **on separate occasions** bei verschiedenen Gelegenheiten

♦ **on two separate occasions** zweimal

to **separate** VERB

> see also **separate** ADJECTIVE

[1] trennen
[2] sich trennen (married couple)

**separately** ADVERB
extra

**separation** NOUN
die Trennung

**September** NOUN
der September ◊ in September im
September

**sequel** NOUN
die Fortsetzung (book, film)

**sequence** NOUN
[1] die Reihenfolge ◊ in the correct
sequence in der richtigen Reihenfolge
♦ **in sequence** der Reihenfolge nach
♦ **a sequence of events** eine Folge von
Ereignissen
[2] die Sequenz (in film)

**sergeant** NOUN
[1] (army)
der Feldwebel (PL die Feldwebel)
die Feldwebelin
[2] (police)
der Polizeimeister (PL die Polizeimeister)
die Polizeimeisterin

**serial** NOUN
die Fernsehserie

**series** SING NOUN
[1] die Sendereihe ◊ a TV series eine
Sendereihe im Fernsehen
[2] die Reihe (of numbers)

**serious** ADJECTIVE
[1] ernst ◊ You look very serious. Du
siehst sehr ernst aus.
♦ **Are you serious?** Ist das dein Ernst?
[2] schwer (illness, mistake)
*Be careful not to translate* **serious** *by*
***seriös.***

**seriously** ADVERB
im Ernst ◊ No, but seriously ... Nein,
aber im Ernst ...
♦ **to take somebody seriously** jemanden
ernst nehmen
♦ **seriously injured** schwer verletzt
♦ **Seriously?** Im Ernst?

**sermon** NOUN
die Predigt

**servant** NOUN
der Diener (PL die Diener)
die Dienerin

to **serve** VERB

> see also **serve** NOUN

[1] servieren (PERFECT hat serviert) ◊ Dinner
is served. Das Essen ist serviert.
[2] aufschlagen (PRESENT schlägt auf,
IMPERFECT schlug auf, PERFECT hat
aufgeschlagen) ◊ It's Agassi's turn to
serve. Agassi schlägt auf.
[3] (prison sentence)

absitzen (IMPERFECT saß ab, PERFECT hat
abgesessen)
♦ **to serve time** im Gefängnis sein
♦ **It serves you right.** Das geschieht dir
recht.

**serve** NOUN

> see also **serve** VERB

der Aufschlag (tennis) (PL die
Aufschläge)
♦ **It's your serve.** Du hast Aufschlag.

**server** NOUN
der Server (computer) (PL die Server)

to **service** VERB

> see also **service** NOUN

überholen (car, washing machine) (PERFECT
hat überholt)

**service** NOUN

> see also **service** VERB

[1] die Bedienung ◊ Service is included.
Die Bedienung ist inklusive.
[2] (of car)
die Inspektion
[3] (church service)
der Gottesdienst (PL die
Gottesdienste)
♦ **the Fire Service** die Feuerwehr
♦ **the armed services** die Streitkräfte

**service area** NOUN
die Raststätte

**service charge** NOUN
die Bedienung ◊ There's no service
charge. Die Bedienung wird nicht extra
berechnet.

**serviceman** NOUN
der Militärangehörige (GEN des
Militärangehörigen, PL die
Militärangehörigen) ◊ a serviceman ein
Militärangehöriger
♦ **He's a serviceman.** Er ist beim Militär.

**service station** NOUN
die Tankstelle

**serviette** NOUN
die Serviette

**session** NOUN
die Sitzung

**set** NOUN

> see also **set** VERB

der Satz (GEN des Satzes, PL die Sätze) ◊ a
set of keys ein Satz Schlüssel ◊ Becker
won the set. (tennis) Becker hat den Satz
gewonnen.
♦ **a chess set** ein Schachspiel NEUT
♦ **a train set** eine Spielzeugeisenbahn

to **set** VERB

> see also **set** NOUN

[1] (alarm clock)
stellen ◊ I set the alarm for seven
o'clock. Ich habe den Wecker auf sieben
Uhr gestellt.
[2] (record)
aufstellen (PERFECT hat aufgestellt) ◊ The
world record was set last year. Der

**S**

☞

Weltrekord wurde letztes Jahr
aufgestellt.

3 (*sun*)
untergehen (IMPERFECT ging unter, PERFECT
ist untergegangen) ◊ *The sun was
setting.* Die Sonne ging unter.

♦ **The film is set in Morocco.** Der Film
spielt in Marokko.

♦ **to set off** aufbrechen ◊ *We set off for
London at nine o'clock.* Wir sind um
neun Uhr nach London aufgebrochen.

♦ **to set out** aufbrechen ◊ *We set out for
London at nine o'clock.* Wir sind um
neun Uhr nach London aufgebrochen.

♦ **to set the table** den Tisch decken

**settee** NOUN
das Sofa (PL die Sofas)

to **settle** VERB
1 (*problem*)
lösen
2 (*argument*)
beilegen (PERFECT hat beigelegt)

♦ **to settle an account** eine Rechnung
begleichen

♦ **to settle down** (*calm down*) ruhiger
werden

♦ **Settle down!** Beruhige dich!

♦ **to settle in** sich einleben

♦ **to settle on something** sich für etwas
entscheiden ◊ *I've finally settled on Crete
for my holidays.* Ich habe mich endlich
dafür entschieden, nach Kreta in Urlaub
zu fahren.

**seven** NUMBER
sieben ◊ *She's seven.* Sie ist sieben.

**seventeen** NUMBER
siebzehn ◊ *He's seventeen.* Er ist
siebzehn.

**seventeenth** ADJECTIVE
siebzehnte

♦ **the seventeenth of August** der
siebzehnte August

**seventh** ADJECTIVE
siebte ◊ *the seventh floor* der siebte
Stock

♦ **the seventh of August** der siebte August

**seventy** NUMBER
siebzig ◊ *She's seventy.* Sie ist siebzig.

**several** ADJECTIVE, PRONOUN
einige ◊ *several schools* einige Schulen
◊ *several of them* einige von ihnen

to **sew** VERB
nähen

♦ **to sew up** (*tear*) flicken

**sewing** NOUN
das Nähen

♦ **I like sewing.** Ich nähe gern.

♦ **a sewing machine** eine Nähmaschine

**sewn** VERB *see* **sew**

**sex** NOUN
das Geschlecht (PL die Geschlechter)

♦ **to have sex with somebody** mit
jemandem Verkehr haben

♦ **sex education** der Aufklärungsunterricht

**sexism** NOUN
der Sexismus (GEN des Sexismus)

**sexist** ADJECTIVE
sexistisch

**sexual** ADJECTIVE
sexuell ◊ *sexual harassment* die sexuelle
Belästigung

♦ **sexual discrimination** die
Diskriminierung aufgrund des
Geschlechts

**sexuality** NOUN
die Sexualität

**sexy** ADJECTIVE
sexy

**shabby** ADJECTIVE
schäbig

**shade** NOUN
1 der Schatten (PL die Schatten) ◊ *It was
thirty degrees in the shade.* Es waren
dreißig Grad im Schatten.
2 (*colour*)
der Ton (PL die Töne) ◊ *a shade of blue*
ein Blauton

**shadow** NOUN
der Schatten (PL die Schatten)

to **shake** VERB
1 ausschütteln (PERFECT hat
ausgeschüttelt) ◊ *She shook the rug.* Sie
hat den Teppich ausgeschüttelt.
2 schütteln ◊ *She shook the bottle.* Sie
hat die Flasche geschüttelt.
3 (*tremble*)
zittern ◊ *He was shaking with fear.* Er
zitterte vor Angst.

♦ **to shake one's head** (*in refusal*) den Kopf
schütteln

♦ **to shake hands with somebody**
jemandem die Hand geben ◊ *They shook
hands.* Sie gaben sich die Hand.

**shaken** ADJECTIVE
mitgenommen ◊ *I was feeling a bit
shaken.* Ich war etwas mitgenommen.

**shaky** ADJECTIVE
zittrig (*hand, voice*)

**shall** VERB

♦ **Shall I shut the window?** Soll ich das
Fenster zumachen?

♦ **Shall we ask him to come with us?**
Sollen wir ihn fragen, ob er mitkommt?

**shallow** ADJECTIVE
flach (*water, pool*)

**shambles** SING NOUN
das Chaos (GEN des Chaos) ◊ *It's a
complete shambles.* Es ist ein völliges
Chaos.

**shame** NOUN
die Schande ◊ *The shame of it!* Diese
Schande!

♦ **What a shame!** Wie schade!

♦ **It's a shame that ...** Es ist schade, dass ...
◊ *It's a shame he isn't here.* Es ist
schade, dass er nicht da ist.

**shampoo** NOUN
das Shampoo (PL die Shampoos) ◊ *a bottle of shampoo* eine Flasche Shampoo
**shandy** NOUN
das Bier mit Limonade

> ❶ **shandy** *is also called **das Alsterwasser** in North Germany and **der Radler** in South Germany.*

**shan't** = shall not
**shape** NOUN
die Form
**share** NOUN
| see also **share** VERB |
[1] (*in company*)
die Aktie ◊ *They've got shares in British Telecom.* Sie haben Aktien der British Telecom.
[2] (*portion*)
der Anteil (PL die Anteile)
to **share** VERB
| see also **share** NOUN |
teilen ◊ *to share a room with somebody* ein Zimmer mit jemandem teilen
♦ **to share out** verteilen ◊ *They shared the sweets out among the children.* Sie haben die Bonbons unter den Kindern verteilt.
**shark** NOUN
der Hai (PL die Haie)
**sharp** ADJECTIVE
[1] scharf (*razor, knife*) ◊ *I need a sharper knife.* Ich brauche ein schärferes Messer.
[2] spitz (*spike, point*)
[3] gescheit (*clever*) ◊ *She's very sharp.* Sie ist sehr gescheit.
♦ **at two o'clock sharp** Punkt zwei Uhr
to **shave** VERB
sich rasieren (*have a shave*) (PERFECT hat sich rasiert)
♦ **to shave one's legs** sich die Beine rasieren ◊ *I don't shave my legs.* Ich rasiere mir die Beine nicht.
**shaver** NOUN
♦ **an electric shaver** ein Elektrorasierer MASC
**shaving cream** NOUN
die Rasiercreme (PL die Rasiercremes)
**shaving foam** NOUN
der Rasierschaum
**she** PRONOUN
sie ◊ *She's very nice.* Sie ist sehr nett.
**shed** NOUN
der Schuppen (PL die Schuppen)
**she'd** = she had, = she would
**sheep** NOUN
das Schaf (PL die Schafe) ◊ *Dozens of sheep were blocking the road.* Dutzende von Schafen haben die Straße versperrt.
**sheepdog** NOUN
der Schäferhund (PL die Schäferhunde)
**sheer** ADJECTIVE

rein ◊ *It's sheer greed.* Das ist die reine Gier.
**sheet** NOUN
das Leintuch (*on bed*) (PL die Leintücher)
♦ **a sheet of paper** ein Blatt Papier NEUT
**shelf** NOUN
das Regal (PL die Regale)
**shell** NOUN
[1] die Muschel (*on beach*)
[2] die Schale (*of egg, nut*)
[3] die Granate (*explosive*)
**she'll** = she will
**shellfish** NOUN
das Schalentier (PL die Schalentiere)
**shell suit** NOUN
der Jogginganzug (PL die Jogginganzüge)
**shelter** NOUN
♦ **to take shelter** sich unterstellen ◊ *They took shelter beneath a bridge.* Sie stellten sich unter einer Brücke unter.
♦ **a bus shelter** eine überdachte Bushaltestelle
**shelves** PL NOUN *see* **shelf**
**shepherd** NOUN
der Schäfer (PL die Schäfer)
die Schäferin
**sheriff** NOUN
der Sheriff (PL die Sheriffs)
**sherry** NOUN
der Sherry (PL die Sherrys)
**she's** = she is, = she has
**Shetland Islands** PL NOUN
die Shetlandinseln FEM PL
**shield** NOUN
der Schild (PL die Schilde)
**shift** NOUN
| see also **shift** VERB |
die Schicht ◊ *His shift starts at eight o'clock.* Seine Schicht fängt um acht Uhr an. ◊ *the night shift* die Nachtschicht
♦ **to do shift work** Schicht arbeiten
to **shift** VERB
| see also **shift** NOUN |
verschieben (*move*) (IMPERFECT verschob, PERFECT hat verschoben) ◊ *I couldn't shift the wardrobe on my own.* Ich konnte den Schrank nicht allein verschieben.
♦ **Shift yourself!** jetzt aber los!
**shifty** ADJECTIVE
[1] zwielichtig (*person*) ◊ *He looked shifty.* Er sah zwielichtig aus.
[2] unstet (*eyes*)
**shin** NOUN
das Schienbein (PL die Schienbeine)
to **shine** VERB
scheinen (IMPERFECT schien, PERFECT hat geschienen) ◊ *The sun was shining.* Die Sonne schien.
**shiny** ADJECTIVE
glänzend

**S**

**ship** NOUN
das Schiff (PL die Schiffe)
**shipbuilding** NOUN
der Schiffbau
**shipwreck** NOUN
der Schiffbruch (*accident*) (PL die Schiffbrüche)
**shipwrecked** ADJECTIVE
◆ **to be shipwrecked** Schiffbruch erleiden
**shipyard** NOUN
die Werft
**shirt** NOUN
1 (*man's*)
das Hemd (PL die Hemden)
2 (*woman's*)
die Bluse
**shit** EXCLAMATION
Scheiße! (*rude*)
to **shiver** VERB
zittern
**shock** NOUN
see also **shock** VERB
der Schock (PL die Schocks)
◆ **to get a shock (1)** (*surprise*) einen Schock bekommen
◆ **to get a shock (2)** (*electric*) einen Schlag bekommen
◆ **an electric shock** ein elektrischer Schlag
to **shock** VERB
see also **shock** NOUN
schockieren (*upset*) (PERFECT hat schockiert) ◇ *They were shocked by the tragedy.* Sie waren über die Tragödie schockiert. ◇ *Nothing shocks me any more.* Mich schockiert nichts mehr.
**shocked** ADJECTIVE
schockiert ◇ *He'll be shocked if you say that.* Wenn du das sagst, wird er schockiert sein.
**shocking** ADJECTIVE
schockierend ◇ *It's shocking!* Es ist schockierend! ◇ *a shocking waste* eine schockierende Verschwendung
**shoe** NOUN
der Schuh (PL die Schuhe)
**shoelace** NOUN
der Schnürsenkel (PL die Schnürsenkel)
**shoe polish** NOUN
die Schuhcreme (PL die Schuhcremes)
**shoe shop** NOUN
das Schuhgeschäft (PL die Schuhgeschäfte)
**shone** VERB see **shine**
**shook** VERB see **shake**
to **shoot** VERB
1 (*gun, in football*)
schießen (IMPERFECT schoss, PERFECT hat geschossen) ◇ *Don't shoot!* Nicht schießen!
◆ **to shoot at somebody** auf jemanden schießen

◆ **He was shot in the leg.** (*wounded*) Er wurde ins Bein getroffen.
◆ **to shoot an arrow** einen Pfeil abschießen
2 (*kill*)
erschießen (IMPERFECT erschoss, PERFECT hat erschossen) ◇ *He was shot by a sniper.* Er wurde von einem Heckenschützen erschossen.
◆ **to shoot oneself** (*dead*) sich erschießen ◇ *He shot himself with a revolver.* Er erschoss sich mit einem Revolver.
3 (*film*)
drehen ◇ *The film was shot in Prague.* Der Film wurde in Prag gedreht.
**shooting** NOUN
1 die Schüsse MASC PL ◇ *They heard shooting.* Sie hörten Schüsse.
◆ **a shooting** eine Schießerei
2 die Jagd (*hunting*) ◇ *to go shooting* auf die Jagd gehen
**shop** NOUN
das Geschäft (PL die Geschäfte) ◇ *a sports shop* ein Sportgeschäft
**shop assistant** NOUN
der Verkäufer (PL die Verkäufer)
die Verkäuferin
◇ *She's a shop assistant.* Sie ist Verkäuferin.
**shopkeeper** NOUN
der Ladenbesitzer (PL die Ladenbesitzer)
die Ladenbesitzerin
◇ *He's a shopkeeper.* Er ist Ladenbesitzer.
**shoplifting** NOUN
der Ladendiebstahl (PL die Ladendiebstähle)
**shopping** NOUN
die Einkäufe MASC PL (*purchases*) ◇ *Can you get the shopping from the car?* Kannst du die Einkäufe aus dem Auto holen?
◆ **I love shopping.** Ich gehe gern einkaufen.
◆ **to go shopping** einkaufen gehen
◆ **a shopping bag** eine Einkaufstasche
◆ **a shopping centre** ein Einkaufszentrum NEUT
**shop window** NOUN
das Schaufenster (PL die Schaufenster)
**shore** NOUN
die Küste
◆ **on shore** an Land
**short** ADJECTIVE
1 kurz ◇ *a short skirt* ein kurzer Rock ◇ *short hair* kurze Haare ◇ *a short break* eine kurze Pause ◇ *a short walk* ein kurzer Spaziergang
◆ **too short** zu kurz ◇ *It was a great holiday, but too short.* Es waren tolle Ferien, nur zu kurz.
2 klein (*person*) ◇ *She's quite short.* Sie ist ziemlich klein.

♦ **to be short of something** knapp an etwas sein ◊ *I'm short of money.* Ich bin knapp an Geld.

♦ **In short, the answer's no.** Kurz, die Antwort ist nein.

♦ **at short notice** kurzfristig

**shortage** NOUN
der Mangel ◊ *a water shortage* ein Wassermangel

**short cut** NOUN
die Abkürzung ◊ *I took a short cut.* Ich habe eine Abkürzung genommen.

**shorthand** NOUN
das Steno

**shortly** ADVERB
1 bald ◊ *He'll be arriving shortly.* Er kommt bald.
2 kurz ◊ *shortly after the accident* kurz nach dem Unfall

**shorts** PL NOUN
die Shorts PL ◊ *a pair of shorts* ein Paar Shorts

**short-sighted** ADJECTIVE
kurzsichtig

**short story** NOUN
die Kurzgeschichte

**shot** VERB *see* **shoot**

**shot** NOUN
1 (*gunshot*)
der Schuss (GEN des Schusses, PL die Schüsse)
2 (*photo*)
das Foto (PL die Fotos) ◊ *a shot of Edinburgh Castle* ein Foto des Edinburgher Schlosses
3 (*injection*)
die Spritze

**shotgun** NOUN
die Flinte

**should** VERB
sollen ◊ *You should take more exercise.* Du solltest mehr Sport machen.

♦ **He should be there by now.** Er müsste jetzt da sein.

♦ **That shouldn't be too hard.** Das dürfte nicht zu schwer sein.

♦ **I should have told you before.** Ich hätte es dir vorher sagen sollen.

*When **should** means "would" use **würde**.*

♦ **I should go if I were you.** Ich würde gehen, wenn ich du wäre.

♦ **I should be so lucky!** Das wäre zu schön!

**shoulder** NOUN
die Schulter

♦ **a shoulder bag** eine Umhängetasche

**shouldn't** = **should not**

to **shout** VERB
see also **shout** NOUN
schreien (IMPERFECT schrie, PERFECT hat geschrien) ◊ *Don't shout!* Schrei doch nicht so! ◊ *"Go away!" he shouted.* "Geh weg!" schrie er.

**shout** NOUN
see also **shout** VERB
der Schrei (PL die Schreie)

**shovel** NOUN
die Schaufel

**show** NOUN
see also **show** VERB
1 (*performance*)
die Show (PL die Shows)
2 (*programme*)
die Sendung
3 (*exhibition*)
die Ausstellung

to **show** VERB
see also **show** NOUN
1 zeigen

♦ **to show somebody something** jemandem etwas zeigen ◊ *Have I shown you my new trainers?* Habe ich dir meine neuen Turnschuhe schon gezeigt?
2 beweisen (IMPERFECT bewies, PERFECT hat bewiesen) ◊ *She showed great courage.* Sie hat großen Mut bewiesen.

♦ **It shows.** Das sieht man. ◊ *I've never been riding before. – It shows.* Ich bin noch nie geritten. – Das sieht man.

♦ **to show off** angeben

♦ **to show up** (*turn up*) aufkreuzen ◊ *He showed up late as usual.* Er kreuzte wie immer zu spät auf.

**shower** NOUN
1 die Dusche

♦ **to have a shower** duschen
2 (*of rain*)
der Schauer (PL die Schauer)

**showerproof** ADJECTIVE
regendicht

**showing** NOUN
die Vorführung (*of film*)

**shown** VERB *see* **show**

**show-off** NOUN
der Angeber (PL die Angeber)
die Angeberin

**shrank** VERB *see* **shrink**

to **shriek** VERB
kreischen

**shrimps** PL NOUN
die Krabben FEM PL

to **shrink** VERB
einlaufen (*clothes, fabric*) (PRESENT läuft ein, IMPERFECT lief ein, PERFECT ist eingelaufen)

**Shrove Tuesday** NOUN
der Fastnachtsdienstag

to **shrug** VERB
♦ **He shrugged his shoulders.** Er zuckte mit den Schultern.

**shrunk** VERB *see* **shrink**

to **shudder** VERB
sich schütteln

to **shuffle** VERB
♦ **to shuffle the cards** die Karten mischen

**S**

to **shut** VERB
zumachen (PERFECT hat zugemacht)
◊ *What time do you shut?* Wann machen
Sie zu? ◊ *What time do the shops shut?*
Wann machen die Geschäfte zu?
◆ **to shut down** schließen ◊ *The cinema
shut down last year.* Das Kino hat letztes
Jahr geschlossen.
◆ **to shut up (1)** (*close*) verschließen
◆ **to shut up (2)** (*be quiet*) den Mund halten
◊ *Shut up!* Halt den Mund!

**shutters** PL NOUN
die Fensterläden MASC PL

**shuttle** NOUN
1 (*plane*)
das Pendelflugzeug (PL die
Pendelflugzeuge)
2 (*train*)
der Pendelzug (PL die Pendelzüge)
3 (*bus*)
der Pendelbus (GEN des Pendelbusses, PL
die Pendelbusse)

**shuttlecock** NOUN
der Federball (*badminton*) (PL die
Federbälle)

**shy** ADJECTIVE
schüchtern

**Sicily** NOUN
Sizilien NEUT
◆ **from Sicily** aus Sizilien
◆ **to Sicily** nach Sizilien

**sick** ADJECTIVE
1 krank (*ill*) ◊ *He was sick for four days.*
Er war vier Tage krank.
2 übel (*joke, humour*) ◊ *That's really sick!*
Das war wirklich übel!
◆ **to be sick** (*vomit*) sich übergeben
◆ **I feel sick.** Mir ist schlecht.
◆ **to be sick of something** etwas leid sein
◊ *I'm sick of your jokes.* Ich bin deine
Witze leid.

**sickening** ADJECTIVE
ekelhaft

**sick leave** NOUN
◆ **to be on sick leave** krankgeschrieben
sein ◊ *Rudi's been on sick leave for three
weeks now.* Rudi ist seit drei Wochen
krankgeschrieben.

**sickness** NOUN
die Krankheit

**sick note** NOUN
1 (*from parents*)
die Entschuldigung
2 (*from doctor*)
das ärztliche Attest (PL die ärztlichen
Atteste)

**sick pay** NOUN
die Bezahlung im Krankheitsfall

**side** NOUN
1 die Seite ◊ *He was driving on the
wrong side of the road.* Er fuhr auf der
falschen Straßenseite. ◊ *He's on my side.*
Er ist auf meiner Seite.

◆ **side by side** nebeneinander
◆ **the side entrance** der Seiteneingang
◆ **to take sides** Partei ergreifen ◊ *She
always takes your side.* Sie ergreift
immer für dich Partei.
2 (*edge*)
der Rand (PL die Ränder) ◊ *by the side of
the road* am Straßenrand
3 (*of pool, river*)
das Ufer (PL die Ufer) ◊ *by the side of the
lake* am Ufer des Sees

**sideboard** NOUN
die Anrichte

**side effect** NOUN
der Nebeneffekt (PL die Nebeneffekte)

**side street** NOUN
die Seitenstraße

**sidewalk** NOUN US
der Bürgersteig (PL die Bürgersteige)

**sideways** ADVERB
1 von der Seite (*look*)
2 zur Seite (*move, be facing*)
◆ **sideways on** von der Seite

**sieve** NOUN
das Sieb (PL die Siebe)

**sigh** NOUN
*see also* **sigh** VERB
der Seufzer (PL die Seufzer)

to **sigh** VERB
*see also* **sigh** NOUN
seufzen

**sight** NOUN
der Anblick ◊ *It was an amazing sight.*
Es war ein irrer Anblick.
◆ **in sight** in Sicht
◆ **out of sight** nicht zu sehen
◆ **to have poor sight** schlechte Augen
haben
◆ **to know somebody by sight** jemanden
vom Sehen kennen
◆ **the sights** (*tourist spots*) die
Sehenswürdigkeiten ◊ *to see the sights
of London* sich die Sehenswürdigkeiten
von London ansehen

**sightseeing** NOUN
das Sightseeing
◆ **to go sightseeing** Sightseeing machen

**sign** NOUN
*see also* **sign** VERB
1 (*notice*)
das Schild (PL die Schilder) ◊ *There was
a big sign saying "private".* Da war ein
großes Schild, auf dem "privat" stand.
◆ **a road sign** ein Verkehrsschild
2 (*gesture, indication*)
das Zeichen (PL die Zeichen) ◊ *There's no
sign of improvement.* Es gibt kein
Zeichen einer Besserung.
◆ **What sign are you?** (*star sign*) Was für ein
Sternzeichen sind Sie?

to **sign** VERB
*see also* **sign** NOUN

unterschreiben (IMPERFECT unterschrieb,
PERFECT hat unterschrieben)
◆ **to sign on (1)** (*as unemployed*) sich
arbeitslos melden
◆ **to sign on (2)** (*for course*) sich
einschreiben
**signal** NOUN
   | *see also* **signal** VERB |
das Signal (PL die Signale)
to **signal** VERB
   | *see also* **signal** NOUN |
◆ **to signal to somebody** jemandem ein
Zeichen geben
**signalman** NOUN
der Stellwerkswärter (PL die
Stellwerkswärter)
die Stellwerkswärterin
**signature** NOUN
die Unterschrift
**significance** NOUN
die Bedeutung
**significant** ADJECTIVE
bedeutend
**sign language** NOUN
die Zeichensprache
**signpost** NOUN
der Wegweiser (PL die Wegweiser)
**silence** NOUN
die Stille ◊ *There was absolute silence.*
Es herrschte absolute Stille.
**silent** ADJECTIVE
still
**silicon chip** NOUN
der Siliciumchip (PL die Siliciumchips)
**silk** NOUN
   | *see also* **silk** ADJECTIVE |
die Seide
**silk** ADJECTIVE
   | *see also* **silk** NOUN |
seiden ◊ *a silk scarf* ein seidener Schal
**silky** ADJECTIVE
seidig
**silly** ADJECTIVE
dumm ◊ *That's the silliest excuse I've
ever heard.* Das ist die dümmste
Ausrede, die ich je gehört habe.
**silver** NOUN
das Silber ◊ *a silver medal* eine
Silbermedaille
**similar** ADJECTIVE
ähnlich ◊ *My sister is very similar to me
in that respect.* Meine Schwester ist mir
in der Hinsicht sehr ähnlich.
**simple** ADJECTIVE
[1] einfach ◊ *It's very simple.* Das ist sehr
einfach.
[2] einfältig (*simple-minded*) ◊ *He's a bit
simple.* Er ist etwas einfältig.
**simply** ADVERB
einfach ◊ *It's simply not possible.* Es ist
einfach nicht möglich.
**simultaneous** ADJECTIVE

gleichzeitig
**sin** NOUN
   | *see also* **sin** VERB |
die Sünde
to **sin** VERB
   | *see also* **sin** NOUN |
sündigen
**since** PREPOSITION, ADVERB, CONJUNCTION
[1] seit ◊ *since Christmas* seit
Weihnachten ◊ *I haven't seen her since
she left.* Ich habe sie nicht gesehen, seit
sie weggezogen ist.
◆ **since then** seither ◊ *I haven't seen him
since then.* Ich habe ihn seither nicht
gesehen.
◆ **ever since** seitdem
[2] da (*because*) ◊ *Since you're tired, let's
stay at home.* Da du müde bist, bleiben
wir doch zu Hause.
**sincere** ADJECTIVE
aufrichtig
**sincerely** ADVERB
◆ **Yours sincerely** ... Mit freundlichen
Grüßen ...
to **sing** VERB
singen (IMPERFECT sang, PERFECT hat
gesungen) ◊ *He sang out of tune.* Er hat
falsch gesungen. ◊ *Have you ever sung
this tune before?* Hast du die Melodie
schon mal gesungen?
**singer** NOUN
der Sänger (PL die Sänger)
die Sängerin
**singing** NOUN
das Singen
**single** ADJECTIVE
   | *see also* **single** NOUN |
allein stehend (*unmarried*)
◆ **a single room** ein Einzelzimmer NEUT
◆ **not a single thing** absolut nichts
**single** NOUN
   | *see also* **single** ADJECTIVE |
[1] (*ticket*)
die einfache Fahrkarte ◊ *A single to
Bonn, please.* Eine einfache Fahrkarte
nach Bonn, bitte.
[2] (*record*)
die Single (PL die Singles)
◆ **a CD single** eine CD-Single
**single parent** NOUN
◆ **She's a single parent.** Sie ist allein
erziehende Mutter.
◆ **a single parent family** eine
Einelternteilfamilie
**singles** PL NOUN
das Einzel (*in tennis*) SING (PL die Einzel)
◊ *the women's singles* das Dameneinzel
**singular** NOUN
der Singular (PL die Singulare) ◊ *in the
singular* im Singular
**sinister** ADJECTIVE
unheimlich

**S**

**sink** NOUN

> see also **sink** VERB

die Spüle

to **sink** VERB

> see also **sink** NOUN

sinken (IMPERFECT sank, PERFECT ist gesunken)

**sir** NOUN

> In German no form of address is normally used apart from **Sie**.
> ◊ Would you like to order, Sir? Möchten Sie bestellen?

♦ **Yes sir.** Ja.

**siren** NOUN

die Sirene

**sister** NOUN

die Schwester ◊ my little sister meine kleine Schwester ◊ I wanted to speak to the sister on the ward. Ich wollte die Stationsschwester sprechen.

**sister-in-law** NOUN

die Schwägerin

to **sit** VERB

[1] (be sitting)
sitzen (IMPERFECT saß, PERFECT hat gesessen) ◊ She was sitting on the floor. Sie saß auf dem Boden.

[2] (sit down)
sich setzen ◊ Sit on that chair. Setz dich auf den Stuhl.

♦ **to sit down** sich setzen

♦ **to be sitting** sitzen

♦ **to sit an exam** eine Prüfung machen

**sitcom** NOUN

die Situationskomödie

**site** NOUN

[1] die Stätte ◊ an archaeological site eine archäologische Stätte

♦ **the site of the accident** der Unfallort

[2] (campsite)
der Campingplatz (GEN des Campingplatzes, PL die Campingplätze)

♦ **a building site** eine Baustelle

**sitting room** NOUN

das Wohnzimmer (PL die Wohnzimmer)

**situated** ADJECTIVE

♦ **to be situated** liegen ◊ The village is situated on the side of the hill. Das Dorf liegt am Berghang.

**situation** NOUN

die Situation

**six** NUMBER

sechs ◊ He's six. Er ist sechs.

**sixteen** NUMBER

sechzehn ◊ He's sixteen. Er ist sechzehn.

**sixteenth** ADJECTIVE

sechzehnte

♦ **the sixteenth of August** der sechzehnte August

**sixth** ADJECTIVE

sechste ◊ the sixth floor der sechste Stock

♦ **the sixth of August** der sechste August

**sixty** NUMBER

sechzig ◊ She's sixty. Sie ist sechzig.

**size** NOUN

> ⓘ Germany uses the European system for clothing and shoe sizes.

[1] die Größe (of object, clothing) ◊ What size do you take? Welche Größe haben Sie?

♦ **I'm a size ten.** Ich habe Größe achtunddreißig.

[2] die Schuhgröße (of shoes)

♦ **I take size six.** Ich habe Schuhgröße neununddreißig.

to **skate** VERB

[1] (ice-skate)
Schlittschuh laufen (PRESENT läuft Schlittschuh, IMPERFECT lief Schlittschuh, PERFECT ist Schlittschuh gelaufen)

[2] (roller-skate)
Rollschuh laufen (PRESENT läuft Rollschuh, IMPERFECT lief Rollschuh, PERFECT ist Rollschuh gelaufen)

**skateboard** NOUN

das Skateboard (PL die Skateboards)

**skateboarding** NOUN

das Skateboardfahren

♦ **to go skateboarding** Skateboard fahren

**skates** PL NOUN

[1] die Schlittschuhe MASC PL

[2] die Rollschuhe MASC PL (roller skates)

**skating** NOUN

[1] das Schlittschuhlaufen

♦ **to go skating** Schlittschuh laufen

♦ **a skating rink** eine Eisbahn

[2] das Rollschuhlaufen (roller-skating)

♦ **to go skating** Rollschuh laufen

♦ **a skating rink** eine Rollschuhbahn

**skeleton** NOUN

das Skelett (PL die Skelette)

**sketch** NOUN

> see also **sketch** VERB

die Skizze (drawing)

to **sketch** VERB

> see also **sketch** NOUN

skizzieren (PERFECT hat skizziert)

to **ski** VERB

> see also **ski** NOUN

Ski fahren (PRESENT fährt Ski, IMPERFECT fuhr Ski, PERFECT ist Ski gefahren) ◊ Can you ski? Kannst du Ski fahren?

**ski** NOUN

> see also **ski** VERB

der Ski (PL die Skier)

♦ **ski boots** die Skistiefel

♦ **a ski lift** ein Skilift MASC

♦ **ski pants** die Skihose SING

♦ **a ski pole** ein Skistock MASC

♦ **a ski slope** eine Skipiste

♦ **a ski suit** ein Skianzug MASC

to **skid** VERB

schleudern (PERFECT ist geschleudert)
**skier** NOUN
  der Skifahrer (PL die Skifahrer)
  die Skifahrerin
**skiing** NOUN
  das Skifahren
  ◆ **to go skiing** Ski fahren
  ◆ **to go on a skiing holiday** in den
  Skiurlaub fahren
**skilful** ADJECTIVE
  geschickt
**skill** NOUN
  das Können ◊ *It requires a lot of skill.* Es
  verlangt viel Können.
**skilled** ADJECTIVE
  ◆ **a skilled worker** ein Facharbeiter MASC
**skimmed milk** NOUN
  die Magermilch
**skimpy** ADJECTIVE
  knapp (*clothes*)
**skin** NOUN
  die Haut (PL die Häute)
  ◆ **skin cancer** der Hautkrebs
**skinhead** NOUN
  der Skinhead (PL die Skinheads)
  *der Skinhead is also used for women.*
**skinny** ADJECTIVE
  mager
**skin-tight** ADJECTIVE
  hauteng
**skip** NOUN
  see also **skip** VERB
  der Container (*container*) (PL die
  Container)
to **skip** VERB
  see also **skip** NOUN
  1 (*with rope*)
  seilspringen (PERFECT ist seilgesprungen)
  2 auslassen (PRESENT lässt aus, IMPERFECT
  ließ aus, PERFECT hat ausgelassen) ◊ *to skip*
  *a meal* eine Mahlzeit auslassen
  ◆ **I skipped the maths lesson.** Ich habe die
  Mathestunde geschwänzt.
**skirt** NOUN
  der Rock (PL die Röcke)
**skittles** SING NOUN
  das Kegeln
  ◆ **to play skittles** kegeln
to **skive** VERB
  faulenzen (*be lazy*)
  ◆ **to skive off** schwänzen (*informal*) ◊ *to*
  *skive off school* die Schule schwänzen
**skull** NOUN
  der Schädel (PL die Schädel)
**sky** NOUN
  der Himmel (PL die Himmel)
**skyscraper** NOUN
  der Wolkenkratzer (PL die Wolkenkratzer)
**slack** ADJECTIVE
  1 locker (*rope*)
  2 nachlässig (*person*)
to **slag off** VERB

◆ **to slag somebody off** über jemanden
herziehen (*informal*) ◊ *She's always*
*slagging me off.* Sie zieht dauernd über
mich her.
to **slam** VERB
  zuknallen (PERFECT hat/ist zugeknallt)
  *For the perfect tense use **haben** when*
  *the verb has an object and **sein** when*
  *there is no object.*
  ◊ *The door slammed.* Die Tür ist
  zugeknallt. ◊ *She slammed the door.* Sie
  hat die Tür zugeknallt.
**slang** NOUN
  der Slang (PL die Slangs)
**slap** NOUN
  see also **slap** VERB
  die Ohrfeige
to **slap** VERB
  see also **slap** NOUN
  ◆ **to slap somebody** jemandem einen
  Klaps geben ◊ *She slapped him.* Sie gab
  ihm einen Klaps.
**slate** NOUN
  1 der Schiefer (PL die Schiefer)
  2 (*for roof*)
  der Schieferziegel (PL die Schieferziegel)
**sledge** NOUN
  der Schlitten (PL die Schlitten)
**sledging** NOUN
  ◆ **to go sledging** Schlitten fahren
**sleep** NOUN
  see also **sleep** VERB
  der Schlaf ◊ *I need some sleep.* Ich
  brauche Schlaf.
  ◆ **to go to sleep** einschlafen
to **sleep** VERB
  see also **sleep** NOUN
  schlafen (PRESENT schläft, IMPERFECT schlief,
  PERFECT hat geschlafen) ◊ *I couldn't sleep*
  *last night.* Ich konnte heute Nacht nicht
  schlafen.
  ◆ **to sleep with somebody** mit jemandem
  schlafen
  ◆ **to sleep together** miteinander schlafen
  ◆ **to sleep around** mit jedem schlafen
  ◆ **to sleep in** verschlafen
**sleeping bag** NOUN
  der Schlafsack (PL die Schlafsäcke)
**sleeping car** NOUN
  der Schlafwagen (PL die Schlafwagen)
**sleeping pill** NOUN
  die Schlaftablette
**sleepy** ADJECTIVE
  schläfrig
  ◆ **to feel sleepy** schläfrig sein ◊ *I was*
  *feeling sleepy.* Ich war schläfrig.
  ◆ **a sleepy little village** ein verschlafenes
  kleines Dorf
**sleet** NOUN
  see also **sleet** VERB
  der Schneeregen
to **sleet** VERB

**S**

see also **sleet** NOUN

♦ **It's sleeting.** Es fällt Schneeregen.

**sleeve** NOUN

[1] der Ärmel (PL die Ärmel) ◊ *long sleeves* lange Ärmel ◊ *short sleeves* kurze Ärmel

[2] (*record sleeve*)
die Hülle

**sleigh** NOUN
der Pferdeschlitten (PL die Pferdeschlitten)

**slept** VERB *see* **sleep**

**slice** NOUN

see also **slice** VERB

die Scheibe

to **slice** VERB

see also **slice** NOUN

aufschneiden (IMPERFECT schnitt auf, PERFECT hat aufgeschnitten)

**slick** NOUN
♦ **an oil slick** ein Ölteppich MASC

**slide** NOUN

see also **slide** VERB

[1] (*in playground*)
die Rutschbahn

[2] (*photo*)
das Dia (PL die Dias)

[3] (*hair slide*)
die Klemme

to **slide** VERB

see also **slide** NOUN

rutschen (PERFECT ist gerutscht)

**slight** ADJECTIVE
klein ◊ *a slight problem* ein kleines Problem ◊ *a slight improvement* eine kleine Verbesserung

**slightly** ADVERB
etwas

**slim** ADJECTIVE

see also **slim** VERB

schlank

to **slim** VERB

see also **slim** ADJECTIVE

abnehmen (*be on a diet*) (PRESENT nimmt ab, IMPERFECT nahm ab, PERFECT hat abgenommen) ◊ *I'm slimming.* Ich nehme gerade ab.

**sling** NOUN
die Schlinge ◊ *She had her arm in a sling.* Sie hatte den Arm in der Schlinge.

**slip** NOUN

see also **slip** VERB

[1] (*mistake*)
der Schnitzer (PL die Schnitzer)

[2] (*underskirt*)
der Unterrock (PL die Unterröcke)

♦ **a slip of paper** ein Zettel MASC
♦ **a slip of the tongue** ein Versprecher MASC

to **slip** VERB

see also **slip** NOUN

ausrutschen (PERFECT ist ausgerutscht) ◊ *He slipped on the ice.* Er ist auf dem Eis ausgerutscht.

♦ **to slip up** (*make a mistake*) einen Fehler machen

**slipper** NOUN
der Hausschuh (PL die Hausschuhe) ◊ *a pair of slippers* ein Paar Hausschuhe

**slippery** ADJECTIVE
glatt

**slip-up** NOUN
der Schnitzer (PL die Schnitzer)
♦ **There's been a slip-up.** Da ist etwas schief gelaufen.

**slope** NOUN
der Abhang (PL die Abhänge)

**sloppy** ADJECTIVE
schlampig

**slot** NOUN
der Schlitz (GEN des Schlitzes, PL die Schlitze)

**slot machine** NOUN

[1] (*for gambling*)
der Geldspielautomat (GEN des Geldspielautomaten, PL die Geldspielautomaten)

[2] (*vending machine*)
der Automat (GEN des Automaten, PL die Automaten)

**slow** ADJECTIVE, ADVERB
langsam ◊ *He's a bit slow.* Er ist etwas langsam.

♦ **to go slow (1)** (*person*) langsam gehen
♦ **to go slow (2)** (*car*) langsam fahren ◊ *Drive slower!* Fahr langsamer!
♦ **My watch is slow.** Meine Uhr geht nach.

to **slow down** VERB
verlangsamen (PERFECT hat verlangsamt)

**slowly** ADVERB
langsam

**slug** NOUN
die Nacktschnecke (*animal*)

**slum** NOUN
der Slum (PL die Slums)

**slush** NOUN
der Matsch

**sly** ADJECTIVE
gerissen (*person*)
♦ **a sly smile** ein verschmitztes Lächeln

**smack** NOUN

see also **smack** VERB

der Klaps (*slap*) (GEN des Klapses, PL die Klapse)

to **smack** VERB

see also **smack** NOUN

♦ **to smack somebody** jemandem einen Klaps geben ◊ *She smacked him.* Sie gab ihm einen Klaps.

**small** ADJECTIVE
klein
♦ **small change** das Kleingeld

*Be careful not to translate* **small** *by* **schmal***.*

**smart** ADJECTIVE
1 schick (*elegant*)
2 intelligent (*clever*) ◊ *a smart idea* eine intelligente Idee
**smash** NOUN
> see also **smash** VERB

der Zusammenstoß (GEN des Zusammenstoßes, PL die Zusammenstöße)
to **smash** VERB
> see also **smash** NOUN

1 (*break*)
kaputtmachen (PERFECT hat kaputtgemacht) ◊ *I've smashed my watch.* Ich habe meine Uhr kaputtgemacht.
2 (*get broken*)
zerbrechen (PRESENT zerbricht, IMPERFECT zerbrach, PERFECT ist zerbrochen) ◊ *The glass smashed into tiny pieces.* Das Glas zerbrach in winzige Scherben.
**smashing** ADJECTIVE
klasse (*informal*) ◊ *I think he's smashing.* Ich finde, er ist klasse.
*klasse is invariable.*
◊ *a smashing film* ein klasse Film
**smell** NOUN
> see also **smell** VERB

der Geruch (PL die Gerüche)
♦ **the sense of smell** der Geruchsinn
to **smell** VERB
> see also **smell** NOUN

1 stinken (IMPERFECT stank, PERFECT hat gestunken) ◊ *That old dog really smells!* Der alte Hund stinkt!
♦ **to smell of something** nach etwas riechen ◊ *It smells of petrol.* Es riecht nach Benzin.
2 (*detect*)
riechen (IMPERFECT roch, PERFECT hat gerochen) ◊ *I can't smell anything.* Ich kann nichts riechen.
**smelly** ADJECTIVE
stinkend
♦ **He's got smelly feet.** Seine Füße stinken.
**smelt** VERB *see* **smell**
**smile** NOUN
> see also **smile** VERB

das Lächeln
to **smile** VERB
> see also **smile** NOUN

lächeln
**smiley** NOUN
das Smiley (PL die Smileys)
**smoke** NOUN
> see also **smoke** VERB

der Rauch
to **smoke** VERB
> see also **smoke** NOUN

rauchen ◊ *I don't smoke.* Ich rauche nicht. ◊ *He smokes cigars.* Er raucht Zigarren.

**smoker** NOUN
der Raucher (PL die Raucher)
die Raucherin
**smoking** NOUN
das Rauchen ◊ *to give up smoking* mit dem Rauchen aufhören ◊ *Smoking is bad for you.* Rauchen schadet der Gesundheit.
♦ **"no smoking"** "Rauchen verboten"
**smooth** ADJECTIVE
1 glatt (*surface*)
2 aalglatt (*person*)
**smudge** NOUN
der Dreck
**smug** ADJECTIVE
selbstgefällig ◊ *He's grown smugger since getting promotion.* Seit seiner Beförderung ist er selbstgefälliger geworden.
to **smuggle** VERB
schmuggeln
**smuggler** NOUN
der Schmuggler (PL die Schmuggler)
die Schmugglerin
**smuggling** NOUN
das Schmuggeln
**smutty** ADJECTIVE
schmutzig ◊ *a smutty story* eine schmutzige Geschichte
**snack** NOUN
der Snack (PL die Snacks) ◊ *to have a snack* einen Snack zu sich nehmen
**snack bar** NOUN
die Imbissstube
**snail** NOUN
die Schnecke
**snake** NOUN
die Schlange
to **snap** VERB
brechen (*break*) (PRESENT bricht, IMPERFECT brach, PERFECT ist gebrochen) ◊ *The branch snapped.* Der Zweig brach.
♦ **to snap one's fingers** mit dem Finger schnipsen
**snapshot** NOUN
das Foto (PL die Fotos)
to **snarl** VERB
knurren (*animal*)
to **snatch** VERB
♦ **to snatch something from somebody** jemandem etwas entreißen ◊ *He snatched the keys from my hand.* Er riss mir die Schlüssel aus der Hand.
♦ **My bag was snatched.** Man hat mir meine Handtasche entrissen.
to **sneak** VERB
♦ **to sneak in** sich hineinschleichen
♦ **to sneak out** sich hinausschleichen
♦ **to sneak up on somebody** an jemanden heranschleichen
to **sneeze** VERB
niesen

**S**

to **sniff** VERB

[1] schniefen ◊ *Stop sniffing!* Hör auf zu schniefen!

[2] schnüffeln an +DAT ◊ *The dog sniffed my hand.* Der Hund schnüffelte an meiner Hand.

♦ **to sniff glue** schnüffeln

**snob** NOUN

der Snob (PL die Snobs)

*der Snob is also used for women.*

◊ *She is such a snob.* Sie ist ein furchtbarer Snob.

**snooker** NOUN

das Snooker ◊ *to play snooker* Snooker spielen

**snooze** NOUN

das Nickerchen (PL die Nickerchen) ◊ *to have a snooze* ein Nickerchen machen

to **snore** VERB

schnarchen

**snow** NOUN

see also **snow** VERB

der Schnee

to **snow** VERB

see also **snow** NOUN

schneien ◊ *It's snowing.* Es schneit.

**snowball** NOUN

der Schneeball (PL die Schneebälle)

**snowflake** NOUN

die Schneeflocke

**snowman** NOUN

der Schneemann (PL die Schneemänner) ◊ *to build a snowman* einen Schneemann machen

**SO** CONJUNCTION, ADVERB

[1] also ◊ *The shop was closed, so I went home.* Das Geschäft war zu, also ging ich nach Hause. ◊ *It rained, so I got wet.* Es hat geregnet, also bin ich nass geworden. ◊ *So, have you always lived in London?* Also, hast du schon immer in London gewohnt?

♦ **So what?** Na und?

[2] so ◊ *It was so heavy!* Es war so schwer! ◊ *It's not so heavy!* Es ist nicht so schwer! ◊ *He was talking so fast I couldn't understand.* Er hat so schnell geredet, dass ich nichts verstanden habe. ◊ *How's your father? – Not so good.* Wie geht's deinem Vater? – Nicht so gut. ◊ *He's like his sister but not so clever.* Er ist wie seine Schwester, aber nicht so klug.

♦ **so much** (*a lot*) so sehr ◊ *I love you so much.* Ich liebe dich so sehr!

♦ **so much ...** so viel ... ◊ *I've got so much work.* Ich habe so viel Arbeit.

♦ **so many ...** so viele ... ◊ *I've got so many things to do today.* Ich muss heute so viele Dinge erledigen.

♦ **so do I** ich auch ◊ *I love horses. – So do I.* Ich mag Pferde. – Ich auch.

♦ **so have we** wir auch ◊ *I've been to Germany twice. – So have we.* Ich war schon zweimal in Deutschland. – Wir auch.

♦ **I think so.** Ich glaube schon.

♦ **I hope so.** Hoffentlich.

♦ **That's not so.** Das ist nicht so.

♦ **so far** bis jetzt ◊ *It's been easy so far.* Bis jetzt war es einfach.

♦ **so far so good** soweit, so gut

♦ **ten or so people** so etwa zehn Leute

♦ **at five o'clock or so** so gegen fünf Uhr

to **soak** VERB

einweichen (PERFECT hat eingeweicht)

**soaked** ADJECTIVE

völlig durchnässt ◊ *By the time we got back we were soaked.* Bis wir zu Hause waren, waren wir völlig durchnässt.

**soaking** ADJECTIVE

völlig durchnässt ◊ *By the time we got back we were soaking.* Bis wir zu Hause waren, waren wir völlig durchnässt.

♦ **soaking wet** patschnass ◊ *Your shoes are soaking wet.* Deine Schuhe sind patschnass.

**soap** NOUN

die Seife

**soap opera** NOUN

die Seifenoper

**soap powder** NOUN

das Waschpulver (PL die Waschpulver)

to **sob** VERB

schluchzen ◊ *She was sobbing.* Sie schluchzte.

**sober** ADJECTIVE

nüchtern

to **sober up** VERB

nüchtern werden (PRESENT wird nüchtern, IMPERFECT wurde nüchtern, PERFECT ist nüchtern geworden)

**soccer** NOUN

der Fußball ◊ *to play soccer* Fußball spielen

♦ **a soccer player** ein Fußballspieler MASC

**social** ADJECTIVE

sozial ◊ *social problems* soziale Probleme

♦ **a social class** eine gesellschaftliche Schicht

♦ **I have a good social life.** Ich komme viel unter Leute.

**socialism** NOUN

der Sozialismus (GEN des Sozialismus)

**socialist** ADJECTIVE

see also **socialist** NOUN

sozialistisch

**socialist** NOUN

see also **socialist** ADJECTIVE

der Sozialist (GEN des Sozialisten, PL die Sozialisten)

die Sozialistin

◊ *She's a Socialist.* Sie ist Sozialistin.

**social security** NOUN

[1] die Sozialhilfe (*money*)

♦ **to be on social security** Sozialhilfe
bekommen
[2] die Sozialversicherung (*organization*)
**social worker** NOUN
der Sozialarbeiter (PL die Sozialarbeiter)
die Sozialarbeiterin
◊ *She's a social worker.* Sie ist
Sozialarbeiterin.
**society** NOUN
[1] die Gesellschaft ◊ *We live in a
multicultural society.* Wir leben in einer
multikulturellen Gesellschaft.
[2] der Verein (PL die Vereine) ◊ *the Royal
Society for the Prevention of Cruelty to
Animals* der Tierschutzverein
♦ **a drama society** eine Theatergruppe
**sociology** NOUN
die Soziologie
**sock** NOUN
die Socke
**socket** NOUN
die Steckdose
**soda** NOUN
das Sodawasser (*soda water*) (PL die
Sodawasser)
**soda pop** NOUN US
die Limo (PL die Limos)
**sofa** NOUN
das Sofa (PL die Sofas)
**soft** ADJECTIVE
weich
♦ **soft cheese** der Weichkäse
♦ **to be soft on somebody** (*be kind to*)
nachsichtig mit jemandem sein
♦ **a soft drink** ein alkoholfreies Getränk
♦ **soft drugs** weiche Drogen
♦ **a soft option** eine bequeme Lösung
**software** NOUN
die Software
**soggy** ADJECTIVE
[1] nass (*soaked*) ◊ *a soggy tissue* ein
nasses Taschentuch
[2] weich (*not crisp*) ◊ *soggy chips* weiche
Pommes frites
**soil** NOUN
der Boden (PL die Böden)
**solar** ADJECTIVE
♦ **solar eclipse** die Sonnenfinsternis
**solar power** NOUN
die Sonnenenergie
**sold** VERB *see* **sell**
**soldier** NOUN
der Soldat (GEN des Soldaten, PL die
Soldaten)
die Soldatin
◊ *He's a soldier.* Er ist Soldat.
**solicitor** NOUN
[1] (*for lawsuits*)
der Rechtsanwalt (PL die Rechtsanwälte)
die Rechtsanwältin
◊ *He's a solicitor.* Er ist Rechtsanwalt.
[2] (*for property, wills*)
der Notar (PL die Notare)

die Notarin
◊ *She's a solicitor.* Sie ist Notarin.
**solid** ADJECTIVE
[1] stabil ◊ *a solid wall* eine stabile Wand
[2] massiv ◊ *solid gold* massives Gold
♦ **for three hours solid** drei geschlagene
Stunden lang
**solo** NOUN
das Solo (PL die Soli) ◊ *a guitar solo* ein
Gitarrensolo
**solution** NOUN
die Lösung
to **solve** VERB
lösen
**some** ADJECTIVE, PRONOUN
[1] ein paar
*Use **ein paar** with plural nouns.*
◊ *I've got some nice pictures of you.* Ich
habe ein paar nette Bilder von dir. ◊ *I
only sold some of them.* Ich habe nur ein
paar verkauft.
♦ **Some people say that ...** Manche Leute
sagen, dass ...
♦ **some day** eines Tages
♦ **some day next week** irgendwann
nächste Woche
[2] einige (*some but not all*) ◊ *Are these
mushrooms poisonous? – Only some.*
Sind diese Pilze giftig? – Nur einige.
♦ **I only took some of it.** Ich habe nur
etwas davon genommen.
♦ **I'm going to buy some stamps. Do you
want some too?** Ich kaufe Briefmarken.
Willst du auch welche?
♦ **Would you like some coffee? – No
thanks, I've got some.** Möchten Sie
Kaffee? – Nein danke, ich habe schon
welchen.
*some is frequently not translated.*
◊ *Would you like some bread?* Möchtest
du Brot? ◊ *Have you got some mineral
water?* Haben Sie Mineralwasser?
**somebody** PRONOUN
jemand ◊ *Somebody stole my bag.*
Jemand hat meine Tasche gestohlen.
**somehow** ADVERB
irgendwie ◊ *I'll do it somehow.* Ich
mache es irgendwie. ◊ *Somehow I don't
think he believed me.* Irgendwie hat er
mir anscheinend nicht geglaubt.
**someone** PRONOUN
jemand ◊ *Someone stole my bag.*
Jemand hat meine Tasche gestohlen.
**something** PRONOUN
etwas ◊ *something special* etwas
Besonderes ◊ *Wear something warm.*
Zieh etwas Warmes an.
♦ **That's really something!** Das ist echt
toll!
♦ **It cost a hundred pounds, or something
like that.** Es kostet hundert Pfund, oder
so in der Gegend.

**S**

☞

◆ **His name is Phil or something.** Er heißt Phil oder so ähnlich.

**sometime** ADVERB

mal ◊ *You must come and see us sometime.* Du musst uns mal besuchen.

◆ **sometime last month** irgendwann letzten Monat

**sometimes** ADVERB

manchmal ◊ *Sometimes I think she hates me.* Manchmal denke ich, sie hasst mich.

**somewhere** ADVERB

irgendwo ◊ *I've left my keys somewhere.* Ich habe irgendwo meine Schlüssel liegen lassen. ◊ *I'd like to go on holiday, somewhere sunny.* Ich würde gern in Ferien fahren, irgendwo in die Sonne.

**son** NOUN

der Sohn (PL die Söhne)

**song** NOUN

das Lied (PL die Lieder)

**son-in-law** NOUN

der Schwiegersohn (PL die Schwiegersöhne)

**soon** ADVERB

bald ◊ *very soon* sehr bald

◆ **soon afterwards** kurz danach

◆ **as soon as possible** sobald wie möglich

**sooner** ADVERB

früher ◊ *Can't you come a bit sooner?* Kannst du nicht etwas früher kommen?

◆ **sooner or later** früher oder später

**soot** NOUN

der Ruß

**soppy** ADJECTIVE

sentimental

**soprano** NOUN

der Sopran (PL die Soprane)

**sorcerer** NOUN

der böse Zauberer (PL die bösen Zauberer)

**sore** ADJECTIVE

see also **sore** NOUN

◆ **It's sore.** Es tut weh.

◆ **That's a sore point.** Das ist ein wunder Punkt.

**sore** NOUN

see also **sore** ADJECTIVE

die Wunde

**sorry** ADJECTIVE

◆ **I'm really sorry.** Es tut mir wirklich Leid. ◊ *I'm sorry, I haven't got any change.* Es tut mir Leid, aber ich habe kein Kleingeld. ◊ *I'm sorry I'm late.* Es tut mir Leid, dass ich zu spät komme. ◊ *I'm sorry about the noise.* Es tut mir Leid wegen des Lärms. ◊ *You'll be sorry!* Das wird dir Leid tun!

◆ **Sorry!** Entschuldigung!

◆ **Sorry?** Wie bitte?

◆ **I feel sorry for her.** Sie tut mir Leid.

**sort** NOUN

die Art ◊ *There are different sorts of mushrooms.* Es gibt verschiedene Arten von Pilzen.

◆ **what sort of ... (1)** was für ein ... ◊ *What sort of cake is that?* Was für ein Kuchen ist das? ◊ *What sort of bike have you got?* Was für ein Fahrrad hast du?

◆ **what sort of ... (2)** was für eine ... ◊ *What sort of school do you go to?* In was für eine Schule gehst du?

to **sort out** VERB

1 (*objects*)

sortieren (PERFECT hat sortiert)

2 (*problems*)

lösen

**so-so** ADVERB

so lala (*informal*) ◊ *How are you feeling? – So-so.* Wie geht's dir? – So lala.

**soul** NOUN

1 die Seele (*spirit*)

2 der Soul (*music*)

**sound** NOUN

see also **sound** VERB, ADJECTIVE

1 (*noise*)

das Geräusch (PL die Geräusche)

◆ **Don't make a sound!** Still!

◆ **I hear the sound of footsteps.** Ich höre Schritte.

2 die Lautstärke ◊ *Can I turn the sound down?* Kann ich die Lautstärke runterdrehen?

to **sound** VERB

see also **sound** NOUN, ADJECTIVE

klingen (IMPERFECT klang, PERFECT hat geklungen) ◊ *That sounds interesting.* Das klingt interessant.

◆ **It sounds as if she's doing well at school.** Allem Anschein nach ist sie gut in der Schule.

◆ **That sounds like a good idea.** Das scheint eine gute Idee zu sein.

**sound** ADJECTIVE, ADVERB

see also **sound** NOUN, VERB

gut ◊ *That's sound advice.* Das ist ein guter Rat.

◆ **to be sound asleep** fest schlafen

**soundtrack** NOUN

der Soundtrack (PL die Soundtracks)

**soup** NOUN

die Suppe ◊ *vegetable soup* die Gemüsesuppe

**sour** ADJECTIVE

sauer

**south** ADJECTIVE, ADVERB

see also **south** NOUN

◆ **the south coast** die Südküste

◆ **a south wind** ein Südwind MASC

nach Süden ◊ *We were travelling south.* Wir sind nach Süden gefahren.

◆ **south of** südlich von ◊ *It's south of London.* Es liegt südlich von London.

**south** NOUN

see also **south** ADJECTIVE

der Süden ◊ *in the south* im Süden
◆ **in the South of Germany** in Süddeutschland

**South Africa** NOUN
Südafrika NEUT
◆ **from South Africa** aus Südafrika
◆ **to South Africa** nach Südafrika

**South America** NOUN
Südamerika NEUT
◆ **from South America** aus Südamerika
◆ **to South America** nach Südamerika

**South American** NOUN
| see also **South American** ADJECTIVE |
der Südamerikaner (PL die Südamerikaner)
die Südamerikanerin

**South American** ADJECTIVE
| see also **South American** NOUN |
südamerikanisch

**southbound** ADJECTIVE
in Richtung Süden ◊ *Southbound traffic is moving very slowly.* Der Verkehr in Richtung Süden kommt nur sehr langsam voran.

**southeast** NOUN
der Südosten
◆ **southeast England** Südostengland NEUT

**southern** ADJECTIVE
südlich ◊ *the southern part of the island* der südliche Teil der Insel
◆ **Southern England** Südengland NEUT

**South Pole** NOUN
der Südpol

**South Wales** NOUN
Südwales NEUT
◆ **to South Wales** nach Südwales

**southwest** NOUN
der Südwesten
◆ **southwest Germany** Südwestdeutschland NEUT

**souvenir** NOUN
das Souvenir (PL die Souvenirs) ◊ *a souvenir shop* ein Souvenirgeschäft

**soya** NOUN
die Soja

**soy sauce** NOUN
die Sojasoße

**space** NOUN
[1] der Platz (GEN des Platzes) ◊ *There isn't enough space.* Es ist nicht genug Platz da.
◆ **a parking space** ein Parkplatz
[2] (*outer space*)
der Raum

**spacecraft** NOUN
das Raumschiff (PL die Raumschiffe)

**spade** NOUN
der Spaten (PL die Spaten)
◆ **spades** (*in cards*) das Pik ◊ *the ace of spades* das Pikass

**Spain** NOUN
Spanien NEUT

◆ **from Spain** aus Spanien
◆ **in Spain** in Spanien
◆ **to Spain** nach Spanien

**Spaniard** NOUN
der Spanier (PL die Spanier)
die Spanierin

**spaniel** NOUN
der Spaniel (PL die Spaniel)

**Spanish** ADJECTIVE
| see also **Spanish** NOUN |
spanisch
◆ **He's Spanish.** Er ist Spanier.
◆ **She's Spanish.** Sie ist Spanierin.

**Spanish** NOUN
| see also **Spanish** ADJECTIVE |
das Spanisch (*language*) (GEN des Spanischen)
◆ **the Spanish** die Spanier MASC PL

to **spank** VERB
◆ **to spank somebody** jemandem den Hintern versohlen

**spanner** NOUN
der Schraubenschlüssel (PL die Schraubenschlüssel)

to **spare** VERB
| see also **spare** ADJECTIVE, NOUN |
◆ **Can you spare a moment?** Hast du mal einen Moment Zeit?
◆ **I can't spare the time.** Ich habe die Zeit nicht.
◆ **There's no room to spare.** Es ist kein Platz übrig.
◆ **We arrived with time to spare.** Wir waren zu früh da.

*Be careful not to translate* **to spare** *by* **sparen**.

**spare** NOUN
| see also **spare** ADJECTIVE, VERB |
das Ersatzteil (PL die Ersatzteile)
◆ **I've lost my key. – Have you got a spare?** Ich habe meinen Schlüssel verloren. – Hast du einen Ersatzschlüssel?

**spare** ADJECTIVE
| see also **spare** VERB, NOUN |
◆ **spare batteries** die Ersatzbatterien FEM PL
◆ **a spare part** ein Ersatzteil NEUT
◆ **a spare room** ein Gästezimmer NEUT
◆ **spare time** die Freizeit ◊ *What do you do in your spare time?* Was machen Sie in Ihrer Freizeit?
◆ **spare wheel** das Reserverad

**sparkling** ADJECTIVE
mit Kohlensäure (*water*)
◆ **sparkling wine** der Sekt

**sparrow** NOUN
der Spatz (GEN des Spatzen, PL die Spatzen)

**spat** VERB *see* **spit**

to **speak** VERB
sprechen (PRESENT spricht, IMPERFECT sprach, PERFECT hat gesprochen) ◊ *Do you speak English?* Sprechen Sie Englisch?

S

◆ **to speak to somebody** mit jemandem reden ◇ *Have you spoken to him?* Hast du mit ihm geredet? ◇ *She spoke to him about it.* Sie hat mit ihm darüber geredet.

◆ **spoken German** gesprochenes Deutsch

to **speak up** VERB
lauter sprechen (PRESENT spricht, IMPERFECT sprach, PERFECT hat gesprochen) ◇ *You'll need to speak up, we can't hear you.* Sie müssen etwas lauter sprechen, wir können Sie nicht hören.

**speaker** NOUN
[1] (*loudspeaker*)
der Lautsprecher (PL die Lautsprecher)
[2] (*in debate*)
der Redner (PL die Redner)
die Rednerin

**special** ADJECTIVE
besondere ◇ *a special occasion* ein besonderer Anlass

**specialist** NOUN
der Fachmann (PL die Fachleute)
die Fachfrau

**speciality** NOUN
die Spezialität

to **specialize** VERB
sich spezialisieren (PERFECT hat sich spezialisiert) ◇ *We specialize in skiing equipment.* Wir haben uns auf Skiausrüstung spezialisiert.

**specially** ADVERB
[1] besonders ◇ *It can be very cold here, specially in winter.* Es kann hier sehr kalt werden, besonders im Winter.
[2] speziell ◇ *It's specially designed for teenagers.* Das ist speziell für Teenager gedacht.

◆ **not specially** nicht besonders ◇ *Do you like opera? – Not specially.* Magst du Opern? – Nicht besonders.

**species** SING NOUN
die Art

**specific** ADJECTIVE
[1] speziell (*particular*) ◇ *certain specific issues* gewisse spezielle Fragen
[2] genau (*precise*) ◇ *Could you be more specific?* Könnten Sie sich etwas genauer ausdrücken?

**specifically** ADVERB
[1] extra ◇ *It's specifically designed for teenagers.* Es ist extra für Teenager gedacht.
[2] genau ◇ *in Britain, or more specifically in England* in Großbritannien, oder genauer gesagt in England ◇ *I specifically said that ...* Ich habe ganz genau gesagt, dass ...

**specs** PL NOUN
die Brille SING ◇ *a pair of specs* eine Brille

**spectacles** PL NOUN
die Brille SING ◇ *a pair of spectacles* eine Brille

**spectacular** ADJECTIVE

spektakulär

**spectator** NOUN
der Zuschauer (PL die Zuschauer)
die Zuschauerin

**speech** NOUN
die Rede ◇ *to make a speech* eine Rede halten

**speechless** ADJECTIVE
sprachlos ◇ *speechless with admiration* sprachlos vor Bewunderung ◇ *I was speechless.* Ich war sprachlos.

**speed** NOUN
[1] der Gang (PL die Gänge)
◆ **a three-speed bike** ein Dreigangrad NEUT
[2] die Geschwindigkeit ◇ *at top speed* mit Höchstgeschwindigkeit
◆ **to speed up** schneller werden

**speedboat** NOUN
das Schnellboot (PL die Schnellboote)

**speeding** NOUN
das zu schnelle Fahren ◇ *He was fined for speeding.* Er hat wegen zu schnellen Fahrens einen Strafzettel bekommen.

**speed limit** NOUN
die Geschwindigkeitsbegrenzung ◇ *to break the speed limit* die Geschwindigkeitsbegrenzung überschreiten

**speedometer** NOUN
der Tachometer (PL die Tachometer)

to **spell** VERB
see also **spell** NOUN
[1] (*in writing*)
schreiben (IMPERFECT schrieb, PERFECT hat geschrieben) ◇ *How do you spell that?* Wie schreibt man das?
[2] (*out loud*)
buchstabieren (PERFECT hat buchstabiert) ◇ *Can you spell that please?* Können Sie das bitte buchstabieren?
◆ **I can't spell.** Ich kann keine Rechtschreibung.

**spell** NOUN
see also **spell** VERB
◆ **to cast a spell on somebody** jemanden verhexen
◆ **to be under somebody's spell** von jemandem wie verzaubert sein

**spelling** NOUN
die Rechtschreibung ◇ *My spelling is terrible.* Meine Rechtschreibung ist furchtbar.
◆ **a spelling mistake** ein Rechtschreibfehler MASC

**spelt** VERB *see* **spell**

to **spend** VERB
[1] (*money*)
ausgeben (PRESENT gibt aus, IMPERFECT gab aus, PERFECT hat ausgegeben)
[2] (*time*)
verbringen (IMPERFECT verbrachte, PERFECT hat verbracht) ◇ *He spent a month in*

*Italy.* Er verbrachte einen Monat in Italien.

> *Be careful not to translate* **to spend** *by* **spenden**.

**spice** NOUN
das Gewürz (GEN des Gewürzes, PL die Gewürze)

**spicy** ADJECTIVE
scharf ◊ *Indian food's much spicier than German food.* Indisches Essen ist viel schärfer als deutsches.

**spider** NOUN
die Spinne

to **spill** VERB
verschütten (*tip over*) (PERFECT hat verschüttet) ◊ *He spilled his coffee over his trousers.* Er hat den Kaffee auf seine Hose verschüttet.
♦ **to get spilt** verschüttet werden

**spinach** NOUN
der Spinat

**spin drier** NOUN
die Schleuder

**spine** NOUN
das Rückgrat (PL die Rückgrate)

**spinster** NOUN
die unverheiratete Frau

**spire** NOUN
der Kirchturm (PL die Kirchtürme)

**spirit** NOUN
[1] der Mut (*courage*)
[2] die Energie (*energy*)
♦ **to be in good spirits** gut gelaunt sein

**spirits** PL NOUN
die Spirituosen PL

**spiritual** ADJECTIVE
geistlich ◊ *the spiritual leader of Tibet* der geistliche Führer Tibets

to **spit** VERB
spucken
♦ **to spit something out** etwas ausspucken
♦ **It's spitting.** Es tröpfelt.

**spite** NOUN
> *see also* **spite** VERB

♦ **in spite of** trotz ◊ *in spite of the bad weather* trotz des schlechten Wetters
♦ **out of spite** aus Gehässigkeit

to **spite** VERB
> *see also* **spite** NOUN

ärgern ◊ *He just did it to spite me.* Er tat es nur, um mich zu ärgern.

**spiteful** ADJECTIVE
[1] gemein (*action*)
[2] gehässig (*person*)

to **splash** VERB
> *see also* **splash** NOUN

bespritzen (PERFECT hat bespritzt)
◊ *Careful! Don't splash me!* Vorsicht! Bespritz mich nicht!

**splash** NOUN
> *see also* **splash** VERB

der Platsch ◊ *I heard a splash.* Ich hörte einen Platsch.
♦ **a splash of colour** ein Farbfleck MASC

**splendid** ADJECTIVE
wunderbar

**splint** NOUN
die Schiene

**splinter** NOUN
der Splitter (PL die Splitter)

to **split** VERB
[1] zerteilen (PERFECT hat zerteilt) ◊ *He split the wood with an axe.* Er zerteilte das Holz mit einer Axt.
[2] zerbrechen (PRESENT zerbricht, IMPERFECT zerbrach, PERFECT ist zerbrochen) ◊ *The ship hit a rock and split in two.* Das Schiff lief auf einen Fels auf und zerbrach in zwei Teile.
[3] (*divide up*)
teilen ◊ *They decided to split the profits.* Sie haben beschlossen, den Gewinn zu teilen.
♦ **to split up (1)** (*couple*) sich trennen
♦ **to split up (2)** (*group*) sich auflösen

to **spoil** VERB
[1] verderben (PRESENT verdirbt, IMPERFECT verdarb, PERFECT hat verdorben) ◊ *It spoiled our evening.* Es hat uns den Abend verdorben.
[2] (*child*)
verwöhnen (PERFECT hat verwöhnt)

**spoiled** ADJECTIVE
verwöhnt ◊ *a spoiled child* ein verwöhntes Kind

**spoilsport** NOUN
der Spielverderber (PL die Spielverderber)
die Spielverderberin

**spoilt** ADJECTIVE
verwöhnt ◊ *a spoilt child* ein verwöhntes Kind

**spoilt** VERB *see* **spoil**

**spoke** VERB *see* **speak**

**spoke** NOUN
die Speiche (*of wheel*)

**spoken** VERB *see* **speak**

**spokesman** NOUN
der Sprecher (PL die Sprecher)

**spokeswoman** NOUN
die Sprecherin

**sponge** NOUN
der Schwamm (PL die Schwämme)
♦ **a sponge bag** ein Kulturbeutel MASC
♦ **a sponge cake** ein Rührkuchen MASC

**sponsor** NOUN
> *see also* **sponsor** VERB

der Sponsor (PL die Sponsoren)
die Sponsorin

to **sponsor** VERB
> *see also* **sponsor** NOUN

sponsern ◊ *The festival was sponsored by ...* Das Festival wurde gesponsert

**S**

☞

von ...

**spontaneous** ADJECTIVE
spontan

**spooky** ADJECTIVE
[1] gruselig (*eerie*) ◊ *a spooky story* eine gruselige Geschichte
[2] komisch (*strange*) ◊ *a spooky coincidence* ein komischer Zufall

**spoon** NOUN
der Löffel (PL die Löffel) ◊ *a spoon of sugar* ein Löffel Zucker

**spoonful** NOUN
♦ **a spoonful of soup** ein Löffel Suppe

**sport** NOUN
der Sport ◊ *What's your favourite sport?* Was ist dein Lieblingssport?
♦ **a sports bag** eine Sporttasche
♦ **a sports car** ein Sportwagen MASC
♦ **a sports jacket** eine Sportjacke
♦ **Go on, be a sport!** Nun komm schon, sei kein Frosch!

**sportsman** NOUN
der Sportler (PL die Sportler)

**sportswear** NOUN
die Sportkleidung

**sportswoman** NOUN
die Sportlerin

**sporty** ADJECTIVE
sportlich ◊ *I'm not very sporty.* Ich bin nicht besonders sportlich.

**spot** NOUN

see also **spot** VERB

[1] (*mark*)
der Fleck (PL die Flecke) ◊ *There's a spot of blood on your shirt.* Du hast einen Blutfleck auf dem Hemd.
[2] (*in pattern*)
der Punkt (PL die Punkte) ◊ *a red dress with white spots* ein rotes Kleid mit weißen Punkten
[3] (*pimple*)
der Pickel (PL die Pickel) ◊ *I've got a big spot on my chin.* Ich habe einen großen Pickel am Kinn.
[4] (*place*)
der Platz (GEN des Platzes, PL die Plätze) ◊ *It's a lovely spot for a picnic.* Es ist ein herrlicher Platz für ein Picknick.
♦ **on the spot (1)** (*immediately*) sofort ◊ *They gave her the job on the spot.* Sie haben ihr den Job sofort gegeben.
♦ **on the spot (2)** (*at the same place*) an Ort und Stelle ◊ *Luckily they were able to mend the car on the spot.* Zum Glück konnten sie das Auto an Ort und Stelle reparieren.

to **spot** VERB

see also **spot** NOUN

entdecken (PERFECT hat entdeckt) ◊ *I spotted a mistake.* Ich habe einen Fehler entdeckt.

**spotless** ADJECTIVE
makellos

**spotlight** NOUN
das Scheinwerferlicht

**spotty** ADJECTIVE
pickelig (*pimply*)

**spouse** NOUN
der Ehemann (PL die Ehemänner)
die Ehefrau

to **sprain** VERB

see also **sprain** NOUN

♦ **I've sprained my ankle.** Ich habe mir den Fuß verstaucht.

**sprain** NOUN

see also **sprain** VERB

die Verstauchung ◊ *It's just a sprain.* Es ist nur eine Verstauchung.

**spray** NOUN

see also **spray** VERB

das Spray (PL die Sprays) ◊ *hair spray* das Haarspray

to **spray** VERB

see also **spray** NOUN

sprühen ◊ *to spray perfume on one's hand* sich Parfüm auf die Hand sprühen ◊ *Somebody had sprayed graffiti on the wall.* Irgendjemand hatte Graffiti auf die Wand gesprüht.

**spread** NOUN

see also **spread** VERB

♦ **cheese spread** der Streichkäse
♦ **chocolate spread** der Schokoladenaufstrich

to **spread** VERB

see also **spread** NOUN

[1] streichen (IMPERFECT strich, PERFECT hat gestrichen) ◊ *to spread butter on a slice of bread* Butter auf eine Scheibe Brot streichen
[2] (*disease, news*)
sich verbreiten (PERFECT hat sich verbreitet) ◊ *The news spread rapidly.* Die Nachricht verbreitete sich schnell.
♦ **to spread out** (*people*) sich verteilen ◊ *The soldiers spread out across the field.* Die Soldaten verteilten sich über das Feld.

**spreadsheet** NOUN
die Tabellenkalkulation (*computer program*)

**spring** NOUN
[1] (*season*)
der Frühling (PL die Frühlinge) ◊ *in spring* im Frühling
[2] (*metal coil*)
die Feder
[3] (*water hole*)
die Quelle

**spring-cleaning** NOUN
der Frühjahrsputz (GEN des Frühjahrsputzes)

**springtime** NOUN

das Frühjahr (PL die Frühjahre) ◊ *in springtime* im Frühjahr
**sprinkler** NOUN
  der Rasensprenger (*for lawn*) (PL die Rasensprenger)
**sprint** NOUN
  _see also_ **sprint** VERB
  der Sprint (PL die Sprints)
  ◆ **a hundred-metre sprint** ein Einhundertmeterlauf MASC
to **sprint** VERB
  _see also_ **sprint** NOUN
  rennen (IMPERFECT rannte, PERFECT ist gerannt) ◊ *She sprinted for the bus.* Sie rannte, um den Bus zu erreichen.
**sprinter** NOUN
  der Sprinter (PL die Sprinter)
  die Sprinterin
**sprouts** PL NOUN
  ◆ **Brussels sprouts** der Rosenkohl SING
**spy** NOUN
  _see also_ **spy** VERB
  der Spion (PL die Spione)
  die Spionin
to **spy** VERB
  _see also_ **spy** NOUN
  ◆ **to spy on somebody** jemandem nachspionieren ◊ *She's spying on me.* Sie spioniert mir nach.
**spying** NOUN
  die Spionage
to **squabble** VERB
  sich kabbeln ◊ *Stop squabbling!* Hört auf, euch zu kabbeln!
**square** NOUN
  _see also_ **square** ADJECTIVE
  1 das Quadrat (PL die Quadrate) ◊ *a square and a triangle* ein Quadrat und ein Dreieck
  2 der Platz (GEN des Platzes, PL die Plätze) ◊ *the town square* der Rathausplatz
**square** ADJECTIVE
  _see also_ **square** NOUN
  ◆ **two square metres** zwei Quadratmeter
  ◆ **It's two metres square.** Es misst zwei mal zwei Meter.
**squash** NOUN
  _see also_ **squash** VERB
  das Squash (*sport*) ◊ *I play squash.* Ich spiele Squash.
  ◆ **a squash court** ein Squashcourt MASC
  ◆ **a squash racket** ein Squashschläger MASC
  ◆ **orange squash** der Orangensaft
to **squash** VERB
  _see also_ **squash** NOUN
  zerdrücken (PERFECT hat zerdrückt) ◊ *You're squashing me.* Du zerdrückst mich.
to **squeak** VERB
  1 quieksen (*mouse, child*)
  2 quietschen (*creak*)

to **squeeze** VERB
  1 pressen (*fruit, toothpaste*)
  2 drücken (*hand, arm*) ◊ *to squeeze somebody's arm* jemandem den Arm drücken
  ◆ **to squeeze into tight jeans** sich in enge Jeans quetschen
to **squint** VERB
  _see also_ **squint** NOUN
  schielen
**squint** NOUN
  _see also_ **squint** VERB
  ◆ **He has a squint.** Er schielt.
**squirrel** NOUN
  das Eichhörnchen (PL die Eichhörnchen)
to **stab** VERB
  ◆ **to stab somebody (1)** (*wound*) jemanden mit dem Messer verletzen
  ◆ **to stab somebody (2)** (*kill*) jemanden erstechen
**stable** NOUN
  _see also_ **stable** ADJECTIVE
  der Stall (PL die Ställe)
**stable** ADJECTIVE
  _see also_ **stable** NOUN
  stabil ◊ *a stable relationship* eine stabile Beziehung
**stack** NOUN
  der Stapel (PL die Stapel) ◊ *a stack of books* ein Stapel Bücher
**stadium** NOUN
  das Stadion (PL die Stadien)
**staff** NOUN
  1 die Belegschaft (*in company*)
  2 die Lehrerschaft (*in school*)
**stage** NOUN
  1 (*in plays*)
  die Bühne
  2 (*for speeches, lectures*)
  das Podium (PL die Podien)
  ◆ **at this stage (1)** an diesem Punkt ◊ *at this stage in the negotiations* an diesem Punkt der Verhandlungen
  ◆ **at this stage (2)** im Augenblick ◊ *At this stage, it's too early to comment.* Im Augenblick ist es zu früh, etwas dazu zu sagen.
  ◆ **to do something in stages** etwas in Etappen machen
to **stagger** VERB
  taumeln (PERFECT ist getaumelt)
**stain** NOUN
  _see also_ **stain** VERB
  der Fleck (PL die Flecke)
to **stain** VERB
  _see also_ **stain** NOUN
  beflecken (PERFECT hat befleckt)
**stainless steel** NOUN
  der Edelstahl
**stain remover** NOUN
  der Fleckenentferner (PL die Fleckenentferner)

**S**

**stair** NOUN
die <u>Stufe</u> (*step*)
**staircase** NOUN
die <u>Treppe</u>
**stairs** PL NOUN
die <u>Treppe</u> SING
**stale** ADJECTIVE
<u>altbacken</u> (*bread*)
**stalemate** NOUN
das <u>Patt</u> (*in chess*) (PL die Patts)
**stall** NOUN
der <u>Stand</u> (PL die Stände) ◊ *He's got a market stall.* Er hat einen Marktstand.
♦ **the stalls** (*in cinema, theatre*) das Parkett SING
**stamina** NOUN
das <u>Durchhaltevermögen</u>
**stammer** NOUN
das <u>Stottern</u>
♦ **He's got a stammer.** Er stottert.
to **stamp** VERB
⎯⎯⎯⎯⎯⎯⎯⎯⎯⎯
| *see also* **stamp** NOUN |
⎯⎯⎯⎯⎯⎯⎯⎯⎯⎯
<u>abstempeln</u> (*passport*) (PERFECT hat abgestempelt)
♦ **to stamp one's foot** mit dem Fuß aufstampfen
**stamp** NOUN
⎯⎯⎯⎯⎯⎯⎯⎯⎯⎯
| *see also* **stamp** VERB |
⎯⎯⎯⎯⎯⎯⎯⎯⎯⎯
[1] die <u>Briefmarke</u> ◊ *My hobby is stamp collecting.* Briefmarkensammeln ist mein Hobby. ◊ *a stamp album* ein Briefmarkenalbum ◊ *a stamp collection* eine Briefmarkensammlung
[2] (*rubber stamp*)
der <u>Stempel</u> (PL die Stempel)
**stamped** ADJECTIVE
♦ **a stamped addressed envelope** ein frankierter und adressierter Rückumschlag
to **stand** VERB
[1] (*be standing*)
<u>stehen</u> (IMPERFECT stand, PERFECT hat gestanden) ◊ *He was standing by the door.* Er stand an der Tür.
[2] (*stand up*)
<u>aufstehen</u> (PERFECT ist aufgestanden)
[3] (*tolerate, withstand*)
<u>aushalten</u> (PRESENT hält aus, IMPERFECT hielt aus, PERFECT hat ausgehalten) ◊ *I can't stand all this noise.* Ich halte diesen Lärm nicht aus.
♦ **to stand for (1)** (*be short for*) stehen für ◊ *"BT" stands for "British Telecom".* "BT" steht für "British Telecom".
♦ **to stand for (2)** (*tolerate*) dulden ◊ *I won't stand for it!* Ich dulde das nicht!
♦ **to stand in for somebody** jemanden vertreten
♦ **to stand out** herausragen
♦ **to stand up** (*get up*) aufstehen
♦ **to stand up for** eintreten für ◊ *Stand up for your rights!* Tretet für eure Rechte ein!

**standard** ADJECTIVE
⎯⎯⎯⎯⎯⎯⎯⎯⎯⎯
| *see also* **standard** NOUN |
⎯⎯⎯⎯⎯⎯⎯⎯⎯⎯
<u>normal</u> ◊ *the standard procedure* die normale Vorgehensweise
♦ **standard German** das Hochdeutsch
♦ **standard equipment** die Standardausrüstung
**standard** NOUN
⎯⎯⎯⎯⎯⎯⎯⎯⎯⎯
| *see also* **standard** ADJECTIVE |
⎯⎯⎯⎯⎯⎯⎯⎯⎯⎯
das <u>Niveau</u> (PL die Niveaus) ◊ *The standard is very high.* Das Niveau ist sehr hoch.
♦ **the standard of living** der Lebensstandard
♦ **She's got high standards.** Sie hat hohe Ansprüche.
**stand-by ticket** NOUN
das <u>Standby-Ticket</u> (PL die Standby-Tickets)
**standpoint** NOUN
der <u>Standpunkt</u> (PL die Standpunkte)
**stands** PL NOUN
die <u>Tribüne</u> SING (*at sports ground*)
**stank** VERB *see* **stink**
**staple** NOUN
⎯⎯⎯⎯⎯⎯⎯⎯⎯⎯
| *see also* **staple** VERB |
⎯⎯⎯⎯⎯⎯⎯⎯⎯⎯
die <u>Heftklammer</u>
to **staple** VERB
⎯⎯⎯⎯⎯⎯⎯⎯⎯⎯
| *see also* **staple** NOUN |
⎯⎯⎯⎯⎯⎯⎯⎯⎯⎯
<u>zusammenheften</u> (PERFECT hat zusammengeheftet)
**stapler** NOUN
die <u>Heftmaschine</u>
**star** NOUN
⎯⎯⎯⎯⎯⎯⎯⎯⎯⎯
| *see also* **star** VERB |
⎯⎯⎯⎯⎯⎯⎯⎯⎯⎯
[1] (*in sky*)
der <u>Stern</u> (PL die Sterne)
[2] (*celebrity*)
der <u>Star</u> (PL die Stars)
*der Star is also used for women.*
◊ *She's a TV star.* Sie ist ein Fernsehstar.
♦ **the stars** (*horoscope*) die Sterne
to **star** VERB
⎯⎯⎯⎯⎯⎯⎯⎯⎯⎯
| *see also* **star** NOUN |
⎯⎯⎯⎯⎯⎯⎯⎯⎯⎯
die <u>Hauptrolle spielen</u> ◊ *The film stars Glenda Jackson.* Glenda Jackson spielt in dem Film die Hauptrolle.
♦ **... starring Johnny Depp** ... mit Johnny Depp in der Hauptrolle
to **stare** VERB
♦ **to stare at something** etwas anstarren
**stark** ADVERB
♦ **stark naked** splitternackt
**start** NOUN
⎯⎯⎯⎯⎯⎯⎯⎯⎯⎯
| *see also* **start** VERB |
⎯⎯⎯⎯⎯⎯⎯⎯⎯⎯
[1] der <u>Anfang</u> (PL die Anfänge) ◊ *It's not much, but it's a start.* Es ist nicht viel, aber es ist immerhin ein Anfang.
♦ **Shall we make a start on the washing-up?** Sollen wir den Abwasch in Angriff nehmen?
[2] (*of race*)

der Start (PL die Starts)
to **start** VERB

see also **start** NOUN

[1] anfangen (PRESENT fängt an, IMPERFECT
fing an, PERFECT hat angefangen) ◊ *What
time does it start?* Wann fängt es an?
♦ **to start doing something** anfangen,
etwas zu tun ◊ *I started learning German
three years ago.* Ich habe vor drei Jahren
angefangen, Deutsch zu lernen.
[2] (*organization*)
gründen ◊ *He wants to start his own
business.* Er möchte ein eigenes
Geschäft gründen.
[3] (*campaign*)
ins Leben rufen (IMPERFECT rief ins Leben,
PERFECT hat ins Leben gerufen) ◊ *She
started a campaign against drugs.* Sie
hat eine Kampagne gegen Drogen ins
Leben gerufen.
[4] (*car*)
anlassen (PRESENT lässt an, IMPERFECT ließ
an, PERFECT hat angelassen) ◊ *He couldn't
start the car.* Er konnte das Auto nicht
anlassen.
♦ **The car wouldn't start.** Das Auto ist nicht
angesprungen.
♦ **to start off** (*leave*) aufbrechen ◊ *We
started off first thing in the morning.* Wir
sind frühmorgens aufgebrochen.
**starter** NOUN
die Vorspeise (*first course*)
to **starve** VERB
verhungern (*die*) (PERFECT ist verhungert)
◊ *People were literally starving.* Die
Menschen sind förmlich verhungert.
♦ **I'm starving!** Ich bin am Verhungern!
♦ **They starved us in prison.** Sie ließen uns
im Gefängnis hungern.
**state** NOUN

see also **state** VERB

[1] der Zustand (PL die Zustände)
♦ **He was in a real state.** (*upset*) Er ist fast
durchgedreht.
[2] (*government*)
der Staat
♦ **the States** (*USA*) die Staaten ◊ *in the
States* in den Staaten
to **state** VERB

see also **state** NOUN

[1] (*say*)
erklären (PERFECT hat erklärt) ◊ *He stated
his intention to resign.* Er erklärte seine
Absicht zurückzutreten.
[2] (*give*)
angeben (PRESENT gibt an, IMPERFECT gab an,
PERFECT hat angegeben) ◊ *Please state
your name and address.* Geben Sie bitte
Ihren Namen und Ihre Adresse an.
**stately home** NOUN
das Schloss (GEN des Schlosses, PL die
Schlösser)
**statement** NOUN

die Erklärung
**station** NOUN
(*railway*)
der Bahnhof (PL die Bahnhöfe)
♦ **the bus station** der Busbahnhof
♦ **a police station** eine Polizeiwache
♦ **a radio station** ein Rundfunksender MASC
**stationer's** NOUN
das Schreibwarengeschäft (PL die
Schreibwarengeschäfte)
**station wagon** NOUN US
der Kombiwagen (PL die Kombiwagen)
**statue** NOUN
die Statue
to **stay** VERB

see also **stay** NOUN

[1] (*remain*)
bleiben (IMPERFECT blieb, PERFECT ist
geblieben) ◊ *Stay here!* Bleiben Sie hier!
♦ **to stay in** (*not go out*) zu Hause bleiben
♦ **to stay up** aufbleiben ◊ *We stayed up till
midnight.* Wir sind bis um Mitternacht
aufgeblieben.
[2] (*spend the night*)
übernachten (PERFECT hat übernachtet)
◊ *to stay with friends* bei Freunden
übernachten
♦ **Where are you staying?** Wo wohnen
Sie?
♦ **to stay the night** über Nacht bleiben
♦ **We stayed in Belgium for a few days.**
Wir waren ein paar Tage in Belgien.
**stay** NOUN

see also **stay** VERB

der Aufenthalt (PL die Aufenthalte) ◊ *my
stay in Germany* mein Aufenthalt in
Deutschland
**steady** ADJECTIVE
[1] stetig ◊ *steady progress* stetiger
Fortschritt
[2] fest ◊ *a steady job* eine feste Arbeit
[3] ruhig (*voice, hand*)
[4] solide (*person*)
♦ **a steady boyfriend** ein fester Freund
♦ **a steady girlfriend** eine feste Freundin
♦ **Steady on!** Immer mit der Ruhe!
**steak** NOUN
das Steak (*beef*) (PL die Steaks) ◊ *steak
and chips* Steak mit Pommes frites
to **steal** VERB
stehlen (PRESENT stiehlt, IMPERFECT stahl,
PERFECT hat gestohlen)
**steam** NOUN
der Dampf (PL die Dämpfe) ◊ *a steam
engine* eine Dampflokomotive
**steel** NOUN
der Stahl ◊ *a steel door* eine Stahltür
**steep** ADJECTIVE
steil (*slope*)
**steeple** NOUN
der Kirchturm (PL die Kirchtürme)
**steering wheel** NOUN
das Lenkrad (PL die Lenkräder)

**S**

**step** NOUN

see also **step** VERB

**1** (*pace*)
der Schritt (PL die Schritte) ◊ *He took a step forward.* Er machte einen Schritt nach vorn.

**2** (*stair*)
die Stufe ◊ *She tripped over the step.* Sie stolperte über die Stufe.

to **step** VERB

see also **step** NOUN

◆**to step aside** zur Seite treten ◊ *She stepped aside to let him pass.* Sie trat zur Seite, um ihn vorbeizulassen.

◆**to step back** zurücktreten

**stepbrother** NOUN
der Stiefbruder (PL die Stiefbrüder)

**stepdaughter** NOUN
die Stieftochter (PL die Stieftöchter)

**stepfather** NOUN
der Stiefvater (PL die Stiefväter)

**stepladder** NOUN
die Trittleiter

**stepmother** NOUN
die Stiefmutter (PL die Stiefmütter)

**stepsister** NOUN
die Stiefschwester

**stepson** NOUN
der Stiefsohn (PL die Stiefsöhne)

**stereo** NOUN
die Stereoanlage

**sterling** ADJECTIVE
◆**five pounds sterling** fünf britische Pfund

**stew** NOUN
der Eintopf (PL die Eintöpfe)

**steward** NOUN
der Steward (PL die Stewards)

**stewardess** NOUN
die Stewardess (PL die Stewardessen)

**stick** NOUN

see also **stick** VERB

der Stock (PL die Stöcke)

to **stick** VERB

see also **stick** NOUN

kleben (*with adhesive*) ◊ *Stick the stamps on the envelope.* Kleben Sie die Briefmarke auf den Umschlag.

◆**I can't stick it any longer.** Ich halte das nicht mehr aus.

to **stick out** VERB
herausstrecken (PERFECT hat herausgestreckt) ◊ *The little girl stuck out her tongue.* Das kleine Mädchen streckte seine Zunge heraus.

**sticker** NOUN
der Aufkleber (PL die Aufkleber)

**sticky** ADJECTIVE
klebrig ◊ *to have sticky hands* klebrige Hände haben

◆**a sticky label** ein Aufkleber MASC

**stiff** ADJECTIVE, ADVERB
steif (*rigid*)

◆**to have a stiff neck** einen steifen Hals haben

◆**to feel stiff (1)** steif sein ◊ *I feel stiff after the long journey.* Ich bin nach der langen Reise ganz steif.

◆**to feel stiff (2)** Muskelkater haben ◊ *I feel stiff after playing football yesterday.* Ich habe gestern Fußball gespielt und habe jetzt Muskelkater.

◆**to be bored stiff** sich zu Tode langweilen

◆**to be frozen stiff** total durchgefroren sein

◆**to be scared stiff** furchtbare Angst haben

**still** ADVERB

see also **still** ADJECTIVE

**1** immer noch ◊ *I still haven't finished.* Ich bin immer noch nicht fertig. ◊ *Are you still in bed?* Bist du immer noch im Bett?

◆**better still** noch besser

**2** trotzdem (*even so*) ◊ *She knows I don't like it, but she still does it.* Sie weiß, dass ich das nicht mag, sie macht es aber trotzdem.

**3** immerhin (*after all*) ◊ *Still, it's the thought that counts.* Es war immerhin gut gemeint.

**still** ADJECTIVE

see also **still** ADVERB

still ◊ *Keep still!* Halt still! ◊ *Sit still!* Sitz still!

**sting** NOUN

see also **sting** VERB

der Stich (PL die Stiche) ◊ *a wasp sting* ein Wespenstich

to **sting** VERB

see also **sting** NOUN

stechen (PRESENT sticht, IMPERFECT stach, PERFECT hat gestochen) ◊ *I've been stung.* Ich bin gestochen worden.

**stingy** ADJECTIVE
geizig

to **stink** VERB

see also **stink** NOUN

stinken (IMPERFECT stank, PERFECT hat gestunken) ◊ *It stinks!* Es stinkt!

**stink** NOUN

see also **stink** VERB

der Gestank

to **stir** VERB
umrühren (PERFECT hat umgerührt)

to **stitch** VERB

see also **stitch** NOUN

nähen (*cloth*)

**stitch** NOUN

see also **stitch** VERB

der Stich (PL die Stiche) ◊ *I had five stitches.* Ich wurde mit fünf Stichen genäht.

**stock** NOUN

see also **stock** VERB

**1** (*supply*)
der Vorrat (PL die Vorräte)

**2** (*in shop*)

das <u>Lager</u> (PL die Lager) ◊ *in stock* auf Lager
♦ **out of stock** ausverkauft
3 die <u>Brühe</u> ◊ *chicken stock* die Hühnerbrühe

to **stock** VERB
| *see also* **stock** NOUN |
<u>führen</u> (*have in stock*) ◊ *Do you stock camping stoves?* Führen Sie Campingkocher?
♦ **to stock up** sich eindecken ◊ *We stocked up with food.* Wir deckten uns mit Lebensmitteln ein.

**stock cube** NOUN
der <u>Brühwürfel</u> (PL die Brühwürfel)
**stocking** NOUN
der <u>Strumpf</u> (PL die Strümpfe)
**stole, stolen** VERB *see* **steal**
**stomach** NOUN
1 der <u>Magen</u> (PL die Mägen) ◊ *on a full stomach* mit vollem Magen
2 der <u>Bauch</u> (PL die Bäuche) ◊ *to lie on one's stomach* auf dem Bauch liegen
**stomachache** NOUN
♦ **to have a stomachache** Bauchschmerzen haben

**stone** NOUN
der <u>Stein</u> (*rock*) (PL die Steine) ◊ *a stone wall* eine Steinmauer ◊ *a peach stone* ein Pfirsichstein

---
🛈 *In Germany weight is expressed in kilos. A stone is about 6.3 kg.*
---

◊ *I weigh eight stone.* Ich wiege fünfzig Kilo.

**stood** VERB *see* **stand**
**stool** NOUN
der <u>Hocker</u> (PL die Hocker)
to **stop** VERB
| *see also* **stop** NOUN |
1 <u>aufhören</u> (PERFECT hat aufgehört) ◊ *He stopped crying.* Er hörte auf zu weinen. ◊ *I think the rain's going to stop.* Ich glaube, es hört auf zu regnen. ◊ *You should stop smoking.* Du solltest aufhören zu rauchen.
♦ **to stop somebody doing something** jemanden daran hindern, etwas zu tun
♦ **Stop it!** Hör auf!
2 (*bus, train, car*)
<u>halten</u> (PRESENT hält, IMPERFECT hielt, PERFECT hat gehalten) ◊ *The bus doesn't stop here.* Der Bus hält hier nicht.
3 <u>stoppen</u> ◊ *a campaign to stop whaling* eine Kampagne, um den Walfang zu stoppen
♦ **Stop!** Halt!
**stop** NOUN
| *see also* **stop** VERB |
die <u>Haltestelle</u> ◊ *a bus stop* eine Bushaltestelle

♦ **This is my stop.** Ich muss jetzt aussteigen.
**stopwatch** NOUN
die <u>Stoppuhr</u>
**store** NOUN
| *see also* **store** VERB |
1 (*shop*)
das <u>Geschäft</u> (PL die Geschäfte) ◊ *a furniture store* ein Möbelgeschäft
2 (*stock, storeroom*)
das <u>Lager</u> (PL die Lager)
to **store** VERB
| *see also* **store** NOUN |
1 <u>lagern</u> ◊ *They store potatoes in the cellar.* Sie lagern Kartoffeln im Keller.
2 <u>speichern</u> (*information*)
**storey** NOUN
der <u>Stock</u> (PL die Stock) ◊ *the first storey* der erste Stock ◊ *on the first storey* im ersten Stock
♦ **a three-storey building** ein dreistöckiges Gebäude
**storm** NOUN
1 (*gale*)
der <u>Sturm</u> (PL die Stürme)
2 (*thunderstorm*)
das <u>Gewitter</u> (PL die Gewitter)
**stormy** ADJECTIVE
<u>stürmisch</u>
**story** NOUN
die <u>Geschichte</u>
**stove** NOUN
1 (*in kitchen*)
der <u>Herd</u> (PL die Herde)
2 (*camping stove*)
der <u>Kocher</u> (PL die Kocher)
**straight** ADJECTIVE
1 <u>gerade</u> ◊ *a straight line* eine gerade Linie
2 <u>glatt</u> ◊ *straight hair* glatte Haare
3 <u>normal</u> (*heterosexual*)
♦ **straight away** sofort
♦ **straight on** geradeaus
**straightforward** ADJECTIVE
<u>einfach</u>
**strain** NOUN
| *see also* **strain** VERB |
die <u>Anstrengung</u> (*stress*)
♦ **It was a strain.** Es war anstrengend.
to **strain** VERB
| *see also* **strain** NOUN |
<u>sich verrenken</u> (PERFECT hat sich verrenkt) ◊ *I strained my back.* Ich habe mir den Rücken verrenkt.
♦ **I strained a muscle.** Ich habe mir einen Muskel gezerrt.
**strained** ADJECTIVE
♦ **a strained muscle** eine Muskelzerrung
**stranded** ADJECTIVE
♦ **We were stranded.** Wir saßen fest.
**strange** ADJECTIVE

**S**

☞

sonderbar ◊ *That's strange!* Das ist
sonderbar!

**stranger** NOUN
der Fremde (GEN des Fremden, PL die
Fremden)
die Fremde (GEN der Fremden) ◊ *a
stranger (man)* ein Fremder
♦ **Don't talk to strangers.** Sprich nicht mit
fremden Menschen.
♦ **I'm a stranger here.** Ich bin hier fremd.

to **strangle** VERB
erwürgen (PERFECT hat erwürgt)

**strap** NOUN
[1] (*of bag, camera, shoe, suitcase*)
der Riemen (PL die Riemen)
[2] (*of bra, dress*)
der Träger (PL die Träger)
[3] (*of watch*)
das Armband (PL die Armbänder)

**straw** NOUN
das Stroh
♦ **That's the last straw!** Jetzt reicht's aber!

**strawberry** NOUN
die Erdbeere ◊ *strawberry jam* die
Erdbeermarmelade ◊ *a strawberry ice
cream* ein Erdbeereis

**stray** NOUN
♦ **a stray cat** eine streunende Katze

**stream** NOUN
der Bach (PL die Bäche)

**street** NOUN
die Straße ◊ *in the street* auf der Straße

**streetcar** NOUN US
die Straßenbahn

**streetlamp** NOUN
die Straßenlampe

**street plan** NOUN
der Stadtplan (PL die Stadtpläne)

**streetwise** ADJECTIVE
gewieft (*informal*)

**strength** NOUN
die Kraft (PL die Kräfte)

to **stress** VERB
see also **stress** NOUN
betonen (PERFECT hat betont) ◊ *I would like
to stress that ...* Ich möchte betonen,
dass ...

**stress** NOUN
see also **stress** VERB
der Stress (GEN des Stresses)

to **stretch** VERB
[1] (*person, animal*)
sich strecken ◊ *The dog woke up and
stretched.* Der Hund wachte auf und
streckte sich.
[2] (*get bigger*)
ausleiern (PERFECT ist ausgeleiert) ◊ *My
sweater stretched when I washed it.*
Mein Pullover ist in der Wäsche
ausgeleiert.
[3] (*stretch out*)

spannen ◊ *They stretched a rope
between the trees.* Sie spannten ein Seil
zwischen den Bäumen.
♦ **to stretch out one's arms** die Arme
ausbreiten

**stretcher** NOUN
die Trage

**stretchy** ADJECTIVE
elastisch

**strict** ADJECTIVE
streng

**strike** NOUN
see also **strike** VERB
der Streik (PL die Streiks)
♦ **to be on strike** streiken
♦ **to go on strike** in den Streik treten

to **strike** VERB
see also **strike** NOUN
[1] schlagen (PRESENT schlägt, IMPERFECT
schlug, PERFECT hat geschlagen) ◊ *The
clock struck three.* Die Uhr schlug drei.
◊ *She struck him across the mouth.* Sie
schlug ihm auf den Mund.
[2] (*go on strike*)
streiken
♦ **to strike a match** ein Streichholz
anzünden

**striker** NOUN
[1] (*person on strike*)
der Streikende (GEN des Streikenden, PL
die Streikenden)
die Streikende (GEN der Streikenden) ◊ *a
striker (man)* ein Streikender
[2] (*footballer*)
der Torschütze (GEN des Torschützen, PL
die Torschützen)

**striking** ADJECTIVE
[1] streikend (*on strike*) ◊ *striking miners*
die streikenden Bergarbeiter
[2] auffällig (*noticeable*) ◊ *a striking
difference* ein auffälliger Unterschied

**string** NOUN
[1] die Schnur (PL die Schnüre) ◊ *a piece
of string* eine Schnur
[2] (*of violin, guitar*)
die Saite

to **strip** VERB
see also **strip** NOUN
sich ausziehen (*get undressed*) (IMPERFECT
zog sich aus, PERFECT hat sich ausgezogen)

**strip** NOUN
see also **strip** VERB
der Streifen (PL die Streifen)
♦ **a strip cartoon** ein Comicstrip MASC

**stripe** NOUN
der Streifen (PL die Streifen)

**striped** ADJECTIVE
gestreift ◊ *a striped skirt* ein gestreifter
Rock

**stripper** NOUN
der Stripper (PL die Stripper)
die Stripperin

**stripy** ADJECTIVE
<u>gestreift</u> ◇ *a stripy shirt* ein gestreiftes Hemd

to **stroke** VERB
| *see also* **stroke** NOUN |
<u>streicheln</u>

**stroke** NOUN
| *see also* **stroke** VERB |
der <u>Schlag</u> (PL die Schläge) ◇ *to have a stroke* einen Schlag bekommen

**stroll** NOUN
♦ **to go for a stroll** einen Spaziergang machen

**stroller** NOUN US
der <u>Sportwagen</u> (*for child*) (PL die Sportwagen)

**strong** ADJECTIVE
<u>stark</u> ◇ *She's very strong.* Sie ist sehr stark. ◇ *Gerry is stronger than Robert.* Gerry ist stärker als Robert.

**strongly** ADVERB
<u>dringend</u> ◇ *We strongly recommend that ...* Wir empfehlen dringend, dass ...
♦ **He smelt strongly of tobacco.** Er roch stark nach Tabak.
♦ **strongly built** solide gebaut
♦ **I don't feel strongly about it.** Das ist mir ziemlich egal.

**struck** VERB *see* **strike**

to **struggle** VERB
| *see also* **struggle** NOUN |
<u>sich wehren</u> (*physically*) ◇ *He struggled, but he couldn't escape.* Er wehrte sich, aber er konnte sich nicht befreien.
♦ **to struggle to do something (1)** (*fight*) kämpfen, um etwas zu tun ◇ *He struggled to get custody of his daughter.* Er kämpfte, um das Sorgerecht für seine Tochter zu bekommen.
♦ **to struggle to do something (2)** (*have difficulty*) Mühe haben, etwas zu tun ◇ *She struggled to pay her phone bill.* Sie hatte Mühe, ihre Telefonrechnung zu bezahlen.

**struggle** NOUN
| *see also* **struggle** VERB |
der <u>Kampf</u> (*for independence, equality*) (PL die Kämpfe) ◇ *It was a struggle.* Es war ein Kampf.

**stub** NOUN
die <u>Kippe</u> (*of cigarette*)

**stubborn** ADJECTIVE
<u>stur</u>

to **stub out** VERB
<u>ausdrücken</u> (PERFECT hat ausgedrückt) ◇ *He stubbed out the cigarette.* Er drückte die Zigarette aus.

**stuck** VERB *see* **stick**

**stuck** ADJECTIVE
♦ **It's stuck.** Es klemmt.

♦ **to get stuck** stecken bleiben ◇ *We got stuck in a traffic jam.* Wir sind im Stau stecken geblieben.

**stuck-up** ADJECTIVE
<u>hochnäsig</u> (*informal*)

**stud** NOUN
1 (*earring*)
der <u>Ohrstecker</u> (PL die Ohrstecker)
2 (*on football boots*)
der <u>Stollen</u> (PL die Stollen)

**student** NOUN
der <u>Student</u> (GEN des Studenten, PL die Studenten)
die <u>Studentin</u>

**studio** NOUN
das <u>Studio</u> (PL die Studios) ◇ *a TV studio* ein Fernsehstudio
♦ **a studio flat** eine Einzimmerwohnung

to **study** VERB
1 (*at university*)
<u>studieren</u> (PERFECT hat studiert) ◇ *I plan to study biology.* Ich habe vor, Biologie zu studieren.
2 (*do homework*)
<u>lernen</u> ◇ *I've got to study tonight.* Ich muss heute Abend lernen.

**stuff** NOUN
1 die <u>Sachen</u> FEM PL (*things*) ◇ *There's some stuff on the table for you.* Auf dem Tisch stehen Sachen für dich.
2 das <u>Zeug</u> (*possessions*) ◇ *Have you got all your stuff?* Hast du all dein Zeug?

**stuffy** ADJECTIVE
<u>stickig</u> (*room*) ◇ *It's really stuffy in here.* Hier drin ist es wirklich stickig.

to **stumble** VERB
<u>stolpern</u> (PERFECT ist gestolpert)

**stung** VERB *see* **sting**

**stunk** VERB *see* **stink**

**stunned** ADJECTIVE
<u>sprachlos</u> (*amazed*) ◇ *I was stunned.* Ich war sprachlos.

**stunning** ADJECTIVE
<u>umwerfend</u>

**stunt** NOUN
der <u>Stunt</u> (*in film*) (PL die Stunts)

**stuntman** NOUN
der <u>Stuntman</u> (PL die Stuntmen)

**stupid** ADJECTIVE
<u>blöd</u> ◇ *a stupid joke* ein blöder Witz
♦ **Me, go jogging? Don't be stupid!** Ich und joggen? Du spinnst wohl!

to **stutter** VERB
| *see also* **stutter** NOUN |
<u>stottern</u>

**stutter** NOUN
| *see also* **stutter** VERB |
♦ **He's got a stutter.** Er stottert.

**style** NOUN
der <u>Stil</u> (PL die Stile) ◇ *That's not his style.* Das ist nicht sein Stil.

**subject** NOUN

**S**

**1** das <u>Thema</u> (PL die Themen) ◊ *The subject of my project was the Internet.* Das Thema meines Referats war das Internet.

**2** (*at school*)
das <u>Fach</u> (PL die Fächer) ◊ *What's your favourite subject?* Was ist dein Lieblingsfach?

**subjunctive** NOUN
der <u>Konjunktiv</u>

**submarine** NOUN
das <u>U-Boot</u> (PL die U-Boote)

**subscription** NOUN
das <u>Abonnement</u> (*to paper, magazine*) (PL die Abonnements)
◆ **to take out a subscription to something** etwas abonnieren

**subsequently** ADVERB
<u>später</u>

to **subsidize** VERB
<u>subventionieren</u> (PERFECT hat subventioniert)

**subsidy** NOUN
die <u>Subvention</u>

**substance** NOUN
die <u>Substanz</u>

**substitute** NOUN
| see also **substitute** VERB |
(*player*)
der <u>Ersatzspieler</u> (PL die Ersatzspieler)
die <u>Ersatzspielerin</u>

to **substitute** VERB
| see also **substitute** NOUN |
<u>ersetzen</u> (PERFECT hat ersetzt) ◊ *to substitute wine for beer* Bier durch Wein ersetzen

**subtitled** ADJECTIVE
<u>mit Untertiteln</u>

**subtitles** PL NOUN
die <u>Untertitel</u> MASC PL ◊ *an English film with German subtitles* ein englischer Film mit deutschen Untertiteln

**subtle** ADJECTIVE
<u>fein</u> ◊ *a subtle difference* ein feiner Unterschied

to **subtract** VERB
<u>abziehen</u> (IMPERFECT zog ab, PERFECT hat abgezogen) ◊ *to subtract three from five* drei von fünf abziehen

**suburb** NOUN
die <u>Vorstadt</u> (PL die Vorstädte) ◊ *a suburb of Berlin* eine Vorstadt von Berlin ◊ *They live in the suburbs.* Sie wohnen in der Vorstadt.

**suburban** ADJECTIVE
◆ **a suburban train** eine S-Bahn

**subway** NOUN
**1** die <u>Unterführung</u> (*underpass*)
**2** die <u>U-Bahn</u> (*underground*)

to **succeed** VERB
<u>Erfolg haben</u> (PRESENT hat Erfolg, IMPERFECT hatte Erfolg, PERFECT hat Erfolg gehabt)

◊ *He succeeded in his plan.* Er hatte mit seinem Plan Erfolg.
◆ **I succeeded in convincing him.** Es ist mir gelungen, ihn zu überzeugen.

**success** NOUN
der <u>Erfolg</u> (PL die Erfolge) ◊ *The play was a great success.* Das Stück war ein großer Erfolg.

**successful** ADJECTIVE
<u>erfolgreich</u> ◊ *a successful attempt* ein erfolgreicher Versuch ◊ *He's a successful businessman.* Er ist ein erfolgreicher Geschäftsmann.
◆ **to be successful in doing something** etwas mit Erfolg tun

**successfully** ADVERB
<u>mit Erfolg</u>

**successive** ADJECTIVE
◆ **on four successive occasions** viermal hintereinander

**such** ADJECTIVE, ADVERB
<u>so</u> ◊ *such nice people* so nette Leute ◊ *such a long journey* eine so lange Reise
◆ **such a lot of (1)** (*so much*) so viel ◊ *such a lot of work* so viel Arbeit
◆ **such a lot of (2)** (*so many*) so viele ◊ *such a lot of mistakes* so viele Fehler
◆ **such as** (*like*) wie zum Beispiel ◊ *hot countries, such as India* heiße Länder, wie zum Beispiel Indien
◆ **not as such** nicht eigentlich ◊ *He's not an expert as such, but ...* Er ist nicht eigentlich ein Experte, aber ...
◆ **There's no such thing.** So was gibt es nicht. ◊ *There's no such thing as the yeti.* So was wie den Yeti gibt es nicht.

**such-and-such** ADJECTIVE
der und der ◊ *such-and-such a place* der und der Ort
die und die ◊ *such-and-such a time* die und die Zeit
das und das ◊ *such-and-such a problem* das und das Problem

to **suck** VERB
<u>lutschen</u> (*sweets*) ◊ *to suck one's thumb* am Daumen lutschen

**sudden** ADJECTIVE
<u>plötzlich</u> ◊ *a sudden change* eine plötzliche Änderung
◆ **all of a sudden** plötzlich

**suddenly** ADVERB
<u>plötzlich</u> ◊ *Suddenly, the door opened.* Plötzlich ging die Tür auf.

**suede** NOUN
das <u>Wildleder</u> ◊ *a suede jacket* eine Wildlederjacke

to **suffer** VERB
<u>leiden</u> (IMPERFECT litt, PERFECT hat gelitten) ◊ *She was really suffering.* Sie hat wirklich gelitten.

♦ **to suffer from a disease** an einer Krankheit leiden ◊ *I suffer from hay fever.* Ich leide an Heuschnupfen.

to **suffocate** VERB
ersticken (PERFECT ist erstickt)

**sugar** NOUN
der Zucker (PL die Zucker) ◊ *Do you take sugar?* Nimmst du Zucker?

to **suggest** VERB
vorschlagen (PRESENT schlägt vor, IMPERFECT schlug vor, PERFECT hat vorgeschlagen) ◊ *I suggested they set off early.* Ich habe vorgeschlagen, dass sie früh aufbrechen sollen.

**suggestion** NOUN
der Vorschlag (PL die Vorschläge) ◊ *to make a suggestion* einen Vorschlag machen

**suicide** NOUN
der Selbstmord (PL die Selbstmorde) ◊ *to commit suicide* Selbstmord begehen

**suit** NOUN
see also **suit** VERB
1 (*man's*)
der Anzug (PL die Anzüge)
2 (*woman's*)
das Kostüm (PL die Kostüme)

to **suit** VERB
see also **suit** NOUN
1 (*be convenient for*)
passen ◊ *What time would suit you?* Welche Zeit würde Ihnen passen? ◊ *That suits me fine.* Das passt mir gut.
♦ **Suit yourself!** Wie du willst!
2 (*look good on*)
stehen (IMPERFECT stand, PERFECT hat gestanden) ◊ *That dress really suits you.* Das Kleid steht dir wirklich.

**suitable** ADJECTIVE
1 passend ◊ *a suitable time* eine passende Zeit
2 angemessen (*clothes*) ◊ *suitable clothing* angemessene Kleidung

**suitcase** NOUN
der Koffer (PL die Koffer)

**suite** NOUN
die Suite (*of rooms*)
♦ **a bedroom suite** eine Schlafzimmereinrichtung

to **sulk** VERB
schmollen

**sulky** ADJECTIVE
beleidigt

**sultana** NOUN
die Sultanine

**sum** NOUN
1 das Rechnen (*calculation*)
♦ **She's good at sums.** Sie kann gut rechnen.
2 die Summe (*amount*) ◊ *a sum of money* eine Geldsumme

to **sum up** VERB

zusammenfassen (PERFECT hat zusammengefasst)

to **summarize** VERB
zusammenfassen (PERFECT hat zusammengefasst)

**summary** NOUN
die Zusammenfassung

**summer** NOUN
der Sommer (PL die Sommer) ◊ *in summer* im Sommer
♦ **summer clothes** die Sommerkleidung SING
♦ **the summer holidays** die Sommerferien

**summer camp** NOUN US
das Sommerlager (PL die Sommerlager)

**summertime** NOUN
der Sommer (PL die Sommer) ◊ *in summertime* im Sommer

**summit** NOUN
der Gipfel (PL die Gipfel)

**sun** NOUN
die Sonne ◊ *in the sun* in der Sonne

to **sunbathe** VERB
sonnenbaden (PERFECT hat sonnengebadet)

**sunblock** NOUN
das Sonnenschutzmittel (PL die Sonnenschutzmittel)

**sunburn** NOUN
der Sonnenbrand (PL die Sonnenbrände)

**sunburnt** ADJECTIVE
♦ **I got sunburnt.** Ich habe einen Sonnenbrand bekommen.

**Sunday** NOUN
der Sonntag (PL die Sonntage) ◊ *every Sunday* jeden Sonntag ◊ *last Sunday* letzten Sonntag ◊ *next Sunday* nächsten Sonntag ◊ *on Sunday* am Sonntag
♦ **on Sundays** sonntags

**Sunday school** NOUN
die Sonntagsschule ◊ *to go to Sunday school* zur Sonntagsschule gehen

**sunflower** NOUN
die Sonnenblume

**sung** VERB see **sing**

**sunglasses** PL NOUN
die Sonnenbrille SING ◊ *a pair of sunglasses* eine Sonnenbrille

**sunk** VERB see **sink**

**sunlight** NOUN
das Sonnenlicht

**sunny** ADJECTIVE
sonnig ◊ *a sunny morning* ein sonniger Morgen
♦ **It's sunny.** Die Sonne scheint.

**sunrise** NOUN
der Sonnenaufgang (PL die Sonnenaufgänge)

**sunroof** NOUN
das Schiebedach (PL die Schiebedächer)

**sunscreen** NOUN
die Sonnenschutzcreme (PL die Sonnenschutzcremes)

S

**sunset** NOUN
der Sonnenuntergang (PL die
Sonnenuntergänge)
**sunshine** NOUN
der Sonnenschein
**sunstroke** NOUN
der Hitzschlag (PL die Hitzschläge) ◊ *to
get sunstroke* einen Hitzschlag
bekommen
**suntan** NOUN
♦ **to have a suntan** braun sein
♦ **suntan lotion** die Sonnenmilch
♦ **suntan oil** das Sonnenöl
**super** ADJECTIVE
klasse
*klasse is invariable.*
◊ *a super film* ein klasse Film
**superb** ADJECTIVE
großartig
**supermarket** NOUN
der Supermarkt (PL die Supermärkte)
**supernatural** ADJECTIVE
übernatürlich
**superstitious** ADJECTIVE
abergläubisch
to **supervise** VERB
beaufsichtigen (PERFECT hat beaufsichtigt)
**supervisor** NOUN
[1] (*in factory*)
der Vorarbeiter (PL die Vorarbeiter)
die Vorarbeiterin
[2] (*in department store*)
der Abteilungsleiter (PL die
Abteilungsleiter)
die Abteilungsleiterin
**supper** NOUN
das Abendessen (PL die Abendessen)
**supplement** NOUN
[1] (*of newspaper, magazine*)
die Beilage
[2] (*money*)
der Zuschlag (PL die Zuschläge)
**supplies** PL NOUN
die Vorräte MASC PL (*food*)
to **supply** VERB
see also **supply** NOUN
[1] liefern (*goods, material*) ◊ *The farm
supplied us with food.* Der Bauernhof
lieferte uns die Lebensmittel.
[2] stellen (*put at somebody's disposal*)
◊ *The centre supplied them with all the
necessary equipment.* Das Zentrum hat
ihnen die ganze notwendige Ausrüstung
gestellt.
**supply** NOUN
see also **supply** VERB
der Vorrat (PL die Vorräte) ◊ *a supply of
paper* ein Papiervorrat
♦ **the water supply** (*to town*) die
Wasserversorgung
**supply teacher** NOUN
der Aushilfslehrer (PL die Aushilfslehrer)

die Aushilfslehrerin
to **support** VERB
see also **support** NOUN
[1] unterstützen (PERFECT hat unterstützt)
◊ *My mum has always supported me.*
Meine Mutti hat mich immer unterstützt.
♦ **What team do you support?** Für welche
Mannschaft bist du?
[2] (*financially*)
sorgen für ◊ *She had to support five
children on her own.* Sie musste allein
für ihre fünf Kinder sorgen.
**support** NOUN
see also **support** VERB
die Unterstützung (*backing*)
**supporter** NOUN
[1] der Fan (PL die Fans)
*der Fan is also used for women.*
◊ *a Liverpool supporter* ein Liverpool-Fan
[2] der Anhänger (PL die Anhänger)
die Anhängerin
◊ *She's a supporter of the Labour Party.*
Sie ist Anhängerin der Labour-Party.
to **suppose** VERB
annehmen (PRESENT nimmt an, IMPERFECT
nahm an, PERFECT hat angenommen) ◊ *I
suppose he's late.* Ich nehme an, er
kommt zu spät. ◊ *Suppose you won the
lottery.* Nimm mal an, du gewinnst im
Lotto. ◊ *I suppose so.* Das nehme ich an.
♦ **to be supposed to do something** etwas
tun sollen ◊ *You're supposed to go
straight home after school.* Du solltest
nach der Schule sofort nach Hause
gehen.
♦ **You're supposed to show your passport.**
Sie müssen Ihren Pass zeigen.
**supposing** CONJUNCTION
angenommen ◊ *Supposing you won the
lottery ...* Angenommen, du gewinnst im
Lotto ...
**surcharge** NOUN
der Zuschlag (PL die Zuschläge)
**sure** ADJECTIVE
sicher ◊ *Are you sure?* Bist du sicher?
♦ **Sure!** Klar!
♦ **to make sure that ...** sich vergewissern,
dass ... ◊ *I'm going to make sure the
door's locked.* Ich werde mich
vergewissern, dass die Tür
abgeschlossen ist.
**surely** ADVERB
sicherlich ◊ *Surely you've been to
London?* Du warst doch sicherlich schon
in London? ◊ *The shops are closed on
Sundays, surely?* Die Geschäfte sind
sonntags doch sicherlich zu, oder?
**surf** NOUN
see also **surf** VERB
die Brandung
to **surf** VERB
see also **surf** NOUN

surfen (PERFECT hat gesurft)
♦ **to surf the Net** im Internet surfen
**surface** NOUN
die Oberfläche
**surfboard** NOUN
das Surfbrett (PL die Surfbretter)
**surfing** NOUN
das Surfen
♦ **to go surfing** surfen gehen
**surgeon** NOUN
der Chirurg (GEN des Chirurgen, PL die Chirurgen)
die Chirurgin
◊ She's a surgeon. Sie ist Chirurgin.
**surgery** NOUN
die Arztpraxis (doctor's surgery) (PL die Arztpraxen)
♦ **surgery hours** die Sprechstunden
**surname** NOUN
der Nachname (GEN des Nachnamens, PL die Nachnamen)
**surprise** NOUN
die Überraschung
**surprised** ADJECTIVE
überrascht ◊ I was surprised to see him. Ich war überrascht, ihn zu sehen.
**surprising** ADJECTIVE
überraschend
to **surrender** VERB
sich ergeben (PRESENT ergibt sich, IMPERFECT ergab sich, PERFECT hat sich ergeben)
**surrogate mother** NOUN
die Leihmutter (PL die Leihmütter)
to **surround** VERB
umstellen (PERFECT hat umstellt) ◊ The police surrounded the house. Die Polizei hat das Haus umstellt. ◊ You're surrounded! Sie sind umstellt!
♦ **surrounded by** umgeben von ◊ The house is surrounded by trees. Das Haus ist von Bäumen umgeben.
**surroundings** PL NOUN
die Umgebung SING ◊ a hotel in beautiful surroundings ein Hotel in wunderschöner Umgebung
**survey** NOUN
die Umfrage (research)
**surveyor** NOUN
[1] (of buildings)
der Gebäudesachverständige (GEN des Gebäudesachverständigen, PL die Gebäudesachverständigen)
die Gebäudesachverständige (GEN der Gebäudesachverständigen) ◊ a surveyor (man) ein Gebäudesachverständiger
[2] (of land)
der Landvermesser (PL die Landvermesser)
die Landvermesserin
to **survive** VERB
überleben (PERFECT hat überlebt)
**survivor** NOUN

der Überlebende (GEN des Überlebenden, PL die Überlebenden)
die Überlebende (GEN der Überlebenden)
◊ There were no survivors. Es gab keine Überlebenden.
to **suspect** VERB
see also **suspect** NOUN
verdächtigen (PERFECT hat verdächtigt)
**suspect** NOUN
see also **suspect** VERB
der Verdächtige (GEN des Verdächtigen, PL die Verdächtigen)
die Verdächtige (GEN der Verdächtigen)
◊ a suspect (man) ein Verdächtiger
to **suspend** VERB
[1] (from school)
verweisen (IMPERFECT verwies, PERFECT hat verwiesen) ◊ He was suspended. Er wurde von der Schule verwiesen.
[2] (from team)
sperren
[3] (from job)
suspendieren (PERFECT hat suspendiert)
**suspender** NOUN US
[1] (for stockings)
der Strumpfhalter (PL die Strumpfhalter)
♦ **suspenders** (braces) US
[2] die Hosenträger MASC PL
**suspense** NOUN
[1] die Ungewissheit (waiting) ◊ The suspense was terrible. Die Ungewissheit war furchtbar.
[2] die Spannung (in story)
♦ **a film with lots of suspense** ein sehr spannender Film
**suspension** NOUN
[1] (from school)
der Ausschluss (GEN des Ausschlusses, PL die Ausschlüsse)
[2] (from team)
die Sperre
[3] (from job)
die Suspendierung
**suspicious** ADJECTIVE
[1] argwöhnisch ◊ He was suspicious at first. Zuerst war er argwöhnisch.
[2] verdächtig (suspicious-looking) ◊ a suspicious person eine verdächtige Person
to **swallow** VERB
schlucken
**swam** VERB see **swim**
**swan** NOUN
der Schwan (PL die Schwäne)
to **swap** VERB
tauschen ◊ Do you want to swap? Willst du tauschen?
♦ **to swap a stamp for a coin** eine Briefmarke für eine Münze eintauschen
to **swat** VERB
totschlagen (PRESENT schlägt tot, IMPERFECT schlug tot, PERFECT hat totgeschlagen)
to **sway** VERB

**S**

☞

schwanken

to **swear** VERB

⟦1⟧ (*make an oath*)
schwören (IMPERFECT schwor, PERFECT. hat geschworen)

⟦2⟧ (*curse*)
fluchen

**swearword** NOUN
der Kraftausdruck (PL die Kraftausdrücke)

**sweat** NOUN
see also **sweat** VERB
der Schweiß (GEN des Schweißes)

to **sweat** VERB
see also **sweat** NOUN
schwitzen

**sweater** NOUN
der Pullover (PL die Pullover)

**sweaty** ADJECTIVE
⟦1⟧ verschwitzt (*person, face*) ◊ *I'm all sweaty.* Ich bin ganz verschwitzt.
⟦2⟧ feucht (*hands*)

**Swede** NOUN
(*person*)
der Schwede (GEN des Schweden, PL die Schweden)
die Schwedin

**swede** NOUN
die Steckrübe (*vegetable*)

**Sweden** NOUN
Schweden NEUT
♦**from Sweden** aus Schweden
♦**to Sweden** nach Schweden

**Swedish** ADJECTIVE
see also **Swedish** NOUN
schwedisch
♦**He's Swedish.** Er ist Schwede.
♦**She's Swedish.** Sie ist Schwedin.

**Swedish** NOUN
see also **Swedish** ADJECTIVE
das Schwedisch (*language*) (GEN des Schwedischen)

to **sweep** VERB
fegen ◊ *to sweep the floor* den Boden fegen

**sweet** NOUN
see also **sweet** ADJECTIVE
⟦1⟧ (*candy*)
das Bonbon (PL die Bonbons) ◊ *a bag of sweets* eine Tüte Bonbons
⟦2⟧ (*pudding*)
der Nachtisch ◊ *What sweet did you have?* Was für einen Nachtisch hattest du?

**sweet** ADJECTIVE
see also **sweet** NOUN
⟦1⟧ süß ◊ *Isn't she sweet?* Ist sie nicht süß?
⟦2⟧ nett (*kind*) ◊ *That was really sweet of you.* Das war wirklich nett von dir.
♦**sweet and sour pork** Schweinefleisch süß-sauer

**sweetcorn** NOUN
der Mais

**sweltering** ADJECTIVE
♦**It was sweltering.** Es war eine Bruthitze.

**swept** VERB *see* **sweep**

to **swerve** VERB
ausscheren (PERFECT ist ausgeschert) ◊ *He swerved to avoid the cyclist.* Er scherte aus, um dem Fahrradfahrer auszuweichen.

**swim** NOUN
see also **swim** VERB
♦**to go for a swim** schwimmen gehen

to **swim** VERB
see also **swim** NOUN
schwimmen (IMPERFECT schwamm, PERFECT ist geschwommen) ◊ *Can you swim?* Kannst du schwimmen? ◊ *She swam across the river.* Sie schwamm über den Fluss.

**swimmer** NOUN
der Schwimmer (PL die Schwimmer)
die Schwimmerin
◊ *She's a good swimmer.* Sie ist eine gute Schwimmerin.

**swimming** NOUN
das Schwimmen
♦**to go swimming** schwimmen gehen
♦**Do you like swimming?** Schwimmst du gern?
♦**a swimming cap** eine Bademütze
♦**a swimming costume** ein Badeanzug MASC
♦**a swimming pool** ein Schwimmbad NEUT
♦**swimming trunks** die Badehose SING ◊ *a pair of swimming trunks* eine Badehose

**swimsuit** NOUN
der Badeanzug (PL die Badeanzüge)

**swing** NOUN
see also **swing** VERB
die Schaukel (*in playground, garden*)

to **swing** VERB
see also **swing** NOUN
schaukeln

**Swiss** ADJECTIVE
see also **Swiss** NOUN
Schweizer ◊ *I like Swiss cheese.* Ich mag Schweizer Käse.
♦**Andreas is Swiss.** Andreas ist Schweizer.
♦**Claudie is Swiss.** Claudie ist Schweizerin.

**Swiss** NOUN
see also **Swiss** ADJECTIVE
(*person*)
der Schweizer (PL die Schweizer)
die Schweizerin
♦**the Swiss** die Schweizer

**switch** NOUN
see also **switch** VERB
der Schalter (*for light, radio etc*) (PL die Schalter)

to **switch** VERB

see also **switch** NOUN
tauschen ◇ *to switch A for B* A gegen B
tauschen
to **switch off** VERB
ausschalten (PERFECT hat ausgeschaltet)
to **switch on** VERB
anschalten (PERFECT hat angeschaltet)
**Switzerland** NOUN
die Schweiz (GEN der Schweiz)

*Note that the definite article is used in
German for countries which are
feminine.*

♦**from Switzerland** aus der Schweiz
♦**in Switzerland** in der Schweiz
♦**to Switzerland** in die Schweiz
**swollen** ADJECTIVE
geschwollen (*arm, leg*)
to **swop** VERB
tauschen ◇ *Do you want to swop?* Willst
du tauschen?
♦**to swop a stamp for a coin** eine
Briefmarke für eine Münze eintauschen
**sword** NOUN
das Schwert (PL die Schwerter)
**swore** VERB *see* **swear**
**sworn** VERB *see* **swear**
to **swot** VERB
see also **swot** NOUN
pauken (*informal*) ◇ *I'll have to swot for*

*the maths exam.* Ich muss für die
Matheprüfung pauken.
**swot** NOUN
see also **swot** VERB
der Streber (PL die Streber) (*informal*)
die Streberin
**swum** VERB *see* **swim**
**swung** VERB *see* **swing**
**syllabus** NOUN
der Lehrplan (PL die Lehrpläne) ◇ *on the
syllabus* auf dem Lehrplan
**symbol** NOUN
das Symbol (PL die Symbole)
**sympathetic** ADJECTIVE
verständnisvoll

*Be careful not to translate **sympathetic**
by **sympathisch**.*

to **sympathize** VERB
♦**to sympathize with somebody** (*pity*)
Mitgefühl mit jemandem haben
**sympathy** NOUN
das Mitleid
**symptom** NOUN
das Symptom
**syringe** NOUN
die Spritze
**system** NOUN
das System (PL die Systeme)

**S**

# T

**table** NOUN
der Tisch (PL die Tische) ◊ *to lay the table*
den Tisch decken
**tablecloth** NOUN
die Tischdecke
**tablespoon** NOUN
der Esslöffel (PL die Esslöffel) ◊ *a
tablespoon of sugar* ein Esslöffel
Zucker
**tablespoonful** NOUN
♦ **a tablespoonful of sugar** ein Esslöffel
Zucker
**tablet** NOUN
die Tablette
**table tennis** NOUN
das Tischtennis (GEN des Tischtennis)
◊ *to play table tennis* Tischtennis
spielen
**tabloid** NOUN
das Boulevardblatt (PL die
Boulevardblätter)
**tackle** NOUN
  see also **tackle** VERB
der Angriff (*in sport*) (PL die Angriffe)
♦ **fishing tackle** das Angelzeug
to **tackle** VERB
  see also **tackle** NOUN
angreifen (*in sport*) (IMPERFECT griff an,
PERFECT hat angegriffen)
♦ **to tackle a problem** ein Problem
angehen
**tact** NOUN
der Takt
**tactful** ADJECTIVE
taktvoll
**tactics** PL NOUN
die Taktik SING
**tactless** ADJECTIVE
taktlos
**tadpole** NOUN
die Kaulquappe
**tag** NOUN
das Etikett (*label*) (PL die Etiketts)
**tail** NOUN
der Schwanz (GEN des Schwanzes, PL die
Schwänze)
♦ **Heads or tails?** Kopf oder Zahl?
**tailor** NOUN
der Schneider (PL die Schneider)
die Schneiderin
◊ *He's a tailor.* Er ist Schneider.
to **take** VERB
  [1] nehmen (PRESENT nimmt, IMPERFECT
nahm, PERFECT hat genommen) ◊ *He
took a plate from the cupboard.* Er
nahm einen Teller aus dem Schrank.
◊ *We took a taxi.* Wir haben ein Taxi
genommen.

  [2] (*take along*)
mitnehmen (PRESENT nimmt mit, IMPERFECT
nahm mit, PERFECT hat mitgenommen)
◊ *Are you taking your new camera?*
Nimmst du deinen neuen Fotoapparat
mit? ◊ *Don't take anything valuable with
you.* Nehmen Sie nichts Wertvolles mit.
◊ *He goes to London every week, but he
never takes me.* Er fährt jede Woche
nach London, aber er nimmt mich nie
mit. ◊ *Do you take your exercise books
home?* Nehmt ihr eure Hefte mit nach
Hause?
  [3] (*to a certain place*)
bringen (IMPERFECT brachte, PERFECT hat
gebracht) ◊ *She always takes her son to
school.* Sie bringt ihren Sohn immer zur
Schule. ◊ *I'm going to take my coat to
the cleaner's.* Ich bringe meinen Mantel
in die Reinigung.
  [4] (*require*)
brauchen ◊ *She always takes hours to
get ready.* Sie braucht immer Stunden,
bis sie fertig ist. ◊ *It takes five people to
do this job.* Für diese Arbeit braucht man
fünf Leute. ◊ *That takes a lot of courage.*
Dazu braucht man viel Mut.
♦ **It takes a lot of money to do that.** Das
kostet viel Geld.
  [5] (*last*)
dauern ◊ *The journey took three hours.*
Die Fahrt dauerte drei Stunden. ◊ *It won't
take long.* Das dauert nicht lange.
  [6] (*tolerate*)
ertragen (PRESENT erträgt, IMPERFECT ertrug,
PERFECT hat ertragen) ◊ *He can't take being
criticized.* Er kann es nicht ertragen,
kritisiert zu werden.
  [7] (*exam, test, subject*)
machen ◊ *Have you taken your driving
test yet?* Hast du deine Fahrprüfung
schon gemacht? ◊ *I decided to take
German instead of French.* Ich habe
beschlossen, Deutsch statt Französisch
zu machen.

to **take after** VERB
nachschlagen (PRESENT schlägt nach,
IMPERFECT schlug nach, PERFECT hat
nachgeschlagen) ◊ *She takes after her
mother.* Sie schlägt ihrer Mutter nach.

to **take apart** VERB
♦ **to take something apart** etwas
auseinander nehmen

to **take away** VERB
  [1] (*object*)
wegnehmen (PRESENT nimmt weg, IMPERFECT
nahm weg, PERFECT hat weggenommen)
  [2] (*person*)

wegbringen (IMPERFECT brachte weg, PERFECT hat weggebracht)
♦ **hot meals to take away** warme Mahlzeiten zum Mitnehmen

to **take back** VERB
zurückbringen (IMPERFECT brachte zurück, PERFECT hat zurückgebracht) ◊ *I took it back to the shop.* Ich habe es in den Laden zurückgebracht.
♦ **I take it all back!** Ich nehme alles zurück!

to **take down** VERB
herunternehmen (PRESENT nimmt herunter, IMPERFECT nahm herunter, PERFECT hat heruntergenommen) ◊ *She took down the painting.* Sie nahm das Gemälde herunter.

to **take in** VERB
verstehen (*understand*) (IMPERFECT verstand, PERFECT hat verstanden) ◊ *I didn't really take it in.* Ich habe das nicht richtig verstanden.

to **take off** VERB
[1] (*plane*)
abfliegen (IMPERFECT flog ab, PERFECT ist abgeflogen) ◊ *The plane took off twenty minutes late.* Das Flugzeug ist mit zwanzig Minuten Verspätung abgeflogen.
[2] (*clothes*)
ausziehen (IMPERFECT zog aus, PERFECT hat ausgezogen) ◊ *Take your coat off.* Zieh den Mantel aus.

to **take out** VERB
herausnehmen (*from container, pocket*) (PRESENT nimmt heraus, IMPERFECT nahm heraus, PERFECT hat herausgenommen)
♦ **He took her out to the theatre.** Er führte sie ins Theater aus.

to **take over** VERB
übernehmen (PRESENT übernimmt, IMPERFECT übernahm, PERFECT hat übernommen) ◊ *I'll take over now.* Ich übernehme jetzt.
♦ **to take over from somebody** jemanden ablösen ◊ *Mr Jones has taken over from Mr Smith as headteacher.* Herr Jones hat Herrn Smith als Direktor abgelöst.

**takeaway** NOUN
[1] (*meal*)
das Essen zum Mitnehmen (PL die Essen zum Mitnehmen)
[2] (*shop*)
die Imbissstube ◊ *a Chinese takeaway* eine chinesische Imbissstube

**takeoff** NOUN
der Abflug (*of plane*) (PL die Abflüge)

**talcum powder** NOUN
der Puder (PL die Puder)

**tale** NOUN
die Geschichte (*story*)

**talent** NOUN

das Talent (PL die Talente) ◊ *She's got lots of talent.* Sie hat sehr viel Talent.
♦ **to have a talent for something** eine Begabung für etwas haben
♦ **He's got a real talent for languages.** Er ist wirklich sprachbegabt.

**talented** ADJECTIVE
begabt

**talk** NOUN
see also **talk** VERB
[1] (*speech*)
der Vortrag (PL die Vorträge) ◊ *She gave a talk on rock climbing.* Sie hielt einen Vortrag über das Klettern.
[2] (*conversation*)
das Gespräch (PL die Gespräche) ◊ *We had a long talk about her problems.* Wir hatten ein langes Gespräch über ihre Probleme.
♦ **I had a talk with my Mum about it.** Ich habe mit meiner Mutti darüber gesprochen.
[3] (*gossip*)
das Gerede ◊ *It's just talk.* Das ist nur Gerede.

to **talk** VERB
see also **talk** NOUN
reden ◊ *We talked about the weather.* Wir haben über das Wetter geredet.
♦ **to talk something over with somebody** etwas mit jemandem besprechen

**talkative** ADJECTIVE
redselig

**tall** ADJECTIVE
[1] groß (*person, tree*) ◊ *They've cut down the tallest tree in the park.* Sie haben den größten Baum im Park gefällt. ◊ *He's two metres tall.* Er ist zwei Meter groß.
[2] hoch (*building*)
*Before a noun or after an article, use* **hohe.**
◊ *a very tall building* ein sehr hohes Gebäude

**tame** ADJECTIVE
zahm (*animal*)

**tampon** NOUN
der Tampon (PL die Tampons)

**tan** NOUN
♦ **She's got an amazing tan.** Sie ist erstaunlich braun.

**tangerine** NOUN
die Mandarine

**tank** NOUN
[1] (*for water, petrol*)
der Tank (PL die Tanks)
[2] (*military*)
der Panzer (PL die Panzer)
♦ **a fish tank** ein Aquarium NEUT

**tanker** NOUN
[1] (*ship*)
der Tanker (PL die Tanker) ◊ *an oil tanker* ein Öltanker
[2] (*truck*)

**T**

☞

der <u>Tankwagen</u> (PL die Tankwagen) ◊ *a petrol tanker* ein Benzintankwagen

**tap** NOUN
[1] (*water tap*)
der <u>Wasserhahn</u> (PL die Wasserhähne)
[2] (*gentle blow*)
der <u>Klaps</u> (PL die Klapse)

**tap-dancing** NOUN
das <u>Stepptanzen</u>
◆ **I do tap-dancing.** Ich mache Stepptanz.

to **tape** VERB
see also **tape** NOUN
<u>aufnehmen</u> (*record*) (PRESENT nimmt auf, IMPERFECT nahm auf, PERFECT hat aufgenommen) ◊ *Did you tape that film last night?* Hast du den Film gestern Abend aufgenommen?

**tape** NOUN
see also **tape** VERB
[1] die <u>Kassette</u> ◊ *a tape of Sinead O'Connor* eine Kassette von Sinead O'Connor
[2] (*sticky tape*)
der <u>Klebstreifen</u> (PL die Klebstreifen)

**tape deck** NOUN
das <u>Kassettendeck</u> (PL die Kassettendecks)

**tape measure** NOUN
das <u>Maßband</u> (PL die Maßbänder)

**tape recorder** NOUN
der <u>Kassettenrekorder</u> (PL die Kassettenrekorder)

**target** NOUN
das <u>Ziel</u> (PL die Ziele)

**tarmac** NOUN
der <u>Asphalt</u> (*on road*)

**tart** NOUN
der <u>Kuchen</u> (PL die Kuchen) ◊ *an apple tart* ein Apfelkuchen

**tartan** ADJECTIVE
im <u>Schottenkaro</u> ◊ *a tartan scarf* ein Schal im Schottenkaro

**task** NOUN
die <u>Aufgabe</u>

**taste** NOUN
see also **taste** VERB
der <u>Geschmack</u> (PL die Geschmäcke) ◊ *It's got a really strange taste.* Es hat einen sehr eigenartigen Geschmack. ◊ *She has good taste.* Sie hat einen guten Geschmack.
◆ **a joke in bad taste** ein geschmackloser Witz
◆ **Would you like a taste?** Möchtest du mal probieren?

to **taste** VERB
see also **taste** NOUN
[1] <u>probieren</u> (PERFECT hat probiert)
◊ *Would you like to taste it?* Möchtest du mal probieren?

[2] <u>schmecken</u> ◊ *You can taste the garlic in it.* Man kann den Knoblauch schmecken.
◆ **to taste of something** nach etwas schmecken ◊ *It tastes of fish.* Es schmeckt nach Fisch.

**tasteful** ADJECTIVE
<u>geschmackvoll</u>

**tasteless** ADJECTIVE
[1] <u>fade</u> (*food*)
[2] <u>geschmacklos</u> (*in bad taste*) ◊ *a tasteless picture* ein geschmackloses Bild ◊ *a tasteless remark* eine geschmacklose Bemerkung

**tasty** ADJECTIVE
<u>schmackhaft</u>

**tattoo** NOUN
die <u>Tätowierung</u>

**taught** VERB see **teach**

**Taurus** NOUN
der <u>Stier</u> ◊ *I'm Taurus.* Ich bin Stier.

**tax** NOUN
die <u>Steuer</u> (*on goods, income*)

**taxi** NOUN
das <u>Taxi</u> (PL die Taxis) ◊ *a taxi driver* ein Taxifahrer

**taxi rank** NOUN
der <u>Taxistand</u> (PL die Taxistände)

**TB** NOUN (= *tuberculosis*)
die <u>TB</u> (= Tuberkulose)

**tea** NOUN
[1] der <u>Tee</u> (PL die Tees) ◊ *a cup of tea* eine Tasse Tee

> *ⓘ Usually, tea is not drunk with milk and sugar in Germany, but is served with lemon, and is referred to as **Schwarztee**. Fruit teas and herbal teas are also very widespread.*

◆ **a tea bag** ein Teebeutel MASC
[2] (*evening meal*)
das <u>Abendessen</u> (PL die Abendessen) ◊ *We were having tea.* Wir saßen beim Abendessen.

to **teach** VERB
[1] <u>beibringen</u> (IMPERFECT brachte bei, PERFECT hat beigebracht) ◊ *My sister taught me to swim.* Meine Schwester hat mir das Schwimmen beigebracht.
◆ **That'll teach you!** Das wird dir eine Lehre sein!
[2] (*in school*)
<u>unterrichten</u> (PERFECT hat unterrichtet) ◊ *She teaches physics.* Sie unterrichtet Physik.

**teacher** NOUN
der <u>Lehrer</u> (PL die Lehrer)
die <u>Lehrerin</u>
◊ *a maths teacher* ein Mathelehrer ◊ *She's a teacher.* Sie ist Lehrerin. ◊ *He's a primary school teacher.* Er ist Grundschullehrer.

**teacher's pet** NOUN
Lehrers Schätzchen NEUT ◊ *She's teacher's pet.* Sie ist Lehrers Schätzchen.

**tea cloth** NOUN
das Geschirrtuch (PL die Geschirrtücher)

**team** NOUN
die Mannschaft ◊ *a football team* eine Fußballmannschaft ◊ *She was in my team.* Sie war in meiner Mannschaft.

**teapot** NOUN
die Teekanne

**tear** NOUN
| see also **tear** VERB |
die Träne ◊ *She was in tears.* Sie war in Tränen aufgelöst.

to **tear** VERB
| see also **tear** NOUN |
zerreißen (IMPERFECT zerriss, PERFECT hat/ist zerrissen) ◊ *Be careful or you'll tear the page.* Vorsicht, sonst zerreißt du die Seite.

*For the perfect tense use **haben** when the verb has an object and **sein** when there is no object.*

◊ *You've torn your shirt.* Du hast dein Hemd zerrissen. ◊ *Your shirt is torn.* Dein Hemd ist zerrissen. ◊ *It won't tear, it's very strong.* Es zerreißt nicht, es ist sehr stark.
♦ **to tear up** zerreißen ◊ *He tore up the letter.* Er zerriss den Brief.

**tear gas** NOUN
das Tränengas (GEN des Tränengases)

to **tease** VERB
⬚1 quälen (*unkindly*) ◊ *Stop teasing that poor animal!* Hör auf, das arme Tier zu quälen!
⬚2 necken (*jokingly*) ◊ *He's teasing you.* Er neckt dich nur.
♦ **I was only teasing.** Ich habe nur einen Scherz gemacht.

**teaspoon** NOUN
der Teelöffel (PL die Teelöffel) ◊ *a teaspoon of sugar* ein Teelöffel Zucker

**teaspoonful** NOUN
♦ **a teaspoonful of sugar** ein Teelöffel Zucker

**teatime** NOUN
die Abendessenszeit (*in evening*) ◊ *It was nearly teatime.* Es war fast Abendessenszeit.
♦ **Teatime!** Abendessen!

**tea towel** NOUN
das Geschirrtuch (PL die Geschirrtücher)

**technical** ADJECTIVE
technisch
♦ **a technical college** eine Fachhochschule

**technician** NOUN
der Techniker (PL die Techniker)
die Technikerin

**technique** NOUN
die Technik

**techno** NOUN

der Techno (*music*)

**technological** ADJECTIVE
technologisch

**technology** NOUN
die Technologie

**teddy bear** NOUN
der Teddybär (GEN des Teddybären, PL die Teddybären)

**teenage** ADJECTIVE
⬚1 für Teenager ◊ *a teenage magazine* eine Zeitschrift für Teenager
⬚2 heranwachsend (*boys, girls*) ◊ *She has two teenage daughters.* Sie hat zwei heranwachsende Töchter.

**teenager** NOUN
der Teenager (PL die Teenager)
*der Teenager is also used for girls.*

**teens** PL NOUN
♦ **She's in her teens.** Sie ist ein Teenager.

**tee-shirt** NOUN
das T-Shirt (PL die T-Shirts)

**teeth** PL NOUN *see* **tooth**

to **teethe** VERB
zahnen

**teetotal** ADJECTIVE
♦ **I'm teetotal.** Ich trinke keinen Alkohol.

**telecommunications** PL NOUN
die Nachrichtentechnik SING

**teleconferencing** NOUN
die Telekonferenzen PL

**telephone** NOUN
das Telefon (PL die Telefone) ◊ *on the telephone* am Telefon
♦ **a telephone box** eine Telefonzelle
♦ **a telephone call** ein Anruf MASC
♦ **the telephone directory** das Telefonbuch
♦ **a telephone number** eine Telefonnummer

**telesales** SING NOUN
der Telefonverkauf (PL die Telefonverkäufe)

**telescope** NOUN
das Teleskop (PL die Teleskope)

**television** NOUN
das Fernsehen
♦ **on television** im Fernsehen
♦ **a television programme** eine Fernsehsendung

to **tell** VERB
sagen
♦ **to tell somebody something** jemandem etwas sagen ◊ *Did you tell your mother?* Hast du es deiner Mutter gesagt? ◊ *I told him that I was going on holiday.* Ich habe ihm gesagt, dass ich in Urlaub fahre.
♦ **to tell somebody to do something** jemandem sagen, er solle etwas tun ◊ *He told me to wait a moment.* Er sagte mir, ich solle einen Moment warten.
♦ **to tell lies** lügen
♦ **to tell a story** eine Geschichte erzählen
♦ **I can't tell the difference between them.** Ich kann sie nicht unterscheiden.

**T**

to **tell off** VERB
schimpfen
**telly** NOUN
der Fernseher (PL die Fernseher)
♦ **to watch telly** fernsehen
♦ **on telly** im Fernsehen
**temper** NOUN
♦ **to be in a temper** wütend sein
♦ **to lose one's temper** wütend werden ◊ *I lost my temper.* Ich bin wütend geworden.
♦ **He's got a terrible temper.** Er ist furchtbar jähzornig.
**temperature** NOUN
die Temperatur (*of oven, water, person*)
♦ **The temperature was thirty degrees.** Es waren dreißig Grad.
♦ **to have a temperature** Fieber haben
**temple** NOUN
der Tempel (PL die Tempel)
**temporary** ADJECTIVE
vorläufig
to **tempt** VERB
in Versuchung führen ◊ *to tempt somebody to do something* jemanden in Versuchung führen, etwas zu tun
♦ **I'm very tempted!** Das reizt mich sehr!
**temptation** NOUN
die Versuchung
**tempting** ADJECTIVE
verlockend
**ten** NUMBER
zehn ◊ *She's ten.* Sie ist zehn.
**tenant** NOUN
der Mieter (PL die Mieter)
die Mieterin
**tender** ADJECTIVE
1 zärtlich (*loving*)
2 empfindlich ◊ *The wound is still tender.* Die wunde Stelle ist noch immer empfindlich.
to **tend to** VERB
♦ **to tend to do something** dazu neigen, etwas zu tun ◊ *He tends to arrive late.* Er neigt dazu, zu spät zu kommen.
**tennis** NOUN
das Tennis (GEN des Tennis) ◊ *Do you play tennis?* Spielst du Tennis?
♦ **a tennis ball** ein Tennisball MASC
♦ **a tennis court** ein Tennisplatz MASC
♦ **a tennis racket** ein Tennisschläger MASC
**tennis player** NOUN
der Tennisspieler (PL die Tennisspieler)
die Tennisspielerin
◊ *He's a tennis player.* Er ist Tennisspieler.
**tenor** NOUN
der Tenor (PL die Tenöre)
**tenpin bowling** NOUN
das Bowling
♦ **to go tenpin bowling** Bowling spielen
**tense** ADJECTIVE

| see also **tense** NOUN |

angespannt ◊ *a tense situation* eine angespannte Situation
**tense** NOUN

| see also **tense** ADJECTIVE |

♦ **the present tense** das Präsens
♦ **the future tense** das Futur
**tension** NOUN
die Spannung
**tent** NOUN
das Zelt (PL die Zelte)
♦ **a tent peg** ein Hering MASC
♦ **a tent pole** eine Zeltstange
**tenth** ADJECTIVE
zehnte ◊ *the tenth floor* der zehnte Stock
♦ **the tenth of August** der zehnte August
**term** NOUN
das Trimester (*at school*) (PL die Trimester)

> ❗ *In Germany the school and university year is divided into two semesters rather than three terms.*

♦ **to come to terms with something** sich mit etwas abfinden
**terminal** ADJECTIVE

| see also **terminal** NOUN |

unheilbar (*illness, patient*)
**terminal** NOUN

| see also **terminal** ADJECTIVE |

das Terminal (*of computer*) (PL die Terminals)
♦ **an oil terminal** ein Ölterminal MASC
♦ **an air terminal** ein Terminal MASC
**terminally** ADVERB
♦ **to be terminally ill** unheilbar krank sein
**terrace** NOUN
1 die Terrasse (*patio*)
2 die Häuserreihe (*row of houses*)
♦ **the terraces** (*at stadium*) die Ränge
**terraced** ADJECTIVE
♦ **a terraced house** ein Reihenhaus NEUT
**terrible** ADJECTIVE
furchtbar ◊ *My German is terrible.* Mein Deutsch ist furchtbar.
**terribly** ADVERB
furchtbar ◊ *He suffered terribly.* Er litt furchtbar. ◊ *I'm terribly sorry.* Es tut mir furchtbar Leid.
**terrier** NOUN
der Terrier (PL die Terrier)
**terrific** ADJECTIVE
super (*wonderful*)
*super is invariable.*
◊ *That's terrific!* Das ist super! ◊ *You look terrific!* Du siehst super aus!
**terrified** ADJECTIVE
♦ **I was terrified!** Ich hatte furchtbare Angst!
**terrorism** NOUN
der Terrorismus (GEN des Terrorismus)

**terrorist** NOUN
der Terrorist (GEN des Terroristen, PL die Terroristen)
die Terroristin
◆ **a terrorist attack** ein Terrorangriff MASC

**test** NOUN
> see also **test** VERB

[1] (at school)
die Arbeit ◊ I've got a test tomorrow. Ich schreibe morgen eine Arbeit.
[2] (trial, check)
der Test (PL die Tests) ◊ nuclear tests Atomtests
[3] (medical)
die Untersuchung ◊ a blood test eine Blutuntersuchung ◊ They're going to do some more tests tomorrow. Sie machen morgen noch weitere Untersuchungen.
◆ **driving test** die Fahrprüfung ◊ He's got his driving test tomorrow. Er hat morgen seine Fahrprüfung.

to **test** VERB
> see also **test** NOUN

[1] probieren (PERFECT hat probiert)
◆ **to test something out** etwas ausprobieren
[2] (class)
abfragen (PERFECT hat abgefragt)
◊ He tested us on the new vocabulary. Er hat uns die neuen Wörter abgefragt.
◆ **She was tested for drugs.** Man hat bei ihr ein Drogentest gemacht.

**test match** NOUN
das Länderspiel (PL die Länderspiele)

**test tube** NOUN
das Reagenzglas (GEN des Reagenzglases, PL die Reagenzgläser)

**tetanus** NOUN
der Tetanus (GEN des Tetanus) ◊ a tetanus injection eine Tetanusspritze

**textbook** NOUN
das Lehrbuch (PL die Lehrbücher)
◆ **a German textbook** ein Deutschbuch

**textiles** PL NOUN
die Textilien FEM PL
◆ **a textiles factory** eine Textilfabrik

**Thames** NOUN
die Themse

**than** CONJUNCTION
als ◊ She's taller than me. Sie ist größer als ich. ◊ I've got more books than him. Ich habe mehr Bücher als er. ◊ more than ten years mehr als zehn Jahre ◊ more than once mehr als einmal

to **thank** VERB
sich bedanken bei (PERFECT hat sich bedankt) ◊ Don't forget to write and thank them. Vergiss nicht, ihnen zu schreiben und dich bei ihnen zu bedanken.
◆ **thank you** danke

◆ **thank you very much** vielen Dank

**thanks** EXCLAMATION
danke
◆ **thanks to** dank ◊ Thanks to him, everything went OK. Dank ihm ging alles gut.

**that** ADJECTIVE, PRONOUN, CONJUNCTION
[1] dieser ◊ that man dieser Mann
diese ◊ that woman diese Frau
dieses ◊ that book dieses Buch
◆ **that one (1)** (masculine) der da ◊ This man? – No, that one. Dieser Mann? – Nein, der da.
◆ **that one (2)** (feminine) die da ◊ This woman? – No, that one. Diese Frau? – Nein, die da.
◆ **that one (3)** (neuter) das da ◊ Do you like this photo? – No, I prefer that one. Gefällt dir dieses Foto? – Nein, das da gefällt mir besser.
[2] das ◊ Did you see that? Hast du das gesehen? ◊ What's that? Was ist das? ◊ Who's that? Wer ist das? ◊ Is that you? Bist du das?
◆ **That's ...** Das ist ... ◊ That's my German teacher. Das ist meine Deutschlehrerin.
◆ **That's what he said.** Das hat er gesagt.

In relative clauses use **der, die** or **das**, depending on the gender of the noun **that** refers to.

[3] der ◊ the man that saw us der Mann, der uns sah
die ◊ the woman that saw us die Frau, die uns sah
das ◊ the child that saw us das Kind, das uns sah
die ◊ the people that helped us die Leute, die uns geholfen haben
[4] dass ◊ He thought that Henry was ill. Er dachte, dass Henry krank war. ◊ I know that she likes chocolate. Ich weiß, dass sie Schokolade mag.
[5] so ◊ It was that big. Es war so groß. ◊ It's about that high. Es ist etwa so hoch. ◊ It's not that difficult. Es ist nicht so schwierig.

**thatched** ADJECTIVE
strohgedeckt

**the** ARTICLE

Use **der** with a masculine noun, **die** with a feminine noun, and **das** with a neuter noun. For plural nouns always use **die**.

[1] der ◊ the boy der Junge
die ◊ the orange die Orange
das ◊ the girl das Mädchen
[2] die ◊ the children die Kinder

**theatre** NOUN
das Theater (PL die Theater)

**theft** NOUN
der Diebstahl (PL die Diebstähle)

**their** ADJECTIVE

**T**

☞

ihr ◊ *their father* ihr Vater ◊ *their mother* ihre Mutter ◊ *their child* ihr Kind ◊ *their parents* ihre Eltern
*Do not use* **ihr** *with parts of the body.*
◊ *They can't bend their arms.* Sie können die Arme nicht bewegen.

**theirs** PRONOUN
[1] ihrer ◊ *This is our computer, not theirs.* Das ist unser Computer, nicht ihrer.
ihre ◊ *It's not our garage, it's theirs.* Das ist nicht unsere Garage, sondern ihre.
ihres ◊ *It's not our car, it's theirs.* Das ist nicht unser Auto, sondern ihres.
[2] ihre ◊ *These are not our ideas, they're theirs.* Das sind nicht unsere Ideen, sondern ihre.
♦ **Is this theirs?** Gehört das ihnen? ◊ *This car is theirs.* Das Auto gehört ihnen. ◊ *Whose is this? – It's theirs.* Wem gehört das? – Ihnen.

**them** PRONOUN
[1] sie ◊ *I didn't see them.* Ich habe sie nicht gesehen.
*Use* **sie** *after prepositions which take the accusative.*
◊ *It's for them.* Es ist für sie.
[2] ihnen
*Use* **ihnen** *when* **them** *means* **to them**.
◊ *I gave them some brochures.* Ich habe ihnen ein paar Broschüren gegeben. ◊ *I told them the truth.* Ich habe ihnen die Wahrheit gesagt.
*Use* **ihnen** *after prepositions which take the dative.*
◊ *Ann and Sophie came. Graham was with them.* Ann und Sophie sind gekommen. Graham war bei ihnen.

**theme** NOUN
das Thema (PL die Themen)
**themselves** PRONOUN
[1] sich ◊ *Did they hurt themselves?* Haben sie sich verletzt?
[2] selbst ◊ *They did it themselves.* Sie haben es selbst gemacht.

**then** ADVERB, CONJUNCTION
[1] dann ◊ *I get dressed. Then I have breakfast.* Ich ziehe mich an. Dann frühstücke ich. ◊ *My pen's run out. – Use a pencil then!* Mein Kugelschreiber ist leer. – Dann nimm einen Bleistift!
[2] damals (*at that time*) ◊ *There was no electricity then.* Damals gab es keinen Strom.
♦ **now and then** ab und zu ◊ *Do you play chess? – Now and then.* Spielst du Schach? – Ab und zu.
♦ **By then it was too late.** Da war es schon zu spät.

**therapy** NOUN
die Therapie

**there** ADVERB
*Use* **dort** *when something is in a fixed position,* **dorthin** *when there is movement involved.*
[1] dort ◊ *Can you see that house there?* Siehst du das Haus dort? ◊ *Berlin? I've never been there.* Berlin? Ich war noch nie dort.
♦ **over there** dort drüben
♦ **in there** dort drin
♦ **on there** darauf
♦ **up there** dort oben
♦ **down there** dort unten
[2] dorthin ◊ *Put it there, on the table.* Stell's dorthin, auf den Tisch. ◊ *He went there on Friday.* Er ging am Freitag dorthin.
♦ **There he is!** Da ist er ja!
♦ **There is ... (1)** Es ist ... ◊ *There's a factory near my house.* In der Nähe von meinem Haus ist eine Fabrik.
♦ **There is ... (2)** Es gibt ... ◊ *There is a lot of poverty in the world.* Es gibt viel Armut auf der Welt.
♦ **There are ... (1)** Es sind ... ◊ *There are five people in my family.* In meiner Familie sind fünf Leute.
♦ **There are ... (2)** Es gibt ... ◊ *There are many schools in this city.* In dieser Stadt gibt es viele Schulen.
♦ **There has been an accident.** Es hat einen Unfall gegeben.

**therefore** ADVERB
deshalb
**there's** = there is = there has
**thermometer** NOUN
das Thermometer (PL die Thermometer)
**Thermos** ® NOUN
die Thermosflasche ®
**these** ADJECTIVE, PRONOUN
[1] die ◊ *these shoes* die Schuhe
♦ **THESE shoes** diese Schuhe hier
[2] die hier ◊ *I want these!* Ich möchte die hier! ◊ *I'm looking for some sandals. Can I try these?* Ich suche Sandalen. Kann ich die hier anprobieren?

**they** PRONOUN
sie ◊ *Are there any tickets left? – No, they're all sold.* Gibt es noch Karten? – Nein, sie sind schon alle verkauft. ◊ *Do you like those shoes? – No, they're horrible.* Gefallen dir die Schuhe? – Nein, sie sind furchtbar.
♦ **They say that ...** Man sagt, dass ...
**they'd** = they had = they would
**they'll** = they will
**they're** = they are
**they've** = they have
**thick** ADJECTIVE
[1] dick (*not thin*) ◊ *The walls are one metre thick.* Die Wände sind einen Meter dick.
[2] dumm (*stupid*)

**thief** NOUN
der <u>Dieb</u> (PL die Diebe)
die <u>Diebin</u>

**thigh** NOUN
der <u>Schenkel</u>

**thin** ADJECTIVE
<u>dünn</u>

**thing** NOUN
das <u>Ding</u> (PL die Dinge) ◊ *beautiful things*
schöne Dinge ◊ *What's that thing called?*
Wie heißt das Ding da?
♦ **my things** (*belongings*) meine Sachen
♦ **You poor thing!** **(1)** (*man*) Du Armer!
♦ **You poor thing!** **(2)** (*woman*) Du Arme!

to **think** VERB
[1] <u>denken</u> (IMPERFECT dachte, PERFECT hat
gedacht) ◊ *I think you're wrong.* Ich
denke, du hast Unrecht. ◊ *What are you
thinking about?* Woran denkst du?
♦ **What do you think about the death
penalty?** Was halten Sie von der
Todesstrafe?
[2] <u>glauben</u> ◊ *I don't think I can come to
the party.* Ich glaube nicht, dass ich zur
Party kommen kann.
♦ **I think so.** Ich glaube schon.
♦ **I don't think so.** Ich glaube nicht.
[3] (*spend time thinking*)
<u>nachdenken</u> (PERFECT hat nachgedacht)
◊ *Think carefully before you reply.*
Denk gut nach, bevor du antwortest.
◊ *I'll think about it.* Ich denke darüber
nach.
[4] (*imagine*)
<u>sich vorstellen</u> (PERFECT hat sich
vorgestellt) ◊ *Think what life would be
like without cars.* Stell dir vor, wie es
wäre, wenn es keine Autos gäbe.
♦ **I'll think it over.** Ich werde es mir
überlegen.

**third** ADJECTIVE
| see also **third** NOUN |
<u>dritte</u> ◊ *the third day* der dritte Tag ◊ *the
third time* das dritte Mal
♦ **He came third.** Er wurde Dritter.
♦ **the third of August** der dritte August

**third** NOUN
| see also **third** ADJECTIVE |
das <u>Drittel</u> (PL die Drittel) ◊ *a third
of the population* ein Drittel der
Bevölkerung

**thirdly** ADVERB
<u>drittens</u>

**Third World** NOUN
die <u>Dritte Welt</u>

**thirst** NOUN
der <u>Durst</u>

**thirsty** ADJECTIVE
♦ **to be thirsty** Durst haben ◊ *Are you
thirsty?* Hast du Durst?

**thirteen** NUMBER
<u>dreizehn</u> ◊ *I'm thirteen.* Ich bin dreizehn.

**thirteenth** ADJECTIVE
<u>dreizehnte</u>
♦ **the thirteenth of August** der dreizehnte
August

**thirty** NUMBER
<u>dreißig</u> ◊ *She's thirty.* Sie ist dreißig.

**this** ADJECTIVE, PRONOUN
[1] <u>dieser</u> ◊ *this man* dieser Mann
<u>diese</u> ◊ *this woman* diese Frau
<u>dieses</u> ◊ *this child* dieses Kind
♦ **this one (1)** (*masculine*) der hier ◊ *That
man over there? – No, this one.* Der
Mann dort? – Nein, der hier.
♦ **this one (2)** (*feminine*) die hier ◊ *That
woman over there? – No, this one.* Die
Frau dort? – Nein, die hier.
♦ **this one (3)** (*neuter*) das hier ◊ *I don't like
that picture over there, I prefer this one.*
Das Bild dort gefällt mir nicht, das hier
gefällt mir besser.
[2] <u>das</u> ◊ *You see this?* Siehst du das?
◊ *What's this?* Was ist das? ◊ *This is my
mother.* (*introduction*) Das ist meine
Mutter.
♦ **This is Gavin speaking.** (*on the phone*)
Hier spricht Gavin.

**thistle** NOUN
die <u>Distel</u>

**thorough** ADJECTIVE
<u>gründlich</u> ◊ *She's very thorough.* Sie ist
sehr gründlich.

**thoroughly** ADVERB
<u>gründlich</u> (*examine*)

**those** ADJECTIVE, PRONOUN
[1] <u>diese</u> ◊ *those shoes* diese Schuhe
♦ **THOSE shoes** diese Schuhe dort
[2] <u>die da</u> ◊ *I want those!* Ich möchte die
da! ◊ *I'm looking for some sandals. Can I
try those?* Ich suche Sandalen. Kann ich
die da anprobieren?

**though** CONJUNCTION, ADVERB
<u>obwohl</u> ◊ *It's warm outside, though it's
raining.* Es ist warm draußen, obwohl es
regnet.
♦ **He's a nice person, though he's
not very clever.** Er ist ein netter Mensch,
auch wenn er nicht besonders klug
ist.

**thought** VERB *see* **think**

**thought** NOUN
der <u>Gedanke</u> (*idea*) (GEN des Gedankens,
PL die Gedanken) ◊ *I've just had a
thought.* Mir ist eben ein Gedanke
gekommen.
♦ **It was a nice thought, thank you.** Das
war nett, vielen Dank.
♦ **It's the thought that counts.** Es war gut
gemeint.

**thoughtful** ADJECTIVE
[1] <u>nachdenklich</u> (*deep in thought*) ◊ *You
look thoughtful.* Du siehst nachdenklich
aus.
[2] <u>aufmerksam</u> (*considerate*) ◊ *She's very
thoughtful.* Sie ist sehr aufmerksam.

**T**

**thoughtless** ADJECTIVE
gedankenlos

**thousand** NUMBER
♦ **a thousand** eintausend ◊ *a thousand marks* eintausend Mark
♦ **two thousand pounds** zweitausend Pfund
♦ **thousands of people** Tausende von Menschen

**thousandth** ADJECTIVE
tausendste

**thread** NOUN
der Faden (PL die Fäden)

**threat** NOUN
die Drohung

to **threaten** VERB
drohen ◊ *He threatened me.* Er hat mir gedroht. ◊ *to threaten to do something* drohen, etwas zu tun

**three** NUMBER
drei ◊ *She's three.* Sie ist drei.

**three-dimensional** ADJECTIVE
dreidimensional

**three-piece suite** NOUN
die dreiteilige Polstergarnitur

**threw** VERB *see* **throw**

**thrifty** ADJECTIVE
sparsam

**thrill** NOUN
der Reiz (*excitement*) (GEN des Reizes, PL die Reize)
♦ **It was a great thrill.** Es war sehr aufregend.

**thrilled** ADJECTIVE
♦ **I was thrilled.** (*pleased*) Ich habe mich unheimlich gefreut.

**thriller** NOUN
der Thriller (PL die Thriller)

**thrilling** ADJECTIVE
spannend

**throat** NOUN
der Hals (GEN des Halses, PL die Hälse)
♦ **to have a sore throat** Halsweh haben

to **throb** VERB
♦ **a throbbing pain** ein pochender Schmerz
♦ **My arm's throbbing.** Mir pocht es im Arm.

**throne** NOUN
der Thron (PL die Throne)

**through** PREPOSITION, ADJECTIVE, ADVERB
durch ◊ *through the window* durch das Fenster ◊ *to go through Birmingham* durch Birmingham fahren ◊ *to go through a tunnel* durch einen Tunnel fahren
♦ **I know her through my sister.** Ich kenne sie über meine Schwester.
♦ **The window was dirty and I couldn't see through.** Das Fenster war schmutzig, und ich konnte nicht durchsehen.

♦ **a through train** ein durchgehender Zug
♦ **"no through road"** "keine Durchfahrt"

**throughout** PREPOSITION
♦ **throughout Britain** in ganz Großbritannien
♦ **throughout the year** das ganze Jahr über

to **throw** VERB
werfen (PRESENT wirft, IMPERFECT warf, PERFECT hat geworfen) ◊ *He threw the ball to me.* Er warf mir den Ball zu.
♦ **to throw a party** eine Party machen
♦ **That really threw him.** Das hat ihn aus der Fassung gebracht.
♦ **to throw away (1)** (*rubbish*) wegwerfen
♦ **to throw away (2)** (*chance*) vergeben
♦ **to throw out (1)** (*throw away*) wegwerfen
♦ **to throw out (2)** (*person*) rauswerfen ◊ *I threw him out.* Ich habe ihn rausgeworfen.
♦ **to throw up** sich übergeben

**thug** NOUN
der Schlägertyp (PL die Schlägertypen)

**thumb** NOUN
der Daumen (PL die Daumen)

**thumb tack** NOUN US
die Reißzwecke

to **thump** VERB
♦ **to thump somebody** jemandem eine verpassen (*informal*) ◊ *I thumped him.* Ich habe ihm eine verpasst.

**thunder** NOUN
der Donner (PL die Donner)

**thunderstorm** NOUN
das Gewitter (PL die Gewitter)

**thundery** ADJECTIVE
gewitterig

**Thursday** NOUN
der Donnerstag (PL die Donnerstage)
◊ *on Thursday* am Donnerstag
◊ *every Thursday* jeden Donnerstag
◊ *last Thursday* letzten Donnerstag ◊ *next Thursday* nächsten Donnerstag
♦ **on Thursdays** donnerstags

**thyme** NOUN
der Thymian (PL die Thymiane)

**tick** NOUN
see also **tick** VERB
1 (*mark*)
das Häkchen (PL die Häkchen)
2 (*of clock*)
das Ticken
♦ **in a tick** in einer Sekunde

to **tick** VERB
see also **tick** NOUN
1 ankreuzen (PERFECT hat angekreuzt)
◊ *Tick the appropriate box.* Kreuzen Sie das entsprechende Kästchen an.
2 (*clock*)
ticken
♦ **to tick off (1)** (*on list*) abhaken

♦ **to tick off (2)** (*scold*) ausschimpfen

**ticket** NOUN
1 (*for bus, tube, train*)
die Fahrkarte ◊ *an underground ticket*
eine Fahrkarte für die U-Bahn
2 (*for plane*)
das Ticket (PL die Tickets)
3 (*for theatre, concert, cinema, museum*)
die Eintrittskarte
♦ **a parking ticket** ein Strafzettel MASC

**ticket inspector** NOUN
der Fahrscheinkontrolleur (PL die Fahrscheinkontrolleure)
die Fahrscheinkontrolleurin

**ticket office** NOUN
1 (*for travel*)
der Fahrkartenschalter (PL die Fahrkartenschalter)
2 (*for theatre, cinema*)
die Kasse

to **tickle** VERB
kitzeln

**ticklish** ADJECTIVE
kitzlig ◊ *Are you ticklish?* Bist du kitzlig?

**tide** NOUN
♦ **high tide** die Flut
♦ **low tide** die Ebbe

**tidy** ADJECTIVE
see also **tidy** VERB
ordentlich ◊ *Your room is very tidy.* Dein Zimmer ist sehr ordentlich. ◊ *She's very tidy.* Sie ist sehr ordentlich.

to **tidy** VERB
see also **tidy** ADJECTIVE
aufräumen (PERFECT hat aufgeräumt) ◊ *Go and tidy your room.* Geh und räum dein Zimmer auf.
♦ **to tidy up** aufräumen ◊ *Don't forget to tidy up afterwards.* Vergesst nicht, nachher aufzuräumen.

**tie** NOUN
see also **tie** VERB
die Krawatte (*necktie*)
♦ **It was a tie.** (*in sport*) Es gab ein Unentschieden.

to **tie** VERB
see also **tie** NOUN
1 (*ribbon, shoelaces*)
zubinden (IMPERFECT band zu, PERFECT hat zugebunden)
♦ **I tied a knot in the rope.** Ich machte einen Knoten in das Seil.
2 (*in sport*)
unentschieden spielen
♦ **They tied three all.** Sie haben drei zu drei gespielt.
♦ **to tie up (1)** (*parcel*) zuschnüren
♦ **to tie up (2)** (*dog, boat*) anbinden
♦ **to tie up (3)** (*prisoner*) fesseln

**tiger** NOUN
der Tiger (PL die Tiger)

**tight** ADJECTIVE

1 eng (*tight-fitting*) ◊ *tight jeans* enge Jeans
2 zu eng (*too tight*) ◊ *This dress is a bit tight.* Das Kleid ist etwas zu eng.

to **tighten** VERB
1 (*rope*)
spannen
2 (*screw*)
anziehen (IMPERFECT zog an, PERFECT hat angezogen)

**tightly** ADVERB
fest (*hold*)

**tights** PL NOUN
die Strumpfhose SING ◊ *a pair of tights* eine Strumpfhose

**tile** NOUN
1 (*on roof*)
der Dachziegel (PL die Dachziegel)
2 (*on wall, floor*)
die Fliese

**tiled** ADJECTIVE
1 gekachelt (*wall*)
2 mit Fliesen ausgelegt (*floor, room*)
♦ **a tiled roof** ein Ziegeldach NEUT

**till** NOUN
see also **till** PREPOSITION

die Kasse

**till** PREPOSITION, CONJUNCTION
see also **till** NOUN

1 bis ◊ *I waited till ten o'clock.* Ich habe bis zehn Uhr gewartet.
♦ **till now** bis jetzt
♦ **till then** bis dann
2 vor

Use **vor** if the sentence you want to translate contains a negative such as "not" or "never".

◊ *It won't be ready till next week.* Vor nächster Woche wird es nicht fertig.
◊ *Till last year I'd never been to Germany.* Vor letztem Jahr war ich nie in Deutschland.

**time** NOUN
1 die Zeit ◊ *It's time to get up.* Es ist Zeit zum Aufstehen. ◊ *It was two o'clock, German time.* Es war zwei Uhr, deutsche Zeit. ◊ *I'm sorry, I haven't got time.* Ich habe leider keine Zeit.
♦ **What time is it?** Wie viel Uhr ist es?
♦ **What time do you get up?** Um wie viel Uhr stehst du auf?
♦ **on time** pünktlich ◊ *He never arrives on time.* Er kommt nie pünktlich.
♦ **from time to time** von Zeit zu Zeit
♦ **in time** rechtzeitig ◊ *We arrived in time for lunch.* Wir kamen rechtzeitig zum Mittagessen.
♦ **just in time** gerade noch rechtzeitig
♦ **in no time** im Nu ◊ *It was ready in no time.* Es war im Nu fertig.
2 (*moment*)

**T**

☞

der <u>Moment</u> (PL die Momente) ◊ *This isn't a good time to ask him.* Das ist kein guter Moment, um ihn zu fragen.
- **for the time being** momentan
  3 (*occasion*)
  das <u>Mal</u> (PL die Male) ◊ *next time* nächstes Mal
- **this time** diesmal
- **two at a time** jeweils zwei
- **How many times?** Wie oft?
- **at times** manchmal
- **a long time** lange ◊ *Have you lived here for a long time?* Wohnst du schon lange hier?
- **in a week's time** in einer Woche ◊ *I'll come back in a month's time.* Ich komme in einem Monat wieder.
- **Come and see us any time.** Besuchen sie uns, wann Sie wollen.
- **to have a good time** sich amüsieren ◊ *Did you have a good time?* Habt ihr euch amüsiert?
- **Two times two is four.** Zwei mal zwei ist vier.

**time bomb** NOUN
die <u>Zeitbombe</u>

**time off** NOUN
die <u>Freizeit</u>

**timer** NOUN
  1 (*time switch*)
  die <u>Schaltuhr</u>
  2 (*for cooking*)
  der <u>Kurzzeitmesser</u> (PL die Kurzzeitmesser)
- **an egg timer** eine Eieruhr

**time-share** NOUN
  das <u>Timesharing-Appartement</u> (PL die Timesharing-Appartements)

**timetable** NOUN
  1 (*for train, bus*)
  der <u>Fahrplan</u> (PL die Fahrpläne)
  2 (*at school*)
  der <u>Stundenplan</u> (PL die Stundenpläne)

**time zone** NOUN
die <u>Zeitzone</u>

**tin** NOUN
  1 die <u>Dose</u> ◊ *a tin of beans* eine Dose Bohnen ◊ *a biscuit tin* eine Keksdose
  2 das <u>Zinn</u> (*type of metal*)

**tinned** ADJECTIVE
in <u>Dosen</u> (*food*) ◊ *tinned peaches* Pfirsiche in Dosen

**tin opener** NOUN
der <u>Dosenöffner</u> (PL die Dosenöffner)

**tinsel** NOUN
die <u>Rauschgoldgirlande</u>

**tinted** ADJECTIVE
getönt (*spectacles, glass*)

**tiny** ADJECTIVE
<u>winzig</u>

**tip** NOUN
see also **tip** VERB
  1 (*money*)

das <u>Trinkgeld</u> (PL die Trinkgelder) ◊ *Shall I give him a tip?* Soll ich ihm ein Trinkgeld geben?
  2 (*advice*)
  der <u>Tipp</u> (PL die Tipps) ◊ *a useful tip* ein guter Tipp
  3 (*end*)
  die <u>Spitze</u>
- **It's on the tip of my tongue.** Es liegt mir auf der Zunge.
- **a rubbish tip** eine Müllkippe
- **This place is a complete tip!** Was für ein Saustall! (*informal*)

to **tip** VERB
see also **tip** NOUN
- **to tip somebody** jemandem ein Trinkgeld geben ◊ *He tipped the taxi driver generously.* Er gab dem Taxifahrer ein großzügiges Trinkgeld.

**tipsy** ADJECTIVE
<u>beschwipst</u> ◊ *I'm feeling a bit tipsy.* Ich bin etwas beschwipst.

**tiptoe** NOUN
- **on tiptoe** auf Zehenspitzen

**tired** ADJECTIVE
<u>müde</u> ◊ *I'm tired.* Ich bin müde.
- **to be tired of something** etwas leid sein

**tiring** ADJECTIVE
<u>ermüdend</u>

**tissue** NOUN
  das <u>Papiertaschentuch</u> (PL die Papiertaschentücher) ◊ *Have you got a tissue?* Hast du ein Papiertaschentuch?

**title** NOUN
der <u>Titel</u> (PL die Titel)

**title role** NOUN
die <u>Titelrolle</u>

to PREPOSITION
  1 <u>nach</u> ◊ *to go to Munich* nach München fahren ◊ *We went to Italy.* Wir sind nach Italien gefahren. ◊ *the train to London* der Zug nach London ◊ *the road to Edinburgh* die Straße nach Edinburgh ◊ *to the left* nach links
- **I've never been to Munich.** Ich war noch nie in München.
  2 <u>in</u> ◊ *to go to school* in die Schule gehen ◊ *to go to the theatre* ins Theater gehen
  3 zu

*Use **zu** when you talk about going to a particular place or person.*

  ◊ *We drove to the station.* Wir fuhren zum Bahnhof. ◊ *to go to the doctor's* zum Arzt gehen ◊ *to go to the baker's* zum Bäcker gehen ◊ *Let's go to Anne's house.* Lass uns zu Anne nach Hause gehen.
- **a letter to his mother** ein Brief an seine Mutter
- **It's hard to say.** Es ist schwer zu sagen.
- **It's easy to criticize.** Es ist leicht zu kritisieren.

♦**something to drink** etwas zu trinken
    ④ bis (as far as, until) ◊ to count to ten bis
zehn zählen ◊ It's ninety kilometres to the
border. Es sind neunzig Kilometer bis zur
Grenze.
♦**from ... to** von ... bis ◊ from nine o'clock
to half past three von neun bis halb vier
♦**ten to nine** zehn vor neun
    *Use the dative when you say or give
something to somebody.*
    ◊ Give it to me! Gib es mir! ◊ That's what
he said to me. Das ist, was er zu mir
gesagt hat. ◊ We said goodbye to the
neighbours. Wir sagten den Nachbarn
auf Wiedersehen. ◊ I sold it to a friend.
Ich habe es einem Freund verkauft.
♦**to talk to somebody** mit jemandem
reden
    *When to is used with the infinitive, it is
often not translated.*
    ◊ I'd like to go. Ich würde gern gehen. ◊ I
don't want to see him. Ich möchte ihn
nicht sehen.
    ⑤ um ... zu (in order to)
    *um ... zu is used with the infinitive.*
    ◊ I did it to help you. Ich tat es, um dir zu
helfen. ◊ She's too young to go to
school. Sie ist noch zu jung, um in die
Schule zu gehen.
♦**the key to the front door** der Schlüssel
für die Haustür
♦**the answer to the question** die Antwort
auf die Frage
**toad** NOUN
    die Kröte
**toadstool** NOUN
    der Giftpilz (GEN des Giftpilzes, PL die
Giftpilze)
**toast** NOUN
    ① der Toast (PL die Toasts) ◊ a piece of
toast eine Scheibe Toast
    ② (speech)
    der Trinkspruch (PL die Trinksprüche)
    ◊ to drink a toast to somebody einen
Trinkspruch auf jemanden ausbringen
**toaster** NOUN
    der Toaster (PL die Toaster)
**toastie** NOUN
    der Toast (PL die Toasts) ◊ a cheese
toastie ein Käsetoast
**tobacco** NOUN
    der Tabak
**tobacconist's** NOUN
    der Tabakladen (PL die Tabakläden)
**toboggan** NOUN
    der Schlitten (PL die Schlitten)
**tobogganing** NOUN
♦**to go tobogganing** Schlitten fahren
**today** ADVERB
    heute ◊ What did you do today? Was
hast du heute gemacht?
**toddler** NOUN
    das Kleinkind (PL die Kleinkinder)

**toe** NOUN
    der Zeh (PL die Zehen) ◊ my big toe mein
großer Zeh
**toffee** NOUN
    der Karamell
**together** ADVERB
    ① zusammen ◊ Are they still together?
Sind sie noch zusammen?
    ② gleichzeitig (at the same time) ◊ Don't
all speak together! Redet nicht alle
gleichzeitig!
♦**together with** (with person) zusammen
mit
**toilet** NOUN
    die Toilette
**toilet paper** NOUN
    das Toilettenpapier
**toiletries** PL NOUN
    die Toilettenartikel MASC PL
**toilet roll** NOUN
    die Rolle Toilettenpapier
**token** NOUN
♦**a gift token** ein Geschenkgutschein
MASC
**told** VERB see **tell**
**tolerant** ADJECTIVE
    tolerant
**toll** NOUN
    die Benutzungsgebühr (on bridge,
motorway)
**tomato** NOUN
    die Tomate ◊ tomato soup die
Tomatensuppe
**tomboy** NOUN
    der Wildfang ◊ She's a real tomboy. Sie
ist ein echter Wildfang.
**tomorrow** ADVERB
    morgen ◊ tomorrow morning morgen
früh ◊ tomorrow night morgen Abend
♦**the day after tomorrow** übermorgen
**ton** NOUN
    die Tonne ◊ That old bike weighs a ton.
Das alte Fahrrad wiegt ja eine Tonne.
**tongue** NOUN
    die Zunge
♦**to say something tongue in cheek** etwas
nicht so ernst meinen
**tonic** NOUN
    das Tonic (tonic water) (PL die Tonics)
♦**a gin and tonic** ein Gin Tonic
**tonight** ADVERB
    ① heute Abend (this evening) ◊ Are you
going out tonight? Gehst du heute
Abend aus?
    ② heute Nacht (during the night) ◊ I'll
sleep well tonight. Ich werde heute Nacht
gut schlafen.
**tonsillitis** NOUN
    die Mandelentzündung ◊ She's got
tonsillitis. Sie hat eine
Mandelentzündung.
**tonsils** PL NOUN

**T**

☞

die <u>Mandeln</u> FEM PL

**too** ADVERB, ADJECTIVE

1 <u>auch</u> (as well) ◊ My sister came too.
Meine Schwester ist auch mitgekommen.

2 <u>zu</u> (excessively) ◊ The water's too hot.
Das Wasser ist zu heiß. ◊ We arrived too
late. Wir sind zu spät gekommen.

◆ **too much** zu viel ◊ too much noise zu
viel Lärm ◊ At Christmas we always eat
too much. Zu Weihnachten essen wir
immer zu viel. ◊ Fifty marks? That's too
much. Fünfzig Mark? Das ist zu viel.

◆ **too many** zu viele ◊ too many
hamburgers zu viele Hamburger

◆ **Too bad!** Da kann man nichts machen!

**took** VERB see take

**tool** NOUN
das <u>Werkzeug</u> (PL die Werkzeuge)

◆ **a tool box** ein Werkzeugkasten MASC

**tooth** NOUN
der <u>Zahn</u> (PL die Zähne)

**toothache** NOUN
die <u>Zahnschmerzen</u> MASC PL ◊ to have
toothache Zahnschmerzen haben

**toothbrush** NOUN
die <u>Zahnbürste</u>

**toothpaste** NOUN
die <u>Zahnpasta</u> (PL die Zahnpasten)

**top** NOUN

see also **top** ADJECTIVE

1 (of tree)
die <u>Spitze</u>

2 (of mountain)
der <u>Gipfel</u> (PL die Gipfel)

3 (of garment)
das <u>Oberteil</u> (PL die Oberteile) ◊ a bikini
top ein Bikinioberteil

4 (of table)
das <u>Kopfende</u> (PL die Kopfenden)

5 (of box, jar)
der <u>Deckel</u> (PL die Deckel)

6 (of bottle)
der <u>Verschluss</u> (GEN des Verschlusses, PL
die Verschlüsse)

◆ **at the top of the page** oben auf der Seite

◆ **to reach the top of the ladder** oben auf
der Leiter ankommen

◆ **on top of** (on) oben auf ◊ on top of the
cupboard oben auf dem Schrank

◆ **There's a surcharge on top of that.** Es
kommt noch ein Zuschlag dazu.

◆ **from top to bottom** von oben bis unten
◊ I searched the house from top to
bottom. Ich habe das Haus von oben bis
unten durchsucht.

**top** ADJECTIVE

see also **top** NOUN

<u>erstklassig</u> (first-class) ◊ a top hotel ein
erstklassiges Hotel

◆ **a top surgeon** ein Spitzenchirurg MASC

◆ **a top model** (fashion) ein Topmodel NEUT

◆ **He always gets top marks in German.** Er
bekommt in Deutsch immer
Spitzennoten.

◆ **the top floor** der oberste Stock ◊ on the
top floor im obersten Stock

**topic** NOUN
das <u>Thema</u> (PL die Themen) ◊ The essay
can be on any topic. Der Aufsatz kann
über ein beliebiges Thema sein.

**topical** ADJECTIVE
<u>aktuell</u> ◊ a topical issue ein aktuelles
Problem

**topless** ADJECTIVE, ADVERB
<u>oben ohne</u> ◊ to go topless oben ohne
gehen

**top-secret** ADJECTIVE
<u>streng geheim</u> ◊ top-secret documents
streng geheime Dokumente

**torch** NOUN
die <u>Taschenlampe</u>

**tore, torn** VERB see tear

**tortoise** NOUN
die <u>Schildkröte</u>

**torture** NOUN

see also **torture** VERB

die <u>Folter</u>

◆ **It was pure torture.** Es war die Hölle.
(informal)

to **torture** VERB

see also **torture** NOUN

<u>quälen</u> ◊ Stop torturing that poor
animal! Hör auf, das arme Tier zu
quälen!

**Tory** ADJECTIVE

see also **Tory** NOUN

<u>konservativ</u> ◊ the Tory government die
konservative Regierung

**Tory** NOUN

see also **Tory** ADJECTIVE

der <u>Konservative</u> (GEN des
Konservativen, PL die Konservativen)
die <u>Konservative</u> (GEN der Konservativen)
◊ a Tory (man) ein Konservativer

◆ **the Tories** die Konservativen

to **toss** VERB

◆ **to toss pancakes** Pfannkuchen in der Luft
wenden

◆ **Shall we toss for it?** Sollen wir eine
Münze werfen?

**total** ADJECTIVE

see also **total** NOUN

<u>gesamt</u> ◊ the total amount der gesamte
Betrag

**total** NOUN

see also **total** ADJECTIVE

1 die <u>Gesamtmenge</u> (amount)

2 die <u>Endsumme</u> (money, figures)

◆ **the grand total** die Gesamtsumme

**totally** ADVERB
<u>völlig</u> ◊ He's totally useless. Er ist völlig
unfähig.

**touch** NOUN

see also **touch** VERB

♦**to get in touch with somebody** sich mit jemandem in Verbindung setzen

♦**to keep in touch with somebody** mit jemandem in Verbindung bleiben

♦**Keep in touch!** Lass von dir hören!

♦**to lose touch** sich aus den Augen verlieren

♦**to lose touch with somebody** jemanden aus den Augen verlieren

to **touch** VERB

see also **touch** NOUN

berühren (PERFECT hat berührt)

♦**"Do not touch"** "Nicht berühren"

♦**Don't touch that!** Fass das nicht an!

**touchdown** NOUN
die Landung

**touched** ADJECTIVE
gerührt ◊ *I was really touched.* Ich war wirklich gerührt.

**touching** ADJECTIVE
rührend

**touchline** NOUN
die Seitenlinie

**touchy** ADJECTIVE
empfindlich ◊ *She's a bit touchy.* Sie ist etwas empfindlich.

**tough** ADJECTIVE
[1] hart ◊ *It was tough, but I managed OK.* Es war hart, aber ich habe es geschafft. ◊ *It's a tough job.* Das ist eine harte Arbeit. ◊ *He thinks he's a tough guy.* Er meint, er sei ein harter Bursche.
[2] zäh (*meat*) ◊ *The meat's tough.* Das Fleisch ist zäh.
[3] fest (*strong*) ◊ *tough leather gloves* feste Lederhandschuhe

♦**Tough luck!** Das ist Pech!

**toupee** NOUN
das Toupet (PL die Toupets)

**tour** NOUN

see also **tour** VERB

[1] die Besichtigung (*of town, museum*)

♦**We went on a tour of the city.** Wir haben die Stadt besichtigt.

♦**a guided tour** eine Führung

♦**a package tour** eine Pauschalreise

[2] die Tournee (*by singer, group*) ◊ *on tour* auf Tournee ◊ *to go on tour* auf Tournee gehen

to **tour** VERB

see also **tour** NOUN

♦**Sting's touring Europe.** Sting ist auf Europatournee.

**tour guide** NOUN
der Reiseleiter (PL die Reiseleiter)
die Reiseleiterin

**tourism** NOUN
der Tourismus (GEN des Tourismus)

**tourist** NOUN
der Tourist (GEN des Touristen, PL die Touristen)

die Touristin

♦**tourist information office** das Verkehrsbüro

**tournament** NOUN
das Turnier (PL die Turniere)

**tour operator** NOUN
der Reiseveranstalter (PL die Reiseveranstalter)

**towards** PREPOSITION
[1] auf ... zu (*in the direction of*) ◊ *He came towards me.* Er kam auf mich zu.
[2] gegenüber (*of attitude*) ◊ *my feelings towards him* meine Empfindungen ihm gegenüber

**towel** NOUN
das Handtuch (PL die Handtücher)

**tower** NOUN
der Turm (PL die Türme)

♦**a tower block** ein Hochhaus NEUT

**town** NOUN
die Stadt (PL die Städte)

♦**a town plan** ein Stadtplan MASC

♦**the town centre** die Stadtmitte

♦**the town hall** das Rathaus

**tow truck** NOUN US
der Abschleppwagen (PL die Abschleppwagen)

**toy** NOUN
das Spielzeug (PL die Spielzeuge)

♦**a toy shop** ein Spielwarengeschäft NEUT

♦**a toy car** ein Spielzeugauto NEUT

**trace** NOUN

see also **trace** VERB

die Spur ◊ *There was no trace of the robbers.* Es gab keine Spur von den Räubern.

to **trace** VERB

see also **trace** NOUN

nachziehen (*draw*) (IMPERFECT zog nach, PERFECT hat nachgezogen)

**tracing paper** NOUN
das Pauspapier

**track** NOUN
[1] (*dirt road*)
der Pfad (PL die Pfade)
[2] (*railway line*)
das Gleis (GEN des Gleises, PL die Gleise)
[3] (*in sport*)
die Rennbahn ◊ *two laps of the track* zwei Runden der Rennbahn
[4] (*song*)
das Stück (PL die Stücke) ◊ *This is my favourite track.* Das ist mein Lieblingsstück.
[5] (*trail*)
die Spur ◊ *They followed the tracks for miles.* Sie folgten der Spur meilenweit.

to **track down** VERB

♦**to track somebody down** jemanden finden ◊ *The police never tracked down the killer.* Die Polizei hat den Mörder nie gefunden.

**tracksuit** NOUN

**T**

der Jogginganzug (PL die
Jogginganzüge)
**tractor** NOUN
der Traktor (PL die Traktoren)
**trade** NOUN
das Handwerk (*skill, job*) ◊ *to learn a
trade* ein Handwerk erlernen
**trade union** NOUN
die Gewerkschaft

> ℹ *Unions in Germany are organized
> within the **Deutscher
> Gewerkschaftsbund (DGB)**.*

**trade unionist** NOUN
der Gewerkschafter (PL die
Gewerkschafter)
die Gewerkschafterin
**tradition** NOUN
die Tradition
**traditional** ADJECTIVE
traditionell
**traffic** NOUN
der Verkehr ◊ *The traffic was terrible.* Es
war furchtbar viel Verkehr.
**traffic circle** NOUN US
der Kreisverkehr (PL die Kreisverkehre)
**traffic jam** NOUN
der Stau (PL die Staus)
**traffic lights** PL NOUN
die Ampel SING
**traffic warden** NOUN
☐1 (*man*)
der Hilfspolizist (GEN des Hilfspolizisten,
PL die Hilfspolizisten)
☐2 (*woman*)
die Politesse
**tragedy** NOUN
die Tragödie
**tragic** ADJECTIVE
tragisch
**trailer** NOUN
☐1 (*vehicle*)
der Anhänger (PL die Anhänger)
☐2 (*caravan*)
der Wohnwagen (PL die Wohnwagen)
☐3 (*advert for film*)
die Vorschau
**train** NOUN
| *see also* **train** VERB |
der Zug (PL die Züge)
to **train** VERB
| *see also* **train** NOUN |
trainieren (*sport*) (PERFECT hat trainiert)
◊ *to train for a race* für ein Rennen
trainieren
♦ **to train as a teacher** eine
Lehrerausbildung machen
♦ **to train an animal to do something** ein
Tier dressieren, etwas zu tun
**trained** ADJECTIVE
gelernt ◊ *She's a trained nurse.* Sie ist
gelernte Krankenschwester.

**trainee** NOUN
☐1 (*in profession*)
der Praktikant (GEN des Praktikanten, PL
die Praktikanten)
die Praktikantin
◊ *She's a trainee.* Sie ist Praktikantin.
☐2 (*apprentice*)
der Lehrling (PL die Lehrlinge)
**der Lehrling** *is also used for women.*
◊ *She's a trainee plumber.* Sie ist
Klempnerlehrling.
**trainer** NOUN
☐1 (*sports coach*)
der Trainer (PL die Trainer)
die Trainerin
☐2 (*of animals*)
der Dresseur (PL die Dresseure)
die Dresseuse
**trainers** PL NOUN
die Turnschuhe MASC PL ◊ *a pair of trainers*
ein Paar Turnschuhe
**training** NOUN
☐1 die Ausbildung ◊ *a training course*
ein Ausbildungskurs MASC
☐2 (*sport*)
das Training (PL die Trainings)
**tram** NOUN
die Straßenbahn
**tramp** NOUN
der Landstreicher (PL die Landstreicher)
die Landstreicherin
**trampoline** NOUN
das Trampolin (PL die Trampoline)
**tranquillizer** NOUN
das Beruhigungsmittel (PL die
Beruhigungsmittel) ◊ *She's on
tranquillizers.* Sie nimmt
Beruhigungsmittel.
**transfer** NOUN
das Abziehbild (*sticker*) (PL die
Abziehbilder)
**transfusion** NOUN
die Transfusion
**transistor** NOUN
der Transistor (PL die Transistoren)
**transit lounge** NOUN
die Transithalle
to **translate** VERB
übersetzen (PERFECT hat übersetzt) ◊ *to
translate something into English* etwas
ins Englische übersetzen
**translation** NOUN
die Übersetzung
**translator** NOUN
der Übersetzer (PL die Übersetzer)
die Übersetzerin
◊ *Anita's a translator.* Anita ist
Übersetzerin.
**transparent** ADJECTIVE
durchsichtig
**transplant** NOUN
die Transplantation ◊ *a heart transplant*
eine Herztransplantation

**transport** NOUN

> see also **transport** VERB

der Transport (PL die Transporte)
◊ *the transport of goods* der
Warentransport

to **transport** VERB

> see also **transport** NOUN

transportieren (PERFECT hat
transportiert)

**trap** NOUN
die Falle

**trash** NOUN US
der Müll

**trash can** NOUN US
der Mülleimer (PL die Mülleimer)

**trashy** ADJECTIVE
schlecht ◊ *a really trashy film* ein
wirklich schlechter Film

**traumatic** ADJECTIVE
traumatisch ◊ *It was a traumatic
experience.* Es war ein traumatisches
Erlebnis.

**travel** NOUN

> see also **travel** VERB

das Reisen

to **travel** VERB

> see also **travel** NOUN

reisen (PERFECT ist gereist) ◊ *I prefer to
travel by train.* Ich reise lieber mit dem
Zug.
♦ **I'd like to travel round the world.** Ich
würde gern eine Weltreise machen.
♦ **We travelled over eight hundred
kilometres.** Wir haben über achthundert
Kilometer zurückgelegt.
♦ **News travels fast!** Neuigkeiten sprechen
sich schnell herum!

**travel agency** NOUN
das Reisebüro (PL die Reisebüros)

**travel agent** NOUN
der Reisebürokaufmann (PL die
Reisebürokaufleute)
die Reisebürokauffrau
◊ *She's a travel agent.* Sie ist
Reisebürokauffrau.
♦ **at the travel agent's** im Reisebüro

**traveller** NOUN

[1] (*on bus, train*)
der Fahrgast (PL die Fahrgäste)
*der Fahrgast is also used for women.*
[2] (*on plane*)
der Passagier (PL die Passagiere)
die Passagierin

**traveller's cheque** NOUN
der Reisescheck (PL die Reiseschecks)

**travelling** NOUN
♦ **I love travelling.** Ich reise sehr gern.

**travel sickness** NOUN
die Reisekrankheit

**tray** NOUN
das Tablett (PL die Tabletts)

to **tread** VERB

**treten** (PRESENT tritt, IMPERFECT trat, PERFECT ist
getreten) ◊ *to tread on something* auf
etwas treten ◊ *He trod on her foot.* Er ist
ihr auf den Fuß getreten.

**treasure** NOUN
der Schatz (GEN des Schatzes, PL die
Schätze)

**treat** NOUN

> see also **treat** VERB

[1] (*present*)
das Geschenk (PL die Geschenke)
[2] (*food*)
der Leckerbissen (PL die Leckerbissen)
♦ **to give somebody a treat** jemandem
eine besondere Freude machen

to **treat** VERB

> see also **treat** NOUN

behandeln (*well, badly*) (PERFECT hat
behandelt)
♦ **to treat somebody to something**
jemandem etwas spendieren ◊ *He
treated us to an ice cream.* Er hat uns ein
Eis spendiert.

**treatment** NOUN
die Behandlung

to **treble** VERB
sich verdreifachen (PERFECT hat sich
verdreifacht) ◊ *The cost of living has
trebled.* Die Lebenshaltungskosten haben
sich verdreifacht.

**tree** NOUN
der Baum (PL die Bäume)

to **tremble** VERB
zittern

**tremendous** ADJECTIVE
[1] fantastisch ◊ *Gordon is a tremendous
person.* Gordon ist fantastisch.
[2] gewaltig ◊ *a tremendous success* ein
gewaltiger Erfolg

**trend** NOUN
der Trend (*fashion*) (PL die Trends)

**trendy** ADJECTIVE
modisch

**trial** NOUN
der Prozess (*in court*) (GEN des Prozesses,
PL die Prozesse)

**triangle** NOUN
das Dreieck (PL die Dreiecke)

**tribe** NOUN
der Stamm (PL die Stämme)

**trick** NOUN

> see also **trick** VERB

[1] der Streich (PL die Streiche) ◊ *to play a
trick on somebody* jemandem einen
Streich spielen
[2] (*knack*)
der Trick (PL die Tricks) ◊ *It's not easy:
there's a trick to it.* Das ist nicht leicht: Da
ist ein Trick dabei.

to **trick** VERB

> see also **trick** NOUN

♦ **to trick somebody** jemanden reinlegen

**tricky** ADJECTIVE

T

☞

knifflig

**tricycle** NOUN
das <u>Dreirad</u> (PL die Dreiräder)

**trifle** NOUN
(*dessert*)
das <u>Trifle</u> (PL die Trifles)

to **trim** VERB
see also **trim** NOUN
[1] (*hair*)
<u>schneiden</u> (IMPERFECT schnitt, PERFECT hat geschnitten)
[2] <u>stutzen</u> ◊ *He trimmed his moustache.* Er stutzte seinen Schnurrbart.
[3] (*grass*)
<u>mähen</u>

**trim** NOUN
see also **trim** VERB
◆ **to have a trim** sich die Haare schneiden lassen ◊ *You need a trim.* Du solltest cir die Haare schneiden lassen.

**trip** NOUN
see also **trip** VERB
die <u>Reise</u> ◊ *to go on a trip* eine Reise machen ◊ *Have a good trip!* Gute Reise!
◆ **a day trip** ein Tagesausflug MASC

to **trip** VERB
see also **trip** NOUN
<u>stolpern</u> (*stumble*) (PERFECT ist gestolpert)

**triple** ADJECTIVE
<u>dreifach</u>

**triplets** PL NOUN
die <u>Drillinge</u> MASC PL

**trivial** ADJECTIVE
<u>trivial</u>

**trod, trodden** VERB *see* **tread**

**trolley** NOUN
[1] (*for shopping*)
der <u>Einkaufswagen</u> (PL die Einkaufswagen)
[2] (*for luggage*)
der <u>Kofferkuli</u> (PL die Kofferkulis)

**trombone** NOUN
die <u>Posaune</u> ◊ *I play the trombone.* Ich spiele Posaune.

**troops** PL NOUN
die <u>Truppen</u> FEM PL ◊ *British troops* die britischen Truppen

**trophy** NOUN
die <u>Trophäe</u> ◊ *to win a trophy* eine Trophäe gewinnen

**tropical** ADJECTIVE
<u>tropisch</u> ◊ *tropical plants* tropische Pflanzen
◆ **The weather was tropical.** Es war tropisch heiß.

to **trot** VERB
<u>traben</u> (PERFECT ist getrabt)

**trouble** NOUN
das <u>Problem</u> (PL die Probleme) ◊ *The trouble is, it's too expensive.* Das Problem ist, dass es zu teuer ist.

◆ **What's the trouble?** Wo ist das Problem?
◆ **to be in trouble** in Schwierigkeiten sein
◆ **stomach trouble** die Magenbeschwerden FEM PL
◆ **to take a lot of trouble over something** sich mit etwas viel Mühe geben ◊ *I took a lot of trouble over that project.* Ich habe mir mit dem Referat viel Mühe gegeben.
◆ **Don't worry, it's no trouble.** Keine Sorge, das macht keine Mühe.

**troublemaker** NOUN
der <u>Unruhestifter</u> (PL die Unruhestifter)
die <u>Unruhestifterin</u>

**trousers** PL NOUN
die <u>Hose</u> SING ◊ *a pair of trousers* eine Hose

**trout** NOUN
die <u>Forelle</u>

**truant** NOUN
◆ **to play truant** die Schule schwänzen

**truck** NOUN
der <u>Lastwagen</u> (PL die Lastwagen)
◆ **He's a truck driver.** Er ist Lastwagenfahrer.

**trucker** NOUN US
der <u>Lastwagenfahrer</u> (*driver*) (PL die Lastwagenfahrer)

**true** ADJECTIVE
<u>wahr</u> ◊ *true love* wahre Liebe ◊ *That's true.* Das ist wahr.
◆ **to come true** wahr werden ◊ *I hope my dream will come true.* Ich hoffe, mein Traum wird wahr.

**trumpet** NOUN
die <u>Trompete</u> ◊ *She plays the trumpet.* Sie spielt Trompete.

**trunk** NOUN
[1] (*of tree*)
der <u>Stamm</u> (PL die Stämme)
[2] (*of elephant*)
der <u>Rüssel</u> (PL die Rüssel)
[3] (*luggage*)
der <u>Schrankkoffer</u> (PL die Schrankkoffer)
[4] (*boot of car*)
der <u>Kofferraum</u> (PL die Kofferräume)

**trunks** PL NOUN
◆ **swimming trunks** die Badehose SING ◊ *a pair of trunks* eine Badehose

**trust** NOUN
see also **trust** VERB
das <u>Vertrauen</u> ◊ *to have trust in somebody* Vertrauen zu jemandem haben

to **trust** VERB
see also **trust** NOUN
◆ **to trust somebody** jemandem vertrauen ◊ *Don't you trust me?* Vertraust du mir nicht?
◆ **Trust me!** Glaub mir!

**trusting** ADJECTIVE
<u>vertrauensvoll</u>

**truth** NOUN
die <u>Wahrheit</u>

**truthful** ADJECTIVE
ehrlich

**try** NOUN
see also **try** VERB
der Versuch (PL die Versuche) ◊ *his third try* sein dritter Versuch
♦ **to have a try** es versuchen ◊ *I'll have a try.* Ich werd's versuchen.
♦ **It's worth a try.** Der Versuch lohnt sich.
♦ **to give something a try** etwas versuchen

to **try** VERB
see also **try** NOUN
[1] (*attempt*)
versuchen (PERFECT hat versucht) ◊ *to try to do something* versuchen, etwas zu tun
♦ **to try again** es noch einmal versuchen
[2] (*taste*)
probieren (PERFECT hat probiert) ◊ *Would you like to try some?* Möchtest du etwas probieren?
♦ **to try on** (*clothes*) anprobieren
♦ **to try something out** etwas ausprobieren

**T-shirt** NOUN
das T-Shirt (PL die T-Shirts)

**tube** NOUN
die Tube
♦ **the Tube** (*underground*) die U-Bahn

**tuberculosis** NOUN
die Tuberkulose

**Tuesday** NOUN
der Dienstag (PL die Dienstage) ◊ *on Tuesday* am Dienstag ◊ *every Tuesday* jeden Dienstag ◊ *last Tuesday* letzten Dienstag ◊ *next Tuesday* nächsten Dienstag
♦ **on Tuesdays** dienstags

**tug of war** NOUN
das Tauziehen

**tuition** NOUN
[1] der Unterricht
♦ **extra tuition** die Nachhilfestunden FEM PL ◊ *She receives extra tuition.* Sie bekommt Nachhilfestunden.
[2] die Studiengebühren FEM PL (*tuition fees*)

**tulip** NOUN
die Tulpe

**tumble dryer** NOUN
der Wäschetrockner (PL die Wäschetrockner)

**tummy** NOUN
der Bauch (PL die Bäuche) ◊ *I've got a sore tummy.* Ich habe Bauchschmerzen.

**tuna** NOUN
der Thunfisch (PL die Thunfische)

**tune** NOUN
die Melodie (*melody*)
♦ **to play in tune** richtig spielen
♦ **to sing out of tune** falsch singen

**Tunisia** NOUN
Tunesien NEUT
♦ **in Tunisia** in Tunesien

**tunnel** NOUN
der Tunnel (PL die Tunnel)
♦ **the Tunnel** (*Chunnel*) der Kanaltunnel

**Turk** NOUN
der Türke (GEN des Türken, PL die Türken)
die Türkin

**Turkey** NOUN
die Türkei
*Note that the definite article is used in German for countries which are feminine.*
♦ **from Turkey** aus der Türkei
♦ **in Turkey** in der Türkei
♦ **to Turkey** in die Türkei

**turkey** NOUN
der Truthahn (PL die Truthähne)

**Turkish** ADJECTIVE
see also **Turkish** NOUN
türkisch

**Turkish** NOUN
see also **Turkish** ADJECTIVE
das Türkische (*language*) (GEN des Türkischen)

**turn** NOUN
see also **turn** VERB
die Abbiegung (*in road*)
♦ **"no left turn"** "links abbiegen verboten"
♦ **Whose turn is it?** Wer ist an der Reihe?
♦ **It's my turn!** Ich bin an der Reihe!

to **turn** VERB
see also **turn** NOUN
[1] abbiegen (IMPERFECT bog ab, PERFECT ist abgebogen) ◊ *Turn right at the lights.* Biegen Sie an der Ampel rechts ab.
[2] (*become*)
werden (PRESENT wird, IMPERFECT wurde, PERFECT ist geworden) ◊ *to turn red* rot werden
♦ **to turn into something** sich in etwas verwandeln ◊ *The frog turned into a prince.* Der Frosch verwandelte sich in einen Prinzen.

to **turn back** VERB
umkehren (PERFECT ist umgekehrt) ◊ *We turned back.* Wir sind umgekehrt.

to **turn down** VERB
[1] (*offer*)
ablehnen (PERFECT hat abgelehnt)
[2] (*radio, TV*)
leiser stellen
[3] (*heating*)
herunterdrehen (PERFECT hat heruntergedreht)

to **turn off** VERB
[1] (*light, radio*)
ausmachen (PERFECT hat ausgemacht)
[2] (*tap*)
zudrehen (PERFECT hat zugedreht)
[3] (*engine*)
ausschalten (PERFECT hat ausgeschaltet)

to **turn on** VERB
[1] (*light, radio*)

**T**

☞

anmachen (PERFECT hat angemacht)
[2] (tap)
aufdrehen (PERFECT hat aufgedreht)
[3] (engine)
anlassen (PRESENT lässt an, IMPERFECT ließ an, PERFECT hat angelassen)

to **turn out** VERB
♦ **It turned out to be a mistake.** Es stellte sich heraus, dass das ein Fehler war.
♦ **It turned out that she was right.** Es stellte sich heraus, dass sie Recht hatte.

to **turn round** VERB
[1] (car)
umkehren (PERFECT ist umgekehrt) ◊ At the end of the street we turned round. Am Ende der Straße kehrten wir um.
[2] (person)
sich umdrehen (PERFECT hat sich umgedreht) ◊ I turned round. Ich drehte mich um.

to **turn up** VERB
[1] (arrive)
aufkreuzen (PERFECT ist aufgekreuzt)
[2] (heater)
höher stellen
[3] (radio, TV)
lauter machen

**turning** NOUN
♦ **It's the third turning on the left.** Es ist die dritte Straße links.
♦ **We took the wrong turning.** Wir sind falsch abgebogen.

**turnip** NOUN
die Steckrübe

**turquoise** ADJECTIVE
türkis (colour)

**turtle** NOUN
die Meeresschildkröte

**tutor** NOUN
(private teacher)
der Lehrer (PL die Lehrer)
die Lehrerin

**tuxedo** NOUN US
der Smoking (PL die Smokings)

**TV** NOUN
das Fernsehen

**tweezers** PL NOUN
die Pinzette SING ◊ a pair of tweezers eine Pinzette

**twelfth** ADJECTIVE
zwölfte ◊ the twelfth floor der zwölfte Stock
♦ **the twelfth of August** der zwölfte August

**twelve** NUMBER
zwölf ◊ She's twelve. Sie ist zwölf. ◊ at twelve o'clock um zwölf Uhr

**twentieth** ADJECTIVE
zwanzigste

♦ **the twentieth of August** der zwanzigste August

**twenty** NUMBER
zwanzig ◊ He's twenty. Er ist zwanzig.

**twice** ADVERB
zweimal
♦ **twice as much** doppelt so viel ◊ He gets twice as much pocket money as me. Er bekommt doppelt so viel Taschengeld wie ich.

**twin** NOUN
der Zwilling (PL die Zwillinge)
*der Zwilling is also used for women.*
♦ **my twin brother** mein Zwillingsbruder MASC
♦ **her twin sister** ihre Zwillingsschwester
♦ **identical twins** eineiige Zwillinge
♦ **a twin room** ein Doppelzimmer mit zwei Betten

**twinned** ADJECTIVE
♦ **Oxford is twinned with Bonn.** Oxford und Bonn sind Partnerstädte.

to **twist** VERB
[1] (bend)
biegen (IMPERFECT bog, PERFECT hat gebogen)
♦ **I've twisted my ankle.** Ich habe mir den Fuß vertreten.
[2] (distort)
verdrehen (PERFECT hat verdreht) ◊ You're twisting my words. Sie verdrehen meine Worte.

**twit** NOUN
der Trottel (informal) (PL die Trottel)
*der Trottel is also used for women.*

**two** NUMBER
zwei ◊ She's two. Sie ist zwei.

**type** NOUN
see also **type** VERB
die Art ◊ What type of camera have you got? Welche Art von Fotoapparat hast du?

to **type** VERB
see also **type** NOUN
Schreibmaschine schreiben (IMPERFECT schrieb Schreibmaschine, PERFECT hat Schreibmaschine geschrieben) ◊ Can you type? Kannst du Schreibmaschine schreiben?
♦ **to type a letter** einen Brief tippen

**typewriter** NOUN
die Schreibmaschine

**typical** ADJECTIVE
typisch ◊ That's just typical! Das ist typisch!

**tyre** NOUN
der Reifen (PL die Reifen) ◊ the tyre pressure der Reifendruck

# U

**UFO** NOUN (= *unidentified flying object*)
das <u>Ufo</u> (PL die Ufos) (= unbekanntes Flugobjekt)

**ugh** EXCLAMATION
<u>igitt</u>

**ugly** ADJECTIVE
<u>hässlich</u>

**UK** NOUN (= *United Kingdom*)
das <u>Vereinigte Königreich</u>
♦ **from the UK** aus dem Vereinigten Königreich
♦ **in the UK** im Vereinigten Königreich
♦ **to the UK** in das Vereinigte Königreich

**ulcer** NOUN
das <u>Geschwür</u> (PL die Geschwüre)

**Ulster** NOUN
<u>Ulster</u> NEUT
♦ **from Ulster** aus Ulster
♦ **in Ulster** in Ulster
♦ **to Ulster** nach Ulster

**ultimate** ADJECTIVE
<u>äußerste</u> ◊ *the ultimate challenge* die äußerste Herausforderung
♦ **It was the ultimate adventure.** Das war das große Abenteuer.

**ultimately** ADVERB
<u>schließlich</u> ◊ *Ultimately, it's your decision.* Schließlich ist es deine Entscheidung.

**umbrella** NOUN
⒈ der <u>Regenschirm</u> (PL die Regenschirme)
⒉ (*for sun*)
der <u>Sonnenschirm</u> (PL die Sonnenschirme)

**umlaut** NOUN
der <u>Umlaut</u> ◊ *The plural of 'Haus' is written with an umlaut.* Der Plural von "Haus" wird mit Umlaut gebildet.
♦ **a umlaut** ä
♦ **o umlaut** ö
♦ **u umlaut** ü

**umpire** NOUN
der <u>Schiedsrichter</u> (PL die Schiedsrichter)
die <u>Schiedsrichterin</u>

**UN** NOUN (= *United Nations*)
die <u>UN</u> PL

**unable** ADJECTIVE
♦ **to be unable to do something** etwas nicht tun können ◊ *I was unable to come.* Ich konnte nicht kommen.

**unacceptable** ADJECTIVE
<u>unannehmbar</u>

**unanimous** ADJECTIVE
<u>einstimmig</u> ◊ *a unanimous decision* ein einstimmiger Beschluss

**unavoidable** ADJECTIVE
<u>umvermeidlich</u>

**unaware** ADJECTIVE
♦ **to be unaware (1)** (*not know about*) nichts wissen ◊ *I was unaware of the regulations.* Ich wusste nichts von den Bestimmungen.
♦ **to be unaware (2)** (*not notice*) nicht merken ◊ *She was unaware that she was being filmed.* Sie merkte nicht, dass sie gefilmt wurde.

**unbearable** ADJECTIVE
<u>unerträglich</u>

**unbeatable** ADJECTIVE
<u>unschlagbar</u>

**unbelievable** ADJECTIVE
<u>unglaublich</u>

**unborn** ADJECTIVE
<u>ungeboren</u> ◊ *the unborn child* das ungeborene Kind

**unbreakable** ADJECTIVE
<u>unzerbrechlich</u>

**uncanny** ADJECTIVE
<u>unheimlich</u> ◊ *That's uncanny!* Das ist unheimlich!
♦ **an uncanny resemblance to** eine verblüffende Ähnlichkeit mit

**uncertain** ADJECTIVE
<u>ungewiss</u> ◊ *The future is uncertain.* Die Zukunft ist ungewiss.
♦ **to be uncertain about something** sich über etwas nicht im Klaren sein ◊ *I'm uncertain about her plans.* Ich bin mir über ihre Pläne nicht im Klaren.

**uncivilized** ADJECTIVE
<u>unzivilisiert</u>

**uncle** NOUN
der <u>Onkel</u> (PL die Onkel)

**uncomfortable** ADJECTIVE
<u>unbequem</u> ◊ *The seats are rather uncomfortable.* Die Sitze sind ziemlich unbequem.

**unconscious** ADJECTIVE
<u>bewusstlos</u>

**uncontrollable** ADJECTIVE
<u>unkontrollierbar</u>

**unconventional** ADJECTIVE
<u>unkonventionell</u>

**under** PREPOSITION
<u>unter</u>

*Use the accusative to express movement or a change of place. Use the dative when there is no change of place.*

◊ *The ball rolled under the table.* Der Ball rollte unter den Tisch. ◊ *The cat's under the table.* Die Katze ist unter dem Tisch. ◊ *children under ten* Kinder unter zehn
♦ **under there** da drunter ◊ *What's under there?* Was ist da drunter?

♦ **under twenty people** weniger als zwanzig Leute

**underage** ADJECTIVE
minderjährig

**undercover** ADJECTIVE, ADVERB
♦ **an undercover agent** (*secret agent*) ein Geheimagent MASC
♦ **She was working undercover.** Sie führte verdeckte Ermittlungen durch.

**underdog** NOUN
der Underdog (PL die Underdogs)
◊ *Arsenal were the underdogs on this occasion.* Arsenal waren diesmal die Underdogs.

to **underestimate** VERB
unterschätzen (PERFECT hat unterschätzt)
◊ *I underestimated her.* Ich habe sie unterschätzt.

to **undergo** VERB
sich unterziehen (*operation*) (IMPERFECT unterzog sich, PERFECT hat sich unterzogen)

**underground** ADJECTIVE, ADVERB
see also **underground** NOUN
1 unterirdisch ◊ *underground water pipes* unterirdische Wasserrohre
♦ **an underground car park** eine Tiefgarage
2 unter der Erde ◊ *Moles live underground.* Maulwürfe leben unter der Erde.

**underground** NOUN
see also **underground** ADJECTIVE
die U-Bahn ◊ *Is there an underground in Bonn?* Gibt es in Bonn eine U-Bahn?

to **underline** VERB
unterstreichen (IMPERFECT unterstrich, PERFECT hat unterstrichen)

**underneath** PREPOSITION, ADVERB
1 unter
*Use the accusative to express movement or a change of place. Use the dative when there is no change of place.*
◊ *I put it underneath that pile.* Ich habe es unter diesen Stapel gelegt. ◊ *It was hidden underneath the carpet.* Es war unter dem Teppich versteckt.
2 darunter ◊ *I got out of the car and looked underneath.* Ich stieg aus dem Auto aus und sah darunter.

**underpaid** ADJECTIVE
unterbezahlt ◊ *I'm underpaid.* Ich bin unterbezahlt.

**underpants** PL NOUN
die Unterhose SING ◊ *a pair of underpants* eine Unterhose

**underpass** NOUN
die Unterführung

**undershirt** NOUN US
das Unterhemd (PL die Unterhemden)

**underskirt** NOUN
der Unterrock (PL die Unterröcke)

to **understand** VERB

verstehen (IMPERFECT verstand, PERFECT hat verstanden) ◊ *Do you understand?* Verstehst du? ◊ *I don't understand this word.* Ich verstehe dieses Wort nicht. ◊ *Is that understood?* Ist das verstanden?

**understanding** ADJECTIVE
verständnisvoll ◊ *She's very understanding.* Sie ist sehr verständnisvoll.

**understood** VERB *see* **understand**

**undertaker** NOUN
der Beerdigungsunternehmer (PL die Beerdigungsunternehmer)
die Beerdigungsunternehmerin

**underwater** ADJECTIVE, ADVERB
unter Wasser ◊ *This sequence was filmed underwater.* Diese Sequenz wurde unter Wasser gefilmt.
♦ **an underwater camera** eine Unterwasserkamera

**underwear** NOUN
die Unterwäsche

**underwent** VERB *see* **undergo**

to **undo** VERB
aufmachen (PERFECT hat aufgemacht)

to **undress** VERB
sich ausziehen (*get undressed*) (IMPERFECT zog sich aus, PERFECT hat sich ausgezogen) ◊ *The doctor told me to get undressed.* Der Arzt bat mich, mich auszuziehen.

**uneconomic** ADJECTIVE
unrentabel

**unemployed** ADJECTIVE
arbeitslos ◊ *He's unemployed.* Er ist arbeitslos. ◊ *He's been unemployed for a year.* Er ist seit einem Jahr arbeitslos.
♦ **the unemployed** die Arbeitslosen MASC PL

**unemployment** NOUN
die Arbeitslosigkeit

**unexpected** ADJECTIVE
unerwartet ◊ *an unexpected visitor* ein unerwarteter Gast

**unexpectedly** ADVERB
überraschend ◊ *They arrived unexpectedly.* Sie sind überraschend gekommen.

**unfair** ADJECTIVE
unfair ◊ *It's unfair to girls.* Es ist Mädchen gegenüber unfair.

**unfamiliar** ADJECTIVE
unbekannt ◊ *I heard an unfamiliar voice.* Ich hörte eine unbekannte Stimme.

**unfashionable** ADJECTIVE
unmodern

**unfit** ADJECTIVE
nicht fit ◊ *I'm rather unfit at the moment.* Ich bin im Moment nicht sehr fit.

to **unfold** VERB
auseinander falten (PERFECT hat auseinander gefaltet) ◊ *She unfolded the map.* Sie faltete die Karte auseinander.

**unforgettable** ADJECTIVE
unvergesslich

**unfortunately** ADVERB
leider ◊ *Unfortunately, I arrived late.* Ich bin leider zu spät gekommen.

**unfriendly** ADJECTIVE
unfreundlich ◊ *The waiters are a bit unfriendly.* Die Kellner sind etwas unfreundlich.

**ungrateful** ADJECTIVE
undankbar

**unhappy** ADJECTIVE
unglücklich ◊ *He was very unhappy as a child.* Er war als Kind sehr unglücklich. ◊ *to look unhappy* unglücklich aussehen

**unhealthy** ADJECTIVE
ungesund

**uni** NOUN
die Uni (PL die Unis) ◊ *to go to uni* zur Uni gehen

**uniform** NOUN
die Uniform ◊ *the school uniform* die Schuluniform

> ℹ *School uniforms are virtually nonexistent in Germany.*

**uninhabited** ADJECTIVE
unbewohnt

**union** NOUN
die Gewerkschaft (*trade union*)

**Union Jack** NOUN
die britische Flagge

**unique** ADJECTIVE
einzigartig

**unit** NOUN
die Einheit ◊ *a unit of measurement* eine Maßeinheit
♦ *a kitchen unit* ein Kücheneinbauschrank MASC

**United Kingdom** NOUN
das Vereinigte Königreich
♦ *from the United Kingdom* aus dem Vereinigten Königreich
♦ *in the United Kingdom* im Vereinigten Königreich
♦ *to the United Kingdom* in das Vereinigte Königreich

**United Nations** PL NOUN
die Vereinten Nationen FEM PL

**United States** NOUN
die Vereinigten Staaten MASC PL
♦ *from the United States* aus den Vereinigten Staaten
♦ *in the United States* in den Vereinigten Staaten
♦ *to the United States* in die Vereinigten Staaten

**universe** NOUN
das Universum

**university** NOUN
die Universität ◊ *Do you want to go to university?* Möchtest du auf die Universität gehen? ◊ *Lancaster University* die Universität von Lancaster
♦ *She's at university.* Sie studiert.

**unleaded petrol** NOUN
das bleifreie Benzin

**unless** CONJUNCTION
es sei denn ◊ *unless he leaves* es sei denn, er geht ◊ *I won't come unless you phone me.* Ich komme nicht, es sei denn, du rufst an.

**unlike** PREPOSITION
im Gegensatz zu ◊ *Unlike him, I really enjoy flying.* Im Gegensatz zu ihm fliege ich wirklich gern.

**unlikely** ADJECTIVE
unwahrscheinlich ◊ *It's possible, but unlikely.* Es ist möglich, aber unwahrscheinlich.

**unlisted** ADJECTIVE US
♦ *to have an unlisted number* nicht im Telefonbuch stehen

to **unload** VERB
ausladen (PRESENT lädt aus, IMPERFECT lud aus, PERFECT hat ausgeladen) ◊ *We unloaded the car.* Wir haben das Auto ausgeladen.
♦ *The lorries go there to unload.* Die Lastwagen fahren dorthin um abzuladen.

to **unlock** VERB
aufschließen (IMPERFECT schloss auf, PERFECT hat aufgeschlossen) ◊ *He unlocked the door of the car.* Er schloss die Autotür auf.

**unlucky** ADJECTIVE
♦ *to be unlucky (1)* (*number, object*) Unglück bringen ◊ *They say thirteen is an unlucky number.* Es heißt, dass die Zahl dreizehn Unglück bringt.
♦ *to be unlucky (2)* (*person*) kein Glück haben ◊ *Did you win? – No, I was unlucky.* Hast du gewonnen? – Nein, ich habe kein Glück gehabt.

**unmarried** ADJECTIVE
unverheiratet (*person*) ◊ *an unmarried couple* ein unverheiratetes Paar
♦ *an unmarried mother* eine ledige Mutter

**unnatural** ADJECTIVE
unnatürlich

**unnecessary** ADJECTIVE
unnötig

**unofficial** ADJECTIVE
[1] inoffiziell (*meeting, leader*)
[2] wild (*strike*)

to **unpack** VERB
auspacken (*clothes, case*) (PERFECT hat ausgepackt) ◊ *I went to my room to unpack.* Ich ging auf mein Zimmer, um auszupacken.

**unpleasant** ADJECTIVE
unangenehm

to **unplug** VERB
**ausstecken** (PERFECT hat ausgesteckt)
◊ *She unplugged the TV.* Sie hat den
Fernseher ausgesteckt.

**unpopular** ADJECTIVE
**unbeliebt**

**unpredictable** ADJECTIVE
**unvorhersehbar** (*event*)

**unreal** ADJECTIVE
**unglaublich** (*incredible*) ◊ *It was unreal!*
Es war unglaublich!

**unrealistic** ADJECTIVE
**unrealistisch**

**unreasonable** ADJECTIVE
**unmöglich** ◊ *Her attitude was
completely unreasonable.* Ihre Haltung
war völlig unmöglich.

**unreliable** ADJECTIVE
**unzuverlässig** ◊ *He's completely
unreliable.* Er ist total unzuverlässig.

to **unroll** VERB
**aufrollen** (PERFECT hat aufgerollt)

**unsatisfactory** ADJECTIVE
**unbefriedigend**

to **unscrew** VERB
**aufschrauben** (PERFECT hat aufgeschraubt)
◊ *She unscrewed the top of the bottle.*
Sie schraubte den Flaschenverschluss
auf.

**unshaven** ADJECTIVE
**unrasiert**

**unskilled** ADJECTIVE
**ungelernt** ◊ *an unskilled worker* ein
ungelernter Arbeiter

**unstable** ADJECTIVE
[1] **nicht stabil** (*object*)
[2] **labil** (*person*)

**unsteady** ADJECTIVE
**unsicher** (*walk, voice*)
♦ **He was unsteady on his feet.** Er war
wackelig auf den Beinen.

**unsuccessful** ADJECTIVE
**erfolglos** (*attempt*) ◊ *an unsuccessful
artist* ein erfolgloser Künstler
♦ **to be unsuccessful in doing something**
keinen Erfolg bei etwas haben ◊ *He was
unsuccessful in getting a job.* Er hatte bei
der Arbeitssuche keinen Erfolg.

**unsuitable** ADJECTIVE
**ungeeignet** (*clothes, equipment*)

**untidy** ADJECTIVE
**unordentlich**

to **untie** VERB
[1] (*knot, parcel*)
**aufmachen** (PERFECT hat aufgemacht)
[2] (*animal*)
**losbinden** (IMPERFECT band los, PERFECT hat
losgebunden)

**until** PREPOSITION, CONJUNCTION
[1] **bis** ◊ *I waited until ten o'clock.* Ich
habe bis zehn Uhr gewartet.

♦ **until now** bis jetzt ◊ *It's never been a
problem until now.* Es war bis jetzt nie
ein Problem.
♦ **until then** bis dahin ◊ *Until then I'd never
been to Germany.* Bis dahin war ich noch
nie in Deutschland gewesen.
[2] **vor**
> *Use* **vor** *if the sentence you want to
translate contains a negative, such as
"not" or "never".*

◊ *It won't be ready until next week.* Es
wird nicht vor nächster Woche fertig
sein. ◊ *Until last year I'd never been to
Germany.* Vor letztem Jahr war ich noch
nie in Deutschland.

**unusual** ADJECTIVE
**ungewöhnlich** ◊ *an unusual shape* eine
ungewöhnliche Form ◊ *It's unusual to
get snow at this time of year.* Es ist
ungewöhnlich, dass es um diese
Jahreszeit schneit.

**unwilling** ADJECTIVE
♦ **to be unwilling to do something** nicht
gewillt sein, etwas zu tun ◊ *He was
unwilling to help me.* Er war nicht
gewillt, mir zu helfen.

to **unwind** VERB
**sich entspannen** (*relax*) (PERFECT hat sich
entspannt)

**unwise** ADJECTIVE
**unklug** (*person*) ◊ *That was rather
unwise of you.* Das war ziemlich unklug
von dir.

**unwound** VERB *see* **unwind**

to **unwrap** VERB
**auspacken** (PERFECT hat ausgepackt)
◊ *After the meal we unwrapped the
presents.* Nach dem Essen haben wir die
Geschenke ausgepackt.

**up** PREPOSITION, ADVERB
**auf**
> *Use the accusative to express movement
or a change of place. Use the dative
when there is no change of place.*

◊ *He drove me up the hill.* Er hat mich
den Berg hinaufgefahren. ◊ *the chapel
up on the hill* die Kapelle auf dem Berg
♦ **up here** hier oben
♦ **up there** dort oben
♦ **up north** oben im Norden
♦ **to be up** (*out of bed*) auf sein ◊ *We were
up at six.* Wir waren um sechs Uhr auf.
◊ *He's not up yet.* Er ist noch nicht auf.
♦ **What's up?** Was gibt's?
♦ **What's up with her?** Was ist los mit ihr?
♦ **to get up** (*in the morning*) aufstehen
◊ *What time do you get up?* Um wie viel
Uhr stehst du auf?
♦ **to go up** **(1)** hinauffahren ◊ *The bus went
up the hill.* Der Bus ist den Berg
hinaufgefahren.

◆**to go up (2)** (*on foot*) hinaufgehen ◊ *We went up the hill.* Wir sind den Berg hinaufgegangen.

◆**to go up to somebody** auf jemanden zugehen

◆**She came up to me.** Sie kam auf mich zu.

◆**up to** (*as far as*) bis ◊ *to count up to fifty* bis fünfzig zählen ◊ *up to three hours* bis zu drei Stunden ◊ *up to now* bis jetzt

◆**It's up to you.** Das ist dir überlassen.

*For other expressions with **up**, see the verbs **go, come, put, turn** etc.*

**upbringing** NOUN
die Erziehung

**uphill** ADVERB
bergauf

**upper sixth** NOUN
◆**the upper sixth** die dreizehnte Klasse
◊ *She's in the upper sixth.* Sie ist in der dreizehnten Klasse.

**upright** ADJECTIVE
◆**to stand upright** aufrecht stehen

**upset** NOUN
see also **upset** ADJECTIVE, VERB
◆**a stomach upset** eine Magenverstimmung

**upset** ADJECTIVE
see also **upset** NOUN, VERB
**1** gekränkt (*hurt*) ◊ *She was upset when he said that.* Sie fühlte sich gekränkt, als er das sagte.
**2** betrübt (*sad*) ◊ *I was very upset when my father died.* Ich war sehr betrübt, als mein Vater starb.
◆**an upset stomach** eine Magenverstimmung

to **upset** VERB
see also **upset** NOUN, ADJECTIVE
aufregen (PERFECT hat aufgeregt) ◊ *Don't say anything to upset her!* Sag nichts, was sie aufregen könnte.

**upside down** ADVERB
verkehrt herum ◊ *That painting is upside down.* Das Bild ist verkehrt herum.

**upstairs** ADVERB
oben ◊ *Where's your coat? – It's upstairs.* Wo ist der Mantel? – Er ist oben.
◆**the people upstairs** die Leute von oben
◆**to go upstairs** hinaufgehen

**uptight** ADJECTIVE
nervös (*nervous*) ◊ *She's really uptight.* Sie ist echt nervös.

**up-to-date** ADJECTIVE
**1** modern (*car, stereo*)
**2** aktuell (*information*) ◊ *an up-to-date timetable* ein aktueller Fahrplan
◆**to bring something up to date** etwas auf den neuesten Stand bringen

◆**to keep somebody up to date** jemanden auf dem Laufenden halten

**upwards** ADVERB
hinauf ◊ *to look upwards* hinaufsehen

**urgent** ADJECTIVE
dringend ◊ *Is it urgent?* Ist es dringend?

**urine** NOUN
der Urin

**US** SING NOUN
die USA PL
◆**from the US** aus den USA
◆**in the US** in den USA
◆**to the US** in die USA

**us** PRONOUN
uns ◊ *They saw us.* Sie haben uns gesehen. ◊ *They gave us a map.* Sie gaben uns eine Karte.
◆**Who is it? – It's us!** Wer ist da? – Wir sind's!

**USA** NOUN
die USA PL
◆**from the USA** aus den USA
◆**in the USA** in den USA
◆**to the USA** in die USA

**use** NOUN
see also **use** VERB
◆**It's no use.** Es hat keinen Zweck. ◊ *It's no use shouting, she's deaf.* Es hat keinen Zweck zu brüllen, sie ist taub. ◊ *It's no use, I can't do it.* Es hat keinen Zweck, ich kann's nicht.
◆**to make use of something** etwas benützen

to **use** VERB
see also **use** NOUN
benützen (PERFECT hat benützt) ◊ *Can we use a dictionary in the exam?* Können wir in der Prüfung ein Wörterbuch benützen?
◆**Can I use your phone?** Kann ich mal telefonieren?
◆**to use the toilet** auf die Toilette gehen
◆**to use up** aufbrauchen ◊ *We've used up all the paint.* Ich habe die ganze Farbe aufgebraucht.
◆**I used to live in London.** Ich habe früher mal in London gelebt.
◆**I used not to like maths, but now ...** Früher habe ich Mathe nicht gemocht, aber jetzt ...
◆**to be used to something** an etwas gewöhnt sein ◊ *He wasn't used to driving on the right.* Er war nicht daran gewöhnt, rechts zu fahren. ◊ *Don't worry, I'm used to it.* Keine Sorge, ich bin daran gewöhnt.
◆**a used car** ein Gebrauchtwagen MASC

**useful** ADJECTIVE
nützlich

**useless** ADJECTIVE
nutzlos ◊ *This map is just useless.* Diese Karte ist echt nutzlos.
◆**You're useless!** Du bist zu nichts zu gebrauchen!

**U**

☞

♦ **It's useless asking her!** Es ist zwecklos, sie zu fragen!

**user** NOUN
der <u>Benutzer</u> (PL die Benutzer)
die <u>Benutzerin</u>

**user-friendly** ADJECTIVE
<u>benutzerfreundlich</u>

**usual** ADJECTIVE
<u>üblich</u> ◊ *as usual* wie üblich

**usually** ADVERB
normalerweise ◊ *I usually get to school at about half past eight.* Ich bin normalerweise um halb neun in der Schule.

**utility room** NOUN
der <u>Abstellraum</u> (PL die Abstellräume)

**U-turn** NOUN
die <u>Wende</u>
♦ **to do a U-turn** wenden
♦ **"No U-turns"** "Wenden verboten"

# V

**vacancy** NOUN
[1] (*job*)
die <u>freie Stelle</u>
[2] (*room in hotel*)
das <u>freie Zimmer</u> (PL die freien Zimmer)
♦ **"Vacancies"** "Zimmer frei"
♦ **"No vacancies"** "Belegt"

**vacant** ADJECTIVE
[1] <u>frei</u> (*seat, job*)
[2] <u>leer stehend</u> (*building*)
[3] <u>leer</u> (*look*) ◊ *There was a vacant look in her face.* Sie hatte einen leeren Blick.

**vacation** NOUN [US]
[1] (*from school*)
die <u>Ferien</u> PL ◊ *They went on vacation to Mexico.* Sie haben in Mexiko Ferien gemacht.
[2] (*from work*)
der <u>Urlaub</u> (PL die Urlaube) ◊ *I have thirty days' vacation a year.* Ich habe dreißig Tage Urlaub im Jahr.

to **vaccinate** VERB
<u>impfen</u>

to **vacuum** VERB
<u>staubsaugen</u> (IMPERFECT staubsaugte, PERFECT hat gestaubsaugt) ◊ *to vacuum the hall* den Flur staubsaugen

**vacuum cleaner** NOUN
der <u>Staubsauger</u> (PL die Staubsauger)

**vagina** NOUN
die <u>Vagina</u> (PL die Vaginen)

**vague** ADJECTIVE
<u>vage</u>

**vain** ADJECTIVE
<u>eitel</u> ◊ *He's so vain!* Er ist so eitel!
♦ **in vain** umsonst

**Valentine card** NOUN
die <u>Valentinskarte</u>

> ℹ *Germans celebrate Valentine's Day by giving flowers rather than sending cards.*

**Valentine's Day** NOUN
der <u>Valentinstag</u> (PL die Valentinstage)

**valid** ADJECTIVE
<u>gültig</u> ◊ *This ticket is valid for three months.* Dieser Fahrschein ist drei Monate lang gültig.

**valley** NOUN
das <u>Tal</u> (PL die Täler)

**valuable** ADJECTIVE
<u>wertvoll</u> ◊ *a valuable picture* ein wertvolles Bild ◊ *valuable help* wertvolle Hilfe

**valuables** PL NOUN
die <u>Wertsachen</u> FEM PL ◊ *Don't take any valuables with you.* Nehmen Sie keine Wertsachen mit.

**value** NOUN
der <u>Wert</u> (PL die Werte)

**van** NOUN
der <u>Lieferwagen</u> (PL die Lieferwagen)

**vandal** NOUN
der <u>Vandale</u> (GEN des Vandalen, PL die Vandalen)
die <u>Vandalin</u>

**vandalism** NOUN
der <u>Vandalismus</u> (GEN des Vandalismus)

to **vandalize** VERB
<u>mutwillig zerstören</u> (PERFECT hat mutwillig zerstört)

**vanilla** NOUN
die <u>Vanille</u>
♦ **vanilla ice cream** das Vanilleeis

to **vanish** VERB
<u>verschwinden</u> (IMPERFECT verschwand, PERFECT ist verschwunden)

**variable** ADJECTIVE
<u>wechselhaft</u> (*mood, weather*)

**varied** ADJECTIVE
<u>abwechslungsreich</u> ◊ *a varied diet* eine abwechslungsreiche Kost ◊ *a varied life* ein abwechslungsreiches Leben
♦ **a varied selection** eine reichhaltige Auswahl

**variety** NOUN
[1] die <u>Abwechslung</u> ◊ *She likes variety in her life.* Sie hat gern Abwechslung im Leben.
[2] die <u>Sorte</u> (*kind*) ◊ *a new variety of rose* eine neue Rosensorte
♦ **a variety of books** eine Vielzahl von Büchern

**various** ADJECTIVE
<u>verschieden</u> ◊ *We visited various villages in the area.* Wir haben verschiedene Dörfer in der Gegend besucht.

to **vary** VERB
<u>schwanken</u> ◊ *It varies between two and four per cent.* Es schwankt zwischen zwei und vier Prozent.
♦ **It varies.** Das ist unterschiedlich.

**vase** NOUN
die <u>Vase</u>

**VAT** NOUN (= *value added tax*)
die <u>Mehrwertsteuer</u>

**VCR** NOUN (= *video cassette recorder*)
der <u>Videorekorder</u> (PL die Videorekorder)

**VDU** NOUN (= *visual display unit*)
der <u>Bildschirm</u> (PL die Bildschirme)

**veal** NOUN
das <u>Kalbfleisch</u>

**vegan** NOUN
der Veganer (PL die Veganer)
die Veganerin
◊ *I'm a vegan.* Ich bin Veganerin.

**vegetable** NOUN
die Gemüsesorte
♦ **vegetables** das Gemüse SING
♦ **vegetable soup** die Gemüsesuppe

**vegetarian** ADJECTIVE
| see also **vegetarian** NOUN |
vegetarisch ◊ *vegetarian lasagne* die vegetarische Lasagne
♦ **He's vegetarian.** Er ist Vegetarier.

**vegetarian** NOUN
| see also **vegetarian** ADJECTIVE |
der Vegetarier (PL die Vegetarier)
die Vegetarierin
◊ *She's a vegetarian.* Sie ist Vegetarierin.

**vehicle** NOUN
das Fahrzeug (PL die Fahrzeuge)

**vein** NOUN
die Vene

**velvet** NOUN
der Samt

**vending machine** NOUN
der Automat (GEN des Automaten, PL die Automaten)

**Venetian blind** NOUN
die Jalousie

**verb** NOUN
das Verb (PL die Verben)

**verdict** NOUN
das Urteil (PL die Urteile)

**vertical** ADJECTIVE
senkrecht

**vertigo** NOUN
das Schwindelgefühl
♦ **He had an attack of vertigo.** Ihm wurde schwindlig.

**very** ADVERB
sehr ◊ *very tall* sehr groß ◊ *not very interesting* nicht sehr interessant
♦ **very much (1)** sehr viel ◊ *He didn't eat very much.* Er hat nicht sehr viel gegessen.
♦ **very much (2)** (*like, love, respect*) sehr ◊ *I love her very much.* Ich liebe sie sehr.
♦ **Thank you very much.** Vielen Dank.

**vest** NOUN
[1] das Unterhemd (PL die Unterhemden)
[2] (*waistcoat*)
die Weste

**vet** NOUN
der Tierarzt (GEN des Tierarztes, PL die Tierärzte)
die Tierärztin
◊ *She's a vet.* Sie ist Tierärztin.

**via** PREPOSITION
über ◊ *We went to Munich via Ulm.* Wir sind über Ulm nach München gefahren.

**vicar** NOUN
der Pastor (PL die Pastoren)

die Pastorin
◊ *He's a vicar.* Er ist Pastor.

**vice** NOUN
der Schraubstock (*for holding things*) (PL die Schraubstöcke)

**vice versa** ADVERB
umgekehrt

**vicious** ADJECTIVE
[1] brutal ◊ *a vicious attack* ein brutaler Überfall
[2] bissig (*dog*)
[3] bösartig (*person*)
♦ **a vicious circle** ein Teufelskreis MASC

**victim** NOUN
das Opfer (PL die Opfer) ◊ *He was the victim of a mugging.* Er wurde das Opfer eines Straßenüberfalls.

**victory** NOUN
der Sieg (PL die Siege)

to **video** VERB
| see also **video** NOUN |
auf Video aufnehmen (PRESENT nimmt auf Video auf, IMPERFECT nahm auf Video auf, PERFECT hat auf Video aufgenommen)

**video** NOUN
| see also **video** VERB |
[1] (*film*)
das Video (PL die Videos) ◊ *to watch a video* ein Video ansehen ◊ *a video of my family on holiday* ein Video von meiner Familie in den Ferien ◊ *It's out on video.* Das gibt's als Video. ◊ *She lent me a video.* Sie hat mir ein Video geliehen.
[2] (*video recorder*)
der Videorekorder (PL die Videorekorder)
◊ *Have you got a video?* Habt ihr einen Videorekorder?
♦ **a video camera** eine Videokamera
♦ **a video cassette** eine Videokassette
♦ **a video game** ein Videospiel NEUT ◊ *He likes playing video games.* Er spielt gern Videospiele.
♦ **a video recorder** ein Videorekorder
♦ **a video shop** eine Videothek

**Vienna** NOUN
Wien NEUT
♦ **to Vienna** nach Wien

**Vietnamese** NOUN
| see also **Vietnamese** ADJECTIVE |
der Vietnamese (PL die Vietnamesen)
die Vietnamesin

**Vietnamese** ADJECTIVE
| see also **Vietnamese** NOUN |
vietnamesisch

**view** NOUN
[1] die Aussicht ◊ *There's an amazing view.* Man hat dort eine tolle Aussicht.
[2] die Meinung (*opinion*) ◊ *in my view* meiner Meinung nach

**viewer** NOUN
der Fernsehzuschauer (PL die Fernsehzuschauer)
die Fernsehzuschauerin

**viewpoint** NOUN
der Standpunkt (PL die Standpunkte)
**vile** ADJECTIVE
ekelhaft (*smell, food*)
**villa** NOUN
die Villa (PL die Villen)
**village** NOUN
das Dorf (PL die Dörfer)
**villain** NOUN
[1] (*criminal*)
der Verbrecher (PL die Verbrecher)
die Verbrecherin
[2] (*in film*)
der Bösewicht (PL die Bösewichte)
**vine** NOUN
die Weinrebe
**vinegar** NOUN
der Essig
**vineyard** NOUN
der Weinberg (PL die Weinberge)
**viola** NOUN
die Bratsche ◊ *I play the viola.* Ich spiele
Bratsche.
**violence** NOUN
die Gewalt
**violent** ADJECTIVE
[1] gewalttätig (*person, film*)
♦ **a violent crime** ein Gewaltverbrechen
NEUT
[2] gewaltig (*explosion*)
**violin** NOUN
die Geige ◊ *I play the violin.* Ich spiele
Geige.
**violinist** NOUN
der Geigenspieler (PL die Geigenspieler)
die Geigenspielerin
**virgin** NOUN
die Jungfrau ◊ *to be a virgin* Jungfrau
sein
**Virgo** NOUN
die Jungfrau ◊ *I'm Virgo.* Ich bin
Jungfrau.
**virtual reality** NOUN
die virtuelle Realität
**virus** NOUN
das Virus (GEN des Virus, PL die Viren)
**visa** NOUN
das Visum (PL die Visa)
**visible** ADJECTIVE
sichtbar
**visit** NOUN
see also **visit** VERB
[1] der Besuch (PL die Besuche) ◊ *my last
visit to my grandmother* mein letzter
Besuch bei meiner Großmutter
[2] (*to country*)
der Aufenthalt (PL die Aufenthalte) ◊ *Did
you enjoy your visit to Germany?* Hat
euer Deutschlandaufenthalt Spaß
gemacht?
to **visit** VERB
see also **visit** NOUN

[1] (*person*)
besuchen (PERFECT hat besucht)
[2] (*place*)
besichtigen (PERFECT hat besichtigt)
◊ *We'd like to visit the castle.* Wir würden
gern die Burg besichtigen.
**visitor** NOUN
der Besucher (PL die Besucher)
die Besucherin
♦ **to have a visitor** Besuch haben
**visual** ADJECTIVE
visuell
to **visualize** VERB
sich vorstellen (PERFECT hat sich
vorgestellt) ◊ *I tried to visualize his face.*
Ich versuchte, mir sein Gesicht
vorzustellen.
**vital** ADJECTIVE
äußerst wichtig ◊ *It's vital for you to
take these tablets.* Es ist äußerst wichtig,
dass du diese Tabletten nimmst.
♦ **of vital importance** äußerst wichtig
**vitamin** NOUN
das Vitamin (PL die Vitamine)
**vivid** ADJECTIVE
lebhaft ◊ *to have a vivid imagination*
eine lebhafte Fantasie haben
**vocabulary** NOUN
der Wortschatz (GEN des Wortschatzes, PL
die Wortschätze)
**vocational** ADJECTIVE
beruflich ◊ *vocational training* die
berufliche Ausbildung
♦ **a vocational college** eine Berufsschule
**vodka** NOUN
der Wodka (PL die Wodkas)
**voice** NOUN
die Stimme
**voice mail** NOUN
die Voicemail
**volcano** NOUN
der Vulkan (PL die Vulkane)
**volleyball** NOUN
der Volleyball ◊ *to play volleyball*
Volleyball spielen
**volt** NOUN
das Volt (GEN des Volt, PL die Volt)
**voltage** NOUN
die Spannung
**voluntary** ADJECTIVE
freiwillig (*contribution, statement*)
♦ **to do voluntary work** ehrenamtlich tätig
sein
**volunteer** NOUN
see also **volunteer** VERB
der Freiwillige (GEN des Freiwilligen, PL
die Freiwilligen)
die Freiwillige (GEN der Freiwilligen) ◊ *a
volunteer (man)* ein Freiwilliger
to **volunteer** VERB
see also **volunteer** NOUN

**V**

☞

◆**to volunteer to do something** sich
freiwillig melden, etwas zu tun
to **vomit** VERB
sich übergeben (PRESENT übergibt sich,
IMPERFECT übergab sich, PERFECT hat sich
übergeben)
**vote** NOUN
⎡ see also **vote** VERB ⎤
die Stimme
to **vote** VERB
⎡ see also **vote** NOUN ⎤

wählen ◊ to vote Labour Labour wählen
◆**to vote for somebody** für jemanden
stimmen ◊ I voted for Bill Clinton. Ich
habe für Bill Clinton gestimmt.
**voucher** NOUN
der Gutschein (PL die Gutscheine) ◊ a gift
voucher ein Geschenkgutschein
**vowel** NOUN
der Vokal (PL die Vokale)
**vulgar** ADJECTIVE
vulgär

# W

**wafer** NOUN
die Waffel

**wage** NOUN
der Lohn (PL die Löhne) ◊ He collected
his wages. Er hat seinen Lohn abgeholt.

**waist** NOUN
die Taille

**waistcoat** NOUN
die Weste

to **wait** VERB
warten
◆ **to wait for something** auf etwas warten
◊ We were waiting for the bus. Wir
haben auf den Bus gewartet.
◆ **to wait for somebody** auf jemanden
warten ◊ I'll wait for you. Ich warte auf
dich. ◊ Wait for me! Warte auf mich!
◆ **Wait a minute!** Einen Augenblick!
◆ **to keep somebody waiting** jemanden
warten lassen ◊ They kept us waiting for
hours. Sie haben uns stundenlang
warten lassen.
◆ **I can't wait for the holidays.** Ich kann die
Ferien kaum erwarten.
◆ **I can't wait to see him again.** Ich kann's
kaum erwarten, bis ich ihn wiedersehe.

to **wait up** VERB
aufbleiben (IMPERFECT blieb auf, PERFECT ist
aufgeblieben) ◊ My mum always waits
up till I get in. Meine Mutti bleibt immer
auf, bis ich nach Hause komme.

**waiter** NOUN
der Kellner (PL die Kellner)

**waiting list** NOUN
die Warteliste

**waiting room** NOUN
das Wartezimmer (PL die Wartezimmer)

**waitress** NOUN
die Kellnerin

to **wake up** VERB
aufwachen (PERFECT ist aufgewacht) ◊ I
woke up at six o'clock. Ich bin um sechs
Uhr aufgewacht.
◆ **to wake somebody up** jemanden wecken
◊ Would you wake me up at seven
o'clock? Könntest du mich um sieben
Uhr wecken?

**Wales** NOUN
Wales NEUT ◊ the Prince of Wales der Prinz
von Wales
◆ **from Wales** aus Wales
◆ **in Wales** in Wales
◆ **to Wales** nach Wales

to **walk** VERB
see also **walk** NOUN
1 gehen (IMPERFECT ging, PERFECT ist
gegangen) ◊ He walks fast. Er geht
schnell.
2 (go on foot)
zu Fuß gehen ◊ Are you walking or
going by bus? Geht ihr zu Fuß oder
nehmt ihr den Bus? ◊ We walked ten
kilometres. Wir sind zehn Kilometer zu
Fuß gegangen.
◆ **to walk the dog** mit dem Hund spazieren
gehen

**walk** NOUN
see also **walk** VERB
der Spaziergang (PL die Spaziergänge)
◊ to go for a walk einen Spaziergang
machen
◆ **It's ten minutes' walk from here.** Von
hier ist es zehn Minuten zu Fuß.

**walkie-talkie** NOUN
das Walkie-Talkie (PL die Walkie-Talkies)

**walking** NOUN
das Wandern
◆ **I did some walking in the Alps last
summer.** Ich bin letzten Sommer in den
Alpen gewandert.

**walking stick** NOUN
der Spazierstock (PL die Spazierstöcke)

**Walkman** ® NOUN
der Walkman ® (PL die Walkmen)

**wall** NOUN
1 die Mauer ◊ There is a wall round the
property. Um das Grundstück ist eine
Mauer.
2 die Wand (PL die Wände) ◊ They have
lots of pictures on the wall. Sie haben
viele Bilder an der Wand.

**wallet** NOUN
die Brieftasche

**wallpaper** NOUN
die Tapete

**walnut** NOUN
die Walnuss (PL die Walnüsse)

to **wander** VERB
◆ **to wander around** herumlaufen ◊ I just
wandered around for a while. Ich
bin einfach eine Zeit lang
herumgelaufen.

to **want** VERB
möchten (PRESENT mag, IMPERFECT mochte,
PERFECT hat gemocht) ◊ Do you want some
cake? Möchtest du Kuchen?
◆ **to want to do something** etwas tun
wollen ◊ I want to go to the cinema. Ich
will ins Kino gehen. ◊ What do you want
to do tomorrow? Was willst du morgen
machen?

**war** NOUN
der Krieg (PL die Kriege)

**ward** NOUN
der Krankensaal (room in hospital) (PL die
Krankensäle)

**warden** NOUN
(*of youth hostel*)
der Herbergsvater (*man*) (PL die
Herbergsväter)
die Herbergsmutter (*woman*) (PL die
Herbergsmütter)
**wardrobe** NOUN
der Kleiderschrank (*piece of furniture*) (PL
die Kleiderschränke)
**warehouse** NOUN
das Lagerhaus (GEN des Lagerhauses, PL
die Lagerhäuser)
**warm** ADJECTIVE
[1] warm ◊ *warm water* warmes Wasser
◊ *It's warm in here.* Hier drin ist es warm.
◊ *It's warmer in the kitchen.* In der Küche
ist es wärmer.
*When you talk about a person being*
*warm, you use the impersonal*
*construction.*
◊ *I'm warm.* Mir ist warm. ◊ *I'm too*
*warm.* Mir ist zu warm.
[2] herzlich ◊ *a warm welcome* ein
herzlicher Empfang
♦**to warm up (1)** (*for sport*) sich aufwärmen
♦**to warm up (2)** (*food*) aufwärmen ◊ *I'll*
*warm up some lasagne for you.* Ich
wärme dir etwas Lasagne auf.
♦**to warm over** aufwärmen

to **warn** VERB
warnen ◊ *Well, I warned you!* Ich habe
dich ja gewarnt.
♦**to warn somebody not to do something**
jemanden davor warnen, etwas zu tun
◊ *He warned me not to go there.* Er
warnte mich davor, dort hinzugehen.

**warning** NOUN
die Warnung
**Warsaw** NOUN
Warschau NEUT
♦**to Warsaw** nach Warschau
**wart** NOUN
die Warze
**was** VERB *see* **be**
**wash** NOUN
*see also* **wash** VERB
♦**to have a wash** sich waschen ◊ *I had a*
*wash.* Ich habe mich gewaschen.
♦**to give something a wash** etwas
waschen ◊ *He gave the car a wash.* Er
hat das Auto gewaschen.
to **wash** VERB
*see also* **wash** NOUN
[1] waschen (PRESENT wäscht, IMPERFECT
wusch, PERFECT hat gewaschen) ◊ *to wash*
*something* etwas waschen
[2] (*have a wash*)
sich waschen ◊ *Every morning I get up,*
*wash and get dressed.* Jeden Morgen
stehe ich auf, wasche mich und ziehe
mich an.

♦**to wash one's hands** sich die Hände
waschen ◊ *Where can I wash my hands?*
Wo kann ich mir die Hände waschen?
♦**to wash one's hair** sich die Haare
waschen ◊ *You should wash your hair.*
Du solltest dir die Haare waschen.
♦**to wash up** abwaschen
**washbasin** NOUN
das Waschbecken (PL die Waschbecken)
**washcloth** NOUN [US]
der Waschlappen (PL die Waschlappen)
**washing** NOUN
die Wäsche (*clothes*)
♦**Have you got any washing?** Hast du
etwas zu waschen?
♦**to do the washing** Wäsche waschen
**washing machine** NOUN
die Waschmaschine
**washing powder** NOUN
das Waschpulver (PL die Waschpulver)
**washing-up** NOUN
der Abwasch ◊ *to do the washing-up*
den Abwasch machen
**washing-up liquid** NOUN
das Spülmittel (PL die Spülmittel)
**wasn't** = **was not**
**wasp** NOUN
die Wespe
**waste** NOUN
*see also* **waste** VERB
[1] die Verschwendung ◊ *It's such a*
*waste!* Es ist so eine Verschwendung!
◊ *It's a waste of time.* Es ist
Zeitverschwendung!
[2] der Müll (*rubbish*) ◊ *nuclear waste* der
Atommüll
to **waste** VERB
*see also* **waste** NOUN
verschwenden (PERFECT hat
verschwendet) ◊ *I don't like wasting*
*money.* Ich verschwende nicht gerne
Geld. ◊ *There's no time to waste.* Wir
haben keine Zeit zu verschwenden.
**wastepaper basket** NOUN
der Papierkorb (PL die Papierkörbe)
**watch** NOUN
*see also* **watch** VERB
die Uhr
to **watch** VERB
*see also* **watch** NOUN
[1] ansehen (PRESENT sieht an, IMPERFECT sah an,
PERFECT hat angesehen) ◊ *Did you watch*
*that film last night?* Hast du dir gestern
Abend den Film angesehen?
♦**to watch television** fernsehen
[2] zusehen (PRESENT sieht zu, IMPERFECT sah
zu, PERFECT hat zugesehen) ◊ *Watch me!*
Sieh mir zu!
[3] (*keep a watch on*)
beobachten (PERFECT hat beobachtet)
◊ *The police were watching the house.*
Die Polizei beobachtete das Haus.

♦ **to watch out** aufpassen
♦ **Watch out! Pass auf!**

**water** NOUN
> see also **water** VERB

das Wasser (PL die Wasser)

to **water** VERB
> see also **water** NOUN

1 (*plant*)
gießen (IMPERFECT goss, PERFECT hat gegossen) ◊ *He was watering his tulips.* Er goss seine Tulpen.

2 (*garden*)
sprengen ◊ *We should water the lawn.* Wir sollten den Rasen sprengen.

**waterfall** NOUN
der Wasserfall (PL die Wasserfälle)

**watering can** NOUN
die Gießkanne

**watermelon** NOUN
die Wassermelone

**waterproof** ADJECTIVE
wasserdicht ◊ *Is this jacket waterproof?* Ist die Jacke wasserdicht?

**water-skiing** NOUN
das Wasserskifahren
♦ **to go water-skiing** Wasserski fahren

**wave** NOUN
> see also **wave** VERB

die Welle (*in water*)
♦ **We gave him a wave.** Wir haben ihm zugewinkt.

to **wave** VERB
> see also **wave** NOUN

winken
♦ **to wave at somebody** jemandem zuwinken ◊ *I waved at my friend.* Ich winkte meinem Freund zu.
♦ **to wave goodbye** zum Abschied winken ◊ *I waved her goodbye.* Ich habe ihr zum Abschied gewinkt.

**wavy** ADJECTIVE
wellig ◊ *wavy hair* welliges Haar

**wax** NOUN
das Wachs (GEN des Wachses)

**way** NOUN
1 die Art und Weise (*manner*) ◊ *That's no way to talk to your mother!* Das ist keine Art und Weise, mit deiner Mutter zu reden!
♦ **She looked at me in a strange way.** Sie sah mich sonderbar an.
♦ **This book tells you the right way to do it.** Dieses Buch erklärt, wie man es machen muss.
♦ **You're doing it the wrong way.** Du machst das falsch.
♦ **In a way you're right.** In gewisser Weise hast du Recht.
♦ **a way of life** eine Art zu leben
2 der Weg (*route*) ◊ *I don't know the way.* Ich kenne den Weg nicht.
♦ **on the way** unterwegs ◊ *We stopped for lunch on the way.* Wir haben unterwegs

angehalten und zu Mittag gegessen.
◊ *He's on his way.* Er ist unterwegs.
♦ **It's a long way.** Es ist weit. ◊ *Berlin is a long way from London.* Berlin ist weit von London entfernt.
♦ **Which way is it?** In welcher Richtung ist es?
♦ **The supermarket is this way.** Zum Supermarkt geht es in diese Richtung.
♦ **Do you know the way to the hotel?** Wissen Sie, wie man zum Hotel kommt?
♦ **"way in"** "Eingang"
♦ **"way out"** "Ausgang"
♦ **by the way ...** übrigens ...

**we** PRONOUN
wir ◊ *We're staying here for a week.* Wir sind eine Woche lang hier.

**weak** ADJECTIVE
schwach ◊ *Maths is my weakest subject.* In Mathe bin ich am schwächsten.

**wealthy** ADJECTIVE
reich

**weapon** NOUN
die Waffe

to **wear** VERB
tragen (*clothes*) (PRESENT trägt, IMPERFECT trug, PERFECT hat getragen) ◊ *She was wearing a hat.* Sie trug einen Hut. ◊ *She was wearing black.* Sie trug Schwarz.

**weather** NOUN
das Wetter ◊ *What was the weather like?* Wie war das Wetter? ◊ *The weather was lovely.* Das Wetter war herrlich.

**weather forecast** NOUN
die Wettervorhersage

**Web** NOUN
♦ **the Web** das Web

**webmaster** NOUN
der Webmaster (PL die Webmaster)
die Webmasterin

**web page** NOUN
die Webseite

**website** NOUN
die Website (PL die Websites)

**webzine** NOUN
das Web-Magazin (PL die Web-Magazine)

**we'd** = we had, = we would

**wedding** NOUN
die Hochzeit
♦ **wedding anniversary** der Hochzeitstag
♦ **wedding dress** das Brautkleid
♦ **wedding ring** der Ehering

**Wednesday** NOUN
der Mittwoch (PL die Mittwoche) ◊ *on Wednesday* am Mittwoch ◊ *every Wednesday* jeden Mittwoch ◊ *last Wednesday* letzten Mittwoch ◊ *next Wednesday* nächsten Mittwoch
♦ **on Wednesdays** mittwochs

**weed** NOUN

**W**

☞

das <u>Unkraut</u> ◇ *The garden's full of weeds.* Der Garten ist voller Unkraut.
**week** NOUN
die <u>Woche</u> ◇ *last week* letzte Woche ◇ *every week* jede Woche ◇ *next week* nächste Woche ◇ *in a week's time* in einer Woche
◆ **a week on Friday** Freitag in einer Woche
**weekday** NOUN
◆ **on weekdays** werktags
**weekend** NOUN
das <u>Wochenende</u> (PL die Wochenenden) ◇ *at the weekend* am Wochenende ◇ *at weekends* am Wochenende ◇ *last weekend* letztes Wochenende ◇ *next weekend* nächstes Wochenende
to **weigh** VERB
<u>wiegen</u> (IMPERFECT wog, PERFECT hat gewogen) ◇ *How much do you weigh?* Wie viel wiegst du? ◇ *First, weigh the flour.* Wiegen Sie zuerst das Mehl.
◆ **to weigh oneself** sich wiegen
**weight** NOUN
das <u>Gewicht</u> (PL die Gewichte)
◆ **to lose weight** abnehmen
◆ **to put on weight** zunehmen
**weightlifter** NOUN
der <u>Gewichtheber</u> (PL die Gewichtheber)
**weightlifting** NOUN
das <u>Gewichtheben</u>
**weird** ADJECTIVE
<u>sonderbar</u>
**welcome** NOUN
| *see also* **welcome** VERB |
◆ **They gave her a warm welcome.** Sie haben sie herzlich empfangen.
◆ **Welcome!** Herzlich willkommen! ◇ *Welcome to Germany!* Herzlich willkommen in Deutschland!
to **welcome** VERB
| *see also* **welcome** NOUN |
◆ **to welcome somebody** jemanden begrüßen
◆ **Thank you! – You're welcome!** Danke! – Bitte!
**well** ADJECTIVE, ADVERB
| *see also* **well** NOUN |
⓵ <u>gut</u> ◇ *You did that really well.* Das hast du wirklich gut gemacht.
◆ **to do well** gut sein ◇ *She's doing really well at school.* Sie ist wirklich gut in der Schule.
◆ **to be well** (*in good health*) gesund sein ◇ *I'm not very well at the moment.* Ich bin im Moment nicht gesund.
◆ **Get well soon!** Gute Besserung!
◆ **Well done!** Gut gemacht!
⓶ <u>na ja</u> ◇ *It's enormous! Well, quite big anyway.* Es ist riesig! Na ja, jedenfalls ziemlich groß.
◆ **as well** auch ◇ *We worked hard, but we had some fun as well.* Wir haben hart gearbeitet, aber auch Spaß

gehabt.
**well** NOUN
| *see also* **well** ADJECTIVE |
der <u>Brunnen</u> (PL die Brunnen)
**we'll** = **we will**
**well-behaved** ADJECTIVE
<u>artig</u>
**well-dressed** ADJECTIVE
<u>gut angezogen</u>
**wellingtons** PL NOUN
die <u>Gummistiefel</u> MASC PL
**well-known** ADJECTIVE
<u>bekannt</u> ◇ *a well-known film star* ein bekannter Filmstar
**well-off** ADJECTIVE
<u>gut situiert</u>
**Welsh** ADJECTIVE
| *see also* **Welsh** NOUN |
<u>walisisch</u>
◆ **He's Welsh.** Er ist Waliser.
◆ **She's Welsh.** Sie ist Waliserin.
◆ **Welsh people** die Waliser MASC PL
**Welsh** NOUN
| *see also* **Welsh** ADJECTIVE |
das <u>Walisisch</u> (*language*) (GEN des Walisischen)
**Welshman** NOUN
der <u>Waliser</u> (PL die Waliser)
**Welshwoman** NOUN
die <u>Waliserin</u>
**went** VERB *see* **go**
**were** VERB *see* **be**
**we're** = **we are**
**weren't** = **were not**
**west** NOUN
| *see also* **west** ADJECTIVE |
der <u>Westen</u> ◇ *in the west* im Westen
**west** ADJECTIVE, ADVERB
| *see also* **west** NOUN |
◆ **the west coast** die Westküste
◆ **a west wind** ein Westwind MASC
<u>nach Westen</u> ◇ *We were travelling west.* Wir fuhren nach Westen.
◆ **west of** westlich von ◇ *Stroud is west of Oxford.* Stroud liegt westlich von Oxford.
◆ **the West Country** der Südwesten Englands
**western** NOUN
| *see also* **western** ADJECTIVE |
der <u>Western</u> (*film*) (GEN des Western, PL die Western)
**western** ADJECTIVE
| *see also* **western** NOUN |
<u>westlich</u>
◆ **the western part of the island** der westliche Teil der Insel
◆ **Western Europe** Westeuropa NEUT
**West Indian** ADJECTIVE
| *see also* **West Indian** NOUN |
<u>westindisch</u>
◆ **He's West Indian.** Er ist aus Westindien.

**West Indian** NOUN

> see also **West Indian** ADJECTIVE

(person)

der Westinder (PL die Westinder)

die Westinderin

**West Indies** PL NOUN

die Westindischen Inseln FEM PL

♦**in the West Indies** auf den
Westindischen Inseln

**wet** ADJECTIVE

nass ◊ wet clothes nasse Kleider ◊ to get
wet nass werden

♦**wet weather** regnerisches Wetter

♦**dripping wet** klatschnass

♦**It was wet all week.** Es hat die ganze
Woche geregnet.

**wet suit** NOUN

der Neoprenanzug (PL die
Neoprenanzüge)

**we've** = we have

**whale** NOUN

der Wal (PL die Wale)

**what** ADJECTIVE, PRONOUN

1 was ◊ What are you doing? Was tust
du? ◊ What did you say? Was hast du
gesagt? ◊ What is it? Was ist das?
◊ What's the matter? Was ist los?
◊ What happened? Was ist passiert?
◊ I saw what happened. Ich habe
gesehen, was passiert ist. ◊ I heard
what he said. Ich habe gehört, was er
gesagt hat.

♦**What?** Was?

2 welcher ◊ What hat do you like best?
Welcher Hut gefällt dir am besten?
welche ◊ What colour is it? Welche
Farbe hat es?
welches ◊ What book do you want?
Welches Buch möchten Sie?
welche ◊ What subjects are you
studying? Welche Fächer studierst du?

♦**What's the capital of Finland?** Wie heißt
die Hauptstadt von Finnland?

♦**What a mess!** So ein Chaos!

**wheat** NOUN

der Weizen

**wheel** NOUN

das Rad (PL die Räder) ◊ the steering
wheel das Lenkrad

**wheelchair** NOUN

der Rollstuhl (PL die Rollstühle)

**when** ADVERB, CONJUNCTION

1 wann ◊ When did he go? Wann ist er
gegangen?

2 als ◊ She was reading when I came in.
Sie las, als ich hereinkam.

**where** ADVERB, CONJUNCTION

wo ◊ Where's Emma today? Wo ist
Emma heute? ◊ Where do you live? Wo
wohnst du? ◊ a shop where you can buy
gardening tools ein Geschäft, wo man
Gartengeräte kaufen kann

♦**Where are you from?** Woher sind Sie?

♦**Where are you going?** Wohin gehst du?

> Be careful not to translate **where** by **wer**.

**whether** CONJUNCTION

ob ◊ I don't know whether to go or not.
Ich weiß nicht, ob ich gehen soll oder
nicht.

**which** ADJECTIVE, PRONOUN

1 welcher ◊ Which coat do you like
better? Welcher Mantel gefällt dir
besser?
welche ◊ Which CD did you buy? Welche
CD hast du gekauft?
welches ◊ Which book do you want?
Welches Buch willst du?
welche ◊ Which shoes should I wear?
Welche Schuhe soll ich anziehen?

> When asking **which one** use **welcher** or
> **welche** or **welches**, depending on
> whether the noun is masculine, feminine
> or neuter.

♦**I know his brother. – Which one?** Ich
kenne seinen Bruder. – Welchen?

♦**I know his sister. – Which one?** Ich kenne
seine Schwester. – Welche?

♦**I took one of your books. – Which one?**
Ich habe eines deiner Bücher
genommen. – Welches?

♦**Which would you like?** Welches
möchtest du?

♦**Which of these are yours?** Welche davon
gehören dir?

> In relative clauses use **der**, **die** or **das**,
> depending on the gender of the noun
> **which** refers to.

2 der ◊ the film which is on now der
Film, der gerade läuft
die ◊ the CD which is playing now die
CD, die gerade läuft
das ◊ the book which I am reading das
Buch, das ich lese
die ◊ the sweets which I ate die
Süßigkeiten, die ich gegessen habe

**while** CONJUNCTION

> see also **while** NOUN

während ◊ You hold the torch while I
look inside. Halt du die Taschenlampe,
während ich hineinsehe. ◊ Isobel is very
dynamic, while Kay is more laid-back.
Isobel ist sehr dynamisch, während Kay
eher lässig ist.

**while** NOUN

> see also **while** CONJUNCTION

die Weile ◊ after a while nach einer
Weile

♦**a while ago** vor einer Weile ◊ He was
here a while ago. Er war vor einer Weile
hier.

♦**for a while** eine Zeit lang ◊ I lived in
London for a while. Ich habe eine Zeit
lang in London gelebt.

♦**quite a while** ziemlich lange ◊ That
happened quite a while ago. Das ist
schon ziemlich lange her. ◊ I haven't

**W**

☞

*seen him for quite a while.* Ich habe ihn schon ziemlich lange nicht mehr gesehen.

**whip** NOUN
see also **whip** VERB
die Peitsche

to **whip** VERB
see also **whip** NOUN
[1] peitschen ◊ *She whipped her horse.* Sie peitschte ihr Pferd.
[2] (*eggs*)
schlagen (PRESENT schlägt, IMPERFECT schlug, PERFECT hat geschlagen)

**whipped cream** NOUN
die Schlagsahne

**whisk** NOUN
der Schneebesen (PL die Schneebesen)

**whiskers** PL NOUN
die Schnurrhaare NEUT PL

**whisky** NOUN
der Whisky (PL die Whiskys)

to **whisper** VERB
flüstern

**whistle** NOUN
see also **whistle** VERB
die Pfeife
♦ **The referee blew his whistle.** Der Schiedsrichter hat gepfiffen.

to **whistle** VERB
see also **whistle** NOUN
pfeifen (IMPERFECT pfiff, PERFECT hat gepfiffen)

**white** ADJECTIVE
weiß ◊ *He's got white hair.* Er hat weiße Haare.
♦ **white wine** der Weißwein
♦ **white bread** das Weißbrot
♦ **white coffee** der Kaffee mit Milch
♦ **a white man** ein Weißer
♦ **a white woman** eine Weiße
♦ **white people** die Weißen MASC PL

**Whitsun** NOUN
das Pfingsten (GEN des Pfingsten, PL die Pfingsten)

**who** PRONOUN
[1] wer ◊ *Who said that?* Wer hat das gesagt? ◊ *Who is Lafontaine?* Wer ist Lafontaine?

*In relative clauses use **der**, **die** or **das**, depending on the gender of the noun **who** refers to.*

[2] der ◊ *the man who saw us* der Mann, der uns gesehen hat ◊ *the man who we saw* der Mann, den wir gesehen haben
die ◊ *the woman who saw us* die Frau, die uns gesehen hat ◊ *the woman who we saw* die Frau, die wir gesehen haben
das ◊ *the child who saw us* das Kind, das uns gesehen hat ◊ *the child who we saw* das Kind, das wir gesehen haben

die ◊ *the people who saw us* die Leute, die uns gesehen haben
*Be careful not to translate **who** by **wo**.*

**whole** ADJECTIVE
see also **whole** NOUN
ganz ◊ *the whole class* die ganze Klasse ◊ *the whole afternoon* den ganzen Nachmittag ◊ *the whole world* die ganze Welt

**whole** NOUN
see also **whole** ADJECTIVE
♦ **The whole of Wales was affected.** Ganz Wales war davon betroffen.
♦ **on the whole** im Großen und Ganzen

**wholemeal** ADJECTIVE
♦ **wholemeal bread** das Vollkornbrot
♦ **wholemeal flour** das Vollkornmehl

**wholewheat** ADJECTIVE US
♦ **wholewheat bread** das Vollkornbrot

**whom** PRONOUN
wen ◊ *Whom did you see?* Wen hast du gesehen?
♦ **the man to whom I spoke** der Mann, mit dem ich gesprochen habe
♦ **the woman to whom I spoke** die Frau, mit der ich gesprochen habe

**whose** PRONOUN, ADJECTIVE
wessen ◊ *Whose book is this?* Wessen Buch ist das?
♦ **Whose is this?** Wem gehört das?
♦ **I know whose it is.** Ich weiß, wem das gehört.
♦ **the man whose picture was in the paper** der Mann, dessen Bild in der Zeitung war
♦ **the woman whose picture was in the paper** die Frau, deren Bild in der Zeitung war
♦ **the girl whose picture was in the paper** das Mädchen, dessen Bild in der Zeitung war

**why** ADVERB
warum ◊ *Why did you do that?* Warum hast du das getan? ◊ *Tell me why.* Sag mir warum. ◊ *I've never been to Germany. – Why not?* Ich war noch nie in Deutschland. – Warum nicht? ◊ *All right, why not?* Also gut, warum auch nicht?
♦ **That's why he did it.** Deshalb hat er es getan.

**wicked** ADJECTIVE
[1] böse (*evil*)
[2] geil (*informal: really great*)

**wicket** NOUN
das Mal (*stumps*) (PL die Male)

**wide** ADJECTIVE, ADVERB
breit ◊ *a wide road* eine breite Straße
♦ **wide open** weit offen ◊ *The door was wide open.* Die Tür stand weit offen. ◊ *The windows were wide open.* Die Fenster waren weit offen.
♦ **wide awake** hellwach

**widow** NOUN
die Witwe ◊ *She's a widow.* Sie ist
Witwe.

**widower** NOUN
der Witwer (PL die Witwer) ◊ *He's a
widower.* Er ist Witwer.

**width** NOUN
die Breite

**wife** NOUN
die Frau ◊ *She's his wife.* Sie ist seine
Frau.

**wig** NOUN
die Perücke

**wild** ADJECTIVE
[1] wild ◊ *a wild animal* ein wildes
Tier
[2] verrückt (*crazy*) ◊ *She's a bit wild.* Sie
ist ein bisschen verrückt.

**wild card** NOUN
die Wildcard (PL die Wildcards)

**wildlife** NOUN
die Tierwelt ◊ *I'm interested in
wildlife.* Ich interessiere mich für die
Tierwelt.

**will** NOUN
see also **will** VERB
das Testament (PL die Testamente) ◊ *He
left me some money in his will.* Er
hat mir in seinem Testament Geld
vermacht.
♦ **He came of his own free will.** Er ist
freiwillig gekommen.

**will** VERB
see also **will** NOUN

*In German the present tense is often
used to express somebody's intention to
do something.*

◊ *I'll show you your room.* Ich zeige
Ihnen Ihr Zimmer. ◊ *I'll give you a hand.*
Ich helfe dir.
♦ **Will you help me?** Hilfst du mir?
♦ **Will you wash up? – No, I won't.**
Wäschst du ab? – Nein.

*Use the German future tense when
referring to the more distant future.*

◊ *I will come back one day.* Ich werde
eines Tages zurückkommen. ◊ *It
won't take long.* Es wird nicht lange
dauern.
♦ **That will be the postman.** Das wird der
Briefträger sein.
♦ **Will you be quiet!** Werdet ihr wohl still
sein!

**willing** ADJECTIVE
♦ **to be willing to do something** bereit
sein, etwas zu tun

to **win** VERB
see also **win** NOUN
gewinnen (IMPERFECT gewann, PERFECT hat
gewonnen) ◊ *Did you win?* Hast du
gewonnen?
♦ **to win a prize** einen Preis bekommen

**win** NOUN
see also **win** VERB
der Sieg (PL die Siege)

to **wind** VERB
see also **wind** NOUN
[1] wickeln (*rope, wool, wire*) ◊ *He wound
the rope round the tree.* Er wickelte das
Seil um den Baum.
[2] sich schlängeln (*river, path*) ◊ *The
road winds through the valley.* Die
Straße schlängelt sich durch das
Tal.

**wind** NOUN
see also **wind** VERB
der Wind (PL die Winde) ◊ *There was
a strong wind.* Es wehte ein starker
Wind.
♦ **a wind instrument** ein Blasinstrument
NEUT
♦ **wind power** die Windkraft

**windmill** NOUN
die Windmühle

**window** NOUN
das Fenster (PL die Fenster) ◊ *to break a
window* ein Fenster kaputtmachen
◊ *a broken window* ein kaputtes
Fenster
♦ **a shop window** ein Schaufenster

**windscreen** NOUN
die Windschutzscheibe

**windscreen wiper** NOUN
der Scheibenwischer (PL die
Scheibenwischer)

**windshield** NOUN US
die Windschutzscheibe

**windshield wiper** NOUN US
der Scheibenwischer (PL die
Scheibenwischer)

**windy** ADJECTIVE
windig (*place*) ◊ *It's windy.* Es ist windig.

**wine** NOUN
der Wein (PL die Weine) ◊ *a bottle of
wine* eine Flasche Wein ◊ *a glass of wine*
ein Glas Wein
♦ **white wine** der Weißwein
♦ **red wine** der Rotwein
♦ **a wine bar** eine Weinstube
♦ **a wine glass** ein Weinglas NEUT
♦ **the wine list** die Getränkekarte

**wing** NOUN
der Flügel (PL die Flügel)

to **wink** VERB
♦ **to wink at somebody** jemandem
zublinzeln ◊ *He winked at me.* Er hat mir
zugeblinzelt.

**winner** NOUN
der Sieger (PL die Sieger)
die Siegerin

**winning** ADJECTIVE
♦ **the winning team** die Siegermannschaft
♦ **the winning goal** das entscheidende
Tor

**winter** NOUN

**W**

☞

der <u>Winter</u> (PL die Winter) ◊ *in winter* im Winter

**winter sports** PL NOUN
der <u>Wintersport</u> SING

to **wipe** VERB
<u>abwischen</u> (PERFECT hat abgewischt)
♦ **to wipe one's feet** sich die Füße abstreifen ◊ *Wipe your feet!* Streif dir die Füße ab!
♦ **to wipe up** aufwischen

**wire** NOUN
der <u>Draht</u> (PL die Drähte)

**wisdom tooth** NOUN
der <u>Weisheitszahn</u> (PL die Weisheitszähne)

**wise** ADJECTIVE
<u>weise</u>

to **wish** VERB
> see also **wish** NOUN

♦ **to wish for something** sich etwas wünschen ◊ *What more could I wish for?* Was mehr könnte ich mir wünschen?
♦ **to wish to do something** etwas tun möchten ◊ *I wish to make a complaint.* Ich möchte mich beschweren.
♦ **I wish you were here!** Ich wünschte, du wärst da!
♦ **I wish you'd told me!** Wenn du mir das doch nur gesagt hättest!

**wish** NOUN
> see also **wish** VERB

der <u>Wunsch</u> (PL die Wünsche)
♦ **to make a wish** sich etwas wünschen ◊ *You can make a wish.* Du darfst dir etwas wünschen.
♦ **"best wishes"** (*on greetings card*) "Alles Gute"
♦ **"with best wishes, Kathy"** "alles Liebe, Kathy"

**wit** NOUN
der <u>geistreiche Humor</u> (*humour*)

**with** PREPOSITION
1 <u>mit</u> ◊ *Come with me.* Komm mit mir. ◊ *a woman with blue eyes* eine Frau mit blauen Augen
♦ **Fill the jug with water.** Tu Wasser in den Krug.
♦ **He walks with a stick.** Er geht am Stock.
2 <u>bei</u> (*at the home of*) ◊ *We stayed with friends.* Wir haben bei Freunden übernachtet.
3 <u>vor</u> ◊ *green with envy* grün vor Neid ◊ *to shake with fear* vor Angst zittern

**within** PREPOSITION
♦ **The shops are within easy reach.** Die Geschäfte sind schnell zu erreichen.
♦ **within the week** innerhalb dieser Woche

**without** PREPOSITION
<u>ohne</u> ◊ *without a coat* ohne einen Mantel ◊ *without speaking* ohne etwas zu sagen

**witness** NOUN
der <u>Zeuge</u> (GEN des Zeugen, PL die Zeugen)

die <u>Zeugin</u>
◊ *There were no witnesses.* Es gab keine Zeugen.
♦ **witness box** der Zeugenstand
♦ **witness stand** der Zeugenstand

**witty** ADJECTIVE
<u>geistreich</u>

**wives** PL NOUN *see* **wife**

**woke up** VERB *see* **wake up**

**woken up** VERB *see* **wake up**

**wolf** NOUN
der <u>Wolf</u> (PL die Wölfe)

**woman** NOUN
die <u>Frau</u>
♦ **a woman doctor** eine Ärztin

**won** VERB *see* **win**

to **wonder** VERB
<u>sich fragen</u> ◊ *I wonder why she said that.* Ich frage mich, warum sie das gesagt hat. ◊ *I wonder what that means.* Ich frage mich, was das bedeutet.
♦ **I wonder where Caroline is.** Wo Caroline wohl ist?

**wonderful** ADJECTIVE
<u>wunderbar</u>

**won't** = **will not**

**wood** NOUN
1 (*timber*)
das <u>Holz</u> (PL die Hölzer) ◊ *It's made of wood.* Es ist aus Holz.
2 (*forest*)
der <u>Wald</u> (PL die Wälder) ◊ *We went for a walk in the wood.* Wir sind im Wald spazieren gegangen.

**wooden** ADJECTIVE
<u>hölzern</u>
♦ **a wooden chair** ein Holzstuhl MASC

**woodwork** NOUN
das <u>Schreinern</u> ◊ *Dieter's hobby is woodwork.* Schreinern ist Dieters Hobby.

**wool** NOUN
die <u>Wolle</u> ◊ *It's made of wool.* Es ist aus Wolle.

**word** NOUN
das <u>Wort</u> (PL die Wörter) ◊ *a difficult word* ein schwieriges Wort
♦ **What's the word for "shop" in German?** Wie heißt "shop" auf Deutsch?
♦ **in other words** in anderen Worten
♦ **to have a word with somebody** mit jemandem reden
♦ **the words** (*lyrics*) der Text SING ◊ *I really like the words of this song.* Der Text dieses Liedes gefällt mir wirklich gut.

**word processing** NOUN
die <u>Textverarbeitung</u>

**word processor** NOUN
das <u>Textverarbeitungssystem</u> (PL die Textverarbeitungssysteme)

**wore** VERB *see* **wear**

**work** NOUN
> see also **work** VERB

die Arbeit ◊ *She's looking for work.* Sie sucht Arbeit. ◊ *He's at work at the moment.* Er ist zur Zeit bei der Arbeit. ◊ *It's hard work.* Das ist harte Arbeit.

◆**to be off work** (*sick*) krank sein

◆**He's out of work.** Er ist arbeitslos.

to **work** VERB

> see also **work** NOUN

1 (*person*)

arbeiten ◊ *She works in a shop.* Sie arbeitet in einem Laden. ◊ *to work hard* hart arbeiten

2 (*machine, plan*)

funktionieren (PERFECT hat funktioniert) ◊ *The heating isn't working.* Die Heizung funktioniert nicht. ◊ *My plan worked perfectly.* Mein Plan hat prima funktioniert.

◆**to work out (1)** (*exercise*) trainieren ◊ *I work out twice a week.* Ich trainiere zweimal pro Woche.

◆**to work out (2)** (*turn out*) klappen ◊ *In the end it worked out really well.* Am Ende hat es richtig gut geklappt.

◆**to work something out** (*figure out*) auf etwas kommen ◊ *I just couldn't work it out.* Ich bin einfach nicht darauf gekommen.

◆**It works out at ten pounds each.** Das macht für jeden zehn Pfund.

**worker** NOUN

der Arbeiter (PL die Arbeiter)
die Arbeiterin
◊ *He's a factory worker.* Er ist Fabrikarbeiter.

◆**She's a good worker.** Sie macht gute Arbeit.

**work experience** NOUN

das Praktikum (PL die Praktika) ◊ *I'm going to do work experience in a factory.* Ich mache ein Praktikum in einer Fabrik.

**working-class** ADJECTIVE

der Arbeiterklasse ◊ *a working-class family* eine Familie der Arbeiterklasse

**workman** NOUN

der Arbeiter (PL die Arbeiter)

**works** NOUN

das Werk (*factory*) (PL die Werke)

**worksheet** NOUN

das Arbeitsblatt (PL die Arbeitsblätter)

**workshop** NOUN

die Werkstatt (PL die Werkstätten)

◆**a drama workshop** ein Theaterworkshop MASC

**workspace** NOUN

der Arbeitsplatz (GEN des Arbeitsplatzes, PL die Arbeitsplätze)

**workstation** NOUN

der Arbeitsplatzcomputer (PL die Arbeitsplatzcomputer)

**world** NOUN

die Welt

◆**He's the world champion.** Er ist der Weltmeister.

**World Wide Web** NOUN

◆**the World Wide Web** das World Wide Web

**worm** NOUN

der Wurm (PL die Würmer)

**worn** VERB *see* **wear**

**worn** ADJECTIVE

abgenutzt ◊ *The carpet is a bit worn.* Der Teppich ist etwas abgenutzt.

◆**worn out** (*tired*) erschöpft

**worried** ADJECTIVE

besorgt ◊ *She's very worried.* Sie ist sehr besorgt.

◆**to be worried about something** sich wegen etwas Sorgen machen ◊ *I'm worried about the exam.* Ich mache mir wegen der Prüfung Sorgen.

◆**to look worried** besorgt aussehen ◊ *She looks a bit worried.* Sie sieht etwas besorgt aus.

to **worry** VERB

sich Sorgen machen ◊ *You worry too much.* Du machst dir zu viele Sorgen.

◆**Don't worry!** Keine Sorge!

**worse** ADJECTIVE, ADVERB

schlechter ◊ *My results were bad, but his were worse.* Meine Noten waren schlecht, aber seine waren noch schlechter. ◊ *I'm feeling worse.* Mir geht es schlechter.

◆**It was even worse than that.** Es war sogar noch schlimmer.

to **worship** VERB

anbeten (PERFECT hat angebetet) ◊ *He worships his girlfriend.* Er betet seine Freundin an.

**worst** ADJECTIVE

> see also **worst** NOUN

◆**the worst (1)** der schlechteste ◊ *the worst student in the class* der schlechteste Schüler der Klasse

◆**the worst (2)** die schlechteste ◊ *He got the worst mark in the whole class.* Er hat von der ganzen Klasse die schlechteste Note bekommen.

◆**the worst (3)** das schlechteste ◊ *the worst report I've ever had* das schlechteste Zeugnis, das ich je hatte

◆**my worst enemy** mein schlimmster Feind

◆**Maths is my worst subject.** In Mathe bin ich am schlechtesten.

**worst** NOUN

> see also **worst** ADJECTIVE

das Schlimmste (GEN des Schlimmsten) ◊ *The worst of it is that ...* Das Schlimmste daran ist, dass ...

◆**at worst** schlimmstenfalls

◆**if the worst comes to the worst** schlimmstenfalls

**worth** ADJECTIVE

**W**

☞

♦ **to be worth** wert sein ◊ *It's worth a lot of money.* Es ist sehr viel Geld wert. ◊ *How much is it worth?* Wie viel ist das wert?

♦ **It's worth it.** Das lohnt sich. ◊ *Is it worth it?* Lohnt es sich? ◊ *It's not worth it.* Das lohnt sich nicht.

**would** VERB
♦ **Would you like ...?** Möchtest du ...?
◊ *Would you like a biscuit?* Möchtest du einen Keks? ◊ *Would you like to go and see a film?* Möchtest du ins Kino gehen?

♦ **Would you close the door please?** Würden Sie bitte die Tür zumachen?

♦ **I'd like ...** Ich würde gern ... ◊ *I'd like to go to America.* Ich würde gern nach Amerika fahren.

♦ **Shall we go and see a film? – Yes, I'd like that.** Sollen wir ins Kino gehen? – Au ja!

♦ **I said I would do it.** Ich sagte, ich würde es tun.

♦ **If you asked him he'd do it.** Wenn du ihn fragen würdest, würde er es tun.

♦ **If you had asked him he would have done it.** Wenn du ihn gefragt hättest, hätte er es getan.

**wouldn't** = **would not**

**wound** VERB *see* **wind**

to **wound** VERB
box: *see also* **wound** NOUN
verwunden (PERFECT hat verwundet) ◊ *He was wounded in the leg.* Er wurde am Bein verwundet.

**wound** NOUN
box: *see also* **wound** VERB
die Wunde

to **wrap** VERB
einpacken (PERFECT hat eingepackt)
◊ *She's wrapping her Christmas presents.* Sie packt ihre Weihnachtsgeschenke ein.

♦ **Can you wrap it for me please?** (*in shop*) Können Sie es mir bitte in Geschenkpapier einpacken?

♦ **to wrap up** einpacken

**wrapping paper** NOUN
das Geschenkpapier

**wreck** NOUN
box: *see also* **wreck** VERB
das Wrack (PL die Wracks) ◊ *That car is a wreck!* Das Auto ist ein Wrack. ◊ *After the exam I was a complete wreck.* Nach der Prüfung war ich ein totales Wrack.

to **wreck** VERB
box: *see also* **wreck** NOUN
[1] (*building*)
zerstören (PERFECT hat zerstört) ◊ *The explosion wrecked the whole house.* Die Explosion hat das ganze Haus zerstört.
[2] (*car*)
kaputtfahren (PRESENT fährt kaputt, IMPERFECT fuhr kaputt, PERFECT hat kaputtgefahren) ◊ *He's wrecked his car.* Er hat sein Auto kaputtgefahren.

[3] (*plan, holiday*)
verderben (PRESENT verdirbt, IMPERFECT verdarb, PERFECT hat verdorben) ◊ *Our trip was wrecked by bad weather.* Das schlechte Wetter hat uns den Ausflug verdorben.

**wreckage** NOUN
[1] (*of vehicle*)
das Wrack (PL die Wracks)
[2] (*of building*)
die Trümmer PL

**wrestler** NOUN
der Ringer (PL die Ringer)
die Ringerin

**wrestling** NOUN
das Ringen ◊ *His hobby is wrestling.* Ringen ist sein Hobby.

**wrinkled** ADJECTIVE
faltig

**wrist** NOUN
das Handgelenk (PL die Handgelenke)

to **write** VERB
schreiben (IMPERFECT schrieb, PERFECT hat geschrieben) ◊ *to write a letter* einen Brief schreiben

♦ **to write to somebody** jemandem schreiben ◊ *I'm going to write to her in German.* Ich werde ihr auf Deutsch schreiben.

♦ **to write down** aufschreiben ◊ *I wrote down the address.* Ich habe die Adresse aufgeschrieben. ◊ *Can you write it down for me, please?* Können Sie es mir bitte aufschreiben?

**writer** NOUN
der Schriftsteller (PL die Schriftsteller)
die Schriftstellerin
◊ *She's a writer.* Sie ist Schriftstellerin.

**writing** NOUN
die Schrift ◊ *I can't read your writing.* Ich kann deine Schrift nicht lesen.

♦ **in writing** schriftlich

**written** VERB *see* **write**

**wrong** ADJECTIVE, ADVERB
[1] falsch (*incorrect*) ◊ *The information they gave us was wrong.* Die Information, die sie uns gegeben haben, war falsch. ◊ *the wrong answer* die falsche Antwort

♦ **You've got the wrong number.** Sie haben sich verwählt.

[2] unrecht (*morally bad*) ◊ *I think fox hunting is wrong.* Ich meine, dass Fuchsjagden unrecht sind.

♦ **to be wrong** (*mistaken*) Unrecht haben ◊ *You're wrong about that.* Sie haben da Unrecht.

♦ **to do something wrong** etwas falsch machen ◊ *You've done it wrong.* Du hast das falsch gemacht. ◊ *Have I done something wrong?* Habe ich etwas falsch gemacht?

♦ **to go wrong** (*plan*) schief gehen ◊ *The robbery went wrong and they got caught.* Der Überfall ist schief gegangen, und man hat sie gefasst.

♦ **What's wrong?** Was ist los?

♦ **What's wrong with her?** Was ist mit ihr los?

**wrote** VERB *see* **write**

**WWW** ABBREVIATION (= *World Wide Web*)

♦ **the WWW** das WWW

**W**

# X

**Xmas** NOUN (= *Christmas*)
 **Weihnachten** NEUT
to **X-ray** VERB
 see also **X-ray** NOUN
 röntgen ◇ *They X-rayed my arm.* Sie

haben meinen Arm geröntgt.
**X-ray** NOUN
 see also **X-ray** VERB
 die Röntgenaufnahme
 ◆ **to have an X-ray** geröntgt werden

# Y

**yacht** NOUN
1 (*sailing boat*)
das Segelboot (PL die Segelboote)
2 (*luxury motorboat*)
die Jacht

**yard** NOUN
der Hof (*of building*) (PL die Höfe) ◊ *in the yard* auf dem Hof

to **yawn** VERB
gähnen

**year** NOUN
das Jahr (PL die Jahre) ◊ *last year* letztes Jahr ◊ *next year* nächstes Jahr ◊ *to be fifteen years old* fünfzehn Jahre alt sein
♦ **an eight-year-old child** ein achtjähriges Kind

> ℹ *In Germany secondary schools, years are counted from the* **fünfte Klasse** *(youngest) to the* **dreizehnte Klasse** *(oldest).*

◊ *the first year* die fünfte Klasse ◊ *the fifth year* die neunte Klasse ◊ *She's in the fifth year.* Sie ist in der neunten Klasse.
♦ **He's a first-year.** Er ist in der fünften Klasse.

to **yell** VERB
schreien (IMPERFECT schrie, PERFECT hat geschrien)

**yellow** ADJECTIVE
gelb

**yes** ADVERB
1 ja ◊ *Do you like it? – Yes.* Gefällt es dir? – Ja. ◊ *Would you like a cup of tea? – Yes please.* Möchtest du eine Tasse Tee? – Ja bitte.
2 doch

> *Use* **doch** *to contradict a negative statement or question.*

◊ *Don't you like it? – Yes!* Gefällt es dir nicht? – Doch! ◊ *You're not Swiss, are you? – Yes I am!* Sie sind nicht Schweizer, oder? – Doch, ich bin Schweizer. ◊ *That's not true. – Yes it is!* Das ist nicht wahr. – Doch!

**yesterday** ADVERB
gestern ◊ *yesterday morning* gestern früh ◊ *yesterday afternoon* gestern Nachmittag ◊ *yesterday evening* gestern Abend ◊ *all day yesterday* gestern den ganzen Tag
♦ **the day before yesterday** vorgestern

**yet** ADVERB
1 noch ◊ *It has yet to be proved that ...* Es muss noch bewiesen werden, dass ...

2 schon (*in questions*) ◊ *Has the murderer been caught yet?* Ist der Mörder schon gefasst worden?
♦ **not yet** noch nicht ◊ *It's not finished yet.* Es ist noch nicht fertig.
♦ **not as yet** noch nicht ◊ *There's no news as yet.* Es gibt noch keine Nachricht.
♦ **Have you finished yet?** Bist du fertig?

**yield** EXCLAMATION [US]
Vorfahrt achten (*on road sign*)

**yob** NOUN
der Rowdy (PL die Rowdys)

**yoghurt** NOUN
der Joghurt (PL die Joghurt)

**yolk** NOUN
das Eigelb (PL die Eigelbe)

**you** PRONOUN

> *Only use* **du** *when speaking to one person, and when the person is your own age or younger. Use* **ihr** *for several people of your own age or younger. If in doubt use the polite form* **Sie***.*

1 Sie (*polite form, singular and plural*) ◊ *Do you like football?* Mögen Sie Fußball? ◊ *Can I help you?* Kann ich Ihnen behilflich sein? ◊ *I saw you yesterday.* Ich habe Sie gestern gesehen. ◊ *It's for you.* Das ist für Sie.
2 du (*familiar singular*) ◊ *Do you like football?* Magst du Fußball? ◊ *She's younger than you.* Sie ist jünger als du. ◊ *I know you.* Ich kenne dich. ◊ *I gave it you.* Ich habe es dir gegeben. ◊ *It's for you.* Es ist für dich. ◊ *I'll come with you.* Ich komme mit dir mit.
3 ihr (*familiar plural*) ◊ *Do you two like football?* Mögt ihr beiden Fußball? ◊ *I told you to be quiet.* Ich habe euch gesagt, ihr sollt still sein. ◊ *This is for you two.* Es ist für euch beide. ◊ *Can I come with you?* Kann ich mit euch mitkommen?

**young** ADJECTIVE
jung ◊ *young people* junge Leute

**younger** ADJECTIVE
jünger ◊ *He's younger than me.* Er ist jünger als ich. ◊ *my younger brother* mein jüngerer Bruder ◊ *my younger sister* meine jüngere Schwester

**youngest** ADJECTIVE
jüngste ◊ *his youngest brother* sein jüngster Bruder ◊ *She's the youngest.* Sie ist die Jüngste.

**your** ADJECTIVE

> *Only use* **dein** *when speaking to one person, and when the person is your own age or younger. For several people of your own age or younger use* **euer***. If in doubt use the polite form* **Ihr***.*

Y

☞

**1** Ihr (*polite form, singular and plural*)
◊ *your father* Ihr Vater ◊ *your mother*
Ihre Mutter ◊ *your house* Ihr Haus ◊ *your seats* Ihre Plätze
**2** dein (*familiar singular*) ◊ *your brother*
dein Bruder ◊ *your sister* deine
Schwester ◊ *your book* dein Buch ◊ *your parents* deine Eltern
**3** euer (*familiar plural*) ◊ *your father* euer
Vater ◊ *your mother* eure Mutter ◊ *your car* euer Auto ◊ *your teachers* eure
Lehrer
*Do not use Ihr, dein or euer with parts of the body.*
◊ *Would you like to wash your hands?*
Möchten Sie sich die Hände waschen?
◊ *Do you want to wash your hair?*
Möchtest du dir die Haare waschen?
◊ *You two, go upstairs and brush your teeth.* Ihr beide geht nach oben und putzt euch die Zähne.

**yours** PRONOUN
*Only use deiner/deine/deines when talking to one person of your own age or younger. Use euer/eure/eures when talking to several people of your own age or younger. If in doubt use the polite form Ihrer/Ihre/Ihres.*
**1** (*polite form, singular and plural*)
Ihrer ◊ *That's a nice coat. Is it yours?* Das ist ein hübscher Mantel. Ist es Ihrer?
Ihre ◊ *What a pretty jacket. Is it yours?*
Was für eine hübsche Jacke. Ist das Ihre?
Ihres ◊ *I like that car. Is it yours?* Das Auto gefällt mir. Ist es Ihres?
Ihre ◊ *my parents and yours* meine Eltern und Ihre
◆ **Is this yours?** Gehört das Ihnen? ◊ *This book is yours.* Das Buch gehört Ihnen.
◆ **Yours sincerely, ...** Mit freundlichen Grüßen ...
**2** (*familiar singular*)
deiner ◊ *I've lost my pen. Can I use yours?* Ich habe meinen Schreiber verlegt. Kann ich deinen benützen?
deine ◊ *Nice jacket. Is it yours?* Hübsche Jacke. Ist das deine?
deines ◊ *I like that car. Is it yours?* Das Auto gefällt mir. Ist das deines?
deine ◊ *my parents and yours* meine Eltern und deine ◊ *My hands are dirty, yours are clean.* Meine Hände sind schmutzig, deine sind sauber.
◆ **Is this yours?** Gehört das dir? ◊ *This book is yours.* Das Buch gehört dir.
◊ *Whose is this? – It's yours.* Wem gehört

das? – Es gehört dir.
**3** (*familiar plural*)
euer ◊ *My computer is broken. Can I use yours?* Mein Computer ist kaputt. Kann ich euren benutzen?
eure ◊ *I haven't got a typewriter. Can I use yours?* Ich habe keine Schreibmaschine. Kann ich eure benutzen?
eures ◊ *Our house is bigger than yours.* Unser Haus ist größer als eures.
eure ◊ *our parents and yours* unsere Eltern und eure
◆ **Is this yours?** Gehört das euch? ◊ *These books are yours.* Diese Bücher gehören euch. ◊ *Whose is it? – It's yours.* Wem gehört das? – Es gehört euch.

**yourself** PRONOUN
*Only use dich/dir when talking to one person of your own age or younger. If in doubt use the polite form sich.*
**1** sich (*polite form*) ◊ *Have you hurt yourself?* Haben Sie sich verletzt? ◊ *Tell me about yourself!* Erzählen Sie etwas von sich!
**2** dich (*familiar form*) ◊ *Have you hurt yourself?* Hast du dich verletzt?
**3** dir (*familiar form*) ◊ *Tell me about yourself!* Erzähl mir etwas von dir! ◊ *If you are not happy with yourself ...* Wenn du mit dir selbst nicht zufrieden bist ...
**4** selbst
◆ **Do it yourself! (1)** Machen Sie es selbst!
◆ **Do it yourself! (2)** Mach's selbst!

**yourselves** PRONOUN
*Only use euch when talking to people of your own age or younger. If in doubt use the polite form sich.*
**1** sich (*polite form*) ◊ *Did you enjoy yourselves?* Haben Sie sich amüsiert?
**2** euch (*familiar form*) ◊ *Did you enjoy yourselves?* Habt ihr euch amüsiert?
**3** selbst
◆ **Did you make it yourselves? (1)** Haben Sie es selbst gemacht?
◆ **Did you make it yourselves? (2)** Habt ihr es selbst gemacht?

**youth club** NOUN
das <u>Jugendzentrum</u> (PL die Jugendzentren)
**youth hostel** NOUN
die <u>Jugendherberge</u>
**Yugoslavia** NOUN
<u>Jugoslawien</u> NEUT
◆ **in the former Yugoslavia** im ehemaligen Jugoslawien

# Z

**zany** ADJECTIVE
irre komisch ◊ *a zany film* ein irre komischer Film

**zebra** NOUN
das Zebra (PL die Zebras)

**zebra crossing** NOUN
der Zebrastreifen (PL die Zebrastreifen)

**zero** NOUN
die Null

**Zimbabwe** NOUN
Simbabwe NEUT ◊ *in Zimbabwe* in Simbabwe

**Zimmer frame** ® NOUN
der Gehapparat (PL die Gehapparate)

**zip** NOUN
der Reißverschluss (GEN des Reißverschlusses, PL die Reißverschlüsse)

**zip code** NOUN US
die Postleitzahl

**zip drive** NOUN
das Zip-Laufwerk (PL die Zip-Laufwerke)

**zipper** NOUN US
der Reißverschluss (GEN des Reißverschlusses, PL die Reißverschlüsse)

**zit** NOUN
der Pickel (PL die Pickel)

**zodiac** NOUN
der Tierkreis (GEN des Tierkreises)
♦ **the signs of the zodiac** die Sternzeichen

**zone** NOUN
die Zone

**zoo** NOUN
der Zoo (PL die Zoos)

**zoom lens** NOUN
das Zoomobjektiv (PL die Zoomobjektive)

**zucchini** PL NOUN US
die Zucchini PL

# LIST OF NEW GERMAN SPELLINGS

▶ GERMAN SPELLING REFORM

In July 1996 all German-speaking countries signed a declaration concerning the reform of German spelling, with the result that a number of new spelling rules were established. These new German spelling rules are now taught in all schools, and are widely used throughout the German-speaking world. In the dictionary we have shown the new spellings where they occur as headwords on the German-English side or as translations on the English-German side. In addition, where the old spelling of a word does not come immediately before or after the new spelling in the dictionary text, the old spelling has been shown in its alphabetical position and a reference has been given to tell you where you can find the new spelling and its translation e.g. **rauh** is cross-referred to **rau**. Of course, you will still come across old spellings in other texts, so to help you recognize them, we have given here a list of new spellings, together with the corresponding old spellings. Words appearing in the dictionary which were previously spelt as one word, and which are now spelt as two words e.g. **fertigmachen – fertig machen** have also been included in this list.

| NEW | OLD | NEW | OLD |
|---|---|---|---|
| Abend | abend | entlässt | entläßt |
| Abfluss | Abfluß | Entschluss | Entschluß |
| Abschlussprüfung | Abschlußprüfung | Erdgeschoss | Erdgeschoß |
| allein stehend | alleinstehend | Erdnuss | Erdnuß |
| allzu oft | allzuoft | Erdnussbutter | Erdnußbutter |
| allzu viel | allzuviel | Erfolg versprechend | erfolgversprechend |
| Anlass | Anlaß | essbar | eßbar |
| Anschluss | Anschluß | Esskastanie | Eßkastanie |
| Ass | As | Esslöffel | Eßlöffel |
| auf sein | aufsein | esst | eßt |
| aufschlussreich | aufschlußreich | Esszimmer | Eßzimmer |
| Aufsehen erregend | aufsehenerregend | Fairness | Fairneß |
| auseinander falten | auseinanderfalten | fallen lassen | fallenlassen |
| auseinander halten | auseinanderhalten | Fass | Faß |
| auseinander nehmen | auseinandernehmen | fertig bringen | fertigbringen |
| Ausschluss | Ausschluß | fertig machen | fertigmachen |
| Ausschuss | Ausschuß | Fitnesszentrum | Fitneßzentrum |
| aus sein | aussein | floss | floß |
| Balletttänzer | Ballettänzer | Fluss | Fluß |
| Balletttänzerin | Ballettänzerin | Flüsschen | Flüßchen |
| Bass | Baß | Flussufer | Flußufer |
| bekannt geben | bekanntgeben | Föhn/Fön | Fön |
| bekannt machen | bekanntmachen | föhnen | fönen |
| Beschluss | Beschluß | frisst | frißt |
| bewusst | bewußt | Gebiss | Gebiß |
| bewusstlos | bewußtlos | gefangen nehmen | gefangennehmen |
| Bewusstlosigkeit | Bewußtlosigkeit | gefasst | gefaßt |
| Bewusstsein | Bewußtsein | geheim halten | geheimhalten |
| biss | biß | gemusst | gemußt |
| Biss | Biß | genau genommen | genaugenommen |
| bisschen | bißchen | genoss | genoß |
| blass | blaß | Genuss | Genuß |
| Brennnessel | Brennessel | genüsslich | genüßlich |
| Cashewnuss | Cashewnuß | geschrien | geschrien/geschrieen |
| dabei sein | dabeisein | Gewinn bringend | gewinnbringend |
| dahinter kommen | dahinterkommen | gewiss | gewiß |
| da sein | dasein | Gewissheit | Gewißheit |
| dass | daß | gewusst | gewußt |
| durcheinander bringen | durcheinanderbringen | goss | goß |
| durchnässt | durchnäßt | grässlich | gräßlich |
| Einfluss | Einfluß | Gräuel | Greuel |
| Engpass | Engpaß | Grundriss | Grundriß |

# GERMAN SPELLING REFORM

**gut aussehend** → **Regenguss**

| NEW | OLD | NEW | OLD |
|---|---|---|---|
| gut aussehend | gutaussehend | misst | mißt |
| gut gehen | gutgehen | misstrauen | mißtrauen |
| gut gemeint | gutgemeint | Misstrauen | Mißtrauen |
| gut tun | guttun | misstrauisch | mißtrauisch |
| Haselnuss | Haselnuß | Missverständnis | Mißverständnis |
| Hass | Haß | missverstehen | mißverstehen |
| hässlich | häßlich | Mopp | Mop |
| Hexenschuss | Hexenschuß | muss | muß |
| Imbiss | Imbiß | musst | mußt |
| Imbisshalle | Imbißhalle | müsst | müßt |
| Imbissstand | Imbißstand | musste | mußte |
| Imbissstube | Imbißstube | müsste | müßte |
| iss | iß | mussten | mußten |
| isst | ißt | müssten | müßten |
| Känguru | Känguruh | musstest | mußtest |
| Karamell | Karamel | müsstest | müßtest |
| Karamellbonbon | Karamelbonbon | musstet | mußtet |
| kennen lernen | kennenlernen | müsstet | müßtet |
| Kokosnuss | Kokosnuß | Nachlass | Nachlaß |
| Kompass | Kompaß | Nacht | nacht |
| Kompromiss | Kompromiß | nahe gelegen | nahegelegen |
| Kontrabass | Kontrabaß | nahe legen | nahelegen |
| Kuss | Kuß | nahe liegend | naheliegend |
| lässt | läßt | näher kommen | näherkommen |
| leicht fallen | leichtfallen | nass | naß |
| leicht machen | leichtmachen | Nebenfluss | Nebenfluß |
| lieb haben | liebhaben | nummerieren | numerieren |
| liegen bleiben | liegenbleiben | Nuss | Nuß |
| liegen lassen | liegenlassen | Obergeschoss | Obergeschoß |
| Maß halten | maßhalten | offen bleiben | offenbleiben |
| Messgerät | Meßgerät | Ölmessstab | Ölmeßstab |
| missbilligen | mißbilligen | Pass | Paß |
| Missbrauch | Mißbrauch | Passkontrolle | Paßkontrolle |
| missbrauchen | mißbrauchen | Passwort | Paßwort |
| Misserfolg | Mißerfolg | patschnass | patschnaß |
| Missgeschick | Mißgeschick | pflichtbewusst | pflichtbewußt |
| misshandeln | mißhandeln | Portmonee/Portemonnaie | Portemonnaie |
| misslang | mißlang | Prozess | Prozeß |
| misslingen | mißlingen | Rad fahren | radfahren |
| misslingt | mißlingt | Rassenhass | Rassenhaß |
| misslungen | mißlungen | rau | rauh |
| missmutig | mißmutig | Regenguss | Regenguß |

| NEW | OLD | NEW | OLD |
|---|---|---|---|
| Reisepass | Reisepaß | tschüss | tschüs |
| Reißverschluss | Reißverschluß | Tunfisch/Thunfisch | Thunfisch |
| riss | riß | übel nehmen | übelnehmen |
| Riss | Riß | Überdruss | Überdruß |
| Rollladen | Rolladen | Überschuss | Überschuß |
| Rosskastanie | Roßkastanie | übrig bleiben | übrigbleiben |
| Russland | Rußland | übrig lassen | übriglassen |
| sauber machen | saubermachen | Umriss | Umriß |
| schief gehen | schiefgehen | unbewusst | unbewußt |
| Schifffahrt | Schiffahrt | ungewiss | ungewiß |
| Schikoree/Chicorée | Chicorée | Ungewissheit | Ungewißheit |
| schiss | schiß | Universitätsabschluss | Universitätsabschluß |
| schlecht gehen | schlechtgehen | unmissverständlich | unmißverständlich |
| schlecht machen | schlechtmachen | Unterbewusstsein | Unterbewußtsein |
| schloss | schloß | Untergeschoss | Untergeschoß |
| Schloss | Schloß | unvergesslich | unvergeßlich |
| Schluss | Schluß | verantwortungsbewusst | verantwortungsbewußt |
| Schlussverkauf | Schlußverkauf | vergesslich | vergeßlich |
| schmiss | schmiß | Vergissmeinnicht | Vergißmeinnicht |
| schnäuzen | schneuzen | vergisst | vergißt |
| Schnellimbiss | Schnellimbiß | verloren gehen | verlorengehen |
| schoss | schoß | verschliss | verschliß |
| Schuss | Schuß | Verschluss | Verschluß |
| Schusswaffe | Schußwaffe | viel versprechend | vielversprechend |
| schwarz sehen | schwarzsehen | Vorhängeschloss | Vorhängeschloß |
| schwer fallen | schwerfallen | Walnuss | Walnuß |
| selbstbewusst | selbstbewußt | wie viel | wieviel |
| selbstständig/selbständig | selbständig | wisst | wißt |
| sitzen bleiben | sitzenbleiben | wusste | wußte |
| Sommerschlussverkauf | Sommerschlußverkauf | wussten | wußten |
| so viel | soviel | wusstest | wußtest |
| so weit | soweit | wusstet | wußtet |
| so wenig | sowenig | Zuckerguss | Zuckerguß |
| spazieren fahren | spazierenfahren | zu Grunde/zugrunde | zugrunde |
| spazieren gehen | spazierengehen | zu Leide/zuleide | zuleide |
| stehen bleiben | stehenbleiben | zu Mute/zumute | zumute |
| Stewardess | Stewardeß | Zungenkuss | Zungenkuß |
| Stress | Streß | zu Stande/zustande | zustande |
| Tipp | Tip | zu viel | zuviel |
| tollpatschig | tolpatschig | zu wenig | zuwenig |
| Trugschluss | Trugschluß | | |